Enlightened Oxford

Enlightened Oxford

The University and the Cultural and Political Life of Eighteenth-century Britain and Beyond

NIGEL ASTON

OXFORD
UNIVERSITY PRESS

Great Clarendon Street, Oxford, OX2 6DP,
United Kingdom

Oxford University Press is a department of the University of Oxford.
It furthers the University's objective of excellence in research, scholarship,
and education by publishing worldwide. Oxford is a registered trade mark of
Oxford University Press in the UK and in certain other countries

© Nigel Aston 2023

The moral rights of the author have been asserted

All rights reserved. No part of this publication may be reproduced, stored in
a retrieval system, or transmitted, in any form or by any means, without the
prior permission in writing of Oxford University Press, or as expressly permitted
by law, by licence or under terms agreed with the appropriate reprographics
rights organization. Enquiries concerning reproduction outside the scope of the
above should be sent to the Rights Department, Oxford University Press, at the
address above

You must not circulate this work in any other form
and you must impose this same condition on any acquirer

Published in the United States of America by Oxford University Press
198 Madison Avenue, New York, NY 10016, United States of America

British Library Cataloguing in Publication Data
Data available

Library of Congress Control Number: 2022946498

ISBN 978–0–19–924683–0

DOI: 10.1093/oso/9780199246830.001.0001

Printed and bound in the UK by
Clays Ltd, Elcograf S.p.A.

Links to third party websites are provided by Oxford in good faith and
for information only. Oxford disclaims any responsibility for the materials
contained in any third party website referenced in this work.

In memoriam

W. Roy Aston (1925–2018) and
Muriel Y. Aston (1925–2018)

Preface

This book has been an unconscionable time in coming to publication and I am greatly indebted to the many people who have helped me achieve my destination. First and foremost are the members of my family who have sustained me in the many years it has taken to complete this book. None of them are historians and by keeping me aware of twenty-first century concerns they kept my eighteenth-century ones refreshed and reinvigorated. For Lydia and Maria, that insistent supper-time question: 'is it finished yet'?—has, I hope, finally been answered. It is a pleasure to record my especial gratitude to my wife, Sarah, for her indefatigable patience and support. Her science background came in particularly useful when I was writing Chapter five.

I wish to thank the librarians and archivists in many repositories in Britain, Ireland, and the United States, who have helped me by providing access to the material in their care, particularly those of the Bedfordshire and Luton Archives; Beinecke Rare Book and manuscript Library, Yale University; Bodleian Library; British Library; Buckinghamshire Archives; Cambridge University Library; Cumbria Record Office (Kendal); Durham University Library, East Suffolk Record Office; Gloucestershire Record Office; Hampshire Record Office; Huntington Library, San Marino; Leicestershire, Leicester, and Rutland Record Office; National Library of Ireland; National Library of Scotland; National Library of Wales; Northamptonshire Record Office; Northumberland Archives; North Yorkshire Record Office; Nottingham University Library; Public Record Office of Northern Ireland; Staffordshire Record Office; The National Archives (Public Record Office); Warwickshire Record Office. Above all, my debt to librarians, archivists, and curators across Oxford should be recorded. Without their help and advice, this book would have been a walking shadow.

I had long sensed that the history of eighteenth-century Oxford and its place and influence in national life was far more dynamic than as conventionally presented, and that its 'orthodoxy' was the product of enquiry and debate and not a state of intellectual torpor. But any historian venturing into a new area of enquiry recognises the need to rely on pointers that others have provided. This wide-ranging book would have been impossible without securing its foundations firmly in the scholarship of a legion of historians living and deceased, as a look at the footnotes and bibliography will reveal. I was fortunate to work for two decades in a largely supportive History Department at Leicester with a distinctive strength in eighteenth-century and early modern studies. It was a pleasure over the years to discuss ideas with Richard Ansell, John Coffey, Sarah Goldsmith, Ian Harris,

VIII PREFACE

Terry Hartley, Steven King, David Manning, Keith Snell, and Roey Sweet, not to mention my own research and taught MA students.

A number of friends and colleagues outside my department at Leicester deserve particular thanks, three in particular: Robin Darwall-Smith (Oxford), William [Bill] Gibson (Oxford Brookes), and Colin Haydon (Winchester). These busy people read draft after draft of successive chapters, made suggestions, offered encouragement, corrected mistakes, and generally kept me going when the resolve to complete was stuttering. Grayson Ditchfield (Kent at Canterbury) and Robin Eagles (History of Parliament) also read over a lot of the material in its earlier guises and were scarcely less helpful and generous with their expert advice. I have also benefitted from discussion with and the advice of Jeremy Black, Michael Brown, James J. Caudle, Elaine Chalus, Jonathan Clark, Simon Dixon, Peter Doll, Roger Emerson, Noelle Gallagher, Malcolm Graham, Derya Gurses, Alastair Hamilton, James J. Harris, Ian Higgins, Neil Hitchin, Michael Honeybone, Joseph Hone, Peregrine Horden, Robert Ingram, Daniel Inman, Harry Johnstone, Peter M. Jones, Wilford Kale, Ian Kelly, Paddy McNally, Jennifer McNutt, Peter Morris, Peter Nockles, Tom O'Connor, Clarissa Campbell Orr, Richard Butterwick-Pawlikowski, Robert Peberdy, Alasdair Raffe, Daniel Reed, Anna Marie Roos, Charles Roundell, Valerie Rumbold, Richard Sharp, Andrew Starkie, Ted Vallance, Peter Walker, and Marcus Walsh. None of these are responsible for errors and misinterpretations that are entirely my respsonsibility.

I acknowledge with thanks research funding from the British Academy and from the University of Leicester, and the generous provision of research leave by the latter. I am grateful to the owners of the manuscripts from which I quote for permission to use their papers: Here I should note especially my thanks to the Duke of Beaufort; Lord Egremont & Leconfield; the Duke of Fife; the Earl of Malmesbury; the Earl of Mansfield; and Lord Lucas.

Everyone at Oxford University Press has been exceptionally helpful and immensely patient. In this regard I wish to thank Cathryn Steele, the Senior Assistant Commissioning Editor for Academic History. Ruth Parr, the History Editor, and her colleagues, particularly Anne Gelling and Seth Cayley, were also encouraging and supportive. Among Ruth's predecessors, Tony Morris helped me formulate a much earlier scheme for this book right at its inception. I would hope that he would still find what we discussed together skeletally recognisable.

Nigel Aston

University of York
Advent 2021

Contents

List of Figures	xiii
Abbreviations and Conventions	xix
A note on dates	xxiii
Introduction	1
1. Fame, form, and function: The University's place and purpose in the long eighteenth century	13

INTELLECTUAL PRESENCE

2. Oxford and British academic contexts after the Glorious Revolution	53
3. The defence of Christian belief and the Church of England	78
Part A: Scripture, sermons, and public theology	78
i) Scriptural politics and production	81
ii) Pulpits, preaching, and publication	90
iii) Professors, parsons, and public theology	100
Part B: The variety of Oxford voices on religion	110
i) Methodists and Roman Catholics	112
ii) Challenges to orthodoxy	115
iii) The reiteration of orthodoxy	119
iv) The decline of patristics	123
v) Church and state aligned?	124
vi) Conclusion	127
4. Oxford and the arts and humanities	131
Introduction	131
i) Polite and impolite verse, the rise of English literary scholarship, and other genres	132
ii) History writing: modern and ancient	144
iii) History writing: medieval and ecclesiastical	152
iv) Studies and controversies in classical literature	159
v) Philosophy and metaphysics	166
vi) Oriental studies	173
vii) Music	182
viii) Conclusion	193

X CONTENTS

5. Oxford and contemporary science: Anxiety, adaptation, and advance 198
   i) The Newtonian challenge 198
   ii) Lecturers, demonstrators, and Hutchinsonians: Newtonianism popularised and resisted 206
   iii) Oxford and the Royal Society after Newton 211
   iv) Oxford science and its reputation in the first half of the eighteenth century: foundations, progress, and obstacles 215
   v) The physical sciences at Oxford: advances, anxiety, and politics in the age of George III 224
   vi) Conclusion 238

INSTITUTIONAL PRESENCE AND INTERACTIONS

6. Oxford personnel: Offices, interest, and the polity 247
   i) Oxford chancellors and the projection and protection of the University, 1715–1809 248
   ii) Vice chancellors and their external impact 260
   iii) College heads: the politically well-connected 269
   iv) Tutors and parents 276
   v) College Visitors and college affairs 281
   vi) Bishops of Oxford and the University 287
   vii) Conclusion 294

7. Oxford and the Crown 298
   Part A: 'The shadow of disloyalty': the University and the monarchy in an era of contested succession c.1700–1760 298
   i) Background 298
   ii) Oath-taking and loyalty 302
   iii) The extent and importance of Jacobitism 306
   iv) Oxford and early eighteenth-century Toryism 314
   v) Whigs and loyalism in early eighteenth-century Oxford 328
   Part B: Loyalism recast and rewarded: Oxford in the age of George III 338
   i) Crown and constitution: the academic affirmation of 'Church and King' in revolutionary times 338
   ii) Conclusion 355

8. Oxford, the world of Westminster, and the defence of the University's interests 358
   Part A: From precarity to prosperity: ministers and the University 360
   i) Working with the Whigs, c.1690–1760 360
   ii) 'The King's friends': ministers and the University in the reign of George III 374

Part B: Defenders of the University's interests in Parliament	379
i) MPs for the University of Oxford	379
ii) Other Parliamentary friends in Lords and Commons	395
Part C: Governmental and legal cross-connections	398
i) Administrative and academic nexuses	398
ii) Lawyers and the University	410
iii) Conclusion	414
9. Beyond the University: Outreach and connections in England, Wales, Scotland, and Ireland	417
Part A: The City and the county	418
i) Beyond the University: the City of Oxford	418
ii) Beyond the University: the county of Oxfordshire	425
Part B: Property, schools, and the Oxford connection	441
i) Beyond the University: land ownership	441
ii) Beyond the University: links with English schools	443
iii) The appeal of school teaching	451
Part C: Oxford and 'Britishness': links to Wales, Scotland, and Ireland	455
i) Beyond the University: Wales	455
ii) Beyond the University: Scotland	461
iii) Beyond the University: Ireland	468
iv) Conclusion	476

CULTURAL CONSTRUCTIONS, CONNECTIONS, AND TENSIONS

10. The University as seen from outside	483
i) Literary and artistic (mis)representations	485
ii) Dissenters and Methodists	496
iii) Graduates of other universities	506
iv) Insiders as outsiders	515
v) The female presence in Oxford	524
vi) Installations, acts, and Encaenias	541
vii) Conclusion	551
11. Oxford and the wider world: The European connections and imperial involvements of the University	553
i) Oxonians in Europe and beyond	554
ii) Europeans in Oxford	563
iii) Oxford and the Republic of Letters	578
iv) Oxford and the British Atlantic: emerging imperial involvements	590
v) Conclusion	597

xii CONTENTS

12. Insider trading: Family, friendship, connection, and culture
beyond the University 599
   i) Patronage and power brokerage 602
   ii) Family, friendship, and academic loyalties 613
   iii) Clericalist culture beyond Oxford: individual endeavours 624
   iv) Clerical culture beyond Oxford: associational 634
   v) Lasting association: the culture of bequests and legacies 642
   vi) Conclusion 654

Conclusion: Oxford variations on an Enlightenment theme 658

Bibliography 677
Index 761

List of Figures

1.1 Map of Oxford, William Faden, 1789, 69 × 58 cm (Oxfordshire County Council—Oxfordshire History Centre). 22

1.2 The North Prospect of the New Quadrangle [Peckwater] of Christs Church in Oxford, 585 × 475 mm (© Governing Body, Christ Church, Oxford). 28

1.3 The South Prospect of the New Quadrangle [Peckwater] of Christs Church in Oxford, 585 × 475 mm (© Governing Body, Christ Church, Oxford). 29

1.4 Queen's College Library, J. C. Buckler, watercolour, 1828, 370 × 270 mm, P1271 (Librarian of the Queen's College, Oxford). 30

2.1 James Butler, 2nd Duke of Ormond, Studio of Michael Dahl, oil on canvas, c.1713, 126.4 × 101.6 cm, NPG 78 (© National Portrait Gallery, London). 66

2.2 Calendar of lectures and the curriculum at Oxford University; in the centre, a sun. Within its concentric circles are listed the various parts of the scholarly curriculum, print, c.1709, 385 × 293 mm (© The Trustees of the British Museum). Museum number: 1977, U. 621. 73

3.1 Humphrey Hody (1659–1707), oil on canvas, c.1695, 73.7 × 61.0 cm, Acc. No. 65 (By kind permission of the Warden and Fellows of Wadham College, Oxford). 85

3.2 Bishop Francis Atterbury, after Sir Godfrey Kneller, oil on canvas, after 1718, 73.7 × 60.8 cm, LP 249 (Bodleian Libraries, University of Oxford). 93

3.3 A View from Trinity College, Oxford [Henry Kett], by and published by Robert Dighton, hand-coloured etching, 1807, 27.0 × 19.8 cm plate size, NPG D13221 (© National Portrait Gallery, London). 121

4.1 Joseph Trapp (1679–1747), unknown artist, oil on canvas, 73.5 × 61.0 cm, LP 249 (Bodleian Libraries, University of Oxford). 139

4.2 Thomas Burgess (1756–1837), Bishop of St David's and Salisbury, William Owen, oil on canvas, copy 1825 of 1817 original at Corpus Christi College, Oxford, 143 × 111 cm, TSD_PCF1 (Trinity St David, Lampeter, Founder's Library). 166

4.3 John Locke, Thomas Gibson, oil on canvas, first half of the eighteenth century, 125 x 101 cm, LP 186 (Bodleian Libraries, University of Oxford). 169

4.4 Sir William Jones, John Flaxman, frieze from the monument in the chapel of University College, Oxford, (The Master and Fellows of University College, Oxford). 178

4.5 Holywell Music Room (© the author). 184

xiv LIST OF FIGURES

4.6 Charles Burney, Sir Joshua Reynolds, oil on canvas, 1781, 749 × 610 cm, NPG D13221 (© National Portrait Gallery, London). 185

4.7 Elizabeth Billington (née Weichsel) ('Clara—A Bravura'), Charles Williams, published by Samuel William Fores, hand-coloured etching, 1802, 37.3 x 24 cm paper size, NPG D34316 (© National Portrait Gallery, London). 190

5.1 George Parker, 2nd Earl of Macclesfield, Benjamin Wilson, oil on canvas, c.1760, 238.7 x 144.8 cm, Acc. No. FM63 (© Coram in the care of the Foundling Museum). 214

5.2 John Freind (1675–1728), Michael Dahl, oil on canvas, c.1720, 125.5 × 101.5 mm, LP 228 (Bodleian Libraries, University of Oxford). 218

5.3 Edmond Halley, Thomas Murray, oil on canvas, gift from the artist 1713, 127 × 101.5 cm, LP 241 (Bodleian Libraries, University of Oxford). 220

5.4 Kitchen and anatomical theatre Christ Church, drawn, engraved, and published by J. Fisher, 1827, 102 × 80 mm (© Governing Body, Christ Church, Oxford). 230

5.5 Oxford Physic Garden, print made by Benjamin Green, after Samuel Wale, line engraving, 1766, 33.7 × 44.1 cm, Acc. No. B2011.14.1 (Yale Center for British Art, Gift of Judith and Norman A. Zlotsky). 234

5.6 Johann Jakob Dillenius, unknown artist, oil on canvas, c.1730, 73 × 63 cm, LP 247 (Bodleian Libraries, University of Oxford). 235

5.7 *Flora Graeca*, Ferdinand Bauer (illustrator), Drawings and Watercolours, MS. Sherard 242, f. 7 Spartium junceum (Bodleian Libraries, University of Oxford). 236

5.8 *Flora Graeca*, Ferdinand Bauer (illustrator), Drawings and Watercolours, MS. Sherard 242, f. 201 Galium graecum (Bodleian Libraries, University of Oxford). 237

5.9 *A description of the passage of the shadow of the moon over England as it was observed in the late total eclipse of the sun April 22, 1715*, E. Halley, printed by J. Senex, printed broadsheet, 43 × 27 cm (University of Cambridge, Institute of Astronomy Library). 240

6.1 Charles Butler, 1st Earl of Arran, Sir James Thornhill, oil on canvas, 1727, 56 × 91 cm (© University of Oxford). 249

6.2 The Coal Wharf, Oxford, Rev. William Henry Barnard, grey wash and graphite print, 1792, 27.3 × 43.2 cm, Acc. No. B1977.14.5408 (Yale Center for British Art, Paul Mellon Collection). 265

6.3 John Wills, Vice-Chancellor and Warden of Wadham College, John Hoppner, oil on canvas, 1792–6, 142.5 × 99.1 cm, Studio Edmark. (By kind permission of the Warden and Fellows of Wadham College, Oxford). 268

LIST OF FIGURES   XV

6.4 Bishop William Cleaver, John Hoppner, oil on canvas, 1800,
141 × 116.2 cm (Reproduced with the kind permission of the Principal
and Fellows of the King's Hall and College of Brasenose in Oxford).   273

6.5 Sir Jonathan Trelawny, Sir Godfrey Kneller, oil on canvas, 1720,
127 × 103.5 cm, NPG 6769 (© National Portrait Gallery, London).   283

6.6 Theophilus Leigh, Master of Balliol College, Oxford, unknown artist,
oil on panel, c.1770, 20.3 × 15.2 cm (Master and Fellows of Balliol
College, Oxford).   285

6.7 Doorway at Christ Church, Oxford, formerly at Cuddesdon Palace, Oxon.
(© the author).   288

6.8 Christ Church Cathedral, Oxford, Richard Gilson Reeve, after
J. M. W. Turner, aquatint, 1807, Acc. No. B1977.14.8368
(Yale Center for British Art, Paul Mellon Collection).   290

7.1 Rev. Sir John Dolben, Robert Taylor, oil on canvas, c.1750,
251.5 × 124.5 cm (Master and Fellows of Balliol College, Oxford).   311

7.2 Thomas Dunster, unknown artist, oil on canvas, c.1690, 73.7 × 59.7 cm
(by kind permission of the Warden and Fellows of Wadham
College, Oxford).   329

7.3 Marble statue of Queen Caroline under cupola at the entrance to the
Queen's College, Oxford, Sir Henry Cheere, 1733–5, OU TQC Art03-001
(Photograph by John Cairns: Librarian of the Queen's College, Oxford).   335

7.4 George Horne, John Bridges, oil on canvas, 140.5 × 109.5 cm (Reproduced
by kind permission of the President and Fellows of Magdalen College).   345

7.5 Robert Nares, by Samuel Freeman, published by Fisher Son & Co, after
John Hoppner, stipple and line engraving, published 1830, 20.7 × 13.1 cm,
D15508 (© National Portrait Gallery, London).   351

8.1 Edward Butler, attributed to Edward Vanderbank, oil on canvas,
233.5 × 142 cm, Acc. No. P00577 (Reproduced by kind permission of the
President and Fellows of Magdalen College).   382

8.2 Prince George of Denmark and George Clarke, Sir James Thornhill, oil
on canvas, 238.7 × 157.4 cm, ASC 051 (by permission of the Warden
and Fellows of All Souls College, Oxford).   385

8.3 Sir Roger Newdigate, 5th Bt., Thomas Kirby, copy after George Romney,
oil on canvas, 1792, 238.8 × 148.6 cm, Acc. No. 52 (University College,
Oxford).   391

8.4 Charles Jenkinson, Lord Hawkesbury, later 1st Earl of Liverpool, George
Romney, oil on canvas, 1786–8, 149.9 × 114.3 cm, NPG 5206
(© National Portrait Gallery, London).   392

8.5 Sir William Dolben, 3rd Bt., after John Opie, oil on canvas, c.1800–18,
60.9 × 73.6 cm (© University of Oxford).   393

xvi   LIST OF FIGURES

8.6 John Wallis, after Sir Godfrey Kneller, oil on canvas, 1701, 74.9 × 62.9 cm, NPG 578 (© National Portrait Gallery, London).   401

9.1 Oxford High Street, Thomas Malton the Younger, oil on canvas, 1798–9, 88.9 × 119.4 cm, Acc. No. B1996.22.26 (Yale Center for British Art, Paul Mellon Collection).   422

9.2 Sir George Rooke, Michael Dahl, oil on canvas, c.1706, 126.5 × 100.4 cm (© National Portrait Gallery, London).   428

9.3 Charles Lawson ('Carolus Lawson'), by and published by James Heath, after William Marshall Craig, line engraving, 1799, 43.8 × 33.4 cm paper size, NPG D37221 (© National Portrait Gallery, London).   454

10.1 Frontispiece to 'The Humours of Oxford', Thomas Cook, after William Hogarth, print, 1807, 18.5 × 12.3 cm, Acc. No. 1949.2 (The Metropolitan Museum of Art, New York: Gift of A. E. Popham, 1949).   487

10.2 Bacon Faced fellows of Brazen Nose, Broke Loose, Thomas Rowlandson, hand-coloured etching, 1811, 23.8 × 32.8 cm, Acc. No. 59.533.1400 (The Metropolitan Museum of Art, New York: The Elisha Whittelsey Collection, The Elisha Whittelsey Fund, 1959).   492

10.3 Mrs Showwell, the Woman who shows General Guise's Collection of Pictures at Oxford, Thomas Rowlandson, hand-coloured etching, 1807, 21.5 x 13.3 cm, Acc. No. 59.533.970 (The Metropolitan Museum of Art, New York: The Elisha Whittelsey Collection, The Elisha Whittelsey Fund, 1959).   526

10.4 University, Thomas Rowlandson, after James Brydges Willyams, hand-coloured etching, 1802, 22.3 × 33.2 cm, Acc. No. 59.533.851(6) (The Metropolitan Museum of Art, New York: The Elisha Whittelsey Collection, The Elisha Whittelsey Fund, 1959).   534

10.5 Love and Learning, or the Oxford Scholar, Benjamin Smith, after Thomas Rowlandson, hand-coloured etching, 1786, 39.3 × 31 cm, Acc. No. 59.533.188 (The Metropolitan Museum of Art, New York: The Elisha Whittelsey Collection, The Elisha Whittelsey Fund, 1959).   536

10.6 Frontispiece to Nicholas Amhurst's 'Terrae-Filius', William Hogarth, print, 1726, 13.9 x 8 cm, Acc. No. 32.35(259) (The Metropolitan Museum of Art, New York: Harris Brisbane Dick Fund, 1932).   545

11.1 Rev. Thomas Shaw, unknown artist, oil on canvas, 75 × 61.7 cm (St Edmund Hall, Oxford).   561

11.2 Duc de Nivernais, Allan Ramsay, oil on canvas, c.1763, 61 × 53.3 cm, NT 1007347 (© National Trust).   568

11.3 Johann Ernest Grabe, Francis Bird, marble monument, 1726, south transept, Westminster Abbey (Copyright: Dean and Chapter of Westminster).   571

11.4 Frontispiece, *Voyage de Cyrus*, Chevalier Ramsay (Bodleian Libraries, University of Oxford).   580

LIST OF FIGURES xvii

11.5 Christopher Codrington, Sir James Thornhill, oil on canvas,
237.5 × 151.1 cm, ASC 032 (by permission of the Warden and Fellows
of All Souls College, Oxford). 591

12.1 5th Lord Digby of Geashill, Sir Godfrey Kneller, attrib., oil on canvas,
1715, 123.2 x 99.6 cm (Reproduced by kind permission of the President
and Fellows of Magdalen College). 610

12.2 Rev. George Fothergill, Principal St Edmund Hall, 1751–60,
unknown artist, oil on canvas, 75 × 60 cm (St Edmund Hall, Oxford). 616

12.3 Richard Roundell and others on the banks of the Isis, a view of Oxford
beyond, John Hamilton Mortimer, oil on canvas, c.1765, 100 × 126 cm
(Dorfold Hall Events Limited). 618

12.4 Statue of John Radcliffe, 1747, Michael Rysbrack, LP 683 (Bodleian
Libraries, University of Oxford). 642

12.5 The library, Christ Church, Oxford, P.TOP.PQ.19 (© Governing Body,
Christ Church, Oxford). 644

12.6 Sir Thomas Cookes Contemplating the Bust of King Alfred, Robert
Edge Pine, oil on canvas, 248 × 195 cm, Acc. No. 356 (The Provost and
Fellows of Worcester College, Oxford). 646

12.7 Canterbury Gate, Christ Church, Oxford before rebuilding, pencil and
watercolour, 1775, John Baptist Malchair, 28.5 × 22.5 cm,
P.TOP.CANT.9 (© Governing Body, Christ Church, Oxford). 647

12.8 A Perspective View of the New [Canterbury] Gate at Christ Church
(Oxford Almanack, 1781), P.TOP.CANT.5 (© Governing Body,
Christ Church, Oxford). 648

Abbreviations and Conventions

AEH	*Anglican and Episcopal History*
AHR	*American Historical Review*
Bart. or Bt.	Baronet
BJECS	*British Journal for Eighteenth-Century Studies*
BJHS	*British Journal for the History of Science*
BJRL	*Bulletin of the John Rylands Library*
Bloxam	J. R. Bloxam, *A register of the presidents, fellows... of St Mary Magdalen College...* (7 vols., Oxford, 1853–85)
Bodl.	Bodleian Library, Oxford
BJHS	*British Journal of the History of Science*
BL	British Library
BLR	*Bodleian Library Record*
Brockliss (1)	ed. L. W. B. Brockliss, *Magdalen College, Oxford. A history* (Oxford, 2008)
Brockliss (2)	Lawrence Brockliss, *The University of Oxford. A history* (Oxford, 2016)
CCEd	Clergy of the Church of England data base
Ch. Ch.	Christ Church
CL	*Country Life*
Crook, *Brasenose*	J. Mordaunt Crook, *Brasenose. The biography of an Oxford college* (Oxford, 2008)
CUL	Cambridge University Library
Curthoys (1)	Judith Curthoys, *The Cardinal's college: Christ Church, chapter and verse* (London, 2012)
Curthoys (2)	Judith Curthoys, *The stones of Christ Church. The story of the buildings of Christ Church* (London, 2017)
Curthoys (3)	Judith Curthoys, *The King's cathedral. The ancient heart of Christ Church, Oxford* (London, 2019)
Curthoys (4)	Judith Curthoys, *Cows & curates. The story of the land and livings of Christ Chgurch, Oxford* (London, 2020)
ECS	*Eighteenth-Century Studies*
EHR	*English Historical Review*
Fasti	John Le Neve, *Fasti ecclesiae Anglicanae 1541–1857,* vol. 8. *Bristol, Gloucester, Oxford and Peterborough dioceses,* ed. Joyce M. Horn (London, 1996)
Foster	J. Foster, *Alumni Oxonienses, the members of the University of Oxford, 1715–1886...* (4 vols., Oxford and London, 1887–8)

xx ABBREVIATIONS AND CONVENTIONS

Gascoigne, *Cambridge*	John Gascoigne, *Cambridge in the age of the Enlightenment. Science, religion and politics from the Restoration.to the French Revolution* (Cambridge, 1989)
GEC	G.E. Cokayne and Vicary Gibbs, *The complete peerage...* (13 vols., London, 1910–59)
GM	*Gentleman's Magazine*
Hearne	*Remarks and collections of Thomas Hearne*, eds. C. E. Doble, D. W. Rannie, and H. E. Salter, [Oxford Historical Society] (11 vols., Oxford, 1885–1921)
HJ	*Historical Journal*
HLQ	*Huntington Library Quarterly*
HMC	Historical Manuscripts Commission
HUO I	*The history of the University of Oxford, Vol. I. The early Oxford schools*, ed. J. I. Catto (Oxford, 1984)
HUO IV	*The history of the University of Oxford, Vol. IV. Seventeenth-century Oxford*, ed. N. Tyacke (Oxford, 1997)
HUO V	*The History of the University of Oxford, Vol. V. The Eighteenth Century Oxford,* eds. L.S. Sutherland and L.G. Mitchell (Oxford, 1986)
HUO VI	*The History of the University of Oxford, Vol. VI. Nineteenth-century Oxford, Part 1*, eds. M. G. Brock and M. C. Curthoys (Oxford, 1997)
Ingamells	*A Dictionary of British and Irish travellers in Italy 1701–1800*, ed. John Ingamells (compiled from the Brinsley Ford Archive) (New Haven, CT, 1997).
JBS	*Journal of British Studies*
JECS	*Journal for Eighteenth-Century Studies*
JHI	*Journal of the History of Ideas*
JMH	*Journal of Modern History*
JMIH	*Journal of Modern Intellectual History*
JOJ	*Jackson's Oxford Journal*
JRUL	John Rylands University Library
JRS	Journal of Religious Studies
JTS	*Journal of Theological Studies*
LLRRO	Leicestershire, Leicester, and Rutland Record Office
LPL	Lambeth Palace Library
Morgan, *Cambridge*	Victor Morgan, *A history of the University of Cambridge,* Vol. 2: *1546–1750* (Cambridge, 2004)
NAS	National Archives of Scotland
Nichols, *Illustrations*	John Nichols, *Illustrations of the literary history of the eighteenth century...* (8 vols., London, 1817–58)
Nichols, *Lit. anecdotes*	John Nichols, *Literary anecdotes of the eighteenth century* (9 vols., London, 1812–15)
NLS	National Library of Scotland
NLW	National Library of Wales

NUL	Nottingham University Library
OHS	*Oxford Historical Society*
OUA	Oxford University Archives
PH	William Cobbett, *The Parliamentary History of England, from the Earliest Period to the Year* 1803 (36 vols., London, 1806–20).
RO	Record Office
SEH	St Edmund Hall
SJC	St John's College
SVEC	*Studies in Voltaire and the eighteenth century*
TCD	Trinity College, Dublin
TLS	*Times Literary Supplement*
TRHS	*Transactions of the Royal Historical Society*
V-C	Vice-Chancellor
VCH Oxon.	*The Victoria history of the County of Oxford,* (22 vols., London, 1907–2022).
Walpole, *Correspondence*	*The Yale edition of Horace Walpole's correspondence,* ed. W. S. Lewis (48 vols., New Haven, CT, 1937–83).
W&MQ	*William & Mary Quarterly*
WHR	*Welsh History Review*
Wood, *Life and times*	*The Life and times of Anthony Wood*, ed. A. Clark (5 vols., Oxford, 1889–1900)
WSRO	West Sussex Record Office
WYAS	West Yorkshire Archive Service

Conventions

All references to the University of Oxford use the 'University' in upper case. A specific College or Hall also uses upper case, while 'a college'/'colleges and 'a hall'/halls refers to colleges and halls within Oxford in general.

A note on dates

Until Britain adopted the Gregorian Calendar in 1752, it used the older Julian calendar, which meant that it was ten days behind continental Europe before 1700, and eleven days behind thereafter. Under the 'Old Style' Julian dispensation, the year was taken to start on 25 March, rather than 1 January (except in Scotland, where 1 January was viewed as the start of the year until the 1707 Act of Union brought the kingdom into conformity with England, Wales, and Ireland). In this work, all dates before 1752 should be assumed to be 'Old Style', but the New Year is taken to begin on 1 January.

Introduction

…a society where emulation without envy, ambition without jealousy, contention without animosity, incites industry and awakened genius; where a liberal pursuit of knowledge and a generous freedom of thought was raised, encouraged, and pushed forward, by example, by commendation, and by authority.

[Robert Lowth], A late Professor in the University of Oxford,
A Letter to the Right Reverend Author of The Divine
Legation … [William Warburton] (London, 1766), 64.

Our Universitys are asleep & the Church snores.

Edward Young to Thomas Tickell, 5 June 1727, quoted in
R. E. Tickell, Thomas Tickell and the Eighteenth Century Poets
(1685–1740) (London, 1931), 131.

I have made another discovery in my travels which you will not consider as a perfectly new one, and that is no less than that Oxford is a very curious place.

Anthony Storer to William, 1st Lord Auckland,
28 September 1790, The Journal and correspondence
of William, Lord Auckland, ed. Bishop of Bath
& Wells (4 vols., London, 1861)

The University of Oxford's reputation as a place of intellectual insignificance in the 'long' eighteenth century was deliberately fostered by contemporaries and in the following centuries on grounds of personal animosity, political antagonisms, a condescension encouraged by the rise and regulation of professional life, and a blindness to cultural contexts. But the advance of scholarship over the last sixty years in our grasp of eighteenth-century institutional and academic life has replaced the (over-) familiar tropes of port, prejudice, and somnolent dons with a more nuanced and compelling picture of the University in all its aspects.[1]

---

[1] As the Young comments indicate, the moaning was well under way in the eighteenth century itself. Richard Polwhele's *The follies of Oxford: or, cursory sketches on a university education* (London, 1785) is a good source of anti-Oxford views, with its lounging Fellows and sporting undergraduates anticipating Wodehouse's Drones Club. See also the *Oxford Magazine* 10 (1773), 365, with its censures on university learning. By the end of the nineteenth century, the tone was comfortably patronising, for instance Charles Grant Robertson's 'blessed euthanasia of eighteenth-century Oxford'; *All Souls College*

Enlightened Oxford: The University and the Cultural and Political Life of Eighteenth-century Britain and Beyond.
Nigel Aston, Oxford University Press. © Nigel Aston 2023. DOI: 10.1093/oso/9780199246830.003.0001

2 ENLIGHTENED OXFORD

Important work on this period is to be found in the *History of the University* in seven volumes,[2] an accessible and detailed survey by Laurence Brockliss,[3] and recent college histories that are based primarily on archival holdings and are much less the self-regarding institutional *hommages* that they have largely superseded.[4] This present book, with its principal perspective on Oxford in relation to the outside world, would not be possible without this accumulation of new studies, any more than it would without the scholarship on those other eighteenth-century worlds—physical, political, religious, and intellectual—in relation to and against which the University, broadly defined, is to be understood.

Of course, not to hear or rationalise away the variously motivated detractors of the University would be not to register the complaints and resentments this complex corporation and its constituent parts could attract. Indeed, that they were made at all is suggestive of the University's failure to live up to what its critics believed it should be doing or thinking, that it appeared to operate within a set of legal, financial, and educational barriers that were considered restrictive, or otherwise as shoring up anachronistic and unwarranted privileges. Correspondingly, its political preferences in this era were a subject of enduring fascination, endorsement, and deprecation for contemporaries and permitted the construction of a monolithic Tory character that was far from the whole story but has had an enduring power. And to deplore its dominant politics was to justify further reducing its influence or instigating external interference and supervision so that it might, as many considered, become as overtly supportive of Hanoverian authority as Cambridge which, without that intervention, Oxford found itself seamlessly attaining from the 1760s.

The primary object of this book is not to offer another history of the University *per se* in the 'long eighteenth century' but to discern, establish, and clarify the multiplicity of connections between the University, its members, and the world outside; to offer readers a fresh, contextualised sense of the University's role in the state, in society, and in relation to other institutions between the Williamite Revolution and the first decade of the nineteenth century, the era that one might loosely describe (though not without much qualification) as England's *ancien régime*. In other words, it seeks to ask where Oxford fitted in to that wider polity, to locate its importance in Church and state and, beyond these, to

---

(London, 1899), 177, and Albert Mansbridge, 'University Life in the middle of the century was at its lowest', *The Older Universities of England. Oxford & Cambridge* (London, 1923), 97. Examples could be multiplied.

[2] HUO I-VIII. The volumes covering the seventeenth to the nineteenth centuries, IV, V, VI, are directly relevant to the current book with V, on the eighteenth century, eds. L. S. Sutherland and L. G. Mitchell, primary to it.

[3] Lawrence Brockliss, *The University of Oxford. A history* (Oxford, 2016).

[4] Scholarly college histories either single/double authored or edited published since 1995 include Brockliss on Magdalen; Catto on Oriel; Charles-Edwards and Reid on Corpus Christi; Crook on Brasenose; several vols. by Curthoys on Christ Church; Darwall-Smith on University College; Davies and Garnett on Wadham; Jones (2nd edn.) on Balliol; Martin and Highfield on Merton.

ponder its place as an institution that upheld confessional entitlement in an ever-shifting intellectual world where national and confessional boundaries were under scrutiny. Patronage, clientage, connection, and, at times, blatant jobbery, figure considerably as they would in any study of an eighteenth-century institution. But, equally, ties of friendship, kinship, and moral obligation are emphasised, all of them having an Oxonian dimension that was commonly just one aspect of a dynamic to be found in many other personal and public spheres of life. Likewise, Oxford-based academics and authors were nurturing ever closer connections with the commercial print world and the public for which it catered on a whole range of subjects. Increasingly, they did not want to stand apart, to restrict consideration of what they wrote to an academic audience at home and abroad, but to create an accessible public profile for educated men and women irrespective of whether they had a degree or not. Oxford quietly cultivated a centuries-old reputation as the 'seat of the Muses' in literature and music. In this century, public accessibility and appreciation could not be ignored if Oxford was to be considered 'enlightened'. For, whatever an author's misgivings in deploying a descriptive term that some would consider teleologically compromised and suspect (though 'an irresistible canvas for historians'),[5] a study of a university in this era cannot neglect its relationship with the multiple contexts of Enlightenment Britain, and with versions of the Enlightenment found elsewhere in Europe. What follows is therefore less an inside history than a consideration of an institutional presence and its place in the life of the country and further afield, assessing what Oxford was supposed to do, what it did, making that wider connection, measuring cultural presence, noting links to the outside. It is a book not about teaching but about the contribution of the university to the advancement of learning broadly imagined.

There are three interconnected sections of this book, 'Intellectual Presence', 'Institutional Presence and Interactions' and, finally 'Cultural Constructions, connections, and tensions'. The first chapter 'Fame, Form, and Function: the University's place and purpose in the long eighteenth century' falls outside all of them but attempts to open up the subject as a whole. It looks broadly at eighteenth-century Oxford's reputation, celebrity, and public standing in relation to Cambridge and the wider British, Irish, and continental higher-education world, noting the retention of the widely perceived archaic Laudian statutes and the decline in student numbers at mid-century, and considering what we should read into these phenomena. Like every institution in the decades after the 'Glorious Revolution', Oxford University was caught up in quite intensive

---

[5] The expression is S. Grote's in 'Review-Essay: religion and Enlightenment', *JHI*, 75 (2014), 137–60. Cf. Jonathan Clark, 'Providence, predestination and progress: or, did the Enlightenment fail'?, *Albion*, 35 (2003), 559–89 with John Robertson, *The Enlightenment. A very short introduction* (Oxford, 2015). See also N. Hudson, 'What is the Enlightenment? Investigating the origins and ideological uses of an historical category', *Lumen*, 25 (2006), 163–74.

4 ENLIGHTENED OXFORD

factional strife that necessarily had an impact on academic life (though one should not assume an inevitably negative one). The argument is made for its vitality as an educational foundation that, once Jacobitism had faded as a viable political choice, deployed the rhetoric of loyalty creatively and intelligently on behalf of the Anglo-Hanoverian state and the confessional regime that pertained in England and Wales. The section on 'form' merely glances at the student body, the curriculum, and the social life of Oxford students, topics well-treated elsewhere;[6] instead of going deeper into them, it emphasises the connection with lay and clerical elites at large and the expectation that the majority of Oxford matriculands would submit to an educational formation that would equip them to undertake that range of public and professional duties discharged by generations before them. In its physical format, however, the University changed appreciably, reflecting an underlying confidence in its future. Dons and students benefitted from improved accommodation; many colleges aped the country-house ideal; the University received a new ceremonial and custodial space in the distinctive shape of the Radcliffe Library (later the Camera). The scale and quality of this building programme that transformed the physical form of Oxford had a national significance that has been insufficiently stressed. The chapter concludes with reflections on the University's function as a necessarily politicised component of the British state, whether this awareness is articulated through manifestations of loyalty, of disloyalty, or just indifference, and broaches the question of how far its functioning intellectual life can be seen through the prism of Enlightenment. John Robertson has noted that Catholic Universities 'were not necessarily well adapted to the sorts of enquiry in which Enlightenment thinkers were engaged, or to the forms in which they wished to publish their conclusions'.[7] Within British, indeed English contexts, that was arguably less the case.

Chapter Two, the first of four covering intellectual presence, provides an overview of Oxford in the decades immediately after the Revolution of 1688 within British academic contexts as a whole, a period when the tight confessional support of the monarchy that the Church had enjoyed from the University in the first half of the 1680s was more fitfully present. It qualifies and, to a degree, repudiates, the prevailing view that Oxford was a Tory bastion unable to adapt to the late Stuart and early Hanoverian order. Scholarship in history and the classics flourished, the Bodleian Library received visitors from across Europe, and the University was substantially rebuilt as a 'new Athens'. Thus without seeking to deny the several varieties of Toryism—and, indeed, of Whiggism—that characterised Oxford, or giving insufficient attention to what many saw as the spread of

---

[6] For the curriculum see L. S. Sutherland in HUO V, 469–92, and E. G. W. Bill, *Education at Christ Church Oxford 1660–1800* (Oxford, 1988), and Midgley for social life.

[7] John Robertson, *The case for the Enlightenment. Scotland and Naples 1680–1760* (Cambridge, 2005), 35.

INTRODUCTION 5

irreligion and the vulnerability of the Church of England, the chapter argues that if Oxford at first adjusted awkwardly to the new dispensation, then that was no less the case for all British universities, especially those in Scotland, where direct government obtrusion in their affairs was more conspicuous. And the traffic between universities north of the border and Oxford gave zest to the latter's intellectual life through the transmission and moderation of Newtonian mathematics.

The third Chapter, on the defence of the Christian faith in its Anglican expression, is foundational to the whole study. The intellectual life of the University pivoted on this theme and a political colouring to it was probably unavoidable. The defence of the University was a defence of the whole Church of England as the University was the cornerstone of the Church-state polity,[8] and the suppression of Convocation as an active institution after 1717—and therefore the exclusion of the Church as a formal, deliberative part of the constitution from public life—conferred more importance on Oxford's status as a corporate voice. The central contention is that University members through a variety of rhetorical strategies displayed a persuasive ingenuity (if not always originality) in protecting the faith upheld by the Established Church in a manner that appealed to audiences beyond Oxford. One can focus readily enough on wrangling and disputation, narrow point scoring, personality clashes, all the exchanges inseparable from the life of Oxford or any other university yet, arguably Oxford, for better or worse, more than any other institution helped to keep the nation recognisably and corporately Christian in this century.

Such centrality within the polity was less evident in the impact of the University's engagement with the arts and humanities where, as in previous centuries, the primary vocation of scholars was to write for and debate with other scholars. Anglo-Latin verse writing continued in full flood during the first half of the century, drawing on a long tradition; it was commonly in manuscript and yet, where it was available in pamphlet format, the desire to attract a wider, metropolitan audience was an obvious inference. At its best, Oxford culture was outward-facing, connected to the book trade of the capital, and the securing of new markets. This emphasis on openness and external links was embodied in Oxford's growing reputation as one of the nation's foremost music-making hubs, and was also visible in the production of vernacular literature that both encapsulated national pride in the achievements of the British state around the time of the Seven Years' War and recognised the strength and breadth of the English literary inheritance down the centuries. Thus Thomas Warton (the younger) and his generation corrected a rather misleading reputation acquired during the Phalaris controversy (itself part of the 'Ancients and Moderns' culture wars that

---

[8] For the University's primary importance as a seminary for the whole Church of England see [L. Bagot], *A defence of subscription to the 39 Articles, as it is required in the University of Oxford;...* (Oxford, 1772), 11.

6 ENLIGHTENED OXFORD

reverberated across Europe at the close of the seventeenth century) that Oxford learning was exclusive, essentially inward-looking, and privileged style over substance. Meanwhile, the increasing demands of empire ensured that the University's seventeenth-century reputation for Oriental languages developed apace and manifested itself inter alia in Arabic studies (well-established since the endowment of the Laudian Chair before the Civil War), as well as in Persian and Sanskrit during the generation of Sir William Jones in the 1770s/80s.

Chapter five moves to an evolving disciplinary area, that of science, however anomalous the descriptive nomenclature in a pre-Darwinian age. Its starting point is Peter Harrison's point that the shift towards a more propositional understanding of religion since the Reformation (thereby reifying religion as a generic term) was accompanied by the growth of the ideal of scientific objectivity, and therefore a potential conflict between religion and science.[9] Despite pioneering activities after the Restoration, symbolised by the foundation of the Ashmolean Museum, eighteenth-century Oxford is often seen as an institution largely at a remove from contemporary science but, as Chapter 5 argues, if science generated concerns for the security of orthodox religion and morality, there were also opportunities to exploit the intellectual capital it offered. Newtonianism had been strong in the university in the 1700s and 1710s,[10] but a dominant claim in the chapter is that Oxford's refusal to collapse its intellectual life into Newtonianism thereafter was as much a sign of intellectual dispassion and openness as of anxiety, though it arguably came at a cost: its own marginalisation in the cultural politics of early Georgian England. Still, as Brockliss has argued, nowhere in Europe was the curricular importance of the natural sciences generally increased before the mid-nineteenth century,[11] Oxford offered gradually improving facilities for experimentation and lecturing in the subject, primarily from collegiate and personal initiatives rather than financed by the University (not that this was an unusual ad hoc arrangement). And if college fellows and tutors lacked the expertise to lead the way then outsiders could be employed. The appetite for these lectures outside the University was acknowledged and regular notice was often given of when and where lectures were being held.[12] Even in medicine, the endowment and opening of the Radcliffe Hospital in 1772 indicates that the 'Medical Enlightenment' manifested itself in the city and, by the end of the century, Oxford was at the forefront of advances in chemistry. The problem was that chemical forces were suggestive of political incandescence and, in the person

---

[9] Peter Harrison, *The territories of religion and science* (Chicago, IL, 2015).

[10] Newton's Oxford supporters portrayed him as a champion of ancient wisdom as well as the leader of the moderns. John Friesen, 'Christ Church Oxford, the ancients-moderns controversy, and the promotion of Newton in post-Revolutionary England', *History of Universities*, 23 (2008), 33–66, at 41.

[11] L. Brockliss, 'Science, the universities, and other public spaces: teaching science in Europe and the Americas', in ed. R. Porter, *The Cambridge history of science*, Vol. 4. *Eighteenth-century science* (Cambridge, 2003), 44–86, at 56.

[12] *JOJ*, 17 Feb. 1758 for John Smith's first series of lectures on anatomy and 'animal economy'.

of Thomas Beddoes, appeared to embody them. His reputation for Jacobinism underlined Anglican anxieties about science in the 1790s and his expulsion from the University indicated that intellectual advance was never politically unconditional. Overall, a scriptural basis for scientific understanding remained commonplace despite challenges, though Oxford University's affirmation of the primacy of theology over diverse forms of natural philosophy was not always sufficiently emphatic for some members.

Four chapters treat themes of institutional presence and interaction. Chapter 6 looks at University officeholders and their connections to the polity and politics of Hanoverian Britain. Because their actions could be crucial to maintaining the influence of the University nationally much rested on their selection and their behaviour in office. The Chancellor and High Steward, as it were, presented the face of Oxford to the outside world; that was barely less the case for the vice chancellor, whose quotidian management of the University might determine the extent of governmental and patronal favour or disapprobation. In such matters, college and hall heads and senior tutors were also potentially in the reckoning. Their incompetence, immorality, and other forms of laxity could inflict serious damage on an institution, especially when it was struggling for tokens of official favour under the first two Georges. Their influence could vary but it reached a climax in the 1790s with Cyril Jackson, Dean of Christ Church, the intimate of many members of Pitt's wartime administration; 'our friend the Dean' is an expression that occurs regularly in the correspondence of ministers. Then there were those with formal roles and power inside the University, the college Visitors and the diocesan bishop (whose jurisdiction extended only to the historic county of Oxford before 1836), whose duties and routines impinged only occasionally on the University but, when they did, could be decisive, especially in the case of the former. All these were, to a greater or lesser degree, power brokers, stood in the centre of intersecting patronage networks, and exercised political influence in and beyond the University.

Office holders and all other members of the University were subjects of the Crown and witnessed to that obligation in oath-taking and other various public actions, some with legal, others with symbolic force. As Chapter 7 considers, the problem for Oxford was that, while it had a reputation for loyalty confirmed by its suffering and status during the first Civil War (1642–6) when the city acted as the king's capital, it found loyalty much harder after the monarchical succession ceased to be strictly hereditary following the flight of James II and the imposition of the Revolution settlement. The irony was that Oxford, notoriously the reputed home of non-resistance and passive obedience, had been in the forefront of objections to James's hasty Catholicising policies and reckoned on their retraction rather than his flight. Relief at William III's rescue soon palled and Anne's reign was a Tory interlude that never quite delivered on expectations. The chapter is

8 ENLIGHTENED OXFORD

insistent on the importance of an influential Whig minority across the University under George I and George II that ensured a limited degree of state largesse despite ministers doing little to downplay Oxford's reputation for Jacobite Toryism that was exaggerated but persistent. It was only after 1760 that those divisions on the underlying issue of monarchy gave way to solidarity of opinion across the University that functioned as a foundational strength of the dynasty and, by extension, the kingdom, in the face of international and internal challenges over the next sixty years.

Beyond the king lay his ministers, and relations with government tended to be unstable and sometimes unseemly until well into the reign of George III (with some interludes of official favour such as 1710–14). This attitude had its roots in corporate independency but, taken too far, it imperilled the functioning of the University by increasing the likelihood of direct ministerial involvement, even an aggressive royal Visitation of the kind narrowly avoided in the late 1710s and late 1740s. Of course, ministers had a legitimate role in exercising royal patronage within the University on behalf of the king, and to appoint loyal clients and placemen was an acceptable mode of building up influence within the University just as it was in other organs attached to the state. Academic relations with the 'world of Westminster' treated in Chapter 8 deal with Parliament as well as the executive and the emphasise the national role assumed by some of the University's MPs, among them Lord Cornbury, Sir Roger Newdigate, Sir William Dolben, and Sir William Scott. The need for them to be distrustful of ministers had largely faded by the 1770s. By then heads of house such as Nathan Wetherell and Jackson were using their considerable range of Westminster contacts to make their colleges virtual antechambers to government service for a select number of undergraduates. It was yet another sign of the reaffirmation of Oxford's centrality to the Georgian constitution, that would only be finally dismantled in the 1830s.

Chapter 9 ranges widely in geography to consider the University's outreach and influence across Britain and Ireland in this period, founded on the premise that the 'long' eighteenth century 'saw the development of a number of discourses, practices, and genres that allowed people to think about place, community, and identity in new ways'.[13] First, the chapter examines engagement with the City of Oxford, with which the University shared so many physical spaces. Beyond that lay the county and the wider south Midlands, all more closely connected through better transport links, including a canal promoted by senior members of the University. Then it looks at the way Oxonian values were connected to the regions, firstly, via the University's land holdings across England and Wales connecting tenants to individual colleges, then through schools and the neglected presence of Oxford graduates (many of them Tories) who functioned as head masters and

---

[13] eds. E. Gottlieb and J. Shields, *Representing place in British literature and culture, 1660–1830: from local to global* (Farnham, 2013), 3.

teachers. The claim is made that these were no less vital than the parish clergy in forming the Anglican identities of the young in their charge. The University's cultural connections via its graduates extended across the realm. Wales had its own particular route to Oxford through Jesus College; there were established reciprocal movements in personnel between Trinity College, Dublin, and the University, and, likewise, for Scotland. Scottish students sympathetic to the episcopalian tradition were naturally attracted to Oxford, and there was a regular traffic between Glasgow, Edinburgh, St Andrews, and Oxford in young men looking to complete their education south of the border via the Snell exhibition at Balliol College. It concludes that, considered numerically on the basis of graduates, Oxford's imprint on the king's non-English subjects may have been small but the University had too great a cultural force field in terms of its values and its history for it to be ignored anywhere in the two kingdoms when educated men encountered each other.

The last of the three overarching themes is that of 'Cultural Constructions, Connections, and Tensions', considered in the three last chapters. The first of these looks at the University as seen from outside, noticing under several headings the different constructions of 'Oxford', some flattering, many derogatory. It begins with the treatment of Oxford literature and art, in guide books, plays, novels, and paintings. The second category consists of Protestant dissenters among whose number non-Trinitarians were particularly vocal in expressing their disdain for Oxford and its high Anglican values—and adept at publicising their criticisms. By contrast, Methodism had Oxford origins in the 1720s and 1730s, but its subsequent loss of currency within the University prompted more regret than anger among its adherents who, themselves, split along Arminian and Calvinist lines later in the century. Then follows the varying attitude of graduates of other universities within Britain with a view to distinguishing the genuinely critical from good-hearted academic one-upmanship, not least the relationship with Cambridge. The fourth category for notice is that of insiders who were technically outsiders, notably college servants, as well as graduates such as Edward Gibbon, who wanted to present themselves as outsiders and had the capacity to damage the standing of the alma mater from which they had distanced themselves. The presence of women across Oxford at every social level receives extended emphasis. By definition, females could not matriculate and so become members of the University, but the degree of female inclusion in university socialisation through kinship, association, and sexual services was not to be under-estimated. Oxford could function as a relatively open cultural space especially on such academic occasions as installations, Encaenia, and the award of honorary degrees, when women had an active consumerist and spectatorial role as well as innumerable opportunities for socialising across the customary gender boundaries.

10 ENLIGHTENED OXFORD

Recent emphasis has been placed on the continuing vitality in seventeenth-century England of a trans-European culture of scholarly humanism that radiated beyond academic communities,[14] and Chapter 11, whose subject is Oxford's continental European connections, finds plenty of vigour discernible in the next century. If Oxford was not primarily a centre for unqualified and uncritical endorsement of progressive thinking, it was one for an admixture of ideas, both 'ancient' and 'modern', and compared favourably with its European counterparts. Even the serious reformer and one-time Cambridge professor, Bishop Richard Watson, observed—with just a hint of complacency—at the turn of the nineteenth century, that whatever their defects, 'our [English] Universities are the best seminaries of education in Europe'.[15] The interaction of Oxford graduates with their counterparts in continental Europe, travelling, working, studying as it might be, on the whole gave a flattering impression of the University's part in their social fashioning, while Oxford dons were generally welcomed irrespective of confessional divergences in libraries and academies, and even in salons from Paris to St Petersburg, Stockholm to Naples. In the reverse direction, Europeans travelled to Oxford, a few matriculating as members of the University, others joining in early or middle career, attracted by the collegiate life, academic initiatives, the Church of England, or a combination of all three. Guests and hosts alike shared in the common culture of eighteenth-century elites, rooted in antiquity and enriched in the Renaissance, a culture that had endured and whose public uses were valued. The chapter also examines imperial connections that linked Oxford to British North America, and the ways in which the Anglo-Hanoverian union provided an important transnational framework for scholarly exchanges.

The final, twelfth chapter is focused on the varied interaction of Oxford graduates with each other and with outsiders through kinship, friendship, and inter-marriage that helps explain the enduring centrality and exceptional leverage of the University in national life. In doing so it rejects the contention (made with Cambridge foremost in mind) that 'the values and intellectual presuppositions of the laity and clergy had so far diverged that universities were commonly regarded as of little value to anyone not intending to embark on a clerical career'.[16] The Beaufort family and the Newdigate/Bagot/Dolben nexus are used to present a different emphasis. Patronage and brokerage are central to the discussion but there were important, non-contractual dimensions operative within this range of networks, those, for instance, that drew on collegiate loyalties as a means of extracting funding to the benefit of Oxford institutions. Fond memories of past associations were likely to be stimulated through social gatherings in London and

---

[14] D. Levitin, *Ancient wisdom in the age of the new science: histories of philosophy in England, c.1640–1700* (Cambridge, 2016).

[15] *Anecdotes of the life of Richard Watson* (London, 1817), 398.

[16] John Gascoigne, *Cambridge in the age of the Enlightenment. Science, religion and politics from the Restoration to the French Revolution* (Cambridge, 1989), 17.

INTRODUCTION   11

the major provincial centres, and such events tended to develop more formally in the course of the century. The chapter also shows how old college connections could bring clergy, otherwise frequently intellectually isolated in rural settings, into contact with each other, from which contact could flow political encouragement, literary creativity, or just enjoyable sociability. For clergy with an Oxford degree, the ultimate sign of their institutional loyalty was to leave to their college or to the whole University a bequest. The sums they could offer tended to be small. The biggest donors tended to come from the laity: the lawyers, the physicians, the gentry, and the nobility, those with cash or chattels to spare or no expectant heir apparent ready to contest any windfall outside the family. Benefactions conferred a sort of immortality, functioned at a level of mutual recognition and the discharge of obligation. Perhaps, above all, they were a token of goodwill and an indicator of contented Oxford memories founded on friendships that had lasted a lifetime, a remittance intended to foster the same sentiments in succeeding generations.

This book insistently emphasises that the University of Oxford was not condemned to marginality in eighteenth-century national and international life because of its apparent reluctance to introduce a modernising curriculum,[17] launch innovative scholarly initiatives, or endorse progressive politics of the kind historians have hailed in some other contemporary British universities. Whatever the degree of corporate inertia found in the University (and few other components of Hanoverian institutional life were immune to that), there was plenty of internal scope for members inclined to be pedagogically creative, to open new research lines, and to be unapologetic Whigs. For if Oxford was a seat of learning rooted in its past—and with an increasing antiquarian awareness of its inheritance—yet it had a capacity for adaptation to an unsuspected degree, with a scope for intellectual and political pluralism that should not be underestimated.[18] We should not therefore fight shy of locating many aspects of University life down the century within what has recently been called 'the Anglican Enlightenment'.[19] It was an enlightenment, as J. G. A. Pocock once put it, 'designed in the defence of

---

[17] For the limited value of examining universities primarily from the perspective of adaptation or non-adaptation to 'modernity' see the essays in eds. F. Cadilhon, J. Mondot, and J. Verger, *Universités et institutions universitaires européennes au XVIIIe siècle: entre modernisation et tradition* (Talence, 1999).

[18] See, for instance, the revised edition of Wood's *The history & antiquities of the University of Oxford and of the colleges and halls* (2 vols., Oxford, 1786–90) by the antiquary John Gutch (1746–1831), also his *History of the University of Oxford* (3 vols., 1792–6). He was Chaplain of Corpus Christi College, 1787–92, Registrar of the University, 1797–1824. Thomas Fowler, *The history of Corpus Christi College* (Oxford, 1893), 304. Rev. Sir John Peshall [or Pechell] (1718–78) *The history of the University of Oxford, to the death of William the Conqueror* (Oxford, 1772).

[19] W. J. Bulman, *Anglican Enlightenment. Orientalism, religion and politics in England and its empire, 1648–1715* (Cambridge, 2015). See also the essential B. W. Young, *Religion and Enlightenment in eighteenth-century England: theological debate from Locke to Burke* (Oxford, 1998).

the magisterial and clerical elites against the claims of the spirit; designed, ... in the defence of law against grace.'[20]

But while one should not underestimate the range of values transmitted to the future graduates of the University (or the scope for extensive cultural outreach they took away from the University with them), Oxford majority opinion at any given time was entirely committed to guarding and protecting the national Church and defeating the cultural and religious alternatives on offer. And it did so successfully, resourcefully, and variously, ensuring a neo-hegemony that endured and offered stability decade after decade. The means, if not the end, were entirely compatible with 'enlightenment', and policed rather than negated existing measures of toleration. What Oxford did less well consistently was to protect the state, despite being so foundational to it as a profoundly royalist entity. The ultimate collective good in the state had to be the protection of the constitution, which was why Oxford, in its inability to align itself comfortably and collectively with the post-Revolution order for decades after its establishment, was at best an unstable, at worst a destabilising presence in the polity. If a narrative of overwhelming, even traitorous Tory domination was partly the construction of its enemies beyond the gates, it was only once loyalty could be aligned with the reigning dynasty without qualification—as it was after c.1760—that the University created the conditions for its own potential flourishing and maximising its influence across the whole country.

---

[20] 'Conservative enlightenment and democratic revolutions: the American and French cases in British perspective', *Government & Opposition*, 24 (1989), 80–105, at 85.

1

Fame, form, and function

The University's place and purpose in the long eighteenth century

OXFORD we know has for some time been used as a term of reproach, and become a byeword among many. Pamphlets have been designedly written, and measures industriously pursued, to lessen her credit.

The Student, or the Oxford Monthly Miscellany (1750), i. 5.

Oxford and Cambridge may be justly considered not only as venerable monuments of antient times, but as a kind of garrisons established by public authority, for the preservation of loyalty, literature, and religion....Take away these memorials of antiquity, those noble and royal testimonies of respect to sanctity of life, and proficiency in learning,...and you weaken one of the great pillars, by which the constitution and spirit of England is supported and perpetuated

[William Thomson], *A Tour in England and Scotland, in 1785/By an English gentleman* (London, 1788), 3–4.

The whole University since I left it had received considerable Alterations. Every College seems to have endeavoured to out-do its neighbours, either in the neatness or magnificence of its buildings.

The Englishman, 19–22 Dec. 1713.

I

Oxford's cultural status within the eighteenth-century polity and its importance—for good or bad—in elite formation was universally acknowledged, conceded even by those. who deprecated its royalist politics, condemned its apparently unprogressive academic curriculum, and rued the confessional blinkers of the men in holy orders who largely staffed it. They were the ones prepared to note how different things were in Cambridge or point out the dynamism of Oxford's Scottish counterparts by the second half of the century. Those voices need to be heard in any assessment of Oxford's national impact, and they are here—both insiders and outsiders—for they backhandedly articulate the sense that whatever

Enlightened Oxford: The University and the Cultural and Political Life of Eighteenth-century Britain and Beyond.
Nigel Aston, Oxford University Press. © Nigel Aston 2023. DOI: 10.1093/oso/9780199246830.003.0002

14 ENLIGHTENED OXFORD

was going on inside Oxford mattered to the world outside: here was an institution
was setting the national tone for the next generation while underpinning the
workings of Church and state or, in the case of the latter between 1714 and 1760,
appearing to undermine it. What happened at Oxford then mattered a great deal
to the rest of the country in terms of cultural and political well-being and
coherence of the whole polity, and therefore the tension that existed for so long
between the post-Revolution Whig state and the majority voice in Oxford was a
cause of vexation and anxiety on both sides. However much early Hanoverian
ministers might attempt to marginalise it, the University's national and international fame acquired over many centuries ensured that it could never be
ignored. That indefatigable author and controversialist, William Warburton,
never ceased to score points on behalf of his Cambridge friends, but even he
could not but (almost) concede in 1754 that Oxford was '...that Athens of loyalty
and learning'. And then, with characteristic archness noted: 'It is hard to say if
Church or State be at present more benefitted by it. For I think the fashionable
divinity of Hutchinson is well matched by the fashionable politics of Filmar [sic].
It is hard to say which has least sense, or more properly the most nonsense. But it
is certain Wiggs [sic] and rational divines are at present the horror of that
renowned university'.[1] Warburton's amusement was exaggerated but it disclosed
an anxiety born of a sense that Oxford's predilection for backward-looking politics
and divinity was both misplaced and more widely destabilising.

This contested celebrity, and Oxford's assured location within the British state
and the international world of letters, has generated surprisingly little scholarly
assessment.[2] By contrast, John Gascoigne thirty years ago produced a critically
acclaimed study of Cambridge that illustrated the power of what he called
'the holy alliance' of Anglicanism and Newtonian science in the period
c.1688–1760, of what, he argued, amounted to a classic manifestation of the
'English Enlightenment'. But far from neglecting wider contexts, *Cambridge in
the age of the Enlightenment* was essentially inward-looking in its treatment of
the University's academic and political activity.[3] One reason for this neglect
of Oxford may be the persuasion that (symptomatic of the search for traces of
Enlightenment trends and tendencies that has dominated late twentieth and early
twenty-first century scholarship), the University stood at a remove that mirrored
its intellectual stagnation,[4] one confirmed by its being less popular and less

---

[1] Warburton to Hon. Charles Yorke, 24 Aug. 1754, BL Egerton MS 1952, f. 35.

[2] J. C. D. Clark has noted that while eighteenth-century English Roman Catholics and the
universities have been largely rehabilitated, Oxford 'has been less well served'. 'Secularization and
modernization: the failure of a "grand narrative"', *HJ*, 55 (2012), 161–94, 186n.

[3] For Cambridge over a longer period see Victor Morgan [with a contribution by C. Brooke],
A history of the University of Cambridge, Vol. 2, 1546-1750 (Cambridge, 2004), and Peter Searby,
A History of the University of Cambridge, Vol. 3: *1750-1870* (Cambridge, 1997).

[4] J. C. D. Clark, regretting the lack of studies of intellectual culture at Oxford and Cambridge in the
early eighteenth century, pointedly observed that '...much of the torpor which seems evident in

populated than previously. Thus in the era of Warburton's regressive castigation, between 1750 and 1759, it has been calculated that only 182 students matriculated at Oxford.[5] There are local reasons behind the mid-century decline in student numbers, but it should not be forgotten that this pattern was a common European phenomenon rather than one peculiar to Oxford, what Jonathan Israel has chosen dramatically to call 'the deepest and most prolonged crisis' in the history of European universities after c.1650.[6] And it has triggered any number of denunciations from a late twentieth-century professoriate committed to a modernising teleology and only too ready to link inadequate recruitment with a faltering intellectual progressiveness. As Notker Hammerstein wrote:[7]

> Insufficient enlightenment, entrenched attitudes, secluded intellectualism and *vis inertiae* were in the eighteenth century enemies of the university in many places, for example, in France, England and Italy, and to some extent also on the Iberian peninsula.

Hammerstein is typical of many in losing no opportunity of insisting that the majority of eighteenth-century universities were 'isolated from the intellectual life of leading figures in the country', and the English universities—'the narrow, somewhat provincial institutions of Oxbridge...' offer any number of opportunities for exaggerated contrasts with their Scottish counterparts.[8] It should hardly need saying that a temporary decline in student numbers is no necessary indicator of a decline in intellectual vitality (whatever the criteria for charting it) let alone national influence per se. Such judgements fail to register the constantly evolving character of eighteenth-century cultural life (and the place of the ancient universities within it), are deaf to the subtle intertwining of 'progressive' with transmitted learning at a university like Oxford, underestimate the dynamic power and capacity for reinvention of some of the traditional elements within the curriculum

---

retrospect reflects only the irrelevance of the pre-occupations of the late-scholastic mind to subsequent problems'. *English Society 1688–1832. Ideology, social structure and political practice during the ancien regime* (1st edn., Cambridge, 1985), 152.

[5] Maria Rosa di Simone, 'Admission', in eds. W. Rüegg and H. de Ridder-Symoens, *A history of the university in Europe*, Vol. 2, *Universities in early modern Europe, 1500–1800* (Cambridge, 1995), 285–325, at 302. For a rough calculation of numbers in colleges in 1759 see OUA: WPa/22/1/30. See also L. Stone, 'The Size and composition of the Oxford student body 1580–1909', in eds. Lawrence Stone at al., *The University in Society*, Vol. 1: *Oxford and Cambridge from the 14th to the early 19th Century* (Princeton, 1974), 3–110.

[6] J. Israel, *Radical Enlightenment. Philosophy and the making of modernity 1650–1750* (Oxford, 2001), 128. For the decline of universities in early eighteenth-century Europe see R. Chartier and J. Revel, 'Université et société dans l'Europe modern: position des problèmes', *Revue d'histoire moderne et contemporaine*, 25 (1978), 353–74; R. Chartier, 'Student populations in the eighteenth century', *BJECS*, 2 (1979), 150–62.

[7] N. Hammerstein,'Relations with authority', in eds. Rüegg and Ridder-Symoens, *Universities in early modern Europe*, 114–53, 123.

[8] Ibid., 137, 140.

16 ENLIGHTENED OXFORD

and, above all, ignore the role of 'unreformed' Oxford (and Cambridge) as loci for the nourishing of the Established Church, the cultural maturation of the social elite, and the defence of the constitution. These dimensions were not, *pace* Maria Rosa di Simone, signs of a 'decadent condition',[9] but central to the role of the English Universities in this era when they were as much constitutional adjuncts as academic institutes.

Those who contested those objectives were understandably uncomfortable with and critical of Oxford's enduring national and international prominence, and obliged to reckon with the weight of the University's fame and breadth of its connections in any attempt to lessen its status or correct its assured *raison d'être*. For Oxford was an institution that, like most others in eighteenth-century Europe looked to history—and its own corporate history in particular—for justification of its contemporary standing, just as did its constituent parts. The University appeared well-protected in a society where precedent was universally presumed to possess a determining force in law, and which was respectful of the continuities evident in Oxford's official past that had given it an extraordinary temporal span of seven centuries (or more, if one reckoned—as most did—that King Alfred was the founder of University College).[10] To its contemporary critics, this longevity could be presented as masking hidebound, antiquated, restrictive, and above all non-progressive practices and procedures that were *démodé*, out of place in an ever more enlightened society. The bibliographer, Thomas Frognall Dibdin (1776–1847, matric. SJC), spoke for many when he recalled how:[11]

> The University partook of... distressing somnolency. There seemed to be no spur to emulation and to excellence. Whatever was done, was to be done only by means of private energy and enthusiasm. The statutes were at that time [end of the eighteenth century] a sort of *caput mortuum*; and yet the members of the University were taught to view and to estimate them as the ancient Roman was taught to look upon the Rubicon, the sacred boundary of his confine – .

Dibdin here represents the classic retrospective view of Oxford as seen from the reforming decade of the 1830s, one that fails to register the scale of pedagogic creativity possible within the Laudian statutes of 1636, for instance, David Gregory's overhaul of the mathematics and sciences curriculum early in the eighteenth century, and William Blackstone's legal advice that allowed the

---

[9] 'Admission', 303; cf. Jonathan Israel, who sees the primary challenge for Europe's universities as finding 'the resources with which to transform them into larger, more diversified, and better funded institutions reflecting the changing requirements and expanding horizons of Early Enlightenment Society'. *Radical Enlightenment*, 129.

[10] For the lawsuit of the 1720s concerning this received notion see Robin Darwall-Smith, *Univ. A history of University College Oxford* (Oxford, 2008), esp. 37–40, 56–7, 251–7, 260–1.

[11] Thomas Frognall Dibdin, *Reminiscences of A Literary Life* (London, 2 vols., 1836), I. 92–3.

University to be bolder in interpreting and even modifying the 1636 code. Opportunities to study science at Oxford were more considerable than commonly recognised, and many students debated scientific questions.[12] Indeed, it has been estimated that Oxford trained thirty-four per cent of all English pioneers of science in the eighteenth century (excluding medics and technicians by definition).[13] Yet a balanced view of eighteenth-century Oxford was increasingly hard to find by the reign of William IV with a reaction against the 'torpor' of unreformed institutions in full spate and the University was predictably found wanting on most counts, particularly the allegedly atrophied state of its intellectual life.[14] With the foundation of new English universities at London and Durham and the model of the German research-orientated university commending itself,[15] 'traditional' Oxford appeared an easy target for early Victorian detraction by outsiders—and its own graduates. From inside the Catholic University of Ireland, John Henry Newman thus used his essay 'The Mission of Saint Benedict' (1858) to set up a comparison between the vast quantity of learned publications generated by the eighteenth-century French Benedictines with the meagre deliveries of his own university in the same period, to the disadvantage of the latter.[16] Newman exaggerated the gap between the Oxonians and the Maurist Benedictines, but such criticisms tell us little about eighteenth-century Oxford, and a great deal about the different educational values of succeeding generations and their consistent conviction that theirs were superior and to be deployed in judgement against their predecessors.[17]

Oxford in the 1830s found itself on the front line against a Whig ministry with a parliamentary majority intent on delivering far-reaching corporate reform in State and Church that had major implications for the University's view of its role, values, mission, government and, above all, its relation to the other major institutions in British public life. And the 'Oxford Movement' that began in that decade was, in large part, a defensive reaction to this challenge that would in itself

---

[12] R .G. Frank, 'Science, medicine and the universities of early modern england: background and sources. Part 1', *History of Science*, 11 (1973), 194–216. Details of the 1636 statutes are in John Griffiths, *The Statutes of the University of Oxford codified in the year 1636* (Oxford, 1888).

[13] N. Hans, *New trends in education in the eighteenth century* (London, 1951), 53.

[14] See W. R. Ward, *Victorian Oxford* (London, 1965); A. Burns and J. Innes, eds., *Rethinking the age of reform: Britain 1780–1850* (Cambridge, 2007). There is little per se on university reform in this last volume or on Oxford but see Arthur Burns, 'English "church reform" revisited, 1780-1840', 136–62).

[15] William Clark, *Academic Charisma and the Origins of the Research University* (Chicago, 2006).

[16] Newman also argued that '...the Colleges in the English Universities may be considered in matter of fact to be the lineal descendants or heirs of the Benedictine schools of Charlemagne'. 'The Benedictine Schools' in *Atlantis*, Jan. 1859. *Travailler à la bénédictine* had become an idiom for undertaking an arduous intellectual task in the later eighteenth century. For the erudite scholarship of the Congregation of Saint-Maur see J. McManners, *Church and Society in Eighteenth-Century France*. Vol. 1: *The Clerical Establishment and its Social ramifications* (Oxford, 1998), 524, 528, 594–600.

[17] For the wider background, B. W. Young, *The Victorian eighteenth century: an intellectual history* (Oxford, 2007).

18 ENLIGHTENED OXFORD

generate a revisionist understanding of the national Church's past (including the pre-Reformation era and, by extension therefore, the University's).[18] Oxford was very used to governmental pressures and those emanating from the administrations of Lords Grey (1830–4) and Melbourne (1834–41) (both products of Trinity College, Cambridge) were arguably not too dissimilar from those facing the University at most junctures in its past. This book's starting point is the Revolution of 1688–9 that refashioned the constitutional understanding of the monarchy along Whiggish lines and broke the hereditary line of succession, actions that obliged the University to rethink its understanding of *iure divino* sovereignty, what it understood by loyalty, and the associated values that had made it the rock and refuge of Charles I during the Civil Wars of the 1640s. Oxford made this adjustment with difficulty, over three generations in fact, so that the overlap between Crown and monarchy was only completely renewed with the accession of George III in 1760. What made the 'abdication' of James II acceptable to the vast majority of University members in 1688–9 was that it lifted the threat to royal violation of its statutes and the intrusion of Roman Catholics into high academic office, and appeared to protect the laws enshrining the supremacy of the Established Church. But relief soon gave way to fresh anxieties as the oaths demanded of the new Williamite regime were unacceptable to about 500 clergy nationally and the nonjuring schism began, depriving the Church of a swathe of its senior leadership cadre, threatening the sacramental Anglicanism the University so much valued, and increasing the allure of Jacobitism for Tory Oxonians, one that remained, to varying degrees, undimmed until the last years of George II in the 1750s.

Of course, there was a vocal, increasingly influential Whig minority in Oxford that immediately qualifies any characterisation of it as a 'Tory University'. Like every institution in the decades after the Revolution, it was caught up in factional strife that necessarily had an impact on academic life (though one should not assume an inevitably negative one). And the fact remains that while a majority in the University could just about admit that the rule of the first two Georges after 1714 as provided for by the Act of Succession 1701 was 'lawful', that it was 'rightful' was another matter. As the law required, all Oxford undergraduates took the oaths that were a condition of entry to the University; how far they dissimulated or mentally qualified their words remains an open question unlikely of final resolution.[19] Which was why the reign of the last of the legitimate Stuarts,

---

[18] P. B. Nockles, 'A disputed legacy: Anglican historiographies of the Reformation from the era of the Caroline divines to that of the Oxford Movement', *BJRL* 83 (2001), 121–67. More generally, Nockles, *The Oxford Movement in context: Anglican High Churchmanship 1760-1857* (Cambridge, 1996). Thus when a widely supported scheme to erect a martyrs' memorial in Oxford was proposed in 1838, Newman and Keble refused to contribute on the ground of their 'view of history'. Nockles, 'A disputed legacy', 132.

[19] Discussed in J. C. D. Clark, *Samuel Johnson, Literature, religion and English cultural politics from the Restoration to Romanticism* (Cambridge, 1994), 89–99.

Queen Anne (1702–14), featured retrospectively as such a refreshing interlude from the vantage point of the Tory wastelands that followed after her death. Thereafter ministerial pressure and interference could be blatant, especially when the Jacobite threat appeared acute, as it did c.1715 and c.1745, and there were plenty of Oxford Whigs and fellow travellers only too willing to stoke the flames of discontent and encourage these interventions; the University's inclinations to Jacobitism made its politics suspect, and the threat of a government-led internal reordering was acute during the late 1710s and late 1740s. It was a backhanded admission that Oxford was simply too important nationally to be allowed to have a political agenda that diverged so significantly from Cambridge's and the Walpole/Pelhamite ascendancy.

After 1760 the tensions between ministers and dons on dynastic grounds disappeared. Instead, such contestation as there was became primarily ecclesiological as pressures mounted externally for an increase in the civil rights of dissenters and Roman Catholics deemed to threaten the legal privileges of the Church of England and, by extension, Oxford's. In 1772–3 Oxford men in Parliament and pamphlets fought hard to stop the dissenters ending subscription to the Thirty-Nine Articles as a legal qualification for office. They succeeded, but subsequently had to concede the less extensive Dissenters' Relief Act 1779 that was, gallingly, supported by the University's Chancellor, the Prime Minister, Lord North. After seeing off successive initiatives between 1787 and 1790 to repeal the Test Acts, the coming of the French Revolution ended parliamentary attempts to legislate for dilution of Anglican privileges, while any number of Oxford graduates lent their voice and/or their pen to the defence of the British constitutional status quo against French republican institutions and beliefs.[20] The turn of the nineteenth century might well be seen as the finest hour of the *ancien régime* University, articulating an intelligent loyalism based on religion that struck a national chord, while displaying a capacity for formulating a response to the arguments of the progressive Whig minority.[21] And, if there was some relief in academic quarters that complete Catholic Emancipation had not formed part of the 1800 Act of Union with Ireland, the capacity of the University to bring in curriculum reforms and other changes while the war with France continued demonstrated that adaptation and improvement generated from within were

[20] For a classic if quite extreme statement see Edward Tatham, *A Sermon Suitable to the Times* (London, 1792). For Convocation in 1792 publishing an address praising Pitt's proclamation against seditious meetings see Bodl. MS Top. Oxon. C. 296, f.7.

[21] For the wider picture see Robert Hole, *Pulpits, Politics and Public Order in England 1760–1832* (Cambridge, 1989), esp. 109–44, 160–73; Hole, 'English sermons and tracts as media of debate on the French Revolution 1789–99', in ed. M. Philp, *The French Revolution and British Popular Politics* (Cambridge, 1991), 18–37. John Dinwiddy argues in the same collection that it was evangelical religion that did most to counter political radicalism in that decade. 'Interpretations of Anti-Jacobinism', 38–49, at 46. Within Oxford evangelicals were a relatively small presence.

20 ENLIGHTENED OXFORD

always a possibility.[22] If Oxford University was infamous according to Whig opinion for the first half of the eighteenth century because of its perceived disloyalty to the monarchy, then it was precisely because of its loyalty to the same institution, at once strident and subtle, that gave it that character for progressive commentators during the era of the American and French Revolutions.

II

> Mrs FOLIO said, that the Radcliff was a good deal like St Paul's, only not half so large or so handsome. A queer sort of building, Ma'am, said young Bonus, - a mere pepper-box,—and there,—(pointing to the turrets of All Souls) there are the sugar-casters.
>
> Terrae-Filius. No. 3, July 7, 1763, 251, in George Colman,
> Prose on Several Occasions; Accompanied with Some
> Pieces in Verse (3 vols., London, 1787), I. 251.

Organisational alterations within the University's established collegiate structures figured rather less in its eighteenth-century development than during previous eras in its history but they certainly occurred. The most obvious sign of change was the creation of new colleges, notably Worcester College in 1714, thanks to a generous personal gift.[23]

Significantly, it was a private bequest rather than a strategically driven corporate initiative, one that colonised existing buildings on the western side of the town and incorporated a private Hall. For the University remained a decentralised, fissiparous entity, proud of its institutional independence, but also protective to and respectful of the independent foundations which made it up. As one Scottish Oxford student considered it in 1772, the University was:

> a great Body consisting of several distinct members; or if we may compare it to so great a Thing I think our State is in some Degree similar to that of Greece in times of old. Thus we may suppose each College to represent a Statea as Athens or Sparta ... [and they answer] ... to the Council of the Amphictyons as we have our Vice-Chancellor ...[24]

---

[22] For the argument that growing tension between undergraduates and tutors influenced the nature and timing of reform at Oxford after c.1800 see Heather Ellis, *Generational Conflict and University Reform. Oxford in the Age of Revolution* (Leiden, Boston, MA, 2012), 5, 7.

[23] Discussed in Chapter 12.

[24] Sir David Carnegie to John Mackenzie, Ch. Ch., 20 Feb. 1772, NLS MS 1248 f. 82, Delvine Papers [Earl of Southesk]. Carnegie (1753–1805), 4th Bt., the *de jure* 7th Earl of Southesk, as a St. Andrews graduate, was well-placed to sense the distinctive structures of Oxford. (The Amphictyons were a league of neighbours arranged among the ancient Greek tribes).

All of which made planning and control by the Vice-Chancellor and senior University officers at moments of public tension, such as the last years of Queen Anne's reign and the '45 Rebellion, difficult to manage, for the varied collegiate political traditions and in-house loyalties of individual establishments made it impossible to achieve a meaningful Oxonian consensus. Unanimity was exceptional, being most nearly achieved in the 1790s and 1800s when the French Revolution appeared to endanger the survival of the national constitution, and by implication the role and purpose of the ancient English universities. In its resistance to centrifugalism, in its spirit of independency on display so noticeably during the first half of the century, Oxford was thus generally reflective of institutional behavioural patterns within the British polity as a whole during 'the long eighteenth century'.

The majority of the Oxford student body made up the future governing elite in Church and state within that polity and the primary socialising function of the University was to fashion their formation and facilitate their friendships. It prepared them for a life of privilege combined with responsibility (they tended to sit together) and did, to varying degrees, its best to complete their education. Oxford was not, at least in its make-up, a cosmopolitan society, but overwhelmingly English in its composition. It has been estimated that in 1735 only three per cent of students were from outside England and Wales, while Irish numbers only reached two to five per cent by the end of the century.[25] In its hegemonic Anglocentricity, Oxford shared in an internationalist diminution that other European higher educational foundations incurred, reflective of deep-rooted confessional divisions that countervailing 'enlightened' influences within the contemporary culture were too weak to overthrow.[26] One should nevertheless be cautious to conclude from this lack of student diversity that Oxford was closed off or necessarily narrow in its exposure to new cultural trends or presences from beyond Britain.

The rumbustious and varied character of social life in eighteenth-century Oxford has been extensively treated and is essentially peripheral to this book.[27] In its sheer variety, it was again reflective of the varying tastes and interests, recreational and educational, of younger members of the propertied elite, and those who aspired to join it.[28] Their schooling had given them the necessary Latin

---

[25] H. Perraton, *A History of foreign students in Britain* (Basingstoke, 2014), 28; Stone, 'Size and composition of the Oxford student body', 68. Irish numbers matriculating at Oxford had been slightly higher earlier in the century. Of ninety-nine active Irish peers 1692–1727, twelve attended Oxford, sixteen Trinity College, Dublin, and only three Cambridge. The comparable figures for 1761–82 are nine at Oxford, twenty-two at TCD, and three at Cambridge. F. G. James, *Lords of the Ascendancy. The Irish House of Lords and its Members, 1600–1800* (Dublin, 1995), 124. See the discussion in Chapter 9.

[26] Brockliss (2), 133, refers to universities as 'confessionally closed'.

[27] Most notably Graham Midgley, *University life in eighteenth-century Oxford* (New Haven and London, 1996).

[28] One should be cautious about over-emphasising social exclusivity. Critics of Oxford may have been too impressed by a perceived 'influx of idle and wealthy students'. Hans, *New Trends in Education*, 53.

Fig. 1.1 Map of Oxford, William Faden, 1789 (Oxfordshire County Council—Oxfordshire History Centre).

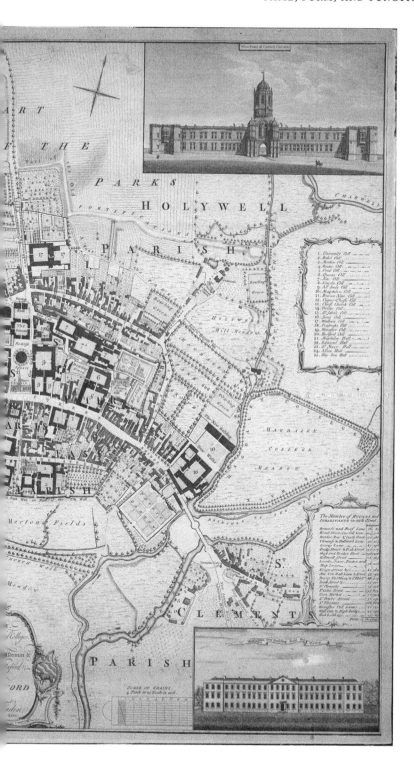

24   ENLIGHTENED OXFORD

to benefit from formal lectures and academic disputations. In collegiate Oxford, tutorial activity was left to the colleges, which were, despite all rumours to the contrary, increasingly diligent in discharging it. At Queen's College, the young don George Fothergill (future Principal of St Edmund Hall) in 1727 wrote home to his family in Westmorland entirely convinced of the efforts he was making to impart knowledge to his charges:

> I sometimes think that Providence may make use of my poor endeavours in this place for the instruction of youth, or some other means for being useful in my generation.
>
> He went on to say that it was undoubted that 'the value of a Liberal education is so great, as to counterbalance a great many difficulties'.[29]

Fothergill appreciated the value of an Oxford education. Of course, from the tutee's perspective, it could appear all too onerous, or, as it was conventionally but poetically rendered:[30]

> At twelve our tutors give the stern command/And each proud chief convenes his subject band;/Then conscious learning puts on all its pride,/And each new frown, each haughty look is tried;/Here musty books with all the dull parade/Of tedious forms before our eyes are laid,...

In fact, most students had considerable time on their hands and, within limits, were left to their own devices. To quote Sir David Carnegie once more, 'In short one may study as much [as one wishes], or be as idle as [one] please[s]'.[31] Parents and guardians gave their sons and charges directions, urged their tutors to monitor their studying, but the students were always ready to send back an account of their activities that was most likely to meet with approval. There were any number of Oxford undergraduate narratives on which to draw, as Walter Stanhope candidly admitted writing home to his mother:[32]

> As to your demand upon me for ye real picture of a College life, do but reverse that I gave you in my last, and it will come pretty near ye Truth: As instead of

---

[29] George Fothergill to his parents, Queen's College, 2 May 1727, Cumbria Record Office (Kendal), WDX 94/acc. 165.

[30] 'Familiar Epistle from an Oxonian to Lady Miller 'on 'A College Life', quoted in Henry Skine, Common Place Book, 42, 24 Nov. 1780, Beinecke Rare Book and Manuscript Library, Osborn Shelves, c509.

[31] Carnegie to John Mackenzie, 31 Dec. 1771, NLS, MS 1248 f. 80, Delvine Papers. For a complaint from Wales that those at Oxford for social not intellectual improvement were damaging it and were 'scholars only in masquerade', see Penrice & Margam MSS, NLW, L 897.

[32] Walter Stanhope to Mrs Ann Stanhope, 14 Mar 1768, Spencer-Stanhope MSS, West Yorkshire Archive Service [hereafter WYRO], (Bradford), Sp/St/6/1/74.

French dishes, & high sauces, a wholesome repast season'd with sententious Aphorisms; instead of Riot & idleness, hard study, or ye lesser accomplishments of drawing, fencing & c., ye exercise of walking, billiards, tennis, riding, rowing.

As Stanhope and any number of other contemporaries attest, urban social spaces outside University bounds were valued, none more so than the taverns and the coffee-houses.[33] There was no theatre in the city and visiting players had to make do with whatever theatrical spaces were available, usually in inns or their court-yards or in the town hall.[34] Performances and actors were monitored by the University authorities and what little drama there was at Oxford was usually attempted during the vacations. As late as 1733 companies had attempted to set up in the city but the authorities here were more successful in enforcing their prohibitions than Cambridge had been. Punitive authority over players was confirmed in the Universities Act, 1737 (10 Geo. II, chap. 19) and a further Act of 1788 banned strolling players performing without permission within fourteen miles of either English university.[35] Nevertheless, on occasion they were admitted, and their rarity value drew in town and gown together.[36] The celebrated Colley Cibber and the Drury Lane theatre company were prohibited from coming into Oxford in 1710, only to have the ban relaxed three years later.[37] They put on daily performances in the second half of June 1713 and all went well. Indeed, they had the thanks of the Vice Chancellor who was also pleased by 'the Decency, and Order, observ'd by our whole Society' during their three-week stay. The and the company reciprocated the goodwill by making a £50 donation towards the repair of St Mary's church.[38]

Student resort to inns and coffee-houses was habitual, especially in the early evening after dinner and before evening chapel.[39] Queen's Lane coffee-house was one of the first in England in the 1650s and it gave rise to a coffee-house culture significant in that it was not within the business-orientated metropolis that is

---

[33] R. Green, and G. Roberson, *Studies in Oxford History, chiefly in the Eighteenth Century*, ed. C. L. Stainer [OHS, 51] (Oxford, 1901), 31–5.

[34] At the end of the eighteenth century, Oxford theatricals were staged in 'The Raquet Court Blue Boar Lane—entrance to Box & pit thro Blue Boar Inn'. The Blue Boar Inn closed in 1818. James Winston (the co-manager of Covent Garden from the early 1800s), Ms for his *Theatric Tourist* (1803), Ms Harvard Theatre Collection TS 1335.211, f.8. Thanks to David Worrall for this information.

[35] See the Vice-Chancellor to the Mayor & Corporation of Woodstock, 21 Apr 1793, John Wills's Letter book. Balliol College Archives and Manuscripts, Jenkyns V.IA LL(2), f. 24.

[36] There was some academic interest inside the University on the theatre. Thomas Hawkins (?1728/9–72), chaplain at Magdalen College from 1754, produced *The Origin of the English Drama, Illustrated... by specimens from our earliest writers...*, which appeared posthumously in 1773.

[37] Midgley, *University Life*, 131. See also Chapter 10, p. 118.

[38] S. Rosenfeld, 'Some notes on the players in Oxford 1661-1713', *Review of English Studies*, 19 (1943), 366–75, esp. 372–4. Around the time of the 1733 Act they were allowed to perform nowhere nearer to Oxford than Abingdon.

[39] Fairer, 'Oxford and the literary world', in HUO V, 779–805, at 793, for details of the coffee-houses and taverns in the city,

26 ENLIGHTENED OXFORD

generally assumed to be the dominant model but in an academic community, Oxford.[40] Every college and hall had its favourite: Wadham men, for instance, went to Bagg's coffee-house on the corner of Holywell every afternoon till Warden Wills's time in the 1790s.[41] In such establishments they met contemporaries from other colleges, refined their pattern of interaction with women (by definition, non-Oxonians) and their male social inferiors, and discussed rather than roistered.[42] There could be a definite academic dimension to Oxford coffee-houses: the antiquarian George Ballard, one of eight clerks at Magdalen College from 1750, could have been found displaying his manuscripts and coins at Clement's Coffee House in Oxford two years previously.[43] Most students and young Fellows used coffee-houses to discover what was happening in the world beyond the University into which most would in due course go; news from family connections and university gossip could be picked up and further filtered by reports and rumour in the press that allowed students to look outwards. One young poetaster thus summarised the addiction of many students to the politics of the day:[44]

> Now crowds to yonder coffee-house repair,/And plan the business of the nation there,/There o'er the vast Atlantic stretch then sail,/And our lost Colonies distress bewail,/Weigh in one scale the Russian & the Turk,/The speech of Mansfield, & the joke of Burke.

These spaces afforded an acceptable opportunity to supplement the otherwise largely homosocial world that Oxford residence required and was certainly not reflective of life afterwards.[45] After graduation and movement into public life, the politically ambitious could be involved nationally and locally at first hand, and would move away from Oxford. But the most socially illustrious products of the University could often be reluctant to stop thinking that if perhaps they had lost their purchase over the college rooms they had occupied while in residence, they possessed residual rights of resort and nomination that the College was bound to

---

[40] Aytoun Ellis, *The penny universities: a history of the coffee houses* (London, 1956), 18. There were approximately thirteen in Oxford *c.*1740 and about twenty in 1800. eds. C. and E. Hibbert, *Encyclopedia of Oxford* (London, 1988), 97.

[41] Joseph Wells, *Wadham College* (Oxford, 1898), 151.

[42] Sheldon Rothblatt, *The Modern University and its Discontents. The Fate of Newman's Legacies in Britain and America* (Cambridge, 1997), 111–12.

[43] Sarah Markham, *John Loveday of Caversham 1711–1789. The Life and Tours of an Eighteenth-Century Onlooker* (Salisbury, 1984), 378. The joke about taverns and coffee-houses being libraries (with journals, gazettes, directories, credit ledgers) was developed in [T. Warton], *A Companion to the Guide and a Guide to the Companion: being a complete supplement to all accounts of Oxford hitherto published...* (3rd edn., London, 1762?), 10–13.

[44] 'Familiar Epistle from an Oxonian to Lady Miller', 43.

[45] It was dons rather than students, for the most part officially celibate while holding a fellowship, who were more likely to court scandal through homosexual activity. For sodomy involving clerics at Wadham see C. S. L. Davies, 'Problems of reform in eighteenth-century Oxford: the case of George Wyndham, Warden of Wadham, 1744–77, *Oxoniensia*, 79 (2014), 61–75, at 62–4.

FAME, FORM, AND FUNCTION 27

honour. Thus the twenty-six year old 3rd duke of Portland (a future Chancellor of the University), a Pelhamite Whig, instructed his former tutor at Christ Church, Edward Smallwell, to stand up for his rights and Smallwell, by then his client, was pleased to do so. He reassured the duke:

> Upon representing your Grace's desire to continue in Possession of the Rooms you liv'd in College, & that Sir Matthew Ridley might live in them, the Dean consents to both... it seem'd to be a point you had much at heart, & as it still preserves you a member of Christ Church. It is presum'd, that none but Nobs [noblemen] and Gen[tlemen] Comm[oners]s will be admitted into those apartments, which are indeed too good for inferior characters.[46]

Christ Church was a grand college that could afford to gratify Portland's wishes because of the extensive building programme that it undertook at intervals through the century. Central to it was the construction of the avant-garde Palladian Peckwater quadrangle that was undertaken early in the century (it was largely completed between 1706 and 1714).[47] It increased the appeal of the House to elite families from dukes downwards on the basis that noblemen and gentlemen commoners would be housed in accommodation that, internally and externally, embodied the country house ideal and might make the college a nursery of future statesmen and men of taste.[48] Successive deans—Aldrich, Atterbury, and Smalridge—strove to raise funds for the project across a wider social basis than the peerage, for they intended that Peckwater should reflect the exalted pretensions of Christ Church, in which all its alumni would have a claim.[49] The quadrangle, when finished, was the last word in Palladian fashion and added

---

[46] Edward Smallwell to Portland, 16 Oct. 1764, Nottingham University Library, PWF8353. [Smallwell had also been tutor to Lord Edward Bentinck, the duke's younger brother].

[47] Curthoys (1), 122–5; W. G. Hiscock, *A Christ Church Miscellany: New Chapters on the Architects, Craftsmen, Statuary, Plate, Bells, Furniture, Clocks, Plays, the Library and Other Buildings* (Oxford, 1946), 40.

[48] Christ Church had consciously aimed to attract this exalted clientele during the deanship of Aldrich's predecessor, John Fell (1660–88), himself an exceptional builder whom Aldrich undoubtedly sought to emulate. Brian Young, *Christ Church 2010* (Oxford, 2011), 20. Young neatly summarises Peckwater's raison d'être: '... something in it of the Palladian English country house transmuted into the similarly domestic requirements of a college building; it demonstrates in stone the role that Aldrich saw to it that the college played throughout the eighteenth century: it was the supremely elegant finishing school for the nobility, in which not only the intellects but also the tastes of the governing classes would be greatly improved'. ibid., 21. Peckwater is further discussed in Chapter 12. The extent to which one can speak of a re-aristocratisation of the universities in eighteenth-century Europe is considered in Willem Frijoff, 'Graduation and Careers', in eds. Rüegg and Ridder-Symoens, *Universities in early modern Europe*, 355–416, at 392.

[49] Among the major benefactors were two royal physicians, Dr. Anthony Radcliffe and Sir Edward Hannes (d. 1710, Student of the House, Reader in Chemistry at Oxford from 1690, and physician to Queen Anne, 1702), as well as scions of great Tory ducal families such as Charles Somerset, marquess of Worcester (1660–98), who had married the daughter of Sir Josiah Childs, former governor of the East India Company. Thomas Salmon, *The Foreigner's Companion Through the Universities of Cambridge and Oxford, and the adjacent Counties* (London, 1748), 85.

Fig. 1.2 The North Prospect of the New Quadrangle [Peckwater] of Christs Church in Oxford (© Governing Body, Christ Church, Oxford).

significantly to the distinction of the University's built heritage that was central to its elevated sense of its identity and ensured its spatial dominance of an otherwise unexceptional small English city with a permanent population of 11,000 by 1770, a regional market centre known for its manufactured gloves, other leather goods, and cutlery.[50] Because of the University, Oxford was a primary site throughout the century for architectural virtuosity, even though only a percentage of the proposals were implemented.[51]

Several Oxford Heads of Houses were as architecturally ambitious as they were academically distinguished and contributed energetically and with distinction to what cumulatively amounted to a rebuilding of the university and, by extension, much of the urban fabric. None more so than the polymath Henry Aldrich, Dean of Christ Church from 1689 until 1710, and Palladian pioneer in the vein of Inigo Jones, who gave architecture an academic presence in Oxford, hitherto dominated

---

[50] q), 74–6, 181. The figure had risen to 12,000 people by 1801, one-tenth members of the University, a similar number associated with it. In 1700, the city's population had been slightly under 2,000. Brockliss (2), 159.

[51] For details see the individual entries under the colleges in eds. H.E. Salter and M.D. Lobel, *VCH Oxon.*, III., *The University of Oxford* (London, 1954); Howard Colvin, *Unbuilt Oxford* (New Haven, CT, 1983).

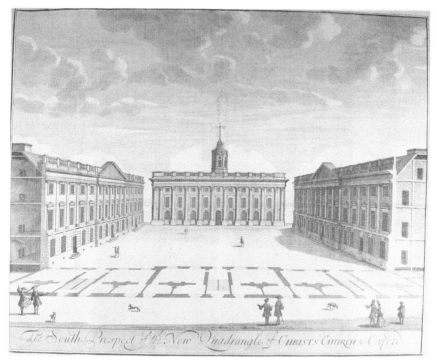

Fig. 1.3 The South Prospect of the New Quadrangle [Peckwater] of Christs Church in Oxford (© Governing Body, Christ Church, Oxford).

by books and music.[52] As well as a practitioner, Aldrich was a notable architectural theorist writing (originally in Latin) *Elementa architecturae* (translated into English in 1789 as *The Elements of Civil Architecture*), a tract whose purpose was to identify the rational origins of the elements of architecture in antiquity.[53] Aldrich did not confine his practice to his own college. He was probably, along with Provost Timothy Halton of Queen's (1632?–1704), primarily responsible for the light Baroque design of the Queen's College Library (1693–6),[54] and both men later worked together on the commission charged with rebuilding All Saints

---

[52] 'Henry Aldrich (1648–1710). An Oxford Universal Man', Exhibition 3 Nov. 2010 to 30 Jan. 2011, at Christ Church. Giles Worsley argued that there may have been 'political overtones' for Aldrich, as for Clarke subsequently, in 'their harking back to the style of early Stuarts...'. Worsley, *Classical Architecture in Britain: The Heroic Age* (New Haven, CT, 1995), 88.

[53] Ibid., 89–90. In the second book he included a selection of villas and palaces copied principally from Palladio and was hopeful that students might imitate them with advantage. As Philip Smyth, in his Introduction to his 1789 *Elements*, wrote: '[Aldrich was] An acute and accurate observer, a patient thinker, a deep and clever reasoner....That the vigour of his conceptions might be transmitted unimpaired by the exposition of them, he sought in a familiarity with classical elegance and propriety, the habit of exhibiting them with force and lustre...'

[54] G. Tyack, *Oxford. An architectural guide* (Oxford, 1998), 139.

Fig. 1.4 Queen's College Library, J. C. Buckler, watercolour, 1828 (Librarian of the Queen's College, Oxford).

Church in the High Street, a project that resulted in another distinguished Palladian edifice.[55] William Lancaster, Halton's successor as Provost of Queen's (1704–17), the protégé and one-time chaplain of Henry Compton, bishop of London, was architecturally ambitious for his college on the grand scale.[56] He was well-known to and influenced by Nicholas Hawksmoor but preferred to produce his own design in conjunction with George Clarke for the educational palace that he planned Queen's to be, a model clearly influenced by the Luxembourg Palace in Paris.[57] Lancaster's aspirations rather outpaced his capacities. While he demolished most of the old buildings in the college their replacements, again in the Palladian style, were largely designed and executed by the

---

[55] R.H. Hodgkin, *Six centuries of an Oxford college. A history of the Queen's College 1340–1940* (Oxford, 1940), 131; H. M. Colvin, 'The architects of All Saints Church, Oxford', *Oxoniensia*, 19 (1954), 112–16.

[56] Hodgkin, *Queen's College*, 132–5.

[57] Tyack, *Oxford*, 152–3; Tyack, 'Majestic architecture': The Queen's College, Oxford', *CL*, 118 (13 Aug. 2014), 58–61.

Oxford master mason, William Townesend (1676–1739), and were incomplete at Lancaster's death.[58]

In terms of architectural competence, expertise, and influence, George Clarke, fellow of All Souls, the University's sometime MP (1717–36), was on a level with Henry Aldrich; Clarke exceeded him in scale, working across several colleges, predominantly in the Palladian style, and devoting to Oxford energies that might have found a metropolitan outlet had it not been for the removal of the Tories from office in 1714.[59] He took over Aldrich's proposal for a monumental work on the southern side of the Peckwater quad, made various adaptations to it, but retained the giant Corinthian order. It was to be the college library and was completed in 1738, two years after Clarke's death.[60] Apart from Queen's, Clarke latterly dedicated himself to working at the new foundation of Worcester. The hall, chapel, and library there were basically constructed to his designs with subsequent modifications by Hawksmoor, 1733–53.[61] Another Oxonian with architectural ambition on the grand scale was Edward Holdsworth, the Nonjuror, with whom originated the design for what became the 'New Building' at Magdalen. In the end, funds could only support the northern range of what was intended to be a new quadrangle.[62]

It was nigh impossible for Heads of Houses looking at what was being done at Christ Church, Queen's, and All Souls not to propose their own construction initiatives as testimony to collegiate pride, stylistic virtuosity (with a nod to avant-gardism), and, not least, to contemporary academic values of form and function. Thus Exeter, Corpus Christi, and New College all had the Townesend builders at work early in the century, often having a hand in design as well as construction.[63] At Balliol, Theophilus Leigh (Master 1726–85) had hopes of completely rebuilding the college. He commissioned the Townesends to execute the designs and, with his

---

[58] Thus the chapel was not consecrated (by the Archbishop of York), until 1 Nov. 1719, and the distinctive gateway to the High Street with its cupola holding a statue of Queen Caroline (by Henry Cheere) standing on a stepped pyramid was not ready until the mid-1730s. Hodgkin, *Queen's College*, 136–7; Tyack, *Oxford*, 155. Lancaster donated £5,000 of his own fortune towards the costs. As Colvin points out, Townesend had a hand in nearly every important building erected in the University c.1720–40. Howard Colvin, *A dictionary of British architects 1600–1840* (3rd edn., New Haven, CT, 1995), 985.

[59] Timothy Clayton has well observed: 'There are few men by whom the appearance of Oxford University was influenced more than by George Clarke'. 'Clarke: father and son', in eds. Green and Horden, *All Souls*, 117–31, at 118; T. Clayton, 'Clarke, George (1661–1736), politician and architect', *ODNB*, online version, 2004. Clarke was a member of the second group of Church Commissioners (1712–14) for constructing the proposed fifty new churches in London. For his role as MP for the University see Chapter 8, pp. 50–3.

[60] Hiscock, *A Christ Church Miscellany*, 52; Tyack, *Oxford*, 156–7. The Upper Library was finally embellished between 1752 and 1762 under the guidance of Dean David Gregory after enough donations had been collected. Tyack estimate is that Thomas Roberts's plasterwork is 'as close as Oxford ever came to capturing the exuberant and evanescent spirit of the Rococo'. ibid., 180.

[61] Colvin, *British Architects*, 250–1.

[62] R. Darwall-Smith, 'The Monks of Magdalen, 1688–1854', in ed. Brockliss (1), 253–386, at 347–52; Colvin, *Unbuilt Oxford*, 81–5.

[63] ibid., 85–6.

32 ENLIGHTENED OXFORD

relation by marriage Sir Edward Turner, 2nd. Bt. (1719–66), as the principal backer, some work was carried out between 1738 and 1743. As ever, funding was the key to completion. In the 1740s, money or enthusiasm at Balliol were in short supply and there was no more building until the late 1760s.[64]

Although the work, both proposed and executed, of Oxford insiders such as Aldrich and Clarke was not short on either inspiration or expertise, the University throughout the century was always ready to commission designs from professional architects. Nicholas Hawksmoor planned to remodel the city of Oxford *tout entire*, creating new visual axes on a classical model with Radcliffe Square as the principal focus, a *Forum Universitatis*.[65] The sum total of his urban, academic accomplishments was more limited but immensely distinguished. He began with the Clarendon Building (1712–15), distinguished for its innovative portico,[66] and ended at All Souls with the north quadrangle, hall, buttery, and Codrington Library, erected between 1716 and 1735.[67] The most distinguished mid-century building in Oxford turned out to be the cylindrical, domed, freestanding Radcliffe Library (it became the Camera after 1862), the work of the Catholic Tory James Gibbs, whose circular plans were given preference over Hawksmoor's when designs for a library were solicited by John Radcliffe's trustees in 1734. Preoccupied over a decade by this commission, Gibbs produced a circular building that looked both to Wrenian and Italian mannerism for inspiration. The end product created a new centripetal presence within the University that astonished and pleased contemporaries and stands comparison with any contemporary European design.[68] Geoffrey Tyack expresses it exactly:

'While elsewhere in England patrons were opting for the prim correctness of Palladianism, Oxford chose for its most prominent public building a full-blooded Baroque which would not have looked out of place in any of the cities of Continental Europe'.[69]

---

[64] John Jones, *Balliol College, 1263-1939. A History* (2nd edn., Oxford, 1988), 169; Colvin, *Unbuilt Oxford*, 105.

[65] Bodl. MS.Top. gen. b. 64, f. 459; Bodl. MS.Top.Oxon.a.26(R); ed. R. White, *Nicholas Hawksmoor and the replanning of Oxford* (Oxford and London, 1997); Vaughan Hart, *Nicholas Hawksmoor. Rebuilding Ancient Wonders* (New Haven, CT, 2002), 185–96, 202–19. There would be a *Forum Civitatis* at Carfax adorned with a commemorative column.

[66] Worsley, *Classical Architecture in Britain*, 101; *VCH Oxon.*, III. 54–5. The work was funded by sales of Clarendon's *History of the Great Rebellion*.

[67] Ibid., III. 190–3.

[68] 'I am no architect but I think Gibb's ye finest building I ever saw by much', opined former Vice-Chancellor, Robert Shippen, 22 Feb. 1740, to Lord Noel Somerset, Badminton Muniments, FmJ 2/22/40; S. G. Gillam (ed.), *The Building Accounts of the Radcliffe Camera* (Oxford, 1958); G. Tyack, 'Gibbs and the Universities', *The Georgian Group Journal* 27 (2019), 57–78; Terry Friedman, *James Gibbs* (New Haven, CT, 1984); Bryan Little, *James Gibbs 1682-1754* (London, 1955).

[69] Tyack, *Oxford*, 171.

Given the furious building activity down to the opening of the Radcliffe Library, it was hardly surprising that construction across Oxford slowed in the second half of the century. The focus tended to be either on completion of work already in progress or specific private commissions. Thus within the first category, Henry Keene undertook the erection of the north range at Worcester College (including the Provost's lodgings) between 1771 and 1776, largely to plans by George Clarke. Keene was an established talent by that date with clients across the country, whereas James Wyatt had shot to fame in the early 1770s for his designs of the Pantheon assembly room in central London. While ready to embrace the fashionable Adam-style of these years, Wyatt was no less at home with a more severe, primitivist originality that looked more to Adam's contemporary Sir William Chambers, as in the Canterbury Quadrangle and Gate at Christ Church (1775–83).[70] As well as work at other Oxford colleges, Wyatt in 1794 completed the Radcliffe Observatory for the University to designs originating with Henry Keene, made memorable by an octagonal tower based on the Tower of the Winds in Athens and surmounted by John Bacon's statue of Atlas holding up the world, 'one of the major monuments of English neoclassicism'.[71] Wyatt's quality of design and accomplished workmanship showed that Oxford's physical presence remained as creatively exceptional at the end of the eighteenth century as it had done at the beginning. And it did so without extinguishing a tradition of accomplished amateurism, perhaps seen at its best in the in the efforts of the ever-versatile Sir Roger Newdigate at University College (1766–8), whose designs (in conjunction with Henry Keene) paradoxically confirmed the vitality and adaptability of the continuing Gothic tradition in Oxford as elsewhere across the country just as it hinted at the Saxon origins of the college.[72]

The built environs of eighteenth-century Oxford constituted an arena of stylistic eclecticism and inspiration, a forum within which international, national, and local influences were creatively blended, that had few European counterparts as a contemporary architectural *locus* recognised for its beauty.[73] One long-term Oxford resident, John Malchair (1730–1812), originally from Cologne, a well-known music and dancing master with many pupils, who first settled there *c.*1760 when appointed leader of the band at the Music Room '...spoke of Oxford as being the most beautiful City in respect of buildings in Europe & said that

---

[70] ibid., 185–6; John Martin Robinson, *James Wyatt (1746–1813). Architect to George III* (New Haven, CT, 2011), 195–7. See Chapter 9.

[71] Tyack, *Oxford*, 184.

[72] ibid., 181–2. Newdigate's remodelling of his seat at Arbury Hall, Warks., also bore evidence of his skills. For the wider Gothic tradition see Worsley, *Classical Architecture in Britain*, 175–95.

[73] Geoffrey Tyack gloomily notes (by reference to the 1700–40 decades) that 'Like Venice in its decadence, Oxford turned in on itself and compensated for the loss of intellectual eminence with the pleasures of magnificent building'. *Oxford*, 149.

34 ENLIGHTENED OXFORD

foreigners (Italians & others) had acknowledged it to Him'.[74] In his many watercolours and engravings Malchair tried to capture some of the hidden corners of a city that was constantly being reconstructed, tidied up, and extended beyond its medieval city walls.[75] He was fascinated, for instance, by buildings such as Friar Bacon's Study, guarding the entrance to Folly Bridge on the south side of the city, that were obstacles to the road improvements Oxford's economic development required. With the city authorities looking (especially after the so-called Mileways Act was passed in 1771) to demolish the remaining gates and widen main roads, and the University and colleges also committed to a reordered landscape, Malchair lost no time in recording a built heritage under threat, demolition actually being carried out (as in the removal of the Canterbury Building at Christ Church, 1783), and some of the new work in progress, as of Wyatt's observatory.[76] A visual record of various colleges and university institutions, in allegorical representations with their founders, was also furnished from the 1670s by the head-piece of the *Oxford Almanack*. In the highly charged political atmosphere of Anne's reign, zealous Whigs were quick to suspect any possible symbols of treason and designs in the Almanacks.[77] And, after 1714, there was a politic movement away from allegories towards depictions of individual colleges and their building proposals notable for their antiquarian accuracy, one encouraged by the Delegates of the Press.[78] These form a core component of the visual Oxford topographical tradition that was well-established *c.*1700 through the delineations and maps of antiquaries such as Anthony Wood and David Loggan;[79] they offer an exceptional opportunity to grasp the physical setting of the University's

---

[74] *The Farington Diary By Joseph Farington, RA*, Vol. 1, *1793 to 1801*, ed. J. Greig, (London, *c.*1922), 290, 1 Aug. 1800. Malchair told Farington that '...Oxford being a National Seminary was a desirable place for an artist to settle in as He might become known, as was His own case, to persons coming from every district in the Kingdom'. Not every foreigner was impressed, even after the great eighteenth-century rebuilding, for instance Pastor Carl Moritz in 1782: 'Only a few of these colleges are modern in construction...Oxford bears a melancholy aspect and I cannot understand how anyone can regard it as one of the finest cities in England next to London'. Moritz, *Journeys of a German in England in 1782*, trans. R. Nettel (London, 1965). See also Chapter 11 for the impression of other visitors from the continent.

[75] Colin Harrison et al., *John Malchair of Oxford. Artist and Musician* (Ashmolean Museum, Oxford, 1998).

[76] Illustrated in ibid., 76, 78, 84. Malchair was not the first to do so. James Green was employed by a member of Queen's in 1750 to draw recently demolished medieval buildings. Julian Munby, 'James (not John) Green (1729-1759, engraver to the University', *Oxoniensia*, 62 (1977), 319–21. Munby argues that many of Malchair's compositions should be regarded as 'essays in picturesque composition'. 'Malchair and the Oxford topographical tradition', in ibid., 55. He was an artist interested in natural phenomena and a friend of the Oxford astronomer Thomas Hornsby.

[77] Illuminatingly discussed in Neil Guthrie, *The material culture of the Jacobites* (Cambridge, 2013), 76–8.

[78] For a descriptive and illustrated list see H.M. Petter, *The Oxford almanacks* (Oxford, 1974). Interestingly, Malchair's designs for the 1767 and 1768 *Almanacks* of the countryside around Oxford were not received well by the Delegates. Harrison et al., *John Malchair*, 14–15.

[79] Munby in 'Malchair and the Oxford Topographical Tradition' in ibid., 45–57, esp. 48–9. Loggan's forty views of the university with a detailed birdseye view of the city were published by him as *Oxonia Illustrata* (Oxford, 1675).

buildings within the wider, rapidly changing urban environment. William Williams brought Loggan up to date with his *Oxonia Depicta* (1733), while John Donowell, in a series of *Perspective Views of the Colleges and other Public Buildings of Oxford* (1755) was a pioneer in depicting the university within the wider townscape and giving a visual sense of an archetypal academic setting (with titles in French and English) to an international as well as a national readership.[80]

III

> The universities, therefore, and the practice which still happily prevails, of educating in those great and ancient seminaries, the British youth of distinction, are of very great political importance: nor would all the consequences that might accompany or flow from their subversion, a matter which has of late been talked of by certain political reformers and other <u>agitators</u>, be for the better'.
>
> Thomas Newte, Prospects and Observations; on a Tour
in England and Scotland: Natural, Oeconomical,
and literary (London, 1791), 4.

The function and purpose of the University tended to be presumed rather than explicated and updated in this era. Oxford's long history as a seat of learning, its built inheritance, and its past and present members were sufficient indicators of what it symbolised, what social and scholastic activities took place within it, and the cultural range and reach of its *alumni*. Any need to offer explanation to outsiders for its actions committed (or omitted) would have been considered both vulgar and redundant. Such ideological reticence was characteristic of English schools and universities more widely and perhaps explains why their sociology has instead been more widely investigated.[81] Oxford's importance in forming the next generation of the governing elite is impossible to underestimate, training leaders for public life, for the professions, for the service of the Crown, all within a context of sociable masculinity. Young noblemen and gentlemen were not necessarily expected to explore the educational pleasures on offer too fulsomely but it is likely to have been only a small minority of them that resisted outright. Thus John, Lord Carteret (1690–1764), one of the most cultivated and accomplished politicians of the first half of the century, took full advantage of Christ Church in the later years of Aldrich. Swift noted wryly in 1730 that Carteret 'with a singularity scarce to be justified, he carried away more Greek, Latin, and

---

[80] Ibid., 50–1.
[81] An observation originally made by Linda Colley thirty years ago (*Britons. Forging the Nation 1707–1837* (New Haven, CT, 1992), 167), which retains some currency.

36 ENLIGHTENED OXFORD

philosophy, than properly became a person of his rank; indeed much more of each than most of those who are forced to live by their learning will be at the unnecessary pains to load their heads with'. Yet Carteret, though exceptional in his responsiveness to what Oxford could offer, was far from unique in the most socially exclusive end of the student body.[82]

External pressures could make institutional defence and justification unavoidable as in the 1690s and then, again, in the 1790s. Oxford was deeply loyal to the Crown and therefore the dynastic Revolution of 1688-9 and the threat of French-style republicanism and democracy a century later were equally destabilising and required a response. The speed with which James II threw away the uncontested authority of the Crown that his brother Charles II had accumulated in the last years of his reign (c.1681-5) and in which Oxford had rejoiced came as a severe shock to the University.[83] Despite its ideological underwriting of non-resistance and passive obedience, as an institution it could not submit to James's attempts to intrude Roman Catholicism into the University and its colleges in defiance of the Test Act (1673). Oxford did resist and initially greeted the Revolution of 1688 and the accession of William III and Mary with relief.[84] It was only subsequently that an essentially High Church and Tory University came to appreciate how far the post-Revolution world was at odds with its own understanding of monarchical and ecclesiastical values and, implicitly, with the kind of educational formation that it offered. Oxford adapted (not always easily) over time; it accommodated itself to the changed public order; it survived. Despite the growth of an influential internal Whig minority, it still suffered official disfavour for several decades in the first half of the eighteenth century: Tory dons could not easily forget the price paid in Church and State for the 1688 Williamite 'deliverance' and the 1714 Protestant Succession as, for instance, in the damage to sacramental Anglicanism and, lying beyond that perceived diminution, the extent to which the Church's legal monopoly had been eroded.[85] That anxiety, which was fully formed by the first decade of the new century, gave rise to recurrent cries of "the Church in danger",[86] and lay behind the major state crisis of 1710 triggered by Henry Sacheverell, a leading Oxonian himself, if never quite part of its establishment.[87]

In some quarters, for all the restored loyalism exhibited by the majority of Oxonians in the reign of George III, that resentment of the swerve in the polity

[82] Jonathan Swift, A Vindication of His Ex[cellenc]y the Lord C[arteret]...(Dublin, 1730), 3.

[83] Grant Tapsell, The Personal Rule of Charles II 1681-1685 (Woodbridge, 2007).

[84] Laurence Brockliss, G. Harriss, and A. Macintyre, Magdalen College and the Crown: Essays for the Tercentenary of the Restoration of the College 1688 (Oxford, 1988); Chapter 2. this title; more generally S. Pincus, 1688. The first Modern Revolution (New Haven, CT, 2009).

[85] M. Pittock, Inventing and resisting Britain. Cultural identities in Britain and Ireland 1685-1789 (Basingstoke, 1997), 100, 104.

[86] J. Innes, 'Jonathan Clark, social history and England's "Ancien Regime", Past and Present, 115 (1987), 165-201, at 181.

[87] Sacheverell was a fellow of Magdalen College, 1703-13, bursar, 1709. Darwall-Smith, 'The Monks of Magdalen', 335-6.

that characterised the 'abdication' of James II and its aftermath was still felt a century and more later. Thus Martin Routh, the long-lived (1754–1854) proto-Tractarian President of Magdalen after 1791, (though no supporter of the doctrine of non-resistance) viewed the Revolution of 1688 and of the men who took part in it with misgivings, drawing on the well-established Tory tradition.[88] Routh and his generation had to steer the University through the shock waves of another international trauma, the French Revolution, a moment when 'Europe has never experienced more alarm and danger...'.[89]

The University's function and purpose could then be reiterated and subsumed within the wider defence of the British monarchical state. That crisis of the 1790s and 1800s, as Linda Colley put it, showed that 'It was patrician patriotism *in the British present* that the public schools and universities sought to inculcate, not just an academic interest in the antique past'.[90] It also confirmed and extended the University's sense of itself as a vital corporate hub in the functioning of the constitution when, in urging the king's subjects to rally to his protection against an external, antagonistic neighbour, the University functioned as both a primary motor and a formulator of loyalist ideologies to underpin the 'historic Constitution' and showed itself ready to adapt its own academic rubrics more systematically than at any point since the 1650s. Ironically, the Constitution that it guarded was essentially that brought in at the 1688 Revolution, as further elaborated a century later by Edmund Burke and others, one that would endure until its own internal dismantling in the late 1820s and early 1830s.[91]

The University's role as a guardian of public stability in the present was one that proceeded seamlessly from its sense of its own antiquity, with institutional origins that predated virtually all others in the kingdom apart from the monarchy and the Church. As Sir Richard Southern articulated it, the University 'was not created; it emerged'.[92] Even putting aside the foundational myths of King Alfred that University College rather perpetuated down the eighteenth century,[93] the University had appointed a Chancellor as early as 1214 as a sign of its incorporation. Cultural confidence born of continuity was primary to the University's identity; tellingly, it took relatively little account of pre- and post-Reformation divergences. Given the appeal to historical precedent as the most accepted means of confirming all manner of contemporary rights and privileges (a resort that managed to survive encroachment across Europe from more utility-based claims popularised by 'enlightened' apologists), it is hardly surprising that Oxonians were

---

[88] Routh's politics are discussed in R.D. Middleton, *Dr Routh* (Oxford, 1938), 148–51. Routh would never describe himself in later life as a Tractarian having a dislike of party labels and party distinctions. Middleton, *Dr Routh*, 142.

[89] John Nichols, in *GM* 63 (1793), ii. 1. [90] Colley, *Britons*, 168.

[91] J. C. D. Clark, *English Society 1660–1832. Religion, ideology and politics during the ancien regime* (2nd edn., Cambridge, 2000), 507–64.

[92] R.W. Southern, 'From Schools to University', in HUO I, 1–36, at 1.

[93] See this chapter, p. 8.

38 ENLIGHTENED OXFORD

resourceful in deploying this approach in both scholarship and apologetics. It was one that was not necessarily unimaginative, obscurantist, or self-serving. And it could sit alongside and temper a variety of more modern attitudes, for instance a growing antipathy to scholasticism in the eighteenth century. There is some validity in the point that 'The universities saw their function as the bulwarks of intellectual tradition'[94] so long as it is not assumed that it amounted to a simplistic dichotomy of stasis versus progress rather than an intellectual eclecticism.

The appeal to history, however, was never neutral. It was fundamental to the functioning of what was a deeply politicised institution at the heart of the national polity, one which was thus susceptible to remodelling and marginalisation in unstable times, such as the Interregnum of the 1650s and the reign of James II. And the University would be threatened with that fate again in the late 1710s and 1740s because of its perceived attachment (more cultural than political but capable of representation as the latter) to the exiled Stuarts. Only with time—from the mid-century—could Oxford revert to supporting and justifying the status quo, taking the lead again in helping to stabilise public culture, interrogating ideas for change, and often questioning the motives of their proponents. In so doing, later eighteenth-century Oxford helped infuse English civil society with values that called attention to why the status quo was worth defending against internal and external challenge, and what the perils of modification and abandonment might be. It is no better than facile to deem such endeavours as academically barren and politically reactionary. To be protective of the polity in 'enlightened' times required particular resourcefulness from its spokesmen, the capacity to articulate new defences, to argue that there was still a strong case to be made for the divine dispensation that underlay the public sphere. To be adaptive, to voice reservations about proposed alterations, to suggest alternatives, were worthy intellectual objectives for an academic society in Revolutionary times. And that message did get across to outsiders, those commentators who were capable of seeing the point, and could come up with their own justification of the English Universities in relation to the constitution, commentators such as Thomas Newte, who wrote in 1791:[95]

Take away these memorials of antiquity, these noble and royal testimonies of respect to sanctity of life, and proficiency in learning, remove every sensible object by which sentiments of early friendship, loyalty, and patriotism are kindled and inflamed in young minds, and disperse our young gentlemen in

---

[94] H. Kearney, *Scholars and Gentlemen. Universities and Societies in Pre-Industrial Britain 1500–1700* (London, 1970), 162.

[95] Thomas Newte, *Prospects and Observations; on a Tour in England and Scotland: Natural, Oeconomical, and literary* (London, 1791), 3–4.

other countries for their education, or even in separate little academies and schools in our own, and you weaken one of the great pillars, by which the constitution and spirit of England is supported and perpetuated.

Within two years of Newte's publication, Britain was at war with Revolutionary France, and the University through its graduates was to the fore in making the case for persistence throughout the war's duration by making clear what the kingdom stood to lose in the event of its defeat. Such a function was not new. Oxford had earlier acted as cheerleader for most of the War of the Spanish Succession until the national consensus over its continuance collapsed in 1709; its endorsement of Pittite patriotism throughout the Seven Years' War (1756–63) helped complete the reconciliation of Jacobite-inclined Tories to the Hanoverian order even before the accession of George III in 1760; and that alignment was so complete by the time of the American War of Independence (1775–83) that, fortified by the arrival of loyalist American refugees, there were barely any dissenting voices from an official bellicosity that corresponded to the sovereign's resolution to make no concessions to the rebellious colonists. Oxford University was thus committed to the war efforts of the state throughout this period and ready to participate distinctively in patriotic causes through recitation, publication, the honouring of martial heroes (it had its favourites such as its Chancellor (1688–1715), the 2nd duke of Ormond), and invocation of the classical past to suggest that the British achievements of the present age equalled or even surpassed them.[96]

Times of war and revolution highlighted the public functions of the University within the monarchy: to uphold the constitution in Church and state, protect it, interpret it, support its current leaders (wherever that could in conscience be done) and form the next generation of them, and defend the faith as proclaimed by the Church of England and embodied in its Supreme Governor, the Sovereign. In so doing, the University might be said to have a quasi-representative role as a great educational foundation within the polity. Or, as Edmund Burke later put it, a collective opinion from Oxford was 'expressive of the sentiments of the People' on a subject within its sphere.[97] Eighteenth-century Oxford, publicly considered, was not an institution for research or disinterested scholarship (any more than Cambridge was) at any price. Neutrality on where evidence and argument

---

[96] War and peace were staple themes in commemorative verses issued by the University to mark the end of international conflicts. In 1713, by contrast with Cambridge—which published a full-scale collection to commemorate the Peace of Utrecht—Oxford delivered a book containing only the verses recited at the Act for the Peace. See *Academiae Oxoniensis comitia philologica in theatro Sheldoniano decimo die Julii a. d. 1713 celebrata: in honorem Serenissimae Reginae Annae Pacificae* (Oxford, 1713); D. K. Money, 'Free Flattery or Servile Tribute? Oxford and Cambridge Commemorative Poetry in the Seventeenth and Eighteenth Century', in ed. J. Raven, *Free Print and Non-Commercial Publishing since 1700* (Aldershot, 2000), 48–66.

[97] Burke to William Windham, 22 Dec. 1790, in Edmund Burke, *Correspondence*, Thomas W. Copeland et al. (eds.), (10 vols., Cambridge, 1958–78), VI. 194–5.

40 ENLIGHTENED OXFORD

might lead and freedom from external interference with the remit of researchers constituted a policy neither central, upheld, nor even imagined until the early twentieth century in English universities. Rather, the University's role was to act as a trustee, a guarantor of orthodoxy in the Church, one of the centres of the ruling order, to act against those who might hazard public tranquillity. It was not until the 1750s at the earliest that University attention, more comfortable in its political affiliations than it had been at any juncture since Queen Anne's death, moved to consider what and how it taught, with Christ Church in the vanguard.[98] Criticism of University examinations began with John Napleton's moderate and intelligent assessment, *Considerations on the Public Exercise for the First and Second Degrees in the University of Oxford* [(Oxford, 1773)], followed soon by Vicesimus Knox in *Liberal Education, or a Practical Treaties on the Methods of acquiring Useful and Polite Learning* (London, 1781).[99] Unfavourable international comparisons were beginning to be made, and rectification required a gradual loosening of the link between scholarship and confessional apologetics.

At no point in this era was Oxford deaf to the political and social risks that subversion was commonly supposed to bring in its train. Vigilance was required by authority figures such as heads of houses, the professoriate, and tutors in being alert guardians of the values of the wider polity, protecting it against openly Jacobite and later Jacobin colleagues, but doing so sensitively and without over-reaction. Occasionally draconian action was deemed necessary. The classic instance occurred during the 'Tory reaction' in the aftermath of the Exclusion Crisis and the Rye House Plot, when Church and state drew together in mutually protective actions designed to repudiate Whig theories of kingship and popular sovereignty, actions that could be deemed either repressive or defensive according to one's perspective.[100] Oxford Convocation had, on 21 July 1683, passed a Judgement and Decree of the University 'against certain pernicious Books, and damnable Doctrines, Destructive to the Sacred persons of Princes, their State and Government, and of all human Society' and, in this series of twenty articles, restated high royalist doctrine.[101] The books thrown on to the pyre outside the Bodleian (the later Old Schools quadrangle) by 'the premier teaching institution in the country'[102] included the writings of John Locke (notably the *Two Treatises on*

---

[98] Ellis, *Generational conflict*, 53ff.

[99] Ibid., 59–62, 67. John Napleton (1738? – 1817, Fellow of Brasenose, 1760), published *Considerations* anonymously; Vicesimus Knox (1752–1821), miscellaneous writer; fellow of SJC, 1775; published *Essays moral and literary* (London, 1778, many reprints); headmaster of Tonbridge School, 1778–1812.

[100] See Tapsell, *Personal rule*; Ronald Hutton, *Charles II. King of England, Scotland, and Ireland* (Oxford, 1989), 404–23.

[101] University of Oxford, *Judicium et decretum universitatis Oxoniensis latum in convocation habita Jul. 21, an 1683, contra quosdam perniciosos libros & propositiones impias* (Oxford, 1683), 1–4; A. Wood, *Athenae* Oxoniensis, ed. P. Bliss, (4 vols., London, 1813–20), IV. 171; J. P. Kenyon, *The Stuart constitution, 1603–1688: documents and commentary* (1st edn., Cambridge, 1966), 471. Discussed in John Spurr, *The Restoration Church of England, 1646–1689* (New Haven, CT, 1991), 261.

[102] J. P. Kenyon, *Revolution Principles. The Politics of party 1689–1720* (Cambridge, 1977), 65.

Government), the key ally of Shaftesbury in the Exclusion campaign and a Student of Christ Church until his abrupt flight into Holland.[103] Whigs never allowed that bonfire to be forgotten in their own party writings and, even in the transformed political culture that followed the 1688 Revolution and the lapsing of the Licensing Act in 1695, would taunt the University that it was itching to replicate its 1683 pyre with new incendiary texts for consignment to the flames.[104] One such text was Benjamin Hoadly's *The Original and Institution of Civil Government* (1709), a challenge to the prolific Nonjuror, Charles Leslie's, views on patriarchalism. In reasserting a people's right of resistance and repudiating divine right to emphasise the legitimacy of the Revolution, Hoadly relied extensively on Locke's views.[105] Buoyed up by the return to power of the Tories in 1710 and concerned by Sacheverell's formal guilt and minimal punishment, the University issued a decree against the book which appeared to threaten Hoadly's writings with the same fate as Locke's. In fact, though *The Original and Institution of Civil Government* was burnt publicly at Exeter, the University authorities resisted the temptation for Oxford to go further and follow this precedent, a counterpart to the state order that Sacheverell's sermons should be burnt by the hangman.[106]

These decrees were neither repealed nor modified after the Revolution and Oxford's custodial role as a censorial authority in Church and state remained formally intact. But it was one that political expediency and the imperative of institutional survival determined should not be deployed after 1714, when the Whig leadership was looking for any excuse to move against the University should its hegemony be confronted. But that academic sense of having the residual role of guardian to protect the core values of the kingdom persisted at Oxford throughout this era and was on show again in the last quarter of the century against external threats, when it was again controversial (during the American

---

[103] M. Goldie, 'John Locke and Anglican royalism', *Political Studies*, 31 (1983), 61–85. Other works burnt were by Thomas Hobbes, John Milton, and Robert Bellarmine. Brockliss, (2), 207. Humphrey Prideaux, a leading anti-deist and Locke's fellow tutor at Christ Church, had spied on the latter for some years prior to Locke's expulsion from Oxford in 1684. For Prideaux ed. Edward Maunde Thompson, *Letters of Humphrey Prideaux, sometime Dean of Norwich, to John Ellis, sometime Under-Secretary of State, 1674–1722* (London, 1875); Alexandra Walsham, *Charitable hatred. Tolerance and intolerance 1500–1700 in England* (Manchester, 2006), 321.

[104] For the wider contexts see eds. G. Partington and Adam Smyth, *Book destruction from the medieval to the contemporary* (Basingstoke, 2014). In 1705 a popularised version of the 1683 decree was drawn up with a plan to circulate it.

[105] Discussed in W. Gibson, *Enlightenment Prelate. Benjamin Hoadly, 1676–1761* (Cambridge, 2004), 100–4; R. Browning, *Political and constitutional ideas of the Court Whigs* (Baton Rouge, LA, 1982), 79.

[106] Apparently, some high Tories would have wished them to do so. Thus, one tract republished the July 1683 decrees and at its foot had an advertisement with a finger pointing to the words 'This is to give notice, that if Mr Hoadley will not Recant his Rebellious and Seditious Principles which he has Borrow'd from the vile Authors here Condemn'd, He may speedily expect the same Censure from both the Universities . . . . Hoadly, *The Oxford Decree: Being an Entire Confutation of Mr Hoadly's Book, of the Original of Government; Taken from the London Gazette* (London, reprinted 1710). It was ordered to be burnt by the hangman. T. Salmon, *The Present State of the Universities and of the Five Adjacent Counties* (London, 1744), 254.

42 ENLIGHTENED OXFORD

War of Independence) and, per contra, helped form and reflect the national consensus in the French Revolution. It partially determined the disdain for radical Enlightenment texts, whether originating domestically or on the continent,[107] for the desirability of taking new ideas seriously had to be set against concerns that they would destabilise legitimately constituted authorities. Though he had Edward Gibbon foremost in mind, the Oxford historian Henry Kett (1761–1825) was thinking more widely when he wrote:[108]

> Any endeavour to loosen the ties of religious duty, is an affront to the pious principles of education implanted in every cultivated mind; and an act of hostility against the general interests of society.

It was impatience with what could be perceived as self-serving caution that drew down such castigation on Oxford and on ancient universities in general, from that unsympathetic Oxford graduate, Adam Smith, when he condemned them in 1776 as

> sanctuaries in which exploded systems and obsolete prejudices found shelter and protection, after they had been hunted out of every other corner of the world.[109]

By that date, Oxford had never given him a doctorate. And it was never going to do so thereafter.[110] Smith had few sympathies for the Church of England and his comments betray his personal unwillingness to acknowledge Oxford's symbiotic relationship to the Established Church. It had a duty of protection that came before all others and reflected its indelible Anglican character, its function as the principal seminary of the Church, and its perceived duty to protect the Church whose priestly orders the vast majority of its resident senior members had taken.[111] Thus there would always be a tendency for their public and personal

---

[107] George Horne condemned 'unlimited free enquiry' as simply 'full permission to attack the church in every possible way. *The Duty of contending for the faith* (Oxford, 1786), 11.

[108] H. Kett, *A Representation of the Conduct and Opinions of the Primitive Christians...* (Oxford, 1791), 156.

[109] Adam Smith, *An Inquiry into the Nature and Causes of the Wealth of Nations*, ed. W.B. Todd (2 vols., Oxford, 1976), II. 772.

[110] Smith was consistently withering (with Oxford in mind). He insisted that opulence enjoyed through privilege was the cause of the 'degradation and contempt' into which he believed most contemporary universities and their teachers had fallen. To William Cullen, 20 Sept. 1774, in eds. E.C. Mossner and Ian Simpson Ross, *The Glasgow Edition of the Works and Correspondence of Adam Smith*, Vol. 6. *Correspondence* (2nd edn., Oxford, 1987), 174. For Oxonian suspicions of Smith's own indifference to Christianity and his amity with David Hume see [George Horne], *A Letter to Adam Smith on the life, death, and philosophy of his friend David Hume... By one of the people called Christians* (Oxford, 1777).

[111] For a jaundiced dismissal of the clergy and the Universities as 'Appurtenances' to 'the Church and the Convocation', see [N. Amhurst] *A letter from a student in Grub-street, to a Reverend high-priest in Oxford. Containing an account of a malicious design to blacken him and several of his friends...* (London [1720]), 12.

FAME, FORM, AND FUNCTION   43

discourses to reflect, and that without any necessary sacrifice of acuteness or adaptability, what John Redwood once called the 'God-ridden' dimension of later seventeenth- and early eighteenth-century thought and, indeed, well beyond.[112] The monarch was the Supreme Governor of the Established Church and the University was bound in at any number of levels with the Crown, which was the primary reason for tensions with Whig ministers and the court for the majority of the decades between 1688 and 1760, difficulties that were absent at Cambridge, certainly from the accession of George I. The majority of Oxonians were not active Jacobites but, as with their counterparts and friends in Parliament, they just longed for recognition. Thus Nicholas Amhurst's factional Oxford doctor was

> zealously affected to the Church, and zealously disaffected to the State for the same Reason that several other pious Doctors are; namely, because one caresses and makes much of him, whilst the other takes no Notice of all his Catholick Merits.[113]

But, in theory at any rate, the Church and state alliance 'was reflected in miniature in unreformed Oxford and Cambridge'.[114] It was here that future lawmakers as well as future clergy were educated, with forty-five per cent of MPs having received an Oxbridge education between 1734 and 1761 (at a time when numbers of matriculands had fallen), and no less than fifty per cent between 1766 and 1812. As John Gascoigne has argued, it is beyond doubt that the concentration of the elite in just two educational institutions 'helps explain the cohesion of the English establishment'.[115] For what undergraduates were likely to find themselves doing soon after they had graduated could never be overlooked, and students could be as aware of those prospects as their teachers. In the words of one prize essayist of the 1780s: 'The great object of education is to prepare us for the due discharge of those various and extensive obligations which belong to us as men and citizens'.[116]

Support of the Church and support of the Crown were overlapping obligations. Thus most Oxonians made the assumption that the Church of England was coterminous with English society as a whole, and that membership of that Church amounted to a fundamental duty of citizenship or, as George Horne put

---

[112] John Redwood, *Reason, Ridicule, and Religion: the Age of Enlightenment in England, 1660–1750* (London, 1976), 9.

[113] [Amhurst] *A letter from a student in Grub-street,* 15.

[114] J. Gascoigne, 'Church and state allied: the failure of parliamentary reform of the universities, 1688–1800', in eds. A. L. Beier, D. Cannadine, and J. M. Rosenheim, *The First Modern Society. Essays in English History in Honour of Lawrence Stone* (Cambridge, 1989), 401–29, at 401.

[115] Ibid., 403.

[116] Charles Thomas Barker (1758–1812, matric. Ch. Ch., 1777; BA, 1781; MA, 1784; BD, 1798; Proctor, 1790; Vicar of St Mary Magdalene, Oxford, 1791–9), his *On the use of history* (Oxford, 1836), originally awarded the Chancellor's English Essay in 1783. Foster, I. 60.

44 ENLIGHTENED OXFORD

it in a sermon on Restoration Day 1760: 'The churchman is the true patriot'.[117] The religious foundations of loyalty that were prominent nationally on display c.1800 are not to be underestimated[118] and if, at that time, both Oxford and Cambridge were facing comparable external pressures to update, much as were other British institutions, they were both capable of making internal changes on their own initiative, while remaining insistent on their underlying and continuing centrality in the polity. Oxford may have been a bastion of orthodoxy in Revolutionary times but it could be dynamic and inventive, and neither then nor earlier did the University cease to engage with the intellectual currents of the age.

IV

[The scholar's] Employment is, first to listen himself attentively to the still voice of Wisdom; and then faithfully to declare her Will to other men,...',

> John Dalton [Fellow of Queen's], Two Sermons preached before the University of Oxford at St Mary's, On Sept 15th, and Oct. 20th, 1745, And now publish'd for the use of the younger students in the two Universities (Oxford, 1745), 4.

It is an age so full of light that there is scarce a country or corner of Europe whose beams are not crossed and interchanged with others – .

> Laurence Sterne, A Sentimental Journey, eds. Tim Parnell and Ian Jack, (Oxford, 2008), 11.

The habitual default usage of 'Enlightenment(s)' as a term of reference when it is actually far more a term of art is to an appreciable degree unavoidable given the wider European contexts within which this book locates the University.[119] Is there any ground then to consider Oxford as, by some token, an institution which reflected and disseminated Enlightenment knowledge and values as, for instance, other British higher educational institutions such as the Universities of Glasgow and Edinburgh are commonly held to have done?[120] Each chapter in this study engages with aspects of that underlying question without claiming to have reached a conclusive answer or one that is anything other than heavily qualified and leaves

---

[117] *The works of the Right Reverend George Horne...*, ed. William Jones (6 vols., London, 1809), III. 136. Quoted in Clark, *English society* (2000), 266.

[118] Matthew McCormack, 'Rethinking "loyalty" in eighteenth-century Britain', *JECS*, 35 (2012), 407–21.

[119] J. G. A. Pocock makes an eloquent, pragmatic case for using 'Enlightenment' and 'Enlightened' in his *Barbarism and Religion*. Vol. 1. *The Enlightenments of Edward Gibbon, 1737–1764* (Cambridge, 1999), 5–9.

[120] For the rather different position at King's College, Aberdeen see ed. Paul Wood, *The Aberdeen Enlightenment. The arts curriculum in the eighteenth century* (Aberdeen, 1993).

space for readerly judgements. If, as John Robertson has it, the Enlightenment was concerned with 'betterment in this world, without regard for the existence or non-existence of the next', then the minority of Oxford writers fell at best on its margins and the majority were not part of it.[121] But this study proceeds on the basis of a much more diffuse conceptualisation, and deliberately fights shy of definitional (over-) exactitude. It chooses to see the pan-European Enlightenment (and Oxford's place, such as it was, within it) as a broad and diverse phenomenon rather than in any sense universally programmatic.[122] It may have witnessed a move away from theology towards philosophy, political economy,[123] and a 'science of man' (Hume's ambition), but most intellectuals continued to believe in the transcendent origin of truth and the providential underpinning of history, and engage the 'new learning' with established authority and religious belief.[124]

But this book is not going to shoehorn a study in Oxford's place in the wider culture into any of the various sub-categories of Enlightenment that have recently been (and not without some plausibility) presented, such as 'theological Enlightenment', 'religious Enlightenment', 'Anglican Enlightenment', and Counter-Enlightenment.[125] They are all serviceable from varied Oxford perspectives but none constitutes an exact paradigm that appropriately labels the dynamism, the cosmopolitanism, the range, and the torpor of the University's life over more than a century.[126] Its collective life defied easy characterisation at any juncture for, as Heather Ellis has reminded us, neither Oxford nor Cambridge made up 'a homogenous cultural space',[127] however much the University's

---

[121] John Robertson, *The case for Enlightenment: Scotland and Naples 1680–1760* (Cambridge, 2005), 8, 47.

[122] For Enlightenment as 'a corpus resembling Borges's Chinese encyclopedia: an apparent jumble, missing a coherent classificatory system', Dan Edelstein, *The Enlightenment. A genealogy* (Chicago, IL, 2010), 7. See also C. Hesse, 'Towards a new topography of Enlightenment', *European Review of History*, 13 (2006), 499–508; eds. Siegfried Jüttner and Jochen Schlobach, *Europäische Aufklärung (en). Einheit und nationale Vielfalt* (Hamburg, 1992). For an emphasis on the Enlightenment as an essentially cohesive European phenomenon in intellectual culture see Israel, *Radical Enlightenment*, vi.

[123] Robertson deems political economy 'the core of the Enlightenment's contribution to Western thought'. *The Enlightenment*, 80.

[124] For Irish and Russian contexts in which these aspects of Enlightenment can be discerned see Michael Brown, 'Was there an Irish Enlightenment? The case of the Anglicans', in eds. Richard Butterwick, Simon Davies, and Gabriel Sánchez Espinosa, *Peripheries of the Enlightenment* [SVEC 2008: 01] (Oxford, 2008), 49–64; Elise Kimerling Wirtschafter, *Religion and Enlightenment in Catherinian Russia. The teachings of Metropolitan Platon* (DeKalb, IL, 2013). And, generally, the landmark eds. R. Porter and M. Teich, *The Enlightenment in National Context* (Cambridge, 1981).

[125] J. D. Burson, *The rise and fall of theological Enlightenment. Jean-Martin de Prades and ideological polarization in eighteenth-century France* (Notre Dame, IN., 2010); David Sorkin, *The religious Enlightenment. Protestants, Jews, and Catholics from London to Vienna* (Princeton, NJ, 2008), esp. 11; William J. Bulman, *Anglican Enlightenment. Orientalism, religion and politics in England and its empire, 1648–1715* (Cambridge, 2015); D. McMahon, *Enemies of the Enlightenment: the French Counter-Enlightenment and the making of modernity* (New York, 2001). S. Grote, 'Review essay: religion and Enlightenment', *JHI*, 75 (2014), 137–60, is an overview of the copious recent literature.

[126] Tim Blanning put it well when he wrote, 'In reality, the Enlightenment was a house with many mansions, with some members occupying more than one simultaneously'. Blanning, *The Romantic revolution* (London, 2010), 57.

[127] H. Ellis, *Generational conflict*, 62.

46   ENLIGHTENED OXFORD

opponents sought to label it as intellectually immutable and politically regressive. And that range was registered by a constituency wider than the members of the University to encompass those who, as Richard B. Sher wrote (with the Scottish Universities in mind) 'read [their] writings, attended their lectures, heard their sermons, and discussed or adopted their ideas and beliefs'.[128]

External outreach was an invariable dimension of Oxford scholarship obscured by a tendency to underestimate the extent of contact between the English universities in the eighteenth century and their continental equivalents.[129] While it might be an exaggeration to call the majority of dons 'transnational agents in an international academic environment',[130] there was a general recognition that cooperation and exchange were essential to scholarship as seen, for instance, in British links to that pioneering Anglo-Hanoverian university, the University of Göttingen.[131] Though confessional and epistemic boundaries remained formidable obstacles to the transmission and increase of knowledge, many Oxford scholars and scientists throughout the 'long' eighteenth century made up part of what Charles J. Withers has called 'Enlightenment traffic',[132] networkers who could, both inside the British Isles and across into Europe, exchange information and assess each other's work in progress without necessarily meeting personally. It was especially important for natural scientists who wanted to map and assess any differences 'between their observations in one place concerning facts in nature and those of different correspondents or between experimental and instrumental results differently arrived at in other places'.[133] These connections did not make these Oxford networkers necessarily classifiable as cosmopolitans,[134] but in the sense that they were balancing local and national preoccupations with a degree of international outreach, then they at least entered into a classic Enlightenment pattern of articulation and reception.

And however much (or how little) Oxford can be considered an academically innovative university,[135] and admits the legitimacy of Foucault's much repeated

---

[128] R. B. Sher, 'Science and medicine in the Scottish Enlightenment', in ed. P. Wood, *The Scottish Enlightenment. Essays in reinterpretation* (Woodbridge, 2002), 110.

[129] For instance S. Conway, *Britain, Ireland, & Continental Europe in the eighteenth century. Similarities, connections, identities* (Oxford, 2011), 136.

[130] Thomas Biskup, 'The University of *Göttingen* and the Personal Union, 1737–1837', in eds. Brendan Simms and Torsten Riotte, *The Hanoverian dimension in British History, 1714–1837* (Cambridge, 2007), 128–60, at 155.

[131] Johann Stephan Pütter, *Versuch einer academischen gelehrten-geschichte von der Georg-August Universität zu Göttingen* (4 vols., Göttingen, 1765–1838), I. 6–7. See also Chapter 11.

[132] Charles J. Withers, *Placing the Enlightenment. Thinking geographically about the age of reason* (Chicago, IL, 2007), 55; David S. Lux and Harold J. Cook, 'Closed circles or open networks? Communicating at a distance during the scientific revolution', *History of Science*, 36 (1998), 179–211.

[133] Withers, *Placing the Enlightenment*, 44.

[134] For the complexities of any concept of Enlightenment as a cosmopolitan movement see Robertson, *The case for Enlightenment*, 72.

[135] Bulman, for one, certainly does: 'Oxford, Cambridge, and many of their counterparts on the continent promoted intellectual innovations far more than they inhibited or opposed them'. *Anglican Enlightenment*, 30.

point about the temporalisation of knowledge in eighteenth-century Europe,[136] the extent to which majority opinion within the University never abandoned a respect for tradition as lying at the heart of intellectual endeavour should not be doubted. It would have endorsed the insistence of that great Oxonian, Samuel Johnson, that anyone who 'hopes to become eminent . . . must first possess himself of the intellectual treasures which the diligence of former ages has accumulated. . . .' And again, 'We cannot make truth, it is our business only to find it'.[137] Such a preference was unsurprising given that Oxford University sat at the heart of an essentially confessionalised state and society,[138] one where religious allegiance to the Established Church was a prerequisite for membership of the University, and dons could not afford to be neutral in protecting their patrimony (and their pupils) from the moral contamination commonly associated with the libertine and immoral strategies of sceptical authors. Oxford became the principal midwife to an intensification of Christian piety through the Methodist movement that was both an offshoot of Anglicanism and a departure from it, and no University member, however nominal their faith, would have considered that they lived in a secular society, not least because the role of the religious establishment in England, as elsewhere across Europe, was too all-pervasive. Thus the term 'secularisation' was restricted to its public-law usage and, as has been well said, '. . . was not used to name a general process of de-Christianization or "disenchantment", that was simply because there was no such process for it to name'.[139] What *could* be found inside and beyond the University were forms of anticlericalism and religious scepticism only later called, for short, "The Enlightenment",[140] and it was on these issues that Oxford graduates involved themselves alongside any number of other Britons with different backgrounds, invariably (but by no means only) from a clericalist and fideist position.

[136] See particularly his *The order of things: an archaeology of the human sciences* (New York, 1970). It may be doubted if Foucault would have conceded the porous boundaries between the secular and the religious in this era.

[137] *The Rambler* 154 (1751), cited in *The Yale Edition of the Works of Samuel Johnson*, eds. W. Jackson Bate and Albrecht B. Strauss, gen. eds. A. T. Hazen and J. –H. Middendorf (23 vols., New Haven, CT, 1958–), III-V. 55. Johnson went on to note: 'The mental disease of the present generation is impatience of study, contempt of the great masters, and a disposition to rely wholly upon unassisted genius and natural sagacity.'

[138] Cf. the slightly different emphasis in Stephen Taylor, 'Un état confessionel? L'Eglise d'Angleterre, la Constitution et la vie politique au XVIIIe siècle', in eds. Alain Joblin et Jacques Sys, *L'Identité Anglicane* (Arras, 2004), 141–54.

[139] Ian Hunter, 'Secularization: the birth of a modern combat concept', *JMIH*, 12 (2015), 1–32, at 9; C. Coleman, 'Resacralizing the world: the fate of secularization in . . . historiography', *JMH*, 82 (2010), 368–96. Cf. John Robertson's argument in *The Enlightenment. A very short introduction* (Oxford, 2015) that the 'high' Enlightenment aided the long-term rise of secularism by subordinating religion to the necessity of civil peace.

[140] J. C. D. Clark, *Our shadowed present. Modernism, postmodernism and history* (London, 2003), 98. For the Enlightenment as more like a heresy than a denial of faith see Derek Beales, 'Religion and culture', in ed. T. C. W. Blanning, *The eighteenth century. Europe 1688–1815* [Short Oxford History of Europe] (Oxford, 2000), 131–77, at 154.

48 ENLIGHTENED OXFORD

V

Oxford's claims to fame in the eighteenth century may have rested in the first instance on its exceptional institutional longevity and constitutional importance rather than on an innovative curriculum, but a glance at any area of its intellectual life down these decades discloses individual initiatives worth notice and recovery. And, considered in cultural terms, the University offered its members, irrespective of their motives for matriculation, opportunities for learning and leisure that remained attractive, despite the reduced number of matriculands at mid-century, not least because of its enhanced physical setting and the comforts on offer. This study therefore challenges the claim of John Gascoigne that 'the values and intellectual presuppositions of the laity and clergy had so far diverged that universities were commonly regarded as of little value to anyone not intending to embark on a clerical career'.[141] For many Oxonians, lay and clerical alike, were entirely capable of communicating their intellectual interests 'across frontiers and language barriers' even as they remained rooted within specifically Oxford contexts and concerns.[142] There was pride in a distinctive academic locale whose learned products and their authors (not to mention gossip and rumour on both headings) could have a national impact, thanks to the easy opportunities for dissemination across the British nation and beyond afforded by print culture; making any number of external connections and representations, in a sense justifying its existence, was arguably more important for the University than at any point in its prior history. Its senior members were a key part, arguably *the* key part, of the English public sphere, as John Pocock has it, '... energetically debating, but as often as not maintaining, the terms of the Anglican supremacy in church and state'.[143] These included mutually contradictory positions, all generally characteristic of this era, 'areas of conflict, tension and crossover', a complex scene best not extrapolated into 'a more abstract model of Enlightenment thought'.[144] But whether well-known authors or not, Oxford dons and indeed their pupils composed an institution at the heart of that nationwide network of

---

[141] Gascoigne, *Cambridge*, 17.

[142] Cf. John Robertson, *The Case for the Enlightenment*, 38. See also Craig Calhoun, 'Imagining solidarity: cosmopolitanism, constitutional patriotism, and the public sphere', *Public Culture*, 14 (2002), 147–71.

[143] *Barbarism and Religion*, I, 299. He insists, correctly, that this public space '... was not occupied by the intellectuals of a new Enlightenment imagining alternative forms of public or cultural order'. Jürgen Habermas has lately reinserted religion into his scheme. See 'Religion and the Public Sphere', in *Between Naturalism and Religion*, tr. C. Cronin (Cambridge, 2008), 114–48.

[144] Paul Giles, 'Enlightenment Historiography and Cultural Civil Wars', in eds. S. Manning and F. Cogliano, *The Atlantic Enlightenment* (Aldershot, 2008), 19–35, at 22. David Manning has shrewdly observed that the rhetoric of enlightenment in the Christian tradition has yet to be both acknowledged and understood. Manning, 'Theological Enlightenments and Ridiculous Theologies: Contradistinction in English Polemical Theology', in *Religion in the Age of Enlightenment*, vol. 2 (2010), 209–41, at 215–27.

patron–client relations that made up the patronage state, wherein the personal and corporate price of non-compliant attitudes and behaviours in regard to the dominant values of that state could be high. Williamite and then Hanoverian suspicions about its loyalties after 1689 and 1714 made that very clear in the face of Oxford's dominant Toryism, even though recurrent ministerial claims 'that the University was a hot-bed of Jacobitism' were 'wholly unwarranted'.[145] And it is now to the distinctive challenges presented to Oxford by the Revolution and the precarious settlement that followed that this book turns.

[145] W.R. Ward, *Georgian Oxford, University Politics in the Eighteenth Century* (Oxford, 1958), 55.

INTELLECTUAL PRESENCE

2

Oxford and British academic contexts after the Glorious Revolution

The last decade of the seventeenth century has been presented as one of painful adjustment for institutions and individuals that were neither complicit in the Revolutionary settlement of 1688–89 nor sympathetic to the cultural values of the House of Orange and its supporters. With the dynastic and religious revolution came in the first fruits of the so-called 'Newtonian Revolution' such as religious toleration, experimental science, and a readiness to debate and publish freely and, where necessary, reject conventions and concepts that appeared either outdated or anomalous.[1] These were the early harbingers of what some historians have chosen to call 'the English Enlightenment'.[2] And they were not—in the first instance—associated with the University of Oxford. In other words one can find at this, the beginning of 'the long eighteenth century', that cultural detachment from the progressive zeitgeist that merely confirmed the University's intellectual marginalisation in the life of state and society in Britain.

This study will challenge every one of these powerful commonplaces and make the case for Oxford's resilience and revival after the ruptures of the 'Revolution'. Despite the depredations attempted by James II, the University continued as a proud, august, self-governing corporation that, after the monarchy and the Established Church, had an unparalleled prestige and importance that it both shared and contested with its slightly junior sister institution eighty miles east in Cambridge. It educated the future leaders of English society, nourished scholarship, and attracted visits and notice from foreign savants that confirmed its international standing and made the university not just a core component of domestic institutional life but a proud member of the republic of letters.

And yet Oxford's relationship *c.*1700 to what might conveniently be labelled the early Enlightenment as generally conceptualised has commonly been deemed one

---

[1] Margaret C. Jacob's *The Newtonians and the English Revolution, 1689–1720* (London, 1976) has been primary to the discussion for over four decades. Her *The Secular Enlightenment* (Princeton, 2019) appeared too late to be considered here. Pincus's *1688* controversially remade the case for the Orange Revolution as a launch pad for modernity.

[2] The term is closely associated with the late Roy Porter (see particularly his essay 'The Enlightenment in England' in eds. Porter and Teich, *The Enlightenment in National Context*, Cambridge, 1981, 1–48, and *Enlightenment. Britain and the Creation of the Modern World*, Harmondsworth, 2000). Since his death in 2002, resort to this currency among historians has been limited.

Enlightened Oxford: The University and the Cultural and Political Life of Eighteenth-century Britain and Beyond.
Nigel Aston, Oxford University Press. © Nigel Aston 2023. DOI: 10.1093/oso/9780199246830.003.0003

54 ENLIGHTENED OXFORD

of stasis, at best marginal, at worst downright hostile. Scholars led by Michael Hunter have looked instead to febrile new spaces of learned sociability in the capital, such as the Royal Society, for signs of intellectual progress and found (by implication) the statutes, composition, and politics of the university more likely to hinder than foster the life of mind and the application of its fruits in society at large.[3] And yet its best tutors were grounded in 'an eclectic, critical form of late humanist erudition' that compared favourably with that of their counterparts anywhere in Europe,[4] neither obscurantist nor unfocused in their learning and, as *érudits*, offering models for acquiring knowledge that endured into the second half of the eighteenth century.[5] They had access to some outstanding resources. This scholarly community could disseminate its work through the University Press, transformed in the late 1660s by Bishop Fell and the Delegates into a learned publishing house with an adventurous programme of new, improved editions of the classics, including mathematical, astronomical, and geographical works[6] and, if they cared to do so, use (as did its many outside academic visitors) the Bodleian Library, one of the finest research libraries in Europe, perhaps the closest that England had to a national library until the foundation of the British Museum in 1753.[7]

In 1690 Fell's executors made over to the University all his interests in the Press (and his equipment) and a University Press in the modern sense finally came into existence. It. led to what Harry Carter has called the 'Augustan Age of the Press', one that lasted until the 1750s, when William Blackstone initiated a series of reforms to overhaul its operations.[8] Arthur Charlett of University College and Henry Aldrich of Christ Church were the key Delegates of the Press in their generation, the former a superb salesman through his ceaseless letter-writing and hospitality, and his assiduity in circulating lists of publications. Charlett was a forceful policer of what the Press published, ever cautious about needlessly

---

[3] See, among other writings, his *Establishing the New Science: The Experience of the Early Royal Society* (Woodbridge, 1989); *Science and Society in Restoration England* (Cambridge, 1981). For Hunter's sophisticated awareness of the wider currents of intellectual life see *Science and the Shape of Orthodoxy: Intellectual Change in late Seventeenth-Century Britain* (Woodbridge, 1995). For learned Societies as cultural rivals to the universities see comments in S. Shapin, *The Scientific Revolution* (Chicago, IL, 1997), 133.

[4] To use William Bulman's phrase. *Anglican Enlightenment*, 30.

[5] For the supposed eclipse of erudition in Enlightenment histories see Pocock, *Barbarism and Religion* (6 vols., Cambridge, 1999–2015), Vol. 1. *The Enlightenments of Edward Gibbon, 1737–1764*, 137–53.

[6] V. Feola and S. Mandelbrote, 'The learned press: geography, science and mathematics', in ed. Ian Gadd, *The History of Oxford University Press: Vol. 1. Beginnings to 1780* (Oxford, 2013), 317–57.

[7] David McKitterick, 'Wantonness and use. Ambitions for research libraries in early eighteenth-century England', in eds. R. G. W. Anderson, M. L. Caygill, A. G. MacGregor, and L. Syson, *Enlightening the British: knowledge, discovery and the museum in the eighteenth century* (London, 2003), 37–48, at 39. Undergraduates were admitted only if they were peers' sons. Brockliss (2), 271.

[8] Harry Carter, *A history of Oxford University Press, Vol. 1: To the year 1780* (Oxford, 1975); I. G. Philip, 'Oxford and scholarly publication in the eighteenth century', *BJECS*, 2 (1979), 123–37.

OXFORD AND BRITISH ACADEMIC CONTEXTS POST-1688   55

offending Whig politicians, and especially watchful of Nonjurors,[9] notably George Hickes—he required the suppression of the Anglo-Saxonist Edward Thwaites's *Heptateuchus* (1698) because it praised Hickes for his academic achievements.[10] But he also recognised true scholarship when he saw it and allowed the publication of Hickes's great *Thesaurus* in 1705 as well as other nonjuring publications, thus acting as something of an academic lifeline when these Nonjurors had no opportunity to hold official posts.[11] Taken together, the Press and the Bodleian, right down the 'long' eighteenth century, would keep scholars in Oxford who might otherwise be tempted to leave its precincts, with Oxford libraries busily acquiring the latest works of science and a range of publications reflecting Enlightenment scholarship. New areas of literary enquiry were opened up by the appearance of guides to its manuscript collections: the University published a catalogue of its manuscript holdings in 1697; in 1767 Oxford University Press published a catalogue of the manuscripts held by Oxford and Cambridge colleges.

Most Oxford academics, down to the mid-eighteenth century, like the majority of Europe's intellectual elite, qualified rather than abandoned scholastic modes of thought and, on that basis at any rate, might be deemed mentally 'unenlightened';[12] they did not consider that scholarly advance had to be at the cost of destabilising or uncoupling Church and state, or that knowledge could come at any price (as an event as fundamental as the Fall of Man had forever shown). The presumption remained that knowledge was already 'known' to men or was there to be recovered, inasmuch as that was possible (or desirable) in a postlapsarian society, with an underlying respect for classical culture as its essential repository. Such was the starting point of the predominantly Oxonian defence of the 'ancients' against those who looked to Richard Bentley and his followers in Cambridge, who had come to believe that thinkers in more recent decades represented the acme of epistemological progress.[13] Neither attitude was in itself unenlightened. Those who argued for the traditional view of the transmission of cultural values were not intellectually deficient or benighted for doing so. On the contrary, they believed that theirs was no less an enlightened attitude (not to be misappropriated in the service of the recklessly innovative) that involved custodianship of received learning and its defence, deployment, and creative restatement and refinement. Knowledge was both validated by and the buttress

---

[9] Thomas Hearne, *Remarks and Collections*, eds. C.E. Doble, D.W. Rannie, and H.E. Salter [Oxford Historical Society] (11 vols., Oxford, 1885–1921), VI. 46–7, 24 Apr. 1717.

[10] D. K. Money, *The English Horace: Anthony Alsop and the tradition of British Latin Verse* (London, 1998), 124–5.

[11] It would do the same for the antiquarian and diarist Thomas Hearne after 1715. Philip, 'Oxford and scholarly publication', 127, 130–1.

[12] Cf. Brown, 'Was there an Irish Enlightenment?', 63.

[13] For the origins and course of this cultural contestation in France in the 1680s, see more widely, the essays in eds. P. Bullard and A. Tadié, *Ancients and Moderns in Europe: comparative perspectives*. Oxford University studies in the Enlightenment (Oxford, 2016).

56 ENLIGHTENED OXFORD

of enlightened Christianity as represented by the Church of England. Only by fully retrieving this perspective can 'enlightenment' be understood in a correct, pre-modern mode that respects the range of contemporary meanings and does not become associated exclusively with the innovative minority attempting to challenge and diversify the meaning and range of knowledge.[14] Above all, it requires a nuanced understanding of the academic purposes of the oldest English university in the early eighteenth century, one which thereby properly allows for a measured estimate of the vitality and diversity of Oxford's intellectual life as well as its national and international impact.

The last two decades of the seventeenth century in western Europe saw the patchy emergence of an intellectual challenge to the predominantly clericalised culture of the universities, one that had religious toleration of Protestant minorities at its core, in part a response to the upsurge in religious violence and persecution across Europe in the 1680s.[15] The involvement of English dissenters in the wider Whig cause at the Revolution gave them some moral entitlement to legal recognition,[16] but opinion in the English universities was apprehensive that concessions to non-Anglicans might undermine academic control over what constituted legitimacy in knowledge as well as creating a probable vehicle for the dissemination of religious heterodoxy.[17] The consequences of the so-called Toleration Act 1689 (1 W&M *c*.18) proved in every way profound and not necessarily intended by its framers. It 'inaugurated a paradigm shift', for it effectively marked the end of the Church of England's claim after almost thirty years of struggle to be the national church, the single all-inclusive church of the English people.[18] And it was used by those who preferred not to go to church anywhere on Sundays to personal advantage. As one Christ Church man, Humphrey Prideaux, could see as early as 1692:

---

[14] As Richard Butterwick has argued, 'the violent language of polemics can lead to the neglect of stances betwixt and between the extremes of radical Enlightenment and apocalyptic Anti-Enlightenment, and evidence of the influence of the methods, priorities, discourses and assumptions of the "enlightened age" upon some of its severest critics is not hard to find.' 'Introduction' in eds. Butterwick, Davies, and Espinosa, *Peripheries of the Enlightenment*, 1–16, at 14.

[15] John Marshall, *John Locke, Toleration and Early Enlightenment Culture* (Cambridge, 2006), 17, 19; P. Zagorin, *How the Idea of Religious Toleration came to the West* (Princeton, NJ, 2003); John Coffey, *Persecution and Toleration in Protestant England, 1558–1689* (London, 2000);); ed. A. Levine, *Early Modern Skepticism and the Origins of Toleration* (Lanham, MD, 1999). Ian Hunter has suggested the late seventeenth century witnessed a 'civil enlightenment'. Hunter, *Rival Enlightenments: Civil and Metaphysical Philosophy in early modern Germany* (Cambridge, 2001). That Anglican Christianity made for the ideal civil religion is foundational to Bulman, *Anglican Enlightenment*.

[16] For the Act of 1689 as a political tactic, a mode of power not a prop to freedom, see ibid., 6, 211.

[17] For attitudes at Cambridge see Gascoigne, *Cambridge*, 75–81; Victor Morgan, [with a contribution by C. Brooke], *A history of the University of Cambridge*, Vol. 2, *1546–1750* (Cambridge, 2004), 526–9, 546.

[18] The quotation is from Ralph Stevens, 'Anglican responses to the Toleration Act , 1689–1714', Ph. D. thesis (Cambridge University, 2014), 4; G. V. Bennett, 'Conflict in the Church', in ed. Geoffrey Holmes, *Britain after the Glorious Revolution, 1689–1714* (Basingstoke, 1969), 155–75; John Spurr, *The Restoration Church of England*, 105 ; Spurr, 'The Church of England, comprehension and the Toleration Act of 1689', *EHR*, 104 (1989), 927–46.

OXFORD AND BRITISH ACADEMIC CONTEXTS POST-1688   57

The Act of Toleration hath almost undon us, not in increaseing ye number of dissenters but of wicked and profane persons; for it is now difficult almost to get any to church, all pleadeing ye licence, although they make use of it only for ye alehouse.[19]

Similarly, the lapsing of the Licensing Act in 1695 unleashed a welter of publication on religious and moral topics that had no particular regard for the Church of England or its vehicle, the University of Oxford.[20] The impact of these changes in public culture was felt quickly by the University which, paradoxically, had initially welcomed the abdication of James II: his attempts at royal absolutism were acceptable on condition that they secured the existing order in Church and State, not, as actually happened, wrought havoc with it through an over-hasty attempt to intrude his Catholic co-religionists into positions of authority, at Oxford as elsewhere.[21] Little wonder that, at the close of 1688, Gilbert Ironside (Vice Chancellor, 1687–9, and Warden of Wadham) collaborated with John, 3rd Lord Lovelace (another Wadham graduate), of Hurley near Henley-on-Thames, commander of the local Williamite forces. Lovelace arrived at Oxford with 300 men to claim Oxford for the Prince of Orange, and Ironside quietly steered the University towards recognising the new regime.[22]

There was relief and apprehension in equal measure at James II's departure. But when William and Mary accepted the Convention's offer of the throne on 13 February 1689, the whole Church of England was plunged into a crisis that directly affected the University. It spoke volumes that three quarters of the bishops did not feel able to assist at the coronation of the joint monarchs. Oxford may have been traumatised by the late king's behaviour, but it suffered another blow in the erection of a replacement regime that was not adequately grounded in heredity to satisfy an institution that felt uncomfortable in a world that had suddenly made the doctrines of passive obedience and non-resistance (reaffirmed in

---

[19] ed. Edward Maunde Thompson, *Letters of Humphrey Prideaux sometime Dean of Norwich to John Ellis sometime Under-Secretary of State 1674–1722* (Camden Society, London, 1875), 154, 27 June 1692. As J. G. A. Pocock has observed, 'Toleration exacts a price of secularisation and politicisation...' *Barbarism and Religion*. Vol. 5. *Religion: The First Triumph* (Cambridge, 2010), 16.

[20] Michael Treadwell, 'The stationers and the printing acts at the end of the seventeenth century', in eds. John Barnard and D. F. McKenzie, *The Cambridge History of the Book in Britain. Vol. IV: 1557–1695* (Cambridge, 2002), 755–76. Robert G. Ingram deems the lapse of the Act to be serving as 'the English Enlightenment's midwife'.

[21] The thirty fellows intruded by the Crown at Magdalen are examined in L.W.B. Brockliss, G. Harriss, and A. Macintyre, *Magdalen College and the Crown: Essays for the tercentenary of the restoration of the college 1688* (Oxford, 1988).

The College did not turn into a Catholic seminary in 1687–8; a hybrid, religiously mixed society resulted but Protestants feared the worst. Similarly, when the king visited University College in 1687 (where the Catholic Obadiah Walker had been intruded as Master), he heard vespers in Walker's Catholic chapel but also made a point of visiting the College's Anglican chapel.

[22] C. S. L. Davies, 'Decline and Revival: 1660–1900', in eds. C. Davies and J. Garnett, *Wadham College* (London, 1994), 36–55, at 38. His work in Oxford done, Ironside became Bishop of Bristol in 1689, tr. Hereford, 1691, d. 1701.

58 ENLIGHTENED OXFORD

proclamations as recently as 1683 and 1685) practically redundant. The University greeted William's accession with deep ambivalence, for it had essentially been wrong-footed.[23] Only a few months previously the birth of a Catholic heir to James on 10 June 1688 was officially recognised in a formal Act on the stage of the Sheldonian Theatre and the publication of a volume of over one hundred poems in honour of the event, including many from Whigs who later supported the Revolution.[24] Once that momentous event had been accomplished the University had to acknowledge that William deserved credit for rescuing the realm from nascent Popish tyranny. The new king stood forth yet more clearly as a Protestant warrior, but Oxford was neither comfortable in celebrating his role as such[25] nor readily able to find any other that would be acceptable. It could only, to a very limited extent, join in the rhetoric of providential deliverance for one who lacked the sanction of hereditary right.[26] For, if 'The Dutch descent [of 1688] was disastrous for James,...it was also a resounding defeat for Anglican royalism',[27] or at least that model of Anglican royalism that had characterised Oxford and, by extension, much of the Established Church since the reign of James I.

The 1690s were a decade in which Oxford adjusted awkwardly to these new religio-political realities,[28] and the disinterested fostering of intellectual discovery was hard to achieve with a new regime struggling to establish itself during the War of the Augsburg League (1689–97) combined with intense party warfare destabilising patterns of patronage. Many alumni, both clerical and lay, who had watched despairingly as James II inflicted such damage on the monarchy, could not in

---

[23] David Money has identified twenty-seven Oxonian 'vicars of Bray' (including the vice chancellor and two heads of houses) who had contributed to a 1688 commemorative book of verse honouring the birth of the (Catholic) Prince of Wales and also to the 1689 volume (the *Vota Oxoniensia*) on the accession of William and Mary. *The English Horace*, 244.

[24] W. Gibson, '*Strenae Natalitiae*: Ambivalence and Equivocation in Oxford in 1688', *History of Universities*, XXXI/1 (2018), 121–40. An annual panegyric in memory of James II was still declaimed at Brasenose College between 1701 and 1711 thanks to a bequest from Sir Francis Bridgeman. Crook, *Brasenose*, 97. For the importance of the Sheldonian theatre as an academic space see Anthony Geraghty, *The Sheldonian Theatre: architecture and learning in seventeenth-century Oxford* (New Haven, CT, 2013).

[25] For William as another Oliver Cromwell see Craig Rose, *England in the 1690s. Revolution, Religion and War* (London, 1999), 33–4.

[26] Ibid., 19–23. For Oxford's initial professions of loyalty to the new king, see Ward, *Georgian Oxford*, 52–3. There was some reluctance among Oxford dons to sign an informal association to protect William after he had landed (drawn up by the Tory Sir Edward Seymour), but most did so when William invited them, even by those who, Gilbert Burnet alleged, '...being disappointed in the preferments they aspired to, became afterwards his most implacable enemies'Burnet, *History of his own time*, ed. M. Routh, (6 vols., Oxford, 1833), III. 350. I am grateful to Tony Claydon for his guidance on this point.

[27] Jacqueline Rose, *Godly Kingship in Restoration England: The Politics of the Royal Supremacy, 1660–1688* (Cambridge, 2011), 274.

[28] See the comments in ibid., 280, on the Church of England as a whole in negotiating Williamite revolution in the 1690s. For the unsuccessful attempts of Oxford MPs to have a bill passed enshrining the University's privileges, and the vindictive requirement in 1694 that members of the University take a special oath of loyalty imposed on no one else, see Bennett, 'Against the tide: Oxford under William III', in HUO V, 31–60, at 32–3, 34, 36, 50.

OXFORD AND BRITISH ACADEMIC CONTEXTS POST-1688   59

conscience take the oaths to William and Mary and withdrew from public life. Though chronically short of funds, such was the choice of Oxford's High Steward in 1689, Henry Hyde, 2nd earl of Clarendon (d. 1709), who at least retained the university office he had held since 1686.[29] Behind the scenes, Clarendon retained respect, loyalty, and influence. He was prominent, for instance, in helping to organise resistance to the cause of Comprehension in the Church of England. Having changed the monarch, the University hierarchy tended to be ultra-protective of the Established Church after the Revolution, none more so than William Jane, canon of Christ Church, Regius Professor of Divinity since 1680, a chaplain of Bishop Compton of London's.[30] Along with William's favourite Whig divines, John Tillotson and Gilbert Burnet, Jane joined a commission of divines to revise the 1662 Book of Common Prayer to make it more acceptable to dissenters and facilitate a Comprehension. In late 1689, it 'produced a carefully devised but generous set of proposals'[31] that were acceptable to a minority of Tories (chiefly, the friends of Secretary of State, Lord Nottingham) but, by then, Jane had already ceased to attend the commission's meetings. Senior Oxonians marshalled their forces to prepare for Convocation. The Hyde brothers, Lords Rochester (who *did* take the oaths) and Clarendon,[32] went to Oxford to devise with Jane a scheme of opposition to Comprehension, and it was a sign of the latter's popularity with the lower clergy that he easily defeated Tillotson to be elected as prolocutor of the Lower House by 55 votes to 28.[33] The vote prefigured the balance of parties in the assembly and the cause of Comprehension was killed off for at least one

---

[29] Henry Hyde, 2nd earl of Clarendon (1638–1709), succeeded his (exiled) father 1674. He was James's former brother-in-law, and uncle of Mary II. See *The Correspondence of Henry Hyde, Earl of Clarendon, and his brother Laurence Hyde, Earl of Rochester, with the Diary of Lord Clarendon from 1687 to 1690*... ed. S. W. Singer, (2 vols., London, 1828). For some time after 1689 (perhaps through the good offices of Clarendon's brother Rochester), leading churchmen who had accepted William and Mary met their nonjuring brethren on a number of occasions at Clarendon's house, and discussed public affairs. His chaplain was the leading nonjuring polemicist, Charles Leslie. W. Gibson, *A Social History of the Domestic Chaplain 1530–1840* (Leicester, 1997), 94.

[30] Jane had sought out the Prince of Orange at Hungerford on his advance east towards London and, in assuring the Prince of the support of the University (though not his coming to the crown), intimated his willingness to succeed to the see of Oxford, vacant through the death of bishop John Fell. On both scores he was unsuccessful. R. A. P. J. Beddard, 'Jane, William (bap. 1645, d. 1707)', *ODNB* (2009), online edn. Jane took the oaths to William and Mary. Despite having framed the Oxford declaration in favour of passive obedience in 1683, he had apparently changed his mind on that score.

[31] Bennett, 'Conflict in the Church', 162; Brent S. Sirota, *The Christian monitors. The Church of England and the age of benevolence, 1680–1730* (New Haven, CT, 2014), 77–80.

[32] The Hyde division over the succession is discussed in G. Tapsell, 'Laurence Hyde and the politics of religion in later Stuart England', *EHR*, 125 (2010), 1415–48, at 142–3.

[33] Nicholas Tyacke, *Aspects of English Protestantism, c. 1530–1700: politics, culture, and society in early modern Britain* (Manchester, 2001), 76–7; T. J. Fawcett, *The liturgy of comprehension, 1689: An abortive attempt to revise the Book of Common Prayer* (London, 1973), 24–46. Significantly, Jane was backed by Bishop Compton. S. Hampton, *Anti-Arminians: the Anglican Reformed tradition from Charles II to George I* (Oxford, 2008), 14–15. The London divine, William Payne, observed that the Church had become fatally divided between 'Janites and Tillotsonians'. Sirota, *The Christian Monitors*, 83.

60   ENLIGHTENED OXFORD

generation. It also revealed the divisions in Tory ranks that mirrored those over the offer of the Crown.[34]

Oxford was not alone in adjusting awkwardly to unpredictable times, and a Revolution that 'was rushed, un-thought-out, and ambiguous'.[35] It shook all aspects of national institutional life and every university in the British Isles suffered upheaval, Oxford rather less than most in its reversion (at least in terms of personnel) to the status quo ante 1685. There was no counterpart to the Catholic Counter-Revolution that Trinity College, Dublin, faced in 1688–9 until William III's victory at the Boyne in July 1690 vindicated the stubborn resistance to King James's suborning of their statutes by the Fellows.[36] Neither was Oxford subject to the investigative commissions that were the lot of the Scottish Universities after the Revolution, a sign of the degree to which the Revolution north of the border was contested.[37] The Episcopalian establishment (composed of very reluctant Revolutionaries in 1688–9) was deemed an unreliable prop for the new regime, many clergy who could not in conscience accept the abolition of the hierarchy were cast adrift, either hanging on precariously in their parishes or moving to England or the American colonies in search of an appointment.[38] Both clergy and laity who shared the same ecclesiology as Oxford dons often sent their sons south to that University rather than have them tainted by Presbyterian teachings. Thus Queen Anne's future doctor, John Arbuthnot (1667–1735), moved within Oxford circles when the young man he was tutoring (Edward Jeffreys, son of a City Alderman) went up to University College in 1694.[39] An altogether exceptional case was Sir George Mackenzie, fearful Scottish law officer during the Stuart reaction of the early 1680s. He retired permanently from Scottish public life after the Revolution and accepting its outcome, came south to matriculate as a very mature student at University College, Oxford in the summer of 1690. He set himself the research project of undertaking a new commentary on Justinian's Digest (the powers required by rulers to preserve

---

[34] More details in Spurr, 'The Church of England, comprehension and the Toleration Act'.

[35] Jonathan Clark, *From Restoration to Reform. The British Isles 1660–1832* (London, 2014), 156.

[36] R. B. McDowell and D. A. Webb, *Trinity College Dublin: an academic history* (Dublin, 2004); J. V. Luce, *Trinity College Dublin: the first 400 years* (Dublin, 1992).

[37] pp. 32–7, this chapter.

[38] Addresses from Episcopalian clergy 'deprived of their charges' to the archbishop of Canterbury and William III, 1695, NAS, Leven & Melville Muniments, GD26/10/79, GD26/10/80; Tim Harris, 'Incompatible revolutions?: the Established Church and the revolutions of 1688–9 in Ireland, England and Scotland', in eds. Allan Macinnes and J. Ohlmeyer, *The Stuart kingdoms in the seventeenth century: awkward neighbours* (Dublin, 2002), 204–25; Jeffrey Stephen, *Defending the revolution. The Church of Scotland 1689–1716* (Farnham, 2013), 25, 123–4, 128. After 1695, there was statutory protection of Scottish Episcopalian clergy still in post. See A. Raffe, *The culture of controversy: religious arguments in Scotland, 1660–1714* (Woodbridge, 2012).

[39] Arbuthnot took his MD at St Andrews but was again regularly in Oxford from the late 1690s. His son Charles became a Student of Christ Church. Lester M. Beattie, *John Arbuthnot: mathematician and satirist* (Cambridge, MA, 1935); *The correspondence of John Arbuthnot*, ed. Angus Ross, (Munich, 2006). For his links to David Gregory see D. E. Shuttleton, '"A modest examination": John Arbuthnot and the Scottish Newtonians', *JECS* 18 (1995), 47–62.

civil order particularly interested him) but he died in London in May 1691 with his project unfinished.

Regime change did not stifle academic enterprise at Oxford but it did little in itself to encourage it. The scholarly consensus is that the early English Enlightenment took shape largely (but not entirely) elsewhere, essentially in civic, urban spaces favourable to its pan-Protestant character and willingness to refashion and reduce Anglican hegemony. In the coffee-houses, taverns, playhouses, private clubs, and societies of early Augustan London, the member-ship of the Republic of Letters underwent subtle reconfiguration rivalling (and, to some extent, eroding) the university as a place of informal learning and politeness.[40] But such cultural spaces existed in Oxford, too. Here the spread of coffee-houses had an irresistible force, and they were as popular with members of the university as townsmen. This growth in civil society allowed for new social diversions and intellectual exchanges on topics most university men might regard as inadmissible, prefer to classify as 'forbidden knowledge', or relate confi-dentially in the privacy of a college setting. For the University traditionally made claim to the sacred character of genuine learning, and knowledge that had the intended or accidental purpose of subverting or scoffing at the providential ordering of the world, the nature of the Godhead, or the character of the Church was not to be lightly admitted into circulation. The embarrassing problem for Oxford was that a minority of its senior members were quite happy to break with that consensus after the Revolution, disregardful of the academic and social penal-ties that would follow.

In William's reign it seemed that heretical teaching and the growth of scepticism *inside* the University were unavoidable by-products of the challenge to adapt quickly to changed times. Arthur Bury's privately printed *The Naked Gospel* [Rector of Exeter College since 1666, and a pro-Vice Chancellor], caused scandal for its apparent Socinianism well beyond Oxford when it appeared in 1690 under the name of 'a true son of the Church of England',[41] but he spoke for many in seeking to set aside allegedly unscriptural Christian dogmas and join in as part of a wider national debate (that Tories did not want) over the next few years, on the politics of Christology. It may be seen as a concomitant of the Established Church's post-Revolutionary repositioning,[42] and an English

---

[40] Cf. Anne Goldgar, *Impolite learning: conduct and community in the Republic of Letters, 1680–1750* (New Haven, CT, 1995).

[41] Expertly discussed in Pocock, *Barbarism and Religion*, I. 105–9, who writes of its 'invective against the Fathers' (I. 106). It was burnt in the Schools Quadrangle by order of the University in August 1690. The barrister and mystical writer William Freke was similarly convicted in 1694 of blasphemy for a tract called a *Brief and Clear Confutation of the Doctrine of the Trinity*, fined £500, and forced to publicly recant. He had ceased to reside at Oxford in 1679 but, embarrassingly for Wadham College, was still connected with the University. Wells, *Wadham College*, 117.

[42] For the wider background see Paul C. H. Lim, *The crisis of the Trinity in early modern England* (Oxford, 2012); B. Sirota, 'The Trinitarian crisis in church and state: religious controversy and the

62   ENLIGHTENED OXFORD

instance of what Pocock has called an Arminian (transmuting into a Socinian) Enlightenment.[43]

Bury's book—he still managed to bring out a second edition of his work in 1691[44]—inaugurated a polemical altercation that rocked (and embarrassed) the University well into the 1690s with the assertive efforts of pro-Trinitarians led by John Wallis, Professor of Geometry and chaplain to William III, doing nothing to stifle the controversy in and beyond Oxford.[45] When, in November 1695, the University found Joseph Bingham (1668–1723), a Fellow of University College, who had preached a sermon at St Mary's Church intended to restate the orthodox position in reply to the Dean of St Paul's, William Sherlock, the jittery Vice Chancellor, Fitzherbert Adams, and half the Heads of Houses found Bingham guilty of heresy for his Trinitarian views. The condemnation was widely adjudged to be an over-reaction and led to the University being rebuked in a royal decree of the following year for usurping the royal prerogative.[46] Otherwise the Crown, remembering the traumatic events of 1687–8 in Oxford, was content to be minimally intrusive in its academic affairs during the 1690s.

The presence of the incendiary anticlerical, antiTrinitarian Irishman, John Toland, in Oxford in 1694–5, making use of the Bodleian Library for materials on 'primitive Christianity' for his *Christianity not Mysterious* (1696) and trading on his growing celebrity status caused further embarrassment.[47] The book's

making of the postrevolutionary Church of England, 1687–1702', *JBS*, 52 (2013), 26–54; S. Trowell, 'Unitarian and/or Anglican: the relationship of Unitarianism to the Church from 1687–98', *BJRL*, 78 (1996), 77–101; Christopher J. Walker, *Reason and religion in late seventeenth-century England. The politics and theology of radical Dissent* (London, 2013), 170–3; John Marshall, 'Socinianism, "Socinianism" and "Unitarianism"', in ed. M. A. Stewart, *English philosophy in the age of Locke* (Oxford, 2000), 111–82.

[43] *Barbarism and religion*, Vol. 2. *Narratives of civil government*, 11, 19, 94–5, 142–3, 150–1, 271, 312; Hugh Trevor-Roper, 'The religious origins of the Enlightenment', in Trevor-Roper, *Religion, the Reformation and social change: the crisis of the seventeenth century* (London, 1967), 179–218. On the different meanings of 'Socinian' in this period see Victor Nouvo, 'Locke's theology', in ed. M.A. Stewart, *English philosophy in the age of Locke* (Oxford, 2000), 183–215, at 211–12.

[44] See his Bury, *The Danger of Delaying Repentance; Set forth in a Sermon Preached to the University, at St Mary's Church on Oxford, On New Year's Day, 1691/2* (London, 1692).

[45] Redwood, *Reason, Ridicule and Religion*, 156–62. That leading member of the 1690s Protestant International, Jean Le Clerc, complained of Oxford's crackdown on Bury and how as earlier '... *Platonic Enthusiasm* was impos'd upon the Word for *Faith, Mystery,* and *Revelation* by cloyster'd Ecclesiasticks'. Le Clerc, *An Historical Vindication of the Naked Gospel, Recommended to the University of Oxford* (London, 1690), 'The Preface to the Reader', sig. A2r.

[46] Abp Tenison to V-C. Adams, 24 Dec. 1695, reporting that the matter had been referred to the judges and their verdict was that the Oxford proceeding was 'unaccountable and illegal', a 'High Usurpation' of the 'king's prerogative' and a 'manifest violation of the laws of this Realm'. William was 'not well pleased' but out of 'his Tender Care for learning' would 'passe by' these proceedings. Bodl. MS Ballard 9, f. 15. The primary target in the Oxford decree was really Sherlock, who had form for High Churchmen for having first refused the oaths to William and Mary and then recanted. The Bingham affair and its aftermath is admirably discussed in Sirota, 'Trinitarian Crisis', 49–51. Adams was Rector of Lincoln College.

[47] Toland was looking at sources on Irish history while in Oxford; he was also an associate of White Kennett and John Aubrey, working with the latter on the history of Druidism. Wayne Hudson, *The English Deists: studies in early Enlightenment* (London, 2009), 85; J. R. Wigelsworth, 'Fashioning Identity in Eighteenth-Century Politics: The case of John Toland', in eds. David A. Valone and Jill

OXFORD AND BRITISH ACADEMIC CONTEXTS POST-1688 63

profound debt to Spinoza was too obvious to be denied.[48] At least Toland was an outsider. It was a Fellow of All Souls College, Matthew Tindal (1657–1733), someone familiar with the High Church position from within, who in Anne's reign proceeded to publish the coruscating *The Rights of the Christian Church Asserted* (1706),[49] an extreme, anti-sacramental and anti-sacerdotal Erastian tract that was burned by the common hangman (along with Sacheverell's notorious 5 November 1709 sermon) by order of the House of Commons in March 1710.[50] It attracted over forty replies led by Thomas Potter, the new Regius Professor of Divinity, but, as Bishop William Wake of Lincoln told Archbishop Tenison, Tindal's book had 'done more hurt among the gentlemen & perhaps nobility too' than any comparable publication of that decade.[51] It also brought All Souls into disrepute despite the efforts of Warden Gardiner to contain his colleague's influence.[52] Tindal meanwhile cultivated a set of connections whose sentiments also did him no favours with mainstream opinion inside Oxford.[53]

When it came to the academic establishment's receptiveness both to new scholarship and treatises offering novel social and institutional perspectives much hung on the personal character and political allegiance of the author.

Marie Bradbury, *Anglo-Irish Identities, 1571–1845* (Lewisburg, PA, 2008), 59–83, at 60–1; Chapter 9, p. 109. Justin Champion noted Toland's early brilliance 'in adapting, expanding and appropriating the commonplace routines of cultural authority to his own purposes', which was precisely what so discomforted University opinion and led to the vice-chancellor ordering him to leave (which he did only to return when the latter was absent). *Republican learning: John Toland and the Crisis of Christian Culture* (Manchester, 2003), 12.

[48] Ian Leask, 'The undivulged event in Toland's <u>Christianity not mysterious</u>', in eds. W. Hudson, D. Lucci, and J. R. Wigelsworth, *Atheism and deism revalued. Heterodox religious identities in Britain, 1650–1850* (Farnham, 2014), 63–80, at 63–75.

[49] It was published anonymously but his authorship was an open secret. Stephen Lalor, *Matthew Tindal, freethinker. An eighteenth-century assault on religion* (London, 2006), 12–16.

[50] William Carroll, chaplain of All Souls (and Tindal's colleague), claimed the *Rights of the Christian Church* was based on Spinoza's *Rights of the Christian clergy* and part of an attempt by 'the deists' or 'Spinozerian atheists' to subvert revealed religion. Locke was also arraigned for his irreligion. Carroll, *Spinoza reviv'd . . .* (Oxford, 1709), 4–15; R. Colie, 'Spinoza in England 1665–1730', *Proceedings of the American Philosophical Society*, 107 (1963), 183–219. For the threat that Spinoza was perceived to pose to scripture and conventional theological hermeneutics see J. Samuel Preus, *Spinoza and the irrelevance of Biblical authority* (Cambridge, 2001). The Sacheverell affair is discussed in Chapter 7.

[51] Wake to Tenison, 24 Sept. 1708, Bodl. MS Eng. C. 3191, ff. 1–2, quoted in Alex Barber, '"Why don't those lazy priests answer the book?" Matthew Tindal, censorship, freedom of the press and religious debate in early eighteenth-century England', *History*, 98 (2013), 680–707, at 705. See also J. A. I. Champion, *The pillars of priestcraft shaken. The Church of England and its enemies* (Cambridge, 1992), 136–8; Dmitri Levitin, 'Matthew Tindal's *Rights of the Christian Church* (1706) and the Church-state relationship', *HJ*, 54 (2011), 717–40.

[52] Thomas Tanner, a former chaplain at All Souls, admitted that the College had 'furnish'd' the nation with 'all sorts of Freethinking'. He hoped people would realise 'that we are not all quite corrupted'. Bodl Ballard MS 4, f. 134r, to Arthur Charlett, 16 Sept. 1717. Quoted in Jeffrey R. Wigelsworth, *Deism in Enlightenment England. Theology, politics, and Newtonian public science* (Manchester, 2009), 59–60. See also 58–64.

[53] Oxford 'Tindalites' included Sedgwick Harrison, a don of indifferent morality, and Blencombe Fisher, who sought to secularise rules for holding fellowships at All Souls. Further afield Tindal was linked with the bookseller and pamphleteer Edmund Curll (1675–1747) and Eustace Budgell (1686–1737), Addison's cousin and miscellaneous journalist, who gave Walpole legal advice on how to drive High Churchmen out of the universities. Hudson, *The English Deists*, 108; Israel, *Radical Enlightenment*, 298.

64   ENLIGHTENED OXFORD

There was a widespread presumption in many quarters of post-Revolution Oxford that Whig principles and libertinism were the real motives of those re-examining the first principles of society, and this conviction became a prima facie basis for damning much of what was being advanced in pamphlet, manuscript, or oral form. Such was not always the case. Certainly Commonwealth Whigs were thriving in this slightly more open public space and they were keen to break or at least reduce Anglican monopolies.[54] There was a neo-republican, dissenting dimension to associative sociability of this sort that limited its appeal and yet, despite small numbers, it was a serious issue for most Oxford-educated dons and clerics by the late 1690s. It was one of the concerns informing the demands for the revival of Convocation to prevent, as leading firebrand Francis Atterbury of Christ Church saw it, the religion of England from being corrupted, and fuelled the cry of the 'Church in Danger'.[55] As one put it, 'whereas our former fears were of Popery and Arbitrary Government now it is of a Commonwealth and the pressure of the Church by the dissenters'.[56]

The changed times demanded that apologists prominent in Oxford appear upon the national stage, which suited the ambitious among them, like Atterbury and William Jane, well enough. The Revolution had given the latter the chance for a political rather than an academic career (though it was rumoured in 1696 that he was to be removed from his chair, as he had not signed the Articles of Association to protect King William), and he was happy, like others before and after, to take his chance and give the world of Lambeth and Westminster priority over professorial duties. Jane was among the most prominent members of the revived 1701 Convocation and under his chairmanship they appointed a committee of Religion 'for the examination of books lately published against the Truth of the Christian Religion'.[57] It extracted five propositions from Toland's *Christianity not Mysterious* but the Upper House (where Whig-inclined prelates had a small majority) decided it had not the legal capacity for judicial censure.[58] A decade on after the Revolution, the University was trying to adjust to a world in which the Church had ceased to be national while remaining established; the hereditary succession to the throne had been broken; dissenters had the legal right to set up

---

[54] In the unstable politics of the 1690s some Commonwealth Whigs in the 1690s were tempted by Jacobitism see M. Goldie, 'The roots of true Whiggism 1688–94', *History of Political Thought*, 1 (1980), 195–236; P. Monod, *Jacobitism and the English people 1688–1788* (Cambridge, 1989), 23–5.

[55] [Atterbury], *A Letter to a Convocation-Man* (London, 1697), 5, 7, 22, 23, 26, 33.

[56] *HMC, Downshire MSS* (6 vols., London, 1924–95), I. 304–5.

[57] Sirota, *The Christian Monitors*, 197. The ambitious Jane's numerous public involvements (he had also been Dean of Gloucester since 1685) gave him little time to function as Regius Professor of Divinity (since 1680). George Smalridge discharged his duties as deputy and, by early in Anne's reign, there was a growing sense across the University that Jane should resign his chair.

[58] Edward Cardwell, *Synodalia. A collection of articles of religion, canons, etc. for the year 1547 to the year 1717* (2 vols., Oxford, 1842), II. 701–5; Justin Champion, *Republican learning: John Toland and the crisis of Christian culture* (Manchester, 2003), 77; M. Greig, 'Heresy hunt: Gilbert Burnet and the Convocation controversy of 1701', *HJ*, 37 (1994), 569–92.

schools and academies with modern curriculum provisions; publication of materials challenging previously sacrosanct views on God, government, and the ordering of society had become much easier, and the commercial interest looking to support from Whigs and dissenters was inexorably rising in the metropolis. It fuelled an emerging consensus inside the elite that there was something wanting in popular religious activity, an anxiety about the erosion of traditional certainties, and a fear of a growth in irreligion.[59] It left the University after 1689 facing unprecedented competition with its standing from the new dissenting academies, learned societies of national and international importance, and the literate public without degrees looking to the unlicensed press for instruction. Oxford's task was thus retrieving intellectual authority and prestige when controls on publishing were eroding and respect for institutional authority was tempered. It would take a variety of imaginative responses to rise to the occasion.

What then was to be Oxford's role in this post-Revolutionary world? It had adapted, not unsuccessfully, to the Commonwealth and interregnum, and there was nothing to stop it being a powerhouse again after 1689. Yet, just as the University feared its own status was being undermined by new social and intellectual forces, so governments were apprehensive and watchful that Oxford had many members who, to a greater extent than Cambridge, had no interest in trying to shore up the values and wider institutional life of the British state, first under William III and then, after the intermission of Queen Anne's reign (when there could be a pretence that the Stuart status quo ante had been restored), under George I (1714–27). It suited Whigs to exaggerate Oxford's character for disloyalty for party political advantage and it generally worked (certainly after 1714–15 when its Chancellor fled and entered the service of 'the [Old] Pretender').[60] Yet the fact was that that Chancellor (1688–1715), the 2nd Duke of Ormond, had been loyal to William and Mary and fought alongside the King at the Boyne and in later military engagements of the Nine Years' War.[61] In Anne's reign, to widespread pleasure in Oxford, he came into his own and controversially succeeded Marlborough as Captain-General of the Queen's forces in 1712.[62] He was an unimpeachable high Anglican and court Tory who had shown imaginative adaptability in the extraordinary circumstances of 1688–90. Here was a model that Oxford men could imitate and look to for protection in the years succeeding it.

[59] See the perceptive comments of Julian Hoppit, *A land of liberty? England 1689–1727* (Oxford, 2002), 208, 225.

[60] Ward, *Georgian Oxford*, 69ff.

[61] Ormond's simultaneous tenure of the Chancellorship of Trinity College, Dublin, made him an immensely powerful patron in British and Irish academic life. See David Hayton, 'Dependence, clientage and affinity: the political following of the second Duke of Ormonde', in eds. Toby Barnard and Jane Fenlon, *The Dukes of Ormonde, 1610–1745* (Woodbridge, 1999), 211–42.

[62] In 1713 the University congratulated itself 'that one of their sacred order, bred amongst us', John Robinson, Bishop of Bristol, was treating for peace on terms dictated by an army under the duke's command. UOA: MS. Conv. Reg. Bd 31, f. 89 (register of convocation, 1704–30).

Fig. 2.1 James Butler, 2nd duke of Ormond, Studio of Michael Dahl, oil on canvas, c.1713 (© National Portrait Gallery, London).

If the realm as a whole had changed course decisively then the oldest University in England could surely do so.

Most academics in the 1690s knew that it made sense for them politically to try to work with the new regime if they were to better themselves professionally, and astute operators with friends in Westminster, such as Henry Aldrich of Christ Church and Arthur Charlett of University College, took care to keep abreast of developments at court, in government, and in Parliament.[63] By comparison with Cambridge, there were relatively few members of the University resigning either their fellowships or their livings to become Nonjurors (though this did not lessen the admiration of many for those who did).[64] Partly as a result of recognising that

---

[63] Charlett was desperate to avoid more royal intervention. Ward, *Georgian Oxford*, 12–13.

[64] Precise numbers vary according to sources. At Cambridge there were reportedly thirty-seven fellows and four scholars ejected as Nonjurors as opposed to twenty-five fellows and one scholar at Oxford. C. Wordsworth, *Social life at the English universities in the eighteenth century* (London, 1874), 603–5; Anthony Wood, *The life and times of Anthony Wood, antiquary, of Oxford, 1632-1695, described by Himself*, ed. Andrew Clark, (5 vols., Oxford, 1891–5), III. 307–9, 9, 31 Aug. 1689. Cf. Brockliss (2), 210. The Oxford figures included the gifted scholar Henry Dodwell (1641–1711), Camden Prof. of History, 1688–91, discussed in Chapter 4, pp. 43-4. Nonjurors among Cambridge

OXFORD AND BRITISH ACADEMIC CONTEXTS POST-1688   67

he had rescued them from the traumas of James II's depredations, they were largely comfortable with recognising William as king *de facto* and not being asked to swear loyalty to him *de jure* following the court Tory example of such as the 2nd Earl of Nottingham.[65] The University formally celebrated victory at the Boyne in 1690 and lamented Queen Mary's death in 1694;[66] its members even turned out in force when the Dutch king appeared briefly in person at the Sheldonian Theatre on 9 November 1695 at the behest of the University's MP and the then Secretary of State for the Northern Department, Sir William Trumbull.[67] Though affection for William III was lukewarm, there was an underlying recognition of what the University owed to him, and addresses in 1696 (abhorring the attempt on his life),[68] 1697, and 1701 were both fulsome and acceptable, and set off with mood music that included bells, bonfires, and illuminations.[69] These were adroit exercises in public relations that were only appropriate for a University with a Chancellor who was one of the kingdom's leading generals in the 1690s and a duke with a Dutch mother who happened to be William's cousin.[70] However, Oxonians who actually joined in the Williamite panegyrics orchestrated by that Tory hate figure, Bishop Gilbert Burnet of Salisbury, were few and far between, though one distinguished defence of the Revolution in print came (anonymously)

---

alumni were 200, as opposed to 157 from Oxford. J. C. Findon, 'The Nonjurors and the Church of England, 1689–1716', unpub. D. Phil. dissertation (Oxford, 1979), Table 1. The removal of all remaining Nonjurors from fellowships was ordered by the government in 1691. Bill, *Christ Church*, 144. But the vice-chancellor, Jonathan Edwards, played for time on the basis that '... the Queen's letter for that purpose was only directed to him, whereas it should have been to him and the Heads of the Universitie [i.e. Houses]'. Wood, *Life and Times*, ed. Clark, III. 373, 15 Oct. 1691.

[65] For Nottingham and the Revolution see H. Horwitz, *Revolution Politicks: the career of Daniel Finch, second Earl of Nottingham, 1647–1730* (Cambridge, 1968), 82–3.

[66] William III had received in person the address from Oxford on the death of Mary as a special favour to Ormond, and it is said to have caused 'teares to stand in his eyes'. Wood, *Life and Times*, ed. Clark, III. 477, 28 Jan. 1695.

[67] *Calendar of State Papers Domestic: William and Mary, 1695 Addenda 1689–1695*, ed. W. J. Hardy (London, 1908), 86–96; Wood, *Life and Times*, ed. Clark, III. 494–5; *HMC*, Buccleuch and Queensberry (Montagu House) *MSS* (2 vols., London, 1897–1903), II, pt. I. 242–55. It was reported that the King had left for Windsor without his dinner because of a warning that he was to be poisoned and that he had been hissed in the Sheldonian Theatre. *The Diary of Abraham de la Pryme, the Yorkshire antiquary*, ed. C. Jackson, (Surtees Soc., 54) (Durham, 1870), 74–6. See also Chapter 7, p. 18.

[68] The Oxford address to the king initially proposed after the 1696 conspiracy was returned by the Lord Chancellor with a demand for a more fervent expression of loyalty, perhaps advisable when one of the leading conspirators was Robert Charnock (executed for treason), the only Fellow of Magdalen not expelled by James II. He had converted to Catholicism under James II and been ejected in 1688. R. Darwall-Smith, 'The Monks of Magdalen, 1688-1854', in ed. L.W.B. Brockliss, *Magdalen College, Oxford. A history* (Oxford, 2008), 253-386, at 334; J.R. Bloxam, *A register of the presidents, fellows... of St Mary Magdalen College* (7 vols., Oxford, 1853–85), VI. 27–36.

[69] *Calendar of State Papers Domestic, 1697*, 479; *HMC*, Downshire MSS, I, pt. ii., 770–1. For the view that most Tories successfully adapted themselves to the break in succession see Tim Harris, *Politics under the later Stuarts. Party Conflict in a Divided Society 1660–1715* (Harlow, 1993), 157.

[70] These connections help explain the laudatory address of congratulation sent up by the University following the Peace of Ryswick (1697) that Lord Macaulay imaginatively considered 'was read with cruel vexation by the nonjurors, and with exultation by the Whigs'. T.B. Macaulay, *The History of England from the Accession of James the Second*, ed. C.H. Firth (6 vols., London, 1913–15), VI. 2726.

68 ENLIGHTENED OXFORD

from the pen of the capable Henry Maurice, Fellow of Jesus College, with *The Lawfulness of Taking the New Oaths Asserted* (London, 1689).[71]

The first problem for dons was always, would the Williamite dispensation last or would they suffer for their apparent treachery if James II was restored, just as they had suffered at his hands when they had resisted his attempts to intrude Roman Catholics in the mid-1680s? And the second was how far, having early on suffered the frustration of Oxonian blocking tactics against Comprehension, would the new regime protect, let alone prefer, those High Churchmen left inside the Established Church? It was disappointment at its failure to do so and the intrusion of latitudinarian, Arminian Whigs into the highest reaches of the hierarchy that had soured the University's relationship with William by the late 1690s, and his with it. For, if the University was indisputably High Church in its ecclesiology, it was also (if to a lesser extent) a stronghold of the Reformed tradition within Anglicanism.[72] In sum, as Steve Pincus has put it, the 'decidedly Low Church' bishops of the post-Revolution episcopate and their 'social connections, ideological pronouncements, and political actions ... reveal a church hierarchy largely committed to Whig politics, comprehension, *and* toleration'.[73] Nevertheless, the pressures to come to terms with the revised order in Church and state during William's reign were insistent (without causing much apparent reduction in the University's intellectual energies, arguably the opposite as its members looked inward). It took time to renegotiate its working arrangements with the monarchy and the protection of the Church was no less actively required than before the Revolution, when the presumption that government would do this had been shattered by James II's incursions.

The University's initial receptiveness to the advent of William of Orange as the undisputed protector of the Protestant interest in 1688 sheltered it somewhat from any shake-up of either its constitution or its membership in the aftermath of the Revolution, as did the predominant presence of the Tories in government down to 1693–4. By contrast, Cambridge, later such a bastion of the Whig interest, was initially hesitant in its embrace of the Orange order, and had to adapt rapidly in the course of the 1690s (which it did quite successfully) so as to avoid forfeiting royal and ministerial patronage.[74] Both English universities fared well in comparison with their Scottish counterparts at St Andrews, Aberdeen, Edinburgh, and Glasgow.[75] The Revolution was forcibly imposed on Scotland and the Restoration political settlement undone: the Episcopalian hold on seats of higher learning accordingly came to an abrupt end because clergy and laity would not break their

---

[71] Tony Claydon, *William III and the Godly Revolution* (Cambridge, 1996). The new king's Calvinism was another impediment to amity.

[72] Hampton, *Anti-Arminians*, 1–38.   [73] Pincus, *1688*, 401, 402.

[74] For Cambridge cross-currents see Gascoigne, *Cambridge*, 772–6.

[75] For the changes within the Scottish universities after the Revolution, see Jennifer Carter, 'British Universities and Revolution, 1688–1718', in eds. Paul Dukes and John Dunkley, *Culture and Revolution* (London, 1990), 8–21, at 15–20.

OXFORD AND BRITISH ACADEMIC CONTEXTS POST-1688   69

oaths of loyalty to James VII.[76] Henceforth, Presbyterianism was the only 'safe' politico-religious profession in Scotland, not because William especially wanted to place power in the hands of Whig Presbyterians but because the formerly dominant party left him no option.[77] Thus on 4 July 1690 the Scottish Parliament passed an act requiring professors, principals, and regents in the universities to swear an oath of allegiance to William and Mary and also subscribe to the Confession of Faith approved a month earlier in Parliament. It was executed by the Committee of Visitation of the university colleges (the task was delegated to local sub-committees) and its extensive brief was not exclusively political. It included special reference to administration, subjects taught, teaching materials and methods, what has been called 'a very serious attempt... to investigate and evaluate the universities in the light of the best contemporary opinion'.[78] With that kind of scope for their operations, all 'Popish' elements and Nonjurors (inevitably Jacobites) were early targets for summary eviction.[79]

The greatest impact was felt at St Andrews, where the Archbishop was both Chancellor and the major patron of the University. Just before James VII's fall, the dons had displayed what Bruce Lenman called 'rare loyalty and abysmal timing' in issuing a laudatory address to him in conjunction with the Scottish bishops. They were purged wholesale in the three colleges by William, 18th Earl of Crawford (d. 1698), a local magnate, ardent covenanter, and President of the Scottish Convention Parliament in 1690; he replaced them with university trained, middle-aged Presbyterians excluded from office since the Restoration.[80]

---

[76] Tim Harris, 'Scotland under Charles II and James VII: in search of the British causes of the Glorious Revolution', in eds. T. Harris and S. Taylor, *The final crisis of the Stuart monarchy. The revolutions of 1688–91* (Woodbridge, 2013), 109–32, at 131–2.

[77] See generally Alasdair Raffe, 'Presbyterians and Episcopalians: The formation of Confessional cultures in Scotland, 1660–1715', *EHR*, 125 (2010), 570–98; Raffe, *Scotland in revolution, 1685–1690* (Edinburgh, 2018). The failure of the new regime to win over the bulk of Episcopalians is considered in T. Clarke, 'The Williamite episcopalians and the Glorious Revolution in Scotland', *Records of the Scottish Church Historical Society*, 24 (1990), 35–51, at 47, 50–1. It has been well said that William III was '... essentially a Latitudinarian who believed that forms of church government were indifferent, but that religious uniformity was desirable'. Clare Jackson, 'The later Stuart church as "national church" in Scotland and Ireland', in ed. Grant Tapsell, *The later Stuart Church, 1660–1714* (Manchester, 2012), 127–49, at 136.

[78] Its work between 1690 and 1695 has been judged 'both severe and ambitious'. Esther Mijers, 'The Netherlands, William Carstares, and the reform of Edinburgh University, 1690–1715', *History of Universities*, 25:1 (2011), 111–42, at 116. The papers are in NAS, PA10. For Principal Gilbert Rule's ultimately unsuccessful attempt at Edinburgh to impose what Episcopalians called a 'Presbyterian Inquisition' see N. Phillipson, 'The Making of an Enlightened University', in Robert D. Anderson, Michael Lynch, and Nicholas Phillipson, *The University of Edinburgh: an illustrated history* (Edinburgh, 2003), 51–102, at 53–8.

[79] Roger L. Emerson comments that the Jacobites purged in 1690 'were almost worshipped in the streets by persons of all ranks', Emerson, *Academic patronage in the Scottish Enlightenment: Glasgow, Edinburgh and St Andrews universities* (Edinburgh, 2008), 276. He argues that the Scottish Enlightenment emerged from the purging of Jacobites and, subsequently, of strict Presbyterians.

[80] St Andrews was left full of discontented ex-academics after the Revolution. while relations with the town were so poor a move to Perth was considered. The election of the 1st Duke of Atholl as Chancellor in 1697 brought some respite. B. Lenman, *The Jacobite Risings in Britain 1689–1746* (London, 1980), 68, 71.

70 ENLIGHTENED OXFORD

It was a reminder of how draconian things could be in 1690 for universities which would not adjust to the new tide and how potentially vulnerable they were to political interference throughout the 'long' eighteenth century. Fortunately for King's and Marischal Colleges at Aberdeen, the Committee of Visitors charged with investigating their affairs was composed of local aristocrats sympathetic to the plight of the Episcopalians (there was no meaningful Presbyterian presence in the city at the Revolution) and there was only one deposition, the King's Professor of Theology, the Jacobite James Garden (1647–1726), in 1697.[81] There were fresh purges at Aberdeen after the abortive '15 Rebellion that further entrenched the new-look Whiggish faculty.

At Edinburgh the Principal and Professors of Divinity, Humanity (that is, Latin), and Philosophy were removed from office, and the affairs of the university were closely watched over by the Town Council; the university's Principal from 1703 to 1715 was no less than William Carstares, formerly William III's main adviser on Scottish affairs, who reorganised teaching along Dutch lines, notably in preparing the ground for the introduction of a medical faculty and curriculum in 1726.[82] Disruption was least evident at the University of Glasgow, where the majority of the governing body was staunchly in favour of the Williamite regime.[83] All the Scottish universities operated on the basis that ministers could and would take a direct hand in their mode of functioning and, by the late 1720s, that controlling presence belonged to the Earl of Islay. His brother, the 2nd Duke of Argyll, was behind the Visitation Commission of 1726–7 at Glasgow that reduced the power of the Chancellor, its Principal John Stirling, and their allies. After 1727 Argyll became Glasgow University's most powerful protector and friend. He had no Oxford counterpart, for Islay and Argyll were then the close allies in Scotland of Sir Robert Walpole.[84]

British universities were required to adapt to the new political landscape and there was pressure on them to adapt to the new rhetorics of learning, not least because of the power and prestige coming to be attached to them. By the Revolution, Isaac Newton's ascendancy was indisputable, his influence pronounced, and yet his University (Cambridge) was slow to trade on the standing of her favourite son as a means of offsetting any sense of tardiness in accommodating

---

[81] D. Findlay and A. Murdoch, 'Revolution to Reform: Eighteenth-Century Politics, c.1690–1800', in eds. E. P. Dennison, D. Ditchburn, and M., *Aberdeen Before 1800: A New History* (East Linton, 2002), 267–86, at 268. The University and local nobles supported Garden in his several appeals to be reinstated during Queen Anne's reign. ed. G. D. Henderson, *Mystics of the North-East* (Aberdeen, 1934), 61–5.

[82] Mijers, 'William Carstares', 121–33; Phillipson, 'The Making of an Enlightened University', 61–3. Carstares was nicknamed 'The Cardinal' among Jacobites.

[83] The Principal and two Professors were jettisoned. It was also visited (if lightly), like Aberdeen, after the '15. A. Skoczylas, *Mr Simpson's Knotty Case. Divinity, Politics and Due Process in early eighteenth-century Scotland* (Montreal, 2001), 166, 185.

[84] Emerson, *Academic Patronage*, 424–5, 85–106.

OXFORD AND BRITISH ACADEMIC CONTEXTS POST-1688   71

politically to William & Mary's joint monarchy.[85] The endowment of the Boyle Lectures in London (first delivered in 1692) in the bequest of Robert Boyle (died 1691) pointed up the marriage of the new physics with Anglican apologetics and Oxford would have been disadvantaging itself not to associate itself with the trend. [86] But the University did so—and early on. Newtonianism caught on readily at Oxford thanks to the advocacy of expatriate Scots, principally David Gregory (1659/61–1708) and his pupil John Keill (1671–1721) in the 1690s, whereas at Cambridge it had to wait for William Whiston's appointment to the Lucasian chair in 1703.[87] Oxford benefitted from Gregory's attachment to his Episcopalian principles; after being unjustly accused of atheism he gave up his chair of Mathematics at Edinburgh after the Revolution and came south to be elected Savilian Professor of Astronomy in preference to Edmond Halley in February 1692, thanks in large measure to Isaac Newton's backing.[88] An unabashed Newtonian who wanted to be the editor of the revised edition of the *Principia*,[89] the productive Gregory was another of Oxford's Fellows of the Royal Society, and found favour with the royal family as tutor to William, Duke of Gloucester, in the year before the Prince's death in 1700.[90] Keill was Scottish Exhibitioner at Balliol College from 1694 and soon teaching experimental physics and chemistry; he succeeded Gregory in the Savilian Chair of Astronomy at the second attempt in 1712, but failed to secure additional employment from the Tory government.[91]

[85] For a shrewd summary of Newton's debt to Cambridge and Cambridge to him see Morgan, *Cambridge*, 501–2.

[86] Geoffrey Holmes's warning against exaggerating the impact of the Boyle Lectures at the time of their delivery is well-made. Holmes, 'Science, reason, and religion in the age of Newton', *BJHS*, 11 (1978), 164–71, at 169. For an authoritative recent biography of Boyle see Michael Hunter, *Boyle: between God and science* (New Haven, CT, 2009).

[87] Anita Guerrini, 'The Tory Newtonians: Gregory, Pitcairne, and their circle', *JBS* 25 (1986), 288–311; ed. W. G. Hiscock, *David Gregory, Isaac Newton and their Circle: Extracts from David Gregory's memoranda 1677-1708* (Oxford, 1937); Gascoigne, *Cambridge*, 142–64.

[88] He became a Fellow of Balliol in 1692, and had Aldrich, Smalridge, and Alsop among his Christ Church friends. Newton called him the 'greatest mathematician in Scotland'. To Arthur Charlett, 27 July 1691, in Newton, eds. H.W. Turnbull et al., *The correspondence of Isaac Newton* (7 vols., London, 1959-77), II. 154–5. See Ch. Ch. MSS 346 for his memoranda and details of his activities at Oxford 1696–1708. Also J. Friesen, 'Archibald Pitcairne, David Gregory and the origins of English Tory Newtonianism', *History of Science*, 46 (2003), 163–91, esp. 170; C. M. Eagles, 'David Gregory and Newtonian science', *BJHS*, 10 (1977), 216–25; P. D. Lawrence and A. G. Molland, 'David Gregory's inaugural lecture at Oxford', *Notes and Records of the Royal Society*, 55 (2001), 185–90.

[89] His most important Oxford treatise was *Astronomiae Physicae et Geometricae Elementa* (1702, trans. 1726), including several unpublished propositions communicated by Newton.

[90] A. G. Stewart, *The academic Gregories* (Edinburgh, 1901), 53, 58, 64, 74; P.S. Gregory, *Records of the Family of Gregory* (London, 1886), 30–6. For Gregory's Jacobite sympathies, see Pat Rogers, *Pope and the destiny of the Stuarts. History, politics, and mythology in the age of Queen Anne* (Oxford, 2005), 56; Money, *The English Horace*, 138–41. For a summary of his career David B. Wilson, *Seeking nature's logic. natural philosophy in the Scottish Enlightenment* (University Park, PA, 2009), 34, 39–44.

[91] Keill is discussed at length in Chapter 5, pp. 6–9. Keill's outstanding student was the precocious James Stirling, a Snell and Warner exhibitioner (and a Jacobite), who produced his *Lineae tertii ordinis Newtonianae* (1717), a commentary on Newton's enumerations of curves of the third degree. John Jones, *Balliol College. A history, 1263-1939* (2nd edn., Oxford, 1988), 149. See also C. Tweedie, *James Stirling. A Sketch of his Life and Works along with his Scientific Correspondence* (Oxford, 1922), 9–10.

Newtonian influences also gradually found a home in the Oxford curriculum but not at the pace seen north of the border:[92] by c.1710 natural philosophy courses in Scottish universities were all fundamentally Newtonian in character. Thus the first Professor of Mathematics at King's College, Aberdeen, Thomas Bower, a protégé of Archibald Pitcairne (1652–1713),[93] was committed to Newtonian science in the 1700s and attempting to equip the college with mathematical instruments for use in both research and teaching. Newtonianism was displacing Cartesianism in the philosophy curriculum at Aberdeen as early as the 1690s.[94] However dubious John Locke's politics, his philosophy became inseparable from Newtonian natural science in the 1690s and Oxford gave him a limited endorsement.[95] In that decade he was taken up by John Wynne of Jesus College (inter alia), who composed an *Abridgement* of the *Essay* for students, considered primarily as a book of logic consistent with scholastic models of training.[96] The leading themes of the *Essay on Human Understanding* continued to be taught in the university even after it was censured by a meeting of Oxford tutors in 1703, and subsequently attacked by the Vice Chancellor, William Lancaster, in 1709.[97] It took until 1744 for the *Essay* to be recommended for undergraduate Collections.[98]

Despite reservations on the basis of novelty, early eighteenth-century Oxford was institutionally quite capable of adapting and adopting the new knowledge and creating what in the end came across as a fusion of the 'ancients' and 'moderns'. There was a general recognition that Aristotelian natural philosophy had a limited currency and that the key battleground was the area of vetting, approving, and policing what would come in its stead. Yet established ways of thinking and

---

Newton was told by John Keill in 1715 that Stirling as an undergraduate had solved a complex problem set by Leibniz to challenge British mathematicians. Tweedie, *James Stirling*, 7; Ian Tweddle, 'Stirling, James (1692–1770), mathematician and mine manager', *ODNB* (2004), online edn.

[92] C. M. Shepherd, 'Newtonianism in the Scottish Universities in the Eighteenth Century', in eds. R. H. Campbell and Andrew S. Skinner, *The Origins and Nature of the Scottish Enlightenment* (Edinburgh, 1982), 62–85.

[93] Pitcairne was one of the celebrated physicians of the age. He studied law at Edinburgh and Paris, but was practising medicine in Edinburgh by the early 1680s. In 1692 he was professor of physics at Leiden but resigned the next year and returned to Scotland. He had a reputation for irreligion and hard drinking. Margaret C. Jacob, *The Secular Enlightenment* (Princeton, NJ, 2019), 130.

[94] Wood, *The Aberdeen Enlightenment*, 3, 6.

[95] That enemies of dogma such as John Toland exploited their familiarity with Locke in the mid-1690s did nothing for the latter's reputation. Champion, *Republican learning*, 3. Locke's respect for Tindal was based on common Oxford ties, despite their differences on the limitations of human reason. J. R. Wigelsworth, '"God can require nothing of us, but what makes for our Happiness:" Matthew Tindal on Toleration', in eds. Hudson, et al., *Atheism and Deism revalued*, 139–55, at 144–6.

[96] Martine Pécharman, 'From Lockean logic to Cartesian(ised) logic: the case of Locke's Essay and its contemporary controversial reception', in eds. P. Bullard and A. Tadié, *Ancients and Moderns in Europe: comparative perspectives* [Oxford University studies in the Enlightenment] (Oxford, 2016), 73–95, at 77–80. Ironically, in the light of Wynne's work, for Locke universities were paralogical institutions.

[97] See Locke to William Molyneux, 2 July 1696, John Locke, *The correspondence of John Locke*, ed. E. S. de Beer (8 vols, Oxford, 1976–89); Maurice Cranston, *John Locke: A Biography* (London, 1968), 384–5.

[98] Kearney, *Scholars and Gentlemen*, 164.

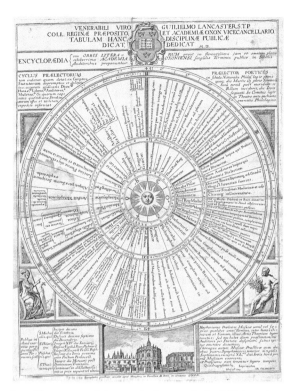

Fig. 2.2 Calendar of lectures and the curriculum at Oxford University; in the centre, a sun. Within its concentric circles are listed the various parts of the scholarly curriculum, print, c.1709 (© The Trustees of the British Museum).

teaching were never hurriedly put aside, not because of indolence or a plodding conformism, but because they were tried and tested. Per contra, 'Enlightenment' influences were never disregarded per se and were especially welcome where they were genuinely serviceable in the cause of religious apologetics. This was, after all, the University's primary *raison d'être* and the perceived growth of irreligion and the aggressive challenge of non-Anglican minorities afforded no reason for donnish complacency by the 1710s. There was a delicate dialectic between 'Enlightenment' and Protestantism (in its various guises always seeking to present itself as a 'reasonable' religion, in contradistinction to almost every other kind of faith found in the world), with the former as a junior partner rather grafted on to the latter.

What raised academic hackles and rather compromised 'Enlightenment' insights was the sense that they had been appropriated and patronised by those who were bent on damaging the institutional standing of the Church (and especially the position of the clergy within it). Moreover, the politics of those committed to progressive epistemologies were invariably Whiggish, enough in itself to upset a University that certainly had Whig enclaves but was essentially a

74 ENLIGHTENED OXFORD

bedrock of court Toryism. The majority of Whigs, of course, proclaimed their attachment to the Church of England and were genuine in their commitment to the Church, but it was the extent to which their party was a stalking horse for radical Whigs, Commonwealth men, and non-Trinitarian Dissenters intent on appropriating 'enlightened' rhetorical tropes and models of lobbying to abuse and undermine both the Established Church and the Christian Gospel as it had been received by that Church that concerned 'high flyers' (and plenty of moderates). In consequence, a lot of the University's intellectual energies (on the whole, success-fully) went into resisting this challenge in the first third of the eighteenth century and indicating how it could function as a veil for the religious indifference and moral relativism that was, according to the classic Oxford conceptualisation that reached back to the Civil War and the English Republic, the enemy of the well-ordered state and a possible harbinger of anarchy. No reader of the great edition of Clarendon's *History of the Great Rebellion*, lovingly prepared by his son Lord Rochester and published in 1702–4, could be left in any doubt about its resonances as party propaganda in the current climate.[99] In its most moderate form, the case for extending limited civil benefits to orthodox dissenters could not be easily denied by High Church commentators, but the risk was always that, once conceded, they would acquire a sceptical and destructive edge in the hands of those who had no wish to endorse the assured position of Oxford University in the British state.

There is nothing paradoxical or inconsistent in arguing that historians have tended to overlook one of the central claims of this book, that Oxford and the moderate Enlightenment (to use Jonathan Israel's phraseology) were comfort-able with each other, even that Oxford was a primary locus for the moderate Enlightenment in England. If it is a truism that the English Enlightenment (like the vast majority of those in other states) had an inherently conservative and Christian character then one can hardly be surprised to find its presence in the primary academic forum of the kingdom,[100] especially where it was denoted less by doctrine but '... as a series of methods or habits of enquiry [in scholarship and criticism], an active way of working, for better or worse'.[101] In Oxford it took a predominantly clerical form, indeed was regulated by the clergy, which could hardly fail to be the case given their overwhelming preponderance among senior resident members, a stewardship and an association that scholars have been

---

[99] Joseph Hone, *Literature and Party Politics at the Accession of Queen Anne* (Oxford, 2017), 143–4. Rochester described Clarendon as 'a Prophet as well as an Historian.' Quoted in James Anderson Winn, *Queen Anne. Patroness of Arts* (Oxford, 2014), 353. For the Hyde brothers and aristocratic history writing see comments in H. Weinbrot, *Literature, Religion, and the Evolution of Culture 1660–1780* (Baltimore, MD, 2013), 32ff.
[100] Such an insistence has become normative in the years since publication of J. G. A. Pocock, 'Clergy and commerce: the conservative Enlightenment in England', in eds. R.J. Ajello et al., *L'Età dei Lumi: studi storici sul settecento europeo in onore di Franco Venturi* (2 vols., Naples, 1985), I, 523–65.; It is a central contention of Young, *Religion and Enlightenment*.
[101] Kristine Louise Haugen, *Richard Bentley. Poetry and Enlightenment* (Cambridge, MA, 2011), 238.

OXFORD AND BRITISH ACADEMIC CONTEXTS POST-1688   75

reluctant to register, perhaps from an excessive willingness to accept at face value the critique of the clergy and clerical values central to the Whig Commonwealth tradition.[102] The Oxford word for 'Enlightenment' had long existed: 'illumination', as found in the University motto, *Dominus illuminatio mea*, the opening words of Psalm 27 and in use since the late sixteenth century.[103] Scholarship, linked with primitive religion of the sort the Church of England claimed to uphold and transmit, was by that definition both an enlightened process and a product, one customarily associated with the metaphor of light as truth that was far more than the unmediated light of reason.[104] And, throughout the century, it was an Oxonian commonplace for preachers to discountenance those philosophers who would set up that 'obscure and imperfect' light 'in competition with the superior advantages of Divine Grace'.[105] Among its several manifestations, Enlightenment could be conservative, cautious, hierarchical, and religious, supplementing and amending disciplines rather than displacing them. Yet, the protean nature of 'enlightened' influences ensured that the phenomenon was constantly threatening to burst its bounds, and its moderate exponents within the University learnt to be watchful, for they were aware that its more extreme apostles wanted to deploy them in the service of irreligion, social reconstruction, and academic upheaval. As John Coffey has argued, there were 'profound tensions within the Enlightenment itself, between its self-consciously Christian proponents and their secular rivals'.[106] Those tensions were disclosed in the rhetorical and publishing freedoms that the Revolution brought in its wake and these required that the University display a cultural adaptability that it found—at least, initially—institutionally awkward to generate and deliver.

Conclusion

The Church of the old royalists had ceased to exist after 1689 and hereditary descent of the monarchy had gone with it.[107] These were painful blows to majority

---

[102] Mark Goldie, 'Priestcraft and the birth of Whiggism', in eds. Nicholas Phillipson and Quentin Skinner, *Political Discourse in Early Modern Britain* (Cambridge, 1993), 209–31.

[103] For contestation regarding the light metaphor within Enlightenment learned culture see eds. Anton M. Matytsin, 'Whose Light is it Anyway? The Struggle for Light in the French Enlightenment', in eds. Anton M. Matytsin and Dan Edelstein, *Let There be Enlightenment. The Religious and Mystical Sources of Rationality* (Baltimore, MD, 2018), 62–85, at 64. For the argument that the metaphor was secularised in the 1750s and 1760s when it lost its original 'religious aura', see Roland Mortier, '"Lumière" et "lumières": histoire d'une image et d'une idée au XVIIe et XVIIIe siecle', in his *Clartés et ombres du siècle des Lumières: études sur le XVIIIe siècle littéraraire* (Geneva, 1969), 13–59, at 25.

[104] With some justice, David Manning has argued that the importance of the metaphor of light makes it needful to use 'the biased descriptive term "enlightenment" to categorize ideas and phenomena;' 'Theological Enlightenments and Ridiculous Theologies', 227.

[105] Timothy Neve, *Eight Sermons Preached before the University of Oxford in the Year 178...* (Oxford, 1781) [Bampton Lectures], III, 57. See also III. 80.

[106] Coffey, 'Milton, Locke and the new history of toleration', *JMIH*, 5 (2008), 619–32, at 629.

[107] G. Reedy, *Robert South (1634–1716). An introduction to his life and sermons* (Cambridge, 1992), 98.

Oxonian sensibilities, ones which some graduates nursed by withdrawing in conscience from both sides in the Nonjuring schism. That said, the great majority did not; the University showed itself capable of blending nostalgia with hard-headedness and in the last two and a half decades of the Stuart monarchy built on its inherited institutional prestige, nationally and internationally. Whatever their reservations (and they were appreciable), the University leadership and most senior members in practice were ready to accept the principle of limited toleration and the Protestant Succession, thereby locating the University within a moderate Enlightenment setting.[108] And if it could not reap the full fruits of that repositioning for decades after 1714, that neglect was due to the general exclusion of Tories and reputedly Tory institutions from power and influence in the kingdom as a whole.

If moderate Protestant Enlightenment can be accurately defined as 'a set of practices and processes of criticism and conversation, enquiry and curiosity',[109] and if these traits were established by the 1730s, then they were hardly less conspicuous in much of the day-to-day life of the University and of its graduates than at comparable foundations at Cambridge, and in Scotland and Ireland.[110] If some Oxford opinion was coy, at times reluctant to embrace these values, it was primarily due to a sense that they could be damaging in relation to religious establishment. While religious apologists in or from Oxford could support and reflect a kind of 'enlightened Anglicanism' (just as there was such a strand in Gallicanism), by the mid-eighteenth century, the enlightenment within England was losing its predominantly moderate, orthodox Christian character.[111] Thus the deist and materialist uses of Newtonian physics encouraged the emergence of a new theologico-political body of learning, Hutchinsonianism, one that was taken up by quite a large proportion of younger members of the University in Oxford during the 1750s. That some influential sections of opinion were inclining towards what one might tentatively call a Counter-Enlightenment agenda by the mid-eighteenth century did not entail the University as a whole's sacrificing its commitment to advanced, moderately progressive learning.[112]

Nevertheless, there was a renewed awareness that 'Enlightened' knowledge could be a formidable weapon that Oxford's enemies could brandish against it,

---

[108] Oxford University certainly does not qualify if one follows Derek Beales and defines 'Enlightenment' as 'a term denoting critical, rationalist, reformist opinion'.

[109] Marshall, *John Locke, Toleration and Early Enlightenment Culture*, 517.

[110] Overblown claims for the achievements of eighteenth-century Scottish universities continue to be made at Oxford's expense. For instance, Wood, *The Aberdeen Enlightenment*, xiii. 'Whereas Oxford proved remarkably resistant to the intellectual ferment of the age of reason, ... Scotland experienced an enlightenment which was predominantly clerical and professorial, ...'

[111] Roy Porter called the reformist spirit of the later eighteenth century the 'second Enlightenment' or 'Enlightenment within the Enlightenment'. See his *Enlightenment. Britain and the creation of the modern world* (Harmondsworth, 2000), 423.

[112] For the concept of Counter-Enlightenment, see the essays by Leighton, 'Hutchinsonianism: A Counter-Enlightenment reform movement', *JRS*, 23 (1999), 168–84.

one that was tied in with weakening the corporate power of the Church of England. This perception induced something of an intellectual defensiveness and caution that, in the eyes of its critics and most commentators, came to characterise the life of the University and its members throughout the eighteenth century. But this is a simplistic distortion. The social and intellectual conservatism of Oxford undoubtedly became more pronounced in the wake of the American and French Revolutions, but in this regard it was only participating in a tendency that was common to institutions in Britain and across Europe, and there is the paradox that serious efforts to tighten academic standards—such as the introduction of honours degrees—were introduced to forestall radicalism.[113] The University was still capable of corporate change at the edges, as were all *ancien régime* institutions, and its learning in these later decades was by no means devoid of moderate enlightened influences. Throughout the century, Oxford showed itself to be a community of communities, with a diverse and dynamic culture containing a range of learned perspectives, and the University's capacity to both reaffirm and reconfigure its intellectual claims against the competition should not be underestimated. But there were two underlying imperatives (or constraints as critics would have deemed them) that consistently informed its functioning. Firstly, like Cambridge and their Scottish and Irish equivalents, Oxford was a core part of the British state and its loyalty to that state was expected to override purely academic considerations or promote intellectual activity of a kind that might end up undermining its own supremacy within the state. Secondly, and supremely, it was a bulwark of Christian belief as embodied in the Church of England, and its discharge of its duties in defending the faith is the subject of the next chapter.[114]

---

[113] See, generally, I. R. Christie, *Stress and Stability in late Eighteenth-Century Britain. Reflections on the British Avoidance of Revolution. [The Ford Lectures 1983–84]* (Oxford, 1984).

[114] J. Mordaunt Crook puts it nicely: 'religiously, culturally, Georgian Oxford embodied the Church of England in academic dress'. *Brasenose. The biography of an Oxford college* (Oxford, 2008), 96.

3

The defence of Christian belief and the Church of England

Be it the permanent glory of this community to maintain inviolate, in union with her renowned sister, the claim and character of bulwarks to a Church in doctrine truly Catholic, in government truly apostolical, in worship truly rational, in temper truly moderate

> Matthew Frampton, LL. D., A Sermon preached
> before the University of Oxford at St Mary's
> on Act Sunday, July 9th 1769 (Oxford, 1769)
> [2 Pet. III. 18, 'Grow in Grace'], 17.[1]

Wisdom herself, which hath builded her House; not vain Pagan wit, but serious Christian Wisdom; not the fabulous Muses, but the truly divine Apostles, who here invite you to her Feast; a Feast . . . of the true JEHOVAH.

> John Dalton, Two Sermons preached before the University of
> Oxford at St Mary's, On Sept. 15th, and
> Oct. 20th, 1745 (Oxford, 1745), 4.

The Ecclesiastical government of this country is an essential part of the great national System established at the Revolution.

> Thomas Burgess, The Divinity of Christ proved from
> his own declarations attested and interpreted by his living
> witnesses, the Jews. A Sermon preached before the University
> of Oxford at St Peter's, February 28th 1790 (Oxford, 1790), 45–6.

Part A: Scripture, sermons, and public theology

Primary to the intellectual life of the eighteenth-century University was the upholding and protection of the Church of England against those who sought to change its structures, its legal entitlements, and its profession of the historic credal

---

[1] The sermon was an explicit response to Francis Blackburne's controversial agenda for religious change, *The Confessional* (1766), from a Wiltshire vicar, the chaplain of Henry, 12th earl of Suffolk (1739–79), a precocious candidate for the Chancellorship in 1762.

Enlightened Oxford: The University and the Cultural and Political Life of Eighteenth-century Britain and Beyond.
Nigel Aston, Oxford University Press. © Nigel Aston 2023. DOI: 10.1093/oso/9780199246830.003.0004

THE DEFENCE OF CHRISTIAN BELIEF   79

formularies. In short, it was to bear witness to the Christian faith, in its public worship,[2] in its teaching, and in its preaching. This mission, coeval with the University's historic identity, was generally judged to be fundamental to its entire *raison d'être*. As one of the earliest Bampton Lecturers put it in 1783:

> For what is that philosophy, which excludes the Supreme Being, from the care and direction of the University? It breaks the bonds,... of piety, sanctity, and religion; and renders worship, devotion, and prayer, needless and unavailing services.[3]

It was the University's competence in discharging this obligation to keep God at its centre by which most of those who held office in other established structures of the British state would measure its institutional success, for Christian belief was embedded in civil society—functioning, to a degree, as a civil religion—and had a secular utility that lent itself to orthodox apologetics.[4] Whatever the risks (even for Whigs of a moderate hue), that a vindication of the Established Church might lapse into the sort of 'priestcraft' immemorially associated with Archbishop Laud, by defending the Church, Oxford University would be, in some sense, defending the state (whatever the dynastic doubts of some of its members).[5] To put it another way, the University was the cornerstone of the Church-state polity, and the suppression of Convocation as an active body after 1717—and therefore the exclusion of the clergy as an estate from their own quasi-parliamentary institution conferred more importance on Oxford's status as a corporate voice.[6] On the face of it, this primary task sounds relatively undemanding, even pedestrian, one that required little more than a restating of familiar claims and arguments in defence of the status quo. And, indeed, it is on such a basis that the eighteenth-century

[2] Worship in college chapels followed the liturgical year with said prayers as laid down in the 1662 Book of Common Prayer and at Christ Church, Magdalen, and New College, was supported by permanent choral foundations.

[3] John Cobb, DD [Fellow of St John's], *Eight sermons preached before the University of Oxford in the year 1783* (Oxford, 1783), 4, Sermon I, 'An Inquiry after happiness'. It contained many references to the Oxford-educated (Wadham) literary theorist and philosopher of language James Harris (1709–80). For the Bampton Lectures see this Chapter, pp. 53–4.

[4] As has been pointed out, '...Christian and monarchist depictions of confessional states as civil religions proliferated during the early Enlightenment'. W. J. Bulman, 'Introduction: Enlightenment for the culture wars', in eds. W. J. Bulman and R. G. Ingram, *God in the Enlightenment* (New York, 2016), 1–41, at 24. For the anticlerical Hume's willingness to uphold the religious establishment in England see R. Susato, 'Taming the "Tyranny of Priests": Hume's advocacy of religious establishments', *JHI*, 73 (2012), 273–93. Hume also upheld corruption in politics.

[5] The difficulty of persuading all parties was not underestimated: 'Those who have a natural Prejudice against Establishments will never give the Arguments used in support of them their due weight. They will shut their eyes against the Truth, and arm themselves at all events against Conviction...' Thomas Griffith, *The Evils Arising from misapply'd Curiosity. A Sermon preached before the University of Oxford*, 9 March 1760 (Oxford, 1760), 17.

[6] Cf. Justin Champion, "'My Kingdom is Not of This World': The Politics of Religion after the Restoration', in ed. N. Tyacke, *The English Revolution c.1590–1720* (Manchester, 2007), 185–202, esp. 196–9.

80 ENLIGHTENED OXFORD

University's reputation for uninspired, underpowered political theology has rested. By contrast, this chapter reveals a richer and more varied story, one in which University members showed persuasive ingenuity in defending the Established Church through a variety of rhetorical strategies coupled with historically validated theological content that appealed to audiences beyond Oxford.

On the whole, the University was successful in ensuring that Anglican legal exclusiveness endured throughout the century despite a plethora of challenges. It won the argument as the motor of that coalition of interests which was determined to protect the status of the Church of England as (re)established in 1660–62 and then confirmed (although amended) in 1688–89. To act in this manner was not *ipso facto* to be unenlightened, for no monarchy in eighteenth-century Europe (including the regimes of 'the enlightened Absolutists') wanted to do without a national Church that would confirm royal legitimacy and entitlement to obedience, thus ensuring a pre-condition of minimal political stability. It was, so it was argued, only through the upholding of the existing Church dispensation that national life could be conducted within a well-ordered society under God and the monarch, whose stability permitted the teaching and learning of the University to flourish. There was nothing within this essentially *ancien régime* framework that precluded intellectual variety, virtuosity, or creativity in revisiting the great questions of religious truth and variously restating them in a manner that stimulated debate and usually made sense to majority opinion. Though some mid century Oxonians such as Thomas Griffith fretted that the 'busy Spirit' of the age would prompt infidels '...to plant new Doctrines in the Church of Christ, [that] will assist the cause of Latitudinarianism, Heresy and Schism;'[7] others, Robert Lowth included, were insistent that without 'freedom of enquiry', there can be no 'advancement of religious knowledge'.

Lowth concluded that:

> It is therefore of the utmost importance to the cause of true religion, that it be submitted to an open and impartial examination; that every disquisition concerning it be allowed its free course; that even the malice of its enemies should have its full scope and try its utmost strength of argument against it. Let no man be alarmed at the attempts of atheists or infidels...[8]

The University's achievement after 1714 was the reconstruction of the concept of 'orthodoxy' following the shock of the Glorious Revolution and the creation of the Hanoverian regime in 1714 in accordance with the terms of the Act of Settlement.

---

[7] Griffith, *The Evils Arising from misapply'd Curiosity*, 20. He also, not untypically, identified 'Infidelity' as also the parent of faction, sedition, and rebellion.

[8] *Sermons and Other Remains of Bishop Robert Lowth, some time Bishop of London*, ed. Peter Hall (London, 1834), 82–3.

THE DEFENCE OF CHRISTIAN BELIEF   81

It posited a Church of England with a distinct sacerdotal character that was both Catholic and Reformed and upheld the pre-Reformation ordering of the ministry with the final authority of scripture and the Thirty-nine Articles under the Supreme Governorship of the sovereign.[9] This was not fashioned without tensions, inconsistencies, difficulties, and embarrassment before 1760, as University members wrestled with questions of loyalty, but it flourished comfortably after the accession of George III when Oxford basked in royal favour for the first time since 1714. At the heart of the problem for some High-Church academics in the time of the first two Georges was trying to square defence of the Church with endorsement of a monarchical succession that they felt was compromising their understanding of the Church as a sacred institution. It led to some confusion but also some stimulating and controversial thinking that captured appreciable attention both during and after the Bangorian controversy of 1717–20.[10] At the same time, the University showed a degree of creative scholarship in scriptural and theological studies that has been insufficiently recognised, one that goes well beyond any narrow High-Church characterisation. In this it is the more remarkable given the loss to official academic life of the Nonjurors after 1689 and, to a lesser extent, after 1714. But before looking at the content of what members of the University were saying in matters of ecclesiology and theology, the chapter considers means of communication and outreach as well as performance and it starts with the foundational text for any defence of Christian truth as received by the Church of England: the Bible.

i) Scriptural politics and production

Most English people encountered 'Oxford' through the Authorized Version Bible [AV] of 1611, used in public worship and in the majority of private houses; the University (from 1632) shared in a monopoly production of the AV in conjunction with the monarch's official Printer and Cambridge University Press, and it never ceased to be keen to retain its market share against these competitors. However, the University's association was somewhat compromised because it was partly complicit in the printing discrepancies that crept into the Bibles that it published under the auspices of its own printing house. Though not of immediate concern to most readers of sacred scripture, in time it generated sufficient

---

[9] As Stephen Hampton has pointed out, the Reformed teaching that justification was by faith alone remained a serious theological option for Anglicans in the early eighteenth century (including many in Oxford). It 'linked the Church of England to its Reformed past, and to the wider world of European Protestantism'. Hampton, *Anti-Arminians: the Anglican Reformed tradition from Charles II to George I* (Oxford, 2008), 127–8, 270.

[10] Andrew Starkie, *The Church of England and the BangoriOan Controversy, 1716–1721* (Woodbridge, 2007).

82 ENLIGHTENED OXFORD

notice (or notoriety) to make it embarrassing beyond scholarly and clerical circles. The great monopolist John Baskett, already in control of the Queen's Printing House, leased Oxford University Press from 1713, giving £2,000 towards the building costs of the new Clarendon Building, half of which (the so-called 'Bible side') was given over to the production of Bibles from its opening in 1712–13.[11] Baskett was concerned primarily with profit (the market in Bibles was always going to be lucrative in a Protestant polity and he aimed to sell plentifully at a low price) and was ready to ride out the rising tide of complaints about the poor quality of the paper used by Oxford University Press and unclear, uneven printing.[12] Even his prestige projects encountered problems, none more calamitously than Baskett's first Bible, a sumptuous two-volume set of 1717 in large folio strewn with misprints, and known as the Vinegar Bible after a glaring typographical error in Luke 20: 9, Christ's parable of the vineyard, that did nothing for the reputation of proofreaders at the Bible Press. The association with Baskett and his family, who contrived (despite much litigation) to hold on to the lease and maximise their profits until 1765, tarnished the University's reputation.[13] Nevertheless, the sale and marketing of the 1611 Bible continued without interruption and the needs of the reader (including the visually impaired) were never lost from sight. Thus the Oxford quarto Bible that was introduced into the SPCK's list in 1798 to provide a Bible in large and clear type 'suitable for old Persons, with weak Eyes'.[14]

The priority for Oxford University was to circulate, explain, and defend the scriptures against the ever-growing number of those who would seize on apparent historical inconsistencies, delight in showing up instances of immorality, and laugh at textual irregularities.[15] And, to meet these challenges unflinchingly, the English Bible had to be based on the latest understanding of the original manuscripts as understood and disclosed by Oxford academics. But careful strategy and timing were necessary, otherwise the Church, by committing itself too publicly to replacing the Authorized Version of 1611, rather than erecting a permanent barrier to heresy, would simply open up the Pandora's Box of what constituted the ur-text in both Testaments. Debate would be reignited on particularly contested parts of scripture (for instance, those commonly held to provide biblical

---

[11] The Press worked here until 1830, with its operations split into the so-called Learned Side and Bible Side in different wings of the building.

[12] Baskett published twelve distinct editions of the Bible at Oxford University Press. Harry Carter, *A history of Oxford University Press, Vol. 1: To the Year 1780* (Oxford, 1975), 168–9, 352–4; R. A. Austen-Leigh, *The Story of a printing house; being a short account of the Strahans and Spottiswoodes* (2nd edn., London, 1912); Robert L. Haig, 'New light on the King's printing office 1680–1730', *Studies in Bibliography*, 8 (1956), 157–67.

[13] G. Campbell, *Bible. The Story of the King James Version 1611–2011* (Oxford, 2010), 129–30; B. J. McMullin, 'The "Vinegar Bible"', *The Book Collector*, 33 (1984), 53–65.

[14] SPCK Minute Books, vol. 32, 140–1, quoted in Scott Mandelbrote, 'The Bible and its Readers in the Eighteenth Century', in ed. Isabel Rivers, *Books and their readers in eighteenth-century England: new essays* (London, 2001), 35–78, at 52.

[15] ed. John Drury, *Critics of the Bible 1724–1873* (Cambridge, 1989).

THE DEFENCE OF CHRISTIAN BELIEF   83

evidence for the Holy Trinity, I Timothy 3:16 and I John 5:7) that would be sure to draw in critics of the Established Church from every compass point: Catholics, dissenters, and 'freethinkers', who would not hesitate to inflict collateral damage on the Church of England. Thus while the objective of revision was desirable (and Oxford scholars paid more than lip service to it), the consequences of achieving it looked politically risky.[16]

The Church's stance in confronting this dilemma was two-fold. First, to go on defending the merits of the Authorized Version, 'the noblest monument of English prose' as Robert Lowth called it;[17] second (and especially from mid-century), to encourage textual scholarship in scriptural manuscripts that might, eventually, offer the basis for a new, official translation of the Bible that could be sanctioned for use in Anglican churches, and would eliminate the errors of translators, transcribers, and printers in the AV. Oxonians were prominent in both strategies. Defence of the Authorized Version could be grounded in its foundational presence in the Anglican formularies alongside the Book of Common Prayer and the Thirty-Nine Articles and Homilies. Thus, there had been a concerted attempt by Bishops Edmund Gibson and White Kennett in the 1720s to shore up the status of the Authorized Version as a sign of royal and episcopal authority and the providential legacy of the English Reformation. This line was popular with orthodox Whigs and low churchmen in Cambridge, and it had much currency in the sister University (where commitment to the Authorized Version never publicly wavered), albeit for more varied motives;[18] more conservative Oxford scholars, such as Thomas Randolph (1701–83),[19] attached to the idea of the providential preservation of the text of scripture down the ages, were comfortable with this approach. For him, ensuring the stability of the received version of the Bible was the priority, for it was on this secure foundation that the defence of orthodoxy would sit. In the light of the contemporary commitment to understanding the prophetic utterances contained in scripture, his point was well made.[20] Undeterred, and with the backing of the archbishop of Canterbury,

---

[16] Especially if Neil Hitchin's point is admitted that the project was part of a 'political agenda to move the Church further along the Protestant road of rational Christianity'. Neil W. Hitchin, 'The politics of English Bible translation in Georgian Britain', *TRHS*, 6th ser., 9 (1999), 67–92, at 81.

[17] Quoted in Alistair McGrath, *In the Beginning. The Story of the King James Bible and how it changed a Nation, a Language and a Culture* (London, 2001), 278.

[18] For the significance of the AV in constructing a (contested) British identity before 1800 see S. Mandelbrote, 'The Bible and national identity in the British Isles, c.1650–c.1750', in eds. T. Claydon and I. McBride, *Protestantism and National Identity. Britain and Ireland, c.1650–c.1850* (Cambridge, 1998), 157–81.

[19] President of Corpus Christi College, 1748–83; Vice Chancellor, 1756–9; Archdeacon of Oxford, 1767–83. Protégé of John Potter, bishop of Oxford, archbishop of Canterbury. Fowler, Fowler, *Corpus Christi College*, 283. For his eccentric character, R.L. Edgeworth, *Memoirs of Richard Lovell Edgeworth, Esq.*, ed. Maria Edgeworth (3rd edn., London, 1844), 56.

[20] Cf. Thomas Randolph, *The Prophecies and other Texts, cited in the New Testament, compared with the Hebrew Original, and with the Septuagint Version* (Oxford, 1782), 52–4, with David Durell, *Critical Remarks on the books of Job, Proverbs, Psalms, Ecclesiastes, and Canticles* (Oxford, 1772).

84 ENLIGHTENED OXFORD

David Durell, during his vice-chancellorship from 1765 to 1768, secured the services of Benjamin Blayney (1728-1801) for collating three editions of the Bible for the OUP delegates,[21] and in 1769 a corrected edition of the Authorized Version appeared with a higher standard of purity in its English text than anything hitherto achieved.[22] His remodelling of the text in accordance with contemporary norms of spelling and punctuation (while retaining a sufficiency of archaic usages) gave it a secure status as a monument of English prose.[23] Blayney's Oxford Bible of 1769 was a kind of revision by default of the Authorized Version that was one of the outstanding scholarly achievements of the eighteenth-century University.[24] More ambitious plans for its replacement never came to fruition, killed off by lack of interest in high places, changing intellectual fashions, and the linking of Biblical reform with liturgical reform.

Despite the public desideratum of upholding a version of scripture that could give believers confidence they had access to an accurate record of divine revelation, Anglican academics nevertheless regarded Biblical textual scholarship as one of the supremely satisfying and demanding career possibilities open to them and the most able among them found it hard to resist testing the waters. Humphrey Hody (1659-1707), sub-Warden of Wadham College, Regius Professor of Greek from 1698, chaplain successively to archbishops Tillotson and Tenison, published his great work *De Bibliorum Textibus Originalibus* [*On the Versions of the Bible* (1705)], in which he mock modestly compared himself to David against the leading Dutch scholar, Isaac Voss, cast as Goliath.[25] John Mill's critical edition of the Greek New Testament published by Oxford University Press in 1707 was a landmark in emerging New Testament criticism and did not occasion slurs on his own orthodoxy.[26] It was widely consulted and reprinted,[27] and constituted a

---

[21] The Cambridge editions of 1743 and 1760 (by F. S. Parris, the University Librarian) were specified by the Press delegates for underpinning Blayney's work. Campbell, *Bible*, 136–7.

[22] Letter from Blayney to the V-C and delegates of the Clarendon Press, 25 Oct. 1769, printed in *Gentleman's Magazine*, 39 (1769), 517–19. Its appearance there is an indicator of educated interest in his efforts. Blayney was Vice-Principal of Hertford College from 1768; Prof. of Hebrew, canon of Christ Church, 1787. Henry Bradley, rev. P. Carter, 'Blayney, Benjamin (1727/8–1801), Hebraist and Church of England clergyman' (ODNB, online edn., 2013).

[23] See David Norton, *The King James Bible. A short history from Tyndale to today* (Cambridge, 2010), 162–73.

[24] Blayney's efforts are summarised in Campbell, *Bible*, 136–42, who credits him with nothing less than 'establishing the text of the modern Bible' and setting an enduring trend by abandoning the practice of capitalising common nouns.

[25] Wells, *Wadham College*, 119. See also Chapter 4, 54–5, 54, n. 136, 64, n. 157.

[26] Mill—'a friend to scholars and an outstanding scholar himself'—was a very moderate Whig in his politics and patronised by the Marlboroughs. He had worked on his edition for thirty years with student assistants to help him collate and transcribe. J.N.D. Kelly, *St Edmund Hall. Almost seven hundred years* (Oxford, 1989), 49; Adam Fox, *John Mill and Richard Bentley. A Study of the Textual Criticism of the New Testament 1675-1729* (Oxford, 1954). Mill, the Principal of St Edmund Hall, neglected his administrative duties, as White Kennett (Vice-Principal, 1691–5), noted: Mill 'was so much taken up with One Thing his Testament that he had not leisure to attend to the Discipline of the House, which rose and fell according to his different Vice-Principals'. BL MS Lansdowne 987, f.187.

[27] It was reprinted in Amsterdam and Rotterdam in 1710; at Leipzig in 1723; and at Amsterdam again in 1746. Philip, 'Oxford and scholarly publication', 130.

Fig. 3.1 Humphrey Hody (1659–1707), unknown artist, oil on canvas, c.1695 (By kind permission of the Warden and Fellows of Wadham College, Oxford)

significant response to textual critics writing after the French Biblical scholar, the Oratorian Richard Simon (1638–1712) had criticised Protestant apologists for their over-reliance on the Bible as the basis of faith.[28] The hope was always that textual finessing would reinforce the witness of the English-speaking faithful, not undermine it. But the risk of doing so inadvertently was never far away and deterred the most talented. Thus the accomplished Cambridge critic Richard Bentley had planned a new edition of the Greek New Testament c.1720, hoping to eliminate errors and interpolations and restore it 'exactly as it was in [th]e best Exemplars at [th]e time of [th]e Council of Nice[a]',[29] in other words before the dispute between Athanasius and Arius shattered the peace of the early Church. Bentley was notoriously not frightened of controversy, yet even he was warned off

---

[28] 'Simon's work was being adapted to counter-orthodox uses in England as early as the mid-1690s. Justin Champion, 'Pere Richard Simon and English Biblical Criticism, 1680–1700', in eds. J. Force and D. S. Katz, *Everything connects. In Conference with Richard H. Popkin. Essays in his Honor* (Leiden, 1999), 38–61, at 60–1; Guy G. Stroumsa, *A New Science. The Discovery of Religion in the Age of Reason* (Cambridge, MA, 2010), 62–76; J. Steinmann, *Richard Simon et les origines de la critique biblique* (Paris, 1960). For the complex responses to Simon in England see G. Reedy SJ, *The Bible and Reason* (Phil., 1985), 107–13.

[29] Bentley to Abp William Wake, 15 Apr. 1716, Christ Church, Oxford, Ms. Wake Letters 20, ff. 76r–7v, cited in Mandelbrote, 'The Bible and its Readers', 41.

86   ENLIGHTENED OXFORD

by those who feared that his efforts would only lead to a repeat of the vituperative polemics of the 4th century AD.[30]

As noted, the main Oxford initiatives at textual revision date from the mid-century and owed much to the encouragement of the head of the hierarchy, Thomas Secker, Archbishop of Canterbury, 1758–68.[31] Secker, a moderate Whig and High Churchman, knew Oxford well, having been bishop of the diocese for over two decades prior to his translation into the primacy, and once ensconced at Lambeth, he lost no time in recruiting Oxford dons into his great project (arguably adumbrated during his last years as Bishop of Oxford):[32] a definitive revision of the Authorized Version that would enhance the intellectual standing of the Church of England that would falter before his death in 1768.[33] Secker had acquired a profound respect for the linguistic and theological scholarship of Oxford scholars (generally other moderate Whigs) in his time as bishop of the see and offered them his trust and his patronage, among them Robert Lowth (1710–87) and Benjamin Kennicott (1718–83), Fellow of Exeter College.

Lowth was an outstanding Hebraist with an international reputation, an expert in translations of the Psalter, and a champion of the correct understanding of Hebrew poetry while he was Professor of Poetry in the University during the 1740s.[34] He also worked at a revision of the whole English Bible, the New Testament part being printed as *An Attempt towards Revising our English Translation of the Greek Scriptures* (1796), not published until after his death.[35] Kennicott made a name for himself as a talented Hebrew scholar under Lowth's auspices and he had made clear his interest in expunging the Old Testament errors in the AV in several publications in the 1750s. As he put it, there was an overriding need 'to compare Scripture with itself—to explain a difficult Phrase or Passage by a clear one, that bears some Relation to it—to consider the natural force of the Original Words, the Tendency of the Context, and the Design of the Writer—to compare the most ancient Editions of the Original, with one another, and with the best Copies of the most celebrated Versions'.[36] In 1758 Kennicott embarked on the collation of all the extant manuscripts of the Hebrew Old Testament in order to

---

[30] Haugen, *Richard Bentley*, 207.

[31] See his *Eight charges...a Latin speech intended to have been made at the opening of the convocation in 1761* (London, 1769).

[32] Hitchin, 'The Politics of English Bible Translation', 80.

[33] Robert Ingram asserts that 'In doing so', Secker set out to use 'the clerical Enlightenment to defeat the radical Enlightenment'. *Religion, Reform and Modernity in the eighteenth century: Thomas Secker and the Church of England* (Woodbridge, 2007), 87.

[34] David Norton, *A history of the Bible as literature* (2 vols., Cambridge, 1993), ii. 97–103; Stephen Prickett, 'Poetry and Prophecy: Bishop Lowth and the Hebrew Scriptures in Eighteenth-Century England', in ed. David Jasper, *Images of Belief in Literature* (New York, 1984), 81–103; Robert G. Ingram, *Religion, Reform and Modernity*, 91–3. Discussed in relation to his work on sacred Hebrew poetry in chaps. 4 and 6.

[35] See Ingram, *Religion, Reform and Modernity*, 87–8.

[36] Benjamin Kennicott, *The state of the printed Hebrew text of the Old Testament considered* (2 vols., Oxford, 1753), I. 12–13.

THE DEFENCE OF CHRISTIAN BELIEF 87

identify variant readings and establish the text that could be used for a new translation.[37] It was an expensive and protracted undertaking—Kennicott's life work. Archbishop Secker turned himself into chief fundraiser for the project, personally contributing ten guineas annually and trying to find his friend and client appropriate preferment in the Church.[38] Kennicott could be relied on to move forward resourcefully and level-headedly without losing his outward show of regard for the Authorized Version. From his base in Oxford he and his assistants set to work issuing ten annual reports between 1760 and 1769 to update subscribers. Though he had his persistent detractors,[39] the end product, the *Vetus Testamentum Hebraicum*, etc. (2 vols., Oxford, 1776–80) confirmed Kennicott as the greatest English biblical scholar of his generation.[40]

Lowth and Kennicott were exceptional scholars, but there were other men of talent in their circle engaged in comparable enterprises during the 1760s, mostly connected with Hertford College, reconstituted as a college in 1740.[41] David Durell (1728–75), its Principal from 1757, was another client of Secker's who helped him identify the least inaccurate printed versions of the AV as an essential preliminary to Blayney's 1769 Bible which, in part, looked to previous Oxford scholarship for inspiration. Thus Durell's translations of the prophetic books of Scripture followed on from Lowth's. William Newcome, fellow (1753) and then vice-principal of Hertford College until his promotion to be Bishop of Dromore in Ireland in 1766, was another outstanding scriptural exegete, both during and after his time in Oxford. He translated the prophets with Blayney and hoped this would

[37] Mandelbrote, 'The Bible and its Readers', 58–9. He eventually outdid Bentley by listing all 683 manuscripts he had collated towards his edition of the Old Testament. See *Vetus Testamentum Hebraicum*, etc. (2 vols., Oxford, 1776–80), I. 70–113.

[38] LPL, Secker Papers, Vol. 2, ff. 1–95, Kennicott and the Hebrew Bible, 1758–66; Secker, *The autobiography of Thomas Secker, Archbishop of Canterbury*, eds. J. S. Macauley and R. W. Greaves (Lawrence, KA, 1988), 170; Ingram, *Religion, Reform and Modernity*, 89–90.

[39] On one side was the truculent, blunt-spoken William Warburton: 'Kennicott is an egregious dunce & I expect little from him. He came to me, but I have demured to subscribe to his pension. I told him no man of sense ever doubted but that collating the Sacred Scriptures proportionately serve[s] the Hebrew text as [much as] it does the Greek text. ... And that he need not have wrote a large book to prove so manifest a thing. ... I held him to be mistaken in his instances. I mentioned several to him, ... ' Uncatl. MS. Letters between the Revd. Mr Warburton and Dr Taylor (later Sir Robert Taylor) from the Year MDCCXXVIII [Harry Ransom Center, the University of Texas at Austin], Vol. 3, no. 57, ff. 93–4, 27 Feb. 1760. Warburton adhered to this view, later writing: 'The two great Quacks of the time, in Church & State, are Kennicott & Wilk[e]s', and expressed surprise that so many of the clergy could not see the former as 'an egregious blockhead'. no. 100, f. 149, 5 Jan. 1769. On the other stood the High Churchmen inclined to Hutchinsonian views on scripture whose long campaign of opposition to Kennicott lasted into the 1770s. See, for instance, George Horne, *An Apology for Certain Gentlemen ...* (Oxford, 1756); *A View of Mr Kennicott's Method* (London, 1760).

[40] His achievement is discussed in F. Deconinck-Brossard, 'England and France in the Eighteenth Century', in ed. S. Prickett, *Reading the Text. Biblical Criticism and Literary Theory* (Oxford, 1991), 136–81, at 151–60.

[41] Scott Mandelbrote, 'Biblical scholarship at Oxford in the mid-eighteenth century: Local contexts for Robert Lowth's *De sacra poesi hebraeorum* (1753)', in ed. John Jarrick, *Sacred conjectures: the context and legacy of Robert Lowth and Jean Atruc* (New York/London, 2007), 3–24. Neil Hitchin refers to it as 'a Hebraists' hive'. Hitchin, 'The Politics of English Bible translation', 80.

'facilitate, an improved English version of the scriptures; than which nothing could be more beneficial to the cause of religion, or more honourable to the reign and age in which it was patronized and executed'.[42] Lowth and the Hon. Shute Barrington (canon of Christ Church in the 1760s) subsequently encouraged Robert Holmes (1748–1805), Fellow of New College, whose collation of the manuscript of the Septuagint (the ancient Greek translation of the OT) received support across the University.[43]

The question remained: if those foundations were in place, would the archbishop still risk sponsoring publication of a revised official Bible?[44] Secker had once been the most promising advocate, yet his enthusiasm gradually diminished after his translation to the primacy.[45] Indeed, as early as 1761 he told his clergy 'the last thing I want is to be the patron of undertakings from which too much quarrelling is likely to arise. These things can wait until an effectual meeting of the synod be called, so that we do not let ourselves stir up internal warfare which will do great harm to the public interest'.[46] It was both a failure of nerve and a backhanded admission that his theological opponents, both inside and outside the Established Church, had the scholarly capacity to be ruthless in exploiting the many opportunities for polemic producing a new official translation would give them, with the added risk that anti-Trinitarianism might be let in through the back door.[47] Secker backed away and his successor, the Hon. Frederick Cornwallis, displayed no interest in persisting with the project. He did not respond to Durell's plea in 1772 for a new translation of the whole Bible on the basis that the AV was vitiated by inappropriate translations and blatant errors.[48]

Nevertheless, Oxford men continued to produce new scholarly translations of sections of the scriptures with the unspoken hope that, cumulatively, they might be the basis for a new Bible.[49] As Kennicott had insisted in the first volume of his

---

[42] William Newcome, *An Attempt Towards an Improved Version, a Metrical Arrangement, and an Explanation of the Twelve Minor Prophets* (Dublin, 1785), xvi. There were other publications issued while he held the archbishopric of Armagh during the last five years of his life (1795–1800). R. Mant, *History of the Church of Ireland from the Reformation to the Revolution*...(2 vols., London, 1840), II. 234.

[43] On Holmes's death, James Parsons of Wadham (1762–1847) was invited by the delegates of the Press to complete his work on the Septuagint (1808–27). Wells, *Wadham*, 140.

[44] Hitchin argues that Secker developed cold feet quite early (perhaps as a result of signs that dissenting aggression was reviving) and 'needing to defuse the situation, he may have prevailed upon the monarch for support in redirecting the energies of his bishops and biblical scholars as a compromise'. Hitchin, 'The Politics of English Bible Translation', 86.

[45] Hitchin argues that he killed the project himself. Ibid., 83.

[46] Secker, *Oratio quam coram Synodo Provinciae Cantuariensis anno 1761...in Records of Convocation*, ed. Gerald Bray (20 vols., Woodbridge, 2005–6), XII. 315–25, 323.

[47] 'The political significance of a new translation was lost on no one. The new reformers saw a reformed bible as a necessary preliminary to the completion of the protestant reformation'. Hitchin, 'The Politics of English Bible Translation', 83.

[48] Durell, *Critical Remarks*, v–vi.

[49] Joseph White, Professor of Arabic, noted the increased knowledge of eastern customs as one reason for a new revision in a sermon of 1778. White, *A Revisal of the English Translation of the Old Testament Recommended* (Oxford, 1779).

THE DEFENCE OF CHRISTIAN BELIEF   89

collation, the *Vetus Testamentum Hebraicum* 'none of the variants was a threat to essential doctrine or increase[d] historical knowledge'.[50] Lowth (translated from Oxford to the see of London in 1777) declared Kennicott's magnum opus to be 'a work the greatest and most important that has been undertaken and accomplished since the Revolution of Letters' (a reference to the early Reformation era),[51] though the bishop was no doubt delighted that his former pupil had seen a project he had first suggested through to completion. Blayney in 1784 produced *Jeremiah, and Lamentations. A New translation with notes critical, philological, and explanatory.* that owed much to the scholarly endeavours of other Hertford men.[52]

Yet the fact remained, without archiepiscopal sanction and encouragement, Oxonian attempts to produce a new English translation of the Bible would come to nothing and University scholars of the last quarter of the century largely moved away from Biblical translation, partly as the project of collecting variant readings 'had also begun to seem flawed as critics realized the inconsequential nature of much of the material being compiled'.[53] With Convocation in abeyance since 1717, the chances of authorising an official commission were anyway much reduced and, though thoughts of reconvening Convocation were entertained by Secker when he became archbishop, they were soon dropped.[54] The contrast with 1604–11, when the Crown threw its weight behind official efforts to produce the AV, were conspicuous. The Church took the easy way out and opted not to expose itself on this front when it was engaged elsewhere with its detractors, and thus the fruits of Oxford scholarship in the form of a new Bible reaching the majority of the English population every Sunday in churches across the land never appeared. At least, thanks to the efforts of Sir William Blackstone and others, the University Press was adapted later in the century so that it could compete on equal terms with other printers. A new 'Bible partnership' with the trade was established, fortified by North's 1775 Act, which maintained Oxford University Press's copyright in the Bible text.[55]

---

[50] D. Patterson, 'Hebrew Studies', in HUO V, 535–50, at 541.

[51] Quoted in Brian Hepworth, *Robert Lowth* (Boston, 1978), 145. See also William McKane, 'Benjamin Kennicott: an eighteenth-century researcher', *JTS*, 28 (1977), 445–64.

[52] It says much that Blayney was unable to use the biblical manuscripts deposited in Lambeth Palace Library because Archbishop Cornwallis was not in residence. Ingram, *Religion, Reform and Modernity*, 96.

[53] Mandelbrote, 'The Bible and its Readers', 63.

[54] Ingram, *Religion, Reform and Modernity*, 157–60. Perhaps surprisingly, given George III's strong faith and Lord North being both Premier and Chancellor, the Crown never moved to appoint a Commission for a revised Bible and the University did not lobby for one in the 1770s. Hopes still lingered in some quarters of the University, qualified by recognition that it would be a long road. Thus John Butler, *A Sermon Preached at the Ordination held at Ch. Ch. Nov. 21. 1779. By John Lord Bishop of Oxford* (Oxford, 1779), 7. '... we shall have a plain road to the doctrines of Christianity, when we are masters of the exact sense of the sacred writings. And that the Scriptures have suffer'd the same corruptions, and abound with the same difficulties as other books of ancient learning, is no matter of argument but of fact'.

[55] See Matthew Kilburn, 'The Blackstone Reforms', in ed. Gadd, *The History of Oxford University Press*, 1. 139–58, at 155–7. Blackstone led a vital enquiry into the University Press in 1756 to

90   ENLIGHTENED OXFORD

A besetting problem for the University and its Press was less the printing of
Bibles than their distribution, especially given that easy access to the scriptures
was central to the activities of the expanding networks of charity, dame, and
Sunday schools, and that they were using the Authorized Version as their primary
text. And yet Oxford academics were not particularly interested in reaching out
to that growing market to buttress the Christian life of the literate public through
the production of such things as dictionaries, commentaries, and scriptural
concordances.[56] That relative omission reflected an underlying caution in the
Church of England (one that was typical of established Churches across Europe)
about unsupervised reading (or instruction at the wrong hands) of the Bible, for
there was a consensus that certain parts of it, prophecy for instance, were
unsuitable reading for ordinary people.[57] Though the numbers of books written
about the Bible with children and young people in mind increased during the
century, the majority of members of the University saw it as no part of their
business to divert their efforts to patronise this market. That was remitted to
voluntary organisations, notably the SPCK, founded in 1698, which concentrated
on the distribution of Bibles along with biblical and religious literature to poor
children, widows, soldiers, seamen, convicts, and other markets hitherto neglected.
Here the University was of material assistance, since the University Press produced
many cheap, small-format Bibles on the Society's behalf.[58] That was about the limit
of the University's involvement. Otherwise it left instruction in scripture to the
catechising initiatives of the parochial clergy without troubling itself to provide
much by way of new written material to underpin that vital dimension of pastoralia,
apart from sermons, that primary vehicle of early modern communication.

ii) Pulpits, preaching, and publication

> The Sermons of our Divines are allowed, by the liberal part of Europe,
> to be the best and purest compositions within the province of
> Theology.
>
> John Langhorne, Letters on the Eloquence
of the Pulpit (London, 1765), 38.

---

professionalise its business habits and reinvigorate the Laudian vision of its furtherance of scholarship.
Wilfrid Prest, *William Blackstone. Law and Letters in the Eighteenth Century* (Oxford, 2008), 134–8,
145–8.

[56] There was, at the Press, an awareness of the need to be proactive in encouraging professorial
outreach into that market. In 1758 the delegates asked three Professors 'to recommend such Books, in
their different Provinces, as they thought would be most acceptable to the Public, & most for the
honour of the University to encourage the Publication of '.' Kennicott to Secker, 7 Mar. 1758, LPL,
Secker Papers 2, f.1, cited in Ingram, *Religion, Reform and Modernity*, 88.

[57] Marcus Walsh, 'Profession and authority: the interpretation of the Bible in the seventeenth and
eighteenth centuries', *Literature and Theology*, 9 (1995), 383–98.

[58] Mandelbrote, 'The Bible and its Readers', 48, 52, 54.

THE DEFENCE OF CHRISTIAN BELIEF   91

Pulpits abounded in eighteenth-century Oxford, testimony to the high value placed on the word in the Anglican tradition (though they were seldom positioned as if to imply that the word was more important than the sacrament).[59] And much care and money was lavished on them as part of the renewal of chapel fittings that took place in several colleges after the Restoration,[60] with advice on refitting the chapels at Merton, All Souls, and St John's being given by that impeccable High Churchman, Sir Christopher Wren.[61] The richness of the decorative woodwork with which many pulpits were constructed was well seen in the new chapel at Trinity College, consecrated in 1694 (thanks to the largesse of its President, the octogenarian Ralph Bathurst),[62] with some of the most delicate carving done by Jonathan Maine, who had honed his skills in some of Wren's London churches. Early in the new century, new pulpits were also installed in the chapels constructed for Corpus Christi (1728–32) and at Queen's. College chapels were quiet, intimate spaces, and private in that they were reserved for members of the college and their guests. They were settings for well-ordered Prayer Book worship, the following of the Christian year, the remembrance of founders and benefactors, and the edification of undergraduates. As preaching spaces, the likelihood of their being used to deliver sentiments and opinions that would resonate with a wider audience was low. Which is not to say that, when discernible, the hortatory capacities of college heads and fellows were not an asset to their foundations. Thus the suave Dr Joseph Smith, Provost of Queen's from 1730 to 1756, came to the college with a reputation for pulpit eloquence built up by his years in the West End as lecturer at St George's church, Hanover Square.[63]

It was from the pulpit of Christ Church cathedral and, above all, from that of St Mary's [University] church, that the preacher would expect his words to have the potential to be heard by larger numbers than those packing the pews and galleries below him. Most Sundays in full term the leading members of the University, including the Vice Chancellor and the Heads of Houses, along with many

---

[59] The pulpit was central to the English public sphere or, as Tony Claydon has put it, one that was predominantly a 'preached public sphere'. 'The sermon, the "public sphere" and the political culture of late seventeenth-century England', in eds. L.A. Ferrell and P. McCullough, *The English Sermon Revised: Religion, Literature and History 1600–1750* (Manchester, 2000), 208–34, at 226.

[60] Studies in sacred spatiality have not so far encompassed academic settings but see generally Nigel Yates, *Buildings, Faith and Worship: The Liturgical Arrangement of Anglican Churches 1600–1900* (Oxford, 1991); Nigel Yates, *Liturgical Space: Christian Worship and Church Buildings in Western Europe 1500–2000* (Aldershot, 2008), chap. 4, which notes that 'The major Anglican contribution to post-Reformation church furnishing was the so-called three-decker pulpit', 73; eds. Andrew Spicer and S. M. Hamilton, *Defining the Holy. Sacred Space in Medieval and Early Modern Europe* (Aldershot, 2005); eds. Andrew Spicer and W. Coster, *Sacred Space in Early Modern Europe* (Cambridge, 2005).

[61] The screens Wren designed for the chapels at St John's and Merton were largely removed in the mid-nineteenth century. Colvin, *Dictionary*, 1089; Kerry Downes, *The Architecture of Wren* (London, 1982), 5, 131.

[62] Thomas Warton, *The Life of Ralph Bathurst* (Oxford, 1761); Clare Hopkins, *Trinity. 450 Years of an Oxford College Community* (Oxford, 2005), 155. See also Chapter 12.

[63] Hodgkin, *Queen's College*, 140.

92 ENLIGHTENED OXFORD

intending ordinands among the undergraduate body, would process to St Mary's to hear a senior cleric offer a carefully constructed (usually) and frequently controversial homily which would generally be printed and appear to represent the opinions of the University to the wider world, however much its first hearers had disagreed with or deprecated its contents. Two official sermons were preached every Sunday, with the exception of Easter Sunday when the morning sermon was replaced by one preached in the chapel of every college at its communion celebration. Other university sermons were delivered on the mornings of feast days occurring in the Book of Common Prayer as well as on key occasions in the Protestant calendar: the accession day of the monarch, the execution of Charles I in 1649 (30 January), the Restoration of the monarchy in 1660 (29 May), and the discovery of the Gunpowder Plot (5 November). There were two sermons on Act Sunday, marking the close of the academic year, an event which had become Commemoration by the second half of the century. The prestigious Sunday morning sermons in term time were delivered from a narrow circle consisting of the Heads of Houses, the two professors of divinity, and the professor of Hebrew (though deputies could be nominated); on all other occasions the list encompassed virtually all in holy orders who had kept their names on their college books, even if they were not usually resident in Oxford (they, too, could name deputies).[64]

Powers of nomination on all these occasions were, under the Laudian statutes, in the gift of the Vice Chancellor, and the usual considerations of patronage applied. It is difficult to be precise about the criteria individual vice chancellors would apply. Considerations of vocal projection probably counted for less than personal ties and a distinct line in churchmanship and party politics. Though the entire body of the University was supposed to be in their seats on a Sunday morning, St Mary's was far too small to accommodate anything like that number. Attendance was likely to be highest when celebrity preachers were down to address the congregation and, in the early eighteenth century, Oxford had two, neither of whom performed regularly in the city: Robert South, Canon of Christ Church, 1670–1716 (and a former Public Orator),[65] and Francis Atterbury, Dean

---

[64] St Mary's was not uniquely the preaching venue. University sermons were preached at Christ Church when the dean or one of the canons was the preacher, and those on Christmas Day, Easter Day, Good Friday, and Ascension Day and a variety of other feast days were allotted to specified colleges. Lent sermons were delivered at St Peter's-in-the-East church. R. Greaves, 'Religion in the University, 1715–1800', HUO, V. 401–24, at 412–13; L. H. Dudley Buxton and Strickland Gibson, *Oxford University Ceremonies* (Oxford, 1935), 106–7; Judith Curthoys, *The Cardinal's college: Christ Church, chapter and verse* (London, 2012), 126; Judith Curthoys, *The King's cathedral. The ancient heart of Christ Church, Oxford* (London, 2019), 124. The office of University Select Preacher with five preachers annually was established in 1801. These would supplement the usual rotation of those on the Vice Chancellor's list. *Historical Register*, 108–14; William Barrow, *An Essay on Education; in which are particularly considered the merits and the defects of the discipline and instruction in our Academies* (2 vols., London, 1804), II. 364.

[65] Reedy, *Robert South, passim*.

of Christ Church, 1711–13.[66] South, 'the implacable Anglican loyalist',[67] had used the pulpit to good effect during the 1690s when he had weighed in against William Sherlock, Dean of St Paul's, with accusations of tritheism implicit in the latter's controversial *A Vindication of the Doctrine of the Holy and Ever Blessed Trinity* (1690).[68] Yet South was best known not as a polemicist but as a pulpit stylist. His reputation and influence were formidable, yet by Queen Anne's reign he was close to decrepit and seldom preached in Oxford, preferring to concentrate on establishing charities in the nearby village of Islip (where he was rector). Atterbury, likewise, found his time in Oxford largely consumed by ferocious rows of his own making within the governing body of Christ Church and his attempt to lead the

Fig. 3.2 Bishop Francis Atterbury, after Sir Godfrey Kneller, oil on canvas, after 1718 (Bodleian Libraries, University of Oxford).

---

[66] Collected in Atterbury, *Sermons on Several Occasions...* (2 vols., London, 1723). James Downey considered that 'in him can be observed the major stylistic trends of eighteenth-century preaching—the lucidity and immediacy of the moralists, the aggressiveness of the polemicists, and the passion of the evangelicals'. James Downey, *The Eighteenth Century Pulpit: Butler, Berkeley, Secker, Sterne, Whitfield and Wesley* (Oxford, 1969), 29; G. V. Bennett, *The Tory Crisis in Church and State 1688–1730. The career of Francis Atterbury, bishop of Rochester* (Oxford, 1975), 35–8.
[67] Hampton, *Anti-Arminians*, 64.   [68] Ibid., 130–6; 143–50.

High Church party nationally.[69] On the whole, University sermons in the eighteenth century produced no Newman. Most Sundays they were competently and dutifully done and, when a sermon made an impact beyond Oxford, it tended to be not on account of the preacher's learning and delivery but because of the rebarbatively controversial note struck, often by a cleric who was both junior and little previously known, who suddenly attracted national attention.[70]

This could be when the preacher chose to use the pulpit to inveigh against his own fellow collegians. Thus John Wesley fully expected, following his 'scarifying denunciation' (as Blackstone put it) of the spiritual apathy and sloth of the senior members of the University in his sermon 'Scriptural Christianity' on St Bartholomew's Day, 24 August 1744, that he would never be asked to preach there again—'I preached, I suppose, the last time at St Mary's', he wrote in his journal, 'Be it so; I have fully delivered my soul.'[71] Or the preacher might asperse his fellow clergy as a caste, a brave, even provocative action in a setting where the defence of the ordained ministry was seen as both a cultural and a political imperative. With the Bangorian Controversy still running at full tilt, Peter Maurice, a young fellow of Jesus College with a reputation for an irregular life, in November 1718 positioned himself squarely behind Bishop Hoadly when he argued—and did so from the pulpit of the University church—that disrespect for the clerical office was owing to the clergy making such high claims for it. He was censured by the two Divinity Professors, Potter (Whig) and Delaune (Tory), convicted of preaching against the twenty-sixth Article of Religion, and forced to recant before Convocation.[72] Per contra, another Whig, (an impecunious Fellow of Exeter) Joseph Betty's heated defence of clerical dignity against 'witty malice, and . . . raging insolence', in a university sermon on 'The Divine Institution of the Ministry, and the Absolute Necessity of Church Government' of 21

---

[69] That said, Atterbury had a careful way of noticing students absent from College prayers when Dean of Christ Church. It was later observed that 'By these gentle means, he governed one of the largest Societies in Europe with ease and pleasure to himself, and greatly to the emolument of this Kingdom, to which many of them still are Ornaments both in Church and State'. A sincere wellwisher to our universities, *Free thoughts upon university education; occasioned by the present debates at Cambridge* (London, 1749), 27–8. Many of his Christ Church contemporaries would have disagreed forcibly with this view of the man.

[70] For the *cause célèbre* of Henry Sacheverell see Chapter 7, pp. 37–9.

[71] John Wesley, *The Bicentennial Edition of the Works of John Wesley* (Oxford, 1975–83; Nashville, TN, 1984-), Vols. I–IV, *Sermons*, ed. Albert C. Outler (1984–7), I. iv; vol. XX. *Journal and Diaries*, III (1743–1754), eds. W. R. Ward and R. P. Heitzenrater, 36–7. Wesley was correct in his presumption. The Vice Chancellor requested his sermon notes and he never preached there again. As a Fellow of Lincoln College, he had preached two previous University Sermons: 'Salvation by Faith' on 11 June 1738 and the 'Almost Christian' on 25 July 1741. The latter was originally intended to be on Oxford's lack of godliness, but he allowed himself to be dissuaded. Vol. XIX. *Journal and Diaries*, II (1738–1743), eds. W. R. Ward and R. P. Heitzenrater, 478.

[72] It turned out to be the last major pro-Hoadly sermon in the Bangorian Controversy. P. Maurice, *The True Causes of the Contempt of Christian Ministers* (London, 1719); Hearne, VI. 255, 261, 262–3; HMC, *Portland MSS*, VII. 246–7, 2 December 1718; Bodl. MS Ballard 20, fo. 117; OUA: Conv. Reg. Bd 31, f. viii. Maurice still secured preferment in the Bangor diocese from Hoadly, became chaplain to the king, and received a Lambeth LL.D. Starkie, *Bangorian Controversy*, 97.

September 1729, stirred up another miniature controversy when he insisted that all opposition to the ministry of the Church was sinful and 'That no excuse can be offer'd by man, which may plausibly be supposed to prevail with God, to pardon those that persevere in the guilt of this abominable sin'. Flattering as it was to Tory majority opinion in Oxford to find a Whig castigating Geneva and stating what, coming from their mouths, would have been less persuasive, pamphlet responses to Betty indicated that his apparent lack of generosity towards non-episcopalian Protestants had been a public relations embarrassment for the University that was compounded by Betty's taking a fatal overdose of laudanum on 1 January 1731.[73]

Occasions of national crisis were supposed to see the clergy use the pulpit to generate and stiffen loyalties.[74] During the vice-chancellorship of the 'peace-loving' Euseby Isham (1744–7),[75] it was Whigs who used the pulpit of St Mary's to proclaim their violent antagonism to Jacobitism, Catholicism, and all things Gallic during the crisis years of 1744–6, years when 'the English papists were the victims of both official suspicion and extraordinary popular hostility—undoubtedly the worst of the century'.[76] Preachers were given an extra wind after the Jacobites advanced into England and Oxford appeared to be right in the rebels' line of march, had they advanced south from Derby. The Rev. Francis Potter, taking his text from Jeremiah in the University church on 24 November 1745, insisted that any prince raised under the influence of France and Rome must indelibly bear the mark of the beast;[77] on the 5th of that month, John Free, vicar of Runcorn, vice-principal of St. Alban Hall, in *The Bloody Methods of Propagating the Popish Religion a Plain Proof that it is not of Divine Original*, indulged in even more rabid sentiments along those lines, casting all those who moaned about excessive taxation in wartime as 'profligate wretches'.[78] The vice chancellor refused him permission to use the University Press to publish his homily, a taken by many Whigs (wrongly) as a sign that the University was indifferent to the dynasty.[79] In fact, majority academic opinion deplored the overstated zeal and

---

[73] This fascinating episode is discussed in Ward, *Georgian Oxford*, 147–8. See also Robert D. Cornwall, *Visible and Apostolic. Constitution of the Church of England in High Church Anglican and Non-Juror Thought* (Newark, DE, 1993), 108.

[74] See generally James Joseph Caudle, 'Measures of allegiance: sermon culture and the creation of a public discourse of obedience and resistance in Georgian Britain, 1714–1760' (Yale Univ. Ph.D, 1996); Gerd Mischler, 'English political sermons 1714–1742: a case study in the theory of the "Divine Right of Governors" and the ideology of Order', *JECS*, 24 (2001), 33–61.

[75] Ward, *Georgian Oxford*, 166.

[76] Colin Haydon, *Anti-Catholicism in eighteenth-century England. A political and social study* (Manchester, 1993), 130.

[77] See also Chapter 7, p. 70. The horrors of Popery past and present were a staple of sermons in 1745–6. See Haydon, *Anti-Catholicism*, 135–6; F. Deconinck-Brossard, 'The churches and the '45', in ed. W. J. Sheils, *The Church and war*, [Studies in Church History, 20], (Oxford, 1983), 253–62.

[78] Ward, *Georgian Oxford*, 167–8, 282.

[79] Frank McLynn argues that the Tories in north Oxfordshire would have turned out for him had the Pretender not retreated. Cf. Haydon, *Anti-Catholicism*, 160–1n.

96 ENLIGHTENED OXFORD

harsh words of Free and his having blatantly (even by eighteenth-century norms) used the pulpit to gain preferment rather than preach the Gospel.

The reception of sermons within Oxford varied on a register that moved from intensity to indifference.[80] Hearing sermons was a regular occurrence for virtually every member of the University irrespective of content and quality, although intending undergraduate ordinands were encouraged to note the conventions of composition and to draw on their contents for inclusion in commonplace books that would be a resource for them in future years.[81] Accessibly delivered, with occasional flourishes of learning and a moralising content rooted in scriptural injunctions often intended to persuade the student body to comport itself decently and harmoniously, and certainly devoid of anything likely to give an impression of 'enthusiasm', homilies delivered within Oxford University were, unsurprisingly, appropriate to their setting and their auditors, and offered focused scriptural exposition without (for the most part) undue political provocation despite the temptation offered by a captive audience.[82] They could be, in their way, moder- ately 'enlightened'. Oxford preachers also functioned as role models for that large part of their congregation (as much as one third) intending to take holy orders themselves and who might in a few years' time be called on to perform in the pulpit. Though many students in the pews might find their attention wandering or even 'express their disapprobation of a preacher in a manner most indecent',[83] at least among a high proportion of those planning a sacerdotal future, sermons might be dutifully discussed.[84] For there were many in the pews who fancied themselves able to see the weaknesses in the preacher's propositions or otherwise to find him wanting and, as Arnold Hunt has argued for an earlier period, it was in the relation- ship between preacher and congregation—their 'interpretative collaboration'— that true meanings lie.[85] On fast days (usually in wartime) and holy days

---

[80] The reception of preaching by the laity in this era remains a complicated issue generally. For a systematic approach in a different context. Arnold Hunt, *The art of hearing: English preachers and their audiences, 1590–1640* (Cambridge, 2010) explores the reception of sermons among congregations through a study of notes taken by hearers. What preachers emphasised was not always that on which parishioners fastened.

[81] Matthew Hawes, commoner of Christ Church, recorded and analysed the arguments of 364 university sermons between 1704 and 1707. Bodl. MS Eng. Th. F.15, 'methods of sermonizing'. Undergraduates were not otherwise taught anything about the arts of preaching.

[82] For characteristics of the eighteenth-century sermon see Downey, *The Eighteenth Century Pulpit*, 1–29; Rolf P. Lessenich, *Elements of pulpit oratory in eighteenth-century England* (Cologne, 1972).

[83] This was the complaint of the Christ Church graduate turned Canterbury parson and school master Edward W. Whitaker. *Sermons on Education* (London, 1788), 64; Nigel Aston, 'Whitaker, Edward William (bap. 1752, d. 1818)', ODNB online version 2012.

[84] J. Spurr, *The Laity and Preaching in Post-Reformation England* [Friends of Dr Williams's Library sixty-sixth Lecture], (London, 2013), 9–10.

[85] One commentator noted of this general tendency in England: '. . . it is the impertinent Humour of the Age to cavil at the best Performances of the Clergy. Their Conceit leads many empty heads to set up for Criticks; and when they go to Church, many times, their thoughts are only engag'd in finding out the imperfections and frailties of the Preacher either in what he says or does . . . It is void of Grace, and good Manners'. Philanthropos, *A Second Plain and Humble Address to the Clergy of all Orders in Great-Britain* (York, 1731), Preface, v. The Hunt ref. is to Hunt, *The art of hearing: English preachers and their*

THE DEFENCE OF CHRISTIAN BELIEF 97

in term time the sermon themes were perhaps more likely to generate controversy than on the average Sunday, and if these fell on a weekday there might be more leisure for informal discussion with the University's teaching round suspended or reduced for the day. Similarly when academic opinion was inflamed and personal animosities threatened to get out of hand as, for instance, when the followers of the Tory William King (Principal of St Mary Hall) and the Whig Henry Brooke (Fellow of All Souls and Regius Professor of Civil Law) were denouncing each other in the late 1740s, a responsible university preacher could try and damp down the flames, as did the orientalist Thomas Hunt (1698–1774), the amiable and well-regarded Regius Professor of Hebrew, with a sermon against defamation in 1750.[86]

News of who was preaching in St Mary's, and what they had said afterwards, could spread rapidly out of the University church into the High Street into the colleges, coffee-houses, and hostelries, making up part of a wider news network. For this was an urban community with a sophisticated, varied geography of oral communication networks that thrived on gossip, where there could be as much interest in the preacher as in what he had preached, with intercollegiate rivalries frequently involved. As one who was no friend to Oxford Toryism observed: 'A bold mettlesome Sermon is of more Value at Oxford than a Quire of Bank Bills,...'[87] One could expect sermons to be discussed by dons and students over meals in hall or holding forth in coffee-houses,[88] and then to be disseminated away from Oxford, perhaps by conversations on the London coaches, or in the form of letters to friends and relations, conveyed later in the century by the mail coaches. George Fothergill, of the Queen's College, writing home to his parents in Westmorland, was quick to tell them how indifferently University pulpit criticism of the lately disgraced Bishop Atterbury had been received. The preacher, said Fothergill:

in the middle of his sermon, began prodigiously to commend the management of the Kingdom by our present Sovereign, and to abuse the Pretender: & spoke very contemptibly & judged very hardly of him, who was lately Bishop

---

audiences, 1590–1640 (Cambridge, 2010), chap. 2. See also John Craig, 'Sermon Reception', in eds. P. McCullough, H. Adlington, and E. Rhatigan, The Oxford handbook of the early modern sermon (Oxford, 2011), 179–93.

[86] Published as an appendix to his Observations on several passages in the book of Proverbs (Oxford, 1775), edited by his pupil Benjamin Kennicott.

[87] [Amhurst] A letter from a student in Grub-street, 41.

[88] The philosopher George Berkeley was typical in his castigation of coffee-house punditry, where (he said) it was 'the custom for polite persons to speak freely of all subjects, religious, moral or political'. Alciphron, or the Minute Philosopher, ed. David Berman (London, 1993), 39. Networks of like-minded scholars all had their favourite venues, though High Churchmen feared that coffee-houses were beyond the control of Church and state. Brian Cowan, The Social Life of Coffee. The Emergence of the British Coffeehouse (New Haven, CT: 2011), chap. 4; Adrian Johns, The nature of the Book: Print and Knowledge in the Making (Chicago, IL, 1998), 553–60.

98 ENLIGHTENED OXFORD

of Rochester, who is, as far as I can gather, by a great many thought to have been innocent as to what was laid against him: for which the Preacher was laughed at by not a few.[89]

News of preachers was also made available unofficially, in the local newspaper, what became *Jackson's Oxford Journal*, founded by the future University printer, William Jackson, in 1753, and, officially, in the *University Almanack*. Good sermons attracted the attention of public and press. They also acted as celebrity fundraisers. In July 1773, a sermon by John Ewer, bishop of Bangor, in support of the Radcliffe Infirmary attracted over £300 in donations from a congregation that included the prime minister, the University's new Chancellor, Lord North, and the 4th Duke of Marlborough. The fundraiser continued with a dinner and an oratorio before 'a most crowded and brilliant audience'.[90]

This conversion of the oral into the written was never slow in Oxford. After all, the preacher was talking from prepared notes and basing his comments on a scriptural text.[91] A preacher with an eye on sales and publicity could speedily turn those notes into a publishable format so that a single University sermon could be available for purchase nationally within a matter of weeks in unbound pamphlet format that allowed reprinting on demand. These one-off print runs would often in due course form part of the collected sermons of an individual divine published in a single or several volumes during or after the subject's lifetime, frequently with a memoir of the author (invariably sympathetic, often panegyrical). Religious works continued to dominate the publishing market. As a core part of these, sermons generated substantial sums of money for publishers throughout the century and remained primary to enlightened communication as a classic form of literature.[92] Sermons constituted a genuinely popular (and therefore lucrative) form that extended the reach of the University to a national and international audience, partly because they were short and serviceable, designed to catch the notice of the reader just as they had earlier sought to keep the congregation in St Mary's attentive. Publishers queued up to secure copyright to the discourses of the most celebrated divines, with many of them appearing under the imprint

---

[89] Cumbria RO (Kendal), WDX 94/acc. 165, 16 Dec. 1725.

[90] *St James's Chronicle*, 8 July 1773.

[91] Yet, as Jenifer Farooq has noted, scholars have only just begun to compare what preachers said in church to their printed sermons. Farooq, *Preaching in Eighteenth-Century London* (Woodbridge, 2013), 5. For an earlier period Hunt, *The Art of Hearing*. He emphasises the rough approximation of the printed version to what would have been heard from the pulpit. Printed sermons tended to be tidied up and perhaps became more cautious.

[92] See generally James Raven, 'Publishing and bookselling, 1660–1780', in ed. John Richetti, *The Cambridge history of English literature, 1660–1780* (Cambridge, 2005), 11–36; John Feather, 'British publishing in the eighteenth century: a preliminary subject analysis', *Library*, 6th ser., 8 (1986), 32–46. Christina Lupton demonstrates that sermons appeared side by side with other forms of reading material and 'routinely slip from reading context to another'. Lupton, 'Creating the writer of the cleric's words', *JECS*, 34 (2011), 167–83, at 173.

THE DEFENCE OF CHRISTIAN BELIEF   99

of Oxford University Press.[93] Authors who were not taken up by the Press, or preferred to arrogate a serious share of royalties for themselves, might look to commercial publishers such as Rivingtons, a firm with enduring High Church preferences, in and out of fashion under its successive chairmen Charles Rivington (1688–1742) and his son John (1720–92).[94] With so many Oxford clerics hoping to make at least some supplementary income from publishing their pulpit offerings, there could be occasional gluts in the market and personal connection with a publisher would help ease the way towards acceptance of a manuscript. It could be more tempting and make more commercial sense for a publisher simply to republish a classic author. There was a constant demand within the University for such texts on a pedagogical rather than a theological basis: the sermons of Tillotson, Atterbury, Samuel Clarke, and others were held up to students as among the finest models of contemporary reasoning and writing, not least in their rhetorical dimensions.[95]

Unsurprisingly, it was not generally the more academic homily that found the widest market, but the most scandalous and controversial, or those that tapped into the national mood as Henry Sacheverell, Fellow of Magdalen College, had managed in 1709–10 with his notorious 'False Brethren in Church and State'.[96] Sacheverell's sermon sold a massive 40,000 copies, more than any other published in the century. His was a *cause célèbre* that was not the lot of most Oxford clerics, who were probably also indifferent to using their physical good looks (if they possessed them) to bolster their sales with the female buying public, as Sacheverell and his apologists managed.[97] Sacheverell's 'False Brethren' sermon ushered in the last four years of contested High Church triumphalism before the cause fell out of official favour with the change of dynasty in 1714, though the market for more sober tracts intelligently pleading the 'honest cause' continued to be Oxford's homiletic stock-in-trade for decades to come.[98] They brought some extra funds into the pockets of their authors and publishers wanted to take them on, sometimes out of loyalty to the cause of the Church but usually from commercial considerations, knowing that Tory parsons, squires, and professional men

---

[93] Matthew Kilburn, 'The Fell Legacy 1686-1755', in ed. Gadd, *The History of Oxford University Press*, 1. 107–38, at 134–5; John Feather, 'A Learned Press in a Commercial World', in ibid., 243–79, at 261.

[94] The latter was publisher to the SPCK from 1760. See Septimus Rivington, *The Publishing Family of Rivington* (3rd ed., London, 1919).

[95] Downey, *The Eighteenth Century Pulpit*, 10. Samuel Johnson called Atterbury's sermons among the best in the English language. Boswell, *The Life of Samuel Johnson*, ed. G. B. Hill, rev. L. F. Powell (6 vols., Oxford, 1934–50), III. 247.

[96] Significantly, Sacheverell's incendiary sermon had been preached in St Paul's Cathedral rather than St Mary's Church, Oxford. See generally Geoffrey Holmes, *The Trial of Doctor Sacheverell* (London, 1973).

[97] See Eirwen E. C. Nicholson, 'Sacheverell's harlots: non-resistance on paper and in practice', in ed. Mark Knights, *Faction displayed: reconsidering the impeachment of Dr Henry Sacheverell* (London, 2012), 69–79.

[98] Farooq argues that the slight decline in the number of sermons published after c.1720 indicates the degree to which multiple editions since the Revolution had been driven by party conflicts. *Preaching in eighteenth-century London*, 57, 95.

100   ENLIGHTENED OXFORD

across the length of England would buy Oxford sermons for comfort as well as edification. The parish clergy would seek to imitate both style and substance, and straightforward borrowing of their contents for use in rural pulpits was quite unexceptionable.[99]

Sermons, however important and influential, were by definition on the short side, and could only deal with individual doctrines or other aspects of belief in an abbreviated format. That was not the case with the core scholarly work of the eighteenth-century University: the production of books systematically expounding, glossing, or defending aspects of the Christian faith and the place of the Church (particularly the Church of England) in the providential scheme of things. These texts were primarily intended for a scholarly readership in and beyond Oxford, but accessibility to the parish clergy as well as interested, educated laymen, an ever-expanding niche market, mattered considerably. What Oxford authors said was always going to be a major factor in judging the success of the defence of orthodoxy in an age when classical Christianity was being repeatedly threatened.

By and large, twentieth-century scholarship disregarded the contributions and impact of Oxford theologians from the Glorious Revolution down to the Oxford Movement.[100] Many individual claims to originality and importance have thereby been either forgotten or underestimated, and that the University between c.1690 and c.1810 nurtured theologians, church historians, biblical and patristic scholars of distinction merits recovery. These scholars produced work of sufficient quality to give the Christian faith its continued status in their own time as the default setting for the majority of the educated. It was their arguments, quite as much as the legal protection it enjoyed, which ensured that the Church of England remained at the heart of national life. And it fell in the first instance to the Divinity Professoriate to express the official voice of the University (inasmuch as it had one) in matters of faith and order. The holders of these Chairs were largely conscious of their duty, but articulation could so easily be compromised by contestation (or its apprehension). But perhaps nothing less was to be expected in an institution where theological considerations were inseparable from political ones.

iii) Professors, parsons, and public theology

Regius Professors of Divinity were well-placed by their office to stand at the forefront of University apologetics, but their success in doing so varied and it

---

[99] A handbook of 1753 advised young clerics 'not to trust at first to their own compositions, but to furnish themselves with a provision of the best sermons, which learned divines of our church have published'. See the useful discussion about the contexts of sermon publishing in Paul Hunter, *Before novels: the cultural contexts of eighteenth-century English fiction* (New York, 1992), 245–50.

[100] The point is of wider applicability. 'These writers [Bernard Bailyn, John Brewer, etc.] accepted the pamphlet, but rejected the sermon'.

could be offset by prior claims of lecturing, politics, or indisposition. For their overriding duty was to ensure that the steady flow of intending ordinands into the University was taught correct theology, even if practical preparations for parish ministry were only gradually catered for. The chair was a Crown appointment, which carried with it a canonry of Christ Church, and therefore party considerations tended to weigh more heavily in appointment than strictly intellectual ones. The predictable result was the exclusion of Tories despite their preponderance in Oxford. The office was held from 1707 to 1737 by a domestic chaplain of Archbishop Tenison's (from 1704) and also of the 1st Duke of Marlborough's, John Potter (1674?-1747), a Whig before he was a High Churchman, and a classicist before he was a theologian. Potter was also an ex-Dissenter who had been imposed on the University, which had wanted George Smalridge, Canon of Christ Church, instead, a man of moderate temper, a lieutenant of Atterbury's in the High Church and Tory interest, and deputy to William Jane, the previous Regius.[101] Potter started promisingly—and reassuringly—enough, bringing out his extensive and systematic *Discourse on Church Government* in the year of his appointment, which functioned as a response to Tindal, a reassertion of the Church's spiritual authority as derived from the Apostles, and a vindication of the rights of princes in the government of the Church, with an emphasis that would have given as much comfort to Gallicans in France as to Queen Anne in England.[102] As a concomitant, and relying on an extensive patristic range, Potter also defended a collegial model of episcopacy and, in a manner that might have disappointed the dissenters, emphasised the exclusive privileges of a regularly commissioned ministry. Potter was a powerful presence in the University and in Church and state at large, a status confirmed when he became Bishop of Oxford in 1715, but he was a disappointment as Regius Professor.[103]

---

[101] Norman Sykes, *Church and State in England in the Eighteenth Century* (Cambridge, 1934), 165; G.V. Bennett, 'The Era of Party Zeal 1702–1714', HUO V, 61–98, at 81. Potter's appointment was part of a compromise package agreed by the Junto Whigs with the Queen over ecclesiastical appointments. Burnet, *History*, V. 340; William Coxe, *Memoirs of John, Duke of Marlborough* (3 vols., London, 1818–19), II. 381. It was reported from Oxford in 1709 that Potter was 'more respected than belov'd among us'. Samuel Palmer to Philip Yorke, 22 Sept. 1709, BL Hardwicke Papers, Add MS 35584, f. 116.

[102] The leading layman, the ex-Nonjuror, Robert Nelson, thought it 'a most admirable performance' and went on 'I am glad such a book comes from that quarter, for I apprehend that set of men [Tindal and his supporters] stand most in need of it. By my consent every candidate of Holy Orders should be obliged to give a perfect account of it, before he is ordained, ...' To Arthur Charlett, Ascension Day [25 May] 1707, in ed. J. Walker, *Letters written by Eminent persons in the Seventeenth and Eighteenth Centuries* ... (2 vols., London, 1813), I. 167–8. Thomas Hearne was less impressed. He considered Potter's response to Tindal dull and ineffectual because he was 'afraid of displeasing some great Men of the same stamp with ye Author of ye wicked tract'. *Remarks and Collections of Thomas Hearne*, eds. C. E. Doble, D. W. Rannie, and H. E. Salter [Oxford Historical Society] (11 vols., Oxford, 1885–1921), VII. 88.

[103] Potter was a frequent preacher at court and was selected to give the sermon at the Coronation of George II in 1727, in itself a signal honour for the University. He attracted controversy for arguing for 'our intire submission to his [the king's] authority,' on the basis that scripture called monarchs 'Vice-regents of God'. J. Potter, *A Sermon Preach'd at the Coronation of King George II and Queen Caroline... October 11 1727* (London, 1727), 3–4. Discussed in Clark, *English Society 1660–1832*, 112–13.

102 ENLIGHTENED OXFORD

Despite his learning being admitted by friends and foes alike, he devoted his time less to the academic opportunities presented by his chair than to the pastoral needs of his diocesan clergy and produced no further scholarly tracts (although retaining the professorship in order to supplement the meagre income of his see until his translation to Canterbury in 1737).[104]

Just as Potter's scholarly interests were properly in Greek antiquities and patristics but he, as with some of his successors, owed his advancement to the Regius Chair of Divinity more to his politics than his intellectual pursuits and the intended duties of the Chair. Potter's next but one successor, John Fanshawe (1741–63), was previously Regius Professor of Greek (1735) and exchanged that crown appointment for Divinity as a result of political services to the Pelhams.[105] Similarly, Edward Bentham (1763–76), had, like Fanshawe, the right credentials for preferment in the eyes of the ministry—court Whiggery ([he] 'hath always been a hearty Friend to the Government;')[106] and moderate High Churchmanship. He was already sub-dean of Christ Church when archbishop Secker persuaded him to accept the chair in 1763 (after immediately suggesting his name to ministers on hearing of Fanshawe's demise as '...a man of character in all respects unblameable, and a very good Scholar and Divine', who had been '... very useful in his present station').[107] He also noted that that the 'promotion' would actually amount to a step back for Bentham, who would have to move from the first to the more junior fifth prebendal stall at Christ Church, because it was annexed to the professorship![108] His interests lay mainly in the field of moral philosophy and logic. His principal theological writings were *De studiis theologicis praelectio* (1764) and *Reflections on the Study of Divinity* (1771). They upheld his moderate, orthodox line and, perhaps partly for that reason, neither could be described as exciting.[109]

Bentham took his professorial duties seriously, and he recognised that the proper formation of the ordained ministry could not be compromised if an

---

[104] It is hard to dissent from Ward's view that Potter, over time, 'to the disgust of majority opinion in the University, turned it [the Regius Chair] into a sinecure'. *Georgian Oxford*, 32. See also John Nichols, *Illustrations of the literary history of the eighteenth century* (8 vols., London, 1817–58), III. 272–3; HMC, *Portland MSS* (10 vols., London, 1891–1913), IV. 320, 386, 473, VII. 24; Bodl. MS. Ballard 21, f. 67; 31.

[105] See BL. Add. MSS. 32711, f. 186; 32716, f. 176, 379; 32887, f.69.

[106] Secker to George Grenville, 10 May 1763. BL, Stowe 119, f.152.

[107] Secker to 2nd Earl of Egremont, 10 May 1763, West Sussex Record Office, [Petworth House Archives], PHA 30.

[108] 'I have got Dr. Bentham against his will, the professorship of Divinity, for who might have got it else, I could not tell... I am sorry for poor Bentham', wrote Secker to the archbishop of York, 'but I am glad for the University' (T. Secker to R. H. Drummond, 31 May 1763, Borthwick Institute for Archives, MS Bp C. & P. VII/175/2). Bentham was fortunate to have the archbishop's backing given that his old patron, the duke of Newcastle, was no longer in favour at the start of George III's reign.

[109] Ward refers to a sermon of Bentham's preached before the Commons on 30 Jan. 1750 with its 'characteristically feeble argument'. *Georgian Oxford*, 181.

THE DEFENCE OF CHRISTIAN BELIEF   103

audience beyond Oxford was to be reached and edified.[110] Thus, with Secker's encouragement,[111] he started a course of lectures in divinity in 1763–4 for intending ordinands, reading three lectures each week during term time without exacting any fee for attendance, 'a striking innovation' as Richard L. Greaves has called it.[112] The year's sixty to seventy lectures formed one continuous course. Surviving undergraduate notes on the lectures make clear that Bentham was not attempting his own *summa* of Anglican doctrine and history, or trying in divinity to rival Blackstone in law. The lectures had a practical edge appropriate for their audience, down to offering guidance on legal questions they might encounter in their parishes. The notes also confirm his doctrinal orthodoxy, and his rehearsal of all the usual objections to those outside the Church of England.[113] Bentham urged a close familiarity with biblical languages to facilitate textual study of scripture for 'the Transcribers were not certainly inspired by the Holy Ghost...often they might be nodding'.[114] The lectures were continued by his successors and, by c.1800, it was claimed that no man could be admitted to holy orders in the Oxford diocese without a certificate stating that he had attended them.[115]

It was not a Regius Professor of Divinity who made the most impact upon theological debate in eighteenth-century England but a holder of the sister chair, whose occupant was not selected by the Crown but elected by all holders of degrees in Divinity, along with college heads. This was the Lady Margaret Professorship, as held by Thomas Randolph, an outstanding exemplar of orthodoxy and theological enlightenment in Oxford. His immediate predecessors were worthy but unexceptional. The companionable William Delaune, the former vice chancellor and President of St John's College, was elected to this chair in 1715, thanks to the votes of bachelors of divinity; only two college heads and six DDs voted for him. Better known as a reformed gambler, and as one who, while vice chancellor, had embezzled the income of the University Press, Delaune

---

[110] Bentham's initiative was a partial recognition that theological training at English universities must be improved. Bishop Gilbert Burnet had previously set up a seminary at Salisbury, but it failed after five years, for which Burnet blamed Oxford opposition. *History*, VI. 308–9. For some unpublished 'thoughts concerning alterations in' the Church that included this initiative see S. Taylor, 'Bishop Edmund Gibson's proposals for church reform', in ed. S. Taylor, *From Cranmer to Davidson. A Church of England miscellany* (Woodbridge, 1999), 169–202, at 181–2.

[111] Within a year of appointment as bishop of Oxford (1738), Secker was canvassing allies to improve clerical education in both universities. Ingram, *Religion, Reform, and Modernity*, 80. See also his sermon on Act Sunday 1733, ibid., 171–2.

[112] Bodl. G.A. Oxon. (b) (19); 'Religion in the University, 1715–1800', 406.

[113] See notes on Bentham's lectures by Henry Hall (1749–1839), Bodl. MS Top. Oxon. c. 226.

[114] Ibid., f. 135.

[115] [James Hurdis], *A Word or two in vindication of the University of Oxford, and of Magdalen College in particular, from the posthumous aspersions of Mr Gibbon* (London, 1800?), 36. It was also a rule enforced by Markham as archbishop of York. Barrow, *An essay on education*, II. 340n. For the wider question of what was expected of candidates for holy orders see J. Gregory, 'Standards of admission to the ministry of the Church of England in the eighteenth century', in eds. T. Clemens and Wim Janse, *The pastor bonus. Papers read at the British-Dutch colloquium at Utrecht, 18–21 September 2002* (Leiden, 2004), 283–95.

104   ENLIGHTENED OXFORD

combined High Churchmanship with a commitment to the Reformed tradition in theology.[116] It took him until he was sixty-nine to publish anything of note: his *Twelve Sermons upon Several Subjects and Occasions* of 1728 (the year before his death) represented a further attempt to relieve his debts rather than to offer a mature theological expression. The tone was moderately anti-Roman, pragmatic, considered, but slightly tired.[117] Delaune's output was immense judged against that of his successor, Thomas Jenner (b. 1687), who held the chair for four decades to his death in 1768 (from 1745 in conjunction with the Presidency of Magdalen College) and in that time offered the public just one infirmary sermon.[118]

Jenner's longevity over four decades ensured that more articulate and arguably more able men were kept out of this senior chair. Thomas Randolph was an obvious choice to succeed him, coming, as he did, with Archbishop Secker's strong endorsement.[119] Already in his late sixties in 1768, he had made a strong impression as President of Corpus Christi College since 1748 and served as vice chancellor from 1756 to 1759 without sacrificing his involvement in current theological controversies and publishing around them. And he saw the desirability of reaching out to the public beyond academe and not underestimating its capacity for grasping the issues contested:

> It is indeed common for persons of superior Learning and Abilities to take up too contemptible an opinion of the vulgar. But when they come to converse with them, they will meet with many of them, who can reason shrewdly enough; and may perhaps find them too hard for them in an Argument. Daily experience shews that People in low Life can reason very justly on the common Occurrences of it.[120]

Randolph was an efficient and methodical man, unphased by hard work or taking on a variety of tasks most men might have shirked. Though a tepid Whig (Potter had been his original patron), he was a committed defender of religious orthodoxy, as his public clash with the heretical Irish bishop, Robert Clayton of Clogher, evidenced.[121] Yet his best theological work was behind him by 1768. It was not so much his concurrent duties as President of Corpus and archdeacon of

---

[116] 'His divinity,... was, by early eighteenth-century standards, just about as conservative as one could get'. Hampton, *Anti-Arminians*, 267.

[117] W. C. Costin, *The history of St John's College, Oxford, 1598–1860* (Oxford, 1958) [Oxford Historical Society, new series, 12], 166–70.

[118] He was also a prebendary of Worcester from 1729. It was customary for the Lady Margaret Professor to hold the 6th prebendal stall in this cathedral annexed to his chair, another instance of Oxford's external outreach.

[119] Secker, *Autobiography*, 67; Ingram, *Religion, Reform and Modernity*, 182.

[120] Randolph, *The Christian's Faith. A Rational Assent. In Answer to a Pamphlet, entitled, Christianity not founded on Argument* (London, 1744), 61.

[121] Randolph, *A Vindication of the Doctrine of the Trinity from the Exceptions of a late Pamphlet Entitled An Essay on Spirit &c.* (Oxford, 1753).

THE DEFENCE OF CHRISTIAN BELIEF   105

Oxford (appointed 1767) that preoccupied him, rather the persistent and pertinent subscription controversy of the 1770s that kept him away from academic divinity.[122]

Randolph's death in 1783 occurred at almost the same juncture as that of the Regius, Benjamin Wheeler. The two vacant Divinity chairs went to two men with pronounced Corpus connections. The Lady Margaret professorship was accepted by Timothy Neve, incument (rector of Geddington, Northants., since 1762), chaplain of Merton College, antiquarian, and Oxford correspondent of the celebrated Spalding Society. Neve's theological and controversial capabilities had been confirmed by his delivering the Bampton Lectures in 1781 and the University wanted him back. But once in harness, inertia and illness were the dominant themes, and his *Seventeen Sermons* were only published posthumously in 1798. Though he was not the first choice, the Regius Chair was collected by Thomas Randolph's third son, John (1749–1813), tutor and censor at Christ Church from 1779 to 1783 and a man who, thanks to his father's influence in Oxford, took possession of his first chair (Poetry) aged just twenty-seven. In his twenty-four years as professor, the younger Randolph imitated Bentham and Wheeler and lectured to ordinands in the theology of the Established Church and published the heads of his divinity lectures in 1784.[123] But he also connected—indirectly—with a wider public via the parochial clergy (many of whom would have attended his classes)[124] offering support of the state in the era of the French Revolution. In 1792 he published a students' compendium which included Bishop Edmund Gibson's four *Pastoral Letters* and Charles Leslie's *Short and Easy Method with the Deists*. He had no hesitation in judging that these works had both a political and a devotional relevance for a new generation.[125] Like Potter, John Randolph held the Regius Professorship in

---

[122] His achievement is assessed in Thomas Charles-Edwards and Julian Reid, *Corpus Christi College, Oxford. A history* (Oxford, 2017), 247–50, 262–3. The controversy centred on relaxing the wide-ranging obligation to take the oath to the 39 Articles of the Established Church and became intermixed with the Dissenters' campaign for the mitigation of their civil disabilities. There was an articulate minority among the dons who wanted change. Benjamin Buckler of All Souls claimed (anonymously) that there was too great a willingness in the majority 'to see every Thing in too *Clerical* a Light' and recommended that undergraduates on matriculation take a straightforward declaration to conform to the worship of the Established Church by constant attendance thereon. *Reflections on the impropriety and Inexpediency of Lay-Subscription to the XXXIX Articles in the University of Oxford* (Oxford, 1772), 13, 18, 21. On 4 Feb. 1773 Convocation rejected such a proposal by 111 votes to 64. *Studies in Oxford History*, 323. Oaths are discussed in Chapter 7.

[123] Randolph lectured on natural religion, both Testaments, ecclesiastical history, doctrine, the Book of Common Prayer, but offered little on ministerial duty and character. F. W. Bullock, *A History of Training for the Ministry of the Church of England in England and Wales from 598 to 1799* (St Leonards-on-Sea, 1969), 116–17; Sara Slinn, *The Education of the Anglican Clergy 1780–1839* (Woodbridge, 2017), 117.

[124] Ibid.

[125] This was the *Enchiridion Theologicum; or, a Manual, for the use of Students in Divinity* (Oxford, 1792, republished 1812, 1825).

106 ENLIGHTENED OXFORD

conjunction with the bishopric of Oxford (from 1799) until he was translated to Bangor in 1807.[126]

Thus at any point in the century, if the public wanted to discover what holders of either of the University's two chairs in divinity had to say on that subject, they would likely be disappointed. It would be to other Oxford representatives that they would have to turn. The workings of the patronage system had failed to throw up a theologian professor who combined talent and communicative skill. When it finally did in 1783 and the Regius Divinity Chair was offered to Thomas Townson (1715–92), senior proctor in 1749–50, widely published former Magdalen fellow and beneficent rector of the lower moiety of Malpas in Cheshire, he turned it down on the grounds of old age (despite being only a year older than Thomas Randolph when he accepted the post). Townson's scholarship was held in the highest regard in Oxford circles, endorsed by no less than the great Hebraist, Robert Lowth, and the publication of his acclaimed and accessible *Discourses on the Four Gospels* in 1778 made him the obvious choice.[127]

The muted public impact of the Divinity professoriate should not conceal the neglected and often distinguished contribution of other Oxford graduates to theological discussion throughout the century. They could be heads of houses, like Jonathan Edwards, Principal of Jesus College from 1686 until 1712 (Vice Chancellor, 1689–92), the author of the magisterial *Preservative against Socinianism*, published in sections over the decade from 1693 who, late in his career, attacked the anti-Romanist Anglican Daniel Whitby (the client of the leading Whig bishop, Gilbert Burnet), for novelty in his *The Doctrine of Original Sin... Asserted* (1711). Edwards's copious *Preservative* was admired and mined rather than read; the same could not be said of the writings of Jenner's replacement as President of Magdalen College in 1768, the High Churchman George Horne (Vice Chancellor, 1776–80). True, he never produced the systematic work of theology anticipated from him, but his engaging and thoughtful sermons were in print throughout his lifetime and his *Commentary on the Book of Psalms* (1776), partly devotional, partly exegetical—the product of twenty years' intermittent preparation—won many admirers from John Wesley to Hannah More for its exemplification of what the latter called his 'sweet and devout spirit'.[128] In 1781 Horne accepted the deanery of Canterbury and the pressures of regular journeys backwards and forwards from Kent to Oxford limited his time for

---

[126] His *Heads of a Course of Lectures* (Oxford, 1784) comprehensively summarised thirty-five of his lectures. Robert Hole, 'Randolph, John (1749–1813)', *Oxford dictionary of national biography*, Oxford University Press, 2004 [http://www.oxforddnb.com/view/article/23120, accessed 13 Oct. 2017]. Randolph was further promoted to the see of London in 1809.

[127] 'Account of the author', in ed. R. Churton, *The works of Thomas Townson* (2 vols., London, 1810), I. v–xcii; N. Aston, 'Thomas Townson and High Church continuities and connections in eighteenth-century England', *BJRL*, 97 (2021), 53–69.

[128] More, *Memoirs of Hannah More*, ed. W. Roberts (4 vols., London, 1834), II. 407.

much beyond occasional writing.[129] One of his predecessors at Canterbury (whom Horne much admired), the emollient High Churchman George Stanhope, dean from 1704 to his death in 1728, had a more settled residence and produced texts that were constantly reprinted.[130] Stanhope published numerous sermons throughout his life as well as the Boyle Lectures he delivered in 1701–2. But it was for his four-volume *Paraphrase and Comment upon the Epistles and Gospels* (1705–8) that he was best known and respected, along with the devotional *Private prayers for every day of the week, and for several parts of the day* (1730).[131]

Stanhope and Horne (who ended his career as Bishop of Norwich, 1790–2) were household names in the Church of England of their day. But the majority of Oxford graduates who took holy orders never gained access to the upper reaches of the hierarchy; among them were an abundance of men who found that learned isolation in rural parsonages offered more scope for writing and instructing their flock than proximity to the Bodleian Library.[132] Such was Dr Edward Wells, a tutor at Christ Church in the 1690s, and subsequently rector of Cotesbach, Leicestershire. He had authored an *Essay on the Trinity* that asserted Christ's divinity against Samuel Clarke in 1712 and then, amid a flurry of assorted texts, produced a pair of instructional manuals of devotion, a *Help for the More Easy Understanding of the Holy Scripture* (1724) and a *Help for the Right Understanding of the Several Divine Laws and Covenants* (1729). According to Hearne's harsh judgement, Wells 'writ & scribbled many books, . . . The truth is, he was a man of great industry, but the books he hath writ & published, as they are very many, so they are inaccurate, & contain very little that is curious'.[133] Wells fell foul of his patron, Browne Willis, while the Yorkshireman, Richard Fiddes (1671–1725), obtained favour for his high-flying views from George Smalridge, Dean of Christ Church, becoming a chaplain to Robert Harley, Lord Oxford, and being awarded an Oxford BD by diploma. The Hanoverian Succession put paid to any realistic hope of rising further and, coming to London, he devoted himself to the production of doctrinal works with a firm High Church leaning such as

---

[129] For Horne see his *Works*; N. Aston, 'Horne and heterodoxy: the defence of Anglican beliefs in the late Enlightenment', *EHR*, 108 (1993), 895–919.

[130] Stanhope was thrice prolocutor of the Lower House of Convocation, a sign of the confidence held in him by a range of clerical opinion. A Cambridge graduate, he was incorporated at Oxford in 1696, and was made DD in 1697.

[131] Weeden Butler, *Some Account of the Life and Writings of the Reverend Dr George Stanhope* (London, 1797).

[132] See Chapter 12.

[133] Hearne, IX. 330; 'curious' in early 18th-century usage implied depth. Wells was nothing if not versatile. As a Christ Church tutor he also produced a mathematical handbook, followed two decades later by his popular *A Treatise of antient and present geography . . .* (Oxford, 1701), *Historical Geography of the New Testament* (1708), and *Historical Geography of the Old Testament* (1711–12). See Robert Mayhew, *Enlightenment geography. The political languages of British geography, 1650–1850* (Basingstoke, 2000), 126–32. The *Treatise* contained maps that Edward Gibbon thought dependable and used in *The Decline and fall*. R. Mayhew, 'Gibbon's geographies', in eds. Karen O'Brien and Brian Young, *The Cambridge companion to Edward Gibbon* (Cambridge, 2018), 41–61, at 45.

A Preparative to the Lord's Supper . . . with Meditations and Prayers (1718) and a systematic defence of orthodox Christianity, Theologia speculative (1718), followed by Theologia practica (1720).[134] With Smalridge dead and the Tories out of favour, Fiddes's exhaustive scholarship afforded scant hope of his winning any substantive reward and he turned largely to non-religious subjects in the 1720s. As in other instances, this priest's political allegiance caused his writings in divinity to be marginalised. But the examples of Wells and Fiddes are a reminder of the importance of both the country parsonage and city lodgings as academic centres in miniature in Georgian England, from which might flow a steady stream of theological production, often from the hands of former Oxford dons displaced by marriage or politics. The quality of their work may have been uneven, but there was a market for it and it generally gave their readers as strong a scent of Oxford values as books originating with resident members of the University.

Parochial clergy with Oxford degrees were as free to contribute to non-scholarly publications—in particular the burgeoning market of newspapers and journals—as resident senior members of the University: reaching out to this huge market was an alluring prospect for dons who wanted to speak up for the Church and try to inform and shape public opinion, that essential component of the 'public sphere'. At the same time, they were unlikely to gain professional kudos as participation was usually occluded and disguised under a pseudonym. It was a breathtaking breach of etiquette for a scholar in holy orders to sign his name under a controversial piece of writing designed for general consumption characterised by the questionable literary device (for a priest) of ridicule. This kind of politically inspired religious journalism could be witty, declamatory, abusive, and potentially libellous, making anonymity doubly necessary.[135] The model during most of the century for like-minded Oxford clergy was the Nonjuror, Charles Leslie's, Rehearsal, which ran from 1704 until closed down in 1709, and was intended as a counterblast to what was perceived as a torrent of Whiggish anticlerical and irreligious publication since the lapsing of the Licensing Act.[136] It sounded the clarion call of Queen Anne's reign of 'the 'Church in Danger' more clearly than any other organ and it harried the Whigs for their perceived

---

[134] For Fiddes's important involvement in challenging Hoadly, see Starkie, Bangorian Controversy, 138–41. Starkie refers to Theologia Speculativa as 'the most thorough critique of Hoadly's view'. ibid., 190. It was dedicated to Archbishop Sir William Dawes who, with Wake and nineteen diocesan bishops, was among its 500 subscribers.

[135] It was the norm anyway. As Jeremy Black observes, 'There was little role for the "journalist", . . . and newspaper reports were largely 'derivative, anonymous and impersonal'. The English Press 1621–1861 (Stroud, 2001), 11.

[136] Ian Higgins makes the good point that 'Leslie's work attacking Whigs and Dissenters also impales the conforming Tories as time-serving apostates from true Church principles of hereditary right monarchy and passive obedience'. 'Jonathan Swift and Charles Leslie', in eds. P. Monod, M. Pittock, and D. Szechi, Loyalty and Identity. Jacobites at Home and Abroad (Basingstoke, 2010), 149–66, at 155. Tory jurors kept their distance from Leslie personally but not from the majority of his output, whose contents and sentiments were in broad agreement with High Church opinion.

endorsement not just of dissent but of deism. In the guise of the 'Observator', the *Rehearsal* characterised the position of their enemies: 'We Whiggs, who are Deists...as to our Common Designs against the Church and Crown'.[137] It may have been *parti pris* but it was effective and in an age of incessant party warfare, clerical journalists could not afford to be defensive.[138]

Since the sense among High Churchmen that the Church was 'in Danger' outlasted the Sacheverell affair and the accession of the new dynasty in 1714, the perceived need to use the press to get this point across and rally national opinion barely waned. And thus engagement in and with it became an insistent option for those looking to make the case for truth and orthodoxy as they perceived them; there was a cultural war to be fought and academics who were masters of the arts of learned polemic might meet the demands of the popular press, while preserving decorum by not officially disclosing their identities. The distinctive voice and politics of Leslie's *Rehearsal* lingered long after the disputes on Occasional Conformity and Sacheverell had faded and it was indeed reprinted in six volumes in 1750. The paper was an inspirational influence on George Horne, Vice- Chancellor in the later 1770s. Horne was an habitual occasional journalist with an arch sense of satirical humour that he could not resist deploying[139] and he was wholly supportive of the arguments of Leslie against infidels, dissenters, and Whigs.[140] When opportunity offered, he was quick to contribute to the *St James's Chronicle*. Oxonians of Horne's kidney during the 1750s also found Richard Nutt's tri-weekly *London Evening Post* much to their taste with its High Church, pro-Convocation, and pro-Tory viewpoint.[141] Newspapers were as popular with clergy readers as they were with any other section of British professional society and it was evidently both a comfort and a source of amusement for country parsons to have the cause of Anglican orthodoxy defended *and* to speculate on which of their friends and colleagues were concealed behind the aliases.

---

[137] *The Rehearsal*, 10 Feb. 1704/05, quoted in Wigelsworth, *Deism in Enlightenment England*, 54.

[138] Bruce Frank, '"The Excellent Rehearser": Charles Leslie and the Tory Party, 1688–1714', in ed. J. D. Browning, *Biography in the 18th Century* (London, 1980), 43–68; Robert Cornwall, 'Charles Leslie and the political implications of theology', in eds. W. Gibson and R. Ingram, *Religious identities in Britain, 1660–1832* (Aldershot, 2005), 27–42.

[139] One commentator of the next generation grandly observed of Horne: 'He loved the press, and published many amusing, if not deep, works, on professional subjects. His imagination rather sparkled than shone, and he was sometimes quaint even to the affectation of prettiness'. *The Autobiography, Times, Opinions, and Contemporaries of Sir Egerton Brydges* (2 vols., London, 1834), I. 124.

[140] J. A. W. Gunn, *Beyond Liberty and Property: The Process of Self-Recognition in Eighteenth-Century Political Thought* (Kingston/Montreal, 1983), 164–5. Horne first read Leslie (the 1721 collected edition) as a young curate in the library of Canon Sir John Dolben' 2nd Bt., protégé of Bishop (Lord) Crew's, at Finedon, Northants., and again at Oxford. Horne, *Works*, I. 65–6.

[141] G. A. Cranfield, 'The London Evening Post and the Jew Bill of 1753', *HJ*, 8 (1966), 16–30; B. Harris, 'The London Evening Post and mid-eighteenth-century British Politics', *EHR*, 110 (1995), 1132–56; James J. Sack, *From Jacobite to Conservative: reaction and Orthodoxy in Britain c.1760–1832* (Cambridge, 1993), 8. Sack notes that the paper retained its Jacobite orientation until at least 1754.

110 ENLIGHTENED OXFORD

Part B: The variety of Oxford voices on religion

At any given point since the Reformation, the energies of most academic clergy were bent towards articulating the economy of salvation for their times and that was no less the case for eighteenth-century Oxonians. They were not unthinkingly restating these concepts when confronted by opponents at home and abroad, and the intelligence they deployed against a constantly changing and formidable range of opponents is not to be underestimated. The best among them were looking for—or stumbling upon—new ways of expressing orthodoxy. Theologians such as the Randolphs, father and son, John Conybeare,[142] and William Dodwell (son of Henry, the Nonjuror, and Archdeacon of Berks) did so with accomplishment: dismissive of novelty for its own sake, concerned to use reason persuasively without exaggerating its reach,[143] protective of the organic development of the faith, and ready to take seriously the charges of heterodox authors before reaching for the label of 'heretic'. And there was a recognition that the Bible contained access to truths that could never be disclosed by unaided human reason. As Conybeare put it:

> The great Truths which we are taught in Scripture are remote from common Conceptions. Some of them, before the Revelation of the Gospel, were entirely unknown; and many others are still mysterious.[144]

He was uncompromising in his commitment to the Church's understanding of the Godhead, a hallmark of Oxford writers. Generally, however many knots could be tied when it was too precisely explicated, the University was a bulwark of Trinitarian Christianity. However much some Cambridge theologians at given points in the century were ready to flirt with some dilution of Athanasian formulae,[145] their Oxonian counterparts had no such interest for, as William Dodwell asserted, the doctrine of the Holy Trinity was 'the very essence of the Christian Religion, the Foundation of the whole Revelation, and connected with every Part of it'.[146]

Oxford theological articulation tended to emerge from the sort of dialectical processes (often in the form of polemical—and highly personalised—exchanges)

---

[142] Rector of Exeter College, 1730–4; rector of St Clement's church, Oxford, 1724–34; Dean of Christ Church, 1733–d.

[143] One of Conybeare's main arguments against Tindal was that the latter overestimated the power of human reason, permanently diminished by the Fall. John Conybeare, DD, *A Defence of Reveal'd Religion against the Exceptions of a late Writer, in his Book, Intituled, Christianity as old as the Creation* (2nd edn., Oxford, 1732), 46. It has been argued Conybeare had the basic material for a theory of progressive revelation but did not develop it.

[144] Sermon preached at Whitehall, 1726, Bodl. MS Eng Th E 49, ff. 61r, 64r.

[145] Gascoigne, *Cambridge*, 118–22, 195–6, 227–8, 247.

[146] William Dodwell, *Sermon on the Practical Influence of the Doctrine of the Holy Trinity* (Oxford, 1745), 19.

that one would expect to find in a university with a range of views on theology, the scriptures, and Church order and history. But Tory and the majority of Whig authors could coalesce and converge around the ideal of orthodoxy, and this was one that the majority had in common, however varyingly expressed, and it was, on balance, compatible with the moderate Enlightenment. There were, admittedly, some intellectual trends in theology that went against this grain, notably Hutchinsonianism. However, that tendency had passed its time of maximum influence by the late 1750s and it is significant that one of its leading spokesmen at Oxford, George Horne, was careful to detach himself gradually from the appellation. For the most part, Oxford's theological attachments were neither deliberately countercultural, nor were they based on some blinkered attachment to a rigid model of an imagined religious past. And they were transferable, ready for reception by the youthful elite who came to Oxford to secure a degree and, indirectly, through books, newspapers, and conversation, to the public at large.

Yet to talk of a monolithic Oxford position in theology is of limited use. If its predominant tendency throughout the century was of a historically conditioned High Churchmanship looking to the past for its legitimation in the present, it never went unchallenged or succeeded in eliminating alternative perspectives. After all, before the 1760s High Church values were commonly allied with varying degrees of Jacobite commitment and these were unlikely to bring their proponents much by way of loaves and fishes in the Hanoverian state. Intellectual enquiry and scholarship tended to create the conditions in any university in which differing standpoints were on display and these could easily spill over into personal invective and political partisanship. Thomas Randolph may have complained in 1752 that such was unworthy of gentlemen, scholars, and Christians, for 'The great Use of Learning and Philosophy is to calm the Mind, to curb the Passions, and teach us the Government of ourselves',[147] but such was a perennial refrain. Religious positioning proceeded from the interconnection of personality, patronage, and academic affiliation. Thus in colleges such as Exeter, Merton, Wadham, and (from the 1720s) Christ Church, one could readily encounter moderate, reasonable voices, articulating content with the Whig settlements of 1689 and 1714 and praising the Church for its primitive adherence to Gospel truths as well as its generosity in respecting the integrity of Protestants outside the establishment fold. By the accession of George III, this somewhat comfortable note was fast falling out of favour as the Tories came out of the cold to take up positions in the new order. A vocal minority among them had impugned the Whig-leaning colleges for complacency and subservience to the Walpole and Pelhamite ascendancy continuously before 1760.

---

[147] Thomas Randolph, *Party Zeal Censur'd. In a Sermon preached before the University of Oxford, at St Mary's, on Sunday, January 19. 1752* (Oxford, 1752), 17. I Cor. ii. 3 was his text.

112 ENLIGHTENED OXFORD

i) Methodists and Roman Catholics

Oxford was the birthplace of Methodism (at least in its Wesleyan format) in the late 1720s with John Wesley of Lincoln College attempting to rekindle what, in his eyes, was a more rigorous and rejuvenated form of Christian practice in daily life and thereby achieve a degree of inner sanctification that his critics alleged was hard to reconcile with the Church's teaching on the sacraments.[148] Wesley came to find Oxford an uncongenial environment and he left in the mid-1730s to try and find his vocation in the wider world, hounded out, as he saw it, by many of those who shared his own High Church origins and whose spiritual disciplines he was trying to enjoin.[149] None of Methodism's apologists came anywhere close to turning Oxford into a powerhouse for the movement, as Wesley's theology—as it had matured by the 1740s—had become excessively suspect and 'enthusiastic' for majority opinion. He had anyway decided that his métier lay in the world beyond Oxford and he took his uncompromising Arminian divinity with him.[150] For Wesley the authority of the Church was a continuous and living force but only so long as the Church was sensitive to the Holy Spirit's guidance in the present age. It was on this key marker that he parted company with his colleagues.[151] Despite his absence and official disapproval, Methodist influences (both in their Arminian and Calvinist manifestations) persisted within the University, articulated by revivalists such as Thomas Haweis (c.1734–1820), curate of St Mary Magdalen from 1758 to 1762.[152] He was deplored in some quarters of the University for his evangelical sermons and for his influence on young men considering ordination. The upshot was that John Hume, bishop of Oxford, refused to license him in 1762.

---

[148] Frank Baker's characterisation of Wesley's 'Holy Club' can hardly be bettered: 'With its devotional time-table and its works of charity, the Holy Club seemed to be a kind of University monastery of the Franciscan Order with John Wesley the acknowledged Superior'. Baker, *A Charge to Keep. An Introduction to the People called Methodists* (London, 1947), 9.

[149] For his indebtedness to Nonjuror theology (as the son of Nonjuring parents) see J. B. Green, *John Wesley and William Law* (London, 1945); T. Dearing, *Wesleyan and Tractarian worship. An ecumenical study* (London, 1966), 91–4. He decided against taking the BD degree in 1741. V. H. H. Green, *The young Mr Wesley. A study of John Wesley and Oxford* (London, 1961), 348, who notes (334ff.) that Wesley's attention to the Holy Club was not at the expense of diligence as a college tutor. Wesley's attitude to Oxford is further discussed in Chapter 10.

[150] Henry D. Rack, *Reasonable Enthusiast. John Wesley and the Rise of Methodism* (London, 1992), 136–7.

[151] G. R. Cragg, *Reason and Authority in the Eighteenth Century* (Cambridge, 1964), 162. From the conference of 1744 (the same year as his notorious St Mary's sermon) Wesley began to regulate the discipline of those in what he now saw as his 'connexion'. J. C. D. Clark, 'The eighteenth-century context', in eds. W. J. Abraham and J. E. Kirby, *The Oxford handbook of Methodist studies* (Oxford, 2009), 3–29, at 8.

[152] A. S. Wood, *Thomas Haweis 1734–1820* (London, 1957), 49–50, for his efforts to establish a second Holy Society in the 1750s. Ingram, *Religion, reform, and modernity*, 154–5. The predestination debate—latterly ratcheted up by Wesley and Whitefield—was by no means exhausted in the 1750s and William Parker, a chaplain-in-ordinary to successive sovereigns and a reputation as a thoroughly orthodox pulpit orator, addressed the University on the subject quasi-authoritatively with his *The scripture doctrine of predestination stated and explained* (Oxford, 1759).

THE DEFENCE OF CHRISTIAN BELIEF   113

It was part of a wider trend. St Edmund Hall had become such a notorious preferred choice for young Methodists by the 1760s that six undergraduates were expelled in 1768 on the authority of the Vice Chancellor, precipitating a minor controversy that confirmed the outside world's persuasion that the University remained antipathetic to both John Wesley and George Whitefield's followers.[153]

'High and dry' opinions and instincts also made the University an uncongenial setting for nascent Anglican evangelicalism;[154] the aims of the Evangelicals were regarded as worthy, their means vulgarly inappropriate for members of the Established Church. They nevertheless maintained a continuous presence at Oxford and were particularly favoured at St Edmund Hall after Isaac Crouch became Vice-Principal in 1783;[155] Crouch was respected in the University as a Church historian and preacher at St Mary's, but he was quietly intent on deepening the evangelical commitment of his students.[156] Overall, it was already evident by the 1770s that Evangelical Anglicans and Wesleyan Methodists were on divergent trajectories.[157]

Contemporaries often found it difficult to distinguish Methodists from Hutchinsonians, a loose movement at its height within the University during the 1740s and 1750s. The founder of this grouping, John Hutchinson, was not an Oxford man and not even a graduate, and yet his *Moses Principia* (1724) influenced an entire generation of dons and students who found in his physico-theology a basis for understanding the world that satisfied their intellect and their souls in a manner no living Oxford theologian apparently could.[158] Hutchinsonianism was appealing on a variety of levels, not least because it provided a systematic, holistic *Weltanschauung* based on a reading of the Hebrew Bible that privileged revelation over natural theology and offered an alternative to the cultural supremacy of Newtonianism. By the 1750s it emerged as a fully fledged Counter-Enlightenment system of natural philosophy that briefly challenged the assumptions of the Biblical

---

[153] Discussed further in Chapter 10, pp. 41–2.

[154] J. D. Walsh, 'The origins of the evangelical revival', in eds. G. V. Bennett and J. D. Walsh, *Essays in modern English Church history in memory of Norman Sykes* (London, 1966), 132–62.

[155] J. S. Reynolds, *The evangelicals at Oxford 1735–1871* (Abingdon, 1975); Slinn, *The education of the Anglican clergy*, 116n. See, generally, K. Hylson-Smith, *Evangelicals in the Church of England, 1734–1984* (Edinburgh, 1988). Evangelical fellows at Lincoln included G. S. Faber (1793–1804), the Bampton Lecturer in 1810, and Thomas Fry (1796–1803), a Church Missionary Society supporter with many youthful followers. V. Green, *The commonwealth of Lincoln College 1427–1977* (Oxford, 1979), 382.

[156] Kelly, *St Edmund Hall*, 70; V.H.H. Green, *Religion at Oxford and Cambridge* (London, 1964), 213–14. Some contemporaries considered that he was Oxford's answer as an evangelical preacher to Cambridge's Charles Simeon.

[157] Ryan Danker, *Wesley and the Anglicans: political division in early evangelicalism* (Downers Grove, IL, 2016).

[158] Nigel Aston, 'From personality to party: the creations and transmission of Hutchinsonianism, c.1725–1750', *Studies in the History and Philosophy of Science*, 35 (2004), 625–44.

114   ENLIGHTENED OXFORD

scholarship of the likes of Lowth, Kennicott, and Durell.[159] It never came near to dislodging their academic ascendancy, but the Christological spiritual values of Hutchinsonianism informed the Christian life of many leading Oxford High Churchmen in the reign of George III, George Horne, Nathan Wetherall, and George Berkeley the younger among them.[160] Significantly, they eventually distanced themselves from Hutchinson's cosmology and idiosyncratic approach to Hebrew.[161]

The principal objective of Oxford divines of all persuasions remained the restatement of Christian orthodoxy as embodied in the teachings of the Church of England. They were all, in varying degrees, antipathetic in principle to Roman Catholicism.[162] This was more than just the Reformation inheritance, for it was based on the fresh collective memory of James II's efforts to intrude papists into several Oxford colleges and the principled obstruction with which they had been greeted.[163] Oxford men habitually drew attention to the errors of Roman teaching that, in their sight, had corrupted that Church and ensured that it could not bear the character of an authentic Catholic communion. The Whigs among them were more vociferous in denouncing Popery, especially at times of national crisis, such as 1714–15 and 1745–6, and shamelessly exploited its resonances in popular culture. Majority Tory, High Church, opinion was more cautious, willing to admit the variants in national expressions of Catholicism such as Gallicanism, and more ready to acknowledge (at least in passing) those elements that the two Churches had in common (such as the historic ministerial ordering of bishops, priests, and deacons) that pre-dated the division of western Christendom.[164] Besides, many Oxford scholars were in contact with continental Catholic scholars and their confessional allegiance was of marginal relevance.[165] All of which rendered Oxford anti-Catholicism arguably as temperate as anywhere in England, perhaps not surprisingly in the light of the attachment of many dons to the Catholic Jacobite dynasty in exile. It says much that the University was very comfortable about the selection of the Catholic James Gibbs as the architect of the

---

[159] Derya Gurses Tarbuck, *Enlightenment Reformation. Hutchinsonianism and religion in eighteenth-century Britain* (London, 2017), esp. 78–81; C. D. A. Leighton, '"Knowledge of divine things": a study of Hutchinsonianism', *History of European Ideas*, 26 (2000), 159–75; Leighton, 'Hutchinsonianism: a Counter-Enlightenment reform movement', *JRS*, 23 (1999), 168–84.

[160] Gurses helpfully calculates that the predominantly Oxonian Hutchinsonians published over 100 pamphlets between 1751 and 1784. *Enlightenment reformation*, 88.

[161] Derya Gurses, 'Academic Hutchinsonians and their quest for relevance, 1734–1790', *History of European Ideas*, 31 (2005), 408–27; Aston, 'From personality to party', 641.

[162] Thomas Hearne was, as so often, an exception. 'Popery' could be an appropriate description of those who subscribed to the errors of the Church of Rome but not a term to describe all Roman Catholics. Gabriel Glickman, *The English Catholic community, 1688-1745* (Woodbridge, 2009), 226. Hearne exchanged medieval manuscripts and martyrologies with the Catholic Charles Eyston. VIII. 258, 389; Geoffrey Scott, *Gothic rage undone. English monks in the age of Enlightenment* (Bath, 1992), 159–62.

[163] Chapter 2, p. 10.   [164] Cf. Farooq, *Preaching in eighteenth-century London*, 164.

[165] Discussed in Chapter 11.

THE DEFENCE OF CHRISTIAN BELIEF   115

Radcliffe Camera. Gibbs himself proudly affirmed his membership of the University in his account of the opening of his masterpiece in which—though a Catholic—he was permitted to matriculate and was mentioned by William King 'in a most honorable manner, in his learned Speech'.[166]

From the mid-century, the fear of 'Popery" was barely articulated within the educated Oxford elite as the plight of the papacy on the continent, losing power relentlessly to aggressive monarchs, was borne in on them.[167] There simply was no threat from that quarter, as Oxonian voices regularly articulated. Thus, William Hawkins observed in his 1787 Bampton Lectures, true Christianity was more in danger 'not so much from the triple-mitre of the Roman pontiff, as from the many headed hydra of infidelity'.[168] A decade later, in the same series, William Finch, doubtless having in mind the travails of Pius VI in the face of the aggressive dechristianising French Republic, went still further arguing that:[169]

> ...the Roman Prelates themselves, even in the worst times of the hierarchy,... have often, where their peculiar interests were not concerned, shewn themselves the patrons of justice, the defenders of the distressed, and the gracious ministers of mercy.

It was during the 1790s that the University welcomed and supported Gallican clergy seeking exile in England, but this was also the decade in which fears were rekindled that Pitt's ministry was too much inclined to favour the claims to full civic equality of native British and Irish Catholics. It would be the prelude to the long struggle against 'Catholic Emancipation' that was finally lost in 1829, and that was played out in Oxford during the heated election for the Chancellorship in 1809 when the pro-emancipation William, Lord Grenville, narrowly secured the post.[170]

ii) Challenges to orthodoxy

Most Oxford religious voices (Hawkins was typical) were far more concerned about the challenge to the status quo posed by Protestant dissenters than they

---

[166] 'James Gibb's notebook', f.52, quoted in William Aslet, 'James Gibb's autobiography revisited', *The Georgian Group Journal*, 25 (2017), 113–30, at 126. He was also delighted in the dedicatory inscription in the legend underneath his bust in the same library.

[167] Haydon, *Anti-Catholicism*, 164–203.

[168] *Discourses on scripture mysteries,...* (Oxford, 1787), 269.

[169] Finch, *The objections of infidel historians and other writers against Christianity, considered in eight sermons* (Oxford, 1797), 87, Sermon 5. He argued more broadly that the contemporary world displayed the dire effects of the extirpation of Christianity. His 7th Sermon contains his reflections on the state of the modern Roman Church.

[170] W. Gibson, 'The election of Lord Grenville as Chancellor of Oxford University in 1809', *Oxoniensia*, 61 (1996), 355–68.

were by papists.[171] Many critics of contemporary Anglicanism (including some within the Church and often Cambridge-educated) longed for, as they saw it, a completion of the Reformation inaugurated two centuries previously and wanted the Established Church to purge itself of non-scriptural remnants in the liturgy and Articles, above all the Athanasian Creed, heard most Sundays during the Litany, and campaigned tirelessly to achieve these goals from the mid-1760s.[172] Though the public culture of eighteenth-century England, however open and contestable, was emphatically Christian,[173] contemporary polemical literature can give the impression that academic clergy conceived themselves as surrounded by a militant coalition of heterodox antagonists. Heretical and overtly non-Christian voices were certainly heard in Oxford and compelled attention. Outsiders such as John Toland in the 1690s and the conspicuous insider, Matthew Tindal, put the defenders of the status quo on their mettle, and encouraged the production of tracts and sermons in reply that, more often than not, showed how formidable the case for orthodoxy could be.[174]

Central to that Oxford understanding of orthodoxy was Trinitarianism and yet, throughout the century, this central Christian tenet was under attack by those who called themselves Christians and contended that the Holy Trinity was unknown in scripture and could not be found in the primitive, pre-Nicene formularies. These took comfort from (and often cited in their cause) Anglican theologians such as Samuel Clarke who also, notoriously, could not wholly endorse the divine status and equality of the Son within the Godhead, and others, including Tillotson, Hoadly, and Edmund Law, whose silence on the subject appeared to give their game away. At least Clarke and his Arian fellow travellers believed in the Trinity, while the Socinians rejected the doctrine outright and deists had no time for revealed religion at all while remaining ready to make common cause—and mischief—with the heterodox.[175] Against this formidable array of opinion were ranged, in successive generations, talented Oxford theologians who were uncompromising in their defence of what for them was both a doctrine and a mystery, and ready to use different ploys to turn the tables on 'infidels'. As John Conybeare, a coming Whig, advised in 1720:

> In our Disputes with Infidels we shall find ourselves oblig'd to use different methods, according as the Principles on which they proceed are different.[176]

---

[171] Edward Tatham was typical in stating bluntly: 'As to myself, I like the papists, I confess, better than Dissenters'. Tatham, *A new address to the free and independent members of Convocation* (Oxford, 1810), 22–3, quoted in in V. Green, *Lincoln College*, 368.

[172] Young, *Religion and Enlightenment*, 62–82.

[173] As was the case in other European monarchical polities, Nigel Aston, 'The Established Church', in ed. William Doyle, *The Oxford Handbook of the Ancien Régime*, (Oxford, 2011), 285–301.

[174] Chapter 2, pp. 22–4.   [175] cf. Clark, *English Society 1660–1832*, 395.

[176] Conybeare was using John 7: 17 as an exposition on the defence of religion and how to go about it, what sort of statements and professions to offer. He preached a sermon on the subject before the University on 2 Oct. 1720. Bodl. MS. Eng., The 49 Sermons of John Conybeare, ff. 89–99, at f. 90.

THE DEFENCE OF CHRISTIAN BELIEF   117

For him as much as for high-flying Tories, theological heterodoxy threatened the religio-political order, theological orthodoxy buttressed it, and the unravelling of society during the mid-seventeenth century proved their point.[177] Arguably, the survival of Trinitarianism as a core doctrine in the Church of England from beginning to end of the eighteenth century was owing principally to Oxford churchmen who through their writings confirmed that Arians and Socinians did not have a monopoly in defining enlightened Christianity. And they did so within a controversial culture in which theological reflectivity was central and therefore bound to lead to flirtation with and even endorsement of heterodoxy.

The University authorities were watchful and passionate on this issue, as well they might be given that even in Oxford, the learned were themselves wittingly and unwittingly capable of falling into error, as the case of William Sherlock had so well shown in the 1690s. He had set out in his *Vindication* to reassert an orthodox understanding of the Trinity in the aftermath of the burning of Bury's *The Naked Gospel*,[178] but a reading of his work led to critics accusing him of falling into the heresy of tritheism.[179] Sherlock's Nicene orthodoxy survived this agitated flurry but it continued to haunt the hierarchy, with Archbishop Wake in 1721 sanctioning a bill against blasphemy that would include those who denied the reality of the Trinity. In the face of advice, Wake stalled, but George Verney, Dean of Windsor and 12th Lord Willoughby de Broke (formerly a fellow of New College), had no such qualms about introducing his own bill to suppress atheism, profaneness, and blasphemy.[180] It fell foul of the Sunderland administration (and a majority on the bench of bishops), a sign of the unwillingness of Whig ministers to antagonise pro-government supporters among Protestant dissenters. Nevertheless, 'It was a measure of the strength of the Trinitarian-dynastic nexus that it held in check for several decades the subversive possibilities of growing Dissenting heterodoxy'.[181]

One reason behind Oxonian dislike of Protestant dissent in its 'rational' guise was the widespread perception that the anti-Trinitarian heresy had increasing numbers of sympathisers in both English universities, mainly Arians but, sometimes, outright Socinians, along with 'antidogmatist quasi Arians' such as Peter Peckard, Edmund Law, John Hey, and Francis Blackburne (Archdeacon of Cleveland), and was fuelling a new wave of heterodox work demanding reform

---

[177] A. M. C. Waterman, *Political Economy and Christian Theology since the Enlightenment: Essays in Intellectual History* (Basingstoke, 2004); Clark, *English Society 1660-1832*, 318–422.

[178] For more on Bury and his book see Chapter 2, 10–11.

[179] Christopher J. Walker, *Reason and religion in late seventeenth-century England. The politics and theology of radical Dissent* (London, 2013), 221. More generally Martin Greig, 'Burnet and the Trinitarian controversies of the 1690s', *JEH*, 44 (1993), 631–51.

[180] Norman Sykes, *William Wake. Archbishop of Canterbury* (2 vols., Cambridge, 1957), ii. 135–8.

[181] Clark, *English Society 1660-1832*, 376.

118 ENLIGHTENED OXFORD

in church and state from the 1760s onwards.[182] University fears about the spread of Socinianism revived in the following decade over the subscription controversy and departure from the Established Church of Theophilus Lindsey and his allies.[183] And conservative dons and others were prominent in 1772–3 and again in 1779 in urging parliamentarians to resist proposals for change associated originally with the Feathers Tavern petition that would irrevocably damage the Anglican establishment.[184] As Lewis Bagot, soon to replace Markham as Dean of Christ Church (1777), anonymously, declared:

> The University hath ever been foremost in Defence of this Church. It is to be hoped she will not now be the first to give way to the violence of an Infidel assault;[185]

In 1779 Bagot was still fretting about how far the Dissenters could concur on the basics of the Christian faith, though he declared they were agreed on one key point, 'that of opposition to the Establishment'. He cited Andrew Kippis, Joseph Priestley, and Richard Price, as ringleaders in chief, and noted that even Bishop Lowth of Oxford '(who is Whig enough in conscience)' had censured Price's latest sermons and his political doctrines.[186]

The militancy of Priestley and his allies intensified the debate over the doctrine of the Trinity. Priestley was a powerful polemicist convinced that his insights into 'primitive Christianity' proved that the later Fathers and Councils were in error and that, as his *History of Corruptions of Christianity* (1782) emphasised, the Trinity was the greatest of all corruptions. And he was not frightened to take on Oxford opinion on the matter by deploying the old charges of 'priestcraft' and 'oppression' in a frontal assault on the ecclesiastical establishment. Though the counter-attack was led by Samuel Horsley, Archdeacon of St Albans, Priestley came up against some redoubtable opponents in Oxford, notably George Horne.[187] Apart from lobbying ministers, the President of Magdalen used his gift for humorous polemic against Priestley and his allies in pamphlet exchanges

---

[182] Michael R. Watts, *The Dissenters* (3 vols. Oxford, 1978–2015). Vol. 1. *From the Reformation to the French Revolution*, 374ff.; E. M. Wilbur, *A History of Unitarianism in Transylvania, England and America* (Cambridge, MA, 1952), 252ff.; Ingram, *Religion, Reform, and Modernity*, 75; J. Gascoigne, 'Anglican Latitudinarianism and political radicalism in the late eighteenth century', *History*, 71 (1986), 22–38.

[183] G. M. Ditchfield, 'Joseph Priestley and the complexities of Latitudinarianism in the 1770s', in eds. I. Rivers and D. L. Wykes, *Joseph Priestley, scientist, philosopher, and theologian* (Oxford, 2008), 144–71, esp. 158–71.

[184] G. M. Ditchfield, 'Feathers Tavern petitioners (act. 1771–1774)', (online edn., *ODNB*, 2005).

[185] [L. Bagot], *A Defence of Subscription*, 26. William Cole noted the 'Torrent of Infidelity, Arianism, Presbyterianism, and Republicanism in the Petitioners, who are bold, forward and arrogant to a Degree to surprise one'. 'Feathers Tavern Petition', BL Add MSS 5873, f.108.

[186] To Sir William Bagot, 14 Mar. 1779, Staffordshire Record Office, D3259/13/18/4.

[187] Aston, 'Horne and heterodoxy', *passim*. For Horne's Cambridge counterpart Samuel Horsley, see Clark, *English society 1660–1832*, 278–82.

and set-piece sermons, such as that delivered in Canterbury cathedral on Trinity Sunday 1786.[188] Thanks to Horne and other compelling Oxford voices heard in the prestigious Bampton Lectures, the pulpit, and the press, this latest threat from anti-Trinitarian 'Christians' was met headlong and contained, with Parliament reaffirming its commitment to upholding the Test and Corporation Acts on three occasions between 1787 and 1790.[189] It was partly a matter of restating the familiar arguments that had been serviceable since the third and fourth centuries and upholding the Anglican persuasion that the Church stood in direct line of descent from the Fathers. If such was the case then the collective, conciliar definitions of the early Church were not to be lightly hazarded. Yet Anglican controversialists like Horne knew that contexts and audiences had changed and he was as determined as Priestley to reach out to the reading public and engage its attention. He died in 1792 (having relinquished the Presidency of Magdalen the previous year) knowing that the Church establishment was in a sufficiently sound shape to resist a religious reform drive at home inspired by the bitterly contested implementation of the Civil Constitution of the Clergy (1790–1) by the Revolutionaries in France.

iii) The reiteration of orthodoxy

The creation of the Bampton Lectures had been one of several means to the end of endorsing orthodoxy afresh for troubled times. One obvious means of combining accessible scholarship in religious apologetics with audience appeal was to establish public lectures, lectures that would quickly be published and disseminated. An opportunity for the University arose in 1751 when, by the will of John Bampton, an annual series of eight lectures was endowed within which the lecturer should 'confirm and establish the Christian Faith and... confute all heretics and schismatics' by speaking on the authority of the scriptures, the Fathers, the primitive Church, and the Articles of Faith found in the Apostles and Nicene Creeds. The Eight Sermons every year were quickly published by the Press and circulated. It took twenty-nine years before the first set of Bampton Lectures was delivered, the honour being accorded to James Bandinel, Public Orator 1776–84, a Fellow of Jesus College. He expressed the hope that they would over time 'answer the pious and generous design of its author, promote the honour of this seat of learning, advance true religion, and effectually secure the bulwarks of Christianity against

---

[188] Horne, *The duty of contending for the faith. A sermon preached at the Primary Visitation of the Most Reverend John, Lord Archbishop of Canterbury, in the Cathedral and Metropolitical Church, on Saturday, July 1st, 1786* (Oxford, 1786). See also Chapter 10.

[189] G. M. Ditchfield, 'The parliamentary struggle over the Test and Corporation Acts, 1787–1790', *EHR*, 89 (1974), 551–77; M. H. Fitzpatrick, 'Heretical religion and radical political ideas in late eighteenth-century England', in ed. E. Hellmuth, *The transformation of political culture: England and Germany in the late eighteenth century* (Oxford, 1990), 339–72.

120 ENLIGHTENED OXFORD

the secret artifices of its concealed and the open attacks of its declared enemies'.[190]

Over the next two decades, some caught public attention more than others sometimes for their subject matter, sometimes because of the preacher's reputation as with George Croft in 1786 (fellow of University College, 1772–80, and a stickler for high clerical standards of learning and scholarship), at least once for scandalous rather than academic reasons, as when controversy engulfed Prof. Joseph White (who lectured in 1784 arguing that Christianity proved its divinity by success while Islam used force)—and, by extension, the University—for failing to declare that he was no more than co-author of his lectures.[191] Otherwise, during the 1780s, the Bampton Lecturers took the opportunity to restate the claims of the Established Church against dissent (George Croft, 1786), and to lambaste Joseph Priestley and Theophilus Lindsey and the former's tendency to make the deity material (Richard Shepherd, 1788). In line with the point just noted, there was a general tendency for the Bampton Lecturers to present their imagined opponents as returning to old arguments rather than stating new ones. As Timothy Neve put it, 'Ancient and exploded objections will be from time to time revived; and the most plausible appearances of truth and beauty will be employed in decorating anew the most offensive opinions'.[192] And this positioning induced lecturers to return to the answers offered to heretics and schismatics by the early Church rather than constructing new ones more suited to the temper of their own century. Yet this rhetorical and dialectical strategy did not preclude either creativity or originality.[193] In 1787 William Hawkins, in his 'Discourses on scripture Mysteries' argued that faith in the Trinity was what the Fathers called 'a standing doctrine of the Christian Church' while, in 1790, Henry Kett of Trinity tried to rehabilitate the Fathers wholesale against Priestley and Gibbon. Hawkins and Kett thus offered indications of a fresh willingness by the late eighteenth century to rehabilitate and deploy patristic sources in a manner that compelled attention before the impact of the French Revolution during the 1790s turned Bampton Lecturers towards prophecy and millennial themes they judged to be nationally apposite.[194]

---

[190] Bandinel, *Eight Lectures*...(Oxford, 1780), VI. 206. His text was I Cor. xi. 19, 'There must be also heresies among you'. The second Bampton Lecturer, Timothy Neve, future Lady Margaret Professor, noted that these Lectures were directed chiefly against those who used an 'artfulness of...mode' in attacking 'some of the leading Articles of Christianity' with a 'colouring' both varied and specious. Neve, *Eight Sermons*...(Oxford, 1781), i–ii.

[191] His title was 'A Comparison of Mahometism and Christianity in their History, their evidence, and their effects...'. One memoir writer wryly noted the '...two usual features of the Bampton Lectures, that of length and dryness'. G. V. Cox, *Recollections of Oxford*, (London, 1870), 217.

[192] Neve, *Eight Sermons*..., Sermon viii, 231. Neve also deplored 'this prurient spirit of controversy,...' for which he blamed rational dissenters. ibid., VI. 164. See also VII. 203.

[193] Though Bandinel, at the beginning, hoped the Lectures would result in Christianity being 'better understood than it was or possibly could be in those ages, when a servile attachment to prescribed opinions kept the intellectual faculties of mankind in a state of perpetual stagnation'. *Eight Sermons*, viii. 210.

[194] Speakers and their topics are detailed in J. Hunt, *Religious Thought in England from the Reformation to the end of the last century* (3 vols., London, 1870–3), III. 338–47.

Fig. 3.3 A View from Trinity College, Oxford [Henry Kett], by and published by Robert Dighton, hand-coloured etching, 1807 (© National Portrait Gallery, London).

Horne, the Bampton Lecturers, and other Oxonian High Churchmen were insistent that theirs was a reasonable faith, one that was not absorbed and lived out unthinkingly but constantly subjected to the scrutiny of their God-given higher faculties. That 'Reason' and Christianity were naturally compatible was a truism for all shades of theological opinion within the eighteenth-century University (including moderate Whigs) and the life of the intellect was to be celebrated and applauded. As James Bandinel put it in 1780:[195]

> God has given us reason that we might be influenced by rational motives: without them our belief, however true, our worship, however pure, cannot properly be called religious;

Mainstream Oxford opinion deplored any suggestion that reason would somehow diminish the truth of the historic faith and was quick to deprecate that growing body of opinion both at home and abroad that was determined to use reason as a

---

[195] *Eight Sermons...*, 6.

means to that end. Such anti-Christian attitudes were denounced as superficial and self-serving and particularly pernicious as they had an impact through print culture on a public likely to be susceptible to their novelty, artfully disguised under the mask of an appeal to 'primitivism'.

Yet this endorsement of reason was never uncritically made, and the majority of Oxford divines were ready to proclaim its limitations, some more than others. As Joseph Butler (before his later eminence, an Oriel College graduate) noted, reason was just one of man's endowments and should not usurp the prerogatives of other faculties.[196] Man's capacity for reasoning was supplemented by what God had revealed of Himself and His plan for the world in Christian revelation. Not to register as much was both pride and folly, as Oxford moralists were quick to point out. John Cobb, Fellow of St John's, in his 1783 Bamptons, thus urged 'the practical and speculative philosopher' to 'pay a just submission to prescription, and bend their ears with equal reverence, to the dictates of their common instructor, redeemer, saviour'.[197] Reason and revelation were not opposites but existed in perfect harmony with each other as pointers towards a higher knowledge that could never be attained in this life. In other words, our understanding was both partial and limited; mankind was to give thanks for what could be understood now of the temporal world and to push forward at its frontiers while accepting that much would never be in our capacity to grasp, thus avoiding the twin perils of rationalism and the intelligent fideism exhibited, for instance, in Henry Dodwell the Younger's (attributed) *Christianity not Founded on Argument... In a Letter to a young Gentleman at Oxford* (London, 1741).[198] Apologists for rational religion, moreover, displayed their own uncertainties, 'nor do any two agree exactly even in the most fundamental particular'.[199] On the whole, Oxford preachers and teachers fought shy of claiming that higher truths were somehow accessible to humanity through mystical experience. In this, they were at one with contemporary religious establishments of all complexions that left it to sectarians and 'enthusiasts' to extend credibility to such encounters. High Churchmen conceded that there was a place for the mystic but read this broadly and symbolically in relation to the worship of the Church militant on earth.

---

[196] Cragg, *Reason and Authority*, 121. Joseph Butler (1692–1752), author of *The Analogy of Religion, Natural and Revealed, to the Constitution and Course of Nature* (London, 1736). Matric. Oriel 1715; BA, 1718; BCL, 1721; DCL, 1733; Bp of Bristol, 1738–50; Dean of St Paul's, 1740–50; Bp of Durham, 1750–d. His attitude to Oxford is discussed in Chapter 10, pp. 67–8.

[197] *Eight Sermons...*, 102. See also, Thomas Randolph's *An enquiry into the sufficiency of reason in matters of religion...* (Oxford, 1738) and his later *The Use of Reasoning in matters stated and explain'd* (Oxford, 1762).

[198] To which his brother, William Dodwell, replied in *Two Sermons on 1 Pet. ii. 15 on the nature, procedure, value and effects of a rational Faith considered; In two sermons preached before the University of Oxford, 11 March and 24 June 1744* (Oxford, 1745).

[199] Cobb, *Eight Sermons*, 35. Cf. William Hawkins, '...you may as well look for one language at Babel as for a catholic system of unbelief,...' *Discourses on Scripture Mysteries*, 5.

iv) The decline of patristics

Many Oxford thinkers throughout the century retained a sense of the Church as a visible corporate body on earth and an entity with divine origins that regained a primitive purity during the Reformation. The sense of identification with the early Christian Church was strong, classically seen in the writings of Joseph Bingham (1668–1723). Bingham, a graduate of University College, was obliged to leave the University after heresy charges were fancifully laid against him during the 1690s but took advantage of a light parochial burden (he was in due course appointed by Bishop Trelawny of Winchester to the Hampshire livings of Havant and Headbourne Worthy), to produce ten volumes of the *Antiquities of the Christian Church* between 1708 and 1722. It was a systematic examination of the customs, usages, and operations of the early Church that stabilised the study of that subject and received near-universal critical acclaim.[200] Bingham was steeped in the study of the Fathers, translating fourteen discourses of St John Chrysostom in 1716, and his work may be said to represent the high-water mark of patristic learning among Oxford scholars in the long eighteenth century.[201] The reasons for this decline (quite marked after the 1740s) are not immediately clear.[202] On the one hand, there was little need of further advance in the subject given the scholarly creativity of the previous century; polemical disputation between Anglicans and Roman Catholics with patristic blows traded also fell out of fashion and, in a British context, study of the Fathers lost its apologetic usefulness.[203] The moderate Whig clerics who dominated the hierarchy during the Walpole and Pelhamite ascendancy had minimal interest in hearing what the Fathers had to say and regarded their 'authority' as suspect and inherently inferior

---

[200] G. V. Bennett adjudged it 'perhaps the most learned work of early ecclesiastical history published before the nineteenth century', 'University, Society and Church 1688-1714', in HUO V, 359–400, at 397; L. W. Barnard, 'Joseph Bingham and the early church', *Church Quarterly Review*, 169 (1968), 192–205; Barnard, 'The Use of the Patristic tradition in the late seventeenth and early eighteenth centuries', in eds. R. Bauckham and B. Drewery, *Scripture, tradition and reason. A study in the criteria of Christian doctrine. Essays in honour of Richard P. C. Hanson* (Edinburgh, 1988), 174–203.

[201] For the flowering of patristic learning in seventeenth-century England see J.-L. Quantain, 'The Fathers in seventeenth-century Anglican theology', in ed. I. Backus, *The reception of the Church Fathers in the west: from the Carolingians to the Maurists* (Leiden, 1996), 987–1008; N. Keene, 'John Fell: education, erudition and the English Church in late seventeenth-century Oxford', *History of Universities*, 18 (2003), 62–101. There is currently no counterpart of Quantain for the eighteenth century.

[202] Robert Cornwall, 'The search for the primitive church: the use of Early Church Fathers in the High Church Anglican tradition, 1680–1745', *AEH*, 59 (1990), 303–29; Peter Doll, 'The idea of the primitive church in High Church ecclesiology from Samuel Johnson to J. H. Hobart', *AEH*, 65 (1996), 6–43; G. V. Bennett, 'Patristic authority in the age of reason', in his *Oecumenica: Jahrbuch für ökumenische Forschung* (1971/2), 72–87; Bennett, 'Patristic tradition in Anglican thought, 1660–1900', in Günther Gassmann and Vajta Vilmos, eds., *Tradition in Luthertum und Anglikanismus: Oecumenica 1971-2* (Gütersloh, 1972), 63–87.

[203] The English term 'patristics' is a coinage of the mid-nineteenth century. Elizabeth A. Clark, 'From patristics to early Christian studies', in eds. Susan Ashbrook Harvey and David G. Hunter, *The Oxford handbook of early Christian studies* (Oxford, 2008), 7–41, at 8.

124 ENLIGHTENED OXFORD

to the scriptures.[204] And therefore for Oxford men to engage in controversy on this ground was never going to carry much persuasive force when there were deists and Arians to be worsted and the language of philosophical divinity was of most use in responding to them. The works of the Fathers (and indeed of the Caroline divines) continued, however, to be reprinted without feeding through into mainstream theological writing even at Oxford. Thus the scholarly tradition was kept alive within the University, and was quietly revived as an appropriate subject of study by Martin Routh at Magdalen in the 1790s, when he began to examine the ante-Nicene Fathers of the second and third centuries.[205]

v) Church and state aligned?

Despite the decline in patristic studies, the Oxford consensus was that there was no purer manifestation of the true Church in its teachings and its ecclesiology than the Church of England and this awareness was the primary motive inspiring its defence in successive generations. Why would any right-minded Christian *not* want to be a member of the *ecclesia anglicana*? This stance was indebted in no small measure to the Caroline divines and the Nonjurors even when these debts were went unacknowledged (as Whig careerists tended to do). And it required a sense (often lightly held) of the national Church's place in relation to the other great communions of West and East, one that came easier with the Orthodox Church in the light of seventeenth-century contacts between Canterbury and Constantinople and the brief establishment of a Greek College at Oxford in the 1700s.[206] This deeply held sense of the Church's institutional identity as something that in the last resort was independent of the state's did not preclude High Church dons from commending their profitable interaction, though foot dragging was never far away in the decades before 1760, given Tory lack of enthusiasm for their Supreme Governor. To call this outlook countercultural in the religious life of mid-eighteenth-century England would be an exaggeration, though it was certainly unfashionable and did nothing to assist an individual's preferment prospects with the Crown. After the accession of George III, with the Tories back in favour and Oxford losing its sense of being 'a beleaguered fortress',[207]

---

[204] John Pocock sees the movement away from patristics to a rational theology as 'part of the Church's patronage of methodical Enlightenment as a means of maintaining the via media...' If that was the case, it must be deemed an essentially Whiggish enterprise with traction largely outside Oxford. 'Conservative Enlightenment and Democratic Revolutions', 88.

[205] Five volumes of his *Reliquiae Sacrae* were published between 1814 and 1848. Middleton, *Dr Routh*, 109–16.

[206] Explored in Chapter 10, pp. 44–8.

[207] Dame Lucy Sutherland's phrase in *The University of Oxford in the Eighteenth Century: A Reconsideration* (Oxford, 1973), 13.

THE DEFENCE OF CHRISTIAN BELIEF   125

it became easier for them to endorse the claims of the state in partnership with a *iure divino* Church.

For the early Hanoverian state was not one that most Oxonians could endorse comfortably without reservation (public or private, and it was usually private) because of what it was not, that is British, of hereditary descent from James II not James I, High Church Anglican, and inclined to Toryism. They had an enjoyed an Indian summer of this imagined monarchy during the reign of Queen Anne and the inflated rhetoric to which the Sacheverell trial gave rise in many quarters was evidence of how deep-rooted such sentiments were.[208] But they were also escapist, because the Queen had no surviving family except for her half-brother, the "Pretender", and conferring on her some kind of earthly immortality, because the hard choice to be made on her demise was, for so many, difficult to confront until it happened and severely disadvantaged the High Church party in the University—as elsewhere—in the 1710s.[209] Oxford political thinkers had a mature political theology, based on the divine right of government, that they stutteringly applied to the post-1714 regime, but neither their heads nor their hearts were in it. Of course, that was not true for moderate Whigs at colleges like Merton, Wadham, and Christ Church, who welcomed the emphatic guarantees for the Church of England that the Protestant Settlement afforded; in many instances, they exploited the discomfiture of academic colleagues and, in return for such government preferment as was going, spoke up in support of the Hanoverian monarchy and its entitlement to loyalty, thereby supplementing a high view of monarchy articu lated by court Whigs elsewhere.[210] It was relatively straightforward to transfer the classic Bible-based justifications for obedience from the Stuart to the Hanoverian dynasty, as Bishop Potter did in his Coronation sermon of 1727, with references to passive obedience and non-resistance either toned down or omitted. Tory clergy generally opted to remain significantly silent on the issue or arouse suspicion from what they chose not to say.

The state services in the Book of Common Prayer were often the flashpoint for rival political theologies to be exhibited, most of all that commemorating the execution of Charles I on 30 January 1649. The King's martyr status triggered all sorts of latter-day associations with their own predicament for Tory preachers in the arid world of the first two Georges and they gloried in denouncing the sectarian 'rebels' who had put the King on trial and then had him judicially executed. Comparisons with the Whig status quo of their own time were implicit even if that could not be spelt out directly. Instead, preachers usually

---

[208] ed. M. Knights, *Faction displayed: reconsidering the impeachment of Dr Henry Sacheverell* (London, 2012), esp. B. Cowan, 'The spin doctor: Sacheverell's trial speech and political performance in the divided society', in ibid., 28–46.

[209] The wistful nostalgia that characterised much Tory political writing in the last years of Anne's life is brilliantly evoked in Pat Rogers, *Pope and the Destiny of the Stuarts*.

[210] Browning, *Political and constitutional ideas of the Court Whigs*, 90.

apostrophised the Church of England with a verve that they would never do for the monarchy of either George I or George II. It was left to Cambridge men to be often openly critical of the martyred Stuart: the Bishop of Peterborough, Richard Terrick, in 1758 called Charles a tyrant and, in 1789, William Pitt's former tutor, George Pretyman of Lincoln, declared the royal martyr was preparing England for absolutism and tyranny.[211] Most Oxford preachers, however, took care not to indulge in excessively fulsome panegyrics for Charles I and his cause lest they be adjudged treasonable.[212] The reawakening of open, unabashed royalist sentiment had to wait for the accession of George III, when Oxonian preachers on 30 January, that day of mourning when the whole nation was called to repent for what its ancestors had done, could really let rip.[213]

Most notoriously, of those who gave voice, attention focused on Thomas Nowell, the Principal of St Mary Hall, Public Orator (to 1776), the Chancellor's secretary, and Regius Professor of Modern History,[214] who, on 30 January 1772, preached before the House of Commons (or, rather, the handful who attended). His endorsement of divine right and submission to a God-given monarchy was so conspicuous that even the Speaker, Sir Fletcher Norton, advised him to tone it down in the printed version.[215] His apparent attempt to present himself as a new Sacheverell and rake over the 1640s once again and (over) develop the analogy with his own time was what principally gave offence to a majority of MPs. Despite Dolben and Newdigate vociferously defending him, the Commons voted to expunge its (conventional) vote of thanks to the preacher on 25 February and a bill to repeal the annual observance of 30 January inspired by Nowell's indiscretions was only defeated by 125 to 97 the following March.[216] Yet Nowell had not knowingly tried to upset MPs and there was an element of political mischief-making by those sympathetic to the dissenters (who were petitioning Parliament against subscription for dissenting ministers and schoolmasters in the early 1770s and were implicit in their hostility to the Test and Corporation Acts) in drawing attention to passages in his sermon that bore with difficulty the weight that they

---

[211] Sack, *From Jacobite to Conservative*, 127–8.

[212] J. C. D. Clark notes that 'the point of these sermons was their publication as texts, not their evocation of any extraordinary veneration for kings'. *English Society 1660–1832*, 271.

[213] The *Morning Post*, on 10 Mar. 1775, declared that passive obedience, non-resistance, and the divine right of kings 'again echo from every corner'. Quoted in Sack, *From Jacobite to Conservative*, 121.

[214] Nowell was a Glamorgan client of the High Tory Dukes of Beaufort. Philip Jenkins, *The making of a ruling class. The Glamorgan gentry 1640–1790* (Cambridge, 1983), 185; Jenkins, 'Jacobites and Freemasons in eighteenth-century Wales', *Welsh History Review*, 9 (1978), 391–406, at 403.

[215] Pasi Ihalainen, 'The sermon, court, and Parliament, 1689–1789', in eds. Francis and Gibson, *Oxford handbook of the British sermon 1689–1901*, 229–44, at 241–4. Ihalainen describes the sermon as 'an anomaly' and compares it to that delivered by Bishop Shute Barrington of Llandaff on the same day which praised civil and religious liberty. Barrington, significantly, was a Merton product.

[216] Ward, *Georgian Oxford*, 251–3, 285. Another attempt to abolish the sermon celebrating King Charles the Martyr failed narrowly in 1774, *GM* 44 (1774), 97. Sermons continued to be preached at Oxford on 30 Jan. into the early nineteenth century. See, as an instance, James Landon, *A Sermon [on 1 Pet. II. 17] preached before the University of Oxford, etc.* (Oxford, 1800).

THE DEFENCE OF CHRISTIAN BELIEF   127

had wanted to put on them. Certainly, when Nowell had delivered his sermon before the University in 1766 it had not stirred up any rancour in an environment where most dons were only too delighted to have a king whom they could unambiguously endorse.[217]

On the face of it, such an attachment to the cult of the Royal Martyr (and Oxford was always one of its bastions, indeed *the* bastion) 123 years after his execution suggests that the University's regard for tradition seen, in this case, in its political theology, stunted any pretensions for it to be considered an enlightened centre of Christian culture.[218] But such a verdict would be predicated on the assumption that the defence of orthodoxy was inherently unenlightened, an assumption that, admittedly, is embarrassingly implicit in the majority of scholarly studies of the eighteenth-century world of ideas: the focus and interest in intellectual history is so often given to the proponents of novelty that the capacities and achievements of those who disagreed with them (usually the majority) tend to be minimised. Thus it tends to be heterodox authors like Tindal who are noticed; an outstanding respondent, the moderate Whig John Conybeare and his 467-page *Defence of Revealed Religion against the Exceptions of a late Writer, in his Book, Intituled, Christianity as old as the Creation* (2nd edn., Oxford, 1732) are neglected, despite his work being an extensive, methodical treatise dealing thoroughly with Tindal almost page by page, thus confirming a Europe-wide reputation gained earlier for his replies to the deists.[219]

vi) Conclusion

Any look at Oxford bears out the recent observation that 'universities and churches remained extremely important to the proliferation of Enlightened theological discourse, as they engaged with a wider reading public, . . . and confronted

[217] The bulk of the sermon's contents were devoted to criticising the Puritans. Its parliamentary censure came as something of a shock to him and to the University. Nowell wrote: 'It gives me the greatest Concern that I should have been even the innocent cause of so much noise and Debate; and that my name should be echoed thro' the Kingdom, as the subject either of praise or censure'. To Sir Roger Newdigate, 28 Feb. 1772, Warks. RO, Newdegate family of Arbury, B. 2027T. Significantly, as George III himself noted, the country gentlemen in the Commons had expected more ministerial support for Nowell and his sermon. See James J. Caudle, 'Preaching in Parliament: patronage, publicity and politics in Britain, 1701–60', in eds. L. A. Ferrell and P. E. McCullough, *The English sermon revised: religion, literature and history, 1600–1750* (Manchester, 2000), 235–65, at 254–7.

[218] Some Oxford eulogists of Charles I, critical of his sentence of execution, became implicitly critical of the death penalty more generally.

[219] This work was dedicated to the then all-powerful Bishop Edmund Gibson, who secured the Deanery of Christ Church for Conybeare in 1733. Warburton called it 'one of the best reasoned books in the world'. See Stephen Taylor, 'The Government and the Episcopate in the mid-eighteenth century: the uses of patronage', in eds. Charles Giry-Deloison and Roger Mettam, *Patronages et Clientélismes 1550–1750 (France, Angleterre, Espagne, Italie)* (Lille/London, 1995), 191–207, at 204. For Conybeare's considerable reputation as a preacher and tutor in Oxford (he could fill St Mary's church), see W. K. Stride, *Exeter College* (London, 1900), 98–104.

128 ENLIGHTENED OXFORD

heterodoxy in public';[220] Oxonian voices in divinity reached out beyond the University and made a major contribution to the manner in which the English received and perceived their religion. And that dissemination began within Oxford itself with clerical formation, as individual professors and tutors tried to motivate their pupils and make clear that it might fall to them in time to give a lead nationally as well as locally.[221] The endowment of the Bampton Lectures attracted considerable attention while, in an urban context, dons got involved as City Lecturers, preaching to the Council and citizens in the city church at St Martin's at Carfax. There and across the huge reach of print culture, even where the Oxford emphasis on and re-presentation of orthodoxy encountered hostility or indifference, its reiteration down the century generated debate about every aspect of the faith that was a token of enlightenment in itself.[222] This was hardly surprising, given the centrality of religion to intellectual life despite competition from secular subjects, and was reflected in publishing patterns: journals, particularly the *Gentleman's Magazine*, made a point of reporting sermons, often generating lengthy correspondence, while in the *Critical Review* reviews of sermons routinely appeared before reviews of novels, suggesting the relative importance and popularity of the genre.[223] For those who were responsive to what the alma mater had to say, especially Tory High Churchmen frozen out of the patronage stakes and isolated in their rural rectories, being able to subscribe to Oxford publications,[224] buy published sermons, or read in the newspapers or in periodicals the gist of what had been preached from the pulpit of St Mary's helped keep them loyal to the 'cause' as well as consolidate a sense of Oxonian identity that was not limited by geographical constraints. And those graduates who were Whigs and not inclined to 'high and dry' theology could also follow their favourite preachers within the stable of competing voices that made up the Oxford divinity spectrum. Whatever their politics, however, educated readers could only follow

---

[220] Bulman, 'Introduction', in eds., Bulman and Ingram, *God in the Enlightenment*, 29. See also Burson, *Rise and Fall of Theological Enlightenment*; Edelstein, *The Enlightenment*.

[221] This responsibility was intended by the University authorities to be discharged to all those *in statu pupillari* under them, not just intending ordinands. As a circular broadsheet issued in the early 1730s by the V-C, College tutors, and Heads of Houses, and Proctors expressed it, tutors were to 'discharge their duty by double diligence in informing their respective pupils in their Christian duty and...in recommending to them the frequent and careful reading [of] the Scriptures and such other books as may serve more effectually to promote Christianity, sound principles and orthodox faith'. Quoted in ed. R. Heitzenrater, *Diary of an Oxford Methodist: Benjamin Ingham 1733-1734* (Durham, NC, 1985), 13.

[222] As Pasi Ihalainen has well said, the eighteenth-century world cannot 'simply be divided into two with traditional religion opposing progressive Enlightenment within religious communities'. 'The Enlightenment Sermon: towards practical religion and a sacred national community', in ed. Joris Van Eijnatten, *Preaching, sermon and cultural change in the long eighteenth century* (Leiden, 2009), 219–60, at 221.

[223] William Gibson, 'The British sermon 1689–1901: quantities, performance, and culture', in eds. Francis and Gibson, *The Oxford handbook of the British sermon 1689–1901*, 3–30, at 5–7.

[224] W. A. Speck, 'Politicians, peers, and publication by subscription, 1700-1750', in ed. Isabel Rivers, *Books and their readers in eighteenth-century England* (Leicester, 1982), 47–68.

THE DEFENCE OF CHRISTIAN BELIEF 129

efforts to secure a new version of the Authorised Version of the Bible at a remove. For though Biblical scholarship in the University was outstanding, it developed without the foundation of a distinctive academic theological journal, such as the *Allgemeine Bibliothek der biblischen Litteratur* in Germany, that might have further stimulated graduate involvement.

The University's contribution to theological debate in the eighteenth century cannot be (mis)represented as regressive and failing to offer anything new to the reformulation of Christianity that apparently excited thinkers and apologists elsewhere. For this is to downplay the continuing appeal of Christian orthodoxy delivered from the full range of theological angles that could be contained *within* orthodoxy. In this sphere, there was a perceived public appetite for the exchange of viewpoints that may have lent itself to the generation of controversy, but also creativity. And within theology, Oxford scholarship reflected that enhanced interest in religious culture with new efforts to understand the beliefs of men and women in the past, for a greater comprehension of *l'homme religieux*, using a much wider range of sources, while contending that there was no necessary incompatibility between orthodoxy and the right use of reason. Throughout this period, public culture in England remained demonstrably Christian in character, with the essential structure of the establishment preserved and the majority of the Church of England not deviating from the Catholic creeds. That such was the case owed more to Oxford divines than any other group, those who stayed in the university, those who took up senior positions in the hierarchy, and those (the majority) whose life was passed serving the people of their parishes. That there may have been no formal preparation for the ordained ministry of the Church of England did not prevent pastorally aware dons doing their best to prepare their charges, as the work of Edward Bentham, Benjamin Wheeler, and John Randolph indicated. That the typical parish priest was one of the best-trained and most highly regulated professionals of the day proves the point.[225]

It has been compellingly said that '...the clerical English Enlightenment was a pugilistic clerical Enlightenment'.[226] And one can readily focus on wrangling and disputation, narrow point scoring, personality clashes, all the exchanges inseparable from the life of Oxford or any other university, yet, arguably Oxford, for better or worse, and more than any other institution, helped to keep the English nation recognisably Christian in this century. It early identified the challenge to Trinitarian beliefs and members engaged in defence of this core doctrine against those who discounted and disbelieved it, especially Socinians, who liked to depict themselves as authentic, primitive Christians: they were seen as as much of a foe in the 1790s as they had been in the 1690s. But there were failures, too, such as

---

[225] W. M. Jacob, *The clerical profession in the long eighteenth century, 1680–1840* (Oxford, 2007).
[226] Robert Ingram's expression in *Religion, reform and modernity*, 76. J. G. A. Pocock, 'Enthusiasm: the anti-self of Enlightenment', *HLQ*, 60 (1998), 7–28; Young, *Religion and Enlightenment*, 6.

130 ENLIGHTENED OXFORD

insufficient use of the resources offered by the treasury of Catholic Christian teaching as tempered by philosophical acuteness. Thus Oxford theologians failed to develop a doctrine of the Godhead that could be an answer to the 'avant-garde doctrine of God'[227] exhibited (to the detriment of his career) by Samuel Clarke in his *Scripture Doctrine of the Trinity* (1712). And, as the role of the Church as a regulator of questions of human conduct receded in the eighteenth century, the English universities arguably failed to hold the line in this area or configure the shape of secularity (the Roman Catholic Church was saved the hard task of regulating morality by its retention of the sacrament of penance). Nevertheless, considered overall from the angle of the defence of orthodoxy, the University's indirect impact on the public could hardly have been greater, as its commitment to the Bible, the creeds, and the national Church—at its best orthodox, creative, and insightful—spread out of its Oxonian heartland to feed into and shape the religious life and culture of the whole country.

[227] The phrase is Stephen Hampton's, *Anti-Arminians*, 220. Hampton considers Clarke as probably 'the most brilliant clergyman of his generation'. Ibid., 162–3, 179–83.

4

Oxford and the arts and humanities

Introduction

... men of sense like what you have done.... if it does not sell well it is
the fault of the times; which relish nothing but wretched politicks, and
contemptible ribaldry; but there is a thirst after Oriental learning, &
ancient history, in Towns, as well as Colleges, greater than it used to be;
John Williams, Gloucester, to Thomas Hunt, Oxford,
6 Feb. 1752, Bodl. MS Eng. lett. d. 145, f. 142.

This chapter argues for the zestiness, vigour, and variety of the arts and humanities in eighteenth-century Oxford, a city closely connected to literary circles in
London (and vice versa), that produced graduates capable of a creativity which
was not, apparently, unduly disadvantaged by being taught according to an
archaic curriculum. In a range of disciplines, Oxford authors attempted to reach
out to a wide public and interest it in the varied literary productions of the
University throughout the decades, without compromising its reputation for
academic learning. Oxford scholars were invariably looking for a publisher and
metropolitan circulation and were far from willing to be left on the sidelines by the
emerging commercial model of publishing. In the ex-weaver's apprentice and
footman, Robert Dodsley, they found one of the best-known, with Dodsley's
friend, Joseph Spence, sometime Professor of Poetry, often introducing the parties,
and making the premises at the Tully's Head inn, London, a congregating point
for Oxonians in the 1740s.[1]

Oxford may not have been a classically defined 'centre of Enlightenment'—
internal respect for its own cultural and religious heritage and the contemporary
establishment saw to that—but it continued, as it had in previous centuries, to
increase the sum of human knowledge and make increasing amounts of it more
accessible to educated audiences in Britain and Europe. Oxford was not an
obscurantist Anglican backwater; it was a university well-connected with the
contemporary world, the one into which its graduates, clerical and lay alike,

---

[1] Harry M. Solomon, *The Rise of Robert Dodsley, Creating the New Age of Print* (Carbondale, IL,
1996), 53, 96.

Enlightened Oxford: The University and the Cultural and Political Life of Eighteenth-century Britain and Beyond.
Nigel Aston, Oxford University Press. © Nigel Aston 2023. DOI: 10.1093/oso/9780199246830.003.0005

132 ENLIGHTENED OXFORD

passed. In the arts and humanities, in an age when discipline, professionalism, and literature were beginning to emerge as historical categories 'through acts of clarification',[2] it was able over time to make its own distinctive contribution to the formation, well-being, and stability of British society so that, as David Fairer has contended, during the last three decades of the century it moved to be 'at the heart of the nation's literary consciousness'.[3] And not just in vernacular literature, taken up with such gusto by Thomas Warton the younger and his generation in a remarkable rejection of the charges of snooty exclusiveness and wrong-headed scholarship, for which its critics had belaboured the University during the Phalaris controversy in the 1690s.[4] Elsewhere, Oxford built on its seventeenth-century reputation for Oriental languages and developed new ties with government as the imperial demands of the British state increased while, nearer to home, a musical culture flourished in the city and gained international notice. And all this in an academic centre where Latin remained officially the language of instruction,[5] and was used also to articulate (often with masterly ambivalence) what remained the overwhelmingly Jacobite character of literature and literary scholarship in early eighteenth-century Oxford.

i) Polite and impolite verse, the rise of English literary scholarship, and other genres

The Anglo-Latinate tradition remained far from torpid for at least the first thirty years of the century at Oxford: tutors propelled and encouraged their most gifted or well-born pupils to seek early fame by submitting Latin verses to greet royal births, marriages, and deaths, and the best of these compositions were generally published.[6] It has been plausibly contended that these constitute, collectively, 'a substantial body of literature, and a major contribution of the university to national cultural life'.[7] But most of the poetry written (whether in Latin or

---

[2] Clifford Siskin, *The Work of Writing: Literature and social change in Britain, 1700–1830* (Baltimore, MD, 1998), 6. In an era of fluid boundaries between the humanities and the sciences, history and natural history, the classifications adopted in this chapter should be regarded as porous, not rigid. D. Woolf, *The Social Circulation of the Past. English Historical Culture 1500–1730* (Oxford, 2003), chap. 5.

[3] 'Oxford and the Literary World', in HUO V, 779.   [4] Discussed in this Chapter, pp. 60–3.

[5] For the decline of spoken Latin within European universities in the eighteenth century see F. Waquet, *Latin or the Empire of a Sign from the sixteenth to the twentieth centuries*, tr. J. Howe (London, 2001), 25–6. The Chancellor's Prize for Latin verse (for junior members) was introduced in 1768 as a means of nourishing a faltering tradition.

[6] See the mordant comments of the mature Jeremy Bentham on being asked by his tutor to write about the death of George II in 1760. *The Works of Jeremy Bentham*, ed. John Bowring, (11 vols., London, 1843), X. 42. The tradition built on college exercises requiring themes, declamations, translations, and verses. D. K. Money, '"A diff'rent-sounding lyre": Oxford commemorative verse in English, 1613–1834', *BLR*, 16 (1997) 42–92; M. L. Clarke, 'Classical Studies', in HUO V, 513–34, at 518.

[7] Money, '"A diff'rent-sounding lyre"', 54.

OXFORD AND THE ARTS AND HUMANITIES   133

English) in Oxford was circulated privately in manuscript between college wits.[8] Intended for private consumption, variously playful, pedantic, and point-scoring, the obscurity of a learned language had its uses for the many Oxonians inclined to Jacobitism. But, by definition, it was not intended for a wide audience (the work was seldom translated, where it was published at all), and its practitioners tended not to be Whigs and were out of favour with ministers after 1714. Latin verse, circulated in manuscript, was, for them, both a consolation and an outlet for amusement, often acerbically at the expense of their enemies. That said, educated public opinion took notice of published commemorative and other verses when they were controversial, amusing, or both. The greatest of the Oxford Latinists, Anthony Alsop, anonymously issued some of his poems (including the odes satirising the fussy, inquisitive, news-gathering moderate Tory Arthur Charlett, Master of University College after 1692) in 1706 in pamphlet form that was plainly designed for the educated London public 'rather than being simply a parochial Oxford exercise with its observation of foibles and good-humoured ridicule'.[9] And there was more than one occasion when university verses were satirised in London. Thus, in 1711, as fears about the security of the Protestant Succession mounted, some of the poems published in Oxford to commemorate the birth of a son and heir to James II in 1688 were mischievously reprinted as part of a wider scheme to satirise the Jacobites as *Select Copies of Amusing Verses, taken out of those two Famous Volumes, intitul'd, Strenae Natalitiae*.[10] Among the Oxford poets were the Hon. Albemarle Bertie (later a Whig MP), Richard Willis and John Wynne (bishops consecrated after 1714), Christopher Codrington (the Whig plantation owner), Samuel Wesley (father of John and Charles Wesley), and the antiquary Edmund Chishull.[11]

However, over time Oxford's commitment to the English vernacular heritage and its contemporary expression developed on an extraordinary scale, and encouraged very senior figures within the University. As Joseph Spence expressed it:[12]

---

[8] See, pre-eminently, Money, *The English Horace*. H. Ravens, 'Manuscript studies and the eighteenth century', *Literature Compass*, 16 (July 2019) for a review of the scholarly consensus that manuscript culture persisted long into the eighteenth century and was interdependent with print culture.

[9] Money, *The English Horace*, 107, 133, 282–3.

[10] Money, '"A Diff'rent-Sounding Lyre"', 50. The full title of the publication that contained them was *State-Amusements, Serious and Hypocritical, fully exemplified in the abdication of King James the Second, to which is added a True List of the Members of Both Universities that Amused his Majesty... with some Select Copies of Amusing Verses, taken out of those two Famous Volumes, intitul'd, Strenae Natalitiae...* (London, 1711).

[11] *State-Amusements* is discussed in Jeremy Black, *Charting the Past. The Historical Worlds of Eighteenth-Century England* (Bloomington, IN, 2019), 83–5.

[12] Spence, *Polymetis, or an enquiry concerning the agreement between the works of the Roman poets, and the remains of the ancient artists* (London, 1747), 287–90. See R. S. Thompson, 'English and English Education in the eighteenth century', in ed. J. A. Leith, *Facets of Education in the Eighteenth Century* SVEC 167 (1977), 66–85, at 74.

134 ENLIGHTENED OXFORD

I do not mean that the classics should be wholly given up; but rather that our own language should not be given up for them: and, indeed, that the study of them need not be so universal.

The value placed on the native tongue was underlined by Robert Lowth's ground-breaking *Short Introduction to English Grammar* (1762), one of the first systematic English grammars for native speakers, and one that sold well across the country to men and women whose only contact with Oxonian culture it might be.[13] But that was increasingly unlikely as from Oxford poured forth verses of all kinds—classical and biblical paraphrase, anacreontics, courtly pastoral poetry—reaching widely expanding readerships. Prose editions and commentaries on English vernacular writings were much fewer until the second half of the century, when the Warton brothers and their circle were to the fore in stimulating interest in the nation's own literary heritage. There were exceptions. John Urry (1666-1715) of Christ Church, a Nonjuror in William III's reign, began work on a new edition of the works of Geoffrey Chaucer in 1711 at Atterbury's behest.[14] This collaborative effort was incomplete on his death but he enjoyed posthumous literary fame for his labours.[15]

Poetic performance certainly flourished in Oxford with Latin and English verses declaimed at Acts, Encaenias, and other grand university *fêtes*, with competitions and prizes available to stimulate competition in this esteemed accomplishment.[16] Some of these efforts, if published, could reach a wider audience as, for instance, did the young Samuel Johnson's verse when John Husbands (his contemporary at Pembroke College) edited *A Miscellany of Poems by Several*

---

[13] Ingrid Tieken-Boon van Ostade, *The Bishop's Grammar. Robert Lowth and the rise of prescriptivism* (Oxford, 2011). It was republished on average every year for the next seventy years. Dodsley was the publisher, and Lowth was delighted with the sales: 'I am very glad to find the Public has so good an Appetite for Grammar', he told Dodsley. *The Correspondence of Robert Dodsley 1733-1764*, ed. James E. Tierney (Cambridge, 1988), 461; Paul Langford, *A Polite and Commercial People. England 1727-1783* (Oxford, 1989), 307. For the pioneering grammatical work of Elizabeth Elstob half a century earlier and her Oxonian circle, see Chapter 10, pp. 85-6.

[14] According to one inside source, Urry was initially unwilling: '...John Urry, because he is an antiquary, must put out a new edition of Cha[i]ucer; John scratches his head, and says he is at [our?] mercy and must not disobey, but he hopes our Governor [Atterbury] he says will be a bishop before he can gather the materials for his work'. 13 Nov. 1711, HMC, *Portland MSS*, VII. 72. The intention was that profits from the book's sales would help pay for the extensive building works in progress at the college. Sarah A. Kelen, 'Cultural capital: selling Chaucer's "Works", building Christ Church, Oxford', *The Chaucer Review* 36 (2001), 149-57.

[15] *The Works of Jeoffrey Chaucer* (London, 1721) was the first edition of Chaucer to be set entirely in Roman type. See W. A. Alderson and A. C. Henderson, *Chaucer and Augustan Scholarship* [University of California Publications in English 35], (Los Angeles, CA, 1970). For the limitations of Urry's edition see Walsh, M., 'Literary Scholarship and the life of editing', in ed. I. Rivers, *Books and their readers in eighteenth-century England: New Essays* (London, 2001), 191-216, at 191-2. The gentleman-scholar, Thomas Tyrwhitt (see this Chapter, p. 71) produced an outstanding and important edition of the *Canterbury Tales* in 1775. ibid., 192-3.

[16] D. K. Money, 'Free Flattery or Servile Tribute? Oxford and Cambridge Commemorative Poetry in the seventeenth and eighteenth centuries', in ed. J. Raven, *Free Print and Non-Commercial Publishing since 1700* (Aldershot, 2000), 48-66.

Hands (1731).[17] Increasingly, tapping in to that wider market was seen to hinge on London publication and access to the particular book distribution channels that it was likely to bring. The quality of such Oxford verse as was available in print varied; sometimes exceptional as in Johnson's translation of Pope's *Messiah*,[18] but generally ephemeral, tucked away in poetic collections that would interest only a minority outside academic circles.

For the first quarter of the new century, Addisonian flavours were pronounced within the literary culture of the University and his influence persisted, despite his hitching his star to the Whigs in the course of Anne's reign. Joseph Addison had originally made his name at Magdalen for his skill in writing entertaining Latin prose and verse but, after being granted leave of absence from the College in 1700, he moved to London and became nationally influential through the distribution of the *Tatler* and the *Spectator*.[19] But his name was constantly before the University and his celebrated play *Cato* (1713) renewed his following among Oxford student poets. Men like Thomas Tickell (1686–1740, Fellow of Queen's, 1709), could ill afford not to court Addison's good offices, while the latter was keen to use his Oxford connections to manage his Whig coterie. While still at Oxford, Tickell, spurred on by Addison, produced a translation of the *Iliad* that deliberately appeared almost concurrently with Pope's more celebrated version.[20] Tickell was keen to attract a patron and that required the maximum projection of his work. He developed a poetic voice (one that brought him considerable personal notice),[21] from his base in the city to make it a site of historical inspiration. Thus in his *On Her Majesty's rebuilding the Lodgings . . . at Queen's Coll.*, Oxford (1733) he adduced such figures as Henry V, the Black Prince, and his mother Phillipa of Hainault as patrons of the university, itself dubbed 'The seat of sages, and the nurse of kings'. There, where the Sheldonian 'Rivals the Stately Pomp of

---

[17] Robert DeMaria, Jr., *The life of Samuel Johnson. A critical biography* (Oxford, 1993), 21–2. His translation of Pope's 'Messiah' was the only Latin verse in a 300-page collection.

[18] Niall Rudd, 'Samuel Johnson's Latin poetry', in eds. L. B. T. Houghton and G. Manuwald, *Neo-Latin poetry in the British Isles* (London, 2012), 105–24, at 117. See also *The Latin & Greek poems of Samuel Johnson. Text, translation & commentary*, ed. Barry Baldwin (London, 1995).

[19] demy (or half-fellow) 1689; fellow from 1697, resigned his fellowship, 1711. Darwall-Smith, 'Monks of Magdalen', 334–5. P. Smithers, *The life of Joseph Addison* (Oxford, 1968), 28–34. For Addison's monumentality in the wider culture see Lawrence E. Klein, 'Addisonian Afterlives: Joseph Addison in Eighteenth-Century Culture', *JECS*, 35 (2012), 101–18.

[20] Pope acknowledged the influence of Oxford in his preface. Addison considered Tickell's *Iliad* to be superior to Pope's version, while Pope himself believed it had in reality been translated by Addison. ed. Sir Richard Phillips, *Addisoniana* (2 vols., London, 1803), I. 97–8. Tickell seems to have been encouraged by Addison to compete deliberately with Pope and damage his subscription for Homer (in which it signally failed). Pat Rogers notes Tickell's influence on the young Pope, *Pope and the destiny of the Stuarts*, 14. Tickell was also an energetic journalist.

[21] His major literary work was *On the Prospect of Peace* (1712), an ambitious poem in anticipation of the Treaty of Utrecht. One admiring reader was Walter Molesworth, who said of Tickell: '. . . as a poet, wherein, if I be not mistaken, he will make as great a figure as any of his contemporaries. He has more of the inventive part (which I take to be the essential of a poet) than any of them;' to the Hon. John Molesworth, 9 Nov. 1721, in HMC, *M.L.S. Clements MSS* (London, 1913), 326.

ancient Rome', as he had written in his earlier his *Oxford. A Poem* (1707), Parnassus is outdone, 'And Isis boasts more Bards than Helicon'.[22]

Tickell achieved a degree of fame by commenting on a major public event of his time from a court Whig perspective; party-political considerations could not be ignored by aspirant Oxford poets in Anne's reign. He served as the model of a patriotic poet for half a century and 'On the Prospect of Peace' went into six editions, praised by Pope and puffed by Addison in the *Spectator*.[23] Another poetic aspirant was Edward Young (1683–1765), future author of *Night Thoughts*, and Tickell's oldest Oxford friend,[24] whose initial verse offerings were forthcoming while he was a Law Fellow of All Souls (1708–30), and producing (among other writings) popular poems, self-published, with copyrights later sold for profit. It offered a model of how an Oxford author might access the London book trade that was being transformed as authors in the wake of the 1710 Copyright Act started to experiment with new ways of profiting from intellectual capital by self-publishing, then trading in copyright. Young's poems included an acclaimed series of seven Horatian-style satires, *The Universal Passion* (1725–8) that made his career: both in verse and play–writing Young was angling for an official post to thereby emulate his friend Tickell (under-secretary of state to Addison, 1717), and created an extensive literary network as a means to that end. He achieved eventual success when he became chaplain-in-ordinary to the Princess of Wales in 1725 and to George II in 1728.[25] On the Tory side John Philips (1676–1709) from Herefordshire won praise for his Miltonic parody *The Splendid Shilling* (1701); *Blenheim* (1705), an unfawning look at Marlborough's victory;[26] and the sub-Virgilian *Cyder* (1708) with its Jacobite undertones, and multiple tributes to Aldrich and other Christ Church Tories.[27] But he died young, before he had any opportunity of attaining public office through his poetic talents.

Oxford figures could play a part in achieving national shifts in poetic trends. One such shift occurred in the 1740s when there was a move away from the 'correctness' associated with Addison to an emphasis on fancy in works that included Joseph Warton's *The Enthusiast, or the Lover of Nature* (1744),

---

[22] Tickell, *The Poetical Works of Thomas Tickell*, ed. C. Cooke (London, 1796), 66, 78. Howard Weinbrot, *Britannia's Issue. The Rise of British Literature from Dryden to Ossian* (Cambridge, 1993), 248.

[23] Dustin Griffin, *Patriotism and poetry in eighteenth-century Britain* (Cambridge, 2002), 50 and n.; S. J. Rogal, 'Thomas Tickell's *Prospect of Peace*', *Illinois Quarterly*, 35 (1973), 31–40. Tickell was part of Addison's so-called Whiggish 'little senate', as was the Oxford poet Henry Carey. A. Williams, *Poetry and the creation of a Whig literary Culture 1681–1714* (Oxford, 2005), 157–8.

[24] John Carswell, *The old cause. Three biographical studies in Whiggism* (London, 1954), 135.

[25] James E. May, 'Young, Edward (*bap.* 1683, *d.* 1765)', *ODNB* (online edn., 2015).

[26] John D. Baird, 'Whig and Tory panegyrics: Addison's The Campaign and Philips's Blenheim reconsidered', *Lumen*, 26 (1997), 163–77.

[27] Christ Church is hailed in Book One of *Cyder* as 'The Muses' fairest Seat,/Where Aldrich reigns, and from his endless Store/Of universal Knowledge still supplies/His noble Care...', Philips, ed. M. G. Lloyd Thomas, *The poems of John Philips* (Oxford, 1927). Matric. Ch. Ch., 1697, and stayed ten years without taking a degree. Three of Philips's six brothers were Nonjurors.

OXFORD AND THE ARTS AND HUMANITIES   137

William Collins's *Odes on Several Descriptive and Allegoric Subjects* (1747), and Thomas Warton's *The Pleasures of Melancholy* (1747).[28] Thomas Warton can lay claim to being the most distinguished Poet Laureate of the whole century, a tenure distinguished by odes that explored the history of his office (1785–90).[29] This multi-talented Oxonian (Fellow of Trinity from 1752 until his death in 1790) acquired a national and international following for his poetry,[30] but also in the emerging field of English literary scholarship. His *Observations on The Faerie Queene of Spenser* (1st edn., London, 1754) pioneered a contextualised approach to Edmund Spenser and his sources;[31] the *History of English Poetry* (3 vols., 1774–81) identified the age of Elizabeth I as that when the relationship between truth and fancy produced the most original poetry, but its appearance unfortunately coincided with Johnson's better-known *Lives of the Poets*. And it came in for some critical disparagement from those ill-disposed to Anglican exclusiveness. Joseph Ritson thus insisted that had the author, a 'thorough-bred Oxonian tory-rory High Churchman' bothered to ask the 'lowest person in Trinity college, the porter, nay, your old bed-maker' for help, he could have avoided errors in glossing old English words.[32] Nevertheless, Warton played a pivotal role second only to that of Johnson in publishing his *History of English Poetry* with its periodisation 'foundational for the emergent discipline of English', a model for narrative literary history, and representing the creation of the canon.[33] An edition of Milton's early verse, *Poems upon Several Occasions* (1785) confirmed the accessibility of his scholarship and his wish both to reach out to the reading public and to emphasise, through the inclusion of his institutional affiliations and academic titles in his literary histories, that a university was the place best suited to the serious discussion of poetry.[34]

Warton also had a less serious side that made him an obvious choice as the (anonymous) editor of *The Oxford Sausage*, a poetical miscellany dating from

---

[28] Fairer, 'Oxford and the literary world', 790.

[29] For the cultural prestige of the Warton brothers, Thomas and Joseph, see David Allan, *Making British Culture. English Readers and the Scottish Enlightenment, 1740–1830* (New York/Abingdon, 2008), 24, 35, 38–9. Not all were impressed. The Rev. Percival Stockdale, the relatively impecunious vicar of Lesbury, Northumberland, and an ambitious author himself, observed: 'I am not mortified with the History of Tom Warton. Alas! £110 a—year would be an Object to me; but I would rather be without it, than be Poet-Laureat: it is the Post of Dullness, and venality'. To Edward Jerningham, 1 June 1785, Huntington Library, CA, Jerningham Papers, Box 5, JE 803.

[30] In 1777 he produced an edition of his *Poems* that nostalgically combined an imagined chivalric past with an elegaic atmosphere. It went into a third edition within two years. The book was the culmination of a career that had begun in the 1740s. Fairer, 'Oxford and the Literary World', 801–2.

[31] See S. Johnson to Warton, 16 July 1754, *The Letters of Samuel Johnson*, ed. R. W. Chapman (3 vols., Oxford, 1952), I. 56.

[32] Ritson, *Observations on the three first volumes of the History of English Poetry. In a familiar letter to the author* (London, 1782), 12, 23.

[33] Deidre Shauna Lynch, *Loving Literature. A Cultural History* (Chicago, IL, 2015), 68–9; R. Wellek, *The Rise of English Literary History* (Chapel Hill, NC, 1941), 201.

[34] The point is well made in Kramnick, *Making the English Canon: Print-Capitalism and the Cultural Past, 1700–1770* (Cambridge, 1999), 144.

138 ENLIGHTENED OXFORD

1764 that had some of the more printable products of the secret Jelly-Bag Society as its principal contents.[35] It good-humouredly parodied the established range of Oxford poetic devices in a manner that perhaps counted against Warton's securing either the Presidency of Trinity or the lasting public recognition that his gifts merited. *The Oxford Sausage* came out at a time when Warton held the chair of Poetry (1757–66) in the University and, to say the least, drew attention away from his four annual lectures on Greek poetry.[36] Nevertheless, it did not diminish the appetite that metropolitan readers had for specimens of Oxford waggery with a satire that was generous, playful, and often with Oxonian practices and attitudes as its subject.[37]

Thomas Warton was the sixth holder of the chair of Poetry since its foundation in 1708.[38] The existence of a chair of this Professorship acted in a small sense as a handmaiden to poetic talent at large in the University, an incentive to write, publish, and have one's work distributed beyond Oxford. But the barriers in practice to reaching a wider audience were formidable: the need for the holder to maintain and extend his academic credentials; the delivery of the lectures in the first instance in Latin; and a preference for taking as one's subject some aspect of ancient, usually classical poetry. The leap from there to public notice, let alone acclamation, was one a minority of Professors managed. The first holder tried hard. This was the Tory pamphleteer, poet, and playwright, Joseph Trapp, fellow of Wadham, who ranged across poetic models from the classical world in his lectures, but was also prepared to suggest subjects suitable for contemporary versifiers.[39]

His successor, Warton's father, had been Professor between 1718 and 1728 and, like some others, did not publish his lectures, and was better known around the University for his Jacobitism.[40] It was not until Robert Lowth became Professor (1741–51) that there were lectures of a calibre that brought lasting renown to

---

[35] See Joseph Warton to Thomas Warton, 5 July [1764], in ed. David Fairer, *The Correspondence of Thomas Warton* (Athens, GA, 1994), 176.

[36] Joan Pittock, *The ascendancy of taste. The achievement of Joseph and Thomas Warton* (London, 1973), 176–214. His forty lectures were never printed, though their influence on reviving an educated interest in Greek literature is commonly presumed. Fairer, 'Oxford and the literary world', 797.

[37] Ibid., 791–4, 800 covers the tradition of Oxford burlesques.

[38] The professorship was set up under the will of Henry Birkhead with revenues from his lands in Berkshire and Durham. Lecturing was obligatory. It was customary to hold the chair for two periods of five years. See J. W. Mackail, *Henry Birkhead and the foundation of the Oxford Chair of Poetry* (Oxford, 1908). See Hal Jensen's 'A self-defining Chair', TLS, 12 June 2015.

[39] Trapp's lectures were translated into English with additional notes and published in 1742. Richard Sharp, 'Trapp, Joseph (1679–1747), Church of England clergyman and writer', *ODNB*, online version, 2004. He had published an heroic tragedy called *Abra-Mulé, Or, Love and Empire* (1704), which played for a while at Lincolns' Inn Fields, starring Anne Bracegirdle in the title role and Thomas Betterton as Mahomet IV. Hal Jensen calls him an 'undaunted pioneer', and comments on how Trapp took aim at a new type of 'dramatic folly', operas starring eunuchs, with an eye no doubt on Handel's *Rinaldo* and its star, the castrato Nicolini, who was packing in the crowds at Vanbrugh's new Queen's Theatre in Haymarket. 'A self-defining Chair', TLS, 12 June, 2015.

[40] cf. J. Pittock, 'Thomas Warton and the Oxford chair of poetry', *English Studies*, 62 (1981), 14–33.

Fig. 4.1 Joseph Trapp (1679–1747), unknown artist, oil on canvas (Bodleian Libraries, University of Oxford).

Lowth and his university, the *De sacra poesi Hebraeorum: Praelectiones Academiae Oxonii Habitae* (Oxford, 1753).[41] Lowth's topic (originally given as lectures in 1741) was the sacred poetry of the Hebrews, a topic that he wanted to understand on its own terms, not according to neoclassical literary canons.[42] It belonged, in his estimate, to a pre-classical tradition that he deemed to contain 'the only specimens of the primeval and genuine poetry', sublime due to the depth and universality of its subject matter, with Jesus as its supreme continuator, and a tradition whose multiple contexts he worked hard to recover. As he put it:

> He who would perceive the particular and interior elegancies of the Hebrew poetry, must imagine himself exactly situated as the persons for whom it was written, or even as the writers themselves; he is to feel them as a Hebrew...[43]

[41] Trans. G. Gregory, as *Lectures on the Sacred Poetry of the Hebrews* (2 vols., London, 1787). They were dedicated to his first patron, Henry Bilson-Legge, the Whig MP and Hampshire landowner, whom he had known from childhood.
[42] Michael C. Legaspi, *The Death of Scripture and the Rise of Biblical Studies* (New York, 2010), 112, 115. He gave thirty-four lectures between 1741 and 1750. ibid., 108.
[43] *Lectures on the Sacred Poetry*, I. 114.

140 ENLIGHTENED OXFORD

In his *Praelectiones*, Lowth acclaimed the Hebrew prophets not as primitives but as men grounded in the arts of music and verse, the inheritors of a highly sophisticated aesthetic tradition.[44] They had produced sublime poetry that was a by-product of divine inspiration.[45] His impact on other English poets, including the Warton brothers, Collins, and Christopher Smart, the Cambridge-educated author *of Jubilate agno*, was pronounced while, in one critical view, his 'influence upon the German Old Testament scholarship of its day has probably never been equalled'. That could not be said of his successor, William Hawkins, who produced nothing memorable in the vernacular unless it be 'Devotion, a Poem', and the 'The Thimble', a poem in the spirit of Pope's 'The Rape of the Lock'.[46] Despite his capacities as an innovative lecturer and minor playwright,[47] Hawkins acquired none of Lowth's continental fame, that was fanned while the latter was still living and endured well beyond his death in 1777.[48] In Oxford, Lowth's exceptional talent could not readily be emulated and, after Warton the younger resigned in 1766, the holders of the Poetry Chair lacked obvious poetic distinction. John Randolph (1776–83) gave lectures on social, intellectual, and linguistic contexts for Homer that were eventually edited by his descendant, Thomas Randolph. These owed much to Lowth's inspiration but Randolph's impact on the scholarly world lay more in divinity, while James Hurdis (1763–1801), the friend of William Cowper (once a candidate for the Poet Laureateship), while he held the chair (1793–1801) found that he became better known as the defender of the University against Gibbon's aspersions than for his own verses.[49]

None of Warton's successors even attempted to eclipse his enduring fame, his efforts to revivify the sonnet form and infuse it with a proto-Romantic nostalgia. His young protégés included Henry Headley (1765–88) and William Lisle Bowles (1762–1850) who, via the monthly magazines and comparable outlets, did their

---

[44] The scale of Lowth's achievement and originality is assessed without exaggeration in Stephen Prickett, 'Poetry and Prophecy: Bishop Lowth and The Hebrew Scriptures in Eighteenth-Century England', in ed. D. Jasper, *Images of Belief in Literature* (Basingstoke, 1984), 81–103. See also the essays in ed. J. Jarick, *Sacred Conjectures: The Context and Legacy of Robert Lowth and Jean Astruc* (New York, 2007).

[45] A point insisted on in *Lectures on the Sacred Poetry*, Lect. 2, I. 48.

[46] In the 'Advertisement' to his *Poems on various subjects* (Oxford, 1781) Hawkins tried hard to distinguish his own work from 'the bulk of modern productions, which are visibly calculated to answer a mere temporary and ungenerous purpose; in the gratification of party rage, popular censoriousness, or personal disgust'.

[47] Hawkins produced two plays—*The Siege of Aleppo* (never performed) and *Alfred* (1770). He also delivered the first academic lectures on Shakespeare, declaring that the playwright's genius, if studied in its proper context, was no less compelling than that of the Greek dramatists. For his classical scholarship see this Chapter, p. 66.

[48] For his international influence see Bodl. Mss. Eng. Lett. C. 573, ff. 39–42; Bodl. Mss. Eng. Lett. C. 574, ff. 32–9, 58–65; J. van den Berg, 'The Leiden Professors of the Schultens family and their contacts with British scholars', *Durham University Journal*, 75 (1982–3), 1–14.

[49] For Randolph's lectures as Professor of Poetry see ed. T. Randolph, *Praelectiones academicae in Homerum* (Oxford and London, 1870). Hurdis matric. at St Mary Hall in 1782; demy of Magdalen College, 1782; probationary fellow, 1788. A. P. Whitaker, *James Hurdis. His life and writings* (Chichester, 1960), 15, 22, 32–41.

OXFORD AND THE ARTS AND HUMANITIES   141

best to perpetuate the influence of the master on an outside world ready to read and respond. The latter's *Fourteen Sonnets, Elegiac and Descriptive, written during a Tour* (Bath, 1789) unquestionably belonged to the so-called 'Warton School' and had an appreciable impact on the poetic formation in the 1790s of the young Coleridge, Southey, and Wordsworth.[50] Southey, at Balliol from 1792 to 1794, was desperate to give vent in his verse to his enthusiasm for the French Revolution,[51] but the University was determined to prevent enthusiastic undergraduates from giving the impression that their elders and betters were somehow sympathetic to 'democracy'. The subject matter of verse became all-important and it was there to hand in the Counter-Revolution, a topic that in the pages of the *Anti-Jacobin*, a periodical to which many young Oxford graduates contributed, brought out again that poetic capacity for disciplined, directed, and amusing satirical invective.[52]

The *Anti-Jacobin* was central to the moulding of British responses to French republicanism in the 1790s but its poetry was, by definition, impolite and though witty, unlearned. It was the informal dimension of Oxford versification in the vernacular inspired by Thomas Warton, with its play on humour and its tendency to the arch and the satirical that primarily commended it to the literate public. Which is not to say that the Anglo-Latin tradition and the revisiting of the poetry of the ancient world (extended to include the Hebrews) through the eyes of successive Professors of Poetry did not continue to arouse interest outside the academy—the level of Latinate literacy retained by a masculine social elite ensured that it would. But considered purely in terms of outreach, its impact was always likely to be restricted.

It would be an exaggeration to say that Oxford literary contributions were excluded from dynamic generic areas of literary expansion, most notably prose fiction, but the fact remains that the University produced no major novelist. The nearest candidate is perhaps Richard Graves (1715–1804), a contemporary of George Whitefield's at Pembroke College (BA 1736, fellow of All Souls, 1736). Graves was frustrated in his academic aspirations and offended his relations by secretly marrying a farmer's daughter and, when it was discovered, he lost his fellowship. As rector of Claverton, Somerset, from 1749 until his death, he was author of *The Spiritual Quixote* (1773), ridiculing the Methodists, and the less well-known *Columella* (1779).[53] Novelists, often female and with a large female readership, operated largely outside the academy. So, too, did linguists.

---

[50] J. B. Bamborough, 'William Lisle Bowles and the riparian muse', in ed. W. W. Robson, *Essays and Poems Presented to Lord David Cecil* (London, 1970), 93–108.

[51] Significantly, Southey did not contribute any of the laudatory verses congratulating Portland on his appointment as Chancellor in 1793 except the facetious 'to a college cat, written soon after the installation at Oxford'. W. A. Speck, *Robert Southey. Entire Man of Letters* (New Haven, CT, 2006), 33–4.

[52] Emily Lorraine de Montluzin, *The Anti-Jacobins, 1798–1800: The Early Contributors to the Anti-Jacobin Review* (Basingstoke, 1987).

[53] Clarence Tracy, *A Portrait of Richard Graves* (Toronto, 1987); J. Butt and G. Carnall, *The Age of Johnson 1740–1789* (Oxford, 1979), 461–2.

142 ENLIGHTENED OXFORD

Given the emerging contemporary interest in the English vernacular, Oxford University could have pioneered the teaching of modern languages. It did not. The intent on the part of the multilingual early Hanoverian state was not lacking. The Crown recognised the importance of equipping likely future members of the royal administration with the language skills required for efficient interaction with their continental counterparts. And the universities, according to this judgement, were the appropriate institutions to undertake this duty, and thereby help in the ongoing business of better aligning talented students (especially needful in Oxford's case) with the interests of the Anglo-Hanoverian polity. Thus when the Professorship of Modern History was inaugurated in 1724 he was placed under an obligation to pay two teachers of modern languages. For a few years after that date about twenty Oxford and Cambridge graduates studied modern History with French and 'High Dutch' with a view to giving them a career path as British diplomats, but the scheme stuttered and eventually halted.[54] It did so for two principal reasons. Firstly, 'the erratic, casual and irrelevant methods by which the British diplomatic service were recruited'; secondly, the absence of enthusiasm among tutors (particularly in Oxford) for either modern language teaching (and the personal benefits thereby accruing to themselves) or the priorities of George I and his Whig ministers.[55]

There was some student interest in the scheme while it lasted: the future traveller and sightseer, John Loveday of Magdalen (1711–89)—who was certainly no Whig—studied the French language diligently with Professor (later Dean) David Gregory's assistant Louis Baillardeau (a Frenchman), undeterred by its not being formally part of the Oxford curriculum.[56] The demand from parents and tutors did not end when the official scheme faltered and folded. Where French was learnt this was achieved through the offices of immigrants (usually of Huguenot extraction) not always employed directly by the University, though first encouraged—though it was not stipulated—to obtain the permission of the Regius Professor of Modern History. Even after the arrival en masse of French *émigrés* escaping the Revolution in the 1790s and mostly desperate for paid employment, the University authorities were still very cautious about offering them work. When one *émigré* applied to teach at Oxford in 1794, the Vice Chancellor rejected him:[57]

---

[54] Samuel Johnson's time at Pembroke coincided with this experimental programme and he certainly read French at Oxford as did (with Italian) his Lichfield compatriot Robert James.

[55] D. B. Horn, *The British diplomatic service 1689–1789* (Oxford, 1961), 179. J. Black, *British diplomats and diplomacy 1688–1800* (Exeter, 2001), 7. Generally J. S. Bromley, 'Britain and Europe in the eighteenth century', *History*, 66 (1981), 394–412, at 402–3. Of course, English schools in the Anglican tradition teaching any modern languages were few and far between.

[56] Sarah Markham, *John Loveday of Caversham 1711–1789. The life and tours of an eighteenth-century onlooker* (Salisbury, 1984), 46.

[57] J. Wills to the duke of Portland, 23 Mar 1794, John Wills Notebook, Jenkyns VI.A (2) Balliol College Archives and Manuscripts. Though Wills shortly afterwards accepted a recommendation by

I represented to him, - that there were already establish'd here two very respectable French Teachers... that it always had been consider'd as improper for us to have, at any one time, in that Situation more than two... under the idea that more than two could not get Bread....

Such language tutors as there were had a steady flow of pupils coming to them for instruction, like William Lee, who in the early 1740s told his father that he was receiving instruction in French from 'a very good operator of that branch of literature in the university'; when John James's son arrived at Queen's College in 1778 he was expected to begin French lessons of three hours weekly.[58] Another alternative for the Oxford undergraduate or graduate was to do as Thomas Beddoes did at Pembroke College in the late 1770s—to teach himself French, German, and Italian by shutting himself in with dictionaries and original works in those tongues.[59]

But the failure of the University to embrace modern language instruction also reflected how far, as Robert Shackleton once noted, '... for centuries past the academic mind appeared to have been closed to French'. It was embarrassingly on display in 1746, when the University Press produced an edition of Corneille's plays and there was a mistake in French on the title page.[60] Other higher-education institutions in the British Isles were much less coy and unconcerned, with Trinity College, Dublin establishing the first chairs in continental languages at any university in Ireland, partly owing to the two-way cultural trade between Ireland and France. Critics of the Oxford curriculum, notably Vicesimus Knox in *Liberal Education* (1781) pleaded for the establishment of a chair in Modern Languages, pointing out the contrast with the Dissenting Academies, where the teaching of foreign languages was central. But not until an endowment announced in the late 1780s was there any prospect of Oxford making formal provision for offering its students instruction in contemporary European languages. This was thanks to the unforeseen generosity of Sir Robert Taylor (1714–88), the successful architect and Sheriff of London 1782-3. In a codicil to his will Taylor left the residue of his large fortune (£180,000) in the first instance to his son and, should he die without issue, to the University of Oxford for buying freehold land and 'erecting a proper edifice thereon, and for establishing a foundation for the

the regional magnate, the Marquess of Buckingham, that the person in question should be a teacher of German in the University. Wills to Bp Cleaver of Chester [the Principal of Brasenose], 31 July 1796, John Wills's Letter book, f. 163. Balliol College Archives and Manuscripts.

[58] W. Lee to Lord Chief Justice Lee, Feb. 7 [1744?], Lee Papers, box 3, folder 2, Beinecke Rare Book and Manuscript Library, Yale University; Brockliss (2), 244.

[59] Kenneth R. Johnston, *Unusual Suspects. Pitt's Reign of Alarm & the Lost Generation of the 1790s* (Oxford, 2013), 96.

[60] R. Shackleton, *British scholarship and French literature: an inaugural lecture* (Oxford, 1981). The paradox is that some of the University's libraries contained strong French collections, the Codrington, for instance, at All Souls. J. S. G. Simmons, *French Publications Acquired by the Codrington Library, 1762–1800* (Oxford, 1978).

144   ENLIGHTENED OXFORD

teaching and improving the European languages'. After various legal complications and the death of Sir Robert's son, Michael Angelo, in 1834, the University finally inherited the sum of £65,000.[61]

ii) History writing: modern and ancient

...if ever an English Writer should arise, who has the Courage equally to displease the Zealots of both Parties, such a one will bid fairest for that Character of Truth, which constitutes the Soul of History.
Reflections on Ancient and Modern History (Oxford, 1746), 29.

'Modern' History in the eighteenth century was written 'by literati, clerics, antiquarians, journalists, and political propagandists, but rarely by full-time professional historians'.[62] It had yet to become a specialised academic discipline and attempts within Oxford to further that process were slow.[63] The historian was not primarily a researcher, though he or she could be and there was plentiful work in archives in the eighteenth century;[64] he or she was a polemicist and a partisan when it came to the recent past, the custodian of a particular way, in Oxford a largely High Church way, of viewing the world, a teleological one. There was invariably a didactic dimension to history writing. For, as Thomas Hearne observed in his *Ductor historicus; or, A short system of Universal History, and an Introduction to the study of it* (London, 1714), reading history should encourage affection for one's ancestors and one's country, offer examples of virtuous conduct, and reveal the manifestation of God in the affairs of mankind. In a university context, where young men were being prepared for lives of public and sacred service, such advantages could not be readily discarded.[65] But Hearne's credibility as an unrepentant Jacobite was unavoidably compromised and Oxford efforts in writing world history from the end of the ancient world

---

[61] http://blogs.bodleian.ox.ac.uk/taylorian/2014/11/13/history-of-the-taylor-institution-library-and-its-collections/; Colvin, *Dictionary of British Architects*, 963.

[62] L. Okie, *Augustan Historical Writing: Histories of England in the English Enlightenment* (Lanham, NY, and London, 1991), 9.

[63] For the variety of forms employable for representing the past see Noelle Gallagher, *Historical Literatures. Writing about the Past in England, 1660–1740* (Manchester, 2012).

[64] As Jeremy Black has pointed out, archival history preceded the professionalisation of historical studies in the nineteenth century. *Charting the past*, 255. It was commonly linked to a commitment to accuracy and impartiality. Cf. A. Pagden, 'Eighteenth-Century anthropology and the "History of Mankind"', in ed. D. R. Kelly, *History and the disciplines: the reclassification of knowledge in early modern Europe* (Rochester, NY, 1997), 223–33.

[65] J. W. Johnson, *The Formation of English Neo-Classical Thought* (Princeton, NJ, 1967), 35. Cf. Hearne with R. Rapin, *Instructions for History* (London, 1680), 28, on the value of history to future leaders for the 'Good of Civil Society', and Bolingbroke's dictum that the purpose of historical research was not meticulous erudition, but prudential instruction.

OXFORD AND THE ARTS AND HUMANITIES   145

were limited. Edward Gibbon, though a graduate of Magdalen, was hardly representative of University opinion with his sneers and his scepticism about the rise of Christianity, such that he provoked several fellow Oxford graduates to answer him, with limited though by no means negligible success.[66] Gibbon's critics were writing, as earlier Oxonian authors had done, primarily to satisfy and sometimes stretch the minds of a graduate elite, clerics naturally a prominent sector, though it was impossible for them not to register that broader readership for history that existed. Gibbon's *Decline and Fall* may have been the greatest ecclesiastical history produced in England since the Reformation but however undeniable his merits as a historian, Gibbon's calling into question a providential reading of the rise of Christianity and his controversial presentation of the formation of theological orthodoxy by the early Church did not go unchallenged.[67]

Readers, new readers especially, were vulnerable and needed guidance. It was understandable that, in a polemical age, Oxford authors might largely satisfy public expectations by appealing to Tory predispositions, for that way sales as well as recognition might lie. And the inspirational figure in the field was an earlier Chancellor of the University, Edward Hyde, 1st Earl of Clarendon, via a posthumous publication overseen by his son Lord Rochester that 'transformed contemporaries' understanding of the Civil War and served as the foundation stone of Hume's and every other history'.[68] Despite a pro-Tory preface to the first volume written by Dean Aldrich designed to draw out the text's relevance to the politics of 1702,[69] Clarendon's *History of the Rebellion and Civil Wars in England* suggested a line of historical writing that might have given rise to comparable exercises examining the English past: its editors appropriated the prestige of the historian

---

[66] David Womersley, *Gibbon and the "Watchmen of the Holy City". The Historian and his reputation 1776–1815* (Oxford, 2002); Pocock, *Barbarism and Religion*. Vol. 5. *Religion: The First Triumph,* 313–72. Gibbon is discussed in Chapter 10.

[67] Tim Stuart-Buttle, 'Gibbon and Enlightenment History in Britain', in eds. Karen O'Brien and Brian Young, *The Cambridge Companion to Edward Gibbon* (Cambridge, 2018), 110–27, at 119, 124; Pocock, *Barbarism and Religion,* Vol. 1, 151, 307. The movement of 'philosophical history' against the Church's theological interpretation of history is sketched out in H. R. Trevor-Roper, *History and the Enlightenment* (New Haven, CT, 2010), 1–16.

[68] Nicholas Phillipson, *Hume* (London, 1989), 78. Cf. John Kenyon, who could say no more than that Clarendon's work is an amalgam of history and propaganda comprising 'personal reminiscence…, accepted chronological fact, and autobiography'. *The History Men: The Historical Profession in England since the Renaissance* (2nd edn., London, 1983), 31.

[69] Rochester (who had left office in 1703) wrote a more incendiary preface to vol. 3 in 1704 to set out the High Church cause, draw analogies between the Civil War and the present, and offer an appeal to the Queen to remind her of the danger, as he saw it, that the Church and the "ancient constitution" faced from Dissent. G. V. Bennett, *White Kennett, 1660–1728, Bishop of Peterborough. A study in the political and ecclesiastical history of the early eighteenth century* (London, 1957), 87–8; M. Neufeld, *The Civil Wars after 1660: Public remembering in late Stuart England* (Woodbridge, 2013), 158–9. His promptings annoyed her, as did Aldrich's preface. Philip Hicks, *Neoclassical History and English culture. From Clarendon to Hume* (Basingstoke, 1996), 71, 73; Edward Gregg, *Queen Anne* (London, 1980), 168.

146　ENLIGHTENED OXFORD

Thucydides and the statesman Cicero as exemplars and equals,[70] while the *History* itself offered a series of Tacitean studies of public men grounded in primary documentation that might have inspired other pens in subsequent productions to develop more sophisticated general concepts of historical analysis. No one within the University, however, took up the challenge to which Hume and Robertson would eventually rise in Scotland.[71]

Instead, when the Oxford Whig cleric, White Kennett, anonymously supplied the seventeenth-century section and preface to the compilation *The Compleat History of England* (3 vols., 1706), he limited himself to contesting quietly some of Clarendon's narrative and identified Charles II and James II as popishly inclined architects of arbitrary government who were providentially confounded by the Glorious Revolution.[72] His authorship quickly discerned, Kennett's thorough work, based on a mass of printed primary sources, won him much prestige (outside Oxford certainly), confirmed his position as a rising pro-Revolution divine, and was popular with the reading public, taking the book into four reprints by 1715.[73] He restated the general idea that knowledge of history is essential to the education of the next generation of politicians.[74] Of course, the content of that history and the party sympathies of the author would give texts a suitably didactic steer, a point on which Kennett had no intention of dwelling any more than necessary. Meanwhile, Clarendon's standing as the greatest English historian was successfully protected by Tories and anti-Walpole 'Patriot' Whigs for most of the century, with Christ Church as the main keeper of the flame.[75] John Oldmixon's bold attempt in his *History of England during the Reigns of the Royal House of Stuart* (1729) to impugn the college's editorial work and Clarendon's royalist bias

---

[70] The title page bore the Greek characters Thucydides had used to describe his own work, 'a possession for all time'. Hicks, *Neoclassical History*, 69, 79. See also the discussion in Karen O'Brien, 'The History Market in Eighteenth-Century England', in ed. Isabel Rivers, *Books and their Readers in Eighteenth-Century England: New Essays* (London, 2001), 105–34 at 110–11. Blackstone proposed a cheap edition of Cicero's works to Oxford University Press Delegates in the late 1750s but it was frustrated by their fussy insistence on collating all the manuscripts of Cicero in the major libraries of England. Prest, *Blackstone*, 170–1.

[71] B. M. G. Wormald, *Clarendon: Politics, Historiography and Religion 1640–1660* (Cambridge, 1951). William Warburton was dumbfounded: 'The world is got into its second childhood', he opined, because Robertson's History [of Scotland] 'good but not better'—had gone into three editions 'whereas Clarendon's remains unsold'. Harry Ransom Center, Uncatl. MS. Letters between the Revd. Mr Warburton and Dr Taylor (later Sir Robert Taylor) from the Year MDCCXXVIII, no. 54, bis. 16 Sept. 1759.

[72] Okie, *Augustan Historical Writing*, 27–32.

[73] Bennett, *White Kennett*, 168–73; Gallagher, *Historical Literatures*, 167–75. Kennett (by then Bishop of Peterborough) revised and added to a new edition in 1719.

[74] Hicks, *Neoclassical History*, 112–14; O'Brien, 'The History Market', 111–12.

[75] Interest in his scholarship and sources developed as memories of the Civil War receded. Thus Thomas Monkhouse (*c.*1726–93, DD Queens 1780), edited the three volumes of *State Papers collected by Edward, Earl of Clarendon...from which his History of the Great Rebellion was composed* (Oxford, 1767–86).

OXFORD AND THE ARTS AND HUMANITIES   147

was counter-attacked with every encouragement from Lord Cornbury, MP for the University, the 1st Earl's great-grandson.[76]

There was an appetite for a new historian on the Clarendon model to emerge: Atterbury was expected to write a study of his own times to inspire Opposition Tories after he was exiled to France in 1723, but nothing was forthcoming or found after his death.[77] As custodian of Clarendon's papers, including the manuscript history of the years 1660–7, when he was Lord Chancellor (that was eventually published as the *The Life of Edward Earl of Clarendon* in 1759), Cornbury was seen by Bolingbroke as the obvious choice based on both status and abilities to write the history of England since the Reformation that he would not compose himself. Cornbury never did so.[78] The shadow cast by Clarendon was so pronounced that it acted as a disincentive to other literate politicians connected to Oxford to emulate him by offering critical accounts of the events they had lived through and may have helped to shape. The Civil War was sufficiently remote by the 1720s for a Tory consensus to have emerged over time that was highlighted annually by the 30 January sermons: there was none such on the Revolution of 1688–9. And, anyway, for Oxford alumni to write about their own times (notwithstanding the public appetite for such accounts) was not encouraged by the University authorities, concerned that historical memoirs offered potential for exploitation by Oxford's enemies. Writings of this nature were best done by social and academic outsiders. Otherwise, sacred, classical, and medieval history were safer options.

If Oxford was short of its own post-Clarendon historians in the first half of the century and lived too long on the cultural prestige of the *Great Rebellion*, what it could offer to Tory penmen was an exceptional distribution and subscription network for historical projects that would help sustain the morale and identity of the politically excluded.[79] It was left to an ordained Nonjuror (who lived as a layman after 1714), Thomas Carte (bapt. 1686–1754, BA Brasenose 1704), to undertake a major study of recent British history, grounding it in original, unpublished sources, particularly those relating to the dukes of Ormond, head

---

[76] Principally in John Burton, *The Genuineness of Ld. Clarendon's History of the Rebellion Printed at Oxford Vindicated. Mr Oldmixon's Slander Confuted* (Oxford, 1744). Preachers also tried, for instance Henry Felton of St Edmund Hall in St Mary's Church, on 31 Jan. 1732, rescuing the *History* 'from the Abusive Invectives raised against it by Oldmixon and others'. ed. C. L. S. Linnell, *The Diaries of Thomas Wilson, DD, 1731–37 and 1750: son of Bishop Wilson of Sodor & Man* (London, 1964), 48. Oldmixon, who acclaimed Locke as the greatest philosopher of the age, has been called 'a brave and imprudent man, not addicted to trimming his sails'.

[77] His former colleague at Christ Church, Canon Stratford, was one of those who never believed the rumours that such an enterprise was in progress—or likely to be. HMC, *Portland MSS*, VII. 465–6.

[78] P. Hicks, 'Bolingbroke, Clarendon, and the role of Classical historian', *ECS*, 20 (1987), 445–71, esp. 451–4; Hicks, *Neoclassical history*, 134–9.

[79] Pat Rogers, 'Book subscriptions among the Augustans', *TLS*, 15 Dec. 1972, 1539–40. The point has been made more recently by Richard Sharp, see Chapter 12, pp. 80–1.

148 ENLIGHTENED OXFORD

of the house of Butler.[80] Carte received the full cooperation of Oxford's Chancellor, Lord Arran (he had published a well-received biography of Arran's grandfather in 1736 with *An History of the Life of James Duke of Ormonde*),[81] several colleges (and the Durham cathedral chapter), and many eminent University members, such as the 4th Duke of Beaufort and John, 5th Earl of Orrery (1707–62) who were anxious to see an authoritative account given of the years before and after the Revolution from an intelligent, high Tory perspective. The end product was much more than that, otherwise it would not have attracted interest in some Whig quarters.[82] Carte gained access to state archives through sympathetic contacts (including the Exchequer via the 3rd Duke of Rutland), while New College, Magdalen, Trinity, Brasenose, and Lincoln were among the five houses making annual donations to fund Carte's research in the early 1740s.[83]

Despite some scepticism among Delegates of Oxford University, they eventually signed up to his plans and Convocation voted him £20 towards his costs in November 1744. The doubters were still vocal: 'There was a long speech made by a Senior Fellow of a College, taking the Proposal to pieces, and complaining that no Specimen of ye Work had been laid before the University'.[84] This prestigious project eventually appeared, printed in London for the author, as (the extremely substantial but still incomplete) *A General History of England* (4 vols., 1747–55). Carte was insistent as to how much his imagination had complemented his research in an effort to produce authentic, readable history: he claimed he had 'judged and wrote of ancient ages, as if I lived only in them'.[85] Some in Oxford were predictably delighted: the Nonjuror Richard Rawlinson opining that Carte's *History* should be honoured by being the first book to be placed in the new Radcliffe Library.[86] Overall, the critical contemporary sense was that, notwithstanding its impressive documentary foundations, Carte's committed Jacobite partisanship had compromised any chance he had of equalling the French writers of classical historiography.[87] He reverted to Filmerian arguments that monarchy

---

[80] Stuart Handley, 'Carte, Thomas (bap. 1686, d. 1754)', *ODNB*, online edn, May 2015 [www.oxforddnb.com/view/article/4780, accessed 10 Nov. 2017]

[81] Thomas Arnold, *Sketches from the Carte papers* (Dublin, 1888), 4.

[82] Details in Okie, *Augustan Historical Writing*, 122, 126, 135.

[83] Bodl., MS Carte 175, f. 105; Okie, *Augustan Historical Writing*, 140.

[84] Thomas Hunt to Richard Rawlinson, 12 Nov. 1744, Bodl., MSS Rawl. letters 96 f. 165.

[85] *General History*, I. 12.

[86] His rationale was that the Radcliffe building was 'designed for the most modern books in all faculties and languages, not in the Bodleian Library'. To Thomas Rawlins, Apr. 1749. Bodl. MS Ballard 2, f. 185.

[87] Thus Carte used the analogy of the Norman Conquest to be scathing about another 'foreign prince', William III, whose legacy was '...the insupportable load of debts and taxes, which have ruined most of the ancient families of our gentry' along with 'the general corruption, with an infinity of other evils, which they have occasioned'. *General History*, I. 450–2. Nevertheless, one critic, Samuel Squire (a court Whig, chaplain to the duke of Newcastle), complained that Carte's undeniable devotion to scholarship was compromised by too many 'fine-spun speculations *a la française* '. *Remarks upon Mr Carte's Specimen of his General History of England*:... (London, 1748), 11. Carte's Jacobite connections and his plans as a Tory political organiser are considered in Linda Colley, *In defiance of oligarchy.*

OXFORD AND THE ARTS AND HUMANITIES   149

was divinely instituted, viewed the modern political order as blatantly corrupt, and condemned Charles I's execution as 'not to be paralleled in all the histories of nations since the creation'.[88] Carte died lamenting that his work was incomplete: he could not take his *History* beyond 1654 and he had no English successors in the second half of the century: the polemical impulse that had driven scholars of his and earlier generations had waned and Oxford threw up no 'philosophical historians' of its own to move away from an understanding of the past where exact scholarship was grounded primarily in erudition, documentation, and a respect for the integrity and superiority of an explicitly Christian culture.[89] And, after Archbishop Wake's death in 1737, the bench of largely Whig bishops had no need to use history as the basis on which to justify their own places and policies.

Modern history was not an element in the Oxford curriculum, whereas in the Scottish universities, history had long been part of the undergraduate experience, and where some of the country's most important historians, such as William Robertson and John Millar, held university posts.[90] Yet Oxford had its own Regius Professorship in the subject after 1724. This innovation was 'a milestone in the association of historical writing with the culture of academe...'[91] though, after its first two appointees, David Gregory (1724–36) and William Holmes (1736–42),[92] the several Professors did little directly to build up the scholarly standing of their subject, and rather treated the post as a sinecure, a means of funding their work in other fields.[93] And this was despite Gregory's early indictment of the Oxford curriculum, one that said more about his Whig politics than his academic finesse:[94]

The Tory Party, 1714–1760 (Cambridge, 1982), 32, 138–40. For Carte's links to the court in exile at Rome in the 1740s see J.C.D. Clark, *English society 1688–1832. Ideology, social structure and political practice during the ancien regime* (1st edn., Cambridge, 1985), 146.

[88] The summary of Carte's work in Hicks, *Neoclassical History*, 159–69, is unsympathetic and presents his oeuvre as 'crashing into the dustbin of history' (168) as public notice turned to David Hume. cf. R. J. Smith, *The Gothic Bequest: Medieval Institutions in British Thought, 1688*–1863 (Cambridge, 1987), 43. Carte's judgements are often acute and his Tory alignment is, in part, a corrective to the prevailing Whig narrative articulated elsewhere by James Tyrrell and Echard.

[89] Bolingbroke's very qualified endorsement of history writing in the *érudit* tradition was normative by mid-century: 'These men court fame as well as their betters by such means as God has given them to acquire it. They deserve encouragement while they continue to compile and neither affect wit nor presume to reason'. 'Study of History', in ed. D. Mallet, *The works of Henry St. John, Lord Viscount Bolingbroke* (5 vols., London, 1754), II. 261.

[90] For Millar see Mark Salber Phillips, *Society and Sentiment. Genres of Historical Writing in Britain, 1740–1820* (Princeton, NJ, 2000), 184–9; O'Brien, 'The History Market', 108.

[91] Daniel Woolf, 'Historical Writing in Britain from the Late Middle Ages to the Eve of Enlightenment,' in eds. J. Rabasa, M. Sato, E. Tortarolo, and D. Woolf, *The Oxford History of Historical Writing. Vol. 3: 1400–1800* (Oxford, 2012), 473–96, at 488. Its political origins are discussed in Chapter 8, pp. 23–4.

[92] Gregory was Dean of Christ Church, 1756–67; Holmes was President of St John's, 1728–48, V-C., 1732–5.

[93] There was a Modern Languages dimension to the post discussed in this Chapter, pp. 23–25.

[94] TNA (PRO) SP 36/6, f. 227, quoted in Ward, *Georgian Oxford*, 132. See Sir C. Firth, 'Modern history in Oxford, 1724–1841', *EHR*, 32 (1917), 3–12.

150   ENLIGHTENED OXFORD

the methods of education in our universities have been in some measure defective, since we are obliged to adhere so much to the rules laid down by our
forefathers...the old scholastic learning has been for some time despised, but
not altogether exploded, because nothing else has been substituted in its place.

In fact, innovation was going on, seen, for instance, in Joseph Spence, the third
holder of the Modern History chair. He was a disciplined, ground-breaking
anecdotist (particularly of Pope, his mentor), who collected and verified (noting
date and informant) information on living people that in time supported a new
kind of biography.[95] Arguably, the Oxford authorities were here supporting a
scholar whose efforts were genuinely important for the history of literature.
Nevertheless, when Spence died in 1768 after having neither resided habitually
in Oxford nor lectured there for the duration,[96] the Heads of Houses were stirred
to produce a memorandum submitted to George III for reform of the Oxford
Professorship and a much stricter remit for its holder: a minimum of fifty lectures
annually and a full term's residence.[97] They were resisted for over two years by
John Vivian, Fellow of Balliol, Regius Professor Designate, but became fully
operative when Thomas Nowell was appointed in 1773. He lectured regularly
but, in terms of publication, his record was scanty.[98]

A move to make office holders more accountable was no guarantee in itself of
increasing their creative scholarship. David Gregory and his successors failed
to engage with the contested history of seventeenth-century England or
challenge the Clarendonian orthodoxy that remained so firmly associated with
Oxford University. Instead, they ignored it, on the questionable basis that the
Revolution of 1688–9 and the change of dynasty in 1714 had made it historically
irrelevant to the educative requirements of later times.[99] And they also declined to

[95] Joseph Spence, *Observations, anecdotes, and characters of books and men collected from
conversation*, ed. James M. Osborn (2 vols., Oxford, 1966).

[96] Spence lived in London from 1741 to 1748 preparing an elaborate, original study—*Polymetis*—of
the relation between Roman art and poetry that brought a new level of evaluation of human beauty that
showed 'le patient travail necessaire à construire la signification de l'oeuvre d'art'. Austin Wright,
Joseph Spence. A critical biography (Chicago, IL,1950), 39, 69, 159. The quotation is from Pascal
Griener, 'Epiphanie et signification. Une révolution dans la contemplation de la sculpture au siècles
des Lumières', in ed. Michel Porret, *Sens des Lumières* (Geneva, 2008), 99–126, at 108.

[97] BL, Add. MS 38334, ff. 149–50.

[98] Full details in ed. Fairer, *Correspondence of Thomas Warton*, Appendix C: 'Thomas Warton, John
Vivian, and the Regius Professorship of History, 1768–1771', 665–7; Lord Lichfield to Warton, 17 Feb.
[1771], BL Add. MS 42561, f. 1. The Regius from 1801 to 1837, Henry Beeke (1751–1837), fellow of
Oriel, 1775; v. of St Mary's, 1782–90, Dean of Bristol 1814 -37, was thorough in discharging his duties,
but he was less of a historian than a financial analyst. His *Observations on the produce of the income tax,
and on its proportion to the whole income of Great Britain* (London, 1799) was held in high regard. He
may have been the first person to teach political economy at Oxford. R. D. Sheldon, 'Beeke, Henry
(1751-1837), writer on taxation and finance', ODNB, online edn., 2004.

[99] Norman Sykes, *Edmund Gibson, Bishop of London, 1669–1748: a study in politics and religion in
the eighteenth century* (Oxford, 1926), 95–105; L. S. Sutherland, 'The curriculum', in HUO V, 469–92,
at 474.

OXFORD AND THE ARTS AND HUMANITIES   151

produce an alternative establishment history: Gregory and Holmes considered that the polemical invective that history writing was likely to encourage made its institutional value negligible, and they received no censure from the Whig establishment for either their failure to produce or their discouragement of others' productions.[100] From the Pelhamite angle, the less Oxford said about the past, the less damage was likely to be done to state stability in the present. Indeed, it was with the present that Gregory concerned himself, writing regularly to the Duke of Newcastle as part of his promotion of the Whig cause.[101] The universities, particularly Oxford, may have played a more direct role in generating historical scholarship and narrative in the reigns of Anne and George I than a century earlier but, despite the Regius Chair, the creative impulse could not be sustained.[102]

Ancient history was a safer academic option. The influence of classical historians in terms of both subject matter and style had profoundly influenced Clarendon in his *History*, and he and his readers alike knew that history's standing as the noblest of prose genres was principally owing to the authors of the ancient world.[103] The well-established Camden Chair in History had long been dedicated almost exclusively to the study of ancient history,[104] giving that subject slightly more locomotion, and most Camden Professors used the statutory method of lecturing on a text as the basis for wider disquisitions on the peoples and institutions of the ancient world.[105] A conspicuous example was Henry Dodwell, from Trinity College, Dublin, in post from 1688 until his ejection as a Nonjuror in 1691. He was an outstanding scholar in search of a polite audience who went on making valuable contributions to ancient chronology even after he was legally required to resign as professor.[106] Dodwell's lustre was immense and none of his successors had a comparable reputation as an ancient historian until William Scott, professor from 1773 to 1785. Scott was the first Camden Professor to lecture in English and his scholarship impressed, among others, even the formidable Cantabrigian Whig critic, Samuel Parr. Scott's refusing of his consent to

---

[100] Holmes took the post but admitted his own unsuitability, insisting that 'there were few less capable' of making a success of it than himself. Sykes, *Gibson*, 94–107; Costin, *St John's College*, 184.

[101] He also wrote much Latin verse. Money, 'The Latin poetry of English gentlemen', in eds. Houghton and Manuwald, *Neo-Latin Poetry*, 125–41, at 136.

[102] Cf. Woolf ', 'Historical writing in Britain', 487.

[103] Hicks, 'Bolingbroke, Clarendon, and the role of Classical historian', *passim*.

[104] As David C. Douglas wrote, 'How far the author of *Britannia* [the great antiquary, William Camden] foresaw this development when he made his benefaction is uncertain,...', *English scholars 1660–1730* (London, 1939), 252.

[105] H. S. Jones, 'The foundation and history of the Camden chair', *Oxoniensia*, viii–ix (1943–4), 170–92.

[106] J.-L. Quantin, 'Anglican scholarship gone mad? Henry Dodwell (1641–1711) and Christian antiquity', in eds. J.-L. Quantin and C. R. Ligota, *History of scholarship. A selection of papers from the seminar on the history of scholarship held annually at the Warburg Institute* (Oxford, 2006), 305–56; C. D. A. Leighton, 'Ancienneté among the Non-Jurors: A study of Henry Dodwell', *History of European Ideas*, 31 (2005), 1–16. Cf. the rather reductionist view of underlying values in A. Ward, 'The Tory view of Roman history', *Studies in English Literature 1500–1900*, 4 (1964), 413–56.

152 ENLIGHTENED OXFORD

publication unfortunately restricted the audience for his elegant and erudite assessments.[107] It was nevertheless indicative of a growing interest in the pedagogic and didactic uses of ancient history at Oxford for students, one pioneered by Dean William Markham at Christ Church (1767–76), who was ever conscious of the need to apprise the next generation of political leaders coming to the House of its uses.[108] Scott's successor, Thomas Warton, promised much as a Greek *littérateur*, yet delivered little. In his inaugural Latin oration he made it clear that he planned to ignore the statutes and in future lectures select one of the ancient historians and discuss his virtues. The problem was that there were no future lectures: Warton was much too absorbed in his new duties as Poet Laureate (1785–90), and he had already discoursed copiously upon the subject as Professor of Poetry.[109] It is a reminder that if post-holders were primarily focused on securing a niche in the public culture rather than putting their prescribed institutional duties first, then efforts to reinforce university teaching risked being a casualty.

iii) History writing: medieval and ecclesiastical

It has long been recognised that Oxford University's contribution to English medieval studies down to the mid-century was profound.[110] Time-worn claims that scholarship suffered because of either the scholastic residue and party feuding, commonly originating in over-reliance on bilious judges such as Hearne and Amhurst. What has been stated less often is the degree to which Oxford medievalists placed their passion for their subject before their political differences or, where politics came into play, stimulated scholarly resourcefulness—often with a polemical edge. Their impact beyond Oxford owed much to their capacity for cooperation among themselves within the University and a range of scholars beyond it. Arguably, this was part of a pan-British and European shift towards moderation and 'trimming' at the close of the seventeenth century.[111] This qualified Whiggish tone was also directly caused by the fallout from the Revolution of 1688-9 and the Nonjuring schism though the impact of the latter should not be exaggerated; if it deprived many of those High Church men of official positions who were most favourable to historical learning and had received

---

[107] W. E. Surtees, *A sketch of the lives of Lords Stowell and Eldon* (London, 1846); L. S. Sutherland, 'The curriculum', 474; Clarke, 'Classical studies', 516.

[108] Markham told young Gilbert Elliot (later the 1st Lord Minto) in 1768 that 'only classical and historical knowledge could make able statesmen'. *Life and Letters of Sir Gilbert Elliot* (3 vols., London, 1874), I. 38.

[109] See this Chapter, p. 16.   [110] Douglas, *English Scholars, passim.*

[111] With its origins in this same trend, Ryan K. Frace thus finds clerical cooperation across the religious spectrum in Anglo-Scottish charitable impulses in the 1700s. 'Religious toleration in the wake of Revolution: Scotland on the eve of Enlightenment (1688–1710s)', *History* 93 (2008), 354–75, at 369.

OXFORD AND THE ARTS AND HUMANITIES 153

Archbishop Sancroft's patronage at Lambeth in the 1680s, it allowed them more time for their studies and informal acceptance on a level of scholarly equality in Oxford. Their successors as senior members at the University in the 1690s looked to the new power-brokers in Church and state to advance themselves and, inasmuch as they were partisan, they were (with the conspicuous exception of Thomas Hearne) court Whigs.

Thomas Tanner (1674–1735) is a classic instance of this tendency.[112] He developed his undergraduate interest, as others did, at the Queen's College, where he became the close friend of Edmund Gibson, also of Queen's, Librarian and Chaplain to Archbishop Tenison. Tanner was a Whig and did well out of the post-1714 dispensation, only returning to Oxford in 1724 as a Canon of Christ Church [Bishop of St Asaph, 1732].[113] In 1695 he made his name with *Notitia Monastica*, that served as a history of all the English and Welsh religious houses with an authoritative bibliography.[114] His industry was immense and he never sacrificed the goodwill of men of all parties. He was heavily involved in all kinds of learned enterprises. With Gibson, he contributed to the latter's edition of Camden's *Britannia* and, again, to the editing of Sir Henry Spelman's English Works. His life's *chef-d'œuvre*, which he would not compromise by excessive haste, a full, updated edition of the great Tudor antiquary, John Leland's *De Scriptoribus*, also appeared only after his demise in 1748 as the authoritative and prestigious, *Bibliotheca Britannico-Hibernica*, an account of all authors flourishing at the end of Tudor England.

Tanner worked in a slightly later period than the majority of Oxford medievalists, whose devotion to Old English studies was well-established by the Glorious Revolution and such that it eclipsed Cambridge as their academic home after the 1690s, with the Queen's College as its particular centre.[115] Edward Thwaites (d. 1711), who came to the college in 1689 and was appointed Anglo-Saxon 'preceptor' ten years later, established his international reputation with the publication of the work of Abbot Aelfric of Eynsham in 1698, and probably had a hand in the edition of King Alfred's *Boethius* ascribed to his student, Christopher Rawlinson, the next year. It was thanks to him that a revised edition of William Somner's great Saxon Lexicon (originally dating from 1659) finally appeared in 1701, one that made Thwaites's hopes of encouraging a School of English

---

[112] Richard Sharp, 'Tanner, Thomas (1674–1735)', *ODNB*, online edn., May 2006 [http://www.oxforddnb.com/view/article/26963]; Douglas, *English Scholars*, 158–64.

[113] John Le Neve, *Fasti ecclesiae Anglicanae 1541-1857*, vol. 8. *Bristol, Gloucester, Oxford and Peterborough dioceses*, ed. Joyce M. Horn, (London, 1996), 93. Having been appointed chaplain and then fellow of All Souls (1695-6), he quit permanent residence in Oxford in 1697 after being named chaplain to the Bishop of Norwich. He later ruefully observed that All Souls had 'furnish'd' the nation with 'all sorts of Freethinking', and hoped that people would appreciate that we 'are not all quite corrupted'. To Charlett, 16 Sept. 1717, Bodl Ballard MS 4, f. 134r.

[114] Tanner was always adding to it so that the 1744 edition was almost fifty per cent longer.

[115] Hearne, IX. 342. Cf. ibid., VII. 327.

154 ENLIGHTENED OXFORD

Language and Literature at the University more realisable.[116] Other aspects of Saxon learning were illuminated by two future Whig prelates: William Nicolson and Edmund Gibson. Nicolson's philological skills were early shown in his making collections for a Saxon grammar, and he took a key role in preparatory studies for a new edition of Anglo-Saxon civil and ecclesiastical laws originally compiled after the Conquest that finally appeared in 1721 with David Wilkins, the Prussian exile (and future librarian at Lambeth Palace), as its titular editor.[117]

The future clerical careerist, Edmund Gibson (1669-1749), was another luminary among the scholars dubbed the 'Septentrionalists' centred on the Queen's College and dedicated to promoting the study of the old northern languages, especially Old English and what would now be called Old Norse. He produced an edition of the Anglo-Saxon Chronicle that treated it, somewhat misleadingly, as a single homogeneous authority but nevertheless was a landmark in early English historical scholarship.[118] And on the fringes of this circle was the remarkable figure of George Hickes (1642-1715), a former fellow of Lincoln College but a leading Nonjuror after the Revolution. Hickes (titular Bishop of Thetford since 1694) could hold no formal position in Queen Anne's Oxford, but his devotion to Anglo-Saxon scholarship bore fruit with his acclaimed *Thesaurus* (1703-5).[119] When a learned German was shown a copy he exclaimed: 'By God, France never produced anything more sumptuous or more magnificent than this, even under the patronage of Louis the Great [XIV].'[120]

Though much Anglo-Saxon research also developed in London (because of Humphrey Wanley, later librarian to the 1st and 2nd earls of Oxford)[121] the part played by Oxford scholars in recovering the Anglo-Saxon past while remaining alert to contexts in its monuments, coins, and other dimensions of its material culture as well as manuscripts was appreciable. Little wonder, then, that, as one

---

[116] Douglas calls Thwaites 'without doubt, one of the most inspiring teachers which Oxford has ever produced'. *English Scholars*, 67. He was deeply loved by his many students and he continued teaching despite having his leg amputated. Nichols, *Literary anecdotes of the eighteenth century* (8 vols., London, 1817–58), IV. 141–9. For his 'nest of Saxonists', see *GM* 156 (1834), II. 262.

[117] Nicolson also wrote a long Latin preface. Douglas, *English Scholars*, 69.

[118] Sykes, *Gibson*, 10. He also produced a revised edition of Camden's *Britannia* in 1695 dedicated to Sir John (later Lord) Somers, the pre-eminent Whig lawyer and Junto member, thereby underlining how he intended to secure his advancement. Mayhew, *Enlightenment Geography*, 101;Mayhew, 'Edmund Gibson's editions of <u>Britannia</u>: dynastic chorography and the politics of precedent, 1695–1722', *Historical Research*, 73 (2000), 239–61. Gibson later acclaimed George I as a living embodiment of shared Saxon origins.

[119] ed. Richard L. Harris, *A chorus of grammars: the correspondence of George Hickes and his collaborators on the "Thesaurus linguarum septentrionalium"* (Toronto, 1992), 3–125.

[120] Quoted in Philip, 'Oxford and Scholarly publication', 132.

[121] Wanley, who matriculated at St Edmund Hall in 1695, was patronised by Arthur Charlett and made an Assistant in the Bodleian Library under Thomas Hyde. However, he never graduated because of his difficulties in mastering the Logic element in the curriculum. Nichols, *Literary anecdotes*, I. 530–42. He failed in an application to become Bodley's Librarian in 1698. Douglas, *English Scholars*, 102. Generally, see Stanley Gillam, 'Humfrey Wanley and Arthur Charlett', *BLR* 16 (1999), 411–29.

OXFORD AND THE ARTS AND HUMANITIES   155

well-wisher observed in 1714 , '...under the kind and generous Influence and Encouragement... of the University of Oxford... the way to the obtaining of this Language is now made easy'.[122] Without these initiatives, the careers of other eighteenth-century Saxon scholars such as Elizabeth Elstob, the 'Saxon nymph', as the Leeds antiquarian, Ralph Thoresby dubbed her,[123] would have been nigh impossible. The dissemination of Oxford learning would also have been hobbled without the technological capacity of the revitalised University Press to express the richness of the northern languages and their literature. Nevertheless, changing intellectual fashions and public taste for the non-philological aspects of the Saxon past ensured that this distinctive dimension of Oxford learning had declined by mid-century.[124]

The Nonjuror and bibliophile, Richard Rawlinson (1681–1755), bequeathed money to the University to establish a chair in Anglo-Saxon studies, but it was not until 1795 that an appointment was made, both a reflection of the decline in the subject's fashionability and the restrictions imposed in the terms of the endowment.[125] The fascination with northern languages remained, but had become tied in with relish for the culturally exotic. There was a market here for speculative antiquarianism rather than exact scholarship, one that the Radcliffe Librarian, Francis Wise (1695–1767), rose to fill without much distinction in his *Some Enquiries concerning the First Inhabitants, Languages, Religion, Learning, and Letters of Europe* (Oxford, 1758) and *The History and Chronology of the Fabulous Ages Considered* (Oxford, 1764).[126]

Oxford Saxonists were politically various; those who worked on ecclesiastical history were often provoked or inspired by considerations of party, especially in the two decades between 1697 and 1717, when the Convocation dispute was raging. To some defenders of the High Church position, it seemed at times as if the Church of England might drift irretrievably into error without the interposition of scholarship. There was, as might have been expected, a default tendency to endorse Nonjuring arguments such as those to be found in Jeremy Collier's *Ecclesiastical History* (2 vols., 1708, 1714) in favour of the Church's divine mandate and its independency from temporal authority of the sort acceptable to most post-Revolution prelates who had no wish to see the Reformation in any way aspersed. If it was slightly embarrassing to the Tories in the University that a

---

[122] Quoted in Douglas, *English scholars*, 71.

[123] Thoresby plainly found himself at a loss in knowing how to a refer to a female scholar. ed. J. Hunter, *The Diary of Ralph Thoresby* (2 vols., London, 1830), II. 131; Nichols, *Literary anecdotes*, IV. 112–40; for Elstob see Chapter 10, 85–6.

[124] The most outstanding contribution to Old English studies in the later eighteenth century was Edward Lye's *Dictionary* (1772), see Chapter 12, 52–3. Cf. D. N. Smith, *Warton's History of English Poetry* (London, 1929), 8.

[125] G. R. Tashjian, 'Richard Rawlinson: A Biographical Study', in eds. G. R. Tashjian, D. R. Tashjian, B. J. Enright, *Richard Rawlinson: a tercentenary memorial* (Kalamazoo, 1990), 83–5.

[126] S. Piggott, 'Antiquarian studies', in HUO V, 757–78, at 766–7; S. Gibson, 'Francis Wise, BD', *Oxoniensia*, 1 (1936), 173–95.

156 ENLIGHTENED OXFORD

ground-breaking work in confessional history came from outside academe, it was partly due to the need for discretion for scholars with careers to run who remained *inside* the Church of England, knew of Queen Anne's lack of sympathy for extreme high-flyers, and could not afford to display Collier's relative sympathy for medieval Catholic Christianity.[127] It was actually Oxford graduates who were court Whigs and moderate churchmen who, through a degree of familiarity with medieval sources that fell little short of Collier's, make the case for a low-level Erastianism in the Church of England in this polemical battle at the turn of the new century with the character of primitive Christianity at its centre.

The dispute over the rights of Convocation, as to its intrinsic constitutional powers and those of the lower vis-à-vis the higher clergy inside it, was essentially Oxonian, with Francis Atterbury and William Wake, Canon of Christ Church (and then a supporter of the Whig Junto Lords), at the head of two embattled factions. Both sides used medieval precedents to press home their respective cases. Atterbury's *The Rights, Powers and Privileges of an English Convocation* (1700) insisted that it was a constitutional requirement to call Convocation every time Parliament sat.[128] Though he had used cathedral archives and diocesan registries, he was ready to sacrifice scholarly depth to make his case and not put off readers who shared his, paradoxically, Whiggish view that the royal supremacy was not unbounded: the fact remained that he was a tough polemical adversary for more erudite medievalists of a Whig dispensation to answer.[129] And there were several of them. White Kennett's precise *Ecclesiastical Synods and Parliamentary Conventions* (1701) sought to make a proper distinction between these two assemblies, and he, with Humphrey Hody,[130] produced the exceptional *History of English Councils and Convocations* the same year, a work that made a signal

---

[127] C. D. A. Leighton, 'The Non-Jurors and their history', *Journal of Religious History*, 29 (2005), 241–57, esp. 251; A. Starkie, 'Contested histories of the English Church: Gilbert Burnet and Jeremy Collier', in ed. P. Kewes, *The uses of history in early modern England* (Huntington Library, San Marino, CA, 2006), 329–47. Thomas Hearne and Richard Rawlinson, Nonjurors with a string of Catholic contacts, had no such hesitation. T. Harmsen, *Antiquarianism in the Augustan age: Thomas Hearne 1678–1735* (Oxford, 2001), 231, 267; Gabriel Glickman, 'The Church and the Catholic community', in ed. G. Tapsell, *The later Stuart Church, 1660–1714* (Manchester, 2012), 217–42, at 233. Williamite Oxonians who clashed with Collier and other Nonjurors in the 1690s were led by Humphrey Hody. Leighton, 'The Non-Jurors and their History', 252.

[128] See the discussion of the historical allusions in Smith, *The Gothic Bequest*, 28–38 and, generally, Jacqueline Rose, 'By law established: the Church of England and the royal supremacy', in ed. G. Tapsell, *The later Stuart Church*, 21–45, at 34–6.

[129] Bennett, *The Tory Crisis*, 52–3; B. S. Sirota, '"The leviathan is not safely to be angered": The Convocation Controversy, Country Ideology and Anglican High Churchmanship', in eds J. B. Stein and S. G. Donabed, *Religion and the state: Europe and North America in the seventeenth and eighteenth centuries*, (Lanham, MD, 2012), 41–61.

[130] Hody also served as Archdeacon of Oxford from 1704 until his death in 1707. See Chapter 3, 14. Frank Stenton called Hody 'one of the ablest members of a very remarkable group of historians', *English Feudalism 1066–1166* (Oxford, 1932), 86. Hody always insisted on his party neutrality— 'I never found in myself any great Inclination to be led about blindfold by any Party;... [Preface to *History of English Councils*], though his patron, Bishop Burnet, enlisted his learning in the cause of Whig polemic. He had earlier been an effective respondent to the Nonjurors in *The Unreasonableness of a separation from the*

contribution to pre-Tudor historical studies, with its striking use of charters, chronicles, and Anglo-Saxon Laws. And he did the job while making every effort to anticipate critics inside the University by avoiding any suggestion of Erastianism.[131]

Added to these texts were two by Edmund Gibson. He used the Lambeth ecclesiastical records to devastating effect against Atterbury with his *Right of the Archbishop to Continue or Prorogue the whole Convocation* (c.1703) and, the culmination of his legal studies on the subject, the *Synodus Anglicana* (1702), with its plentiful references to medieval scholarship.[132] The most exceptional of the scholarly responses to Atterbury's Rights of Convocations was William Wake's *The State of the Church and Clergy of England... Historically deduced from the Conversion of the Saxons to the Present Times* (1703). Its 800 erudite pages showed conclusively, by reference to all the Church assemblies that had ever been held in medieval England, that there was at that time no close interrelation between Convocation and Parliament, and that the final authority to decide whether or not Convocation should meet lay with the sovereign. The book was five years in the making (and owed much to Kennett) but it confirmed Wake's standing as the leading medievalist in England despite his over-willingness to accept the whole period as one in which royal supremacy over the Church was little different from that asserted by Henry VIII after the Submission of the Clergy in 1532.[133] Wake was conversant with much continental scholarship on Church Councils (through his familiarity with the interest in conciliarism that ultra-Gallicans had in France), and it gave him an edge over all his contemporaries.

Oxonian scholarship in medieval and ecclesiastical history entered a prominent period after 1714. With Convocation indefinitely prorogued after 1717 (apart from a brief recall in 1741) the indirect impetus to archival research it had offered ceased to be operative. There was complacency on one side, resignation and vexation on the other. The emergent Whig status quo in Church and State invested little in stirring up debate about historical interpretations of the English past that might undercut its power base in the present, and aspirants to high office among the clergy could see how any such efforts might work against them. No such restraints were operative among Tory authors. The Nonjuror, Thomas Hearne (1678–1733), was pre-eminently an editor of English medieval texts, held no academic offices after 1715 (when he refused the oaths to George I), and was denied access to the Bodleian. But that did not prevent him from publishing thirty-seven editions with the Oxford University Press between 1703

New Bishops... (London, 1691), based on his edition of a Greek treatise on schism—attributed to Nicephorus—from one of the Barocci MSS in the Bodleian. Wells, *Wadham College*, 119. It did nothing to enhance his popularity in Oxford. Ward, *Georgian Oxford*, 40, 72–3.

[131] Bennett, *White Kennett*, 39–44, 167.　　　[132] Sykes, *Gibson*, 31–52.

[133] Thomas Lathbury, *A History of the Convocation of the Church of England* (2nd edn., London, 1853), 392–4; Sykes, *Wake*, I. 107–16; Sykes, *Church and State*, 302; Douglas, *English Scholars*, 213–5.

158   ENLIGHTENED OXFORD

and 1735, for instance, Leland's *Itinerary* (1710) and *Collectanea* (1715), Camden's *Annales* (1717), and many English chronicles.[134] For these labours, as Thomas Warton later remarked, all antiquaries must be indebted.[135] But, for a variety of reasons, Hearne stayed aloof from the movement in Old English studies and he was unappreciative of Saxonists (including Elizabeth Elstob), and his critical judgements could be both wayward and eccentric. Nevertheless, without distractions inside a college, or hunting for preferment, Hearne had scope for doing things differently and had many supporters within the colleges. Among Tories of Hearne's generation, the tendency was to use historical scholarship as a refuge from the Whig present rather than riposte to it. The demoralising impact of official disfavour and the attraction of academic politics and, sometimes, other disciplines, supplemented inertia most effectively. Moreover, in most parts of Catholic and Protestant Europe, the reaction against the whole *érudit* tradition of the previous century was well under way by the 1740s. And with it a readiness to undervalue the antiquarian learning fostered in Oxford via the material resources available in the Ashmolean Museum (1683) that too often came to be seen as collectable curiosities.[136]

Oxford thus gave up encouraging its best graduates to engage in the editing of medieval texts while the early Hanoverian bishops interested themselves less in ecclesiastical history. Thus William Warburton, thoroughly Whig, newly appointed bishop of Gloucester, looking back in 1760, favourably contrasted the polemical abilities of Atterbury with the profound learning of Wake and Kennett, 'two of the dullest fellows in the world to combat'.[137] Their scholarship had been not enlightened, but clericalist, humanist, and solid, then suddenly it became unfashionable, an unwanted presence in the *siecle des lumières*. Instead, the finest fruits of early eighteenth-century Oxford historical exchanges were to be found not among the University's products looking to write national surveys, but out in the provinces among graduates refining antiquarian studies to a high point of historical methodological sophistication.[138] Theirs was, in itself, a reaction to Whiggish relegation of rigorous medieval studies. Otherwise, scholarship based on historical research and evaluation was put aside in favour of literary history, elegancy was preferred to erudition, and it was an Oxford layman, Edward Gibbon, who, notoriously without any desire to vindicate the Church's past,

---

[134] Figure given in Philip, 'Oxford and scholarly production', 130.

[135] Cf. Gibbon: 'His editions will be always recommended by their accuracy and use'. Address recommending Mr Pinkerton, in *The Miscellaneous Works of Edward Gibbon, Esq.,* ed. John, Lord Sheffield (5 vols., London, 1814), III, 567; Douglas, *English Scholars*, 184–94.

[136] The popularity of these resources in Tory and Nonjuring circles lent itself to detraction. T. Harmsen, 'Bodleian imbroglios, politics and personalities, 1701–1716: Thomas Hearne, Arthur Charlett, and John Hudson', *Neophilologus*, 82 (1998), 149–68. Cf. Piggott, 'Antiquarian studies', 758–9.

[137] [William Warburton], *Letters from a Late Eminent Prelate to one of his Friends* (2nd edn., London, 1809), to Richard Hurd, no. cxlv, 314. Smith, *The Gothic Bequest*, 56, notes the importance of feudalism to Warburton earlier in his influential *The Alliance between Church and State* (London, 1736).

[138] See Chapter 12.

aroused sufficient antagonism inside the University to lead some scholars again to consider afresh the English medieval past. Not that Gibbon disclaimed erudition, far from it. As John Pocock has put it:

> It is crucial to the understanding of Gibbon as an Enlightened figure that he pursued erudition and laboured at it, in defiance of the contempt which the polite and philosophical sometimes displayed.[139]

iv) Studies and controversies in classical literature

> All Europe admires the fine editions of ancient authors which from time to time are published in these Universities [Oxford and Cambridge], and it is certain that when the English do seriously apply themselves to anything they succeed perfectly in what they undertake;
>
> Jean Le Clerc, The life of Dr Burnet, late Bishop of Sarum...
>
> (London, 1715).

The interest of the wider world in Oxford editions of classical texts was most famously expressed in a controversy at the turn of the eighteenth century that turned on a fake edition, and showed Oxford academics to be such entertaining controversialists that their scholarship was of secondary importance. It also underlined the University's apparent preference for the philosophical and ethical superiority of the ancient authors over their modern equivalents, and set Christ Church against its sister Cambridge college, Trinity, in the so-called 'Battle of the Books', a core component of the culture war between 'ancients' and 'moderns' that reached its peak in western Europe c.1700.[140] Tutors may not have published much themselves, but there were occasions when they sought applause for themselves in the world of letters by encouraging a well-born and gifted pupil to show his own scholarly aptitude through precocious publication. Such was the background to the dispute in the 1690s around the authenticity of the epistles of Phalaris, one which had resonances far beyond the world of classical letters.[141]

---

[139] *Barbarism and Religion*, I. 108.

[140] eds. Bullard and Tadié, *Ancients and Moderns in Europe*; ed. M. Fumaroli, *La Querelle des Anciens et des Modernes, xvii*^{e}*–xviii*^{e}* siecles* (Paris, 2001). The point has been well made that it was not so much 'a debate or conflict between Ancients and Moderns, but a public spat between two Modern factions'. Levent Yilmaz, *Le temps moderne: Variations sur les anciens et les contemporains* (Paris, 2004), 29 [my translation].

[141] Joseph M. Levine, *The Battle of the Books: History and Literature in the Augustan Age* (Ithaca, NY, 1991) is an assured guide to the controversy. Phalaris (d. 554 BC) was tyrant of Acragas (modern Agrigento) in Sicily.

160 ENLIGHTENED OXFORD

The pre-Revolutionary practice at Christ Church was for the dean to give a young scholar the task of editing a classical text that would, once completed, go on general sale. The scholar selected by Dean Aldrich in 1693 was the Hon. Charles Boyle (later 4th Earl of Orrery, nephew of the chemist, Robert Boyle), who had the (often very amusing) epistles of Phalaris allotted to him and, with unmerited self-confidence in what he might accomplish, set to work. The choice of Phalaris was heavily freighted, for Sir William Temple, the retired elder statesman, had within the previous twelve months, published his rambling, controversial *Essay on Ancient and Modern Learning*, which had held up Phalaris as a model letter-writer, and used the latter's excellence as the basis for his claim that, in sentiment and style, the ancient writers were superior to the modern. Two years later, in 1695, Charles Boyle's edition was released. It provoked an immediate rumpus both for its endorsement of Temple's contention and for its scholarship. It was not that Boyle asserted the authenticity of the epistles; it was his slighting reference to the ex-Oxford classicist, Boyle Lecturer, and current Keeper of the Royal Library, Richard Bentley,[142] that induced the latter to over-react and publish a dissertation (1697) that in just seventy-eight pages offered accumulated proofs sufficient to show the epistles of this 6th-century BC tyrant to be spurious and, in the process, embarrassed the Christ Church dons whom he rightly suspected were the real authors of Boyle's edition. That was the signal for Aldrich to authorise what was in effect a collective Christ Church riposte that attempted to demolish Bentley's particular arguments, pushing Boyle to the margins while retaining his name on the cover as the author of *Dr Bentley's Dissertations on the Epistles of Phalaris and the Fables of Aesop Examin'd* (London, 1698), a text that was actually the joint product of a group of Christ Church dons (all ex-Westminster School products, including the Freind brothers, George Smalridge, and Anthony Alsop) led by Francis Atterbury.[143]

The Atterburians took their stand on Bentley's literary critical methods (presented implicitly as a threat to Christianity), ignored Boyle's original thesis, and shamelessly (and brilliantly) pitched their appeal at the literary coffee-houses and social gatherings. It went into two editions and entertained the public not for its persuasive scholarship but for its witty implication that Cambridge dons were a danger to the survival of the faith; for the Bible itself could become victim of this forensic criticism just as, in France, Homer's prestige was being called into question. It also offered a shamelessly snobbish excoriation of Bentley as a rough Yorkshire clown, a mere pedant guilty of 'Written Illbreeding',[144] a 'library-keeper' who (in a resourceful comic twist) could not possibly be the author of the

---

[142] Bentley had lent the Royal Library's manuscript of Phalaris to be collated for the Oxford project, and then requested its return before Boyle and his collaborators had completed using it. Haugen, *Richard Bentley*, 112–13.

[143] Bennett, *Tory Crisis*, 38–43; Money, *The English Horace*, 78–9.

[144] Charles Boyle, *Dr. Bentley's Dissertations on the Epistles of Phalaris...Examin'd* [with the assistance of F. Atterbury, G. Smalridge, R. Freind, J. Freind, W. King, and A. Alsop] (London, 1698), 93, better known as *Boyle against Bentley*. For King's brilliant use therein of a mock index see Dennis

OXFORD AND THE ARTS AND HUMANITIES   161

Dissertation circulating under his name. For his part, Bentley joshed Boyle as author of *Dr Bentley's Dissertations . . . Examin'd* as someone who knew his materials at second hand, an Oxford scholar unfamiliar with books even in 'the publick Library at *Oxon*', one who does not know how to use a catalogue, dependent on 'his Assistant [. . .] *that consulted Books for him*'.[145] The consensus at the time was that Boyle and his backers had triumphed, so much so that Atterbury brought out his *A Short View of the Controversy* that rehearsed all the points made earlier laced with additional pleasantries and mockery. It was a premature celebration of success for Bentley's monumental [second] *Dissertation on Phalaris* (1699), returning to the original subject of the controversy, in fact routed Boyle and Atterbury in scholarly terms. Written with quotations in English and despite being 540 pages long, it was designed for a much larger audience than Latin specialists, and marked a milestone in Bentley's becoming what Kristine Louis Haugen has called 'a public intellectual'.[146]

But the attention of the interested public to the Christ Church wits during the so-called 'Battle of the Books' was never scornful, despite their *de haut en bas* rhetoric. In deploying it, the wits had, in an important sense, won one part of the exchange with Bentley.[147] And the fact that the whole 'Battle' could not be confined within the academy, indeed that Oxonians pitched hard for sympathisers in both town and country, was successful in generating notice for the University. Irrespective of whether an individual considered the Epistles were a forgery or not, the exchanges in themselves grabbed attention. They confirmed that Oxford graduates (certainly those from Aldrich's Christ Church) could be playful, communicative, and (counter-intuitively) modern in reaching out to an audience much wider than the 'Republic of Letters', one that got the joke and enjoyed rebarbative sallies at the expense of Bentley and his friends.[148] For both sides recognised that responses would owe much to the politics of those who read them and those who read about them: for Atterbury and his allies were Tories, in favour of the rights of Convocation, whereas Bentley was a Whig with the Whig Bishop of Worcester, Edward Stillingfleet, his leading patron in this decade. As Haugen nicely puts it: 'The Phalaris controversy, . . . was thus in part a proxy war for a

---

Duncan, *Index, A History of the . A Bookish Adventure* (Harmondsworth, 2021), 146–50. As J. G. A. Pocock observes more widely, 'The Battle of the Books in England was on one level the conflict between the amateur and the pedant;' *Barbarism and Religion*, I. 108.

[145] Bentley, *A Dissertation upon the Epistles of Phalaris with an answer to the objections of the honourable Charles Boyle, Esq.* (London, 1699), 378.

[146] Haugen, *Richard Bentley*, 121. Money tellingly observes that the debate might have been settled with less rancour were it not for Bentley's 'sordid combativeness'. *The English Horace*, 77. See also G. Highet, *The Classical Tradition* (Oxford, 1949), 284–6.

[147] Cf. Jonathan Brody Kramnick, who concluded that the fight over Phalaris showed ' . . . the clergy and the academy were bereft of the open and worldly language of the periodical and the salon'. *Making the English Canon*, 89.

[148] This wit is well-described in C. J. Horne, 'The Phalaris controversy: King versus Bentley', *Review of English Studies*, 22 (1946), 289–303.

162 ENLIGHTENED OXFORD

contemporary political issue of very serious implications'[149]—the validity of the Revolution settlement and the recast public culture that underpinned it.

Over time, any adverse effects of the controversy on Oxford's standing soon faded and do not appear to have significantly damaged the University's reputation for classical scholarship. Unlike history, classical literature was an essential part of Oxford studies, and the staple of such teaching as the colleges provided. Oxford had no equivalent to Cambridge's Richard Bentley or Richard Porson at any point in the century.[150] There was a Regius Chair of Greek, yet those who filled it between 1688 and 1800 added little lustre to the University's reputation in terms of either publishing much or building on the work of their illustrious humanist predecessors,[151] with the definite exception of Humphrey Hody, William III's choice as professor from 1698 to 1705 and someone with a passion for serious Greek scholarship,[152] and the possible exception of Cyril Jackson's younger brother, William (1751–1815), who held the chair from 1783 to 1811, when he was appointed to the see of Oxford. At the time of his death, Hody (also a formidable Biblical scholar) was engaged on a lecture course covering figures such as the Greek Renaissance humanists, Bessarion, and Theodorus Gaza, though these lectures were not published until 1742. Otherwise, many of the chair-holders contented themselves with delivering an inaugural lecture or remained better-known for other exploits, such as Thomas Milles (1705–08), author of an edition of St Cyril of Alexandria's oeuvre, who attempted to make the actress Anne Bracegirdle lead a more respectable life and had episcopal success as Bishop of Waterford after the 8th Earl of Pembroke preferred him in 1708;[153] or Thomas Shaw (1694–1751), (Regius Professor of Greek 1741; Principal, SEH 1740), a North African traveller and former chaplain to the English Factory in Algiers.[154]

Otherwise, it was left to those who were professors in other subjects to offer some erratic leadership in classical studies, just as their interests took them.

---

[149] Haugen, *Richard Bentley*, 123.

[150] Bentley actually spent a year in Oxford (he was incorporated at Wadham in 1689) as tutor to the son of Bp Stillingfleet, and undertook some scholarly work in conjunction with Hody, in connection with the *Epistola ad Joannem Millium* (London, 1691); Haugen, *Richard Bentley*, 81–99.

[151] Lord Chesterfield, only half-jestingly, when considering a career choice for his (natural) son, suggested in 1748: 'What do you think of being Greek Professor at one of our Universities? It is a very pretty sinecure, and requires very little knowledge (much less than, I hope, you have already) of that language', ed. B. Dobrée, *The letters of Philip Dormer Stanhope, 4th Earl of Chesterfield* (6 vols., London, 1932), IV. 1084..

[152] Cf. Clarke, 'Classical Studies', 514, deems the eleven appointees to be 'undistinguished as scholars'.

[153] Milles was chaplain at Christ Church in 1694 and vice-principal of SEH from 1695 to 1707. Hearne was his scathing critic: 'The Court could not have put a greater affront upon us than pitching upon a Person void of Integrity, Parts, or Learning,...he not understanding the Rudiments of the Greek Tongue,...'. I. 326. He is considered 'A scholar of ability' in the *ODNB*. See G. Le G. Norgate, 'Milles, Thomas (1671-1740), Church of Ireland bishop of Waterford and Lismore', rev. Julian C. Walton, *ODNB*, online edn., 2004.

[154] Shaw's importance is set out in Chapter 11.

OXFORD AND THE ARTS AND HUMANITIES   163

Thus Joseph Trapp, the first Professor of Poetry, was preoccupied with the Roman classical poets, as reflected in his authorship of a verse translation of Virgil;[155] William Hawkins (1751–6) was an authority on Greek drama, and had an admiration for Aeschylus that distinguished him from those who preferred the more polished Sophocles and Euripides;[156] Thomas Warton, Hawkins's successor, published a lecture on Theocritus and, in his two-volume edition of the *Idylls* (1770), he made his case for preferring this Greek poet over Virgil.[157] The realisation that a non-University-educated public wanted to know more in general terms about Greek and Roman societies occasionally surfaced in Oxford. The young John Potter, the future Primate, when a Fellow of Lincoln, brought out *The Antiquities of Greece* (1697–8) with the intention of unlocking the treasures of Greek literature.[158] He had a career to make, early public notice would do him no harm. But his was a rare instance of a primer, and his example failed to inspire future generations of young Fellows to do likewise as they waited for a living to become vacant.

Despite the unexceptionable impact of the Oxford Professoriate, the University was a place of some talented classical scholarship throughout the long eighteenth century, thanks to the textual editions of leading Greek and Latin authors produced (mainly) by industrious college tutors and published by the University Press. Their quality—and their reception—were predictably varied. Two industrious Magdalen fellows, Richard West and Robert Welsted, produced an edition of Pindar (1697) that contained an embarrassing number of errors,[159] John Shaw's *Argonautica* of Apollonius Rhodius (2 vols., Oxford, 1779) received an international mauling,[160] but Thomas Robinson's (Merton) Hesiod of 1737 was, by contrast, well regarded, and Thomas Fenton (Ch. Ch.) produced a Greek edition of Homer—*Ilias* (Oxford, 1714)—that over half a century later was adjudged by one critic to be 'one of the most correct Editions of Homer'.[161]

---

[155] *Praelectiones poeticae* (3 vols., Oxford, 1711–19).

[156] Hawkins, *Works* (3 vols., London, 1758). See also pp. 19–20, this chapter. Samuel Musgrave (1732–80), the physician and classical scholar, one-time Radcliffe travelling Fellow of Corpus Christi College, later (1778) produced an outstanding edition of the plays of Euripides with foundations laid through his work in Paris libraries that has been hailed as 'one of the greatest achievements of English classical scholarship of the eighteenth century'. M. L. Clarke, *Greek Studies in England* (Cambridge, 1945), 61–2.

[157] Warton's *Theocritus* received a muted scholarly reception. Whereas he made no attempt to offer his own biography of the poet, he generously acknowledged the editorial scholarship of Jonathan Toup (1713–85). Clarke, 'Classical Studies', 528. Toup was a parish priest in Cornwall, discussed in Chapter 12, p. 59.

[158] R. Anderson, *Memoirs of the Life and Writings of John Potter* (Edinburgh, 1824), iv–v.

[159] Hearne, I. 153; Richard Dawes, *Miscellanea critica* (Cambridge, 1745), section ii.

[160] For the comments of the Dutch based scholar Daniel Albert Wyttenbach in *Bibliotheca critica* (3 vols., Amsterdam, 1779–1808), I. pt. 3, 113–17, see Clarke, 'Classical Studies', 528n.

[161] Edward Harwood, *A View of the Various Editions of the Greek and Roman Classics, with remarks* (London, 1775), 3. Fenton had the assistance of his contemporary, Lewis Stephens. HMC, *Portland MSS*, VII. 72.

164 ENLIGHTENED OXFORD

Interest moved after *c.*1750 to the dramatists and the needs of students were not forgotten by dons. John Burton of Corpus Christi College indefatigably promoted the benefits of Greek and Roman literature throughout his life.[162] His *Pentalogia* (five Greek plays published in 1758) included what was in effect a manifesto urging their reading in universities and schools. Of the Greek historians, only Thucydides was accorded an edition, but that a serviceable one produced in 1696 by John Hudson, fellow of University College (later Bodley's Librarian).[163] And the complete works of Xenophon appeared between 1690 and 1703, edited rather slightly by Edward Wells of Christ Church.[164] Of the Latin historians, however, the only new edition was Hearne's of Livy (1708), characteristically thorough, with variant readings from six Oxford manuscripts collated by Hearne himself. Latin verse writers were neglected. Over the 'long eighteenth century', there were new editions of Ovid's *Metamorphoses* (1696, one that did not impress Bentley), Lucretius (1695), and Virgil (1795). Of these, it was Thomas Creech's translation in his early twenties of *De Rerum natura* (1682) that most struck critics for its brevity, clear organisation, and useful notes.[165] Creech, first at Wadham, later a Fellow of All Souls (1683) and the friend of Christopher Codrington, committed suicide in 1700 after moving from Oxford to Welwyn as incumbent only the previous year, before he could make further contributions to scholarship.[166] But his English Lucretius was the standard full-length edition throughout the next century.[167] Creech, it has been claimed, was a key figure in a group of scholars active in Oxford during the 1680s seeking to follow the French lead in making the classics available in the vernacular to a wide public.[168]

Oxford bucked the wider trend of neglecting Plato as individual dialogues, or groups of dialogues, were edited by various scholars throughout the

---

[162] *Memoirs of the Late Rev. and Learned John Burton, D.D. of Eaton, GM* 41 (1771), 305–8, is a short English translation of Edward Bentham's essay on his friend.

[163] A 1706 plan for an edition of Polybius never materialised. Carter, *History of O.U. Press*, I. 335.

[164] Wells was honest about his minimal input in the preface to the complete edition of 1703. Clarke, 'Classical Studies', 528 and n.

[165] When a third edition was published in 1683, John Dryden, the Poet Laureate, led the way in a prefix that included thirteen commendatory poems by Aphra Behn, John Evelyn, and Thomas Otway, recognising Creech's achievement. For Creech's work within the wider Epicurean revival see C. Wilson, *Epicureanism at the Origins of Modernity* (Oxford, 2008); R. Kroll, *The Material World: Literate Culture in the Restoration and Early Eighteenth Century* (Baltimore, MD, 1991); T. F. Mayo, *Epicurus in England (1650–1725)* (Dallas, TX, 1934). Creech also translated Theocritus (1684); and his translation of Manilius was published posthumously in 1700. Wells, *Wadham College*, 97–9.

[166] [John Froud], *Daphnis: Or, a Pastoral Elegy upon the unfortunate and much-lamented Death of Mr Thomas Creech* (London, 1700); Scott Mandelbrote, 'The Vision of Christopher Codrington', in eds. Green and Horden, *All Souls under the Ancien Régime*, 132–74, at 169–70.

[167] D. Hopkins, *Conversing with Antiquity. English Poets and the Classics from Shakespeare to Pope* (Oxford, 2010), 91–2, 122. Creech took care in his preliminaries and notes to distance himself from many of Lucretius's views.

[168] Ibid., 122–3. White Kennett was also prominent, with composite versions of Anacreon (1683) and the Roman historian Cornelius Nepos (1684), as well as a translation of Erasmus's *Praise of Folly* (1683).

century.[169] The outstanding Platonist in the University was a Prussian émigré, John William Thomson (St Edmund Hall, 1725), whose *Parmenides* (1728)—one that included his own *Prolegomena*—fell victim to fashion and received little contemporary notice, despite its many merits.[170] Aristotle still secured attention, though the relative dearth of new editions is suggestive of how far Oxford had distanced itself from this once ascendant philosophical school.[171] High points were an anonymous 1759 edition of the *Rhetoric* aimed at students; the author (William Holwell of Christ Church) furnished it with extensive notes aimed at explaining difficult passages. Thomas Winstanley of Brasenose produced an unexceptional edition of the *Ethics* in 1780,[172] though it was generally reckoned to be outshone by that of Thomas Tyrwhitt (1730–86, Clerk to the House of Commons, a fellow of Merton, 1755–62), published posthumously in 1794.[173]

In the second half of the century two deans of Christ Church, William Markham and Cyril Jackson, promoted the revival of Greek studies,[174] but it was perhaps Thomas Burgess (1756–1836) of Corpus Christi who was outstanding in the field. He precociously made his name while still an undergraduate in 1778 by editing a new edition of John Burton's *Pentalogia*, then followed it three years later with one of Richard Dawes's *Miscellanea critica* that included extensive additional notes. These texts received critical acclaim from scholars outside Oxford, including Wyttenbach and Villoison abroad, and Charles Burney (the younger) and William Vincent at home.[175] Burgess was keen to publish Oxonian work in a quarterly classical journal, but the nearest to it he managed was the *Museum oxoniense literarium* (first volume published 1792, the second in 1797), an attempt at a latter-day reinvention of the Republic of Letters, defined on a more generous scale.[176] Thus classical studies were being regularly invigorated in later

[169] For Plato (and Aristotle) at Oxford see P. R. Quarrie, 'The Learned Press: Classics and Related Works', in ed. Gadd, *The History of Oxford University Press*, 1. 371–84, at 374–5; F. B. Evans, 'Platonic scholarship in eighteenth-century England', *Modern Philology*, 41 (1943), 103–10.

[170] Martha K. Zebrowski, 'John William Thomson's 1728 Edition of Plato's "Parmenides": A Calvinist humanist from Königsberg reads Platonic theology in Oxford', *JECS* 30 (2007), 113–31. See also Chapter 11.

[171] 'Terrae-Filius', aka Nicholas Amhurst, was characteristically exaggerating the reality when he castigated the University in 1721 because it '... by statute obliged her *matriculated* issue to defend and maintain all his [Aristotle's] *peripaterical* doctrines, right and wrong together, to the last gasp of their breath, and the last drop of their ink'. *Terrae-Filius, or, the secret history of the University of Oxford (1721; 1726)*, ed. William E. Rivers (Newark, DE, 2003), no. xxi, 183, 28 Mar. 1721.

[172] Wyttenbach, *Bibliotheca critica*, II. pt. 3, 114–16.

[173] See generally Clarke, 'Classical studies', 529. For Tyrwhitt's considerable and versatile scholarship see R. M. Ogilvie, *Latin and Greek: a history of the influence of the classics on English life from 1600 to 1918* (London, 1964), 70 G.H. Martin and J.R.L. Highfield, *A History of Merton College, Oxford* (Oxford, 1997), 261–2, 278. It was he who detected Thomas Chatterton's forgeries.

[174] Bill, *Education at Christ Church*, 281–5, 288.

[175] John S. Hardford, *The life of Thomas Burgess, DD, FRS, FAS, & c., late Lord Bishop of Salisbury* (2nd edn., London, 1841), 11–20.

[176] Clarke, 'Classical Studies', 530.

Fig. 4.2 Thomas Burgess (1756–1837), Bishop of St David's and Salisbury, William Owen, oil on canvas, copy 1825 of 1817 original at Corpus Christi College, Oxford (Trinity St David, Lampeter, Founder's Library).

eighteenth-century Oxford through the enterprise of individual scholars but, in other subject areas, particularly philosophy, in an atrophied state in the University, as it appeared to its critics, that was rather less the case.

v) Philosophy and metaphysics

Philosophy (as opposed to 'natural philosophy' that looked to the natural sciences) referred to the ancients, the scholastics, and to modern writers such as Bacon, Descartes, and Oxford's own John Locke, and there was no discrete discipline so named in the eighteenth-century University, when so much intellectual activity fell under the penumbra of divinity.[177] Whyte's Chair of Moral Philosophy (endowed 1621) certainly existed but, as far as lecturing was concerned, had fallen into desuetude, a sinecure for one of the Proctors, usually the

---

[177] See, generally, J. Yolton, 'Schoolmen, Logic and Philosophy', in HUO V, 565–92.

OXFORD AND THE ARTS AND HUMANITIES   167

Senior one.[178] Similarly, the influential moral thought of the 3rd Earl of Shaftesbury (1671–1713) was largely overlooked at Oxford: his Whiggish pedigree and his aversion to clericalist universities help explain the neglect.[179]

The University gave a low priority to investing in a subject that was the handmaiden of theology and could have functioned as an agency in inculcating raised standards of public morality, the degeneration of which conservative commentators never ceased to bemoan down the 'long eighteenth century'. Students were taught the subject, but most tutors were cautious and conservative in their approach, rather less so when it came to logic. Standard manuals of scholastic logic within a loose Aristotelian framework were still in intensive use among the students; these prepared them academically for the undemanding public exercises in the subject that did so much to sink Oxford's reputation among progressive educationalists from the 1750s onwards (its own graduates among them, such as Vicesimus Knox).[180] But it is easy to overlook the fact that up-to-date logic manuals by Isaac Watts (1746) and William Duncan (professor of natural philosophy at Aberdeen) (1748) were sometimes read independently by undergraduates with initiative.[181]

These public exercises had a remarkable longevity and were still in place for the BA degree c.1800.[182] At the close of the Stuart era, their existence was taken for granted on a variety of grounds. John Wallis, for instance, in 1700 argued that those entering public life would find training in logic and philosophy far more valuable than equestrian skill. And dons in that era were still spending time and trouble on updating scholastic manuals for their students, among them Dean Aldrich at Christ Church, whose *Artis logicae compendium* (1691) was to determine the terms of reasoning for most Oxford men for over a century. The talented polymath and pipe smoker, Henry Aldrich, certainly did not find his mathematical aptitude at all incompatible with the subtlety of scholastic logic.[183] Nevertheless, by the middle decades of the following century, this pedagogy was appearing increasingly unfit for purpose. It was not that logical disputations per se were considered inappropriate by its critics (and anyone who claimed credibility

---

[178] Moral philosophy contained elements of what would subsequently be classified as psychology, logic, ethics, jurisprudence, history, and rhetoric. See R. B. Sher, 'Professors of virtue: the social history of the Edinburgh moral philosophy chair in the eighteenth century', in ed. M. A. Stewart, *Studies in the philosophy of the Scottish Enlightenment*, (Oxford, 1990), 87–126.

[179] Discussed in I. Rivers, *Reason, grace and sentiment. A study of the language of religion and ethics in England, 1660–1780* (2 vols., Cambridge, 1991–2005), II. 195–9. Where his influence was discernible at all, it was largely mediated through Francis Hutcheson.

[180] See Chapter 1, pp. 47–8.   [181] Darwall-Smith, 'Monks of Magdalen', 261.

[182] G. V. Cox, *Recollections of Oxford* (London, 1870), 38–9, and n.; John Gascoigne, 'The role of the universities in the Scientific Revolution', in eds. David C. Lindberg and Robert S. Westman, *Reappraisals of the Scientific Revolution* (Cambridge, 1990), 207–60, at 225.

[183] For Henry Aldrich see Stuart Handley, 'Aldrich, Henry (1648–1710)', ODNB, online edn., 2004. W. G. Hiscock, *Henry Aldrich of Christ Church, 1648–1710* (Oxford, 1960) remains useful. Aldrich's papers were destroyed at his request on his death.

168   ENLIGHTENED OXFORD

as a logician took aim at them, including Isaac Watts and Edward Bentham), for their prominence reflected a concern to train clergy in the skills of controversy;[184] it was rather, as John Napleton, for one, pointed out, that the University seemed incapable of implementing the minor changes to the examination process that would restore academic value for the students and cease to generate unfavourable notice from the University's watchful critics.[185] Indeed, new logics were coming in ineluctably and, it has been argued, 'became the instruments by which the important issues' in science, religion, and ethics 'came into the Oxford curriculum'.[186] But not quickly enough for some. Edward Tatham, the consistently anti-Aristotelian Lincoln don, early in the nineteenth century was adamant that 'the old moral philosophy of Aristotle, Cicero, and Epictetus, however admirable in their days, is at this day not worth a louse'. According to him, 'Everything is sacrificed to your *Dear Dialectica*, that is, to Aristotle. A Young man must devote himself to dialectic for the whole of his four years—and he will be an Egregious Blockhead at the end'.[187] Tatham, however, embarrassed the majority of his college colleagues and was widely resented across the University. But his hopes were set on reaching the public outside Oxford.

Of course, Bentham and Napleton were following in the footsteps of one who had begun the attack on school logic and philosophy: John Locke.[188] They were happy to own his name and extend his influence, and many college tutors included Locke's foundational *Essay concerning Human Understanding* on their reading lists, while others, unhappy at his Whiggish politics and dubious Trinitarianism, opted not to engage with his work too closely.[189] In 1703 Oxford college heads collectively attempted to suppress the *Essay* along with titles by the Huguenot radical, Jean Le Clerc, probably from the twin motives of concern that the students were reading too much of the 'new philosophy' that was undermining scholastic logic and disputations.[190] After further deliberation, following the suggestion of Jonathan Edwards, Principal of Jesus, they opted to advise tutors

---

[184] I. Watts, *The Improvement of the Mind: Or a supplement to the art of logick* (London, 1741); E. Bentham, *Reflexions upon the nature and usefulness of logick as it has been commonly taught in the schools* (2nd edn., Oxford, 1755); W. M. Jacob, *The Clerical Profession in the Long Eighteenth Century 1680–1840* (Oxford, 2007), 45.

[185] See Chapter 1, pp. 47–8; Rothblatt, *The modern university and its discontents*, 161–2.

[186] Yolton, 'Schoolmen, Logic and Philosophy', 591.

[187] *Oxonia purgata, consisting of a series of addresses on the subject of the new discipline in the University of Oxford* (London, 1812), 89. And see Green, *Lincoln College*, 371–5.

[188] Some of his withering criticisms made in the *Essay* are summarised in Yolton, 'Schoolmen, Logic and Philosophy', 570–2.

[189] For the subject generally see Alan P. Sell, *John Locke and the Eighteenth-Century Divines* (Cardiff, 1997), esp. chap. 2. Keith Feiling's description of him 'almost the official interpreter of the Revolution' is to be commended. *In Christ Church Hall* (London, 1960), 34.

[190] J. Yolton, *John Locke and the Way of Ideas* (Oxford, 1956), 3–4, 11–12; John Marshall, *John Locke, Resistance, Religion and Responsibility* (Cambridge, 1994), 452. Locke's psychologising of personal identity also called into question the resurrection of the dead, and came in for much criticism in the 1700s and 1710s.

Fig. 4.3 John Locke, Thomas Gibson, oil on canvas, first half of the eighteenth century (Bodleian Libraries, University of Oxford).

not to recommend or use these titles but little seems to have been done in practice.[191] Diligent students, particularly those of Whiggish inclination, wanted to read him, among them Henry Egerton of New College (b. 1689), future Bishop of Hereford, who systematically set out the fruits of his reading in an unpublished manuscript, 'Notes & Observations upon Mr Lock's Essay Concerning Human Understanding'.[192] Oxford critics of Locke were never readily silenced. Winch Holdsworth of St John's College in a sermon of 1720 imputed to Locke denial of bodily resurrection and kept up his sniping. In his *A Defence of the Doctrine of the Resurrection of the Same Body* (1727), he insisted that 'Mr Lock hath Usurped in the Empire of Learning too Much and too Long. It is Time he should be deposed from his Tyranny; And brought down to his Proper Sphere'.[193] And, as late as 1790, Henry Kett (Fellow of Trinity, a diligent tutor and sympathetic to

---

[191] James Tyrrell asked Locke not to 'impute the indiscreet zeal of a few men to the whole University...', letter of 28 Feb. 1704, quoted in Cranston, *John Locke*, 467. Warden Dunster of Whiggish Wadham was one Head of House ready to vindicate Locke's book at the meeting. See also ibid., 468–9.

[192] Hertfordshire Archives and Local Studies, Ashridge Papers, AH1934-1936.

[193] *A defence of the doctrine of the resurrection of the same body* (London, 1727), Preface, v.

170   ENLIGHTENED OXFORD

academic reform) accused Locke of scepticism, and proposed the Scottish 'Common Sense' approach as the antidote.[194]

But Kett was in a minority. Edward Bentham, a follower of Bishop Joseph Butler, did as much as any Oxonian to complete Locke's rehabilitation. He was epistemologically engaged with Locke, never in any doubt about his exceptional influence or the way that the *Essay* had opened up the natural history of man in a way that made it impossible to retain the old logic without recognising Locke's recasting of the nature and function of the human understanding. As John Yolton has justly said of Bentham's *Reflexions upon the Nature and Usefulness of Logick, with a Vindication*, (1740, 2nd ed., 1755), he offers a 'well written and succinct' text that takes full account of Locke and offers the reader 'a thoughtful account of old and new' approaches to the subject.[195] Here and in the more pedestrian, posthumous *An Introduction to Logick (Scholastick and Rational)* (1773) Bentham moderated Locke's dismissal of scholastic logic by preferring not to condemn the subject as wholly unworthy of academic attention. Bentham's earlier *An Introduction to Moral Philosophy* (Oxford, 1745) was not original but offered a clear account of the subject that fully registered the impact of Locke.[196] Bentham opted for ease of access and invited his intended student audience to think with some modern authorities in mind rather than follow a new set of formal rules. It was up to date, included a list of contemporary authors in moral philosophy (among them Samuel Clarke, Francis Hutcheson, and Thomas Rutherforth), and had an extensive list of topics with recommended reading.[197] And all within an explicitly theistic framework, with Bishop Butler recommended in the Preface.

Other colleagues were not far behind. Thus John Burton, the highly regarded Corpus tutor, tried to insert Locke alongside other moderns into the philosophical curriculum, and the Christ Church collections books confirms the frequency with which his *Essay* appeared on reading lists for students.[198] It was indeed Dean John Conybeare of the House who acclaimed Locke as the 'glory of that age [the seventeenth century], and the instructor of the present'.[199] The literature reaching

---

[194] Cranston, *John Locke*, 42. Horne and Napleton were among other later Oxford critics of Locke's philosophical position (and, by implication, of his theology). For Kett, see *GM* 95 (1825), 184.

[195] 'Schoolmen, logic and philosophy', 574.

[196] In two tables presenting a huge range of material, Bentham cited Locke on the gospel as the perfect body of ethics. *An Introduction*, 102.

[197] 'Schoolmen, logic and philosophy', 582–3. See also Yolton's essay on Bentham in eds. John W. Yolton, John Valdimir Price, and John Stephens, *The Dictionary of eighteenth-century British philosophers* (2 vols., Bristol, 1999), I. 76–7. For Bentham's intellectual abilities see Gibbon's *Memoirs of My Life*, ed. Betty Radice (Harmondsworth, 1984), 90; ed. George Birkbeck Hill, rev. L. F. Powell, *Boswell's Life of Johnson* (6 vols., Oxford, 1934–50), II. 445, 20 Mar. 1776.

[198] Fowler, *Corpus Christi College*, 271.

[199] Conybeare, *A Defence of Reveal'd Religion against the Exceptions of a late Writer, in his Book, Intituled, Christianity as old as the Creation* (2nd edn., Oxford, 1732), 167. Christ Church was, under Conybeare, ever more comfortable with the memory of Locke. It said much that a life-size statue of Locke was installed in a niche in the stairwell of the College's new Library building in 1759 when it was still under construction.

students came to reflect his omnipresence. In 1755 the late Daniel Waterland's (the highly esteemed Cambridge controversialist) *Advice to a Young Student, with a method of study of the first four years* went into a second edition with Waterland commending not just Locke, but recommending other recent titles, among them Butler's *Analogy of Religion* (1736).[200] Locke was too strong a cultural force in eighteenth-century society at large to make direct rejection of his epistemology a realistic proposition for his Oxford critics. Their tactics were instead to ignore his work, downplay its significance, or just sneer. Meanwhile, the majority of tutors saw that he had his pedagogic uses and recognised that for them to omit the *Essay* from their teaching would be both perverse and a disservice to their students.

David Hume, however, was another matter. Horne of Magdalen and William Adams of Pembroke (*An Essay on Mr. Hume's Essay on Miracles*, 1752) wrote against him and their challenges generated a certain amount of outside interest before silence descended again.[201] Hume's challenge to the Christian basis of ethics was not systematically answered in Oxford and it was principally William Warburton who rallied affronted clerical opinion after the appearance of *The Natural History of Religion* in 1757 and forced Hume to make a tactical retreat,[202] seen in his decision not to publish the *Dialogues on Natural Religion* in his lifetime. Horne, in his anonymous *Letter to Adam Smith on the life, death, and philosophy of his friend David Hume...By one of the people called Christians* (Oxford, 1777) did not examine Hume's philosophical principles directly but condemned him as one '...who seems to have been possessed with an incurable antipathy to all that is called RELIGION'. [203] He was content to rely on what James Beattie, the Scottish poet and 'Common Sense' philosopher from Aberdeen University, in his *Essay on Truth* (1770), had suggested of Hume's scepticism in the *Treatise* and *Enquiries*,[204] and deplore Smith's depiction of his friend as wise and virtuous, approaching death with scandalous equanimity, bantering Charon in an imaginary dialogue before boarding the boat across the Styx.[205] And young

---

[200] Yolton, 'Schoolmen, logic and philosophy', 589–90; Rivers, *Reason, grace and sentiment*, II. 196.

[201] Ibid., II. 272–3; R. M. Burns, *The Great Debate on Miracles* (Lewisburg, PA, 1981), 239–44. William Adams (1706–89) was Master of Pembroke College, 1775–89. For doubts about his strict orthodoxy see Robert Burns, 'William Adams', in eds. Yolton et al., *Dictionary of eighteenth-century British philosophers*, I. 4–6. His sentiments in religion were said to be 'liberal'. *GM* 59, (1789), I, 176.

[202] See Evans, *Warburton and the Warburtonians*, 216; Robert Ingram, 'William Warburton, Divine Action, and Enlightened Christianity', in eds. Gibson and Ingram, *Religious Identities*, 97–117.

[203] *A Letter to Adam Smith LL.D. on the Life, Death, and Philosophy of his Friend David Hume Esq., by one of the People called Christians* (2nd edn., Oxford, 1777), 10–11. Horne's authorship was scarcely veiled. He returned to consider aspects of Hume's work in *Letters on Infidelity* (2nd edn., Oxford, 1786).

[204] According to David Allan, this was 'the key dispute framed by the mature Scottish Enlightenment'. *Making British Culture*, 128–9.

[205] Discussed in Rivers, *Reason, Grace and Sentiment*, II. 263–4. It impressed Warburton's circle. See Bishop Hurd to Balguy, 21 Apr. 1777, Balguy Correspondence, Beinecke Library, Box 1, Folder 24: 'Dr Horn[e]'s little tract is admirable, & will do much good, besides mortifying that first-rate coxcomb, Adam Smith, on whom the full patrimony of his friend's impiety has descended'.

172 ENLIGHTENED OXFORD

William Agutter (1758–1835), a committed anti-slaver and demy of Magdalen College, preaching before the University in 1786 on 'the difference between the death of the righteous and the wicked, illustrated in the instance of Dr Samuel Johnson and David Hume, Esq.', was at pains to emphasise that 'the confidence or the tranquillity of the infidel are no arguments in his favour'.[206]

Majority opinion resisted the various attempts to produce a wholly naturalistic ethics. Even so, a precocious George Horne found such student exposure as there was to the study of metaphysics and ethics dangerously tempting them to deism, first through the 'heathens', after which an undergraduate probably proceeded to William Wollaston, Shaftesbury, and others; and was at length fixed in the opinion 'that reason is sufficient for a man without revelation'.[207] Toland, Tindal, and Anthony Collins might as readily have been held up as exemplars of this trend. It was actually the Oxonian, Matthew Tindal's *Christianity as Old as the Creation* (1730) that afforded a sustained, systematic attempt to show the extent of its viability.[208] He offered the orthodox abundant embarrassment in arguing that revelation added nothing to discerning the laws of nature not already imparted by reason, and that as much guidance was provided for the moral man in Confucius as in the Sermon on the Mount. It was cold comfort for High Churchmen that Tindal showed how, on the latitudinarians' own terms, natural religion was sufficient and a special revelation through the Bible was redundant.

Tindal's writings were influential enough to infect this subject area for a century after his death, and the University discouraged engagement on it. Majority opinion within it would not concede the ground but the price paid was a degree of intellectual sclerosis in moral philosophy that contrasted with a willingness to be developmental despite the Laudian Statutes in matters of logic. There were honourable exceptions. William Adams's *The Nature and Obligation of Virtue* (1754), a relatively neglected text, insisted on the primacy of the moral law for all religions, but still argued that although 'belief of a God and a future state, though no way necessary to the nature or obligation of virtue' these beliefs are 'without question of absolute necessity to support it in practice' because '...merit and happiness, virtue and prudence, will at last coincide in the next life'.[209] And late eighteenth-century Oxford had no equivalent to Cambridge's William Paley and his moderate endorsement of utility; Joseph Butler's *Analogy* was consistently preferred for teaching purposes. Moreover the ambivalence about John Locke's

---

[206] Agutter, *The difference between the death of the righteous and the wicked, illustrated in the instance of Dr Samuel Johnson and David Hume, Esq. A sermon* (London, 1800), 11.

[207] Horne, ed. Jones, *Memoirs of the life, studies and writings of Horne* (London, 1799), I. 31, 34 (letters to Horne's father, 1749).

[208] Isabel Rivers has pointed out that, in *Christianity as Old as the Creation* Tindal 'does not really deal with ethics although his whole approach to religion is ethical', *Reason, Grace and Sentiment*, II. 76–83, at 83. There were 150 replies to his book. See also Chapter 2, pp. 22–4, for Tindal.

[209] Adams, *The Nature and Obligation of Virtue. A sermon preached in the parish church of St Chad, Salop, . . .* (London, 1754), 45–6, 54.

OXFORD AND THE ARTS AND HUMANITIES 173

standing that was never wholly dissipated in this era—in such contrast to the wider, favourable public reception—confirmed the (otherwise quite misleading) impression for many that Oxford was tangential to the *siècle des lumières*. It stood in sharp contrast to the University's high profile across the continent in Oriental studies.

vi) Oriental studies

In terms of its institutional provision, Oxford was one of the foremost centres for Oriental learning in the world, a subject that even Gibbon could describe as 'the pride of Oxford',[210] with as many as two professorships (the Laudian and Lord Almoner's) in the subject area.[211] It had an uneven descent of academics holding the Laudian Chair of Arabic (1640) in the century after the death of the great Edward Pococke in 1691,[212] three of them—Thomas Hyde (1691–1703);[213] Thomas Hunt (1738–74), and Joseph White (1774–1814)—making some contribution to the very broad subject area stipulated by Laud: showing the similarities between Arabic, Syriac, and Hebrew, explaining points of grammar, and expounding the work of an ancient and approved author.[214] These three figures—all of them primarily Old Testament Bible scholars—were conscious of being the keepers of the flame that Pococke had originally illuminated,[215] and they had the riches of the Bodleian's manuscript collections from which to draw. For the most part, they satisfied the prevailing demand in the University for instruction in Hebrew[216] (essential in understanding the origins and early contexts of

---

[210] Gibbon once expressed an inclination to study Arabic, but his tutor discouraged him. *Memoirs*, 82.See Chap. 10, p. 77, n. 181.

[211] It could easily have had a third with proposals afoot early in the reign of George III to set up a chair in Persian. See 'A proposal for establishing a Professorship of the Persian language in the University of Oxford', printed pamphlet, probably by Warren Hastings. BL, India Office Records, Mss Eur B77, dated *c*.1767– 9. Cf. P.J. Marshall, 'Warren Hastings as scholar and patron', in eds. A. Whiteman, J. S. Bromley, and P. J. M. Dickson, *Statesmen, Scholars, and Merchants: Essays in Eighteenth-Century History presented to Dame Lucy Sutherland* (Oxford, 1973), 242–62, at 245. It was an indicator of the prestige of Persian as the best language for an ambitious cadet or junior writer in the East India Company's service.

[212] P. M. Holt, 'Edward Pococke (1604–91), the first Laudian Professor of Arabic at Oxford', *Oxoniensia*, 56 (1991), 119–30.

[213] John Wallis, who held the post between 1703 and 1738, was scorned by Hearne (II. 63) as one who 'if ever he understood' Arabic 'may be suppos'd now to have forgott it, he having the Character of one that keeps much Company and few Books, intirely neglecting his Studies'. He is dismissed as a 'disastrously bad' Professor by G. J. Toomer, *Eastern wisedome and learning. The study of Arabic in seventeenth-century England*(Oxford, 1996), 298.

[214] Arabic chairs were founded at Leiden (1613) and Cambridge (1632).

[215] Marshall, 'Oriental studies', in HUO V, 551–64, at 554.

[216] Hyde, Hunt, and White were also, during some part of their tenure as Laudian Professor, concurrently holders of the Regius Chair of Hebrew to which the Laudian chair, in effect, stood in reversion. Hyde was Bodley's Librarian from 1665 to 1701, and held positions at Salisbury and Gloucester cathedrals (archdeacon) as well as Oxford.

174 ENLIGHTENED OXFORD

Christianity) as well as Arabic and other eastern languages, and equipping future clerks in holy orders to defend its historical claims against its contemporary detractors.[217] Any other approach could invite criticism from the intellectually conventional. Thus Hunt's published comments to the effect that Hebrew and Arabic were sister languages, both descended from a common 'oriental' original, brought him censure from the Hutchinsonians in the University in the 1750s, who were determined to assert both the superiority and the antiquity of Hebrew vis-à-vis the Arabic.[218] The other chair, what would eventually become known as the Lord Almoner's Professorship (1699),[219] was more closely bound up with the teaching of contemporary Turkish and Arabic, undertaken primarily to be of service to the government in the translation of diplomatic and commercial correspondence with constituent parts of the Ottoman Empire.[220] Because of the uncertain funding of the post, it could operate either as a non-professorial endowment (as seems to have been the case when Jean Gagnier was lecturing and writing between 1714 and 1740), or held jointly with the Laudian chair, as Thomas Hunt did between 1740 and 1748.[221]

None of these professors were particularly interested in contextually reconstructing the intellectual culture of Arab societies over time; they were not attempting to make a case—as others increasingly were—for a neglected civilisation from which enlightened Europeans had much to gain.[222] In Oxford there was limited recognition that there was a republic of Arabic letters, a working community of scholars of 'different languages, political affiliations, and traditions of belief".[223] There was no

---

[217] Cf. Pocock, *Barbarism and religion*, I, 41.

[218] See Benjamin Holloway, *The Primaevity and Pre-eminence of the sacred Hebrew... vindicated from the repeated attempts of the Reverend Dr Hunt to level it with the Arabic, and other Oriental dialects* (Oxford, 1754). Holloway had elsewhere written on the age of Middle Eastern tongues, and appealed to divines (Hunt was clearly in his sights), not to 'mix, and yoke themselves unequally with Unbelievers; and even leave that contumacious Herd to write and Act in their own way'. *Remarks on Dr Sharp's Pieces on the Words Elohim and Berith* (Oxford, 1751), 34.

[219] L. S. Sutherland, 'The origin and early history of the lord almoner's professorship in Arabic at Oxford', *BLR*, 10 (1978–82), 166–77. John Fell had been keen to establish a school where prospective missionaries could master Arabic. C. G. D. Littleton, 'Ancient languages and new science: the Levant in the intellectual life of Robert Boyle', in eds. A. Hamilton, M. H. van den Boogert, and B. Westerweel, *The Republic of Letters and the Levant* (Leiden, 2005), 151–71, at 160.

[220] For government interest in the Lord Almoner's chair and the production of linguists, Marshall, 'Oriental Studies', 552–3.

[221] Hunt (1696–1774), fellow of Hart Hall, 1721, gave up the Lord Almoner's post on becoming Regius Professor of Hebrew in 1747. His career was facilitated by his being chaplain to the 1st Earl of Macclesfield (the disgraced Lord Chancellor) and tutor to his sons. The Laudian Professor (1703–38) was John Wallis, an absentee. After 1728 all his teaching was given to Gagnier. For Gagnier see Michael J. Franklin, 'Gagnier, John (c.1670–1740) ODNB, online edn., 2004. Also p. 92 in this chapter, and Chapter 11, p. 34.

[222] As Noel Malcolm has remarked, '...the antiquarianism of the scholar was, for a long time, blocked by the ethnography of the observer'. Malcolm, 'The Study of Islam in Early Modern Europe: Obstacles and Missed Opportunities', in eds. P. Miller and F. Louis, *Antiquarianism and Intellectual life in Europe and China, 1500–1800* (Ann Arbor, MI, 2012), 265–88, at 279.

[223] Alexander Bevilacqua, *The Republic of Arabic Letters. Islam and the European Enlightenment* (Cambridge, MA, 2018), 3.

Oxford equivalent to Simon Ockley's (chaplain to Robert Harley) *History of the Saracens*, based on hitherto unused source material and published in two volumes in 1708 and 1718 (for which Cambridge would take the credit),[224] unless it be an edition of the description of Egypt in the early thirteenth century by Abd al-Latif of Baghdad that was finally completed in 1800, edited by Joseph White.[225] Hunt had collected the materials for an edition, even issued a prospectus but, characteristically diffident in his immense learning, never took the project any further forward.[226] White intended his edition to be the outrider of an ambitious 'General History of Egypt', but that, too, was never forthcoming.

On the whole, for the Oxford professoriate, whatever the Arabs had managed in the medieval centuries in terms of sound learning had been either transmitted back to Christendom or consigned to appropriate neglect, save in the case of astronomy and medicine. Hunt did concede that medical treatises written in Arabic contained much that was still important, and it was on his recommendation that the University Press brought out a Latin text in 1778 of the *De chirurgia* of 'Abulcasis' (al-Zahrawi), a medieval Arab physician (died 1098).[227] There was also a readiness to work on new editions and translations of Arabic historians, following the pioneering work of Pococke. Hyde, an extraordinarily gifted polyglot, made a breakthrough into the contemporary understanding of Zoroastrianism, thanks to making contacts with learned Parsis in Surat, obtaining their scriptures, and translating them. The end product was his masterly *Historia religionis veterum Persarum eorumque Magorum* (Oxford, 1700), a considerable advance on the previous accounts that had relied exclusively on Greek tradition, and a work that would be used by Montesquieu.[228] According to Guy G. Stroumsa, '...it shows in exemplary manner how a scholar with only limited access to the

---

[224] For Ockley's equal regard for the cultural achievements of the Arabs as well as for their military deeds, and his many research visits to use the Arabic manuscripts in the Bodleian, see ibid., 139–40, 146–7, 153; Cornel Zwierlein, *Imperial Unknowns. The French and British in the Mediterranean, 1650–1750* (Oxford, 2016), 202–4, 229–30.

[225] John Swinton, the Keeper of the University Archives, claimed authorship of several articles which appeared in the last of seven volumes of the 'ancient' part of *An Universal History from the Earliest Account of Time to the Present* (London, 1736–44) and in a volume of *Additions to the Universal History* (London, 1750), GM 54 (1784), 892. They are generally judged not to be distinguished productions. Marshall, 'Oriental Studies', 560–1.

[226] *Proposals for Printing by Subscription, Abdollatiphi historiae Aegypti compendium* (Oxford, 1746). In 1750 it was reported by a visitor that his translation into Latin from the Arabic of the Egyptian history had made him put aside his 'papers relating to a future Grammar of the Arabic;' John Williams to Gregory Sharpe, n.d. [mid-1750], Bodl. MS Eng. lett. d. 145. f. 16. Williams also noted: 'His wine was very good; we had a great deal of Greek, the natural consequence of a bottle'.

[227] Hunt, *De antiquitate, elegantia, utilitate, linguae arabicae, oratio* (Oxford, 1739); Marshall, 'Oriental studies', 555.

[228] Stroumsa, *A New Science*, 101–13; J. Duchesne-Guillemin, *The Western response to Zoroaster* (Oxford, 1958); Norah Kathleen Firby, *European travellers and their perception of Zoroastrians in the 17th and 18th Centuries* (Berlin, 1988); M. Strausberg, *Fascinazion Zarathustra: Zoroaster und die europäische Religionsgeschichte der frühen* (Berlin, 1998). Zoroastrian studies were not a priority for Hyde's successors in Oxford.

176 ENLIGHTENED OXFORD

necessary sources can still deal significantly with a historical phenomenon'.[229] Nevertheless, it had few initial subscribers, and Hyde's contemporary reputation (salted by stories of his private life), descended to a 'mixture of amusement and contempt'.[230] It was only in the mid-century that international esteem rose for Hyde's *Historia*; it was republished in 1760 in Oxford through Hunt's efforts, and his collected papers appeared in two volumes in 1767.[231]

Studies of Islam as a religion and in the life and writings of the Prophet existed on a limited scale in eighteenth-century Oxford. Humphrey Prideaux's 1697 biography (which had no access to untranslated Arabic works) was much republished but his main purpose was polemical: to warn against the errors of the deists and to show how the enemies of Christianity could exploit divisions within the Church.[232] As G.J. Toomer put it:

> Everything is grist to his mill, provided that it presents the subject of his biography in a bad light.[233]

The most dispassionate academic was Jean Gagnier (a French Roman Catholic convert to Anglicanism), who produced an edition of *Ismael abu'l-Feda, De vita, et rebus gestis Muhammedis* (Oxford, 1723) that at least took the Prophet's historical standing seriously and was the basis for his *Vie de Mahomet* (3 vols., Amsterdam, 1731). This accessible text, with long passages translated from the Muslim sources, turned out to be the last word on the subject from an Oxonian of this era, and was the basis of most other European writing on Muhammad until the publication of Gustav Weil's *Mohammed der Prophet* over a century later.[234] Gagnier's was, in every sense, an enlightened work, for he was trying to cater sympathetically for the growing curiosity in the west about the Prophet's life and religion and attempting

---

[229] *A new science*, 103. Stroumsa argues for Hyde's 'deep influence' on Pierre Bayle.

[230] Toomer, *Eastern wisedome*, 297. Nevertheless, on hearing of his death, a Dutch professor exclaimed 'Decessit Hydius, stupor mundi! (Hyde is dead, the world is numb)'. Quoted in Stroumsa, *A New Science*, 103.

[231] Carter, *History of O.U. Press*, I. 390. Hyde also had an awareness of the major significance of Chinese culture and even brought a Chinese Christian to Oxford. Toomer, *Eastern wisedome*, 248–9. Toomer considers Hyde's output 'substantial' but 'erratic'. ibid.

[232] Prideaux, *The True Nature of Imposture fully Display'd in the Life of Mahomet... Offered to the Consideration of the Deists of the Present Age* (Oxford, 1697); P. M. Holt, 'The treatment of Arab history by Prideaux, Ockley, and Sale', in eds. B. Lewis and P. M. Holt, *Historians of the Middle East* (Oxford, 1962), 290–302.

[233] Toomer, *Eastern wisedome*, 292. According to Toomer, Prideaux's book bears witness to the decline of Arabic studies in England.

[234] Gibbon considered Gagnier as the 'best and most authentic of our guides' in understanding the Prophet. *The History of the Decline and Fall of the Roman Empire*, ed. David Womersley (3 vols., Harmondsworth, 1994), III. 190. See B. Lewis, 'Gibbon on Muhammad', in eds. G. W. Bowerstock, J. Clive, and S. R. Graubaud, *Edward Gibbon and the Decline and Fall of the Roman Empire* (Cambridge, MA., 1977), 61–73, at 65. Gagnier still described Muhammad as 'the greatest villain of mankind, and the most mortal enemy of God'.

to see him from a distinct Muslim viewpoint.[235] Oxford produced no work of importance on Muslim sacred texts. There was no equivalent to George Sale's 1734 translation of the Qur'an into English that located Islam 'as a system of belief rooted in time, place, and, most significantly, [in] the text of the Qur'an'.[236] Though Sale's translation was commissioned by the SPCK, this may have been because he was caught up in the Spinozist current of Enlightenment thought (his was the translation read by Voltaire) and Anglican Oxford opted to stand well back from such a double (if interrelated) challenge to orthodoxy. The temptation to confirm the moral supremacy of Christianity against this belated version of monotheism had a strong attraction at Oxford. Joseph White's 1784 Bampton Lectures—'a Comparison of Mahometism and Christianity'—took this line and represented something of a regression to a pre-Enlightenment disdain for Islamic ethics, and rowed back against the generally increased recognition of the cultural and religious sophistication of Arab cultures. Nevertheless, White made the conservative case eloquently only to attract criticism for plagiarism.[237]

Hyde's published work on various oriental religions, like his successors', was predominantly in Latin, and their sense of a wider audience beyond the academy was not well developed. That attitude was reflected in the inability of either Hyde or Hunt to transmit their undoubted interest in Arabic and Persian poetry into a serviceable, accessible English translation.[238] And Hyde never brought out his promised Arabic-English dictionary, that would have stimulated exploration of the literature. The scholar who really brought Orientalist writings to public attention and secured the plaudits of his Oxford coevals and abundant international esteem was [Sir] William Jones (1746–94), fellow of University College from 1766, 'Persian Jones', whose curiosity was early awakened from his reading while at Harrow School of the *Thousand and One Arabian Nights* in Antoine Galland's twelve-volume French translation (1704–17).[239]

Jones, who became the foremost Orientalist of his generation,[240] brought Mirza, a Syrian he had met in London, with him to Oxford in order to imitate (and,

---

[235] Marshall, 'Oriental studies', 553, 560. For this wider tendency to dispassionate comprehension of the world's religions see eds. Lynn Hunt, Margaret C. Jacob, and Wijnand Mijnhardt, *The Book that changed Europe. Picart & Bernard's religious ceremonies of the world* (Cambridge, MA, 2010).

[236] Ziad Elmarsafy, *The Enlightenment Qur'an: the politics of translation and the construction of Islam* (Oxford, 2009), 24.

[237] Bevilacqua, *The Republic of Arabic Letters*, 69–72, 84–9. See Chapter 10, p. 38, for White's 'plagiarism'.

[238] Hyde left in manuscript translations of Sa'di and Hafez, but, tellingly, they were in Latin. Marshall, 'Oriental studies', 556.

[239] Such was the popularity of the Nights that Marina Warner called the eighteenth century 'The Century of the Arabian Nights'. *Stranger Magic: Charmed states and the 'Arabian Nights'* (London, 2012).

[240] For what follows I am particularly indebted to Michael J. Franklin, *Sir William Jones* (Cardiff, 1995), 5–13, 15–24; Franklin, 'Orientalist Jones' (Oxford, 2011); G. Cannon, *The life and mind of Oriental Jones: Sir William Jones, the Father of Modern Linguistics* (Cambridge, 1990); ed. A. Murray, *Sir William Jones 1746–1794: A commemoration* (Oxford, 1998).

Fig. 4.4 Sir William Jones, John Flaxman, frieze from the monument in the College of University College, Oxford (The Master and Fellows of University College, Oxford).

sometimes, correct) his native pronunciation; he also set about intensifying his studies in (pre-Islamic) Arabic and Persian literature (principally from manuscripts held in the Bodleian), inspired by Robert Lowth's poetic insights into Hebrew and measured by his own precocious linguistic talents. Jones's relentless stream of publications in the early 1770s brought him into contact with admiring scholars across the continent while tapping into a market-tested subject from a wide range of domestic readers who associated Persia with romantic tales. Jones was actually working to disabuse them, to get away from the tradition of Eastern personae that had flourished since Montesquieu's *Lettres Persanes* was first published (1721).[241] Drawing on an Enlightenment sense of criticism through the comparative method, he was insistent that the preoccupation with fantastic Oriental imaginings were distorting perceptions of Middle Eastern cultures at every level, and determined on putting the best of Classical Arabic literature before the public. To stimulate educated taste, he stressed the exceptional similarities between Homer and his Persian counterparts by, for instance, offering both verse and prose translations of *Ten Odes* by Hafez, giving readers a comparative perspective that respected the textual integrity of the original version.[242]

---

[241] Clare Brant, *Eighteenth-Century Letters and British Culture* (Basingstoke, 2006), 218–20.
[242] In his short *Dissertation sur la littérature orientale* (London, 1771) Jones thus juxtaposed French prose versions of Hafez's 10th Ode and Horace's 32nd Ode.

OXFORD AND THE ARTS AND HUMANITIES   179

Jones packed his *Grammar of the Persian Language* (1771) with poetic examples (including the 'Song of Hafez', the first translation of a Persian song into English) to reflect the sophistication of its literary culture,[243] and his book had an impact on a vastly wider range of readers than grammarians or lexicographers forming,[244] as it did, the taste of the next generation of English poets, Romantic poets.[245] The preface has been deemed a 'turning point in the history of humane studies, for it comprises the most eloquent *apologia pro litteris orientalibus* which had yet been penned, perhaps that has ever been penned'.[246] In *Poems, consisting chiefly of translations from the Asiatick languages* (1772), Jones produced his best-seller, one which featured close translations many of his own verses, loosely based on Asian models, that dynamically and originally created the basis of the Oriental verse tale, and delighted a public ready for anything Ossianic, especially another version of Fingal the Caledonian hero, coming out of the east.[247] It was a growing market, one that consumed the recent writings 'recovered' by Thomas Percy, Thomas Chatterton, James Macpherson, and, most recently, the Aberdonian, James Beattie's, *The Minstrel* (1771), a Celtic version of Jones's primitive, proto-Romantic aesthetic. As Elizabeth Montagu, the 'Queen of the Blues', rapturously observed, following publication:

> The descriptions are so fine, & all the objects so brilliant, that the sense aches at them, and I wish'd that Ossians poems had been laying by me, that I might sometimes have turn'd my eyes from ye dazzling splendor of the Eastern noon day to the moonlight picture of a bleak mountain. Every object in those pieces is blooming and & beautiful; the passions too are of the sort which belong to paradise.[248]

---

[243] The preface, Jonathan Israel observes, stands out 'for the eloquence and cogency of its plea for the study of eastern languages and literatures', *Democratic Enlightenment. Philosophy, Revolution, and Human Rights 1750–1790* (Oxford, 2012), 599.

[244] Jones took care to notify the public in his advertisement to the Grammar that he had secured the patronage of Cambridge as well as Oxford, stating, 'The protection of the most celebrated Universities in the world, sufficiently proves its high importance to the progress of learning; . . .', quoted in Cannon, *Oriental Jones*, 41.

[245] Jerome J. McGann appropriately offers Jones's later (1785) Sanskrit-inspired *A Hymn to Na'ra'yena* as the first poem in his *The New Oxford Book of Romantic Verse* (Oxford, 1993). The last edition of the Persian Grammar (the 8th) appeared only in 1828. See also V. de Sola Pinto, 'Sir William Jones and English literature', *Journal of the London School of Oriental Studies*, 11 (1946), 686–94.

[246] A. J. Arberry, *Asiatic Jones: the life and influence of Sir William Jones* (London, 1946), 33.

[247] J. Yohannan, 'The Persian poetry fad in England, 1770–1825', *Comparative Literature*, 4 (1952), 137–60.

[248] To James Beattie, quoted in ed. G. Cannon, *The Letters of Sir William Jones* (2 vols., Oxford, 1970), I. 111. Jane, Duchess of Gordon's comment that 'often have I heard verses of his *Minstrel* brought in, &, repeated with such enthusiasm as brought tears into my eyes-' could well be applied to much of Jones's 'Persian' verse of the early 1770s. To Sir William Forbes, [26 Oct. 1789], NLS Fettercairn MSS, ACC.4796/41.

180 ENLIGHTENED OXFORD

In the first of two persuasive and influential essays appended to *Poems*, 'On the Arts, Commonly Called Imitative', Jones reflected on the processes of transmitting literature from one culture to another, rejected Aristotle's supposed doctrine that all poetry is imitative, and instead emphasised the role of the passions in an original attempt to justify Oriental literary sublimity.[249] In the second, 'On the poetry of the Eastern nations', Jones claimed that European poetry had 'subsisted too long on the perpetual repetition of the same images, and incessant allusions to the same fables' to drive home his broadly Lowthian contention that the sophisticated Persian civilisation and its letters could be no less inspiring to the cultivated mind than either Athens or Rome, and worthy of study in its own right.[250] He was also concerned to show that Persia, far from being a despotic polity, actually had a preoccupation with liberty, property rights, and reason that compared favourably with the European record. He instanced the Persian poet, Sa'di, who would likely have been suppressed in Europe for 'spreading with too strong a glare the light of liberty and reason'. Such convictions fanned the growth of his own republican Whiggism in the course of the 1770s in a manner that lessened the number of his friends (if not his admirers) at Oxford.[251] Jones's extraordinary early flowering was recognised by his election to the Royal Society in 1772 aged just twenty-six, and he became a member of Johnson's Literary Club the following year.[252] In an Oxford context, Jones owed much to the support of University College under Nathan Wetherell, and he shone out as one of its academic stars alongside Robert Chambers and William Scott. Weeks before his death, Hunt, too, gave his blessing to Jones's *Poeseos Asiaticae Commentariorum* (1774), a learned if uneven treatment of Asiatic poetry in 473 pages, that was very well received by English and continental orientalists.[253]

Jones had no interest either in Christian apologetics or in using his knowledge of Asiatic language as the basis for a career in the Established Church.[254] He might

---

[249] Cannon, *Oriental Jones*, 51.

[250] *Sir William Jones: Selected Poetical and Prose Works*, ed. Michael J. Franklin, (Cardiff, 1995), 336.

[251] He was an independent Whig candidate for the University against Sir William Dolben at the general election of 1780. Jones considered the charge unjust 'if they mean one, who wishes to see a republick in *England*;' but just 'if they mean one, who thinks a republick in the abstract the only rational, manly, intelligible form of government'. *Letters*, II. 499.

[252] Franklin, *Sir William Jones*, 30.

[253] Hunt (who had criticised the manuscript), hoped the book would be 'an happy instrument in the hands of learned and inquisitive men, for unlocking the rich treasures of wisdom and knowledge' contained in eastern languages. 2 Mar. 1774, Lord Teignmouth, *Memoirs of the life, writings, and correspondence of Sir William Jones* (2 vols., London, 1804), I. 209. Gibbon in the *Decline & Fall* claimed he had read with much pleasure this work 'of that wonderful linguist'. ed. Womersley, III. 353.

[254] Jones considered the truth of Christianity to be highly probable, if incapable of demonstration, and a part of English law. Cannon, *Oriental Jones*, 60. His colleague and first biographer, John Shore, 1st Lord Teignmouth, Governor-General of India (1793–8), did his best to fit Jones into what Cannon calls 'a near-model of Clapham evangelicalism', *Oriental Jones*, xi. Lowth's *Isaiah. A New Translation* (Oxford, 1778) was admittedly an important influence on him.

have made an appreciable income from his book sales but, short of both monied and learned patrons, he opted instead for a legal career (he was called to the Bar in 1774) to give him the financial independence that his fellowship would never give him. He eventually turned away from Persian to Sanskrit and Indology once he secured a judgeship in India in 1783, a year after the publication of his translation of the *Mu'allaqát, or Seven Arabian Poems*, brought his Bedouins to public attention for the last time. Before he was thirty he had received international recognition as Britain's leading philologist, but the University was unable or unwilling to retain him, and Jones's interests were anyway turning to law and politics. Beyond his loyal core of friends at University College (he was senior fellow there by 1780), the University as a *corps* found it hard to claim fully as its own son one so committed to radicalism and universalism by the later 1770s, and somewhat detached from theology.[255] Despite an early admiration for Blackstone,[256] Jones had been unwilling to defer to the temper of the academic establishment and support the American War, and his alma mater reciprocated the favour in what was something of a lost opportunity for them both.

State pressures arising from intensified imperial responsibilities in India after the end of the Seven Years' War were the constant backdrop to Jones's work and offered non-academic career paths for scholars such as Jones. Though he turned down the Duke of Grafton's government offer of a post as interpreter for Eastern languages in 1767 (he subsequently expressed regret at his decision),[257] his utility to the East India Company was obvious and was early recognised when the Company attempted to pirate *Grammar of the Persian language* (1771) in proof (and would later adopt it as its standard training manual). Jones was by no means alone in being courted by the East India Company. Nathaniel Halhed (1751–1830) was a classically educated Christ Church graduate who joined its service and was appointed by the Governor-General of Bengal, Warren Hastings, to make a compilation of Hindu law and translate it into English, despite Halhed's limited knowledge of Sanskrit and dependence on Bengali or Hindustani explanations of passages in the text by the pandits. He was the translator of *A Code of Gentoo Laws* (1776) and author of the first English grammar of Bengali (1778). He connected the latter to Sanskrit and anticipated Jones's statement on the relation of Sanskrit to Latin and Greek.[258]

---

[255] Franklin, *Sir William Jones*, 16. Indications of his very Whiggish attachment to liberty were apparent in the planned Oration for Encaenia, 1773, which he chose not to deliver rather than amend. Cannon, *Oriental Jones*, 61–2.

[256] Peter Brown, *The Chathamites. A study in the relationship between personalities and ideas in the second half of the eighteenth century* (London, 1967), 361.

[257] Cannon, *Oriental Jones*, 7–8, 12, 57.

[258] R. Rocher, *Orientalism, Poetry, and the Millennium: The Checkered Life of Nathaniel Brassey Halhed* (Delhi, 1983). Jessica Patterson, *Religion, Enlightenment and Empire: British interpretations of Hinduism in the eighteenth century* (Cambridge, 2002) appeared too late for me to notice it.

182   ENLIGHTENED OXFORD

These growing needs of state also stimulated the engagement of other Oxford figures in Persian (the language of cultured Indian Muslims). Thus Joseph White between 1780 and 1783 prepared an edition of the Persian text of the *Institutes of Timur*, the whole appearing in 1783 at the expense of the East India Company, with a translation into English by Major William Davy, Persian secretary to Warren Hastings. Despite the blow to his reputation from the way his 1784 Bampton Lectures were composed, White was one of the most outstanding linguists of the late eighteenth century, and was in contact with international orientalists, among them Silvestre de Sacy (a leading member of the *Académie Royale des Inscriptions et Belles-Lettres* in Paris during the second half of the century). John Richardson of Wadham toiled many years while still in his twenties to produce a Persian Dictionary, that was completed and published in two volumes in 1776 and 1780. He was no less committed than Jones to appealing to men and women of taste rather than blinkered, inelegant 'editors and commentators' with their 'addiction to' 'an unnecessary display of learning', and his work advanced knowledge of the language in England.[259] Though showing some credulity regarding Persian writers, Richardson was a considerable talent in his own right whose labours in the Bodleian and other libraries were extensive, yet the riches of the University's Oriental manuscripts remained under-exploited in the 1780s and 1790s.[260] Other scholars were, on the whole, slow in responding to Jones's exhortations to study and translate the available holdings, while the original Pockockian themes in oriental scholarship had not been displaced by either the new literary studies Jones had pioneered or the turn of the British imperial state towards the Indian subcontinent. Though at best partially acknowledging him, Oxford University's reputation for encouraging scholarship in Oriental languages benefitted significantly from William Jones's high standing and its international renown was boosted accordingly.[261] Such a trend was also evident in the musical life of the University, one that it shared with the city.

vii) Music

Oxford was one of the greatest musical centres in Europe, open and accessible to all comers: it sent its musicians out to London and beyond to sing, perform, and

---

[259] J. Richardson, *A Grammar of the Arabick Language* (London, 1776), viii, quoted in Marshall, 'Oriental studies', 562; Wells, *Wadham College*, 141. Wadham also had William Austin as an assistant lecturer in Arabic for a short period starting in 1776.

[260] There were regular additions to the corpus of materials in the University's holdings. Thus, on the death in 1754 of James Fraser, a factor in the East India Company's service in Surat in the 1740s, his widow sold his collection of Sanskrit manuscripts to the nascent Radcliffe Library. Cohn, *Colonialism and its Forms of Knowledge*, 97–8.

[261] For Jones's defence of Oxford scholarship against French detractors, see Cannon, *Oriental Jones*, 42–4; Brown, *The Chathamites*, 352.

OXFORD AND THE ARTS AND HUMANITIES   183

compose, while the extensive music-making public joined celebrities national and international in flocking to Oxford to join in its musical life.[262] College choirs and chapel organists in three colleges (Christ Church, Magdalen, and New College) provided musical accompaniment to daily Anglican services,[263] and some of the first purpose-built facilities for concerts became available with the opening of the Holywell Music Room in 1748. In terms of musical geography, the Oxford musical nexus looked not just to London and west to the Three Choirs Festival, but also into the West Midlands to Lichfield and Birmingham, and south to Salisbury. Music thus constituted a critical part of Oxonian life and was relatively accessible to outsiders, with some of it part of a repertoire they might encounter elsewhere but that could be heard to advantage in a university centre and place of exceptional culture. Academically, the study of music figured no more than nominally in the curriculum, and suppliants for the degrees of either Bachelor or Doctor of Music only needed to matriculate at one or other college to take their degree without proceeding through a course of formal instruction.[264] There was a Heather Professor of Music but his official duties were light and centred on delivering a lecture in English on the Saturday before the Act[265] and on composing ceremonial works for University events, especially for the Act when it was such a centrepiece of the University's festive year, before c.1710. The holder of the Chair at the Revolution, Richard Goodson senior, was Professor for thirty-six years until his death in 1718. Rather than securing fame for any composition of exceptional distinction, he was adept at the production of various *pièces d'occasion* such as his 'Ode for the visit of William III' in 1695 with its choral setting of the words

---

[262] S. Wollenberg, *Music at Oxford in the Eighteenth and Nineteenth Centuries* (Oxford, 2001); idem., 'Music in Eighteenth-Century Oxford', *Proceedings of the Royal Musical Association*, 108 (1981–2), 69–99. Cyril Ehrlich, *The Music Profession in Britain since the Eighteenth Century. A Social History* (Oxford, 1985), 19–25, discusses English musical life in the provinces with barely a mention of Oxford.

[263] The traveller, the Hon John Byng, was not impressed with the New College choir: 'the service most idly perform'd, by such persons as I should suppose had never learnt to sing or read.' John Byng, 5th Viscount Torrington, *The Torrington Diaries (1781–94)*, ed. C. Bruyn Andrews (4 vols., New York, 1935–8), I. 55.

[264] The BMus tended to be taken mainly by cathedral and church organists and choirmasters; the DMus was rarely awarded and usually only to the most distinguished musicians, such as William Croft, Charles Burney, and William Crotch. Further details of recipients are given in S. L. F. Wollenberg, 'Music and musicians', in HUO V, 865–88, at 867–8.

[265] It had evidently become a concert by the time Richard Goodson senior was Heather Professor. See generally H. Watkins Shaw, 'The Oxford University Chair of Music, 1627–1947, with some account of Oxford degrees in music from 1856', *BLR*, 16 (1998), 233–70; *The Heather Professor of Music, 1626–1976: exhibition in the divinity school October 1976* (Bodleian Library, Oxford, 1976). The lecture was subsequently detached from the chair and allotted to an individual elected annually by the vice chancellor and the proctors. C. F. A. Williams, *Degrees in music* (London, 1893), 35. The lecture was offered in the Sheldonian in 1733 with a view to entertaining the ladies. See Bodl. MS Top. Oxon. e.214.

Fig. 4.5 Holywell Music Room (© the author).

'Plaudite regi, plaudite Gulielmo'. His son, Richard junior (d. 1741), succeeded him in his chair on his death.[266]

Then came another father and son pair. These were the two Hayeses, William and son Philip. It was the elder who made the greater impact because of his more emollient personality and his greater distinction as a composer.[267] William Hayes's (1708–78) setting of William Collins's *The Passions* was a contemporary success when first performed in the Sheldonian on 6 July 1750. He followed it up with two other major works, *Peleus and Thetis*, and the 1751 Commemoration Ode, *Where shall the muse* (a setting of a Thomas Warton text), which was far more than a slavish Handelian imitation (though he was a warm admirer of the composer). Hayes had an exceptional all-round talent. He was a composer, singer, music director, writer and academic, organist and 'informator choristarum' of Magdalen College chapel in 1734. As Professor of Music from 1741, he was the first such to have any known role in the examination of exercises for music

---

[266] Wollenberg, 'Music and Musicians', 870n. Both men were also organists of Christ Church. Robert Thompson, 'Goodson, Richard (c.1655–1718)', ODNB, online edn. 2008; htttp://library.chch.ox.ac.uk/music

[267] For an authoritative study Simon Heighes, *The Life and Works of William and Philip Hayes* (New York, 1995). For Philip Hayes, Heather Professor 1777–97, see Paul R. Hale, 'Music and Musicians', in eds. J. Buxton and P. Williams, *New College, Oxford 1379–1979* (Oxford 1979), 267–93, at 273–4; J. S. Bumpus, *History of English Cathedral Music, 1548–1889* (London, 1908), 215.

Fig. 4.6 Charles Burney, Sir Joshua Reynolds, oil on canvas, 1781 (© National Portrait Gallery, London).

degrees.[268] He was also the principal moving force behind the construction of the Holywell Music Room. Hayes produced English chamber cantatas, organ-accompanied anthems, and convivial vocal music, and was much admired by the pre-eminent critic, Charles Burney. He combined a deep antiquarian bent (his *Catches, Glees, and Canons* of 1757 was the first extant publication devoted to the subject)[269] with an awareness of the latest styles and forms, and his writings on music cover aesthetics, and the business of organising concerts and music festivals (he conducted regularly himself for the Three Choirs festival). Other works included an oratorio, 'The Fall of Jericho', and 'Six Cantatas'. *The Passions* became a readily imitative piece of work that lived on in the repertoire, being revived by the composer himself at the Three Choirs Festival in Gloucester in 1760.[270]

---

[268] Watkins Shaw, 'University Chair of Music', 247.
[269] Oxford had one of the earliest catch clubs in the country. See Brian Robins, 'The Catch and Glee in Eighteenth-Century Provincial England', in eds. S. Wollenberg and S. McVeigh, *Concert Life in Eighteenth-Century Britain* (Aldershot, 2004), 141–60, esp. 143–5.
[270] Ibid., 882–3; CD notes by Anthony Rooley and Simon Heighes to Hayes, *The Passions*, Schola Cantorum Basiliensis (2010).

186   ENLIGHTENED OXFORD

Of all the Heather Professors, it was William Crotch (1775–1847) who turned out to be the major talent and celebrity.[271] As a musical prodigy, he had been involved in concerts at Oxford since 1779, when he had sat on his mother's knee to give an organ recital and encouraged Burney to make comparisons with Mozart in his *Account of an Infant Musician* (London, 1779).[272] Crotch was the first Heather Professor of the century to give regular lectures (1800–4), and in published format they make clear that the historical study of music in the University was under way; he had a talent for combining academic example with material from different countries and eras.[273]

The choral tradition that centred on college chapels and the performance of daily worship was strong; the Heather Professor was customarily organist of the university church, and all of them (with the exception of Goodson junior and Hayes senior) had acted as organist at Christ Church before appointment to the chair. They severally, through their composition of church music and work with choristers, both preserved and strengthened the English choral tradition, sending out many of their pupils to take up positions in provincial cathedrals and parish churches,[274] and developing an awareness of how Oxford music might have its uses for provincial congregations.[275] Thus William Hayes's *Sixteen Psalms... set to music for the use of Magdalen College, Oxford* (1776), included a score without an organ part for country churches. The Heather Professors ignored neither developments in liturgical musical settings on the continent nor the rich heritage of their predecessors since the Reformation, and made the choirs of Christ Church, New College, and Magdalen centres of choral excellence for most of the century.[276]

These collegiate services certainly had their share of visitors from outside (Christ Church cathedral was, after all, the mother church of the Oxford diocese) yet it was the set-piece academic occasions of the whole university that brought in outsiders and music to match for Oxford *en fête*. Music was played and heard on ceremonial academic festival occasions such as the Act and Encaenia in the summer, when the official ceremonial in the Sheldonian was supplemented by regular concerts. In the early eighteenth century, one could expect to hear an ode

---

[271] Technically speaking, he was the first-recognised 'professor', rather than just 'Music Master' under Heather's Ordinances of 1626, Watkins Shaw, 'University Chair of Music', 249. He was appointed at the tender age of twenty-two in 1797.

[272] For Crotch in Oxford see Cox, *Recollections*, 149–50.

[273] Wollenberg, 'Music and Musicians', 885.

[274] It seems likely that some of the earliest provincial musical societies of the eighteenth century were started by clergy in cathedral cities and modelled on those of Oxford, as in Hereford.

[275] Sally Drage, 'A Reappraisal of Provincial Church Music', in ed. D. Wyn Jones, *Music in Eighteenth-Century Britain* (Aldershot, 2001), 172–90, at 183.

[276] Wollenberg, 'Music and musicians', 886–7. Learned sacred works from the contemporary Catholic Church were performed in Oxford concerts. The Stabat Mater *c.*1710 of Emanuele d'Astorga (1686–1757?) was one such. William Weber, *The Rise of Music Classics in Eighteenth-Century England. A Study in Canon, Ritual, and Ideology* (Oxford, 1992), 184–5.

for solo voices, chorus, and instruments or a mixture of overtures, symphonic style pieces, songs, and choruses. The Heather Professor had final responsibility for deciding on the choice of pieces and choreographing the event and he might call on other colleagues to supplement his own music for the occasion. Thus Henry Aldrich supplemented Goodson's musical offerings at the Act in 1703 with his own small-scale compositions.

The Act of 1713 to celebrate the Treaty of Utrecht saw the University excel itself in proclaiming its fulsome loyalty to the Queen and the Oxford ministry, and music was used to get the message across to everyone gathered. William Croft, Organist and Master of the Choristers at Westminster Abbey, and Organist and Composer of the Chapel Royal, was called in to set to music two Odes (*Laurus cruentas* and *With noise of cannon*) written by Joseph Trapp, the Poetry professor, to celebrate the Peace.[277] The occasion, according to one London paper, was a great success, and Croft stood triumphant for his *Musicus Apparatus Academicus*: 'The Harmony, Solemnity, and Variety of which Piece, has given all that are Judges an unspeakable Esteem for that exquisite and inimitable Master'.[278] Croft received his doctorate for these accomplished pieces. The Act and, subsequently, Encaenia, often elicited some fine submissions from intending doctoral gradu-ands. An instance of an outstanding Oxford exercise for the DMus was Charles Burney's Haydnesque anthem 'I will love Thee, O Lord my Strength' (1769) with its subtle phrasing and sensitive word-setting,[279] one subsequently heard at Hamburg under the direction of C. P. E. Bach in 1773, as well as 'repeatedly performed at Oxford, after it had fulfilled its original destination'.[280] It was by no means only English church musicians who were honoured with the award of the D.Mus. The University looked to recognise academically both native composers writing significant amounts for the theatre, such as Thomas Arne (his Roman Catholicism proved no obstacle) and Samuel Arnold in 1759 and 1773,

---

[277] For the extent of this practice see T. A. Trowles, 'The musical ode in Britain, *c*.1670–1800', DPhil diss., University of Oxford, 1992.

[278] *The British-Mercury*, 15 July 1713, quoted in H. Diack Johnstone, 'Music and Drama at the Oxford Act of 1713', in eds. Wollenberg and McVeigh, *Concert Life*, 199–218, at 209; M. Tilmouth, 'The beginnings of provincial concert life in England', in eds. C. Hogwood and R. Luckett, *Music in Eighteenth-Century England. Essays in Memory of Charles Cudworth* (Cambridge, 1985), 1–19, at 9. For details of the verse see OUA: NW/1/1 *Lemmata et Quaestiones, etc. In Comitiis et Ecaeniis, etc, 1677–1733*. Much was made of 'Ormondus Imperator', very little of his predecessor as Captain-General, currently in exile, the Duke of Marlborough. A.D. Godley, *Oxford in the eighteenth century* (London, 1908), 188–9.

[279] Burney expressed his pleasure that in the performance of his anthem there was 'not one mistake of consequence'. To Esther and Fanny Burney, Oxford, 22 June 1769, in ed. A. Ribeiro, SJ, *The Letters of Charles Burney vol. 1, 1751–1784* (Oxford, 1991), 52–3. See Roger Lonsdale, *Dr Charles Burney. A literary biography* (Oxford, 1965), 77–9.

[280] Charles Burney, *A General History of Music* (4 vols., London, 1776–89), III. 329; *Memoirs of Dr Charles Burney 1726–1769*, eds. S. Klima, G. Bowers, and K. S. Grant, (Lincoln, NE, 1988), 178; Wollenberg, 'Music and musicians', 869 and n.

188 ENLIGHTENED OXFORD

respectively, as well as distinguished foreign musicians, among them the virtuoso flautist Friedrich Hartmann Graf in 1789 and the renowned Joseph Haydn in 1791.[281]

After the 1713 Act, it took the University another two decades to develop the institutional confidence to celebrate on such a grand scale again and, for the 1733 Act, it had what it believed to be a trump celebrity card: an invitation to the leading court composer, Georg Friedrich Handel. He accepted. It was personally lucrative to him because of the number of expensive benefit concerts staged at the Sheldonian, though the University was miffed when he snubbed it over the award of an honorary DMus.[282] Tickets for the performances were not cheap, beyond the price bracket of many university members and perhaps a disincentive to academic outsiders to attend: a satirical ballad-opera, *The Oxford Act, . . . as it was perform'd by a company of students at Oxford* (London, 1733), includes in its cast a scholar called 'Thoughtless' who had to sell his furniture in order to afford tickets for one of the Handel benefits, and Hearne grumpily bemoaned the concerts 'given by one Handel, with his dirty crew of foreign fidlers, in the Theatre and in Christ-Church hall, at five shilling tickets'. The great man produced one remarkable example of his genius for Oxford. This was his *Athalia*—'the work that is', according to Donald Burrows, 'arguably Handel's first masterpiece of English theatre oratorio'[283]—and one that premiered not in London but at the Sheldonian on 10 July 1733.

Though that occasion proved to be the final Act, music set pieces and spectaculars continued and were principally connected with the Encaenia (a lower-key version of the Act without any danger of intervention by the unruly *Terrae Filius*), cancellarial installations[284] and, from 1770, the annual Radcliffe Infirmary meeting.[285] Commemoration concerts celebrating benefactors at the end of the academic year tended to be primarily Handelian festivals, and that composer could dominate the repertoire on the most grand occasions. His brief 1733 visit reverberated for another two decades, enthusiastically celebrated by the elder Hayes.[286] Thus the award of the latter's doctorate and the celebrations for the opening of the Radcliffe Library in April 1749 were accompanied by a three-day Handel festival at the Sheldonian Theatre, conducted by Hayes himself, when *Esther, Samson, Messiah,* and several anthems were heard on three afternoons.

---

[281] Deborah Rohr, *The careers of British musicians, 1750–1850* (Cambridge, 2001), 67.

[282] H. Diack Johnstone, 'Handel at Oxford in 1733', *Early Music,* 31 (2003), 248–60.

[283] See W. Dean, *Handel's Dramatic Oratorios and Masques* (2nd edn., Oxford, 1990), 247–64.

[284] Both Hayeses, father and son, composed such odes for University ceremonial occasions as William's 'Hark! hark, from ev'ry tongue' for the installation of Westmorland as Chancellor in 1759. Watkins Shaw, 'University Chair of Music', 247.

[285] There is also the likelihood that concerts on or near to St Cecilia's Day (22 November) were a regular and significant feature of the Oxford musical calendar during the 1730s and 1740s.

[286] D. Burrows, 'Sources for Oxford Handel performances in the first half of the eighteenth century', *Music & Letters,* 61 (1980), 177–85; S. Wollenberg, 'Handel in Oxford: The tradition c.1750–1850', *Göttinger Händel-Beiträge,* 9 (2002), 161–76.

OXFORD AND THE ARTS AND HUMANITIES   189

In their way, some of the contents of the libretti for these works offered almost as much scope for political complications as William King's 'Redeat' invocations, such as the phrase 'Mercy to Jacob's Race God Save the King' in *Esther*.[287] Oxford consistently took the lead among English provincial centres in performing complete oratorios by Handel.[288]

It was not until the last decade of the century that Oxford found a celebrity composer to outshine Handel. This was Joseph Haydn—'this musical Shakespeare' as one journal called him[289]—who was as eager to take the proffered honorary DMus (a rare award) in 1791 as Handel had been to decline it. It was Charles Burney who had suggested to him that he should take the degree soon after his arrival in England in January that year. His fame had gone before him, thanks in large measure to the promotional efforts of his friend, and the organiser of his trip, Johann Peter Salomon, who had been actively involved in Oxford concerts from 1781.[290] So much so that when his scheduled opening performance in in the city scheduled for 18 May 1791 was cancelled at the last moment, the audience erupted into a riot. It was some consolation that he did appear for three grand concerts in July to huge applause, a recognition both popular and academic that he charmingly reciprocated to the University.[291] His symphony no. 92 in G major, the so-called 'Oxford' symphony, then received its first Oxford performance, though it had probably been introduced earlier to London audiences.[292]

Improving travel meant that London performers (including many of the continental stars) could easily make trips to Oxford even during the winter season, and no Encaenia was complete without a leading role for a well-known impresario. Thus the castrato Giusto Ferdinando Tenducci, idol of London society, appeared several times; the June 1789 Commemoration was graced by the singing of the Mozartian stars Francesco Benucci (the first Guglielmo in *Così fan tutte*) and Nancy Storace, the original Susanna in Mozart's *Marriage of Figaro*.[293] The fervour that greeted their public appearance could easily boil over into public

---

[287] See Bodl. MS Top. Oxon. b.43. f. 21. For King's notorious 'Redeat' oration with its Jacobite undertones at the opening of the Library, see Chapter 7, 28–9.

[288] Wollenberg, '"So much rational and elegant amusement, at an expence comparatively inconsiderable": The Holywell Concerts in the Eighteenth Century', in eds., Wollenberg and McVeigh, *Concert Life*, 243–59, at 253.

[289] *European Magazine*, 15 July 1791, quoted in H. C. Robbins Landon, *Haydn: Chronicle and Works* (5 vols., London, 1976–80), III.. *Haydn in England 1791–1795*, 93. See generally eds. R. Chesser and D. Wyn Jones, *The Land of Opportunity: Joseph Haydn and the British* (London, 2013).

[290] Wollenberg, 'Music and musicians', 873 and n.

[291] He later reckoned that the visit brought him 'the acquaintanceship of the most prominent men and the entree into the greatest houses'. Landon, *Haydn*, III. 92.

[292] Wollenberg observes that 'It represented Haydn at the height of his technical powers'. 'Music and musicians', 874. He also sent the canon 'Thy voice O harmony' (later part of his setting of the Ten Commandments) to the university.

[293] *JOJ*, 26 June 1789. She made British (chiefly London-based) tours in 1784–7 and 1790–2.

Fig. 4.7 Elizabeth Billington (née Weichsel) ('Clara—A Bravura'), Charles Williams, published by Samuel William Fores, hand-coloured etching, 1802 (© National Portrait Gallery, London).

disorder incidents, as when the celebrated German vocalist, Madame [Gertrude Elizabeth] Mara, was at the centre of a riot in the Sheldonian in 1785.[294] Elizabeth Linley (the playwright and politician Richard Brinsley Sheridan's first wife) and Elizabeth Billington (née Weichsel, a native of Freiberg, Saxony) were regular guest performers, and the latter's status was confirmed when she was the star turn at an evening concert on 2 July 1793 for Portland's installation as Chancellor when 'by her angelic strains [she] proved herself worthy of the popularity she has obtained at Oxford'.[295] Likewise Oxford-based musicians often performed in the capital. One such was Thomas Norris (1741–90), organist of Christ Church (1776–90) and of St John's College (1765). As a tenor soloist

---

[294] *Morning Post*, 30 June 1785. Wollenberg, 'Music and musicians', 877, for a note on other internationally accomplished performers who appeared.
[295] Bodl. MS Top. Oxon. d. 174, f. 238 quoted in ibid., 872. The scurrilous *Memoirs of Mrs Billington* by James Ridgway, published in 1792, had done nothing to dampen public acclaim for the singer.

OXFORD AND THE ARTS AND HUMANITIES   191

and glee writer, he sang at festivals such as the Handel commemorations in Westminster Abbey.[296]

Music-making was not at all reserved for these great festival days and the arrival of prima donnas on circuit. Without any academic intervention, gathering to share and make music had long flourished in college rooms and taverns as part of the essential sociability of Oxford life.[297] And, emulating royal ceremonial occasions, students could take to the river in summer. On 10 June 1754 the young Cornish undergraduate, Edward Giddy, could be found taking part in a concert on the river where fourteen musicians from several Oxford colleges performed as they floated along the Thames. The 'water music' was provided by horns, violins, hautboys, basses, flutes, and drums (Giddy played the violin).[298] These were occasional outings. Slightly more formalised was the Oxford musical club (it lasted three decades from the 1690s) that met monthly at Hall's tavern, with a membership of about forty that included Daniel Purcell, the organist of Magdalen College, James Brydges, later 1st Duke of Chandos, and Anthony Alsop, Anglo-Latin poet and librettist.[299] It was because concerts there and at the King's Head tavern and benefit concerts in college halls under the aegis of the Musical Society and other groups were so popular that the need for purpose-built premises became urgent in the 1740s as Oxford, like other urban centres, became a setting for the public concert.

These were the origins of the Holywell Music Room, opened in 1748, a venue designed to accommodate 400 people where visiting soloists were frequently invited to accompany the resident orchestra.[300] The initiative threw the door open for concert life to be organised semi-independently of the University, though the Professor of music was generally on the management committee. Holywell quickly became a place where town and gown met in an atmosphere of social ease for the Monday evening subscription concerts.[301] For the rest of the century, concertgoers at the Room could expect to hear many of the performers from the metropolitan pleasure gardens at Vauxhall and Ranelagh, as well as instrumentalists such as the gamba-player Karl Friedrich Abel and the foremost London

---

[296] Curthoys (3), 207; Weber, *The Rise of Musical Classics*, 171, 187
[297] Thus James Woodforde of New College was devoted to music and enjoyed attending concerts and playing music until he ceased to be a resident member in 1776. See many instances given in ed. W. N. Hargreaves-Mawdsley, *Woodforde at Oxford 1759-1776* (OHS., XXI, 1969). And John Free, *Poems, and Miscellaneous Pieces formerly written by John Free, DD* (London, 1751), for a brilliant satire on an Oxford musical party at Christ Church.
[298] Cornwall Record Office, CRO DG 25, Scrapbook of Catharine Davies.
[299] M. Crum, 'An Oxford music club, 1690-1719', *BLR*, 9 (1974), 83–99; Money, *The English Horace*, 61.
[300] J. H. Mee, *The Oldest Music Room in Europe: A Record of Eighteenth-Century Enterprise at Oxford* (London, 1911).
[301] W. Hayes, 'History of the Music Room', Bodl. MS Top. Oxon. D. 337; *Wood's Antient and Present State of the City of Oxford*, ed. Sir John Peshall (London, 1773), 247–8; Wollenberg, '"The Holywell Concerts in the Eighteenth Century'.

192 ENLIGHTENED OXFORD

violinist, Wilhelm Cramer, and, above all, vocalists from abroad. The stewards of the Musical Society responsible for the Room were responsible for drawing up programmes (they used *Jackson's Oxford Journal* for publicity purposes from its inception in 1753) and engaging performers and, on the whole, discharged their duties inspiringly, keeping audiences happy and coming through the doors, hiring many gifted foreigners for the house orchestra, and snapping up the services of virtuosi soloists.

What did they play? The Holywell band certainly performed a lot of Handel (*Messiah* and *Acis and Galatea* were predictable favourites) but showed an awareness of the developing repertoire in the second half of the century with Arne, Charles Avison, and William Boyce well represented. Pieces by Abel and J. C. Bach were popular, as well as contemporary music from Italy (Cimarosa, Gazzaniga, Sarti), Germany (notably Franz Xaver Richter, Stamitz), and Austrian (Vanhal and Dittersdorf).[302] By the 1790s, concertgoers could expect 'ancient' and modern music comfortably juxtaposed: Stamitz symphonies and Haydn quartets alongside Handel's choruses and Corelli's concertos typically featured. Glees could be heard there and the new genre of keyboard concerto, as well as audience favourites, for instance, Philip Hayes's 'Farewell to the Rocks of Lannow' (a setting of Anna Seward's verses) during the late 1780s and early 1790s.[303]

Wherever one looks, eighteenth-century Oxford was musically part of a flourishing national and international network of musical performers. These offered an ever more varied repertoire of both 'ancient' and modern compositions, to be heard in the college choirs, the Holywell Music Room, the Sheldonian Theatre, and scores of ad hoc venues across the University. Exchange was central to this dynamic culture, from the mutual pleasure of having Haydn in residence in the city to those playing in the Holywell band heading out of Oxford to make up numbers elsewhere. Thus many Oxford musicians went to perform in Salisbury concerts from time to time, while the Salisbury trumpeter William Biddlecombe was a regular performer at Oxford concerts from the mid-1750s onwards.[304] Oxford music brought in visitors (and their money) year after year, the most committed among them taking home some of the modest amounts of British music published in the city by Philip Hayes and Paul Alday. Oxford may have fed on celebrity musicians but it nurtured a quotidian musical culture unsurpassed in its variety that had no contemporary equivalent outside the metropolis and acted as an inspiration and example to other towns and cities.[305]

---

[302] Wollenberg, 'Music and musicians', 879–80.   [303] Wollenberg, 'Holywell concerts', 253–4.
[304] See correspondence in D. Burrows and R. Dunhill, *Music and Theatre in Handel's World: The Family Papers of James Harris 1732–1780* (Oxford, 2002).
[305] For an exhaustive survey of manuscripts written by Oxford composers and copyists c.1740–80, see P. Ward Jones and D. Burrows, 'An inventory of mid-eighteenth-century Oxford musical hands', *Royal Musical Association Research Chronicle*, 35 (2002), 61–139.

viii) Conclusion

There were three audiences for the cultural products of Oxford University in the long eighteenth century: the University itself, the wider 'republic of letters' (to use a phrase losing its currency after the mid-century), and new markets. Its record of achievement within each was mixed, with stellar performers such as Robert Lowth in poetry and William Jones in Eastern languages who captured attention and plaudits, to be set against other academics who had minimal interest in reaching a non-traditional audience (or even a traditional one). The majority of scholars who wrote and composed were arguably more conscious of the world beyond Oxford than in any previous age. The London market loomed larger but publication in Oxford was far from in itself condemning an author to an exclusively academic market and limited sales. And a slowly increasing number of Oxford graduates were interested in making careers as authors, and often showing their paces before they left the University. The appearance of more and more nationally distributed periodicals such as the *Gentleman's Magazine* (started in 1731) aroused widespread interest in Oxford,[306] and a desire to either contribute or emulate among both dons and students. Two of the latter, George Colman and Bonnell Thornton, while still at Christ Church produced a periodical paper called *The Connoisseur* that appeared from 31 January 1754 to 30 September 1756, and found that it was widely read and admired beyond Oxford.[307]

In history, the University was associated for better or worse throughout this era with Clarendon's *History*. The work defined its values in the reign of Queen Anne and these still carried weight when confronting the revolutionary challenges of the 1790s. Yet, without denying its many exceptional qualities, it was a product of the essentially polemical nature of English history-writing in the century after the Civil Wars and was perhaps a disincentive to creativity in modern history that, among Oxonians, only Thomas Carte—partially—attempted to surmount. Ironically, it was Gibbon's *Decline and Fall* that, in a sense, constituted the acme of Oxford history writing, yet the University distanced itself and Gibbon returned the favour.[308] Given the University's commitment to ancient history, upheld by successive holders of the Camden chair,[309] that failure to connect came at a high

---

[306] 'I congratulate you on your Magazine's gaining Ground in this University'. 'Philo-all-souls' to Edward Cave, the editor, *GM* 8 (1738), 206.

[307] *European Magazine* (5) 1785, 83. For *The Student, or the Oxford and Cambridge Monthly Miscellany,* that originated around the same time see Chapter 10, p. 55.

[308] Charlotte Roberts notes how each time Gibbon uses 'pious' and 'piety' to describe his relationship with his father and with Oxford 'they fall into the sentence with a more hollow and uncomfortable ring'. *Gibbon and the Shape of History* (Oxford, 2014), 162–3.

[309] James Moore and Ian Macrgregor Morris, 'History in Revolution? Approaches to the Ancient World in the Long Eighteenth Century', in eds. James Moore, Ian Macgregor Morris, and Andrew Bayliss, *Reinventing History. The Enlightenment Origins of Ancient History* (London, 2008), 3–29, unaccountably does not mention Oxford.

194   ENLIGHTENED OXFORD

institutional price. Two generations earlier, Oxford's excellence in Anglo-Saxon studies of every kind stimulated antiquarian initiatives across the country and also encouraged an interest in more recent vernacular literature that, in the middle decades, became vigorous just as early medieval studies faltered under what John Pocock has called 'the disdain of a new spirit'.[310]

Yet that 'new spirit' did not disdain the inheritance of vernacular literature, one that Oxford came to embrace wholeheartedly by the mid-century with Thomas Warton in the vanguard. His prominence underscores the justifiable claim made by David Fairer that one should view that period quite as much as the Age of Warton as the Age of Johnson.[311] However, despite Warton's considerable involvement, Oxonian scholars did not play much part in the development of a nascent professional critical practice in the century's course. Their focus lay elsewhere, though it was far from having a solely internal gaze.[312] And if, as Anne Goldgar has argued,[313] there was a mid-century shift within a new culture of politeness when the scholar's social status fell while the author's rose, then Warton's career surely demonstrates that a university professor could be both a scholar and an author with a readership inside and outside the academy. Moreover, Warton in his way cheerfully demonstrated the artificiality of distinctions between 'politeness' and 'impoliteness'. He was fascinated by changes over time to English usages, as was Robert Lowth, who exhibited yet another side of his talents with the publication of his *English Grammar* of 1762. Its phenomenal sales confirmed the willingness of the University to serve the contemporary needs of the English-speaking peoples—most of whom would have no connection with Oxford—in a serviceable and accessible way. In contrast to the vitality of academic interest in the native vernacular, studies and publications in modern languages, despite the royal encouragement in the 1720s, remained lack lustre. But that being the case, Oxford was not out on a limb with the majority of British schools or universities.

If ever one name resonated approvingly in Whig circles for a century after his death it was John Locke; if there was an exception to that level of recognition and endorsement it was in Oxford. Here the University was and remained out of kilter with most reaches of British, European, and North American opinion. That is not to say that many dons and students did not read him, teach him and own him, but

---

[310] *Barbarism and Religion*, I. 149.

[311] 'Introduction' to ed. Fairer, *Correspondence of Thomas Warton*, xix. See also Steve Newman, '"The Maiden's Bloody Garland": Thomas Warton and the Elite Appropriation of Popular Song', in eds. P. Fumerton, A. Guerrini, and K. McAbee, *Ballads and Broadsides in Britain, 1500–1800* (Farnham, 2010), 189–205 for the range of Warton's interest in popular culture in Oxford and far beyond.

[312] Fairer notes the power (and the inaccuracy) of Pope's creation of an Oxford removed from the world, with Addison and Richard Steele before him jibing at it from the metropolis. 'Oxford and the literary world', 780–1, 782–3.

[313] Goldgar, *Impolite learning*, 226–42.

OXFORD AND THE ARTS AND HUMANITIES   195

there was an abiding suspicion at large of what he represented (itself a backhanded compliment) that was never wholly overcome and the possibility that there could be a cult of Locke in Oxford to balance that of Newton at Cambridge was negligible. William Adams—despite his amity with Samuel Johnson, another member of Pembroke College—was one of those who did have time for Locke and was ready to engage with Hume on the question of miracles and contribute to the contemporary perception that the latter's scepticism on that subject was unpersuasive.[314] But Adams was not much known to the public outside Oxford. Neither was Edward Bentham, but he proved an energetic professor who had student needs in mind throughout his tenure and to some degree made up for the empty White's chair in Ethics by publishing philosophical works that ranged widely. But Bentham was no Paley, and if Oxford did produce a philosopher comparable in standing to Locke it was Joseph Butler, whose major works appeared after his connection with the University had ceased. Despite his disinclination to associate with his alma mater, on Butler's death in 1752 the University was quick to make the connection and his *Analogy of Religion* became a core teaching text.[315] And, up to a point, it stuck with Aristotle for all his contemporary detractors. His continuing philosophical utility in teaching was confirmed by Aldrich's *Artes logicae compendium*, published in long and short form in fourteen editions between 1691 and 1801.

In philosophy, the 'Ancients' may have remained dominant, but that was consistent with an educational culture where the study of the ancient world was primary on the basis less of aesthetic delight than as one offering the most appropriate framework within which to tune the academic and moral formation of the next generation of the elite. The Phalaris controversy in part reflected the opportunities people like Henry Aldrich wanted to give their young charges, being an early opportunity to show their paces.[316] It showed the University engaged in a literary exercise that was unashamed of social exclusiveness, but it was relieved by humour and some fine comedic jibes at Bentley's expense. And it was another form of bidding for public notice. Efforts to keep classical scholarship reconciled with gentility did not cease as a result of Bentley's 'victory' and it remained eminently compatible with the ordained ministry of the Church.[317] Thus even

---

[314] See John Earman, *Hume's abject failure: the argument against miracles* (New York, 2000).

[315] P.B. Nockles, '"Lost causes and...impossible loyalties": the Oxford Movement and the University', in HUO VI, 195–268, at 210. See Chapter 10, pp. 66–7 for Butler and Oxford.

[316] The practice did not end with Phalaris. Thus Canon William Stratford of Ch. Ch. to Edward Harley: 'We now talk of setting our young men at work; a good thing if proper hands are employed on subjects that may be of use. Broxholme is to put out a new edition of Virgil, I know not though how he will mend those we have. Fairfax to put out the Iliads, to answer the late Dean's edition of the Odyssey'. HMC, *Portland MSS*, VII. 72, 13 Nov. 1711.

[317] cf. Joseph Levine, 'By 1700, the learning of a gentleman and the learning of a scholar had come to seem incompatible'. 'Swift and the Idea of History', 82.

196 ENLIGHTENED OXFORD

when the level of classical editing and publishing inside the University was challenged (as, arguably, it was for much of the early Georgian era),[318] work by scholars in holy orders up and down the country might be prospering, sometimes remarkably so. Such were often previously college Fellows heading into the countryside for matrimony and taking their talent with them.

That was not the case with Oriental languages, where scholars either stayed in Oxford or sought posts that brought them directly into contact with the cultures whose linguistic inheritance they were studying. There was an emerging recognition that these languages were no less worthy of study than Greek or Latin, though not all agreed with such claims. Thus Warton considered that Arabic poetry was 'extravagant and romantic' while Gibbon thought that Eastern authors lacked 'the temperate dignity of style, the graceful proportions of art, [and] the forms of visible and intellectual beauty'.[319] It was such reservations as these that William Jones devoted his career to overcoming, convinced as he was that eastern voices could rejuvenate European art and letters. And Jones's own voice commanded international esteem in the 1780s and 1790s. His career as an Indian judge from 1783 highlighted the new opportunities for Oxford graduates which empire opened up. These were built on academic foundations that nurtured the attempt, as much as contemporary values allowed, to study Oriental cultures on their own terms without the missionary purpose that would soon be inseparable from this scholarship.[320] Though the process was halting in this period, holders of the Oxford chairs in Arabic helped facilitate a more contextualised perception of Islam by western Europeans, part of the continual alterations in 'the changing consciousness of the "Other", of that Arabic-speaking, mainly Muslim world'.[321]

At its best, Oxford culture was outward-looking and open to new audiences and markets, setting the pace in international scholarship, and that free flow and accessibility was nicely embodied in its reputation as a music-making centre. Was this a culture of nostalgia debilitating current intellectual endeavour? Emphatically not, though it was rooted in that cultural deposit and unashamed of defending its values in the current age. While there can be no doubt that the Laudian Statutes were a formal barrier to any sort of progressive manifestations

---

[318] A perception that generated a distinctive humour, as in Richard West's writing on Oxford in 1735: 'a country flowing with syllogisms and ale where Horace and Virgil are alike unknown', quoted in Ogilvie, *Latin and Greek*, 41. Scholars whose careers did not depend on it could justifiably judge that there was no sense in replacing a standard classics edition if it was reliable.

[319] Quoted in P. J. Marshall and G. Williams, *The Great Map of Mankind. British Perceptions of the World in the Age of Enlightenment* (London, 1982), 73.

[320] Nile Green, *Terrains of Exchange. Religious economies of global Islam* (London, 2014), 43, calls the early nineteenth century the 'Parnassus of the Evangelical Empire'.

[321] A. Hourani, *Islam in European Thought* (Cambridge, 1991), 4; M. Wintle, 'Islam as Europe's "other" in the long term: some discontinuities', *History*, 101 (2016), 42–61, at 44.

in the arts and humanities, there is likewise none that the University in all sorts of ways was adaptable in circumventing them (not least, through individual initiatives), admittedly more successfully in some subject areas than others.[322] And that would be much the same balance sheet in natural philosophy and the sciences.

[322] In 1759, counsel's opinion was sought on whether a Laudian statute could be modified. And the reply was in the affirmative. On that basis, in July 1760 the hebdomadal board successfully promulgated two explanatory statutes, one dealing with the franchise, the other prohibiting University members from becoming burgesses of the City. Griffiths, *Statutes*, xvi–xix, 310–13.

5

Oxford and contemporary science

Anxiety, adaptation, and advance

The Works of God, are manifest to all men with Reason and Understanding, from the Contemplation of those Works, to discover the Wisdom and Glory of their Maker.

Samuel Clarke, 'Men have Natural Abilities of Knowing God'
[I Corinthians 1.21], *Sermons* (10 vols., London, 1730/1),
ix. 17. 'Preface' by B. Hoadly.

'True and genuine Science...will always contribute to the support and advancement of Religion, and the religious mind will always be best able to correct and amend the sallies and deficiencies of human learning'.

Benjamin Buckler, 'The Alliance of Religion and Learning
considered: A Sermon preached before the Right Honourable John
Earl of Westmorland, Chancellor, and the University of Oxford,
at St Mary's, on Act Sunday, viii July 1759' [Ephesians 2:21],
(Oxford, 1759), 10.

i) The Newtonian challenge

The death of Sir Isaac Newton on 20 March 1727 and his burial in Westminster Abbey on 4 April (after the body had lain in state in the Jerusalem Chamber on 28 March) underlined the national status and European celebrity of the greatest lay natural philosopher in England, renowned for his long presidency of the Royal Society, his innovative theories in gravity and optics, his public service as Master of the Mint, and (by scholars) for his adjustments to ancient chronology.[1] The great man's funeral was choreographed with an attention usually reserved for the sovereign, the cortège being followed by the Fellows of the Royal Society, among

---

[1] While mindful of the risk of anachronism, 'science' is used here to signify a specific branch of study based primarily on observation and experiment. On the terms *science* and *natural philosophy* see A. Cunningham, 'Getting the game right: some plain words on the identity and invention of science', *Studies in History and Philosophy of Science*, 19 (1988), 365–89.

Enlightened Oxford: The University and the Cultural and Political Life of Eighteenth-century Britain and Beyond.
Nigel Aston, Oxford University Press. © Nigel Aston 2023. DOI: 10.1093/oso/9780199246830.003.0006

OXFORD AND CONTEMPORARY SCIENCE   199

them Lord Chancellor King (the friend of John Locke), two dukes (Montrose and Roxburgh) and three earls (Pembroke, Sussex, and Macclesfield) as the pallbearers.[2] Unsurprisingly, the event attracted international attention. As Voltaire observed:

> Sir Isaac Newton was rever'd in his Life-time, and had a due respect paid to him after his death; the greatest men in the nation disputing who shou'd have the honour of holding up his pall.[3]

His demise completed Newton's establishment as the dominant cultural icon of the early eighteenth century and confirmed the science associated with his name as a model for future advances.[4] Colin Maclaurin (1698–1746), Professor of Mathematics at Edinburgh University and member of the Royal Society, Newton's friend and client, hailed him as one who had 'opened matter for the enquiries of future ages, which may confirm and enlarge his doctrines, but can never refute them'.[5] More importantly, he had given his successors 'the excellent models' that might enable them to 'make farther advances'.[6] And indeed, as David Spadafora has observed, 'for the most part, the Augustan fear of science' ended with his death.[7] Yet that qualification, 'for the most part', is important. Even in his lifetime it did not escape notice that his commitment to experiment implied a rejection of Biblical doctrine and Aristotelianism *tout court*. Some of the most telling assaults on selected aspects of the Newtonian programme had emanated from Cambridge itself in the 1720s in the writings of Robert Greene, fellow and tutor of Clare Hall, though these were far from a general indictment.[8]

---

[2] *London Gazette* 6569, 1–4 Apr. 1727 in www.newtonproject.sussex.ac.uk/view/texts/normalized/ OTHE00002 Talbot, 1st Earl of Sussex (1690–1731), was the sole Oxonian among them, having been educated at Christ Church. Pembroke, the 8th Earl, was the dedicatee of Locke's *An Essay upon the Human Understanding*. For his learning (by no means untypical of peers who were FRS) see eds. D. and M. Honeybone, *The Correspondence of William Stukeley and Maurice Johnson 1714–1754* (Woodbridge, 2014) [Lincoln Record Society, vol. 104], 44.

[3] Voltaire, *Letters Concerning the English Nation*, ed. Nicholas Cronk (Oxford, 1994), 193. 'His Countrymen ... interr'd him as tho' he had been a King who had made his People happy', ibid., 62.

[4] As Patricia Fara has claimed, his burial in the Abbey ensured 'the continuity and consolidation of Newton's social persona despite the disintegration of his physical body'. P. Fara, 'Faces of Genius: images of Isaac Newton in eighteenth-century England', in eds. G. Cubitt and A. Warren, *Heroic Reputations and Exemplary Lives* (Manchester, 2000), 57–81, at 65. See also Fara, *Newton. The Making of Genius* (London, 2002); 'Apotheosis', in Mordechai Feingold, *The Newtonian Moment. Isaac Newton and the making of modern culture* (New York, 2004), 169–80.

[5] He never held an Oxford post but was in the running for one at least once. The influential John Conduitt (married to Newton's niece) told him that he had been mentioned to 'several proper persons' as a successor to Halley in his chair should the latter die. To Maclaurin, 10 Mar 1732/3, in ed. S. Mills, *The Collected Letters of Colin MacLaurin* (Nantwich, 1982), 47.

[6] Colin Maclaurin, *An Account of Sir Isaac Newton's Philosophical Discoveries* (2nd ed., London, 1750), 10, 14.

[7] David Spadafora, *The Idea of Progress in Eighteenth-Century Britain* (New Haven, CT, 1990), 9.

[8] Iliffe, 'Philosophy of Science', in ed. Porter, *Eighteenth-century science*, 267–84, at 277; J. Gascoigne, 'Ideas of Nature', in ed. Porter, *Eighteenth-century science*, 285–304, at 293. For earlier warnings about the Newtonian philosophy in Cambridge from Richard Marsh (1699) and John Edwards (1714) see Gascoigne, *Cambridge*, 164–74.

200 ENLIGHTENED OXFORD

Oxford University was certainly not in denial about admitting the level of Newton's remarkable genius, indeed it has been claimed that '…it was in Oxford that his ideas were actively fostered and disseminated'.[9] Newton himself had even ventured over to Oxford in August 1720—to considerable acclaim—to meet his indefatigable Oxonian defender, the Savilian Professor of Astronomy since 1712, John Keill.[10] By then, Newtonian insights had been part of the University's pedagogy for a quarter of a century. According to his successor as a lecturer on experimental philosophy at Hart Hall (1710), John Theophilus Desaguliers, Keill was one of the first men to teach Newtonian physics by experiments in a mathematical manner from the mid-1690s to 1709.[11] From Balliol, Keill had first lectured in natural philosophy at Hart Hall and contributed frequently to the *Philosophical Transactions* of the Royal Society.[12] He explicitly denounced Cartesian mechanism and reasoning and declared that all the efforts of all the mechanical philosophers did 'not amount to the tenth part of those Things, which Sir Isaac Newton alone, through his vast Skill in Geometry, has found out by his own sagacity'.[13] Newton had been closely concerned in Keill's early involvement in the dispute on calculus in the 1710s, with the latter defending the Newtonian position via a vitriolic attack on Leibniz in 1713 in the new *Journal littéraire de La Haye*,[14] only to find his character used against him by opponents.[15]

---

[9] Allan Chapman, 'Oxford's Newtonian school', in eds. John Fauvel, Raymond Flood, and Robin Wilson, *Oxford figures: eight centuries of the mathematical sciences* (2nd edn., Oxford, 2013), 166–71, at 165.

[10] For Keill he was the 'divine Newton', *An introduction to the true astronomy: or, astronomical lectures, read in the Astronomical School of the University of Oxford*, (2nd edn., London, 1721)., vi (originally published in Latin). Mordechai Feingold dubs him Newton's 'pitbull'. *The Newtonian moment*, 46. The extent to which Keill's views correspond to Newton's is discussed in James E. Force, *William Whiston. Honest Newtonian* (Cambridge, 1985), 60–2. See also E. W. Strong, 'Newtonian explications of natural philosophy', *JHI*, 17 (1957), 49–83. Keill's importance is well-summarised in Gregory Lynall, *Swift and science. The satire, politics, and theology of natural knowledge, 1690–1730* (Basingstoke, 2012), 57–64.

[11] L.W.B. Brockliss, 'Science, the universities, and other public spaces: teaching science in Europe and the Americas', in ed. Porter, *Eighteenth-century science*, 44–86., at 63. For Desaguliers, see this Chapter, pp. 25–7. The lecture notes of John Ivory (matric. Ch. Ch., 1707) afford evidence of Keill's teaching at Oxford between 1704 and 1712. CUL, MS Add. 9317.

[12] These lectures (in which he attacked Thomas Burnet's *Theory of the Earth* (1698) for its Cartesian shortcomings) were published in 1701 as *.Introductio ad Veram Physicam*. (Eng. trans. 1736). David B. Wilson, *Seeking Nature's Logic: Natural Philosophy in the Scottish Enlightenment* (University Park, PA, 2009), 35, 50–1. It has been called 'arguably the first popular expositions of Newtonian philosophy ever published'. D. Kubrin, 'John Keill', in Charles C. Gillespie, ed.-in-chief, *Dictionary of Scientific Biography* (16 vols., New York, 1970–80), VII. 275–7.

[13] Quoted in Feingold, *The Newtonian Moment*, 42.

[14] J. B. Shank, *The Newton Wars and the Beginning of the French Enlightenment* (Chicago, 2008), 184, 216. See generally A. Rupert Hall, *Philosophers at War: The Quarrel between Newton and Leibniz* (Cambridge, 1980).

[15] eds. H.W. Turnbull et al., *Correspondence of Isaac Newton* (7 vols., London, 1959–77), VII. xxx-xxxv. Keill was a heavy drinker, married a servant (daughter of a bookbinder and his former mistress), and was, according to Hearne, 'a man of very little or no Religion'. *Reliquiae Hearnianae* (London, 1857; rev. 1966), ed. J. Buchanan-Brown, 237–8, 1 Sept. 1721, quoted in Money, *The English Horace*, 159, 162–3.

OXFORD AND CONTEMPORARY SCIENCE 201

Not that these slurs shadowed his high profile in the international scientific community, which was reinforced by the publication in 1721 of *An introduction to the true astronomy*, whose thesis was that astronomy established God's existence, and scripture instructed man that the heavens declared the glory of God.[16] In this work, Keill drew on a concept he had received from Newton via Gregory, that of a *prisca philosophia*, an 'ancient wisdom', and contended that knowledge came to the Greeks this way.[17] But, as David B. Wilson has pointed out, Keill was an eclectic thinker for whom Newtonianism was but one source of knowledge. His was 'a theological Newtonianism, modified and strengthened by Aristotelian considerations'.[18] Keill had indeed announced in his *An introduction to the true physics* that, though Newton's genius had accomplished more than all the rest of human history combined, he would incorporate ideas from four other groups that had made useful contributions: Plato, Aristotelian peripatetics, experimenters, and the mechanical philosophers.[19] Such a range was an obvious consequence of physics being still taught within the arts or philosophy faculty. It essentially covered the material covered in Aristotle's *Physics* and *De caelo*, but studied mathematically and phenomenologically under the shadow of Newton.[20]

Yet Newton's astonishing record had generated a degree of anxiety among some senior members about its potentially unsettling impact on classical Christianity, and what had happened since the Revolution in the perceived growth of unbelief apparently bore out these forebodings.[21] Critical attention was less on Newton than on his forthright, aberrant disciples such as William Whiston, who had descended from being the great man's chosen successor in the Lucasian Chair at Cambridge and the reputable author of *The New Theory of the Earth* (1696) to

---

[16] Keill, *An introduction to the true astronomy,*, ii, dedicated to the 1st Duke of Chandos, the vastly wealthy patron of natural philosophers. Keill also brought out two mathematical textbooks in 1715.

[17] The idea was a commonplace in Christ Church during the period c.1690–1720 and not unacceptable to Atterbury himself. Gregory had previously endorsed the work of ancient mathematicians when, in 1703, he had published an edn. of Euclid's elements. Friesen, 'Christ Church Oxford, the Ancients-Moderns Controversy', *History of Universities*, XXIII/I (2008), 33–66; 48, 55.

[18] Wilson, *Seeking Nature's logic*, 53.

[19] *An introduction to the true physics*, 1–3, 9–10. This was the vernacular translation from the Latin original. See this Chapter p. 7, n. 13.

[20] Brockliss, 'Science, the universities, and other public spaces', 79–80. Aristotelianism retained an honoured place on the margins of the Oxford curriculum, by no means all its insights considered outmoded. See C. Mercer, 'The Vitality and Importance of Early Modern Aristotelianism', in ed. T. Sorell, *The Rise of Modern Philosophy. The Tension Between the New and Traditional Philosophies from Machiavelli to Leibniz* (Oxford, 1993), 33–67, at 54.

[21] George Hickes, Nonjuring bishop of Thetford, complained in 1713 that it was 'Newtonian philosophy which has made so many Arians and Theists, and that not only among the laity but I fear among our divines'. Letter to Roger North, 23 May 1713, quoted in Larry Stewart, 'Samuel Clarke, Newtonianism, and the factions of post-Revolutionary England', *JHI*, 42 (1981), 53–72, at 61. A case in point might be John Toland, who had learned Newtonianism at Edinburgh from David Gregory; and it was partly owing to his reading of Newton that he left the Christian camp. Anita Guerrini, 'John Keill, George Cheyne, and Newtonian physiology, 1690–1740', *Journal of the History of Biology*, 18 (1985), 247–66. See generally J. R. Wigelsworth, 'A sheep in the midst of wolves: reassessing Newton and English Deists', *Enlightenment and Dissent*, 25 (2009), 260–86.

202 ENLIGHTENED OXFORD

becoming (undeservedly) something of a laughing-stock and public heretic.[22] Optimistically, Whiston had tried on a visit to Oxford in 1712 to find possible recruits for his 'Society for Promoting Primitive Christianity'. Thomas Rennell of Exeter College and his pupil, Thomas Rundle, were sympathetic, but Rennell advised Whiston that Oxford was not cultivable soil.[23] It never had been: back in 1698 Keill, in his *An Examination of Dr Burnet's Theory of the Earth*, had attacked Whiston's *New Theory of the Earth* (which confirmed the narrative of Genesis on Newtonian grounds) for an excessive reliance on mechanical causes, a denial of special providence, and a faulty naturalistic explanation for the Flood that rested on incorrect observation and numerical calculation.[24] Everything Whiston did from that date confirmed him as a marked man in the sight of Oxford high churchmen.

Newton's friend, Samuel Clarke, and his allies had proclaimed that there was no cause for concern about the implications for revealed religion as received by the Church from Newtonian science, yet the Boyle Lecturers, all of them clergy, hardly came across either to the lay public or to their colleagues in holy orders as, to a man, uncompromised champions of orthodoxy;[25] of seventeen between 1692 and 1714 only three—Francis Gastrell (1697), Offspring Blackall (1700), and George Stanhope (1701)—could be called high church in their sympathies.[26] And if the perennial task of the Boyle Lecturers was to re-establish Protestantism upon the 'new science' while arguing against the supposed evils of hyperrationalism, these were, in themselves, for Oxford Tories, questionable strategies.[27] This disquiet was

[22] Newton had kept Whiston out of the Royal Society for proclaiming his anti-Trinitarianism in public. Force, *Whiston*, 23–4;

[23] Thomas Rennell, Fellow of Exeter College, MA 1699; BD and DD 1710; later rector of Bishop's Leighton, Devon. Published two sermons. Nichols, *Lit. anecdotes*, IX. 486n. Speaking of the poet, James Thomson, Rundle wrote: 'his [God's] works are his words; he speaks his sublime wisdom and goodness to us in them, and NEWTON is his interpreter'. To Mrs Barbara Sandys, Mar. 1729, *Letters of the late Thomas Rundle*, ed. James Dallaway [of Trinity College, Oxford] (2 vols., Gloucester, 1789), II. 77. Rundle's reputation as a theological disciple of Clarke cost him the see of Gloucester in 1733–4.

[24] Anita Guerrini, 'Newtonianism, medicine and religion', in eds. Ole Peter Grell and Andrew Cunningham, *Religio Medici: Religion and Medicine in Seventeenth-Century England* (Aldershot, 1996), 293–313, at 298; For the unfolding exchanges see Peter Harrison, 'Newtonian science, miracles, and the Laws of Nature', *JHI*, 56 (1994), 531–53, at 541n.

[25] John Hedley Brooke, *Science and Religion. Some Historical Perspectives* (Cambridge, 1991), 160. Clarke translated *Opticks* into Latin and defended the Newtonian notion of 'absolute space' against Leibniz. His underlying purpose was to demonstrate the crucial presence of God in a Newtonian universe. Scott Mandelbrote notes that not all Boyle lectures consisted of physico-theology, let alone in its Newtonian version. 'Early Modern Natural Theologies', in ed. Russell Manning, *The Oxford Handbook of Natural Theology* (Oxford, 2013), 75–99 at 90.

[26] N. Tyacke, 'From Laudians to Latitudinarians: a shifting balance of theological forces', in ed. Tapsell, *The Later Stuart Church*, 46–70, at 58. Of these three only Gastrell was an Oxford graduate (Christ Church). Cf. John Gascoigne's insistence that a fair number of Boyle Lecturers were unwilling to affirm the link between Anglicanism and Newtonianism. Gascoigne, 'From Bentley to the Victorians: the rise and fall of British Newtonian natural theology', *Science in Context*, 2 (1988), 219–56, at 222–4.

[27] Jan W. Wojcik, 'The theological Context of Boyle's Things above Reason', in ed. M. Hunter, *Robert Boyle reconsidered* (Cambridge, 1994), 139–55; Betty Jo Teeter Dobbs and Margaret C. Jacob, *Newton and the Culture of Newtonianism* (Atlantic Highlands, NJ, 1995), 68. For High Church

OXFORD AND CONTEMPORARY SCIENCE   203

seldom publicly voiced in the 1720s. The 'Newtonians' were in favour both in government and at court and Oxford was all too conscious of its vulnerability to external audit and intervention: Clarke's eventual fall from grace and Walpole's determination to keep him out of a bishopric owed little to any pressures emanating from Oxford University. Clarke's ingenuous inability to veil his variance with credal orthodoxy worked against him, though his enlightened version of Christianity held considerable appeal despite (or perhaps because of) its semi-Arianism;[28] it was more than tolerated by the majority of clerics cultivating the favour of the new Hanoverian establishment who were by and large careful to steer well clear of overt theological lapses that would play into the hands of their Tory enemies.

By the time of his death in 1727, his respectable apologists had largely shielded Newton's high-riding reputation from any slurs on the basis of his personal religious beliefs; he had lived long enough to distance himself from his refusal to subscribe to the Thirty-Nine Articles and that moment in his career over a generation earlier when his hostility to Athanasius had leaked out.[29] The question of Newton's personal orthodoxy was one that barely figured in any quarter, no doubt facilitated by there being no whiff of anticlericalism in any of his published speeches and writings.[30] Yet, arguably, Oxford opinion stood at something of a remove from offering incense to the memory of the great man. University academics were not thereby intellectually out of the swim; they registered the seminal importance of Newton's work and his bequest, while also recognising its current modishness and appeal to the Whig establishment.

readings of the early Newtonian agenda see S. Snobelen, 'Caution and conscience, and the Newtonian reformation: the public and private heresies of Newton, Clarke, and Whiston', *Enlightenment and Dissent*, 16 (1997), 151–84, at 160–4. John Friesen has argued that for High Churchmen 'Newton's mathematical methods could serve to justify an ordered society based on hierarchy'. 'Archibald Pitcairne, David Gregory and the Scottish origins of English Tory Newtonianism, 1688–1715', *History of Science*, 41 (2003), 163–91, at 184.

[28] J. P. Ferguson, *Dr. Samuel Clarke. An Eighteenth Century Heretic* (Kineton, 1976), 208–9. For most Oxonians, his *Scripture-Doctrine of the Trinity* (1712) and his censure by the Lower House of Convocation had fatally compromised Clarke's standing as a Christian apologist. It was hard for his orthodox enemies to trounce him because his semi-Arianism was a minor component of his religiosity. Dobbs and Jacob, *Newton and the Culture of Newtonianism*, 98. Clarke emphasised morality rather than sacred rites in his 'resolute Protestant anti-sacerdotalism'. J. Gascoigne, 'Science, religion and the foundations of morality in Enlightenment Britain', *Enlightenment and Dissent*, 17 (1998), 83–103, at 88–103.

[29] For Newton's religion generally see Frank E. Manuel, *The Religion of Isaac Newton* [The Fremantle Lectures 1973], (Oxford, 1974); John Brooke, 'The God of Isaac Newton', in eds. John Fauvel, Raymond Flood, Michael Shortland, and Robin Wilson, *Let Newton be!* (Oxford, 1988), 169–83; Scott Mandelbrote, *Footprints of the lion. Isaac Newton at work* (Cambridge, 2001), 115–30; S. D. Snobelen, 'Isaac Newton, heretic: the strategies of a Nicodemite', *BJHS*, 32 (1999), 381–419, esp. 396–412. Several of Newton's detractors detected anti-Trinitarianism in the 'General Scholium' added to the 2nd edn. of the *Principia* in 1713 and lumped him in with the materialists he despised. L. Stewart, 'Seeing through the Scholium: religion and reading Newton in the eighteenth century', *History of Science*, 34 (1996), 123–64; Iliffe, 'Philosophy of Science', 276.

[30] Privately, Newton compared the Anglican clergy favourably with those of the age of Constantine. Mandelbrote, *Footprints of the Lion*, 7–8.

204   ENLIGHTENED OXFORD

This studied coolness does not appear to have disadvantaged the University in public perceptions or exposed it to embarrassment. There were many other grounds, after all, on which its detractors could subject Oxford to excoriation rather than its low-key endorsement of Newton. The range of opinion in Oxford reflected the astonishing plasticity of Newton and his inheritance, more widely evident in British society,[31] as well as a wariness about going too far in its endorsement of the values that had come to be attached to Newton and their potentially troubling consequences. What his followers were doing with his work, both in his lifetime and post-mortem, was to be scrutinised for two related reasons: the likelihood that their findings were erroneous and the damage this could do to the related causes of true learning and religion. Though Newton himself had to be presented as by and large beyond reproach, the first critiques were appearing. Thus, in his lectures of 1727–8 in St Paul's Cathedral, endowed under Lady Moyer's will, the Oxonian Henry Felton attacked Newton's *Chronology*; Joseph Trapp in 1729–30 (assisted by Daniel Waterland, the outstanding Cambridge apologist of orthodoxy) in the same series also struck a critical note.[32] For the most part, what struck contemporaries as more information about his religion trickled out, was less Newton's (disputed) Arianism than his Biblicism and prophetic faith, apparently confirmed by the publication (also in 1733) of his (heavily edited) *Observations on the Prophecies of Daniel, and the Apocalypse of St John*. Even so, the number of British readers who considered Newton's scriptural views were likely to lead to heretical conclusions gradually increased. His tendency to bend the Bible to conform with other ancient traditions prompted Arthur Young to opine that he was 'sorry to see Principles so favouring the Schemes of the Deists, with so great a name affix'd to them'.[33] Even Whiston in due course began to state publicly that Newton held anti-Trinitarian views.[34]

In the contest over Newton's religious affiliation three sides can be broadly identified.[35] The first were those who were trying to associate Enlightenment

---

[31] Scott Mandelbrote, 'Eighteenth-century Reactions to Newton's Anti-Trinitarianism', in eds. J. E. Force and S. Hutton, *Newton and Newtonianism. New Studies* (Dordrecht/Boston/London, 2004), 93–111. As Brian Young has judiciously observed, 'No simple demarcation of attitudes to Newtons and Newtonianism can be constructed by historians'. *Religion and enlightenment*, 162–3.

[32] Later published as . *The Christian Faith asserted against Deists etc.* (London, 1732). Scott Mandelbrote justly calls Trapp 'a subtle reader of Newton, alert to the chance to turn a nuanced argument on its head'. He gained his Oxford DD in 1728. Mandelbrote, 'Eighteenth-century reactions to Newton's Anti-Trinitarianism', 101–2.

[33] Arthur Young, *An Historical Dissertation on Idolatrous Corruptions in Religion* (2 vols., London, 1734), II. 1077, quoted in Force, *Whiston*, 140.

[34] ibid., 140–1; Mandelbrote, *Footsteps of the Lion*, 135. Voltaire (who was fascinated by Newton's character and private life) had no hesitation in making no secret of his hero's Arianism in his *Letters on the English Nation* (1734) and his *Elements of Newton's Philosophy* (1738). 'The celebrated Sir Isaac Newton honour'd this opinion [Arianism] so far as to countenance it', he reported with splendid understatement in 1733. Voltaire, *Philosophical Letters Or, Letters Regarding the English Nation* (Indianapolis, IN, 2007) [trans. Prudence L. Steiner], ed. John Leigh, 21, 22.

[35] cf. H. Guerlac, 'Where the Statue Stood: Divergent Loyalties to Newton in the Eighteenth Century', in ed. E. R. Wasserman, *Aspects of the Eighteenth Century* (Baltimore, MD, 1965), 317–34.

insights with anticlerical and even anti-Christian attitudes and saw Newton as a
fellow-traveller and an inspiration; the second were high churchmen (largely
Oxonians) who were ready to admit that the first party were in essentials right,
that Newton was indifferent to revelation and that his physics was much harder to
reconcile with Christian orthodoxy than had been generally claimed; the third
group, and by far the most significant in England during the 1730s and 1740s,
were publicly insistent that Newtonian science and orthodoxy were in essentials
wholly compatible and that the charge made against Sir Isaac of espousing
Arianism as one convinced of the corruption of the Christian religion could not
be substantiated. What could be said—and this view always had its Oxford
supporters, especially at Christ Church[36]—was that Newton was committed to
the tradition of *prisca sapientia*, of 'ancient wisdom', a perspective entirely compatible with faith in Christ.[37] Whatever their private opinions, the majority in this
diverse third group attempted to project an appearance of doctrinal solidarity and
prevent overt non-Trinitarians from winning major pieces of patronage in the
Church of England. This last perspective was widely held and difficult to dislodge
by either deists or the ultra-orthodox and it was the backbone of what has been
called the 'holy alliance' of Newton's natural philosophy and the apologetics of
low-church Anglicans, especially those in or from Cambridge, the Hanoverian
establishment's university of preference before *c*.1760.[38]

Thanks to David Gregory and John Keill, Newtonianism had been strongly
positioned within the teaching of the Professoriate earlier in the century, when the
University felt unable to ignore its accumulating cultural force. But these men had
no obvious successors and there was no attempt in the 1730s to try and trump
Cambridge by encouraging Oxford academics to launch into Newton-inspired
studies or to poach practitioners established elsewhere.[39] This omission needs
explaining. It may be represented as intellectual retreat, a sign that Oxford was
entering the middle decades of the century when its reputation as a centre of
academic endeavour was waning, but this perception is unconvincing. The fact
that Oxford was less absorbed in Newtonian culture than Cambridge or the Royal
Society actually suggests intellectual independence rather than intellectual decline,

[36] John Friesen's argument is that the promotion of a favourable image of Newton at Christ Church
as 'a modest natural philosopher who respected the ancients' acted as a decisive weapon in the College's
concern to counter the claims of the moderns, at least while Aldrich, Atterbury, and Smalridge held the
Deanship in succesion. 'Christ Church Oxford, the Ancients-Moderns Controversy', 41, 58.

[37] Richard H. Popkin, 'Polytheism, deism, and Newton', in eds. James E. Force and R. H. Popkin,
Essays on the context, nature and influence of Isaac Newton's theology (Dordrecht, 1990), 27–42.

[38] The 'holy alliance' is a central element in John Gascoigne, *Cambridge*; Gascoigne, 'Politics,
patronage and Newtonianism: the Cambridge example', *HJ*, 27 (1984), 1–24. See also Larry Stewart,
*The Rise of Public Science: Rhetoric, Technology, and Natural Philosophy in Newtonian Britain,
1660–1750* (Cambridge, 1992). Cf. Margaret Jacob in *The Newtonians and the English Revolution*,
whose unstated principle was that Newtonianism and latitudinarianism were identical.

[39] In Cambridge, Robert Smith, Master of Trinity College (1742–68), helped make Newton a major
attraction for his college. Fara, 'Faces of genius', 67.

206 ENLIGHTENED OXFORD

a refusal to honour the zeitgeist that was grounded in conviction rather than incuriosity.[40] If Newton became slightly marginal to Oxonian concerns, it reflected both the confidence of natural philosophers within the University in their own independent experimental undertakings, the academic priority that was accorded to *literae humaniores*, and an undeniable sniffiness about the links between Newton's science and his somewhat cranky prophetic findings.[41] But, Newton and the 'Newtonians' apart, other cultural anxieties about the 'new learning' persisted in terms of its proponents, their image, and the extent to which the marketing of science fell outside traditional academic controls.

ii) Lecturers, demonstrators, and Hutchinsonians: Newtonianism popularised and resisted

It was less Newton than the ever-expanding social and academic range of those proud to call themselves his disciples that lay at the root of the University's difficulty in embracing the growing diversity of cultural and commercial enterprises being undertaken in the name of science, itself part of a much wider wave of sociability.[42] As Paul Langford wrote, 'It was middle-brow science and there was a serious market for it'.[43] The coffee-house demonstrations of Newton's optics and physics that were part of this 'public science' were often advertised in provincial papers and together they raised all sorts of questions among the majority of university-based scholars who shunned and derided them.[44] There appeared to be a diminishing overlap between the role of the cleric and that of the natural philosopher, with the attendant fretting about dissonances that could follow

[40] As one Oxford graduate, John, 5th Earl of Orrery (1707–62), told his son (making reference to Swift): '...those determinations in philosophy, which at present seem to the most knowing men to be perfectly well founded and understood, are in reality unsettled, or uncertain, and may perhaps some ages hence be as much decried, as the axioms of Aristotle are at this day. Sir Isaac Newton and his notions may hereafter be out of fashion. There is a kind of mode in philosophy, as well as in other things...' John Boyle, Earl of Orrery, *Remarks on the life and writings of Dr. Jonathan Swift...In a series of letters from John Earl of Orrery to his son* (London, 1752), 97.

[41] Michael Byrne, 'Alternative cosmologies in early eighteenth-century England', Ph.D. thesis (University of London, 1998) details the variety of challenges to the Newtonian model.

[42] Mary Fissell and Roger Cooter, 'Exploring natural knowledge. Science and the popular', in ed. Porter, *Eighteenth-century science*, 129–58, at 158.

[43] Langford, *A Polite and Commercial people*,, 279. See also S. Pumfrey, 'Who did the work? Experimental philosophers and public demonstrators in Augustan England', *BJHS*, 28 (1995), 131–56; G. Bowles, 'The place of Newtonian explanation in English popular thought, 1687–1727', D. Phil. thesis (Oxford University, 1977); essays in ed. Alan Q. Morton, 'Science lecturing in the eighteenth century', special issue of the *BJHS*, 28 (1995).

[44] Jeffrey R. Wigelsworth, *Selling science in the age of Newton. Advertising and the commoditization of knowledge* (Aldershot, 2010), for the way in which advertisements in newspapers helped sell science as a commodity. These included Tory newspapers like the *Post Boy*, which sold in large numbers from the late 1690s onwards. ibid., 43.

OXFORD AND CONTEMPORARY SCIENCE   207

when this form of learning escaped the control of gentlemen virtuosi and clerks in holy orders.

For a start, the moral character of the 'scientist' operating outside a university or a learned society was seen as inherently and dangerously unreliable, his work often questionable, distinguished less by the empirical than by the madcap. And some critics noted how these tendencies could even be found within the Royal Society. The miscellaneous writer and civilian lawyer William King (1663–1712),[45] whose Christ Church connections and loyalties had led him to attack—with some panache—Richard Bentley in his *Dialogues of the Dead* (1699),[46] next targeted Hans Sloane, the physician, indefatigable collector, and secretary of the Royal Society (1693–1712), as part of a wider satire on the *Philosophical Transactions*, the journal of the Royal Society. King used Sloane's exotic natural histories as evidence of the corruption of learning that such influential figures as Sloane appeared happy to engineer and encourage. In his anonymous *The Transactioneer* (1700) (which proceeded from his series of sarcastic *Useful Transactions*), King mocked the way this man who, in his estimation, had 'neither parts nor learning', and functioned as 'the master of only scraps'. On this reading, Sloane had wrecked the Royal Society's credibility, as editor of its *Transactions*, with his conspicuous credulousness.[47] King's excoriation mirrored Jonathan Swift's anti-scientific philippics in *The Battle of the Books* and, later, in *Gulliver's Travels*.[48] This exposure of quackery calling itself natural philosophy gratified scholars who shared Swift's epistemological traditionalism (if not his outright pessimism) and were wary of groundless intellectual pride.[49]

---

[45] educ. Westminster and Christ Church, MA, 1688, DCL and admitted advocate at Doctors's Commons, 1692. D. Engel, 'The ingenious Dr King', Ph.D. thesis (Edinburgh University, 1989; Hugh de Quehen, 'King, William (1663–1712)', *ODNB* online edn., 2008. For his collected output see *The Original Works in Verse and Prose of Dr William King* (3 vols., London, 1776).

[46] Levine, *Battle of the Books*, 102–5, for details.

[47] *The Transactioneer, with Some of His Philosophical Fancies: In two dialogues* (London, 1700) took the form of a dialogue between 'A Gentleman' and 'a Virtuoso' suggesting the social gulf that lay between them in a manner that echoed the exchanges between the Christ Church wits and Richard Bentley. See Chapter 4, pp. 61-4. Details of King's attack on Sloane are in Duncan, *Index*, 150-2; James Delbourgo. *Collecting the world. The life and curiosity of Hans Sloane* (Harmondsworth, 2017), 64–8, 183. In 1710 King attacked Sloane again in *A voyage to the island of Cajami*. Ibid., 169–70.

[48] Swift himself was technically a member of Oxford University after his matriculation at Hart Hall in 1692. See Chapter 9. His hostility to scientists (above all, to Newton) extended to Descartes, Gassendi, and Hobbes. See Lynall, *Swift and science*, and Richard Olson, 'Tory-High Church opposition to science and scientism in the eighteenth century: the works of John Arbuthnott, Jonathan Swift, and Samuel Johnson', in ed. John G. Burke, *The uses of science in the age of Newton* (Berkeley, CA, 1983), 171–204.

[49] Tita Chico, *The experimental imagination. literary knowledge and science in the British Enlightenment* (Stanford, CA, 2018), 48–63; Marjorie Nicolson and Nora M. Mohler, 'The scientific background of Swift's "Voyage to Laputa"', in ed. A. Norman Jeffares, *Fair Liberty was all his cry. A tercentenary tribute to Jonathan Swift 1667–1745* (London, 1967), 226–70, esp. 250–69; David Nokes, *Jonathan Swift. A hypocrite reversed* (Oxford, 1985), 323; Patrick Reilly, *Jonathan Swift: the brave desponder* (Manchester, 1982), 214.

208   ENLIGHTENED OXFORD

If ridicule of the virtuosi and the Royal Society was thus widespread, it was particularly concentrated on the mountebank or the 'gimcrack', those who, in their person, appeared to confirm that one could not be both polite and 'scientific',[50] Foolish and delusional they might be, but their comic character was not to offset the risk they posed to upsetting the Christian beliefs of those before whom they appeared and offered scientific 'demonstration' as performance art.[51] The 'empyric' was thus readily linkable with the eccentric and the socially base; for Samuel Johnson, as late as the 1750s, the term still connoted quackery.[52] These public demonstrators appeared ready to invite untutored audiences (including women) to challenge the penalty of the Fall by offering a facile and factitious understanding of the physical nature of the universe, when its cautious exposition properly belonged to the ordained ministry. In their hands learning was likely to be a means of undermining intellectual and political authority.

There were models to show how academics might manage the leap into a world outside eager to be impressed by all things Newtonian. One such was John Theophilus Desaguliers (1683–1744) who came close to joining the vulgar popularisers but adroitly retained his respectability.[53] Inspired by the lectures given at Oxford by Keill (to whom he acted as an assistant), he had done the same at Hart Hall until 1713 when he went to London and became famous for his lectures and demonstrations at the Royal Society, for an easy-reading primer called *The Newtonian System of the World* (1728), and for his accessible books on experimental science, especially his *Course of Experimental Philosophy*.[54] But his career raised concerns that beneficed clergy who delighted in natural philosophy were putting demonstrations and personal research far ahead of their pastoral duties. Desagulier's apparent lack of involvement in his parish at Whitchurch, Middlesex, was such that his patron, the 1st Duke of Chandos,[55] (for whom he acted as an engineering consultant in matters of irrigation, hydraulics, and steam devices),

---

[50] Chico, *The experimental imagination*, 122–9; Al Coppola, *The theater of experiment. Staging natural philosophy in eighteenth-century Britain* (Oxford, 2016).

[51] Simon Schaffer, 'Natural philosophy and public spectacle in the eighteenth century', *History of Science*, 21 (1983), 1–43.

[52] Samuel Johnson, *A dictionary of the English language: An anthology*, ed. D. Crystal, (Harmondsworth, 2005), 213.

[53] Matric. Ch. Ch., 1705, awarded an Oxford BCL and DCL in 1719. Bodl., Rawlinson MSS, J. 4°.3. Desaguliers was incorporated at Cambridge, 1726.

[54] A. T. Carpenter, *John Theophilus Desaguliers. A natural philosopher, engineer and Freemason in Newtonian England* (London, 2011), 18–19 Desaguliers has been credited with 'a vision that may be called proto-industrial'. Dobbs and Jacob, *Newton and the culture of Newtonianism*, 76. Carpenter, *Desaguliers*, and P. Boutin, *Jean-Théophile Desaguliers. Un Huguenot, philosophe et juriste, en politique* (Geneva, 1999) explore the breadth and achievement of his career. See an undated, unnamed notebook on 'Mechanicks, Hydrostaticks and Pneumaticks' likely to reflect his Oxford research interests at Bodl. MS. Add. *c*.272.

[55] He was the Duke's personal chaplain from 1710. Chandos was an undergraduate at New College, 1692–4. Carpenter, *Desaguliers*, 153–76. Larry Stewart, 'Public Lecture and Private Patronage in Newtonian England', *Isis*, 77 (1986), 47–58, at 52–3; C. H. Collins Baker and Muriel I. Baker, *The life and circumstances of James Brydges, First Duke of Chandos* (Oxford, 1949), 47–62.

OXFORD AND CONTEMPORARY SCIENCE   209

rebuked him thus: '... the inhabitants ... have been forced to go a begging to other ministers to bury their dead. This is a very shameful neglect & what I have more than once complained to you of'.[56]

Desaguliers was perhaps the most prominent among Newtonian popularisers entertaining and instructing the public up and down Britain, cashing in on the marketing opportunity and, it has been claimed, representative of 'a broad European movement'.[57] Oxonian disquiet over this aspect of the Newtonian inheritance simmered away among a minority down to the 1760s. During his long career as a controversialist, William Jones of Nayland, the arch-Hutchinsonian, never tired of complaining about the rage for experimentalism in texts such as *An Essay on the First Principles of Natural Philosophy* (Oxford, 1762).[58] For Jones, the unstructured aspects of this learning admitted too many models for establishing truth. He was among those who believed that it had contributed to an excessive emphasis in the contemporary Christian economy of salvation on natural theology at the expense of revelation, in effect modifying theological tradition to suit the new revealed order of physics and mathematics.[59] Jones was an uncompromising High Churchman who gloried in his distinctive spiritual inheritance, yet he deplored the impact he adjudged Newton to have had on a correct understanding of the faith. He was representative of the surfacing of anti-Newtonian anxieties within such academic circles in Oxford during the 1740s and 1750s that was at odds with the University's earlier willingness overall to embrace first-generation Newtonianism through the likes of Gregory, Keill, and Freind, all well-disposed to the High Church cause.

In their intellectual and spiritual disquiet, anti-Newtonian Oxonians in the reign of George II sought a new source of authority and believed they had found one in the physico-theological writings of John Hutchinson.[60] The publication of his collected works between 1737 and 1749 would usher in a decade of debate in Oxford about the extent to which true enlightenment could be associated with Newtonian physics and the creation of what was, in effect, a Hutchinsonian party.[61]

---

[56] Huntington Library, San Marino, CA, Stowe MSS. 57, xli, ff. 131–2, Chandos to Desaguliers, 20 Mar. 1738/9, quoted in Stewart, *The rise of public science*, 219. Desaguliers was, admittedly, a demonstrator at the Royal Society itself.

[57] Geoffrey V. Sutton, *Science for a polite society. gender, culture, & the demonstration of Enlightenment* (Boulder, CO, 1995), 192; Stewart, *The rise of public science, passim*.

[58] L. Stewart, 'The trouble with Newton in the eighteenth century', in eds. Force and Hutton, *Newton and Newtonianism*, 221–37, at 230–1, 235. George Horne had earlier complained about the 'stupid admiration' of men of genius making experiments that degraded 'the philosopher into the mechanic'. *A fair, candid and impartial state of the case between Sir Isaac Newton and Mr Hutchinson* (Oxford, 1753), 54.

[59] See generally A. J. Kuhn, 'Nature spiritualised, aspects of anti-Newtonianism', *Journal of English Literary History*, 41 (1974), 400–12.

[60] For exemplary contextualisation see Philip Connell, *Secular chains. Poetry and the politics of religion from Milton to Pope* (Oxford, 2016), chap. 5, 'The Literature of physico-theology', esp. 177–97.

[61] Nigel Aston, 'From personality to party: the creation and transmission of Hutchinsonianism, c.1725–1750', *Studies in the History and Philosophy of Science*, 35 (2004), 625–44.

210 ENLIGHTENED OXFORD

Its early influence in Oxford in the 1730s was primarily via Benjamin Holloway, a Cambridge graduate but Rector of Middleton Stoney, ten miles north of the city, with friends in the University that included Walter Hodges, Provost of Oriel College, and George Watson, who tutored George Horne at University College.[62] Holloway was a prolific author and gifted admirer of Hutchinson and his circle of followers while '... claiming his independence'.[63] In his *Experimental Philosophy Asserted and Defended against Some Attempts to Undermine It* (1740), he contended that Hutchinson's cosmological system was compatible with experimental science and saw no necessity to resort as per the Newtonian paradigm to unseen forces to explain or justify natural phenomena. He rejected what he called 'occult qualities' in favour of a mechanical model where the function of fire, light, and spirit was sufficient for the operation of the universe.[64]

The cultural and intellectual credibility this revsionary tendency sought was hard won. It confronted a professorial corps in mathematics and the sciences loosely describable as Newtonian in its academic underpinnings, while the readiness of many Hutchinsonians to be *ad hominem* in their criticisms united a range of Oxonians, including the influential Thomas Hunt and Benjamin Kennicott, against them.[65] And then, in 1759, the return of Halley's Comet in 1759 appeared to be irrefutable confirmation of the universal law of gravitation, in short, of Newton's mathematical system of the universe.[66] Nevertheless, Oxford's scientific culture was by that date sufficiently diverse and well established for Newtonian and anti-Newtonian viewpoints to be vigorously debated even as attention turned away from physics.[67]

Hutchinsonianism, it might be said, was for most who engaged with it at Oxford more of a corrective than an alternative to Newtonian physico-theology. Perhaps the majority, like John Wesley, that displaced Oxonian, saw something

---

[62] Robin Darwall-Smith, *Univ. A history of University College Oxford* (Oxford, 2008), 271–3. Holloway was Horne's 'dearest friend and kind instructor'—as the latter put it in 1759. CUL MS Add. 8134 A (2)90. For Holloway see also Chapter 12, pp. 52–4.

[63] Tarbuck, *Enlightenment Reformation*, 30, 39–41, 125.

[64] Ibid., 57, 87. Tarbuck judges his attempt 'to promote Hutchinsonian cosmology as a pure scientific method, without the aid of its biblical backing,... a remarkable effort, attempting to tackle opponents on their own ground'. For Horne, Jones, and their own Hutchinson-inspired work on sciences, ibid., 20. For worries that Newton's philosophy might be another form of materialism see J. C. English, 'John Hutchinson's critique of Newtonian heterodoxy', *Church History*, 68 (1999), 581–97.

[65] Hunt took the attacks on his position phlegmatically. He told Richard Rawlinson after one assault. 'You see my last Speech is attack'd by the Hutchinsonian Julius Bate; but he has done me no more harm, than Hutchinson and his other followers had done me before, who have been pelting me ever since I publish'd Bp Hooper *De Benedictione Patriarcha Gen.*, wch is now above 20 years'. 20 Mar. 1749, Bodl. MSS Rawl. letters 96 f. 303.

[66] S. Schaffer, 'Comets & idols: Newton's cosmology and political theology', in eds. Paul Theerman and Adele F. Seeff, *Action and reaction: Proceedings of a symposium to commemorate the tercentenary of Newton's Principia* (Newark, DE: 1993), 206–31.

[67] Newton had his uses as a philosophical authority when the occasion demanded. William Adams of Pembroke did so when he argued that whether a course of nature was ever interrupted was still an open question. *An essay on Mr Hume's essay on miracles* (London, 1752), 20–1.

in Hutchinsonianism without becoming discipular.[68] However, for men like Horne and William Jones, making their academic mark in the 1750s, a more aggressive anti-Newtonianism seemed appropriate as they returned to scripture and Hutchinson's own emphasis on Moses as the archetypal scientist, whom Newton and his followers had dared to supplant.[69] On this reading Newtonianism tended to undermine the grammar and rhetorical structures of religious language; a multiple hermeneutics appeared to encourage doubt, with empiricism and error dangerously entangled. Watson and Holloway, Jones and Horne, and others worried that with doctrine played down in favour of natural theology, the risks of compromising the Old Testament and rendering revelation superfluous were considerable, and this apprehension contributed to the renewed mid-century emphasis on salvation through faith in Christ and a more biblically based understanding of divine Creation that, in the country at large, Methodism was fanning.

As Horne put it to his patron in Kent:[70]

...Sir I. N. Dr C. and all their mathematical and Metaphysical Followers are the Innovators [not Hutchinson], who have trumped up Systems of Religion and Philosophy out of their own Brains, and set afoot a false scheme of both to the Exclusion of the S[acred] S[criptures]. which alone is true in either...Damnable Billets are every Day popping out in the infidel Way-against the Trinity, ye Pentateuch, & ye Canticles, which shew plain enough which way we are going— The Lord preserve us all faithful unto Death, that we may receive a Crown of Life'.

iii) Oxford and the Royal Society after Newton

The emerging Oxford interest in what became known as Hutchinsonianism and other anti- or counter Newtonian systems was not lessened by developments within the Royal Society after Newton's death.[71] Of course, Oxford graduates

---

[68] While Wesley praised Newton's genius in observing the laws of nature, yet he retained some Cartesian sympathies, and was somewhat attracted to Hutchinsonianism (although by no means adopting it) because it seemed more theologically orthodox. J. C. English, 'John Wesley and Isaac Newton's "System of the World"', *Proceedings of the Wesley Historical Society*, 48 (1991), 69–86.

[69] D. S. Katz, 'Moses's *Principia*: Hutchinsonianism and Newton's critics', in eds. J. E. Force and R. H. Popkin, *The books of nature and scripture: Recent essays on natural philosophy, theology and biblical criticism in the Netherlands of Spinoza's time and the British Isles of Newton's time* (Dordrecht, 1994), 201–11.

[70] Horne to Rev. Denny Martin, 22 Jan. 1751, Kent Archives U23 C21/8. For a more mature perspective admitting that Newton had settled 'laws and rules in Natural Philosophy' see Horne's *A fair, candid and impartial state of the case between Sir Isaac Newton and Mr Hutchinson* (Oxford, 1753).

[71] T. Birch, *The history of the Royal Society of London*, (4 vols., London, 1756–7), repr. with introduction by A. R. Hall (London, 1968); C. R. Weld, *History of the Royal Society* (2 vols., London, 1848); Sir Henry Lyons, *The Royal Society, 1660–1940: a history of its administrations under its charters* (Cambridge, 1944).

212 ENLIGHTENED OXFORD

had been prominent within the Royal Society since its foundation and there were established networks of cultural sociability between the Society and the colleges grounded in Anglican sociability.[72] And the turn of the Society away from mathematics and astronomy towards applied science (evidenced by the publication of its widely read *Philosophical Transactions*, including various abridged editions), with collecting, surveying, and applied mechanics all prioritised, was also non-controversial. The recipients of its prestigious Copley Medal, awarded annually from the 1730s to the 1780s, all tended to come from these fields.[73] This turn in the century towards technological innovation and experimental precision reflected the value accorded to the useful by the Enlightenment, and that the Society was in a position to sponsor them was achieved through internal realignments in personnel and policies brought forward by its talented leadership cadre, some of whom were quite indifferent about whether their views and prominence offended the Established Church.[74]

Some of the private noises coming out of the Society during the presidency of Martin Folkes (1741–53) were disquieting. The antiquarian William Stukeley reported in the 1730s that in the private dining rooms of the Society, Folkes and his 'junto of sycophants' 'scoffed at religion' and that 'when any mention is made of Moses, of the deluge, of religion, scriptures... it generally is received with a loud laugh'.[75] Folkes was a thorough-going Newtonian, Deputy Master of the Premier Grand Masonic Lodge of England,[76] and a nominal churchman. Despite having archbishop William Wake as his uncle by marriage, allegations of his materialist

---

[72] Of the forty-one founding members of the Royal Society, twenty-two were Oxford graduates, five were from Cambridge, ten had attended both universities. K. Theodore Hoppen, *The common scientist in the seventeenth century: a study of the Dublin Philosophical Society* (London, 1970), 70.

[73] M. Yakup Bektas and Maurice Crosland, 'The Copley Medal: the establishment of a reward system in the Royal Society, 1731–1839', *Notes and Records of the Royal Society of London*, 46 (1992), 43–76.

[74] G. S. Rousseau and D. A. B. Haycock, 'Voices calling for reform: the Royal Society in the mid-eighteenth century, Martin Folkes, John Hill, and William Stukeley', *History of Science*, 37 (1999), 377–406; Richard Sorrenson, 'Towards a history of the Royal Society in the eighteenth century', *Notes and Records of the Royal Society*, 50 (1996), 29–46; 'Did the Royal Society matter in the eighteenth century?', *BJHS*, 32 (1999), 130–2.

[75] Quoted in James E. Force, 'The breakdown of the Newtonian synthesis of science and religion: Hume, Newton, and the Royal Society', in eds. Force and Popkin, *Essays on Isaac Newton's theology*, 143–64, at 143; David Boyd Hancock, '"The cabal of a few designing members": the presidency of Martin Folkes, PRS, and the Society's first charter', *Antiquaries Journal*, 80 (2000), 273–84; Force, *Whiston*, 195. Stukeley was in no doubt about Folkes's irreligion: 'in matters of religion an errant infidel & loud scoffer. Professes himself a godf[athe]r to all monkeys, believes nothing of a future state, of the Scriptures, of revelation... He thinks there is no difference between us & animals; but what is owing to the different structure of our brain, as between man & man'. *The family memoirs of the Rev. W. Stukeley*, ed. W. C. Lukis (3 vols., Durham, 1882–7) [Surtees Soc., vols. 73, 76, 80], I. 99–100. Stukeley had once been friends with Folkes and had himself flirted with deism before his own religious conversion.

[76] Ric Berman, *The foundations of modern Freemasonry. The grand architects—political change and the scientific Enlightenment, 1714–1740* (2nd edn., Brighton, 2014), for details on Folkes's Masonic background and its significance.

OXFORD AND CONTEMPORARY SCIENCE   213

inclinations were never dispelled, while his interest in Roman ancestral cults, and his sympathy for pagan religions of antiquity were no secret.[77] It has been claimed that under Folkes the Society's apologetic goal during its first forty years of promoting 'a strong conception of generally provident nature and regular natural law while also retaining God's special providence via miracles or prophecies' was abandoned.[78] That such a man as he should succeed Newton and Sir Hans Sloane as president of the Royal Society (PRS) suggested the degree to which scepticism and freemasonry had become acceptable within the early Hanoverian learned establishment.[79] The choice, as Folkes's successor, of the astronomer and Cambridge graduate George Parker, 2nd Earl of Macclesfield (1697–1764), came as something of a relief to many Oxford academics, particularly those who knew Macclesfield, a learned peer known to be well-disposed to the University, with his seat and observatory (established by James Bradley in 1739) at Shirburn Castle less than twenty miles away from Carfax.[80] One FRS noted:[81]

> we have got a very good president at the R.S. Lord Macclesfield, & he is a man of religion (as I think) & thats a great rarity among our philosophers. they are generally great enemys to Moses, the prophets, & apostles. our late president Folkes a deplorable spectacle.

Folkes's presidency also partly explains the tension between the metropolitan intellectual elite and the clergy during the 1730s and 1740s that often appeared in the guise of anticlericalism. Nevertheless, he had enough friends within the University to be awarded a doctorate of laws in July 1746. The gesture was a reminder of the range of political opinions held by academics plus the pressures coming from outside Oxford making for cultural conformity (not least, continued patronage deprivation); the University authorities were obliged to register (however grudgingly) that, despite the running made by Oxford through the likes of

---

[77] Bodl MS Eng. Misc. e. 135, p. 3; Anna Marie Roos, 'Taking Newton on tour: the scientific travels of Martin Folkes, 1733–1735', *BJHS*, 50 (2017), 569–601. Her intellectual biography, *Martin Folkes (1690–1754). Newtonian, Antiquary, Connoisseur* (Oxford, 2021), appeared too late for me to notice it.

[78] Force, *Whiston*, 128, 136–7, 154, who also contends that this 'shift' 'seems to have been accomplished within the Society itself more through ridicule and mockery than because of explicitly argued tracts and pamphlets', ibid., 129. Generally, J. Force, 'Whiston, Hume and the relation of science to religion among certain members of the Royal Society', *JHI*, 45 (1984), 517–36.

[79] 45% of Royal Society Fellows were Masons in the 1720s. P. Elliot and S. Daniels, 'The "school of true, useful and universal science"? Freemasonry, natural philosophy and scientific culture in eighteenth-century England', *BJHS*, 39 (2006), 207–29.

[80] Thomas Hunt, the future Professor of Hebrew, was another don regularly at Shirburn Castle, probably helping to build up the book collections there. Macclesfield's son and heir, Lord Parker, was his pupil and went up to Hart Hall in 1740. Hunt to Richard Rawlinson, 8 May 1740, Bodl. MSS Rawl. letters 96, f. 7r.

[81] William Stukeley to Maurice Johnson, 9 Apr. 1753, quoted in eds. D. and M. Honeybone, *Correspondence of Stukeley and Johnson*, 185. Macclesfield was largely responsible for the adoption of the 'New Style' calendar in 1752.

Fig. 5.1 George Parker, 2nd Earl of Macclesfield, Benjamin Wilson, oil on canvas, c.1760 (© Coram in the care of the Foundling Museum).

Gregory and Keill in Queen Anne's time, the Whig establishment had appropriated Newton to itself and deference was non-negotiable.[82]

For all the uncertainties the new physics had triggered, these should not obscure the extent to which the University had made its own discrete contribution to scientific progress by the reign of George II. If, in the heyday of Gregory and Keill, Oxford bid fair to rival Cambridge as a Newtonian nexus, that moment passed as the uses of the new physics for Christian heterodoxy disclosed themselves, and those who flocked around the great man in his last years, like James Jurin (Secretary of the Royal Society 1721–7), were markedly latitudinarian.[83] What survived into the middle of the eighteenth century has been called a

---

[82] '...the Newtonians were increasingly identified with the rise of a Whig oligarchy...'.It [1688–9] was thus not merely a political or intellectual revolution: for Newton and many of his enthusiastic followers, it was both'. Stewart, 'Samuel Clarke, Newtonianism, and the factions of post-Revolutionary England', 54.

[83] James Jurin (1684–1750), fellow of Trinity College, Cambridge, 1708; physician to Guy's Hospital, 1725–32; President of the Royal College of Physicians, 1750.

OXFORD AND CONTEMPORARY SCIENCE 215

'sanitized version of Newtonianism'[84] and, in this format, it was broadly accept-able to majority Oxford opinion, the Hutchinsonians apart. But then there were many strands to Oxford natural philosophy other than its Newtonian aspects.

iv) Oxford science and its reputation in the first half of the eighteenth century: foundations, progress, and obstacles

Eighteenth-century science, as understood and practised at Oxford, was academ-ically eclectic.[85] Tellingly, the Savilian Professors in Astronomy and Geometry, under their foundational statutes of 1619, were expected to lecture on both ancient and modern topics as well as practical mathematics.[86] Thus John Wallis, Professor of Geometry, may have widened the range of higher algebra and invented the symbol for infinity, but he also spent the years between 1676 and 1688 editing classical mathematicians' writings. It was indicative, as Vittoria Feola has argued, of the underlying assumption in Oxford 'science' that knowledge could be advanced only through a 'cooperation' of Ancients and Moderns.[87] It was also sufficiently grounded in the studies of Sir Christopher Wren, Robert Boyle, Robert Hooke, and others that there was no overriding intellectual imperative to swerve in an exclusively Newtonian direction.[88] Its empirical, experimental dimension was well established and relatively unclouded by religious controversy (unless it be Edmond Halley's alleged unbelief).[89] During the Commonwealth and early Restoration John Wilkins (himself a future Anglican bishop)[90] and his circle at Wadham College had made the University the major centre for experimental studies when the city was full of displaced London intellectuals.[91] Though this

[84] Gascoigne, *Cambridge*, 142–84; Mandelbrote, 'Eighteenth-century reactions to Newton's anti-Trinitarianism', 111; Force, *Whiston*, 91.

[85] For some helpful thoughts on pre-disciplinarity see G. S. Rousseau, *Enlightenment borders: pre-and post-modern discourses: medical, scientific* (Manchester, 1991), 217–18.

[86] John Friesen, 'Christ Church Oxford, the ancients-moderns controversy', 37, 53.

[87] Vittoria Feola, 'The Ancients "with" the Moderns: Oxford's approaches to publishing ancient science', in eds. P. Bullard and A. Tadié, *Ancients and Moderns in Europe: comparative perspectives* [Oxford University studies in the Enlightenment] (Oxford, 2016), 19–35, at 19. For Wallis, see Chapter 8, p. 78.

[88] Robert G. Frank, *Harvey and the Oxford Physiologists* (Berkeley, CA, 1980). Of the dozen or so later seventeenth-century Oxford 'scientists' charted by Frank, Boyle is the best-known. Ibid., 44ff. See Hunter, *Boyle, passim*.

[89] For this reputation, like David Gregory before him, see Manuel, *The religion of Isaac Newton*, 7.

[90] Allan Chapman, 'The first professors', in eds. Fauvel, Flood, and Wilson, *Oxford figures: eight centuries of the mathematical sciences*, 92–113, at 101–5. For Wilkins and the origins of latitudinar-ianism in the Church, see H. R. McAdoo, *The spirit of Anglicanism: a survey of Anglican theological method in the seventeenth century* (London, 1965), chap. 6.

[91] Mark Curtis, *Oxford and Cambridge in transition, 1558–1642. An essay on changing relations between the English universities and English society* (Oxford, 1959), chap. 9; C. Webster, *The Great Instauration: science, medicine and reform 1626–1660* (London, 1975), 51–7, 153–74; Hunter, *Science and society in Restoration England*, 23. R. T. Gunther, *Early science in Oxford* (14 vols., Oxford, 1923–45) remains indispensable.

216 ENLIGHTENED OXFORD

provincial momentum could not be sustained when the initiative and the cachet passed to the Royal Society after its foundation in 1660, the work of Hooke and Wallis inter alia signified that Oxford science 'abounded with gifted men who could turn their hands to anything and make original contributions' in the University as much as in London.[92] The original, mid-century dynamism was also upheld by the Oxford Philosophical Society, established in the city in 1683. Its members performed experiments, presented and discussed papers (particularly those given at the Royal Society), and kept in touch with a kindred society in Dublin.[93]

Related cultural developments in Oxford engendered new scholarly opportunities. Famously, when the antiquary, alchemist and astrologer Elias Ashmole inherited the plantsman John Tradescant's 'rareties' museum (itself reflecting the popular link between Noah and natural history) as a deed of gift it was placed in a building designed specifically for that purpose, opened in 1683. It housed a display of objects on the top floor, a lecture room at ground level, two libraries (one of chemistry, one of natural philosophy), and a chemistry laboratory in the basement.[94] Its Keeper was Robert Plot (1640–96), also the University's first Professor of Chemistry (1683–9).[95] Plot also edited the *Philosophical Transactions of the Royal Society* from Oxford between 1684 and 1686, and had an opportunity to place work originating in the University before an international audience; more locally, the Philosophical Society met at the Ashmolean, for it was in part expected to function as a centre for study and teaching.[96] And outsiders visited keen to update an Oxford audience with the latest developments in natural philosophy elsewhere. In October 1695 a remarkable Irishman, Dr Bernard [O']Connor (b. 1666), arrived from the continent and gave a course of lectures in which he

---

[92] Chapman, 'The first professors', 113.

[93] Its ethos owed much to 'coffee-house culture'. John Wallis and Robert Plot were its principal members. *The life and times of Anthony Wood, antiquary, at Oxford, 1632–1695, described by himself,* ed. Andrew Clark (5 vols., Oxford, 1891–5), III. 76–8; Gunther, *Early science,* IV; Webster, *The Great Instauration,* 81–2. A. M. Roos, 'The Oxford Philosophical Society and the Royal Society: a meeting of minds?', podcast 23 July 2013 http://podcasts.ox.ac.uk/oxford-philosophical-society-and-royal-society-meeting-minds. The orientalist, Robert Huntington, and the distinguished Irish doctor, Charles Willoughby, co-founded the Dublin Society, and were former Fellows of Merton. Martin and Highfield, *Merton College,* 219–20.

[94] A. MacGregor, *Tradescant's Rarities: essays on the foundation of the Ashmolean Museum 1683, with a catalogue of the surviving early collections* (Oxford, 1983); Gunther, *Early science,* I. 43–51; A. V. Simcock, *The Ashmolean Museum and Oxford science, 1683–1983* (Oxford, 1984), 7–10. A. MacGregor and A. J. Turner, 'The Ashmolean Museum' in HUO V, 639–58, discuss successive Keepers and their erratic curatorial records. Eds. O. Impey and A. MacGregor, *The origins of museums. the cabinet of curiosities in sixteenth- and seventeenth-century Europe* (Oxford, 1985) for the wider context.

[95] Magdalen Hall; Secretary of the Royal Society; founder of the Oxford Philosophical Society; historiographer-royal, 1688. See also Chapter 12, pp. 64, 81. He had only one successor as professor after 1689. Brockliss (1), 242n. This was the physician Edward Hannes (c.1664–1710), apptd. 1690, resigned 1704, when the chair lapsed. He was named a royal physician, 1702, knighted 1705. His alcaic odes in the Horatian vein draw on his medical experience. Money, *The English Horace,* 55; Leicester Bradner, *Musae Anglicanae: A history of Anglo-Latin poetry, 1500–1925* (New York, 1940), 208–10, on medical learning and literature.

[96] A.G. MacGregor and A.J. Turner, 'The Ashmolean Museum', in *HUO* V, 639–58, at 643, 644.

described the new discoveries in anatomy, physiology, and medicine by Marcello Malpighi (the pioneer of microscopical anatomy), Lorenzo Bellini (in the structure of the kidneys), and Francesco Redi (the founder of experimental biology).[97] [O']Connor had originally studied medicine at Reims, where he may have encountered the work of Descartes. Once in England he had converted to Anglicanism but may have reverted to his old faith on his deathbed in 1698.[98]

The enduring power and appeal of Noachian geology and Plottian natural history throughout the eighteenth century are striking. In the hands of individuals as different as Plot and, later, (Sir) Hans Sloane, these offered a cultural counterpart to Newtonian mathematical physics. Sloane, the second President of the Royal Society, was not an Oxford graduate but well-connected to and, by that date, well-thought-of by most in the University. As PRS, he raised the prominence of natural history after 1727 (as opposed to mathematical demonstration) and encouraged the Oxonian emphasis on that subject area (and botany in particular) that endured for decades.[99] It was an emphasis that counsels against exaggerating the extent to which Newtonianism displaced other, older rhetorics of natural philosophy, theology, and history: Newtonianism was not even positioned to act as a full-blown alternative to them.

The Ashmolean laboratory contained some expensive experimental apparatus that was soon well-used. Thus John Whiteside, an avowed Newtonian, and Keeper of the Ashmolean (1714–29), chaplain of Christ Church, taught Newtonian mechanics in the lecture room at the Ashmolean with a privately owned, expensive collection of apparatus. He impressed Halley and his course in experimental physics, like those that followed in the course of the century, had no shortage of subscribers.[100] But the use of apparatus was not at all in the early eighteenth century the determining sanction for confirming hypotheses. For instance, the relevance of microscopic forces for chemical phenomena was restated in John Freind's *Chymical lectures*, given in the basement of the Ashmolean in 1704, first published in Latin in 1709, and translated into English and published by 'JM' as *Chymical Lectures* (1712).[101] Freind set them out in the form of axioms

[97] His book *Dissertationes medico-physicae* had been published in Oxford in 1693. M. T. Pugh, 'Bernard Connor (1666–1698)', *Rheumatology*, 41 (2002), 942–3.

[98] He was briefly court physician (1694–5) to John III, king of Poland. Appointed FRS after lecturing at Oxford and moving to London. .Brown, *The Irish Enlightenment*, (Cambridge, MA, 2016), 148–56; A. H. T. Robb-Smith, 'The life and times of Dr Richard Frewin (1681–1761): medicine in Oxford in the eighteenth century', [15th Gideon de Laune lecture, Worshipful Society of Apothecaries of London, 19 Apr. 1972] https://practitioners.exeter.ac.uk/wp-content/uploads/2014/11/Frewin.pdf, 9.

[99] Iliffe, 'Philosophy of Science', 281. For William King's [of Christ Church] attack on Sloane a quarter of a century earlier see this Chapter, p. 22.

[100] Chapman, 'Oxford's Newtonian School', 170–1. For his 'Philosophical Lectures', *c.*1720 see CUL MS Add. 6301; also Bodl. MS Bradley 48 'Whitesides Opticks, very full', *c.*1720–5, 'a course of mathematical lectures'.

[101] G. L.'E. Turner, 'The physical sciences', in HUO V, 659–81, at 663. Freind (1675/6/7–1728), the associate of Atterbury, studied at Christ Church under Aldrich and was appointed a lecturer on chemistry at Oxford in 1704. He was a popular physician in Tory high society at the close of Anne's reign and became implicated in the Atterbury Plot. An indication of his exceptional range as one who

Fig. 5.2 John Freind (1675–1728), Michael Dahl, oil on canvas, c.1720 (Bodleian Libraries, University of Oxford).

and deductions, and the axioms were made to depend on the personal authority of Newton (to whom the lectures were dedicated).[102] Freind, part of the remarkable Christ Church circle that included Gregory and Keill, asserted that Newton's experiments were 'evident to the Sense of all Mankind', and that the principles he drew from them were 'demonstrative Conclusions'. The thesis that Newton had demonstratively established the existence of chemically active forces was also stated in John Keill's 1708 paper in the *Philosophical Transactions*, only for it to be scorned by Leibniz as a return to scholastic philosophy. Not that Aristotelianism had entirely gone away. Traditionalist physics was still expounded

---

'combined polite learning with Newtonian science' is given in Money, *The English Horace*, 150–4; C. O. Brink, *English Classical scholarship. historical reflections on Bentley, Porson and Housman* (Cambridge, 1985), 55. He was a member of the influential Tory-leaning Brothers Club with Swift and Matthew Prior. Olson, 'Tory-High Church opposition to science and scientism', 178. Generally J. S. Rowlinson, 'John Freind: physician, chemist, Jacobite and friend of Voltaire's', *Notes & Records of the Royal Society*, 61 (2001), 109–27.

[102] Freind was celebrated as a medical scholar. Doubtless aware of the condition of the heir presumptive, William, Duke of Gloucester, while at Oxford he published on 'Hydrocephalus' in *Philosophical Transactions* of the Royal Society in 1699 and on *Spasmi rarioris historia* (physical disturbances or 'fits' in the 'animal spirits') in the same journal two years later.

OXFORD AND CONTEMPORARY SCIENCE   219

alongside Newtonian courses, and colleges often laid on their own courses in non-mathematical physics.[103]

Oxford was certainly not a university that eschewed mathematics.[104] Its study had long been encouraged there on the basis of its usefulness for landowners, army and naval officers, and others. No less a figure than Henry Aldrich acted as a mathematics tutor and a key patron of the subject while, for over almost a century, John Wallis (1616–1703) and Edmond Halley (1656-1742) brought Oxford recognition as a locus for mathematical and astronomical work, both men teaching the subjects, recognising the need to educate the public, and personally involved in affairs of state. Wallis, Savilian Professor of Geometry from 1649 and an active and early Fellow of the Royal Society, was, by the Revolution, as a committed Whig and brilliant cryptologist, more concerned to spend his time deciphering intercepted dispatches for William III.[105] He had just produced *A Treatise of Algebra, Both Historical and Practical* (London, 1685), the first substantial history of mathematics in the English language, running to one hundred chapters. And he also found time to publish a collection of his mathematical works between 1693 and 1699 as an inspiration for the next generation.[106] The widely travelled Halley succeeded to John Wallis's chair (appointed January 1704) when his own international reputation as an astronomer was already secure,[107] additionally enhanced by the publication of Newton's *Principia* at his own expense in 1687.[108] Not that his achievements to date entirely offset his reputation as a very rough diamond. The astronomer John Flamsteed (admittedly his grievous enemy) complained that Halley 'talks, swears and drinks brandy like a sea captain', and he notoriously still insisted on using the title 'Captain' rather than 'Professor' for years afterwards.[109]

Though an observatory was built in 1705 on the roof of his house in New College Lane,[110] Halley's Oxford post turned out to be slightly marginal to the celebrity he consolidated in the following decades as a mathematical astronomer,

---

[103] See Brockliss, 'Science, the universities, and other public spaces', 60; Bill, *Christ Church*, 308–10.

[104] M. Feingold, 'Mathematical Sciences and new philosophies', in HUO IV, 359–48.

[105] D. E. Smith, 'John Wallis as a cryptographer', *Bulletin of the American Mathematical Society* 24 (1917), 82–96.

[106] R. Flood and J. Fauvel, 'John Wallis', in eds. Fauvel, Flood, and Wilson, *Oxford figures: eight centuries of the mathematical sciences*, 114–39.

[107] The Royal Society elected him a Fellow when he was just 22, and Charles II ordered the University to grant Halley his MA degree by Royal Mandamus rather than requiring him to be examined for it. Chapman, 'Edmond Halley', in ibid., 140–64, at 144.

[108] He took care to praise Newton and then Wallis and Gregory in his inaugural lecture as Savilian Professor in May 1704. ed. E. F. MacPike, *Correspondence and papers of Edmond Halley* (Oxford, 1932), 251.

[109] Letter to Abraham Sharp, 18 Dec. 1703, quoted in J. and M. Gribbin, *Out of the shadow of a giant. Hooke, Halley and the birth of British science* (London, 2017) 263.

[110] Arthur Charlett called it 'very commodious and well constructed' and forecast it would produce 'discoveries and improvements in the mathematical sciences equal if not superior to any in Europe'. To

Fig. 5.3 Edmond Halley, Thomas Murray, oil on canvas, gift from the artist 1713 (Bodleian Libraries, University of Oxford).

calculator of planetary transits, and expert in cometary orbits, recognised in his appointment as secretary to the Royal Society (1713) and Astronomer Royal (1721).[111] Nevertheless, his fame attracted distinguished foreign visitors to Oxford, he lectured as his chair required, and some of his lectures, on solutions of polynomial equations, were published. His Oxford years as Savilian Professor, before he succeeded Flamsteed as Astronomer Royal, coincided with his papers on the physical composition of deep space, stellar distribution, and the proper motion of stars.[112]

Ormond, 27 June 1705, HMC, *Ormonde MSS* (New Series, London, 1920), VIII. 162; H. E. Bell, 'The Savilian professors' houses and Halley's observatory at Oxford', *Notes and Records of the Royal Society*, 16 (1961), 179–86.

[111] He was asked to offer advice to ministers and the House of Commons in 1712 and 1714, respectively. Alan Cook, *Edmond Halley. charting the heavens and the seas* (Oxford, 1998), 331.

[112] Halley's Oxford career is considered in Cook, *Edmond Halley*, 321–53; Chapman, 'Edmond Halley', 156–61. See also C. A. Ronan, *Edmond Halley: genius in eclipse* (London, 1970). For his successor as Savilian Professor of Geometry, the undersung Oxford teacher, Nathaniel Bliss, see Chapman, 'Oxford's Newtonian school', 177–9.

OXFORD AND CONTEMPORARY SCIENCE   221

James Bradley (1693–1762), Halley's protégé and Keill's successor as Savilian Professor of Astronomy after 1721,[113] conducted most of his significant astronomical studies at an observatory at Wanstead in Essex, having complained that there were neither enough instruments owned by the University nor a building capable of housing his own instruments in Oxford sufficient for him to carry out his research.[114] Bradley's nomination as the third Astronomer Royal following Halley in 1742 conferred immense prestige on the University—and showed that the early Hanoverian establishment was ready to reward loyalists within it—and his importance as an astronomer outside the University only redoubled his celebrity within it.[115] He retained his Oxford chair after 1742, kept up two houses in Greenwich and Oxford, and travelled up to the University to offer a popular course in experimental physics, which he taught from 1729 to 1760 in the Ashmolean museum.[116] Bradley seems to have lectured on average to fifty-seven students per session, an exceptionally high number.[117] Since he charged attendees, it was well worth his while to keep giving his lectures.[118] Undergraduates flocked to hear him, knowing of his reputation—the 'living embodiment of the Newtonian tradition'—and capacity for holding their interest.[119] As one wrote to his father: 'I intend shortly by my Tutor's advise [sic] to subscribe 3 guineas to dr Bradley's Lectures in natural philosophy, they are by all accounts very curious, instructive and entertaining'.[120] And the Church establishment could be confident that in his hands (he was, of course, ordained) this learning would not be directed towards undermining the clerical, Christian culture that was for majority opinion

[113] There were nine electors to the Savilian Professorship, including Cabinet ministers and the archbishop of Canterbury. He was appointed at the behest of Lord Chancellor Macclesfield and Martin Folkes (then vice-president of the Royal Society), neither especially well-affected to Oxford. See ed. S. P. Rigaud, *Miscellaneous works and correspondence of the Rev. James Bradley* (Oxford, 1832).

[114] Gunther, *Early science*, II. 85.

[115] A. Chapman, 'Pure research and practical teaching: the astronomical career of James Bradley, 1693–1762', *Notes and Records of the Royal Society*, 47 (1993), 205–12. John Fisher, 'Astronomy and patronage in Hanoverian England: The work of James Bradley, Third Astronomer Royal of England', (London, Ph.D. thesis, 2004) argues that the scale of his achievement surpassed anything Halley did. For technical details of his observing procedures see Allan Chapman, *Dividing the circle: the development of critical angular measurement in astronomy 1500–1800* (Chichester, 1995). The 2nd Earl of Macclesfield at Shirburn Castle was Bradley's key patron.

[116] MacGregor and Turner, 'The Ashmolean Museum', 650; Turner, 'The physical sciences', 674; 'Dr Bradley's mathematical lectures abridged November 1747', an abstract or notes from a course of twenty lectures on experimental philosophy. Museum of the History of Science, Oxford, MSS Museum 3.

[117] Gunther, *Early science*, XI. 65–80: Bodl. MS. Bradley 3.

[118] Allan Chapman has calculated that by 1752 he was making around £650 per annum, an income larger than the Bishop of Oxford's. 'Pure research and practical teaching', 210.

[119] Chapman, 'Oxford's Newtonian school', 175. Newton once described him as the best astronomer in Europe. R. Woolley, 'James Bradley, third Astronomer Royal', *Quarterly Journal of the Royal Astronomical Society*, 4 (1963), 47–52. He discovered the aberration of light, the apparent displacement of a star's position due to the Earth's movement through space, the first observational proof of terrestrial motion.

[120] W. Lee to Lord Chief Justice [Sir William] Lee, Oxon., Feb. 7 [1744?], Lee Box 3, folder 2, Beinecke Rare Book and Manuscript Library, Yale University.

222 ENLIGHTENED OXFORD

the only authentic model usable to deliver and disclose enlightened knowledge to young men.

Despite these commanding figures being on its books, Oxford was never quite the rival to Cambridge as a mathematical centre in these decades; it lagged behind the competition in medicine from Scottish and Dutch institutions as well.[121] Apart from the London hospitals there was only one centre of medical instruction in eighteenth-century Britain: Edinburgh. The latter attracted students away from Oxford (and Cambridge), notably those who either were dissenters or wished to obtain some practical clinical teaching unavailable in the English universities where, as late as 1702, the University calendar noted that:

> A Student of medicine in this University is not required to attend any lectures but is left to acquire his knowledge from such sources as his discretion may point out.[122]

It also simply took longer to study for a medical degree. The situation was not improved by Oxford's possessing a powerful group of resident physicians reluctant to recognise outsiders, for instance by awarding them Oxford medical degrees either by creation or by incorporation. These made the most of their prescriptive rights as *doctores alentes*, doctors living within the university precincts.[123] Yet there was movement of sorts and, despite the vagaries of the Regius Professor of Medicine and other official post-holders, plus apprehensiveness around the association of medicine and atheism,[124] students were trained up. Though Oxford doctors of medicine were required to expound passages from Galen throughout the eighteenth century under the framework of the Laudian statutes, minor modifications were introduced within the faculty from the 1760s, even if the Bachelor of Medicine degree still offered no on-the-job instruction and involved a compulsory examination in at least two out of four ancient authors: Hippocrates, Galen, Celsus, and Aretaeus.[125] The advantage of this 'traditional' curriculum was

---

[121] Scotland became more of a magnet than the United Provinces after *c*.1750. Steven Shapin, 'The audience for science in eighteenth-century Edinburgh', *History of Science*, 12 (1974), 95–121, at 102. For background surveys of Oxford medicine see C. Webster, 'The medical faculty and the physic garden', in HUO V, 683–723; ed. K. Dewhurst, *Oxford medicine. Essays on the evolution of the Oxford Clinical School to commemorate the bicentenary of the Radcliffe Infirmary 1770–1970* (Oxford, 1970); M. Davidson, *Medicine in Oxford* (Oxford, 1953).

[122] See M. G., *Mercurius Oxoniensis, or the Oxford intelligencer, for the year of our lord 1707* (London, 1707) for a list of such lecture times as there were and summaries of their contents.

[123] eds. R. G. W. Anderson and A. D. C. Simpson, *The early years of the Edinburgh Medical School* (Edinburgh, 1976) for the background. Webster, 'The medical faculty'. 688–9, considers the restrictive practices of the *doctores alentes*.

[124] Andrew Cunningham, 'Where there are three physicians, there are two atheists', in eds. Ole Peter Grell and Andrew Cunningham, *Medicine and religion in Enlightenment Europe* (Aldershot, 2007), Int., 1.

[125] T. N. Bonner, *Becoming a physician: medical education in Britain, France, Germany and the United States, 1750–1945* (Baltimore, MD, 2000), 39–40. The Regius Professor of Medicine was expected to lecture on Hippocrates or Galen twice a week during term time. Webster, 'The medical faculty and the physic garden', 702.

OXFORD AND CONTEMPORARY SCIENCE   223

that Oxford medical graduates became familiar with a range of medical texts thanks to their skills in latinity,[126] but it seems to have done nothing to stem the flow of Oxford graduates to the Scottish and Dutch universities to study medicine within a comparable or superior medical faculty—as well as allowing an uncomplicated opportunity for the University's detractors to score easy points. Those that did stay to take the MD had the incentive of knowing that one could not be a member of the Royal College of Physicians without being either an Oxford or a Cambridge medical graduate.

And there were brilliant Oxford-educated physicians working in the city who won fame outside it and provided role models for the next generation. Perhaps the most gifted was Richard Frewin (1681?–1761). He combined medicine with classical scholarship. He was a Westminster student at Christ Church, a younger member of the Freind circle, and an outstanding Latinist acknowledged by his readership in rhetoric (he welcomed Francis Atterbury to the House as Dean in 1711). But he also took the MB and MD degrees (1707 and 1711), and spent the next five decades practising medicine across Oxford (he attended Henry Aldrich) while also holding the Camden Professorship of History after 1727 (there were no other candidates). Frewin had a lifelong interest in the medicinal uses of plants and left £2,000 in trust for the physicians of the Radcliffe Infirmary.[127]

There was an anatomy school in the Schools quadrangle but it was more of a museum than a recognisable anatomical theatre of the sort to be found in, for instance, Padua.[128] Nevertheless private lectures and demonstrations were offered on the premises at intervals in the first half of the century by such as Frank Nicholls (1699?–1778), son-in-law of the society physician, Richard Mead, styled 'praelector in anatomy' in his published works. He lectured at Oxford on anatomy and demonstrated the minute structure of blood vessels before he, too (c.1720), moved to London.[129] Thereafter Nathan[iel] Alcock (1707–79), with an Edinburgh and Leiden background (he was the pupil of Herman Boerhaave), offered lectures from the late 1730s by private arrangement in anatomy and chemistry despite the sniffiness of the Oxford medical establishment. He was popular with students. But his liberal Calvinism and freemasonry retarded his incorporation (Jesus, 1741) and it was not until 1742 that he was admitted as an

---

[126] See N. Vickers, *Coleridge and the doctors: 1795–1806* (Oxford, 2004).

[127] Jean Loudon, 'Frewin, Richard (1680/1–1761)', ODNB online edn., 2008; Robb-Smith, 'The life and times of Dr Richard Frewin (1681–1761) http://practitioners.exeter.ac.uk/wp-content/uploads/2014/11/Frewin.pdf www.oxfordhistory.org.uk/doctors/index.html for 'physicians, surgeons, apothecaries, dentists, [in Oxford] 1621–1850.'

[128] Frances Valadez, 'Anatomical studies in Oxford and Cambridge', in ed. Allen G. Debus, *Medicine in seventeenth-century England* (Berkeley, CA, 1973), 393–420, for the background.

[129] Exeter College, MA, 1721, MD, 1729. Nicholls had Jacobite sympathies and was the leading teacher of anatomy in England between 1730 and 1740, influencing both William Hunter and William Smellie. H. M. Sinclair and A. H. T. Robb-Smith, *A short history of anatomical teaching in Oxford* (Oxford, 1950), 26ff.; Anita Guerrini, 'Nicholls, Francis [Frank] (bap. 1699–?1778), anatomist and physician', ODNB, online edn., 2004.

224 ENLIGHTENED OXFORD

MA and made Praelector in Chemistry.[130] Alcock was followed in 1758 by John Smith, who consolidated a reputation as a minor medical writer, and held the Tomlins readership.[131]

They alike faced the besetting problem that scientific instruments were either not widely available or inaccessible, and remained associated with artisan efforts rather than being appropriate for genteel learning. Though there was a mathematical-instrument maker trading in Oxford in William III's reign,[132] that situation changed only slowly as the social elite began to treat these instruments as prestige objects, men of rank such as Charles Boyle, 4th Earl of Orrery (1676–1731), who donated to Christ Church the mathematical and optical instruments he had collected between 1690 and 1710.[133] It was not until the mid-century that this major hiatus and disincentive to Oxford science was gradually remedied, mainly through appreciable benefactions, such as that of the 5th Lord Leigh. Leigh left to the Vice Chancellor and Provost of Oriel College £1,000 for purchasing models and a proper apparatus 'for exemplifying and illustrating the Mathematical Lectures and Experiments formerly read and explained in the Museum by Doctor Bradley and Mr Bliss.'[134]

v) The physical sciences at Oxford: advances, anxiety, and politics in the age of George III

Astronomy now turns her globe,/Now through her tube triumphant soars,/Expatiates o'er heaven's azure robe/And every burning gem explores.

Musaeus, 'On a view of Oxford', *GM*, 22 (1752), 379.

---

[130] FRS 1750; DM 1749; left Oxford 1759. He declined the Regius Chair of Medicine on the death of William Woodforde in 1758. To his credit, Alcock nursed no sense of grievance and praised his adopted university unstintingly in 1740 for what it did get right:

> The advantages of learning in every branch particularly the Belles Lettres, and a taste for fine writing are so far superior here to anything that can be met with abroad, that it would provoke one's indignation and contempt to hear of any comparison.

Turner, 'The Physical Sciences', 663–5; Peter J. T. Morris, 'The eighteenth century: chemistry allied to anatomy', in eds. R. J. P. Williams, A. Chapman, and J. S. Rowlinson, *Chemistry at Oxford. A history from 1600 to 2005* (London, 2009), 52–78, at 63; N. Hans, *New trends in education in the eighteenth century* (London, 1951), 48–9.

[131] For the occasional anatomy lectures in the century see Sinclair and Robb-Smith, *A short history of anatomical teaching in Oxford*, 18–26; Webster, 'The medical faculty and the physic garden', 703–5.

[132] For John Prujean and his workshop in New College Lane, see Willem Hackman, 'Mathematical instruments', in eds. Fauvel, Flood, and Wilson, *Oxford figures: eight centuries of the mathematical sciences*, 74–90, at 86–9.

[133] Ibid., 89; A. J. Turner, 'Mathematical instruments and the education of gentlemen' *Annals of Science*, 30 (1973), 51–88. The Orrery Collection of instruments was moved to the Museum of the History of Science in the 1930s. Gunther, *Early science*, I. 380.

[134] OUA: WPb/2/2, Lord Leigh's bequest to Ashmolean, 1767. Will proved London 22 July 1786. Oriel College was left the peer's own mathematical instruments, apparatus, and books.

OXFORD AND CONTEMPORARY SCIENCE 225

I went this morning...to Lectures on natural Philosophy, was extremly entertained for two hours, with explanations and Experiments upon the Microscope, Colours, the rainbow imitated, and the causes of all these things distinctly Explained.

Lord Granville Leveson-Gower to Lady Stafford, 20 May 1789, *Private correspondence of Lord Granville Leveson Gower: 1781 to 1821,* ed. Castalia, Countess Granville (2 vols., London, 1916), I. 16.

In these decades Oxford science made some advances and cross-institutional connections were made. It was also an era in which the gradual breakdown of the traditional general categories of 'natural philosophy' and 'natural history' in favour of a range of specialist disciplines accelerated.[135] Representative of these years was *the* commanding Oxford figure *c.*1800—Dean Cyril Jackson—who had first made his academic name as a mathematician and botanist.[136] Always concerned with the practical application of knowledge, and one who helped to remove obstacles in developing the steam engine when patents were required, Jackson welcomed Joseph Black (1728–99), professor of medicine and chemistry at Glasgow and then at Edinburgh, as a visitor to Christ Church in 1788 when he came south to meet James Watt and his former pupil, Thomas Beddoes.[137] But if there were some material improvements to facilities for science practitioners that aided intellectual advance, they were counterbalanced by barriers that in this era were less religious than political. Here, as in the rest of Oxford life, the shadow of the French Revolution was in due course inescapable and worked against career progression for any don inclined to countenance, let alone embrace, its values, as the departure of Thomas Beddoes from the University disclosed.

The growth of experiment owed much to the advent of more sophisticated scientific instruments, primarily for astronomy, and these, by definition, were not

[135] J. Gascoigne, 'The eighteenth-century scientific community: a prosopographical study', *Social Studies of Science,* 25 (1995), 575–81; J. Gascoigne, 'The role of the universities in the Scientific Revolution', in eds. David C. Lindberg and Robert S. Westman, *Reappraisals of the scientific revolution* (Cambridge, 1990), 207–60.

[136] Bodl MS Top Oxon. d.174, f. 48. As Nicholas Tyacke points out (noting an omission in the ODNB), Jackson was elected FRS in 1772. 'From *Studium Generale* to modern research university: eight hundred years of Oxford history' [review of Brockliss (2)], *History of Universities,* XXX/1–2 (2017), 205–25, at 209. For Jackson's contacts with Matthew Boulton and the Lunar Society see Chapter 12, p. 79.

[137] ed. Robert G. W. Anderson, *Correspondence of Joseph Black* (2 vols., Farnham, 2012). In the opinion of the Edinburgh professor, Dean Jackson lived 'very soft'. D. Stansfield, *Thomas Beddoes MD. 1760–1808: chemist, physician, democrat* (Dordrecht, 1984), 45. Black also met William Thomson, Dr Lee's Reader in Anatomy from 1785, who had studied with him at Edinburgh in 1781–2 and became a friend of James Hutton. Thomson researched the action of heat in geology in support of Hutton's theories of slow geological change. Paul Kent, 'Oxford and the industrial age: another dimension', in *Christ Church Matters,* Issue 29, Trinity 2012, 6–8. See also A. L. Donovan, *Philosophical chemistry in the Scottish Enlightenment: the doctrines and discoveries of William Cullen and Joseph Black* (Edinburgh, 1975).

226   ENLIGHTENED OXFORD

destined for the Ashmolean Museum. By the mid-century, it had a dated, neglected air that pushed it to the margins of progressive science, as what its collections could offer in terms of teaching aids diminished. William Huddesford (1732–72), Keeper of the Ashmolean from 1755 until his early death, son of Vice Chancellor George Huddesford, did what he could to modernise by rearranging the natural history collections better to classify and present natural as opposed to artificial exhibits.[138] His fresh approach, coupled with a willingness to seek advice from naturalists more experienced than himself, encouraged many fresh donations, including a whole mineralogical collection from the celebrated Cornish antiquarian, William Borlase. Huddesford, however, sensed that he could expect little encouragement from the University, telling Borlase:[139]

> You will perhaps laugh to see me tri[f]ling about a Place now despised and undervalued—and when soe little encouragement is give[n] *here* to labours of this kind.

He also amassed an impressive publication list to his name, particularly by bringing into print new editions of works (including those by Martin Lister and Edward Lhuyd) based on specimens that had become part of the Ashmolean's collections.[140]

Huddesford's early death marginalised the Ashmolean once more just at the point when it was moving again towards the centre of Oxford scientific life. Instead academic and public attention focused on the provision of a new university observatory, another project funded by the legacy of John Radcliffe, constructed along the Woodstock Road. The post of Radcliffe Observer was created in 1772 for Thomas Hornsby (1733–1810), the tenth Savilian Professor of Astronomy from 1763 in succession to Bradley,[141] and the best-known Oxford 'scientist' of his generation (despite having no astronomical discovery to his name), 'the eye of Oxford', as Edward Tatham called Hornsby in his Address to

---

[138] Huddesford's significance is established in Arthur MacGregor, 'William Huddesford, (1732–1772): his role in reanimating the Ashmolean Museum, his collections, researches and support network', *Archives of Natural History*, 34 (2007), 47–68. For Keepers of the Ashmolean in this century see David A. Berry, 'Collecting at Oxford: a history of the University's museums, gardens, and libraries', (unpub. Oxford D.Phil. thesis, 2 vols., 2004), I. 164–71.

[139] MacGregor and Turner, 'The Ashmolean Museum', 652–7, for the quotation and Huddesford's tenure. Public admission to the Museum, however, declined during his Keepership. Letter of 4 Dec. 1760 to Borlase, quoted in ibid., 657. For Borlase, see Chapter 12, pp. 70–1.

[140] Anna Marie Roos, 'Fossilized remains: The Martin Lister and Edward Lhuyd ephemera', in eds. V. Keller, Anna Maria Roos, and Elizabeth Yale, *Life, death, and knowledge-making in Early Modern British scientific and medical archives* (Leiden and Boston, MA, 2018), 150–72, at 151–7.

[141] Hornsby was, as with Bradley, the personal preference of the 2nd Earl of Macclesfield and this connection proved decisive. Joseph Browne to Earl of Egremont, Queen's College, 24 July 1762, West Sussex Record Office, [Petworth House Archives] PHA 27; Archbishop Secker to Egremont, Lambeth, 13 Dec. 1762, PHA 30.

OXFORD AND CONTEMPORARY SCIENCE   227

Convocation in 1810 on the great astronomer's decease.[142] Hornsby was aware that, rather than relying on ad hoc viewing points in Oxford or using Shirburn Castle, the University urgently required a major observatory equipped with a full set of instruments, and successfully petitioned the Radcliffe trustees to that end in 1768.[143] Bradley had a new house built for his work adjacent to the site of the Observatory and this investment was welcomed in the London press as a means of exciting, as one paper put it, ' a spirit of emulation among the younger students. This is the more to be desired, as it has been long been a complaint, that mathematical studies are not so much encouraged in this University, as philological and polite-literature'.[144] The Radcliffe Observatory, designed originally by Henry Keene and completed by the young James Wyatt on a strikingly Grecian neo-classical plan,[145] when completed was better equipped than any of its European counterparts with lecture rooms and spaces for valuable instruments,[146] and it soon became an essential port of call for those visiting the city, such as Edward Pigott in 1776, the year which saw the greater part of the exterior completed:[147]

Saw the observatory, very well situated; having the best and biggest instruments that are made; and altogether I think much compleater than that at Greenwich: Mr Hornsby the Observer is very civil; and is known to be very understanding in that part; . . .

The following October brought an eight-day visit from Thomas Bugge (1740–1815), the newly appointed Professor of Mathematics and Astronomy at the University of Copenhagen. He made many technical observations about the apparatus and concluded the whole was ' . . . the best in Europe, both as regards the

[142] Cox, *Recollections,* 136n. Fellow of Corpus Christi College; Professor of Experimental philosophy, 1763–1810; FRS, 1767; Radcliffe Librarian, 1783; Sedleian Professor of Natural Philosophy, 1782. See A. Chapman, 'Thomas Hornsby and the Radcliffe Observatory', in eds. Fauvel, Flood, and Wilson, *Oxford figures: eight centuries of the mathematical sciences,* 202–20; Ruth Wallis, 'Cross-Currents in astronomy and navigation: Thomas Hornsby FRS (1733–1810)', *Annals of Science,* 57 (2000), 219–40; H. Knox-Shaw, J. Jackson, and W. H. Robinson, *The observations of the Reverend Thomas Hornsby, DD* (Oxford, 1932).
[143] Chapman, 'Thomas Hornsby', 203–4; A. D. Thackeray, *The Radcliffe Observatory, 1772–1792* (Oxford, 1972).
[144] *General Evening Post,* 18–23 Sept. 1773.
[145] G. Tyack, 'The making of the Radcliffe Observatory', *The Georgian Group Journal,* 10 (2000), 122–40. He deems the external sculpture of the tower, carried out in the 1790s, 'one of the few coherent neo-classical programmes of sculptural embellishment in an English public building of its date.' ibid., 133.
[146] Chapman calls it 'the finest and best-equipped observatory' of its date in Europe. 'Thomas Hornsby', 216; Wallis, 'Cross-Currents', 227–30; Brockliss, 'Science, the universities, and other public spaces', 82.
[147] Edward Pigott (1753–1825), July 1776, in Diary, 2 vols., *c.*1764–85, Osborn MS Fc 80, Beinecke Rare Book and Manuscript Library, Yale University. It was not entirely finished until 1794, the cost of the building and instruments being a hefty £28,000. It was completed by Wyatt after Henry Keene's death in 1776. Colvin, *Biographical dictionary,* 1111.

228 ENLIGHTENED OXFORD

arrangement and the instruments'.[148] For Bugge as for other visitors, Hornsby was as much of a draw as his Observatory. This was the consequence of his efforts to observe the transit of Venus, first in 1761 (when it was hampered by cloudy conditions) and then, more famously, in 1769. There were 149 observing stations around the world for the 1769 transit and in Oxford (where Hornsby took charge) there was a multi-national team of six different observers stationed at six different places;[149] Hornsby himself conducted his observation from the Tower of the Five Orders in the Old Schools Quadrangle.[150]

Hornsby worked closely with the greatest instrument-maker of the age, John Bird, in a good-humoured rivalry turning on speculation as to whether it would be the observatory or the instruments that would be first completed.[151] If the instruments available in the Observatory were of exceptional quality, they reflected a trend within the University as a whole. Some of the best of the century were produced by George Adams the elder and younger, both in their time mathematical-instrument makers to George III. Adams senior (1720–73) was also an optical designer and writer, the author of *A Treatise on the Construction and Use of Globes* (1766). He produced terrestrial and celestial globes probably commissioned for Christ Church Library in the 1760s.[152] These were becoming as much teaching aids as trophy items as the amount of organised teaching done by holders of 'scientific' chairs increased after *c*.1760, for instance the lectures on 'experimental philosophy' given by Hornsby's predecessor as Sedleian Professor of Natural Philosophy, Benjamin Wheeler, in the early 1770s.[153] Hornsby continued the trend 'instituting courses of lectures at which attendees were expected to be more than passive observers'.[154] Thus in May 1769 he put on a special course of

---

[148] Bugge inspected eleven observatories, two in the United Provinces and nine in England. eds. K. M. Pedersen and P. de Clercq, *An observer of observatories. the journal of Thomas Bugge's tour of Germany, Holland and England in 1777* (Aarhus, 2010), 105–29, at 128.

[149] Wallis, 'Cross-Currents', 222, 224; ed. A. Goudie, *Seven hundred years of an Oxford college: Hertford College, 1284–1984* (Oxford, 1984), 35.

[150] For his results see Museum of the History of Science, Oxford, MSS Radcliffe, MS 7, Observations, computations, and notes by Hornsby (including the 1769 Transit of Venus). Other schedules of his transit observations are in MSS 20–21.

[151] See Museum of the History of Science, Oxford, MSS Radcliffe, MS 29 agreement between John Bird and the Delegates for the supply of five observatory instruments, 1771; invoice from P. & J. Dollond for two achromatic telescopes, 1774. Also J.A. Bennett, 'Equipping the Radcliffe Observatory: Thomas Hornsby and his instrument makers', in eds. R. G. W. Anderson, J. A. Bennett, and W. F. Ryan, *Making instruments count* (Aldershot, 1993), 232–41, at 239; I. Guest, *Dr John Radcliffe and his trust* (London, 1991), 240, n. 27; Wallis, *Cross-Currents*, 239; Chapman, 'Thomas Hornsby', 206–10.

[152] J. Millburn, *Adams of Fleet Street, instrument maker to King George III* (Aldershot, 2000).

[153] Fellow of Magdalen Hall who concurrently held a chair in Divinity. Magdalen College MS.4990, notes taken by anonymous student *c*.1772. Neither of Wheeler's immediate predecessors as Professor (the chair was endowed in 1619), the Hon. Charles Bertie and Joseph Browne (the latter Provost of Queen's from 1750 and V-C, 1759–65), had lectured. Assistant lecturers were still called upon to act as substitutes. Israel Lyons thus lectured from 1764 to a class of 60 plus. Hans, *New trends in education*, 52.

[154] Charles-Edwards and Reid, *Corpus Christi College*, 240; Chapman, 'Thomas Hornsby', 214–16.

OXFORD AND CONTEMPORARY SCIENCE 229

lectures in the Ashmolean about the imminent transit of Venus (for which he charged a guinea), and his philosophy course of 1785 included the theory of balloons. Hornsby's genuine topicality ensured there was no shortage of attendees from inside and outside the University. Here was another Oxford scientist who understood the need to foster a public understanding of his research.[155]

Bradley and Hornsby made Oxford an international astronomical centre to complement the significant advances in anatomy and chemistry, too.[156] Oxford was caught up in the great wave of hospital building going on in eighteenth-century Britain based largely on private and voluntary initiatives, in this case funding coming from the Radcliffe trustees.[157] In 1758, £4,000 was made available to build an Infirmary constructed on land north of St Giles, donated by Thomas Rowney MP. This state-of-the-art hospital opened on St Luke's Day 1770 and was from the beginning a University institution, including governors and senior medical staff. Accommodation was provided for sixty-eight patients in four wards, and there were six physicians, six nurses, an apothecary, servants, and porters. The opening of the Infirmary proved a lure to talented Oxonian medical tyros who might once have headed for Edinburgh, most notably William Austin (1754–93) who, having lectured on Arabic after taking his BA in 1776, returned to Oxford in 1780 (MD, 1783), where he lectured in physiology and became Professor of Chemistry in 1785 and physician to the Radcliffe Infirmary.[158] Its governors and senior medical staff were members of the University by the 1780s, and senior members were using it as an informal teaching and socialising centre.[159] This status was reflected and sustained in the annual payment usually made to the Infirmary by the vice chancellor on behalf of the whole University and by some colleges. St John's offered five guineas each year from 1799, a sum increased to eight when a chaplain was appointed.[160]

A further sign of progress came in 1767 when the Anatomy School at Christ Church (commissioned by the Dean and Chapter, designed by Henry Keene) was

---

[155] Gunther, Oxford science, II. 407, 410–11.

[156] See Morris, 'The eighteenth century: chemistry allied to anatomy', for a more balanced perspective than the gloomy view offered in Jan Golinski, Science as public culture. chemistry and Enlightenment in Britain, 1760–1820 (Cambridge, 1992), 53–4.

[157] C. Stevenson, Medicine and magnificence: British hospital and asylum architecture, 1660–1815 (New Haven, CT, 2000). For the politics of charitable giving see A. Wilson, 'Conflict, consensus and charity: politics and the provincial voluntary hospitals in the eighteenth century', EHR, 111 (1996), 599–616.

[158] Wells, Wadham College, 141–2. He was appointed physician at St Bartholomew's Hospital, London in 1786, and was the first to offer regular chemistry lectures there. Norman Moore, 'Austin, William (1754–1793), physician', rev. Claire L. Nutt, ODNB online edn., 2004.

[159] A. H. T. Robb-Smith, A short history of the Radcliffe Infirmary (Oxford, 1970); A. G. Gibson, The Radcliffe Infirmary (London, 1926).

[160] He also took the liberty of offering ten guineas each from the Chancellor (Portland) and the latter's eldest son, Lord Titchfield. V–C Wills to Portland, 12 Sept. 1796, Letter book. Balliol College Archives and Manuscripts, Jenkyns VI.A (2), f. 62. See also Chapter 3, pp. 40–1 for an instance of a charity sermon raising funds for the Radcliffe Infirmary.

Fig 5.4 Kitchen and anatomical theatre Christ Church, drawn, engraved, and published by J. Fisher, 1827 (© Governing Body, Christ Church, Oxford).

opened. It was funded by a £1,000 benefaction from John Freind and supplemented by a further £2,300 from Matthew Lee, the prosperous royal physician.[161] It contained a chemical laboratory and a museum and was used by John Parsons (1742–85) for his anatomical lectures. There were two public human dissections held there annually; the fee-paying public could come in, many of them doubtless curious to see the inside of 'skeleton corner', with its cadavers from Oxford Prison stored ready for use in teaching.[162] The energetic Parsons became Reader in anatomy (a post funded by Matthew Lee) in the University in the late 1760s,[163] was physician to the new Radcliffe Infirmary from 1772, and was first Clinical Professor from 1780 until his death under a £7,000 bequest of the University's late

---

[161] It is now the Lee Building. Curthoys (1), 151–2; Brockliss (2), 313. The 'laboratory' style was reminiscent of a contemporary gentleman's house. P. J. T. Morris, *The matter factory. a history of the chemical laboratory* (London, 2015), 69.

[162] Christ Church Library, MS. lii.b.i, 'Annual visitation of Dr. M. Lee's anatomical theatre, accounts etc. 1796–1860' has details of Parsons's large collection of specimens used as aids in his lectures.

[163] Lee's will stipulated that his Reader was not to be in holy orders and was to be a product of Westminster School and Christ Church. The school stipulation soon lapsed. Morris, 'The eighteenth century: chemistry allied to anatomy', 64–5.

OXFORD AND CONTEMPORARY SCIENCE   231

Chancellor and chairman of the Radcliffe trustees, the 3rd Earl of Lichfield.[164] Parsons followed the 'phlogiston' theory of combustion and thus implicitly endorsed the similar work being done by Oxford's theological *bête noire* of the 1780s, the Unitarian minister, Joseph Priestley.[165] It set both of them apart from Lavoisier's work in Paris with his new model for matter based on chemically interactive 'elements' such as sulphur, iron, and 'oxygene', one that only gradually became known outside France.[166]

Thanks to Lee and Parsons, there was scope in the 1790s for the University to gain comparable recognition for its emerging prowess in chemistry by the endowment of a Regius Chair in the subject—if ears could be bent and funding found.[167] The obvious candidate was Thomas Beddoes (1760–1808), a Pembroke graduate (1779) connected to provincial dissenting communities, whose distinction as a chemist taught by William Cullen and Joseph Black at Edinburgh was recognised by the creation of a 'readership' for him at Oxford in 1788, with Dean Cyril Jackson acting as his patron.[168] Beddoes also owed much to Martin Wall (1747–1824), a fellow of New College and a pioneer in his chemistry lectures (these were published in 1782) who wrote *Dissertations on Select Subjects in Chemistry and Medicine* the following year.[169] Beddoes was still more popular and more obviously talented. He believed that pneumatic chemistry, the chemistry of gases, could serve as the basis for a revolution in medicine, and his erudition, charisma, and knowledge of French and German research brought crowds into his Oxford chemistry lectures, explicitly modelled on Joseph Black's, with an emphasis on technical inventiveness and experimental demonstration.[170] Thus, in June 1790, in conjunction with James Sadler (1753–1829), the Oxford

---

[164] Brockliss (2), 276.

[165] Priestley was a major supporter of phlogiston into the 1800s after it had been generally abandoned by other chemists. To a degree, his scientific standing was recognised in Oxford. Thus Hornsby in 1785 advertised a course of philosophical lectures at the museum on 'The different Kinds of Air, Natural and Factitious, in which the principal Discoveries of Dr Priestley and others will be introduced and proved by actual Experiment'. Quoted in Turner, 'The physical sciences', 674.

[166] Thomas L. Hankins, *Science and the Enlightenment* (Cambridge, 1985), 100–10.

[167] 'We have no kind of Establishment or Endowment for a Chemical Professor; & on that account the Study of Chemistry is not pursued with that attention, which so useful a Science deserves:' V-C Wills to Portland, 10 Feb. 1796, Letter book. Balliol College Archives and Manuscripts, Jenkyns VI.A (2), ff. 128–9.

[168] Golinski, *Science*, 158–64. Beddoes Papers, OUA: Dep. C. 134/1(a)/8. For the debate on whether he held an established post within the University see F. W. Gibbs and W. A. Smeaton, 'Thomas Beddoes at Oxford', *Ambix*, 9 (1961), 47–9.

[169] Wall attracted many students to his lectures and succeeded Parsons as Lichfield Clinical Professor in 1785. Turner, 'The Physical sciences', 666; Webster, 'The medical faculty', 709. Though also accepting of phlogiston, he may have mentioned Lavoisier's theory in his second or later course of lectures. He complained that, by comparison with Germany, in England 'Chymystry...was neglected for Newtonism'. 'Minutes of Dr. Wall's lectures in chemistry', 1781, Bodl. MS Radcliffe Trust e.9, p. 5, quoted in Morris, 'The eighteenth century: chemistry allied to anatomy', 66.

[170] Bob Harris, *A tale of three cities: the life and times of Lord Daer 1763–1794* (Edinburgh, 2015), 204.

232 ENLIGHTENED OXFORD

balloonist and technician in the chemistry laboratory,[171] Beddoes constructed a sphere filled with inflammable airs that, once lit, shot up in the air above Oxford, and its fiery trails made an artificial comet.[172]

With that reputation, Beddoes was the obvious name for the University to forward to the Home Secretary, Henry Dundas, for presentation to the king with professorship in view. As further enquiries were made regarding his political suitability, it became known in both Westminster and Oxford that Beddoes's pro-Revolutionary politics had inclined him to oppose the May 1792 Royal Proclamation issued by the government against seditious writings (and the second part of Thomas Paine's *The Rights of Man* in particular).[173] Beddoes, a chemist when Priestley had associated the subject with the subversion of establishments (a point Burke took the lead in driving home after the outbreak of the French Revolution),[174] could not be trusted, and his impetuosity did not work in his favour. Beddoes had meanwhile made matters worse by writing and circulating a handbill or 'fly sheet' arguing against raising money for the relief of the suffering French clerical refugees by suggesting that these clerics were not the victims of the recent September Massacres, and had shown themselves prejudiced against the Revolution in every aspect. And he dared to attack Pitt's government for stoking up enmity against France. This stance made him notorious as a 'democrat' in his politics and students were consequently warned off his lectures that autumn (1792). He left the University shortly afterwards aware that there was a real threat of Crown prosecution against him. As one relieved Oxford don intimated, 'in his political character he is a most violent democrat [who] takes pains to seduce young men to the same political principles'.[175]

---

[171] Eleven months after the Montgolfier brothers, Sadler, in Oct. 1784, had reportedly made the first balloon flight in England from Christ Church meadows. He used a basic (and unsafe) 170-foot hot air balloon, flew for half an hour, and landed six miles away, near Wood Eaton, north of the city. *JOJ*, 9 Oct. 1784; Mark J. Davies, *King of all balloons. the adventurous life of James Sadler the first English aeronaut* (Stroud, 2015). See also Clare Brant, *Balloon madness. flights of imagination in Britain, 1783–1786* (Woodbridge, 2017), 69–73.

[172] M. Jay, *The atmosphere of heaven: the unusual experiments of Dr Beddoes and his sons of genius* (New Haven, CT, 2009); E. Robinson, 'Thomas Beddoes, M.D., and the reform of science teaching at Oxford', *Annals of Science*, 9 (1955), 137–41.

[173] J. Mori, *William Pitt and the French Revolution 1785–1795* (Edinburgh, 1997), 108, 112–13; F. O'Gorman, 'Pitt and the Tory reaction to the French Revolution, 1789–1815', in ed. H. T. Dickinson, *Britain and the French Revolution* (Basingstoke, 1989), 21–37.

[174] M. Crosland, 'The image of science as a threat: Burke versus Priestley and the "Philosophic Revolution"', *BJHS*, 20 (1987), 277–307.

[175] His future father-in-law, Richard Lovell Edgeworth, summed up Beddoes and his prospects thus: 'A little fat Democrat of considerable abilities, of great name in the Scientific world as a naturalist and Chemist—good humored good natured—a man of honour and Virtue, enthusiastic & candid—...if he will put off his political projects till he has accomplish'd his medical establishment he will succeed and make a fortune, but if he bloweth the trumpet of Sedition the Aristocracy will rather go to hell with Satan than with any democratic Devil'.

Postscript to a letter from Maria Edgeworth to Mrs R. Clifton, 21 July 1793, quoted in Marilyn Butler, *Maria Edgeworth. a literary biography* (Oxford, 1972), 110.

OXFORD AND CONTEMPORARY SCIENCE   233

The rationale for the putative chair evaporated with his departure, as he was the only serious candidate for it.[176] The whole embarrassing episode was a reminder that, in a Revolutionary age, no amount of academic flair could offset perceived disloyalty to Church and state, and that it would be predominantly in dissenting circles that advanced scientific experimentation would occur. As Stephen Shapin has written, '… if gentlemanly politeness substantially defined the central value system, then science was a mode of cultural self-expression that could be used symbolically to challenge traditional canons of politeness'.[177] But, in the Revolutionary decade, more than politeness was at stake. It was the whole Anglican higher educational establishment that had to be protected (including student admissions).[178] Beddoes was soon replaced as a 'chemical reader' by Robert Bourne, Fellow of Worcester College (1762–1829), who offered the first of a series of courses of chemical lectures in the Ashmolean the same year, and steered clear of politics and religion. In the circumstances, and playing to his own strengths, he shrewdly adopted a 'highly practical' approach to the subject, offering his audience a basic knowledge of the properties of matter.[179]

At least Oxford botany remained uncontaminated by political considerations and, in John Sibthorp (1758–96), produced an original scientist to set alongside Beddoes in terms of his international importance in his subject. The University had possessed a Physic Garden since 1621, one of the oldest in Europe, considered by Linnaeus (who visited it in 1736) to be superior to those of other European universities,[180] but plagued by poor management and underfunding.[181] Its founder,

[176] T. H. Levere, 'Dr Thomas Beddoes at Oxford: radical politics in 1788–1793 and the fate of the Regius Chair in Chemistry', *Ambix* 28 (1981), 61–9; T.H. Levere, 'Dr Thomas Beddoes: science and medicine in politics and society', *BJHS*, 17 (1984), 187–204; T.H. Levere, 'Dr Thomas Beddoes: chemistry, medicine and the perils of democracy', *Notes & Records of the Royal Society*, 63 (2009), 61–9; Kenneth R. Johnston, *Unusual suspects. Pitt's reign of alarm & the lost generation of the 1790s* (Oxford, 2013), 98–100. See generally Stansfield, *Thomas Beddoes MD*. For details of funds deemed available in early 1796 for professorships of Botany and Chemistry, and the efforts of the Vice Chancellor to sort out with Dean Jackson the problems caused by Beddoes and the sudden death of John Sibthorp (Sherardian Professor of Botany), see Wills's Letter book. Balliol College Archives and Manuscripts, Jenkyns VI.A (2), ff. 133, 136.
[177] Shapin, 'The image of the man of science', in ed. Porter, *Eighteenth-century science*, 159–83, at 177–8.
[178] The future high Tory poet Robert Southey, a reader of Bishop Richard Watson's *Chemical essays* (1781) and hoping 'to practice a little chemistry at Oxford when I get there', was kept out of Christ Church by Cyril Jackson after the headmaster of Westminster, William Vincent, in Sept. 1792 alerted the Dean to Southey's essay in the School periodical critical of Burke (and flogging in the 5th form). Speck, *Robert Southey*, 20–6.
[179] Turner, 'The physical sciences', 668. These were published as *A syllabus of a course of chemical lectures, read at the Museum, Oxford, in seventeen hundred ninety four* [Oxford, 1794].
[180] Webster, 'The medical faculty', 711–23; Mavis Batey, *Oxford gardens. The university's influence on garden history* (Amersham, 1982), 31–3, 137–9; R. T. W. Gunther, *Oxford gardens* (Oxford, 1912), 17; W. Blunt, *The compleat naturalist: a life of Linnaeus* (London, 1971), 114–15. Its layout was changed in the 1720s with funds provided by Sherard. The Garden was renamed the Botanic Garden in the 1840s. Its Cambridge equivalent only dates from 1762.
[181] Nevertheless, it benefitted from bequests. Thus Henry Compton, bishop of London and an accomplished amateur botanist, on his death in left his plant collection to Oxford, on a scale that

Fig. 5.5 Oxford Physic Garden, line engraving, Print made by Benjamin Green, after Samuel Wale, 1766 (Yale Center for British Art, Gift of Judith and Norman A. Zlotsky).

Henry Danvers, 1st Earl of Danby (1573–1644), had intended that a professorship of Botany should be established to complement it but that did not occur until well after the Civil War, in 1669. Financial consolidation of the chair and its endowments occurred in the late 1720s as a result of arrangements made by William Sherard to donate his library and herbarium to the University, have his protégé Johann Jakob Dillenius installed as Sherardian professor, and bring about better academic management of the garden.[182]

Dillenius's successor, Humphrey Sibthorp (1713–97), lacked the character or the academic distinction to give Oxford botany international allure or entice students to come and hear him (he was a reluctant lecturer), but at least he had

---

required the construction of a special house in the Physic Garden. Hearne, V.122. Further exotic plants were given in 1715 by his successor in the see, John Robinson (an Oriel benefactor). Berry, 'Collecting at Oxford', I. 92.

[182] Webster, 'The medical faculty', 717–18. The erudite Sherard was particularly fascinated by the flora of the Middle East. He had studied in Paris and Leyden, travelled widely on the continent, and acted as British consul at Smyrna in 1703–15. The first professor would be Sherard's nominee, thereafter he would be selected neither by Convocation nor by the Crown but by the Royal College of Physicians. See Chapter 11 for Sherard and Dillenius. Sherard's library was housed in a building erected on the High Street near the Physic Garden.

Fig. 5.6 Johann Jakob Dillenius, unknown artist, oil on canvas, c.1730 (Bodleian Libraries, University of Oxford).

the foresight to encourage Joseph Banks. Banks had already developed a lifelong interest in botany when he came to Christ Church in 1760 (he left Oxford in 1763 without taking a degree as he was already an independently wealthy man following the death of his father in 1761).[183] Though not at the time reputed to be a very talented student, he botanised and fossil-hunted on Shotover Hill and in Headington Quarry, and encouraged Sibthorp to pay Israel Lyons the younger (1739–75) to travel across from Cambridge and revive interest in botanical studies at Oxford.[184] Sibthorp's successor, his son John, by comparison, was energetic, forceful, and cosmopolitan, and regularly abroad in pursuit of his herborising

---

[183] Banks had other contemporaries who shared his passion for botany, for instance, John Stackhouse, Fellow of Exeter College, 1761–4, who studied seaweeds and was an early Fellow of the Linnean Society. Stride, *Exeter College*, 108.

[184] ed. J. C. Beaglehole, *The Endeavour journal of Joseph Banks 1768–1771* (2 vols., Sydney, 1962), I. 8; H. C. Cameron, *Sir Joseph Banks. The autocrat of the philosophers* (London, 1952), 2–3; Simon Werrett, 'Introduction: rethinking Joseph Banks', *Notes and Records of the Royal Society*, 73 (2019), 425–9, for the latest assessment of Banks in context. Lyons offered an Oxford lecture course in 1774. Lynn B. Glyn, 'Israel Lyons: a short but starry career. The life of an eighteenth-century Jewish botanist astronomer', *Notes and Records of the Royal Society*, 56 (2002), 275–305.

Fig. 5.7 *Flora Graeca*, Ferdinand Bauer (illustrator), Drawings and Watercolours, MS. Sherard 242, f. 7 Spartium junceum (Bodleian Libraries, University of Oxford).

obsession.[185] He researched and lectured in Oxford from 1787 to 1794. Apart from his magnum opus—the *Flora Graeca*, uncompleted at his death—he produced a *Flora Oxoniensis* (1794) based entirely on his own observations, added many specimens to the Sherardian herbarium, and completed his father's catalogue of the Physic Garden.[186] He subscribed unreservedly to the advanced taxonomy of Linnaeus (he was a founder member of the Linnean Society in 1788) and had an interest in the applied aspects of botany that would lead in time to the establishment of the Sibthorpian chair of rural economy. His premature death from tuberculosis deprived the University, in the mid-1790s, of an outstanding, innovative scientist just as, in very different circumstances, had its de facto expulsion of William Beddoes.

Academic caution in sponsoring new 'scientific' subjects was by no means at an end in the last quarter of the century. Though botany advanced, thanks to the energies of the Sibthorps, the emerging interest in fossils was resisted by the

---

[185] For John Sibthorp, see also Chapter 11, p, 14 and n.
[186] Bodl. MS Sherard 229; Webster, 'The Medical Faculty', 721–2; Green, *Lincoln College*, 359. In *Flora Oxoniensis* he added more than 400 species to the 330 already listed in the county, as well as more than 100 bryophytes, 200 fungi, and several algae and lichens.

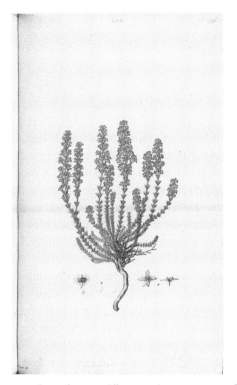

Fig. 5.8 *Flora Graeca*, Ferdinand Bauer (illustrator), Drawings and Watercolours MS. Sherard 242, f. 201 Galium graecum (Bodleian Libraries, University of Oxford).

University. Thomas Hornsby was approached by the naturalist Emanuel Mendes da Costa FRS (1717–91), one of the leading fossil experts of his time, hoping to secure permission in 1774 to lecture on that subject in the University.[187] However, the Vice Chancellor adjudged such a course 'could not be read here with propriety'. Hornsby opined that there would be insufficient demand for it, and the opportunity was lost.[188] Despite the lack of official sanction, the enthusiasm of bright students for the subject did not evaporate and was fostered at a distance by Mendes da Costa. He gave the future prelate William van Mildert (1765–1836) letters of introduction to those keen on geological pursuits, and received news

---

[187] Da Costa studied conchology and published treatises on fossils and shells, 1757–78. Yolanda Foote, 'Mendes da Costa, Emanuel (1717–1791), naturalist', *ODNB*, online edn., 2008. For recent work on Da Costa see the Royal Society online guide https://artsandculture.google.com/story/emanuel-mendes-da-costa-1717-1791-the-royal-society/mAWBb0daZKtiIA?hl=en and PhD work of Aron Sterk at https://history.lincoln.ac.uk/2018/12/11/cultural-assimilation-of-portuguese-jews-in-18th-century-london-and-portugal/.

[188] Nichols, *Illustrations*, IV. 516–9. It did not help his cause that Mendes da Costa had been dismissed as clerk and librarian of the Royal Society in 1767 for misappropriating about £1,500 of the Society's funds. He was incarcerated in the King's Bench prison between 1768 and 1772.

back from his young follower that he had purchased a job lot of fossils from a labourer at Headington, who frequently brought them to the colleges and sold them for next to nothing.[189]

vi) Conclusion

The conferment of an honorary degree on Martin Folkes in 1746 suggests that Oxford opinion was insufficiently agitated about the private speculations of any public intellectual, however eminent his standing as a natural philosopher and antiquarian, to breach the conventions of learned politeness by withholding from him an honorary degree. Folkes's redeeming aspect was that he was only distantly connected to Oxford, held sway in nominating new Fellows to the Royal Society (and Oxonians were as anxious as any to be admitted), kept his opinions on Christianity predominantly to himself and made sure he did the minimum publicly to acknowledge them. In this, he was following the precedent set by Newton himself as PRS. It also indicates that the University had become relatively comfortable with the ways of natural philosophers and historians and took some care to guard against wayward teaching and instruction (especially of the young) by confining the 'scientific' parts of the curriculum to a minor part of the University's intellectual life. That curb did not stop keen students and other interested parties from attending such lectures and other forms of demonstration in Oxford that officially and unofficially existed, often farmed out to individuals not holding University posts. The price paid for this relative caution unavoidably allowed for the passing of many new discoveries to agencies and individuals beyond the University and gave the false appearance of an over-cautious academy. The Beddoes affair in the 1790s reinforced the impression, perhaps exaggerated it.

But University opinion had to balance the desirability of formulating new knowledge and discerning its practical applications—as initiatives such as the Radcliffe Infirmary and the Lee Building underlined—against entrusting exposition to the wrong hands, that is to those like Beddoes, whose religious heterodoxy and political convictions (and his willingness to articulate them) necessarily made him *persona non grata*. Majority opinion in Oxford generally recognised the damage that empirical science in the wrong hands could do to a publicly Christian culture that appeared threatened. But it was not a reaction based on

---

[189] Van Mildert to Mendes da Costa, 10 June 1784, Durham University Library, Add MS 419. He also reported that two gentlemen at Pembroke were 'assiduous' in their study of fossils, and Dr [John] Parsons observing that 'the study of Natural history is very little pursued in Oxford....' Van Mildert had just arrived at Queen's College from Merchant Taylors' School, London, and was sympathetic to Hutchinsonianism. He was Boyle lecturer, 1802–4; Bampton lecturer, 1813; Regius Professor of Divinity, 1813–19; ended his career as Bishop of Durham, 1826–36, and was instrumental in founding Durham University. E. A. Varley, *The last of the Prince Bishops: William Van Mildert and the High Church movement of the early nineteenth century* (Cambridge, rev. edn., 2002).

ignorance, complacency, or a desire to preserve unchanged an outmoded Aristotelian status quo, as the flourishing mathematics culture early in the century indicated. As Vittoria Feola has put it: '...Oxford scientific authors remained calm, and calmly advanced knowledge.'[190] And that remained broadly the case in the decades that followed.

For a while in the early part of the century, the diffusion of Newtonian science among the laity was a nagging cause of anxiety in some academic quarters, and with it the associated worry that the culture of natural philosophy would cease to be presided over by clergymen; that, in the early Hanoverian era (as the example of the Royal Society apparently showed), the new physics was acting an agency of laicisation within the academy. There was a possibility that the cause of the faith was in danger of passing into Arian hands and the challenge for the orthodox by the late 1720s was how to wrest it back. But they did so successfully and remained vigilant, correctly concluding that there were always those (usually outside) who would use natural philosophy and the science associated with it as a means of assailing the Established Church and Oxford in particular.

Inside the University, apart from some initial disquiet regarding Halley, successive Savilian and Sedleian Professors avoided any taint of infidelity and, for the most part, showed a vigour in their research and teaching that fed an ever-increasing public appetite for scientific understanding. These were men—at any rate, in the Savilian cases—whose national profile commanded attention and they wanted to inform and involve that public where possible.

Thus Halley, having calculated that on 22 April 1715 London would experience its first total eclipse of the sun since 20 March 1140, had maps distributed all over England to solicit observations of local eclipse conditions, as well as assuring the new king's subjects that it was a natural event and would do no harm to them.[191] In Oxford, Halley's contemporaries and their successors advertised their lectures, for the most part welcomed non-members of the University (so long as they paid the fee) who came to them, and marketed their work and celebrity. In sum, they were as much demonstrators as those outside an academic setting were in London. But they were the 'right sort' of demonstrator from the University's perspective.

Clergy (including perhaps the majority of Oxford graduates who actively considered the matter) came to be reconciled—to greater or lesser degrees—with the fresh understanding of the world and its natural, physical, and political ordering afforded by Francis Bacon, Isaac Newton, and John Locke: enlightened divines took their stand on reason, pointing to the just life under natural law as

---

[190] 'The Ancients "with" the Moderns', 35. Feola's readiness to recognise the level of scientific achievement in eighteenth-century Oxford and its openness to external influences corresponds with the view of Nicholas Tyacke in his review of Brockliss (2), 'From *Studium Generale* to modern research university', 208–14.

[191] Chapman, 'Edmond Halley', 140.

240 ENLIGHTENED OXFORD

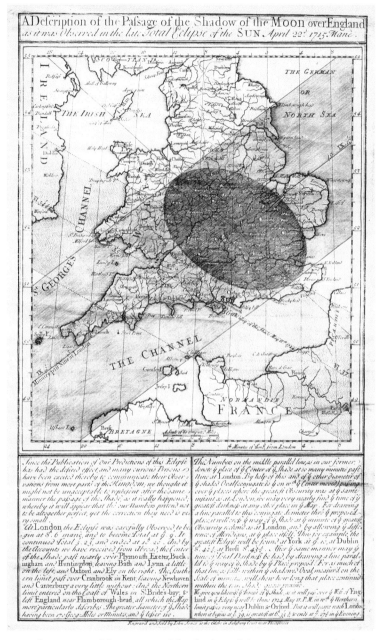

Fig. 5.9 *A description of the passage of the shadow of the moon over England as it was observed in the late total eclipse of the sun April 22, 1715*, E. Halley, printed by J. Senex, printed broadsheet (University of Cambridge, Institute of Astronomy Library).

OXFORD AND CONTEMPORARY SCIENCE   241

confirmed by revelation and the moral law that was commonly believed to be imprinted in every man's heart.[192] Arguably, much of the rhetorical emphasis on natural theology in eighteenth-century discourse *c*.1700–50 should be seen as a means of reconnecting with the natural order according to Newtonian lights. If Oxford opinion was never wholly at ease with this strategy (and, in some cases, vehemently rejected it), there might be a case for claiming that its clerical seminarians inclined back towards it as their years in parochial ministry increased and their ties to Oxford became enervated.[193]

It has been recently argued that a 'scientific' modernity was 'often explicitly, [formed] by religious considerations: Christianity set the agenda for natural philosophy in many respects and projected it forward...'.[194] That had been the rationale adopted in the early 1690s by Richard Bentley and the other Boyle Lecturers, but it never received more than a lukewarm endorsement at Oxford: University opinion was not persuaded that Bentley and his friends had quite got it right and that doubt manifested itself in various Oxonian contexts throughout the eighteenth century. But the practical problems inherent in establishing an alternative to the cultural hegemony of Newtonianism were insuperable, even in those quarters where the volition existed. The epistemological dominance of Newtonian 'method' (and, indeed, the Newtonian 'brand') was everywhere discernable across Europe after 1740, be it in medicine, 'science of man', even religion.[195] Most Oxonians just accepted the reality, took little or no interest in Newton's personal religion (in as much as it was known), and carried on with their studies and publishing.

If one exclusively identifies Enlightenment values as predominantly Newtonian, then Oxford clearly cannot be listed without qualification. The indicators while Gregory and Keill held sway were that it *could* have been but, thereafter, physico-theological reservations made it at best guardedly Newtonian. On the other hand, majority Oxford opinion was cautious about attaching itself hard and fast to overtly Counter-Enlightenment attitudes, such as Hutchinsonianism. The University constructively mediated between the alternatives and kept its options

---

[192] John Henry, *The scientific revolution and the origins of modern science* (Basingstoke, 1997), 85. This sense of compatibility drives home the underlying point that there were only the binary alternatives in this era of a reified 'science' and a reified 'religion'...' J. C. D. Clark, '"God" and "the Enlightenment"', in eds. W. J. Bulman and R. G. Ingram, *God in the Enlightenment* (New York, 2016), 215–35, at 215.

[193] The point merits further research. David Pailin asks for a more nuanced disclosure of meaning in 'natural religion'. Pailin, 'The confused and confusing story of natural religion', *Religion*, 24 (1994), 199–212. But cf. Scott Mandelbrote, 'Early Modern Natural Theologies', in ed. Russell Manning with J.H. Brooke and Fraser Watts, *Oxford Handbook of Natural Theology* (Oxford, 2013), 75–99, esp. 89–99.

[194] Stephen Gaukroger, *The collapse of mechanism and the rise of sensibility: science and the shaping of modernity, 1680-1760* (Oxford, 2011), 3.

[195] Iliffe, 'Philosophy of science', 281; Brockliss, 'Science, the universities, and other public spaces', 80. For the many brands of Newtonianism see R. E. Schofield, 'An evolutionary taxonomy of eighteenth century Newtonianisms', *Studies in Eighteenth-Century Culture*, 7 (1978), 175–92.

242 ENLIGHTENED OXFORD

open. And, as developments in George III's reign showed, Oxford was capable of projecting itself to the outside world beyond the learned public, publishing lectures in the vernacular, inviting non-members of the university into its chemical and anatomical theatres, and treating them when sick in the Radcliffe Infirmary. And at the highest levels of the state, the increased scope of government activity made calling on the services of men holding University posts (including Oxonians) ever more desirable. Thus successive professors of astronomy became ex officio members of the Board of Longitude and when Bradley became Astronomer Royal he succeeded in obtaining a £1,000 grant from the Admiralty to re-equip the Greenwich Observatory in 1748, 'perhaps the largest single government grant to British science up to that point'.[196]

Intellectual anxieties could be managed even if the figure of the 'man of science' was never quite rescued from impolite and vulgar imputations in the course of the 'long' eighteenth century, especially in a scholarly community where social graces were privileged, and 'to demur about your scientific knowledge was to show your social knowledge'.[197] Indeed, in the person of Thomas Beddoes he was reimagined all over again. But vexation and embarrassment were quickly laid aside as Oxford reaffirmed its commitment to the methodology he and his (non-suspect) colleagues had embraced through the social prominence of individuals such as Sir Christopher Pegge (1764/5–1822), Dr Lee's Reader in Anatomy (1790), Regius Professor of Medicine, 1801–22,[198] and the accomplishments of John Kidd (1775–1851), his more energetic successor in that last post (1818), previously chemical Reader (1801), professor (1803), and physician to the Radcliffe Infirmary, 1808–26.[199] It was a sign of the times that, in 1810, experimental philosophy was formally incorporated into the University, with a Readership in chemistry subsequently paid for by a grant from the Crown (1813).[200] Even more significantly, in 1803 the three praelectorships (professorships) established by the generous will of George Oakley Aldrich (a Nottinghamshire physician and Merton graduate, 1722–97) in medicine, anatomy, and chemistry, were filled.[201] And it was another sign of the times that Oxford-educated individuals, and clergy

[196] John Gascoigne, 'The Royal Society and the emergence of science as an instrument of state policy', *BJHS*, 32 (1999), 171–84, at 180 notes the crucial role of Sir Joseph Banks in that respect. The quotation is from Chapman, 'Oxford's Newtonian school', 177.

[197] A point well made in Susan Scott Parrish, *American curiosity: cultures of natural history in the colonial British Atlantic world* (Williamsburg, NC, 2006), 117.

[198] W. Tuckwell, *Reminiscences of Oxford* (London, 1900), 60–1; Robert Fox, 'Science at Oriel', in ed. Jeremy Catto, *Oriel College. A History* (Oxford, 2013), 645–77, at 652–3. George III commended Prime Minister Addington for appointing Pegge to the Regius chair for 'merit not solicitation'. Hon. G. Pellew, *The life and correspondence of Lord Sidmouth* (3 vols., London, 1847), I. 429.

[199] J. F. M. Clark, 'Kidd, John (1775–1851), physician', *ODNB* online edn., 2007.

[200] *Oxford University calendar* (1817), 65.

[201] Turner, 'The physical sciences', 668. It is probably no coincidence that Aldrich was a neighbour and leasee of the University Chancellor, the Duke of Portland, in north Nottinghamshire. John S. Rowlinson, 'Chemistry comes of age: the 19th century', in eds. Williams, Chapman, and Rowlinson, *Chemistry at Oxford*, 79–130, at 79–80. Kidd was named to the Chemistry chair.

at that, were starting to make an impact on the gathering pace of industrialisation. It was nowhere better glimpsed than in the inventor and agricultural innovator, Edmund Cartwright (1743–1823), who took out a patent for a power-loom in 1785 when rector of Goadby Marwood, Leicestershire. It revolutionised the weaving industry (despite the clamour of aggrieved workers), and Cartwright received the thanks of the House of Commons and a grant of £10,000 in June 1809 for his services to the community.[202]

---

[202] Entered University College, Fellow of Magdalen College, 1764. He was also an accomplished minor poet, an honorary member of the Board of Agriculture from 1804, and superintendent of the Duke of Bedford's model farm at Woburn from 1801. David Hunt, 'Cartwright, Edmund (1743–1823), Church of England clergyman and inventor of a power loom', *ODNB*, online edn., 2015.

INSTITUTIONAL PRESENCE AND INTERACTIONS

6

Oxford personnel

Offices, interest, and the polity

Oxford University was one of the oldest corporations in the country with a founding myth that its academic residents preferred not to dispel wholly lest exactitude displace mystique.[1] Its prestige in a society that valorised institutional longevity and the force of custom was never in doubt and the University exerted a correspondingly powerful hold (both directly and indirectly) on national life in eighteenth-century Britain. Civil society in Georgian England (and beyond) took its tone from Oxbridge graduates and thus the influence of Oxford fed into innumerable social circles beyond the University in ways that are highlighted in this study. Key to this process of elite preparation, integration, and acculturation were the officers of the University, those who were connected by patronal and political ties to non-academic individuals of equivalent or superior status or rank. This chapter's starting point is the claim that the influence of the University via its members past and present in every reach of Church and state was mediated as much by the actions and milieu of its leading officers as it was by the cultural and educational formation of its graduates. A great deal therefore hinged on their selection and their behaviour in office. They, as it were, presented the face of Oxford to the outside world, connected directly to it by virtue of the posts they held, the vice chancellorship, college headships, and tutorial positions within them. Then there were those with formal roles and power inside the University, the college Visitors and the diocesan bishop (with his cathedral doubling as a college chapel), whose duties and routines impinged only occasionally on Oxford but, when they did, could be decisive. They were all, in varying degrees, power brokers, stood in the centre of intersecting patronage networks, and exercised political influence in and beyond the University. This chapter, through a selective and representative study of some of them, attempts to measure their presence and influence, and gauge and assess their connection to the wider polity. And it begins with an office that stood at the apex of the hierarchy, one that, in the eighteenth century, was far from being merely either decorative or honorific: the Chancellorship of Oxford.

---

[1] See Chap. 1, p. 8.

Enlightened Oxford: The University and the Cultural and Political Life of Eighteenth-century Britain and Beyond.
Nigel Aston, Oxford University Press. © Nigel Aston 2023. DOI: 10.1093/oso/9780199246830.003.0007

248 ENLIGHTENED OXFORD

i) Oxford chancellors and the projection and protection of the University, 1715–1809

The office of Chancellor was critical to the University's well-being as its public face in national life, charged with defending its institutional integrity through the channels of influence available to the office-holder: the court, the government, the House of Lords, and informal exchanges with other members of the elite. It conferred extensive powers of patronage that made it immensely attractive to politicians, including nomination of the Vice Chancellor and appointment of all Principals at Oxford's Halls except one (St Edmund Hall). In the world of the first two Georges, where royal and ministerial offices were largely denied to Oxonian Tories, posts in the gift of Oxford's Chancellor were a limited form of compensation for clergy and other professionals whose principles kept them out in the cold. Thus it was crucial to Oxonian stability that whoever held it was a friend to majority Tory interests in the University. Thanks to astute politicking and fast manoeuvring, whenever there was a vacancy in the eighteenth century, Convocation managed to avoid the upheaval that any out-and-out Whig Chancellor would have brought in his wake. All six Chancellors from Arran to Grenville discharged their duties with a quiet competence and intelligence that has seldom been acknowledged. The incumbent on the death of Queen Anne was James, 2nd Duke of Ormond (1665–1745), who had succeeded his deceased grandfather in the post just months before the Revolution. The Duke—whose 'good nature and charming manner were universally remarked on by contemporaries'[2]—cut a grand figure, and the bulk of the University adored him for it, ever ready to heap praises on their Tory head as a way of cutting his martial and political rival, Marlborough, down to size.[3] But Ormond's priorities lay at court, with the army, and in Ireland, and the new dynastic order after 1714 entailed a loss of favour and, worse, income from office, that looked set to ruin him.

When the Duke left hastily for France in August 1715 (and was subsequently attainted),[4] Convocation acted to forestall a candidate being intruded on the University by the predominantly Whig ministry. And it had one to hand:

---

[2] Hayton, 'Dependence, clientage, and affinity', 236.

[3] For instance, Arthur Charlett likened Ormond to the Elizabethan Sir Francis Drake and compared the victory the Duke and the Tory Admiral, Sir George Rooke, had won at Vigo in 1702 to that over the Armada in 1588. BL Add MS. 28889, f. 384.

[4] David Hayton describes his flight in 1715 as probably 'a blessing in disguise for the estate'. 'Dependence, clientage and affinity', 219. He estimates the ducal debt at a staggering £110,500. He lived on until 1745, spending his later years in some splendour in the papal enclave of Avignon (though remaining an Anglican) and continued to attract loyal notice in some Oxonians' quarters. It was reported in 1738 that, of many 'honest gentlemen' collected at Leiden (many no doubt Grand Tourists), 'Most of Them are still Members of the University of Oxford, and have the most profound Respect for their ever honour'd Lord and Chancellor, as They always stile Your Grace:' Ezekiel Hamilton to Ormond, Leyden, 22 Apr. 1738, HMC, *Weston Underwood MSS* (London, 1885), 519.

Fig. 6.1 Charles Butler, 1st Earl of Arran, Sir James Thornhill, oil on canvas, 1727 (© University of Oxford).

Ormond's brother, Charles, 1st Earl of Arran (1671–1758), who now stepped out from under the Duke's shadow for the first time and was elected with alacrity.[5] Arran, a distinguished army officer and nephew by marriage of Nathaniel, 3rd Lord Crew (1633–1721), the long-serving bishop of Durham, had the right Tory credentials and had lately (1712–14) served as Master-General of the Ordnance in Ireland.[6] He took up his office at once despite infuriated Whigs threatening him with the complete loss of his property.[7] The Earl, a low-key, wily Jacobite related by birth to the Orange family, had a part in the Atterbury Plot to bring in the exiled Stuart monarchy (he was promoted Duke of Arran by James III in the

---

[5] His moderate Whig opponent, Thomas, Lord Pembroke, collected only three votes. Hearne Collections, V. 110–11, 115. For the election see Bodl. MSS. Ballard 38, ff. 224–7; Ward, Georgian Oxford, 57–8; Nigel Aston, 'The Great survivor: Charles Butler, Earl of Arran and the Oxford Chancellorship, 1715–1758', in eds. R. Darwall-Smith and P. Horden, 'Oxford: The Forgotten Century', in History of Universities XXXV, 1 (2022), 348–69.

[6] Summary in Eveline Cruickshanks and Howard Erskine-Hill, The Atterbury Plot (Basingstoke, 2004), 95–6.

[7] The choice, wrote one, was 'in contempt of the Court and common sense'. [John Toland,] The State-Anatomy of Great Britain. Containing a Particular account of its several Interests and parties... (9th edn., London, 1717), 73.

250 ENLIGHTENED OXFORD

Jacobite peerage but never used the title in England) while still being far from *persona non grata* to Princess Caroline of Wales and her circle.[8] After the failure of the 1722 Plot, Arran saw the expediency of distancing himself from treasonable projects for the sake of the University, a tacking that was reflected inter alia in the greater diversity of some of his nominations to the Vice Chancellorship.

Remarkably, despite his fringe involvement in a treasonable enterprise and the permanent residence of his elder brother, the Duke, on the continent openly promoting the interests of James III, Arran was left alone by the Walpole government, as was his sister-in-law, Mary, Duchess of Ormond (daughter of the 1st Duke of Beaufort), who came and went in London society from her house in Chelsea with no apparent limitations, often visiting the Earl and Countess at their residence in Grosvenor Street.[9] Arran was consistently conscious of his obligations towards the wider Butler clan (he had no children), the majority of them Roman Catholics,[10] to the point of admitting at least one and possibly two of his 'papist' great-nephews into the University (though they could not lawfully graduate).[11] If he could only do a certain amount to push the University into the centre of national life during his forty-three years as Chancellor, he also turned out to be politically untouchable, thanks principally to the Butler family's record of service to William III and, probably, the protection of his sister, Henrietta (d. 1724), and her husband, Henry de Nassau, 1st Earl of Grantham, and Lord Chamberlain to Caroline, as both Princess of Wales and Queen consort after her husband's accession to the throne, 1717 37.[12]

As with all Oxford's Chancellors, Arran was only occasionally in residence. His main function was to work for the best interests of the University (which he was too fly to conflate exclusively with those of the Tory party) and that usually entailed spending most of the year at Westminster and in London society. In

[8] Arran was personally close to Atterbury. Ibid., 106, 110, 116, 119; Linda Colley, *In Defiance of Oligarchy. The Tory Party 1714–1760* (Cambridge, 1982), 198. In 1716 he was appointed Commander-in-Chief of all the Pretender's land and sea forces in England. Ward dryly notes that this was 'an empty honour indeed'. Ward, *Georgian Oxford*, 59. Eveline Cruickshanks emphasised that Arran was dealing directly with 'James III' about a restoration at one point. Royal Archives, SP 52/100, Mar 1721. It could be argued that this was a tactical ploy out of primary loyalty to his brother, the Duke, rather than to the Pretender in the first instance.

[9] The Duchess never saw her husband again after his flight into what proved permanent exile in 1715. *A short Memorial and Character of that most noble and illustrious Princess Mary Dutchess of Ormonde* (s.n., 1735).

[10] His heir until 1738 was Col. Thomas Butler [of Kilcash, co.Tipperary], who had been a colonel in the Jacobite forces and who remained an active supporter of the exiled Stuarts well into the 1720s.

[11] One of these is certainly Richard Butler, son of James, County Longford, Ch. Ch., matric. 1719, aet. 18, like Arran a kinsman of the Barons Cahir [I], Foster, I. 203. Other kinsmen included James Butler, son of James, St Margaret's, Westm., matric. Ch. Ch. 1718, aet. 19. He graduated BA 1722, MA, 1725, Foster, I. 202; Somerset Hamilton Butler (1718–74), 8th Viscount Ikerrin, cr. Earl of Carrick [I], 1748. Matric. Ch. Ch., July 1735, aet. 17; LL.D., TCD, 1747, Foster, I. 204.

[12] His survival is discussed in Aston, 'The Great survivor'. It says much that he gave up hopes of regaining Ormond's residence at Richmond Lodge, Surrey, when the Prince of Wales bid on it at auction. There were no further bids after the Prince raised his hand and he acquired it for a sum well below its market value. Information gratefully received from Ruth Musielak.

OXFORD PERSONNEL 251

that connection it helped that Bishop Atterbury's influence with the Dean and Chapter propelled Arran—standing against the Duke of Newcastle—into the influential post of High Steward of Westminster (as successor to his brother) in early 1716.[13] Arran thereby accrued appreciable electoral influence in the key constituency, though he omitted to capitalise on it. Instead, he opted for contented seclusion at Bagshot Park in Surrey (where he was Ranger and Keeper under the Crown) and made the recovery of Ormond's confiscated estates his priority.[14] Arran walked the tightrope between loyalty and disloyalty with consummate mastery, carefully supported in his act by his intelligent wife, Elizabeth (1679–1756).[15] Contemporaries did not underestimate him: the moderate Tory and ex-Speaker, William Bromley, opining that he 'would as soon take the word of Lord A[rran] as of any man alive'.[16] His years of work as President of the Westminster Infirmary and his reputation for charity brought him plaudits in later life from most of his contemporaries.[17]

The greatest service that Arran did for Oxford was to live on to the immense age of 87 and hold office as Chancellor for forty-three years, a record that still stands. He was replaced by another vigorous geriatric Jacobite, John Fane, 7th Earl of Westmorland (1685–1762), whom he had appointed as High Steward in 1754.[18] Westmorland (like Arran not an Oxford graduate) was another military man, a friend of the 1st Viscount Cobham of Stowe and married to a Cavendish [Mary, only daughter of Lord Henry Cavendish, brother of the 2nd Duke of Devonshire], one who had come late to the 'honest' cause, only gradually discarding his Whig ties. By the later 1730s Westmorland had gravitated towards the Opposition and the Leicester House Circle of Prince Frederick of Wales and paid a high price for his preference soon after inheriting the earldom from his brother in 1736, when Walpole ensured that he lost his colonelcy of the 1st Troop of Horse Guards

[13] *British Weekly Mercury*, 7–14 Mar. 1716, issue 559: Surrey History Centre, Thomas [Brodrick] to Alan, Lord Brodrick, 29 Mar. 1716, Brodrick MSS vol. 3, 1248/3/346–7.
[14] Bagshot Park was Crown land, previously the seat of Richard, 1st Earl of Ranelagh, and reverted to the Crown on Arran's death. *Universal Chronicle or Weekly Gazette*, 16 Dec. 1758. For a description dated 1736, see Markham, *John Loveday*, 243. That Arran took care to reclaim Ormond's Irish property only and his refusal to seek the restoration of the Ormond dukedom in his favour after his brother's death in 1745 further smoothed his path. More details in Chapter 7, p. 24.
[15] Bagshot Park was close to Pope's residence at Hall Grove. The poet seems to have teased Lady Arran about her hypochondria. Rogers, *Pope and the Destiny of the Stuarts*, 27n.
[16] Northamptonshire Record Office [hereafter NRO], Isham MSS. 1869.
[17] 'It may very well be said, that this most excellent Earl, was both honoured and esteemed by all when living, for those shining, charitable, great and good qualities, which were so peculiar and similar to his great Ancestors'. *London Evening Post*, 23 Dec. 1758, issue 4858. Even Horace Walpole conceded he had become 'an inoffensive old man'. Horace Walpole, *Memoirs of King George II*, ed. John Brooke (3 vols., New Haven, CT, 1985), III. 42. Not quite all of them. The court Whig, John, 5th Lord Berkeley of Stratton (a Christ Church product), considered that Arran had been made Chancellor 'by the foolish faction there [at Oxford] for fear they should have been suspected of not being Jacobite', and wondered if the choice of the next Chancellor would suggest that 'Oxford has acquired more prudence since that Period'. Lincolnshire Archives, Berkeley Diaries, BQ2/6/14 & 15, 11 Dec. 1758.
[18] Ward, *Georgian Oxford*, 200.

252   ENLIGHTENED OXFORD

(Arran had been colonel of the 3rd Troop in his time). Westmorland thereafter remained in cantankerous opposition, continuing to cultivate Prince Frederick while also discovering Jacobitism in the 1740s with all the passion of a convert, being present among the leadership cadre when the 'Young Pretender' met them in Pall Mall on his furtive visit to London in September 1750.[19] He was unusual, both for keeping communications open in two directions and for seeing Jacobitism as a potentially viable alternative to the dynasty in situ despite Prince Charles Edward's defeat at Culloden as recently as 1746.

Politics and the army apart, Westmorland was a civilised man with an interest in antiquities and an important architectural patron of Colen Campbell.[20] As if any doubts remained that he was not well qualified for the Chancellorship because unlearned, he delivered himself of an unscripted Latin oration at his installation in 1759 that won even the Whig Kennicott's admiration.[21] His combination of personal dignity and a propensity for bibulous conviviality was a winner. After seeing off a challenge from the ministry's preferred candidate, Bishop the Hon. Richard Trevor of Durham, 'in an election of great consequence & importance to the University',[22] he was installed Chancellor 'with a magnificence which set a standard for all subsequent entertainments'.[23] These abundant social graces were just what the University needed as its new Chancellor led it into the new reign that commenced on 25 October 1760. With first-hand experience of Prince Charles Edward's leadership deficiencies, Westmorland was unsurprisingly delighted with his new sovereign, George III. But bitterness over his past treatments still rankled and he declined to head the University delegation to court to present its loyal address on George's accession, as he could not stomach its flattering words about the late king and his administrations. This attachment to principle (born of disappointments nearly three decades old) did neither Westmorland nor Oxford much harm as they more or less accorded with George III's own view of his grandfather's reign. Westmorland was too old to reap (he was 74 when elected Chancellor) the benefits of royal favour himself but his unbridled loyalty worked

---

[19] Sir Charles Petrie, 'The Elibank plot, 1752–3', *TRHS*, 14 (1931), 175–96, at 179. See also D. Zimmermann, *The Jacobite movement in Scotland in exile, 1746–159* (Basingstoke, 2003).

[20] For Westmorland's architectural projects other than the celebrated Mereworth Castle, Kent, see Nigel Aston, 'Dual loyalties? John, 7th Earl of Westmorland, Jacobitism, and the Leicester House connection', unpublished paper.

[21] William King, *Political and literary anecdotes of his own times* (London, 1818), 172–3; Clark, *Samuel Johnson*, 102.

[22] Dean David Gregory [to Lord Ilchester?], Christ Church, 20 Dec. 1758, BL, Holland House Papers, Add MS 51349. There were those who considered Convocation's choice tactically inept: 'If they have wantonly set the Govt at Defiance, & thrown themselves out of the Channel of Preferment, they are poor Politicians. If there remains among them any Remnant of the Old Leaven of Jacobitism, they are not only bad men, but little better than natural fools.' Lord Berkeley of Stratton, Lincolnshire Archives, Berkeley Diaries, BQ2/6/17, Jan. 1759.

[23] Richard Sharp, 'The Oxford Installation of 1759', *Oxoniensia*, 56 (1991), 145–53; *The Harcourt papers*, ed. E. W. Harcourt (14 vols., Oxford, 1880–1905), VII. 223. See also OUA: NW/1/29, printed orders for the reception of Lord Westmorland as Chancellor.

OXFORD PERSONNEL   253

wonders for others, not least his heir and nephew Sir Francis Dashwood, who
came into government as Chancellor of the Exchequer under Lord Bute.[24]

Westmorland died on 26 August 1762, his three years as Chancellor having
turned out to be the culmination of a remarkable career.[25] With his main estates at
Mereworth in Kent and Apthorpe in north-east Northamptonshire, he had been
at a slight disadvantage in exercising influence in Oxfordshire. That could not be
said of either of his successors. The first of these, George Lee, 3rd Earl of Lichfield
(1718–72), had long sought the chancellorship, having mustered all the grace he
could in the 1759 election and withdrawn from the cancellarial poll rather than
split the Tory vote.[26] Lichfield's credentials were impeccable: a direct descendant
of Charles II with a Nonjuring and Catholic background, a graduate of St John's
College, possessed of a major estate in the county at Ditchley Park near Charlbury
and, as Viscount Quarendon, knight of the shire for Oxfordshire from 1741 to
1743 before he inherited the earldom.[27]

The Earl was part of the 'Old Interest' (a loose coalition of Tory connections
and anti-Pelhamite malcontents) in a way that Westmorland had never been, and
yet the latter's prominence in Jacobite counsels in the 1750s plus a greater degree
of antipathy to the Pelhams than Lichfield possessed gave him the edge as a
candidate. There were also, well-founded as it transpired, suspicions that the latter
was just a touch too close to the new court for comfort in an institution that was
still coming to terms with the emerging axis of royal favour and its implications.
Both earls were good natured—except towards each other—and it rather showed:
witness Westmorland's first offering the High Stewardship to Thomas, 2nd Lord
Bruce of Tottenham (1729–1814), before doing the honourable thing and
appointing Lord Lichfield in September 1760.[28] Electing the latter as Chancellor

---

[24] Betty Kemp, *Sir Francis Dashwood: an eighteenth-century independent* (London, 1957), 1–80 for
his early career.

[25] Jonathan Spain, 'Fane, John, seventh earl of Westmorland (bap. 1686–d. 1762), army officer and
politician', *ODNB*, online edn., 2009.

[26] Ward, *Georgian Oxford*, 208–9.

[27] Lichfield had a reputation for enjoying the bottle, no necessary disadvantage in either academic or
county circles. Archbishop Secker wrote of him, 'he sometimes drinks too much: but [I] have been
assured that he doth it not habitually; and have never heard, that he delights in tempting others to
excess; nor do imagine, that his House will be open to Oxonians for that purpose'. W. J. Smith, *The
Grenville Papers* (4 vols., London, 1852–3), II. 5, 7. One squib was less polite:
Quoted in William Wing, *Oxfordshire in the Eighteenth Century, and the County Election of 1754*
(Bicester, 1881), xii.

> First, in support of interest old,
> From Ditchley staggers Lichfield bold,
>   An hardy chief for drinking;
>   His glass he fills up to the brim,
>   And thinks by making his head swim
>   He keeps his cause from sinking.

[28] Ward, *Georgian Oxford*, 212. The High Stewardship was essentially an honorific office within the
University that often functioned as a steppingstone to the Chancellorship and 'He is Judge in Capital
Cases where a student is a party'. Markham, *John Loveday*, 119.

254   ENLIGHTENED OXFORD

made political sense as Lichfield was in high favour at court, becoming a Lord of the Bedchamber in December 1760 and being subsequently appointed a Privy Councillor and Captain of the Gentlemen Pensioners (July 1762).[29] There was some talk of Lord Bute, the first minister, King's favourite, and Lichfield's patron, coming forward, but in the end the only other candidate was the Worcestershire grandee, Thomas, 2nd Lord Foley (1703–66), who attracted votes from unconvinced Tories. They saw with some consternation that Lichfield had received extensive backing from Whigs. These may have hoped that, in the transformed political landscape of the early 1760s, with Lichfield talking publicly of his pleasure in the redundancy of the old party distinctions, they might lose less official patronage *within* the University than anticipated.[30]

And thus the University secured a Chancellor who was the first to hold a court appointment at the time of his election since the seventeenth century. Not that it counted for too much. Lichfield had the goodwill of the king, but stayed loyal to Bute too long and had drifted into inconsequence by the late 1760s as a taste for the bottle gained the upper hand.[31] His death ten years after his assumption of office gave the University scope to secure itself the king's first minister, Frederick, Lord North, MP, as Chancellor and the opportunity could not have occurred at a more opportune moment with the Church of England (and, by extension) the University, under immense parliamentary and outdoor pressure to relax the laws on subscription.[32] North's appropriateness for the office was not limited to his being Premier. His family were in direct descent from the founder of Trinity College and had been generous benefactors to it: his father (the 1st Earl of Guilford) was Lord Chamberlain to Queen Charlotte and resided at Wroxton Abbey in the north of the county. North was personally delighted when the invitation to put his name forward came from Trinity College on receipt of the news that Lord Lichfield was dying:[33]

> So public & eminent a testimony of so respectable a lady as the University of Oxford can never be declined by any man, who is, in the least degree, able to judge of the value of distinctions, & to esteem those, which are truly honourable.

As a loyal servant of the Crown North appealed to Tories and court Whigs alike; and he was by nature good-humoured, intelligent, and amiable. He was also a

---

[29] Roland Thorne, 'Lee, George Henry, third earl of Lichfield (1718–1772), ODNB, online edn., 2006; G.E. Cokayne and Vicary Gibbs, *The complete peerage*... (13 vols., London, 1913–59), VII. 647.

[30] Ward, *Georgian Oxford*, 219–22.

[31] Ibid., 222. Letters regarding Lord Lichfield's Chancellorship are in Oxfordshire Archives, DIL XXIII/a–j. For his institution of the Chancellor's Prizes and his personal graciousness of manner see *GM* 43 (1772), 349. For the sale of his house to fund a chemistry professorship see Lord Grantham to Hon. Frederick Robinson, 21 Feb. 1779, Beds and Luton Archives Services, Wrest Park Papers, L30/15/54/120.

[32] pp. 17–21, this chapter.

[33] North to Dr Bartholomew Peisley, 29 Aug. 1772, Beinecke Rare Book and Manuscript Library, Yale University, OSB MSS file 16852. Peisley (c.1723–81) was senior Fellow of Trinity College at his death. Foster, III. 1090.

strong practising Anglican and had been since his undergraduate days at Trinity when he and his half-brother, Lord Dartmouth, were reputed to have been 'as regular as Great Tom . . . they never missed early prayers in their college chapel *one* morning, nor any evening when not actually out of Oxford'.[34] And he proclaimed his commitment in the strongest terms in his letter confirming his candidature:[35]

> The support of the established church is not more the duty, than it is the interest of every Englishman; I am happy in thinking that such are the sentiments of much the greater part of the nation, & there is, I believe, nobody who does not see how intimately the prosperity of the Church is connected with that of the two Universities.

His eventual uncontested election as Chancellor came as no surprise and pleased almost all parties from the king downwards.[36] A very contented Fellow of New College expressed the consensus thus:

> Never was an election conducted with more honour and good humour, nor can the Annals of the University produce such another affectionate and respectable testimony to the public and Private Virtues of the Chancellor.[37]

The arrival of delegates of Convocation for his installation at 10, Downing Street dramatically symbolised the University's move to the centre stage of British public life and unequivocally underlined its cultural importance. Oxford had finally selected one who was both 'A devout Anglican and warm admirer of the settlement of 1688'.[38] As one Oxonian pointed out:

> Surely all things considered, the great Figure he now makes, and what an Ornament he was formerly to this Place, there could not have been a properer Candidate offered;[39]

---

[34] *GM* 68 (1798), 282–3.

[35] North to Peisley, 29 Aug. 1772, Beinecke Rare Book and Manuscript Library, Yale University, OSB MSS file 16852. Great Tom was the bell in Wren's bell tower above the main gate of Christ Church.

[36] L.G. Mitchell, 'Politics and Revolution 1772–1800', in HUO V, 163–90, at 169–71.

[37] Fiennes Eddowes to Thomas Harris, 8 Oct. 1772, Hampshire Record Office, 9M73/G425. Oxford's astute choice was favourably contrasted with Cambridge's recent election as its Chancellor in 1768–9 of the dissipated 3rd Duke of Grafton, North's predecessor as first Minister. Grafton's installation there in July 1769 led the acerbic contemporary commentator, Junius, to suggest the time was approaching when 'the venerable tutors of the university will no longer distress your modesty, by proposing you for a pattern to their pupils' and added sarcastically: 'Yet for the benefit of the succeeding age, I could wish that your retreat might be deferred, until your morals shall happily be ripened to that maturity of corruption, at which the worst examples cease to be contagious'. *The letters of Junius*, ed. John Cannon (Oxford, 1978), 85–6.

[38] John Cannon, *Lord North. The Noble Lord in the Blue Ribbon* (London, 1970), 13.

[39] Academicus, in *Public Advertiser*, 2 Oct. 1772, issue 11717. Cf. the reflection in the *General Evening Post*: 'The Tories now seem the most desirous to support the Brunswick line, and the Whigs seem to think that line has lost its merit, in proportion as they are excluded from the loaves and fishes. Interest, interest, how greatly dost thou constitute the springs of human action', 6 Oct. 1772, issue 6083.

256   ENLIGHTENED OXFORD

North was delighted with his appointment even if he turned out to be not quite the bulwark against religious change that his sponsors had hoped for. Certainly, he was immediately urged to take up the cudgels by his academic backers as they fought to preserve the subscriptional status quo. As the President of Magdalen put it, 'To you my Lord, your orthodox university looks up . . . to preserve her dignity and her utility inviolate'.[40]

Despite his professions of unqualified loyalty to the Established Church, North was not unbending in the defence of subscription (there were fears in Oxford that relaxing lay subscription might cause irresistible pressure to end clerical subscription). He privately and personally favoured the relaxation of lay subscription on matriculation (as did some other senior members), but when a move to enact it failed in the House of Commons in February 1772, there was no suggestion on that occasion that his behaviour and sentiments had somehow disqualified him for selection as Chancellor. Yet alarmist opinion was gathering, ready to assume the worst. As one writer put it (after North had replaced Lichfield):

> A Public Attack was made in the House of Commons upon our Subscription. It had not one Advocate. The Friends, and even the Representatives of the University gave it up as indefensible, our Chancellor intends to recommend an Alteration; the Bishops concur; and all our Friends are alarmed for the Fate of the University.[41]

Preoccupied by state business and still adjusting to his new academic appointment, North absented himself from the debates on the Dissenters' relief bill in early 1773 while encouraging prominent churchmen in Parliament to resist it and rely on the House of Lords to quash the proposal.[42] Six years later, the orthodox party at Oxford were confronted with another bill for relieving dissenting ministers and school masters. This time the Chancellor, to the surprise and relief of

---

[40] [George Horne], *A Letter to the Right Hon. The Lord North, Chancellor of the University of Oxford, concerning Subscription to the XXXIX Articles* (Oxford, 1773).

[41] *A Collection of papers, designed to explain and vindicate the present mode of subscription required by the University of Oxford* (Oxford, 1772), 23. The claim that North was making a 'quiet attempt to remove the Anglican monopoly of Oxford University' as soon as he became Chancellor is, however, an overstatement. Peter D. G. Thomas, *Lord North* (London, 1976), 148. Cf. John Cannon, *Lord North*, 13, who argues that 'North was firmly opposed to alterations in the basic structure of church or state'. See also Chapter 8, pp. 3, 36–8. Before the vote in the Commons on 6 Feb., Oxford Convocation had also reaffirmed its commitment to subscription on the existing basis though the Vice Chancellor, Nathan Wetherell, had proposed to recommend repeal of a part of the 39 Articles relating to faith and religion and substituting some other 'test in their room'. ed. A.W.A. White, *The Correspondence of Sir Roger Newdigate of Arbury Warwickshire* [Dugdale Society Publication, xxxvii] (Hertford, 1995), 186.

[42] However, in defending subscription at the University of Oxford at this time, North rose to the occasion, remarking that 'The reforming notions of this age are dangerous in their tendency', for 'something more than reformation is intended . . . to which if we give way, adieu to religion, adieu to everything dear to us as men and as Christians!' 23 Feb. 1773, *PH*, 17, col. 757.

some like Dean Lewis Bagot of Christ Church,[43] exerted himself on behalf of the University, and presented its petition in the Commons on 20 April, requesting that a declaration of Christianity should accompany any relief from subscription to the Church of England's Thirty-Nine Articles.[44]

North's value to Oxford, however, diminished after he resigned as Premier in March 1782; his Coalition with Charles James Fox and the Portland Whigs in 1783 was an embarrassment to Oxonian court loyalists that nothing could quite expiate. Oxford's Chancellor (who finally succeeded as 2nd Earl of Guilford in August 1790) was in parliamentary opposition after his removal from office by the king in December 1783; his marginalisation appeared physically confirmed through his fast descent into blindness by 1787.[45] That North was associated with the Foxites was embarrassing for Oxford opinion and, though there continued to be much affection for him personally (especially as his sight and general health declined), in political terms the gap that had opened up in 1783-4 only gradually closed again, strengthened by North's opposition to Pitt's April 1785 Parliamentary reform Bill, and his speeches against Henry Beaufoy's motions to repeal the Test and Corporation Acts in 1787 and 1789.[46] The first was on 28 March 1787, when he endeared himself afresh to the University and even Pitt paid him high compliments;[47] the second was on 8 May 1789, his last appearance in the Commons. On that occasion, he characteristically insisted that he honoured and respected the Dissenters, but argued 'that if the House weakened the Church, they weakened themselves; and that if they abandoned the wise precautions of their ancestors, they endangered the constitution of their country'.[48] He died much regretted in August 1792, as attached to his *alma mater* as ever, and looking during his last illness for a young University man who might read to him.[49]

---

[43] 'It was thought a good argument for making him our Chancellor, that it would engage him firmly in support of the Establishment. Now is the Crisis'. Lewis Bagot to Sir William Bagot, 14 Mar. 1779, Staffs RO, D3259/13/18/4. Dean Bagot was the leading campaigner in Oxford in 1779 to stop the Dissenters. He collected their tracts and was fed information by his brother, Sir William, and Sir Roger Newdigate from the Commons.

[44] U. R. Q. Henriques, *Religious Toleration in England, 1787-1833* (London, 1961). Discussed further, Chapter 8, p. 38.

[45] Peter Whiteley, *Lord North. The Prime Minister Who Lost America* (London, 1996), 220.

[46] *PH.*, xxvi, 818-23; 28, 16-27. That said, the two University MPs in 1783-4 kept their distance from Pitt: Francis Page was in Opposition after 1784, and Sir William Dolben had voted for Fox's East India Company bill (though he soon returned to support of the king's government). J. J. Sack, *From Jacobite to Conservative: Reaction and Orthodoxy in Britain c.1760-1832* (Cambridge, 1993), 81-2.

[47] The Principal of Magdalen Hall (1786-8), Matthew Lamb, reported to North's father:
'We all felt ourselves so much obliged to his Lordship [North], & I fancy the Vice Chancellor will be desired to return our Thanks in form. Even Dr Priestley is said to have commended Lord North's Speech in the highest terms, & to have declared that he "honored Lord North above any man in England, because he spoke with the most perfect knowledge of the subject, & directly from the heart"'. Bodl. MS. North d.21, f. 114, 1 Apr. 1787. Lamb was not an uncommitted party, since North had appointed him to his headship, and he also acted as North's constituency manager at Banbury.

[48] *PH*, 26, 818-23; 28, 16-27; W. Belsham, *Memoirs of the Reign of George III... to the Commencement of the Year 1799* (6 vols., London, 1801), IV. 128.

[49] *Memoirs of Richard Cumberland* (2 vols., London, 1807)., II. 253.

258   ENLIGHTENED OXFORD

North's nomination signalled the final realignment of Oxford with the Hanoverian polity; the election of his successor, William, 3rd duke of Portland (1738–1809), both confirmed that positioning and, for the first time, gave the University a chancellor from an impeccable Whig background, the head of one of the great 'Revolutionary' families. It was both an astonishing and an explicable choice given the circumstances of the early 1790s. Portland had formally presided over the Fox-North Coalition down to its dismissal in December 1783 and thereafter (with, of course, Lord North) been in opposition to Pitt. But the turbulent and violent course of the French Revolution threw the Opposition into disarray, and, by August 1792 (the date of North's death), Portland and a very sizable proportion of his following had shown their willingness to support Pitt's ministry on key security issues, despite their continuing distrust of the Premier and personal attachment to Fox.[50] The Cabinet, however, had worked to hook in the Portland Whigs, not least by patronage. The duke turned down the ministerial offer of a Garter ribbon in July 1792, but then came the vacancy at Oxford. His nomination and successful election to the Chancellorship was sanctioned and supported by the Cabinet to entice him further into the ministerial orbit, one step nearer to breaking with Fox. It was another reminder of what a vital piece of state patronage the Oxford Chancellorship constituted and this time, for once, ministers fostered the whole process and got their man installed.[51] The University did little to rebuff this sign of government high favour and, anyway, had no obvious alternative candidate to hand from a hereditary Tory family. The 5th Duke of Beaufort half-heartedly put his name forward for the poll but Portland swept all before him and the outcome at the election in September 1792 was never in serious doubt.[52] Oxford, it seemed, was finally ready to have a Whig as its head, admittedly one who was fast taking on the high Tory character that would colour the last fifteen years of his political life.

The Duke's election was for, the second successive time, the result of close coordination—a 'fix' one might reasonably call it—between the hebdomadal board and the ministry. In this case the vital point of academic contact was Cyril Jackson, Dean of Christ Church, the colossus of academic politics in the 1790s,[53] who at once saw that Portland, as a graduate of Christ Church, could

---

[50] Such as the royal proclamation against seditious writings issued on 21 May 1792. David Wilkinson, *The Duke of Portland. Politics and party in the age of George III* (Basingstoke, 2003), 84–9. See also L. G. Mitchell, *Charles James Fox* (Oxford, 1992), 120–6. In the debate on the proclamation Fox had singled out the growth of 'a high church spirit' as 'a serious threat to liberty'. Charles James Fox, *The speeches of the Rt. Hon. C. J. Fox in the House of Commons* (6 vols., London, 1815), ed. J. Wright, IV. 441, 25 May 1792.

[51] 'They suggested his name, countenanced his nomination and watched the progress of the election anxiously', F. O'Gorman, *The Whig Party and the French Revolution* (London, 1974), 103.

[52] He was privately installed by an 'adjourned convocation' in an elaborate ceremony at his Buckinghamshire seat of Bulstrode Park on 5 Oct. 1792 described at length in the *GM* 64 (1794), 404–6. See also Chapter 12, pp. 21–2.

[53] For Jackson see also this chapter, pp. 48–9.

surely be expected to favour the House.[54] Jackson's presumption was quite right. As he told a college alumnus and MP, Christ Church thereby intended 'nothing of Party or Hostility to Government...', but there was the need to have someone educated at Oxford (which ruled out the 4th Duke of Marlborough) and, in his (Jackson's) view Portland rather than the Foreign Secretary, Lord Grenville, best served the 'interests of the Country'. To appoint him would in effect be a 'compliment paid to his late manly & constitutional Conduct', an act of good faith that would require him in future to show 'his attachment to the present system of things against innovation'.[55] Even so, Portland's hesitations over abandoning Fox and his reluctance to commit himself wholeheartedly to the government tried the patience of some Oxonians between his appointment and installation in July 1793. One noted:

> The installation went off upon the whole much better than was expected, the Duke of Portland was under great apprehensions of a more cold reception, & from his late conduct had good reason to be so, it is certain that had Ld Guildford died 4 months later he would have had no chance of being elected.[56]

Christ Church thus became the centre of state *and* university power in Oxford for the first time since the days of Harley, Bolingbroke, and Atterbury seventy years previously when, as they were in the 1790s, college and government patronage networks had become enmeshed. Exactly two years after becoming Chancellor of Oxford, the Duke joined Pitt's government as Home Secretary, bringing with him the bulk of the Whigs in both Houses of Parliament. From 1794 to 1801 Portland and Jackson saw to it that young products of Christ Church were enlisted into the service of the British state on an exceptional scale, working particularly in the Home Office and in the clandestine services it was supporting in the war against Revolutionary France.[57] But Christ Church was not the only beneficiary of the Duke's patronage. Within the University itself, the Chancellor held out the hand of friendship to colleges of a prevailing Whig tradition to the point of nominating some of their heads to the Vice Chancellorship as the academic establishment closed ranks in the face of a formidable external enemy that made Whig and Tory divisions, for the time being, of nominal relevance. That situation could not

---

[54] It also constituted something of a return of favour on Jackson's part for Portland, in 1783, when First Lord of the Treasury during the Fox-North ministry, had been instrumental—with the endorsement of the Prince of Wales (later George IV)—in appointing Jackson to the Deanery. For Jackson as Portland's confidante see Michael Durey, *William Wickham, Master Spy* (London, 2009), 191.

[55] C. Jackson to Isaac Hawkins Browne, Ch. Ch., 9 Aug. 1792, OSB file 7942, Beinecke Rare Book and Manuscript Library, Yale University. Jackson intimated that the choice of Portland had approval at the highest level (including Grenville and William Markham, Archbishop of York), and urged Browne to canvas pro-Portland votes in Shropshire.

[56] Lewis Way to a friend at Glasgow University, 1793, Hants RO 75M91/B19/1.

[57] Discussed in Chapter 8, pp. 83–4.

260   ENLIGHTENED OXFORD

endure indefinitely and, sure enough, party animus resurfaced following the next national political realignment—that of 1801—brought on by Pitt's resignation following the king's refusal to approve Catholic Emancipation. Portland was one of those who stayed in office under Henry Addington in ostentatious support of the Crown and the Established Church, but he was no longer a chancellor who commanded a consensus within the University as the election of Pitt's pro-Catholic cousin, the bibliophile William, Lord Grenville (1759–1834), in the bitterly fought contest of 1809, vividly displayed. Portland had latterly excluded Whiggish academics from cancellarian patronage and resentment among the growing numbers of the excluded was enough to tip the balance in Grenville's favour, despite Oxonian doubts about removing the last legal disabilities affecting Roman Catholics.[58]

ii) Vice chancellors and their external impact

Oxford chancellors were public figures, non-academics, and power brokers with extensive gifts of patronage. And the most important piece of patronage they had in their gift was the nomination of the Vice Chancellor, the academic head of the University chosen from the list of college principals, the man called on to handle Oxford's often fraught internal politics and, no less demandingly, second (and often spearhead) the Chancellor's efforts to protect and extend the University's interests in the outside world. Given that, until late in the century, the Vice Chancellor tended to be a Tory called upon to operate occasionally but efficiently in the Whig world outside, the diplomatic demands imposed on the office-holder were of a high order. And, consequently, they were variously discharged.

Vice chancellors were always in holy orders and expected to defend the Church establishment on the basis that it was coterminous with the interests of Oxford. To undermine one was, by definition, to undermine the other in a primarily confessional constitution. Connections to the Tory party carried as much weight as administrative competence in the appointment of vice chancellors during the reigns of the first two Georges. However, the intense external scrutiny and suspicion Oxford faced in the decade after 1714 ensured that expediency, pragmatism, and the courtly virtues of a *politique* were also placed in the job description. No vice chancellor's links to the Tory party in Parliament were closer than those of Dr Robert Shippen (1675–1745), Principal of Brasenose College, who was the longest-serving holder of that office in this era between 1718 and 1723

---

[58] See BL Add. MS 37909; Add. MS 51530, ff. 97–100; W. Gibson, 'The Election of Lord Grenville . . .';
Peter Jupp, *Lord Grenville 1759–1834* (Oxford, 1985), 304–5, 414–17. For Grenville as Chancellor see
ibid., 459–60; Crook, *Brasenose*, 181 and n., 182n.

OXFORD PERSONNEL   261

(the customary term was three years, but he was Arran's favourite).[59] Robert was the brother of William Shippen, MP, and married to the daughter of Peter Legh of Lyme Park in Cheshire, a high Tory. At Oxford, in Queen Anne's last years, he was identified with the Harcourt interest led by William Delaune, Vice Chancellor 1702-6,[60] and was recommended as a suitable candidate by the then powerful Dr William King, Arran's controversial and often cantankerous secretary and registrar.[61] Shippen's Jacobite links stood out dramatically.[62] Indeed, the years in office of this high-flying cleric coincided with his brother's scarcely concealing his efforts in the Commons and beyond to restore the 'Pretender', culminating in the Atterbury Plot.[63] To his credit, Robert Shippen showed himself able to weather the storm of criticism hurled at the University for its allegedly treasonable politics during these years. He came in for particular criticism after Thomas Warton the elder, the Professor of Poetry, preached a sermon on Restoration Day 1719 deeply critical of virtually every aspect of King George's reign to date. Whigs in the University urged Shippen to proceed against Warton in the Chancellor's Court on charges that the sermon was seditious and the matter was brought before the Lords Justices that summer during the king's absence in Hanover.[64] He did not. Partly from tactical skill, partly from good luck, Shippen kept external interference at bay: he had to endure some ferocious criticism from the government, but he got away with it.[65]

Almost despite himself, Shippen had exhibited a studied moderation in the face of provocation on both sides that may have surprised all parties. Arran, with William King at a distance, no longer his secretary, thereafter signalled his

[59] His Oxford career is summarised in Crook, *Brasenose*, 123-41. Much of the information regarding Shippen comes from Hearne. He was unmarried and his lecherous disposition seems undeniable. See R. W. Jeffery, 'An Oxford Don Two Hundred Years Ago', unpub. MS, Brasenose College Archives, MPP 56F4/10.

[60] Ward, *Georgian Oxford*, 115 and n., 123-4.

[61] David Greenwood, *William King. Tory & Jacobite* (Oxford, 1969), 17-19, 29. King was installed as Principal of St Mary Hall in late 1719.

[62] cf. Mordaunt Crook's designation of Robert Shippen as 'a Hanoverian Jacobite'. *Brasenose*, 127.

[63] Cruickshanks and Erskine-Hill, *The Atterbury Plot*, 52, 71, 157, 189. *The Spiritual Intruder unmask'd: in a letter from the orthodox in White-Chappel to Dr Shippen* (London, 1716) offers a powerful critique of Robert Shippen's churchmanship following his appointment as rector of Whitechapel in 1716.

[64] BL Add MS 29604 [Carewe Papers], contains details of the Chancellor's Court at Oxford for the period 1707-21 (the Vice Chancellor acted as his commissary), mainly drafts, plaints, cases, and dispensations for individual degree candidates. The Court (dating from the thirteenth century) had jurisdiction over all matriculands, and a large number of tradesmen as well. It was usually presided over by the Vice Chancellor, with Proctors acting for the defence and prosecution. Actions for debt remained important. One of the more bizarre cases was the suit of Henry Thornowitz (1717-19) against John Acland, fellow of All Souls, for failure to recompense him for lute lessons. Ibid., ff. 41-57. The correctional side of the court had largely disappeared after the Civil War and that aspect was dealt with by the hebdomadal board instead. For its medieval heyday see W. A. Pantin, *Oxford Life in Oxford Archives* (Oxford, 1972), 54-65.

[65] For details see TNA (PRO) SP 36/16, ff. 170, 322-32, 356:/17, ff. 102, 103, 108-14, 139, 143-60, 196-7, 219-21:/18, ff. 14, 90-1, 254:/19, ff. 346-7:/21, f. 342. He was also widely disliked by other Tories on personal grounds. Crook, *Brasenose*, 124, 130-1.

262 ENLIGHTENED OXFORD

intention of pushing for stability in the management of the University through a prudent nomination of successive vice chancellors who were careful to avoid any confrontations with ministers, as far as was possible. The awkward Shippen was replaced in 1723 by the less rebarbative John Mather, President of Corpus Christi College, before whom in committee Dr George Coningsby, King's Vice-Principal at St Mary Hall, was summoned in 1727.[66] His offence, another provocative 30 January sermon comparatively unflattering to George I; his punishment, prohibition from preaching to the University for two years, a verdict which led Lord Townshend, the senior Secretary of State, to thank the University authorities.[67]

Mather was succeeded by Edward Butler (1728–32), President of Magdalen from 1722 to 1745, and William Holmes (1732–5), President of St John's, men no less committed to this policy of rapprochement. Butler was wealthy, a layman, a Tory married to Sacheverell's sister-in-law (Mary Tate, of Burleigh Hall, nr. Loughborough, Leics.) but, by the date of his appointment, had turned from Jacobitism to being a Hanoverian loyalist.[68] Arran, for all his personal residual Jacobitism, could see no reason by this date not to invite one of those best described as court Whigs from the larger colleges (Christ Church being a conspicuous exception) to serve as his deputy. Holmes was certainly a courtier, appointed a king's chaplain in 1734, close to George II's son-in-law, William IV, Prince of Orange, and an obvious choice—except on the grounds of his scholarship—as second Regius Professor of Modern History in 1736.[69]

The challenge to display Oxford as loyal at a time of national crisis was the central issue confronting Euseby Isham (1697–1755) (Rector of Lincoln College, 1731–55) during his vice chancellorship from 1744 to 1747, one that coincided with the Jacobite Rebellion of 1745–6. Oxford might very easily be deemed a security risk once the army of Prince Charles Edward Stuart began its advance south of Manchester in October 1745. Only a minority of senior members of the University had signed the Association rapidly set up to preserve the constitution in Church and State (with all its Whiggish connotations) as it was circulated in both the city and the county. Isham, a moderate Tory from a well-connected Northamptonshire family (his brother, Sir Edmund, the 6th Baronet, a Fellow of Magdalen from 1720 to 1736, was MP for the county) felt discretion required that

---

[66] Shippen continued to be an influence on Arran, not always a helpful one. In 1728 he apparently encouraged the Earl to write a letter to George II protesting at the University's loss of the Visitorship of University College, which the Heads of House then rejected by two to one. Darwall-Smith, *University College*, chap. 12.

[67] He commended Charles I as 'a Prince that was not alien by birth, & that he preferred to dignities in the Church men of true worth and learning'. TNA (PRO), SP 35/17/1, ff. 44, 57; R. Greaves, 'Religion in the University', 414–15; Ward, *Georgian Oxford*, pp. 134–5; Charles-Edwards and Reid, *Corpus Christi College*, 233.

[68] ed. Brockliss (1), 262–3. He was close to the distinguished Nonjuror, Edward Holdsworth. ibid., 337. For his election as one of the MPs for the University see Chapter 8, p. 48.

[69] For Holmes, see Chapter 4, p. 39. The actions of his successor, Stephen Niblett, Warden of All Souls, are considered at Chapter 8, p. 60.

his name be among them. Consistency was at stake here (as well as political expediency) as the University had earlier pledged itself to resist the rebellion in an Address to George II, and any tokens of overt disloyalty would be mercilessly seized on by Whig critics of Oxford.[70] The scholarly, courteous Isham judged the situation well, preferring to protect the University and risk the aspersions of its committed Jacobite minority and rowdy undergraduate sympathisers, guessing correctly that most moderate Tories would uphold his actions.[71]

Isham had left office by the time his successor, John Purnell (Warden of New College, 1740–64), faced the prospect of legal action sponsored by the Pelham ministry's law officers to combat the University's apparent inability to prevent its members from seeking publicity for their unsubtle Jacobite roistering *after* the '45 was over.[72] Hard though it was, both men had sought to keep the University at a distance from public events that were unlikely to work to its advantage and Dr George Huddesford (1699–1776), President of Trinity and Vice Chancellor from 1753 to 1756, had the same strategy in the notorious Oxfordshire election of 1754 when the Whig interest made a determined bid to seize the county's parliamentary seats from the Tories. With the University containing dons who were fierce partisans on both sides and seeing personal advantage from the victory of either the 'Old Interest' or 'New Interest' candidates, Huddesford (an Associator in 1745) would have his work cut out, despite the astute guidance of William Blackstone. With the backing of the hebdomadal board, the University imposed severe restrictions on political activities while the election was taking place. However, the prestige of his office counted for little in restraining academic-conviction politicians, and it was not until 8 October 1754 when, on reappointment to office, he pointedly excepted one college (everyone knew he meant Exeter, the nerve centre of the 'New Interest' during the election) from his compliments to the student body for its behaviour during the poll and the electoral scrutiny that followed it. This College, he declared, had 'opened its gates, and its cellars to the Refuse of mankind, to be the shop of Corruption, and the factory of Perjury'. The speech was repeated in the press and triggered an exchange of pamphlets that drew in Huddesford, spun out the electoral agitation, and did nothing for the University's reputation nationally.[73] Huddesford was unfortunate that his term of

---

[70] Ward, *Georgian Oxford*, 166.

[71] Hearne (X. 434) had called him 'good-natured' and 'honest' in 1731. See also XI. 129, 140–1, 155 for the cordial relations between them. He had acted as Arran's key adviser for many years. See NRO, Isham MSS 2980, Arran to Dr Isham, 2 Aug. 1730: 'I received your letter of the 28 of last month concerning a Vice Chancellor. I shall continue Dr Butler and desire you will prepare a letter to that purpose'. A female admirer considered Isham's 'Accomplishments are numerous, & his Manners the most polite,...NB his nose is too little for the Breadth of his face which is pink...his height is the tallest of any pate in Oxford...'. 'Shepilinda', *Memoirs*, 17–18.

[72] Chapter 8, p. 29.

[73] *London Evening Post*, 8 Oct. 1754; R. J. Robson, *The Oxfordshire Election of 1754: A Study in the Interplay of City, County and University Politics* (London, 1949); Ward, *Georgian Oxford*, 192–206; L.S. Sutherland, 'Political Respectability 1751–1771', in HUO V, 129–62, at 132–7. *Jackson's Oxford Journal* was founded to publish election material from both sides.

264   ENLIGHTENED OXFORD

office coincided with an Oxfordshire election that attracted huge press interest across the country, but his attempt to be a restraining influence, however well meant, was always going to be a precarious exercise and, as his heated public words indicated, he was furious at the way some of his colleagues had so blatantly and extravagantly involved Oxford in a bitter electoral episode.[74]

After 1760, the vice chancellorship assumed an enhanced public importance that reflected the University's favourable new standing with the ministers of George III. Vice chancellors were tasked with building on the official cordiality extended towards the University, evident early in the reign, and ensuring that it endured and brought with it both institutional benefits and protection. Assured of royal goodwill and set free from newly defunct Jacobitism, vice chancellors became comfortable with their novel prominence as natural insiders rather than establishment outcasts. Nathan Wetherell, Master of University College, and Vice Chancellor between 1768 and 1772, destroyed any veneer of independency from ministers. W. R. Ward uncharitably described Wetherell as 'full of oily obsequiousness to the great' but he exaggerated, made light of Wetherell's talents as a networker, and was unwilling to concede this distinguished Oxonian's own intellectual capacity.[75] Despite being a Hutchinsonian in the 1750s as well as a friend of Sir Roger Newdigate, Wetherell had no hesitation in attaching himself in the late 1760s to such as Charles Jenkinson, whose connections lay essentially with the 'New Interest', but who had emerged more recently as leader of the 'king's friends' with a reputation for 'secret' influence with George III.[76] With Whig–Tory divisions counting for less, Wetherell emolliently cast himself as the reconciler of all those who would serve the interests of the king and, by extension, those of the University. But if Wetherell turned himself into a successful courtier as well as a sound administrator, the material interests of the University were admirably served, and that combination of roles characterised the discharge of his duties. Wetherell had force of personality as well as diplomatic talents. He worked energetically during the subscription crisis of 1772–3 to keep Charles Jenkinson (and through him, the wavering Premier and Chancellor, Lord North) and the University's MPs (Newdigate and Page) up to the mark, and left them in no doubt that the University would not easily tolerate concessions to Dissenters that weakened the Church.[77] A sure mark of royal favour was the conferring on

---

[74] Whig partisans were equally scornful of him, presenting him—unfairly—as a paid-up ally of William King's. '...Dr Huddesford is a most stupid Thing', wrote one anonymous newspaper writer. 'Extract of a Letter from a Fellow of a College in Oxford to his Friend at Lostwithiel in Cornwall', *London Evening Post*, 17 Apr. 1755. At his own college, Trinity, Huddesford supported literary pursuits, and was responsible for encouraging Thomas Warton the younger on his way.

[75] Ward, *Georgian Oxford*, 231. Darwall-Smith more accurately accords Wetherell the accolade of being 'arguably the ablest and most-active Vice-Chancellor of the century', *University College*, 291. He found time during his four years in post to lay the foundation stone of the Radcliffe Observatory, inaugurate the new market in 1772, and speculate successfully on Oxford canal shares. Cox, *Recollections*, 169.

[76] The Jenkinson connection is discussed in Chapter 8, pp. 63, 88–91.

[77] BL Add MS 38207, ff. 85, 90, 100, 184, 190, 197, 239; this chapter, pp. 19–21.

Fig. 6.2 The Coal Wharf, Oxford, Rev. William Henry Barnard, grey wash and graphite print, 1792 (Yale Center for British Art, Paul Mellon Collection).

Wetherell in October 1771 of the Deanery of Hereford, which he held in plurality. For an Oxford vice chancellor to receive such preferment, unimaginable earlier in the century, was a sure sign of changed times. And Wetherell repaid the favour in full by masterminding the election of North as the University's Chancellor in the autumn of 1772 only days before his term of office came to an end.[78] As well as his gifts as an astute political operator, Wetherell was a man of practical intelligence who moved with the times. Thus in 1767 he was conferring with Sir Roger Newdigate about the possibility of linking Oxford with Coventry by canal.[79]

After four years under Thomas Fothergill, North's first selection as Vice Chancellor (1776–80) was George Horne, President of Magdalen College since 1768. Horne was a talented controversialist with a nice line in irony, an academic of unimpeachable orthodoxy who, like Wetherell (they had been contemporaries at University College), had started his career as a pronounced Hutchinsonian.

---

[78] BL Add MS 38470, ff. 43–95; Mitchell, 'Politics and Revolution', 169–71; Ward, *Georgian Oxford*, 256–9. For North's election to the Chancellorship, see this chapter, pp. 15–19. Wetherell's political activities are considered in Darwall-Smith, *University College*, 284–5, 287.

[79] Warks. RO, Newdegate family of Arbury Papers, CR0136/B3716a. See also draft letter of Newdigate to Wetherell on the route of the Coventry Canal, 7 Sept. 1767, in ed. White, *Newdigate Correspondence*, 145., 145; VCH Oxon., IV. 208–9, 293–4. The corporation of Oxford petitioned for a bill in 1769 for a canal connecting Coventry to Oxford (mainly for the movement of coal) that was eventually completed in 1790 with a new wharf opened at Hythe Bridge. Langford, *Polite and Commercial People*, 414, 416; Judith Curthoys, *Cows & curates. The story of the land and livings of Christ Church, Oxford* (London, 2020),74. Oxford quickly became dependent on the Canal for the supply of coal and when it was frozen for ten days in 1795 the price locally rose over 200%. Cox, *Recollections*, 20.

266 ENLIGHTENED OXFORD

Since those early days in the 1750s, his intellectual range had increased and his reputation as an outstanding preacher had grown. Horne was neither an administrator nor a scholar of the very first rank, but he was far from being a fumbler, and North acted responsibly in preferring him to the Vice-Chancellorship. His court connections were less extensive than Wetherell's, for Horne was not driven by career ambitions and he relished his home life with his wife and daughters in the President's Lodgings. Jenkinson, by 1776 a major confidant of George III, liked him, and North also saw his worth as a churchman of considerable moral influence. But his impact in governing the University was limited. As one acute observer noted:[80]

> Perhaps there never was a man in a station so reverenced as Dr Horne appears to have been; but his mildness and benevolence – his *leniores virtutes* – were better calculated to acquire the affections than promote the good of our University.

Yet Horne was nothing if not dutiful and he never shirked the need to put his talents to the service of his faith and his University, both of which he believed were being pummelled by a growing number of detractors. Horne was the enemy of the radical Enlightenment in all its manifestations. His latest target was David Hume, whose controversial deathbed in 1776 confirmed the arch-sceptic's lack of faith down to his dying breath, scandalously so as Horne viewed matters, and his riposte humorously made clear his moral objections in *A Letter to Adam Smith... by one of those People called Christians*.[81] The tract was published anonymously to avoid any embarrassment to the University but, had he signed it, it would likely have increased his public recognition. Though not intolerant, Horne shared the reluctance of his predecessors to make concessions to the Dissenters, who made another parliamentary attempt at extracting concessions in 1779, and this time it was rightly predicted that North's government would be unable to prevent Parliament allowing them limited relief from subscription. In the light of the willingness of both Houses to pass a modest measure, Horne cannot be personally blamed for a failure of leadership. The University had sent up a petition against it (that the Premier had supported) and, amid the distractions of the American War of Independence and a Spanish declaration of war, the Vice Chancellor's concern for the well-being and security of the Established Church were judged untimely even by moderates on the bench of bishops.[82]

---

[80] J. James, jnr. to J. Boucher, 19 May 1781, in ed. M. Evans, *Letters of Richard Radcliffe and John James of Queen's College, Oxford 1753–1783* [Oxford Historical Society, 9], (Oxford, 1888), 140.

[81] Nigel Aston, 'Horne and heterodoxy: the defence of Anglican beliefs in the late Enlightenment', *EHR*, 108 (1993), 895–919.; D. C. Rasmussen, *The Infidel and the Professor. David Hume, Adam Smith and the Friendship that shaped Modern Thought* (Princeton, NJ, 2017), 199–214. See also Chapter 4, pp. 81–2.

[82] Ward, *Georgian Oxford*, 273. For the attitude of the bishops, see Martin Fitzpatrick, 'Toleration and truth', *Enlightenment and Dissent*, 1 (1982), 3–31, at 7.

Horne ended his stint in office with some relief, his efforts acknowledged by the award of the deanery of Canterbury in 1781 on Lord North's recommendation.[83]

Horne turned out to be the last Vice Chancellor of the eighteenth century to secure the wider recognition that the award of a plum piece of preferment in the Church of England conferred. It did not help Oxford office holders' prospects that the Chancellor, Lord North, ceased to be head of the Treasury in March 1782 and that his eventual, long-term successor from the end of 1783, Pitt the Younger, was a Cambridge man whose bestowal of ecclesiastical offices depended on the guidance of his former tutor, George Pretyman, Bishop of Lincoln and Dean of St Paul's from 1787.[84] The advancement of the Duke of Portland to the Chancellorship in 1792 gave a new political flavour to appointments. John Wills, the Warden of Wadham College (1783–1806), and Vice Chancellor from 1792 to 1796, was the first (very mild) out-and-out Whig to hold the office for several decades,[85] and took great care to acclaim the Duke's new academic status in accepting his own new dignity:

> Your Grace's Goodness in accepting an office, which must have so great a share in forming the minds & influencing the morals of the rising generation, can not but give pleasure to every Friend of Learning, Order, & Constitutional Principles, throughout the Kingdom.

While holding the Vice-Chancellorship, Wills visited Portland from time to time at his palatial London residence to keep the Duke in touch with the life of the University at second hand, on occasion setting up dining arrangements on behalf of the Heads of Houses and the Proctors with their Chancellor at Burlington House.[86] It was a solid working relationship. Wills naturally endorsed his patron's commitment to the war with Revolutionary France. He did not disappoint expectation as a cheerleader for patriotism in time of war,[87] or clamp down on any activities that looked even mildly seditious: when, in 1794, eleven undergraduates sought to establish a Society for 'Science and Literary Disquisition'

---

[83] Darwall-Smith, 'The monks of Magdalen', 266.

[84] Pitt and Pretyman were nevertheless careful to honour precedents which gave both English universities an approximate balance of numbers when appointments were made to senior offices in the Church. Thus on the death of Bishop Robert Lowth of London in 1787, Pitt, anxious to be fair to Oxford, promised his cousin, the 1st Marquess of Buckingham, that after Pretyman's promotion to Lincoln, William Cleaver should have the next see, which turned out to be Chester. East Suffolk RO, HA 119 (T108/42), Pitt to Pretyman, 4 Nov. 1787; Buckingham to W. W. Grenville, 8 Nov. 1787, HMC, *Fortescue MSS* (3 vols, London, 1892–99), I. 289.

[85] To Portland, 29 Sept. 1792, Balliol College Library, Jenkyns papers, VI.A (2), letter-book of John Wills. Wells, *Wadham College*, 155-5.

[86] Wills to Portland, 20 Nov. 1795, Balliol College Library, Jenkyns papers, VI.A (2), f. 118–19.

[87] Mitchell, 'Politics and Revolution', 188–9. He reassured Portland that 'the sole purposes of our academical Institutions' are the 'maintenance of Order, the Advancement of Learning, and the furtherance of Religion and morality'. To Portland, 25 Sept. 1793, Balliol College Library, Jenkyns papers, VI.A (2), f. 34.

Fig. 6.3 John Wills, Vice-Chancellor and Warden of Wadham College, John Hoppner, oil on canvas, 1792–6 (By kind permission of the Warden and Fellows of Wadham College, Oxford).

(politics and religion would not be discussed) and applied for sanction from Wills and the Proctors, it was ruled that they could only meet in each other's rooms for fear of inciting unrest.[88] Unsavoury characters considered to be of a 'bad character', such as one Monsieur de la Sol, were carefully monitored and, in his case, turned away. Wills reported that: 'In his Lectures with Gownsmen, he was accused of studiously introducing Politicks & endeavouring to inculcate republican Principles, & of treating Religion in general with ridicule, & the Christian with something worse'.[89] This policing was still not enough to win him promotion outside Oxford. Portland, however, did do something for Michael Marlow, President of St John's 1795–1828, and Vice Chancellor in the

---

[88] Thus, Members would later be known as the 'Lunatics.' Wells, *Wadham College*, 155–6. For University authorities working in the 1790s to curb attempts by students to organise themselves in groups or societies see Ellis, *Generational Conflict*, 72–5.

[89] To Thomas Carter (for the attention of Portland), 21 Feb. 1796, Balliol College Library, Jenkyns papers, VI.A (2), f. 132. De la Sol threatened to appeal to the public against Wills but appears not to have done so.

1798 to 1802 quadrennium, when he became Premier in 1807 by securing a prebendal stall at Canterbury.[90]

iii) College heads: the politically well-connected

As vice chancellors were essentially the nominees of the Chancellor, they tended to be academic insiders with some gift—however limited—for administration, as their house headships suggested. Certainly in Arran's time, his vice chancellors were unlikely to be viable candidates for the kind of patronage that would give them much public notice beyond Oxford; whereas those college principals who never became vice chancellor and yet *were* well-connected to the monarch and ministry could turn that status to personal and institutional advantage. The deanery of Christ Church was a particularly prized asset for clerical careerists, frequently leading to an even more prestigious and lucrative destination. Appointment to it was in the gift of the Crown and the 'House' itself was, of course, a royal (re)foundation of Henry VIII's, and the Canons in the Chapter, like the Dean, held office only as a result of their acceptability to the ministry of the day.[91] The nomination of Francis Atterbury, High-Church firebrand, as Henry Aldrich's successor in early 1711, brought Christ Church publicity for all the wrong reasons. On the face of it, his presence there aptly symbolised the triumph of the Tories, who had taken power a year earlier under the loose direction of Robert Harley. Yet through the Oxfordshire landowner and lawyer, Lord Keeper Harcourt, Atterbury was much more beholden to Harley's colleague and rival, Henry St John, (created Viscount Bolingbroke in 1712). The divisions in the 'House' came to reflect those within what turned out to be Queen Anne's last ministry, a deeply unstable, deeply factional period in the history of Christ Church, that riveted attention from way beyond Oxford. In casting himself as a second Cardinal Wolsey, Atterbury found it inherently impossible to avoid a quarrel, as he had done when holding his previous deanery, at Carlisle. Canons and Students at Christ Church both found it impossible to work with someone who was frustrated by the limitations for independent action of a Dean when confronted with capitular resistance; it soon became a priority to move him out of

---

[90] BL Add. MS, 37909, f. 44. Marlow had a reputation as a sporting man with a forceful musical wife. Cox, *Recollections,* 199–200.

[91] Appointments to the eight Christ Church Canonries (two attached to professorships) were plum gifts after 1714 for Whig ministers trying to ensure committed Whigs could be either confirmed or intruded into the University. Thus when Edward Bentham was named canon of the first prebend in 1754 (he also acted as Sub-Dean) it gratified Archbishop Herring, who had told Newcastle the year previously that 'I find the best of our Oxford friends think his Majesty can't do a better thing for that place, than to give this worthy man this particular preferment'. 30 Apr. 1753, BL, Add. MS 32731, f. 395. Within the University they had the standing of heads of Houses. See, generally, Curthoys (3), 129–30.

270 ENLIGHTENED OXFORD

Oxford to a setting where his talents and copious energies could be more evidently on display.[92] That proved to be the bishopric of Rochester and the deanery of Westminster in 1713, causing a collective sigh of relief in the college and much pleasure at his replacement by a more emollient Tory, George Smalridge.[93]

Like so many eighteenth-century Deans, Smalridge held Christ Church in commendam (in conjunction) with the bishopric of Bristol, an under-endowed see but nevertheless one whose possession conferred additional laurels on a dean of Christ Church and gave him a platform in the House of Lords.[94] Smalridge's modest hopes of becoming Archbishop of Canterbury were wrecked by Thomas Tenison's longevity (d. 1715) and the change of ministry in 1714,[95] and his conscientious, moderate Toryism, on display in his refusal to sign the declaration of his brother bishops condemning the Jacobite rising of 1715-16, placed him permanently on the political sidelines, and cost him his post as Lord High Almoner.[96] Such marks of royal favour would thereafter, for half a century, be reserved to conformist court Whigs including, indeed, his immediate successor, the intelligent and able Hugh Boulter, a man of trenchant anti-Jacobite convictions recommended by Bishop Edmund Gibson of Lincoln. He also received the see of Bristol as part of the Whig leader, Lord Sunderland's, drive to strengthen the party's presence in the House of Lords.[97] Boulter disappointed his Whig sponsors, including Lord Townshend, by doing little to strengthen that same interest in Oxford.[98] As it was reported:

---

[92] Curthoys (1), 147–53; Bennett, *Tory Crisis*, 143–60, 168–72; Ward, *Georgian Oxford*, 45–6, 49. 'Students' at Christ Church were members of the foundation and the approximate equivalent of Fellows elsewhere.

[93] The anti-Atterburian canon, William Stratford, thus reported the news to his pupil Lord Harley: 'Upon the report here of what Lord Chancellor had said to Blechingden [his chaplain, Richard Blechinden, later first Provost of Worcester College] when he asked him whether he had been to ask blessing of the new bishop [i.e. Atterbury], White, the censor, and some others threw up their caps in the quadrangle and huzza'd to a new dean. Some of the present Dean's friends got together upon it; much bickering there was, but no blows'. 9 June 1713, *HMC*, Portland MSS, VII. 138–9. See also Chapter 8, pp. 72–3.

[94] The see of Bristol has been wryly described as 'for most of the eighteenth century...almost a pocket borough of Christ Church'. Bill, *Education at Christ Church*, 54.

[95] His principal advocate was one of the few Tories in the government between 1714 and 1716, the veteran statesman Daniel Finch, 2nd Earl of Nottingham. See his anonymous memo 'Ye approaching death of Archbp Tenison' [1715], Leicestershire, Leicester, and Rutland Record Office, Finch Papers, D57, Box 4765, ecc. 6.

[96] Bill, *Education at Christ Church*, 44. Despite the disfavour of George I and his minister, Smalridge was supported by the King's daughter-in-law, Princess Caroline. To his credit, he preserved his stance as the most judicious senior Tory in Oxford down to his death.

[97] Graham M. Townend, 'The Political career of the 3rd Earl of Sunderland', (Edinburgh Ph.D. thesis, 1985), 268. For Boulter's anti-Jacobite leanings see his *Foundation of Submission to our Governors Considered: A Sermon Preached at St Olave's, Southwark, 26 November, 1715* (London, 1715), 20, in which 'James III' was denounced as the 'popish bigotted Pretender'.

[98] Canon Stratford had predicted as much on Smalridge's demise: 'Whoever comes will not make many converts among the present set, and it may require more time than may come to his share to raise up a new generation. I fear more for the Chapter than the students. Some of our brethren are old and dropping. I am likely to be here in a comfortable post'. To Lord Harley, 5 Oct. 1719, *HMC*, Portland MSS, VII. 261.

the bishop tho' a zealous Whig carries himself so well both at the University and at Bristol that he is very well esteemed by the Tories at both places. His endeavour is by gentleness and all the fair ways possible to win the affection of everyone to the present establishment.[99]

Boulter left Christ Church in 1724 for a bigger prize in Ireland: the archbishopric of Armagh.[100] As the followers of Robert Harley, like senior canon Dr William Stratford, died off in the 1720s, party divisions continued to soften. The Christ Church chapter was steadily appropriated by tepid Whigs acceptable to the Walpole administration who could be expected to stand up for its interests within the University.[101] Dean John Conybeare (rector of Exeter College from 1730 until he moved to the House in 1733) neatly embodied this new profile, one that he attempted to associate with unimpeachable religious orthodoxy through, for instance, his comprehensive reply to Tindal's *Christianity as old as the Creation* in 1732. That text was dedicated to his main patron Edmund Gibson, by that date the Bishop of London and the most politically significant member of the hierarchy.[102] It was thanks to Gibson's backing that this distinguished if unexciting theologian was awarded the Deanery in 1733. The Bishop of London's fall from Walpole's favour as main adviser on ecclesiastical preferment later put the brakes on Conybeare's fervent hopes of a bishopric, and it was not until 1750 that he was able to supplement the income of Christ Church with the meagre revenues of Bristol.[103]

Conybeare was arguably the outstanding Whig presence in Oxford in George II's reign. He turned Christ Church into a bastion of Hanoverian loyalism, 'an almost exclusive club of ministerial Whiggism',[104] and that status continued into the post-1760 era when Tories took a full part in the work of monarchical consolidation. William Markham, a former headmaster of Westminster and governor to George, Prince of Wales (later George IV), combined the Deanery with the Bishopric of Chester, and left both in 1776 for the Archbishopric of York;[105] his successor, Lewis Bagot, (the first Tory Dean since Smalridge) held it in conjunction with the See of Bristol before resigning both on promotion to

---

[99] Egmont to William Perceval, 3 Mar. 1722, BL Add MS. 47029, f. 109–10.

[100] His successor as Dean, William Bradshaw (1671–1732), was also bishop of Bristol. His was an unfortunate name borne by a regicide, which his critics did not hesitate to invoke. See Chapter 7, p. 66.

[101] Ward, *Georgian Oxford*, 108.   [102] Lalor, *Matthew Tindal*, 128–31.

[103] It was a belated recognition of Conybeare's service in supporting the Whig interest.

BL Add MS 32721, ff. 424–5, Herring to Newcastle, 22 July 1750; Add MS 32722, ff. 63–4, T. Secker to Newcastle, 7 Aug. 1750. For some highlights of his career see Ward, *Georgian Oxford*, 137–8, 180; Bill, *Education at Christ Church*, 51–4.

[104] Ward, *Georgian Oxford*, 141.

[105] Markham's work commitment kept him away from Christ Church with what became embarrassing conspicuousness. One undergraduate complained—a touch harshly—of the 'neglect of all order' that followed from 'the absence of our Dean, the Bishop of Chester, who is so much taken up with his royal Pupil that we are favoured with very little of his Company. One would think that in such a situation he would give it up, however he does not seem to be the least inclined that way at present

272   ENLIGHTENED OXFORD

Norwich in 1783. He was replaced by the outstanding figure of Cyril Jackson, Dean from 1783 to 1809, who refused all offers of a mitre and, instead, used his position and his gifts for discreet leadership as Dean to maximise the influence of Christ Church at the highest levels of the British state (and across the University) during the French Revolutionary and Napoleonic Wars. Jackson had no wish to win a public name for himself but he was deeply respected by those who had been educated at the House in his time, for he had offered them, gentleman commoners and noblemen included, the future leaders of the country, a better-than-average higher education.[106] Jackson even won a rare compliment from the Greek scholar, pedagogue, and Foxite, Samuel Parr, in 1800:[107]

> I have long thought, and often declared, that the highest station in the church would not be more than an adequate reward for Cyril Jackson ... he has qualities of head and heart to adorn the primacy of all England, and to protect all the substantial interests of the English church.

Jackson was exceptional in his connection to government circles in George III's time, mainly through the respect he commanded with former pupils, including George Canning and William Wickham;[108] such access to ministers had not been known at Christ Church since Atterbury's troubled time at the Deanery when his behaviour had limited his usefulness to the Harley administration. Jackson was run close by William Cleaver, the Principal of Brasenose from 1785 to 1809 and from 1787 Bishop of Chester (later translated to Bangor (1800) and St Asaph (1806)).[109] Cleaver had taught Pitt's cousins, the Grenville brothers, in the 1770s,[110] and both of them protected their former tutor in later decades, mainly via the good offices of William, Lord Grenville, Foreign Secretary from 1791 to 1801.[111] Pitt's Cabinet could rely on Jackson and William Cleaver working quietly but sedulously for the interests of the government in Oxford and took seriously

---

until he gets a better Bishopric; while in the mean time Ch. Ch. dwindles away in numbers & seems much on the decay from no other apparent cause than his neglect of it'. Sir David Carnegie to John Mackenzie Esq., 11 Apr. 1772, MS 1248, f. 84, NLS Delvine Papers [Earl of Southesk].

[106] For more on Jackson's ministerial connections, see this chapter, pp. 25–6.

[107] Quoted in Clarke, *The Georgian era: memoirs of the most eminent persons, who have flourished in Great Britain, from the accession of George the First to the demise of George the Fourth* (4 vols., London, 1832–4), I. 515.

[108] There are many references to Jackson in *The Letter-Journal of George Canning, 1793–1795*, ed. Peter Jupp [Camden, 4th series, 41] (London, 1991). For Wickham see Durey, *William Wickham*. He acted as Grenville's electoral agent in the 1809 contest for the Chancellorship against Lord Eldon and the 6th Duke of Beaufort. Ibid., 194.

[109] The younger Cleaver brother was Euseby, bishop of Ferns and then archbishop of Dublin in Ireland, who looked more to Charles, 3rd Earl of Egremont at Petworth as his patron. Both tutor and student were Christ Church graduates. Bill, *Education at Christ Church*, 232.

[110] *Grenville Papers*, IV. 257. For Cleaver as the energetic Principal of Brasenose, see Crook, *Brasenose*, 161–2.

[111] For Lord Grenville's influence on the 1787 and 1800 promotions see James J. Sack, *The Grenvillites, 1801–29. Party Politics and Factionalism in the Age of Pitt and Liverpool* (Urbana, IL, 1979), 82. See also this chapter, p. 40, n. 85.

Fig. 6.4 Bishop William Cleaver, John Hoppner, oil on canvas, 1800 (Reproduced with the kind permission of the Principal and Fellows of the King's Hall and College of Brasenose in Oxford).

the recommendations from these College Heads regarding the talent and capacities of graduates desirous of attracting the attention of ministers.[112] By the late 1790s Grenville was evincing interest in the welfare and revitalisation of the Church of England, a concern that led him in time to offer himself as a candidate for the Chancellorship on Portland's death in 1809.[113] Among other turn-of-the-century prelates, William Cleaver was foremost in nurturing these

---

[112] It did not always operate in the opposite direction. In 1795 Jackson was grumbling to Portland about the calibre of appointments to Christ Church canonries. Nottingham University Library, Portland papers, PlC 51/5/1, 15 Mar. 1795. And he does not seem to have thought much of Pretyman personally. 23 Oct. 1794 NUL, PwF 5765/1: 23 Oct. 1794. See Reider Payne, 'George Pretyman, bishop of Lincoln, and the University of Cambridge 1787–1801', http://theclergydatabase.org.uk/cce_a3-html/ for hints of a perceived tendency of Pitt and Pretyman to neglect Oxford University. Cf. this chapter, p. 40, n. 85.

[113] See this chapter, p. 25, and associated correspondence in BL Add MSS, 59001–3. John Randolph (his former tutor at Christ Church), Henry Bathurst, Charles Moss, and Edward Vernon were other Oxford-educated prelates of the 1800s who looked to Grenville and vice versa. ed. C. Stray, *Oxford classics: Teaching and Learning, 1800–2000* (Oxford, 2007), 32.

274 ENLIGHTENED OXFORD

inclinations despite being unable to endorse Grenville's willingness to back Catholic Emancipation.[114]

Cleaver was a High Churchman who had, shortly before his death in 1815, drifted into becoming a pro-Tory supporter of Lord Liverpool's administration in the Lords.[115] In an earlier age, when most Oxford Tories were vulnerable to accusations of Jacobitism, most college heads could never aspire to a bishopric. Many simply settled down to enjoy their patrimony without risking political retaliation from the Whig interest and made their peace as best they could. Thus Richard Newton, Principal of Hart Hall from 1710, then best classified as a "Whimsical Tory" (one of those unequivocally committed to the Hanoverian Succession),[116] subordinated all other considerations to securing full collegiate incorporation for the Hall. For this he needed an endowment, a royal charter, and the endorsement of his most celebrated alumnus, Henry Pelham (Premier, 1743–54).[117] After a protracted struggle, he succeeded in 1740 when a charter was granted and Hertford College was formed with himself as its first Principal. Newton remained an ally of the Pelhams, and wrote against the Tory interest in the University for the last few years of his life.[118] He was one of the keenest academic reformers in the University of his generation.

By contrast, Dr William King, the equally long-lived Principal of St Mary Hall (1717–63), was neither whimsical nor any friend to the Pelhams. He was a maverick power broker in the Tory interest as secretary to Lord Arran for the first half of George I's reign, before his determination to stand as a candidate for a University seat in the General Election of 1722 made former allies desert him. King slowly returned from the sidelines as an academic politician in the 1740s, as yet steadfast in his Jacobitism. That commitment wavered in the next decade and he began to place his hopes in the young Prince George of Wales (later George III) as a future sovereign who might reasonably be expected to end what King viewed as the corrupt Whig oligarchy that had kept power exclusively in its own hands for much too long. After 1760, everything changed, but it was too late for him to benefit personally. In his prime, King creatively opted to channel his energies into

---

[114] Sack, The Grenvillites, 120.

[115] For Cleaver's political tergiversations between 1805 and 1815 see ibid., 104–5, 162, 221n.

[116] Robson, The Oxfordshire Election, 173. Newton had a reputation among some alumni as a (respected) disciplinarian, Private Thoughts on Religion, ... extracted from the diary of the Rev. Thomas Adam, ed. James Stillingfleet, (2nd edn., York, 1795), iii.

[117] Pelham matriculated at Hart Hall in 1710, having been recruited from Westminster School by Newton (who had been his personal tutor earlier in life in his father's [Thomas, 1st Lord Pelham of Laughton] household). Henry followed Newton after the latter's appointment at Hart Hall 'for the purpose of continuing his studies under the superintendence of so able an instructor'. William Coxe, Memoirs of the Administration of the Right Honourable Henry Pelham... (2 vols., London, 1829), I. 6–7; S. G. Hamilton, Hertford College (London, 1903), 41. His brother Thomas Pelham-Holles, 1st Duke of Newcastle, was at Clare Hall, Cambridge (University Chancellor from 1748) and Newton was naturally no less desirous of the duke's support.

[118] S. G. Hamilton, 'Dr Newton and Hertford College', in ed. M. Burrows, Collectanea, 3rd Ser., (Oxford, 1896), 285–6; Hamilton, Hertford College, 41–63; Ward, Georgian Oxford, 143–5.

literary composition using Latin to mock his adversaries; he also gained a reputation for daring polemic in the press that brought him quite a following beyond Oxford, (even if he often discretely veiled his authorship).[119]

King was a divisive presence in and beyond Oxford. A more temperate post-Revolution Tory, Thomas Turner, President of Corpus Christi College (1688–1714), won respect from a wide range of views because of his government of his college and his unwillingness to court the powerful. Despite his Nonjuring sympathies, he was 'too wary a man to enter into an open opposition of anyone unless the occasion should be very extraordinary'.[120] As a prebend of St Paul's, his official presence when in residence in the City of London afforded a personal point of contact between the University and the merchants that could improve their better mutual understanding at a time when Tories were disquieted by the rise of the 'monied interest'. Turner had his Whig counterparts as college heads in the eighteenth century though, certainly before 1760, a majority of them felt obliged to counteract Tory preponderance with overt demonstrations of loyalty to the new monarchical order in the state. This posturing served to confirm their own importance to ministers, counteracted any impression that the University was an unqualified nest of Toryism, and encouraged Whig families across Britain to send their sons to Oxford.

Whig efforts to intrude their supporters could be aggressive and attracted press attention. At Whiggish Merton, where the final choice of three candidates as Warden was the Archbishop of Canterbury's as the College's Visitor, one of the strongest Whigs in Oxford, John Holland, was elected in 1709.[121] His controversial attempt, in cooperation with other fellows of his persuasion, to fill six vacant fellowships exclusively with other Whigs in 1716 delighted the pro-Hanoverian press, a true display of 'English Spirit' according to *The Flying Post* of 12 March.[122] Like him or loathe him, Holland was a fixture in early Georgian Oxford. Some of his contemporaries looked on a College Headship as just another piece of patronage accrued and left when they received a better offer. This was the case with

[119] Greenwood, *William King, passim*; W. King, *Political and Literary anecdotes,*, 150–1; Money, *The English Horace*, 201–2. For Anglican interest in the press, see J. Black, *The English Press in the Eighteenth Century* (London, 1987), 250.

[120] Stratford to Edward, Lord Harley, 2 Sept. 1711, *HMC*, Portland MSS, VII. 53; Narcissus Luttrell, *A Brief Historical Relation of state affairs, from September 1678 to April 1714* (6 vols., Oxford, 1857), V. 201. For a summary of his career see Charles-Edwards and Reid, *Corpus Christi College*, 206–15, 223–3. His elder brother, Francis Turner, bishop of Ely, refused the oaths to William and Mary, was deprived, and spent much of the 1690s hidden by Thomas at Oxford. Despite some uncertainty, Thomas Turner did take the oaths. ibid., 212–13.

[121] Martin and Highfield, *Merton College*, 237–9; B. W. Henderson, *Merton College* (London, 1899), 153–4. Its members were disparagingly cast by their political enemies as 'Lollards' for their allegiance, evoking (unfavourable) academic memories of the reformist, anti-sacerdotal Wycliffites of the early fifteenth century. John Holland, matric. Magdalen Hall, 1682; Proctor, 1700; Fellow of Merton, 1691; Warden, 1709–34; chaplain to the king and canon of Salisbury, 1716, and of Worcester, 1723. https://www.british-history.ac.uk/alumni-oxon/1500-1714/pp706-747.

[122] Merton elections to fellowships in the 1720s were further complicated by Whig fault lines over attitudes pro and con in relation to Bishop Hoadly and the Bangorian Controversy. Ward, *Georgian Oxford*, 99–103.

276 ENLIGHTENED OXFORD

William Baker, a client of the 1st Duke of Marlborough, who overcame Tory opposition within Wadham College to be elected Warden in 1719. He was a confirmed Whig but, already holding posts as Archdeacon of Oxford (from 1715), Rector of St Giles-in-the-Fields, London, and chaplain to George I on his Hanover progresses, his sights were set unwaveringly on a mitre. It duly materialised in 1723 when Baker was named to the see of Bangor, and he resigned as Warden.[123]

As previously noted, it was John Conybeare who was in the front line of efforts to expand Whig interests in Oxford. Before he went to Christ Church, he had dedicated himself similarly at Exeter, and kept an eye on it after his move.[124] Francis Webber, Principal of Exeter from 1750 to 1771, was friend and protégé of Conybeare, kept his college steadfastly loyal to the Whig cause, and endorsed it with some aggressive pamphleteering. For both services (and for his part in managing the 'New Interest' in the 1754 Election) he received the Deanery of Hereford in 1756.[125] Deaneries and bishoprics therefore were conditionally available to Oxford men between 1714 and 1760—so long as one was a Whig.[126] At the inception of the new order, in 1715, one who was barely describable as such, John Wynne, the Principal of Jesus, received the See of St Asaph, largely as a concession to his patron Sir Roger Mostyn, 3rd Bt. (1673-1739), the son-in-law of Daniel, Earl of Nottingham, the Hanoverian Tory then in government as Lord President of the Council. Wynne had been the most moderate of Harleyites before 1714; afterwards, he trimmed with his patron, received his reward, and became a reliable prop in Oxford of the new order.[127] Wynne's career trajectory in Hanoverian Oxford summarises *in nuce* the path to ministerial favour that was expected in Whitehall and St James's. It says much that Wynne was one of only three Heads of House who wanted to send a loyal address on the King's safe return from one of his regular excursions to Hanover.[128]

iv) Tutors and parents

Public recognition, even celebrity of an Oxonian, beyond the University might also come from the patronage of a powerful pupil. A relationship that might begin

---

[123] Ibid., 104-5.

[124] His immediate successor as Rector in 1737, James Edgcumbe (1705-50), continued, in a minor key, Conybeare's defence of orthodoxy and helped thereby to associate it (and Exeter College) with mainstream Whig allegiance. J. Foster, *Alumni Oxonienses, the members of the University of Oxford, 1715-1886*...(4 vols., Oxford and London, 1887-8), II. 407. Conybeare's capacity for nurturing younger controversialists such as Edgcumbe and Leonard Twells (DD, 1740) would repay further research. For the latter see ed. Linnell, *The Diaries of Thomas Wilson*, 57.

[125] *Biographia Britannica*, eds. W. Oldys and A. Kippis (6 vols., London, 1747-66), IV. 92; Robson, *The Oxfordshire Election*, 164-5; Ward, *Georgian Oxford*, 204.

[126] See Chapter 7.

[127] He was Principal from 1712 to 1720. W. Gibson, 'A Welsh bishop for a Welsh see: John Wynne of St Asaph', *The Journal of Welsh Ecclesiastical History*, 1 (1984), 28-43.

[128] Abel Boyer, ed., *The Political state of Great Britain* (60 vols., London, 1711-40), XIII. 235-6.

as one of tutor and student could mutate in time into one of client and patron and even the projection of one who had started as a don into the life of the state. With the majority of University figures frozen out by their Toryism from royal and official patronage prior to 1760, that offered them by individual peers and gentlemen assumed an unprecedented significance. An ambitious college fellow who acted as a tutor to a nobleman or gentleman commoner while the latter was resident thereby supplemented his income, enhanced his prospects of receiving a living faster than his colleagues waiting for college preferment, and might have opportunities to cut a more prominent figure on the public stage through his association with his former pupil than colleagues who remained behind in Oxford. So much depended on ministerial survival and, in this regard, the consignment of the Tory party to permanent opposition for two generations after 1714 wrecked or reduced the career hopes of those who had been educating the sons of those who came to power in the political upheaval of 1710. Dr William Stratford, Canon of Christ Church, and Robert Harley's chaplain when he was a secretary of state (1704–08), taught the latter's eldest son, Edward, Lord Harley, when his father was Lord Treasurer. For all that Stratford acted (with Francis Gastrell) as one of 'the great man's agents' in Oxford,[129] his dutifulness brought Stratford no benefits in further ascending the hierarchical ladder: Lord Oxford was impeached after the death of Anne and Lord Harley never immersed himself in active Tory politics.

Tutor and pupil would in most cases get to know each other well while the younger man was an Oxford undergraduate. Thus Stratford's relationship with Lord Harley evolved from a tutorial one into an avuncular, gossipy friendship. Like and respect could bloom on both sides and constitute lifelong memories— good and bad.[130] Bishop John Douglas recalled in his autobiographical notes under the year 1738 that George Drake, Fellow of Balliol, an active teacher, Dean, and Bursar, was one 'whom I shall always have an affectionate Rememberance of as I profitted much by his superintending my studies'.[131] Tutors, generally not much older than the students and waiting for a benefice to fall vacant, were likely to be informally in company with them, sometimes dining together or riding out into the country. A typical tutor might on average have half a dozen pupils in his care, seeing them each perhaps twice a week,[132] but singling out a nobleman or gentleman commoner for special notice was both appropriate and irresistible. It may have been a counsel of perfection, but there was a working presumption that if tutor and parents coordinated their efforts in forming the

---

[129] Bennett, *Tory Crisis*, 144.

[130] Patrons could be generous in acknowledging what they owed their tutors. For example Arthur Onslow's didactic autobiography (written *c*.1760) emphasised his tutor's 'more than ordinary pains with me' between 1708 and 1710 despite deficiencies in his own studies. HMC, *Onslow MSS* (London, 1895), pt ix, 2, n. 8.

[131] BL Egerton MS. 2181, f.6. Douglas, a Scotsman, attended Balliol College, MA, 1743.

[132] Jones, *Balliol*, 142–4, gives the example of Jeremiah Milles, Fellow after 1697, Vicar of Duloe, Cornwall, 1705–46, based on Balliol College MS 461, his diary for 1701–2.

278 ENLIGHTENED OXFORD

young man in question, then the time and the cost would all have been worth-while. Or, as Cyril Jackson expressed it, writing *c*.1768 to Lady Charlotte Finch about her son, George:[133]

> I wd hope that we shall all go hand in hand together towards forming him in every particular—that we may have the satisfaction of seeing him hereafter step forth into the world completely finish'd in every respect as a good man, a scholar, & a Gentleman—this cannot be the work of any one person; & if we do not all cooperate, we must necessarily hinder one another—'

Failure to abide by any educational stipulations offered by a powerful father could damage any don's prospects of worldly progress. When the princely 1st Duke of Chandos presented his son and heir, John, Earl of Carnarvon, aged fourteen, to Balliol College, he told the boy's tutor that Carnarvon was to receive 'a thorough knowledge of the excellency of our Ecclesiastical constitution'. Nothing was to be allowed 'in his way which may lead him to think amiss of our happy Establishment in State', so he would in time emerge a 'Strict Churchman, and a Sincere Friend to our present settlement'.[134] Carnarvon was pulled out after eighteen months and no one gained immediately at Balliol from his brief presence.[135] On occasion, a tutor (acting in effect as a domestic 'bear-leader') was intruded into Oxford by a family who had paid for him to accompany his pupil, with all parties anxious not to disrupt a relationship that could have all-round advantages. Thus the Scot David Mallet, while still mixing with his London acquaintances, attended Oxford with his pupil, James Newsham, as a gentleman commoner.[136] The position changed somewhat during the middle and later decades of the century, when the trend was for only two Fellows at most who would act as tutor in a single college, and would usually act together, so that a tutor in a large College (or a successful tutor like William Scott at University College) could have at least two dozen students under his control at any one time. That did not, of course, preclude other Fellows from privately assuming a supervisory role of an undergraduate in response to a parental request.

Some tutors accepted an invitation to leave the University, either temporarily or permanently, to accompany their charges on the Grand Tour after graduation.

---

[133] LLRRO, DG7 Box 4953 Bundle 31/62. Jackson had just returned to Oxford from London as a guest of Lady Charlotte and her family. In this letter he quoted Montesquieu about the three key influences on a boy: his father, his mother, and the world.

[134] Jones, *Balliol*, 154; Joan Johnson, *Princely Chandos. James Brydges 1674–1744* (Stroud, 1984), 82–3. Joseph Hunt, Senior Fellow, Master after 1722, was named tutor to Carnarvon for a fee of £200. Jones, *Balliol*, 140.

[135] Lord Carnarvon's capacity for undistracted study appears to have been limited and his father, the Duke, was vexed that his heir, as a gentleman commoner, did not dine as a matter of course at High Table as he had done at New College in the early 1690s. Johnson, *Princely Chandos*, 82–3.

[136] James Newsham, matric. St Mary Hall, 1736, aet. 19. Foster, III. 1018.

OXFORD PERSONNEL 279

Those in that category could include professors. Thus Joseph Spence, Professor of Poetry from 1728, made three journeys to the Continent, but returned afterwards to the University and his other preferments. His second Tour, to the Low Countries and France as governor to John Morley Trevor (1716–43), led to his receiving in 1754 a prebend of Durham from its Bishop, Richard Trevor, John Morley Trevor's cousin.[137] Leading a young milord on a Tour could be the beginning of a lifelong connection, as between Thomas Townson, Fellow of Magdalen, and William Drake (the elder) of Shardloes in Buckinghamshire (1722–96), later MP for Amersham. Here clientage turned into amity in a manner that brought Townson into convivial contact with any number of Midlands families that had a Tory past, including the Bagots, Norths, Legges, and Newdigates.[138] Hospitality was invariably on offer to tutors like Townson, who could converge independently on the same country house. Thus, in 1757, when Townson called at Arbury Hall, Newdigate's seat in Warwickshire, he found another Fellow of Magdalen, his brother-in-law, Dr Thomas Winchester,[139] already taking his ease:

> It was a week before I could disingage the Doctor [Winchester] from the enchantments of Molly Coneyers, and get him to Blithfield; where however he found abundance of fair ladies, beside those of the family, to console him; Lady Dartmouth, Lady North, and the two Miss Legges, the latter of whom endeavour'd to sooth his sorrow with an Italian song excellently sung.[140]

The number of chaplaincies in the hands of individual peers was formidable and staying thus in the entourage of a grandee was an odds-on path to securing a head start in the preferment stakes.[141] A tutor who chose to remain in Oxford to pursue his ambitions might also look to a powerful ex-student for protection, especially when that pupil's interest in the University remained formidable. Such was the case for William Denison of University College, who had been tutor there to

---

[137] John Morley Trevor (1716–43), matric. Ch. Ch., 1734; MP Lewes, 1738–43; Commsr. of the Admiralty, 1742–3. Foster, IV. 1438. For Spence's convivial, educative relationship with the Earl of Middlesex of Ch. Ch. (heir to the 1st Duke of Dorset), on tour together 1730–3, see Spence, *Observations*, I. xxvi-vii.

[138] See Nigel Aston, 'Thomas Townson'.

[139] Winchester's career is a reminder that a tutor that did not always derive benefit from propinquity to his charges. Gibbon was briefly Winchester's pupil and thought little of him: '[Winchester] well remembered that he had a salary to receive, and only forgot that he had a duty to perform. Instead of guiding the studies, and watching over the behaviour of his disciple, I was never summoned to attend even the ceremony of a lecture; and, excepting one voluntary visit to his rooms, during the eight months of his titular office, the tutor and the pupil lived in the same college as strangers to each other'. *Memoirs*, 83. For a salutary, balanced corrective of Winchester see Ian Doolittle, 'William Blackstone, Edward Gibbon and Thomas Winchester: The Case for an Oxford Enlightenment', in eds. W. Prest and A. Page, *Blackstone and his Critics*, (London, 2018), 59–75, at 62–8, 75.

[140] Townson to Drake, Blithfield 5 Oct. 1757, Magdalen College, Oxford, Drake MSS, D/DR/8/16. Mary [Molly] Conyers (d. 1797) was the unmarried sister of Newdigate's first wife, Sophy, and also his tenant and neighbour. White, ed., *Newdigate Correspondence*, 288n.

[141] See William Gibson, *A Social History of the Domestic Chaplain* (Leicester, 1997).

280 ENLIGHTENED OXFORD

Henry, 3rd Duke of Beaufort (and his brother, Lord Noel Somerset MP, later 4th Duke),[142] the great-nephews of Ormond and Arran. Denison's bid to become Master of University College after Charlett's death in 1722 was acrimoniously contested and resulted in complicated litigation that gave neither Denison nor the Duke anything to show for it.[143] Denison had to wait until 1745 for a headship, when Lord Arran nominated him as Principal of Magdalen Hall.[144] Throughout that interval, the Somerset brothers stood by him, with Denison on the lookout for preferment, and quick to bring it to ducal attention. When the opening at Magdalen Hall appeared he wrote, with some slight presumption, to Lord Noel:

> ...I shall accept of it [the Principalship] with some pleasure, & with a due sense of gratitude to my Lord Duke & you for applying to the Chancellor on my behalf, & getting me a promise from him of the first Hall that should become vacant.[145]

Denison betrayed his desperation in ending with a not-so-gentle nudge to Lord Noel to remind Lord Arran of his promise if necessary. It is a reminder of how quickly some clients expected their supporters to jump when the moment to swoop on an office arrived.

Similarly, well-placed former pupils could rally to a tutor whom they suspected had been unfairly treated and exert pressure if the matter came to the notice of ministers. The Whig Richard Meadowcourt, Fellow of Merton College, was the subject of a steady stream of criticism within Oxford for his defence of the government in Walpole's time, including one that 'he had wrongfully aspers'd the University in relation to their Behaviour in the Excise Riot'.[146] Spencer Cowper, future Dean of Durham, who had known him for six years, insisted on his character as a good man and

> As a Tutor I think I can safely answer for his Care, I never saw him one day but he had some one or other of his Pupils with him, and generaly the greatest Part

---

[142] The 3rd Duke matriculated aged just 13 in 1720. Denison had also been 'a sort of governor to him at Westminster'. Stratford to Ld Harley, 26 Oct. 1720, *HMC*, Portland MSS, VII. 280. William Denison (d. 1756) matric. University College, 1693; BA, 1697; MA, 1700; Proctor, 1710; BD, 1715. https://www.british-history.ac.uk/alumni-oxon/1500-1714/pp366-405.
  Rector of several Hampshire benefices, Clanfield, 1736–56; rector of Chalton with Idsworth, 1736–56. CCEd Person ID: 92871.
[143] After a long judicial process, Denison was obliged to yield up the Mastership in 1729. Darwall-Smith, *University College*, 247–59, observes that the great Mastership dispute left the College 'in a wretched condition', ibid., 259; Ward, *Georgian Oxford*, 114–16.
[144] He held it until 1755 when his son succeeded him. Hamilton, *Hertford College*, 126, 155–86.
[145] Oxford, 17 Jan. 1744, Badminton Muniments, FmJ 2/34, f.10. Denison's plan was for Lord Noel to send on the nomination form to the Chancellor for his signature and then its return to him. Denison to Somerset, 22 Jan. 1744, ibid., f. 11.
[146] For his letter to Charles Delafaye, Under-Secretary of State, see William Coxe, *Memoirs of the Life and Administration of Sir Robert Walpole* (3 vols., 1798), III. 137.

spent their evenings in his Company, and for his Learning or abilityes I never yet heard either call'd in question.[147]

Ministers took Meadowcourt's side and he was awarded a canonry of Worcester in 1734. His fate showed that government patronage could occasionally manifest itself when private patronal possibilities faded. Nevertheless, the tutor-student relationship locked senior University members into what, if it was functional, would yield benefits on both sides. It was an informal marker of the University's association with lay and clerical members of the elite. At a formal level, that was also incorporated into the College Visitatorial system.

v) College Visitors and college affairs

Eighteenth-century Oxford was a more litigious university than Cambridge (certainly down to the mid-century) and, when it did attract extensive outside notice, it could be through journalistic reports of personal contestation rather than additions to learning. The phenomenon may be in part explained because of fewer opportunities for patronage elsewhere until the 1760s, so something like a College Headship became fought for that more keenly. When College Heads and fellows could not settle their own affairs, resort was frequently made to higher authority, usually the College Visitor, who acted as a final court of appeal. The Visitor held a prestigious title that conferred on him both patronage and juridical rights within Oxford that ensured the office kept its currency throughout the century. And the powers it conferred offered scope for some sort of protection against perceived ministerial aggression. The aging Bishop Trelawny of Winchester, in the early years of George I's reign, considered that moderate Tories like himself who happened to be College Visitors, could guard the University against the reformist intentions of the Stanhope-Sunderland ministry, for Visitors 'have power enough to make a terrifying example of all free talkers...', be they Jacobites or 'free-thinkers'.[148]

Visitors had the last word on a college's internal affairs and could determine how open it was to external influences, such as in accessibility to and eligibility for fellowships. In the course of the century, the more daring among them were prepared to make imaginative, even creative interpretation of a college's statutes, often dating from the Middle Ages. Such an exercise lay at the heart of how to

---

[147] S. Cowper to 2nd Earl Cowper, Exeter College, 23 Oct. 1735, *Letters of Spencer Cowper Dean of Durham 1746–74*, ed. Edward Hughes, [Surtees Society, vol. clxv] (Durham/London, 1956), 4.

[148] On that basis, he implored Archbishop Wake not to support the legislation ministers were known to be preparing (he was responding to a paper on the state of St John's College that Wake had sent him). To Wake, 17 Feb. 1717, quoted in Costin, *St John's College*, 173. See Chapter 8 for these planned incursive reforms.

282 ENLIGHTENED OXFORD

make 'ancien régime' Oxford work most effectively in the current age, but it was, by definition, contentious, and it increased the likelihood of the Visitor being dragged into the public gaze for the wrong reason. Beyond him lay the public courts of law. To resort to them could be a disruptive, expensive process from which no one emerged with much credit,[149] George Clarke, for one, was so annoyed at an expensive lawsuit and an appeal to the Visitor at All Souls over Hawksmoor designs to be funded by himself and the duke of Wharton that, in his bequest to Worcester College, he inserted a special clause against any resort to the Visitor(s) in an appeal from the election of a fellow 'to avoid the shameful and unnecessary expenses which I have seen some Visitors put some Colleges to upon such occasions'.[150] Similarly, in some other colleges, incoming fellows were asked to take an oath not to appeal against internal decisions.[151]

The legitimacy and reach of Visitatorial powers had been confirmed in a judicial decision of the House of Lords in 1694. The case of Phillips v. Bury determined that university jurisdiction was a branch of ecclesiastical law so that the Court of King's Bench had no right to extend its jurisdiction into that area.[152] The vindication of the rights of the Bishop of Exeter aroused interest in Europe, where the Protestant juridicist, Pierre Jurieu, claimed that Bishop Trelawny had done more to combat latitudinarianism in Holland than anyone else. The Bishop himself, in having Visitors' rights secured by a judicial judgment of the country's highest court, had also struck a decisive blow for the preservation of orthodoxy in Oxford at a time when anticlericalism among Whig common lawyers was marked.[153]

Collegiate harmony was unlikely when the Visitor's politics and preferences were calculated to set him on a collision course with a senior governing body. The chances of that happening were quite high when a Visitor of a Tory college was a Whig prelate. Party politics inevitably obtruded and was particularly vicious in the first quarter of the century. There was a ferocious contest in 1703 for the Wardenship of New College, between Thomas Braithwaite and Charles Trimnell, ex-tutor to Marlborough's son-in-law, the Junto Whig 3rd Earl of Sunderland. A technicality over procedures devolved the decision to Bishop Peter Mews of Winchester; counsel on both sides appeared before him and he

---

[149] The cause célèbre was the Bury Affair involving Exeter College and Trelawny (then Bishop of Exeter) as its Visitor in the early 1690s when efforts were underway to remove Bury from his Rectorship. See Chapter 2, pp. 19–20.

[150] Quoted in Montagu Burrows, *Worthies of All Souls: four centuries of English history, illustrated from the College archives* (London, 1874), 384.

[151] I.G. Doolittle, 'College Administration', HUO V, 227–68, at 228–9.

[152] HMC, *House of Lords MSS, 1693–1695* (New Series, London, 1900), I. 393–6; Bp Trelawny to Charlett, 15 Dec. [1694], Bodl. MS. Ballard 9, f. 75; Stride, *Exeter College*, 78–9.

[153] The Lords' proceedings are considered in M. G. Smith, *Fighting Joshua. A Study of the Career of Sir Jonathan Trelawny, bart., 1650–1721, Bishop of Bristol, Exeter and Winchester* (Redruth, 1985), 89–91, who notes that peers were influenced by the opinion of Edward Stillingfleet, Bishop of Worcester, who delivered a detailed argument in favour of the powers of a visitor.

Fig. 6.5 Sir Jonathan Trelawny, Sir Godfrey Kneller, oil on canvas, 1720 (© National Portrait Gallery, London).

eventually ordered the Tory, Braithwaite, to take office. Two leading lights in the University, Aldrich and Atterbury, both became embroiled. As the latter observed to the Bishop of Exeter (Trelawny): 'Your Lordship can hardly imagine how far this matter was driven into a party cause, and how much the great men of both sides were for the event of it'.[154]

Most Visitors were non-elected, with Balliol being anomalous in having scope to elect its own Visitor. In the first instance, college statutes (and foundational intentions) provided that a prelate or the monarch would always be the Visitor; the Bishop of Winchester held no fewer than five Visitorships. Jesus College was unusual in having an hereditary peer who represented the family associated with the College's foundation.[155] This was the Earl of Pembroke & Montgomery, head

---

[154] Atterbury to Bp Trelawny, *The epistolary correspondence of the Right Reverend Francis Atterbury, DD.*, ed. J. Nichols (2nd edn., 4 vols., London, 1789–90), I. 222–36; R. K. Pugh, 'Post-Restoration bishops of Winchester as Visitors of Oxford colleges', *Oxoniensia*, 43 (1978), 170–87; Penry Williams, 'From the Reformation to the era of Reform, 1530–1850', in eds. Buxton and Williams, *New College*, 44–72, at 60, citing New College MSS. 5063, 5079.

[155] It was not always straightforward to establish who the College Visitor actually was. For the case of Oriel College, see this chapter, p. 71.

284 ENLIGHTENED OXFORD

of the Herbert family, who held the Visitorship.[156] When in 1712 the College divided along party lines in a disputed election to the Principalship, it was the 8th Earl who decided that John Wynne, the Lady Margaret Professor of Divinity (1705–16), who had enjoyed the 'honour and happiness of conversation' with him as his chaplain, should become Principal. The Earl made every effort to proceed impartially.[157]

At Christ Church, a royal foundation, the sovereign was the Visitor. Elsewhere, holders of a bishopric commonly held the office, the Archbishop of Canterbury at All Souls and Merton, the Bishops of Exeter and Lincoln at the eponymous colleges. Other colleges, Balliol, for instance, elected their Visitor with a clear eye on the material advantages he could offer them. In 1691 the College broke with tradition and named the wealthy Dr Richard Busby, the celebrated schoolmaster, as Visitor. He was known to be contemplating endowment of a post in the University, and did indeed, four years later, settle a catechetical lectureship (on orthodox Christianity) on Balliol.[158] Nomination as Visitor could give that office-holder a commanding influence in Balliol's workings. In the 1720s the College was only too keen to receive attention from the extraordinarily wealthy 1st Duke of Chandos, and contentedly installed his brother, the Hon & Rev Henry Brydges, Archdeacon of Rochester, as its Visitor in 1723. Three years later, on the death of the Duke's client, Joseph Hunt, the Mastership fell vacant and the Duke urged his brother to put his name forward. Archdeacon Brydges (who died in 1728) was reluctant to comply, perhaps swayed by the public insistence of four Fellows that it was infra dig for the Visitor to become Master, but at least he did all he could to have his nephew, Theophilus Leigh, fellow of Corpus Christi College (and the Duke's nephew), chosen instead.[159]

In occasional instances, there was legal uncertainty as to the identity of the Visitor. At Oriel, the fellows in the 1720s looked again at the College's first and neglected set of statutes in their dispute with Provost George Carter, went to the Court of Common Pleas, and had their argument that the Crown and not the bishop of Lincoln was their proper Visitor upheld.[160] The Oriel experience can

---

[156] 'a Family to which we are devoted'. Thomas Pardo and Fellows to Henry Legge and Richard Arundell, n.d. [c.1750], Jesus College OA, Box 150. Thanks to Colin Haydon for this reference.

[157] 'Lord Pembroke has been at Oxford and received the appeals of both parties; ordered the government to be carried on by the other officers, till he had decided their differences; told them he would decide them when he returned to London with all the impartiality he could and should have regard to merit'. *HMC, Portland MSS,* VII. 88, letter of 10 Sept. 1712; W. Gibson, 'A Whig principal of Jesus', *Oxoniensia,* 52 (1987), 204–8, and this chapter, p. 56.

[158] See his will in G. F. Russell Barker, *Richard Busby DD (1606–1695)* London, (1895); Jones, *Balliol College,* 129–30. Busby was headmaster of Westminster School for the extraordinary length of fifty-seven years (1638–95).

[159] Ibid., 154ff., for the bitter election of 1726. By contrast with Oriel and University College, there was nothing the Balliol malcontents could do about it. Leigh could be pompous, but he promoted the academic life of Balliol even in old age, trying to encourage a more studious regime. ibid., 173.

[160] P. Seaward, 'Politics and interest, 1660–1781', in ed. Catto, *Oriel College* (Oxford, 2013), 160–92, at 176–83; F. J. Varley, 'The Oriel College lawsuit, 1724–6', *Oxoniensia,* 6 (1941), 56–69.

Fig. 6.6 Theophilus Leigh, Master of Balliol College, Oxford, unknown artist, oil on panel, c.1770 (Master and Fellows of Balliol College, Oxford).

usefully be compared with the contemporary one at University College, where the dispute over the Mastership could not be resolved for so long because each side claimed a different Visitor, and the matter also went to a court of law. It showed how destructive uncertainty about the Visitor could be.[161]

Where Visitors were *ex officio* appointees, the burden could be unwanted, unprofitable, and time-consuming. At Merton the frequency of appeals to the Archbishop of Canterbury as Visitor in ostensibly trivial internal questions caused Archbishop Potter in 1737 to send five commissioners to hold a long, searching enquiry into the causes that lasted nearly a year. Exhortations to forget and forgive, observe civility, courtesy, and good fellowship gradually bore fruit, and the Archbishop of Canterbury's Right of Visitation was also confirmed by the Court of King's Bench.[162] At All Souls, successive archbishops became embroiled in test cases over non-residency and fellows' obligation to take holy orders over

---

[161] For the University College wrangling see this chapter, pp. 62–3.
[162] Henderson, *Merton College*, 157–8, 159. Earlier in the century, William Delaune, President of St John's, thought that all government was weakened in those colleges whose Visitors were too ready to

286 ENLIGHTENED OXFORD

which Warden Gardiner (1702–26) was reluctant to compromise.[163] Archbishop Tenison held a formal visitation of the College in 1710 through the agency of the Dean of Arches. The turbulence continued and Wake felt obliged to hold a second Visitation in 1719, which was considered to have come down against the reforming Warden.[164] Wake insisted he had tried his utmost to be fair:

> I have spared no trouble, I have stuck at no cost to get the best advice and direction I could; and I have clearly satisfied my own conscience that I have done impartially what I thought truth, justice and the welfare of that Society required.[165]

Archbishops also courted opprobrium from the College because of the primary claims of Archbishop Henry Chichele's (the College's founder in the early fifteenth century) descendants to most of the College fellowships, thereby disadvantaging intellectually meritorious candidates. In 1723 Archbishop Wake decided that the founder's wishes must be literally accepted, despite the growing antipathy of progressive opinion in All Souls to the deleterious consequences of unbridled nepotism.[166] But then Wake's descendants, thanks to his wife, could claim Founders' Kin at All Souls, and so his decision might be considered hardly disinterested. This case also illustrates the degree to which a college was pinned in when a Visitor, as it were, jumped the wrong way. For there was nothing that Warden Gardiner could do by way of appeal to a higher authority. And so matters continued. By the 1770s, with three out of four vacancies being filled by founders' kinsmen, Archbishop Frederick Cornwallis cast himself in the unlikely role of educational reformer, determining that the fellows were not required to give preference to Chichele's kin while there were ten such kinsmen among the forty fellows in the College.[167]

His attitude was not untypical, for Visitors were landed with the task of interpreting foundational College statutes that no longer made sense for current requirements. At Trinity, as elsewhere, ways were increasingly found to bend the rules of the founder's statutes, and Visitors were pragmatic over their literal enforcement. In 1713, the Bishop of Winchester, Sir Jonathan Trelawny, spoke authoritatively on the college pecking order, with the object of protecting those

---

listen to private complaints: 'God grant it may never be so in St John's'. Visitor's Letter Bk no 144, quoted in Costin, *St John's College,* 180. Delaune was later the subject of damning personal criticism when accused of embezzling university funds.

[163] For the background see J. Clarke, 'Warden Gardiner, All Souls, and the Church, c.1688–1760', in eds. Green and Horden, *All Souls under the Ancien Régime,* 197–213.

[164] *HMC,* Portland MSS, VII. 21–2, 257, 263, 275.

[165] Quoted in Burrows, *Worthies of All Souls,* 380. See also Sykes, *Wake,* II. 241–5.

[166] ibid., II. 245–6.

[167] Archbishop Moore confirmed the injunction in 1792. G. D. Squibb, *Founders' Kin. Privilege and Pedigree* (Oxford, 1972), 44–6, 60–8.

who could not afford to take the expensive DD from losing their seniority when officers were elected, in effect allowing the statute on taking higher degrees to be dispensed with: 'I cannot but think, considering the tenor of your statutes, that poverty or the meanness of a man's circumstances should be a good reason for his not proceeding to that chargeable degree'.[168]

At Balliol, Bishop the Hon. Shute Barrington of Durham (Visitor, 1805–26), acted in the same spirit in the first decades of the nineteenth century. He was a constitutional Tory, yet one who upheld the Master's (Isaac Parsons) plans for open fellowship elections despite the 1507 Statutes which gave existing Scholars of the College an advantage.[169] These were tokens of the difference that episcopal intervention could make in the affairs of a constituent part of the University. That allowed to the diocesan bishop within whose see the University was located was rather less, despite the Bishop's episcopal throne being set down in Christ Church cathedral.

vi) Bishops of Oxford and the University

The see is so poor, it is hardly worth solicitation, unless for a circumstance—its vicinity to Mag. Coll. & <u>a good country house in a salutary air</u>, which is of much consequence to me & mine;
George Horne to George Berkeley, 13 Oct. 1788, BL Add.
MS 39312, f. 79.

Five miles south-west of Oxford was the village of Cuddesdon, an unexceptional country parish save for its containing the palace of the Bishop of Oxford. It could be presumed that the proximate presence of this ecclesiastical dignity, with his cathedral at Christ Church and his place in the House of Lords, would have suited and served the University in protecting and projecting its interests, but it seldom happened thus. Until mid-century, the Bishop of Oxford and the University of Oxford tended to co-exist as neighbours with only occasional bursts of congeniality. Of course, the bishops professed the best interests of the University, but they could be slow to take them up and, where they did, their relative episcopal insignificance counted against their catching either public or ministerial notice.[170] The see could be difficult to fill. For Oxford was a poor bishopric, worth less than £600 pa and a small one (roughly coterminous with the county), founded by

---

[168] Trinity College Archives, A Register B. f. 61, quoted in Hopkins, *Trinity*, 175. For Hoadly's attitude as Visitor of Trinity see ibid., 182.

[169] Jones, *Balliol*, 177, 80.

[170] Their powers within the University were minimal. As Bp John Butler put it, 'he could almost as soon recommend to a Bishoprick, as to a studentship [at Ch. Ch.] ...', J. Boucher to J. James, snr. [Dec. 1780], in ed. Evans, *Letters of Richard Radcliffe and John James*, 137.

Fig. 6.7 Doorway at Christ Church, Oxford, formerly at Cuddesdon Palace, Oxon. (© the author).

Henry VIII in 1542 during the Reformation, and its incumbents were considered as on the first rung of preferment, men who would, if fortune favoured them, secure translation to a more prestigious and certainly a more lucrative see.[171] As William Wake confided to Arthur Charlett, Master of University College, when his name was being mentioned as a potential successor to Bishop John Hough on his translation to Lichfield in 1699:

> But if I would alter my condition, Oxford is the bishopric of all England that I should the least desire to fix upon. To say nothing of the revenue, which is yet but mean, other reasons there are enough to make a man unwilling to come to it;
> ...I have heard yourself named; but in truth I love you too well to wish it to you, who want some further help to keep it warm.[172]

---

[171] Sykes, *Church and State*, 63. For the efforts of Thomas Secker's well-wishers to secure his translation in the 1740s see Ingram, *Religion, Reform and Modernity*, 65.

[172] Bodl. MS Ballard MSS 3, f. 34, 31 Mar. 1700. The diocese was not actually offered to Wake by Abp Tenison. He was asked if he would take the similarly 'small' see of Bristol and he declined. Bishop Hough, who had held the see since 1690, hoped for a limited tenure. When some of his friends

OXFORD PERSONNEL   289

After Samuel Parker (d. 1688) all ten successive holders of the see before Charles Moss (consecr. 1807) apart from Edward Smallwell (Bishop 1788–99) moved on to fresh pastures, two of them in succession, Potter and Secker straight to the primacy of All England after two decades at Oxford.[173] Clearly the allure of being some sort of representative of the University was never enough to offset the ambition of further promotion and, in fairness to the majority of bishops, they had talent enough to take them on to London or Canterbury (as four of them managed).

Then there was the question of how much time the diocesan was expected to devote to the interests of the University, the major corporation within the see, to be set in the balance with the 176 parishes that looked to him for pastoral oversight. John Hough, bishop from 1690 to 1699, was awarded the see in grateful recognition of his services in defying James II's incursions at Magdalen and was allowed to retain its Presidency until 1701;[174] Potter, as has been seen,[175] was a diocesan first and a Regius Professor only second, holding on to his chair in order to boost his income.[176] The poverty of the see generally disposed its holders to seek out supplementary in commendam posts. William Talbot (bishop, 1699–1715) retained the Deanery of Worcester throughout his Oxford years;[177] Secker was elected to the Deanery of St Paul's in 1750 and an extra £2,000 in income; his successor at Oxford likewise replaced him at St Paul's.[178] All of them used Christ Church Cathedral for occasional services.[179] Because of the large number of graduates taking holy orders, ordinations in the Oxford diocese were frequent,

---

congratulated him upon his accession to the Bishopric of Oxford, it was reported 'Prithee', says he, 'I did not take this for a saddle, I only meant it for a stirrup'. 'Table-Talk and papers of Bishop Hough. 1703–1743', in ed. W. Burrow, *Collectanea. Second Series, OHS*, 16 (1890), 380–416, at 393.

[173] John Potter was a follower of William Wake, became friendly with George II and Queen Caroline in the 1720s, and was named archbishop, largely through the Queen's influence, in 1737. He supposedly gave the Queen a favourable regard for Christ Church. ed. Linnell, *The Diaries of Thomas Wilson*, 188, Oct. 1736; John, Lord Hervey, *Some materials towards memoirs of the reign of King George II*, ed. R. Sedgwick (3 vols., London, 1931), II. 398, 547–8; Anderson, *Memoirs of Potter*, ix. The equally long-serving Secker sought quietly to reform the Oxford diocese in cooperation with Daniel Burton, its chancellor, and a canon of Christ Church, 1760–75. *Fasti*, viii. 104.

[174] Darwall-Smith, 'The Monks of Magdalen', 259–60. For the minimal impact of Bp Hough on cathedral and diocese in the 1690s see Curthoys (3), 128.

[175] See Chapter 3, pp. 45–7.

[176] He still presided in person at the Divinity Acts. Anderson, *Memoirs of Potter*, vii. His continuing academic influence is not to be entirely discounted. The measured Thomas Randolph, President of Corpus, 1768–83, was a client of Potter and, in the dedication of an early work, thus acknowledged his debt: 'If I have shewn any skill in unravelling his sophistry, or any knowledge in the doctrines of the gospel, I have learnt it from your Grace's Example and Instructions' [Potter became Abp of Canterbury, 1737]. *The Christian's Faith. A Rational Assent*, iv. Randolph was replying to Henry Dodwell the younger's *Christianity not founded on Argument . . . In a Letter to a young Gentleman at Oxford* (1741).

[177] Talbot was no scholar but he carried out diocesan visitations in person in 1701, 1704, and 1707. Oxfordshire Archives, ORO, MS Oxf. Dioc. e.6, e.7, e.8. He was married to Sarah, Duchess of Marlborough's cousin and his nomination was intended as a means to moderate the University's politics.

[178] Ingram, *Religion, Reform and Modernity*, 66–7.

[179] For the bishops and Christ Church, see Curthoys (3), 134.

Fig. 6.8 Christ Church Cathedral, Oxford, Richard Gilson Reeve, after J. M. W. Turner, aquatint, 1807 (Yale Center for British Art, Paul Mellon Collection).

three or four times annually at mid-century, and invariably in the cathedral.[180] Technically, the Dean and Chapter had to give leave to bishops to ordain there, but tensions were negligible except, briefly, in 1711 when the Tory Atterbury was Dean and the Whig Talbot bishop.[181] And, in 1783, when the College refused Bishop John Butler permission to prepare his ordinands in the Chapter House, this caused much episcopal annoyance.[182]

Above all, there was the distinct likelihood of a political fissure between the Bishop and the University: bishops were likely to be Whigs, the University predominantly Tory. That trend was confirmed with the appointment of the Low Church, court preacher William Talbot in 1699,[183] though there was an easing when he was replaced by John Potter, the insider, in 1715, whose triennial

---

[180] Oxford Episcopal Registers, cited in W. M. Marshall, 'The Dioceses of Hereford and Oxford, 1660–1760', in eds. J. Gregory & J. S. Chamberlain, *The National Church in Local Perspective. The Church of England and the Regions, 1660–1800* (Woodbridge, 2003), 197–221, at 205–6. Most of Hough's ordinations were held in Magdalen College Chapel. W. M. Marshall, *Church Life in Hereford and Oxford 1660–1760. A Study of Two Sees* (Lancaster, 2009), 200.

[181] Ibid., 174–5.   [182] Curthoys (1), 88.

[183] Cf. W. Gibson, 'William Talbot and Church parties, 1688–1730', *JEH*, 58 (2007), 26–48. Talbot was an enemy of Sacheverell. See his *The Bishop of Oxford his speech* (London, 1710).

charge to his clergy (1719) took a firm anti-Hoadly stance.[184] It could still be hard going for all parties. As Bishop Secker reminded Lord Hardwicke in 1753, 'the small property I have in Oxfordshire lies either in the hands of, or in the neighbourhood of persons whom I cannot influence'.[185] An invariable duty of an incoming prelate, as ministers like the Duke of Newcastle saw it, was to try and advance the interests of the King in the University. Where that had been done steadfastly, it gave any bishop some claim to preferment in more tranquil reaches of the Church. Recommending Secker to Newcastle, Hardwicke reminded the duke:[186]

> Your Grace knows the worthy & strong part, the Bishop acted the last year, in the affair of the University of Oxford, tho' a Standard was set up for them in a certain place; and I know that He has been since very ill-treated & run upon at Oxford for his Behaviour on that occasion.

For the Bishop to be both principled and effective in his relations with the University presupposed suppleness and goodwill on both sides, a willingness to work with the other party, and a refusal to press a point where circumstances required it. These were demanding *desiderata* and a falling out was not uncommon, over patronage as much as politics. Colleges could be jealous of diocesan intrusion. There was, for instance, a protracted dispute involving Lincoln College as to whether the chaplaincies of All Saints and St Michael's churches (normally held by fellows) were exempt from archidiaconal jurisdiction. It came to a head in 1739 when Secker was Bishop and rumbled on into the 1750s with the college standing its ground against the Bishop.[187] Secker had led a charm offensive towards the whole University soon after his appointment to promote dicocesan and academic unity. At his Primary Visitation of 1738 he invited 'all the Heads of Houses, & all the Clergy of the Diocese who resided in Oxford, to dine with me', and there were regular 'public days' (usually a Thursday) at Cuddesdon thereafter for town, county, and University figures to mingle.[188] With many dons holding Oxfordshire livings and a majority of the county clergy Tories it could be uphill work, as Secker's patron, Lord Hardwicke observed: 'I have long seen that spirit and great industry has been used to keep up that spirit, where you see the exertion

---

[184] Anderson, *Memoirs of Potter*, vii–viii.   [185] BL Add MSS. 35592, f. 30, 8 Feb. 1753.

[186] BL Add MSS. 32721, f. 418, 20 July 1750. Secker's varying at Oxford of the toast 'Church and King' brought Samuel Johnson's ire: 'The Archbishop of Canterbury', said he (with an affected smooth smiling grimace), 'drinks, "Constitution in Church and State". Being asked what difference there was between the two toasts, he said, 'Why, Sir, you may be sure he meant something'. ed. Birkbeck Hill, rev. Powell, *Boswell's Life of Johnson*, 1780, IV. 29.

[187] Green, *Lincoln College*, 312–18.

[188] *The Autobiography of Thomas Secker, Archbishop of Canterbury*, ed. John S. Macauley and R. W. Greaves, (Lawrence, KA, 1988), 19; BL Add MS 46689, f. 3, Berkeley Papers, vol. II, journal of George Berkeley, Jr. Hospitality at Cuddesdon in Potter's time was meagre. Marshall, *Church Life in Hereford and Oxford*, 203.

292 ENLIGHTENED OXFORD

of it, in order to hold out that place [Oxford] as the garrison and fortress of Toryism and Jacobitism'.[189] The cultural gap that existed was graphically illustrated on 15 October 1745 when Bishop Thomas Secker presided at a city meeting over the 121 signatories of an Association for the preservation of the Constitution in Church and State (against the Jacobite threat), one largely declined and boycotted by the Tories in the county, and attracting the signatures of only seven heads of colleges and halls.[190] He later encouraged George II not to receive the University's tardy address on the Treaty of Aix-la-Chapelle, and identified himself openly in the 1754 Oxfordshire election with support for the 'New Interest' and the cause of its candidates, Lord Parker and Sir Edward Turner.[191]

The diocese and University might have been umbilically connected if, as was at least twice seriously mooted, the Bishop of Oxford had also been the Dean of Christ Church. That deanery was considered a superior prize to a poor bishopric, yet a combination of the two made probable a burden of business that offset any financial advantages Thus Bishop John Potter resisted the powerful and varied coalition—Archbishop Wake, Lord Chancellor Macclesfield, and Bishop Atterbury among them—all urging him to be a candidate for the Christ Church Deanery in 1719. Half a century later, on Dean Gregory's death in 1767, rumours flew around that John Hume, Bishop of Salisbury, freshly translated from Oxford,[192] would be the next Dean. Again, nothing came of it, Hume probably considering the deanery would require the resignation of his lucrative Durham prebend in return for demanding academic duties.[193]

In George III's reign relations between the University and the Bishop eased significantly.[194] Cooperation became less unusual. It was a sign of the times that when Sir William Dolben, an 'Old Interest' candidate and son and heir of the former Tory Visitor of Balliol, Canon Sir John Dolben, was first elected as a University MP (for seven weeks only in 1768), he, unusually, enjoyed episcopal backing. The Bishop, the great Hebraist, Robert Lowth, was a Whig, but that they were both kinsmen also did no harm in bringing them together.[195] Lowth was

---

[189] P. C. Yorke, The life and correspondence of Philip Yorke, Earl of Hardwicke, Lord High Chancellor of Great Britain (3 vols., Cambridge, 1913), II. 134.

[190] Paul Langford, 'Tories and Jacobites', in HUO V, 107–22, at 120; Ward, Georgian Oxford, 166. The University, guided by V-C Isham, had signed an Address of Loyalty to George II. See this chapter, pp. 32–3.

[191] Secker, Autobiography, 27; Robson, The Oxfordshire election, 83; Ingram, Religion, reform and modernity, 179–80.

[192] Hume [Corpus Christi, BA, 1724] had succeeded Secker as Bp of Oxford in 1758 (he had begun his episcopate at Bristol, 1756–8), and was translated to Salisbury in 1766. Foster, II. 713.

[193] Ward, Georgian Oxford, 107; NUL, Portland MS, PWF8369, Smallwell to 3rd Duke of Portland, 18 Sept. 1767. Four Christ Church deans did hold bishoprics, but not of Oxford: Smalridge, Bradshaw, Conybeare, and Bagot received Bristol, Markham went to Chester.

[194] There were signs of it even in the last years of George II. Secker was optimistic: 'And though I be among the Children of men that are set on Fire, they have given me but little disquiet and one may hope will grow cooler than hotter'. LPL, Secker Papers 7, f. 92, to Archbishop Thomas Herring, 12 May 1755.

[195] BL Add. MS. 38305, f. 51.

translated to London in 1777, as was, in 1809, John Randolph, talented don and Bishop of Oxford from 1799.[196] Both men's intellectual capacities and standing within Oxford had brought them a mitre in the first place. Randolph's services to Oxford in the House of Lords were conspicuous.[197] Thus he fully supported the University Advowsons Bill in Parliament in spring 1805. It aimed to remove a restrictive clause in the Mortmain Act of 1736 in order for colleges to purchase a higher proportion of livings for their fellows, so as to increase their opportunities of finding a benefice and making a clerical career. Thus it was hoped this relief to the colleges would also work for the benefit of the parishes.[198]

Not all Bishops of Oxford were Oxford graduates. John Butler, the 'sleek and subtle' Archdeacon of Surrey, who received the see in 1777 (and really wanted it, as a colleague noted),[199] was neither an Oxford nor a Cambridge graduate, and was seen in some quarters as an odd choice. Butler himself seems to have sensed his good luck in a letter to his colleague, the archdeacon of Winchester:[200]

It happens fortunately for me, that your being a son of Cambridge excluded you from the situation, in which I am placed, else I must have been hurt by the opinion, which would have been justly formed by all the world, that there was a mistake in the promotion ... [I] shall labor hard to give my friends no occasion to repent of it'.

When he was not pushing his own career forward through the influence of the powerful Onslow family, Butler cultivated Oxford scholars. Within a few days of taking up the see, he was dining with the Dean and Chapter of Christ Church and holding a public reception, optimistically opining that 'My Life will probably be very comfortable in the intercourse I shall have with the University.'[201] His public anti-American stance (confirmed by the pamphlets he wrote under the signature of "Vindex") made majority Northite University opinion overlook his previous anti-Bute Whiggism and he reciprocated this goodwill before his translation to

---

[196] Within a year of his becoming a bishop Randolph was offered the Primacy of Ireland by the Duke of Portland, the Home Secretary, with the approval of the King. It was a critical appointment with the Act of Union only months from implementation, but Randolph declined to give up his 'present situation for one in Ireland.' Letter of 1 Feb. 1800, Bodl. MS Top. Oxon. d. 355, f.1. The primacy had also been offered to Cyril Jackson.

[197] And inside the University as Bishop. On his own admission, Randolph may have continued for a time to lecture in the University (and reside in Christ Church) three evenings a week, after resigning the Regius Chair of Divinity in 1799. Letter of 20 Nov. 1800, Bodl. MS Top. Oxon. d. 355, f. 19.

[198] Hansard, *Parliamentary Debates*, 1st ser. (1805), IV. Col. 142, V. cols. 5–6; Diana McClatchey, *Oxfordshire Clergy 1777–1869* (Oxford, 1960), 8–9.

[199] It 'is the very thing in the world that he would have chosen & I believe he is now very well pleased that he did not go to Chester'. Beilby Porteus to 2nd Lord Grantham, 10 Aug. 1777, Bedfordshire Archives and Record Services, Lucas Papers, L230/14/315/17. Porteus had been given Chester.

[200] Beinecke Library, Yale University, Balguy Correspondence, OSB MSS 127, Butler to Thomas Balguy, 1777–89, 14 Apr. 1777.

[201] Butler to Lord Onslow, 16 June 1777, Surrey History Centre, G173/2/1/138.

294 ENLIGHTENED OXFORD

Hereford in 1787 by helping Carl Gottfried Woide transcribe the *Codex Alexandrius* and publish a text of the New Testament from it in 1786.[202] Butler was both reasonably dutiful as a diocesan, and ready to take up the cudgels against commonly perceived detractors of the faith, writing to his patron, George, 4th Lord Onslow: 'I am engaged for six Sundays to come to preach about the diocese for the Society for propagating the Gospel, lest Mr Gibbon should intirely stop the progress of it'. Yet it says much about Butler's unfortunate scholarly judgement that he considered that the unfortunate young Oxford graduate, Henry Edward Davis, afterwards witheringly disposed of by Gibbon in his *Vindication*, had 'demolished' the latter 'as an original historian'.[203]

Butler was keen enough to move on to Hereford when an opportunity for translation arose in 1787 and his successor in the see of Oxford, somewhat surprisingly, Edward Smallwell, was a follower and former tutor of the 3rd Duke of Portland, then in opposition to Pitt's government.[204] Smallwell, though Bishop of St Davids since 1783, had retained as bishop his canonry at Christ Church (since 1775) and, despite an annual income reckoned at £900 in 1762, had likely had a sufficiency of making the long journey to and from his 'vast and unwieldy' see in the west of Wales.[205] He was a known quantity at Christ Church and ministers were ready to allow him to retain his stall in the cathedral,[206] and in the 1790s, to quote Leslie Mitchell, Smallwell acted as 'a major channel for the preferment of Oxford men'.[207] The institutional incorporation of the diocesan bishop into the cathedral chapter at this juncture (though, in another sense, he had been part of it since 1775) symbolically illustrates the degree to which tensions between the Ordinary and the University had eased three decades into George III's reign.

vii) Conclusion

Smallwell's translation to Oxford suited Christ Church interests and, irrespective of Dean Jackson's loose connections to the Portland interest at that time, it suited

---

[202] Butler's character and career is engagingly discussed in C. E. Vulliamy, *The Onslow Family 1528–1874 with some account of their times* (London, 1953), 179–95. He was an unlikely candidate in the early nineteenth century for the authorship of the *Letters of Junius*. Horace Walpole disliked him, mainly for his politics: '... is there a yard of lawn in England more dirty than Butler's?' To William Mason, 25 Apr. 1781, Walpole, *Correspondence*, XXIX, 134.

[203] Quoted in Vulliamy, *The Onslow Family*, 191.

[204] His career is summarised in Foster, IV. 1308.

[205] Smallwell's connection with the college lasted almost all his adult life and he was trying for a canonry as a young man as early as 1765. 'My years, & singular knowledge of Christ Church, my life & attachment to the Place, my wishes to be in a station, where I might still drudge on in its service might all plead for me'. To Portland, NUL, PWF8361, 29 July 1765.

[206] Lord Chancellor Thurlow wanted the see of St Davids for Samuel Horsley, having been impressed with his qualities as a talented controversialist in exchanges with Priestley. F. C. Mather, *High Church Prophet. Bishop Samuel Horsley (1733–1806) and the Caroline Tradition in the later Georgian Church* (Oxford, 1992), 63, 163, 177. For Canons and political patrons see Bill, *Education at Christ Church*, 126–7.

[207] 'Politics and Revolution', 188.

Pitt's government to recognise them, too. The appointment was indicative of the extent to which majority opinion among senior University office-holders once more had a decisive presence in and purchase on the polity on the eve of the French Revolution. The lean decades had gone. Having a Chancellor in state office, such as Ormond before 1714 and North during the 1770s, could not help but give the University a compelling stake in official patronage—so long as there was no clash of interests between ministerial policy and Oxford's preferences. Where there was tension, as with attitudes towards subscription and enhanced civil freedom for dissenters during North's years at the Treasury, having an Oxford Chancellor in the Cabinet was no guarantee that the University's stated interests would be upheld in their entirety. Arran had no such influence. But, at least after the Atterbury fiasco, he had played a quiet defensive game that went some way to ensure that Walpole and then the Pelhams were unwilling to take up the more enthusiastic Whig schemes for curtailing Oxonian vested interests by statute. It was enough for the Crown in these years to use its many channels of patronage to appoint thoroughgoing Hanoverian loyalists to Oxford posts in the hope that over time Oxford would become more like Cambridge, where Newcastle held the Chancellorship from 1748 to 1768.[208] Some, by no means all, of Arran's nominees as Vice Chancellor worked astutely to shore up Oxford's credibility and therefore protect its external interests. Thus William Holmes's charm offensive of the mid-1730s built on the goodwill that the Act of 1733 and the visit of the Prince and Princess of Orange (son-in-law and daughter of George II) had generated.[209] It did no harm to the University's brilliant efforts, masterminded by his successor in post, to limit the damage the Mortmain Bill could do to the University's propertied interests. After him, Euseby Isham's behaviour in the '45 somehow combined expediency and principle so as to limit the scope Oxford's external critics could plausibly have for hostility to the University's perceived lack of energies during the Jacobite incursion.[210] From 1760, successive Vice Chancellors operated in the comfortable knowledge that University interests were not just broadly safe, but were favoured and could be extended. How ingeniously that could be done was best exemplified by Nathan Wetherell between 1768 and 1772.

Wetherell's amity with Charles Jenkinson was a vital component of his leadership strategy, in relation to both his own college and the University as a whole. He was an outstanding college head under whose aegis the later eighteenth-century establishment was peopled by many University College alumni who had been resident in the 1760s and 1770s. But, once his career and financial ambitions had been satisfied, and with a large family to look to, Wetherell rather lost interest in

---

[208] For the powers of the Crown in nominating to Studentships exercised by Newcastle see Bill, *Education at Christ Church*, 122.

[209] Bodl MS Top Oxon. d.174, 149–50.   [210] See this chapter, pp. 32–3.

296   ENLIGHTENED OXFORD

his Mastership. The key player in Oxford's relationship with the world beyond in the 1790s and 1800s was Cyril Jackson, Dean of Christ Church, who never looked elsewhere for preferment (though he was never short of offers).[211] Jackson's establishment contacts were remarkable. For the most part, college heads mediated their external influence through their own student body and, beyond that, the families from which they originated. Historic links with different regions could count here for as much or more as political loyalties. Influence was therefore local rather than metropolitan for college heads, though they almost all had their patrons in government and Opposition and might, where they were in holy orders, hope at some point for preferment beyond Oxford. That might mean a deanery, a canonry, or an archdeaconry; for the very fortunate, even a bishopric, such as those held successively by William Cleaver, the able Principal of Brasenose, and Grenville client. And former Oxford Heads of Houses moving on to govern dioceses elsewhere—such as John Hough and George Horne at Magdalen, and William Markham and Lewis Bagot at Christ Church—would often have places in their episcopal gift to offer, should they feel so disposed, to former college colleagues.

Within colleges and halls, the tutor-student relationship was pedagogic (especially as matriculation ages steadily rose and tutors needed to behave less as schoolmasters) and potentially patronal. At no point in the 'long' eighteenth century did it lose its instrumentality in building up mutual loyalties that could last lifetimes and bring benefits to both parties. These associations could be seen in embryo across the university at any point in time, and could be generational. They were foundational to the University's multiple connections to the social and political elite in the world outside.

The Visitatorial system was a primary, formal instance of that symbiotic relationship. There was, at any given point, usually one College Visitor willy-nilly involved in adjudicating in a foundation's contested internal affairs that divided competing parties and individuals. Their unedifying wrangling did Oxford's image with the outside world no favours, but where personality differences could be veiled by principle, any consideration of how it all looked to outsiders was a secondary consideration. Of course, a lot could be at stake in terms of power and place, and it is striking how unwilling to compromise both sides could be in most of these altercations. Though they had their counterparts in other Hanoverian institutions, disputes involving Visitors were likely to damage the University's collective influence if only because they were such obvious ammunition for its many critics. When called upon to intervene, Visitors were

---

[211] Smaller College heads were resentful at the extent to which Jackson had, to their mind, converted Oxford into a fiefdom. Thus Edward Tatham, Rector of Lincoln: 'The University had become somewhat like the government of the great Monarch of the East, administered by a Bassa [bashaw]with the help of Sazesacks of his own choice and promotion, in the most arbitrary way'. [Anon.], *A New Address* (1810), 7.

therefore engaged in a form of damage-limitation exercise and it is to their credit how constructively and with minimal *parti pris* most of them seem to have discharged their responsibilities. What John Jones said of Balliol can be also be said generally:

> Visitors, whose misfortune it was to have all this squabbling thrust upon them, emerge with much credit: they ... exercised their authority with patient and impartial wisdom.[212]

Many of the episcopal Visitors—Canterbury at All Souls, Winchester at Corpus Christi, Lincoln and Exeter at the eponymous colleges among them—were prelates. The Bishops of Oxford held no such jurisdiction and were something of a poor relation to the University. After all, the latter had been in existence for almost four centuries before the diocese of Oxford was created. It was still in the best interests of both parties that they co-existed constructively and, for the most part, that was the case in this period. Ministers may at times have wished for the Bishop to be their stalking horse within the University (that was the expectation with Talbot, Potter, and Secker initially), but he was usually too busy with the diocese or in Parliament to fulfil these excessive hopes more than partially. Relations, were on the whole, good, even harmoniously so, and mutual respect was never particularly hard to generate. It helped that Potter and Randolph held University chairs in addition to their see, and that Robert Lowth was an internationally acclaimed Hebraist. Apart from John Butler, all the eighteenth-century bishops were Oxford graduates, all used Christ Church cathedral regularly, all knew that, in the end, their episcopal influence would be maximised by working with moderate opinion across the University. And for the latter, the place of the diocesan bishop within the wider polity was an opportunity to project the place of the University within the state in a positive light. As with other intersecting patronage networks, mutual respect was essential if reciprocity was to thrive.

[212] *Balliol College*, 160.

7

Oxford and the Crown

... the Interests of the University are intimately connected with those
of the Crown; and the shadow of Disloyalty in such a Body is most
unnatural.

Edward Bentham, *A Letter to a Fellow
of a College* (Oxford, 1749), 64.

God bless the King, I mean the Faith's Defender,
    God bless – no harm in blessing – the Pretender,
    But who Pretender is, or who is King,
    God bless us all – that's quite another Thing.
'Intended to allay the Violence of PARTY-SPIRIT',

John Byrom, *Miscellaneous Poems*
(2 vols., Manchester,), I. 342.

Part A: 'The shadow of disloyalty': the University and the monarchy in an era of contested succession *c.*1700–1760

i) Background

Oxford was 'the loyal city', and the University was explicitly attached to the royal
supremacy under the statutes of 1636. It was a reputation that had been hard won
and confirmed when the city and University had served as the de facto capital
of England during the monarch's residence in the first Civil War between 1642
and 1646,[1] and it was tenaciously upheld throughout the 'long eighteenth century'.
That the University was almost entirely inimical to any manifestation of republicanism or commonwealth sentiments was a given; the divisions within the
University were rather about what sort of monarchy and who should be king.
And it was only after 1760 that those divisions gave way to solidarity of opinion
across Oxford that functioned as a foundational strength of the dynasty and, by

---

[1] J. Barratt, *Cavalier Capital: Oxford in the English Civil Wars* (Solihull, 2016); Jerome de Groot,
'Space, Patronage, procedure: the court at Oxford, 1642–46', *EHR*, 117 (2002), 1204–27; I. Roy and
D. Reinhart, 'Oxford and the Civil Wars', in HUO IV, 687–732; I. Roy, 'The city of Oxford, 1640–1660',
in ed. R. C. Richardson, *Town and Countryside in the English Revolution* (Manchester, 1992), 130–68.

Enlightened Oxford: The University and the Cultural and Political Life of Eighteenth-century Britain and Beyond.
Nigel Aston, Oxford University Press. © Nigel Aston 2023. DOI: 10.1093/oso/9780199246830.003.0008

OXFORD AND THE CROWN   299

extension, the polity in the face of international and internal challenges over the next sixty years. For in George III the University finally had again its *summum bonum*: a king who was as dedicated to discharging conscientiously his responsibilities as Supreme Governor of the Church of England as much as he was to being the sovereign of his people.

Seventeenth-century Oxford was loyal to the Stuarts as the family providentially allocated the throne by an all-wise Providence, and Oxford men died in their hundreds on the battlefields of the 1640s because of their unwillingness to allow Charles I's critics to dismantle his prerogative and destroy his distinctive construction of a powerful monarchy and a Church which he had rebuilt.[2] That loyalty was not uncritical, as the productions of those in Lord Falkland's Great Tew Circle outside the university pointed up,[3] and the primary importance of one of its products, Edward Hyde, 1st Earl of Clarendon, in government under the restored monarchy between 1660 and 1667, brought with it a bid to inject some of those perceptions into the operation of the state.[4] Clarendon eventually floundered and was brought low,[5] a fate he bore in his French exile with a loyalty that, in its way, mirrored the faithfulness of his late royal master, Charles I, to his ultimately divisive vision of Church and state. The king's faithfulness and his blood sacrifice, as his followers saw it, reflected the ambitions of 'wicked men' who had brought in their dominance through a turbulent upheaval in the life of the nation. That experience of disruption to the established order, Oxford preachers insisted in their sermons of 30 January and on innumerable other occasions, must never be repeated.[6] No wonder that the University rallied unconditionally behind Charles II during the Whig onslaught of the Exclusion Crisis (1678–81), which prompted the king's decision to hold what turned out to be the last Exclusion Parliament in the city, in 1681.[7]

There followed, in quick succession, the royalist reaction (1681–5), the Catholicising trauma of James II's reign (1685–8), and the Glorious Revolution (1688–9).[8] Oxford had issued proclamations against resistance to the crown in 1683 and again in 1685 (these also functioned as an endorsement of the Anglican

---

[2] It is also the case that many Oxford men died for Parliament during the Civil War, most famously John Hampden (Magdalen), mortally wounded at the battle of Chalgrove in 1643.

[3] S. Mortimer, *Reason and Religion in the English Revolution* (Cambridge, 2010), 63–87; S. Mortimer, 'Great Tew circle (*act.* 1633–1639)', *ODNB*, online edn., 2007; H. Trevor-Roper, *Catholics, Anglicans and Puritans* (London, 1987), 166–230.

[4] B.H.G. Wormald, *Clarendon: Politics, History and Religion 1640–1660* (Cambridge, 1951); R. Ollard, *Clarendon and his Friends* (Oxford, 1988).

[5] R. Hutton, *Charles II. King of England, Scotland, and Ireland* (Oxford, 1989), 250–1; Ollard, *Clarendon*, 285–317.

[6] Andrew Lacey, *The cult of King Charles the Martyr* (Woodbridge, 2003); M. Knights, 'The Tory interpretation of history in the rage of parties', *HLQ*, 68 (2005), 353–73.

[7] Dubbed by Tim Harris '...a piece of political theatre orchestrated by the king for public consumption'. *Politics under the later Stuarts*, 201.

[8] G.V. Bennett, 'Loyalist Oxford and the Revolution', in HUO V, 9–30; Beddard, 'James II and the Catholic Challenge', in HUO IV, 907–54. See also discussion in Chapter 2.

300   ENLIGHTENED OXFORD

character of the University), but the Revolution insistently raised the question of dynastic loyalties. This was the issue that would not go away for the next three-quarters of a century. Put simply, if an hereditary monarch, by his policies and actions, was adjudged to be endangering the institutional vitality of the Crown and subverting the Established Church, could he be displaced? Such was the question that many Tories preferred instinctively not to confront.[9] Those who did face it and answered in the negative became Nonjurors; the majority, with the best grace they could muster, went along with William III's coup and the breach of the hereditary succession (which they hoped would be temporary).[10] The Revolution had, at a stroke, rescued the institutional life of the kingdom from being engulfed by Catholicism, but, by the same token, it had delivered the leadership of the Established Church largely into the hands of those who unambiguously declared themselves supporters of the new dispensation, court Whigs, 1690s style, and mainly Cambridge men.[11] Loyalty was required after the Act of Settlement of 1701 less to an hereditary succession than to a parliamentary and Protestant succession, and it was an adjustment that numerous Oxonians in all walks of life did not find easy to make or admit, one in which public commitment was offset by private doubts (or even treason). After the twelve-year interlude (1702–14) in which dynastic and monarchical loyalties were once more felicitously conflated, a lasting rupture occurred in 1714. The University did its best to be loyal to the early Hanoverians without ever persuading the new dynasty and its advisers that it actually was. This hesitant endorsement of the holders of the crown between 1714 and 1760 resulted in a large section of the University being pushed to the fringes in the life of the state and Cambridge in consequence basking in official favour.

Divisions and tensions on the central issue of sovereign power in eighteenth-century England gave birth to a rich seam of discussion and debate in the University in which models of monarchy were scrutinised in sermons, pamphlets, lectures, taverns, and coffee-houses, sometimes in an abstract, non-specific manner to protect controversialists from official sanctions, but not at the cost of

---

[9] As Mark Goldie has argued, Tories preferred to look back to what had happened in the 1640s rather than to examine too determinedly what had taken place in 1688. See Goldie, 'The Revolution of 1689 and the structure of political argument', *BIHR*, 83 (1980), 473–521.

[10] While travelling east from Torbay to London in late 1688, at Hinton St George, Somerset, the Prince of Orange had received the Hon. Leopold Finch, Warden of All Souls (1686–1702), who declared that the University was strongly in his support. That was, of course, prior to William's taking of the Crown. Finch, the younger son of the 3rd Earl of Winchilsea, had been head of a company of scholars formed to oppose the Duke of Monmouth's rebellion in 1685, and had gained the Wardenship with the backing of James II. Despite that background, he was still rewarded for his minor part in the Revolution with a prebend of Canterbury in 1689. That same year his father was restored as Lord-Lieutenant. of Kent. Wigelsworth, *All Souls College, Oxford in the early eighteenth century: piety, political imposition, and legacy of the Glorious Revolution* (Leiden, 2018), 13, 19. CCEd Person ID: 35521 for his ecclesiastical career.

[11] T. Claydon, *William III* (Harlow, 2002), 104–5; Rose, *England in the 1690s*, 182–9. For the King's efforts to reassure the Church party through the efforts of his propagandists see T. Claydon, *William III and the Godly Revolution* (Cambridge, 1996), 164–77.

OXFORD AND THE CROWN   301

dialectical vigour. For everything was fluid after 1714; there could be no assurance that the dynastic beneficiaries of the Revolution would survive if 'James III' was obtruded into Britain, a possibility that neither Whigs nor Tories ever doubted. It gave an edge to polemic about the Crown and its powers that made ministers abidingly watchful and was itself a backhanded tribute to Oxford's importance in shaping the character of national debate on the topic; members of the University offered some of the most intellectually creative (and often covert) defences of their chosen royal option, whether Hanoverian or Stuart. To discuss monarchy, however codedly, was to discuss where power lay in the polity and, by extension, who should exercise it. With royal successions disputed in Spain, France, and the Habsburg Empire in the first half of the century as well as in Britain, nothing mattered more in any European state in terms of its character and operation than who presided over it, given the powers available to him or her; Oxford's willingness to posit and argue for an alternative vision to that articulated by the new Whig establishment of the 1710s and 1720s made it a dangerous, predominantly countercultural presence in the Georgian state, one that was never readily controlled. In a bid to counter it, ministers used every weapon of preferment, conferred or promised, to encourage Whig counter-discourses within the University that made for a rich and contested series of political exchanges. Inasmuch as there was a public debate about power in Britain c.1714–60, it owed much to Oxford's unwillingness to accept uncritically the new conformity and to continue to offer and justify a legitimist political theology that could be suitably tweaked and updated.

Party leaders in Parliament, both Whig and Tory, on occasion looked to Oxford academics to supply them with new or revivified arguments that would buttress the status quo and, more commonly, justify its modification, alternative operation, or outright replacement. Wherever they stood on the central issue of royal allegiance, they could not be other than watchful about what was said on the matter in the universities, however much some Whigs might insist that majority opinion in Oxford would never wean itself away from an attachment to hereditary monarchy. For what came out of the University could have a major impact on what was said and thought at Westminster. It must be emphasised that the Whig voice in Oxford since the 1680s had always been considerable and had never been silenced. Indeed, by the 1750s, any description of Oxford as a Tory, let alone as a Jacobite stronghold without qualification (though these were still being made),[12] was palpably inaccurate for two reasons: first, moderate Whig voices such as John Conybeare, John Burton, and his cousin, Edward Bentham, had become ever more

---

[12] Most famously, Pitt the Elder (matric. Trinity College, 1726, studied for a year) denounced Oxford in the Commons on 25 Nov. 1754 as a 'seminary' of disaffection where he had lately heard treasonable views expressed. P. Palmer to unknown, 27 Nov. 1754, Bodl. MS Top. Oxon. C. 209, ff. 25–6; R. Blacow to T. Bray, Exeter Coll, Bray MSS, 3 Dec. 1754; Walpole, *Memoirs...George II*, II. 27–8.

302 ENLIGHTENED OXFORD

persuasive with the passage of time, assisted by the failure of the '45 Rebellion; secondly, the future of the Hanoverian dynasty was embodied in George II's son and heir, Frederick, Prince of Wales, and he was showing himself willing to reach out and assure Tories that, when he became king in the fullness of time, there would be room for them in the new dispensation - a realm ruled by a 'Patriotic King'.[13] Frederick's premature death in 1751 shut down debate on the issue of allegiance for a few years but, after his son George reached his majority in 1756, and gave every sign via his political mentor, Lord Bute, that all critics of the Pelhams would be welcomed after George II's demise, Tories in the University recovered their voice (if not their name, given the familiarity that the looser term, the 'Old Interest', had accumulated) and saw their deliverance as imminent. After 1760, it would be this interest that pledged itself without qualification to the Hanoverian regime, leaving Whigs to adopt a more detached position vis-à-vis the monarchy as they adopted reformist policies that George III and his ministers could not endorse. By the 1790s, it was only the small number of Foxite Whigs in Oxford who were—to a greater or lesser degree—uncomfortable with the revived 'Church and King' values endorsed by the vast majority in the University (and in the country at large). These loyalists applauded in the person and prejudices of George III a salutary antithesis to the values upheld by Revolutionary France, and drew on a rich, mature, and eclectic vein of monarchist rhetoric that was rooted in historical awareness and made allowance for the importance of constitutional continuities at a time of disruption. It was always more than patriarchal posturing.

ii) Oath-taking and loyalty

The eighteenth-century monarchy for its protection relied less on the threat of coercion than on the word of honour of any future member of the elite as expressed in the taking of a solemn oath. Oaths were, in fact, ubiquitous across the social order, part of the fabric of life throughout the country in parishes, municipal corporations, in the armed services, a kind of extension 'of swearing to observe the customs and obligations of one's own community',[14] and oaths had a particular importance when applied to the propertied and their scions. Oaths were, prima facie, intended to root out disloyalty to the regime since a subscriber was pledging allegiance to the king and abjuring rival claimants to the throne.[15]

---

[13] G. Glickman, 'Parliament, the Tories and Frederick, Prince of Wales', *PH*, 30 (2011), 120–41; Robin Eagles, 'Frederick, Prince of Wales, the "Court" of Leicester House and the "Patriot" Opposition to Walpole, c.1733–1742', *The Court Historian*, 21 (2016), 140–55.

[14] Paul Langford, *Public Life and the Propertied Englishman 1689–1798* (Oxford, 1991), 102.

[15] For the confusing subject of oaths of allegiance, see ibid., 101–16. For the sheer numbers that could be involved in the emergencies of 1689, 1696, and 1723, ibid., 104–5; Edward Vallance, 'Women, politics, and the 1723 oaths of allegiance to George I, 1723', *HJ*, 59 (2016), 975–99.

And yet a charge repeatedly levelled at Oxford by outsiders, Whig outsiders, was that the University was full of at best, dissimulators, at worst, outright liars and men of bad faith. Such critics found it hard to contain their fury at the way in which controls intended by Parliament to flush out the enemies of the Hanoverian Succession were apparently non-functional within the University, conveniently forgetting that the scope for sophistry when taking a politicised oath had always been considerable, as the several reactions to the accession of William and Mary in 1689 had shown. In this way, with some dramatic irony, Oxonians were obliged to admit the value of dissenters' 'mental reservations' in the matter of oath-taking.[16] Whig pamphleteers regularly vented their patriotic spleen on alleged Oxonian dissimulation after occasions such as the '45 Rebellion and the opening of the Radcliffe Library and depicted it as a conspiracy against the new dynasty from within the establishment. One critic, with an eye cast back to the '45, noted that no oath had been more profaned than that of allegiance:

> It is remembered how Persons, of all Conditions and Denominations, flocked in Crowds to make this faithless Test of their Allegiance; and yet, after all this wise Precaution, could the King count one Friend more? Were there not as evident marks of Disaffection after, as before; and even by those who had made this mock Testimonial of their Loyalty?[17]

There were three oaths relating to the state in question. On matriculation all new undergraduates took the Oath of Supremacy, denying the authority of the see of Rome to depose any prince to whom his subjects otherwise owed obedience. There was mention of a 'Foreign Prince', but that would never be how a Jacobite would view the *de jure* sovereign authority of the 'Old Pretender'. However, under I William & Mary, s.1, c.8, Heads of Houses, Fellows, and Professors were required to take the Oath of Allegiance alongside that of Supremacy and, under I Geo I, s.2, c.13, it was reasserted and extended to cover all on the Foundation (scholarship holders were included here) and Exhibitioners over eighteen. In effect, the oath required of an Oxford graduate was that of allegiance to King George by name and, if he was to be awarded a fellowship or any further preferment within the University he would also take the draconian Act of Abjuration against the Stuarts and updated to include 'James III'.[18]

---

[16] For the early modern era as an age of dissimulation see P. Zagorin, *Ways of lying: dissimulation, persecution and conformity in early Modern Europe* (Cambridge, MA, 1990); J. R. Snyder, *Dissimulation and the culture of secrecy in early modern Europe* (Berkeley, CA, 2009).

[17] *A treatise concerning Oaths and Perjury* (London, 1750), 607.

[18] Clark, *Samuel Johnson*, 93–4, citing I Geo I, s. 2, c. 13.

For the average Oxford student still in his teens or the College fellow in his twenties, such pledges were not to be lightly made,[19] for these oaths were designed to be a *sine qua non* in legitimising the role of an individual, however young, as full participant in the life of the state by acknowledging a named monarch from whom all temporal authority descended. That said, in a culture where oath-taking was ubiquitous, it was all too easy (should one want to) to see oaths as formalities, taken as a matter of course. But, as far as the University's detractors were concerned, it was impossible for there to be such manifest disloyalty to the Protestant Succession, unless the majority of senior members were perjurers and, in effect, blasphemers. Thus there existed 'a major problem for the intellectual integrity of a large section of the English intelligentsia' that they appeared to be bringing the obligation of oaths into general disregard through their 'perjury'.[20]

Were these allegations justified? Certainly, there were relatively few men of conscience who, after the great time of trial for the Tories of 1689 was passed and the Nonjurors had consolidated a semi-distinct identity, abandoned a promising university career for the wilderness. Yet those who did quit the academic scene near the beginning of George I's reign included men of talent and seniority:[21] William Marten (Vice-Principal) of Hart Hall; Richard Middleton Massey, (Under-Keeper of the Ashmolean); and Ralph Sheldon, steward of Christ Church. Twenty-two Fellows (including Students of Christ Church) in all became Nonjurors. Among the best-known names were Thomas Hearne, the gossipy sub-librarian of the Bodleian (despite many who urged him to subscribe and not wreck his career), Edward Holdsworth, Fellow of Magdalen and classicist;[22] both these (among others) remained caught up in the life of the University and its graduates through the good offices of their friends who remained on the books. Hearne was always ready to point the finger at Tories in the University whose sense of specific allegiance had been diluted, and it is likely that the total number of those unreservedly committed to the Stuart succession after 1714 was small. If there was a Jacobite majority in Oxford, as the Whigs were ready to insist, then it was a

---

[19] Jeremy Bentham claimed he had been excused from subscribing in 1760 because of his very tender age—twelve. His Victorian editor, Sir John Bowring, noted, '"Loyalty and virtue", I have heard him say, "were then synonymous terms."' Quoted in Clark, *English Society 1660–1832* (2000 edn.), 52.

[20] Clark, *Samuel Johnson*, 93. For semiotic opacity in an earlier era in response to demands of transparency and public accountability see A. Hadfield, *Lying in Early Modern English Culture. From the Oath of Supremacy to the Oath of Allegiance* (Oxford, 2018).

[21] Obtained from J. H. Overton, *History of the Nonjurors* (London, 1902), 471–96. Cf. their counterparts a generation earlier in 1689–91, Chapter 2, pp. 28–30.

[22] Jonathan Clark has controversially presented Samuel Johnson as another such in due course. Clark, *Samuel Johnson*, 93–9, 114–24. He left Pembroke in 1731, compelled by 'irresistible necessity'. ed. Birkbeck Hill, rev. Powell, *Boswell's Life of Johnson*, I. 79. Clark argued that Johnson only accepted the degrees of Hon. MA (1755) and DCL (1775) from Oxford as he was not required to take an oath on the occasions. Other scholars disagree, Robert Folkenflik stating, *pace* Clark, 'there is no reason to believe he either refused to take them or that he avoided putting himself in a position where he would be required to take them'. 'Johnson's Politics', in ed. Greg Clingham, *The Cambridge Companion to Samuel Johnson* (Cambridge, 1997), 102–13, at 103.

very qualified Jacobitism. Nevertheless, the departures of 1714–16 could not help but reawaken memories of the 'Great Rebellion' and the fate of clerics loyal to Charles I and episcopacy in the Established Church. Only weeks before the Hanoverian Succession, John Walker (sometime Fellow of Exeter College) had published *Sufferings of the Clergy* to commemorate the 'victims' of republicanism and regicide, and it could not but find an echo among those called upon in their time to make a choice one way or the other.

There were always those for whom the logic of the cooking-pot would trump every other consideration, whose need for a place and remuneration was the priority. But even these careerists could staunch their consciences with unexpressed mental reservations: there would be the intention to be loyal to the first two Georges *ceteris paribus*, subject to the notion of 'customary oaths' by which oaths required within the academy might be taken without moral commitment,[23] indeed with any number of casuistical reservations and qualifications as refined by Tories since the Revolution. That there was a degree of disingenuousness in the Oxford of 1714 to 1760 seems undeniable; false swearing was probably inevitable in a time of highly charged party conflicts. Oxford was an institution where the hedging of political bets had become part of the fabric, supplemented in some cases by cussedness, a resolve not to give up office just so that some time-server to the new order could be moved in, justified by the widely held Tory view that these oaths were 'simply weapons of proscription'.[24] And the qualifiers could always draw on the old Tory doctrine of passive obedience to the existing authority (though its corollary of non-resistance was rather less serviceable). It was an important, often neglected distinction.

Subscription to the Hanoverian regime ceased to be either controversial or contumacious. By the mid-century, what was believed to be happening in Oxford was presented by commentators as part of a wider problem in the kingdom of a perceived decline in reverence for oath-taking. The blame was laid not at the door of individual perjurers but on post-Revolutionary parliamentary initiatives in extending and imposing so many oaths. These could be deemed an encouragement to imperilling an individual's immortal soul and thus a sin and a disgrace in a Christian society. There was also a cynicism about the rehearsal of spiritual penalties for those who perjured themselves, invoking the deity for reasons that could not disguise expediency dressed up as principle. Blasphemy and perjury had been too easily imported into the system. And it was observed both that Whig careerists in the Church had suppressed personal credal misgivings rather than jeopardise their own preferment, and (particularly during the Occasional Conformity crises in Anne's reign) that the Test Act itself prostituted the Holy Sacrament.[25]

The arguments about the Oxford oaths fuelled the wider debate about the extent to which individuals were bound by the laws under which they lived.

---

[23] See Langford, 'Tories and Jacobites 1714–51', 109.
[24] Langford, *Public Life and the Propertied Englishman*, 103.   [25] Ibid., 109–10.

306 ENLIGHTENED OXFORD

Both were inconclusive; neither side could be said to have won. And the accession of George III in 1760 and the death of 'James III' in 1766 effectively brought the controversy about academic perjury to an end. The debate was moving away from the Crown to the way in which the Church of England was upheld on oath by officeholders, ushering in the controversies of the 1770s over religious subscription, debates that were primarily concerned with theological heterodoxy rather than politics. The conclusion must be that these oaths made to uphold the Hanoverian Crown had been broadly successful in acting as a clamp against disloyalty at Oxford and preventing such disaffection as there was from being any worse. Significantly, where Association had been *voluntary*, as in 1745, the number of Oxonians who had come out and pledged support was not high.

iii) The extent and importance of Jacobitism

> One of the principal coffee-houses in the *highstreet* is called *James's* coffee-house. Can anything be more flagrantly jacobitical?
>
> Dr William King, quoted in Murray Pittock,
'The Culture of Jacobitism', in ed. J. Black,
Culture and Society in Britain, 1660–1800
(Manchester, 1997), 124–45, at 140.

> Oxford is paved with Libels; and the very Stones in the streets, whenever they open their Lips, speak Treason.
>
> [Thomas Bray], Mr Boot's Apology for the conduct
of the late H—gh S—f (1754)

Oxford was in no sense an unambiguously Jacobite university between 1689 and 1714. Confirmed Jacobites were always a minority within Oxford, despite endless allegations to the contrary, but qualified, cultural Jacobitism abounded for many decades after 1689, and was perhaps to the taste of a majority in the University until the 1740s. The flight and 'abdication' of James II at the end of 1688 had actually come as something of a relief to the majority of the University, and William III (and certainly Queen Mary) were sufficiently authentic Stuarts to make the 1690s a decade in which overt Jacobite demonstrations were a rarity; the traumas of the late king's reign were still too close to be readily forgotten, and Tory opinion in the University, looking forward to the accession in due time of Princess Anne and, beyond her, William, Duke of Gloucester (b. 1689),[26]

---

[26] Anne wished to have George Hooper, Dean of Canterbury (Student of Christ Church and former chaplain to Abp Sheldon) as Gloucester's Preceptor, but William III insisted on Burnet. Hester W. Chapman, *Queen Anne's Son. A Memoir of William Henry, Duke of Gloucester 1689–1700* (London, 1954), 133.

remained non-committal towards James II and the putative 'Prince of Wales' in exile at St. Germain-en-Laye, and tepid towards his son-in-law and daughter, the successor sovereigns. Cajoled along by the example of their Chancellor, the 2nd Duke of Ormond, one of William's comrades in arms in Flanders, Oxonians did their best: the high point of cordiality between Oxford and King William occurring in the aftermath of Sir William Trumbull's election as an MP for the University in October 1695. Though William talked much with Ormond in the Sheldonian and accepted from him specimens of the books printed by the University,[27] the king's sense that he was not among friends was palpable, and was reflected in his hasty departure without a tour of the colleges and, over the medium term, in the lack of enthusiasm for appointing Oxonians to bishoprics in his reign.[28]

Anne's accession in March 1702 was greeted with relief and pleasure and she was given a rapturous reception when she visited Oxford in August that same year.[29] In that hope Oxonians were disappointed, for the Queen for the most part looked to act as a political moderate who, on balance, had only a marginal preference for Tories over their Whig counterparts, and increasingly found their hard-line policy emphases vexatious, as her impatience with the 'Tackers' (Tory MPs determined to end Occasional Conformity by doubtful parliamentary means) in 1705 intimated.[30] Yet she was a Stuart, she was devoted to the Established Church, she was protective of the sovereign's prerogative powers, and was a very suitable subject for Stuart typology.[31] There was no chance of Oxford turning Jacobite while she lived, despite the blow of her surviving son's predeceasing her in 1700.[32] It was only as her health worsened after 1710 that the University at last started to confront the impact on itself and the Church of the implementation of the Protestant succession under the 1701 Act of Settlement. And being persuaded that the *de jure* 'James III' would never renounce his

---

[27] Wood, *Life and Times*, III. 494–6; BL Add MS. 28879, f. 289. Discussed in Chapter 2, p. 30.

[28] [E. Bernard]—T. Smith [10 Nov. 1695], Bodl. MS Smith 47, f. 183; G.V. Bennett, 'Against the Tide: Oxford under William III', in HUO V, 31–60 at 49–51; Chapter 2, passim. For the ecclesiastical commission's appointments see G. V. Bennett, 'King William III and the episcopate', in eds. G. V. Bennett and J. D. Walsh, *Essays in modern English Church history in memory of Norman Sykes* (London, 1966), 104–32; G. V. Bennett, 'Conflict in the Church', in ed. G. Holmes, *Britain after the Glorious Revolution* (London, 1969).

[29] Hone, *Literature and Party Politics*, 85–92; Hone, 'Politicising praise: panegyric and the accession of Queen Anne', *JECS*, 37 (2014), 147–58; N. Aston, 'Queen Anne and Oxford: the royal visit of 1702 and its aftermath', *JECS*, 37 (2014), 171–84.

[30] Gregg, *Queen Anne*, 155–7, 192, 196; Anne Somerset, *Queen Anne. The Politics of Passion. A Biography* (London, 2012), 275–6, 280. 'Moderation' was not a popular term in the high Tory lexicon. She visited Cambridge in 1705, an indicator of changes in the political wind. R. O. Bucholz, 'Queen Anne and the limitations of royal ritual', *JBS*, 30 (1991), 288–323, at 310.

[31] K. Sharpe, *Rebranding rule. The Restoration and revolution monarchy 1660–1714* (New Haven, CT, 2013), 578–615.

[32] Daniel Szechi notes that 'At the start of her reign the Jacobite movement as a whole was virtually inert.' 'Jacobite Politics in the Age of Anne', in ed. C. Jones, *British Politics in the Age of Holmes. Geoffrey Holmes's British Politics in the Age of Anne 40 Years On* (London, 2009), 41–58, at 46.

308 ENLIGHTENED OXFORD

Catholicism, the leaders of the University and their patrons in 1713–14 (with one or two exceptions)[33] did not intend to be the losers when the Elector of Hanover reached British shores to claim his inheritance. There were crypto-Jacobite murmurings and grumblings audible in Oxford common rooms between 1710 and 1714, but that was always going to be the case with the University lined up behind Harley's 'Great Ministry' and looking to hold on to its advantage when the Queen finally succumbed. Under Vice Chancellor Gardiner of All Souls, ever keen to cultivate the goodwill of Harley,[34] expressions of Jacobitism among the undergraduate body were frowned upon and an appearance by the *Terrae Filius* at the Act of 1713 was banned because of Gardiner's fears that he would use it to celebrate the wrong sort of loyalism.[35]

Oxford was emphatically not a predominantly Jacobite university on George I's accession, yet the sense persisted that the majority of its members were embracing the post-Stuart era with a palpable lack of enthusiasm: Queen Anne's demise was lamented with a degree of threnody that intimated that, however disappointed many had been at the late monarch's studied moderation, Tory Oxonians—newly 'homeless in the state'[36]—sensed they were likely to be pushed further still from royal favour under the Hanoverian dispensation. Whig determination not to tolerate a mixed-party administration on the model of the early 1690s was confirmed after the outbreak and course of the '15 Jacobite Rebellion gave the party the excuse it needed to exclude the Tory remnant in government, thereby greatly increasing the appeal of a Stuart restoration for ambitious Tories, and those who feared for the safety of the Church of England in Whig hands.[37] It was above all the flight abroad of Oxford's Chancellor, the Duke of Ormond, and his subsequent involvement in the '15 that gave the Whigs all the ammunition they needed to ignore (and ask the King and the public to ignore) the numerous and complicated fault lines of Oxford's politics and drive home the simple message that Oxford and Jacobitism were synonymous, that this was a disloyal university.

---

[33] Significant among them was Henry, 2nd Duke of Beaufort, nephew of the 2nd Duke of Ormond, discussed in Chapter 12, pp. 12–13.

[34] Gardiner was in post between 1712 and 1715. William Bromley reported to Harley that Gardiner was 'full of acknowledgements for the Favours he has received from you'. Letter of 17 Nov. 1710, BL Add MS, 70287, unfoliated.

[35] A pamphlet purporting to be the prohibited speech went on sale, much to Gardiner's fury, who wanted this 'Scandalous Libel' ceremoniously burnt in the Schools quadrangle. Willes, *The speech that was intended to have been spoken by the Terrae-Filius* (London, 1713); *The University Miscellany, or more burning work for the Oxford Convocation* (London, 1713); Hearne, IV, 243–4. The historian and future Nonjuror Thomas Carte spoke for many when he wrote to Arthur Charlett of the ban setting 'a very good Precedent &, I hope, will be always followed, all men of sense & goodness having long complained of the intolerable license therein taken of throwing scandal abroad without distinction of persons, regard to truth or even any wit to recommend it & make it palatable.' Bodl MS Ballard 18, f. 51, letter of 8 July 1713.

[36] Murray Pittock, *Jacobitism* (Basingstoke, 1998), 133.

[37] For the range of Tory responses to proscription see Colley, *In Defiance of Oligarchy*, 26–41.

OXFORD AND THE CROWN 309

Ormond's hasty exit was a shock to most in the University, but the hasty election of his younger brother, Lord Arran, as the new Chancellor in September 1715 was less a Jacobite gesture than a determination not to have a Whig grandee like Marlborough or his son-in-law, Sunderland, intruded into that key leadership position.[38] But its timing, at the height of the Rebellion, and the blatant refusal to consider the Prince of Wales as a plausible candidate, sent out the wrong signals to moderate opinion beyond Oxford, as did the failure to transmit a loyal address on the King's return from Hanover in October 1716 with Gardiner, for once, leading the opposition to the proposal.[39] As Paul Langford shrewdly observed: 'Even if Oxford harboured few rebels for practical purposes—the temper and tone of life there were difficult to explain except in relation to a powerful swell of Jacobite sentiment'.[40] Popular Tory demonstrations fuelled by alcohol took to the streets on the long evenings of early summer (28, 29 May, 10 June). Student disaffection and rioting (however provoked and taking however much satisfaction in tweaking the noses of authority) were eagerly reported in the Whig press and apparently offered further evidence of disloyalty to George I that stemmed from the alleged Jacobitism of the teachers and governors. It was on the basis of an unfounded allegation that the Pretender had been proclaimed as King in Oxford on 27 October 1715, and a regiment of students had been formed to rise under disaffected officers, that the military occupation of the city was ordered.[41]

The fact was that the leaders of the University could restate the desirability of declaring themselves loyal to the new order in Church and state while nursing a series of grievances against George I and his Whig advisers that grew ever more numerous as one-party hegemony increased. They understandably looked to Italy and saw a young Stuart claimant to the throne, a man born in England, whose assurances of protection for the Church and power for the Tories grew steadily more attractive.[42] Jacobite propensities grew among a range of Tories, especially the younger MAs who stood to lose much less than more senior members, knew that their chances of obtaining preferment from the Whigs were scanty, but whose

[38] See Chapter 6, p. 5.

[39] Ward, *Georgian Oxford*, 65, 280, points out that the refusal was intended as a ploy by Oxford court Tories to arouse the interest of George, Prince of Wales.

[40] 'Tories and Jacobites 1714–51', 105. Cf. Ward, who, in explaining such disaffection as Oxford exhibited, noted '...it is also impossible to overlook the provocation to which the University was exposed'. *Georgian Oxford*, 67.

[41] HMC, *Stuart papers* (7 vols., London, 1902–23), I. 438; Boyer, ed., *The Political state of Great Britain*, X. 536, 585–6. There can be little doubt that a sizable body of undergraduate opinion in 1715–16 was militantly pro-Jacobite. For one of them from Christ Church captured at the battle of Preston in 1715 see William Gibson, *The Church of England 1688–1832. Unity and Accord* (London, 2001), 139.

[42] 'James III' wrote to both universities (20 Oct. 1715) to allege that the Whigs were planning to ruin them by depriving them of their lands and reducing their privileges, which he promised he would defend. HMC, *Stuart papers*, I. 438. His letter had little immediate impact.

310 ENLIGHTENED OXFORD

gauge of the Pretender's capacity to achieve a restoration was not necessarily acute. Some followed the example of Lord Arran and played a dangerous double game: just at the time (March 1721) that the Earl was dealing directly with 'James III' about a restoration, he was allowed to purchase the forfeited estates of his brother, the 2nd Duke, by private Act of Parliament dated July 1721.[43] Though not prosecuted for his subsequent involvement in the Atterbury Plot, the effect of his close shave and the failure of the Plot made Oxford Jacobites extremely circumspect in disclosing themselves for upwards of a decade.[44] There had never been many of them among the Heads of Houses and one who was, the turbulent William King of St Mary Hall, was unsuccessful in challenging the moderate Harleian Tory, George Clarke, for one of the University seats in the General Election of 1722, despite a range of MA followers in most colleges and a fiercely fought campaign.[45]

The fiasco of the Atterbury Plot made the bulk of the University's upper ranks more determined than ever to appear distanced from Jacobitism,[46] especially as they anticipated a warmer welcome at court for Tories after George I's death in 1727. When that event happened, there was a welcome of sorts, but it soon faded. Privately, with their friends, in their families, senior Oxonians, marginalised since 1714-16, kept faith with the 'honest cause' (as Jacobitism was euphemistically termed) as best they could, while keeping public embarrassment to the University to a minimum. Despite the efforts of successive vice chancellors to steer the University away from public and ministerial notice for the wrong reasons, Oxford, institutionally, retained many characteristics of a crypto-Jacobite resort in the first half of George II's reign.[47] Thus Sir John Dolben, the Visitor of Balliol (though primarily resident at a safe distance in his Durham canonry, courtesy of his patron, Bishop Crew), paid an annuity to Bishop Atterbury in exile, and happily accepted the gift of a portrait of Charles Edward Stuart in the 1740s.[48] Commemorative preaching, especially 30 January sermons, offered another opportunity to celebrate values of true loyalty and kingship that, by definition, critiqued the current order in Church and state. Most preachers took care not to overstep the mark, let the mask slip too much, and risk official disavowal by the

---

[43] *Lords Journal*, xxi. 549–50, https://www.british-history.ac.uk/lords-jrnl/vol21/pp547-556. It seems likely that ministers sold him the forfeited property for a low price in appreciation of the family's long service to the crown. F. G. James, *Lords of the Ascendancy. The Irish House of Lords and its Members 1600–1800* (Dublin, 1995), 115–16.

[44] For Arran, see Chapter 6, pp. 5–10, and Aston, 'The Great survivor'.

[45] Ward, *Georgian Oxford*, 123–8. Paul Kléber Monod pointedly notes that 'Oxford was perhaps the sole constituency in England where a staunch Tory could be opposed on the basis of his not being enough of a Jacobite'. *Jacobitism and the English People*, 277.

[46] There appear to be no subscription returns for 1723 in Oxfordshire, so the resources are lacking for determining how individual college fellows responded to the demands to proclaim loyalty to the Hanoverian dynasty. I am grateful to Edward Vallance for this information.

[47] The problem of which Tories were Jacobites and what their Jacobitism signified defies precise adjudication. See the comments of I. R. Christie, 'The Tory Party, Jacobitism and the '45: a note', *HJ*, 30 (1987), 921–31.

[48] Philip Thicknesse, *Memoirs and Anecdotes* (3 vols., London, 1788–91), I. 209–11.

University authorities, ever apprehensive of intervention from ministers listening to Whigs determined to find evidence of treason.[49] Thus, when Walpole's contentious Excise Bill was withdrawn in 1733, the indefatigable Jacobite hunter Richard Meadowcourt, at Merton, alleged he saw students in the streets 'throwing money among the rabble, and reviving the old cries of Ormon[de], Bolingbroke, king James for ever, &c.'[50]

During the '45, however tepid private regard for George II may have been, the academic authorities did certainly not encourage overt commitment to Prince Charles Edward Stuart.[51] It was perhaps just as well for the University that the

Fig. 7.1 Rev. Sir John Dolben, Robert Taylor, oil on canvas, c.1750 (Master and Fellows of Balliol College, Oxford).

---

[49] For the Coningsby affair see Chapter 6, p. 31.
[50] Coxe, *Memoirs of Walpole*, III. 137, quoted in George Hilton Jones, *The Main Stream of Jacobitism* (Cambridge, MA, 1954), 187; J. Oates, *Jacobitism in eighteenth century English schools and colleges* [The Royal Stuart Society, Paper LXXII] (London, 2007), 9.
[51] For the duration of the rebellion and beyond, the Vice Chancellor, Euseby Isham, withheld his consent to the publication of an ultra-loyalist sermon preached by the Rev John Free, Chaplain of Christ Church, when the Prince's army was at Derby and might be expected in Oxford. John Free, DD, *A Volume of Sermons preached before the University of Oxford* (London, 1750), xii–xiv. The offending item was Sermon X. For official attitudes see Chapter 6, pp. 32–3, 89.

312 ENLIGHTENED OXFORD

Stuart army advanced no further south into the Midlands than Derby.[52] After Culloden, dons and their Tory patrons may have been looking increasingly to Prince Frederick of Wales as an alternative focus for their loyalist instincts, but an undergraduate admiration for the pluck shown by Prince Charles Edward Stuart in 1745–6 was constantly manifesting itself in the years following; the Blacow affair of 1747–8 revealed the reluctance of the University authorities to take a firm hand against intoxicated students abusing George II and his ministers.[53] A proportion of Oxonians could not quite bring themselves to break with the Stuarts and the chance to express their cultural sympathies for the cause (as opposed to their political commitment) was invariably irresistible.

Members of the University and their guests crammed into the Radcliffe Library for its opening on 13 April 1749 and heard William King use his official oration— just three years after Culloden—to stirring, suggestive effect. There were no fewer than five REDEAT apostrophes in his speech ('Restore that great *genius* of Britain'), all delivered in support of 'Astraea' (who, by association, was intended as the Young Pretender, though many others in his audience may have heard an acclamation of Prince Frederick) and the return of rightful kingship, castigating the corruption of recent times.[54] It was a learned, Latin oration that caught national attention, reinforced perceptions of Oxford as the Jacobite epicentre, provoked apologists both pro and anti the Prince, with propagandists riffing on the words of King's speech. His sheer daring was breathtaking and commanded admiration and anger in equal measure.[55] The young poet, Thomas Warton of Trinity College, was in no doubt:

---

[52] For a later claim made by Dr Thomas Brookes, the pluralist rector of Shipton-under-Wychwood (1773–1814), matric. Magdalen Hall, 1749, that the north Oxfordshire squires (probably led by Sir Robert Jenkinson, 5th Bt. (1720–66) (matric. SJC, 1738, DCL, 1749) of South Lawn Lodge in Wychwood Forest (brother of the future Cabinet minister, Charles Jenkinson) would have joined any southward march from Derby, see E. Marshall, *The early history of Woodstock Manor and its environs* (Oxford, 1873), 270n. Neither Jenkinson nor others supportive of the 'honest' cause in the county appear to have tried to contact Prince Charles Edward. Thomas Rowney, one of the MPs for the city of Oxford, who, according to Lord Egmont, had 'drunk ye Pretender's health 500 times', was 'frightened out of his wits' when 'the Pretender's Son came into England ... and ordered his chaplain to pray for King George'. BL Add MS 47012, D 12, Earl of Egmont, 'notes on the Tories'.

[53] Richard Blacow, *A Letter to William King, LL.D. Principal of St Mary Hall in Oxford. Containing a particular account of the treasonable riot in Oxford in Feb. 1747* (London, 1755); Ward, *Georgian Oxford*, 169–71; Chapter 8, pp. 29–32. For good liquor as the alleged life and support of Jacobitism see Edward Bentham, *A Letter to a Fellow of a College* (Oxford, 1749), 53. Certainly Arthur Charlett was once caught out disclosing his Jacobite preferences after a few drinks. Frank McLynn has claimed that 'The English Tories were merely Jacobites of the mouth or the wine-bottle'. *Charles Edward Stuart. A Tragedy in Many Acts* (London, 1988), 189.

[54] For the text, in Latin and English, see Bodl. Gough Oxf. 81 (5) and GA Oxon. 8vo 62 (3); *Translation of a Late Celebrated Oration occasioned by a Libel [sic] entitled 'Remarks on Dr King's Speech'* (Oxford, 1749); 'The Opening of the Radcliffe Library in 1749', *Bodleian Quarterly Record* 1 (1915), 165–72; Greenwood, *William King*, 197–203; Colley, *In Defiance of Oligarchy*, 257. It may be that King wrote his speech in such a way that it could be open to either interpretation.

[55] For opponents, see *A friend to Mr Kennicott* [Benjamin Kennicott], *A letter to Dr King occasion'd by his Late apology, . . .* (London, 1755), 32.

He [King] blends the speaker's with the patriot's fire...
What Britons dare to think, he dares to tell.
Bids happier days to Albion be restored
Bids ancient Justice rear her radiant sword;
From me, as from my country, claims applause,
And makes an Oxford's, a Britannia's cause.[56]

King was almost taunting the government to prosecute him as a Jacobite yet in 1749, he had the luxury, which he would not have had in 1745, of knowing that his invocations would not have the corollary of a call to arms. And with that room for reserve that Oxford Jacobites even of his dye left themselves, he could, if pressed, insinuate that his words had Hanoverian connotations. That scope soon came to an end. The death of Frederick, Prince of Wales, in 1751, and the longevity of George II arguably reinforced Jacobite inclinations among a hard core of Tories in the short term, even if they were only too aware at first hand of the personal unsuitability of Prince Charles Edward for the duties of kingship: with other Jacobite sympathisers, King had met the Prince secretly in London in September 1750, and the Young Pretender's conversion to Anglicanism was not enough to offset his absence of regal potential.[57] He and they came away disappointed that Prince Charles Edward post-Culloden was by character and temperament unsuited to witness to what might be deemed the best in Jacobite values; which was not to say that those values could not be transferred to endorse Hanoverian kingship—on the proviso that it was not that embodied in George II.

For most of the 1750s, therefore, Oxonian Jacobites comfortably subsumed their identities within the broad banner of the 'Old Interest'.[58] Though essentially marking time, they were pleased to draw on the heritage of Stuart loyalty, privately

---

[56] Quoted and discussed in Murray Pittock, *Poetry and Jacobite Politics in Eighteenth-Century Britain and Ireland* (Cambridge, 1994), 89–90. One present reported that Dr King 'Described bad Kings & Ironically excepted his Majesty. Drew ye character of military Hero's without mentioning the Duke of Cumberland...he pray'd that in case we lost our Chancellor we might cho[o]se another of a particular Character which he described & intended to have understood as a Compliment to ye Duke of Beaufort, put a severe Satyr on the D. of New Castle by way of opposition & contrast'. Letter of Thomas Breary, Driffield, Yorks., 24 Apr. 1749, Bodl., Radcliffe (Library) Papers, MS Top Oxon. b. 43, ff. 19–20. King was arguably mindful of the court's refusal of the first Oxford address the previous December. See this Chapter, pp. 71–2.

[57] King, *Political and Literary anecdotes*, 196–209. He deplored his avariciousness, 'the certain index of a base and little mind'. Ibid.,, 201–2. Cf. McLynn, *Charles Edward Stuart*, 399. Tellingly, his address at the Commemoration of July 1754 (when Lord Westmorland took office as High Steward at the end of the academic year) similarly lamented the condition of society and politics without discernible Jacobite connotations. Greenwood, *William King*, 267–9. For Prince Charles's lack of interest in the University, see Ward, *Georgian Oxford*, 150.

[58] The comments of James J. Sack on the protean party nomenclature of the 1750s are exemplary. *From Jacobite to Conservative*, 50–63. As Sack notes (52), by the 1750s 'whatever enthusiasm there may have been for Jacobitism among the Tories was exceedingly tempered'.

314   ENLIGHTENED OXFORD

celebrate it,[59] and openly witness to it when opportunity offered, as in John, 7th Earl of Westmorland's installation as Chancellor in succession to Arran in July 1759.[60] But they knew that, barring an unwanted miracle, their Prince would not return and that, in point of fact, they did not want him back when the choice lay between a royal, middle-aged inebriate given to beating up his mistresses, born in Italy, and George, Prince of Wales, the virtuous heir presumptive, born at Kew in 1738. The Westmorland installation was, arguably, at the time as well as retro-spectively, a last hurrah for Jacobitism, and even then not unambiguously so, for Westmorland was a nobleman whose connections with Leicester House and Prince Frederick had been enduring.[61] And, in that sense, the University was turning to embrace the future in the person of that Prince's son and heir. After his accession in 1760, Jacobitism quickly became, in Jonathan Clark's words, 'a harmless Oxford mannerism',[62] one that nodded to the past but offered not the slightest indicator of an individual's undoubted loyalty to the person and rule of George III. Even William King, in his last years, was a welcome presence at court levées, and became a supporter of Lord Bute's Peace of Paris (1763) and George Grenville on his succeeding the latter as premier the same year.[63]

iv) Oxford and early eighteenth-century Toryism

Jacobitism was a recurrent but essentially incidental presence in eighteenth-century Oxford, and is best regarded as just one aspect of the predominant Toryism of the University: dangerous, fascinating, exciting, scandalous, diverting, noteworthy, an after-dark diversion. Otherwise University Tories had many other aspects of their beliefs to temper and refine to fit the post-Revolutionary age, and their willingness to make Toryism progressive and patriotic as the century wore on can be underestimated. Theirs was not a static, reactive, reactionary perspective. In one sense the Toryism of the 1730s and 1740s was countercultural, in another it was a generous creed for the future, that was ready to sink party difference for the national good, row back on Anglican exclusiveness in the

---

[59] For Edward Gibbon's observing the fellows of Magdalen toasting the Stuarts see *Memoirs*, 76–80. Oxford toasts in the 1750s were often drunk in Jacobite glasses, most of which, indeed, are now considered to postdate 1745. G. B. Seddon, *The Jacobites and their Drinking Glasses* (London, 2015). I am grateful to Richard Sharp for this reference.

[60] See Chapter 6, pp. 9–12.

[61] Sharp, 'The Oxford Installation of 1759', 149, argues for the 'overwhelmingly Tory complexion of the week's celebrations', noting (149) the presence of the Jacobite hostess, Anne Drelincourt, Viscountess [of] Primrose.

[62] J. C. D. Clark, *The Dynamics of Change. The Crisis of the 1750s and English Party Systems* (Cambridge, 1982), 10. For George III's unconcern about Jacobitism, *The Devonshire Diary. William Cavendish Fourth Duke of Devonshire, Memoranda on State Affairs 1759-1762*, eds. Peter D. Brown and Karl W. Schweizer [Camden, 4th Ser., 27] (London, 1982), 171.

[63] BL Egerton MS 2136, f. 67, William King to Lord Le Despenser, 7 Sept. 1763.

OXFORD AND THE CROWN   315

interests of all the King's subjects in the projected brave new monarchical world that never was of Frederick, Prince of Wales, then of George III. Whigs appeared as the party of vested party interests; Tories offered another, more generous vision of the future that drew on the best of the past.

Oxford was the powerhouse of Toryism. If, in the 1690s, the temptation to retreat into nostalgia for a lost pre-Revolutionary golden age was sometimes overwhelming for dons, those who had not become Nonjurors (ie. the vast majority) were required to work with the new status quo in Church and state and, so long as it persisted, make the best of it. The adjustment was not easy. Accepting the legitimacy of what had taken place in 1688–9 could never be ungrudgingly given when Tories had so long upheld the principles of indefeasible hereditary succession, non-resistance, and the inviolability of oaths.[64] Arguments that denied these had been breached were, with varying degrees of plausibility, developed, but Oxonian attention was more directed to the threat from relatively unfettered press freedoms in the wake of the lapsing of the Licensing Act (1695), the growth of Dissent, the sense that deism was on the march, and involvement in a costly foreign war.

With Atterbury and the Christ Church circle to the fore, the University led the way in arguing for the summoning of Convocation in 1697 as a barrier to the perceived threat to the Church from the likes of Lord Somers, the legal luminary of the Whig Junto. It was that proud, aging Oxonian, Lord Rochester, who eventually persuaded William III in early 1701 to consent to the call.[65] In one light, it was a familiar, but newly defensive clericalism, but it was offset by adoption of Country party rhetoric arguing for lower taxes and a respect for the liberties of the subject. The appeal of this programme as a viable alternative to that of the new Whig establishment could not be ignored by the turn of the eighteenth century.

The assaults of James II were too recent and too painful for Jacobitism to be a viable option for the majority of Oxford Tories in the 1690s, who would mostly have conceded that the Prince of Orange's arrival had gone a long way towards 'saving' the Church from the depredations of its then Supreme Governor, his father-in-law, and, in that limited sense, subscribed to a providentialist theory of 1688. Yet, for all the masterly management of moderate Tories in Oxford by such as Arthur Charlett and Henry Aldrich in negotiating post-Revolutionary realities, by the late 1690s, the strain felt by University Tories in cooperating with the King on a range of his policies was becoming unsupportable.[66] They looked

[64] Tim Harris, Revolution. The Great Crisis of the British Monarchy, 1685–1720 (Harmondsworth, 2006), 359.
[65] Sykes, Church and State, 297 et seq.; Bennett, Tory Crisis, 48–56. See also Chapter 2. Rochester was concurrently trying to bring in a Tory ministry, in conjunction with Bishops Compton, Thomas Sprat, and Trelawny. Many discussions occurred in Christ Church itself during the later 1690s, courtesy of Dean Aldrich. Smith, Fighting Joshua, 100.
[66] The early death of the accessible, charming and Anglican Queen Mary from smallpox in Dec. 1694 had not helped. Rose, England in the 1690s, 41–7.

316 ENLIGHTENED OXFORD

increasingly towards the new Country party axis that Robert Harley, Paul Foley, and their Oxfordshire ally, Simon Harcourt, lawyer and landlord (who had been at school with Harley), along with William Bromley, Warwickshire squire and Christ Church graduate (MP for the University from early 1701), were steadily building.[67] The young Duke of Gloucester's death in 1700 meanwhile reopened the Succession question and, though Tories largely went along with the Act of Settlement (June 1701) vesting the Crown after Anne in the Hanoverians (not least because its provisions included much of the 'Country' programme and other parts of it were 'an indictment of William's reign'),[68] the death of James II the following September again brought the question of allegiance to the fore. A new oath of abjuration was brought into Parliament, requiring Tories to renounce the new Stuart Pretender, 'James III', and his title.[69] What alone sweetened this crisis of conscience for some was the sure prospect of Princess Anne's imminent accession and the unlikely one that she would conceive afresh and render the Act of Settlement redundant.[70]

Anne's succession to the throne in March 1702 ended a time of enormous strain on the Tory ideology of Church and Crown in the years following the Revolution, in that the 'two elements of that creed, wrenched apart by James II, [had] remained sundered'.[71] In 1702 it might be hoped that they could be reunited. The new reign prompted an initial Tory resurgence across the nation fanned by Oxonian flames that began to blow themselves out by 1704–5 as the party registered its disappointment at the Queen's unwillingness to endorse either their men or their measures unconditionally, including the shrill High Churchmanship of which Oxford remained the epicentre.[72] Anne's growing removal from high Tory attitudes was in evidence on 4 January 1705, when Vice Chancellor Delaune with several Heads of Houses and the Proctors attended the Queen with a printed copy of the speeches and verses spoken in the Sheldonian Theatre that New Year's Day. Their equal bias towards Admiral Sir George Rooke as much as the duke of Marlborough was embarrassingly out of kilter in a court dominated by the latter's wife and

---

[67] David Hayton, 'The "Country" interest and the party system, 1689–1720', in ed. C. Jones, *Party and management in Parliament 1660–1784* (Bath, 1984), 37–85. For Bromley's early career see Keith Feiling, *A History of the Tory Party 1640–1714* (Oxford, 1924), 310; Ward, *Georgian Oxford*, 20–1. Bromley's publications of the early 1690s detailing his travels in Europe were presented by his enemies as a sure sign that he had connections with the Pretender. Edward Chaney, 'The Grand Tour and the evolution of the Travel Book', in eds. Andrew Wilton and Ilaria Bignamini, *Grand Tour. The Lure of Italy in the Eighteenth Century* (London, 1996), 95–7, at 95.

[68] Evelyn Cruickshanks, *The Glorious Revolution* (Basingstoke, 2000), 87; Harris, *Politics under the later Stuarts*, 164–5. Only one Tory MP, John Granville, spoke in favour of a Jacobite successor during the debate on the Bill. *The Parliamentary Diary of Sir Richard Cocks 1688–1715, ed.* D. W. Hayton (Oxford, 1996), xlvii.

[69] Kenyon, *Revolution Principles*, 33–4, 89–90.

[70] For an emphasis on Anne's contested right to the throne see Hone, *Literature and party Politics*, 2, 167–8.

[71] Rose, *The 1690s*, 268.

[72] Holmes, *Politics in the Age of Anne*, 194–5; Gregg, *Queen Anne*, 177–81.

followers. Anne returned what was described as 'a dry answer' telling Delaune 'how kindly she took this Instance of their Zeal' and added 'as they might be assured of her Protection, so she would not doubt of their Care to encourage PRINCIPLES, which would promote the Peace and Welfare of her self, and all her Subjects'.[73]

In Tory terms, her reign is indelibly associated with one Oxonian—Henry Sacheverell, the high-flying, incendiary Fellow of Magdalen. And it is the case that Sacheverell articulated (and ranted on) uncompromisingly Tory concerns and anxieties about Dissenters, the role of the Established Church in the post-Revolutionary state, and the manifold challenges confronting a publicly Christian polity.[74] Interestingly, until his trial, the Doctor had relatively little to say himself about the monarch or the monarchy, as opposed to the Church. It was left to his defenders at his trial to develop, sometimes stumblingly, the implications for the Crown of his rhetoric. As a brilliant self-publicist, Sacheverell came across to the country at large as *the* voice of Oxford. Yet, apart from the heady days of his trial and the advent of a Tory administration when the University dispatched an address to the queen in favour of his principles,[75] senior Oxford academics were wary of Sacheverell, kept him at a distance, offered him no preferment, and were somewhat embarrassed by his antics.[76] Certainly, he passed through Oxford on his way north after his trial was over, read prayers at Magdalen College, and was warmly received by the Vice Chancellor, William Lancaster (who had stood bail for him).[77] But the 'Doctor' was not invited back. This omission suggests, correctly, that there was a moderate current of Toryism within the University, influential disproportionately to its numbers within the Heads of Houses and

[73] A. Boyer, *The History of the Reign of Queen Anne* (London, 1733), 168. Boyer added: 'And as the University of Oxford spoke the sense of the whole High-Church party, so it was not long before the Court, who now espoused the opposite Interest, shew'd their Resentment of it'. ibid. See also Winn, *Queen Anne. Patroness of Arts*, 397.

[74] His career before the St Paul's sermon of 5 Nov. 1709 is summarised in W. A. Speck, 'The Current State of Sacheverell Scholarship,', in ed. Knights, *Faction Displayed*, 16–27, at 19.

[75] The address reflected a decree in Convocation. Whigs and Jacobites were equally condemned in the document which abhorred 'that Popish Republican Doctrine of Resistance of Princes', UOA: MS. Conv. Reg. Bd 31, f. 62. Whigs in the Lords were aghast and on 22 March 1710 ordered what they called the decree of the University of Oxford in favour of passive obedience and non-resistance to be burnt by the hangman. Luttrell, *Historical Relation*, VI. 56, 23 Mar. 1710. Tindal's *The Rights of the Christian Church Asserted* was condemned by the Commons the same month. See Chapter 2, pp. 22–4.

[76] It says much that, when in 1708 Sacheverell decided to take his DD—something which was usually done only by Heads of House and canons of Christ Church, several senior Fellows of Magdalen decided that, because Sacheverell was quite a junior Fellow, they had better go through the trouble and expense of taking their own DDs to stop him leaping over them in the pecking order. Thanks to Robin Darwall-Smith for this information.

[77] Lancaster was later accused of 'turning Cat in Pan, and deserting the Doctor, and his Cause' when he had personally received Sacheverell warmly, and 'was more frequent in his Visits to him at his own Appartments, than some People, who had no great Friendship for the Doctor, . . .' J. K., *Dr Sacheverel's Progress from London, to his Rectory of Salatin [Selattyn] in Shropshire* (London, 1710), 5–6. For Lancaster, 'smooth boots', taking a Whiggish address to the Queen from the University, see Hearne, II. 384 (2 May 1710). *A Letter from Oxford* (Aug. 1710) mentions the money raised for Sacheverell in the colleges, and for Oxford celebrations on his acquittal see Wigelsworth, *Deism in Enlightenment England*, 114–15.

318   ENLIGHTENED OXFORD

the professoriate by men like Aldrich, Charlett, Delaune, and Gardiner (all of whom, except the first, presided over remarkably disunited colleges), that was determined to avoid an overheated rhetoric that would only play into the hands of the Whigs. And there was always the possibility, as one Oxford poet wryly intimated, that preferment, might change Sacheverell's own outlook:[78]

> Among ye high Church men I find there are severall,
> Do swear to ye merits of Henry Sacheverell.
> Amongst ye low Church men too I see yet as oddly,
> Some pin at their faith on one Benjamin Hoadly,
> But we moderate men our judgment suspend,
> For God only knows how these matters will end;
> For Sal'bury Burnet & Kennet White show;
> That Doctrines may change as preferments do go,
> And twenty years hence for what you or I know,
> It may be Hoadly ye high, and Sacheverell ye low.

The question remains, did this moderate Toryism have its own distinctive programme and values, or was it just a matter of academic pragmatism and politeness? Moderate Oxonians by 1710 had rallied to Harley (created Earl of Oxford in 1711), became courtiers and benefitted from his patronage of the University over the four years of his ministry.[79] But Tories still struggled to produce, certainly within Oxford, enough unequivocal ideological indicators to suggest that they were comfortable in a pluralist, post-Revolutionary state, ready to receive the House of Hanover unreservedly, and to endorse a powerful monarchy when its crown was not worn by a Stuart. Aldrich died in 1710 better known for his architectural and aesthetic interests, while other moderate Tories either were too caught up in college business or lacked the inclination to make the case for an updated Toryism that was comfortable with the post-1688 state and could endorse the importance of a monarchical polity for the new century that went beyond an exercise in nostalgia.

Sacheverell's chief counsel, the Oxford lawyer and former Attorney-General Sir Simon Harcourt,[80] tried at his client's trial to broaden out the meaning of the words 'the supreme power' (as used in the notorious sermon of 9 November) to mean something more than the monarch. The term, Harcourt contended, also

---

[78] The James Marshall and Marie-Louise Osborn Collection, Beinecke Rare Book & Manuscript Library, Yale University, Osborn Shelves fc24, ff. 19–20.

[79] His insertion of Anne's statue in Tom Tower at Christ Church was a public sign of his affection for the Queen. Judith Curthoys, *The stones of Christ Church. The story of the buildings of Christ Church, Oxford* (London, 2017), 114. At University College, Charlett allowed a Fellow's brother to pay for a statue of the Queen above the main entrance. Thanks to Robin Darwall-Smith for this information.

[80] His career is summarised in Stuart Handley, 'Harcourt, Simon, first Viscount Harcourt (1661?–1727), lawyer and politician', ODNB, online edn., 2004.

OXFORD AND THE CROWN 319

denoted 'the legislative power' which had substantially effected the Revolution of 1688–9 (he used the words 'the Lords and Commons concurring and assisting in it', Harcourt was trying desperately to deny that the Revolution had overturned the principle of non-resistance by placing all his emphasis on the legitimising actions of the Convention Parliament of 1689. This interpretation was stretching credibility, but Harcourt was insistent: 'We are hearty well-wishers to the Revolution, and to the happiness of England that is in a great measure built upon it'.[81] The problem for Harcourt and the like-minded was to break down the Whig insistence that such a claim was either disingenuous or a lie and this they never succeeded in doing between 1710 and 1714. Whigs could thus point to pro-Sacheverell academics such as Joseph Trapp (chaplain to Bolingbroke from 1713) peddling a Filmerite line and castigating those who would make the people 'sovereign, the representative' over their natural governors;[82] they reminded the public of the book-burning decrees of 1683,[83] and the wording of documents such as the 1710 Oxford Address constructed in the triumphal aftermath of the Sacheverell affair with its reference to never questioning 'any title by which your Majestie holds your Crown, particularly that which is hereditary.' It all seemed to add up to an evasion of the parliamentary basis of the Queen's title, thereby disclosing that the good faith of the Tories and their friends in the University was negligible.[84]

And yet an explicitly 'Hanoverian Toryism' was emerging by 1712 which tried to accept the foundational status of the Revolution in the constitution and the legislation that had followed from it. But it struggled to be fully persuasive and its rhetoric was still under construction when the Queen died on 1 August 1714.[85] Anne's demise devastated Tory political prospects and internal party discords, already under acute strain, weakened them further. It was in this depressing atmosphere that Oxford Tories, reflecting the wider mood, took their threnodic leave of the Queen, more conscious than ever of what she symbolised and what they owed to her goodwill and her patronage (qualified though it was). As Dean Smalridge poetically lamented:[86]

[81] *The Tryal of Dr Henry Sacheverell* (London, 1710), 126, 127, 140; Kenyon, *Revolution Principles*, 136–8. Harcourt's careful management of the arguments is discussed in Brian Cowan, 'The Spin Doctor: Sacheverell's Trial Speech and Political Performance in the Divided Society', in ed. Knights, *Faction Displayed*, 28–46, at 43–6.

[82] [Joseph Trapp?], *The Character and Principles of the Present Set of Whigs* (London, 1711), 5. Trapp's authorship was quickly discerned.

[83] Chapter 2, p. 11.

[84] *An Answer to the Address of Oxford University* (London, 1710); *University Loyalty, or the Genuine Explanation of the Principles and Practices of the English Clergy* (London, 1710).

[85] For its Jacobite detractors, see for instance, George Lockhart, *The Lockhart Papers: containing memoirs and commentaries upon the affairs of Scotland from 1702 to 1715*, ed. Anthony Aufrere (2 vols., London, 1817), I. 475–6.

[86] A Society of Gentlemen. *The Loyal Mourner For the Best of Princes: Being a Collection of Poems sacred to the Immortal Memory of Her late Majesty Queen Anne* (London, 1716), 23. Smalridge's poem was called 'The Muses' Memorial of her late Majesty', addressed to the Duke of Buckingham, a member of Harley's government. Anne had promised a large donation for the new quadrangle at Christ Church. There were many Oxonian contributors to this collection.

320 ENLIGHTENED OXFORD

> O had but envious Death made some Delay,
> And not so hasty snatched the Royal Prey:
> Then, (may Her Promises to me be shown!)
> Thy Muses, Oxford, had Her Blessings known.
> What Domes, O Sacred Mother, hadst thou seen,
> The Pious Gift of a Religious Queen!

Anne had come to Oxford just once (as had William III before her), George I and George II never contemplated a visit to the University on the model of 1695 and 1702, though foreign princes were honoured and entertained.[87] Despite this deliberate and enduring royal snub, Oxford Tories in positions of influence were, for the most part, overwhelmingly Hanoverian. Their private opinions of the first two Georges might not have been high, but there was a hard-headed acknowledgement that if William III could be recognised, no less was due to his successors. For the leaders of the University, too much was at stake to do otherwise. The Whigs were constantly alert to the possibility of playing the Jacobite card against majority opinion in Oxford and it says much for the constructive leadership of the University that, despite slips, it was quite careful not to give them much of a handle after the lessons of the Atterbury Plot had been absorbed. In any event, the primary quarrel of the Tories was not with the king but with his ministers, the closing down of constitutional options, and the construction of a Whig oligarchy that would brook no Tory competition. Oxford Tories were frustrated and angered by this exclusion. If the impatient and disappointed among them (usually the younger and older men with less materially at stake) occasionally gave vent (often in their cups) to anti-Hanoverian sentiments then, though embarrassing and counterproductive, it was hardly unexpected. This was a loyalist University, it was loyal to the Hanoverian dynasty, and yet this loyalty was both denied and spurned.[88]

It could have been otherwise. Oxford pledged its allegiance unequivocally to George I on his arrival in England with Chancellor Ormond, Vice Chancellor Gardiner, William Bromley, and the 2nd Earl of Rochester (High Steward) presenting 'The Humble Address of the Chancellor, Masters, and Scholars

---

[87] George I made a highly successful visit to Cambridge in 1717, as did George II in 1728. R. J. White, *Dr. Bentley. A Study in Academic Scarlet* (London, 1965), 111, 164, 204. George II also visited the new (1734) university of Göttingen in Hanover amid much fanfare in 1748. Andrew C. Thompson, *George II. King and Elector* (New Haven, CT, 2011), 185. For rumours of George I coming to see Oxford in late summer 1724 see John Stone to Lord Fermanagh, 1 Aug. 1724, *Verney Letters of the Eighteenth Century from the MSS at Claydon House*, ed. Margaret Maria, Lady Verney (2 vols., London, 1930), II. 115. See Chapters 6, pp. 88–9 and 11, pp. 32–3 for the successful entertainment of the Prince and Princess of Orange at Oxford in 1733.

[88] W. R. Ward was driven to the conclusion that it is 'impossible to overlook the provocation to which the University was exposed'. *Georgian Oxford*, 67.

of the University of Oxford' to George I on 24 September 1714 supplicating royal favour:[89]

> We have been always educated in those principles of loyalty and obedience which are taught by the Church of England and enforced by the laws, which . . . strictly enjoyn us to support the right of your Ma[jes]tie and royal house to the imperial crowne of this realm'.

For his part, Dean Smalridge praised the King's 'mighty mind' and invited him to Christ Church.[90] Leaders of official Oxford opinion like these men were natural courtiers, though Tory courtiers, and were desperate for royal recognition. But Whig journalists were no less keen to uphold their party advantage and flag up any celebration of Tory principles as outright disloyalty. Admittedly, the University gave them the ammunition they were looking for when it conferred a doctorate in civil laws on Sir Constantine Phipps, Lord Chancellor of Ireland since 1710 (and previously one of Sacheverell's counsel) on the very day of George I's crowning in what was easy to present as a countercultural gesture or even an alternative coronation.[91] Provocative, even tactless it might have been, but at that juncture the outright exclusion of all Tories seemed unlikely. But within a year of the King's accession following defeat in a general election, the impeachment of Oxford and Strafford, the flight of Ormond and Bolingbroke, and the construction and aftermath of the '15, the screws were being turned ever tighter on the Tories and Oxford moderates were summarily cast aside: Smalridge was deprived of his place as Lord Almoner to George I after refusing to sign the declaration of the episcopal bench against the Jacobite rebellion; Charlett and Stratford lost office as King's chaplains, while Charlett and Gardiner were dismissed from the Commission of the Peace.[92]

---

[89] George I acknowledged it with some grace: 'I am highly pleased with the Assurances of Duty so Affectionately express'd in your Address. You could not have given me a more satisfactory Instance of it'. Quoted in Bernard Gardiner, *A Plain Relation of Some Late Passages at Oxford* (Oxford, 1717), App. 4, a letter written deliberately to restore the University's credibility with George I. Wigelsworth, *All Souls College*, 152.

[90] OUA: MS. Conv. Reg. Bd 31, ff. 112–13; George Smalridge, *Miscellanies* (London, 1715); Ward, *Georgian Oxford*, 53. Smalridge had been, politically if not personally, an Atterbury and Sacheverell ally.

[91] The oration was given by Joseph Trapp. BL Add. MS. 6116, f. 33. With gleeful irony, the Whig Edmund Gibson called it a Tory 'masterpiece' in which Trapp made 'a florid speech in which he call'd Dr Sacheverel the Oxford Heroe, and said that in him, Con Phipps—habuit Clientes, Ecclesiam & Academicam'. To Bp William Nicolson, 30 Oct. 1714, Bodl. MS. Add. A. 269, f. 36; [John Toland], *Patricola, The State-anatomy of Great Britain. Containing a Particular account of its several Interests and parties* . . . (9th edn., London, 1717), 52, 72. As David Hayton notes, the event was 'a mini-festival of Sacheverelliana', 'Irish Tories and Victims of Whig Persecution: Sacheverell Fever by Proxy', in ed. Knights, *Faction Displayed*, 80–98, at 96. The University's failure to produce a loyal address on the King's return from Hanover in 1716 served a comparable purpose for its enemies.

[92] For Whig pleasure at Smalridge's dismissal see Bodl. MS. Add. A. 269, f. 45, Gibson to Bishop Nicolson, 13 Nov. 1715; ibid., f. 46, 19 Nov.; Ward, *Georgian Oxford*, 67, 112–13. For the purge of magistrates see Lionel K. J. Glassey, *Politics and the Appointment of Justices of the Peace, 1675–1720* (Oxford, 1979), chap. 8; Norma Landau, *The Justices of the Peace 1679-1769* (Berkeley, CA, and

322 ENLIGHTENED OXFORD

These were calculated marks of disfavour against men who were moderates in most respects, who longed for the King to extend his confidence to Oxford Tories, the natural supporters of monarchy. As one sympathetic to their plight put it:

> ...as for our divisions, murmuring, aversions, and political feuds, there is one infalliable cure... viz. A convenient sphere in Church or State wherein we might gloriously display our most loyal and truly Protestant affections.[93]

It was a vain appeal. And then Smalridge's death in 1719 further weakened both the Oxford and the reversionary interest.[94] He was the last Tory prelate whom Caroline, Princess of Wales incorporated into her sparkling circle of often heterodox divines, a figure who might—given time—have developed a mature Hanoverian Tory discourse that could have been deployed within court and government.[95] His removal curtailed hopes that differences within the royal family might somehow benefit the University and, by extension, the Tory party.

Despite repeated snubs and disappointments, the dominant note of Oxonian Toryism in the 1720s remained moderation rather than a recourse to that fatal attraction: Jacobitism. Though their Chancellor was in the game and their ex-Chancellor a key player, Oxford Tories by and large steered clear of involvement in the Atterbury Plot,[96] but it did them no good in royal estimation, let alone that of Walpole. And so they waited for better times (or most of them did), enjoyed the realisation that Oxford as well as Cambridge had benefitted from royal largesse when new Regius professorships of History were created in 1724,[97] and did not demur from the loyal petitions that were still sent up to George I, including an expression of concern at the peril in which George I's person stood from the Pretender, carried, by a small majority, in March 1727.[98] George I was not incapable of other benefactions to Oxford. Thus when the burning of Christmas decorations by choristers in the open central grate in Christ Church Hall in 1720 made Wolsey's roof catch fire and required it to be almost entirely reconstructed, it was funded largely by a gift of £1,000 from George I.

London, 1984), 86–95. Charlett had a discrete revenge: in 1719, when the Radcliffe Quadrangle at his college was nearing completion, he had installed, not a statue of the reigning monarch, but one of Mary II. Thanks to Robin Darwall-Smith for this information.

[93] *The Muses' Fountain Clear, or the Dutiful Oxonian's Defence of his Mother's Loyalty to His Present Majesty King George* (London, 1717).

[94] Boyer, ed., *The Political state of Great Britain*, XVIII. 233–5; TNA (PRO) SP 35/17, f. 159:/18, f. 14; HMC, *Portland MSS*, VII. 220; *The Muses' Fountain Clear*, 19.

[95] For suspicions about Smalridge's own orthodoxy see W. Gibson, 'Altitudinarian Equivocation: George Smalridge's Churchmanship', in eds. W. Gibson and R.G. Ingram, *Religious Identities in Britain, 1660-1832* (Aldershot, 2005), 43–60.

[96] Chapter 6, p. 6.

[97] Chapter 4, pp. 23–4, 39. For the king's personal interest in the professorships see R. Hatton, *George I. Elector and King* (London, 1978), 369.

[98] Hearne, IX. 288, 292.

OXFORD AND THE CROWN   323

And he could be sensitive about his interventions in the University's internal affairs. When the Tory Thomas Cockman surprised his supporters by appealing to the king for help during University College's disputed Mastership election of the 1720s, George behaved very properly.[99] Unsurprisingly, reflecting a national trend, a few well-established Tories with deep Oxford connections, driven by ambition or avarice, could wait no longer and effectively left the party. Most notably, Lord Harcourt, who was rewarded for his departure from the ranks of the self-styled 'honest' party with an increased pension, a step up in the peerage to a viscountcy in 1721, and readmission to the Privy Council the next year.[100] Old Tory fault lines were showing once more and maintaining the resemblance of a common front in the 1722 General Election was not straightforward, evident not least in the contest to represent the University.

The accession of George II in mid-1727 did not end the exclusion, though the University looked forward to the day when, 'upon a nearer and more intimate experience', the King would 'more fully discover in her, the genuine character of an undissembled loyalty, a loyalty . . . arising from the pure fountains of reason and revelation'.[101] Warm coronation addresses submitted included one from the Professor of Poetry (1718–28) Thomas Warton the elder, who accorded Queen Caroline almost equal weight to the new King.[102] The sentiments were high-flown, the reality dismal: Tories came initially in some number to court to kiss the new King's hand, and left empty-handed.[103] George and Queen Caroline may briefly have entertained thoughts of ignoring Walpole and asking a favoured few into the royal service, but they soon thought better of it: Oxford Tories remained outcasts as long as he reigned (thirty-three years). Neither would the King come to them, though he visited Cambridge to award honorary degrees.[104] Again, it is Tory Oxford's acceptance of that situation (however grudging), its adhesion to the principles of non-resistance, that is striking. It was, to all intents and purposes, loyal to the dynasty in the 1730s. No wonder that Dean Swift in 1732 thought court politics entirely triumphant in Oxford, which he claimed to find 'wholly changed, and entirely devoted to new Principles . . . a most corrupt seminary the two last times I was there'.[105] Had Swift looked harder, he would have found the principles not too

---

[99] Curthoys (1), 51–2; Darwall-Smith, *University College*, 251–3.
[100] Archibald S. Foord, *His Majesty's Opposition 1714–1830* (Oxford, 1964), 68.
[101] OUA: MS. Conv. Reg. Bd 31, ff. 242, 246.
[102] *Verses on the Coronation of their late Majesties King George II and Queen Caroline, October 11, MDCCXXVII* (London, 1761), xv. Warton was Fellow of Magdalen, 1717–24, and had circulated Jacobite verses in 1717–18.
[103] 'We are all in haste to make our compliments', reported Canon Stratford, 26 June 1727, HMC, *Portland MSS*, VII. 448, 451. Leading high-flying peers, including Lichfield, Gower, Scarsdale, and Strafford, kissed hands at court on 15 June, *Mist's Weekly Journal*, 17 June 1727. See also *Lockhart Papers*, II. 51; Charles B. Realey, The *Early Opposition to Sir Robert Walpole*, 1720–1727 (Philadelphia, PA, 1931), 219–20.
[104] C. H. and J. W. Cooper, *Annals of Cambridge* (5 vols., Cambridge, 1842–1908), IV. 196–7.
[105] To John Gay, 4 May 1732, in ed. David Woolley, *The Correspondence of Jonathan Swift, D.D.*, (5 vols., Frankfurt am Main, 1999-2007), III. 468. He visited Oxford in the summers of 1726 and 1727.

324 ENLIGHTENED OXFORD

different from those of Queen Anne's time,[106] even as Toryism glimpsed yet another possible new dawn, could the Robinocracy but be overthrown.

When Walpole fell in 1742, leaving his constitutional system intact, Oxford Tories experienced the same disgust as many others did across Britain. These coincided with misfortunes in the War of the Austrian Succession and a revival in Jacobite hopes associated with the coming of age of 'James III's' eldest son, the vigorous Prince Charles Edward Stuart, determined on taking action to regain his father's throne. Oxonian Tories were fascinated but treated the possibility of the Stuart heir ending their political frustration as unlikely. Instead, the main Tory refrain during the 1740s was the persistence of 'corruption' and the need for a post-Walpolian regeneration of national life though, for some among them, it acted as something of a proxy for Jacobitism. Opposition leaders in both Houses were invited to the University for the conferring of honorary degrees that gave the Public Orator, Dr William King (more of a Jacobite admittedly than most Tories), the opportunity of making elegant, ambiguous anti-ministerial speeches in Latin, decrying the vacuity of modern patriotism and the likelihood of impending state destruction if the Old Corps Whigs remained in power, in effect, advocating something like a reversion to the old Country programme around which most Tories and many disgruntled Whigs could rally.[107] Yet the presence of a few Tories like Lord Gower and Sir John Hynde Cotton in the so-called 'Broad Bottom' administration of 1744–6 required Oxonian Tories to reconsider their presentiment that there was no prospect for their party so long as George II either lived or reigned, and made University support of the Hanoverian dynasty during the '45 difficult to avoid. Throughout the crisis years of 1742–6 (after Britain had officially gone to war), the University officially assured the King of its loyalty. For instance, when there was a threat of invasion in 1743-4, Convocation promised every assistance, noting that:[108]

> The solid & disinterested principles of Piety & Loyalty have ever engag'd your University of Oxford in the defence of their Sovereigns upon all important emergencies, & Your Majesty may securely rely upon the steady & inviolable attachment of those persons, who will ever be guided by the uniform influence & direction of such laudable rules of conduct & action.

---

[106] See the readiness in principle of some Tories to pay homage to George II, in [John Campbell], *The Case of the Opposition Impartially Stated* (London, 1742), 15–16.

[107] See, for instance, his three speeches collected in *William King's Speeches* (Bodl. Gough Oxf. 144); eds. L. Dickens and M. Stanton, *An Eighteenth-century correspondence: being letters...to Sanderson Miller, Esq of Radway* (London, 1910), 95. Tory pamphleteering in 1742–3 arguing for the party's disinterested, public-spirited service to the constitution are discussed in Foord, *His Majesty's Opposition*, 234–5. For an alternative view of the 'ideological fuzziness' of Toryism, with the holding in tension of 'contradictory goals and hopes', see Bob Harris, *Politics and the Nation. Britain in the Mid-Eighteenth Century* (Oxford, 2002), 44–6.

[108] OUA: Wpy/22/1p, Humble Address to the King.

OXFORD AND THE CROWN   325

Later, following the outbreak of the Jacobite Rebellion in 1745, Ligonier's Horse was entertained by some members of the University on its way north towards the combat zone (a far cry from the garrisoning of Oxford in 1715–17); after victory at Culloden, the Convocation lavished praise on the Duke of Cumberland for his suppression of the Rebellion and celebrated with fireworks and loyal health.[109] Hanoverian Toryism had, it seemed, finally come of age.

This professed loyalism was not enough to win round the court or break the Pelhamite stranglehold on power. Whig apologists seized on compromising incidents, such as tardiness in joining the national subscriptional community and signing the County Association in 1745 or the way the University dealt with the Blacow affair in 1748, to damn the whole institution as still untrust-worthy, still essentially Jacobite despite all signs to the contrary.[110] Such a narra-tive fitted readily into what Henry Fielding called that 'strange Spirit of Jacobitism, indeed of Infatuation' which 'discovered itself at the latter End of the Year 1747' and which led him to produce his satirical *Jacobite's Journal* of 1747–8.[111] In fact, Tory Oxonians had by this date more or less committed themselves to the King's cultivated son and heir, Frederick, Prince of Wales, as a true friend of the University, and professions of Hanoverian loyalty in the 1740s were directed as much to him, another enemy of the Old Corps' monopoly of power, as to his father. The cultivation of the heir apparent had begun early with many congratu-latory verses offered to him in on his engagement (1734) and his marriage to Princess Augusta of Saxe-Gotha in 1736.[112] Frederick, never his father's favourite, was always happy to cultivate those excluded from royal patronage, and he saw early on the personal advantage of cultivating non-Jacobite Oxford Tories.[113] They, in turn, saw the value of gaining the Prince's attention, with Vice Chancellor Stephen Niblett leading the way.

Mutual admiration grew over time. By 1748 leading Tory patrons of Oxford, including the 4th Duke of Beaufort, the 3rd Earl of Lichfield, and Thomas, 2nd Lord Foley, were happy to negotiate a working arrangement with the Leicester

---

[109] Details in Ward, *Georgian Oxford*, 166.   [110] See Chapter 8, pp. 28–34.
[111] No. 49 (5 Nov. 1748) in Fielding, *'Jacobite's Journal' and Related Writings*, ed. W.B. Coley (Middletown, CT, 1975), 424.
[112] *Epithalamia Oxoniensia* (Oxford, 1734); *Gratulatio Academiae Oxoniensis…*(Oxford, 1736), discussed in D. Money, 'The Latin Poetry of English gentlemen', eds. L. B. T. Houghton and G. Manuwald, *Neo-Latin Poetry in the British Isles* (London, 2012), 124–41. There had been some desire among his British advisers even in the 1710s that Frederick should be brought from Hanover either to Oxford or (more likely) to Cambridge to be trained for his future role as king. William King, Abp. of Dublin to Abp. Wake, 26 June 1717, BL Add MS 6117, f. 40.
[113] HMC, *Egmont diary* (3 vols., London, 1920–23), I. 160. Among them may have been the young Oxford historian, James Hampton (1721–78), who drew on his expertise on the Greek historian Polybius to produce *A Parallel between the Roman and British Constitution…*(London, 1747), a serious work of political analysis. Hampton was, it was claimed, '…the first man of the age to undertake a non-partisan appraisal of the actual operation of political parties in Britain'. Foord, *His Majesty's Opposition*, 268–9. Hampton was accused of violence and expelled from his fellowship at Corpus in 1749. Charles-Edwards and Reid, *Corpus Christi College*, 253–4.

326 ENLIGHTENED OXFORD

House Whig opposition on the basis of an updated country-party programme and look forward, between them, to ousting the Old Corps and their Cambridge favourites in what could be presented as the rebirth of the monarchy and the Tory party.[114] This possibility inspired Oxonian Tories during the late 1740s and sharpened Whig resentments. In 1749, Oxford offered verses to Prince Frederick, and Theophilus Leigh, Master of Balliol, assured him of the University's political support whenever it might be needed.[115] That hour never came. The Prince predeceased George II in March 1751 and the University lost its leading Hanoverian patron since 1714. It occasioned, as one correspondent remarked, 'general and real concern' at Oxford and the loss fell 'very heavily upon individuals'. When a consolatory address was sent up there was 'hardly a member of the University, who has not already put himself into mourning, and if I may judge from appearances, I believe no prince ever died more sincerely lamented than His Royal Highness'.[116] Such had been its commitment to Frederick that there was no prospect of any official forgiveness for the University so long as George II survived, for he professed to the University's retiring MP, Lord Cornbury, that Oxford's behaviour throughout his reign had been unreasonable.[117] Oxford Tories and the Crown were once more poles apart. Oxford, like so many other institutions and people, was confounded by George II's exceptional longevity. By 1751, only a handful of kings of England (Henry I and Elizabeth I among them) had lived as long. So his survival and Frederick's premature death were two unexpected setbacks for the Tories.

Bereft of its Hanoverian Prince of Wales and disillusioned after first-hand encounters with his Stuart equivalent, despite his professed conversion to Anglicanism,[118] Oxonian Toryism had no princely object of devotion for several

---

[114] The Prince's position as a rallying point for the Opposition is discussed in Glickman, 'Parliament, the Tories and Frederick, Prince of Wales'; Aubrey Newman, 'Leicester House politics, 1748–51', *EHR*, 76 (1961), 577–89, who noted (579) that High Tories were drawn in by intended moves against the University in the late 1740s—'a coalition for certain purposes, with aims fixed in advance.' Tory numbers in the Commons actually dropped after the 1747 General Election, from 136 MPs to 117.

[115] Ward, *Georgian Oxford*, 173.

[116] Bodl. MS Eng. lett. d. 145, f. 102 Ch. Ch., 31 Mar. 1751, F. W. Sharp to Thomas Sharp. For an instance of informal, pro-Frederick verses from Oxford on his death, see Bodl. MS Ballard 29, f. 137: 'The following Copy was lately directed to Ld Robert [Manners-] Sutton, Lord of the Bed Chamber, and directed to P of Wales'. It includes the verse:

> Deny'd our gracious Sovereign's Sight,
> Pursu'd by Bedford's ire,
> Poor Oxford mourns in doleful Plight,
> Nor dares to string the Lyre.

[117] Cornbury noted that George made this comment with a smile. 'I repli'd Sir, ... your Interests could not be much affected by what they could do, But their own suffer'd essentially. The King said indeed they have hurt themselves more than me. They have hurt themselves very much'. Letter to Arthur Onslow, 27 Jan. 1750, quoted in ed. Mary Clayton, *A Portrait of Influence. Life and Letters of Arthur Onslow, the Great Speaker* [Parliamentary History: Texts & Studies 14] (London, 2017), 163–73, at 171.

[118] Cf. Guthrie, *Material Culture of the Jacobites*, 136.

years, while the equally uninspiring figures of George II and 'James III' lived on. With leading figures in the University such as Thomas Randolph urging an end to obsolete party rigidities,[119] the old networks of friendship and association were transmuted into the 'old interest'. Pride in the cultural heritage of Toryism still persisted and (in both its Jacobite and Hanoverian manifestations) was the dominant note of Oxford Toryism between 1754 and 1760, splendidly on display in such festival occasions at the election of Lord Westmorland as Arran's successor in the Chancellorship in 1759.[120] But there was also inspired constitutional engagement. It was a Hanoverian court Tory, Sir William Blackstone, who produced the *Commentaries* that are the defining document of contemporary jurisprudence yet, in another sense, they represent a further phase in the accommodation of Tory-Jacobite Oxford with the Hanoverian regime around the middle of the century.[121] Toryism as a contemporary political force was starting to make little political sense, though Oxford Tories hoped for the future even as the party organisationally withered away, its leadership evaporated.[122] As the spectre of Jacobitism faded so did the Whig-Tory distinction, as factions contemplated a future without George II under a young prince whose goodwill could be anticipated more fervently and hopefully with every passing year.[123] Party distinctions were further dissolved by William Pitt's overwhelming personal impact on national politics from 1756–7 onwards, as 'Patriotism' became all the rage as the Seven Years' War moved to a triumphant British outcome. Even *Jackson's Oxford Journal* had turned Pittite by the late 1750s.[124] And with the accession of Prince Frederick's eldest son as George III in October 1760, Oxford-educated Tories throughout the country expected him to wear his late father's patriotic mantle, end the proscription of the Tories, and at last throw the full weight of the

---

[119] See Randolph, *Party zeal censured. In a Sermon preached before the University of Oxford, at St Mary's, on Sunday, January 19. 1752* (Oxford, 1752) and the replies. Mark Knights has shrewdly noted the paradox whereby 'the passion of party provoked *partisan* condemnations of party zeal'. Knights, *Representation and Misrepresentation in Later Stuart Britain. Partisanship and Political Culture* (Oxford, 2005), 181, 204. Incivility and impoliteness compounded the offence. Ibid., 244.

[120] See Chapter 6, pp. 11–12.

[121] J. C. D. Clark, 'Religion and Political Identity: Samuel Johnson as a Nonjuror', in eds. J. Clark and H. Erskine-Hill, *Samuel Johnson in Historical Context* (Basingstoke, 2002), 79–145, at 123. See David Martin-Jones, *Conscience and Allegiance in seventeenth-century England: the political significance of oaths and engagements* (Rochester, NY, 1999), 234–5, for Blackstone's acceptance of de facto arguments about the descent of the Crown. However, he made nothing of any right of popular resistance. See also this chapter, pp. 89–90.

[122] The aged ex-Jacobite, Dr William King, derided the Tories to a young protégé for not having one man amongst them capable of being put at their head. BL Bowood Papers Vol. 10, f. 59, Col. Robert Clerk to Lord Fitzmaurice, London, 15 Sept. 1759.

[123] A Tory polemicist noted in the mid-1750s that Tories 'now defend the royal house on the throne, with as much zeal as the Whigs'. B. Angeloni [John Shebbeare], *Letters on the English Nation*, (2 vols., London, 1755), I. 22.

[124] As one pamphleteer noted early in George III's reign of the Tory party's 'vagrant state': 'You have been wandering about, gentlemen, for some years past, in search of a minister, under whom you might recover your importance, without giving up the absurdities of your ancestors'. [John Butler], *An Address to the cocoa-tree, from a Whig* (London, 1762), 6.

328　ENLIGHTENED OXFORD

Crown behind the University of Oxford as a national force for good, and end the virtual monopoly of royal favour enjoyed by an exceptionally influential minority—Oxford Whigs.

v) Whigs and loyalism in early eighteenth-century Oxford

The University of Oxford 'would not be known if it were not for the treasonable spirit publicly avowed and often exerted there'.

Philip Stanhope, Lord Chesterfield, Letters from
Lord Chesterfield to Alderman George
Faulkner, etc. (London, 1777), 23.

Whigs were a constant and increasing presence in eighteenth-century Oxford. Their importance makes any unqualified description of the University as 'Tory Oxford' entirely misleading. Yet it benefitted Whig interests and justified a case for receipt of patronage to depict Oxford as an incorrigible Tory redoubt, compromised in the post-Revolutionary polity by its attachment to Jacobitism, and themselves heroic witnesses and victims in a wilderness. And it generally suited ministers to give credence to this dramatic licence. Just as the Tories battled to overcome their opponents' persistent misrepresentations vis-à-vis the Hanoverian monarchy (without ever quite succeeding), so the challenge to the Whigs was to persuade the public that the Church of England was as safe in their care as was the Revolution settlement. In that objective, they proved eventually successful, even to the point (once the Bangorian controversy had run its course and thanks, in the first instance, to Edmund Gibson, the Oxonian called by Walpole to be his ecclesiastical minister)[125] of making it possible to be both a High Churchman and a Whig by the 1730s—an implausible and eccentric combination a generation earlier. Court Whiggism, too, had matured sufficiently by the 1710s to make the habitual Tory charges of republicanism and fanaticism levelled at the party of limited leverage.[126] Against that cultural shift, and with Tory politicians out of Crown favour, the temptation for younger Oxonians (including many outside the predominantly Whig colleges) to sing the new tune and get a career started in the Church or the law increased. Enough did so steadily to increase the share of Crown patronage accorded to Oxford men by the mid-century, though the University never eclipsed Cambridge as the Crown's academy of choice as long as George II survived and the Duke of Newcastle retained his political prominence.

---

[125] Stephen Taylor, '"Dr. Codex" and the Whig "Pope": Edmund Gibson, Bishop of Lincoln and London, 1716–1748', in ed. R. W. Davis, *Lords of Parliament. Studies, 1714–1914* (Stanford, CA, 1995), 9–28, at 15–17, 27. If Gibson's hope was thereby to neutralise the Tories, he did not succeed. Cf. Gibson, *The Church of England*, 87.

[126] See Browning, *Political and Constitutional Ideas of the Court Whigs*.

Fig. 7.2 Thomas Dunster, unknown artist, oil on canvas, c.1690 (By kind permission of the Warden and Fellows of Wadham College, Oxford).

At the Revolution, as was only to be expected, a Whig in a position of prominence at Oxford was a *rara avis*. Wadham College was their main bastion, presided over by Hearne's *bête noire*, Dr Thomas Dunster,[127] while, at Pembroke, a latitudinarian Calvinist, John Hall, the long-serving Master (1664–1710), was promoted to the see of Bristol in 1691.[128] Also sent to Bristol as Dean in 1694 was George Royse, careerist Provost of Oriel (elected 1691), and domestic chaplain to Archbishop Tillotson. His appointment showed early on in the new order that even a loyalist college of Oriel's character was open to Whig and Low Church influences.[129] However, court Whiggism of the sort associated with the Junto developed fast in the 1690s and, on the whole, without much reference to Oxford.

---

[127] Thomas Dunster, (c.1657–1719), matric. Wadham, 1673; MA 1679; Fellow, 1681; Proctor, 1688; DD, 1690; Warden of Wadham, 1689–1719. https://www.british-history.ac.uk/vch/oxon/vol3/pp279-287 Wadham was the only college to hang portraits of William III and George I in its hall. Ward, *Georgian Oxford*, 103–4. See also Martin and Highfield, *Merton College*, 255.

[128] Bishop Gilbert Burnet preached at Hall's consecration. There were rumours that Hall's orders were Presbyterian, dating from 1655. He was elected Lady Margaret Professor of Divinity in 1676 and even Hearne admitted his professorial lectures were highly regarded. Douglas Macleane, *Pembroke College* (London, 1900), 150–1.

[129] P. Seaward, 'Politics and Interest, 1660–1781', 168–71.

330 ENLIGHTENED OXFORD

But already there were intellectually gifted, younger clergy from Oxford, such as Gibson and White Kennett (looking to William Wake as their exemplar), aligned with King William and the Revolution settlement, and determined to stand up to Atterbury and the Tory firebrands over the Convocation dispute launched in 1697.[130] They made that wrangle very much an Oxford exchange. Throughout the twelve years of Anne's reign, Oxford Whigs were on the back foot, but they played a skilful defensive game, making the most of their three principal assets: the goodwill of the Junto Whigs, a Whig majority on the bench of bishops under Archbishop Tenison, and the importance for the Whig cause in the county and the University of the impending arrival of the Duke and Duchess of Marlborough in the vicinity, following the duke's victory at Blenheim in 1704.[131] The duke's power was promptly on display in 1707 when he secured the Regius Chair of Divinity for John Potter.[132] A courtier rather than a strict party man, Marlborough's ecclesiastical patronage amounted to little,[133] but with Tenison as Metropolitan for two decades, Whigs had other means of securing prominence within the University, as at Merton where the Archbishop as college Visitor made the final selection of Warden from three candidates nominated by the senior fellows.[134]

Whig defensiveness ended with the accession of George I. By Christmas 1714 it was plain that he was to be the champion of the Whigs, their king, and that he and his ministers would both defend and advance the cause of Whiggism pretty well exclusively within Oxford. Where there was Crown patronage, Whigs would be preferred and Tories excluded. All Oxford Whigs, and those who decided it was advantageous to be Oxford Whigs, had to do was to laud the Protestant Succession. Close association did no harm. Thus Daniel Lombard, fellow of St John's until 1719, who had been on the Hanover embassy to Princess Sophia in 1701, was named chaplain to Caroline, Princess of Wales, soon after George I's accession.[135] Denunciation of the full register of the new dynasty's perceived antagonists was also

---

[130] It was left to Cambridge to give an honorary doctorate to Kennett and incorporate Gibson in 1705. Ward, *Georgian Oxford*, 29. The latter had received his DD originally at Oxford in 1702.

[131] The Marlboroughs did not finally move into the east wing at Blenheim palace until 1719, but their presence was a reality in local politics for over a decade previously. Holmes, *Marlborough*, 473; Frances Harris, *A Passion for Government. The Life of Sarah Duchess of Marlborough* (Oxford, 1991), 221, 222, 225. Duchess Sarah early made a point of sending gift of venison to Whig Heads of Houses. It was reported that when some of them, led by Warden Dunster of Wadham, went to Blenheim to wait on the Duke and offer thanks, they received a dismissive reception: the Duchess had expected the University officially to come and compliment the Duke on gracing his country and their neighbourhood. Hearne, I. 169–70, 26–27, Jan. 1706. See also Chapter 9, pp. 21–3.

[132] Chapter 3, pp. 45–6. Ward pointed out that Marlborough never created a solid following in the University, *Georgian Oxford*, 39.

[133] For a duke, Marlborough had few benefices to offer ambitious clergy. He gave Bladon and Woodstock to his Oxford ally, Dr William Baker, Warden of Wadham, and Archdeacon of Oxford, 1715–23. Ward, *Georgian Oxford*, 104.

[134] See Chapter 6, p. 54.

[135] He was possibly one of those stirring up trouble for Oxford with the new ministers. Costin, *St John's College*, 173–4. W. P. Courtney, 'Lombard, Daniel (1678–1746), Church of England clergyman and author', rev. Philip Carter, ODNB online edn., 2013.

de rigueur in these quarters. Many Oxonian students were ready for pro-Whig militancy. The Constitution Club, a body of young Whigs formed by some New College students led by Henry Thomas and the Hoadlyite ordinand George Lavington (a future bishop of Exeter), warmly celebrated the King's birthday on 28 May 1715, under their president, William, Lord Hartington (1698–1755), grandson of the 1st Duke of Devonshire, one of the 'Immortal Seven' who had invited the Prince of Orange to England in July 1688, and son and heir of the 2nd Duke, Lord Steward of George I's household.[136] They were aggressive, socially confident, well connected, and ready to intrude their principles in Oxford when opportunity offered and publicise them in the London press. Their activities were less constitutional and lawyerly than devoted to drinking and womanising in city taverns and then at Merton College on George I's birthday in 1716. The club steward, Richard Meadowcourt of Merton, was constantly running afoul of the University authorities, and no less sedulously put it about that his graduation had been delayed only because of his loyalty to King George. It was ill-advised brinkmanship that led to the break-up in confusion of the Constitution Club in 1718, having caused the Whigs more embarrassment than good publicity.[137]

Older men were no less ready to prepare their own martyrology and publicise it. They included John Ayliffe, Fellow of New College, whose *The Antient and Present State of the University of Oxford* (2 vols., 1714) and its anti-Stuart line led to his being deprived of his degrees by the Chancellor's Court and banished.[138] Nothing daunted, he publicised his case in a pamphlet of 1716—*The Case of Dr Ayliffe*—and demanded a royal visitation of the University, as was the fashion at that moment. Another expelled, disgruntled Whig, Nicholas Amhurst of St John's College, produced the most copious of all the press attacks on Oxford in his *Terrae Filius* of 1721 with the strap line that Oxford was chock full of papists who wanted to live under a popish king.[139] This sort of negative publicity was directed primarily at securing a ministerial intervention in remodelling the government of the University and, when that was not obtained and the Sunderland-Stanhope ministry imploded, so Whig animadversions—for the time being—faltered.[140] But when further, preferably official opportunities presented themselves to highlight

---

[136] For its members see Philoxon [Richard Rawlinson], *A Full and Impartial Account of the Oxford Riots* (London, 1715), 8–9.

[137] Ward, *Georgian Oxford*, 57, 61, 88–90, discusses the legal proceedings brought against them in 1716–17. Meadowcourt was the nephew of Warden Holland of Merton. Martin and Highfield, *Merton College*, 242.

[138] The ostensible reason was his criticism of the Clarendon Press and misappropriation of funds by successive Vice Chancellors. *The Antient and Present State* only goes as far as the mid-seventeenth century. Vol. 2, chap. 2 of the book considers the powers of Visitors and there is a section on the Chancellor and Vice Chancellor. J. H. Baker, *Monuments of Endlesse labours. English Canonists and their work, 1300–1900* (London, 1998), 87.

[139] Amhurst is further discussed in Chapter 10.

[140] Ward, *Georgian Oxford* 71, 79; Penry Williams, 'From the Reformation to the Era of Reform, 1530–1850', 60–1.

332 ENLIGHTENED OXFORD

their unqualified Hanoverian loyalism, as they did in abundance in the aftermath of the Atterbury Plot, Oxford Whigs were not slow to seize them. The vigorous anti-Jacobite sermon preached at St Mary's church in 1723 by John Wynne of Jesus College (Fellow 1718–25), published as *The Duty of Studying to be Quiet, and to do our own Business, Explain'd and Recommended* (London, 1724), is a good instance of that reflex.

The gradual growth of Whig influence in the colleges occurred after it became clear that the party's interest in Oxford was also the court interest, one that by the 1720s had largely discarded the hectoring ideological tones of an Ayliffe or an Amhurst. Temporal advancement was a ready inducement for well-placed Whigs to act when opportunity offered. Thus, in 1721, the chaplains of Bishop White Kennett of Peterborough and Earl Cowper (the former Lord Chancellor), both fellows of Merton, were mobilised to ensure that the Whig candidate for a vacancy at the college would succeed. Afterwards, both were rewarded with a living and a canonry apiece.[141] But the centre of court interest was neither Merton nor Wadham but Christ Church, unsurprisingly, given the Crown's power of appointment to its canonries and deanery. As its Harleyite stallholders died off, so they were replaced by moderate Whig loyalists acceptable to Walpole and Newcastle, men whose precursor had been Thomas Potter back in 1707. William Bradshaw, Dean of Christ Church from 1724 to 1732, had different priorities from those of Atterbury or Smalridge, but, like them, he was expected to act as the principal representative of the court in the Oxford of his day, supporting the polite Whig interest in and beyond the House, in effect a rival to the succession of Tory vice chancellors named by Lord Arran.[142] He had his work cut out inside Christ Church. One who was less than well-disposed to Bradshaw reported in 1726:[143]

> The governor's [Bradshaw] jealousy of designs in his subjects to affront him in everything they do or say and their contempt of him increase every day. And this is the formidable man that was to convert and new model the whole society. He will I am afraid be the occasion of dividing it.

Such was the price of dislodging the old Harleyite ascendancy inside the college. Vicious in-fighting, adroit manoeuvring, and good fortune saw the Whigs also gain the upper hand in Jesus College by 1726, though Wadham became less important to them after the Warden, Robert Thistlethwayte (1724–39) fled to Brussels after a charge was laid against him at the Assizes for sodomising a

---

[141] Gibson, *A Social History of the Domestic Chaplain*, 94.

[142] Hearne (III. 120; also V. 361 and XI. 138) called Bradshaw 'a vile Whigg' but grudgingly admitted he was 'a man of Parts'. He was a Fellow of New College, 1695–1718. While Dean he did his best to drum up support for Walpole's hugely controversial Excise Bill of 1733—unavailingly, even among Whigs. Ward, *Georgian Oxford*, 149.

[143] Stratford to Lord Oxford, 18 July 1726. HMC, *Portland MSS*, VII. 441.

OXFORD AND THE CROWN   333

student.[144] Instead, Exeter, under successive Rectors from 1730—John Conybeare, Joseph Atwell, James Edgcumbe, and Francis Webber—moved closer to centre stage.

A decade later, and Conybeare had emerged as the most important Whig in Oxford, writing sensibly and accessibly in the party cause much as he did theologically, and had received the Deanery of Christ Church (in 1733) for his pains.[145] Heads of House who saw the change in the political wind were quick to trim their sails, like the Provost of Oriel, Dr George Carter, controversially (and erroneously, as the courts at length judged) claiming Visitatorial powers for the Bishop of Lincoln properly belonging to the Crown to secure the election of Whig fellows in the early 1720s, and anticipating the goodwill of successive bishops of that see, Edmund Gibson and Richard Reynolds, both of them Whigs.[146] Senior Oxonians wanting to secure something like national prominence for most of these two reigns stood minimal chance without establishing a character as moderate Whigs. There was no other way to royal preferment or to challenge Cambridge cronyism.

And recognition would be forthcoming. Thus it was John Potter, the High Church Whig Bishop of Oxford, so long associated with the University, who was accorded the honour of preaching at the coronation of George II and Queen Caroline in 1727 and acclaimed unequivocally their royal heritage and authority.[147] Similarly, Robert Clavering, the Bishop of Peterborough and Regius Professor of Hebrew, used his 30 January sermon before Parliament in 1731 to praise the king and queen and 'their illustrious Progeny'.[148] And, for their pains in the party—and, by extension, the royal interest—at Christ Church, both Bradshaw

---

[144] Anonymous, College-wit sharpen'd: or, the Head of a house, with, a sting in the tail... (London, 1739); C. S. L. Davies, 'Thistlethwayte, Robert (bap. 1690, d. 1744), college head and subject of sexual scandal', ODNB, online edn., 2008; G. Rousseau, 'Privilege, Power and Sexual Abuse in Georgian Oxford', in ed. George Rousseau, Children and sexuality: From the Greeks to the Great War (Basingstoke, 2007), 142–69.

[145] See Chapter 6, pp. 46–7, 55 for further details of Conybeare at Christ Church and the Whig interest at Exeter College.

[146] Carter had cultivated episcopal and ministerial connections without undue obsequiousness from George I's accession and was rewarded with appointment as a royal chaplain as early as Feb. 1717. Seaward, 'Politics and Interest', 172. See also Chapter 6, p. 71.

[147] Potter, A Sermon [on 2 Chron. ix. 8] preach'd at the Coronation of King George II., and Queen Caroline, ... Oct. 11, 1727 (London, 1727). Clark, English Society 1660–1832 (2000 edn.), 102, notes the key significance of his 'willingness to compromise on the dynasty' as a way of protecting the Established Church. His predecessor, William Talbot, a stronger Whig, had preached at George I's coronation on 20 Oct. 1714. He urged (in vain, and with a touch of the disingenuous), 'Let all our party-quarrels be buried in oblivion, all distinguishing names and characters be forgotten'. Talbot, A Sermon [on Ps. cxviii. 24, 25] preach'd at the Coronation of King George, ... October the 20th, 1714 (London, 1714), 28. Talbot was translated to Salisbury the following year. Margot Johnson, 'Talbot, William (1659–1730), bishop of Durham', ODNB online edn., 2004.

[148] Clavering, A Sermon preach'd before the Lords Spiritual and Temporal... on Saturday, January XXX. 1730 (London, 1731) [The great duty and happiness of living quiet and peaceable]. It was a moderate sermon that called Charles 'this glorious Martyr' but offered no general condemnation of dissenters. Weinbrot, Literature, Religion, 122–3. Robert Clavering (1671–1747) MA, Lincoln College, 1696; fellow and tutor of University College, 1701; Canon of Christ Church and Regius Professor, 1715–47; Bp of Llandaff, 1725; trans. Peterborough, 1729. Scott Mandelbrote, 'Robert Clavering (1675/6–1747), orientalist and bishop of Peterborough', ODNB online edn., 2004.

334   ENLIGHTENED OXFORD

and Conybeare, received (as Smalridge had done before them), the modestly endowed see of Bristol held *in commendam*; and Warden Baker of Wadham left the University to become bishop of Bangor in 1723.[149] There were also occasional royal donations to individual colleges. Thus the statue of Queen Caroline that graces the entrance to Queen's was to acknowledge her donation of £1,000 (in response to a request from the provost, Joseph Smith, to complete the replacement of its medieval buildings) to mark the laying of the foundation stone of the screen wall on the High Street under the supervision of Nicholas Hawksmoor to a George Clarke design of 1708/9.[150]

After a few wobbles once Sir Robert Walpole had quit the Treasury in 1742 and it seemed, for a brief moment, that the Tories might find favour, the court Whigs regrouped, and the threat to Hanoverian survival posed by the '45 confirmed the exclusive appeal of Oxonian Whigs to the Pelhamite power brokers at Westminster. Conveniently ignoring the partisan character of the county Association for the preservation of the constitution in Church and state, produced in 1745, that had guaranteed even the most moderate of Tories would think twice about signing it, and huffing and puffing in indignation at every sign of student unrest or bad behaviour that could be dressed up as Jacobitism, Whigs with an eye to the main chance seized the moment.[151] Francis Potter, vicar of Burford, in effect made his case for an archdeaconry with his St Mary's church sermon of 24 November 1745 on Jeremiah 22. v. 30—'For the children of Israel have only provoked me to anger with the work of their hands saith the Lord'—with the clear implication that the University had increased the risk of the twin perils of Popery and persecution coming in through its lingering attachment to indefeasible hereditary right.[152] And Edward Bentham, the Whitehall preacher, within the University urged junior members to respect the holders of legitimate authority, the kind of injunction he hoped that Lord Chancellor Hardwicke and Bishop Secker of Oxford would also read.[153]

---

[149]   Chapter 6, p. 47 for Conybeare's promotion; Ward, *Georgian Oxford*, 104–5, 108.
[150]   Matthew Dennison, *The First Iron Lady. A Life of Caroline of Ansbach* (London, 2017), 333–4; Hodgkin, *Queen's College*, 141.
[151]   One commentator noted with some justice that 'there seldom wants hungry courtiers in any reign, who hope, by misrepresenting these seats of learning, to get their Houses dissolved, in order to share the plunder among themselves'. *The Gentleman and Lady's Pocket companion for Oxford* (London, 1747), 20–1.
[152]   F. Potter, *A Sermon preached before the University of Oxford... on the present Rebellion* (London, 1745).
[153]   See *A Letter to a Young Gentleman of Oxford* (London, 1749). Bentham's efforts were ridiculed by Dr. William King in a series of verse lampoons.

> 'Men of Oxford, I tell you, (and faith! it is true)
> Not a page of this work did I write with a view
> To inflame our great folk, or to hurt one of you.
> But howe'er, to cajole my good friends at Whitehall,
> And to find out the way to some pretty near stall,
> Let me roundly declare ye are Jacobites all'.

King, *A Poetical Abridgement both in Latin and English of the Rev. Mr. Tutor Bentham's Letter to a Young Gentleman of Oxford...* (London, 1749). For rumours that Bentham was to receive a Durham canonry see Spencer to 2nd Earl Cowper, in ed. Hughes, *Letters of Spencer Cowper*, 156, 3 Nov. 1752.

Fig. 7.3 Marble statue of Queen Caroline under cupola at the entrance to the Queen's College, Oxford, Sir Henry Cheere, 1733–5 (Photograph by John Cairns: Librarian of the Queen's College, Oxford).

336 ENLIGHTENED OXFORD

Whig pressure on the University only intensified in the late 1740s, precisely at the moment when the Duke of Newcastle had been elected as Chancellor of Cambridge. It was tactically sensible of Convocation to give thanks for the Peace of Aix-la-Chapelle (1748), and to promise to enforce peace within the University 'by example, by exhortation, by discipline, by severity...and to give a right and loyal direction to the warmth of youth'. Singling out the sovereign, the University had expressed its wish that the new year [1749] 'may begin with choice and lasting Blessings, upon your Sacred Person and Royal House for many Generations'.[154] Such a submission was still deemed insufficient by Dean Conybeare of Christ Church, a man basking in official favour as his appointment to preach before the Commons on the day of public thanksgiving for the Peace confirmed.[155] He persuaded Secker to put the worst possible gloss on it to the ministry so that George II would, as he duly did, declare the Address improper, perhaps because of its invocation of the wider 'Royal House'.[156]

Yet, by the late 1740s, the revival of father-son enmity in the royal family was posing a dilemma for Whigs: should they support the King or, with an eye on the future, align themselves behind Frederick, Prince of Wales, who was far from inclined to sanction the perpetuation of abuse and the ostracism of either the Tories or Oxford University. On the contrary, he was trying to reconcile party interests in a constructive attempt by Leicester House to widen the basis of royal patronage that anticipated developments in his son's reign.[157] There remained a strong Pelhamite following in Oxford that would not tack with the 'Patriot' breeze, with old hands like the *provocateur* and informer Richard Blacow of Brasenose, and the up-and-coming Hebraist, Benjamin Kennicott of Exeter, prominent among them, and they were given an extended lease of life when the Prince's unexpected death in 1751 temporarily rescued the Whigs from a crisis of royal loyalties. In the guise of the 'New Interest', University Whigs gave their all to winning the celebrated county election of 1754, with Exeter College serving as a kind of headquarters in the city from which Thomas Bray, Fellow (and later Rector) of the College, coordinated the press campaign on the 'New Interest''s behalf.[158]

---

[154] Address to the King from Oxford, 28 Dec. 1748. Newcastle Papers, BL Add MS 32717, f. 554. William King's speech at the opening of the Radcliffe Library the following April did little to confirm the sincerity of these sentiments.

[155] His subject was given in the title: Conybeare, *True Patriotism. A sermon preach'd before the Honourable House of Commons*... (London, 1749). It included a fulsome panegyric to George II.

[156] *GM* 19 (1749), 20–1; *London Evening Post*, 17–19 Jan. 1748/9; BL Add MS. 35590, f. 230. His *Sermons* (2 vols.), published posthumously in London in 1757, with his widow's [Jemima Conybeare] good offices, were also dedicated to the monarch. The opening of the Radcliffe Library might be seen as part of the University's attempt at a broadly based counter-attack against this kind of Whig aggression.

[157] See this chapter, pp. 53–6.

[158] He was not alone. Edward Bentham was belatedly awarded a canonry at Christ Church because of his articles on behalf of the 'New Interest'. See Chapter 6, p. 42, n. 92. Blacow was given a Windsor canonry, and Kennicott was made a Whitehall preacher. Ward, *Georgian Oxford*, 197, 200.

Whig energies and animosities were not easily dissipated for the remainder of the decade, with the election of Arran's successor as Chancellor, Lord Westmorland, showing that the Whig strongholds of George I's reign—Exeter, Merton, and Wadham—remained the party's power bases nearly forty years later. Christ Church had also come over to the cause of the court, Hertford had been secured, but there were few inroads in other colleges. The balance sheet suggests Whig underperformance at Oxford, given the unambiguous commitment of the dynasty to that party in every decade since the 1710s. Whig academics had held their ground, but no more than that, as the comfortable defeat of the court candidate in the cancellarial contest of 1758, Richard Trevor, Bishop of Durham, confirmed.[159] In earlier centuries Heads of Houses had been imposed on colleges regardless of the view of the fellows; in the eighteenth, the Whigs had been unable to do anything significant to displace Cambridge as the Hanoverian Crown's English university of choice. They were, of course, up against statutes, college tradition, and the weight of opinion among old members and their allies in public life, and the political consequences of hitting the Tories too hard—or in the wrong place—were never lost on Walpole or his Pelhamite successors. And there is another possibility. It was simply not in the material interests of Cambridge-educated Whigs, with most of the best places in the Church, to bring Oxford in from the cold, as it would only increase competition for them.

Instead, Whig Oxonians such as John Free fell back too readily on the old commonplaces of martyrdom in a hostile environment, when most of the political advantages lay with them. Throughout these decades Whig Oxonians had not really formulated any new theoretical propositions for envisaging or presenting the institutional or constitutional position of the Crown that went beyond well-established apostrophes to the Revolution and William III. They could do that well enough, as Kennicott latterly demonstrated from the pulpit of St Mary's church in January 1757, preaching on Christian fortitude and emphasising (with such a conspicuously critical subtext meant for Tory consumption that the Vice Chancellor refused his imprimatur) that 1688 was 'an event ever to be mentioned by true Englishmen and true Protestants with transports of gratitude'.[160] Otherwise, Oxford Whiggery seldom reached beyond personal panegyrics of the monarch. It was an essentially reactive rhetoric that too easily chose the easy option of point-scoring rather than trying to introduce new ways of looking at monarchy that built on those handed down by the Revolutionary generation of 1688.

---

[159] [G. Allan], *A Sketch of the Life... of Richard Trevor, Lord Bishop of Durham* (Darlington, 1776). Cf. King, *Political and Literary anecdotes*, 183.

[160] B. Kennicott, *Christian Fortitude* (Oxford, 1757).

338   ENLIGHTENED OXFORD

Part B: Loyalism recast and rewarded:
Oxford in the age of George III

i) Crown and constitution: the academic affirmation of 'Church and King' in revolutionary times

The Tories are all at court, and Oxonians are made Bishops. The Cocoa-Tree is running a race with Arthur's towards the golden goal of St James's.

'Terrae-Filius', Number 4, July 8, 1763, in George
Colman (the Elder), *Prose on Several Occasions; Accompanied with Some Pieces in Verse* (3 vols., London, 1787), I. 259

It is in our universities that the rising generation, amidst the decay and downfall of the academical establishments on the continent, may learn to resist and refute the metaphysical subtleties, which have thrown half the nations of Europe into confusion

William Barrow, *An Essay on Education*, II. 308

The race as to which party would do better in a world without George II started before the old king was dead. Oxonian loyalty in the year of victories—1759— transcended party differences in a manner that was almost unprecedented; no wonder that Tory Heads of Houses unanimously agreed with their Whig counterparts in November 1759 over an address stating that the old king might be succeeded by a line of princes inheriting his virtues as well as his crown, and reigning like him in the hearts of his people.[161] If any diehard Jacobites nursed disappointment that the French-sponsored invasion attempt of 1759 intended to seat the Young Pretender belatedly on the throne of his ancestors had been utterly defeated, it was not displayed.[162] The Jacobite option as a serious political alternative turned out to have expired well before George II. Instead, Tories/the Old Interest to a man welcomed the accession of his grandson, George III, on 25 October 1760 with pent-up loyalty. His advent represented a fresh start, a turning away from the old Pelhamite oligarchy that Pitt the Elder had worked with rather than dismantled. Knowing whose son he was, aware of George's aversion to

---

[161] OUA: MS. Conv. Bh 35, ff. 133 et seq. The University's efforts to court favour unequivocally with George II had begun again after Prince Frederick's demise. In 1756, on the outbreak of the Seven Years' War, there were unblushing references to his 'most sacred person' in a staunchly patriotic address. OUA: Bg 34, f. 226. The King seems to have been unmoved, and remained hostile to Oxford in 1758. Sutherland, 'Political respectability', 143.

[162] C. Nordman, 'Choiseul and the last Jacobite Attempt of 1759', in ed. E. Cruickshanks, *Ideology and Conspiracy. Aspects of Jacobitism, 1689–1759* (Edinburgh, 1982), 201–17; Jeremy Black, *Pitt the Elder* (Cambridge, 1992), 187–8.

OXFORD AND THE CROWN   339

factional and party distinctions,[163] Tories hoped that old wounds would be bound up, that Oxford would at last receive its due share of court notice, and that its graduates (irrespective of their political persuasion) would again predominate in the councils of the British nation.[164]

Oxford Whigs and the beneficiaries of the old regime were, understandably, apprehensive about the likelihood of seismic changes coming soon in the public sphere, and these were reflected in arguments in Convocation on the question of whether to draw up an address to the throne condemning the published effusions of loyalty (many with party-political undertones) emanating from urban and corporate meetings being held across England.[165] In these circumstances, would the University 'not be exposed to just censure for entering into the views either of a successful or a disappointed faction.' But then again, were these outpourings 'of sufficient consequence to deserve the serious opposition of so respectable a body?' And was it 'not peculiarly unbecoming a Literary Body officiously to take the lead in Political Disputes which it knows only by report?' And even if Cambridge had already sent in its address, should 'any arguments drawn from the example of our sister University ... influence the conduct of a body, which justly values itself upon its Independence?'[166]

But the tide of opinion was too strong to resist, Oxford Tories could hardly contain themselves, and an address of loyalty to the young sovereign was speedily got ready, albeit with concessions to Whigs still lamenting the late king's demise. The Chancellor, Lord Westmorland, found his profound approval of George III offset by these complimentary references in the address to the new sovereign's grandfather, and tellingly absented himself from the blue-blooded party that took it to St James's Palace, headed by Lord Lichfield, the High Steward, and Joseph Browne, the Vice Chancellor (and Provost of Queen's).[167] In terms of party affiliation, it was actually a representative delegation calculated to upset neither Newcastle

[163] As Paul Langford put it, 'Exorcising the spirit of party was a high priority in mid-century, and synonymous with a new brand of patriotism on offer. George III, as a fervent advocate of its miraculous properties, sold this elixir with conviction.' *Public Life and the Propertied Englishman*, 124.

[164] Gibbon noted that 'The accession of a British King reconciled them [the country gentlemen] to the government and even to the court: but they have been since accused of transferring their passive loyalty from the Stuarts to the family of Brunswick; and I have heard Mr Burke exclaim in the house of Commons "They have changed the idol, but they have preserved the idolatry!"' *Memoirs*, 124.

[165] Convocation singled out the Chelmsford address for particular censure. Of the address of the Canterbury diocesan clergy one correspondent noted wryly: '... if his Majesty will follow the advice of that learned reverend body, without reserve, I doubt not but the everlasting crown they promise him would be such a one as Laud provided for Charles the First'. Thomas Percival to unknown, 20 Nov. [1760], HMC, *Kenyon MSS*, (London, 1894), 497.

[166] The arguments are summarised in Badminton Muniments, FmL 4/2/1. Voting was surprisingly close.

[167] OUA: Bh 35, ff. 209 et seq. For Westmorland's castigation of the 'whole tenor of administration in the last reign' see his letter to V-C Browne, Bodl. MSS. D.D. Dashwood (Bucks.) A.4/2; Badminton Muniments, FmK 1/3/36. Joseph Browne (1700–67), Sedleian Prof. of Natural Philosophy, 1741-d; Provost of Queen's, 1756-d.; V-C, 1759–65. William Hunt, 'Browne, Joseph (1700–1767), college head', rev. S. J. Skedd, ODNB, online edn., 2004.

340 ENLIGHTENED OXFORD

nor Hardwicke unduly. Yet the Tories were back at court, indeed welcomed there and, unlike 1727, they had no plans to go away empty-handed. Aware of young George's antipathy to party, they rallied around the person of the King and the prospects his reign appeared to hold out for them.[168] There was certainly plenty of scope for official congratulations in the years immediately following, beginning in September 1761 with the king's marriage (the 8th) and coronation (the 22nd). And, this time around, Westmorland went with a University delegation that included 150 students, all of them led up by the Master of Ceremonies to the throne, where the Earl rather muddled his lines. As one witness reported:[169]

He [the Chancellor] was very old, and, even with the help of spectacles, could not read well, so it took rather a long time. The King answered, without reading, with grace and fluency. They were then all allowed to kiss his hand.

Nothing daunted, the University was corporately back at court with an address on the birth of the Prince of Wales in 1762, insisting that 'the interests of Prince and people are so intimately and inseparably connected with each other' that the prosperity of all must be enhanced by the King's happiness in paternity.[170] But it reserved its grandest display (a retinue of 200) for the presentation of its official congratulations in 1763 on the controversial Treaty of Paris, the conclusion to the Seven Years' War, that was opposed so publicly by Oxford's old hero, the great War Minister, William Pitt. But, by this date, Oxford had for some time been committed to a Buteite agenda, that endorsed by the king's favourite, Newcastle's replacement as First Lord of the Treasury in May 1762. The prevailing sentiments of the address, that the war had been 'necessary' but was also 'expensive and destructive', might have been drafted by Bute himself.[171] And throughout this decade, Oxford dons moved sedulously into royal circles hunting for and receiving patronage. Cyril Jackson's contacts with the royal family began in the 1760s when he was tutor at Christ Church to George Finch, later 9th Earl of Winchilsea, whose mother, Lady Charlotte Finch, was governess to George III's young children.[172]

---

[168] Cf. Clark, 'Religion and Political Identity', 121: 'The initial effect of the eirenic policy of the young George III was not to produce a mood of tranquil reconciliation, but to heighten tensions as winners and losers at court eyed each other with jealous watchfulness'.

[169] Count Frederick Kielmansegge, *Diary of a Journey to England in the years 1761–1762* (London, 1902), 22. At the Drawing-room that followed the marriage the day afterwards, Westmorland's poor eyesight had led to an even more celebrated gaffe, when he mistook the King's old flame, the beautiful Lady Sarah Lennox, for Queen Charlotte and tried to kiss Lady Sarah's hand. The wit, George Selwyn, observed: 'Oh, you know he always loved Pretenders!', and Walpole cattily observed: 'People think that a Chancellor of Oxford was naturally attracted by the blood of a Stuart'. Walpole, *Correspondence*, XXI. 531, to Sir Horace Mann, 10 Sept. 1761.

[170] OUA: Conv. Bh 35, ff. 393 et seq.

[171] Ibid., Bh 35, fol. 430 et seq.; *GM* 33 (1763), 40, 181–2.

[172] Jackson stayed regularly in London with Lady Charlotte and her family. See his letter to her of c.1768, LLRRO, DG7/Bundle 31/62, Box 4953.

It was principally via this channel that Jackson duly became sub-preceptor to George, Prince of Wales.[173]

Oxford was avid for a visit in person from King George and Queen Charlotte to show its loyalty on the spot, just as it had done soon after Queen Anne's accession in 1702. Rumours of an imminent visit were triggered when the University spent heavily on renovation of the Sheldonian Theatre in the spring of 1762. As one don informed a former minister:[174]

> I can assure you that the University were never better disposed to shew their Duty to his Majesty & his Family, & indeed they never had greater Reason. We have great numbers of Youth of Genius & Learning & only want Encouragement to stir their Emulation. His Majesty's great Love of ye fine Arts & Literature raise ye highest Expectations in this Place, . . .

But George did not appear. And the same was frustratingly true in 1763, when the press reported in April that the visit would occur when Parliament rose; then it was postponed to the great Peace Encaenia of July 1763, at which William King delivered his last oration; then in September, till sometime in the unspecified future.[175]

That day turned out to be over two decades distant,[176] when the middle-aged monarch, Queen Charlotte, Princes Ernest, Augustus, and Adolphus, and Princesses Royal, Augusta, and Elizabeth visited the University privately on 13 September 1785. They travelled in five carriages with their friends George, the 2nd Earl and (Elizabeth) Countess Harcourt, from nearby Nuneham Courtenay to attend morning prayers at Christ Church Cathedral, to be waited on (after inspecting the House) at Corpus Christi College by its President, John Cooke, and the recent Vice Chancellor, Samuel Dennis (President of St John's).[177] An extemporised levee was held in the Sheldonian, where William Hayes played the organ, while the Vice Chancellor (Joseph Chapman, President of Trinity College),

---

[173] George Croly, *The Life and Times of His Late Majesty, George the Fourth* (London, 1830), 19, 26. Jackson remained in contact with the Prince in adulthood and was a regular visitor to Brighton as the latter's guest. Ibid., 116–17.

[174] Dr Thomas Wilson to Edward Weston, 1 Oct. 1762. Wilson was hoping that the Royal Family would attend the Public Act for the Peace planned for the following July. HMC, *Weston Underwood MSS* (London, 1885), 345.

[175] *JOJ*, 13 Mar., 2 Oct. 1762: 9 Apr., 18 June, 17 Sept. 1763: 5 May 1764: 8, 15 June 1765: 17 Sept. 1768. See below for King's oration.

[176] Rumours frequently surfaced, as in 1777 when one correspondent told the American Secretary of State, Lord George Germain, one was likely soon, observing that George showed a predilection for Oxford at the expense of Cambridge, and 'it will shock the prejudices of many of his most respectable subjects'. 24 May 1777, HMC, *Stopford-Sackville MSS* (2 vols., London, 1904–10), I. 71–2.

[177] John Cooke (c.1735–1823), matric. Hertford Coll., 1749; BA, 1753, Corpus Christi; MA, 1757; BD, 1765; DD, 1782; President, Corpus Christi, 1783-1823; V-C, 1788–92. Foster, I. 289; Samuel Dennis (c.1739–95), matric. SJC, 1757; MA, 1765; DD, 1774; President, SJC, 1772–95; V-C, 1780–4. Foster, I. 363.

342   ENLIGHTENED OXFORD

Proctors, and Heads of Houses kissed the sovereign's hand.[178] They also visited the Bodleian, the Picture Gallery, the Pomfret and Arundel marbles, New College, St John's College, the Observatory, All Souls, Queen's, and Magdalen Colleges. The King and Queen presented their portraits to St John's College and met the municipal officials in the Council Chamber where the King knighted the mayor. The University apparently only had two hours' notice that the royal party was on its way, yet crowds gathered in Oxford quickly, 'but they were so civil there was not the least confusion'.[179]

The visit was repeated by another one, celebrated on an elaborate scale on 13 August the following year (partly as a sign of collective relief that the stabbing of the king by the lunatic Margaret Nicholson on 2 August had not been more serious).[180] Fanny Burney reported that people thronged to see the king, queen, and princesses, but that 'was still the genteelest and most decent crowd I ever saw'. After delivering his Address on behalf of the University,[181] Vice Chancellor Chapman made an unexpected reference to the recent tribulations and tribulations of Queen Charlotte in a manner that required her to disguise her tears with her fan and the royal princesses cried openly.[182] After the extended college visiting and an elaborate collation in Christ Church Hall,[183] the King and Queen, with the Princess Royal, and Princesses Augusta and Elizabeth in attendance, went on to stay with their friends, the 4th Duke and Duchess of Marlborough at Blenheim Palace (who had attended them at the academic ceremonies,[184] a token of the harmony prevailing between the Churchill family and the University by the 1780s).[185]

---

[178] *European Magazine* 8 (1785), 238; Edward Holt, *The Public and Domestic Life of his late Gracious Majesty George the Third* (2 vols., London, 1820), I. 281–2; J. R. Green, *Studies in Oxford History, chiefly in the Eighteenth Century*, ed. C. L. Stainer [OHS, 51] (Oxford, 1901), 211–13; Godley, *Oxford in the eighteenth century*, 136; John Richard Green, *Oxford during the last century* (Oxford, 1859), 120.

[179] Letter of Col. Manners, 18 Sept, [1785], Journal of Lady Mary Coke, Lewis Walpole Library, Yale University.

[180] See Holt, *Public and Domestic Life*, I. 288–90; *Diaries and Letters of Madame d'Arblay*, ed. Charlotte Barrett (7 vols., London, 1854), III. 78–90; *European Magazine* 10 (1786), 238.

[181] Of all the Addresses that the King had received, that from Oxford University was the only one to which he made a formal reply delivered verbally in person. Holt, *Public and Domestic Life*, I. 287. Joseph Chapman. (*c.*1743–1808), matric. Trinity, 1759; MA, 1766; Proctor, 1775; DD, 1777; President, Trinity, 1776–1808; V-C, 1784–8. Foster, I. 239.

[182] Burney noted ' . . . I question if there was one dry eye in the theatre.' *Diaries and Letters of Madame d'Arblay* III. 81.

[183] It was an occasion when the royal family banqueted and their entourage, including Fanny Burney, went unfed.

[184] The heir to the dukedom, George, Marquess of Blandford (1766–1840), was an undergraduate. He was stationed in a position of honour, along with other members of his family, in the Sheldonian. *Diaries and Letters of Madame d'Arblay*, III, 79.

[185] Joseph Chapman apologised that the heads of Houses and Convocation had sent a corporate address of thanks for the visit without having previously consulted the Chancellor. To Lord North, BL North (Sheffield Park) papers, Add MS. 61869, f. 159; John Moore, Abp of Canterbury to Dcss of Marlborough, 10 Aug. 1786, BL Blenheim papers Add MS. 61670, ff. 139–40; and return, 16 Aug. 1786; *The Journal and Correspondence of William, Lord Auckland*, ed. Bishop of Bath & Wells (4 vols., London, 1860–2), I. 386–7.

Even before it hailed the King in person, the University had no doubts about George's personal commitment to fostering learning[186]—and to Oxford learning in particular—on show only a few months into his reign when Kennicott was awarded a royal bounty of £200 per annum, completing a public subscription of £800 per annum to take forward his collation of the Hebrew MSS. of the Old Testament.[187] This display of generosity was by no means unusual. For instance, in 1783 Samuel Dennis, the Vice Chancellor, notified the Chancellor of a warrant for the delivery of a copy of the Doomsday Book ordered by the King for the University, having already advised college heads and proctors of 'this fresh mark of the Royal Bounty and Regard to this place, ... '[188] And it was not just a matter of gift giving. Typically, of his general concern for the Crown as the fount of honour, the King evinced a pronounced personal interest in appointment to Regius chairs. As he was quick to tell Lord North soon after the latter's election to the Chancellorship:

> I am certain this will stimulate you to recommend on vacancies none but men of character and abilities for the Regius Professorships, and I can assure you that I shall expect all those I appoint to perform such duties as the heads of houses shall require of them.[189]

Unsurprisingly, the University was to the fore in formulating and producing a rhetoric of royal acclamation that drew on rich seams of monarchical loyalism that had seldom been openly paraded since Queen Anne's death. Oxford loyalty to and liking for George III never wavered at any point during his long reign, and members of the University played an overlooked part in creating a cult of the King that came to its full flowering in the 1790s.[190] Prints and portraits of the young King and Queen abounded and were to be found in premises across the University, in imitation of Chancellor Lichfield's presentation of a full-length portrait of the King for the University picture gallery. Books of verses were offered whenever an occasion seemed propitious, starting with a book 'of condolence and

---

[186] For the King as a book collector see J. Marsden, 'Books and binding', in ed. J. Roberts, *George III & Queen Charlotte. Patronage, Collecting and Court Taste* (London, 2004), 221–43.

[187] Ward, *Georgian Oxford*, 216. However, the King was privately criticised by Bishop Barrington for his failure to contribute to a later scholarly labour: 'You suppose that much may be done by Royal patronage, and subscription of the Bishops. The former was tried without success in support of one of the most important undertakings, since that of Dr Kennicott's, to the cause of Revelation, viz, Dr Holmes's collation of the 70 MSS;' To Rev. J. H. Hindlay, 24 Oct. 1800, The James Marshall and Marie-Louise Osborn Collection, Beinecke Rare Book & Manuscript Library, Yale University, Osborn Shelves fc 142, letter book of Bishop Shute Barrington, 1799–1811, f. 34.

[188] Dennis to Lord North, 25 Mar. 1783, BL North (Sheffield Park) papers, Add MS 61869, f. 149.

[189] George III to Lord North, 5 Oct. 1772, ed. Sir John Fortescue, *The Correspondence of King George the Third* (6 vols., London, 1927–8), II. 400.

[190] Linda Colley, 'The apotheosis of George III: loyalty, royalty and the British Nation 1760–1820', *P&P*, 102 (1984), 94–129.

344   ENLIGHTENED OXFORD

congratulation' that included rhymes of exceptional adulation,[191] and evidence of unconfined joy (especially among junior members) at having once again at an *English* king, the heir to his father's 'Patriotic' agenda, with pro-court journals such as the *Auditor* soon hailing him as 'a Patriot King'.[192] There were more laudatory verses for the great Encaenia of July 1763 on the signing of the Peace of Paris when William King, with—for once—virtually the whole University behind him '...complimented his majesty for his particular regard to Arts, to Literature, and to the University of Oxford'.[193] Such tributes were well reported nationally and helped confirm public partiality for the youthful sovereign.

Oxford clergy had vied with each other in the early 1760s to show that George was the pattern of what a Christian king should be, and how much the whole country owed him their duty. For dons with Hutchinsonian sympathies, particularly George Horne, Fellow of Magdalen, for whom the royal supremacy was not a political settlement but a Scriptural injunction, it was impossible to resist dipping into the treasury of royalist commonplaces bequeathed them by an earlier Tory generation. From the pulpit of St Mary's church on 30 January 1761, he reminded his congregation that non-resistance to government in Church and state was a non-negotiable concept, and did not find it difficult to imagine that young King George would soon be imitating Charles I's 'god-like virtues' as benevolent ruler.[194] It was all too easy for Oxonian preachers to fall back on this well-worn comparison when occasion offered every 30 January, and the mark could be overstepped, as Thomas Nowell famously found out on in 1772,[195] when, juxtaposing the virtues of George III with those of Charles I, Nowell prayed that 'the guilt of an ungrateful abandoned people may not cause this sun to be withdrawn from us'.[196] Another Oxonian (though one having the additional latitude that not holding a post within the University gave him), the leading Hutchinsonian and Horne's friend, William Jones of Nayland, went further than Nowell in his claims regarding was owed in obedience to George III, taking his rejection of resistance to

[191] *GM* 31 (1761), 90.
[192] The University also published Latin verses on George II's death, George III's marriage, and the birth of the Prince of Wales (1762), from a range submitted by undergraduates and vetted by inspectors that included Prof Thomas Warton the younger. Fairer, 'Oxford and the Literary World', 797n.
[193] *JOJ*, 9 July 1763. There was, of course, no *Terrae Filius* present in person, but an entertaining journal was published that summer under that 'nom de plume' by George Colman. *Prose on Several Occasions*, I. 221–62.
[194] 'What a noble subject is Christianity seated upon a throne!', apostrophised Horne. 'The Christian King', in G. Horne, *Sermons on various subjects and occasions* (London, 1793), 17.
[195] Nowell's sermon is fully discussed in Chapter 3, pp. 94–5.
[196] *PH*, XVII. 312–31; *GM* 42 (1772), 134–5. Nowell had many sympathisers outside Parliament for the censure of this sermon. James Boswell observed that it was the effect of 'that turbulence and faction which disgraced a part of the present reign...Dr Nowell will ever have the honour which is due to a lofty friend of our monarchical constitution', ed. Birkbeck Hill, rev. Powell, *Boswell's Life of Johnson*, IV. 296, 11 June 1784. Sack perceptively notes that the King failed to offer Nowell any royal patronage—despite parallels the preacher had drawn between George III and Charles I. *From Jacobite to Conservative*, 123–4, 129.

Fig. 7.4 George Horne, John Bridges, oil on canvas (Reproduced by kind permission of the President and Fellows of Magdalen College).

civil government directly from the nonjuring tradition he and Horne so venerated, above all from Charles Leslie, when he wrote in 1776:[197]

> If it be a truth that laws (however originated) bind a people, the people of England are bound not to resist with force the king, or those commissioned by him, in any case or upon any pretence whatsoever.

Here was a case of old wine in very new bottles.

Yet these were sentiments that would have pleased George III (though they did no good for Jones in terms of his ascent in the Church) coming, as they did, in the year when the Declaration of Independence by the Thirteen Colonies posed an unparalleled internal challenge to the monarchical basis of the Hanoverian monarchy.[198]

---

[197] Jones, *A Discourse on the English Constitution; Extracted from a Late Eminent Writer, and Applicable to the Present Times* (London, 1776), text, 1.

[198] For clerical support for the war generally see Paul Langford, 'The English Clergy and the American Revolution', in ed. E. Hellmuth, *The Transformation of Political Culture: England and Germany in the Late Eighteenth Century* (Oxford, 1990), 275–308.

346   ENLIGHTENED OXFORD

Having just elected Lord North as its Chancellor, the majority of University members were always going to throw their weight behind his government's policy of reducing the King's rebellious subjects to obedience. This preference was entirely consistent with the thrust of the immensely authoritative—and Oxonian—constitutional handbook, Blackstone's *Commentaries* (originally published between 1765 and 1769 and dedicated to his royal employer, Queen Charlotte) that had proclaimed the absolute sovereignty of the King in Parliament in all matters concerning the state. Blackstone, the great court lawyer, was intelligently insistent on the need for reverence, loyalty, and obedience, and had thus acclaimed George III:

> a sovereign, who, in all those public acts that have personally proceeded from himself, hath manifested the highest veneration for the free constitution of Britain; hath already in more than one instance remarkably strengthened its outworks; and will therefore never harbour a thought, or adopt a persuasion, in any the remotest degree detrimental to public liberty.[199]

In line with this strand of thinking that on 26 October 1775, after a warm debate in Convocation,[200] the University sent up an address to the King which declared its abhorrence of misuse of freedom of the press, 'licentious' criticism of King and parliament, and 'illegal associations' fermenting rebellion in Britain during wartime. These amounted to 'seditious proceedings' and the University declared in favour of coercive measures.[201] Edmund Burke, the leading Rockingham Whig and supporter of conciliation, then in intemperate language accused Oxford of 'advising a civil war, and calling those that opposed it rebels and traitors'.[202] Most members of Convocation were in no mood to listen to 'the specious sophistry of this frothy orator',[203] and his intervention deepened the rift between Burke and his leading Oxford acquaintance, Bishop William Markham, Dean of Christ Church. The Regius Professor of Divinity, Edward Bentham, ever the loyalist, offered a defence in Latin of government policy in *De tumultibus Americanis* (1776) and, from St Mary's and other pulpits, numerous sermons drew on the deep wells of Oxonian loyalty, and urged the Americans to surrender in good faith and see what

---

[199] William Blackstone, *Commentaries on The Laws of England*, gen. ed. Wilfrid Prest, *Book I: Of the Rights of Persons*, ed. David Lemmings (Oxford, 2016), I. 216. For Blackstone's influence on George III's education, J. L. McKelvey, *George III and Lord Bute: the Leicester House years* (Durham, NC, 1973), 84–5. And also J. W. Cairns, 'Blackstone, an English Institutist: legal literature and the rise of the nation state', *Oxford Journal of Legal Studies*, 4 (1984), 318–60.

[200] '…I should think it unlikely that Cambridge would follow our example in addressing His Majesty…. There were only three Non-Placets—…' William Jackson to Lord Lewisham, Staffs RO D(W)1778/V/852.

[201] OUA: MS Conv. Reg. Bi, f. 363. See also TNA (PRO) HO 55/11/32; 11/53; ed. Peter Force, *American Archives…*, (4th ser., 6 vols., Washington, 1837–46), III. 1188.

[202] *PH*, XVIII. 854.

[203] [E. Bentham], *The Honor of the University of Oxford Defended against the Illiberal Aspersions of E[dmun]d B[urk]e Esq.* (London, n.d.) [1776], 1. Bentham's was the leading riposte.

a magnanimous, benevolent sovereign George III could be. Myles Cooper, the Oxford-educated, dispossessed president of King's College, New York, pleaded with the rebels in a St Mary's Fast Day sermon of December 1776 to obey the powers 'ordained of God', and derided 'Original Compacts which never existed'. Such orthodox sentiments invited and received plenty of Whig opprobrium, but they accurately reflected majority opinion in the University.[204] Oxford also tried to make practice compatible with principle: it was relatively speedy to give refuge and relief to several colonial clerics who had suffered hardship and depredation because they would not renounce their king.[205]

The Rockingham Whigs, averse to Blackstone personally, and with Burke as their principal spokesman, echoed the traditional Country claim that 'the power of the crown, almost dead and rotten as Prerogative, has grown up anew, with much more strength, and far less odium, under the name of Influence'.[206] And this conviction, by the late 1770s, sounded a chord with a minority of Oxonians (particularly non-resident members) that believed the University was uncritically close to the court. They were increasingly disinclined to follow the King and his government in prosecuting the war that by 1779 had become a global conflict; it was evidenced by such as the circular sent to members of Convocation on 20 July 1779 opposing a scheme of voluntary payments for the war effort.[207] In 1780 the Commons passed John Dunning's celebrated motion that the power of the Crown ought to be diminished, and its echo was heard for a while in Oxford in what was an updated country party, commonwealth Whiggism. William Jones, the immensely talented lawyer and orientalist, fellow of University College, the friend of John Wilkes, stood as a candidate for the University in the 1780 General Election,[208] and was the exponent of a mild Miltonic republicanism that, nevertheless went far beyond anything the Rockinghamites advocated.[209]

---

[204] Myles Cooper, *National Humiliation and Repentance Recommended and the Causes of the Present Rebellion in America Assigned* (Oxford, 1777), 22; [A. M. Shore], *A Letter to the Rev. Dr. Cooper on the Origin of Civil Government* (London, 1777). Cooper's sermon caused controversy by implying that the power of the King and Parliament was divinely ordained. Discussed in Gunn, *Beyond Liberty and Property*, 174; Sack, *From Jacobite to Conservative*, 126.

[205] Most refugee priests were quick to head to London and not Oxford. In the second half of 1777 there were seven from Maryland alone.

[206] *Burke's Thoughts on the cause of the Present Discontents*, ed. F.G. Selby (London, 1951, originally pub. 1902), 9. Gunn argues that the claim of the divine right of kings was 'extremely resilient' during George III's reign. *Beyond Liberty and Property*, 136.

[207] Bodl. G. A. Oxon. b 111 (n. 62).

[208] Peter Brown, *The Chathamites. A study in the relationship between personalities and ideas in the second half of the eighteenth century* (London, 1967), 363–5. The bishop Jones most admired was Jonathan Shipley of St Asaph, his future father-in-law, the friend of Benjamin Franklin, and one of the few prelates to speak and vote against the American War. Ibid., 325–38, 371–2.

[209] For Jones's insistence that he was '... certainly the only Whig candidate', see Cannon, ed., *The Letters of Sir William Jones*, I. 377. Jones's political reputation preceded him at the General Election: his support for the American colonists and a rejected speech for North's installation at the 1773 Encaenia were well known.

348 ENLIGHTENED OXFORD

Apart from Jones and his young friends, dissident, unappeased Whigs were few and far between in the Oxford of the 1770s and early 1780s. There were nearby Whig grandees with some residual influence in the university—William, 6th Lord Craven and the maverick 4th Earl of Abingdon (a minor patron of Kennicott in the 1760s) were prominent among them,[210]—who opposed the American War in Parliament, and espoused progressive causes such as the Association Movement with some verve, but they had a tiny number of clients at a senior level in the University. Most older academics, usually with a Pelhamite pedigree, had tended to do quite well out of royal patronage after 1760, and were predisposed to slip their moorings and become out-and-out courtiers (often through the offices of that supreme 'King's Friend', Charles Jenkinson).[211] These types had little or nothing to say publicly about political theory, especially when it concerned the Crown of England, but their wish to please the King and his advisers when opportunity offered was very evident. Their silence did them no harm: that inveterate place hunter, Edward Bentham, became Regius Professor of Divinity in 1763 during George Grenville's administration with little fuss about his previous political obligations to Newcastle's allies;[212] Benjamin Kennicott's nomination as Radcliffe Librarian in 1766 was confirmed by George III on the recommendation of the Duke of Grafton;[213] and Christ Church made a seamless transition from the old reign to the new as a bastion of courtiers and placemen whose commitment to Whiggism became less its defining tone. The House remained a nursery of future prelates. John Moore, client of the 4th Duke of Marlborough (George III's friend and contemporary), went from a Christ Church canonry to become bishop of Bangor and then (1783) to the metropolitan see itself. Another canon picked out personally by George for lawn sleeves was the Hon. Shute Barrington, younger brother of Lord North's Secretary-at-War, both of whom had distanced themselves from a distinctly Whiggish family background.[214]

Though the Rockingham Whigs had a cluster of supporters connected with Oxford in the 1770s (notably through the 3rd Duke of Portland, Rockingham's successor as party leader after 1782), their principal academic following lay in Cambridge. Thus the revival of political heat on substantive issues was less divisive in loyalist Oxford than in most other parts of England: Oxford was comfortable with George III and the court, and the court with Oxford, allowing both moderate Tories and moderate Whigs room to flourish, terms that persisted, though

[210] For Abingdon's excoriation of Toryism, associating it with tyranny, see his *Thoughts on the Letter of Edmund Burke, Esq.* (6th edn., Oxford, 1777), lii.

[211] See Sack, *From Jacobite to Conservative*, 76–7.

[212] For Bentham, see Chapter 3, pp. 47–50. It was an explicable choice if only on the basis that Oxford was Bentham's world, and he never missed one term's residence from matriculation to his death.

[213] Ingram, *Religion, Reform and Modernity*, 181–2.

[214] Ward, *Georgian Oxford*, 216, 220, 226. For Moore, N. Aston, 'Moore, John (bap. 1730, d. 1805)', ODNB online version, 2008. See also Chapter 8, p. 23.

OXFORD AND THE CROWN   349

lacking stable explication.[215] With few exceptions, these supported Lord North's Premiership (and thereby the King's express preference) until his final resignation in March 1782. Political embarrassment for the University arose less then but a year later when North made his notorious junction with George III's *bête noire*, Charles James Fox, and formed the famous Coalition. The King's loathing of a government foisted upon him was public knowledge, as was his resentment of North personally for making the arrangement possible in the first place.[216] When it came to a choice between what the King wanted, and what its Chancellor was doing, there was never going to be much doubt where most University loyalties would lie. Even so, there were some surprises among the dons when Thomas Nowell, Principal of St Mary Hall, refused to sign the loyal address to George III in 1784, a reflection of the renewed political confusions brought about the advent and dismissal of the Coalition, and the arrival of 'Pittite' and 'Foxite' labels.[217]

If this political divergence about the use of the royal prerogative and personalities accentuated the distance between the University and its Chancellor for the remainder of his life (North, by then, 2nd Earl of Guilford, died in 1792), it was more than compensated for by the visits to Oxford of George III, Queen Charlotte, and some of their children during the 1780s. This new association anticipated the loyalism of the Revolutionary decade and found further expression in the appointment of a senior Oxonian - Thomas Warton of Trinity College—to be the new Poet Laureate in 1785 and his regular production of odes honouring the King until Warton's death in 1790.[218] Thus the University underscored its respect not just for the principles of monarchy but also for the sovereign's own paternal commitment to his family and thus, by extension, to the nation at large. Even Vicesimus Knox, a former fellow of the Whig society at St John's College, could, by 1787, 'venture to pronounce George the Third a Patriot King'.[219] During the Regency Crisis of 1788–9 the University—despite the anomaly of having a Chancellor in Opposition—was unswervingly Pittite.

The king's recovery from illness in 1789 was greeted with relief, the local newspaper noting that the colleges as well as the houses of the citizens were illuminated, and New College, Queen's, All Souls, University, and Trinity Colleges were 'particularly distinguished for their judicious Arrangement of Lights'.[220]

---

[215] Toryism, wrote Paul Langford, had become little 'more than a shorthand for describing supporters of Lord North, whatever their beliefs and connections'. *Public Life and the Propertied Englishman*, 134.

[216] Foord, *His Majesty's Opposition*, 386–7; Whiteley, *Lord North*, 216; Thomas, *Lord North*, 144–5.

[217] *Whitehall Evening Post*, Mar 13–16, 1784.

[218] Fairer, 'Oxford and the Literary World', 801.

[219] Knox, *Essays Moral and Literary* (2 vols., 9th edn., London, 1787), I. 29. For the monarchy's growth in popularity, the *locus classicus* is Colley, 'The Apotheosis of George III'.

[220] *JOJ*, 14 Mar. 1789. George III did not visit Oxford that year. However, in November the King's brother, the Duke of Gloucester, and his children Prince William Henry and Princess Sophia visited. They were received by the Vice Chancellor at the Star Inn, toured the colleges, met the Dean and

350 ENLIGHTENED OXFORD

In due course, the University sent up an address of congratulation to St James's Palace on the King's recovery in 1789, presented by Lord North, Lord Dartmouth (High Steward), Vice Chancellor Cooke, President of Corpus, and a full delegacy.[221]

These loyal sentiments remained the official line of the University throughout the French Revolutionary War (1793–1802). Even before it broke out on 1 February 1793 the Royal Proclamation of May 1792 had initiated the first campaign against reform and revolution, and helped provoke a wave of loyal responses, with the University vaguely blasting the 'intemperate Zeal of wild Theorists'.[222] Oxford-educated apologists throughout the kingdom thereafter drew on layers of accumulated royalist rhetoric to make George III central to the contest many in Britain felt they were engaged in against the twin perils of republicanism and democracy, atheism and anarchy.[223] As counterpoises, there was a commitment to the principle of monarchy and to the King personally, drawing on any number of instances of George's personal piety to support varying notions of benign patriarchy and national unity.[224] The sovereign represented a barrier to the possibility of mob rule that would overthrow the established Constitution in Church and state (including, of course, Oxford), and deprive Britons of the benefits they derived from it. The Duke of York's chaplain, the philologist and future editor of the *British Critic*, Robert Nares (1753–1829; MA, Ch. Ch., 1778), thus argued in 1792 that the sanctity of the king, as expressed in the coronation, was vital to the preservation of the Constitution. He was God's vicegerent, who upheld the laws that God had established to maintain harmonious societies, and the removal of a king ushered in the worst possible political dangers. Nares conceded that the king's power came from his people but, given his sanctity, it did not follow that their arbitrary will could overstep his wisdom.[225]

resident Canons in Christ Church library, where young noblemen were presented to them. D. Wauchope to William Clerk, Edinburgh, Oxford, 9 Nov. 1789, National Archives of Scotland, GD18/5542; Bodl. MS Top Oxon. d.174, f. 225.

[221] Cox, *Recollections*, 3. It waspishly noted that 'it was singular that Ld North as Chancellor of the University chose to come up with it, & as being blind was led in by Ld Dartmouth. – The sight would have been affecting if he last winter had shewn more sensibility for the King's misfortune'. West Yorkshire Archives Services, Diaries of Lady Amabel Yorke, Vyner Add. MS. 2299, Vol. II, f. 27, 28 Mar 1789.

[222] *London Gazette*, 16 June 1792.

[223] See Marilyn Morris, *The British Monarchy and the French Revolution* (New Haven, CT, and London, 1998), esp. 104–8. For clerical responses in general to the French Revolution see Emma Vincent Macleod, *A War of Ideas. British attitudes to the Wars against Revolutionary France, 1792–1802* (Aldershot, 1998), 135–49; R. Hole, 'English Sermons and Tracts as Media of Debate on the French Revolution', in ed. M. Philp, *The French Revolution and British Popular Politics*, (Cambridge, 1991), 18–37. For the millennial dimension C. D. A. Leighton, 'AntiChrist's revolution: some Anglican apologists in the age of the French wars', *Journal of Religious History*, 24 (2000), 125–42.

[224] G. M. Ditchfield, *George III. An Essay in Monarchy* (Basingstoke, 2002), 77–108.

[225] Nares still defended a qualified and necessary right of resistance. *Principles of Government Deduced from Reason, Supported by English Experience, and Opposed to French Errors* (London, 1792), esp. 81–99, 137–43. He was a committee member of the ultra-loyalist Association for the Preservation of Liberty and Property against Republicans and Levellers. E. C. Black, *The Association.*

Fig. 7.5 Robert Nares, by Samuel Freeman, published by Fisher Son & Co, after John Hoppner, stipple and line engraving, published 1830 (© National Portrait Gallery, London).

Sermons along these lines indicate the centrality of the religious idiom to the often frenetic loyalism of the 1790s.[226]

The University's interventions in the national debate on the Constitution during these years were controversial in some quarters and did nothing for its reputation among Dissenters, Foxites, and other state reformers. Yet the University and its graduates had become an essential component of the late Hanoverian polity by the late 1790s, in sermons and abundant loyalist and patriotic journalism putting their talents at the service of the dynasty, making an intellectual case for establishment, able both to justify monarchy to most of the nation and to work within the state not just for the Crown's institutional survival

---

British Extraparliamentary Political Organisation 1769-1793 (Cambridge, MA, 1963), 243. For Robert Nares see R. Hole, 'British Counter-Revolutionary Popular Propaganda in the 1790s', 59–83, in ed. Colin Jones, *Britain and Revolutionary France: Conflict, Subversion and Propaganda* (Exeter, 1983).

[226] Nancy U. Murray, 'The Influence of the French Revolution on the Church of England and its Rivals, 1789–1802', (D.Phil., Oxford, 1975), 95–103 for the marginal position of liberal Anglicanism after 1789.

352 ENLIGHTENED OXFORD

but for its prospering. Oxford pride in the monarchy in the 1790s was far from unthinking, and more than a reactionary repetition of constitutional clichés. On the contrary, it made the case for stability on the British model of 1688 overwhelmingly attractive when set against the experimentation that characterised French republicanism. This revivified defence of monarchy within the [1688] Revolutionary framework could at last receive near unanimous Oxonian endorsement during the Portland Chancellorship (1793–1809) and beyond.

During wartime from 1793 onwards, most Oxford graduates were as ready as any other section of the population to play their patriotic part. There were many kinds of practical responses undertaken in response to the emergency. The University found £2,449 as voluntary aid for the government towards the raising of troops 'for the Internal Defence of the Country', as part of a nationwide appeal in 1794.[227] This was just the start. The following year the Vice Chancellor organised a fund for recruiting men for the Navy, and expected the colleges and their members to contribute generously: St John's gave £11 4s, Christ Church offered £49.[228] The student body across the University responded to the government's call to create a national defence force with some fervour, and the Oxford University Volunteers was formed and drilled regularly in the late 1790s under the command of Col. John Coker of Bicester, formerly a Fellow of New College, with the Vinerian Professor of Law (James Blackstone) as Lieutenant-Colonel.[229] College servants enlisted, as did many clergy—patriotically determined to defy the ban on persons in holy orders bearing arms—led by the Rev. Frederick Barnes (Canon of Christ Church, 1810–59). He served as Major, and the Rev. Theophilus Leigh Cooke, Fellow of Magdalen, was acting Adjutant.[230] The possibility of a French invasion in the late 1790s and early 1800s was no idle threat and University members of all ages were caught up in the craze for amateur soldiering. As one reported it:

Why does the Drum & Fife precede the College Bells, why are the Caps and Gowns laid aside for a more Military Dress, and why does the Musket and

---

[227] For some initial hesitation on the part of the University authorities as to endorsing subscription to this fund officially see Vice Chancellor Wills to Francis Page, MP, 12 Apr. 1794, Balliol College Archives and Manuscripts, Jenkyns VI.A (2), f.62.

[228] Cox, *Recollections*, 17; Ch. Ch., D&C i.b.7, 646 quoted in Curthoys (1), 195.

[229] Individual colleges became heavily engaged with the Volunteers. Jesus College students flocked to the colours and the College made large payments to the support of the Corps in the later 1790s. *VCH Oxon.*, III. 267; J. N. L. Baker, *Jesus College Oxford 1571–1971* (Oxford, 1971), 27, 28. John Coker (b. c.1751), matric. New Coll., 1769, MA, 1776; Proctor, 1786; called to the Bar, 1779; DCL, 1798. Foster, I. 273.

[230] A City Loyal Volunteer Corps (250 men) under Sir Digby Mackworth was also formed. Cox, *Recollections*, 36; Crook, *Brasenose College*, 177–8. Sir Digby Mackworth, 3rd Bt. (1766–1838), matric. Magd. Coll., 1788, DCL, 1799, of New College; Lt.-Col. of Oxford City Loyal Volunteers, 1798, 1803–4. Foster, III. 896. Also J. E. Cookson, *The British Armed Nation 1793–1815* (Oxford, 1997), 8–9, 24–8; Austin Gee, *The British Volunteer Movement, 1794–1814* (Oxford, 2003).

Bayonet supply the Place of Books, while beneath each Oxford Parson's Wig lurks a Captain or Lieutenant; and no longer ago than this morning I saw a Doctor of Divinity knock down an Under Graduate with his Musket;[231]

During the 1798 invasion scare, the governing body of St John's College spent £220 7s 9d 'in arming the college' and gave £200 'towards the exigencies of the State'. The University, as a body, raised a total of £4,000 to that end in what was, nationally, a troubled year, with rebellion in Ireland and a heavy tax burden to meet wartime exigencies.[232] Invasion threatened despite Nelson's victory at the Nile in August 1798. Oxford was identified by the government as a place for holding prisoners and as an evacuation centre for south-coast inhabitants should the French make a landing. To prepare for the possibility an Association was formed in the city to reinforce the existing authorities involving both the University and the corporation.[233] Its student members were placed under the obligation to repair back to the city in its defence should the French land in England. By July 1798 nearly 500 men across the University had enrolled and exercised daily in four divisions: St John's, Trinity, Magdalen, and New College, as part of the Oxford Loyal Volunteers [OLV].[234] They received their colours from the Chancellor and Home Secretary, the Duke of Portland, on 2 July 1798, in a colourful spectacle that, in John Randolph's words, 'such as has never before been seen & probably will not be again'.[235] But it would be—only the following year.

Despite wartime hardships, the University reflected British patriotism as vigorously as any other institution. For instance, Admiral Adam Duncan's victory over the Dutch fleet at Camperdown in October 1797 was celebrated with special illuminations at Christ Church.[236] If Oxonian apologists were disappointed that

---

[231] Godschall Johnson the younger to his stepmother, Oriel College, 18 May 1798, in eds. B. Francis and E. Keary, *The Francis Letters...* (2 vols., London, 1910), II. 424–5.

[232] Musical concerts were a favoured means of raising funds. An advertisement in *JOJ* (3 Mar.) for a concert in the Holywell Music Rooms for 8 Mar. 1798 announced that all the profits would go to a patriotic subscription to Exchequer funds (the musicians offered their services gratis); after the Nile, a concert at the Town Hall attended by the musicians of the Music Room in combination with Volunteer Military bands was held to contribute to the relief of widows and orphans. Details in Susan Wollenberg, '"Thus we Kept Away Bonaparte:" music in Oxford at the time of the Napoleonic Wars', in ed. M. Philp, *Resisting Napoleon: The British response to the threat of invasion 1797 to 1815* (Aldershot, 2006), 173–204 at, 193–4.

[233] Costin, *St John's College*, 239; Cox, *Recollections*, 35; H.F.B. Wheeler and A.M. Broadley, *Napoleon and the Invasion of England. The Story of the Great Terror* (London, 1908, repr., Stroud, 2007), 106–8.

[234] Cambridge by comparison allowed a term's grace to undergraduates who enrolled as Volunteers not in the University city but in their counties of domicile. For Bishop Samuel Horsley's criticism of the Oxford scheme as 'perfect madness', see his letter to his son Heneage Horsley (at Christ Church), 30 Apr. 1798, quoted in Mather, *High Church Prophet*, 257. Dean Jackson strongly disagreed.

[235] Randolph to Thomas Lambard, 10 July 1798, Bodl. MS Top. Oxon. d.354/2, ff. 36–7.

[236] Ch. Ch., D&C i.b.7, 669 quoted in Curthoys (1), 195. The Heather Professor, William Crotch, wrote pieces for both Duncan's and Nelson's victories. Wollenberg, '"Thus we Kept Away Bonaparte'", 194. Crotch became an Ensign in the Oxford Loyal Volunteers in 1803. Mee, *The Oldest Music Room*, 145, n.2.

354   ENLIGHTENED OXFORD

George III did not grace the University personally with his presence during the Revolutionary War, there was some compensation by way of visits from other members of the royal family. In 1799 Frederick, Duke of York, came to the city and its freedom was presented to him in a gold box. He was received at Christ Church by Portland and Cyril Jackson as a prelude to receiving the diploma degree of Civil Law, and a great ball was held at the town hall. Patriotic spirits flowed freely the next day when the Duke reviewed the Oxford Loyal Volunteers on Port Meadow.[237]

But these were also tense times, when wartime shortages stretched loyalty to the Crown to breaking point and the University could be in the front line when disturbances erupted, as they did nationally in the winter of 1799–1800. There were riots in Oxford over the high price of bread: Volunteers had to be placed within the walls of New College to protect university property, the Vice Chancellor Michael Marlow (President of St John's, 1795–1828) read the Riot Act on Carfax,[238] and David Hughes of Jesus College (its Principal from 1802), fearing an attack on the premises, urged Home Secretary Portland to send in the dragoons. In the event, Special Constables kept order sufficiently.[239] The University and the City Volunteer Corps were both temporarily disbanded during the Peace of Amiens (1802–3) but, with the resumption of the war in May 1803, the threat of invasion loomed larger than ever until Nelson's victory at Trafalgar. The whole of Oxford prepared for the worst and cooperation between the city and University reached new levels of efficiency. A public subscription raised the huge sum of £6,500 locally, the University and the Corporation leading the subscription with the pledge of £500. The money was partly for the national exchequer, partly for the reconstitution of the Volunteers into one Oxford corps. There were field days in Port Meadow, skirmishes on Shotover, with University members soldiering on a larger scale than ever, so much so that 'a Term' was granted in 1803 to those members who might be prevented from being in residence by their military duties in other parts of the kingdom.[240] There was also the distinct possibility that George III and the royal family might retreat to Oxford should a French invasion occur, if only as a staging post on the road to Weedon in Northamptonshire, the military hub earmarked for their residence. His absence in the event was a disappointment that could be borne with equanimity by the University.

---

[237] ed. M. G. Hobson, *Oxford Council Acts 1752–1801* (Oxford, 1962), 269; *JOJ*, 22 June 1799; Cox, *Recollections*, 41.

[238] Michael Marlow (*c.*1759–1828), matric. SJC, 1776, Fellow, 1779, MA 1784, BD 1789, DD, 1795; V-C., 1798–1802, Select Preacher, 1805, 1817; Vicar of St Giles', Oxford, rector of Handborough, Oxon., 1795; preb. of Canterbury, 1808. Foster, III. 913.

[239] Cox, *Recollections*, 42–3; *VCH Oxon.*, III. 267; W. Thwaites, 'Oxford's Food Riots', in eds. A. Randall and A. Charlesworth, *Markets, Market Culture and Popular Protest in Eighteenth-Century Britain and Ireland* (Liverpool, 1996), 137–62, at 154–5.

[240] Cox, *Recollections*, 50, 52–3. For a balanced assessment of the fighting value of the Volunteer Corps of 1803–5 see R. Glover, *Britain at Bay. Defence against Bonaparte, 1803–14* (London, 1973), 44–7.

ii) Conclusion

If loyalty to the Crown as an institution was perceived as the primary duty of subjects and essential to the preservation of the Constitution,[241] then Oxford University never wavered in that attachment throughout the long eighteenth century. Gifted individuals incapable of attachment to the status quo for the sake of it, such as the jurist William Jones, may have flirted with republican values as mediated via the commonwealth tradition, but there was never any prospect of this perspective taking hold at large, not least because royalism reached a fresh crescendo in the 1790s and 1800s. For all that Oxford was and remained unbendingly monarchist, it had soon become apparent after the 1688 Revolution that the nature of the attachment to the throne had changed irrevocably: the uneasy combination of relief over an end to Catholic intrusions and anxiety about the status of the Established Church was nicely represented by the degree of caution with which the King and the University regarded each other when William III briefly appeared in the Sheldonian Theatre in November 1695. Despite tacit acceptance of the Revolution, Oxford was obviously more comfortable with the political thinking that had helped it achieve pre-eminence before 1688 in its relationship with the monarchical state.

The acclamation of Queen Anne in 1702 powerfully underlined the fact. If her own disposition tended towards moderation in politics, what she symbolised as a Stuart sovereign more emotionally committed to her role as supreme governor of the Established Church than any monarch since her grandfather Charles I had immense resonance inside Oxford. These years, 1702–14, turned out to be an Indian summer for Oxonian royalism. If Atterbury became the nationally prominent exemplar of Tory church politicians, it was Sacheverell who stole the limelight, and too easily conveyed the impression that he (and, indeed, Atterbury) was typical of Oxford in his principles and purposes. Outwardly, the University warmly welcomed 'the Doctor' on his travels northwards in 1710, but its moderate Tory leaders neither rewarded him nor wanted him back in Oxford. Charlett, Gardiner, Smalridge, Bromley, Clarke, and the rest were bent on keeping the University under their control as the most assured way of making a relatively smooth transition into the new dynastic era that the Act of Settlement had provided for. If, at one level, they recognised the need to look to the era after Anne, they still found it hard to craft and articulate a Toryism that reflected that expectation and would commend it to the incoming House of Hanover.

The scale and degree of party exclusion became apparent within the first two years of the new king's reign and it caused both disappointment and resentment within the ranks of the excluded. The University was subject to the law of the land

---

[241] H. T. Dickinson, *The Politics of the People in Eighteenth-Century Britain* (Macmillan Press, Basingstoke, 1994), 258.

356   ENLIGHTENED OXFORD

and its members largely took the oaths of loyalty to the Crown after 1714, whatever they thought of George I or George II as individuals. Addresses were sent up to St James's Palace at regular intervals and their importance should not be discounted: they are helpful as corporate statements regarding political positioning and, though primarily 'boilerplate' expressions of loyalty, the detail of what they praise or neglect to mention can be important. This keeping up of legal appearances also ensured some kind of protection for the Church of England. Of course, the Jacobite cause elicited the cultural sympathies of innumerable senior members in these decades without ever making them overt, uncompromising adherents of the 'honest cause'. Caution, self-preservation, and perks of office saw to that. Undergraduates and younger dons with not much materially at stake were less restrained and their activities in the 1710s, early 1720s, and late 1740s allowed Whigs to exaggerate the extent of Jacobitism within Oxford for their own political advantage. For many, perhaps the majority, Jacobitism was something of a defiant pose, a means to indicate dissatisfaction with the Whigs at being excluded from power, but one which concealed some nervousness at the possibility of actually being put into power. Loyalty was, in reality, protean, multipurpose, and forbearing, so that even the occasional Nonjuror like Thomas Hearne was allowed to remain quietly in residence. In the earlier Hanoverian era, Tory politics and Tory attitudes were recast for use in the new order and transmuted into the 'Old Interest'.[242] Rooted in the past, it was yet an evolving and adaptable creed (even a modernising one), an alternative to the sometimes-stifling hegemonic Whig political and cultural dominance.

Though assured of royal favour after 1714, Oxford Whigs for years afterwards presented a defensive posture to the wider world. To them came the chaplaincies, canonries, deaneries, and bishoprics in ecclesiastical life, and the full range of legal and civil preferment in the temporal sphere. They were the King's friends within the fortress: their task to speak out, speak up, and bring reformation. And yet their discharge of those duties generally disappointed ministers in that they failed to create in the University a fervent sense of obligation to the family in possession until after the death of George II. It said much that the Whigs were incapable of inducing either George I or George II to visit Oxford, and that the heir to the latter, Prince Frederick, was on much better terms with Oxford Tories in the 1740s than the official Whig interest. Had Whigs of the capacity of Conybeare been more willing to attempt amity with academic Tories it might have been a different story but to have done so would have resulted in a more even share of patronage and shown Whig rhetoric about the extent of Tory Jacobitism to be misleading. And that was too high a price for Whigs to pay. Overall, between 1714 and 1760,

---

[242] One correspondent of Speaker Onslow noted that, for Tories in Oxfordshire '... the jingle of the Old Interest and the Old Style [calendar change] serves their purpose wonderfully'. Thomas Edwards to Arthur Onslow, 22 Dec. 1752, Bodl. MS Bodley 1012, ff. 37–9.

Oxford was never close to replacing Cambridge either as a nursery of Whig talent or as the King's English university of choice.

That situation was entirely reversed under George III when University and monarch appeared harmoniously matched. The University was relieved and delighted at his accession in equal measure, for it opened up the length and breadth of Crown patronage; furnished it with a sovereign of quiet Anglican piety who painstakingly discharged his duties as protector of the Church; gave Oxford men of Higher Churchmanship opportunities to be its bishops, and proved to be a king who revered learning and would visit in person. Politically, his view and the majority in the University coincided: over John Wilkes and his provocative popular politics in the 1760s;[243] over the American rebellion and War; over the French Revolution. His reign and his longevity brought greater security for the University than Anne's had done, and Oxford played a neglected part in fostering an outpouring of national loyalty even before the country's obvious affection for its king was articulated during the Regency Crisis of 1789 and then sustained over the next two decades in wartime. The University and its graduates acted as cheerleaders for British institutions throughout those years, generally resourcefully, occasionally intolerantly, but unswerving in a projection of monarchy as foundational to the constitution for which many of its sons were fighting and dying.[244]

---

[243] For University attitudes to Wilkes see Ward, *Georgian Oxford*, 218, 237; Sack, *From Jacobite to Conservative*, 121; Costin, *St John's College*, 221.

[244] Though the actions of some Oxonians prominent in French Revolutionary and Napoleonic Wars (such as General Thomas Graham, later 1st Lord Lynedoch) are relatively well-known, the subject of wartime service in the regular armed forces of the Crown by Oxford matriculands and the casualty rate among them awaits systematic exploration.

8

Oxford, the world of Westminster, and the defence of the University's interests

> Tho it will be a work of time, no way seems so likely to bring that University into a wise way of thinking and acting as to pick out and distinguish those valuable men in it who are Friends to his Majesty and the Protestant succession.
>
> Archbishop Thomas Herring to Newcastle,
> 1750, BL Add MS 32721, f. 425

Though Oxford University was legally a discrete corporate entity, it was a strikingly porous one: it was open to various kinds of external involvement (or interference, depending on one's perspective) in its internal affairs, principally from the Crown and its advisers.[1] As England's oldest higher-educational institution, one that functioned as a clerical seminary, a finishing school for the governing elite, a doctrinal source for Anglican teaching, a centre of scholarship ancient and modern, and a major component of the patronage nexus, its place in the early modern kingdom was too considerable for it not to be subjected to political pressures. That the state would not hesitate to intrude on an extensive scale had been indicated within recent memory in the wholesale purges of royalist personnel made during the Interregnum of the 1650s,[2] and James II's pro-Catholic intrusions of the 1680s. Oxford may have been a profoundly royalist institution, but it was never comfortable when the monarchy was advancing policies that seemed both inimical to its own and, by definition, the sovereign's best interests. From 1714 until the 1750s, the University knew, and the politicians knew, that just as James II had attempted to benefit his co-religionists, the Whigs might try for an equivalent coup that would give their academic clients an uncontested domination of Oxford along the lines that they had largely achieved at Cambridge.

Ministers throughout the 'long' eighteenth century could use just the threat of a Visitation or an unsympathetic remodelling of the Laudian statutes to ratchet up the pressure on the University to have a care about how far it indulged Jacobite or

---

[1] Broadly delineated in Brockliss (2), 150–8. See also Peter A. Vandermeersch, 'Teachers', in ed. Hilde de Ridder-Symoens, *A history of the university in Europe. Vol. 2. Universities in early modern Europe (1500–1800)* (Cambridge, 1996), 210–55, at 224.

[2] Details in Blair Worden, 'Cromwellian Oxford', in HUO IV, 733–72.

Enlightened Oxford: The University and the Cultural and Political Life of Eighteenth-century Britain and Beyond.
Nigel Aston, Oxford University Press. © Nigel Aston 2023. DOI: 10.1093/oso/9780199246830.003.0009

OXFORD AND THE WORLD OF WESTMINSTER   359

neo-Jacobite sympathisers within its walls. It was not until the long reign of George III that there was a comfortable convergence of regalian and academic interests though, even then, the University authorities could take nothing for granted. There were ungrounded apprehensions in the 1770s that where the Cabinet's policy did not match Convocation's over subscription, Lord North would act as Premier first and Chancellor of Oxford second, whereas he characteristically walked that tightrope with aplomb.[3] Later, during the 1790s, Heads of Houses acted just as the government and public expected to ensure that any Jacobin sympathisers were either silenced or expelled during the prolonged threat to national security posed by the French Revolutionary Wars. In that troubled decade, the links between Oxford and the world of Westminster were perhaps more intimate and extensive than at any point since the Harley/St. John ministry of 1710–14, but the point should not be overplayed. At every juncture, politicians and academics gossiped and tittle-tattled about each other, sedulously fed the rumour mill, second-guessed intentions, speculated about appointments and policies, and met personally in the common rooms, taverns, churches, and libraries of Oxford, London, and everywhere in between. Whig politicians sought to bend the University to reflect the policy preferences of the Hanoverian state; the University did its not inconsiderable best to temper them and defend its interests by lobbying its own well-placed Westminster allies. At general election times, the University might be said to function as the centre of a network of publicists and propagandists with an influence that fanned out well beyond Oxford.[4] And the average Oxford student followed politics at the centre keenly, especially if their father was in government, like Simon Harcourt in 1704, who was tracking the parliamentary battle over Occasional Conformity. Yet, as he admitted to his friend, 'tis as ridiculous to hear an upstart Oxonian talk of politics, as 'tis to see an unpowdered periwig and dirty boots in a drawing room.'[5]

Ministerial involvement through patronage was, in one sense, entirely legitimate, because of Crown appointments, particularly to Regius professorships, canonries, and to some college headships, of which Christ Church was the most prestigious. Oxford was also a central hub in nationwide patronage networks and, if on no other basis than that, the importance of the relationship between the University and whatever administration held sway can hardly be underestimated. If Oxford wanted to achieve institutional stability in order to carry out its primary educative functions, then the University authorities had no choice but to try and work with the ministry (however distasteful that quotidian imperative was to dons and junior members with less at stake and inclined to put principle on parade).

---

[3] See Chapter 6, pp. 19–21.
[4] Hone, *Literature and Party Politics,* considers this angle in Anne's reign.
[5] NLW, Ottley correspondence (Pitchford Hall) (hereafter Ottley Corresp.) Vol. 1, 1983, Harcourt to Ottley, 9 Nov. 1704.

360 ENLIGHTENED OXFORD

Much depended on how closely ministers wanted to become involved in in Oxford's internal affairs, make academic politics an extension of national concerns, and show the country that they would bend a recalcitrant Oxford to the greater needs of the state. It might be so much posturing but, at such moments, the University needed all the friends it could draw on. The lobbying powers of the University's two MPs in the Commons and behind the scenes could be a vital supplement to any protective efforts of its own officers; they were invariably respected figures, men of competence, whose broad commitment to Toryism was never at the expense of intelligent manoeuvring designed to maximise cross-party support. They could also appeal to the goodwill of the University's graduates in both Houses of Parliament and across the country, often liaising closely with college officers such as Nathan Wetherell of University College in the 1760s/70s and Cyril Jackson of Christ Church in the years around the turn of the nineteenth century. At that date, during the Portland Chancellorship, Oxford and Westminster were a harmonious whole at the centre of the British establishment. The contrast to the unease of a century earlier—in the aftermath of the 1688 Revolution—was pronounced.

Part A: From precarity to prosperity: ministers and the University

i) Working with the Whigs, c.1690–1760

...a proud, Popish, fierce, and unsociable spirit, a spirit of narrowness, party, censoriousness, and bigotry, has prevail'd there, ever since the Reformation,...
> [John Toland,] *The State-Anatomy of Great Britain*
> (9th edn., London, 1717)

I have nothing at present to Recommend to You but that You will persevere in Promoting Religion, Loyalty, Learning and good Manners, and carefully instill those Principles into the Youth committed to your Care, whereby the laudable Ends of Your Institution will be happily answered.[6]
Lord Hardwicke to the Principal and Fellows of Jesus College, 16 Feb.
> 1749 (?) Jesus College Oxford Archives, Box 150

Having relished the Tory reaction of Charles II's last years and resisted the 'Popish' strategies of his brother, Oxford was confronted with another potentially traumatic challenge after 1688: working with the Whigs in government,

---

[6] Thanks to Colin Haydon for this reference.

OXFORD AND THE WORLD OF WESTMINSTER   361

sometimes, as during the Junto years (1695–99), the dominant element in William III's administration. Whatever the personal disappointments about the need for the Revolution in the first place and their extensive reservations about the persons and policies of William III's Whig ministers, the Oxford academic establishment gave government little trouble in the 1690s. The Chancellor, the 2nd Duke of Ormond, fighting alongside the King in Flanders during the War of the Augsburg League, embodied in his person an irrefragable emblem of the University's commitment to the new order.[7] Meanwhile, the Junto, though watchful, was too busy winding down the war and fighting for its own parliamentary survival against the 'Country party' in the Commons to contemplate complicating matters further by mounting a frontal assault on predominantly Tory Oxford. The idea certainly appealed to Lord Somers in the last months of the Junto in 1699–1700 as the Convocation controversy intensified and the nuisance value of Oxford mounted with it. Sir John Holt, LCJ, wondered about the legality of a visitation of the universities, while the influential court Whig, Charles, 1st Duke of Shrewsbury (1660–1718) argued against its expediency.[8] Other Whigs noted that Oxford was anyway being sapped on its flanks by the emergence of Dissenters into public prominence and the appointment of moderate Whigs to the episcopal bench.

After Anne's accession in 1702, the University found itself with innumerable friends in high places as the Tories returned, initially, to royal favour. In return, Oxford dons committed to the party, men such as Roger Altham, Charles Jones, John Mather, William Tilly, and John Willett, endorsed Tory parliamentary and mayoral candidates, and used University and Assize sermons to get across the High Church message.[9] In Harley, Harcourt, and Bolingbroke, Oxford had three power brokers whom University members courted vigorously and the favour was reciprocated;[10] Harley's choice of name for his earldom in 1711 was widely assumed to be more a mark of his regard for the University and the city than his familial claims to the title.[11] There was some disappointment in academic

---

[7] Chapter 2, pp. 27–8. Ormond was not alone in going to the wars in the 1690s. Christopher Codrington, Fellow of All Souls and its future great benefactor, saw distinguished service at the Siege of Namur, 1695, and was promoted colonel by William III. The Whigs James Stanhope (Trinity), Secretary of State 1714–21, and Richard Steele (Merton), playwright and pamphleteer, ended their studies prematurely to do likewise.

[8] *The Life of Humphrey Prideaux, D.D.* (London, 1748), 192; BL Egerton MS. 2618, f. 219; Ward, *Georgian Oxford*, 23.

[9] Nicholas Tyacke, 'From Laudians to Latitudinarians: a shifting balance of theological forces', in ed. Tapsell, *The later Stuart Church,*1660–1714 (Manchester, 2012), 46–67, at 61.

[10] Financial gift giving towards the University as a client was always anticipated from ministers, Harley towards Christ Church, for example. 'Mr Secretary Harley, as he passed last week through Oxford, dined with the Dean and gave him a bill of 100£ towards their building, as a testimony of his special respect to that society'. Charlett to Ormond, 27 June 1705, HMC, *Ormonde MSS*, VIII. 162.

[11] His full title (to distinguish him from the previous de Vere holders of the earldom, dormant after 1703) was Earl of Oxford & Mortimer. HMC, *Ancaster MSS* (London, 1907), 442, for objections to Harley's choice of title by the Bertie family, Marquesses of Lindsey. Lord Keeper Harcourt, addressing the new Lord Oxford at the Court of Chancery on his also being made Lord Treasurer, having noted

362   ENLIGHTENED OXFORD

quarters by 1705–6 that the Queen preferred 'mixed ministries' to full-blooded Tory ones and there is a sense in which the notorious Sacheverell sermon of 5 November 1709 can be read as a lament that Anne and her governments to date had rather let down the 'true blue' cause. By that date, the 'duumvirs'—Godolphin and Marlborough—were kept in office by Whig Junto ministers and, luckily for Oxford, they were soon swept away by Harley's brilliant political manoeuvrings in the wake of the Sacheverell impeachment that led to the formation of his 'Great Ministry' of 1710–14.

These were four years when Oxford's centrality to national life was beyond dispute, with each of the leading ministers—Harley, Rochester, Bolingbroke, Harcourt—seeking the advancement of their clients in the University. There were three besetting background issues: could the ministry remain united, how long would the Queen live given her invalid status by 1713, and, behind everything, were the Tories committed to the Protestant Succession? For the most part, the answer to that last question was an affirmative, but it was not an unambiguous affirmative and, despite the determination of Vice Chancellor Bernard Gardiner in 1713–14 to give no official countenance to Jacobitism, his efforts were undermined by the attachment of many Oxonians to Stuart loyalism, the religiosity and (sometimes) the politics of the Nonjurors, and dislike of everything the Revolution had come to represent.

The Queen's death on 1 August 1714 brought a pause to a few years of intensive party strife in which Oxford had become generally associated in the public mind with a Toryism that everywhere shaded into Jacobitism. It was a flagrantly politicised representation brilliantly adumbrated by publicists such as Richard Steele, working for the Whigs in Opposition. And when the Whigs took power on George I's arrival, it suited their party interests to sing the same refrain and turn every slight token of apparent Oxonian disloyalty into yet more evidence that the Tories could not be trusted in power. That Oxford under Gardiner had made great strides to display its loyalty to the Protestant Succession by striking the note of 'Hanoverian Toryism' could be downplayed because it was in the party interests of the Whig leaders (by 1715 Stanhope and Sunderland, Townshend and Walpole) to question Tory good faith. As W. R. Ward splendidly put it, the Whigs intended 'butchering their opponents to make a party holiday' and barring the Tories from the bulk of Crown preferment in Church and State.[12] And thus it followed that, if the Tories en masse were to be excluded from the public weal, so would the

that some of his blood derives from the Veres, played up the connection between Harley and academic life: 'Nor is that title less suited to you, as it carries in it a Relation to one of the chief Seats of Learning: For, even your Enemies, My Lord, if any such there still are, must own, That the Love of Letters, and the Encouragement of those who excel in them, is one distinguishing Part of your Character'. [Thomas Salmon], *The Life and reign of her late Excellent Majesty Queen Anne* (London, 1738), 579–80; ed. Harcourt, *The Harcourt Papers*, II. 38; GEC. X. 261n., 264n.

[12] *Georgian Oxford*, 55.

University of Oxford be. The University's nurturing of Sacheverell, its festive endorsement of the Treaty of Utrecht, the sporadic rioting that occurred following George I's accession, the flight into exile of its Chancellor in July 1715 and, above all, the intensely clerical character of the University, were charges that could be and were used by Whig apologists in the later 1710s in their denunciation of the High Church party and its allies as 'the faction'.[13] That it was far from a hotbed of Jacobitism was beside the point. In a precarious regime, made more precarious by its one-party character, Oxford might plausibly be deemed a security risk.[14]

If presenting it in that light made the chances of the Whigs engrossing power to themselves more tenable, their leaders were ready to do so and, playing on the hysterical reports emanating from party supporters in Oxford hoping for intervention from outside, opted for confrontation over conciliation. The Riot Act of 1715 was occasioned by minor disturbances in the city that May that centred around the installation of the youthful grandee, the Marquess of Hartington, to the Presidency of the Constitution Club.[15] Viscount Townshend, the senior Secretary of State, did not mince his words to Arthur Charlett, Pro-Vice-Chancellor, after the Oxford riots of 28 and 29 May 1715:

> your behaviour ... has been very remiss upon this extraordinary occasion, and by no means suitable to that Zeal and Duty that Persons in your Station ought to have shewn towards his Majesty and his Government.

Ostentatiously, the government required Oxford JPs to search for weapons and gunpowder as a security measure before the first anniversary of the King's accession on 1 August.[16] During the course of the '15, fears that a rising was imminent in Oxford led to letters to and from dons being opened,[17] claims that the Pretender had been proclaimed on 27 October, and the quartering by William Pulteney, the Secretary-at-War, of General John Pepper's regiment in what would

---

[13] Gunn, *Beyond Liberty and Property*, 51.

[14] Whiggishly inclined journals made the most of cases such as that reported in Mar. 1716 of seven scholars at a coffee-house who drank the Pretender's health and cast aspersions on the Hanoverians. *St James's Evening Post*, 3471, 31 Mar. 1716.

[15] TNA (PRO) SP/44/116, f. 293. See also Townshend's letters of 3, 6, 14 June 1715, TNA (PRO) SP 44/117; 3 June 1715, TNA (PRO) SP 44/117. He wrote in comparable terms to the Mayor of Oxford. There was actually nothing amounting to corporate disobedience, and the rioting was confined. Crook, *Brasenose*, 142; John Miller, *Cities Divided: Politics and Religion in English Provincial Towns, 1660–1722* (Oxford, 2007), 284–5. Details of the Constitution Club are in Chapter 7, pp. 63–4.

[16] TNA (PRO) SP 35/2, ff. 45–6, 125; HMC, *Townshend MSS* (London, 1887), 157. Nothing was discovered apart from a few sporting guns. However, later in the year, a consignment of arms *was* found that helped to vindicate Whig charges. Boyer, *Political State*, X. (1715), 536.

[17] Even the Vice Chancellor, John Baron (1715–18), complained of interference with his mail. He insisted to a correspondent that he never had and never would correspond with the enemies of government. NLW, Ottley Correspondence 2413, Baron to Adam Ottley, 1 Jan. 1716/7.

be, in effect, the military occupation of the city.[18] They stayed for a year in what was billed as a peacekeeping initiative but functioned as a blatant exercise in political intimidation against the Tories.[19]

The Whig split of 1717–20 did little to change this aggressive, anti-Oxford agenda, one kept constantly heated in pro-ministerial papers and pamphlets[20] and designed to provoke and afford the excuse for coercion, even if, in Parliament, Tory peers and MPs frequently found themselves working in alliance with Walpole and Townshend.[21] Their rivals, Stanhope and Sunderland, were determined to reduce the leading institutions of the kingdom into docile Hanoverian loyalty and used the 'Commonwealth' Whig tradition as an ideological vehicle to achieve an authoritarian objective, urged on by those who hoped to benefit. The Septennial Act of 1716 had already provided for general elections at seven-year rather than three-year intervals; the Convocation of the Church of England had been prorogued in 1717 following an incandescent reaction in its Lower House ending in its levelling of charges of heresy against Bishop Hoadly (for his sermon 'My Kingdom is not of this world' preached before the King suggesting that Christ had not laid down a single form of Church government; a Peerage Bill was presented to Parliament in February 1719, that would have limited the Crown's power to create new peerages;[22] and there was every prospect that, in the aftermath of the repeal of the Occasional Conformity and Schism Acts via the Act to Strengthen the Protestant Interest in 1718, a direct assault on the Test & Corporation Acts would follow to gratify the wishes of Whigs' vital dissenting allies.[23]

And, with such a programme, it was no surprise that as early as spring 1717, ministers were considering a bill for reform of the two universities, designed particularly to reframe the statutes of Oxford University to draw the fangs

[18] The troops were ordered not to offend either scholars or townspeople, but neither officers nor soldiers should be 'corrupted' by Oxonians. TNA, WO4/17/261.

[19] Boyer, *Political State*, X. 343–6; HMC, *Stuart papers*, I. 438; Hearne, V. 125. The troops probably initiated a minor riot on 28–29 May 1716 involving themselves, townsmen, and a few students, when the Mayor of Oxford was beaten up. There were other disturbances on 30 Oct. 1716, when troops were provoked into aggressive retaliatory action. Monod, *Jacobitism and the English People*, 222–3; Miller, *Cities Divided*, 291–3. The City authorities made an official protest and there was a debate in the Lords on 30 Mar. 1717 on the role of the University in the disturbances when Tory peers mustered no less than thirty-three votes in the pro-Oxford minority. *PH.*, VII. 431–4; Ward, *Georgian Oxford*, 62–4. Cf. Monod, *Jacobitism and the English People*, 276, which argues that 'government fears of disaffection were not groundless' and talks of 'Oxford's disloyalty to the Hanoverians'.

[20] Discussed in detail in Ward, *Georgian Oxford*, 69–82. Charlett and Gardiner were both struck off as Justices in 1718 as part of a nationwide purge of magistrates. See Chapter 7, p. 46.

[21] Jeremy Black notes the large attendance of Tory MPs in the Commons in Jan.–Feb. 1718 as a sign of their determination to block any pro-Dissenter legislation. Black, 'Parliament and the political and diplomatic crisis of 1717–18', *PH*, 3 (1984), 77–102, at 93, 95.

[22] Sykes, *Wake*, I. 141–2; C. Jones, '"Venice preserv'd; or a plot discovered": the political and social context of the Peerage Bill of 1719', in ed. C. Jones, *A pillar of the Constitution: The House of Lords in British politics, 1640–1784* (London, 1989), 79–112.

[23] G. M. Townend, 'Repeal of the Occasional Conformity and Schism Acts', *PH*, 7 (1988), 24–44; Black, 'Parliament and the political and diplomatic crisis of 1717–18', 93.

OXFORD AND THE WORLD OF WESTMINSTER 365

permanently of the principal academic animator of the Church of England.[24] Prominent commonwealth men such as Robert Molesworth and John Toland urged them on as a crucial means of reducing what they saw as the dominant Tory clericalism of the Universities, leading to a regressive intellectual life and political disaffection. 'Why may not Oxford, for example, be reformed or purged by a royal commission tomorrow, as Aberdeen was the other day, or as Oxford itself was at the Reformation?', asked Toland.[25] It might stop the corrosive effect of the 'Turbulence and sedition' of the tutors. For clergy dabbled too much in politics as 'veriest bunglers' and the clerical qualification for teaching fellowships should go.[26]

Lord Townshend, someone disposed to play up security considerations,[27] had, as early as November 1715, received a blueprint for university reform drawn up at his request by his Norfolk neighbour and friend, the Christ Church graduate and Arab historian, Humphrey Prideaux, Dean of Norwich. His proposal ran to fifty-seven Articles, and key to it was Article thirty, that recommended that at the beginning of each parliament each House should name six commissioners, and the King six. This body would constitute (together with both English archbishops and the Lord Chancellor or Lord Keeper), a standing Committee to be Curators of the two Universities with Visitatorial powers. Dons were to be productive, and for those that were not, as a concession, Drone Hall would offer a sanctuary, with each member receiving a salary of £20. The caveat was that this sum would be paid by the college to which the member belonged.[28] Prideaux disarmingly stated that he was looking to 'make these noble Schools of learning best answer the end, for which they are appointed', offering their students lessons in uncorrupted morality and improvement in their knowledge, and better equipping the clergy in the defence of 'our Holy Christian Religion'.[29] Prideaux let it be known what was

---

[24] The Whig press had begun to make the case for a royal visitation of the universities in the autumn of 1716. Ward, *Georgian Oxford*, 74. The subject is authoritatively considered in Gascoigne, 'Church and state allied', 407–17.

[25] [Toland], *State-Anatomy*, 71. For Toland and most Whigs Cambridge was '...a hundred times less guilty...', ibid., 73. Some Oxford Tories were also suspected of wanting to lure the Crown into a visitation so that the errors of James II might be repeated. Crook, *Brasenose*, 130n.

[26] [Toland], *Reasons for enabling Protestant Dissenters to bear publick office* (London, 1717), 70, 74. Reform of the clergy and clerical culture was fundamental to many advocates of an overhaul of the English universities and Oxford in particular. See *Reasons for a Royal Visitation. Occasion'd by the Present Great Defection of the Clergy from the Government* (London, 1717).

[27] Ward talks of his 'pathological fear of their [the universities'] politics'. Ibid., 136; Coxe, *Walpole*, II. 122.

[28] *Life of Humphrey Prideaux*, 199–237, for the full 57 Articles (*c*.1715). Prideaux had been known for his attention to academic discipline while a tutor at Christ Church in the 1680s and had hoped for the succession of a Comprehension measure in 1689. *Life of Humphrey Prideaux*, 14, 58–9; R. W. Ketton-Cremer, *Humphrey Prideaux* (Norwich, 1955), 28–9. The Prideaux scheme is discussed in Gascoigne, 'Church and state allied', 410–13.

[29] Prideaux to Townshend, 26 Nov. 1715, in *Life of Humphrey Prideaux*, 188–9, 193, 198. Prideaux privately set out his rationale in a letter of 26 Oct. 1716 to his long-time patron, Lord Nottingham: 'If ever a Reformation be attempted it must begin at the two Universitys wch are both exceedingly out of Order. Those whom they now order for the Clergy can never support the Church for only one in four

366 ENLIGHTENED OXFORD

afoot and tried to move neutral opinion his way. He even sent Archbishop Wake a copy of his 'Articles', urging him to see a royal visitation as a means of improving the working life of the Established Church, partly by asserting the authority of the bishops over the restless lower clergy.[30]

Townshend's objectives were more immediately political, and the subject had higher backers than the likes of Prideaux. At the head of the power brokers urging action without further delay was the Oxfordshire magnate Lord Chief Justice Parker (later 1st Earl of Macclesfield), previously prominent in the prosecution of Sacheverell, and using his patronage to unscramble High Church networks.[31] According to legislation he personally designed, building on and modifying what Prideaux had originally proposed,[32] the autonomy of the University had to yield to the greater good of the realm. It was predicated on the basis, as the preamble said, that Oxford had become 'infected with principles of sedition'. There was a corresponding need, in the interests of 'peace and tranquillity,' to stop the infection of 'false principles utterly inconsistent with our happy establishment in church and state'.[33] The plan would have deprived for a term of years the Universities and their component colleges of all rights of appointment and patronage; these rights would be vested in royal commissioners with extensive powers of enforcing their decisions, while the Chancellors of each could be removed at the King's pleasure, and their successors appointed by the Crown.[34] A comparable process was, after all, under way in Scotland in the aftermath of the

that come for Orders being fit for them. The method of Study & ye method of discipline[e] is quite wrong in both those places of publick Education & both must be reform'd before they can answer ye end of their institution'. LLRO DG7/Bundle 24, Box 4950.

[30] Wake wavered on the issue but took Prideaux's case seriously, at least initially. Sykes, *Wake*, II. 109, 115, 133; Gascoigne, 'Church and state allied', 412–13. Further discussed this Chapter, p. 19, n. 39.

[31] For Parker's extensive Cambridge connections (he was a Trinity College graduate) who did not, on the whole, fear a visitation, see Gascoigne, *Cambridge*, 92–3. Parker (1666?–1732) was in high favour at court, being created a baron in 1716 and an earl in 1721. He was Lord Chancellor 1718–25. A. A. Hanham, 'Parker, Thomas, first earl of Macclesfield (1667–1732), lord chancellor', *ODNB*, online version, 2009.

[32] Parker had slightly earlier produced (c.1717) 'A Memorial Relating to the Universities, suggesting amendments in the statutes' [BL MS Stowe 799, ff. 1–13], which Gascoigne considers may have been stimulated by his involvement in the Sacheverell prosecution of 1710. 'Church and state allied', 413. See also a draft petition in Lord Cowper's papers from the Commons to the Crown, proposing discipling of the universities to prevent disaffection, c.1716/17. Hertfordshire Archives, Panshanger Papers, D/EP F138. These two lawyers may have been keeping up pressure on Townshend. It was reported by the king's mistress, Mme von der Schulenburg, in Mar. 1717 that the former's ardour for tackling the university problem had waned, though she intimated that George I remained keen on reform. Hatton, *George I*, 369.

[33] Edmond Miller, in *An Account of the University of Cambridge, and the Colleges there* (London, 1717), insisted that Oxford was more the guilty party for its subversion. Other pro-visitational pamphlets made the same point.

[34] Full details of this 'Bill for the Reformation of the two Universities' in J. Gutch, *Collectanea Curiosa; or miscellaneous tracts, relating to the history of England and Ireland, . . .* (2 vols., Oxford, 1781), II. 53–73; Ward, *Georgian Oxford*, 86–7; Gascoigne, 'Church and state allied', 414–15; B. Williams, *Stanhope: a Study in 18th-Century War and Diplomacy* (Oxford, 1932), 401–2, 456.

OXFORD AND THE WORLD OF WESTMINSTER   367

'15 through the Visitation Commissions to the Universities of Glasgow, Aberdeen, and St Andrews in 1716–18.[35] Why should not England be subjected to a similar overhaul? It was the very question that John Toland had framed.

Neither of the King's leading ministers had any sense of obligation to either English university. Sunderland, one of the greatest bibliophiles of the age,[36] had been at Utrecht University with the leading English Dissenter, Edmund Calamy, while Stanhope, who resumed the office of Secretary of State in April 1718 with an earldom, had been briefly an undergraduate at Trinity College in the early 1690s before quitting prematurely to fight in Flanders. Oxford left little mark on him. He was passionately committed to religious toleration as a means of strengthening what was often referred to as 'the Protestant Interest'.[37] Though he welcomed the Universities bill, he appears to have had no part in drafting it. Other Whigs were not enthusiasts. Motives were not disinterested. Thus the Earl of Islay, in Opposition and affronted by the exclusion of his allies from the Scottish Commission on Universities, stood at a remove on the question of the independence of English corporate bodies such as the two universities and the Crown's interest in them.[38] With the (2nd) Duke of Devonshire, the Duke of Newcastle, and Archbishop Wake also urging delay, and the Whig split also intervening, no further progress in bringing the bill forward was made in the spring of 1717.[39] In May 1718, the Attorney-General, Sir Nicholas Lechmere (a leading spokesman for Sunderland in the Commons), was reported to be at work on a fresh version of the project.[40] As external pressures mounted, University grandees began to organise and marshal arguments that, had ministers been sufficiently determined to impose wholesale remodelling on Oxford, would have proved flimsy barriers. A note of desperation was creeping in. Charlett, for instance, put his faith in the rights of local visitors:

---

[35] Discussed in Chapter 2, pp. 32–7.

[36] A. K. Swift, 'The Formation of the Library of Charles Spencer, 3rd Earl of Sunderland (1674–1722): A Study in the Antiquarian Book Trade' (unpub. Oxford D.Phil. thesis, 2 vols., 1986).

[37] Aubrey Newman, *The Stanhopes of Chevening. A Family Biography* (London, 1969), 75–6; T. Claydon, *Europe and the Making of England 1660–1760* (Cambridge, 2007), 200–1, 202–3.

[38] Emerson, *Academic Patronage*, 414–16.

[39] Townend, 'Repeal of the Occasional Conformity and Schism Acts', 28–9. Despite Prideaux's earlier lobbying, Wake had come down against what he called 'Knight Errantry against the Universities' and claimed most of the bishops felt likewise. Wake to Cowper, 14 Mar. 1717, Hertfordshire Archives, Panshanger Papers, D/EP F62, f. 37 quoted in ibid., 29. He had received an address from senior members of the University (including Smalridge) designed to avert it. LPL, MS 941/42. John Baron, as Vice Chancellor on behalf of the University, had also called on the Archbishop (letter of 18 Mar. 1716/17, Christ Church, Oxford, Wake MS 15, nos. 24, 25) to use all his influence to prevent a royal visitation of the universities. Wake was sympathetic, knowing how ferociously the bishops would be blamed should it proceed. Gascoigne, *Church and state allied*, 416.

[40] Interested parties on the reforming side were busy submitting their ideas to ministers, for instance, John Taylour, of Calverton, Bucks., to Ld Macclesfield, with his suggestions for *Rendering the Universities more usefull.* 13 Sept. 1718. Hertfordshire Archives, D/EP F57.

368 ENLIGHTENED OXFORD

all Colliges, who have local visitors, are certainly free from all other Visitations, Regal or otherwise: I am sure Ld Somers, was very clear, both before the Revolution, and after it, that the University was a Lay Body, and not subject to any Royal Visitation, any more than other Lay Bodys, that subsist by Charters, as London, Oxford, or any other Corporate Towns: But on these Heads, we must consult, the best Counsill;[41]

Legislation was finally brought forward late in 1719 in an atmosphere whipped up by extreme anticlericalist authors such as Thomas Gordon and John Trenchard, who were ready to accuse Oxford of sins rivalling those of the anti-Christ.[42] In May, at a Privy Council meeting, a commission was appointed to prepare for a visitation of Cambridge, with Sunderland especially hoping to reunite the Whig factions through partisan legislation.[43] The universities' legislative initiative proposed in 1719 had at its core the redrafting of their statutes by a royal commission.[44] Oxford escaped this legislative infliction more by chance than by resourceful negotiation: the ministry was unable to overcome the combined votes in the Commons against the Peerage Bill of the dissident Whigs, the Tories, and independent MPs,[45] and gradually drew back from what was left of this intensive and coherent remodelling initiative in the winter of 1719–20.[46] Instead, conciliatory feelers were put out to the Tories (Harcourt alone succumbed).[47] Then, in the summer of 1720, the bursting of the South Sea Bubble monopolised ministerial attention.

Oxford turned out to be the indirect beneficiary of the reordering of the king's government after the deaths of Stanhope in 1721 and Sunderland the year following.[48] Robert Walpole, newly installed as First Lord of the Treasury, put aside any further enactment of proposals designed to anchor Whig supremacy in the state on a conspicuously authoritarian basis. Instead, there would be an attempt at building an institutional consensus. Coercion would become a weapon of last resort. Central to this moderate Whiggery was the rebuilding of a partnership with the Church of England on the basis of the legal status quo that Walpole implemented through the good offices of the moderate Oxonian Whig, Edmund Gibson, Bishop of London.[49] Extreme Hoadlyian latitudinarianism was repudiated and no further statutory concessions to the Dissenters were foreseen.

---

[41] BL Egerton MS 2618, f. 219, Charlett to George Clarke, 11 Dec. [1718].

[42] J. Black, 'Regulating Oxford: ministerial intentions in 1719', Oxoniensia, 50 (1985), 283–5.

[43] See Sunderland to 3rd Earl of Carlisle, 18 Nov. 1719, HMC, Carlisle MSS (London, 1897), 23.

[44] BL Add MS 61495, ff. 92–3, plans for a visitation of the Universities, 1719.

[45] Interestingly, Lechmere was one of those who joined Walpole in speaking decisively against it. PH, VII. 609–27; Williams, Stanhope, 415–16.

[46] Wigelsworth, All Souls College, 175–6.   [47] HMC, Portland MSS, VII. 266–74.

[48] Canon Stratford was curious to know how the freethinking Sunderland had faced death and 'whether he showed any sense of religion; I suppose not'. HMC, Portland MSS, IV. 321–2.

[49] Taylor, '"Dr. Codex" and the Whig "Pope": Edmund Gibson'.

OXFORD AND THE WORLD OF WESTMINSTER   369

Anglican monopolies would stay in place and the threat of remodelling was, for the time being, lifted from Oxford. Walpole and Townshend had not given up their reservations about the University's loyalty to the Hanoverian dynasty, but they opted instead to elicit its members' cooperation via the enticements of a patronage system rather than looking to penal sanctions that would destroy the University's independence. It says much for Walpole's tactical skills that, despite almost certainly knowing the considerable extent of the Earl of Arran's knowledge of the Atterbury Plot (1722–3), he chose to leave the University's Chancellor undisturbed in office rather than turning him into yet another Tory martyr.[50]

A further sign of a pragmatic consensus was given in 1723–4, when the government established a range of academic posts in Oxford designed in the first instance to reward loyalty rather than talent. In 1723, Gibson instituted an inexpensive scheme for twelve Whitehall Preachers from both English universities, to be selected from among college fellows for their scholarship and gifts of exposition, and deliberately intended it to be a link between the government and the universities, an incentive to ambitious Oxonian clergy to subscribe to Whig principles.[51] In 1724, a Regius professorship of History was established, intended to train up young men for the King's service, instructing them in both history and contemporary foreign languages.[52] It was, at one level, intended to widen the curriculum and encourage careers in the service of the Crown along the lines of the (short-lived) *Académie Politique*, established in France in 1712; at another, it opened the way to instruction in a thoroughly Whiggish version of the recent past.[53] Some Oxonians wondered what was meant by the démarche, Dr Stratford of Christ Church speculating: 'Surely somewhat more than appears is aimed at by this great profusion of favours on a sudden. I wish they may be distributed with such prudence as not to defeat what is aimed at by them.'[54] That this was in essence an academic device designed for political engineering did not escape the notice of Convocation which, in response, offered an unenthusiastic letter of

---

[50] See Aston, 'Great survivor', in eds. Darwall-Smith and Hordern, *Oxford: The Forgotten Century*, 348–69.

[51] Gibson intended these preachers to 'answer objections against the administration, and confute the lies and misrepresentations of the enemy upon their own knowledge and observation'. Sykes, *Gibson*, 92–4. Canon Stratford of Christ Church presciently foresaw how it would be: 'The project for preachers at Whitehall is managed in such a way as is not likely, I am afraid, to work the wonders expected from it. No indifferent men, none that would go many though not all lengths perhaps, are to be taken notice of [in] it. It is declared none must hope for a share in this bounty but they who are staunch Whigs, and openly profess themselves to be so. I am afraid this will not increase the number of honest thorough Whigs; rather unite and confirm, than break the perverse Tories. You will allow me some concern to see so great a project, through ill management, not likely to be improved to the ends it was designed for'. 3 Apr. 1724, to Lord Harley, HMC, *Portland MSS*, VII. 377.

[52] BL Add. MSS 5843, f.255 ff. The uses of the chair for historical scholarship are discussed in Chapter 4, pp. 39–40.

[53] There is no supporting evidence for W. M. Marshall's claim that George I intended to consult George Hooper, octogenarian Tory bishop of Bath & Wells (DD, 1677) over the appointments. Marshall, *George Hooper 1640–1727 Bishop of Bath and Wells* (Milborne Port, 1976), 175.

[54] 21 May 1724, to Lord Harley, HMC, *Portland MSS*, VII. 378.

370 ENLIGHTENED OXFORD

thanks for the royal largesse.[55] Townshend was not impressed by such a jejune offering. The University would have to try again to show its gratitude convincingly. The Dean of Christ Church was told insistently that there had to be a suitably gracious address. It was expediently offered despite initial resistance by John Mather, the Vice Chancellor, and two powerful college heads: Gardiner of All Souls and Shippen of Brasenose. And so a delegation composed of the Vice Chancellor, several Heads of Houses, the proctors, additionally 'accompanied by a great number of Bishops of the said University', was duly sent to London on 9 November and the King's speech in response was 'full of grace and favour'.[56]

The mid-1720s was the beginning of two decades in which the Whigs learnt to live with Oxford and Oxford with the Whigs, to put up with each other's ways, however vexatious. There was also a growing perception within academe of a reduced threat to the Church from that so recently apprehended. Indeed, Walpole had no intention of deliberately provoking a head-on confrontation with the University,[57] and he strove, where he could safely do so and where his legislative commitments would not be unduly compromised, to reassure the academic establishment that his government would act in good faith towards it. Thus, in 1725, ministers moved in the Commons to prevent a debate when Arthur Onslow, an Old Whig, made a motion 'to restrain the two Universities... from purchasing new Advowsons and Presentations to Benefices'.[58] There would be no revival of Convocation as an efficient legislative body for the Church of England, but Oxford men would be eligible for senior appointments in Church and state—so long as their loyalty to the existing order was absolutely beyond dispute, preferably by being good court clerics. And, as the Act of 1733 showed, the University was ready to reciprocate the olive-branch, and even awarded the Lord Chancellor, Charles, 1st Lord Talbot, an honorary degree in 1735.[59]

Such mutual cosying up only extended a certain distance. Gibson and Walpole agreed that ecclesiastical patronage was essentially for the exclusive benefit of the Whig clergy.[60] Outright Tories however, remained ineligible, even unambiguously non-Jacobite ones. So, too, were those attached to the accumulating numbers of Whigs in opposition to the ministry after the failure of the Excise Bill in 1733

---

[55] UOA: MS Conv. Reg. Bd 31, f. 208, quoted in Ward, *Georgian Oxford*, 134. A comparable chair was awarded to Cambridge.

[56] Boyer, *Political State*, XXVIII. 479–82; Stratford to Lord Harley, 12 and 17 Nov. 1724, HMC, *Portland MSS*, VII. 387.

[57] There was more talk of a royal visitation for Oxford in 1723. HMC, *Portland MSS*, VII. 351–2. But ministers were going in another direction. As Lord Townshend put it in a draft to George I, *c.*1723: '... The Universities have behaved themselves at least inoffensively, & some Steps have been taken by Your Maty to make it no less their Interest than Duty to cherish & propagate Principles of Loyalty & Affection to Your Person & Government'. HMC, *Weston Underwood MSS*, 429.

[58] ed. Richard Chandler, *The History and Proceedings of the House of Commons from the Restoration to the Present Time* (14 vols., London, 1742–4), VI. 337.

[59] Earl of Ilchester, *Lord Hervey and his Friends* (London, 1950), 227.

[60] Ward, *Georgian Oxford*, 142.

OXFORD AND THE WORLD OF WESTMINSTER 371

(particularly the clients and allies William Pulteney and John, Lord Carteret). By that date, the working relationship of Oxford with the First Minister had lost something of its lustre. Walpole appeared newly prepared to countenance measures to benefit Dissenters that, while not amounting to a direct threat to Oxford, were hazarding the material well-being and lawful privileges of the Established Church. Once again it looked as if the Church was 'in Danger', and as if the Whigs could never be regarded as its trustworthy custodians.[61] Oxonians were in good company: most of the Bishops voted against the ministry on the proposal to exempt Queen Anne's Bounty from the Mortmain Bill in 1736 and Bishop Gibson, Walpole's principal adviser on Church management since 1723, was denounced as the 'Ringleader of Sedition' by government loyalists, and lost that status.[62]

Calmer waters were navigated after Gibson was superseded as Church 'manager' by Thomas Pelham-Holles, 1st Duke of Newcastle, in the late 1730s. His, on the whole, benign dispensation of ecclesiastical patronage lasted for the remainder of George II's reign.[63] Despite being an active Chancellor of Cambridge University (elected after the death of the 6th Duke of Somerset in December 1748),[64] the Duke had no desire to pick a quarrel with the sister university. As a seriously observant churchman who set his face against heterodoxy in candidates for episcopacy,[65] it was hard for Tory high-flyers to offer any persuasive moral objections to Newcastle's management of the Church. By the mid-1740s, he had built up a formidable connection within Oxford composed both of principled Whig churchmen and those who realised that, unless they were exceptionally fortunate, there was no way up the *cursus honorum* without Newcastle's good offices.

The revival of Jacobitism in that decade, however, rekindled in the Pelhamite Ascendancy something of the old anxieties and trepidation about Oxford's loyalty that their ministerial predecessors had felt after the '15. With the survival of the regime in the balance during the '45, Oxford's tepid endorsement of the status quo—judged by the numbers signing the Articles of Association—was not quickly forgotten at Westminster. Newcastle and his brother, Henry Pelham, came to consider that, despite the gentle nurturing of a ministerial party inside the

---

[61] There was also periodic Whig sabre-rattling from the pulpit. Thus Dr Richard Banner (brother-in-law of Sacheverell) used an Assize sermon of 27 July 1732 to preach against 'the Privileges of the University which were intended to be taken away etc'. ed. Linnell, *The Diaries of Thomas Wilson*, 62.

[62] John, Lord Hervey, *Memoirs of the Reign of King George II*, II. 536. See also Taylor, '"Dr. Codex"', 13.

[63] Edward Young, Fellow of All Souls, archly observed in 1743, to the Duchess of Portland: 'The Duke of Newcastle is our Pope. Ecclesiastics are under his thumb, and he is fixed as St Paul's by his own weight in spite of all the revolutions of the little court buildings round about him'. HMC, *Bath MSS* (5 vols., London, 1904–80), 280; S. J. Taylor, 'The factotum in ecclesiastical affairs? The Duke of Newcastle and the Crown's ecclesiastical patronage', *Albion*, 14 (1992), 409–33.

[64] For details Morgan, *Cambridge*, 538–9.

[65] Sykes, *Church and state*, 278–82, 437–9; S. Taylor, 'Church and state in England in the mid-eighteenth century: the Newcastle years 1742–62', Ph.D. dissertation, University of Cambridge, 1987, 103–5.

372 ENLIGHTENED OXFORD

University and despite the official protestations of loyalty to George II, there were still too many in Oxford incorrigibly sympathetic to the 'honest cause' and the appeal of Prince Charles Edward Stuart. And, even when the latter was back in France, a substantial proportion of Oxonians could not give up the wider anti-establishment values that he represented. Hence the popularity in the University of both the 'Patriot' programme and the person of Frederick, Prince of Wales.[66]

It was against this background and regular display of undergraduates flaunting the white cockade and shouting their Jacobite slogans that the government opted for intervention. The occasion was offered when Richard Blacow, Fellow of Brasenose, reported what he considered a serious breach of public order by Jacobite students in February 1748, and Vice Chancellor John Purnell decided on not punishing the culprits beyond fines and deferring of degrees. Despite the advice of the Attorney-General, Sir Dudley Ryder, who doubted the soundness of Blacow's evidence, ministers stepped in.[67] Amid a glare of national publicity, two Balliol College and one St Mary Hall students—Charles Luxmore, John Whitmore, and James Dawes—were arrested, tried for uttering treason, and the last two were convicted. Charges were also laid against Purnell with a view to prosecution.[68] The reaction in Oxford was rioting, but the authorities were undeterred.[69] As the alarm was sounded about the continuing contamination of Oxford, one Cambridge man (who happened to be one of the King's chaplains) noted with horror: 'I am in attendance with a very clever man of that university, who tells me that Jacobitism at Oxford at this time wears less reserve, & cares less about the decency of the exterior than in the year 15. God save us'.[70]

For a while in the winter of 1748–9 the Cabinet thought seriously about proceeding with a visitation of Oxford followed by legislation that would transfer at least the nomination of the Chancellor to the Crown. A series of meetings occurred involving Lord Chancellor Hardwicke, the Attorney General and Solicitor General, Archbishop Herring and five bishops, to draft a bill for reform of Oxford as a way of dealing with Jacobite infestation.[71] Hardwicke wanted to act, Newcastle too, provided that Cambridge was exempt from any such measure

---

[66] Chapter 7, pp. 9, 28, 30.   [67] Ward, *Georgian Oxford*, 171.

[68] Jones, *Balliol College*, 163–4. In the event, Purnell's trial was countermanded on the basis of insufficient evidence to proceed. *GM* 18 (1748), 281; Ward, *Georgian Oxford*, 174. The future Lord Chancellor, Robert 'Bob' Henley, represented the defence most effectively at the trial of the three students. George Bingham, *Dissertations, Essays, and Sermons, to which are prefixed Memoirs of his Life, & c. By his son Peregrine Bingham, LL.B* (2 vols., London, 1804), xxviii.

[69] Richard Blacow, *A Letter to William King, LL.D. Principal of St Mary Hall in Oxford. Containing a particular account of the treasonable riot in Oxford in Feb. 1747* (London, 1755), 7–13; M. Sharpe to Hardwicke, 4 Nov. 1748, BL Add MS 35887, f. 24.

[70] Pyle to Samuel Kerrich, 24 Mar. 1749, in ed. A. Hartshorne, *Memoirs of a Royal Chaplain, 1729-1763. The Correspondence of Edmund Pyle, DD . . .* (London, 1915), 147. Cf. Thomas Edwards to Arthur Onslow, 17 Nov. 1748: 'surely it is high time that some how or other a check were put to that impudent Spirit of Rebellion which poisons the Sources of Education in that University', in ed. Clayton, *Life and Letters of Arthur Onslow*, 145.

[71] Harrowby MSS Trust, vol. 430: diary of Sir Dudley Ryder, 12 Apr. 1748.

OXFORD AND THE WORLD OF WESTMINSTER 373

(which would be hard to justify publicly);[72] Lord Chesterfield (Secretary of State for the Northern Department, 1746–8), gave his fiat to a political intervention at Oxford. So, too, did Bishop Thomas Sherlock of London (a man with extensive Tory contacts and a former Cambridge Vice Chancellor), who stood so high in Newcastle's favour that he was made a Privy Councillor in 1749;[73] Granville (the former Carteret), was more cautious.[74] In the end, with some significant Whig voices urging restraint,[75] nothing was done. As William Blackstone relayed the news to his friend and fellow collegian, the serving Proctor:[76]

> ...it is with great satisfaction...that after all the big words and blusterings of our great men, after all the abuse that has been so plentifully scattered both on the university and on its magistrate, and (what is the worst circumstance of all) after a very heavy expence with which an innocent man has been saddled, the prosecution is at last dropt,...

Despite the provocation of the Blacow incident and William King's incendiary speech at the official opening of the Radcliffe Library, ministers, it seemed, were ready to let sleeping dogs lie. Bishop Secker—with somewhat excessive optimism—reassured Lord Hardwicke, however, that Oxonians 'have certainly been put in Fear: enough I believe to make all of them present cautions of affronting the Government and some of them careful to pay it Respect'.[77]

Veiled threats to the University did not entirely recede, even after Prince Frederick's premature death in 1751 deprived the Hanoverian reversionary interest of its leader. It occurred only months after Prince Charles Edward Stuart, on an

---

[72] '...I can never admit, That if the late and notorious Conduct of the University of Oxford, should make a Visitation or Enquiry there advisable, That will be any Reason for the same at Cambridge whose Behaviour is as meritorious, as the other is justly to be censured'. Newcastle to Bishop Sherlock, BL Add MS 33061 f. 31.

[73] See Sherlock to Newcastle, 20 Jan. 1749, BL Add MS 32718, f. 29, and the Duke's reply of 21st, f. 31. Edward Carpenter, *Thomas Sherlock 1678–1761* (London, 1936), 90–2.

[74] Granville advised Newcastle against or 'he would soon kindle a flame in the Kingdom, that he would never see extinguished'. Lincolnshire Archives, Berkeley of Stratton MSS, 4/63/38ff. Diary entry of 16 Apr. 1756.

[75] Horace Walpole, the Premier's son, adopting a Tory voice for his own ends in his pamphlet *Delenda est Oxonia*, reminded the Pelhams that the Glorious Revolution had been precipitated by James II's assault on Oxford University and that Oxford merely wished 'to have it reconciled to their apprehensions, how affection to the eldest son of the Elector of Hanover should be a mark of Jacobitism; how attachment to the House of Pelham is whiggism & loyalty'. Paget Toynbee, 'Horace Walpole's *Delenda est Oxonia*', *EHR*, 42 (1927), 95–108. The pamphlet was seized before it could be circulated.

[76] To George Bingham, 17 Nov. 1748, in Bingham, BD, *Dissertations*, xxvii. Perhaps in a final effort to drum up public opinion to pressure ministers to do something, Richard Newton of Hart Hall urged reform of the universities to improve their role as places of moral and theological formation, insisting that Parliament's assistance was essential for Oxford's reformation. See his *A Series of papers on subjects the most interesting to the nation in general and Oxford in particular*...(London, 1750). They were mostly published anonymously in the *General Evening Post* between Jan. and July 1751. See Gascoigne, 'Church and state allied', 418–9.

[77] BL Add MS 35590, f.301, quoted in Ingram, *Religion, Reform and Modernity*, 175.

374 ENLIGHTENED OXFORD

incognito visit to London, had been unable to persuade a select group of English well-wishers (including the 4th Duke of Beaufort and Dr William King) that his plans for a restoration without foreign assistance were unrealistic.[78] The controversy over the Jewish Naturalisation legislation (the so-called 'Jew Bill') and the Oxfordshire county election in 1753–4 revived party heats and ministerial anxieties, though this time lacking any threat to state survival from either insurgency or invasion.[79] Hardwicke (whose apprehensions about Oxford rivalled Townshend's earlier feelings in their intensity) relied on Bishop Secker's monitoring of the situation in the aftermath of these events for some reassurance—and found none:[80]

> As to a certain party, which your Lordship describes, I am sorry they have deceived your hopes, but am glad you now see them in their true colours....
> I have long seen that spirit; and great industry has been used to keep up that spirit, where you see the exertion of it, in order to hold out that place as the garrison and fortress of Toryism and Jacobitism.

In those unpropitious circumstances, it was hard for the government to revert to Newcastle's preferred, quieter style of management. It was the patriotic response of the University to the Seven Years' War that really calmed down party heats and ministerial anxieties. The Elder Pitt may have been unkind in his parliamentary comments about Oxford's disloyalty (to the House of Hanover) but that did not preclude the University's, like the majority of the country's, embracing what turned out to be the triumphant cause of 'Pitt and Patriotism' once the Seven Years' War erupted in 1756. With Jacobitism expiring as a realistic political creed, Pitt's sort of Whiggism was one that fitted even Tories.

ii) 'The King's friends': ministers and the University in the reign of George III

> Under the auspices of the sacred Gospel of Christ, we investigate the nature of the Laws of [our] Country, we make our youth sensible of the excellence of the English Constitution, and we teach them a due obedience to its statutory ordinances;
>
> [Edward Bentham], The Honor of the University of Oxford defended, against the illiberal Aspersions of E—d B—e, Esq.; with pertinent observations on the present rebellion in America (London, 1775), 4.

---

[78] See Chap. 7, pp. 30–1.

[79] For the University and the 'Jew Bill', see Ingram, *Religion, Reform and Modernity*, 175–8; T. W. Perry, *Public Opinion, Propaganda, and Politics in Eighteenth-Century England. A Study of the Jewish Naturalization Act of 1753* (Cambridge, MA., 1962), 95–100, 135–7.

[80] Hardwicke to Secker, 3 Sept. 1754, BL Add MS 35593, f. 3, quoted in Ingram, *Religion, Reform and Modernity*, 180.

OXFORD AND THE WORLD OF WESTMINSTER 375

The contrast between academic-ministerial relations in the half-century after 1760 and the one that preceded it could hardly be more pronounced. The new king loathed what he perceived to be the Whig Pelhamite stranglehold over his grandfather and bringing the Tories in from the cold was consonant with his determination to end factional favour and feuding. The objective was easier for George III to articulate than to achieve and the first ten years of his reign were characterised by extreme ministerial instability at Westminster.[81] But if the Tories came in from the cold, so did the University of Oxford, an institution that sang a theme of loyalty to the young King from the day of his accession. Though its rhetoric may have occasionally still resonated in popular protest thereafter, for the propertied, Jacobitism was, to all intents and purposes, an extinct cause from the day George became king (22 October 1760), and entirely so after 'James III' expired on 1 January 1766. Any notion of governmental tampering in Oxford's affairs became utterly pointless and irrelevant. The Crown and the University had become two institutions that wanted to work together, whose ideological preferences were closely aligned, despite lingering 'Old Interest' hesitations. On the two key issues of the 1760s—American taxation and the Wilkes affair—majority opinion in the University stood four-square behind George Grenville (Premier, 1763–5, and a Christ Church man) in upholding the Stamp Act and deprecating John Wilkes's demagoguery. Grenville was alone among politicians of national eminence in the 1760s in taking much interest in his old University; Chatham had no time for his alma mater; Bute was academically inclined and took a major interest in University affairs and appointments, but Scottish ones, continuing an enlightened tradition inherited from his uncle, the 3rd Duke of Argyll (d. 1761);[82] Rockingham did not go to university, and Grafton was a Cambridge graduate. But in Lord North (Trinity College; Premier 1770–82), Oxford found its eighteenth-century political apotheosis, in his person, anchored the University at the heart of the King's government.

North, like his father the 1st Earl of Guilford, was a court Whig, but he had sufficient Tory ancestors to reassure the old Tory families who backed his coercive policies against the American colonists so that they would more than treat him as one of their own.[83] He assumed the Chancellorship in October 1772, eight months after the Feathers Tavern petition urging a relaxation in subscription had been defeated in Parliament. It was typical of him that he both warned that the petitioners were acting in the spirit that motivated the Fifth Monarchists and would overthrow the Church of England and *tried* to be accommodating and generous in reassuring the petitioners that there was plenty of room for all inside

---

[81] P. D. G. Thomas, *George III. King and Politicians 1760–1770* (Manchester, 2002); Jeremy Black, *George III. America's last King* (New Haven, CT, 2006), 43–95; Ditchfield, *George III*, 49–68.

[82] Roger L. Emerson, 'Lord Bute and the Scottish Universities 1760–1792', in K. W. Schweizer, *Lord Bute. Essays in Re-interpretation* (Leicester, 1988), 147–79.

[83] P. Langford, 'Old Whigs, Old Tories and the American Revolution', *Journal of Imperial and Commonwealth History*, 8 (1980), 123–7.

376 ENLIGHTENED OXFORD

and on the perimeters of the national Church, citing the open, though strictly illegal questioning of the doctrine of the Trinity.[84] North had some part in advising its rejection in the Commons, enough at any rate to confirm the desirability to the electors of making him head of the University as well as the Treasury. Nevertheless, academic worriers could not rid themselves of the uneasy prognostication that instead of defending the ecclesiastical status quo, he might use his combination of offices to pressurise Oxford into modifying its official attitude.[85]

Such apprehensions were not realised: for North, as for the majority of the political elite, state policy still required adherence to the status quo. He was ready to join Sir Roger Newdigate and Sir William Dolben in opposing Sir William Meredith's motion for the relaxation of subscription in the Commons in February 1773,[86] and generally

used his parliamentary tactical skills to the University's advantage. In April 1779 Sir Henry Hoghton MP again brought forward a bill to exempt dissenting ministers and schoolmasters from subscribing to the 39 Articles. North knew the balance of opinion in the Commons meant it was likely to pass. Thus, in Committee on the bill he introduced a petition from Oxford University asking that Dissenters should instead make a declaration of Trinitarian Christianity. The amendment was accepted. This new clause, particularly aimed at Socinianism, slightly wrong-footed Hoghton and his friends. It was carried in the Commons against their wishes, and this helped secure the bill's passage through the Upper House.[87] Hard-line Tories may have grumbled that concessions were being made when so many Dissenters sympathised with the rebellious colonists but, considering that 1779 was a year when invasion threatened Britain and North appeared incapable of giving a lead to Cabinet colleagues, the University could consider itself lucky in the exertions he then made on its behalf. Academic opinion was also reassured that he and his father

---

[84] The petition was lost on 6 Feb. 1772 by 217 votes to 71. *PH*, 17, cols. 274, 296, 6 Feb. 1772; Parliamentary Diary of Sir Henry Cavendish, BL Egerton MSS 232, 155–69; G. M. Ditchfield, 'The subscription issue in British parliamentary politics, 1772–9', *PH*, 7 (1988), 53–64.

[85] G. M. Ditchfield, 'Ecclesiastical policy under Lord North', in eds. John Walsh, Colin Haydon, and Stephen Taylor, *The Church of England c.1689–c.1833. From toleration to Tractarianism* (Cambridge, 1993), 228–46, at 231. Also discussed in Chapter 6.

[86] See also Chapter 6, pp. 20–1. The instance of Meredith is a reminder that proponents of change included Oxonians. He was a Christ Church graduate, early inclined to Jacobitism, awarded a DCL in 1749, then became a Rockingham Whig who drifted away again towards the court. Patrick Woodland, 'Meredith, Sir William, third baronet, (bap. 1724, d. 1790), politician' *ODNB*, online version, 2004.

[87] John Almon, *The Parliamentary Register...* (17 vols., London, 1775–80), XII. 100–108, 308–18, 353–4; Warks. CRO, CR136, Newdigate Diary, Mar.–Apr. 1779; *London Chronicle*, 20 Apr., issue 3492. The amendment ran: 'I, A.B. do solemnly declare, in the presence of Almighty God, that I am a Christian and a Protestant; and as such that I believe that the Holy Scriptures of the Old and New Testaments as commonly received in Protestant churches, do contain the revealed will of God, and that I do believe the same as the rule of my Doctrine and Practice'. Henriques, *Religious toleration in England, 1787–1833*, 56–7.

subscribed generously to the financial relief of the 'distressed' American episcopalian clergy[88] and, in making recommendations for Crown patronage within the Church, there was no danger of Oxford's not receiving its fair share of plum posts (though North was scrupulously fair in trying to treat the two universities equally). However, once North left office in March 1782 and, the following year, served as Home Secretary in the Fox-North Coalition, relations between him and the University were never quite the same again. When Pitt the Younger took office, the vast majority of academics transferred their allegiance to him as the defender of the king's prerogative to select his own ministers, against the claims of what might be perceived as an aristocratic faction that spoke of defending the 'interests of the people' while in reality defending their own.

Pitt's relationship with the University was never close. He was, of course, a Cambridge graduate himself, one of that university's two MPs and elected its High Steward in 1790. He had no deliberate policy of favouring Cambridge at the expense of Oxford in patronage terms but, with his former tutor, Bishop George Pretyman, acting as his main ecclesiastical adviser, the affairs and well-being of Cambridge had assumed an institutional prominence by the 1790s that they had not known since the end of George II's reign.[89] At least Oxford could detect that his administration had become, by the late 1780s, generally well-disposed towards preserving existing constitutional arrangements in Church and state,[90] with the Premier disappointing his many Dissenting allies by not lending his support in Parliament to repeal of the Test and Corporation Acts. Pretyman may have drawn the reprint of Thomas Sherlock's 1718 work *Vindication of the Corporation and Test Acts* to his master's attention, though the evidence that it carried anything like decisive evidence with him is 'slender indeed'.[91] More pragmatic policy considerations applied.

After the French Revolutionary Wars began in 1792/3, Pitt's government needed all the ideological buttressing of the British Constitution that Oxford and its graduates could offer the nation. There was never any likelihood that such endorsement would not be forthcoming, though it was never uncritical of government slackness in being seen to support the Established Church.[92] Through its personnel and their publications, Oxford University did as much as any

[88] Ditchfield, 'Ecclesiastical Policy under Lord North', 242–3. North gave £25, Guilford £20.
[89] Payne, 'George Pretyman, bishop of Lincoln, and the University of Cambridge'. See Chapter 6, pp. 40, 50, n. 113.
[90] G. M. Ditchfield, 'Ecclesiastical legislation during the ministry of the younger Pitt, 1783–1801', *PH*, 19 (2000), 64–80.
[91] Ibid., 74.
[92] In 1799 Bp Cleaver was trying to persuade Lord Grenville for a legislative initiative to stunt sectarian growth caused by the rising number of Meeting Houses being licensed under what bishops considered to be an abuse of the Toleration Act. Details in ibid., 76.

378 ENLIGHTENED OXFORD

institution in the country to motivate Britons by merging the survival of religion, monarchy, and the rule of law in an accessible patriotic rhetoric that laid out the issues deemed to be at stake in the struggles against Revolutionary and then Napoleonic France. The University's central importance in the life of the polity was underscored when the kingdom stood needful. Ministers gave it every encouragement in 1792 by facilitating the election of the Whig grandee, the 3rd Duke of Portland, to succeed Lord Guilford as Chancellor.[93] Portland may have been, formally, the leader of the Foxite Whigs, but he and the majority of his party were being lined up to join the government in a coalition and the Oxford appointment was an early inducement to have him consider that prospect seriously.[94] Many of the Duke's most influential advisers (with William Windham, MP, of University College, to the fore) were Oxford graduates and they mended fences with the University with alacrity between 1790 and 1793.[95] Windham and his allies were arch-defenders of the 1688 settlement and staunch monarchists (though they understandably lacked a soft spot for George III personally because of his sabotage of the Coalition).

During Portland's Chancellorship (1792–1809), there was a faintly Whiggish tinge to the leadership of Oxford. For Portland had been Lord Chamberlain in the Rockingham ministry of 1765–6, in which the veteran Duke of Newcastle had been Lord Privy Seal, and then been in Opposition for most of the time since (1782, 1783 apart). But what mattered in the 1790s was (from July 1794) his place as Home Secretary in Pitt's cabinet restoring to Oxford a voice at the top table that could be relied on to represent its interests directly in policy-making for the first time since North left office in 1782. As one of the leading pro-War ultras in government, alongside Windham and the 2nd Earl Spencer, Portland was a key patron in Cabinet of High Church opinion that was increasingly characterised by a distinctly defensive Protestant tone at the close of the century, as Oxford voices raised alarm at any inclusion of Catholic emancipation in legislation for an Act of Union with Ireland.[96] The Duke's national and academic standing in the 1790s and 1800s fostered a combination of established 'Tory' opinion in Oxford[97] with an implicit commitment to the recently commemorated achievements of the Williamite Revolution symbolised by having a Bentinck at its head. It made for a redoubtable intellectual bulwark that showed

---

[93] See Chapter 6, pp. 23–5.

[94] John Ehrman, *The Younger Pitt.* Vol. 2. The *reluctant transition*, (London, 1983), 176–7, 183–5.

[95] Fox, by comparison, though a Hertford College product, detested Oxford as 'the capital of Toryism', and commiserated with his nephew, the 3rd Lord Holland, for being 'obliged to be at Oxford for your various nonsenses'. Letter of 5 May 1792, BL Add. MSS 47571, f. 9.

[96] Mather, *High Church Prophet*, 109; Wilkinson, *Portland*, 149–55.

[97] Thus the *Anti-Jacobin*, 5 (Feb. 1800), 290: 'We profess ourselves to be Tories and High-Churchmen. Let our adversaries make the most of this declaration...,' Gunn noted that 'As the reaction to the French Revolution swept a whole generation to the right, High-Toryism all but disappeared as a separate cause'. *Beyond Liberty and Property*, 190.

Part B: Defenders of the University's interests in Parliament

i) MPs for the University of Oxford

Portland's appointment was the third time since 1689 that an Oxford Chancellor had been in the Cabinet. To have such a voice in the executive was an exceptional piece of fortune, though one that potentially set up a conflict of interests between national and academic considerations. That was less likely to be a problem for the average Oxford graduate who was a member of the legislature and would be likely, in most cases, to be protective of the interests of his alma mater. For those Oxonians who were not peers, the turnaround time between graduation and membership of the House of Commons could be brief and it was a commonplace progression. A total of 945 MPs in the Parliaments of 1790–1820 had matriculated at one of the two English universities and, of those, no fewer than 285 were Christ Church men (its nearest competitor, Trinity College, Cambridge, had only 151).[99] At any given point in this period, the likelihood was that half of Oxford MPs came from that same college. Smaller ones could be strongly represented in the legislature. Thus, during Wetherell's Mastership at University College after 1764, thirty-seven old members sat in the Commons (as opposed to just twenty-five MPs between 1689 and 1764), including the future Burkeite apologist, and Cabinet minister from 1794, William Windham.[100]

The majority of MPs made up a silent majority who seldom if ever contributed to debate. Those who did so were likely to exhibit a rhetorical distinctiveness that was the product of its academic formation. At Christ Church Dean Jackson modelled his noblemen and gentlemen commoners as future national leaders, able to command a seat in either House of Parliament early in their lives, and likely to support the government of the day.[101] It is therefore unsurprising that the

---

[98] Interestingly, George III shifted his position slightly, telling Portland in 1801 that he was 'an old Whig; that he considered the statesmen who made the barrier treaties, and conducted the last years of the [Spanish] succession war [1702–13/14], the most able ones we ever had'. ed. 3rd Earl of Malmesbury, *Diaries and Correspondence of James Harris, First Earl of Malmesbury* (4 vols., London, 1844), IV. 44.

[99] C. Reid, *Imprison'd Wranglers. The Rhetorical Culture of the House of Commons 1760–1800* (Oxford, 2012), 127. This discussion relies heavily on Dr Reid's findings.

[100] Darwall-Smith, *University College*, 283.

[101] Not every product of Christ Church in Jackson's time leaned towards a pro-Pittite line. Thus the maverick baronet, Sir Francis Burdett (1770–1844) (matric. Ch. Ch., 1785, though an unmotivated student), MP for Boroughbridge 1796–1802, Middlesex 1802–6, Westminster, 1807–37, while keeping himself a little aloof from the Foxites, made a reputation for favouring parliamentary reform and denouncing the war with France. Marc Baer, 'Burdett, Sir Francis, fifth baronet (1770–1844), politician', *ODNB*, online version, 2009; M. W. Patterson, *Sir Francis Burdett and his Times* (2 vols.,

380 ENLIGHTENED OXFORD

Collections Book at the House shows that classical rhetoric and oratory were widely studied. Between 1785 and 1820 some fifty-seven per cent of undergraduates adopted Aristotle's *Rhetoric* for intensive study in their third year.[102] University occasions such as the Act or the Encaenia gave favoured undergraduates the opportunity for first efforts at speech-making and they might bring to that performance an existing familiarity with adapting their speech to arguing for or against a proposition. Thus at New College declamations were given in Latin on general ethical questions, such as whether a wise man changes his mind or whether courage in wartime or justice in peacetime deserves more praise.[103] Conscientious students would practise hard for set-piece occasions—to the vexation of neighbours who did not share their enthusiasm. At Christ Church, George Colman the Younger had to put up with the declamatory practice of Richard, Viscount Wellesley (1760–1842), in rooms adjacent to his own on Tom Quad, reading aloud from Cicero and Demosthenes as part of a training for public performance in debate that Dean Bagot encouraged. It was, he recalled—'characterized by a most wearing and dismal uniformity of sound!—calculated either to irritate the nerves of a next neighbour, or to lul him to sleep'.[104]

The University's principal spokesmen and its first line of defence at Westminster were its own two MPs. Commentators considered that, as constitutional redoubts, these were institutions that were fitly represented in Parliament. In Blackstone's words, they embodied 'useful members of the community' and their MPs were there to 'protect in the legislature the rights of the republic of letters'.[105] All doctors and Masters of Arts had the franchise and the total number of electors in the early eighteenth century was around 350 (493 voted in the election of 1768).[106] Unlike Cambridge, the Crown had no power to influence the outcome of elections by the creation of honorary doctors. To be one of the University's two MPs conferred a prestige that was nationally admitted and,

London, 1931). The 3rd Lord Holland (1773–1840) [MA, Christ Church, 1792], Fox's nephew, was another uncompromising Whig.

[102] Reid, *Imprison'd Wranglers*,130; R. M. Wyland, 'An archival study of rhetoric texts and teaching at the University of Oxford', *Rhetorica*, 21 (2003), 175–95; J. Mahoney, 'The Classical tradition in eighteenth-century English rhetorical education', *History of Education Journal*, 9 (1985), 93–7. Charles Fox, for instance, studied rhetoric with William Newcome soon after matriculating at Hart Hall in 1764. ed. Earl of Ilchester, *Letters to Henry Fox Lord Holland...* (London, 1915), 204.

[103] For instances see ed. Hargreaves-Mawdsley, *Woodforde at Oxford*, 3 (26 Oct. 1759), 159–60 (2 Mar. 1764), 222 (3 May 1774).

[104] Colman, *Random Records* (2 vols., London, 1830), I. 308–9. Educ. Eton and Ch. Ch., suc. as 2nd Earl of Mornington 1781, cr. Marquess Wellesley, 1799; Governor-General of India, 1797–1805; Foreign Secretary, 1809–12; Lord-Lt. of Ireland, 1821–8, 1833–4; Lord Steward, 1832–5; Lord Chamberlain, 1835.

[105] William Blackstone, *Commentaries on the Laws of England* (originally published Oxford, 1765–9), gen. ed. W. Prest. Book 1: *Of the Rights of Persons*, ed. David Lemmings (Oxford, 2016), Bk. 1, chap. 2, 115.

[106] M. B. Rex, *University Representation in England 1604–1690* (New York, 1954); www.his toryofparliamentonline.org/volume/1754-1790/constituencies/oxford-university.

invariably, they were men of talent and capacity drawn from leading Tory families.[107] Their views were often articulated in the Commons and, when publicised in the press, gained significant notice. Overall, their attendance records compare favourably with those of other members, though age, illness, and sheer disinclination could take their toll. Thus Peregrine Palmer, MP 1745–62, was denoted as follows by the 2nd Lord Egmont in his electoral survey of c.1749–50: 'an honest plain man, much affected with the gout and wont attend often, a Tory...'.[108] Competition to be selected as a candidate for what was to all intents and purposes the most prestigious Tory constituency in the country was generally intensive. Thus in 1793, when Francis Page, one of the sitting MPs, was believed to be mortally ill, candidates being lined up to succeed him included Thomas Wenman, Regius Professor of Civil Law; the Marquess of Worcester, heir of the 5th Duke of Beaufort; the Speaker (and future Premier), Henry Addington; and Sir William Scott, KC (who had stood previously at the 1780 General Election).[109]

Elections tended to be dominated by the larger, richer colleges, especially Christ Church, Magdalen, and All Souls, foundations that were anyway proximate to the political world of the metropolis through a whole series of alumni networks.[110] Weeks of horse trading, intrigue, intercollegiate alliances, and misinformation were all part of the process, though candidates were not allowed in the city during the election campaign and could not canvass in person. Electors faced one crucial question that could never be finally resolved. was it in the best interests of the University to select a 'court' candidate, a man who was—or could be 'an insider'— or opt instead for a figure whose appeal lay in his independency? Before the Tory proscription of 1714-16, during the quarter of a century when the Tories were in power regularly, there was much to be said for backing a minister, or one of his closest connections, as one of the two University MPs (or 'burgesses'); for the other seat, a backbencher with 'country' instincts might offer a suitable balance, such a man as Sir William Whitelocke (1636–1717) of Henley-on-Thames, one of those 'honest toilers in the cause of the University and of high-church politics'

---

[107] The Whigs did put up an able and moderate candidate, the Hon. Robert Trevor, of Queen's and All Souls, envoy to the United Provinces, in a by-election for the University in 1737, but he was decisively defeated. Ward, *Georgian Oxford*, 153–5. As William Jones told Wilkes in 1780, 'A Whig candidate for Oxford will never have any chance except at a time (if that time should ever come) when the Tory interest shall be almost equally divided.' 7 Sept. 1780, BL Add. MS 30877, f. 90.

[108] Quoted in www.historyofparliamentonline.org/volume/1715-1754/member/palmer-peregrine-1703-62.

[109] www.historyofparliamentonline.org/volume/1790-1820/constituencies/oxford-university Page survived his malady and remained as a University MP until 1801.

[110] Christ Church gradually pulled ahead in numbers of voters. In 1805 it had 213 of them, compared with the next college, Magdalen, with 97. Ibid; Thomas H.B. Oldfield, *An entire and complete history, political and personal of the boroughs of Great Britain History of Boroughs* (2 vols., London, 1792), II. 22.

Fig. 8.1 Edward Butler, attributed to Edward Vanderbank, oil on canvas (Reproduced by kind permission of the President and Fellows of Magdalen College).

elected in this era.[111] Alternatively, a lawyer connected with the University, possibly a civilian like George Clarke, had much to commend them. On only one occasion in this period did a serving Head of House and former Vice Chancellor (1728-32) represent the University. This was Dr Edward Butler, the President of Magdalen, who held a seat from 1737 to his death in 1745. He put up for it when William Bromley the younger (bap. 1699) died suddenly a few weeks after his election.[112]

It was a reassurance for the University in the aftermath of the Revolution that the brother of Lord Nottingham (William III's principal Secretary of State in 1690), the Hon. Heneage Finch, a staunch Anglican (he was a counsel with Somers and others at the trial of the Seven Bishops in 1688 and had previously served as

---

[111] MP for Oxford University, 1703-17. The phrase is W. R. Ward's, *Georgian Oxford*, 26, who highlighted Whitelocke's persuasive ridiculing of the 1709 bill to relax college statutes on the taking of holy orders. See this Chapter, p. 50.

[112] HMC, *Weston Underwood MSS*, 487, 490; www.historyofparliamentonline.org/volume/1715-1754/member/butler-edward-1686-1745.

OXFORD AND THE WORLD OF WESTMINSTER   383

Solicitor-General from 1679 to 1686), continued to serve as a burgess.[113] In 1695 the University went one better and elected a Secretary of State in the person of Sir William Trumbull, a courtier and former Fellow of All Souls, though a controversial figure in some Oxford quarters because of his tepid Toryism (Trumbull enjoyed considerable Tory backing, even from Queen Mary's uncle, the Nonjuring Lord Clarendon). The experiment was not a success: Trumbull had neither been able to moderate the growing dominance of the Junto Whigs in William's administration (he resigned as Secretary of State in December 1697 complaining of being 'treated more like a footman than a secretary'),[114] nor work closely enough with his constituents to make the majority of them enthusiasts for his standing at the 1698 election. However, the return of William Bromley (Christ Church, BA 1681) as an MP in 1701 turned out to be a brilliant move. For, perhaps than any other man in this period, Bromley proved able to maintain his principled Toryism alongside dutiful attention to his constituents until his death in 1732 and service in government during Queen Anne's reign.[115] Between 1704 and 1714 he acted, in Geoffrey Holmes's phrase, as 'the chief standard-bearer for the High Churchmen' in the Commons. Most Oxford electors delighted in his conspicuous profile: Bromley was one of the leading 'Tackers' in 1705 (indeed he had moved that the Occasional Conformity bill be tacked to the Land Tax on 28 November) and his commitment to the cause of Sacheverell in 1710 (however unwelcome to vice chancellors Lancaster and Gardiner) was conspicuous.

He was ever vigilant in protecting Oxford's interests, and could be both subtle and stern, depending on the tactics an occasion demanded. When a Junto-dominated government allowed its supporters to publish a draft bill early in 1709 to repeal college statutes in both English universities that stipulated the taking of holy orders for fellows, Bromley initially laboured behind the scenes to neutralise the initiative. Enlisting the help of George Clarke and knowing that All Souls lawyers in London favoured the scheme,[116] Bromley and his allies proposed the abandonment of any bill with a promise that he would use every influence to ensure reasonable requests for dispensations were granted. He then found

---

[113] Ward, *Georgian Oxford*, 15–16. Finch, discussed in this chapter, pp. 100–2, was also the cousin of Dr Leopold Finch, then Warden of All Souls.

[114] James Vernon, *Letters Illustrative of the Reign of William III from 1696 to 1708, addressed to the Duke of Shrewsbury*, ed. G. P. R. James, (3 vols., London, 1841), I. 391, 404, 432; J. P. Kenyon, *Robert Spencer, Earl of Sunderland 1641–1702* (London, 1958), 295–6.

[115] A. A. Hanham, 'Bromley, William (bap. 1663, d. 1732), speaker of the House of Commons', *ODNB*, online version, 2011. Typically, on 22 Feb. 1707, as the House was about to go into committee on the bill to ratify the Union with Scotland, Bromley, ever mindful of his constituents' interests, moved that consideration be given to an additional clause protecting Oxford and Cambridge universities, that they 'may continue for ever, as they are now by law established'. eds. C. Jones and G. Holmes, *The London Diaries of William Nicolson, Bishop of Carlisle 1702–1718* (Oxford, 1985), 393.

[116] For the 3rd Earl of Sunderland's (Secretary of State for the North, 1706–10) pressurising the University and All Souls, see Jeffrey R. Wigelsworth, *All Souls College, Oxford in the Early Eighteenth Century: Piety, Political Imposition, and Legacy of the Glorious Revolution* (Leiden, 2018), 66–7, 91–3.

384   ENLIGHTENED OXFORD

Warden Gardiner's face set against any compromise. That left Bromley (ably seconded by Whitelocke in the House) with no choice but to rally sufficient opinion (including the Speaker) to induce ministers to drop it.[117] None of this lessened Bromley's professional dedication to the Queen's service and, having held the office of Speaker with some distinction since 1710, he was a competent choice to succeed William Legge, 1st Earl of Dartmouth, as a Secretary of State in 1713. He tried hard if unavailingly in the thirteen months he held that office to keep the allies of Lords Oxford and Bolingbroke on good terms with each other.[118] Throughout his thirty-one years of service to Oxford University in the Commons, no one endeavoured more to preserve Tory unity or better preserved his popularity with backbenchers, thanks to his 'short and clear' manner of speaking.[119]

Bromley embodied Oxonian Toryism at its creative best. His parliamentary career under Anne showed that it was possible for an Oxford University MP to exhibit the skills that might reconcile the competing claims of court and country. Before his adoption he had proved his Tory mettle by not signing the Association for the protection of William III in 1696, and that gave him the edge in his selection two years later. Conversely, when grandees tried to intrude a junior minister's candidature for a university seat, the attempt could backfire. Ormond thus failed to have his client, the Whiggish under-secretary, John Ellis (he had served under Trumbull), adopted in 1698.[120] Likewise the moderate Tory, George Clarke, Fellow of All Souls from 1680, Judge Advocate 1682–1705, joint Secretary at War 1693–1704, Joint Secretary to the Admiralty 1702–5 (concurrently Secretary to Prince George of Denmark, Queen Anne's husband) was not endorsed in 1705. Clarke was offered his opportunity in 1717 when Whitelocke died in harness.[121] At that moment of acute stress for the academic establishment, it was judged vital not to give Whig ministers further excuses to justify remodelling the University by selecting a firebrand Tory. It was Clarke, the man of business and supremely gifted amateur of the arts, who was judged by most University politicians sans pareil as a candidate. He had always been among the University's eyes and ears in London (Laurence, 1st Earl of Rochester, was his early patron) reporting on political developments and the public mood and

---

[117] John Clarke, 'Warden Gardiner, All Souls, and the Church, c.1688–1760', in eds. Green and Horden, *All Souls under the Ancien Régime*, 197–213, at 200–1; Nichols, *Illustrations*, III. 280; HMC, *Downshire MSS*, I. pt. ii. 871. See also BL Lansdowne MS. 1013, f. 120.

[118] Ward, *Georgian Oxford*, 50.   [119] Holmes, *Politics in the Reign of Queen Anne*, 277–8.

[120] BL Egerton MS. 2618, f. 182. John Ellis, student of Ch. Ch., 1664; under-secretary of state, 1695–1705; a relative of the Jesuit priest, Philip Ellis; generous benefactor to his college in the construction of Peckwater quadrangle. Stuart Handley, 'Ellis, John (1642x6), government official', *ODNB*, online version 2008.

[121] Clarke was the relative by marriage of Bernard Gardiner of All Souls, the recent Vice Chancellor, who championed his claims to the seat. Ward, *Georgian Oxford*, 112, 121–2. Clarke had earlier been returned for Oxford University in James II's Parliament of 1685. He sat for East Looe in 1702, Winchelsea in 1705, and Launceston in 1711. He served as a Lord of the Admiralty in the Harley ministry, 1710–14.

Fig. 8.2 Prince George of Denmark and George Clarke, Sir James Thornhill, oil on canvas (by permission of the Warden and Fellows of All Souls College, Oxford).

working with artists and booksellers.[122] As Smalridge (Bishop of Bristol, Dean of Christ Church) wrote to the previous Vice Chancellor, Bernard Gardiner:[123]

> It will become all, who wish well to the university, to have our thoughts upon a proper successor, a person of experience and gravity, one who is entirely in our interest, and able to support it, one against whom the Government can have no exception, and who will be acceptable to, and agree with, his colleague. I believe you are of the same sentiment with me, that no one better answers this character, no one at any time, and especially at this juncture, could be more proper for us to pitch upon than our worthy friend Dr. Clarke.

Despite an attempt by Dr William King to gain election in 1722, Bromley and Clarke represented the University without interruption until the former's death in 1732.

---

[122] Clayton, 'Clarke: Father and Son', 124.
[123] Nichols, *Illustrations*, III. 282–3. In 1710 he had exerted influence to prevent a visitation of All Souls and would duly do so again behind the scenes of the whole University in 1718.

386 ENLIGHTENED OXFORD

Bromley was offered a minor office by George I in the autumn of 1714, which he refused because most Tories were ignored by the new monarchy. It was a fateful decision, and it remains hard to dissent from the late Geoffrey Holmes's judgement that Bromley was the 'man incomparably best fitted to lead the Tory party through the wilderness'.[124] His parliamentary probity and unwillingness to be bought over by any faction always commanded admiration. It was typical of him that an attempt by Lord Harcourt (who was quietly aligning himself with the Whigs in 1719–20) to prevail on Bromley to support a Whig administration was unavailing; equally representative was Bromley's studied but polite rebuff to his erstwhile colleague by always being absent when Harcourt called at his lodgings.[125] Though he intervened regularly in Commons debates with the authority owing to him as a Privy Councillor and former Secretary of State, Bromley never ceased to make the defence of Oxford's interests his parliamentary priority; even the captious Hearne could express admiration for 'an honest man...reckoned by some to have died a martyr in the service of our university'.[126] Bromley and Clarke did not shirk their duties in the Commons toiling away year after year on the floor of the House and in committee, despite the odds that the Tories faced in both Houses in making their opinions count for anything in Whig government policy-making.[127] For both of them, the honour of representing the University to the best of their abilities (Clarke found age and the loss of his left eye an increasing affliction in the early 1730s) afforded them a satisfaction that outweighed office-holding at any price.

Bromley's death opened the way for the electors in convocation to jump two generations and opt in February 1732 to return a candidate who had just attained his legal majority. It was his name and his pedigree that made him the obvious symbolic choice, if no more. This was Henry Hyde, Viscount Cornbury (1710–53), son and heir of the 4th Earl of Clarendon and 2nd Earl of Rochester (1672–1753), and great-grandson of Charles II's Lord Chancellor. Cornbury was a man of taste who acted as pallbearer at John Gay's funeral in 1732, and was later praised by Pope and Swift.[128] That he was a Jacobite and had been appointed a

---

[124] G. Holmes, 'Harley, St John and the Death of the Tory Party', in ed. G. Holmes, *Britain after the Glorious Revolution 1689–1714* (London, 1969), 216–37, at 230.

[125] HMC, *Portland MSS*, V. 557, 625.

[126] Hearne, XI. 32–34. Holmes considered his last eighteen years in the Commons 'a slow downward drift into relative obscurity'. 'Harley, St John and the Death of the Tory Party', 230.

[127] Clarke once, with excessive modesty, said of himself: '...for, tho' I am very uselesse in Parliament, I think my self oblig'd to attend,...' To Edward Nicholas, BL MS 2540, f. 250, Oxford, 9 Jan. 1724.

[128] See the reference in the 6th epistle of the first book, in the *Imitations of Horace*, Maynard Mack, *Alexander Pope. A Life* (New Haven, CT, 1985), 688, to Cornbury's reputation for probity as it stood in the late 1730s for having earlier refused a government pension:

> Would ye be blest? Despise low Joys, low gains;
> Disdain whatever CORNBURY disdains –.

Discussed in C. Brant, *Eighteenth-Century Letters and British Culture* (Basingstoke, 2006), 261–4. He was praised by Swift in a letter to John Gay, 4 May 1732, in ed. Woolley *Correspondence of Swift*, III. 468.

OXFORD AND THE WORLD OF WESTMINSTER 387

Lord of the Bedchamber by his cousin 'James III' in Rome the previous year was not adjudged a disadvantage either by his sponsor, George Clarke, or by voters.[129] This early allegiance was a false indicator of his maverick politics. After sponsoring the abortive eponymous plot in the early 1730s,[130] Cornbury abandoned Jacobitism and by the end of the 1730s (after an interlude in opposition) moved to backing Walpole's troubled administration.[131] He thereafter endorsed its Pelhamite replacement, but by the late 1740s was widely considered to have returned to opposition again.[132] With his health also failing, and living much abroad, he had no difficulty in securing royal and ministerial approval for his promotion to the Upper House under a writ of acceleration in his father's barony of Hyde of Hindon.[133] Most leaders of the University were piqued that Cornbury's action precipitated a by-election. There were no official thanks. Instead, unofficial relief that its maverick representative, whom many had come to feel had irrevocably sullied his escutcheon by abandoning his ancestral Toryism, was quitting the scene.[134] The honour also seemed embarrassingly inconsistent with his earlier ostentatious rejection of political patronage that Pope had lavishly praised.[135]

With this record, the fact that the University continued to nominate and elect Lord Cornbury demands explanation. It shows the power of ancestral obligation, of what could be allowed to the heir of what was left of the Hyde inheritance (Cornbury sold much land to settle accumulated family debts),[136] a sort of shadow endorsement of what could be allowed as heredity in the absence of a Stuart on the throne. It was also a tacit realisation that having as one of its MPs someone who offered conditional support to the government might not be such a bad thing. Cornbury had played a constructive role in the University's campaign against the

---

[129] Cornbury had several meetings with the Pretender who, it was reported, wept on recalling the loyalty of the Hydes to the Stuarts. TNA (PRO) SP 98/32, f. 238 (John Walton, 11 Aug. 1731). [This was the pseudonym of the Hanoverian Baron Philip von Stosch, appointed by ministers to report on the Stuarts in Rome].

[130] D. Szechi, *The Jacobites, Britain and Europe 1688–1788* (Manchester, 1994), 93–4; Eveline Cruickshanks, *Political Untouchables. The Tories and the '45* (London, 1979), 12.

[131] Coxe, *Walpole*, III. 519. See also J. B. Owen, *The Rise of the Pelhams* (London, 1957), for his progress.

[132] Keith Feiling, *The Second Tory Party 1714–1832* (London, 1938), 32. Cornbury himself retrospectively saw consistency in his conduct, telling Speaker Onslow: '...the confusion & destruction of their [both Partys] several Factions Distinctions and Divisions were ever the first and Greatest Rules of my Conduct & the most desired Effects of my Endeavours for the Public Welfare'. Lord Hyde [Cornbury] to Arthur Onslow, Berkeley Square, 27 Jan. 1750/1. BL Add. MS 52474, ff. 86–97.

[133] NLW, Glynllifon Estate Papers, 714. Cornbury might have considered that his peerage (which would have been his anyway on the death of his father [whom he actually predeceased]) could be reconciled with his earlier comment to his cousin: 'Every thought of mine is now confined to serve this country while I live, and manure it when I die'. Quoted in Maynard Mack, *Pope*, 700. Few in Oxford would have viewed it thus.

[134] Langford, *A Polite and Commercial People*, 213; Ward, *Georgian Oxford*, 161–2, 282. Some electors got together to offer their personal thanks and insisted that he had 'the Esteem and Reverence of all Parties', particularly as Oxford's protector 'While Report was making so free with the Character of the University'. [Some Oxford Electors], *A Letter to the Right Honourable Henry Lord Viscount Cornbury, occasioned by a Letter from his Lordship to the Vice-Chancellor of Oxford in Convocation* (London, 1751), 11, 13, 14.

[135] Spence, *Observations*, I. 145.   [136] Details in Chapter 9, p. 34.

388 ENLIGHTENED OXFORD

anticlericalism of the Commons evident in 1736 when the ministry (though opposing a motion for repeal of the Test Act) endorsed the Quakers' tithe bill and the Mortmain bill. Both eventually passed.[137] The latter aimed at restricting bequests of lands and the number of livings owned by charitable bodies in inalienable possession. It amounted to 'a significant attack on corporate Anglican philanthropy' and was motivated by fears of the Church acquiring an excessive accumulation of wealth.[138] But its effect would also be to so complicate such benefactions as Oxford had received from John Radcliffe and George Clarke as to deter future major legators. Given that most colleges in both universities were steadily increasing the number of livings in their gift,[139] they were furious at the threat to their autonomy on the dubious grounds that not to legislate would lead to that perennial Whig nightmare—an increase in independent clerical power.[140]

Oxford organised quickly to protect its endowments with the ailing George Clarke (Cornbury was also helping to concert resistance) hosting a meeting at his London lodgings of prominent Tories including William Shippen, Sir William Wyndham, Sir Watkin Williams-Wynn, and the lawyer and MP Nicholas Fazakerly (the latter charged with drawing up the University's petition against the proposal).[141] Cornbury presented an exemption clause based on the petition and, to the surprise of many MPs, Walpole's ministry accepted it.[142] These concessions owed much to the inspired preliminary lobbying of Vice Chancellor Stephen Niblett, who ignored Cornbury's warnings and solicited favours at Walpole's levée while at the same time collecting statistics for his parliamentary friends on college endowments and livings.[143] In the Commons, the universities were exempted from the restrictions on endowments but gained minimal

---

[137] S. Taylor, Sir Robert Walpole, the Church of England and the Quakers Tithe Bill of 1736, *HJ*, 28 (1985), 51–77.

[138] Egmont Diary, in HMC, *Egmont diary*, II. 256; Hervey, *Memoirs*, II. 530–1. Governments throughout Europe were anxious to curtail mortmain, and it was prohibited in most states irrespective of religious confession by c.1750, with the Austrian Netherlands (1753), Austria and Venice (1767) and Naples (1769–72) duly following on.

[139] Oxford possessed around 290 c.1730, Cambridge around 230. Some colleges held no livings. Bernard Palmer, *Serving two masters. Parish patronage in the Church of England since 1714* (Lewes, 2003), 102.

[140] Cambridge lobbied no less fervently than Oxford. Gascoigne, *Cambridge*, 102.

[141] Colley, *In Defiance of Oligarchy*, 70. It was presented alongside those emanating from the Sons of the Clergy and the Governors for Queen Anne's Bounty on 25–26 Mar. 1736. 'William Hay's Journal' in eds. S. Taylor and C. Jones, *Tory and Whig. The Parliamentary Papers of Edward Harley, 3rd Earl of Oxford, and William Hay, MP for Seaford 1716–1753* (Woodbridge, 1998), 137.

[142] 'Many thought they did not deserve such Exemption, on Account of the little Zeal they had always shewn to the Family on the Throne. And indeed such large Societies with a great Property are a sort of *Imperium in Imperio*. And when disgusted may distress a Government'. ibid. One unidentified peer in favour of the exemption (and the bill overall) noted that university revenues ought to increase: '...for as every other channel for death-bed devises will from henceforth be shut up, I must think it will cause the more to flow into that channel'. *PH*, ix.1156.

[143] John Clarke, 'Warden Niblett and the Mortmain Bill', in eds. Green and Horden, *All Souls under the Ancien Régime*, 217–32. Fourteen draft amendments were produced to cover every conceivable turn of the debate, and two printed papers were produced for distribution among MPs: *Reasons Humbly offered to the House of Commons against the Bill now depending for restraining the*

concessions on advowsons. It was stipulated, firstly, that the colleges should not be able to increase the total number of advowsons owned and, secondly, that they could not exchange one living for another that was more valuable.[144]

Despite his proven capacities, by the time he left the Commons in 1750 Cornbury had largely lost his previously accumulated electoral goodwill in Oxford circles. Instead, the dominant 'Old Interest' (as it was becoming customary to refer to the Tories) in the University opted instead to elect as his replacement in January 1751 a man of undoubted Tory instincts: Sir Roger Newdigate, 6th Bt. (1719–1806), of Arbury hall, north Warwickshire, an alumnus of University College. Newdigate was no Squire Western. His antiquarian, artistic, and architectural interests, and his high Anglicanism, complemented and enhanced rather than distracted him from serving the University as its burgess for three decades.[145] Until his last few years in the Commons, Newdigate was the most diligent of parliamentarians, possessed of a willingness to engage in the various business of the Commons (including election disputes) that compelled respect. He enjoyed his service in the militia during the latter part of the Seven Years' War and was one of those country gentlemen who in November 1761 discussed with Pitt and Charles Townshend (Secretary-at-War) a petition to put the militia raised in wartime on a permanent footing Newdigate's endorsement of annual parliaments, weekly pay for MPs, and the exclusion of placemen from the Commons were at one with the Country Party Tories of William III's reign and in principle aligned him behind some of the Old Whig/Wilkesite radicals of his own day. But, in his implacable opposition to any encroachment on the Church of England, he could not have been further from them.[146] He held out against all the alterations

---

Disposition of Lands ... as far as Relates to the University of Oxford [London], (1736?); *Some Plain Reasons humbly offer'd against the Bill now Depending in Parliament & c.* (London, 1736). Ibid., for difficulties in concerting tactics with Cambridge.

[144] 'William Hay's Journal', 138. The colleges were ultimately allowed by Parliament to continue to purchase advowsons up to a maximum of half as many livings as there were fellows. The restrictive clauses were repealed in 1805 under the University Advowsons Act on the ground that such an artificial restriction made the succession to livings of fellows excessively slow. Palmer, *Serving Two masters*, 102–3; Cooper, *Annals of Cambridge*, IV. 482–3. Cornbury had expected a motion to forbid colleges to expel fellows who had refused to take orders and was relieved at its absence. Ward, *Georgian Oxford*, 159.

[145] Newdigate also had a considerable estate at Harefield, Middx., and had represented that county until defeated in the 1747 General Election. William Frederick Vernon, *Notes on the Parish of Harefield, county of Middlesex* (London, 1872) 9, 23, 24; C. Musgrave, 'Arbury Hall, Warwickshire', *Country Life*, 8, 15 and 29 Oct. 1953. His benefactions to the University included the Newdigate Prize. For a discussion of why Newdigate was elected rather than the Hon. Robert Harley, the 1st Earl of Oxford's great-nephew, see eds. Taylor and Jones, *Tory and Whig*, liv. For an abstract of the poll at Oxford, 31 Jan. 1751, see Newcastle papers, BL Add MS 30661, f. 365.

[146] Newdigate had by *c.*1760 come to disdain the nomenclature of Whig and Tory, much preferring 'a nobler name—the country party'. See P. D. G. Thomas, 'Sir Roger Newdigate's essay on party, c.1760', *EHR*, 102 (1987), 394–400, at 396–7, and the sophisticated discussion of Newdigate's politics in Sack, *From Jacobite to Conservative*, 51–2. Newdigate was the centrepiece of Sir Lewis Namier's classic essay, 'Country gentlemen in Parliament 1750–1783', *History Today*, Oct. 1954, 676–88.

390 ENLIGHTENED OXFORD

proposed to subscription and to relief for dissenters,[147] defended the continued observance of the 30 January commemorations of Charles I, and spoke out against a bill to repeal them in 1772.[148] Towards the end of that year, after Newdigate had reported to the Vice Chancellor (Thomas Fothergill, youngest brother of George) on recent proceedings (and his part in them) in the House relating to the Test Act and subscription, as they potentially threatened 'the wellbeing of the University', Fothergill, speaking for the Heads of Houses and Proctors, responded with thanks for 'yr affectionate regard for the safety & welfare of the university'.[149] In all this, Newdigate's studied independency allowed him to be more uncompromising than suited Lord North.[150] Thus he opposed the Dissenters' relief bill of 1779 (which passed) on the basis that any man should 'who held the constitution of his country sacred, and who regarded the religion of his country . . . as the foundation of all our liberties'.[151]

Newdigate was at once loyal and independent, delighting in the accession of George III yet still watchful. As he put it: ' . . . men proscribed and abused for 50 years together [should] be presented with fools caps if they make ladders for tyrant Whigs to mount by. I like the King and shall be with his ministers as long as I think an honest man ought, and believe it best not to lose the country gentleman in the courtier'.[152] Years of mutual suspicion with government verging on disaffection made it strategically difficult for the University in the early years of George III to nominate courtiers as candidates to represent it alongside Newdigate. Thus at the 1768 General Election, the Grafton government's choice, Charles Jenkinson, was unsuccessful and an 'Old Interest' squire, Francis Page, was chosen instead. Jenkinson's (admittedly, occluded) talents were already conspicuous,

---

[147] Ian R. Christie noted that some men with Tory pedigrees (and Oxford degrees) did not share Newdigate's commitment. Thus Sir Charles Mordaunt, MP for Warwickshire, voted for the abolition of clerical subscription, and Sir John Molesworth, MP for Cornwall, in 1773 supported the Meredith motion on University subscription. Thomas, 'Politics in the age of Lord North', *PH*, 6 (1987), 47–68, at 59; this Chapter, pp. 36–7, 37 n. 88.

[148] His reference to the royal martyr as 'the only canonized saint' of the English Church caused laughter in the House. 3 Apr. 1772, *PH*, xvii, 435–8.

[149] Newdigate to V-C Fothergill, 18 Nov. 1772, in ed. White, *Newdigate correspondence*, 187–8; Fothergill to Newdigate, Warks. RO, Newdegate family of Arbury Papers, 24 Nov. 1772, B. 1676. Newdigate was in close communication with successive vice chancellors, not least during Nathan Wetherell's tenure in office, Master of his own college. Newdigate was proud of his University College pedigree, and Wetherell was always ready to exploit that bond.

[150] Newdigate's attendance in the 1774–80 Parliament was fitful and suggestive of a growing disenchantment with North's governmental policy that may have led to his decision to resign his seat in 1780. Announcing his decision to the Vice Chancellor, he mentioned the problems that had resulted from 'majorities implicitly following the dictates of the ministers of the day, changing their opinions as the minister was changed . . . the people at large more corrupt than even the representative body, and that more corrupt than even the minister himself'. 18 June 1780, in ed. White, *Newdigate Correspondence*, 227. Earlier in the decade, before the war erupted, the University was hopeful that the Premier and the University's MPs would work hand in glove. Thus the Vice Chancellor wrote in late 1772: 'In Hopes that, if you repair to Parliament soon, our Chancellor and You & Mr Page may perhaps have a conference together'. Warks. RO, Newdegate family of Arbury Papers, CR0136/B1673.

[151] Almon, *Parliamentary Register*, XII. 106–7.

[152] Memorandum *c*.Nov. 1762, quoted in Namier, 'Country Gentlemen in Parliament', 685.

Fig. 8.3 Sir Roger Newdigate, 5th Bt., Thomas Kirby, copy after George Romney, oil on canvas, 1792 (University College, Oxford).

Page's were limited,[153] though his supporters cried up his independence from ministerial influence, and he carried the day easily. Pressure from the other political direction—from committed Whigs—was similarly resisted, and it doomed the brave attempt of William Jones of University College to win the seat on Newdigate's eventual retirement in 1780.[154]

Instead, the prize went to another High Church Midlands baronet, Sir William Dolben, (1726–1814) [Christ Church] of Finedon, Northamptonshire, who was the grandson of an Archbishop of York, and the son of a Visitor of Balliol (Sir John Dolben) who had been the protégé of Lord Crew, Bishop of Durham. Sir William (who had sat for the University for a few weeks in 1768) turned out to be as dutiful and able in discharging his parliamentary duties as Newdigate.[155]

---

[153] Francis Page (1726–1803) [New College, MA 1747; DCL 1749]. Johnson exaggerated Page's deficiencies when he adjudged him 'an Oxfordshire [Middle Aston] gentleman of no name, no great interest, nor perhaps any other merit, than that of being on the right side'. *Letters of Samuel Johnson*, ed. Chapman, I. 208–9. For Charles Jenkinson see also Chapter 6, pp. 36, 38, 89 and this Chapter, 90–2.

[154] See Chapter 7, p. 93.

[155] Dolben had been initially one of those urging Newdigate not to retire into private life, writing on 11 May 1780: 'I protest, when I consider the critical situation of our constitution in Church as well as

Fig. 8.4 Charles Jenkinson, Lord Hawkesbury, later 1st Earl of Liverpool, George Romney, oil on canvas, 1786–8 (© National Portrait Gallery, London).

Ever watchful in his protection of Oxford's interests, he generally intervened whenever there appeared a challenge to the existing rights of the Established Church. Thus when John Pollexfen Bastard brought forward a bill to regulate the church courts in 1787 (it eventually became 27 Geo. III, c. 44), which would forbid the bringing of prosecutions there for immorality after a lapse of six months, Dolben was its unrelenting critic.[156] Ministers could generally rely on his support, though it was never uncritical or suggestive of dependency, and he thus considered each of the anti-government censure motions made between Yorktown (19 October 1781) and North's eventual resignation in late March 1782 on its merits, though profoundly opposed to conceding American independence. Likewise, on the French Revolutionary War and Pitt's administration,

---

State, I am frighten'd at my own insufficiency for such a station, and shall most sincerely rejoice to see it filled by one who has been so long tried and so generally approved in it.' Warwickshire RO, Newdegate family of Arbury Papers, B.1635.

[156] *PH*, XXII. (20 Apr. 1787), 127–32. Despite the opposition of Abp Moore, ministerial acquiescence allowed its passage. Ditchfield, 'Ecclesiastical Legislation during the Ministry of the Younger Pitt', 67.

Fig. 8.5 Sir William Dolben, 3rd Bt., after John Opie, oil on canvas, c.1800–18 (© University of Oxford).

though well-disposed in principle,[157] his vote could not be taken for granted. And, remarkably, for a University MP, he voted for parliamentary reform in the votes of 1783 and 1785, and on Charles Grey's motion for reform in 1797.

It was above all Dolben's Christian humanity that stood out. Having become shocked at the conditions in which slaves were transported from Africa to the West Indies, Dolben in 1788 introduced a bill that stipulated minimal conditions of comfort for shipping them over and steered what became the Slave Trade Regulation Act on to the statute books principally through his own efforts. So often popularly considered to be a centre of opposition to reform of all kinds, the first move in the British Parliament for statutory control of the slave trade had come from one of the representatives for Oxford University.[158] Every year Dolben

---

[157] In Nov. 1795 he and Windham were alone in offering a defence of John Reeves's High Tory pamphlet *Thoughts on the English Government* (denounced as a seditious libel by R.B. Sheridan, a view from which Pitt did not demur) and he was teller in a division against Reeves's prosecution on 14 Dec. D. Eastwood, 'John Reeves and the contested idea of the Constitution', *JECS* 16 (1993), 197–212.

[158] J. Stockdale, *Debates and Proceedings... during the Sixteenth Parliament of Great Britain* (19 vols., London, 1785–90), XV. 69–70, 71, 72, 75, 76; John Brooke, *The House of Commons 1754–1790. Introductory Survey* (Oxford, 1968), 270. The African author of *Thoughts and Sentiments on the Evil and Wicked Traffic of the Slavery* (London, 1787), Ottobah Cugoano, predicted that in time 'your noble

394   ENLIGHTENED OXFORD

acted to prevent the legislation from expiring and was regularly chairman at the committee stage of slave-trade abolition bills. He also supported William Wilberforce's peace motion in May 1795.[159]

Though the low-profile Page finally abandoned his seat in 1801 (in came Sir William Scott without a contest) the vigorous Dolben stayed on as University burgess until 1806 (a few weeks short of his 80th birthday),[160] with the way just about clear for the Speaker of the Commons, Charles Abbot, to take the vacated seat.[161] That election was dominated by the 'Catholic Question' and repeated insinuations that Christ Church and the government had become excessively influential, both in lobbying for their preferred candidate and in securing his return.[162] Scott (1745–1836), considered in his time the finest of Oxford tutors (even Edward Gibbon approved of him), a civil lawyer, MP for Downton between 1790 and 1801, had more than once shown his alertness in the Commons to any intended encroachment on Anglican interests. Thus on 24 Feb. 1797 he had opposed James Adair's Quaker Relief Bill by making a telling comparison with the French attack on ecclesiastical rights of property in 1789–90.[163] He was also the de facto senior legal guardian of the Established Church as judge of the consistory court of London and vicar-general of the province of Canterbury (1788–1820);[164] his brother was Lord Chancellor Eldon and both men had been well-known to Oxonians for decades as outstanding conservatively minded lawyers. Scott further articulated his concerns on ecclesiastical questions between the by-election of 1801 and the General Election of 1806. Thus, he sponsored the Clerical Residency Act through the Commons during 1803 and spoke against Catholic claims on 14 May 1805.[165] Some opined that he was going a little too far

name shall be revered from shore to shore' (Northants. RO, Dolben (Finedon) collection, D(F) 39, n.d., probably 1788). See also J. W. LoGerfo, 'Sir William Dolben and "The Cause of Humanity": the passage of the Slave Trade Regulation Act of 1788', *Eighteenth-Century Studies*, 6 (1973), 431–51.

[159] See *GM* 84 (1814), I. 417; Nigel Aston, 'Dolben, Sir William, third baronet (1727–1814), politician and slavery abolitionist', *ODNB*, online version, 2004, for a summary of his career.

[160] Dolben 'relinquished that honourable station, only from a conscientious fear that increasing years and probable infirmities might render him less capable of filling it with that energy and activity which he had unremittingly exerted'. *JOJ*, 2 Apr. 1814.

[161] Charles Abbot (1757–1829), educ. Westminster and Ch. Ch.; lawyer; Chief Secretary for Ireland, 1801–2; Speaker, 1802–16; cr. 1st Baron Colchester, 1816. For complaints in 1806 that the University's MPs had become too dependent on ministers, see Crook, *Brasenose*, 180–1.

[162] ed. R. H. Cholmondeley, The *Heber Letters: 1783–1832* (London, 1950), 197–200, 214.

[163] *PH*, XXXII. 1512; G. M. Ditchfield, 'Parliament, the Quakers and the tithe question 1750–1835', *PH*, 4 (1985), 87–114, at 103–6.

[164] In 1798 he also became judge of the Admiralty court and a privy counsellor. Henry J. Bourguignon, *Lord Stowell: judge of the High Court of Admiralty, 1798–1828* (Cambridge, 1997), 40–1. For his pre-eminence as a civilian lawyer, see W.C. Townsend, 'Life of Lord Stowell', in *The Lives of twelve eminent judges of the last and of the present century* (2 vols., London, 1846), II. 305.

[165] *PH*, XXXV. 1549 (1801); XXXVI. 463, 492, 889, 1559 (1802–3); Warks RO, Newdegate family of Arbury Papers, B.3729, Dolben to Newdigate, 14 May 1803. His principal speech was published as a pamphlet, *Substance of the speech of . . . Sir William Scott . . . upon a motion for leave to bring in a bill relative to non-residence of the clergy* (London, 1802). The Act did not outlaw plurality but laid down

OXFORD AND THE WORLD OF WESTMINSTER   395

in his zeal in promoting the pastoral efficiency of the parish clergy and hazarding their material well-being. The University, however, stood solidly by him.

The two Sir Williams—Dolben and Scott—were as capable a pair of parliamentarians as any in Britain, both committed, intelligent churchmen, whose support was cultivated by ministers (Pitt regularly offered George III information on what Dolben had said in Parliament) and whose influence extended well beyond Westminster. Dolben, a humane country gentleman to the fore with Wilberforce in his moral and practical condemnation of the slave trade;[166] Scott, the brilliant civilian lawyer and don, intent on making the Church of England pastorally efficient as a means of strengthening its establishment when Catholic and dissenting claims were becoming insistent. These two personified the University in the House of Commons in a manner which compelled respect. In so doing, they showed a commitment to the existing political order that was far from uncritical, marked themselves out as enlightened lay Anglicans, and appeared in direct line of succession to the best of their predecessors: Trumbull, Clarke, Bromley, Cornbury, and Newdigate.

ii) Other Parliamentary friends in Lords and Commons

By contrast with the Commons, the defence of the University in the House of Lords fell upon none officially charged with representing its interests, but there was seldom any shortage of temporal peers well-disposed to the place (often because it was their alma mater) who spoke and acted for it. Its Chancellors, all of them peers between 1688 and 1772 and 1790 and 1809, who might have been expected to be prominent in this role, for one reason or another, tended to make their influence felt in other ways: Ormond was essentially a courtier and a soldier; Arran appears to have made the avoidance of being publicly outspoken a golden rule; Westmorland was too old and had too short a time in office to make his voice heard; Lichfield was another courtier and, much later, Portland, besides being famously mute as a debater, found his duties as Home Secretary in wartime took

---

that clergy who were non-resident in their parish parsonage had to obtain a licence from their bishop. Critics noted that while the lower clergy would be compelled to reside in their parishes, the same stipulation would not apply to the bishops. The latter were lukewarm about the legislation, and it proved difficult to enforce. J. Gregory, *Restoration, Reformation and Reform, 1660–1828. Archbishops of Canterbury and their Diocese* (Oxford, 2000), 172. On Catholic emancipation, ed. T.C. Hansard, *The Parliamentary Debates from the Year 1803 to the Present Time* (22 vols., London, 1812), IV, 966.

[166] Dolben's interest in sponsoring improvements in public morality mirrored those of Wilberforce. Thus he was a strong supporter in 1787 of the Royal Proclamation against Vice and Immorality and, in 1795, displayed a strong interest in a bill that would have given more teeth to the Lord's Day Observance Act by making sabbath-breaking a breach of the peace. J. Innes, 'Politics and Morals: The Reformation of Manners Movement in Later Eighteenth-Century England', in ed. E. Hellmuth, *The Transformation of Political Culture: England and Germany in the Late Eighteenth Century* (Oxford and London, 1990), 57–118.

396 ENLIGHTENED OXFORD

up all his waking hours. In the absence of the Chancellor and the High Steward (himself invariably a peer) and given the high levels of parliamentary attendance expected of the episcopal bench, it might have been anticipated that successive Bishops of Oxford would have been to the fore in standing up for this epicentre of their diocese. Having their cathedral in a college was a visual symbol of how much the protection of Oxford's interests were subsumed in those of the wider Church of England, so that the affairs of the two institutions could not readily be prised apart. But, as discussed, for their career's sake, Bishops of Oxford (all of them moderate Whigs in the eighteenth century) had to be circumspect when there was any prospect of a conflict between ministerial and ecclesiastical interests.[167] It famously took years for Secker to recover his reputation from his flirtation with the 'Patriot' opposition to Walpole in the late 1730s, yet he eventually was awarded the primacy, as was his predecessor, John Potter, who never lost his High Church instincts and was not afraid, when the issue demanded it, to associate himself in the division lobby with Tories who had minimal prospects of promotion. Thus when the Quakers bill was laid before the Lords in January 1722, offering them new forms of affirmation and declaration, Potter (and Archbishop Wake) joined a protest against its passing at third reading alongside Archbishop Dawes, and Bishops Atterbury and Gastrell (of Chester), Oxonians all.[168]

Such Oxford-educated prelates had established themselves over the previous decade as ready to speak and vote in the Lords on causes dear to the Church, to the University and, more likely than not, to the Tory party. Thus all the bishops opposed the 1709 bill relating to the obligation of fellows to take holy orders, Bishop Trelawny of Winchester lashed out at lawyers, observing that its passing would turn the colleges into 'nurserys of lawyers & attorneys' and expose them to litigation in Westminster Hall 'where atheism, socinianism & a proper detestation of ye principles & government of ye universitys is allowed and justify'd'.[169] Successive Deans of Christ Church, Atterbury (as Bishop of Rochester), and Smalridge (as Bishop of Bristol), were as prominent as any of the Tory lay peers in the House of Lords between 1714 and 1720. Atterbury was the brilliant orator and party leader who neither had nor wanted any [Hanoverian] court interest;[170] Smalridge—a finer speaker from the pulpit than in the Upper House—combined judicious protectiveness of the University's interests (cracking down on neo-Jacobite *provocateurs*) with opposition to the impeachment of Lord Oxford and

---

[167] Chapter 6, pp. 74–87.

[168] J. Disney, *Memoirs of the life and writings of Arthur Ashley Sykes* (London, 1785), 130. There were fears that the concession would permit Quakers to evade tithe payments. The Protest was later expunged from the Lords Journals because of the 'high-flying' language used about the powers of Convocation. *PH*, VII. 938–46.

[169] Bodl. Ballard MS 9, ff. 69, 73.

[170] Bennett, *Tory Crisis*, 195–9; Cruickshanks and Erskine-Hill, *The Atterbury Plot*, 71–3.

repeal of the Schism and Occasional Conformity Acts, plus popularity at the court of the Prince and Princess of Wales.[171]

It tended, however, to be temporal rather spiritual peers who were the most prominent defenders of the Church and the University in the Upper House after 1714, among them Charles, 4th Earl of Orrery, who led the Tories in the Lords between 1725 and 1731, and cut a more impressive figure at the end of his life than in the 1690s when he stood in eye of the Phalaris storm.[172] The classic profile was to combine a committed Toryism with previous experience of the more rumbustious political encounters in the House of Commons. Two such were Edward Harley (1699–1755), a Christ Church man and nephew of Anne's Premier, who succeeded as 3rd Earl of Oxford in 1741 and Lord Noel Somerset (1709–56), 4th Duke of Somerset from his brother's death in 1745. Oxford's importance as a Tory leader increased steadily during the 1740s in proportion to his involvement in Lords' business.[173] His capacities so endeared him in some Oxford circles that his name was mentioned in 1751 as a successor to Lord Arran upon the next vacancy in the Chancellorship.[174] However, the failure of his son and heir, Roger, Lord Harley, to secure victory over Newdigate in the Oxford by-election of January 1751 lowered the Earl's level of interest in the University, and it confirmed a diminution of his Tory instincts and an increase in his ministerial connections, primarily through Lord Hardwicke.[175]

There was no danger of Beaufort's Tory instincts falling away, though his susceptibility to gout, coupled with the time required to manage the recently inherited ducal patrimony hindered his commitment to parliamentary duties. If Beaufort's Jacobite predilections were never in doubt, neither was his grasp of the art of the politically possible in attempting a restoration.[176] Indeed, his spirited opposition in the Commons to the Mortmain bill in 1736 confirmed his

[171] For Bishop Smalridge's decisive influence (as a Tory) on Archbishop Wake at this time see Gibson, 'Altitudinarian Equivocation', 46.

[172] For his post-1714 career see the summary in Lawrence B. Smith, 'Boyle, Charles, fourth earl of Orrery (1674-1731)', *ODNB*, online edn., 2008.

[173] No one signed more protests during his time in the Lords (1741–55) than the 3rd Earl of Oxford. ed. Taylor, *Tory and Whig*, lii.

[174] Hearne, XI. 37. He had succeeded Bromley as a Radcliffe Trustee in 1732, and his name appeared as a possible Lord Privy Seal in a prospective Leicester House ministry of 1750. See the discussion about his role and capacities in ed. Taylor, *Tory and Whig*, li–lii. Colley harshly deemed him 'unqualified for partisan activity on behalf of the Tory parliamentary party as a whole.' *In Defiance of Oligarchy*, 68.

[175] ed. Taylor, *Tory and Whig*, liv–lv.

[176] Cf. Eveline Cruickshanks, who notes that both the 3rd and 4th Dukes of Beaufort were committed to the '45, the one being privy to the project, his successor sending assurances of support to France in August 1745. No contacts were made between him and Charles Edward Stuart during the '45. www.historyofparliamentonline.org/volume/1715-1754/member/somerset-lord-charles-noel-1709-56 The Welsh Jacobite lawyer, David Morgan, who had been the 4th Duke's secretary, during interrogation after capture plausibly insisted that Beaufort would never give up any part of his estate. Frank McLynn, *The Jacobite Army in England 1745. The Final Campaign* (2nd edn., Edinburgh, 2001), 15. He was, however, the leader of the 'Remitters', that group of English Jacobites that continued to contribute funds to 'James III' after Culloden. D. Zimmermann, *The Jacobite Movement in Scotland and in Exile, 1746-1759* (Basingstoke, 2003), 82.

398 ENLIGHTENED OXFORD

dedication to the University's interests and merited the bestowal on him of a DCL for services rendered in July the same year. After John, 2nd Lord Gower defected from the party to serve in government in 1742–3 and 1744, the 4th Duke quietly assumed the role of principal Tory leader in the Lords and held it for almost a decade, though incapacitated by gout by the early 1750s.[177] Beaufort used his Presidency of the Honourable Board of Loyal Brotherhood (founded by his father, the 2nd Duke) as a vehicle to facilitate convivial communication between Tory drawn from both Houses. He addressed a meeting of thirteen peers and 103 MPs (both Tories and Leicester House Whigs) at the Loyal Brotherhood's London headquarters, the St Albans Tavern, on 1 May 1749, to concert parliamentary tactics when a visitation of Oxford appeared imminent.[178] By that date, he was on excellent terms with virtually the entire range of Tory opinion.[179] Had Lord Arran expired during that period, the Duke of Beaufort might well have taken precedence over the claims of Lords Westmorland and Oxford to the University Chancellorship.

As it was, he and the University saw out the several threats to its integrity and, in the reign of George III, the protection of the University was caught up generally in the defence of the Church of England against those who sought changes to subscription, extended relief for Protestant Dissenters, and the repeal of the Test and Corporation Acts. Inasmuch as those issues came before the House of Lords, it tended to be the bishops who took the lead in arguing against them rather than the temporal peers. There was little point in looking to those nominally charged as High Steward of Oxford with defending the University from their seat in the Lords: the erudite Edward, 5th Lord Leigh (1767–86) was insane for the last decade of his life, and the 2nd Earl of Dartmouth (1786–1801), Lord North's half-brother, an evangelical with Methodist sympathies, had effectively retired from public life by the time of his appointment.

Part C: Governmental and legal cross-connections

i) Administrative and academic nexuses

As an institution intertwined with most aspects of eighteenth-century public life, it could be anticipated that the formal and informal ties of the University of Oxford with the state would be both various and extensive. The state increasingly needed the services of highly educated graduates to operate it. The several French

---

[177] Colley, *In Defiance of Oligarchy*, 252.
[178] Ibid., 72; Theophilus Leigh to Dowager Duchess of Chandos, 5 May 1749, Balliol College, Oxford, MS. 403. Lord Oxford also played a prominent role at that gathering. Walpole to Sir Horace Mann, 3 May 1749, *Correspondence*, XX. 50–1.
[179] NLW, Badminton MS 2215.

OXFORD AND THE WORLD OF WESTMINSTER 399

Wars gave rise to sophisticated financial and administrative apparatus, with the proliferation of boards, committees, and sub-departments staffed by skilled men. In this world patronage could be vital to obtaining an initial appointment, though a talent for business as well as the right connections was a requisite for most men seeking promotion or perhaps a secretarial post with a minister.[180] Scholarship too, as in the case of Thomas Tyrwhitt, who served as under-secretary to Newcastle between 1756 and 1762 before becoming Clerk of the Commons.[181] Oxford also produced clergy expected to endorse the polity's legitimacy, lawyers who would support its best interests in court, and army officers who would risk their life for it. Even when there was a stand-off between ministers and Oxford in George I's time, it was unrealistic to imagine that Cambridge alone could provide men who could be relied on to serve the state loyally. By the 1770s Oxford graduates were helping to build up a distinctive ethos of public service that remained intimately connected with the customary patronage networks and their personal career advancement.

Apart from serving in government offices and often sponsoring improved working practices, many came straight from college into wartime intelligence-gathering and security operations. The most suitable graduates for this demanding kind of employment were generally singled out and recommended by senior dons who had ties to ministers, men who were trusted to work hand in glove with the national power brokers, Arthur Charlett of University College, for instance, in the first two decades of the century and, pre-eminently, Cyril Jackson of Christ Church, in the last two. Then there were the Oxford lawyers whose advice might be sought by ministers informally to supplement or replace that of their own law officers. The most notable was William Blackstone in the 1750s and 1760s. And there were the connections on which so much of this activity was erected, on lines that bisected the Georgian state, between the educators of the sons of the king's ministers (or would-be ministers), and their fathers, a vital position of trust on which so much depended, and for which some material reward might be expected—and its absence possibly resented. The goodwill of the government was not to be bought at any price—though there were always the ambitious, the unscrupulous, and the fawning who believed it could—and yet, when it was in place, when Oxford was comfortably settled within civil society, it made for academic flourishing and social well-being.

---

[180] Bishop John Moore observed archly of two such Oxonian appointees:

I saw Lord Temple on his way [to Ireland as lord-lieutenant]. He seems perfectly happy, & dreams of no difficulties. Should any arise, his two Secretaries, who have had the peculiar advantage of imbibing all their Politicks at Oxford, uncontaminated with embarrassments of official knowledge or Parliamentary experience, will soon enable him to get the better of them. BL Blenheim Papers, Add MS. 61670, f. 132, to Duchess of Marlborough, 30 Sept. 1782.

[181] Chapter 4, p. 71.

100   ENLIGHTENED OXFORD

Governments looked to the universities to provide them with learned clerks who could decipher letters, a matter of state security in wartime, a vital responsibility in Queen Anne's reign, when Jacobite plans for a landing in favour of 'James III' intensified the menace posed by French European aggrandisement. There was a marked dynastic and Oxonian aspect to cryptography which, in the light of the University's appreciable interest in Jacobitism and, for a minority, outright involvement in it, might appear a risk. Cambridge men should have been obvious candidates for this kind of work when Oxford was, for half a century, considered by Whig power brokers (men who stood to benefit from depicting Oxford as an internal security liability) to have more than one foot in the Jacobite camp.

But such was not the case. In fact, with one short interlude, the intercepting and reading of correspondence was entrusted to loyal Whig hands in the University.[182] They worked largely at home under an oath of secrecy. John Wallis (1616–1703), Savilian Professor of Geometry, had, as a young man, decoded intercepted messages from Charles I for the Parliamentarians and, after the Restoration, he continued to act as the government's official cryptographer.[183] He passed his skills on to his grandson, William Blencowe, a barrister and 'a proud fanatical Whig' (a fairly extreme labelling even for Thomas Hearne),[184] a protégé of Archbishop Thomas Tenison, and a (lay) fellow of All Souls from 1703.[185] His grandfather's post reverted to him at an initial salary of £100 per annum from the Secret Service fund to undertake much of this code-breaking activity. He was the first Englishman to be the official Decypherer and did so well at his duties that his salary was doubled after six years in service.[186] However, his work was affected by the efforts of the Junto Ministers in 1708–9 to dispense him from taking holy orders as the All Souls statutes required and Warden Gardiner's efforts to thwart them.[187] Blencowe committed suicide in August 1712 after two blows. First, once the Tory government of Robert Harley was installed in 1710, the Queen had personally sent a letter to Archbishop Tenison saying that 'she did not approve Mr Blencowe's insisting on his being in her service to excuse him from conforming to the Statutes of his College' and any dispensation from his taking holy orders was revoked (confirmed after complicated legal proceedings). Second, ministers ended his employment with the winding down of the war, and gave his post to

---

[182] For what follows see K. Ellis, *The Post Office in the Eighteenth Century. A Study in Administrative History* (Oxford, 1958), Appendix 1, 127–31.

[183] See Chapter 5, pp. 37, 44–5.   [184] Hearne, III. 439.

[185] Edward Carpenter, *Thomas Tenison Archbishop of Canterbury. His Life and Times* (London, 1948), 278. Blencowe was no friend to Warden Gardiner and was well inclined to Matthew Tindal in the Fellowship. Wigelsworth, *All Souls College*, chap. 4; Clarke, 'Warden Gardiner, All Souls, and the Church', 203ff.

[186] Wigelsworth, *Deism in Enlightenment England*, 63; D. Kahn, *The Codebreakers: the Comprehensive History of Secret Communication from Ancient Times to the Internet* (London, 1996), 169; Burrows, *Worthies of All Souls*, 356.

[187] Clarke, 'Warden Gardiner, All Souls, and the Church', 196–205.

Fig. 8.6 John Wallis, after Sir Godfrey Kneller, oil on canvas, 1701 (© National Portrait Gallery, London).

John Keill, Professor of Astronomy, who was undistinguished in his efforts, and lost the place to a much younger man in May 1716.[188]

This was Edward Willes (1693-1773), who had graduated from Oriel in 1712, was subsequently a member of the stridently Whig Constitutional Club, and had been taught cryptography by William Blencowe. He immediately showed his qualities when, in 1716, he broke the code of the Görtz-Gyllenborg correspondence and accessed 300 letters from pro-Jacobite Swedish diplomats revealing their efforts to bring about a Jacobite uprising in Britain; he later (1719-22) deciphered correspondence between Atterbury and Jacobite exiles, and it was crucial evidence at Atterbury's trial. Along with his colleague in the Decipherer's office, Anthony Corbiere (a Cambridge graduate), Willes appeared on several occasions before the Lords in 1723 and attested on oath to the veracity of their findings, despite the efforts of Atterbury and his counsel to present objections.[189] He was rewarded with a canonry of Westminster Abbey and, later, the Deanery of Lincoln in 1730.

---

[188] HMC, *Portland MSS*, VII. 529-31; Carpenter, *Tenison*, 280-1; Kahn, *The Codebreakers*, 169-70.
[189] Bennett, *Tory Crisis*, 236, 268.

102 ENLIGHTENED OXFORD

He continued to undertake important work for the administration even after being appointed Bishop of St David's in 1742, and three of his grandsons, Edward, William, and Francis Willes were undertaking deciphering work for Pitt's government during the 1790s.[190]

The security of the state in wartime required a trusted cadre of staff whose bona fides and competence could be guaranteed. Ministers during the French Revolutionary Wars would invariably look towards the universities for their supply of young men from the right sort of social background, those untainted by the slightest whiff of French republican sympathies, who could get on with the job given them. In 1793 Pitt's administration secretively established a central registry within the Alien Office (in itself a new creation), whose purpose was to collect and co-ordinate intelligence received from a wide variety of sources, and the majority of those working in this centre had academic and social connections to Christ Church.[191] Among them William Wickham, John King (Under-Secretary at the Home Office, 1791–1806), Thomas Carter, and George Canning, were some of the many young men cast by Jackson (an expert talent-spotter) for a life in the public service, a destination for which he had been 'moulding, encouraging, and supporting' them during their years at the House and after graduation.[192] Neither was it a coincidence that Jackson was a client and a friend of the 3rd Duke of Portland, the Chancellor of the University, Home Secretary from 1794, and himself a Christ Church graduate.[193] More than any other minister, the under-estimated Portland made certain that it was predominantly Christ Church graduates who were earmarked for employment in what became the secret service sub-department housed inside the Alien Office, itself reporting to the Home Office.

Portland was kept au fait with security developments by his private secretary, Thomas Carter (c.1761–1835), but all intelligence roads in Britain in these years eventually led to William Wickham, another of Jackson's prize pupils, who held office officially as superintendent of aliens.[194] Between 1798 and 1799 Wickham

---

[190] Kahn, *The Codebreakers*, 171. His career is summarised in W. Gibson, 'An eighteenth-century paradox: the career of the decipherer-bishop Edward Willes', *JECS*, 12 (1989), 69–76.

[191] What follows relies heavily on Michael Durey, 'William Wickham, the Christ Church connection and the rise and fall of the security service in Britain, 1793–1801', *EHR*, 121 (2006), 714–45; Durey, *William Wickham, master spy*, 8–14. See generally E. Sparrow, *Secret service. British agents in France 1792–1815* (Woodbridge, 1999); Sparrow, 'The alien office', *HJ*, 33 (1990), 361–84. Jackson's influence with ministers is discussed more fully in this chapter, pp. 91–6.

[192] Durey, 'The Christ Church Connection', 717. One obituary talked of how he inspired his pupils 'with a lively sense of the nature and importance of their future duties', *GM*, 89 (1819), II. 459–63, at 462. For Jackson's influence on Canning who, while at Ch. Ch., helped form a debating society which sported a uniform, see Sir Charles Petrie, *George Canning* (London, 1946), 19–21, Also Roger Knight, *Britain against Napoleon. The Organization of Victory 1793–1815* (Harmondsworth, 2013), xxxiii–xxxiv.

[193] The 3rd Duke's son and heir, the Marquess of Titchfield (b. 1768), was also at Christ Church during the 1780s, and became Canning's brother-in-law. Titchfield was awarded a DCL by his father at his installation in 1793.

[194] These appointments made up, in Durey's words, 'nearly a full "House" in the Home Office'. *William Wickham*, 44.

OXFORD AND THE WORLD OF WESTMINSTER   403

was to all intents and purposes head of the secret service, turning the inner office into 'a genuine national intelligence centre'[195] and, perhaps more than anyone, helping to prevent external invasion and internal insurrection.[196] However, after Pitt left office in 1801 and the Treaty of Amiens was signed in 1802, this Christ Church circle evaporated, a victim of the new Premier, Henry Addington's, reduction of secret service funds by one third.[197] When Pitt resigned over the King's unwillingness to concede full Catholic emancipation there also went, as Michael Durey has expressed it,. '...the idea of a comprehensive, integrated and centralised intelligence centre...It was not to be revived until the twentieth century'.[198] And when it was, it would be indelibly associated with Oxford's sister university. Wickham himself had concluded the game was over not when Pitt quit office but before that, after First Consul Napoleon Bonaparte had beaten the Austrians at Marengo on 14 June 1800, and he had twice sent in his resignation as Under-Secretary to Portland.[199]

These intimate connections with government were nothing new. Early in the century three Heads of Houses—Arthur Charlett, Henry Aldrich, and Francis Atterbury—had all acted as power brokers whose good offices were courted by Tory ministers. Charlett's was the most invisible presence of the three in the Oxford/Westminster world, an irrepressibly curious individual whose network of correspondents ensured that he fulfilled a role that satisfied him hugely: a one-man clearing house of information that was *generally* reliable and often influential at the highest level.[200] In short, as Richard Rawlinson called him—he was 'that generous universal correspondent'.[201] As rector of Hambleden, not far from Henley-on-Thames, from 1707 to 1722, he was placed in a parish that was placed approximately halfway between Oxford and the capital, politically convenient and symbolically appropriate. Charlett, however, was far more than an ineffectual gossip and a political weathercock, being active between 1690 and 1715 in the University's political affairs as a kind of Oxford 'fixer'. Thus he had an important role in the selection of candidates for the University seat in 1701; secured Sir William Whitelocke's candidature in 1703 for the same (as a replacement for

---

[195] Durey, *William Wickham, master spy*; Durey, 'The Christ Church Connection', 717, 737.

[196] Ibid., 737. He was officially Under-Secretary at the Home Office. How much Jackson knew of his activities as a master of espionage must remain an open question.

[197] Philip Ziegler, *Addington. A Life of Henry Addington First Viscount Sidmouth* (London, 1965), 152.

[198] Durey, 'The Christ Church Connection', 745.

[199] Remarkably, and in recognition of Jackson's unique advisory position, the Duke refused to accept it unless it was endorsed by 'our good friend the Dean'. Quoted in Sparrow, *Secret Service*, 214.

[200] For Charlett see Luttrell, *Historical Relation*, II. 355, IV. 142; Darwall-Smith, *University College*, 219–46, esp. 227–8. He was brilliantly sent up (because of his reputation for tipsyness) in *The Spectator*, no. 43, by Richard Steele, as 'Abraham Froth', satirising Oxford's political influence in 1711 via its armchair statesmen. See *The Spectator*, ed. Donald F. Bond, (5 vols., Oxford, 1965–87), I. 180–5. See also J. G. Jenkins, *The Dragon of Whaddon: Being an account of the life and work of Browne Willis (1682-1760). Antiquary and Historian* (High Wycombe, 1953), 144–5.

[201] Bodl. MS Ballard 2, f. 10.

104   ENLIGHTENED OXFORD

Heneage Finch on his elevation to the peerage as Lord Guernsey) with the *fiat* of the Tory grandee, Thomas, 1st Viscount Weymouth at Longleat; and cultivated a warm relationship with Robert Harley after his emergence as a Tory leader.[202] Though Pro-Vice-Chancellor and a long-time royal chaplain, Charlett's influence was in free fall after 1714 as rumours, essentially groundless, circulated about his allegiance and that of his College.[203]

Aldrich and Atterbury, both conspicuously different Deans of Christ Church, were more in the political maelstrom than Charlett. Aldrich emerged in the 1690s as Oxford's most prominent High Tory lobbyist, making the deanery 'almost a headquarters of Toryism'.[204] Working alongside William Jane, he had shown his power in thwarting the plans for Comprehension in 1689 and confirmed his standing as a figure of influence with any number of clergy whom Tory politicians at Westminster needed to cultivate in order to strengthen their own position. Aldrich (Vice Chancellor, 1692–5) encouraged and helped to form the political outlooks of the young men who filled the House in his time, and maintained contacts with them after they had 'gone down'.[205] The College, as he saw it, could only benefit from the good offices of those likely to be future Tory leaders, such as Sir Thomas Hanmer, 4th Bt. (1677–1746), the tutee of Robert Freind and a kinsman of the Duke of Ormond, whom Aldrich particularly cultivated.[206] The cautious and reserved Hanmer's acceptance of the Speakership in 1713 delighted a later Dean as 'so much to the Honor & Advantage of this Society'.[207] Aldrich shared confidences with Lord Rochester, his frequent guest at the Deanery, as Rochester looked for clerical propagandists and anticipated the time when the Church party would sweep all before it on his niece, Princess Anne's, accession.[208]

---

[202] Ward, *Georgian Oxford*, 14, 19, 26, 33, 42. Charlett never became one of Harley's intimates. Weymouth's Tory status as a friend of the Nonjurors was impeccable, though his electoral influence was in decline in the 1690s.

[203] Charlett wrote to Lord Arran in July 1717 that University College was 'intirely devoted and attached to the Illustrous House of Hanover'. Quoted in Darwall-Smith, *University College*, 243. Hearne (VI. 75-6) claimed the letter was 'much laugh'd at'. Attempts by Bromley to secure Charlett a prebendal stall in Worcester Cathedral predictably came to nothing in the new reign. Bromley to Lord Aylesford (formerly Lord Guernsey), 1 Nov. 1714, Chatsworth MS FCH/6/22. For his previously unsuccessful effort pointing out that Oxford senior members who were royal chaplains had not been preferred ('...which is discouraging to them and to the University,...), see Bromley to Oxford, 27 Oct. 1712, HMC, *Portland MSS*, V. 240.

[204] Bennett, *Tory crisis*, 30.

[205] As most peers who came to Oxford in the 1690s and 1700s attended Christ Church, Aldrich's scope for influence was unparalleled. Bennett, 'Against the tide', 38–9; V.H.H. Green, 'The University and Social Life', in HUO V, 309–58, at 311.

[206] Their opportunities for socialising in Shropshire as well as London and Oxford were increased when Aldrich became rector of Wem. John, Lord Hamer, *A Memorial of the Parish and Family of Hanmer in Flintshire* (London, 1876), 253n. Freind lived to compose Hanmer's Latin epitaph, which Samuel Johnson turned into English.

[207] Smalridge to Hanmer, 3 Sept. 1713, NLW Bettisfield MSS [Hanmer], No. 6. He replaced William Bromley, MP for the University, as Speaker. Unfortunately for Ch. Ch., Hanmer only held the chair for just over a year. J. A. Manning, *The Lives of the Speakers of the House of Commons...* (London, 1851), 423–31.

[208] G.V. Bennett, 'Conflict in the Church', 165.

Though Aldrich duly became Prolocutor of the Lower House of Convocation in 1702, events did not quite fall out that way: Rochester quit office as Lord President in a huff midway through 1703, having accomplished little. Had he stayed on longer Aldrich's political influence might have endured and he might have received a bishopric. As it was, when Rochester did return to office after the Tory landslide of 1710, Aldrich had just died, and Rochester followed him a year later.

His successor at the Deanery, Francis Atterbury, though talented enough, lacked Aldrich's finesse and adroit touch in politics (the two men, with fifteen years' age difference between them, cooperated uneasily). He returned to Oxford as the veteran and storm petrel of the Convocation campaign, determined to act as standard-bearer for the Church interest under Harley and Bolingbroke, and to work personally with them to vindicate it. It suited all parties, as Harley, together with Sir Simon Harcourt (Solicitor-General 1702-7, Attorney-General 1707-8), had been looking to court and cultivate senior Tory clerics from early in Queen Anne's reign. It was a means of building up their own interest among churchmen and securing Atterbury's good offices was a key part of that strategy. By 1705 he had emerged as Harley's acknowledged lieutenant in ecclesiastical affairs, 'indefatigable in his master's service'.[209] Brilliant, restless, and ambitious, Atterbury lapped up this attention and demanded influence on Tory policy formation in 1710-14, for instance, in ensuring the place of Convocation within the Constitution as the most effective vehicle for countering heresy and, at the same time, securing the integrity of ecclesiastical power against encroachment from the state.[210] His expectations of Harley as chief minister after 1710 were soon disappointed, and Atterbury switched his attention to Lord Bolingbroke as the man most likely to usher in what Gary Bennett famously referred to as an 'Anglican counter-revolution' [vis-à-vis that of 1688].[211] Much to the relief of his colleagues at Christ Church, Atterbury resigned the Deanery in 1713 (to be succeeded by a new dean in the Aldrich mould—George Smalridge) for a diocese and his own place in Parliament as Bishop of Rochester, acting as Bolingbroke's ecclesiastical lieutenant. If there was a principal author of the contentious Schism Act of 1714 to repress dissenting academies it was Francis Atterbury.[212]

---

[209] Bennett, *Tory Crisis*, 83, 86. Harley in 1704 promised him the succession to the Deanery of Christ Church whenever Aldrich should die. ibid., 128.

[210] Mark Goldie has argued that this position originated in his endorsement of the views of Henry Dodwell and similar Nonjurors. Goldie, 'The Non-Jurors, Episcopacy, and the Origins of the Convocation Controversy', in ed. E. Cruickshanks, *Ideology and Conspiracy: Aspects of Jacobitism, 1689-1759* (Edinburgh, 1982), 15-35.

[211] While still Prolocutor of the Lower House of Convocation (before he became a bishop), Atterbury also tried to concert his plans for the Church with William Bromley, by then the Speaker. Bennett, 'Conflict in the Church', 171-2. It was Bromley who later took the Schism bill through its Commons stages.

[212] Bennett, *Tory Crisis*, 176-7. See also Dickinson, *Bolingbroke*, 111, 120, 129. He worked in conjunction with his key Oxford ally, Lord Chancellor Harcourt. Holmes, 'Harley, St John and the Death of the Tory Party', 225.

406   ENLIGHTENED OXFORD

Atterbury's ministerial influence collapsed upon Queen Anne's death, and it was many decades before another senior Oxford academic had a corresponding degree of influence with ministers. This came in the shape of Nathan Wetherell, Master of University College, a far less mercurial personality than Atterbury. Though personally a High Tory with Hutchinsonian sympathies, he made his College central to realigning the Oxford 'New Interest' with George III's court and administrations in the 1760s and 1770s.[213] Wetherell's main point of contact in both was Charles Jenkinson, scion of an old Oxfordshire family,[214] and a University College graduate himself.[215] The two men established a friendship that worked in the University's favour well into the 1780s. Jenkinson made himself a master of networking in the new reign, starting out with holding the post of Lord Bute's private secretary from 1760. In 1763 he was appointed joint Secretary to the Treasury by George Grenville, a place he held for two years; he slowly emerged as leader of the 'King's Friends' after Bute's retirement, an inchoate grouping whose loyalties were determined by whoever the monarch deemed fit to serve him in office.[216] As far as Oxford was concerned, Jenkinson had two problems: firstly, his zeal on behalf of the Whigs in the 1754 county election had not been forgotten by the University Tories;[217] secondly, he was just a little too close to government. That past and that proximity worked against him when he stood for the University on a vacancy in February 1768 (when he was obliged to withdraw), and in the general election the next month, when his opponents successfully cast him as a ministerial dependent.[218] Jenkinson's importance only increased after Wetherell became a reforming vice chancellor (1768–72) and Lord North became Premier in 1770; it was Jenkinson who helped induce North to allow his name to go forward as a candidate for the Oxford Chancellorship in 1772.[219] When Jenkinson took office in 1778 as Secretary-at-War it was a non-Cabinet appointment, but his personal influence 'behind the curtain' with George III

---

[213] See Chapter 6, pp. 35–7.

[214] Jenkinson angrily insisted in debate on 12 Feb. 1770 on his genteel origins, when it was claimed his pompous manner did not become 'a gentleman risen from the situation he has done'. 'The Parliamentary Diary of Sir Henry Cavendish, 1768–74', quoted in L.B. Namier, *The Structure of Politics at the Accession of George III* (2nd edn., London, 1957), 11. Richard Pares argued that his 'total lack of personal charm' did Jenkinson's career no favours. *King George III and the politicians* (Oxford, 1953), 12n.

[215] Darwall-Smith, noting Wetherell's limited interest in scholarship, refers to Jenkinson as the former's 'true soulmate'. *University College*, 301.

[216] Black, *George III*, 68.

[217] See Ward, *Georgian Oxford*, 197, 205. Yet he had been a friend at Charterhouse of the Hutchinsonian Tory Jones of Nayland and would be the dedicatee of one of the latter's books. Sack, *From Jacobite to Conservative*, 76–7.

[218] ed. N. S. Jucker, *The Jenkinson Papers: 1760–1766* (London, 1949), xxi, 47–60. Both Wetherell of University College and Horne of Magdalen supported his candidature. BL Add MS 38457 *passim*.

[219] See Chapter 6, pp. 15–16.

OXFORD AND THE WORLD OF WESTMINSTER 407

outweighed his official status.[220] Jenkinson's interest in distinctively Oxford concerns and electioneering gradually tailed away in the early 1780s, and he thus refused Wetherell's blandishments and declined to put his name forward to replace Sir Roger Newdigate as a possible replacement burgess in 1780.[221] Though employed again in office by Pitt the Younger (especially after he took a peerage in 1786),[222] Jenkinson had far less influence over him as Premier than he had when North filled that role. Wetherell would have to look elsewhere.

The Master kept up his political interests principally through the talented classical scholar and Portland Whig, William Windham (1750–1810, matric. Univ., 1767), who, curiously enough, also held the office of Secretary-at-War (from 1794). Both men were profoundly committed to the struggle against Revolutionary France. They differed, however, on Catholic emancipation, with Windham resigning with Pitt over the issue in 1801 because it was not included with the Irish Act of Union. Wetherell gave no encouragement to Windham when, in 1801 and 1805–6, Windham was sniffing around to see if he might secure nomination when one of the University's parliamentary seats next fell vacant (Jackson was no less determined to keep him out). The ageing Master of University College (he died in 1807 after a forty-three year tenure) declared that he could not endorse someone who supported Emancipation, a measure that was 'pregnant with inevitable evils of the greatest magnitude both to Church & State'.[223]

Wetherell was too old, Windham too much his own man, for their relationship ever to make the impact on the life of the British state that the Jackson-Portland one delivered over two decades.[224] Jackson always took care to try and rise above narrowly Pittite and Foxite partisanship during his deanship, '...the man of all others' with his erstwhile charges who had progressed at his direction into public life, 'notwithstanding his great wig and short cassock, to whom a matter of feeling may be confided with perfect security of his entering into and understanding it'.[225] And, while Portland was in Opposition (1783–94), Jackson had other connections at a junior level in administration. For instance, Matthew Lewis (b. c.1750),

---

[220] For North's reliance on capable subordinates of non-Cabinet rank see Thomas, *Lord North*, 67, 108. For Jenkinson's confidential communications with the King between 1778 and 1782, often behind North's back, '...in tones that no one else presumed to use – rather like those of a tactful tutor helping his pupils along with advice and encouragement', see Stanley Ayling, *George III* (London, 1972), 278; Herbert Butterfield, *George III, Lord North and the People 1779–1780* (London, 1949), 31–2; Pares, *King George III and the politicians*, 171–2.

[221] Ward, *Georgian Oxford*, 276.

[222] cr. 1st Baron Hawkesbury, 1786; President of the Board of Trade, 1786; Chancellor of the Duchy of Lancaster, 1786; cr. 1st Earl of Liverpool, 1796. John Cannon, 'Jenkinson, Charles, first Earl of Liverpool (1729–1808), politician', *ODNB*, online version, 2013.

[223] BL Add MS 37909 f. 38, quoted in Darwall-Smith, *University College*, 300.

[224] See Chapter 6, pp. 25–7.

[225] Canning *Letter-Journal*, 112, 29 May 1794. Cf. the comment of Thomas Dibdin: 'few men could dress themselves in the robes of authority with greater dignity and effect'. *Reminiscences*, I. 80n.

408   ENLIGHTENED OXFORD

Deputy secretary and First Clerk at the War Office from the early 1770s, was 'from his earliest years' his 'most intimate friend';[226] the two men met regularly when Jackson was in London (he was a preacher at Lincoln's Inn). But it was particularly after Portland very slowly gravitated towards Pitt and away from Fox, that the Dean was able to make a further range of contacts in the ministerial team during the 1790s (often with young ministers who were Christ Church graduates themselves). It increased his influence across a range of government departments beyond the Home Office and its secret sub-department to create in time 'a Christ Church phalanx in government administration, with Christ Church patrons in the Cabinet'.[227] Between 1794 and 1802, the college acted as a kind of anteroom to state employment in a surveillance capacity.

In terms of influencing patronage and appointments in both Church and state, Cyril Jackson eventually acted as an Oxford counterbalance to George Pretyman, Bishop of Lincoln, Pitt's original clerical adviser. His commanding position in the University ensured that his 'influence...extended way beyond the walls and out into wider society where a Christ Church nomination could easily forestall any contest for a prime position'.[228] Jackson's opinion counted. He was universally respected and was on occasion willing to initiate delicate negotiations at the highest level; in May 1803 he produced an unsuccessful plan to bring Pitt back into the ministry, using the Dukes of York and Portland as intermediaries with Henry Addington.[229] Neither did he follow fashionable opinion, for he was, in his way, an old-fashioned Whig, who originally looked to Lord Rockingham's followers for preferment. Thus, when Burke's *Reflections on the Revolution in France* were being acclaimed across the nation in 1791 by everyone from the King down, Jackson took a different line. As the young 3rd Lord Holland reported: 'The Dean of X Church is very violent against Burke, & seems to treat him & his opinions as either mad or something worse'.[230] Over the next few years he adopted more authoritarian views and never strayed too far from Portland in politics. When Portland was Premier (1807–09) Jackson was a frequent, informal visitor to Downing Street. On the Duke's death, Jackson regretted he had lost a friend to whom 'next to my duties at Christ Church, my whole mind and its affections were chiefly directed—'.[231] Cyril Jackson was but the latest in a long line of Oxonian

---

[226] Canning, *Letter-Journal*, 34, 2 Dec. 1793; 100, 12 May 1794; 112, 29 May 1794.

[227] Durey, 'The Christ Church Connection', 723.   [228] Curthoys (1), 210.

[229] Addington declined. Malmesbury, *Diaries and Correspondence,*, IV. 255–6, 259; ed. Lord Colchester, *The Diary and Correspondence of Charles Abbot, Lord Colchester, Speaker of the House of Commons 1802-1817*, (3 vols., London, 1861), I. 422–4; John Ehrman, *The Younger Pitt: The Consuming Struggle* (London, 1996), 605n. Lord Hawkesbury (2nd earl of Liverpool from 1808), son and heir of Charles Jenkinson, Addington's Foreign Secretary 1801–4, had been at Christ Church under Jackson in the late 1780s. Canning, *Letter-Journal*, 253, 16 May 1795.

[230] BL Add MSS 51731, f. 4,1 12 May [1791] Holland to Caroline Fox. Jackson adopted more authoritarian views in the course of the decade. Bill, *Education at Christ Church*, 79.

[231] To William Howley, LPL, MS 2186, f. 10, quoted in Bill, *Education at Christ Church*, 66.

OXFORD AND THE WORLD OF WESTMINSTER   409

eminenti whose connections with ministers linked the University to the centre of power, though his reach was exceptional.[232] He acted more as a fellow patron alongside ministers than as their client, a position of de facto equality that had never quite been equalled earlier.

The extent of his prominence and patronage as dean eclipsed anything that would have been available to him in any but the most senior bishoprics and he was never much tempted to accept any of the senior appointments in the hierarchy that were dangled before him. In 1794 he refused the offer of the 'poor' see of Bristol;[233] then, on Bishop Smallwell's death in 1799, he advised the government to give the vacant Oxford diocese to his younger brother, William Jackson (1751–1815) rather than himself;[234] the following year he was offered the see of Armagh (and thus the Primacy of the Irish Church) on the death of another Oxford man, Archbishop William Newcome, and was one of several who turned down the honour, for all that it was a critical moment in the life of Ireland with the Act of Union on the statute book and the associated (and rather sudden) declining likelihood of Catholic emancipation in the immediate future.[235] Apart from his nurture of talent, a further reason behind Jackson's pre-eminence in government circles was his first-hand familiarity with the state of the country. With British travellers largely cut off from the Continent after the French Revolutionary Wars began, Jackson, most summers, toured one region or other of the British Isles, gaining instruction and knowledge in addition to visiting friends and pupils.[236] And, though committed (not uncritically) to maintaining the status quo in Church and state,[237] Jackson took care to cultivate friendships with Dissenters and others of differing views.

---

[232] See the discussion of his career in Ibid., 64–84, who, unaccountably claims that Jackson had 'little political influence'. Ibid., 67.

[233] Jackson to Pitt, 2 Mar. 1794, TNA (PRO) 30/70/3/182. However, in 1787 he had applied to the Earl of Lonsdale when the see of Carlisle fell vacant. He knew of Lonsdale's influence in the appointment and hoped that the Earl would confirm Pitt's understanding that it was Oxford's turn for an episcopal vacancy. BL Egerton MS 2181, f.54, Autobiography of Bishop John Douglas.

[234] For the Dean's rather dismissive view of his brother, see Bill, *Education at Christ Church*, 78. The younger Jackson had to wait until 1812 before becoming Bishop of Oxford. Bishop Cleaver of Chester, the Principal of Brasenose, was also considered by his brother Euseby, Bishop of Ferns (Ireland) to be interested in translation to Oxford. WSRO, Petworth House Archives, PHA57/17, E. Cleaver to 3rd Earl of Egremont, early 1799. In 1799 the Regius Professor of Divinity, John Randolph (1749–1813), was eventually named to the vacancy.

[235] He might also have followed his predecessor but one in the Deanery, William Markham, as Archbishop of York in 1807. Bill, *Education at Christ Church*, 68.

[236] 'He sought for information, and obtained it, from every one that came in his way, from sailors, fishermen, workmen, and artisans'. GM, 89 (1819), II. 460. He was even famously arrested as a spy in 1804! Bill, *Education at Christ Church*, 75. Commending Dean Jackson to his brother, the Cornish baronet, Sir Christopher, the author and traveller John Hawkins wrote in 1792: 'He is a man of eminent classical learning and better informed upon general subjects than any priest I ever knew with the most liberal manners.' WSRO, J/1/2246c.

[237] For Jackson being 'mightily pleased that his advice and Mr Pitt's [to Canning] should have so exactly tallied' (on a pragmatic approach to resisting repeal of the Test Act), see Canning, *Letter-Journal*, 97–100, 12 May 1794.

410 ENLIGHTENED OXFORD

ii) Lawyers and the University

Jackson had the ear of ministers as an exceptional college head driving forward the reform of the curriculum and producing gifted elite graduates, many of whom had gone on to the Inns of Court after Oxford.[238] It had become a well-trodden path: Oxford graduates who were the sons of country gentlemen and clergy returned in large numbers to practice at the Bar after 1760 and were apparently more prepared to protect clerical interests than their predecessors of the first half of the century.[239] The rise in the number of qualified barristers drawn from both English universities (a cause dear to Blackstone),[240] was also the fruit of a diverse if not dynamic legal culture in Oxford, for the cult of the English common law was already well-established at the beginning of the century and was further refreshed by publication of Sir Matthew Hale's posthumous *The History of the Common Law of England* (1713).[241]

Meanwhile, the civil-law tradition continued to be upheld at Oxford, with a small number of students studying for the BCL degree. Few of these planned to become advocates of Doctors' Commons, still less to a pursue political careers.[242] But the politics of those who held the Regius Chair in Civil Law (attached to Corpus Christi College) were generally a consideration in their appointment. Among its more distinguished holders (from 1796) was Burke's younger friend (and his literary executor), French Laurence (1757–1809), who had helped prepare Warren Hastings's impeachment a decade earlier. His appointment before the era of the Portland Chancellorship would have been improbable.[243] All Souls was a particular centre for civilians, but formal teaching of the subject was really pioneered by Robert Eden and Francis Walwyn from the 1730s at University College. Eden, (he was later Archdeacon of Winchester), expounded elements of the civil law according to the method and order of Justinian in a textbook published in 1743 and designed with the students he was already teaching in mind.[244] That classic organisational model of Justinian's *Institutes* drawn from

---

[238] See Chapter 6, pp. 27–8.

[239] P. Lucas, 'A collective biography of the students and barristers of Lincoln's Inn, 1680–1804: A study in the "Aristocratic Resurgence" of the eighteenth century', *JMH*, 46 (1974), 227–61.

[240] In 1768 the four Inns of Court decided to allow Oxford and Cambridge graduates to qualify in three instead of five years. Paul Lucas, 'Blackstone and the reform of the legal profession', *EHR*, 77 (1962), 456–89. For reflections on legal pedagogy as it stood at the start of the century see T. Wood, *Some Thoughts Concerning the Study of the Laws of England in the Two Universities* (London, 1708).

[241] Jonathan Clark, *From Restoration to Reform. The British Isles 1660–1832* (London, 2014), 195.

[242] See J. L. Barton, 'Legal Studies', in HUO V, 593–605, at 594–600.

[243] For Bishop Warburton's amusement at a previous Civil Law Professor being made Professor of Arabic see Uncatalogued MS. Letters between the Revd. Mr Warburton and Dr Taylor (later Sir Robert Taylor) from the Year MDCCXXVIII [Harry Ransom Center, University of Texas at Austin], no. 96, 7 Feb. 1768. Lectures in civil law ceased to be delivered around this date.

[244] Darwall-Smith, *University College*, 263. Scholarship in Roman Law continued into the second half of the century. Thus Alexander Crowcher Schomberg, probationer Fellow of Magdalen from 1782 until his death, produced *An historical and chronological View of Roman Law*, 1785 (translated into

OXFORD AND THE WORLD OF WESTMINSTER   411

late antiquity also inspired those engaged with the native common-law tradition led by Thomas Wood (1661–1722), Fellow of New College, who in 1720 published his *Institute of the Laws of England*.[245] But it was the foundation of the Vinerian chair in 1753 under the bequest of Charles Viner that underlined the University's commitment to legal scholarship that would most benefit future practitioners at the English bar. For the first time students could hear lectures and be taught in the English common law as well as in Roman Law, and thus be of immediate value to those undergraduates considering using the law as a means to a parliamentary career.[246] For a while, the first holder of the chair (1758–66), William Blackstone, had hopes of turning the study of the common law into a university discipline, with New Inn Hall becoming exclusively a lawyers' college, but his ambition never gathered sufficient traction.[247] However, there were unofficial lawyerly collaborations within Oxford, notably the University College Club (founded in 1792), presided over by William Scott.[248] One of its leading luminaries, William Jones, demonstrated how readily politically ambitious lawyers could combine their ambitions with academic study of the law with his brilliant *An Essay on the Law of Bailments* (1781) with its arguments for the integration of Roman and Common law ideas.[249]

Unsurprisingly, many Oxonian lawyers, once qualified, rose, like William Jones, to the top of their profession as legal practitioners and developed client links to government, as he did, briefly, while the 2nd Earl of Shelburne (1737–1805) was Premier (1782–3). They were thus well-placed to try and make

---

French), and *A Treatise on the Maritime Laws of Rhodes* (1786). Thompson Cooper, 'Schomberg, Alexander Crowcher (1756–92), poet and writer on jurisprudence', rev. Rebecca Mills, *ODNB*, online version, 2004.

[245] Brockliss (2), 280. He had previously produced a *New Institute of the Imperial or Civil Law* (London, 1704).

[246] H. G. Hanbury, *The Vinerian Chair in English Legal Education* (Oxford, 1958). The chair was elective and attracted a lot of interest from voters when there was a vacancy, as in 1777. William Jackson gleefully noted to his pupil: 'I hope you took notice what a respectable minority I was in on the Vinerian Election. We are getting into a dreadful way of canvassing on every occasion—almost as bad as a Cornish Borough'. 29 Apr. 1777, Jackson to Lewisham, Staffs RO, Dartmouth MSS, D(W)1778/V/ 862. The successful candidate with 236 votes was Richard Woodoeson (1745–1822), previously deputy to Robert Chambers. He narrowly defeated Giles Rooke, the future judge, who had 231. Wooddeson lectured and published on English law while holding the chair and acted as counsel to the University. GM 47 (1777), 194.

[247] Brockliss (2), 276, 312. Blackstone's successor as second Professor, Robert Chambers, was a largely absentee Principal of New Inn Hall from 1766 to 1803. He became a member of the Supreme Court of Bengal in 1777 and persuaded the University to allow him to go to India with permission to reoccupy his chair if he found the conditions unsuitable. T. M. Curley, *Sir Robert Chambers: Law, Literature, and Empire in the Age of Johnson* (Madison, WI, 1998), 32, 43, 69, 71; Hanbury, *The Vinerian Chair*, 52–4.

[248] Curley, *Sir Robert Chambers*, 65.

[249] 'It is startling for its daring and innovative use of Natural [law] methodology, and without overstatement it can be said to have heralded a new era in treatise-writing in the Common law'. Jean Meiring, 'Conversation in the Law: Sir William Jones's Singular Dialogue', in eds. K. Halsey and J. Slinn, *The Concept and Practice of Conversation in the long Eighteenth Century, 1688–1848* (Newcastle-on-Tyne, 2008), 128–50, at 146.

ministers aware of academic opinion and then reiterate at Oxford what was said at Westminster, in effect, act as mediators between two different but related worlds of mutual influence and intrigue. In the dramatically changed landscape of the 1690s, Heneage Finch, MP for the University 1689–98 and 1701–03,[250] exhibited a constructive, Tory influence in national politics that reflected the willingness of the Finch family to work with the new Williamite regime (embodied in his brother, Daniel, 2nd Earl of Nottingham, serving as senior Secretary of State, 1689–93). Heneage was a sufficient force in the Commons that his keenness to throw the weight of the Church party behind the government in 1690 was vital in stabilising the new status quo. The divergence between the two Finch brothers, Daniel and Heneage, neither standing aloof from state affairs (despite both voting for a Regency in the 1689 Convention Parliament),[251] and the two Hyde brothers, Henry and Laurence, the one a Nonjuror, the other in injured Opposition, made for a striking dynastic contrast in Toryism in William's reign.

Heneage Finch had a sharp intellect that was reflected in his parliamentary interventions and a capacity for advancing himself at court because of his talents as an advocate and a parliamentarian. There were regular rumours over several years that he would be named as Attorney-General or even Lord Chancellor, but it never happened. Nottingham's loss of office in late 1693 removed one obvious springboard; Heneage Finch's public refusal in the Commons, alongside the High Tory leader, Sir Edward Seymour, to accept William as 'rightful and lawful king' in February 1696, did him no favours at court;[252] and his declining influence as the Augsburg League War ended was compounded by poor health. Finch made a comeback and re-entered the Commons in 1701 with a fresh interest in 'country party' issues, though he was firmly identified with the court again after Anne's accession. Though never a minister himself between 1689 and 1702 (his slightly uneasy stand-off symbolised the University's post-Revolutionary dynamic), he was an accomplished legal operator that ministers could never comfortably overlook.

When Anne was queen another Oxford lawyer, Simon Harcourt (Pembroke College), was the most important Tory counsel of his day, acting as a counter-weight to a distinguished phalanx of Whig rivals and holding the offices of Solicitor-General between 1702 and 1707, and then Attorney-General, 1707–08 and 1710. He endeared himself to majority Oxford opinion by his canny defence of Sacheverell at his trial in Westminster Hall. Once the Harley government was formed, he was sent to the House of Lords with a barony as Lord Keeper (Lord Chancellor from 1713), and gradually aligned himself with the Bolingbroke/

---

[250] Hon. Henege Finch, educ. Westminster and Ch. Ch. Paul D. Halliday, 'Finch, Heneage, first earl of Aylesford (1648/9–1719, lawyer and politician', *ODNB* online version, 2008.

[251] M. B. Rex, *University Representation in England* (London, 1954), 313–18.

[252] Burnet, *History*, IV. 306. He was one of eighty-nine MPs who refused to swear the association oath in 1696.

OXFORD AND THE WORLD OF WESTMINSTER   413

Atterbury wing of the party. And with Christ Church. His son and heir, Simon Harcourt (b. 1684) was taught there in Aldrich's time, and the ambitious father kept up the connection and favoured the 'House'. Its tutors were part of a plan to have the younger Simon (MP for Wallingford in the 1710 Parliament) selected as a candidate for the University in 1713 in lieu of Sir William Whitelock. The plan withered, because of the father's poor relations with Vice Chancellor Gardiner and the Harleyite resentment at a vulgar intrusion sanctioned by Atterbury.[253]

Another legal well-wisher to Oxford in a later generation was Dr George Lee, MP (?1700–58), an admirer of Earl Granville's, who developed a close association with Leicester House and Prince Frederick in the late 1740s.[254] Had both he and his princely patron lived longer, then Lee's star might have risen well beyond the orbit it actually achieved in his lifetime: Dean of Arches (with a knighthood and Privy Councillorship) from 1751, indicating his status as the senior 'civilian' lawyer in the country, a position he held concurrently with that of Treasurer of the Household to Princess Augusta, Prince Frederick's widow.[255] When MP for Brackley, he had been one of the counsel offering legal advice to the University in March 1736 as it confronted the challenge that the Mortmain Bill offered and, thereafter, though a moderate Whig and place-hunter, he continued to function as a protector of the Church's interests and, by extension, Oxford's.[256]

It was, however, another lawyer who, at one time, nurtured his Leicester House connections, William Blackstone, the first Vinerian Professor 1758–66, who, more than any other legal figure, straddled the Oxford/Westminster divide. He had a capacity for contemporary constitutional analysis that transcended party affiliation and, by the 1760s, gave him a status, in Jonathan Clark's phrase, as 'the country's quasi-official legal oracle'.[257] Blackstone was pre-eminently an All Souls academic lawyer rather than a practitioner, and one whose ambition was knowingly tempered by his commitment to mid-century Tory politics. Thus he, a strong organiser for Newdigate's candidature for a University seat in 1750–1,[258] would not endorse the Pelhamite ascendancy, and it may have cost him his chances of taking up the Regius Chair of Civil Law in 1753, despite—or perhaps

---

[253] Ward, *Georgian Oxford*, 49. Simon Harcourt senior had himself thought of being adopted as a University candidate at the 1698 General Election. http://www.historyofparliamentonline.org/volume/1690-1715/member/harcourt-simon-i-1661-1727 He is further considered in Chapter 7, pp. 40–1.

[254] For his rivalry with the 2nd Earl of Egmont as Prince Frederick's adviser, see ed. A. Newman, 'Leicester House politics, 1750–60, from the papers of John, second earl of Egmont', *Camden Miscellany*, XXIII, CS, 4th ser., 7 (1969), 85–228.

[255] Frederick had earmarked Lee to be Chancellor of the Exchequer in any administration formed after his accession. Foord, *His Majesty's Opposition*, 275. Along with most of Prince Frederick's followers, Lee made his peace with the Pelhams in 1751, and was again talked of by Newcastle as a possible Chancellor. Clark, *The dynamics of change*, 34, 112, 132–3, 162–4. He resigned his position in Princess Augusta's household shortly before his death as, with the rise of Lord Bute and a 'new' Leicester House opposition, his own influence tailed off. Walpole, *Memoirs of George II*, III. 28; McKelvey, *George III and Lord Bute*, 19–21, 123.

[256] Ward, *Georgian Oxford*, 157. Lee was a Ch. Ch. graduate, BCL 1724, DCL., 1729.

[257] *English Society 1660–1832*, 34.   [258] Prest, *William Blackstone*, 100–5.

414 ENLIGHTENED OXFORD

because of—the endorsement of William Murray (Lord Mansfield, LCJ from 1756) with his hereditary Jacobite background.[259] He got his own back in the county election of 1754 when he backed the 'Old Interest', produced a signed treatise denying the right of copyholders to a freehold vote, and wrote pseud-onymously against the Whigs.[260] Like so many Oxonians, he came into his own in the new reign when, newly appointed Principal of New Inn Hall, he became a King's Counsel and Solicitor General to Queen Charlotte (1763–70), the model of a court lawyer. The appointments were something of a reward for Blackstone's services in aligning Tory support behind the Bute government, on whose behalf he was quite prepared to negotiate with non-Old Corps Whigs such as Henry Fox and Lord Shelburne, elder brother of his former pupil, Thomas Fitzmaurice.[261] Blackstone was by no means the last Oxford lawyer to assume pre-eminence as the century drew to a close, as the exceptional careers of the two Scott brothers, Sir William and Sir John (respectively Lords Stowell and Eldon), testified. The former, in the first half of his career, gave the University exceptional service, and the latter, in his unwavering and eloquent commitment to the pre-reformed status quo in Church and state, acquired a totemic significance for Oxford ultra-Tories.

iii) Conclusion

> ... it seems to me the farthest thing in the world from what ought at least to be the design of a seminary of Learning, that any animosity shou'd arise there against any man's sentiments in the search of knowledge; which can only be had by the freedom of debate, & without which an University wou'd contradict its nature & shall I say its name.
>
> Arthur Onslow to Conyers Middleton, 6 July 1733, in ed.
> Mary Clayton, *A Portrait of Influence. Life and Letters of Arthur Onslow, the Great Speaker* [Parliamentary History: Texts & Studies 14] (London, 2017), 67.

---

[259] Ibid., 108–9; D. A. Lockmiller, *Sir William Blackstone* (Chapel Hill, NC, 1938), 39; L. S. Sutherland, 'William Blackstone and the Legal Chairs at Oxford', in eds. R. Wellek and A. Ribeiro, *Evidence in Literary Scholarship: Essays in Memory of James Marshall Osborn* (Oxford, 1979), 230–5.

[260] W. Blackstone, *Considerations on Copyholders* (London, 1758); *JOJ*, 12 May 1753; Clark, *English Society 1660–1832*, 242; Ward, *Georgian Oxford*, 196–7, who notes that Richard Blacow considered him to be the anonymous pro-Tory 'Coryphaeus' in the *London Evening Post*.

[261] Ward, *Georgian Oxford*, 216, 219–20. Bishop Warburton, for one, was unimpressed: 'I am returned to my first opinion of Blackstone, which was that he had a mean servile ambition that dispose[s] him to betray his principles, whether they were good or bad; he was first a Tory with his better knowledge of the Law, & [an] enlarged prospect of preferment made him a Whig...' Uncatl. MS. Letters [Harry Ransom Center, University of Texas at Austin], no. 105, 13 Nov. 1769.

If Abuse of this University is with some People become a fashionable Topick of Conversation; it is no less fashionable with others to admit every new-invented Story against it as an incontestable Truth, I had almost said, as an Article of Political Faith.

> [A.M.], A Letter from A Member of the
> University of Oxford, to a Gentleman in the Country;
> Containing a Particular Account of a Watch-Plot (London, 1754), 4.

There may have been occasional threats of visitation, ministers may have been vexed by the behaviour of ill-disposed dons and riotous, irresponsible students, but the two-way relationship between Oxford and Westminster was a fundamental aspect of public culture, its synergies apparent in every direction. The going for the University was certainly not easy at Westminster before the 1730s with the 'Robinocracy' and then the Pelhamites entrenched in power. Whig supremacy was riveted on to Britain after 1714 despite the strength of Tory sentiment in the country at large, and the Whigs did not hesitate to take advantage of the other party's difficulties in crafting and articulating a Toryism that reflected national endorsement and might commend the party to the incoming dynasty. Given that political reality for the incoming Townshend-Stanhope ministry, the University might have hoped for conciliation from the new Whig government instead of confrontation and the ever-present possibility of coercion and a clean sweep of Tories in the colleges. It survived, and Walpole had no intention—if he could possibly avoid it—of imitating Stanhope and Sunderland and planning a full-blown visitation of Oxford with a view to statutory overhaul of its constitution. In his mind, the Established Church, through the patronage system, the prorogation of Convocation, and the repeal of the contentious legislation of Anne's reign, had been sufficiently brought to heel. And if the Church had been institutionally weakened and shown its dependence on Whig politicians and Whig politics, then Oxford by definition had been weakened.

It is here perhaps that the answer lies to the insistent question of why the Whig Ascendancy never in the end reformed Oxford. Such a policy was liable to divert government energies needlessly and attract a wide-ranging opposition in the Commons as a reflection of the University's influence over the MPs it had educated. Oxford was never short of defenders at Westminster, several of them, such as Bishop Atterbury or William Bromley, household names. Even when times were unpropitious, as they were for so much of the first half of the century, the University could rely on its graduates, wherever they were placed—in Britain or abroad, as landowners, clergy, ministers, members of either House of Parliament—making the best interests of Oxford a rule of conduct throughout life. That was supremely the case for MPs for the University and, invariably, one or both of them were among the most prominent and accomplished performers in the Commons, on whom the national spotlight often fell. Moreover, given that

Cambridge was not really considered to require externally imposed remodelling, singling out Oxford was rendered additionally awkward. Even the intended policy of re-educating the University in a Whig version of the recent past, intimated by the creation of the Regius Professorships in 1724, was not purposefully followed up by ministers, whose enthusiasm was less marked than their master's.[262] Oxford was thus left to its own devices until the 1850s, more by good fortune than by conscious policy.

That said, ministers were not beyond encouraging Oxford Whigs to be aggressive within the spectrum of University politics and beyond, and to project an increasingly implausible martyred image. For party warfare remained intensive right up to the late 1750s with bouts of intensive exchanges (particularly when an election was imminent) that could present an immensely disputatious and litigious scene. And the aftermath of the '45 for a while showed that not much was required to rekindle all the old Jacobite suspicions in government circles. That Oxford was synonymous and coterminal with Toryism (and, by extension, with Jacobitism) remained central to Whig apologetics until the middle of the century. If, after the accession of George III, the old suspicions of ministers were not extinct in some academic quarters until the 1770s, they were on their last gasp: by the last quarter of the century, Heads of House such as Wetherell and Jackson were using their considerable range of Westminster contacts to make their colleges virtual antechambers to government service for a select number of undergraduates. It was yet another sign of the reaffirmation of Oxford's centrality to the Georgian constitution that would only be finally dismantled between 1828 and 1832.

[262] Ward, *Georgian Oxford*, 133–4.

9

Beyond the University

Outreach and connections in England, Wales, Scotland, and Ireland

Away from St James's and Westminster, there were multidirectional human and cultural movements between Oxford and other parts of the country, making nowhere in Britain potentially beyond the influence of the University and its colleges. Its graduates are the obvious cases in point, representing, consciously or otherwise—and for better or worse—the values of the University some distance away from its purlieus, where Oxford was known by reputation rather than first-hand familiarity. Locally and regionally, the University was woven into the fabric of day-to-day life. It occupied much the same physical space as the City of Oxford, and thus relations with the municipality had constantly to be (re)negotiated to facilitate the optimum working of both institutions. Beyond the urban centre was the county of Oxfordshire, where the scale of the University's status as a patron and employer gave it a presence in the management of county affairs; it looked reciprocally to the major landowners and boroughs in Oxfordshire to confirm and uphold its importance, culturally and politically. This hinterland extended into Buckinghamshire, north and west Berkshire, and much of Northamptonshire and Warwickshire where, often literally, all roads led to Oxford. The University's extramural involvement was always most in evidence (often dramatically so) at election times when many of the colleges—not least because of family connections and (related) political concerns—exercised an influence pro or contra a particular candidate in several constituencies, notably the county of Oxfordshire itself. And the university, the city, and the county were ever more au fait with each other's life through press reports, especially after the inauguration of *Jackson's Oxford Journal* in 1753 by William Jackson, printer, a title that publicised information and carried reports (and gossip) about local worthies.[1]

Nationally, Oxford's influence was ubiquitous as a major landowner, but extended beyond acreage and income: the ties between individual colleges such as Queen's, Exeter, and Wadham with the regions were enduring, especially in education, where particular schools expected to send their pupils on to their 'own' Oxford college. Considered generally, Oxford graduates as schoolmasters and

---

[1] Oxford had acquired its first newspaper in 1737. Black, *The English Press 1621–1861*, 9.

Enlightened Oxford: The University and the Cultural and Political Life of Eighteenth-century Britain and Beyond.
Nigel Aston, Oxford University Press. © Nigel Aston 2023. DOI: 10.1093/oso/9780199246830.003.0010

118   ENLIGHTENED OXFORD

ushers could play a considerable educational role in the formation of their charges through curriculum preferences and pedagogic talents and were at least as vital as the parish clergy in forming the Anglican identities of the young entrusted to them. The University's cultural connections via its graduates extended to all parts of the kingdom. Wales had its own route to Oxford through Jesus College; there were established reciprocal movements in personnel between Trinity College, Dublin, and the University, and, likewise, for Scotland. Scottish students committed to the episcopalian tradition were naturally attracted to Oxford, and there was a regular traffic between Glasgow and Oxford in young men looking to complete their education south of the border, via the Snell exhibition at Balliol College. Whether considered in terms of physical space or cultural connection and educational formation, Oxford's presence in provincial England and in aspects of Welsh, Irish, and Scottish life, was never far away.

Part A: The City and the county

i) Beyond the University: the City of Oxford

... the small but complex society, set in an equally small and beautiful, but very dirty and unsalubrious, town, ...

> Lucy Sutherland, *The University of Oxford in the Eighteenth Century. A Reconsideration* [James Bryce Memorial Lecture, 1972] (Oxford, 1973), 12.

Ever since the City has been patronized by the Two Noble Families of Blenheim and Whytham, it has done well. Its Trade has flourished, and its Inhabitants have been revered.

> 'To the Worthy Freemen of the City of Oxford', 29 Mar. 1784, Bodl. MS Top Oxon. c. 280 f. 115.

The complicated collective identities within the city required much cultural negotiation. In past centuries, the University and the corporation had had their differences and their confrontations, but in this era, there was an underlying effort at institutional cooperation, and a readiness not to meddle unhelpfully in each other's affairs.[2] It helped that Oxford was a Tory-controlled corporation until after the accession of George III. It also suited the majority of the University that the

---

[2] For jockeying between the mayor and vice chancellor in the seventeenth century, see Alan Crossley, 'City and University', in HUO IV, 105–35, at 120–1. The Freemen of the town (sometimes called 'Hanasters') were all members of one or more Guilds and had the exclusive right to constitute the 'Commons' of Oxford. They elected twenty-four Councillors (for life) on to the Common Council; the Cabinet or 'Thirteen' was composed of the Mayor, four Aldermen, and eight assistants. All members forming the 'Thirteen' also held office for life. The franchise was burgage tenure of the Corporation and Freeman type.

BEYOND THE UNIVERSITY 419

heads of a cadet branch of the Bertie family, the 1st and 2nd Earls of Abingdon from nearby Rycote Park, were high stewards of the borough, kept a magisterial eye on municipal affairs, and worked to ensure Tory party advantage in elections both to the mayoralty and to the city's two seats in Parliament.[3] In 1695, Thomas Wharton, the aggressive Whig 'fixer', put up a candidate as mayor to challenge the influence of his despised brother-in-law, Lord Abingdon, but it was rebuffed.[4] The Whigs also made occasional efforts to nominate a parliamentary candidate for the city, with nothing much to show for it until a municipal financial crisis opened the way to their infiltration. A cash shortage in 1766–8 necessitated a search for ready money, and at last gave an entrée to the powerful Blenheim interest in the form of the 4th Duke of Marlborough and his family connection.[5] Tories were not unduly troubled since the Duke was a pre-eminent courtier and personal friend of King George; they were less comfortable with the other joint patron, Willoughby Bertie, 4th Earl of Abingdon, a bitter opponent of the North government. The two noblemen put up their brothers to represent the City of Oxford: Lord Robert Spencer (Ch. Ch., 1762–5), 1771–90, and the Hon. Peregrine Bertie (a retired naval officer, of Weston-on-the-Green), 1774–90. Both (especially Lord Robert) were, after 1784, ready to give their votes to the Opposition. Spencer's total commitment to Fox had, by 1790, made him persona non grata to the city, the University, and his embarrassed brother, the Duke.[6]

Irrespective of political differences, successive earls of Abingdon were generally trusted by both dons and freemen and could act as intermediary in any minor constitutional squabbles between the two. There were occasional spats between individual colleges and the Council over matters such as rights of way, but nothing that commanded wider attention. The relationship was formally governed by past precedents and customs that were usually respected and were formalised by the annual commemoration of the St Scholastica's Day Riot 1355. Every 10 February the Mayor and Bailiffs (together with sixty-three citizens representing the alleged number of scholars slain on that day) would march 'in penance' to St Mary's Church to swear to uphold the University's privileges.[7] Here the Vice Chancellor, the Vicar of St Mary's, the Proctors, and the University Registrar received sixty-

[3] R. Fasnacht, *A history of the city of Oxford* (Oxford, 1954), 128. In 1749 Thomas Rowney became High Steward, to be succeeded by Sir James Dashwood in 1759. Both were Tory MPs for the City and the first commoners to hold the office since 1605. *Wood's Ancient and Present State of the City of Oxford*, ed. Peshall, 361.

[4] Christopher Robbins, *The Earl of Wharton and Whig Party Politics 1679–1715* (Lewiston, NY, 1991), 94.

[5] Fasnacht, *City of Oxford*, 127ff. Cox, *Recollections*, 68, noted the city's reputation as 'a Blenheim Borough'. For the corporation's unsuccessful attempt to bribe its sitting MPs in 1766 to pay off its accumulated debts see Thomas, *George III*, 184. See generally R. Sweet, 'Freemen and independence in English borough politics c.1770–1830', *P&P*, 161 (1998), 84–115.

[6] John Cannon, 'The Parliamentary representation of the City of Oxford 1754–90', *Oxoniensia*, 10 (1960), 102–8; eds. Green and Roberson, *Studies in Oxford history*, 214–15.

[7] Pantin, in *Oxford Life in Oxford archives*, 98–104, argued that the death toll in 1354 was much less than sixty-three, so the reasons for choosing that number are by no means clear.

120   ENLIGHTENED OXFORD

three pennies, usually in small silver coins.[8] It was a well-rehearsed ceremony with a sermon and litany that caused minimal friction in this era.[9] The Mayor and the Vice Chancellor also acted jointly to enforce the Assize of Bread at the city's market until it was abolished in 1813.[10] Nevertheless, disputes between town and gown over quotidian matters such as market supervision, street maintenance, alehouses, building developments, and noctivagation, were part of the background to Oxford life. For its part, the University had historically used its court leet (jurisdiction over petty offences) to dampen civic pride and register complaints over encroachments on the city waste (undeveloped land), though the court gradually fell into disuse from the late seventeenth century.[11] Eventually, in 1768, the University set up a permanent body of Delegates of Privileges to ensure its interests were protected vis-à-vis the municipality.

Issues of status still occasionally rankled, especially over 'privileged persons'. These were matriculated local tradesmen (usually barbers, booksellers, and college servants),[12] sworn to the service of the University, and largely exempt from municipal jurisdiction. In any disputes—and these tended to be over financial services and payments—a claimant was obliged to seek redress in the Chancellor's Court.[13] Fresh mutual misunderstanding about spatial presence and control also occurred from time to time. The result could be a furious iteration of perceived rights and angry exchange of correspondence often threatening resort to the law courts or even the Privy Council. When Queen Anne visited the University on 26 August 1702 the Delegates of Convocation required that Heads of Houses make clear 'that no Scholar (during her Majesties stay) presume to appear about the Court, Street, Inns or any public houses whatsoever' with any offender's name to be entered into 'the Black-Book, and kept back from his Degree'.[14] The plan was defective. The University and the corporation had not liaised over the order of their respective processions, and they had collided and jostled near St Peter's-

---

[8] *VCH Oxon.*, IV. 53–6, 159–60, 246; L.H. Buxton and Strickland Gibson, *Oxford University Ceremonies* (Oxford, 1935), 153–5.

[9] In 1690 the city attacked the ceremony as 'too great a badge of popery to be required in a protestant university', but it was shrugged off by the University and not repeated. Crossley, 'City and University', HUO IV, 105–35, at 121–2. A committee was appointed in Jan. 1793 to go into the question of the St Scholastica's Day payment, but it lasted only a month. And in 1800 the Mayor failed to attend the ceremony. C. J. Day, in 'The University and the City', HUO VI, 441–76, at 441. It was abolished in 1825. Cox, *Recollections*, 112–14.

[10] See this chapter, p. 11. The 1771 Improvement Act provided for the continued appointment by the University of Clerks of the Market (a title first used in 1513) to control it.

[11] *VCH Oxon.*, IV. 130–40; I. G. Philip, 'The Court Leet of the University of Oxford', *Oxoniensia*, 15 (1950), 81–91; Pantin, *Oxford life in Oxford archives*, 91–6. The city's court leet survived until 1839.

[12] Members of the Company of Barbers (which had been incorporated by the Chancellor of the University as early as 1348 and existed until 1859) dined once a year with the Vice Chancellor and supped annually with the Proctors.

[13] The most celebrated dispute in this era concerned the barber, William Taman. See ed. Hobson, *Oxford Council Acts 1752–1801*, 184, 223, 252–4.

[14] *Advertisements from the Delegates of Convocation for her Majesties Reception, to be delivered by Heads of Houses with great charge to their Respective Colleges and Halls*, OUA: WPy/28/8/37.

BEYOND THE UNIVERSITY   421

in-the-East church and again in the High Street. Chaos briefly ensued, causing what the University called 'a publick & notorious disturbance in the presence of the Queen's most excellent majesty'. The incident created vexation among senior academics and protests were lodged with the city Council, the University angrily contrasting the two corporations, one 'engaged in the profession of the most noble and useful sciences; the other consisting partly of creditable retail tradesmen, but for the most part of the lower rank of mechanics'.[15] The corporation responded thus to the Vice Chancellor's complaint issued through Convocation on 11 Sept. 1702: '... the Citty would have been well pleased if any Expedient could have been found to prevent the mixture of their body with the Members of the University; Itt not appearing to the Citty that the order of proceeding of the Members of the University and Citty in such processions, hath ever yett been settled'.[16] Neither party was prepared to contemplate easily sacrificing its prominence on a state occasion. However, once tempers had cooled on both sides, a plan to govern future processions was worked out to mutual satisfaction in 1703.

Oxford's built environment outside the University and the colleges, like that of many larger English towns, was considerably renewed during the century,[17] and the trend was variously encouraged by some senior members of the University. Levels of expectation rose over time as other cities 'improved' and an 'enlightened' public came to see uncleanliness and squalor as incompatible with civic life, prompting a form of partnership between the University and the Mayor and Corporation in the management of the townscape. Largely because of the lobbying of Vice Chancellor Wetherell,[18] a 1771 Act of Parliament (the first of the Oxford Mileways Acts) allowed for many improvements on the main streets of the city, sweeping away jumbled buildings and alleys (especially in and around the High Street), through the auspices of a Paving Commission with power to raise income through the rates.

Down went the remaining North and East Gates, and in went a wider and grander entrance over Magdalen Bridge (1779) to improve the flow of long-distance traffic coming into the city from the east. Further regenerative work took place to pave all the thoroughfares and streets of the town after a further statute was passed in 1781.[19] The conduit on Carfax that had served the University

---

[15] OUA: register of convocation 1693–1703, NEP/*subtus*/30, register bc, minutes at end, quoted in Crossley, 'City and University', 121; T. Wood, *A vindication of the proceedings of the University of Oxford* (Oxford, 1703).

[16] OUA: SP/D/9. Common Council insisted the disorders were caused 'by the Crowd of persons of all sorts at that time of night as well as Strangers as Cittyzens pressing to see her Majesty, without any Intension to disturb the procession, or to raise disputes concerning itt; and without the Consent or allowance of this Citty'. OUA: SP/D/9.

[17] Langford, *A polite and commercial people*, 424–32, for the numerous 'Improvement Acts' obtained by urban councils across the nation.

[18] See Sutherland, 'The administration of the University', in HUO V, 205–26, at 222–4.

[19] For the city's petition to Parliament in Nov. 1770 see ed. Hobson, *Oxford Council Acts 1752–1801*, 86; Midgley, *University Life*, 92–5. For financial irregularities following the 1771 Act see England, *An*

Fig. 9.1 Oxford High Street, Thomas Malton the Younger, oil on canvas, 1798–9 (Yale Center for British Art, Paul Mellon Collection).

since 1617 had become an obvious obstruction to traffic (especially on market days) and did not survive these alterations, though it was not removed from its central location until 1787, despite sustained municipal grumbles.[20] Street paving, cleaning, and lighting were all reorganised by the commissioners, to general approval.[21] The University and the city were equally committed to these improvements as the membership of the 1771 Paving Commission suggested, with the Vice Chancellor (he usually presided at meetings of the Commission until the late 1780s) and University officers, Heads of Colleges and Halls, and fifty-two Doctors of Divinity having places on it. The Commissioners were empowered by the 1771 Act to set up the Market Committee, another Town and Gown body (six members of the Corporation and six members of Convocation) that drove forward the construction of the new covered market in the centre of the town,

---

Attempt to state the accounts of receipts and expences relative to the Oxford Paving Act: with remarks (Oxford, 1774), quoted in R. Sweet, *The English Town 1680–1840. Government, Society and Culture* (Harlow, 1999), 108.

[20] C. Cole, 'Carfax conduit', *Oxoniensia*, 29–30 (1964–5), 142–66, at 144, 147, 149, 150; *Wood's history of the city of Oxford. Vol. 1: the city and suburbs*, ed. A. Clark, (Oxford, 1889), 63; H. E. Salter, *Oxford city properties* (Oxford, 1926), 355–6.

[21] *VCH, Oxon.*, IV. (1979), 232; Emily Cockayne, *Hubbub. filth, noise & stench in England 1600–1770* (New Haven, CT, 2007), 246–7. For earlier complaints see 'A Citizen', *A candid remonstrance* (London, 1764).

BEYOND THE UNIVERSITY 423

opened in 1774.[22] Similarly, in October 1795 a committee was set up to discuss with the Vice Chancellor the trades and professions which should be considered as privileged by each body.[23] These changes amounted to a shift in power in Oxford towards bodies on which Town and Gown were represented equally and which they jointly financed.

No one took a greater interest in town planning than Edward Tatham, Rector of Lincoln College from 1792. In his *Oxonia Explicata et Ornata* (1773) he produced a detailed improvement blueprint which, he prophesied, if adopted, would one day see 'Oxford the most splendid spot of ground, of its extent, in the European nations'. His wish list included placing 'a grass plot with shrubs' in St Giles, 'or a piece of water extended down the centre with a road for carriages and foot path on either side, which will carry with it an air of elegance'. St Mary's church was daringly slated for removal as it 'is not equal to so venerable and august an assembly as that of this University, and is inferior to other buildings'.[24] Tatham was delighted when the local Improvement Commission in Oxford initiated a major street-clearance programme, observing:

> Our forefathers seem to have consulted petty Convenience and monastic Reclusiveness, while they neglected that Uniformity of Design, which is indispensable to Magnificence, and that Elegance of Approach, which adds half the Delight.[25]

The Oxford Common Councillors were from the elite of the citizenry, but it was with those lower down the social scale that dons such as Tatham would be likely to have first-hand dealings. College servants (including women) connected them to the life of the town; Oxford shopkeepers sold them personal items; innkeepers and coffee-house waiters supplied them with wine, beer, and coffee. Given that University members were obliged to wear academic dress when out in the city it was hard for them to merge into the mass of urban faces. There were occasions when distinctions melted. Riots were one but, more convivially, town and gown blended in one crowd celebrating the (false) news of Admiral Edward Vernon's victory of 1741 over the Spanish defenders of Cartagena.[26] Only a few University

---

[22] ed. Hargreaves-Mawdsley, *Woodforde at Oxford*, 188. Profits from the market were to be divided equally between the University and the town. The City of Oxford had serious financial problems in the 1760s and 1770s and these acted as an incentive to cooperation. In 1772 the city, with the University, borrowed £5,000 on the security of the new market. ed. Hobson, *Oxford Council Acts 1752–1801*, 93.

[23] Ibid., 237. The arrangement with the Company of Barbers in Jan. 1796 might have been a positive result of this meeting. ibid., 241.

[24] Tatham, *Oxonia Explicata et Ornata. Proposals for the disengaging and beautifying the University and City of Oxford* (Oxford, 1773), cited in ed. Hobson, *Oxford Council Acts 1753–1801*, App. iii, 301, 303, 305; Green, *Lincoln College*, 361.

[25] *Oxonia Explicata et Ornata* quoted in P. J. Corfield, *The Impact of English Towns 1700–1800* (Oxford, 1982), 176.

[26] Bodl. MS. Rawlinson Letters 96, f. 50. In Nov. 1740 the Welsh Red Herring Club had met to celebrate the birthday of Admiral Vernon, as the hero of the victory at Porto Bello: the King's Head's windows were illuminated and there was a bonfire outside. Bodl. MS. Top. Oxon. f. 49, 29.

men nursed the desire to go academically undressed and incognito in the city, though Thomas Warton the Younger was one such. The Professor of Poetry was fascinated by 'the theatre of death', as were so many of his contemporaries. Warton had a 'propensity to be present at public exhibitions, as to have induced him at a time, when he was desirous of not being discovered, to attend an execution in the dress of a carter'.[27] Other gownsmen were more interested in visiting the prisoners at Oxford gaol in the Castle, such as James Woodforde of New College, who sought out the condemned awaiting execution.[28] The young John Wesley and other members of the 'Holy Club' went to the gaol regularly in the early 1730s to minister to the incarcerated (with the permission of the governor and the chaplain) and encourage offenders to repent through reading prayers, taking services, and distributing pious books such as *The Whole Duty of Man* and Nathaniel Lardner's *The Christian Monitor*.[29] Wesley also made a point of visiting the debtors' prison in the North Gate known as Bocardo, attempting to instruct the prisoners' children and making over to them small sums for their immediate needs.[30]

At the level of the middling sort, the relative compatibility of University members with the citizens and their families came to be less problematic, though there could be occasional flare-ups and townsmen tended to be intolerant of insults, real or threatened. Thus when George Monk Berkeley, the grandson of the philosopher, said he would not 'put on his best clothes to speak ye prologue at Blenheim before such rabble as the Oxford Citizens. This got about, & the town had like to have been too hot for him.'[31] Generally, the fashionability of politeness reduced the social distance between the two sectors. Indeed, it was remarked by some outsiders that the reputation of Oxford townsfolk for politeness arose because of the frequent opportunities they had of conversing with scholars and students.[32] It might be exampled in the Oxford dancing master Matthew Towle, who made a living instructing or writing about the finer points of deportment, posture, and movement, and provided exhaustive rules for genteel behaviour in

---

[27] ed. Richard Mant, *Poetical Works of... Thomas Warton, B.D.....* (5th edn., Oxford, 1802), ciii.

[28] ed. J. Beresford, *The Diary of a Country Parson: The Reverend James Woodforde. 1758–1781* (5 vols., London, 1924–31), 2 Feb. 1761, 28 Feb. 1763, 22 Mar. 1762, 13 Mar. 1775, cited Midgley, *University Life*, 146.

[29] V. H. H. Green, *The Young Mr Wesley. A study of John Wesley and Oxford* (London, 1961), 141, 157–9, 162, 171, 181, 185. His father, Samuel Wesley, had done the same himself as an undergraduate. The SPCK had long had a policy of sending each county jail in England a package of religious literature, including (the Nonjuror) and a Bible.

[30] Ibid., 160, 181. For Bocardo see *VCH Oxon.*, IV. 334–5.

[31] George Horne to George Glasse, 22 Oct. 1787, Houghton Library, Harvard University, MS Hyde 61 (1.27).

[32] See N. Spencer, *The Complete English Traveller, or a new survey and description of England and Wales* (London, 1771), 464. The adult male literacy rate in the city was running at 77% (1799–1804). Corfield, *The Impact of English Towns*, 142.

varied circumstances.[33] Townsfolk could also be tempted to ape the literary styles and concerns of the educated. Thus N. Elliot, 'Shoe-maker, in St Ebb's-Lane, Oxford', produced his *The Atheist* (London, 1770), a poem that ranges discursively around contemporary society in a loosely Popean manner, and attracted many Oxonian subscribers, including Bishop Lowth and the traveller James, Lord Deskford (later 7th Earl of Findlater, 1750–1811). Certainly, there was an increasing overlap and convergence in the places town and gown might frequent. This propinquity acted as a fillip to share physical spaces with each other (not necessarily at the same time), such as in the Oxford Physic Garden which acquired more significance as a pleasure garden and place of common recreation than as a centre of medical botany.[34] It could be included in any perambulation as part of the water meadows east of Magdalen College surrounded by branches of the River Cherwell and associated with Addison, who, partly inspired by them, had composed the first version of his *Pleasures of the Imagination* in 1712.[35]

ii) Beyond the University: the county of Oxfordshire

> In this part of our county, there are more fine houses near each other than in any, I believe, in England.
>
> Passages from the Diaries of Mrs Philip Lybbe Powys
> of Hardwick House, Oxon, AD 1756 to 1808 (London, 1899),
> ed. E. J. Climenson (London, 1899), 194–5, 12 Aug. 1778.

The county of Oxfordshire, along with adjacent parts of Berkshire and Buckinghamshire, was particularly familiar to those dons who, in conjunction with their fellowships, held rural livings (usually within a ten-mile radius of the University) and did their pastoral duties in person rather than appoint a curate, though many did just that.[36] Christ Church, for example, offered twelve perpetual curacies (in effect, vicarages paid by stipend from a trust or endowment fund) in 1778 that could be held with Studentships, most of which were within easy riding distance of Oxford.[37] On Saturday evenings or very early on Sunday mornings such individuals could be seen leaving the city and hacking across country to hold services and thereby become familiar at first hand with these parishes and

---

[33] Towle, *The young gentleman and lady's private tutor* (Oxford, 1771). See Philip Carter, 'Polite "Persons": character, biography and the gentleman', *TRHS*, 6th ser., 12 (2002), 333–54, at 340.

[34] Chapter 5, pp. 73–4.

[35] Paul A. Elliott, *Enlightenment, modernity and science. Geographies of scientific culture and improvement in Georgian England* (London, 2010), 130–2.

[36] Bodl. MS Rawl. J. 4°.24 lists benefices belonging to the University and Colleges in the 1740s. Fifty-seven were in their gift in Oxfordshire (including nine in the city). There were also many in contiguous Northamptonshire and Berkshire, as well as Hampshire and Wiltshire, slightly further afield.

[37] Curthoys (4), 47, 218.

426 ENLIGHTENED OXFORD

their people.[38] Not all of these men were necessarily parish priests in their own right. Thus Isaac Crouch, as Vice-Principal of St Edmund Hall between 1783 and 1807, did Sunday duty at Chislehampton and Stadhampton for the absent incumbent.[39] The task of preaching the word and administering the sacraments required a capacity for adaptability rather than academic credibility,[40] and it was met in every generation by a handful of Oxford scholars, including men of the eminence of John Mill at Bletchingdon and Robert South at Islip, in their person, however indirectly, taking the scholastic world out into the countryside, and their corner of the county back into their colleges. Those who were not interested in such a ministry either did not take a local living or nominated a deputy to do the duty, but the experience could also act as a 'taster experience' for young dons who might, in the normal course of things, get married and move to a parish in another region of England. In practice, combining non-residence with the proficient undertaking of pastoral work appears to have been hit and miss, and a Christ Church parish such as Drayton St Leonard (Oxon.) was often held by Students who employed a curate. In such circumstances, parishioners might feel hard done by, though grievances were seldom publicly aired.[41]

Some men, however, became quite acclimatised. Edward Tatham, the Rector of Lincoln College, came to enjoy rural living so much that he scarcely ever resided in Oxford, farmed his own glebe at Combe along the Evenlode valley, prided himself on his pigs, and often brought them into the city to market with him.[42] Others used their parish as a seed ground for antiquarian scholarship. Thus White Kennett's reputation as a teacher of history inside the University in the 1690s was enhanced by the work on the tenurial history of north-east Oxfordshire that he undertook while holding the living at Ambrosden. His *Parochial Antiquities attempted in the History of Ambrosden, Burcester, and other Adjacent Parts in the Counties of Oxford and Bucks* (Oxford, 1695) has been called 'a microcosm of feudal history' based on the rich layers of new documentation he had collected from the late Saxon era.[43] It was not his antiquarianism but his politics that brought Kennett into conflict with the squire of Ambrosden, Sir William

---

[38] The nearer a parish was to Oxford the more convenient it tended to be. For the unsuccessful efforts in 1769 of John Warneford, Camden Professor of History since 1761, to obtain the living of Garsington in preference to his resident curacy at Wappenham, south Northants., see ed. G. Eland, *Shardeloes papers of the Seventeenth and Eighteenth Centuries* (Oxford, 1947), 43–5.

[39] Kelly, *St Edmund Hall*, 70. He was also a regular preacher at St Mary's university church.

[40] Bishops could be insistent on emphasising the need for pastors to moderate the content and tone of their sermons according to the composition of their congregation. See, for instance, Gibson, *The charge of Edmund lord bishop of Lincoln, at his primary visitation, in the year 1717* [London, 1717], 13–19.

[41] Curthoys (4), 50.

[42] Cox, *Recollections*, 234; Green, *Lincoln College*, 378. For his argumentative wife see *Procs. Oxf. Arch & Hist Soc.*, VI (1894), 3–4.

[43] Bennett, *White Kennett*, 159, 163. Bennett deemed it 'a clear and sober book unmarred by a polemical purpose'. In Jack Simmons's view, Kennett merited the appellation of 'the Father of Parish History'. Simmons, *Parish and Empire: Studies and Sketches* (London, 1952), 119.

Glynne, briefly a burgess for the University.[44] He came to detest White Kennett as his parish priest at Ambrosden (he had been nominated by Glynne's father), following his 30 January sermon to the House of Commons in 1704, critical of Charles I and fervently in favour of the War of Spanish Succession. Francis Wise (1695–1767), the Keeper of the University's archives (from 1726) and Radcliffe Librarian, 1748–67, had a more congenial relation with his patrons, the North family of Wroxton. From them in 1726 he received the donative (in effect, a stipendiary curacy) of the benefice of Elsfield on the edge of Otmoor, where he improved the manor house, kept his fine library, and transformed the garden with cascades and triumphal arches, as well as replicas of the tower of Babel, an Egyptian pyramid, and a Druidic temple.[45]

The Cherwell took the traveller west into the Oxfordshire countryside and, as on the other points of the compass, out into the land holdings of the University's elite neighbours whose influence was appreciable and whose goodwill could not be presumed.[46] The ties of family, friendship, and clientage between the University and the nobility and gentry of the county oiled their dealings, and Oxford offered honorary degrees and college invitations to satisfy cravings for status and conviviality among the non-clerkly. Many senior dons served as Justices of the Peace in the county, such as Theophilus Leigh and John Cooke, President of Corpus after 1783, latterly the 'Father of the University', whose obituary described him as an 'upright and attentive magistrate'.[47] Politics, of course, was likely to be decisive in determining the relationship, for whereas the majority of country gentleman and beneficed clergy in the county were Tories, the leading peers and major landowners were Whigs. When party hostilities were at their most intensive in the first half of the century, that alignment was a material consideration both for the University corporately and for its senior members individually, who might forgivably covet the offices and livings in the gift of the grandees.

The point was driven home in 1705 when a grateful monarch awarded the 1st Duke of Marlborough the royal manor of Woodstock, the land on which the vast Blenheim Palace (always known as 'Blenheim House' in the eighteenth century)

---

[44] Sir William Glynne, 2nd Bt., a Tory. MP Oxf. Univ. 1698–1701; Woodstock 1702–5; DCL 1706. Other dons, including Thomas Tanner, worked on the manuscript collection housed in Glynne's library at Ambrosden. www.historyofparliamentonline.org/volume/1690-1715/member/glynne-sir-william-1663-1721

[45] Alexandra Walsham, *The Reformation of the Landscape. Religion, identity & memory in early modern Britain & Ireland* (Oxford, 2011), 321; Sir George Clark, *Elsfield church and village* (Oxford, 1975); S. Gibson, 'Francis Wise, BD, Oxford antiquary, librarian and archivist', *Oxoniensia*, 1 (1936), 173–95. He also held the rectory of Rotherfield Greys in the south of the county (1745–67).

[46] Land in the ownership of individual colleges in the county was also appreciable. Adderbury, south of Banbury, was one such college-owned village (New College). eds. Buxton and Williams, *New College Oxford*, 31.

[47] *GM*, 93 (1823), I. 281. For his involvement in the Oxford food riot of 1800, see Charles-Edwards and Reed, *Corpus Christi College*, 271.

Fig. 9.2 Sir George Rooke, Michael Dahl, oil on canvas, c.1706 (© National Portrait Gallery, London).

would be built, a mere eight and half miles away from Carfax.[48] The Marlborough influence (there were no other dukes primarily resident in Oxfordshire) almost overnight became the determining factor in county politics, given the 1st Duke's status as commander-in-chief of the allied forces in Flanders 1702–12 and Duchess Sarah's place as Queen Anne's Groom of the Stole and Mistress of the Robes.[49] However much Tories sneered and hymned their heroes Sir George Rooke and the Duke of Ormond, the Marlboroughs commanded too much influence at court (except between 1710 and 1714) for the University leadership to ignore them, and it was drawn into an enduring symbiotic relationship born out of topographical proximity rather than natural affection.[50] Dr William Lancaster of Queen's, for one, took no time in realising the value of having Marlborough as

---

[48] £260,000 had been spent on its construction by 1716, when Blenheim was still far from complete. David Green, *Sarah, Duchess of Marlborough* (London, 1967), 204. The total cost was eventually £300,000. James Lees-Milne, *English Country Houses: Baroque* (London, 1970), 183.

[49] But it did not confer an immediate advantage: both Duke and Duchess were vexed by the Tory landslide in Oxfordshire in the 1710 General Election. Harris, *The General in Winter*, 318.

[50] 'Blenheim is a curse upon this place', observed the Harleyite Tory Canon Stratford of Ch. Ch. in 1711. HMC, *Portland MSS*, VII. 55.

his patron and was ready to risk accusations of toadying while Vice Chancellor (1706–10) to ease the trials and tensions of these first years of the new Blenheim-Oxford axis.[51] They could have been worse. But the 1st Duke's commitment to commanding the Queen's armies, his absence abroad for much of the year, the unfinished state of Blenheim, Duchess Sarah's indifference to the vast pile, and, above all, his own diffidence about the learned, limited his impact on the University and reduced his appeal as a patron.[52]

The 1st Duke was moribund from strokes for some time before his eventual death in 1722. He may have gone, Blenheim remained, along with the ducal influence that came back in full flood locally after the thoroughly Whiggish Charles, the 3rd Duke (1706–58), bent on securing a predominant county interest vis-à-vis the Tory 3rd Earl of Abingdon once and for all, took reluctant possession of the house on his grandmother's demise in 1744.[53] As part of that campaign, the new duke and his followers joined in the general hue and cry against Oxford in the wake of the Blacow incident and Dr King's speech in the late 1740s without academe being unduly troubled by their involvement.[54] But, by the time of his death, in 1758, the asperities of party warfare were beginning to be downplayed, and the relationship between Oxford and the long-lived George, 4th duke (1739–1817) was cordial:[55] his tutor and chaplain, John Moore (Archbishop of Canterbury from 1783), was warmly received in Christ Church upon nomination by the Crown to a canon's stall in 1763, when Marlborough was the King's Lord Chamberlain.

It helped that the Duke and George III were both contemporaries and temperamentally akin; it was irksome from an academic vantage point that, despite being Lord Lieutenant of the county, Marlborough from the late 1770s retreated into private life with ever more application, and viewed the affairs of Oxford University with relative passivity—except for his astronomical passion.[56] Marlborough was a

[51] Lancaster was essentially a courtier but worked for the Whig interest in Oxfordshire during the 1710 General Election. Ward, *Georgian Oxford*, 39. For the 1st Duke's support of John Potter for the Regius Professorship of Greek in 1707 in defiance of University majority opinion, see Chapter 3, pp. 45–6. Lancaster failed to gain either the see of Chichester or an Irish bishopric, which he believed might be the prizes on offer for his following the Duke.

[52] Winn, *Queen Anne. Patroness of Arts*, 413.

[53] Sarah had earlier strengthened her interest as a result of the quarrel between Lord Abingdon and the Oxford freemen. Harris, *A Passion for Government*, 269.

[54] The Duke was quite frank: 'I hated . . . Oxford for being so near Blenheim'. Marlborough to Henry Fox, Blenheim, 13 July 1749, Holland House papers, BL Add MS 51386, f. 48. See also f. 58. He also disliked Cambridge on other grounds. And this was despite his being awarded a complimentary DCL. Thomas Hunt to Richard Rawlinson, 6 June 1746, Bodl. MSS Rawl. letters 96, ff. 235–5.

[55] For George III's visit to Blenheim in 1786, see Chapter 7, p. 84; M. Fowler, *Blenheim. Biography of a Palace* (Harmondsworth, 1989), 112–16.

[56] 'The Duke', wrote John Byng, 'lives the life of a quiet domestic gentleman, surrounded by his children', *Torrington Diaries*, I. 192. That ideal appealed equally to King George. cf. Marlborough's brother-in-law, the Earl of Pembroke: The duke 'will hardly stir any more. He is so benothinged, and so beset . . . that His Grace's oysterical apathy is baneful to all near him as well as to himself'. Pembroke to Lord Herbert [1781], ed. Lord Herbert, *Pembroke papers (1780–1794)*, *Letters and diaries of Henry, tenth earl of Pembroke and his circle* (London, 1950), 177. There is a jaunty account of him in A. L. Rowse, *The later Churchills* (London, 1958), 87–160.

competent amateur astronomer who built a private observatory, and produced reams of mathematical calculations, corrected by the Savilian Professor, Thomas Hornsby.[57] Other dons who appeared as guests at Blenheim when the chance arose included such as John Randolph, Regius Professor of Divinity, who was happy to dignify some dull but fashionable amateur theatricals in October 1787 with an excessively deferential epilogue to a performance of *The Guardian*, followed by the Vice Chancellor himself (in company with two bishops and three deans) to view the Spencer family and their friends act out *False Delicacy* and *The Liar*.[58] They gained little for their pains. For the Duke had minimal interest left in the world beyond Blenheim, Woodstock, and the city of Oxford. One Oxonian whom he judged ill-suited actually became his son-in-law. This was the amateur thespian, Edward Nares (1762–1841), fellow of Merton College from 1788, Bursar after 1794,[59] who had the cheek—or the daring—to court and secretly marry the Duke's favourite daughter, Lady [Georgina] Charlotte Spencer.[60]

Blenheim hemmed in the University to the north; to the south was the Whiggish enclave of the Harcourt family at Nuneham Courtenay, acquired in 1710 (their original landholding locally had been at Stanton Harcourt, six miles to the west).[61] The Harcourts were newly minted Whigs. Simon, 1st Lord Harcourt, had been one of the staunchest Tories in the county and a friend of the University on a basis of mutual interest during the Harley/St John ministry; he also turned out to be one of the many fair-weather Tories who could not resist Whig blandishments after 1714.[62] Such a volte-face naturally induced the Harcourt family to view the predominant Tory interest at Oxford differently and the 2nd Viscount (1714–77) (created 1st Earl Harcourt 1749), as a lifelong

---

[57] The Duke was elected FRS in 1786, and presented Oxford University with a large telescope and a number of paintings. Rowse, *The later Churchills*, 160 and n.

[58] 'Blenheim House Theatre', in *Town and Country Magazine or Universal Repository* 18 (Oct. 1787), 437–8; Fowler, *Blenheim. Biography of a Palace*, 84. For the Duke himself serving refreshments on an occasion when the Corporation of Oxford attended the Blenheim theatre, see *The Life and Times of Frederick Reynolds* (2 vols., London, 1826), I. 8.

[59] He was vicar of St Peter's-in-the-East, Oxford from 1792, Bampton Lecturer in 1805, and Regius Professor of Modern History from 1813. G. Cecil White, *A Versatile Professor. Reminiscences of the Rev. Edward Nares, DD* (London, 1903); A. P. Ledger, *A Spencer Love Affair. Eighteenth-Century Theatricals at Blenheim Palace and Beyond* (Fonthill, 2014). Nares as historian is discussed in Black, *Charting the Past*, 229–32.

[60] Fowler, *Blenheim*, 117–19. Lady Charlotte ran off to meet him unannounced at Henley-on-Thames in 1797, prompting him to express anxiety and embarrassment in equal measure to the Duke.

[61] *VCH, Oxon.*, XII., ed. Alan Crossley (Oxford, 1990), 274–81; *VCH, Oxon.*,V., ed. Mary D. Lobel (London, 1957), 234–49. They made many real estate purchases in and around the county on the basis of the 1st Lord's income at the bar.

[62] For his earlier career see Chapters 7, 8. Harcourt did not forget his ties to the University. See HMC, *Portland MSS*, VI. 345, 19 Jan. 1723, for Harcourt setting up as a benefactor to Oriel. For the distrust of his new allies see Nicholas Papers, BL Egerton MS 2540, f. 283, George Clarke to Edward Nicholas, 23 June 1724: 'Our malicious Whigs, who don't love him; set about a groundless story, I dare say, that his pension is stop'd, wch I believe they wish, for they don't love him; tho' he has been so serviceable'.

BEYOND THE UNIVERSITY   431

court Whig, worked to advance the 'New Interest' with energy and consistency. He was never quite able to disassociate the University from treason until the accession of George III made the presumption entirely implausible.[63] Harcourt had been the future king's governor in 1751 and dominated Queen Charlotte's household in the 1760s (first as her Master of the Horse, then as her Lord Chamberlain).[64]

Such contacts with the new royal family made a rapprochement with the Harcourts more than expedient for the University authorities. The initial beneficiary of this refreshed relationship was Harcourt's chaplain, Joseph Hoare, Principal of Jesus College (1768–1802), who was made a prebendary of Westminster Abbey in 1762.[65] When the 2nd Earl inherited the estates and titles in 1777, the Harcourts had become a generally benign presence in south Oxfordshire, politically marginal, personal friends—and loyal servants—of the King and Queen from the 1780s, and the proud possessors in Nuneham Park of the Carfax Conduit (moved there in 1787).[66] A peerage family that did hold fast to their Hanoverian Toryism were the Anglo-Irish Annesleys, earls of Anglesey, of Bletchingdon Park on the north-east side of Oxford. For all his proven capacities in office and parliament, Arthur, the 5th Earl (suc. 1710), was eventually marginalised in public life after the Hanoverian succession and the earldom passed to one distant cousin and the Bletchingdon estate to another.[67]

The last of Oxford's immediate four noble neighbours—the Bertie family— moved more slowly from Toryism to Whiggery than the Harcourts and ended the century with a decidedly non-court version of it. The Berties, earls of Abingdon (1682), owned extensive estates at Rycote Park near Thame and Wytham Abbey (three miles away from Oxford but just inside Berkshire). They were, at the Revolution, the principal power brokers in the county but could not, in terms of money and influence, compete with their great ducal rivals at Blenheim and were, a century later, a waning force in Oxford and neighbourhood. Their political allegiances varied but, for the most part, they interacted cordially with the

---

[63] He told Newcastle, 'Tory or Jacobite, which are so much alike that I could never distinguish the difference'. BL Add MSS. 32728, f. 364, 24 July 1752. For his role in the 1754 Oxfordshire election, see this Chapter, p. 43, n. 107. Neither the 1st nor the 2nd Earl Harcourt followed the 1st Viscount to Pembroke, or indeed any other Oxford college.

[64] Martyn J. Powell, 'Simon, first Earl Harcourt (1717–1777), politician and administrator in Ireland', *ODNB* online version, 2006.

[65] *Fasti*, VIII. 83–97. Hoare was notable as the only Head of House who had wanted to relax subscription in the early 1770s. Brockliss (2), 216. Thomas Bray, Rector of Exeter College (1771–85), was another academic favoured by the 1st Earl. When the latter was appointed Lord Lieutenant of Ireland in 1772 he awarded Bray the deanery of Raphoe, which he quickly exchanged for a canonry of Windsor in 1774. *GM* 55 (1785), 324.

[66] The 2nd Earl had a private key giving him access to Christ Church Walk. He also sponsored an Oxford poetry prize.

[67] Anglesey's Oxford connection was tenuous. He was a Cambridge graduate, sat as one of its MPs between 1702 and 1710, and acted as High Steward between 1722 and his death. http://www.histparl.ac.uk/volume/1690-1715/member/annesley-hon-arthur-1678-1737

432   ENLIGHTENED OXFORD

University.[68] The 1st Earl (1653–99), a committed Tory commanding a county elite dominated by Tories, was reinstated as Lord Lieutenant after the Revolution and held that commanding role in Oxfordshire life until 1697 when he was dismissed for failing to sign the Association in defence of King William.[69] His son, however, Montagu Venables-Bertie, the 2nd Earl (1673–1743), could expect no easy reversion to that office with the Marlboroughs recently domiciled at Blenheim. His politics (he was a Hanoverian Tory), his lesser land holdings, and his bank balance counted against him and he was Lord Lieutenant only between 1702 and 1706, and 1712 and 1715, when the Marlboroughs were out of favour during the Harley administration. The 2nd Earl proved unequal to the pressures of sustained opposition, and his previously assertive leadership of the Tory county interest languished post-1715.[70] Their common exclusion from royal esteem in the early Hanoverian decades positioned the University with the Abingdons, and that situation continued after Montagu's nephew, Willoughby, succeeded as 3rd Earl (1692–1760).[71]

Willoughby, 4th Earl of Abingdon (1740–99), was an independent Whig who was profoundly opposed to the American War. His politics set him at odds with majority opinion in the University, but his encumbrance with debts generated by his addiction to the pleasures of the turf (despite marrying an heiress, he died insolvent) limited his public impact locally and nationally; he abandoned Rycote to his creditors in the early 1770s in favour of Wytham.[72] Abingdon's passionate lifetime musical interests both as a minor composer himself and as patron of Karl Friedrich Abel and J. C. Bach reached its apogee when Haydn visited England in the 1790s. Abingdon, who had known him for many years, was as instrumental as anyone in bringing Haydn to England and so to Oxford for his degree.[73]

Beyond the inner ring of aristocratic landowners were other landed peers whose interest in favour of the University could not be presumed. The Parker family at Shirburn Castle (acquired in 1716) near Watlington was not at first easily

---

[68] The earls of Abingdon had the right to name one of the forty Students of Christ Church. Salmon, *The Foreigner's Companion*, 80.

[69] Paul Monod, 'Jacobitism and country principles in the reign of William III', *HJ*, 30 (1987), 289–310, at 296; Robin Eagles, 'A man subject to vapours': James Bertie, Earl of Abingdon, and his brothers, c.1670–1699', in https://digital.bodleian.ox.ac.uk/collections/rediscovering-rycote/

[70] HMC, *Portland MSS*, VII. 115, 139; Colley, *In defiance of oligarchy*, 181. This despite his brother, the Hon. Charles Bertie, being a fellow of All Souls and Sedleian Professor in the 1720s. It was reported that 'by removing the Bucks and Does from Oxford to Cumnay [sic] . . .' Abingdon's influence in Oxford urban elections was also declining, for all that he was High Steward and Recorder of the Borough. ed. Linnell, *The diaries of Thomas Wilson,* 6 Dec. 1732, 82.

[71] He refused to join the Oxfordshire Association in 1745. R. J. Robson, *The Oxfordshire Election of 1754: A Study in the Interplay of City, County and University Politics* (London, 1949), 2.

[72] There were sales of goods and furnishings at Rycote Park in 1779 and 1780. See Bodl. MS. Top. Oxon. b.121, f.65.

[73] George Colman, the Younger, *Random Records* (2 vols., London, 1830), II. 284n; R. Hughes, *Haydn* (London, rev. edn., 1974), 68–9, 90–1; R. Leppert, *Music and Image. Domesticity, ideology and socio-cultural formation in eighteenth-century England* (Cambridge, 1988), 139–143.

courted.[74] Lord Chancellor Macclesfield, the 1st Earl (in office 1718–25), had been a proponent of subjecting the University to a governmental Visitation until the confirmation of Walpole in power in 1721 and his own disgrace four years later on charges of peculation wrecked his hopes. Macclesfield had no sympathies for high-flying clergy, as his devastating speech against Sacheverell at his impeachment only confirmed. But then he had been the friend of Bernard Mandeville, the quondam patron (at a distance) of John Toland, and had made Pierre Des Maizeaux, the Huguenot journalist and talented networker with a personal interest in heterodox religion, tutor to his heir.[75] Though publicly favouring the Low Church party,[76] Macclesfield was comfortable giving the impression that he leaned towards deism or even atheism.[77] His son, the 2nd Earl, a highly competent mathematician, astronomer, and President of the Royal Society from 1752, built a superb library and observatory at Shirburn Castle.[78] As the patron and friend in succession of Bradley and Hornsby, he ensured that the Parker family came to stand at much less of an academic and social remove from the University by the mid-century. The conferring of an hon. DCL on Macclesfield on 3 July 1759 was both a recognition of his intellectual distinction and a gesture towards neighbourly harmony.

The Parkers were newcomers to Oxfordshire and had a reduced impact on county affairs because of the burden placed on their finances by the £30,000 fine imposed on the 1st Earl when he was convicted on impeachment of corruption charges in 1725. And his family had no connection with Oxford University through educational formation. The same could hardly be said for the Hydes at Cornbury Park though, like the Parkers, they had only acquired their principal

---

[74] See M. F. Parker, *Scattered Notices of Shirburn Castle, Oxfordshire* (London, 1887).

[75] Des Maizeaux supplied Macclesfield with books and papers and passed the summer of 1716 at Shirburn. He promoted the work of Toland and Anthony Collins, the latter being his friend and another patron. E. Grist, 'Pierre Des Maizeaux and the Royal Society', in eds. A. Thomson, S. Burrows, E. Dziembowski, and S. Audidière, *Cultural transfers: France and Britain in the long eighteenth century* (Oxford, 2010), 33–42, at 36, 39–40; S. Mandelbrote, 'Pierre Des Maizeaux: History, Toleration, and Scholarship', in eds. C. Ligota and J.-L. Quantin, *History of Scholarship: A Selection of papers from the Seminar on the History of Scholarship held annually at the Warburg Institute* (Oxford, 2006), 385–98.

[76] In Oxford terms, Conybeare was his most important client. Macclesfield as Lord Chancellor awarded him the rectory of St Clements in the city. Ward, *Georgian Oxford*, 138. The Lord Chancellor was also an amateur astronomer (though nothing like as proficient as his son would prove) who had observed with interest the eclipse of 1715, acted as Halley's patron, and successfully canvassed his claim to succeed Flamsteed as the Astronomer Royal. Cook, *Edmond Halley*, 347.

[77] W. Prest, 'Law, lawyers and Rational Dissent', in ed. K. Haakonssen, *Enlightenment and Religion: Rational Dissent in Eighteenth-Century Britain* (Cambridge, 1996), 173–82; J. Rudolph, *Common Law and Enlightenment in England, 1689–1750* (Woodbridge, 2013), 201–2; A. Mitchell, 'Character of an independent Whig—"Cato" and Bernard Mandeville', *History of European Ideas*, 29 (2003), 291–301. Zachary Pearce, Dean of Westminster, in his unpublished autobiography, defended Macclesfield's '... constant sense of Religion as a Christian;' Westminster Abbey Muniments, 64856A.

[78] Paul Quarrie, 'The scientific library of the Earls of Macclesfield', *Notes and Records of the Royal Society*, 60 (2006), 5–24; Quarrie, *The library of the Earls of Macclesfield, removed from Shirburn Castle, Part One: natural history* (12 parts, London, 2004), Introduction, 8–21. In 1761 Thomas Hornsby observed the Transit of Venus from the castle grounds.

434 ENLIGHTENED OXFORD

estate (in their case, Cornbury Park) within relatively living memory - 1661. They might have been expected to act as the natural leaders of Tory society across the county, but the withdrawal of the 2nd Earl from public life at the Revolution put paid to that and ownership was transferred to his brother, Laurence, Lord Rochester, the leading High Tory, in 1700. For several years, Rochester entertained his University friends there. Charlett and Aldrich thus stayed with the Earl at Cornbury for nearly a week in 1704. The former told a friend that he had encountered 'Gentlemen of admirable Shining Parts & Good Sense', and a 'noble Collection of Pictures & Books...'.[79] On the whole Rochester never seems to have spent much time at Cornbury, for all his prestige within the University. The same was the case for his less prominent son Henry, the 2nd Earl, High Steward of the University, in succession to his father from 1711.[80] Both men preferred their estate near Wootton Bassett in west Wiltshire and in 1751 the family was obliged to sell the entire Cornbury estate and the Rangership of Wychwood Forest for £61,000. The purchasers were their self-aggrandising Whig neighbours at Blenheim, the 3rd Duke of Marlborough's trustees.[81]

The 2nd Earl of Clarendon was not the only county magnate to disengage at the Revolution and become a Nonjuror. The 1st Earl of Lichfield (1663–1716), whose seat was at Ditchley Park, did likewise. He was a Lee, descendant of Elizabeth I's Champion, Sir Henry Lee, and married to a natural daughter of Charles II by the Duchess of Cleveland. Lichfield was a Tory through and through, but the instincts of the courtier were embedded in the Lee lineage, and his successors were gradually drawn back to St James's. It was his ancestry, his politics, and his taste that endeared Lichfield and his descendants to the eighteenth-century University, plus their family association with St John's College; in these and other ways they felicitously mirrored each other. The 1st Earl was no scholar but he was a man of taste, and commissioned James Gibbs to rebuild Ditchley shortly before his death.[82] Gibbs's Catholicism was no barrier to this project, indeed the 2nd Earl's wife, Frances Hales, was a member of the same communion. This Lord Lichfield was nominated DCL 1732, and the same degree was awarded to his son, the 3rd Earl, in the year of his succession to the estates and title—1743. It was this Lord Lichfield (d. 1772) who displayed the greatest appetite for public affairs of any of the Lee earls. Throughout his life, he interested himself in the life of the University

---

[79] Charlett to Humfrey Wanley, 13 Oct. 1704, Bodl. MS Ballard 13, f. 114, 13 Oct. 1704, cited in Stanley Gillam, 'Humfrey Wanley and Arthur Charlett', *BLR*, 16 (1999), 411–29, at 423.

[80] 'A good, simple, civil man'. Jonathan Swift, *Journal to Stella. Letters to Esther Johnson and Rebecca Dingley, 1710–1713*, ed. Abigail Williams (Cambridge, 2013), 479, Jan. 1713.. The 2nd Earl of Rochester succeeded his cousin as 4th Earl of Clarendon in 1723.

[81] V. J. Watney, *Cornbury and the Forest of Wychwood* (London, 1910), 191–4. For a contemporary description of Cornbury and its lord, and the apartments for the 2nd Earl of Rochester's daughter, the Duchess of Queensberry, see Mary Delany, *The Autobiography and Correspondence of Mary Granville, Mrs Delany* (3 vols., London, 1861), ed. Lady Llanover, II. 441–3.

[82] C. Christie, *The British Country House in the Eighteenth Century* (Manchester, 2000), 50.

which, for its part, courted him, and enjoyed his largesse as a host. He served as one of the Radcliffe trustees,[83] became High Steward, and then Chancellor, acting as an advance guard in securing the realignment of Oxford with the court.[84]

The Norths' Oxfordshire estate lay in the north-west corner of the county up against the Warwickshire border, at Wroxton Abbey, three miles beyond Banbury, a one-member constituency over which they had a commanding influence. Francis, later Lord Chancellor Guilford, inherited the property from the Pope family (the original founders of Trinity College, Oxford, in 1555) in 1677, and the connection between the Norths and Trinity was nurtured on both sides throughout the eighteenth century, for the family were leaseholders from the College. The Norths were Tories by descent, but the 2nd Lord Guilford was one of those who transferred his allegiance to the Whigs after 1714, and it was upheld on his death in 1729, by Francis, the 3rd Lord; it stayed there throughout his life in a manner that resembled the trajectory of the Harcourts. And this new commitment persisted despite his inheriting in 1734 the older barony of North from his first cousin once removed, the 6th Lord North & Grey, a key player in the Atterbury Plot. The new Lord North was a loyal follower of Frederick, Prince of Wales, but came back to the Pelhams, like so many, on the Prince's death, and was duly rewarded with the Earldom of Guilford for his initiative and for losing out to the 1st Earl Harcourt on the post of governor to the thirteen-year-old Prince George. He was one of the greatest courtiers of the century, originally appointed a Gentleman of the Bedchamber to the Prince of Wales in 1730 and still in service with Queen Charlotte as her Treasurer on his death a full sixty years later aged eighty-six.[85]

Interaction with Trinity College was central to the management of Wroxton, and Guilford took pains early on to show himself a generous benefactor (and in so doing intimate that the family finances had made something of a recovery from the time of his first succeeding): in 1737 he gifted a wrought-iron gate to beautify the Broad Street entrance, and thereby overcame the problem of the impractical and narrow medieval gateway.[86] Relations between leasor and lessee were not always harmonious: Guilford and his heir, Lord North, were both at odds with Trinity in the 1770s over the college's right to mark and fell trees on the Wroxton estate. It was not resolved until 1780 when a 'benefaction' of £100 arrived from

---

[83] Oxfordshire Archives, DIL XXIII/2a-I, accts and letters re Dr Radcliffe's estate.

[84] See also Chapter 6, pp. 13–15. The 3rd Earl and his wife, Diana Frankland (a descendant of Oliver Cromwell), had no children. He was succeeded as 4th Earl (1706–76) by his uncle, a son of the 1st Earl, who had also been MP for Oxford (1754–68). When the latter was mortally injured after being thrown off his horse, Ditchley passed through the female line to the Viscounts Dillon. See generally E. Corbett, *A History of Spelsbury* (Banbury, 1962).

[85] For the 1st Earl of Guilford and Wroxton, see C. D. Smith, *The Early Career of Lord North the Prime Minister* (London, 1979), 27–30, 60–2, 259–67.

[86] Trinity College Archives Benefactors' Book III, 61, quoted in Clare Hopkins, *Trinity*, 173. Carriages could henceforth be conveniently driven up around an elegant oval lawn in front of the chapel.

436 ENLIGHTENED OXFORD

Wroxton, and an agreement that the terms of the lease could be changed.[87] Guilford extended his hospitality at Wroxton to members of other colleges, welcoming, for instance, his step-grandsons from Christ Church, Lord Lewisham and the Hon. William Legge, along with Cyril Jackson, in 1774.[88] The underlying point was that Oxford University and the North family were aligned in property as well as in politics, for when the University opted for North as its Chancellor, it selected someone who was heir to an Oxfordshire estate on lease from one of the colleges.[89]

Finally, the interests of three peerage families with estates not too far from Oxford occasionally impinged on events in that county and, by extension, in the University. The first property was leased by a bishop closely involved in the life of Oxford throughout his life: Nathaniel, 3rd Lord Crew, Bishop of Durham (1633–1721). Steane Park, near Brackley, just over the county border in Northamptonshire, made a useful base for the Bishop on his numerous visits to the University and in entertaining county families supportive of his interest. On more than one occasion the Vice Chancellor and senior dons travelled there in some state, keen not to lose the good offices of that remarkable prelatical survivor and eventual great benefactor to the whole University, and to Lincoln College in particular.[90]

The two other families were predominantly Whigs and stood at a remove to majority academic opinion, emphatically so in the case of the Junto magnate, Honest 'Tom' Wharton, 1st Earl of Wharton (1648–1716), the great electoral manager of the Whigs in several counties, with his main Buckinghamshire estate at Nether Winchendon between Aylesbury and Oxford.[91] He actually served as Lord Lieutenant of Oxfordshire between 1697 and 1702 (replacing his brother-in-law Abingdon in that post and as Chief Justice in Eyre)[92] without having long enough to much extend his patronage, though he purged Tory JPs and put in his friends.[93] However, his efforts to put up Whigs for the county failed in 1698 and he seems never to have concerned himself with city, county, or university much again.[94] The Wharton interest briefly re-emerged after Thomas, Lord Wharton's sudden death in 1715 and his extraordinarily gifted frenetic son, Philip, later 1st Duke of Wharton, inherited, and placed his influence—and his

---

[87] Ibid., 177.   [88] Staffs RO D(W)1778, V. 853, Dartmouth to Lewisham, 27 June 1774.

[89] Guilford even required his son—as Chancellor of Oxford—to oblige him. For example, BL Add MS. 61874, f.9 29 June 1779, a request to North on Guilford's behalf to vote for William Carter of Oriel, the nephew of one of the Earl's Kent tenants, at the next election of Radcliffe Travelling fellows.

[90] He was appointed Rector of Lincoln in 1668. As an instance of his rural hospitality, in August 1719 Bishop Robinson of London, Vice Chancellor Shippen, and others were greeted at Steane by Lord Crewe in 'his princely robes' and dined on a fat buck with copious French wine. C. E. Whiting, *Nathaniel Lord Crewe Bishop of Durham (1674–1721)* (London, 1940), 305.

[91] W. A. Speck, *Tory & Whig. The Struggle in the Constituencies, 1701–1715* (London, 1970), 11.

[92] Luttrell, *Historical Relation*, IV. 298; www.oxfordhistory.org.uk/people_lists/oxon_lord_lieuten ants/index.html

[93] Glassey, *Justices of the Peace*, 126, 137–9.   [94] Robbins, *Earl of Wharton*, 95.

BEYOND THE UNIVERSITY 437

cash—at the disposal of the high Tories looking to the 'king over the water.' But, after his largesse towards All Souls, the young Duke threw away his fortune and his estates,[95] and went into exile and to his death abroad. From time to time, the Lords Craven also took an interest in Oxford affairs. William, 6th Lord Craven (succeeded to the barony, 1769), was periodically involved in Oxfordshire county politics, but it was hard for him to focus his efforts in one place when he owned 70,000 acres stretching over four counties.[96] Inasmuch as he did, it was Berkshire that was the priority, where he inclined to opposition, like the 4th Lord Abingdon.

As a centre of intense party-political agitation in its own right, both Tories and Whigs in the county had their champions within the University. With the city of Oxford as the main polling centre, on which candidates and voters alike converged, members of the University were inevitably caught up in the often frenzied, hard-fought proceedings of county elections. The main objective of all Tory gentlemen and their academic allies in the county in the later 1690s was directed towards keeping out Wharton and his Whigs and limiting his influence during the years he was Lord Lieutenant of Oxfordshire. In that exercise of containment, they were largely successful (partly because Wharton had so many electoral commitments nationwide). It could not be readily repeated when a new, double-headed political colossus—the 1st Duke and Duchess of Marlborough and their family— arrived in the shire during Anne's reign. The national power that the couple commanded was immediately registered in Oxfordshire through the Duke's support for his son-in-law, Viscount Rialton, when he successfully stood for a county seat in the 1708 General Election. Rialton was a victim of the pro-Sacheverell Tory tide in 1710, but he was back (having succeeded his father, the Lord Treasurer, as 2nd Earl of Godolphin) in the driving seat as Lord Lieutenant of Oxfordshire, 1715–35, in effect the guardian of the Marlborough family interest, his importance a reminder of the steadily declining competition offered by the Abingdons.

Godolphin proved lacklustre in his party zeal for the Whigs, a disappointment to his formidable mother-in-law, Sarah, Duchess of Marlborough, and it was not until the 3rd Duke took up residence at Blenheim on her death in 1744 that the Churchill family could act as the principal motor of (Whig) court interests in the county. As it was, Tories represented the county unopposed between 1715 and 1754, among them the wealthy Sir James Dashwood, 2nd Bt (1715–79), knight of the shire from 1740 to 1754 and, again, from 1761 to 1768. With his extensive land

---

[95] Winchendon was bought by the trustees of the Duke of Marlborough in 1726, and Wharton's large picture collection was sold to Sir Robert Walpole. L. Melville, *The Life and Writings of Philip Duke of Wharton* (London, 1913), 144. For his generous patronage at All Souls see Chapter 12, pp. 87–8.

[96] In Berkshire he owned Morewood House, Hampstead Marshall, south-west of Newbury; also Ashdown House; he built Benham Park, near Speen, in 1775. The Cravens' principal residence was at Coombe Abbey, Warwickshire.

438   ENLIGHTENED OXFORD

holdings stretching from Kirtlington north to Banbury,[97] he was the cynosure of
Tories locally and, though not an Oxford graduate, among Tory partisans he was
the University's most favoured country gentleman after Sir Roger Newdigate.[98] In
1754, however, Dashwood and the Tory predominance in the county faced the
most determined challenge to date at the General Election from the Whig 'New
Interest', so concerted that it gained enduring national notoriety as a frenzy of
expense and 'corruption', one that 'engaged the energies, pockets, and interests of
Tories and Whigs nationally'.[99]

It was led by the Duke of Marlborough (who had decided on breaking the
county peace back in 1752) in cahoots with his fellow magnates—Harcourt,
Macclesfield, and Guilford—accorded the blessing of the diocesan bishop,
Secker, and urged forward by Newcastle and Henry Fox.[100] The Whig intention
to wrest both county seats from a Tory stranglehold was evidenced through an
outpouring of pamphlets, squibs, journalism, verses, and lavish hospitality on
behalf of their candidates, the Pelhamite Viscount Parker (eldest son of the 2nd
Earl of Macclesfield) and the immensely wealthy Sir Edward Turner, 2nd Bt., of
Ambrosden, a major investor in Government and East India Company stocks, and
an unsuccessful candidate for a University seat in 1750.[101] Against them were
arrayed Dashwood and his cousin, the 3rd Viscount Wenman of Thame Park (the
holder of an Irish peerage, MP for Oxford City, but ready to stand for the county).
The Tory pair secured a majority on the poll (their election expenses were said to
be over £20,000), but a double return was made and the Commons seated the
Whig candidates in April 1755. It was a deeply divisive contest for the county, the
high point of party warfare before it died away.[102] For the University, however,
with just over twenty senior members having the vote as freeholders, the involvement was somewhat indirect.[103] The majority wished Dashwood and Wenman
well, expected them to be returned, and only gradually woke up to the formidable
threat posed by the 'New Interest'.

Both 'Interests' relied on dons for contributions in the war of ideas, and
Thomas Randolph, President of Corpus, in particular, was a known supporter

---

[97] J. Townsend, *The Oxfordshire Dashwoods* (Oxford, 1922), 24.

[98] For Dashwood's familial and Jacobite connections see Robson, *Oxfordshire Election*, 7–9. He was
an able estate manager with a varied portfolio of investments, including the Royal African Company, but
he 'never made any attempt to cultivate an interest in the University. His excursions into academic
politics were as unimportant as they were infrequent'. Ibid., 64–5, 71. Inasmuch as he had academic
connections, they were with All Souls.

[99] Harris, *Politics and the Nation*, 46.   [100] Robson, *Oxfordshire Election*, 15–16.

[101] His father had been Chairman of the Company. Robson, *Oxfordshire Election*, 13. His name and
career lent themselves to easy ribaldry at his expense. http://www.histparl.ac.uk/volume/1715-1754/
member/turner-sir-edward-1719-66

[102] Oxfordshire County Council, *The Oxfordshire Election of 1754*, Record Publication No. 6
(Oxford, 1970).

[103] For the voting record of freeholder dons in 1754, see the table in Robson, *Oxfordshire Election*,
76: 12 for the Old Interest, 11 for the New (5 of them cast by Ch. Ch. men).

of Turner as the 'New Interest' candidate for the county, much as he had come out in favour of the baronet at the by-election for a University seat in 1751.[104] He tried three years later to stay grandly and unconvincingly aloof from the taunts and name-calling on both sides,[105] with the 'New Interest 'raising the old Jacobite and papist canards and their opponents resorting to anti-Semitism as the election campaign became embroiled in the debate on the Jewish Naturalisation Bill.[106] Another senior don, Thomas Bray, turned Exeter College into the campaign headquarters of the 'New Interest 'in Oxford writing in *Jackson's Oxford Journal*, the *Gentleman's Magazine*, and other organs[107] and coordinating his electioneering with the endlessly resourceful Lady Susan Keck out in the county.[108] She was the wife of Anthony Keck of Great Tew and aunt of the 6th Duke of Hamilton (d. 1758, St Mary Hall, DCL 1743), and the real organising energy of the 'New Interest'. The ambitious Hebraist, Benjamin Kennicott, also willingly lent his services, both out of conviction and the prospect of the preferment that victory might bestow on him.[109]

A less likely backer of the 'New Interest' was Theophilus Leigh, Master of Balliol, a man with a fair income and light duties of office, but one who, as he aged, had developed a keen appetite for royal largesse and looked to county society for career satisfaction.[110] With Turner (who had married into the Leigh family) standing he needed no further inducement to show his hand, and suffer the taunts

---

[104] Ward, *Georgian Oxford*, 193. Professor Thomas Hunt was another anti-Tory patron. He attended a large meeting on 15 Feb. 1753 for nominating candidates for the county and reported his house full of —'New Interest'—company for days afterwards. Hunt to Dr Gregory Sharp, Bodl. Ms Eng. lett. d. 146, f. 39.

[105] He insisted in a sermon of 1752 that such conduct was seasonable in Oxford where 'we are not only members of the Publick Community, and liable to join in the *Party-Distinctions*, which divide the rest of our Fellow-Subjects, but are all of us incorporated into one Body here'. *Party Zeal Censur'd*, 4.

[106] There was little public comment from the dons on the matter or any attempt by them to adopt anti-Semitic slogans as 'Old Interest' campaigners in the county were doing. In one sense that omission could be deemed enlightened, in another self-serving as it kept ministers at bay. The Whig John Free in Oct. 1753 preached and published in St Mary's church in favour of the Jews, and that was about it. 'Academicus' in the *London Evening Post* grieved 'to find both our Universities quite silent in a matter of such infinite moment and importance'. Robson, *Oxfordshire Election*, 92–3.

[107] Ibid., 74–5. Lord Harcourt thanked Bray fulsomely for his efforts thus: 'All the Gentlemen that I have seen declare that we would not have polled a hundred votes, without the assistance of your College. But however we may be indebted to your Society, we are undoubtedly more so to you, than to almost any other person of the Party. It is a piece of justice I shall allways do you to acknowledge it, wherever I have an opportunity of mentioning Mr Brays name.' Exeter College MSS, Bray Papers, 30 Apr. 1754, quoted in Greenwood, *William King*, 266–7.

[108] Exeter College MSS, Bray Papers, letters to Thomas Bray from Lady Susan Keck. 'Old Interest' publicists dubbed her 'Lord Sue'. E. Chalus, '"My Lord Sue": Lady Susan Keck and the great Oxfordshire election of 1754', *PH*, 37 (2013), 443–59; Elaine Chalus, *Elite Women in English Political Life, c.1754–1790* (Oxford, 2005), 199–205, 213–16 For two other women campaigners, ibid., 202, 213.

[109] For William Blackstone's involvement on the opposite side, see Chapter 8, p. 104.

[110] Leigh in 1769 was acting as chairman of Quarter Sessions, supporting the claims in a letter to the Duke of Marlborough of two clergy to be appointed JPs, and seems also to have nominated two more. Details in P. Virgin, *The Church in an age of negligence. Ecclesiastical structure and problems of Church reform 1700–1840* (Cambridge, 1989), 117.

440 ENLIGHTENED OXFORD

of 'the Rev. Dr. Twister' and worse.[111] Apart from Blackstone, the 'Old Interest''s paper champions were—inevitably—Dr William King, seconded by Benjamin Buckler of All Souls.[112] Much of what they wrote was anonymous, as they had no wish to run the risk of a royal visitation for a third time in the course of half a century.[113] There was also perhaps a sense that the county Tories were quite capable of running their own campaign as successfully as they had done in the past. In line with this concern for the wrong sort of headlines, the University in a *Programma* on the eve of the poll (15 April 1754) appointed wardens of the streets, confined undergraduates without votes to college, and ordered college gates to be shut. The principal contravention was made by Exeter College on polling day opening its front gate to a party of 'New Interest' voters.[114]

That infringement stoked the fires for further internal feuding within the University for another year,[115] but, as far as county elections went, there would be no more contests until 1826, no opportunity for academic animosities to be given an outlet in that particular format. Shocked by the expense of the 1754 contest, the two 'Interests' were averse to any repetition.[116] Instead, it was agreed that the Marlborough family should put their name to one county seat and the gentry would have the other. Such a carving up was initially resented by many in the county (especially the Whigs) who felt themselves thereby marginalised, but the concordat stuck. Back, in 1761, came Sir James Dashwood, who gave way graciously in 1768 to the 4th Viscount Wenman, an Oriel graduate, who generally followed his brother-in-law, Abingdon, though with few of that Earl's radical propensities. The other seat was continuously occupied by the 4th Duke of Marlborough's brother, Lord Charles Spencer, from 1761 to 1790. For the University in the new reign, in general as happy as the Blenheim dynasty to support the governments of George III, it was an unexceptionable arrangement that tended to county harmony. And whatever misgivings University sympathisers for the 'Old Interest' might have entertained about admitting the

---

[111] Bodl. MS Dep. C.577, ff. 26, 59; *The Election Magazine, or the Oxfordshire Register...* (Oxford, 1753), 41–2; Jones, *Balliol College*, 159. The 'Old Interest' compared him to the two-faced pump in the High Street near Carfax. John Freinshemius, *Threnodia, or an Elegy on the Unexpected and Unlamented Death of the M[aster] of B[alliol], faithfully done into Modern English...* (Oxford, 1753), 16.

[112] Robson, *Oxfordshire Election*, 78–9.   [113] Ward, *Georgian Oxford*, 198–9.

[114] Ibid., 199–200; Robson, *Oxford Election*, 107–9; Greenwood, *William King*, 265–6. The extreme partisanship of Exeter College and the moral character of so many on its governing body caused ructions for some months after the election was over. The Vice Chancellor, George Huddesford, on 8 Oct. 1754 in his annual speech to Convocation complimented the members of the University on their behaviour during the poll, with the exception of those from one college, which had been a hotbed of political agitation. His words were repeated in *JOJ* and the *London Evening Post* and led to further exchanges between the principal parties that generated publicity outside Oxford. The Rector of Exeter, Dr Francis Webber, was duly favoured by the ministry with the Deanery of Hereford in 1756, for what Newcastle had called his 'distinguished merit'. To Harcourt, BL Add MS 32857, f.231, 19 July 1755.

[115] Robson, *Oxford Election*, 109–14.

[116] The astronomical expenses are estimated of at least £40,000 for each side. Frank O'Gorman, *Voters, Patrons and Parties. The Unreformed Electorate of Hanoverian England, 1734–1832* (Oxford, 1989), 146.

Marlborough interest into a half share of the county's representation after half a century of keeping it out, they were powerless to change the situation. Indeed, they could go the extra mile to defend it, as on 13 March 1784, when an Oxfordshire county meeting at the Town hall adopted an address unreservedly critical of the Foxite Opposition. Only the Vice Chancellor, Samuel Dennis, tried to defend Lord Charles Spencer from the Pittite majority criticising the principle of making Addresses as a party device, and was excoriated by Lord Abingdon for his pains.[117]

Part B: Property, schools, and the Oxford connection

i) Beyond the University: land ownership

Oxford's association with the city and county was predominantly political. Further afield, it was encountered by any number of men and women as a landowner. Oxford colleges and halls possessed land all over England and Wales, either acquired at foundation or bequeathed or purchased in the following centuries. They all, to a greater or lesser degree, had estates to be supervised, leases to be negotiated, rents to be collected, and improvements (where funds allowed) to be initiated.[118] An interest and involvement in provincial life was therefore primary to sustaining materially the collegiate life of the University, with tenants and dependents to be found in most counties. As college incomes derived mostly from property, these were subject to the variations that all landlords, secular, ecclesiastical, and educational, faced. Prolonged warfare and high taxation brought inevitable problems. For instance, in the 1690s there were alternating gluts and scarcities in agricultural commodities with wartime land taxes driving down the value of land and leases with a deleterious impact on the incomes of both colleges and individual fellows. When land prices rose, so college members were the direct beneficiaries. And new gifts in the form of land were being made year after year. At St John's College, during President Holmes's time, notable benefactions included Dr Charles Woodroffe's bequest of the manor of Middleton Winterslow, Wiltshire, and a farm in the parish, to augment small livings in St John's gift.[119] A gift could come from an unanticipated direction. An illustrative

---

[117] *Whitehall Evening Post,* 13–16 Mar. 1784, which noted: 'Almost everyone present reprobated the behaviour of the Vice Chancellor and some jokes were passed on Abp. Laud's heart and night-cap being deposited in the College where the Reverend Doctor presides'. The high-flying Dr Thomas Nowell was interestingly one of the few who refused to sign the Address.

[118] This subject is treated in most of the 'new' college histories (see Introduction) though there is no systematic comparative study and the personal interactions implicit in the connection between the colleges and the provinces have seldom been brought to life. Curthoys (4) is an attempt to give the subject the attention it inherently merits. For a fine study showing the location of one college's holdings see D. H. Fletcher, *The Emergence of Estate Maps. Christ Church Oxford, 1600 to 1840* (Oxford, 1995).

[119] Costin, *St John's College,* 185–7.

442 ENLIGHTENED OXFORD

case is that of Edward Careswell, a wealthy Shropshire landowner. He left six farms in that county and in Staffordshire to Christ Church to fund eighteen exhibitions for boys from Shropshire's grammar schools, despite having no known connections with the College.[120]

The priority of a college was of course to maximise the income from its material assets, but initiatives directed to that end might adversely affect the interests of those who lived on their estates. And conflict could arise, particularly on the sensitive subject of land enclosures. In 1773, at Braunston, Northamptonshire, 115 inhabitants—half of whom were illiterate—petitioned against Jesus College's enclosure plan, which threatened to impoverish most of the parishioners and be the 'entire ruin' of most of the labourers and of the rural poor. But the principal and the College sanctioned the scheme, which went ahead on the primary basis that it would increase the living's value.[121] On the other hand, well-established tenants could also expect to make money from their leases. These were made for twenty-one years at Trinity College where, as across the University as a whole, they were usually renewed after seven, when a 'fine' was paid. That was calculated as a multiple of the land's 'clear value' in the knowledge that the College tenants (who generally bequeathed their leases and sublet the land as de facto owners) made far more from it than the 'reserved rent' they paid to the College landlord.[122]

Colleges admitted the need for senior members (usually the Head of House himself) to make regular summer journeys or 'progresses' out into the counties to see for themselves how their estates were being maintained and the level of stewardship services provided. They invariably felt particularly dutiful in maintaining and nurturing connections with those places connected with their founders. Thus the tomb of Edward II in Gloucester cathedral, which had fallen into neglect after the Reformation, was rescued in the 1730s as a result of interest in their supposed founder by the fellows of Oriel College. In 1755 the President of Corpus Christi, Thomas Randolph, was inspecting college estates in Lincolnshire and came across the house in Ropsley where its founder, Bishop Richard Foxe, had been born. In an act of filial piety, with the consent of the owner of the house, Lord William Manners, a stone was put up in the wall with the inscription: 'Richard Fox, Bishop of Winchester and founder of Corpus Christi College Oxford was born in this house'.[123]

Management of these holdings required senior college members to display a level of administrative and financial competence not always evident in scholars.

---

[120] The Dean and Chapter commissioned an 'atlas' to enable them to plan improvements to the estate. Details in Curthoys (2), 160–1.

[121] Jesus College OA, LV, Braunston, Petition, 26 Nov. 1773. Thanks to Colin Haydon for these details.

[122] Hodgkin, *Trinity*, 176.

[123] Fowler, *Corpus Christi College*, 289. It may have been as much an act of atonement as of piety, for the College had sold the remains of Foxe's mitre in President Mather's time (1715–48), and the house in Ropsley earlier in Randolph's.

BEYOND THE UNIVERSITY   443

Some individuals, however, found their forte in this field, men such as Thomas Hayward, Warden of New College (1764–8), who put the estates on a sounder footing, and died in a fall from his horse while out on a visit to one of them.[124] At Christ Church the well-housed and well-paid Canons often took responsibility for managing the House's estates through personal visits and met regularly in Chapter to discuss business. They were perhaps surprisingly adept at ensuring the flow of rents and profits with dividends and windfalls shared among all foundationers in what was a unique, double foundation of college and cathedral.[125] Estate management became ever more organised as the century went on and the role of bursar as a college officer correspondingly more demanding. As senior bursar at Trinity, the literary scholar Thomas Warton the younger rose to the challenge, writing numerous notebooks detailing the names of sub-tenants, the size and location of their holdings, and the condition of their cottages.[126]

It helped if college heads had an early grounding in property stewardship through their own family holdings. Such was the case with Cyril Jackson, whose family was clearly involved at mid-century in making the most of their inheritance in the West Riding through such measures as continuing the colliery on Shipley Moor, and endorsing the Calder & Hebble Navigation canal, and the turnpike road from Keighley to Halifax.[127] Jackson, once Dean of Christ Church and as befitted an individual with connections to the Lunar Society, took a personal interest in using the latest technologies to develop the industrial potential of college estates. From the 1780s, with the increased use of steam power, the need for coal grew nationally, and Christ Church explored fresh sources in north Somerset where it owned land. The Dean and Chapter appointed a clerk or manager to each colliery; new shafts were sunk reserving to Christ Church the 'coleage', i.e. the mineral rights, when land in the Mendip Hills was leased out. That left the difficulty of transporting coal away from the collieries. Jackson, a canal enthusiast, supported steps to build the North Somerset Coal Canal, which would link his collieries to the Kennet and Avon Canal, the latter being operational by 1794.[128]

ii) Beyond the University: links with English schools

Oxford University's place in the cultural topography of England as a whole was transmitted both formally and associationally through education and the University's involvement in schooling, especially the public schools and grammar schools. Pupils there were offered a predominantly classics-orientated curriculum

---

[124] Nichols, *Lit. anecdotes*, IX. 256.   [125] Curthoys (3), 129–30.
[126] Hopkins, *Trinity*, 178.   [127] West Yorkshire Archives Service (Calderdale), RP 2404, 2477.
[128] More details in Curthoys (4), chap. 7.

444 ENLIGHTENED OXFORD

that would be the foundation of their studies as undergraduates,[129] but more than that, their educational formation would take place within an Anglican setting and ethos, one where intellectual progress and ambition were combined with a stress on loyalty to the Church and the monarchical constitution. The great public schools were there for the primary benefit of higher society, but their academic demands were considerable, encouraging their pupils to gain 'command of a patrician culture of late humanism' still highly esteemed, and commence that acquisition of formal oratorical skills designed to appeal 'to parents hoping for a distinguished public career for their sons'.[130] These establishments fostered a sense of identity that often extended into adult life and could transcend political differences.[131]

The best grammar schools were not far behind, though given their slightly different social range, they tended to incur similar criticisms to those increasingly made of Oxford, that they were circumscribed by their charters and statutes and so kept from adapting to evolving pedagogical needs.[132] Defenders of the study of the ancient authors and the value of learning more than one language were, however, neither silent nor unconvincing, such as George Croft (1747–1809), fellow of University College (1772–80) and a career as teacher as Master of Beverley Grammar School 1768–80, and Headmaster of Brewood School, Staffordshire, 1780–91.[133] Croft was a serious educationalist who took on detractors like Vicesimus Knox in his *A Plan of Education, delineated and vindicated...* (1784), which aimed to 'remove the prejudices of those, who think the education of a grammar school too circumscribed'.[134] Indeed, at their best—usually when there was an outstanding headmaster at the helm ready to supplement the subject prescriptions handed down from their foundation[135]—grammar schools produced pupils able to extract maximum value from their teaching, who went on

---

[129] For the limitations of Greek teaching in English schools until the nineteenth century see Ogilvie, *Latin and Greek*, 83–5.

[130] Clark, *English Society 1660–1832*, 223; Paul Langford, *Englishness Identified. Manners and Characters 1650–1850* (Oxford, 2000), 205. See also Chapter 8, pp. 44–5 for oratory.

[131] Henry French and Mark Rothery, *Man's Estate. Landed Gentry masculinities c.1660–c.1900* (Oxford, 2012), 75.

[132] See Langford, *A Polite and Commercial People*, 80–1. There were between 1,000 and 1,200 grammar schools in England in 1727 in corporate boroughs and many market towns. The *locus classicus* of a new vision that might be offered by the older foundations was contained in Vicesimus Knox's *Liberal Education: or, A Practical Treatise on the Methods of Acquiring Useful and Polite Learning* (London, 1781), a book that went through ten editions. Knox was headmaster of Tonbridge School.

[133] Darwall-Smith, *University College Oxford*, 324.

[134] George Croft, *A Plan of Education, delineated and vindicated...and a short Dissertation upon the stated provision and reasonable expectation of Public Teachers* (Wolverhampton, 1784), 12.

[135] The same applied to public schools. At Rugby, the educational talents of Thomas James as headmaster over a sixteen-year period were only made possible after the school trustees secured an Act of Parliament in 1777 enabling them to update the curriculum with 'modern' subjects. Langford, *A Polite and Commercial People*, 82.

to do likewise at Oxford.[136] The prestige that the best of them retained was easily obscured by the failings of others unable to adapt sufficiently to the competition offered by newer, private schools.

Schools up and down the country had historic connections with particular colleges within the University, with dons often reciprocally found as members of their governing bodies, able to influence the curriculum used in schools and the individuals teaching it. Schools would tend to send their best pupils to that College (often via closed scholarships and exhibitions) which, in turn, might well send back its own graduates to teach in them, so setting up a circular cultural vector. Thus Sherborne School, like so many establishments in the south-west, had major connections with Wadham.[137] Pembroke had strong links with Gloucestershire. The College awarded scholarships to boys from Gloucestershire schools, and the Master held a reserved prebend in the Cathedral. When in residence there the Master of Pembroke was invited to inspect the school ['The Crypt'], report to the cathedral chapter, and meet boys who wished to go on to Oxford.[138]

Nowhere was the relationship more symmetrical and intimate than that between Westminster School (by general consent the foremost school in England) and Christ Church: the majority of the Deans and Canons between 1660 and 1760 were educated at the school,[139] and the (head) Master of Westminster was chosen alternately by the Dean of Christ Church and the Master of Trinity College, Cambridge (with the consent of the Dean of Westminster).[140] As the young, home-educated Lord Fitzmaurice suggested—with some pardonable exaggeration—in coming up in 1755: 'Christ Church is composed, nineteen out of twenty, of those who have been bred at Westminster'.[141] Former pupils of Westminster had their own Studentship category in the college, and were elected annually by the Dean after a public examination.[142] A stellar performance was not necessarily the only criterion for election; the claims of kindred, political considerations, and financial necessity also commonly entered the equation.[143] Ex-Westminster pupils were also increasingly colonising the Canoneer Studentships

---

[136] R. S. Tompson, 'The English grammar school curriculum in the 18th century: a reappraisal', *British Journal of Educational Studies*, 19 (1971), 32–9. Anthony Fletcher, *Gender, sex, and subordination in England 1500–1800* (New Haven, CT, 1995), 300, notes the diversification of grammar schools after 1700 in terms of their curriculum.

[137] A. B. Gourlay, *A History of Sherborne School* (Winchester, 1951), 62.

[138] Charles Lepper, *The Crypt School Gloucester 1539–1989* (Gloucester, 1989), 17–19; Bennett, 'The Era of Party Zeal', 97.

[139] Bill, *Education at Christ Church*, 87–8.

[140] E. C. Mack, *Public Schools and British Opinion 1780 to 1880* (London, 1938), 7; F. H. Forshall, *Westminster School. Past and Present* (London, 1884), 87ff.

[141] Quoted in Lord Fitzmaurice, *Life of William Earl of Shelburne* (2nd edn., 2 vols., London, 1912), I. 13.

[142] Forty Students were named by Westminster, the rest (Canoneer Students) by the Ch. Ch. Chapter. The Earls of Abingdon also chose one. Salmon, *The Foreigner's Companion*, 80.

[143] Christ Church and its sister Cambridge college, Trinity, were required to elect no fewer than three candidates annually from Westminster. The colleges chose in rotation in alternate years, and also

446   ENLIGHTENED OXFORD

reserved for the rest of the Christ Church chapter, and they also benefitted from the foundation of additional exhibitions and scholarships for their school by Robert South and, later, by Matthew Lee.[144]

A creative interchange of staff between the college and school was operative. Early in the century it was neatly embodied in John Nicholl (*c.*1683–1765), who 'coxed and boxed' with Robert Freind. Nicholl was a Christ Church tutor in 1713 who, the next year, became Under (or deputy head) master at Westminster under Robert Freind. Nicholl succeeded the latter in the Headmastership (1733–53) before returning to the 'House' as Canon of the eighth prebend, 1751–65 again as Freind's replacement.[145] In the next generation William Markham went directly from being headmaster of Westminster (1753) to the Deanery of Christ Church (1767–77) and was closely involved in the reforms of undergraduate studies that his predecessor, David Gregory, had pioneered. Under his aegis, many Westminster scholars went on to the 'House' as Students or Commoners.[146] The Westminster influence at the 'House' fell away somewhat before the end of the century in favour of George's III preferred academy—Eton—though its eclipse cast a relatively small shadow.[147]

The links between New College and Winchester College as a double foundation were at least as historically entwined with personnel traffic in both directions.[148] The relationship had come to exhibit a structural inflexibility that worked against intellectual achievement at degree level and beyond in several regards. As so many Wykehamists came on to New College as undergraduates and had an exclusive right to New College fellowships, their academic abilities at school—or the lack of them—would likely be reflected at the University.[149] And there was educational dynasticism in the form of Founders' Kin privileges (for those who could claim it

---

selected candidates alternately during the election itself. Candidates could express a preference for one university over the other. Far more Students were elected to Christ Church than Scholars elected to Trinity: 429 to 368 in the century. Bill, *Education at Christ Church*, 93–4, 95–6.

[144] Ibid., 99, 103–6.

[145] Freind was Under master, 1699–1711; Head Master, 1711–33; canon of Ch. Ch., 1737. *GM* 21 (1751), 380; 35 (1765), 443; G. Russell Barker and Alan H. Stenning, *Record of old Westminsters* (2 vols., London, 1928), I. 352–3, II. 692; John Sargeaunt, *Annals of Westminster School* (London, 1898), 138–9, 165–70.

[146] Bill, *Education at Christ Church*, 60–1.

[147] '...by my accounts from Ch. Ch. the Etonians have had much the advantage of us of late years. On the other hand, I understand that [William] Vincent has taken great pains & has sent off of late some boys well finished & who probably will restore the Credit of the School'. Welbore Ellis to Abp Charles Agar of Cashel, 3 Jan. 1791, Hants RO, Normanton Papers 21M57/C27/1. The Ellises were a well-established Anglo-Irish, Westminster and Christ Church kinship network. Vincent was Headmaster at Westminster, 1788–1802.

[148] Many boys began their education at New College School around the age of 8 or 9 and only later moved to Winchester. It was, as Warden Purnell put it, 'the best nursery for Winchester foundation'. Purnell to Lord Noel Somerset, 6 Feb. 1740, Badminton Muniments FmJ 2/22/29. See also FmJ 2/22/59, 22 Feb.

[149] Barry Shurlock, *The Speaker's Chaplain and the Master's Daughter. A Georgian Family & Friends* (Winchester, 2015), 13, 17, 25; Squibb, *Founders' Kin*, 42; Bennett, 'University, society, and Church', 367, for New College admissions and privileges.

on the basis of blood descent from both Colleges' founder, Bishop William of Wykeham) that operated in an exclusionary manner and kept out such talented individuals as Joseph Warton (headmaster of Winchester College, 1766–93) as the poet William Collins from admission to New College. Moreover, early eighteenth-century Winchester had masters who were few and underpaid, with most of the income going to the College Fellows there, who had minimal duties. Not surprisingly, pupil numbers at Winchester tailed off.

Neither did squabbles over patronage serve as a beneficial advertisement for either institution.[150] The Wardenship of Winchester was £300 per annum more valuable than the New College equivalent at mid-century and was bound to be tempting when a vacancy occurred. In 1712, Thomas Braithwaite, then a lacklustre vice chancellor, had gone to Winchester without a stir.[151] Not so in 1757. Warden John Purnell wanted to go; though Purnell was an ex-vice chancellor, the Bishop of Winchester, the octogenarian veteran Whig, Benjamin Hoadly, sought to keep him out. The reasons were political: to Hoadly's mind, Purnell had tolerated drunken Jacobites, and now was the time of reckoning. He exercised his power of veto and installed Dr Christopher Golding (d. 1764) instead.[152] New College also had a disputatious connection with Bedford School over its power of nominating both master and usher, a right contested by Bedford Corporation, which sought to have the appointment of the Master in its own hands. When Matthew Priaulx, a Fellow of New College, took up the post in 1717 to marry a well-off bride he found the corporation bent on hindering him at every turn, and he did not receive a penny of his salary between 1717 and 1725, when the court of Chancery decreed that the right of nomination to both posts lay with New College, and that the Corporation should pay all Priaulx's arrears.[153]

Brasenose College had connections with schools across the north-west of England, particularly in Lancashire and Cheshire, most notably with Manchester Grammar School.[154] A high percentage of incoming students were undoubtedly reassured by the cultural Jacobitism they were likely to encounter at the College, and brought their own along to reinforce it.[155] When Brasenose renewed itself under the enlightened Principalship of William Cleaver (himself

---

[150] Williams, 'From the Reformation to the era of reform', 52, 65.

[151] Bennett, 'The era of party zeal', 92.

[152] CCEd Person ID: 23733. For the resultant controversy see [Statutophilus] *An impartial bystander's review of the controversy concerning the wardenship of Winchester College* (London, 1759); Williams, 'From the Reformation to the era of Reform', 62. That Purnell had been awarded a rectory in 1754 by the 4th Duke of Beaufort said everything about his Tory allegiances (and his relative material well-being). Badminton Muniments, FmJ 2/7, Memoranda Book.

[153] New College had sustained him in the interim with a payment of £40 annually for himself and the usher. Priaulx was part author of the satirical poem *Merton Gardens*. Ibid., 37.

[154] The Grammar Schools at Manchester, Middleton, and Whalley between them held thirty-four scholarships to Brasenose at one point. Jan Maria Albers, *Seeds of Contention: Society, Politics, and the Church of England in Lancashire, 1689–1780* (Yale, Ph.D., 1988), 176.

[155] Crook, *Brasenose*, 97, 102–3, 116–20, 168.

448 ENLIGHTENED OXFORD

made Bishop of Chester in 1787) after 1785, it did so without abandoning those regional roots.[156] Bequests in the shape of scholarships and exhibitions in this era only served to reinforce these geographical linkages. Thus Pembroke offered five Bishop Morley scholarships (endowed in 1678) for Channel Islanders to be nominated by the Dean, Bailiff, and Jurats of Jersey and Guernsey. There was a proviso: the Morley scholars were obliged to return to the Islands 'to serve the publick as preachers, schoolmasters, or otherwise'.[157] Balliol accumulated a number of exhibitions allocated to particular schools, for instance the Greaves exhibition, for the benefit of Ludlow Grammar School products in the first instance.[158] That was one of the tidier bequests. When Magdalen Hall in the 1730s accepted the benefaction of Dr William Lucy, a former alumnus, it was on the basis of four scholarships for pupils of Hampton Lucy Grammar school, Warwickshire (with a preference for the founder's family), and for natives of Kilton, Somerset, with one Scholar always coming from Scotland.[159] And conditions of tenure of awards could, over time, become distinctly embarrassing. At the Queen's College, Bridgeman exhibitions worth £20 annually for natives of Lancashire and Cheshire stipulated that each of the holders should deliver a yearly panegyric on James II. Not until 1734 was a Chancery decree obtained nullifying that proviso.[160]

Awards were not given exclusively by old members. Sarah, Duchess of Somerset (died 1692, widow of the 4th Duke), was an outstanding benefactress to Brasenose in the 1680s, the place of her first husband's education. She bequeathed the manor of Thornhill, Wiltshire, for the foundation of scholarships to Brasenose, principally through Marlborough Grammar School. As her Latin inscription in Westminster Abbey put it, the Duchess upheld ' the education and nourishing of youth in piety and good literature'.[161] Her example was followed by another high-born woman, Lady Elizabeth Hastings, to the advantage of the Queen's College, like Brasenose drawing many of its junior members from the north of England. By a codicil to her will of 1739, Lady 'Betty' endowed five Hastings exhibitions at Queen's (primarily to sponsor improvements in the educational standards of the clergy) with an elaborate entrance procedure that required the nominated schools to send their candidates to the best inn at Aberford in Yorkshire one day each Whitsun week.[162] As judged by seven local incumbents, the names of the ten candidates who performed best in the exercises would be sent

---

[156] Ibid., 163.

[157] Macleane, *Pembroke College*, 157–8. Not all opted to do so, Thus a one-time Morley Scholar, David Durell (1728–75), stayed in Oxford and rose to become Principal of Hertford and subsequently Vice Chancellor. Ibid., 87.

[158] Jones, *Balliol College*, 132; D. J. Lloyd, *Country Grammar School: History of Ludlow Grammar School* (Ludlow, 1977).

[159] Hamilton, *Hertford College*, 124.   [160] Hodgkin, *Queen's College*, 143.

[161] She was also, because of family connections, a benefactor to St John's College, Cambridge.

[162] The schools were the Grammar Schools of Leeds, Wakefield, Beverley, Skipton, Sedbergh, Ripon, and Sherburn-in-Elmet in the West Riding; Haverthwaite in Lancashire (Furness); Appleby in

BEYOND THE UNIVERSITY 449

on to the College. These would then be put in an urn and the first five names drawn out would receive an award.[163] Once her students had taken their degrees and holy orders, then a decent career path was guaranteed them; her will laid down that her advowsons were to go in the first instance to ministers who had been her exhibitioners so long as they could provide a testimonial of 'their orthodox principles, their pious and prudent behaviour during their stay there [at Oxford], of their diligence in prosecuting their studies, of their performing their exercises in Publick with Credit Reputation'.[164]

These awards potentially offered a way into Oxford not just for the sons of the urban elites but the sons of a few from poorer families whose Grammar School education might have been a financial struggle for their parents. A limited degree of social mobility was thus frequently built into the school-college relationship.[165] Thus Queen's accepted talented boys from Westmorland and Cumberland as battelers on probation—they had to battel, or pay, for most of their food. The next stage for some of them would be promotion to status of a 'Poor Boy' and becoming a member of the Foundation.[166] The endowment of awards could make an appreciable difference both in consolidating an existing topographical identity and in extending outreach. At Lincoln College, the extraordinary generosity of Lord Crew in establishing exhibitions for boys from Northumbria had brought over forty of them to Oxford by c.1760, well beyond the College's usual areas of intake in the east Midlands.[167] School staff could also help out gifted impoverished pupils even when there was no scholarship for them. At Newcastle Royal Grammar School, the scholarly talents of the Rev. John Brand (1744–1806), the future historian of the town, were recognised by an outstanding Headmaster (1749–87), the Rev. Hugh Moises, who rescued him from a career as a cordwainer, to send him on to Lincoln College with the financial backing of some local

---

Westmorland; St Bees and Penrith in Cumberland. [F. Wrangham], *A brief history of the Free Grammar School at Leeds* (Leeds, 1822), 20–2. The school at St Bees was headed by a succession of Queen's graduates.

[163] A note in her codicil justified this unusual criterion thus: 'And though this method of choosing by lot, may be called by some superstition or enthusiasm, yet as the advice was given me by an orthodox and pious prelate of the Church of England, as leaving something to providence, and as it will be a means of saving the scholars the troubles and expense of a journey to Oxford, under too great an uncertainty of being elected, I will this method of balloting be ever observed'. It was ended in 1859. Hodgkin, *Queen's College*, 144–5.

[164] Will and codicils in Borthwick Institute, University of York, LEF/4; Abstract of will 23 Apr. 1739, WYAS (Leeds) LD 235, 236, 239. As a leading supporter of the SPCK, she was particularly anxious that they should go as missionaries to the East Indies with which her estate had some connection. She had originally been in discussion with the Principal of St Edmund Hall on the subject in 1730, but the appointment of a favourite cleric, Joseph Smith, to the Provostship of Queen's that year made her change her mind. George Hastings Wheler, *Hastings Wheler Family Letters 1693–1704. Lady Betty Hastings and her Brother* (2 vols., London, 1929), II. 73–101; Sirota, *The Christian Monitors*, 249.

[165] Grammar schools were less exclusive than they became after the nineteenth-century reforms. W. J. Reader, *Professional Men: The Rise of the Professional Classes in Nineteenth-Century England* (London, 1966), 198. See generally R. S. Tompson, *Classics or Charity? The Dilemma of the 18th Century Grammar School* (Manchester, 1971).

[166] Hodgkin, *Queen's College*, 124.   [167] Green, *Lincoln College*, 306.

450 ENLIGHTENED OXFORD

sponsors.[168] It was also quite common for the family of an Oxford tutor to bring to his attention a promising pupil back home, especially those from humbler backgrounds. Thus Richard Fothergill in Westmorland to his brother Thomas, the future Provost of Queen's:

> Mr Williamson a mercer in Kendal desired me when I wrote to let you know he had a son which he intended for Queens, about 17 years of age, that had been two or three years in Greek, & desired to know when would be a proper time to enter him,... and whether you would be willing after he was entered to let him spend the winter in Kendal, all which I promised to do & to let him [know] as soon as I got an answer from you. The man has the character (& I believe deserves it) of an honest sensible, able man, & this is his only child, so I beg you'll be so good as to give it a place in your consideration, & to let me know the result as soon as you well can.[169]

With many colleges (especially the smaller foundations) recruiting in particular zones, there was a direct correlation between the calibre of student produced by the Grammar Schools and the academic attainment that could be anticipated after arrival in Oxford. The University recruitment crisis of the 1750s was in part triggered by the perceptible decline and falling numbers of many provincial Grammar Schools due to increasing obstacles for entry to them for gifted poor boys.[170] But these schools still took advantage of the closed awards system to send on such pupils as they could enrol to their usual Oxford college, despite the risk of choking off its intellectual vitality. Also, Fellowships were often attached to those educated at certain schools, as at St John's where several fellowships were exclusively reserved for the products of Merchant Taylors; others were restricted to certain parts of the country.[171] Thus, such was the power of the Blundell's School, Tiverton, connection with Balliol College that in 1732 seven of the fourteen Fellows were from Blundell's, because of the interconnection of the closed scholarships with the fellowships. As Sir John Dolben, the Balliol Visitor, complained, the old Blundellians 'habitually voted for their compatriots without regard to the more important questions of good conduct and scholarship'.[172] Parents of the middling support, confronted with uninspired teaching and a narrow curriculum

---

[168] Eneas Mackenzie, *A Descriptive and Historical Account of the Town and County of Newcastle Upon Tyne* (Gateshead, 1827), 339. For Moises see John Brewster, A *Memoir of the late Reverend Hugh Moises* (Newcastle, 1823).

[169] Cumbria Record Office (Kendal), WDX 94/acc. 165, Richard to Thomas Fothergill, 16 Nov. 1751.

[170] For changing recruitment patterns see Stone, 'The size and composition of the Oxford Student Body 1580–1909'.

[171] Sutherland, *Oxford in the Eighteenth Century*, 11.

[172] H.W. Davis, *A History of Balliol College*, rev. R.H.C. Davis and Richard Hunt (Oxford, 1963), 158.

at too many Grammar Schools, increasingly looked to place their sons at the public schools or one of the newly created private classical schools with masters intent on sending pupils on to both English universities.[173] Colleges like Queen's, that had an established catchment area, were materially affected: Provost Smith tried with small success to take boys from some of the County Durham schools in order to widen the College's geographical cohort of 'Poor Boys' who might be able to go on and secure a fellowship.[174]

iii) The appeal of school teaching

Masters at these schools often maintained a close relationship with Oxford. Most had taken holy orders, much as would have been the case were they bent on obtaining a parochial benefice, but instead, for a variety of motives, had opted to teach boys rather than take on what might be ordinarily an unstimulating round of pastoral duties in a village. Politics could matter when appointments were made. Thus when Bishop Hare of St Asaph (1727–31) sought a master from Principal Thomas Pardo of Jesus College for Wrexham School it was because he was confident that the College's Whig loyalties would produce just the man.[175] Per contra, convinced Jacobites who might find high preferment hard to come by in the Hanoverian Church had an opportunity through schoolmastering to hand on their Stuart loyalism to the next generation and that could be incentive enough to look for a pedagogic career.[176] One such was John Hunter, the 'very severe and wrong-headedly severe' master of Lichfield Grammar School, who educated Samuel Johnson.[177] The latter may arguably have learned from him to associate the Latin culture, semi-clerical status and moral rigour of schoolmastering with an attachment to the exiled king.[178] Many younger Oxonians with fellowships gave up waiting for a college living to fall vacant and took up schoolteaching instead, despite counsel in some quarters not to do so. A disappointed Whig careerist, Dr John Free, a former Chaplain of Christ Church, insisted that that school teaching was not suited

---

[173] Hans, *New Trends*, 117–35. There is a useful list of school masters who kept private schools in ibid., App. 1, 221–42.

[174] Hodgkin, *Queen's College*, 161.

[175] The bishop observed that 'among other proper Qualifications [the College] is well affected to the Govermt', JCOA PR. PARDO/1, 9 Mar. 1729 (?). Thanks to Colin Haydon for this reference.

[176] Jonathan Oates notes that Winchester was still thought of in some quarters as essentially Jacobite as late as 1758. Oates, *Jacobitism in eighteenth century English schools and colleges* [The Royal Stuart Society, Paper LXXII] (London, 2007), 10–12.

[177] A. L. Reade, *Johnsonian gleanings* (11 vols., London, 1909–52), III. 153; Robert DeMaria, Jr., *The life of Samuel Johnson. A critical biography* (Oxford, 1993), 10.

[178] Paul Monod, 'A Voyage out of Staffordshire', in eds. J. Clarke and H. Erskine-Hill, *Samuel Johnson in historical context* (Basingstoke, 2002), 11–43, at 21; Craig Rose, '"Seminarys of Faction and Rebellion": Jacobites, Whigs and the London charity schools, 1716–1724', *HJ*, 34 (1991), 831–56.

452 ENLIGHTENED OXFORD

to the Purpose, and Business of a Clergyman. It has in it all the Tameness, Meanness, and Confinement of the lowest Servility; ... though it may advance the Learning of a Boy, it is nothing but Destruction and Distraction to the Learning of a MAN.[179]

Free's views carried only so much weight. Certainly towards the end of the century, teaching carried a new veneer of social respectability, with grammar schools occasionally placing recruitment advertisements in *Jackson's Oxford Journal* and other local papers, including salary and curriculum details.[180] In some cases, school appointments lay in the gift of an Oxford college and brought with them more money and more prestige than the average benefice. James Woodforde, for instance, fellow of New College, was disappointed not to be elected Headmaster of Bedford School in 1773, what he called the 'third best thing in the gift of New College'.[181] Woodforde, in his early thirties, was a decade older than John Wesley of Lincoln College who, in 1727, nearly put his name forward for the mastership of Skipton Grammar School (Lincoln could nominate if the vicar and wardens failed to do so).[182] A generation later, in 1751, Wesley's own pupil, Richard Bainbridge (fellow 1736–52), was interested in the appointment for himself and made plain its attraction for a young don short of money and anxious to move away from the confines of college. He called Skipton [Ermysted's] Grammar School:

A charming piece of preferment, especially to a person who is not averse to ye charges, attendance, and duty of a school; it is one of ye best endowed schools, not only in ye north but in England.[183]

A move into schoolmastering could also be born of desperation if one had to leave Oxford quickly, as was the case for Thomas Paget, Fellow of Corpus Christi College, and a proctor, when his secret marriage was unearthed by the college authorities. Necessity compelled him to start a small private school which he kept going after taking the helm at Sherborne School (1743–51). He was not a social success either in the school or in the town; gossip about his shadowy time in Oxford was probably unavoidable, but plausible accusations that he was diverting boys to his own school completed the damage and made it expedient for him to take the living of Mells in Somerset.[184]

---

[179] Free, *Sermons preached before the University of Oxford*, Preface, viii.
[180] Tompson, *Classics or Charity?*, 30, 30 n.5, 31.
[181] See ed. Beresford, *Diary of a Country Parson*, I. 119, 1 Sept. 1773. It went to John Hooke, fellow of New College 1757–73, Headmaster of Thame School, Oxon., 1768–73.
[182] See A.M. Gibbon, *The Ancient Free Grammar School of Skipton in Craven* (Liverpool, 1947).
[183] *The Letters of the Rev. John Wesley*, ed. J. Telford (8 vols., London, 1931), I. 42–3.
[184] Gourlay, *Sherborne School*, 52.

At the highest level, the scholarly interconnection between Westminster School and Christ Church making William Markham's move from the Headmastership to the Deanship appear natural and desirable suggested that one could take up teaching as a career and still rise to the heights of the establishment. The eighteenth century was no less the century of great headmasters than the nineteenth. Queen's College had a distinguished record in this regard. Richard Yates, nominated by the college to Appleby Grammar School, was fifty-eight years in office from 1723 till his death in 1781, and was correcting Latin translations up to a fortnight prior to his death. He made concessions to modern subjects and attracted pupils from outside Westmorland. Half a guinea from every leaver who could afford it built up a Library Fund, including science textbooks, Molière, Addison, English grammars, and a list of 'recommended reading' by Archdeacon John Law of Carlisle for 'students of divinity'.[185] St John's College produced in one generation Alexander Stopford Catcott of Bristol Grammar School, 1722–44, John Jones of Oundle, 1718; and Matthew Smith of Merchant Taylors, 1720, all of them differently distinguished.[186] Catcott was able to confound critics of Free's opinions by combining headmastering with distinctive scholarship. Inspired by John Hutchinson, he looked again at the etymology of the Hebrew word *Elahim* in his sermon preached before Bristol Corporation, *The Supreme and Inferior Elahim* (1735/6), a homily that emphasised the Trinitarian insistence of early Hutchinsonianism and inspired the next generation of Oxonians who took up this anti-Newtonian physico-theology with extreme seriousness.[187] Catcott was far from alone. Another product of St John's, John Hildrop, took over the Headmastership of the Marlborough Grammar School (where Sacheverell had been a pupil in the 1670s) and spent most of Queen Anne's reign running the school and completing a project that drew heavily on the Oxonian patristic learning he had accumulated, *God's Judgments upon the GENTILE Apostatized Church, Against the Modern Hypothesis of some Eminent Apocalyptical Writers* (in four parts), published anonymously in 1713, appearing with the endorsement of Archbishop John Sharp of York.[188] Charles Lawson, High Master of Manchester Grammar School, 1764–1807, promoted the study of mathematics at the school in a manner that foreshadowed Cyril Jackson's promotion of the subject. The resemblances did not stop there. Zealous to a fault as a teacher even in old age, Lawson balanced his pedagogy with a swagger that bordered on the vainglorious, fancying himself in an Oxford quadrangle, and the master of a college, even keeping a hunter and a horse for his groom, though

---

[185] E. Hinchliffe, *Appleby Grammar School—from Chantry to Comprehensive* (Appleby, 1974), 45–8, 52–3.

[186] Costin, *St John's College*, 178.

[187] M. Neve and R. Porter, 'Alexander Catcott: glory and geology', *The British Journal for the History of Science*, 9 (1977), 37–60; Gurses Tarbuck, *Enlightenment Reformation*, 68–75.

[188] Hildrop was Headmaster from 1703 to 1733 continuously. Stedman, *Marlborough*, 193–6.

Fig. 9.3 Charles Lawson ('Carolus Lawson'), by and published by James Heath, after William Marshall Craig, line engraving, 1799 (© National Portrait Gallery, London).

they were hardly ever employed.[189] Headmasters, in short, were powerful figures in channelling pupils through to Oxford, and could be influential in favouring one college over another. Sir Justinian Isham of Lamport's consultation of the Head of Rugby school in 1707 for advice about the placing of his son at the most suitable college, was replicated in most schools.[190]

It was not unknown for the learning of an outstanding school master alumnus to be recognised by the University with an invitation to return and deliver lectures. Such was the call that came for Dr John Bidlake (1755-1814) when it was almost too late. He was the Headmaster of Plymouth corporation Grammar School (1779-1810) who encouraged artistic talent, including Benjamin Haydon and Charles Locke Eastlake. His capacities were recognised by his being named Chaplain to William, Duke of Clarence, and by his University asking him to give the 1811 Bamptons Lecture, published as *The Truth and Consistency of Divine Revelation, With Some Remarks On The Contrary Extremes of Infidelity*

---

[189] J. A. Graham and B. A. Phythian, *The Manchester Grammar School 1515–1965* (Manchester, 1965), 24–8; W. R. Whatton, *The History of Manchester School...* (2 pts., Manchester, 1825), 115–23; Hans, *New Trends*, 40.

[190] Sutherland, *Oxford in the Eighteenth Century*, 8.

and Enthusiasm (London, 1813), with an emphasis on the consistency of the Mosaic and Christian revelations that the Hutchinsonians might have appreciated. Bidlake unfortunately suffered a cerebral stroke while delivering the third lecture.[191] Men like Bidlake were precisely those who nurtured boys ready to go up to Oxford to take advantage of the curriculum reforms being seen through by Cyril Jackson and John Eveleigh of Oriel.[192] And the favour could be returned if the school in question was reasonably accessible from Oxford. Thus Reading Grammar School under Richard Valpy (1781–1830) was visited triennially by the Vice Chancellor of Oxford when plays by Plautus or Sophocles and Euripides (the latter in Greek costume) were performed in aid of local or public charities.[193] A more common form of approval for the scholastic endeavours of an Oxonian headmaster was for those who had known him at University—and had in most cases remained at Oxford themselves—to donate books to his school library, a complimentary gesture that invited emulation in the next generation. When Richard Pococke was Head Master of the Grammar School (King Edward VI's) at Southampton (*c.*1690-1710), the donors of books to the library included such eminent contemporaries as John Hudson, the Bodleian librarian; Thomas Bisse, Fellow of Corpus Christi and Chancellor of Hereford cathedral, and Edward Thwaites, fellow of Queen's, Regius Professor of Greek and White's professor of moral philosophy, 1708–11.[194] It was typical of the host of educational threads criss-crossing the country and linking Oxford with most parts of England, connections which, on a different scale, were no less operative across the rest of Britain and Ireland.

Part C: Oxford and 'Britishness': links to Wales, Scotland, and Ireland

i) Beyond the University: Wales

The failure of Owain Glyndwr in the early fifteenth century to secure an independent principality with two universities[195] meant that the closest such establishment to Wales was, from 1571, Oxford. And therefore the sons of gentlemen,

---

[191] Nigel Aston, 'Bidlake, John (1755–1814), schoolmaster and Church of England clergyman', *ODNB* online version, 2004.

[192] John Eveleigh (1748–1814), fellow of Oriel, 1770; dean, 1775–81; provost, 1781–1814; vicar of St Mary's, Oxford, 1778–81; prebendary of Rochester, 1781. Brockliss (2), 157, notes how Eveleigh in the 1790s was 'anxious to fill the University with intellectual heavyweights who could fight the Church of England's corner'.

[193] T. A. B. Corley, 'Valpy, Richard (1754–1836), schoolmaster', ODNB online edn., 2006; C. F. Russell, *A History of King Edward VI School Southampton*(Cambridge, 1940), 251.

[194] Ibid., 216.

[195] I am indebted to Colin Haydon for a draft copy of his chapter , 'Two Hundred Years: From "The Glorious Revolution" to the Tercentenary c.1688–c.1871', in eds. F. Heal, R. Darwall-Smith, R.J. B. Bosworth, and C. Haydon, *Jesus College Oxford of Queen Elizabethes Foundation. The first 450 Years* (London, 2021). See also Baker, *Jesus College*.

clergymen, and yeomen attached to the established Church—many of whom had come through Wales's academically impressive grammar schools—came to converge on the Elizabethan foundation of Jesus College.[196] In the course of the eighteenth century, Jesus's supremacy was contested and young Welshmen fanned out across the colleges, encouraged by changing patterns of patronage. Increasingly, the upper levels of the gentry from a county like Glamorgan—the Mansells, Stradlings, and Gwyns—went on from Westminster school to Christ Church rather than Jesus.[197] Of the smaller foundations, Pembroke College offered one fellowship and one scholarship for natives of Pembrokeshire or, failing that, any South Wales county. These were founded by a former gentleman commoner from a familial Jacobite background in west Wales, Sir John Phillips, 6th Bt. (c.1701–64).[198] Cultural Jacobitism was strong in the principality and the Beauforts were among its patrons, much as they were in Oxford: in 1745 the 3rd Duke of Beaufort established a scholarship at Oriel that was a prize attraction for Tory families drawn in large part from Swansea and the zone of the ducal estates in Monmouthshire.[199]

Entrants to Jesus College came from across the principality though, after 1713, more from the northern counties (Denbighshire supplied the greatest number of Jesus students) because of endowed scholarships and exhibitions.[200] Though many sons of Wales's landowners and gentlemen still continued to matriculate, other Jesus students tended to hail from less socially privileged backgrounds and those from the same locality or county might band together.[201] Some undergraduates were not even in permanent residence. Thus William Jones, an assistant teacher at Abergavenny School, was concurrently an undergraduate at Jesus and could manage no more than occasional presence on cost grounds.[202] But has been noted by one historian, the cultural and social capital that accrued to curates

[196] P. Jenkins, 'The Anglican Church and the unity of Britain: the Welsh experience, 1560–1714', in eds. Steven G. Ellis and Sarah Barber, *Conquest & Union. Fashioning a British State 1485–1725* (Harlow, 1995), 115–38, at 129.

[197] Jenkins, *The making of a ruling class*, 156–7. The proportion of leading gentry attending Jesus in 1621–1700 was 55%; between 1701 and 1780 it fell to 32%. Ibid., 216, 224; A. G. Prys-Jones, 'Carmarthenshire and Jesus College, Oxford', *The Carmarthenshire Antiquary*, 4 (1962), 16–25.

[198] Macleane, *Pembroke College*, 200. The Fellow had the benefit of the perpetual curacy of West Haroldston with Lambton in Pembrokeshire. Phillips provided a stipend as title for the future evangelist George Whitefield to be ordained by Bishop Martin Benson of Gloucester.

[199] P. D. G. Thomas, 'Jacobitism in Wales', *Welsh Historical Review*, 1 (1962), 279–300. At least thirteen Glamorgan men attended Oriel College 1741–80, about 16% of total county matriculands. The appointment involved the exercise of influence by county magnates such as George, 2nd Lord Vernon (1735–1813) and Sir Charles Kemys Tynte, 5th Bt. (1710–85). Academic considerations took second place. Glamorgan RO, Cardiff, D/DKT/1/7, 79, quoted in Jenkins, *The making of a ruling class*, 229. See also ibid., 154–5, 172, 176. For the 5th Duke's connections with Jesus College, Crook, *Brasenose College*, 153n.

[200] See R. Gilbert, *Liber Scholasticus* (London, 1829), 313–17.

[201] Between 1690 and 1719, Jesus annually provided the largest quota of freshmen who matriculated as plebians. Bennett, 'University, society and Church 1688–1714', 385. In the later years of the century, friends from North Wales rode in groups for safety on horseback to and from Oxford.

[202] ed. O. F. Christie, *The diary of the Revd William Jones, 1777–1821* (London, 1929), 83.

BEYOND THE UNIVERSITY   457

such as Jones from attending Oxford 'had a high value when it came to competing for employment, preferment, and social regard'.[203]

These trends could not prevent Welsh stereotyping (not always good-humoured) from being fostered among students and dons alike, elegantly articulated in the much-read Edward Holdsworth's mock-heroic poetic satire, *Muscipula Sive Cambro Muo Machia* (1709), wherein Taffy, the inventor of the mousetrap, was subjected to ridicule. It did not go unanswered: at the behest of the fellows of Jesus, Thomas Richards of Llanfyllin, another competent young Latin poet, produced *Hoglandiae Descriptio* (1709), a poem that critics considered the equal of Holdsworth's.[204] The fact was that Oxford attracted talented Welsh students from a range of schools, who returned home (usually having taken orders) with a range of literary skills that they could deploy as readily in Welsh as in English. Their Oxford experience did not make them devalue the richness of their own native vernacular inheritance in both prose and verse, it gave them more ways in which to develop it, as with the Rev. Ellis Wynne's *Visions of the Sleeping Bard* (1703), a satirical and often scabrous commentary on the follies and iniquities of Welsh and London life.[205] Wynne went back to Wales; so did other graduates from a landed background who did not take orders but might, in later life, join the Welsh lieutenancy, shrievalty, or bench. Many other students took either English livings or the road to London after graduating, aware that English was the language of advancement.[206] Those who, usually for academic reasons, stayed on in Oxford, appear to have kept up a degree of socialisation based on the ties they had developed while undergraduates. Such was the basis of the Red Herring Club (1694–1774), probably founded by the great Welsh scholar, Edward Lhuyd, unmistakably Welsh in its ethos, though numbering many Englishmen among its members. Several Herringites were from Jesus, the distinguished names including David Parry (Keeper of the Ashmolean, 1709–14), Henry Fisher (University Registrar, 1737–61), Eubule Thelwall (Principal of Jesus 1725–7), and Humphrey Owen, steward of the club and Bodley's librarian, 1747–68.[207]

---

[203] Slinn, *The education of the Anglican clergy*, 126.

[204] Leicester Bradner, *Musae Anglicanae: A History of Anglo-Latin Poetry, 1500–1925* (New York, 1940), 228; W. J. Hughes, *Wales and the Welsh in English Literature* (London, 1924), chap. 3; G. H. Jenkins, *The Foundations of Modern Wales 1642–1780* (Oxford, 1993), 213, 232–3. For the argument that *Muscipula* was about more than mocking the Welsh and the wider references to Sacheverell both there and in *Hoglandiae* see W. Gibson, '*Muscipula* and *Hoglandia*. Sacheverell's literary battle, 1709–1711', *Welsh Journal of Religious History*, 7 & 8 (2012–13), 39–50. Richards's work was corrected by Edward Lhuyd and Anthony Alsop.

[205] Jenkins, *Modern Wales*, 234–6. He notes that at least thirty-two editions of this work had been published by 1932.

[206] Of Jesus College's twenty-two livings only seven were in Wales. Jacob, *The Clerical Profession*, 83. Welsh livings were notoriously poor.

[207] 102 members have been identified between those dates. See Bodl. MS. Top. Oxon. f.49; MS Top. Oxon. e.281. Owen was Principal of Jesus, 1763–8. For the Red Herring's Jacobite nature see Greenwood, *William King*, 77. It appears to have met initially for academic discussion but over time became more political and sociable. Baker, *Jesus College*, 34.

458   ENLIGHTENED OXFORD

Despite producing firebrand Jacobites like Sir Watkin Williams-Wynn, 3rd Bt. (1693?–1749), the greatest landowner in the principality and leader of the Cycle of the White Rose (a Welsh Jacobite Society),[208] Jesus College moved gradually in the first half of the century from being a High Church bastion to one fairly evenly divided between Whigs and Tories.[209] It was testimony to a collegiate spirit based on a common Welsh identity that tended to diffuse the worst party feuding.[210] Not even the Whigs among them took pride in the appointment of Benjamin Hoadly to the see of Bangor in 1715. A few years later it was reported that the Jesus men in Oxford were furious with Hoadly for preferring Peter Maurice, the author of a sermon censured in Oxford, to several appointments in the Bangor diocese.[211] And this solidarity persisted, indeed was made easy as party animosities cooled in George III's reign, with Jesus students and fellows taking pride in keeping up their contacts in the province, a camaraderie fictionally represented in Tobias Smollett's 1771 novel *The expedition of Humphrey Clinker*, many of the letters it contained written by one J. Melford to 'Sir Watkin Phillips, Bart. of Jesus College, Oxon.'[212] It was this spirit of collegiate interconnection that made possible the outstanding scholarship of Edward Lhuyd, one whom Hans Sloane later described as 'the best naturalist now in Europe'.[213] Lhuyd—the natural son of an impoverished Welsh gentleman, Fellow of the College, Keeper of the Ashmolean Museum, 1691[214]— was more than a naturalist and antiquary. He had a grasp of many disciplines, and was an energetic, diligent, and inspirational character.

The Principal and Fellows of Jesus in the early 1690s were keen on producing a history of Wales on the Robert Plot model and, having been impressed by the detailed information of Welsh counties Lhuyd sent for use in Gibson's edition of Camden's *Britannia* in 1695, thought that he might be just the man for the job.[215] Lhuyd was more than receptive, issued proposals for a 'British Dictionary,

---

[208] Tellingly, the third baronet's inheritor son and grandson were educated at Oriel and Christ Church, respectively.

[209] For the High Church dominance in Wales 1690–1714 see Jenkins, 'The Anglican Church and the unity of Britain', 136–7.

[210] Thus Principal Thomas Pardo's letters contain news about Wales, remarks about visits there, and comments on 'our Countrymen'. Thanks to Colin Haydon for this information.

[211] Browne Willis to Bp Adam Ottley, 13 Feb. 1720/1, NLW Ottley Corresp., vol. 1, 1824; Starkie, *The Church of England and the Bangorian Controversy*, 97–8.

[212] Baker, *Jesus College*, 45.

[213] R. T. Gunther, *Early Science in Oxford, Vol. XIV, Life and Letters of Edward Lhwyd* (Oxford, 1945); B. F. Roberts, *Edward Lhuyd: the making of a scientist* (Cardiff, 1980); F. Emery, *Edward Lhuyd, FRS, 1660–1709* (Cardiff, 1971); G. Daniel, 'Edward Lhuyd: antiquary and archaeologist', *WHR*, 3 (1966), 345–59. WHR 25 (2010), 1–115, was a special issue to mark the tercentenary of Lhuyd's death.

[214] A. MacGregor, 'Edward Lhuyd, museum keeper', *WHR*, 25 (2010), 51–74. Lhuyd had first been Assistant Keeper under Plot, whom he disliked. Jenkins, *Modern Wales*, 218.

[215] G. Walters and F. Emery, 'Edward Lhuyd, Edmund Gibson, and the printing of Camden's *Britannia*, 1695', *Library*, 5th series, 32 (1977), 109–37. Lhuyd's contempt for Plot can be seen in the design of the *Archaeologia Britannica*, which avoids Plot's error-prone attempts to reconcile natural history and antiquarianism. R. F. Ovenell, *The Ashmolean Museum, 1683–1894* (Oxford, 1986), 3–63 (Plot); 64–107.

BEYOND THE UNIVERSITY   459

historical and geographical' (that would also take in parts of Scotland and Ireland, Cornwall and Brittany), and was urged on by supporters such as John Williams, Archdeacon of Cardigan (fellow 1670–81), who lauded 'so good and learned a design and [one] so much for the reputation of our country'.[216] Williams worked hard to secure patronage and subscriptions across the principality for Lhuyd, enlisting inter alia the antiquarian Humphrey Humphreys, bishop of Bangor (1689–1701),[217] and Thomas Mansell (later 1st Baron Mansell of Margam), both Jesus men. The next step in the mid-1690s was to send out about 4,000 'Parochial Queries' with thirty-one questions concerning the geography, natural history, and antiquities of Wales.[218] The whole network of Anglican squires, clerics, and farmers responded enthusiastically to 'dear Ned' or 'Honest Gabriel', in effect acting as his field workers and supplying him with copious amounts of information at a parish level.[219]

Lhuyd himself did not stay in Oxford all the time writing. He set off in 1697 on a four-year, 3,000-mile expedition (1697–1701) into Wales, Scotland, and across to Brittany in pursuit of natural knowledge, wanting to see sites and curiosities for himself, recording as he went, and using his gift for teasing out information from among the common people to good effect.[220] His thoroughly researched, detailed, and recondite *Archaeologia Britannica* (the first of an intended multivolume work) appeared in 1707 two years before his premature death; it was dubbed 'one of the major achievements of the age in the fields of philology and antiquity', one which made the case for a sophisticated early British civilisation on the basis of artefactual evidence. It exhibited an exacting philological and lexicographic rigour that was typical of Oxford scholarship of its time.[221] For all his accessibility, Lhuyd would not cut one corner, proceeding on the basis of the rule that he would countenance no theories 'for which I have

---

[216] MS Ashmole, 1817b, f. 200, cited in Baker, *Jesus College*, 32. For the detailed background and the subscription problems Lhuyd had experienced with his *Lithophylacii Britannici ichnographia* (1699), a geological field guide with a focus on fossils see Elizabeth Yale, *Sociable Knowledge. Natural History and the Nation in Early Modern Britain* (Philadelphia, PA, 2016), 179–201.

[217] G. White, 'Humphrey Humphreys, bishop of Bangor and Hereford 1648–1712', *Anglesey Antiquarian Society and Field Club* (1949), 61–76.

[218] Jenkins, *Modern Wales*, 241. Lhuyd was also involved in corresponding with antiquaries working on similar subjects in other parts of the British Isles, for instance the Gaelic antiquary Roderick O'Flaherty in Galway. ed. R. Sharpe, *Roderick O'Flaherty's letters to William Molyneaux, Edward Lhwyd, and Samuel Molyneaux, 1696–1709* (Dublin, 2013). See generally Adam Fox, 'Printed questionnaires, research networks and the discovery of the British Isles, 1650–1800', *HJ*, 53 (2010), 593–621.

[219] Over 2,000 letters to and from Lhuyd are online as part of the Oxford Early Modern Letters Online Project. See http://emlo-portal.bodleian.ox.ac.uk/collections/?catalogue=edward-lhwyd

[220] N. Edwards, 'Edward Lhuyd and the origins of early medieval Celtic archaeology', *Antiquaries Journal*, 87 (2007), 165–96; eds. J. L. Campbell and D. Thomson, *Edward Lhuyd in the Scottish Highlands 1699–1700* (Oxford, 1963). Lhuyd even spent two weeks incarcerated at Brest on suspicions of being a spy. Yale, *Sociable knowledge*, 80–1.

[221] For Lhuyd's creation of 'Britain' as both a topographical object and a political object see ibid., 38–9, 194.

460 ENLIGHTENED OXFORD

no warrant from my own reasoning'.[222] Without his pioneering work, largely directed from his rooms in Jesus College, the subsequent cultural revival in eighteenth-century Wales would have taken very different forms.[223] And Lhuyd was very proud of his Celtic origins, proclaiming his Welsh separateness from England in British terms: 'I don't profess to be an Englishman, but an old Briton'.[224]

Lhuyd died in debt, some of it to the University and its printer, primarily for the printing of the *Archaeologia Britannica*, whose costs had not been fully covered by subscription. He left behind a vast corpus of unpublished manuscripts and other materials,[225] but the able pupils he collected at Jesus College in his lifetime were largely unable to build on his initiative. Only five years after his death, one of them, the Rev. John Morgan, newly removed from Merionethshire to take up the rectory of Matching in Essex, was complaining in 1714 that 'there peeps not a penny paper from Jesus College for the use of their country'.[226] The brightest hope in the generation after Lhuyd was Moses Williams (1685–1742), FRS, scholar, translator, and collector, whose ambition was to publish ancient Welsh manuscripts held in libraries across Britain. In 1717 he brought out in Welsh a register of all printed books published in that language, and his *Repertorium Poeticum* (1726) was a useful alphabetical list of celebrated odes. That was the limit of his achievement. Williams was brimful of ideas for arousing Wales from its economic torpor, which included setting up a university,[227] but he was unable to win over backers, and died a disappointed man. When the Welsh cultural renaissance got under way around the middle decades of the century through such outlets as the Society of Ancient Britons and the Gouge Trust (both supported in Oxford), the Jesus College contribution was arguably less than might have been expected given Lhuyd's pioneering scholarship. Nevertheless, as Philip Jenkins's work has underlined, the clergy of the Welsh Church, many of them educated at Jesus College, 'would be central to every movement [in the 'long' eighteenth century] to promote

---

[222] Quoted in Emery, *Edward Lhuyd*, 27. For his rigorous methodology see also Jenkins, *Modern Wales*, 218; Rosemary Sweet, *Antiquaries. The Discovery of the Past in Eighteenth-Century Britain* (London, 2004), 125–7.

[223] For the Welsh cultural revival Sweet, *Antiquaries*, 139–41; Jenkins, *Modern Wales*, 244–6; Sam Smiles, *The Image of Antiquity: Ancient Britain and the Romantic Imagination* (New Haven, CT, 1994), 16–17.

[224] S. Piggott, *William Stukeley* (Oxford, 1950), 8. One of Lhuyd's most conspicuous achievements was to confirm the close linguistic relationship between the Welsh and Irish languages. Clare O'Halloran, *Golden Ages and Barbarous Nations. Antiquarian Debate and Cultural Politics in Ireland, c.1750–1800* (Cork, 2004), 20–1.

[225] The University took into its ownership most of the books he owned and sold off the manuscripts. E. Rees and G. Walters, 'The dispersion of the manuscripts of Edward Lhuyd', *WHR*, 7 (1974), 148–78.

[226] Prys Morgan, A *New History of Wales: The Eighteenth-century Renaissance* (Llandybie, 1981), 21. For Morgan's Anglo-Welsh literary importance in the generation after Lhuyd's death see J. Saunders Lewis, *A School of Welsh Augustans, Being a study in English influences on Welsh literature during part of the 18th century* (Wrexham/London, 1924), 27–9.

[227] Jenkins, *Modern Wales*, 244, 248–9; Sir L. T. Davies and A. Edwards, *Welsh Life in the Eighteenth Century* (London, 1939), 85.

learning and literature in the Welsh language'.[228] And pride in Welsh culture continued to be exhibited at Oxford down the century. George Richards (1767–1837), a fellow of Oriel, 1790–6, produced the prize-winning poem *The Aboriginal Britons*, performed at the Sheldonian Theatre in July 1791 and published later that year; his pamphlet collection, *Songs of the Aboriginal Bards of Britain* (1792) was also well-received. Richards played on the idea of Wales as a historical home of liberty and defiance that helped shape a British common identity, a theme that caught the national mood as the country prepared for war with France.[229]

ii) Beyond the University: Scotland

Scotland had four universities, but many native Scots still came on to Oxford, usually to complete their studies, others going to Cambridge, the Dissenting Academies, or the Inns of Court and the anatomy schools in London. And there was traffic, too, in senior academics, usually southbound. Exchanges became slightly more problematic after 1689, with the abolition of episcopacy in the Kirk, and it took at least two generations for the residual hostility towards Scottish Presbyterians intending to study at Oxford to subside.[230] In the aftermath of the change in the person of the sovereign and the upheaval in the government of the Kirk, in the 1690s there was quite an exodus south to the English universities (largely Oxford) of talented Scots with episcopalian convictions, including John and James Keill, the Arbuthnots father and son, academic refugees unable to subscribe to the Westminster Confession of Faith (in some cases, 'rabbled' or evicted from their churches in the southern Lowlands in the winter of 1688–9),[231] making up a select Caledonian diaspora in the university.

The Tory majority at Oxford down to 1714 worried over the fate of the appreciable numbers of Scottish Nonjuring clergy trying to secure a future for themselves and willy-nilly drifting into Jacobitism. While these had contacts with the English Nonjurors at large, they also had friends and well-wishers in the University working for their legal toleration north of the border (the 1712 Toleration Act was the main fruit of their efforts, restoring an unrestricted right of public worship for those willing to swear loyalty to the Queen).[232] These

---

[228] Jenkins, 'The Anglican Church and the unity of Britain', 129.

[229] Elizabeth Edwards, *English Language Poetry from Wales* (Cardiff, 2013), 16, 84, 87, 270–1. In 1793 he published the poem *Modern France*, a pamphlet-length poem deploring French violence.

[230] T. Clarke, 'Nurseries of Sedition?: The Episcopal Congregations after the Revolution of 1689', in ed. J. Potter, *After Columba—After Calvin, Community and Identity in the Religious Traditions of North East Scotland* (Aberdeen, 1999), 61–9.

[231] Harris, *Revolution*, 372–8; A. Raffe, *The Culture of Controversy: Religious Arguments in Scotland, 1660–1714* (Woodbridge, 2012), 219–24.

[232] Ryan K. Frace, 'Religious toleration in the wake of revolution: Scotland on the eve of Enlightenment (1688–1710s)', *History*, 93 (2008), 354–75, is useful on the willingness of some kirk

462 ENLIGHTENED OXFORD

welcomed the visits, long or short, of their Scottish brethren to Oxford, and looked out for English benefices to which they might be preferred. The Scottish episcopalian James Greenshields was the particular hero of Oxford Tories as a kind of Sacheverell in a minor key, who had suffered imprisonment by the Edinburgh town council for using an Anglican liturgy in defiance of the local presbytery.[233] He was semi-officially received in person in Oxford during May 1711 after the House of Lords had upheld his appeal.[234] Many in the colleges offered support for his promotion of the English liturgy north of the border by holding collections for Prayer Books.[235] William Bromley (his particular patron) called him 'a great sufferer in a very good cause' and Greenshields received an honorary MA for his pains.[236] After his return north, Oxford efforts concentrated on the production at the Press of Prayer Books (primarily '... for the better sort' in Scotland). There were 1,300 copies ready stored at Oxford University Press in October 1712, of which 500 were despatched to Aberdeen the following January.[237]

While Anne lived and the Tories were in power, such initiatives were favourably received if not always speedily acted upon; all that changed once the Hanoverians came in and Scottish episcopalians became too closely identified with militant Jacobitism after the '15 for the authorities to sanction their official presence. However repugnant it was (not least because some feared it foreshadowed the future for the English Church), in the reign of George I Oxford had to accept that Presbyterianism in Scotland was entrenched beyond displacement while 'James III' remained a *de jure* king, and looked on with trepidation while the Whigs set up commissions to purge its Universities of episcopalians.[238] Oxford's quiet alliance with the Nonjurors of north-east Scotland who had kept up their presence and influence at Aberdeen University was dissolved,[239] and there were prominent individual casualties, including the mathematician James Stirling (at Oxford from 1711 on a Snell Exhibition),[240]

---

leaders, such as Robert Wodrow, Keeper of Glasgow University's Library, to move towards better relationships with deposed Episcopalians. But it went little further than sharing information and being civil.

[233] J. Stephen, 'English Liturgy and Scottish Identity: The Case of James Greenshields', in eds. Allan I. Macinnes and D. J. Hamilton, *Jacobitism, Enlightenment and Empire* (London, 2014), 59–74.

[234] Ben Rogers, 'The House of Lords and religious toleration in Scotland: James Greenshield's Appeal, 1709–11', in eds. R. McKitterick, C. Methuen, and A. Spicer, *Studies in Church History*, 56: *The Church and the Law*, (Cambridge, 2020), 320–37.

[235] BL MS 22908, f. 95.

[236] T. M. Clarke, 'The Scottish Episcopalians 1688-1720' (Edinburgh, Ph.D., 1987), 246, 333. He also received an honorary Cambridge degree the same year, ibid., 342.

[237] Ibid., 343, 363.   [238] Discussed in Chapter 2, pp. 32–6.

[239] K. German, 'Jacobite Politics in Aberdeen and the '15', in eds. P. Monod, M. Pittock, and D. Szechi, *Loyalty and Identity. Jacobites at Home and Abroad* (Basingstoke, 2010), 82–97; R. L. Emerson, *Professors, Patronage and Politics. The Aberdeen Universities in the Eighteenth Century* (Aberdeen, 1992), 18–34.

[240] He reported to his father on arrival: 'We have very much to do, but there is nothing here like strictness. I was lately matriculate, and with the help of my tutor I escaped the oaths, though with much ado.' Letter of 20 Feb. 1711, quoted in Tweedie, *James Stirling*, 3.

who left Balliol in the winter of 1716–17 after refusing the oath of allegiance to George I.[241]

For all these setbacks, Oxford High Churchmen throughout the century looked with affection on the Scottish Nonjurors as possessing a similar descent to themselves, one that, for ecclesiological purity, was worthy of admiration, and transcended any narrow notions of state-Church allegiance. These Scots in their sight embodied respect for the Christian mysteries and orthodox Trinitarian belief. George Berkeley (the younger), canon of Christ Church, with a son at St Andrews University, son of the great philosopher, devoted his later life to nurturing contacts between the Church of England and the Scottish Nonjurors when, by the 1780s, it was politically safe to do so.[242] Berkeley even wrote from St Andrews that he would submit to the Scottish bishops if he knew how he could do so. One correspondent admitted, 'I do not fully comprehend what the Dr. drives at'.[243] George Horne, President of Magdalen College, seconded his friend's efforts to bring them out of the cold. Their lobbying, taken up by Bishop Samuel Horsley, would find its fruit in the Relief Act of 1792, made possible by the death of Prince Charles Edward Stuart ['Charles III'] in 1788 and the willingness of the moderate majority among the Scottish Nonjurors, led by Bishop John Skinner (the younger), thenceforth to pray for George III.[244]

The presence of Scottish students in Oxford was a small token of Britishness that the University nurtured, a socialising dimension of the gradual construction of Anglo-British identity, with Scottish professional and elite families recognising the personal advantage derived from political and cultural integration.[245] Before 1707 relatively few members of the Scottish aristocracy received an English education. Thereafter, numbers steadily increased.[246] Of course, after the Union, a high proportion of the Scottish nobility and gentry attending university in England came up to Oxford via English public schools. They included the Gaelic-speaking Sir James Macdonald, 8th Baronet of Sleat (1742–66), an old

---

[241] He may have been expelled or quit prior to that. For Stirling's mathematical capacities see Chapter 2, p. 40, n. 92. Upon leaving Balliol he had the offer of a professorship at an Italian university that he declined. He later ran a mine for a Whig peer and made about £2,000 per annum. Tweedie, *James Stirling*, 8, 10n.

[242] There was considerable interest at Lambeth over these initiatives. See the correspondence between Granville Sharp and Robert Findlay, Regius Professor of Divinity at Glasgow University, on the legitimacy of the Scottish Episcopal church (Nonjurors) in 1785. LPL, Moore Papers Vol. 6, 111–16.

[243] Bp Skinner to Bp Petrie, 29 Oct. 1782, Aberdeen University Library MS 3320/6/97, f. 21.

[244] F. C. Mather, 'Church, Parliament and penal laws: some Anglo-Scottish interactions in the eighteenth century', *EHR*, 92 (1977), 540–72; Mather, *High Church prophet*, 116–38, esp. 121–3.

[245] C. Kidd, *Subverting Scotland's past. Scottish Whig historians and the creation of an Anglo-British identity, 1689–c.1830* (Cambridge, 1993).

[246] Keith M. Brown, 'The origins of a British aristocracy: integration and its limitations before the treaty of union', in eds. Ellis and Barber, *Conquest & union*, 222–49, at 233–4. For Scottish MPs, especially from noble families, who had attended either Oxford or Cambridge see Brooke, *The House of Commons 1754–1790*, 164.

Etonian who went on to Christ Church,[247] the 'Marcellus of the North' as James Boswell called him, an unpriggish model of youthful probity and learning that won him many admirers and invited comparisons with Sir Philip Sidney. Macdonald's comparable premature death caused much distress.[248] Another was David, Viscount [of] Stormont (1727–96), later ambassador to Maria-Theresa of Austria and then Louis XV of France and a cabinet minister in North's government, a product of Westminster and Christ Church. He and his uncle, Lord Chief Justice Mansfield, were occasionally subject in Oxford to the same mid-century 'Scotophobia' that their countrymen in England often had to bear,[249] and a willingness to find even a trace of a Scottish accent risible was still current in the 1790s, as James Boswell reassured his discomposed son, Jamie:

> Perhaps there being an erroneous account of your birth may be ominous of your rising high in the Law; for when Lord Mansfield went to Oxford some scotch connection who accompanied him upon being asked the place of his birth which was Perth by his pronunciation Parth made it be thought Bath and he is accordingly enrolled at Christchurch as a native of that place.[250]

Other Scots from a landed background, such as John Sinclair of Ulbster (1754–1835), attended Oxford (Trinity College in his case) as part of the process of British elite socialisation, after going first to both Edinburgh and Glasgow Universities.[251] To send a son to Oxford could still be a controversial choice for a Scot from a mercantile background. One such claimed that at Oxford they 'look back with a wishful eye and would willingly reclaim the antient splendour of Mother Church's pretentions to power dominion and state independency'. But he still preferred that his son should go there rather than one of Scotland's four.[252]

---

[247] He and his brother were under government pressure to attend an English university to ensure their clan loyalty. His widowed mother, Lady Margaret, and sister were also in favour, with the former insistent on the superiority of an Oxford education for him. His younger brother Alexander, who succeeded to the title and estates, was educated at Westminster, St Andrews, and Oxford, and qualified for the English bar. He married an English wife. Stana Nenadic, *Lairds and Luxury. The Highland gentry in Eighteenth-century Scotland* (Edinburgh, 2007), 52–3, 66.

[248] 'a remarkable young man of good parts and great application', Boswell noted on 26 Nov. 1762, *London Journal 1762–1763*, ed. Gordon Turnbull (Harmondsworth, 2010) 12. They met for the last time in Oxford in April 1763, ibid., 204–6. For Macdonald and his circle of friends in Oxford see *Memoirs of Richard Lovell Edgeworth*, 55ff.

[249] Mansfield, then the Hon. William Murray, was first on a list of King's Scholars admitted to Christ Church from Westminster in June 1723. For a discussion of his studies and his distancing himself from any hint of Jacobitism see Norman S. Poser, *Lord Mansfield. Justice in the Age of Reason* (Montreal & Kingston, 2013), 30–3.

[250] Boswell to James ('Jamie') Boswell the younger, 6 Dec. 1794, Beinecke Rare Book and Manuscript Library, Yale University, Boswell Collection (GEN MSS 89), L 154.

[251] He also entered for the English bar at Lincoln's Inn and intended a career south of the border. R. Mitchison, *Agricultural Sir John. The Life of Sir John Sinclair of Ulbster 1754–1835* (London, 1962), 23–4.

[252] John Black, Bordeaux, to Robert Black, London, 12 Feb. 1746, Black family Papers, Huntington Library, HM 49167, quoted in James Livesey, *Civil Society and Empire. Ireland and Scotland in the Eighteenth-Century Atlantic World* (Yale, 2009), 140.

And then there were Englishmen who, for one reason or another, went to Oxford *after* attending a Scottish University. Among them was the Hon. Thomas Fitzmaurice (strictly speaking, an Anglo-Irishman), brother of the 2nd Earl of Shelburne, who upon matriculating at Glasgow in 1759 had Adam Smith as his tutor. Shelburne's own experience at Christ Church had put him off the place, yet he was happy (as was Smith) that the willing Fitzmaurice should go on to Oxford in 1762 to take further his legal studies by attending Blackstone's lectures on the laws of England.[253] Smith also took students who came on to Glasgow to complete their education. The Hon. Henry Herbert, Eton and Christ Church, arrived at Glasgow in 1762 and, while at the College, was introduced by his tutor to leading members of the Scottish Enlightenment, David Hume in Glasgow, and Thomas Reid and George Campbell in Aberdeen among them.[254] And there were also the small number of those who started at Oxford before deciding (or having it decided for them) that a Scottish higher education would be more suited to their aptitudes. One such was Charles Darwin (1758–78), the precociously talented son of the botanist, poet, and religious radical, Erasmus Darwin, who left Christ Church a year after joining in October 1774 to go and study medicine at Edinburgh, having found the college's classics emphasis uncongenial;[255] by contrast, George Colman the younger spent so much time in London at the theatres that his father sent him north to King's College, Aberdeen.[256] Scots were thinly spread compared with the number of Welshmen in Oxford, though the University was ready to be generous in incorporating as MAs academic Scots who conformed once in England to the established Church. Thus the Rev. William Braisbridge, vicar of Newchurch, Isle of Wight, who taught mathematics at Edinburgh 1724–31 and became MA and DD of Aberdeen, was admitted as a Master in Oxford in 1740.[257]

The Snell exhibition at Balliol College brought in a steady stream of Scottish graduates from Glasgow University, men of roughly the same age as Oxford undergraduates when they arrived, because higher education north of the border generally commenced when a boy was thirteen or fourteen rather than seventeen or eighteen. The Snell exhibition was originally to provide ordinands for the episcopal Church in Scotland when it was tottering on the verge of disestablishment in the late seventeenth century. In the Hanoverian era, its primary cultural purpose became integrating Scots into the British whole (ostensibly by giving

---

[253] N. Aston, 'Petty and Fitzmaurice: Lord Shelburne and his Brother', in eds. N. Aston and C. Campbell Orr, *An Enlightenment Statesman in Whig Britain: Lord Shelburne in Context* (Woodbridge, 2011), 29–50, at 33–4; Ian Simpson Ross, *The Life of Adam Smith* (Oxford, 1995), 134–6.

[254] Ibid., 137–8.

[255] J. Uglow, *The Lunar Men: the friends who made the future 1730–1810* (London, 2002), 271.

[256] Colman resided in Aberdeen with two other Englishmen sent there for much the same reason. Jeremy F. Bagster-Collins, *George Colman the Younger, 1762–1836* (New York, 1946), 13–16.

[257] The documents had to be signed by Lord Arran, which he did on 17 Mar. 1740, Northumberland Archives, SANT/BEQ/4/16/084/B.

them an entrée into English life as priests or chaplains), and presbyterian members of the Kirk were obliged like everyone else at matriculation at Oxford to subscribe to the Thirty-Nine Articles of the Church of England.[258] The first election was made in 1699. They thereupon became (if they were not so already by baptism and episcopal confirmation) honorary Anglicans and were required to attend chapel services at Balliol.[259] Though some of the award-holders claimed to find the Oxford experience disappointing, others found it all too easy to confine their intimacy to their fellow countrymen or other members of the College. There were those who wanted to break out, like the Exhibition holder, Charles Robertson, in the late 1780s. One friend agreed to send Robertson letters of introduction to people outside Balliol but advised against straying too far beyond its walls: [260]

> ...this last part of my advice may perhaps be different from what you have received from some of your friends, but I give it you on the strength of my own experience of the good effects of following it, both while I was at College, & since I left it.

But there was no shortage of Glasgow students applying to come south (the draw of John Locke, the great Oxford philosopher with whom all Scottish students engaged, may have played its part), and nominations—one on merit, one on patronage grounds—were decided at the highest levels of the Scottish administration.[261] Thus in the 1730s, Walpole's leading power broker in Scotland, the Earl of Islay (3rd Duke of Argyll from 1743) assisted by his henchman, Lord Milton, had a major influence on Glasgow University's choice of the exhibitioners.[262] Their involvement betokens the significance of the Snell award in fostering a sense

---

[258] See William Innes Addison, *The Snell Exhibitions: From the University of Glasgow to Balliol College, Oxford* (Glasgow, 1901); Aberdeen University Library MS 3320/6/111: 'Right of Principal & other members of the College to nominate students from Scottish Universities to 10 Exhibitions at Balliol' (notification from the Master of Balliol, 1809); Gleig Papers, NLS MS 3872, ff. 61, 67, 81–2.

[259] Exhibitioners were obliged to give a bond for £500 that they would be ordained. L. Stones, 'The life and career of John Snell (c.1629-1679)', *Stair Society Miscellany*, 2 (1984), 148–85. In 1738 a lawsuit was begun in Chancery to compel the exhibitioners to enter the Church of England. The Lord Chancellor rejected the case in 1744 and called for the overhaul of the legal basis of the Snell charity. Edinburgh University Library MS La. II.99⁷, quoted in Ross, *Adam Smith*, 79.

[260] William Gregory to Charles Robertson, 9 Jan. 1788, NAS, Robertson of Lude, GD132/776/5.

[261] Demonstrated academic capacity in Greek as well as Latin excluded many potential Scottish students and the insistence rankled. See John Stirling to 1st Duke of Montrose, 18 Jan. 1717, Montrose Muniments. NAS, GD220/5/713.

[262] NLS MS 16671, Saltoun Papers. Islay took a dim view of the English universities, which he thought only taught classics well. He attacked 'their sinecure Professors' in the House of Lords in 1736. Islay to Milton, 29 May 1736, NLS MS. 16564, Saltoun Papers. Islay, 'a man of sense and learning', as David Hume later called him, was an old Etonian who was set apart by then proceeding to Glasgow rather than Oxford or Cambridge, 'a fairly authoritarian Whig' at ease with Jacobites and Tories. Roger L. Emerson, *An Enlightened Duke. The Life of Archibald Campbell (1682-1761), Earl of Ilay, 3rd Duke of Argyll* (Kilkerran, 2013), 18, 107.

of British identity through a cross-national educational experience, a crucial dimension in eighteenth-century state formation.

Among the Exhibitioners, heading south on the six- or eight-day journey from Edinburgh was Adam Smith (Balliol, 1740–6), whose time there coincided with an appeal by the Snell exhibitioners to the Glasgow Senatus Academicus (winter 1744–5) to put pressure on Balliol to improve the treatment meted out by the College to them, especially regarding the way they were assigned the worst rooms. The Glasgow governing body duly contacted Theophilus Leigh, the Master, but he was reluctant to do anything, accusing the Snell students of having a 'total dislike of the college'.[263] If they so deprecated living conditions, they could move elsewhere. On the one hand, Leigh welcomed Scots on Snell or Warner exhibitions, while on the other, once in residence, he did them no favours. There was litigation over financial arrangements, and the College tried to divert exhibition moneys into general purposes.[264] Smith was critical not of Oxford's social life but of the intellectual life he encountered there.[265] And, though he had disliked the fierce Calvinist tradition he encountered at Glasgow, all this did nothing to endear Oxonian Anglicanism to him.[266]

Adam Smith's acerbic comments on Oxford's meagre provision for his instruction while in residence in comparison with the pedagogic rigours of Glasgow are usually taken to be typical of Snell award-holders generally. Whatever the curricular deficiencies, the idea that Oxonian culture had no trace of the Enlightenment values of improvement, virtue, and practical benefit most scholars find in its mid-century Scottish counterparts is not sustained on closer examination.[267] Part of the culture

---

[263] Addison, *Snell Exhibitions*, 19–22.

[264] Jones, *Balliol College*, 164. The situation does not appear to have eased over time. It was reported in 1772 that there was a virtual civil war in Balliol between the college and the Glasgow exhibitioners insistent on their grievances. Sir David Carnegie to John Mackenzie Esq., 11 Apr. 1772, Delvine Papers, NLS, MS 1248, f.84. That same year a son of the 8th Earl of Dundonald was expelled from Balliol and intended to appeal. Carnegie to Mackenzie, f. 87, 30 June 1772.

[265] For instance, 'It will be his own fault if anyone should endanger his health at Oxford by excessive study, our only business here being to go to prayers twice a day, and to lectures twice a week'. Smith, 24 Aug. 1740, *Correspondence*, eds. Mossner and Ross, 1. Per contra, it has been argued that Smith's mind was primarily formed at Oxford in the 1740s so that it was understandable if he should conclude 'a commercial society was perfectly consistent with patrician hegemony'. Clark, *English Society 1660–1832* (2000), 150; Donald Winch, *Adam Smith's politics: an essay in historiographic revision* (Cambridge, 1978), 181ff. Nicholas Phillipson considers the copious reading Smith undertook at Oxford in *Adam Smith. An Enlightened Life* (Harmondsworth, 2010), 56–64.

[266] Ross, *Adam Smith*, 60–80. For the claim that religion was crucial to Smith's later work see P. Minowitz, *Profits, priests and princes. Adam Smith's emancipation of economics from politics and religion* (Stanford, CA, 1993), and for Smith's religious position generally see Gavin Kennedy, 'Adam Smith on Religion', in eds. Christopher J. Berry, Maria Pia Paganelli, and Craig Smith, *The Oxford Handbook of Adam Smith* (2013); online edn., Oxford Academic, 1 July 2013, https://doi.org/10.1093/oxfordhb/9780199605064.013.0023, accessed 2 Feb. 2023, and the essays in ed. P. Oslington, *Adam Smith as Theologian* (London & New York, 2011).

[267] For Scottish universities in an Enlightenment context see T. M. Devine, *The Scottish Nation 1700–2000* (Harmondsworth, 1999), 77–80; R. B. Sher, *Church and University in the Scottish Enlightenment. The Moderate Literati of Edinburgh* (Princeton, NJ, 1985), 28–31; R. L. Emerson, 'Scottish Universities in the eighteenth century, 1690–1800', *SVEC*, 167 (1977), 453–74.

468 ENLIGHTENED OXFORD

clash was actually political, with Scots at Tory Balliol presumed to be Whigs and unreservedly in favour of the Hanoverian Succession. In fact, men from episcopalian backgrounds willing to take the oaths of commitment to the Hanoverian monarchy still came south and took up the Snell award. One such was Smith's contemporary at Balliol, John Douglas (1721–1807), son of a Fife merchant, who, with the patronage of Walpole's parliamentary opponent, William Pulteney, later Earl of Bath, and then of George III himself, rose to be Bishop of Carlisle, Dean of Windsor, and, finally, Bishop of Salisbury. He moved from St Mary Hall to Balliol in 1738 and held a Snell award from 1745 to 1748 after having first been ordained in the Church of England and served as a chaplain at the battle of Fontenoy (1745). Unlike Smith, he had nothing but praise for his Balliol tutor, George Drake.[268] And some Snell exhibitioners liked Oxford so much that they stayed there, notably John Smith (Balliol, 1744), who taught anatomy and chemistry and held the Savilian Chair of Geometry from 1766 to 1797.[269] Scots such as Smith encouraged their fellow countrymen to join them in Oxford and exercise patronage opportunities as they arose. He was the client of Abraham Robertson, who came with empty pockets out of Duns in Berwickshire to be a servitor at Christ Church and tried to finance himself by opening an evening school for mechanics in London that failed. John Smith stepped in and appointed Robertson as his professorial deputy in 1782, while he was also favourably noticed by Dean Jackson and nominated as college Chaplain. It was no surprise that, on Smith's death, Robertson followed him in the same Savilian chair (to 1810).[270] The connection between the University of Aberdeen and Oxford also endured into the second half of the century. It was well seen in the person of James Williamson (c.1740–1813) who came from Marischal College (where he had been taught by James Beattie) as a mature student (matric. 1769, St Alban Hall) and soon made his mark as an outstanding mathematician. He was the author of *Elements of Euclid* (Clarendon Press, 1781).[271]

iii) Beyond the University: Ireland

Of all the other universities in the British Isles (Cambridge apart), Oxford was most closely linked with Trinity College, Dublin [TCD], on account of their established, exclusively Anglican basis. It made it, for instance, much easier for a Dublin graduate coming to Oxford with a Master's degree or equivalent to be made a member of the University, in what was called incorporation *ad eundem gradem*. To some extent, Trinity in its first century of life had been under the wing

---

[268] BL Egerton MS 2181, ff. 4, 6, 12. Douglas wrote against Hume but also aided him. He was friendly with many of the Scottish literati.

[269] eds. Fauvel, Flood, and Wilson, *Oxford Figures*, 185; Morris, 'The Eighteenth Century: Chemistry allied to Anatomy', 64. Smith wrote about the benefits of taking the waters at Cheltenham.

[270] Cox, *Recollections*, 144–7.   [271] ed. Goudie, *Hertford College*, 34–5.

BEYOND THE UNIVERSITY 469

of its much older English sisters. Thus, until St George Ashe's appointment in 1692, Oxford or Cambridge graduates had always been named as Provosts of Trinity.[272] There was institutional overlap even higher up the *cursus honorum*. For Oxford was presided over continuously for eighty-nine years by a senior member of one of the greatest Irish families, the Butlers, in the persons of the 1st Duke of Ormond (1669–88), his son the 2nd Duke (1688–1715), and the latter's brother, the 1st Earl of Arran (1715–58). The Ormonds, father and son, held the Oxford Chancellorship contemporaneously with the Dublin one (the 1st Duke received his Dublin post in 1660)[273] though, when George, Prince of Wales (the future George II) was elected to succeed the 2nd Duke at Trinity on his attainder, Dublin signalled a desire to court the goodwill of the new ruling house in a manner that Oxford was unwilling at that date to do.[274] Thereafter they were set on quite different paths vis-à-vis the Hanoverian establishment, confirmed by the installation of Richard Baldwin, a firmly Whig Provost, at Trinity, Dublin, in 1717.[275]

Anglo-Irish families sending their sons to Oxford either sent them via Trinity College, Dublin, or missed the latter out altogether in their concern that these youths should mingle in the best circles at the earliest opportunity. As Rachel Wilson has put it, 'An English education 'created a sense of belonging, to think of themselves as extensions of the English elite, equally sophisticated and able to pursue opportunities no both countries.' Jonathan Swift was one such. Having matriculated at Hart Hall in early summer 1692 to read to for a Master's degree the weeks that he kept term for incorporation gave him the utmost satisfaction, as he wrote to his uncle:

> I was never more satisfied than in the behaviour of the University of Oxford to me. I had all the civilities I could wish for, and so many favours, that I am ashamed to have been more obliged in a few weeks to strangers, than ever I was in seven years to Dublin College.[276]

[272] J. V. Luce, *Trinity College, Dublin. The first 400 years* (Dublin, 1992), 36. Kearney described Trinity, Dublin as 'Oxford's Irish offshoot', *Scholars and Gentlemen*, 153. Cf. the considerable overstatement in R. B. McDowell and D. A. Webb, *Trinity College Dublin 1592–1952. An academic history* (Cambridge, 1982), 519: 'There is no evidence whatsoever for any Oxford influence in TCD after 1688'.
[273] David Hayton, *The Anglo-Irish Experience, 1680–1730. Religion, Identity and Patriotism* (Woodbridge, 2012), 68. For the 1st Duke's typically lavish entourage of fourteen coaches filled with dignitaries and dependents, when he arrived at Oxford to be installed as Chancellor in 1678 en route to Dublin, see Thomas Carte, *An history of the Life of James, Duke of Ormond* (originally published, 1736, 6 vols., Oxford, 1851), IV. 536. For Lord Arran's election as Oxford Chancellor in 1715, see Chapter 6.
[274] Dr Samuel Molyneaux, the Prince of Wales's secretary, was on hand in Dublin to achieve a smaller-scale Hanoverian Succession at Trinity. T. Barnard, *A New Anatomy of Ireland. The Irish Protestants, 1649–1770* (New Haven, CT, 2003), 108–9.
[275] J. W. Stubbs, *The History of the University of Dublin* (Dublin, 1889), 153–60. In the words of a 1783 pamphlet, since 1714 'the College of Dublin has ever peculiarly merited the name of a Whig university'. John Forsayeth, *Thoughts on the present state of the College of Dublin*, 11, quoted in McDowell and Webb, *Trinity College Dublin*, 72.
[276] To William Swift, 29 Nov. 1692, *Correspondence*, ed. Woolley, I. 22. Swift ever after made the most of his Oxford connections, and gratifyingly reported in 1712 that Atterbury and friends regarded

470 ENLIGHTENED OXFORD

The 1st and 2nd Dukes of Ormond deliberately tried to popularise Oxford as a destination for the sons of Irish notables.[277] Annesleys, Veseys, Boyles, Percevals, and Southwells all came over in successive generations, usually heading to the 'House',[278] the most celebrated among them the Hon. Charles Boyle, part of the literary set fostered by Henry Aldrich during the 1690s, engaging on behalf of the 'Ancients' in the cultural warfare of that decade.[279] There were other good reasons why Oxford was an attractive alternative to Dublin. TCD was institutionally stagnant under the early Hanoverians and not a single publication by a fellow of the college appeared between 1722 and 1753, even though their numbers had increased from nineteen in 1700 to twenty-eight by mid-century. Student discipline was deteriorating and the curriculum made Oxford's appear positively progressive. It was only after John Hely-Hutchinson was appointed Provost in 1774 that TCD gradually began a systematic attempt at structural overhaul.[280]

In those circumstances, it was considered by many Ascendancy families that the despatch of their sons to England might encourage decreased dissipation and scholastic as well as social progress, though unfamiliarity with the Oxford collegiate system could generate its own perplexities. In 1766 Arthur Pomeroy in Dublin was keen to place his eldest son at Oxford. In a letter asking for assistance he said that it was 'a point of much consequence and difficulty to me, as from my remote situation it is no easy matter for me to determine what College to put him to, . . . '[281] Richard Lovell Edgeworth (1744–1817), of Edgworthstown, county Longford, was pulled out of Trinity by his dissatisfied father on account of his drunken idleness and sent on to Corpus Christi College, Oxford in 1761.[282] Paternal hopes were half satisfied: the young Edgeworth combined creative intelligence with sporting interests, being induced to invent a plan for telegraphing by a desire to know the result of a race at Newmarket. The slightly older Henry Flood

---

him as a 'Christchurch man.' *Journal to Stella*, ed. Williams, II. 514, 15 Mar. 1712. Hamilton, *Hertford College*, 38. Swift's picture was given to the Bodleian gallery in 1739. Thomas Hunt to Richard Rawlinson, 13 Mar. 1741, MSS Rawl. letters 96, f. 51, for details of the inscription.

[277] Toby Barnard, 'Introduction', in eds. Barnard and Fenlon, *The Dukes of Ormonde*, 37–8. Seventy-nine individuals whose birthplace was listed as 'Ireland' entered Ch. Ch. between 1660 and 1727; nineteen were noblemen, thirteen gent commoners. Ch. Ch. Oxford, Dean's Register 1660–1757, DP i.a.3, quoted in Richard Ansell, 'Irish Protestant Travel to Europe, 1660–1727' (Oxford, unpub. D. Phil., 2014), 21.

[278] Thanking the 2nd Duke for securing his son a place at Christ Church, John Vesey, Archbishop of Tuam) wrote in 1699: 'It is not enough, it seems, that I wear the marks of your most noble grandfather's favour. It is hereditary in your family to oblige from generation to generation.' NLI Ms. 2456, f. 391, quoted in Barnard, 'Dependance, clientage and affinity', 235n.

[279] Toby Barnard, *Making the Grand Figure. Lives and Possessions in Ireland, 1641–1770* (New Haven, CT, 2004), 51–2, 64, 314; Lawrence Berkley Smith, Jr., 'Charles Boyle, 4th Earl of Orrery, 1674–1731', (unpub. Edinburgh Univ. Ph.D., 1994), 14–37.

[280] McDowell and Webb, *Trinity College Dublin*, 39, 43, 45–9, 60; Michael Brown, *The Irish Enlightenment* (Cambridge, MA, 2016), 212–16.

[281] To 8th Earl of Abercorn, 7 Apr. 1766, PRONI D623/A/37/21.

[282] Uglow, *The Lunar Men*, 128. Another reason was apparently the proximity at Black Bourton, Oxon., of his father's friend, Paul Elers, a barrister. *Memoirs of Richard Lovell Edgeworth, Esq.*, 46–7.

(1732–91), the future 'Patriot' orator in the Dublin House of Commons and agitator for Irish legislative independence (achieved in 1782), found Oxford to his taste in a way that Dublin had not been. Because he had applied himself so little to his studies in three years at Trinity College, young Flood was despatched by his family to Christ Church in 1750 as a gentleman commoner, and it proved his educational making. Flood was fortunate to find in William Markham (the future dean), college lecturer in rhetoric (1747–50) and junior censor (1751), one of the outstanding teachers of the age, and he resumed his studies with renewed enthusiasm, an example of how stimulating a mid-century Oxford education could be where there was a genuine meeting of minds. For both men (Markham had Irish origins himself), and despite their political differences, it was the beginning of an enduring friendship. Flood's achievement was recognised by the unusual award (to a gentleman commoner) of an honorary MA at Oxford in 1752.[283]

Another beneficiary of Oxford was John Fitzgibbon (1749–1802), the future Lord Chancellor of Ireland at the passing of the Act of Union (1800), and the fierce opponent of any incorporation of Catholic Emancipation within it. He came on to Christ Church (MA, 1770) after a distinguished academic progress at Trinity, and stood out for ability as much in Oxford as he had in Dublin.[284] Edgeworth, Flood, and Fitzgibbon arrived at Oxford having tasted—too much tasted in the case of the first two—university life in Dublin, and half knew what was expected of them. The same was not always the case for their fellow countrymen who had not had the socialising experience of an English school and brought to Oxford boisterous attitudes that were almost too much for young Englishmen. The retired Cabinet Minister, Welbore Ellis (1713–1802), remembering his time at Kilkenny before going on to Westminster School, alluded to the 'mutinous ferocity of spirit cultivated among even the little boys' in Ireland, and knew his nephew, archbishop Charles Agar of Cashel, grasped his meaning only too well:

> You have seen enough of this in those who having receiv'd their School education in that country & have come to Oxon who were dreaded in every College where they offer'd themselves, & were after many disorders sent away.[285]

---

[283] James Kelly, *Henry Flood. Patriots and Politics in Eighteenth-Century Ireland* (Dublin, 1998), 31–4; Warden Flood, *Memoirs of the life and correspondence of Henry Flood* (Dublin, 1838), 14.

[284] Cf. Ann Kavanaugh, 'Fitzgibbon, John, first Earl of Clare (1748–1802), lord chancellor of Ireland', ODNB online edn., 2008. In the early 1770s the College apparently decided for the time being to take no more graduates *ad eundem* from Dublin. Hon. Edward Ward (at Ch. Ch.) to Lord Bangor, 2 May [1771?], PRONI D2092/1/9/21.

[285] Welbore Ellis to Abp Agar, 20 Sept. 1790, giving advice on the education of the latter's younger sons. Hampshire Record Office, Normanton Papers, 21M57/C24/8. Cf. comments from a Scottish baronet at Christ Church almost two decades earlier: '... it is much more the Fashion to study at Ch. Church than most People imagine. We have to be sure (& what Society is free of them) a Sett of idle Fellows, chiefly Irish, but they seem rather to be despised than admired by the Society in general'. Sir David Carnegie to John Mackenzie Esq., 31 Dec. 1771. NLS, Delvine Papers, MS 1248, f. 80.

472   ENLIGHTENED OXFORD

In the security-obsessed University of the 1790s it was less the roistering tendencies of Irish students that concerned the authorities than apprehensions that Irish subversives intent on overthrowing the established order in that kingdom would continue their machinations if they tried to matriculate at Oxford. When the Duke of Portland received a warning from the zealous Protestant, Lord Chancellor Clare, that some among the nineteen United Irishmen he had expelled from Trinity College, Dublin were planning to take that path, he lost no time in alerting the Vice Chancellor to be on his guard.[286]

Scholarly contacts between Dublin and Oxford were long-established and it was natural that there should be mutual interest in each other's libraries and special collections. John Toland's original justification for his time in Oxford in 1693 was to spend time in the Bodleian working on an Irish dictionary and a dissertation designed to prove that the Irish were originally a colony of the Gauls.[287] Often, when one scholar sought to consult manuscript collections held in Oxford, exchanges still had to be negotiated. There could be difficulties. When in 1784 the Chevalier O'Gorman, the Irish soldier, genealogist (he researched the lineage of expatriate Irishmen seeking to acquire nobility in France), and antiquarian, wanted to use the Bodleian to consult manuscripts relating to Irish history, the astronomer Dr Henry Usher (Senior Fellow and first Andrews Professor of Astronomy at TCD, 1783) went over in person to secure permission and temporary possession. The problem was less that the Chevalier had soldiered with the Irish Brigade in the French army than that he was a Roman Catholic and manuscript collector with valuable estates in France. Usher's 'embassy' gave the still-nervous Oxford authorities evidence of the Chevalier's bona fides and allayed any apprehension that he might want to add some of the manuscripts into his private collection surreptitiously.[288]

Oxford churchmen took much interest in the affairs of their sister Church after the Revolution and those who went out to Ireland from Oxford understandably wanted other graduates to join them. William Perceval was unrestrained when he told Arthur Charlett '... such are much wanted here and wished for by us who know the difference between an Oxford and an Irish education',[289] as high flyers in

---

[286] Portland to vice chancellor, 30 Apr. 1798, PRONI T2905/22/102; www.bonhams.com/auctions/25354/lot/28/ For TCD as a seedbed of student activism for the United Irishmen movement see Brown, *The Irish Enlightenment*, 413.

[287] Discussed in Chapters 2 and 10. Toland came to Oxford via Glasgow and Edinburgh. A Donegal man he only went to Dublin after this sojourn in Oxford.

[288] To Chevalier Thomas O'Gorman, Belanagare, 28 July 1784, BL Add MS 21121, cited in eds. Robert E. Ward, John F. Wrynn, SJ, and Catherine Coogan Ward, *Letters of Charles O'Conor of Belanagare. A Catholic Voice in Eighteenth-Century Ireland* (Washington DC, 1988), 444; R. Hayes, 'A forgotten Irish antiquary: Chevalier Thomas O'Gorman 1732–1809', *Studies: An Irish Quarterly Review*, 30 (1941), 587–96.

[289] Perceval to Arthur Charlett, 10 May 1707, Bodl. MS Ballard 36, f. 39, quoted in T. C. Barnard', '"Almoners of Providence", the clergy, 1647 to c.1780', in eds. T. C. Barnard and W. G. Neely, *The clergy of the Church of Ireland 1000–2000* (Dublin. 2006), 78–105, at 96.

BEYOND THE UNIVERSITY   473

both Churches mutually tried to encourage each other. The High Church cause in Ireland may have been select but it was vociferous and with Oxford's Chancellor as Irish Lord-Lieutenant between 1703 and 1707 and 1710 and 1713, and the Irish convocation meeting alongside the Dublin parliament between 1704 and 1713, its supporters were well-placed to maximise their influence.[290] Encouragement from Oxford was an important morale-booster for the Irish while, on the other side of St George's Channel, 'honest' Oxonians could congratulate themselves that the High Church interest was making progress beyond England. Sacheverell had his own Irish equivalent in the person of Francis Higgins, whose uncompromising anti-Dissenting sermons were scarcely less forceful than his own,[291] while Atterbury made good use of his cousin (and vice versa), Thomas Lindsay, bishop of Killaloe (1656–1724), and a former fellow of Wadham College, in lobbying ministers and advancing their mutual high-flying interests. Given the unambiguously Protestant nature of the Revolution Settlement in Ireland and the tiny number of non-Catholic Jacobites,[292] Irish High Churchmen were never close to achieving a majority in their Church, even with Ormond's endorsement. They had, for instance, little to show for their exertions in the Irish Convocation, which suffered much the same inconclusive wrangling as its English counterpart.[293] And the death of Queen Anne in 1714 and Ormond's flight in 1715 pushed their party completely to the margins without even the prospect of any support for their plight from Trinity College, set, as it was, on an impeccably Whig course.[294]

Oxford-educated Tories trying to advance their careers in the Church of Ireland were thereby stymied. While their patrons Rochester and Ormond had served as Irish viceroys, they had their share of the ecclesiastical plums; a classic beneficiary was Charles Hickman (1648–1713) of Christ Church, Lord Rochester's domestic chaplain 1684, and later chaplain to both William III and Queen Anne. It was

---

[290] D. W. Hayton, 'The High Church party in the Irish Convocation, 1703-1713', in eds. H. J. Real and H. Stover-Leidig, *Reading Swift: papers from the 3rd Münster symposium on Jonathan Swift* (Munich, 1998), 117–40. The sacramental and ceremonial life of the Church had historically interested fewer in Ireland than in England. F. R. Bolton, *The Caroline tradition of the Church of Ireland* (London, 1958).

[291] Higgins was a regular visitor to England. Alex W. Barber, 'Censorship, salvation and the preaching of Francis Higgins: a reconsideration of High Church Politics and theology in the early eighteenth century', *Parliamentary History*, 33 (2014), 114–39; D.W. Hayton, 'Irish Tories and victims of Whig Persecution: Sacheverell fever by proxy', in ed. Knights, *Faction displayed* (2012), 80–98, at 84–92; D.W. Hayton, *Ruling Ireland, 1685-1742. Politics, politicians and parties* (Woodbridge, 2004), 137, 143, 156–7.

[292] Eamon O Ciardha, *Ireland and the Jacobite cause, 1685-1766. A fatal attachment* (Dublin, 2004), 115, 173–6; T. Doyle, 'Jacobitism, Catholicism, and the Irish Protestant elite, 1700–1710', *Eighteenth-Century Ireland*, 12 (1997), 28–59; S. J. Connolly, *Religion, law, and power. The making of Protestant Ireland 1660-1760* (Oxford, 1992), 240–1.

[293] Hayton, *Ruling Ireland*, 134–5, 138, 143. Hayton points out that in Ireland there were more Tory bishops in the Convocation than in its English equivalent, though the balance of parties negated any chances of lasting legislative achievements. Ibid., 135–6.

[294] For Oxford defiantly registering its approval of what the recently dismissed Irish Lord Chancellor, Sir Constantine Phipps, had attempted while in office, through the award to him of an honorary degree, see Chapter 7, p. 45.

474   ENLIGHTENED OXFORD

thanks to Rochester's influence that the see of Derry came his way in 1703.[295] Similarly, Welbore Ellis (1652?–1734), a former army chaplain and Student of Christ Church, Oxford, was chaplain to Ormond's household from 1700 to 1705 which cleared his path to progress to the Deanery of Christ Church, Dublin, and on to the sees of Kildare and Meath.[296]

After 1714 Oxford men might be tempted to consider senior posts in the Church of Ireland if they were sufficiently lucrative (witness Hugh Boulter's translation to Armagh in 1724 when he relinquished the 'poor' see of Bristol and the Deanery of Christ Church, Oxford) or felt inclined to follow a patron if he were named Lord Lieutenant. But these individuals were invariably part of the Whig minority in the University for whom removal to Ireland would allow less political confinement than in the embattled Oxford of the first two Georges. Boulter, who had the confidence of Bishop Gibson of London and therefore of Sir Robert Walpole, took care to recommend Englishmen for Irish episcopal vacancies on the majority of occasions and Christ Church men in particular: the proviso was that they had to be dependable Whig courtiers.[297] Perhaps following his experience of life in Oxford, as late as 1727 Boulter still feared Trinity could be 'a seminary to Jacobitism'.[298] The two successors of Boulter at Armagh but one were contemporaries at 'the House': first, George Stone (Archbishop, 1747–64), a key political manager in mid-century Ireland;[299] second, Richard Robinson (Archbishop, 1765–94), a much poorer politician but a primate whose interests lay in building, improvement, and regeneration.[300]

There was, very briefly, a low-key Tory revival in the Church of Ireland during Lord Carteret's viceroyalty (1724–30) when moderate High Churchmen with Oxford pedigrees were among the beneficiaries of another Christ Church product.[301] Among them was William Perceval, Archdeacon of Cashel (1671–1734), who had originally returned to Ireland with Rochester. He was one of Higgins's

---

[295] Hayton, *Ruling Ireland*, 143.

[296] For the Whig writer Richard Steele's admiration for his old Oxford tutor, see ed. R. Blanchard, *Tracts and Pamphlets by Richard Steele* (Baltimore, MD, 1944), 9. For more details on Bp Ellis and Steele at Oxford see Calhoun Winton, *Captain Steele. The Early Career of Richard Steele* (Baltimore, MD, 1964), 33–9, 43.

[297] Richard Holmes, 'English Whigs and Irish Patriots: Archbishop Boulter and the politics of party in Hanoverian Ireland', *Eighteenth-Century Ireland*, 31 (2016), 75–93; P. McNally, '"Irish and English interests": national conflict within the Church of Ireland episcopate in the reign of George I', *Irish Historical Studies*, 29 (1995), 295–314; J. Falvey, 'The Church of Ireland episcopate in the eighteenth century', *Eighteenth-Century Ireland*, 8 (1993), 103–14, at 109.

[298] To Archbishop Wake, 6 July 1727, in *Letters written by His Excellency Hugh Boulter, D.D., Lord Primate of all Ireland & c.*, (2 vols., Oxford, 1769), I. 180.

[299] See E. Magennis, *The Irish political system, 1740–1765: the golden age of the undertakers?* (Dublin, 2000).

[300] A. P. W. Malcolmson, *Archbishop Charles Agar: churchmanship and politics in Ireland, 1760–1810* (Dublin, 2002), 139–40. Agar himself went up to Christ Church in 1755 and there developed the scholarly habits that remained an important part of his character, ibid., 37–8; A.P.W. Malcolmson, *Primate Robinson 1709–94: 'a very tough incumbent in fine preservation'* (Belfast, 2003).

[301] Hayton, 'Irish Tories', 92.

BEYOND THE UNIVERSITY 475

cheerleaders in his heyday, and his hopes of a bishopric had shrivelled upon Anne's demise. But under the well-disposed Carteret, Perceval enjoyed a last hurrah of official favour and was an active member of the Dublin Society after 1731 when also incumbent of St John's church in the city with a prebendal stall at Christ Church Cathedral.[302] Perceval may never have worn a mitre, but he found some compensation in a passion for classical architecture that was widely shared and drew on the influence of Oxford designs sponsored and authored by Henry Aldrich, Dean of Perceval's old college. And he was aware of more recent building in the University and city through his own Oxford contacts. Perceval's architectural enthusiasm grew as his ecclesiastical importance in Ireland diminished, in some sense trying to incorporate into the building plans of his own circle a flavour of remembered Oxford Palladianism. He happily shared his passion with his friends and neighbours, especially the Vesey family, fellow Oxonians and connoisseurs, headed by Sir Thomas Vesey, Bt., (Bishop of Ossory, 1714–30) who built at Abbey Leix, County Laois.[303] As Toby Barnard has elegantly argued, the recollection of the architecture at Christ Church (above all, Peckwater Quadrangle) was one of the most significant classical influences on the many Irish clergy (mainly but not exclusively from Oxford backgrounds) building or renovating their churches and residences.[304]

And not just the clergy. Oxford-educated Anglo-Irish landowners were no less inspired. Barnard points to the figure of Colonel William Flower (1685–1746) at Castle Durrow, county Laois, building there from 1712 on the basis of estate rentals drawn from Wales as well as Ireland. As another product of Tory Christ Church under Aldrich, Flower built while his political career languished: the sophisticated, spacious design of Castle Durrow suggested that Flower was both well-informed about the latest architectural fashions in Oxford and continental Europe and still aspiring to public notice.[305] Given this distillation of Christ Church architectural and cultural influences in Ireland, it was only appropriate that Archbishop Robinson, that great builder, should give funds to his old college to allow the Chapter to commission the young James Wyatt to seal off the east end of the Peckwater quad at Christ Church with what would be known as the Canterbury quadrangle, built 1773–83 in a slightly more severe classical style than that of its neighbour, complete with a triumphal arch entrance and residential block.[306] The design expresses the importance of Oxford as an institution at

---

[302] For Perceval's career see T. C. Barnard, '"Almoners of Providence"', 95–7.

[303] Barnard, *Making the Grand Figure*, 22, 51–2. Vesey was educated at Eton and Christ Church and had also been a fellow of Oriel College, 1695. He was an Ormond client.

[304] Toby Barnard, 'Improving clergymen, 1660–1760', in eds. A. Ford, J. McGuire, and K. Milne, *As by Law Established. The Church of Ireland since the Reformation* (Dublin, 1995), 136–51, at 146.

[305] He received some recognition when an Irish barony was conferred in 1733. Barnard, *Making the Grand Figure*, 62–5.

[306] The Archbishop initially made two separate gifts of £1,000 towards its cost. A further £4,000 was awarded by him for costs to cover construction of the S-W corner of the quadrangle on condition that it was used only by undergraduates of the highest social standing. Curthoys (2), 147–51; Malcolmson, *Primate Robinson*, 45; H. L. Thompson, *Christ Church* (Oxford, 1900), 165–6.

476 ENLIGHTENED OXFORD

the heart of eighteenth-century Anglo-Irish cultural exchanges which, while not lessening an informal sense of English superiority among the majority of University members, did not undercut the underlying inference of formal academic equality among matriculands irrespective of rank and nation. It was well seen in the early 1740s when Convocation in Oxford debated whether the sons of Scottish and Irish noblemen should be on the same footing as the English, and carried it in their favour despite the display of 'Scotophobic' sentiments among some in the minority.[307] In return, a sense of what Irish members of the University owed to their teachers and their college was generously on display. One such occasion came in May 1813 when an expensive silver Warwick vase was presented to Dean Jackson 'By a numerous and distinguished body' of Irish Christ Church Oxonians 'Who have been members of that Society since the commencement of the present century, . . .'[308]

iv) Conclusion

University interests extended way beyond the confines of Oxford. This was an institution rooted in town, county, and country through ideas and individuals, and it was one that gained rather than lost influence in the British state. Most immediately, within the confines of the borough, town and university relations were relatively trouble-free in most years, with each other's status and traditions seldom contested and cooperation normative. The University was not sealed off from the world beyond, outreach took a variety of forms. To give an obvious example, citizens could freely hear ordained Oxford collegians preaching regularly in the city's parish churches. Inherited customs acted out, such as the Assize of Bread, had their eighteenth-century uses in symbolising equity and mutual goodwill. As has been well said, the Assize, 'by bringing University, trade and the poor together . . . may have helped to promote a degree of understanding between them'.[309] The University was, in its guarded way, generally ready to support endeavours to improve the material well-being of the city's population. Christ Church had consistently maintained Almshouses for twenty-four paupers as part of Cardinal Wolsey's original foundation and when the pious high Churchman, Robert Nelson, sponsored Charity Schools in Oxford,[310] members

---

[307] Staffs. RO, D1057/M/I/14/15, Congreve Papers, Thomas Townson to Rev Richard Congreve, 6 June 1744.

[308] Bodl. MS Top Oxon. d.174, f. 83.

[309] W. Thwaites, 'The Assize of Bread in eighteenth-century Oxford', *Oxoniensia*, 51 (1986), 171–81, at 181; Sweet, *The English Town*, 108.

[310] Curthoys (1), 57–62; Nelson to Charlett, St Simon & St Jude, 1707, in ed. J. Walker, *Letters written by eminent persons in the seventeenth and eighteenth centuries* . . . (2 vols., London, 1813), I. 170.

of the University were ready to help him raise funds.[311] University officers additionally offered periodic charitable distribution to the poor of the town, while individual colleges did much the same. Thus, during the long Presidency of John Cooke, Corpus Christi could be found subscribing £6 16s 6d to the 'Indigent Poor of Oxford'. His benevolence extended to prisoners housed in Oxford gaol. On one occasion, he asked his college to make available funds for seventy-four prisoners, men who depended on public benevolence. The sum was spent on fuel and meat for them.[312] And that academic largesse was not confined to the borough. When smallpox erupted in Burford in summer 1758, the University collected £122 and sent it to the overseers of the poor in that town to be distributed among the sufferers.[313]

As in any English county, the social elite naturally had interests in the county town that brought most of them—even the grandest—into Oxford regularly, and contacts with the University were sought after on both sides. Some grandees, not necessarily Oxford graduates, were courted and rewarded through the award of an honorary BCL; others, of a Tory disposition, came in for the drinking and the feasting at the High Borlace meetings. This summer festive gathering held between the 1720s and the 1750s was only connected at a distance with the University, for it occurred in August (usually on or around the 18th), during the long vacation.[314] Nevertheless, its fascination for sociable Tories *inside* the University was indubitable. Grandees, dependents, and well-wishers convened inside the city, drank and dined convivially, going so far as to pass a motion in 1738 to 'adopt a new restoration attempt'. Its more serious purpose was to ensure the success of Tory candidates for the borough and the county.[315] Over the course of the century, the loosely Whiggish county elite gradually became aligned with the University: the close involvement of the 1st Lord Harcourt in academic patronage was diluted into the courtly involvement of his successors at Nuneham Courtenay; the anticlericalism of the 1st Earl of Macclesfield at Shirburn Castle was transmuted into the astronomical expertise of his son, to the great benefit of Oxford; and, after the death of Sarah Marlborough, successive dukes maintained the curious detachment of Blenheim, however determinedly individual dons courted the goodwill of the Churchills. But, as the 1754 election showed clearly, the gentry of the county and its environs were more reluctant to discard their Toryism, men like Walter

---

[311] See, for instance, Edmund Archer, *A sermon preach'd at the parish church of St Martin October the 21st 1712. At the anniversary meeting of the Mayor, aldermen, and other trustees, for the charity schools of the City of Oxford* (Oxford, 1713). Archer was a Fellow of St John's, recently named Archdeacon of Taunton.

[312] Fowler, *Corpus Christi College*, 295, 296. Between 1757 and 176 St John's donated five guineas annually to Oxford's poor. Costin, *St John's College*, 212.

[313] *London Evening Post*, 7–10 Oct. 1758.

[314] Colley memorably dubs it an 'annual alcoholic romp'. *In Defiance of Oligarchy*, 71.

[315] ed. Linnell, *The Diaries of Thomas Wilson*, 66, 18 Aug. 1732; Oates, *Jacobitism in eighteenth century English schools and colleges*, 9; F. Madan, *A Century of the Phoenix Common Room, 1786–1886* (Oxford, 1888), 9–10. Also discussed in Chapter 10.

478 ENLIGHTENED OXFORD

Pryse, a Welsh high Tory (d. 1745) with a house in Woodstock who, in the 1730s, received regular visits from undergraduates and, as Hearne reported, 'hath abundance of MSS papers relating to the late horrid Revolution, more he saith than any one hath besides'.[316]

Oxford academic opinion could take comfort from the knowledge that, whatever the political differences of the place, the nobility and gentry of the county were almost to a man united behind the cause of the Established Church. Thus when there was a meeting of gentlemen and clergy at Thame from across Oxfordshire, Berkshire, and Buckinghamshire in 1732 to voice opinions and subscribe to the view that the repeal of the Test and Corporation Acts would assist 'the increasing & further corroborating the Liberties of the Protestant Dissenters in particular; & to the better Uniting Protestants with one another', the Irish peer, John, 1st Viscount Barrington (a long-standing Dissenting apologist), of Shrivenham, Berkshire, was the only peer to sign.[317] And the social elite vied with each other—and with the University—in their commitment to philanthropy and charitable causes such as the Radcliffe Hospital, and criss-crossed each other in social life, including Freemasonry. Politics could never be wholly put aside in these interactions, but they counted for relatively little when Oxford races were running and much of the county turned up to enjoy the events. Annual race meetings were held in Port Meadow every August throughout the century, when county society mingled socially and easily with the University, often with festivities in the town hall and cockfighting at the cockpit at Holywell.[318] These events were regularly reported in *Jackson's Oxford Journal*. To take one year—1767—one finds attending and circulating the Duke and Duchess of Marlborough, Lord Charles Spencer, Lord and Lady Wenman, Sir Thomas Stapleton, 5th Bt., (MP for the city, of Greys Court, Rotherfield Greys), and Sir James Dashwood, 2nd Bt., of Kirtlington. The races and their popularity were commonly represented as a sign of Oxford's widespread appeal and the generosity of racegoers:

A stronger Proof [of this flourishing] cannot be brought forward than the brilliant Assemblage of Personages who croud, annually, to the Races, to manifest their Respect, and contribute to the Prosperity of the Place. Large as it may appear, yet true it is, that £2000 was left in Oxford at the last Anniversary [meeting].[319]

---

[316] Hearne, X. 255, 19 Oct. 1731.
[317] BL Add MS 33052, Newcastle Papers, ff. 84–5, 1 Nov. 1732.
[318] Midgley, *University Life*, 111–13.
[319] Bodl MS Top Oxon. c. 280 f. 115, 'To the Worthy Freemen of the City of Oxford', 29 Mar. 1784. Another visitor, in 1790, noted that the 'Town was in a glorious confusion'. Travel diary of Mary Shiffner, East Sussex RO, SHR830A, f. 7, 8 Aug., return journey from Sussex to Pontrilas.

BEYOND THE UNIVERSITY 479

The races may have taken place during the long vacation, but college fellows and others in residence commonly joined in the festivities, some with a genuine interest in the sport, others to seek out female relations or spectators, or just catch up with their patrons in a convivial setting.[320] Many of the young Oxford men hoping to gain notice from those with well-endowed livings or other places in their gift would be unsuccessful and, though they were likely to take holy orders, would end up as schoolmasters. It was not a calling to be derided. If they did well in their profession—apart from the likelihood of being offered places outside it— they would be well-placed to attract notice from individual Oxford colleges who wanted to attract their pupils. As headmasters they were in a strong position to direct traffic (or not) in a particular direction and their good offices were solicited by dons. To be headmaster of one of the great schools of England—Westminster, Eton, Winchester, Merchant Taylors—gave an individual a major stake in the nation's patronage nexus and established connections with Oxford colleges. Strings were shamelessly pulled when a prestigious principalship became vacant and could hinge on party allegiance and connection.[321] These schools tightened rather than lessened their domination of entry to the ancient universities in the course of the century and their products often brought with them to Oxford a loyalty to their school that was further nurtured as young men by the presence of so many of them in one *locus*. Thus many undergraduates who were old Etonians frequently high-tailed it off from Oxford to take part in their old school's Montem ceremonies,[322] patronised by the monarchy and forming what has recently been argued to be 'a public expression of public social identity'. By comparison, Grammar Schools lost some ground academically and socially in the Oxford stakes. That said, the system of closed scholarships kept them in the game, the link of some establishments such as the Welsh Grammar Schools with a college like Jesus remained solid, and they were capable of curriculum modernisation on a scale that has seldom been admitted, often introduced by Oxford graduates.

The Welsh collegial connection was well-established by the eighteenth century (and by no means confined to Jesus College) but the possibility of setting up a comparable college for students from either Scotland or Ireland or both was an idea that seems to have occurred to nobody. The confessional boundaries between Presbyterian Scotland and episcopalian England ensured that only a minority of

---

[320] Thomas Townson, for instance, of Magdalen College. To Rev Richard Congreve, 29 Aug. 1738, Congreve Papers, Staffs. RO, D1057/M/I/14/9. The letter makes specific mention of Grace Gardiner, the daughter of Warden Gardiner.

[321] Thus William Adams of Welton, Northamptonshire, in 1731 asked the Tory Sir Justinian Isham, 5th Bt., MP for the County, to put in a word with William Bromley, MP for the University and one of the trustees of Rugby School, on behalf of his kinsman John Plomer if, as seemed likely, the current headmaster (Henry Holyoake) died. That event duly occurred and Plomer got the post. Adams to Isham, 28 Feb. 1730/1. NRO, Isham Papers: 2864.

[322] For instance, George Finch to Ly Charlotte Finch, Ch. Ch., 19 May 1771, LLRRO, DG7 Box 4953, Bundle 31/66.

Scottish graduates would contemplate continuing their studies at Oxford and, while that barrier did not operate between Dublin and Oxford, Trinity College wanted to nurture young Irish Anglicans itself, not see them take their talents and their fees across the water. That successive dukes of Ormond served concurrently as Chancellor of both universities facilitated a degree of academic connection that endured but, throughout these decades, the Irish community at Oxford remained 'small but well-documented', and mainly aristocratic, with incomes to match.[323] Considered numerically on the basis of graduates, Oxford's imprint on the King's non-English subjects may have been small, but the University had too great a cultural force field in terms of its values and its history for it to be ignored anywhere in the two kingdoms when educated men encountered each other. Oxford may have been off the centripetal print axis of Edinburgh-London that was a key component of British cultural formation,[324] but England's oldest centre of higher learning constructed its own discrete cultural vector that insistently registered its presence across the Anglo-Hanoverian polity.

[323] Ansell, 'Irish Protestant Travel', 20, 21; T. Barnard, 'Protestantism, ethnicity and Irish identities, 1660–1760', in eds. T. Claydon and I. McBride, *Protestantism and national identity: Britain and Ireland, c.1650–1850* (Cambridge, 2004), 206–35, at 217.

[324] For this axis see Richard B. Sher, *The Enlightenment and the Book. Scottish Authors and their Publishers in Eighteenth-Century Britain, Ireland, and America* (Chicago, IL, 2010).

CULTURAL CONSTRUCTIONS, CONNECTIONS, AND TENSIONS

10

The University as seen from outside

At Oxford the people are all either mad or asleep, and it is hard to say which sort one could learn most from: only the former sort break out sometimes into flights, which, because the by-standers laugh at them, their fellows take for wit.

Thomas Secker to John Fox, 28 July 1716, quoted in *Monthly Repository* (Oct. 1821), 569.

Ah! Oxford is a wondrous place,
Wondrously crammed with Quizzes;
Full of grave gowns, and grave grimace,
Strange forms, and stranger Phizzes

Richard Laurence, 'The Wonders of Oxford', in H. Cotton, Poetical Remains of French Laurence, DCL, MP, and Richard Laurence, DCL, Archbishop of Cashel (Dublin, 1872), 8.

Its past and present members imagined that they knew Oxford, that they both owned and guarded the University's identity. Yet the sense of 'Oxford' that most Britons entertained was one derived from a physical or associational distance, a detachment that did not always make for a balanced perspective on this educational and clerical powerhouse, central to the functioning of the eighteenth-century establishment. Thus many outsiders, Dissenters for instance, tended to be forceful critics for whom the University and its ways presented a tempting target as a regressive and exclusionary institution. That said, the majority of non-Oxonians—of whom females by definition made up the majority—were ready to view it either sympathetically or at any rate neutrally. Women might be indirectly attached to the University via their male relations, who might entertain and display them on the great social days of the academic calendar, notably at Oxford 'Acts' and subsequently Encaenias. And, irrespective of family connections, visitors and tourists from Britain and abroad put the city down on their itineraries as an unmissable attraction.

This chapter therefore considers a range of reactions to 'Oxford' from outsiders and attempts to assess their influence on opinion at large in imagined constructions of a distinctive academic community, as well as asking how successful were those who wanted to put forward an alternative 'image' of the University. Some openings for detractors could not be disguised, principally the static recruitment

Enlightened Oxford: The University and the Cultural and Political Life of Eighteenth-century Britain and Beyond.
Nigel Aston, Oxford University Press. © Nigel Aston 2023. DOI: 10.1093/oso/9780199246830.003.0011

of George II's reign and the decline in plebeian numbers that only underlined the University's apparent social exclusivity and the increased problem of access for unprivileged Anglicans.[1] If Oxford was an aspirational object for this category, then their relative absence (reflected in the falling number of servitors down the years)[2] called into question Oxford's effectiveness in educating a sufficiently wide social range of male Anglicans for the leadership of Church and state to be replenished in succeeding generations. Early in the century, Oxford was an easy target for Whig controversialists of all kinds looking for an obvious location for Jacobite scare stories. That Oxford education was 'entirely tending to the extirpation of the Protestant Religion' was a charge originally levelled in *University Loyalty* (1683), reprinted in 1710 as a sensationalist response to the Sacheverell agitation with the subtext that restoration of the 'Pretender' was endorsed at Oxford, a typical polemical product of the kind that looked for quick political gain.[3] Here the emphasis fell on disloyalty; an alternative critical theme was that in its curriculum and intellectual preferences Oxford was unenlightened, not doing what a contemporary university should be doing (according to changing definitions), perhaps by comparison with its Scottish counterparts. Those who expected more personally from it could dress up disgruntlement by making such allegations. For instance, someone disappointed in their expectation of an honorary degree, such as William Warburton who had his offer of an honorary doctorate of divinity withdrawn by the University in 1741. In solidarity with his editor and friend, Alexander Pope thereupon turned down his own honorary doctorate of laws.[4] At least Warburton, who had a friend in John Conybeare, Dean of Christ Church, tried to make clear that the personal affront to himself had not been made by the University but by his personal enemies within it.[5]

Six loose categories have been adopted for consideration of this external gaze, beginning with creative literature and art, the depiction of Oxford in guidebooks, plays, novels, and paintings. Secondly, Protestant dissenters and Methodists, the one excluded from Oxford because of its subscription requirements and their own confessional allegiance, the other able to matriculate and graduate though

---

[1] Plebeian matriculands are estimated at 17% in 1760, 1% in 1800. Brockliss (2), 163n. See an attempt at a statistical survey covering 1752 to 1886 in C. A. Anderson & M. Schnaper, *School and Society in England: Social backgrounds of Oxford and Cambridge Students* (Washington, 1952), 7.

[2] Brockliss (2), 228–9. These were positions which provided a small stipend in return for work in Hall or Chapel.

Only seven students were admitted as Servitors or as 'Bible-Clerks' at Wadham College in the 1790s, compared to forty-two in the 1690s. Davies, 'Decline and Revival', 40–1.

[3] The full title was *University loyalty: or, the genuine explanation of the principles and practices of the English clergy, as established and directed by the decree of the University of Oxford, past in their convocation 21 July 1683. and republish'd at the trying of Dr. H. Sacheverell* ... (London, 1710).

[4] Pope famously insisted, '...I will be Doctor'd with you, or not at all'. *The Works of Alexander Pope*, eds. W. Elwin and W.J. Courthorpe (10 vols., London, 1871–89), IX. 217; Mack, *Alexander Pope*, 745. For the furore generated in Oxford see Greenwood, *William King*, 124–6.

[5] A.W. Evans, *Warburton and the Warburtonians. A study in some eighteenth-century controversies* (London, 1932), 85–6.

THE UNIVERSITY AS SEEN FROM OUTSIDE   485

increasingly uncomfortable as the distance between the Established Church and the Wesleyan and non-Wesleyan variants within Methodism widened. Dissenters, particularly non-Trinitarians, could be vociferous in expressing their disdain for Oxford and its High Anglican values and adept at publicising their criticisms. The specific objects of their attacks are identified, and the political and cultural costs of their exclusion are weighed up in an assessment of damage inflicted on the University. After that, the varying attitude of graduates of other universities within Britain are examined with a view to distinguishing the genuinely critical from good-hearted academic one-upmanship. Then, those who were connected to the University but were either non-matriculands in the case of servants whose labour was indispensable to the functioning of the entire institution, or Oxford graduates who coyly or publicly positioned themselves at a critical distance and had the capacity to tarnish the standing of their alma mater. Feminine angles on Oxford make up the fifth category, paying regard to the considerable extent of female inclusion in university socialisation at every level but the formally academic. The chapter ends with notice of the (usually) annual summer festivities that were the Act and, later, Encaenia, when the University and Oxford at large were en fête, and town and gown and men and women mingled in partying, and issues of status and association could be briefly played down if never entirely forgotten. These were occasions that heightened familial awareness of Oxford's standing in national life.

i) Literary and artistic (mis)representations

'O! These strolling collegians are never abroad, but upon some mischief'.

Parly, in Farquhar, *The Constant Couple*,
ed. W. Myers (Oxford, 1995), 45.

Oxonians in residence were no less keen theatregoers than the rest of the country and relative proximity to the capital made it easy for them to make short visits to watch their preferred performance: the young Cornishman Edward Giddy was not untypical when he went to Hammersmith by coach in May 1754 and saw Garrick perform in *King Lear* and another play, *The Mourning Bride*.[6] Oxford scholars and students themselves had a long literary pedigree. The stock types—the unworldly don, the frustrated but lubricous undergraduate, the cunning college servant— were well-known characters to eighteenth-century readers and theatre-goers and continued to keep them entertained. A university setting within which ideas and opinions could be explored was, by contrast, generally avoided by either novelists

---

[6] A. C. Todd, *Beyond the blaze: a biography of Davies Gilbert* (Truro, 1967), 14. He also visited Vauxhall and Ranelagh pleasure gardens.

486 ENLIGHTENED OXFORD

or playwrights, in favour of the picaresque and the comedic. One author, the eminent physician Archibald Pitcairne, in an obscure Scottish comedy of 1691, *The Phanaticks*, bucked the trend and brought in his old friend, David Gregory (1661–1708), the astronomer and brand-new Oxford academic,[7] in a play that aimed to explain why Jacobites were quick to embrace Newtonian physics while Whigs were stuck with the syllogistic scholasticism of Aristotle. Such efforts were rare.

Dramatists largely shied away from academic themes and, especially after the passing of the Licensing Act in 1737, learnt to present the politically controversial in different ways (censorship tended to happen at the level of interdicting individual expressions or words rather than by wholesale prohibition of the plays).[8] The need to generate audience numbers and ensure financial returns both for themselves and for theatre managers was always the priority. And an Oxford setting contained a risky element of unfamiliarity that might not appeal, quite apart from the limited opportunities that a predominantly masculine institution afforded for including a 'love interest' that would allow celebrity actresses to shine. And thus characters were usually depicted as types against a loosely academic backdrop and suggested, rather than impersonated, the latter a general tendency in early eighteenth-century English theatre.[9] One exception was arguably John Gay, Alexander Pope, and John Arbuthnot's *Three Hours after Marriage* (1717), which had its own Complete Key that identified Fossile as Dr John Woodward, the collector and classifier of fossilised remains, with a consuming interest in the Noachian Flood, here mocked as the epitome of bad scholarship.[10] The Scriblerian play with its farcical ritual and mockery of false learning was part of a tradition dating back to at least Shackerley Marmion's *The Antiquary* (published 1641). And this one, Al Coppola has recently argued, was 'a distinct throwback', one that was 'very nasty and personal ...' at Woodward's expense.[11]

Thomas Baker's popular *An Act at Oxford* (London, 1704), revealed the comic possibilities of Oxford rituals when placed before an outside audience and, for understandable reasons, located the action within the great if occasional summer

---

[7] For Gregory and Pitcairne see Chapter 2, pp. 38–40. There is an edition by John MacQueen of *The Phanaticks* (Woodbridge, 2012).

[8] Cf. M.J. Kinservik, *Disciplining satire. The censorship of satiric comedy on the eighteenth-century London stage* (Lewisburg, PA, 2002).

[9] Ibid., 137.

[10] Coppola, *The Theater of experiment*, 103–9; Ashley Marshall, *The Practice of satire in England 1658–1770* (Baltimore, MD, 2013), 175; J. M. Levine, *Dr Woodward's Shield. History, Science, and Satire in Augustan England* (Berkeley, CA, 1977), 40–1, 238–52.

G. Sherburn, 'The fortunes and misfortunes of *Three Hours after Marriage*', *Modern Philology*, 24 (1926–7), 91–109.

[11] Coppola, *The Theater of experiment*, 103. Coppola argues that Woodward was, for the Scriblerians, 'an avatar of ill-founded empiricism and hasty hypotheses, one whose naïve certainty about nature leads him into manifest absurdities'. Ibid., 109. Woodward had several academically respectable friends in the University, notably John Hudson, Bodley's Librarian. Levine, *Dr Woodward's shield*, 165–6.

THE UNIVERSITY AS SEEN FROM OUTSIDE 487

Fig. 10.1 Frontispiece to 'The Humours of Oxford', Thomas Cook, after William Hogarth, print, 1807 (The Metropolitan Museum of Art, New York: Gift of A. E. Popham, 1949).

celebration of the 'Act'. Non-academic characters—women in particular—could be shown engaging with the usual Oxford cast, and play could be made with the part of the *Terrae Filius*, who, immediately before he delivered an 'anti-panegyric', was introduced to spectators by Bloom, the Gentleman Commoner, as 'the University Jester,—the Terrour of fudling Doctors, and fornicating Commoners, a Serviter in Scandal,—and Harliquin of the Sciences', etc.[12] But *An Act at Oxford* did not have a long stage run. The University authorities took offence and Baker was obliged to change the location and the names of the characters.[13] For all that it was a racy intrigue, his play was essentially a rumbustious entertainment that was hard to criticise, but dramas that exhibited more edge could cause problems for their author, especially when they happened to be insiders like the Rev. James Miller (1706–44), lecturer at the Trinity Chapel in Conduit Street, London, who

---

[12] [Thomas Baker], *An Act at Oxford* (London, 1704), 49. See this Chapter, pp. 115–17 for more on the *Terrae Filius*.
[13] It was reworked as *Hampstead Heath* (1705), 'which is altogether inferior'. Robert D. Hume, *The development of English drama in the late seventeenth century* (Oxford, 1976), 463.

488 ENLIGHTENED OXFORD

wrote to bolster his income. With an instinct for guarding his back, he located himself behind the nom de plume 'A Gentleman of Wadham College' when he brought out *The Humours of Oxford* in 1730 (it opened at the Drury Lane theatre that January), and tried to pass it off as an outsider's offering.[14]

One female character was called Lady Science who appears retrospectively as a pseudo-scientific prototype for Mrs Malaprop);[15] a more notable one was a woman of wit, Clorinda, played by Anne Oldfield (1683–1730), a co-owner of Drury Lane for a short time. In the cast list also appears 'Kitty, an Oxford Jilt,' played by Catherine Raftor (1711–85), later better known under her married name and nickname as 'Kitty' Clive. Both were amongst the highest-paid actresses of their time.[16] It tells us something about the significance of the play to theatre managers and the audiences they bought it for. Clorinda was given some of the best lines, for instance when she speculated:

> 'What a lovely Age t'would be, Aunt, if all the pretty Gentlemen, and fine Ladies, were to turn Stargazers and Philosophers.—to see a Beau encompass'd with Telescopes and Globes, instead of Looking-Glasses, and Peruke–Blocks; and a Coquette with Euclid and Newton on her Toilet, instead of Waller and Congreve; and stripp'd of all her Patches, to mark the Planets in the Solar System, ha, ha!'[17]

But the Oxford characters, Haughty and Conundrum the fellows, Apeall, an affected scholar, hit somewhat too close for home to pass without disgruntled academic murmurings.[18] Lines reproving Fellows for an unprofitable existence came too near to denigration not to be controversial when uttered before a fashionable audience at the Theatre Royal, perhaps fitting this theatrical definition of one: 'A Rude, Hoggish, Proud, Pedantick, Gormandizing Drone—a dreaming, dull, Sot that lives and rots like a Frog in a Ditch'.[19]

Miller found his anonymity hard to sustain and his diocesan, Edmund Gibson of London, took umbrage. As if Miller's ribald aspersions were not enough, what may have been an astute sales ploy in giving the published version a frontispiece by William Hogarth had the unintended effect of increasing curiosity about the

---

[14] Marshall, *The Practice of satire*, 210.

[15] Discussed in Chico, *The experimental imagination*, 54–8.

[16] Thanks to David Worrall for this information.

[17] [James Miller], *The humours of Oxford* (Dublin, 1730), 13.

[18] Haughty corresponded approximately to Joseph Trapp and Conundrum to Robert Thistlethwayte. See Paula Joan O'Brien, 'The life and works of James Miller, 1704–1744, with specific reference to the satiric content of his poetry and plays', Ph.D. thesis (University of London, 1979), 17, 19, 23.

[19] Ibid., Act II., scene i. Hannah Cowley later in the century offered acceptably gentle satire in her *Who's the Dupe?* (1779) in which the character of Gradus of Brasenose College (she daringly named a real setting) is laughed at for his pedantry, provincial manners, and unfashionable dress. Crook, *Brasenose*, 102.

THE UNIVERSITY AS SEEN FROM OUTSIDE   489

play's author. He may have considered that he had nothing to lose in preferment terms given his status as a High Churchman and an enemy of Walpole in a Whig college, yet he never ventured into academic theatricals again, instead producing plays such as *The Coffeehouse*, which hit out at standard targets such as fops, hackney poets, and Italian opera via characters that were largely abstracts.[20]

George Colman (himself a product of Westminster and Christ Church) the Elder's *The Oxonian in Town* of 1767 attempted to disarm censure in advance by putting two Oxford students, Frank Careless and Charles Knowell, in a metropolitan setting and generating sympathy for them by making the London characters—Sharp, Rook, and M'shuffle—the comic villains.[21] It was by no means the first such exercise: George Farquhar in *Sir Harry Wildair* (1701) had sent Banter, the pseudo-Oxonian, up to town boasting he can 'dance a minuet, court a mistress, play at picquet, or make a paroli with any Wildair in Christendom'.[22] As Careless and Knowell go in search of their old cronies, Bob Lounge and Dick Scamper, Careless delights at being in the capital, demanding of his friend:

'Is not this a chearful square beyond the dull gloom of a melancholy quadrangle? and the gay appearance of every one you meet, a more pleasing sight, than a few solemn faces in starched bands and grizel wigs?'[23]

He heartily relishes his false freedom: 'Rot the Proctors and Oxford all together; with all my heart. London shall be my university, and here I'll take my degrees in mirth and jollity', and there are the obligatory tavern scenes and some gentle exchanges with the women they meet there. One of the 'ladies' relates that her father was a barber and mayor of Oxford. Even if she was ruined by a gentleman commoner of Marlin's College, she takes care to mention that he had since been a good friend to her.[24] The satirical intent of this two-act comedy was really aimed at the Irish card sharpers who exploited the high spirits of undergraduates out on the spree.[25] In *The Oxonian in Town*, it is Knowell who steps in to prevent the ruin of his more innocent, good-natured friend. Indeed, Colman hit home so accurately that on the third night, the performance had to be halted temporarily

[20] Kinservik, *Disciplining Satire*, 129. For a full treatment see O'Brien, 'The life and works of James Miller'.

[21] G. F. A. Wendeborn remarked in 1791 that this frequently acted drama represented Oxford undergraduates' ways 'in lively colours, but it is said, that they are not yet sufficiently strong'. *A View of England towards the close of the eighteenth century* (2 vols., London, 1791), II. 160.

[22] Cf. young Bookwit in Richard Steele's comedy *The Lying Lover* (1704), another student quickly turned into a town spark.

[23] *The Oxonian in town. A comedy* (London, 1767), 11.   [24] Ibid., 1–2, 11.

[25] Paul Goring, '"John Bull, pit, box, and gallery, said no!": Charles Macklin and the limits of ethnic resistance on the eighteenth-century London stage.' *Representations*, 79, (2002), 61–81.

because of catcalls in the theatre instigated, it has been suggested, by some of the card tricksters in the audience.[26]

The construction of Oxford on the eighteenth-century stage was essentially tolerant, no more than half-heartedly antagonistic, and certainly not calling into question the University's historic right to go about its business. Indeed, it was the very stability of its institutional presence that made possible its humorous dramatic construction on stage. The same could be said of much versifying about the University coming from outsiders. One of the most celebrated offerings of its time, *Academia, or the Humours of Oxford* (1691), was written by an obvious outsider—a woman. She was Alicia D'Anvers, the wife of Knightley D'Anvers of Trinity College, and daughter of Samuel Clarke, Esquire Bedel of the University, and therefore close enough to insiders to give her work comic credibility as she related the account of Oxford's sights given by the manservant, John Blunder, on returning home from a visit to his master at Queen's College.[27] Oxford was presented and marketed to the public quite widely in the eighteenth century less as 'the English Athens' than as a centre of japes, jokes, pleasantries, and quick-wittedness. Jest Books originating in or claiming to depict Oxford had an appreciable market share in what some disparagingly dubbed 'coffee-house literature'. For instance, William Hickes's *Oxford Jests, Refined and Enlarged* (London, 1671), designed to appeal to a wide proportion of the literate public (women as well as men), had a perennial popularity as its periodic reissue with new witticisms—1686, 1688, 1733, and 1760—indicated. Despite the disdain of the high-minded Addison, collections of such witticisms abounded and sold well.[28] Thomas Sheridan and Jonathan Swift even included this pun in a volume dedicated to the subject:

A scholar, passing through a street, made to a fellow who had a hare swinging on a stick over his shoulder, and accosted him as follows: 'prithee, friend, is that thy own hare or is it a periwig?'[29]

The eighteenth century was not a time for novels set in a university. The nearest approximation would be the anonymous *The Adventures of Oxymel Classic, Esq: Once an Oxford Scholar* of 1768 about a dunderhead scholar.[30] More usually, a

---

[26] One spectator, the young dissenter, Sylas Neville, was delighted that Colman did not cancel the performance. 'I think it contains many good sentiments and excellent instruction to young men and is not unworthy of Mr Colman'; ed. B. Cozens-Hardy, *The Diary of Sylas Neville 1767–1788*, 10 Nov. 1767 (London, 1950), 27.

[27] Godley, *Oxford in the Eighteenth Century*, 112–13. Extracts are given in Samuel F. Hulton, *The Clerk of Oxford in Fiction* (London, 1909), 228–41.

[28] S. Dickie, *Cruelty & laughter. Forgotten comic literature and the unsentimental eighteenth century* (Chicago, IL, 2011), 16–44, esp. 22–3.

[29] 'Tom Pun-Sibi', *Ars pun-ica, sive flos linguarum: the art of punning; or, the flower of languages; in seventy-nine rules: for the farther improvement of conversation and help of memory* (Dublin, 1719; repr. London, 1720?), 3.

[30] Dickie, *Cruelty & laughter*, 256.

THE UNIVERSITY AS SEEN FROM OUTSIDE   491

character with Oxford connections or a visit to the city could form part of a text. Thus in Tobias Smollett's *Peregrine Pickle* (1751), the eponymous hero kept his own horses, attended all the races within fifty miles of Oxford, and used to make frequent incognito visits to London. It was not far from the non-malign send-up of undergraduates contained in the abundant periodical literature. In *The Guardian* (no. 24), Jack Lizard, returning home from Oxford, told the company when a dish of wildfowl was served at dinner 'that, according to the opinion of some natural philosophers, they might be lately come from the moon'. Jack, the unrepentant smart alec, lost no opportunity of making his family wiser, telling his mother, Lady Lizard, when she burnt her finger in lighting the lamp for her teapot, that there was no such thing as heat in fire. *The Babbler* (no. 77) depicts another over-confident young Oxonian, Tom Welbank, lodging at an uncle's near the Haymarket, who is depicted as daring to disagree with Lady Mary Wortley Montagu that London is a much finer place than Oxford, and then offer a eulogy on classical literature as part of an 'harangue upon the benefits of education' which invoked 'all the celebrated authorities of antiquity, as if the company required any proof of that nature to support the justice of the argument'. The embarrassing sketch ends with the comment that 'it was the general opinion of the table that Tom would make a pretty fellow when he knew a little more of the world'.[31]

If the stage was an appealing medium for the dramatic depiction of Oxonian characters, artists who had visited the University city created a personal, pictorial impression of the milieu in which dons, undergraduates, and townsfolk lived.[32] Official images of Oxford abounded, from engravings of the various kinds of academic costume to the high-quality, much admired artwork that adorned each annual University *Almanack*, the calendar of university events.[33] The artists who supplied the designs for the latter were, in fact, outsiders themselves, at least inasmuch as they were not Oxford graduates, and included some prominent contemporaries, among them the map-maker turned landscape artist, Paul Sandby, who supplied the annual illustration for the *Oxford Alamanack* for twenty years. In 1769 Edward Rooker and his son Michael Angelo Rooker provided a heading that broke with the dominant allegorical design that had predominated as a frontispiece since the *Almanack*'s first publication in 1671 and depicted a University institution in detail (All Souls), viewed from an oblique angle, with small figures in the foreground. Michael Angelo Rooker produced this kind of exterior view for the next twenty years.[34] These were highly competent drawings, but they lent themselves to parody. Thomas Rowlandson painted watercolours

---

[31] Discussed in Mortimer Robinson Proctor, *The English University Novel* (Berkeley, CA, 1957), 38–9; Hulton, *The Clerk of Oxford*, 269–71.

[32] For plans in the 1780s to establish an Academy of Painting in Oxford, see Harrison et al., *John Malchair of Oxford*, 18.

[33] Chapter 1, pp. 36–7.

[34] Patrick Conner, *Michael Angelo Rooker 1746–1801* (London, 1984), 23, 33, 106–12.

Fig. 10.2 Bacon Faced fellows of Brazen Nose, Broke Loose, Thomas Rowlandson, hand-coloured etching, 1811 (The Metropolitan Museum of Art, New York: The Elisha Whittelsey Collection, The Elisha Whittelsey Fund, 1959).

based on *Almanack* designs in which human activity is more a feature and humour conspicuous. Thus in a view of Magdalen College a dog has overturned a milkmaid, causing a hod-carrier up a ladder to tip his bricks on to the man below. An artist like him, officially unconnected with Oxford, had more scope for presenting its less heroic aspects as part of the place's social performance in the *comédie humaine*. Rowlandson also used Oxford as a general backdrop in his 'Love and Learning, or the Oxford Scholar' (print, 1786) where an undergraduate and his girlfriend are spied on by his angry jilted sweetheart.[35] Later work moved into specific academic spaces. His graphic 'Brazen Nose Chaple Broke Loose' (c.1800–5) captures the pompous postures of the dons leaving Brasenose chapel, gowns flowing as they pass by unconcerned bystanders, in a 'masterpiece of controlled caricature'.[36] Here their pretensions to social dominance are punctured and shown up as cosmetic artifice through Rowlandson's brilliant draughtsmanship.

He had no chance of being approached by the Delegates of the Clarendon Press for a design. Instead it was the much younger and outstandingly talented J. M. W. Turner who gained a commission to supply watercolour views for the *Almanack* as early as 1799, the year before he was elected to the Royal Academy.

---

[35] R. Paulson, *Rowlandson. A new interpretation* (London, 1972), 82.
[36] John Hayes, *Rowlandson Watercolours and Drawings* (London, 1972), 183.

THE UNIVERSITY AS SEEN FROM OUTSIDE   493

The debt to Rooker is apparent in the ones he painted for the *Almanack* for engravings between 1801 and 1811, with designs that were 'clear and plainly spoken, and suggest a degree of emotional detachment'.[37]

Those who saw Oxford characters and ways depicted artistically, dramatically, or read about the University in print were likely to join the throng of tourists who were a constant presence in the city, able to travel there with relative ease thanks to the improved road system of the county facilitated by the General Turnpike Act 1773 that gave incentives to build and maintain roads.[38] As British tourism grew, as hostelries, coffee-houses, and taverns sought to benefit from the trade that it generated, businesses in the city expanded.[39] Oxford became an essential destination with daily coach departures for London and elsewhere that allowed for every sort of curious traveller irrespective of whether they had one day or several at their disposal.[40] Oxford could easily be followed by other feature items of this expanding trade—Blenheim, Stowe, and Ditchley—and possibly then on to Stratford-on-Avon.[41] No sooner was construction of the Marlboroughs' grand seat under way than the number of summer visitors pouring into Oxford grew so fast that one canon complained:[42]

I will never pass the months of July and August here again. I am almost foundered with showing sights to people, that take us in their way to Bath or Blenheim. That Blenheim is a curse upon this poor place, I would at any time make one in a rising of the University, town and county, to raze it to the ground.

Even for those who opted not to leave their own armchairs, there was no shortage of descriptive literature to guide them around the sights of the university, its buildings and its gardens, most of it enthusiastic in its tone and sentiments. Numbers of visitors entering the city needed directions and the oldest surviving

---

[37] James Hamilton, *Turner's Britain* (London, 2003), 56–60.

[38] The term 'tourist' came into currency in the last quarter of the eighteenth century. Ian Ousby, *The Englishman's England. Taste, travel and the rise of tourism* (London, 2000), 14. For Oxfordshire's impressive network of turnpike roads by *c*.1800, see J. Cary, *Cary's traveller's companion, or, a delineation of the turnpike roads of England and Wales* (London, 1791); W. Albert, *The turnpike road system in England 1663-1840* (Cambridge, 1972). Foreigners' observations are treated in Chapter 11.

[39] The jumbled buildings and alleys of much of the town centre counted against its attractions. For the 1771 Improvement Act that initiated major changes in the urban landscape, Chapter 9, pp. 10–12.

[40] Well before the turnpikes, William Haynes's flying coach did the journey in a day *c*.1700 for 12 shillings. Services from Oxford to Bath and Bristol were established in 1702, to Gloucester in 1713, and to Birmingham, Hereford, Warwick, and Worcester by 1753. The University claimed an exclusive right to license stagecoaches throughout this century. OUA: CC/134/2/2.

[41] Blenheim was the most popular of all English country houses for visitors throughout the century. Visitors were received every afternoon (Sundays excepted) between 2 and 4 in the 1780s. Ousby, *The Englishman's England*, 53–4, 61, 62.

[42] Canon Stratford in HMC, *Portland MSS*, VII. 55, 11 Sept. 1711.

494   ENLIGHTENED OXFORD

street map in a guidebook to any British urban centre is the one of Oxford found in Green's *A Pocket Companion for Oxford*, 1762 edition.

The pioneering travel accounts covering England that Celia Fiennes (1698) and Daniel Defoe[43] included in their published tours were widely imitated over the following decades.[44] Extended references to Oxford could be presumed in geographical descriptions of the whole of England such as Aiken's *England Delineated* in which Oxford is familiarly presented as '...a seat of learning, with the reputation of which the whole literary world is sufficiently acquainted'.[45] It was not unusual to find literary tourists and guides hazarding an opinion as to whether Oxford or Cambridge was the more visually distinguished. Defoe gave Oxford the prize for 'the largeness of the place, the beauty of situation, the number of inhabitants, and of scholars', and was in no doubt that it was 'a noble flourishing city'.[46] He singled out the Sheldonian Theatre as, 'in its grandeur and magnificence, infinitely superior to any thing in the world of its kind'.[47] Celia Fiennes also considered that Oxford offered more pleasure to the visitor than Cambridge, where the 'buildings are old and Indifferent'. She considered Trinity College, Cambridge to be the finest in the city but here praise was qualified, for it was 'not so Large as Christ-church College in Oxford'.[48] Fiennes, using William Camden's *Britannia* as a travel guide, prided herself on her scrupulous honesty. For later authors, too much frankness might limit their market value. Mild hyperbole became the norm in works looking to entice tourists to see for themselves and, as part of the process, purchase the book.

A minority opted for the candid assessment. The Tory apologist (a non-Oxbridge historical geographer) Thomas Salmon,[49] in his *The Foreigner's Companion Through the Universities of Cambridge and Oxford*, may have described the colleges and public buildings, along with 'An Account of their respective Founders, Benefactors, Bishops, and other Eminent Men educated in

---

[43] ed. E. Wingfield Griffiths, *Through England on a Side Saddle in the Time of William and Mary, Being the Diary of Celia Fiennes* (London, 1888). Defoe's *A Tour through the Whole Island of Great Britain* was published in 3 vols. between 1724 and 1726. It purports to be a record of seventeen 'Circuits or Journeys' made by an anonymous Gentleman. Pat Rogers claims it should be reckoned both the 'liveliest [guidebook] ever written' and the ultimate Augustan expression of the English epic. Daniel Defoe, *A tour through the whole island of Great Britain*, ed. P. Rogers (Harmondsworth, 1971), 33.

[44] John Byng declared in 1782, 'Tour writing is the very rage of the times' [West Country tour, 1782]. For his comments on Oxford see *The Torrington Diaries*, I. 5–6, 119.

[45] [John Aiken], *England delineated; or, a geographical description of every county in England and Wales:...for the use of young persons* (2nd ed., London, 1788), 183.

[46] Defoe, *A tour*, 350, 351.

[47] Ibid., 352. The superb acoustic was widely acknowledged. As one Cambridge undergraduate admitted: '...the Theatre far outdoes ours for the design of it, for a word spoken anywhere in it may be heard all over;...', H. Partridge to Henry Partridge, Esq., 22 July 1730, Norfolk Archives, MC55/23, 506 x 2.

[48] ed. Griffiths, *Diary of Celia Fiennes*, 49.

[49] Information on Salmon, a minor historian and polemicist, formally unconnected with Oxford, is limited. Okie, *Augustan Historical Writing*, 99–113; R. Mayhew, *Enlightenment Geography: The Political Languages of British Geography, 1650–1850* (London, 2000), 132–40.

them', but he wanted foreign visitors to be in no doubt about blemishes. Thus he told them that the Butchers' market every Wednesday and Saturday disfigured the High Street, a thoroughfare whose occupants also took the dirt out of their houses on a daily basis and dumped it in the middle of the street.[50] Similarly, *The New Oxford Guide* boasted that it was

'... founded on actual observation, and compiled from a real and attentive survey of every particular which it describes ... We have nothing in common with others, but the subject; the colouring will be found to be different, and the execution new'.[51]

The plethora of guides and companions led one Oxford wag (almost certainly Thomas Warton), to produce anonymously *A Companion to the Guide, and A Guide to the Companion: Being a Complete Supplement to all the Accounts of Oxford hitherto published* (3rd edn., 1762?), a brilliant tongue-in-cheek assemblage spoofing antiquarians and others on the basis laid out in the Preface:

> It is become an universal Complaint, that the accounts of OXFORD, hitherto published, are full of Mistakes and Misrepresentations.—ANTHONY WOOD was an Antiquarian and an Old Woman: Mr Salmon, Author of the Present-State of th Universities, is a Cambridge-Man: and that the Reverend Mr Pointer, Rector of Slapton in Northamptonshire, was but little acquainted with our Academical Annals. is evident, from his supposing the MALLARD of All-Souls College to be a Goose.

Irrespective of whether they had bought a 'companion', a 'guidebook' (or which particular one), travellers throughout the century communicated their own impressions to personal letters or to a private journal.[52] They were often of a fairly conventional sort, especially from young visitors on an extended journey with a limited comparative repertoire and a busy schedule to follow. Other, more mature visitors might have a special reason for coming to the city, in the case of James Boswell's lifelong friend, the Rev William Johnston Temple (1739–96), a

---

[50] *The Foreigner's Companion*, 21. Private visitors corroborated the scruffiness of much of the urban environment. Sylas Neville observed, 'The houses of the inhabitants at Oxford serve as a foil to the public buildings. They are in general of wood covered over with plaister'. *The Diary of Sylas Neville 1767–1788*, 283, 4 Nov. 1781.

[51] A Gentleman of Oxford, *The New Oxford Guide: or, Companion through the University*. (Oxford, 1759), v–vi. It covered pictures, statues, and buildings and had gone into 7 editions by 1787. Stephen Bending has shown how in a publication like the *New Oxford Guide* (6th edn., 1778) a popular guidebook negotiates different kinds of audiences by describing the differences between the 'antiquarian' and 'the mere spectator', the former a more polite figure. The latter is likely to be easily bored, but still a curious traveller, in search both of 'entertainment and information'. '"The true rust of the Barons' Wars": gardens, ruins and the national landscape', in eds. M. Myrone and L. Peltz, *Producing the Past. Aspects of Antiquarian Culture and Practice 1700–1850*, (Aldershot, 2001), 83–94, at 84.

[52] The full term 'guidebook' only dates from the early nineteenth century, but the concept and the colloquialism 'guide' appeared in the previous century, Ousby, *The Englishman's England*, 12. See also J. Vaughan, *The English Guide Book c.1780–1870: An Illustrated History* (Newton Abbot, 1974).

496 ENLIGHTENED OXFORD

'Cantab', and Cornish parish priest, a curiosity to see how the sister university looked. He professed himself 'enchanted':[53]

> I am...humbled to think how much it exceeds Cambridge, indeed they will not bear a comparison in any light whatever. Kings Chapel & Trinity are all we can boast of. Our Theatre & Library too exceed theirs, tho' the stile of architecture is far from pure. How the arts embellish the world!

Others might come to hear some preaching of quality or controversy. One anonymous Irish cleric, on an excursion to Oxford from Bristol in 1772, timed his visit to coincide with a sermon preached at St Mary's church by William Hawkins of Pembroke College (the former Poetry Professor), who combined a defence of the Thirty-nine Articles with an attack on Francis Blackburne's controversial revisionist tract, *The Confessional*. The visitor reported that Hawkins had rebutted criticisms of the ecclesiastical status quo 'in a clear & masterly style'.[54] In fact, the issue remained a live one.

ii) Dissenters and Methodists

> The body of the clergy seem to be more orthodox than they were in the last reign, and more bigotted. We see what a court and an establishment can do.
>
> Joseph Priestley to Theophilus Lindsey, 22 Jan. 1790.

In 1773, following the failure of the Feathers Tavern petition, some of those in Francis Blackburne's circle, led by his son-in-law, the Cambridge-educated Theophilus Lindsey, left the Church of England in despair at its institutional unwillingness to adopt a more eirenic attitude to Protestant dissenters.[55] Few of those who resigned and became Nonconformists had any connection with Oxford University which, consistently in this period, indeed all the way down to the eventual repeal of the Test Act in 1828, deployed a formidable array of arguments against making further concessions to those who would not accept the existing

---

[53] Letter to Boswell of 12 May 1790. Beinecke Library, Yale University, C 2885. Temple, on the same date, elsewhere commented that he was: '...surprised at the spaciousness of the Streets and the magnificence of the Colleges". *Diaries of William Johnston Temple 1780–1796*, ed. Lewis Bettany (Oxford, 1929), 72.

[54] BL Add MS 27951, Journeys from Dublin to London [by an Irish cleric], f. 92, 9 Aug. 1772.

[55] There is a fine summary of Lindsey and his circle in the 1770s in S. Andrews, *Unitarian radicalism. Political rhetoric, 1770–1814* (Basingstoke, 2003), chap. 2. And see the introductory essays in each volume of ed. G. M. Ditchfield, *The letters of Theophilus Lindsey (1723–1808)* (2 vols., Woodbridge, 2007, 2012). Other high-profile Cambridge resigners included John Jebb of Peterhouse (but only in 1775). Anthony Page, *John Jebb and the Eighteenth-Century Origins of British Radicalism* (Westport, CT, 2003), chaps. 5, 6.

THE UNIVERSITY AS SEEN FROM OUTSIDE   497

establishment. Though there were friendships that crossed confessional lines between Oxford Anglicans and Dissenters,[56] majority opinion in the University regarded the latter as, at best, stiff-necked malcontents, barely Christians with a neo-republican pedigree, at worst, subversive malcontents who would stop at nothing to achieve civil and religious parity with Anglicans, in the process smashing episcopacy and Trinitarian belief.

When a young Oxford graduate and baronet opted to become a Dissenting minister in the 1770s it became a *cause célèbre*. This was Sir Harry Trelawny, 7th Bt. (1756–1834), descendant of one of the seven bishops who had defied James II in 1688 by resisting his Declaration of Indulgence in favour of non-Anglicans. Young Trelawny had only taken his BA and accepted the Book of Common Prayer after much heart-searching and advice.[57] Affection for Oxford and his friends there held him back from committing himself to Presbyterian ordination, but he eventually took the plunge in 1777, when he deplored the dominance of heathen authors at universities and the way pulpits were filled with 'the same stuff— Divinity, I dare not call it'.[58] His punishment was to have his name removed from the college books. He held out for three years before returning to the fold.[59] The more mature William Tayleur of Shrewsbury (1712–96) drifted into Unitarianism from his Westminster (where he was Captain of the school in 1730) and Christ Church background—and stayed with it. In time he became a trustee of Lindsey's Essex Street chapel and proved one of Priestley's most munificent financial benefactors, with regard to both his scientific work (in which Lindsey took hardly any interest) and his theological publications.[60]

Though Oxonians came in time to countenance the Toleration Act 1689, its speedy impact in diluting uniform religious observance across England and Wales afforded a salutary precedent regarding the likely consequences of further eroding Anglican privileges. Protestant Dissenters returned the favour: most expected nothing from Oxford and were incurious about either visiting the city or

---

[56] Thus William Adams, Master of Pembroke College, had maintained a friendship with Richard Price after the publication of the latter's *Review of the principal questions and difficulties in morals* in 1758. Lindsey to William Tayleur, 27 Mar. 1779, in ed. Ditchfield, *Letters of Lindsey*, II. 290 and n.2.

[57] Jerom Murch, *A History of the Presbyterian and General Baptist Churches in the West of England* (London, 1835), 541–2.

[58] Edward Ashburner, *A sermon at the ordination of the Rev. Sir Harry Trelawny, Baronet, and A.B. (late of Christ Church, Oxford)...preached at Southampton, April 22, 1777...Together with an introductory discourse, and questions...Sir Harry Trelawny's answers, and confession of faith...* (Southampton, 1777?), 26.

[59] He later explained how '...the fervour of inexperienced youth, a scrupulous mind, and conversation with enthusiastical dissenters, conspired to produce all that religious frenzy, which, for many months, hurried me into excesses that I shall not justify. May all this space be considered as a parenthesis in the history of my life!' *A Letter from the Rev. Sir Harry Trelawny, Bt., to the Rev. Thomas Alcock, vicar of Runcorn and of St Budeaux* (London, 1780), 17. Trelawny's tergiversations continued: he was subsequently ordained in the Church of England before later becoming a Catholic priest.

[60] G. M. Ditchfield, 'William Tayleur of Shrewsbury (1712–96): A case study in eighteenth-century lay religious leadership,' *Enlightenment and Dissent*, 26 (2015), 3–23.

498 ENLIGHTENED OXFORD

attempting to engage with its members. Instead they consolidated their own further and higher educational arrangements. Their schools and academies at Daventry, Warrington, and Hackney, with their 'modern' curriculum, came to be widely regarded as exemplifying 'Enlightened' values more convincingly than either of the ancient universities, especially Oxford.[61] Where they bothered at all, eighteenth-century Dissenters in their sermons, addresses, and prolific polemical writings were generally adept at presenting an 'Oxford experience' as one that was blindly rooted in the past, prejudicial to civic well-being, and essentially inimical to human progress. Thus Priestley, in a public letter to Pitt the Younger (a Cambridge product), lauded the Dissenting Academies, 'being formed in a more enlightened age', 'while your Universities resemble pools of stagnant water, ours are like rivers, which, taking their natural course, fertilize a whole country'.[62] His ally, the lapsed Anglican, the Unitarian and former Cambridge fellow, Gilbert Wakefield, looked across to Oxford, and he expressed relief at never having studied there, and deplored what he thought he saw:[63]

> Their [Oxford academics] powers of invention are unexerted, their ambition is at rest . . . orthodox theology, high church politics, and passive obedience to the powers that be, sit enthroned there; and spread their stupifying influence through the atmosphere around them.

These were not impartial sentiments, but because the majority of resident Oxford scholars preferred to ignore them and let them go by default (engaging in controversy with Dissenters could generate wearingly protracted exchanges), Dissenters had more success in getting across their outsiders' perspective on Oxford as a cradle of Toryism and pedagogic obscurantism than they might otherwise have done.

Dissenters were—with some reason—at their most antagonistic towards Oxford in Queen Anne's reign as they defended themselves against the wave of support for Sacheverell and the rhetoric of the 'Church in Danger' (he intemperately claimed the Dissenters were infiltrating everywhere), and warned, as stalwart Whigs, of the threat to the Protestant Succession. After George I was safely installed, and the place of Dissenters in the life of the state was safeguarded (so

---

[61] Daventry was the principal Dissenting academy in the Midlands, originally founded in Northampton in 1729, moving to Daventry in 1752 and subsequently moving back to Northampton. Priestley was its most famous pupil. See www.qmul.ac.uk/sed/religionandliterature/dissenting-academies/dissenting-academies-online/

[62] *Letter to the Right Honourable William Pitt . . .* (1787), in ed. J. T. Rutt, *The theological and miscellaneous works of Joseph Priestley, LLD FRS & c.*, (25 vols., New York, NY, 1817–31), XIX.. 128; *GM* 57 (1787), 423. As John Money has well said, Priestley's theology 'promised salvation by Progress, not by Grace'. 'Joseph Priestley in cultural context: philosophic spectacle, popular belief and popular politics in eighteenth-century Birmingham', *Enlightenment and Dissent*, 8 (1989), 69–89, at 74.

[63] *Memoirs of the life of Gilbert Wakefield, BA, formerly fellow of Jesus College, Cambridge. Written by himself* (2nd edn., 2 vols., London, 1804), 59–60.

THE UNIVERSITY AS SEEN FROM OUTSIDE 499

long as he and his successors remained on the throne),[64] these minority Protestants became increasingly absorbed in doctrinal disputes and lost numbers to an Established Church whose leadership was unambiguously court Whig.[65] Thereafter relations between moderate, Trinitarian dissenters and members of the University with a comparable faith were by no means normatively hostile and the steady growth of the Whig presence in Oxford in the reign of George II contributed to at least two decades of relative harmony.

Dissenters with the national status and reputation for learning of the Independent Isaac Watts (1674–1748) and Philip Doddridge (1702–51) did not go uncourted. Despite its perceived Arian tendencies, the University adopted Watts's *Logick, or The Right Use of Reason . . .* (1724) as a foundational educational manual. John Wesley read Watts extensively while a tutor at Lincoln College and thought highly of his theology, notably his teaching on original sin, while his capacities as an hymnologist were no less praised and culturally influential. In the next generation, Doddridge of Northampton, an eirenic moderate Calvinist, was treated by his many admirers virtually as an honorary Anglican. As a theologian and educationalist he was regarded as a force for good by such contemporary figures in Oxford as George Costard, Fellow of Wadham, James Merrick, Fellow of Trinity and versifier of the Psalms, Richard Newton of Hart Hall, and Thomas Hunt, Professor of Hebrew and Canon of Christ Church.[66] There were always non-Arian Dissenters ready to acknowledge generously Oxford's achievements. The Presbyterian minister at Bristol, Edward Harwood, classical scholar and Biblical critic, friend of Priestley, with an Edinburgh DD, educated in Dissenting academies and a semi-Arian himself, thus applauded Oxford's production of classical Greek texts. In 1775 he published *A view of the various editions of the Greek and Latin classics*, several times reprinted, and writes thus:

> The University of Oxford has produced more splendid and accurate editions of the Greek classics than all the other Universities in Europe. West's Pindar, Hudson's Dionysius, Dr Mill's Greek Testament, Jebb's Aristides, Warton's Theocritus, and several other Greek Authors published at Oxford are superior to any Editions other countries have published, in correctness of text, splendour of execution, and sagacity of criticism.[67]

---

[64] eds. N. Aston and B. Bankhurst, B., *Negotiating Toleration. Dissent and the Hanoverian Succession, 1714–1760* (Oxford, 2019).

[65] The impact of theological liberalism on eighteenth-century religion is discussed in Watts, *The Dissenters*, I. 386–92, 488–90.

[66] ed. T. Stedman, *Letters to and from the Rev. Philip Doddridge, DD* (Shrewsbury, 1790), 147–57, 333–47; G.F. Nuttall, *Philip Doddridge, 1702–51: his contribution to English religion* (London, 1951).

[67] Edward Harwood, DD, *A view of the various editions of the Greek and Latin classics*. With remarks (2nd edn., London, 1778), xiv. See also ibid., xxvi.

500 ENLIGHTENED OXFORD

Aggression towards Oxford, and what, for Dissenters, it represented, erupted again in George III's reign as the University returned to royal favour: Archbishop Secker (himself an ex-Dissenter) patronised its clergy, and it stood firm against (in a way that Cambridge did not) changes to the liturgy and, above all, to subscription.[68] The belligerent 'Rational Dissenters', whose identity was firmly established in the 1770s, gave epistemic significance to individual enquiry and private judgement.[69] They were, it has been claimed, 'the dominant force in the late-eighteenth-century Enlightenment',[70] and, certainly, they constituted a formidable network loosely and ably marshalled by leaders of the calibre of Richard Price (an Arian) and Joseph Priestley (a Socinian).[71] These two had a public importance disproportionate to the numbers who followed them and, with their pro-American[72] and then pro-French Revolutionary politics to counterpart their theological heterodoxy,[73] became 'hate figures' for most of Oxford's academic luminaries. Personal friendships apart, Price ignored Oxford,[74] where Priestley was viewed, as George Horne put it, as 'a Volcano, constantly throwing out matter for the increase of heresy, schism, or sedition, and never to be quenched by disputing'.[75] Priestley was tactically adept, abandoning the tradition of invective and victimisation in the late 1780s in favour of one that was more emollient, an attempt to persuade Oxford dons and students that they need not be apprehensive about the repeal of the Test Acts.[76] It was a tactic also used in the

---

[68] See generally James E. Bradley, *Religion, revolution, and English radicalism. Nonconformity in eighteenth-century politics and society* (Cambridge, 1990); A. Lincoln, *Some political and social ideas of English Dissent, 1763–1800* (Cambridge, 1938), 27. Norman Sykes considered that the anti-subscription campaign, inasmuch as it was supported by Anglicans, was 'largely a Cambridge campaign'. *Church and State*, 84.

[69] M. Fitzpatrick, 'Toleration and truth', *Enlightenment & Dissent*, 1 (1982), 3–31, esp. 29–30; Cragg, *Reason and authority in the eighteenth century*, 259–60.

[70] M. Fitzpatrick, 'Enlightenment', in ed. I. McCalman, *An Oxford companion to the Romantic age: British culture 1776–1832* (Oxford, 1999), 299–310, at 307.

[71] The literature on both is vast. On Price see D. O. Thomas, *The honest mind: the thought and work of Richard Price* (Oxford, 1977); on Priestley the essays in eds. I. Rivers and D. L. Wykes, *Joseph Priestley, scientist, philosopher, and theologian* (Oxford, 2008) are a sound starting point. Other no less belligerent Dissenting leaders of the 1770s, including Caleb Evans, James Murray, Joshua Toulmin, and George Walker, and their pulpit critiques of the clerical establishment are treated in Valerie Smith, 'Rational Dissent in England c.1770–c.1800: Definitions, Identity and Legacy' (Univ. of Kent Ph.D., 2017); Bradley, *Religion, revolution, and English radicalism*, 127–47, 170–2.

[72] C. Bonwick, *English Radicals and the American Revolution* (Chapel Hill, NC, 1977); Bonwick, 'English Dissenters and the American Revolution', in eds. H. C. Allen and R. Thompson, *Contrast and Connection: Bicentennial Essays in Anglo-American History* (Athens, OH, 1976), 88–112.

[73] Andrews, *Unitarian Radicalism*, 9, 31–40, 85–7; J. Creasy, 'Some Dissenting attitudes towards the French Revolution', *Transactions of the Unitarian Historical Society*, 13 (1966), 155–67.

[74] Price's stated intention was one of 'separating religion from civil policy, and emancipating the human mind from the chains of church-authority, and church establishments'. *Evidence for a future period of Improvement in the State of Mankind... in a Discourse delivered on Wednesday the 25th April 1787, at the Meeting-house in the Old Jewry London...* (London, 1787), 32.

[75] ed. W. Jones, *Memoirs of the Life, Studies, and Writings of the Right Reverend George Horne, D.D., late Lord Bishop of Norwich* (London, 1795), 141.

[76] Bernard Lord Manning, *The Protestant Dissenting Deputies*, ed. O. Greenwood (Cambridge, 1952), 217ff.

THE UNIVERSITY AS SEEN FROM OUTSIDE   501

Commons by the Whig dissenting MP and Warrington graduate, Henry Beaufoy, when he introduced the motion for repeal in the Commons, on 27 March 1787. The Dissenters were neither Levellers nor republicans, he insisted, only to be countered by Sir William Dolben quoting from Priestley's *Reflections on the Present State of Free Inquiry in this Country* (Birmingham, 1785), and pointing its subversive 'gunpowder' image'.[77]

What particularly incensed senior Oxford academics was a parallel attempt to address University students directly in a bid to persuade them that the great mass of early Christians were Unitarians and that they should not take their oaths on matriculation and graduation too hastily. This campaign began with Priestley's *Defences of Unitarianism for 1786* (1787), which contained letters to the 'Young Men, who are in a Course of Education for the Christian Ministry, at the Universities of Oxford and Cambridge.'[78] He brought out a second set of letters attacking subscription to 'the Candidates for Orders in the Two Universities' in his *Defences of Unitarianism for 1787* (1788) and Lindsey joined in with his *Vindiciae Priestleianae: An Address to the Students of Oxford and Cambridge* (1788).[79] It was a bold, outflanking strategy that reinforced Oxford's sense of being under siege in the late 1780s, a pressure that only eased after the outbreak of the French Revolution.[80] It did not go unanswered. The Oxford counteroffensive (part of a wider riposte reaffirming Trinitarian orthodoxies) recognised the threat to the allegiance of entrants to Anglican orders. What most caught attention was a stinging anonymous reply to Priestley's *Letters* from 'An Undergraduate', quickly and rightly ascribed to the President of Magdalen College, that denounced Priestley as 'an enemy to authority'.[81] Horne and his allies outside the University managed at least to divert Priestley's attention to other targets.

---

[77] Priestley rushed out *A Letter to the Right Honourable William Pitt* (1787) almost immediately as a means of correcting many of the false impressions his earlier work had created. H. Braithwaite, *Romanticism, Publishing and Dissent. Joseph Johnson and the Cause of Liberty* (Basingstoke, 2003), 80–1. It formed part of the campaign for repeal of the Test and Corporation Acts. Robert Schofield, *The Enlightened Joseph Priestley. A Study of His Life and Work from 1773 to 1804* (Philadelphia, PA, 2004), 268–9. For Dolben, *PH*, 26, col. 831.

[78] He had first criticised University subscription as early as 1769 with his *View of the Principles and Conduct of the Protestant Dissenters*. Discussed in Rivers, *Reason, Grace, and Sentiment*, II. 348–9. In a wider context, these letters constituted part of the ongoing controversy relating to his high Socinian *A History of the Corruptions of Christianity*, first published in 1782. Schofield, *The Enlightened Joseph Priestley*, 228.

[79] Braithwaite, *Romanticism, Publishing and Dissent*, 84. Priestley's *Letters . . . to the Young Men* was addressed by name to Horne. Lindsey's work in reality was targeted at Horne by undermining his scholarship and Hutchinsonian insights.

[80] Priestley made more of an impression at Cambridge. In Dec. 1787 a Grace was presented in the University Senate signed by many BAs and MAs asking that subscription be eliminated for advancement to the MA. It was not adopted. Schofield, *The Enlightened Joseph Priestley*, 269n.

[81] *A Letter to the Rev. Dr Priestley. By an Undergraduate* (2nd edn., Oxford, 1787), 28. Lindsey was predictably unimpressed with it. Horne 'followed the illiberal practice introduced by those controversial bravadoes, who having first entered the lists with Dr Priestley, soon discovered that it was by much the easiest and shortest method of dealing with their formidable antagonist to assume a lofty and

502   ENLIGHTENED OXFORD

It was also, perhaps, a sign of frustration on the part of Priestley and his militant colleagues that the academic establishment had to date both absorbed their attacks and—without douceurs—persuaded many of the Nonconformist gentry to send their sons to Oxford and in time conform to the state Church.[82] Lindsey, an ex-Anglican himself and with many Anglican friends, never doubted the obstacle that Oxford's predominant ecclesiology posed to granting the concessions the Protestant dissenters craved. Though he was ready to acquit the bulk of the clergy from being as 'illiberal' as in 'the days of Sacheverel' he exempted from that judgement 'what are called the Tory-Gentry in general, and your Oxonian clergy in particular:...' Significantly, this grudgingly generous spirit predated the Birmingham riots of 1791 directed against Priestley by eighteen months, the same year that, at a meeting of the Unitarian Society chaired by Priestley, the toast was 'May the sun of liberty rise on Oxford, as it has on Cambridge, and long since on the Dissenters'.[83] Given aggressive sentiments of that sort, it is not surprising that Oxford dons regularly directed their homiletic fire at Priestley and his ilk immediately before and after the outbreak of the French Revolution.[84]

Moderate Dissenters of learning were still prepared to cooperate academically with Oxonians—and vice versa—even in a decade marked, as the 1780s were, by renewed denominational tensions. Thus Dean Cyril Jackson of Christ Church is known to have attended meetings of the Lunar Society, became friends with the chemist Joseph Black, and did much to support Matthew Boulton and James Watt in their experiments.[85] The rising Oxford luminary, Joseph White, Laudian Professor of Arabic, negotiated the services of Samuel Badcock, Dissenting minister at South Molton, Devon, in preparing material for his Bampton Lectures of 1784—just as he did those of Samuel Parr. Badcock was willing to conceal the extent of his contribution provided he was paid—and he was not. White (who was habitually in debt) failed to honour the financial arrangements made with Badcock and, immediately after the latter's premature death, these became the subject of gossip in the University and the press that did White's reputation (and, by extension, Oxford's) no favours. As one critic put it:

---

supercilious air, and to arraign his literary character, instead of disproving his stubborn facts, and refuting his potent arguments'. Thomas Belsham, *Memoirs of the late Reverend Theophilus Lindsey, MA* (London, 1812), 196–7.

[82] D. L. Wykes, 'The Contribution of the Dissenting Academy to the Emergence of Rational Dissent', in ed. Haakonssen, *Enlightenment and Religion*, 99–139, at 132–4, 136.

[83] Lindsey to William Tayleur, 10 Feb. 1790, in ed. Ditchfield, *The Letters of Theophilus Lindsey*, II. 38; *GM* 61 (1791), 321.

[84] For instance, R. Shepherd, DD, *Sermons on Several Occasions* (London, 1803), 306–9, Sermon XIII, preached at Oxford on 30 Jan., no year given but dating from the early 1790s. See generally Arthur Sheps, 'Sedition, Vice, and Atheism: The Limits of Toleration and the Orthodox Attack on Rational Religion in late Eighteenth-Century England', in eds. R. Hewitt & P. Rogers, *Orthodoxy and heresy. Essays from the DeBartolo conference* (Lewisburg, PA, 2002), 51–68.

[85] eds. C. Butler, J. Curthoys, and B. Young, *Christ Church, Oxford, a portrait of the house* (London, 2006), 165. Further discussed in Chapter 5, pp. 56–7 and Chapter 12.

THE UNIVERSITY AS SEEN FROM OUTSIDE 503

He has exalted himself above the level of common praise and common distinction, by means the most intriguing, and by artifices the most unmanly. He has done what in the eye of an honest man cannot be excused.[86]

Parr became caught up in the charges and countercharges and in 1790 White was more or less forced to be entirely honest and publish *A Statement of Dr White's Literary Obligations to the late Rev. Mr Samuel Badcock, and the Rev. Samuel Parr, LL.D* (Oxford, 1790). His reputation never entirely recovered whereas the Dissenter, Badcock's, emerged untarnished. The whole affair did nothing to lessen the indifferent standing of the University in the eyes of Nonconformists.[87]

Methodists were not part of that revisionist assault. They might easily have been, given the breakdown of relations between John Wesley and his own university in the mid-1740s but, thereafter, tempers on both sides subsided. Methodism was, vis-à-vis Oxford, both an internal and external phenomenon. The University was inseparable from its origins; it had nurtured, in some sense, the *first* Oxford Movement. And, like its nineteenth-century successor, it quickly aroused suspicion and hostility (as well as evoking commitment and endorsement) among academics and undergraduates, becoming something of a sectarian challenge in the 1740s, with implausible claims to divine commission from such a dynamic preacher as George Whitefield, himself an Oxford graduate.[88] Whitefield's claims were met head on by Joseph Trapp in writings such as *The True Spirit of the Methodists, and Their Allies...Fully Laid Open*, wherein Whitfield stood accused of 'Quakerism, Enthusiastic Madness and Malice'.[89] Methodism polarised mid-century Oxford opinion and, like Tractarianism a century later, it only secured scope for growth and evangelistic impact once it had moved away from its academic origins. Yet it was and remained in John Wesley's lifetime essentially an *Anglican* reform movement, though one whose insistent separatist tendencies became gradually harder to restrain, especially on the issues of episcopal ordination, lay itinerancy, extempore preaching, and the

[86] Anon., *An Appeal to the Members of the University of Oxford relating to the Rev. Dr White's Bampton Lectures. By no Academic* (London, 1789), 4–5; Lord Boringdon to Hon. Frederick Robinson, 1 Dec. 1789, West Devon RO, 1259/1/115.

[87] The damage might have been greater had Badcock not died in 1788 and had he not sought ordination in the Church of England, immediately prior to his demise serving as curate of Broad Clyst.

[88] Whitefield saw his Oxford experience at Pembroke College as foundational to his spiritual and theological development. Mark K. Olson, 'Whitefield's Early Theological Formation', in eds. G. Hammond and D. Ceri Jones, *George Whitefield, Life, Context, and Legacy* (Oxford, 2016), 29–45, at 30.

[89] Trapp, *The True Spirit of the Methodists, and Their Allies...Fully Laid Open* (London, 1740), 26. It followed on from his *The Nature, Folly, Sin, and Danger of being Righteous Over-much* (London, 1739). Trapp urged people not to seek out 'these imposters and seducers' and to 'shun them as you would the plague.' See Brett C. McInelly, 'Whitefield and His Critics', in eds. Hammond and Jones, *George Whitefield*, 150–66, at 156–7; Clark, 'The Eighteenth-Century Context', in eds. W.J. Abraham and J. E. Kirby, *The Oxford Handbook of Methodist Studies* (Oxford, 2009), 3–29, 15; Albert M. Lyles, *Methodism Mocked: The Satiric Reaction to Methodism in the Eighteenth Century* (London, 1960), 18.

creation of an independent set of organisational structures looking to Wesley for sanction rather than to a bishop or archdeacon.[90] Methodism was half in and half out of the Church of England, a force for Protestant renewal within Britain, but the plebeian character it assumed in the process ensured that most Oxonians were far from endorsing the means it was using to achieve that desirable end.

At least the disdain of most Heads of Houses for Methodists was offset by the willingness of many incumbents with Oxford degrees across England to act as key allies for Wesley, men such as Henry Piers (Bexley, 1739–69) and Vincent Perronet (Shoreham, 1728–85), both in Kent.[91] Their presence in the movement allowed Wesley to encourage his supporters to keep on attending their parish churches wherever feasible. In Oxford itself, the Methodist society was dominated by townsfolk with only a smattering of gownsmen, and Wesley, on his occasional visits to Oxford between 1751 and his death in 1791, preached to them in private premises or in their new preaching house.[92] He always regretted that he could not recruit more Oxford graduates to become field evangelists but the fact was, as Henry Rack has concluded, 'Methodism in its earliest form and original home was a failure'.[93]

Evangelicals who were not Methodists (but were often depicted as such, partly because the demarcation lines could be so nebulous) found Oxford uncongenial territory until the last years of the century,[94] their sympathies for the Established Church often being represented as tepid and suspect. But if they sought ordination in the Church of England, it was expedient for them come to up Oxford (judged by Evangelicals as being theologically less rationalising than Cambridge) and put up with slurs along the lines that they were outsiders masquerading as insiders. The Cornishman, Thomas Haweis, arrived in Oxford in the 1750s (matric. Christ Church, 1755, Magdalen Hall, 1757) as a product of the Methodist revival based on Truro around the Rev. Samuel Walker (1714–61) [Exeter College, BA 1736]. It took some time for Haweis to persuade Bishop Secker to ordain him and doubts were not overcome when his sermons at St Mary Magdalen attracted unfavourable

---

[90] J. Gregory, 'In the Church I will live and die: John Wesley, the Church of England and Methodism', in eds. W. Gibson and R. Ingram, *Religious Identities in Britain, 1660-1832* (Aldershot, 2005), 147–78. Wesley was automatically president of the annual Methodist conference until his death in 1791. Nigel Yates, *Eighteenth-Century Britain. Religion and Politics, 1714-1815* (Harlow, 2008), 90.

[91] N. Yates, 'The Anglican Establishment and its Critics 1714–1830', in eds. N. Yates, R. Hume, and P. Hastings, *Religion and society in Kent, 1640-1914* (Woodbridge, 1994), 22–52, at 42–3.

[92] Green, *The young Mr Wesley*, 257, 269ff., 300–2 He was encouraged to note in the 1780s the increase 'in zeal as in number' of Oxford Methodists. *Journal of John Wesley*, ed. N. Curnock (8 vols., London, 1916, repr., 1938), VI. 454. Wesley remained a fellow of Lincoln until his resignation in 1751, his leave of absence renewed each Chapter Day, his stipend drawn, his rooms let out for rent. Green, *Lincoln College*, 347.

[93] Rack, *Reasonable enthusiast*, 105.

[94] For the gap between Wesley and those whom John Kent called 'the more sophisticated evangelical Anglicans', see his *Wesley and the Wesleyans: religion in eighteenth-century Britain* (Cambridge, 2002), 73–8.

THE UNIVERSITY AS SEEN FROM OUTSIDE 505

notice from the University, with riots led by students in his church by the end of December 1761. He left Oxford for London in 1762.[95]

The dubious compatibility of Methodism with membership of Oxford University was highlighted when six students were expelled from St Edmund Hall in 1768. The affair caught national attention.[96] Under the Principalship (from 1760) of George Dixon, numbers matriculating at the Hall had steadily climbed. So had the numbers of those who deprecated the presence of those with Calvinist Methodist affiliations (many bankrolled by Wesley's rival, the semi-separatist Selina, Countess of Huntingdon) and their talk of 'regeneration, inspiration, and drawing nigh to God'. The vice-principal, John Higson, decided to act. Without waiting for Dixon's approval—which he would never have granted—seven young Methodists were reported to Vice Chancellor Durell (acting in a Visitatorial capacity) in February 1768 for investigation. An internal enquiry took place and, despite Dixon's testifying as to their orthodoxy, six of the seven were expelled for hostility to the doctrine and discipline of the Church of England by praying and preaching in private houses that were regarded as conventicles. Higson thereupon found himself commended for his public spirit in bringing the matter to the attention of the authorities.[97] Commentators were divided. Samuel Johnson approved, and so, at first, did the arch-Arminian Wesley, delighted to see Lady Huntingdon's protégés condemned,[98] but George Whitefield wrote to the Vice Chancellor saying that if it was disgraceful for ordinands to be caught singing hymns, praying extempore, and expounding verses of scripture, the question in the ordination rite: 'Do you trust that you are inwardly moved by the Holy Ghost?' should be amended to: 'Do you trust that you are NOT moved by the Holy Ghost?'[99]

As it was, with remarkable aplomb, Dixon still admitted students with pronounced evangelical leanings to the Hall, Lady Huntingdon continued both to send and to pay for them,[100] and there was no repetition of a *cause célèbre* that had not, on the whole, been sympathetically received by the public. Nevertheless, the affair had shown up a widespread Oxonian perception that Methodist

[95] Discussed in Chapter 3, p. 68.

[96] Kelly, *St Edmund Hall*, 62–5; Green, 'Religion in the Colleges', 458–64; Green, *Religion at Oxford and Cambridge*, 204–13; Reynolds, *The evangelicals at Oxford*, 37–40; Ward, *Georgian Oxford*, 239–45; S. L. Ollard, *The six students of St Edmund Hall* (Oxford, 1911).

[97] Most historians have had little time for Higson. The Methodist Gordon Rupp called him 'a psychological case'. Gordon Rupp, *Religion in England, 1688–1791* (Oxford, 1986), 476. Contemporaries were more understanding.

[98] Wesley, *Journal*, V. 293. It was falsely alleged that the Countess was funding their education at Oxford. A. M. W. Stirling, *The annals of a Yorkshire house from the papers of a macaroni and his kindred* (2 vols., London, 1911), I. 227–8.

[99] Whitefield, *Letter to the Reverend Dr Durell, Vice Chancellor of the University of Oxford* (London, 1768).

[100] Thus John Eyre, first editor of the *Evangelical Magazine*, went up to the Hall in 1779 after a spell as an itinerant preacher and some time at her Trevecca college from 1776. Alan Harding, *The Countess of Huntingdon's connexion. A sect in action in eighteenth-century England* (Oxford, 2003), 182, 300–1.

506   ENLIGHTENED OXFORD

sympathisers were infiltrating the University and aimed to subvert the order and authority of the Established Church; Lady Huntingdon certainly drew that conclusion and made Trevecca a substitute for Oxford for those entering the ministry under her colours.[101] Wesley, too, invested more time in his plans for a preachers' training institution at Kingswood near Bristol, and he was explicit about the differences he wanted between Oxford and this new academy.[102] He had no time for the view held by some of his followers that scholarship and training were dangerous because preachers would be less concerned about evangelism, saying:

> 'I trust there is not one of them who is not able to go through such an examination in ... practical, experimental Divinity as few of our candidates for holy orders, even in the University ... are able to do'.[103]

As long as the connection, however tenuous, between Methodism and the Established Church remained intact, the followers of John Wesley continued to matriculate at Oxford and take holy orders. Their presence acted as an effective gag against Methodists who might want to inveigh against the University in the years after the St Edmund Hall expulsion. If anything, the situation for Methodists at Oxford, covert or open in their practice, eased from the early 1780s. By then John Wesley's celebrity status as a Methodist *and* a continuing Anglican was almost universally recognised (despite his controversial 'ordination' of presbyters for North America in 1784). And the de facto withdrawal of legal recognition of Lady Huntingdon's connection as a constituent of the Church of England was also reassuring for stalwart churchmen.

iii) Graduates of other universities

> ' ... whereas Oxford is an University within a Town; Cambridge is a Town within an University; ... And in point of Situation, it [Oxford] has the Advantage of Cambridge both for Health and Pleasure.
>
> G. Miege, The present state of Great Britain and Ireland ... (London, 1719), 23, 61.

---

[101]   Ibid., 181.

[102]   R. P. Heitzenrater, 'Wesley and education', in ed. S. J. Hels, *Methodism and education from roots to fulfillment* (Nashville, TN, 2000), 1–13; M. Bishop, 'Wesley and his Kingswood schools', in ed. John Lenton, *Vital Piety and Learning: Methodism and Education—Papers given at the 2002 Conference of the Wesley Historical Society* (Oxford, 2005), 16–24.

[103]   ed. Curnock, Wesley, *Journal*, VIII. 219, 221.

THE UNIVERSITY AS SEEN FROM OUTSIDE 507

Graduates of other universities were another constituency who might be expected to be uncharitable in their views on Oxford which was largely articulated through a chaffing rivalry of the sort that had prevailed for centuries, most obviously with Cambridge. It was seen immediately after the Revolution in the 'Battle of the Books' that pitched Whiggish moderns, especially those of Trinity College, Cambridge, against Tory ancients at Christ Church, described, neatly, as a symbolic contest 'expressing not merely two different styles of classical scholarship but two conflicting religious and political traditions'.[104] Comfortable in the plenitude of royal favour before 1760, Cambridge men could afford to be magnanimous, though they could seldom resist jibes (meant with greater or lesser degrees of seriousness) about Oxford's Jacobite reputation. It was returned in kind. Literary one-upmanship was a predictable feature of the Oxford 'Act' where the presence of a sizable Cambridge contingent in the academic crowd could be assumed.[105] They were fair game for an in-form *Terrae Filius*, such as the one who in the 1703 Act set up a beauty contest between the Oxford Latinist Anthony Alsop and Gabriel Quadring, Master of Magdalene College, Cambridge, with these words:[106]

> But you gentlemen of Cambridge are very unkind, you must pardon us if we shew you some little resentment; 'tis very hard you bring competitors for our Poëtick Lectures; For thô the great Quadring has wrote a Tetrasticon Heroïcum, yet our Alsop votidem versus conscripsit, suos Butleros: See whether Quadring or Alsop has the best on't.

Such tribal banter was always readily found among graduates of both universities with a literary bent. Samuel Johnson was thus reminded by Hester Thrale (later Piozzi) that he had ridiculed William Mason's *Caractacus* as coffee-house entertainment. In response: 'Why child (said he), what harm could that do the fellow: I always thought very well of Mason for a *Cambridge* man:'[107]

Where exercises in institutional one-upmanship did occur, the intention was often to gain favourable ministerial notice as when, in the aftermath of the furore following the opening of the Radcliffe Camera in April 1749, Cambridge sent up an early address (breaking the convention of waiting for Parliament to meet and

---

[104] Clark, *Samuel Johnson*, 78.

[105] For the Oxford/Cambridge rivalry at the 'Act' see Money, *The English Horace*, 230–1.

[106] He then quoted some verses and translated them. *Terrae Filius*: speeches by Roberts of St Mary's Hall, 12 July, *c*.1703, Badminton Muniments, FmH 4/4. For later scoffing at Cambridge verses see Stratford to Lord Harley, 23 June 1713, HMC, *Portland MSS*, VII. 146.

[107] Hester Lynch Piozzi, *Anecdotes of the late Samuel Johnson during the last twenty years of his life* (London, 1786), 37–8. Piozzi also recalled: 'Dr Johnson delighted in his own partiality for Oxford; and one day, at my house, entertained five members of the other University with vigorous instances of the superiority of Oxford, enumerating the gigantic names of many men whom it had produced, with apparent triumph. At last I said to him, Why there happen to be no less than five Cambridge men in the room now. "I did not (said he) think of that till you told me; but the wolf don't count the sheep". Ibid., 35, 36.

508 ENLIGHTENED OXFORD

do so) to congratulate George II on the making of the Peace of Aix-la-Chapelle at the close of the War of the Austrian Succession. As the Master of Balliol observed:

'I can't think Cambridge would have taken this new and extraordinary Step, without some Intimation from Great Persons (to whom They have easy access) that such measure would be agreeable'.[108]

Oxford followed suit only to suffer the exceptional embarrassment of having its address rejected on the grounds that it was insufficiently obsequious. It betokened the real possibility that Newcastle (elected as Cambridge's Chancellor in 1748 in succession to the duke of Somerset) was preparing a commission of inquiry and redress in the English universities, with the focus falling principally on Oxford.[109] The political ructions at mid-century with Oxford backing Prince Frederick and Cambridge his father's leading minister, Newcastle, stimulated other lesser inter-varsity spats that spilled over into the arts, notably the poetic contest between Thomas Warton (Oxford) and William Mason (Cambridge), initiated in 1749 when Mason, in his *Isis* (written in heroic couplets), attacked Oxford for its Jacobitism and alleged dissipation,[110] and was answered by Warton in *The Triumph of Isis*, in which he hailed Oxford as a bastion of enlightenment and a haunt of the Muses.[111] Other Oxford outsiders could not disagree more strongly with the Warton perspective and saw only a series of provocative behaviours during the later 1740s condoned and encouraged within the University, thereby cocking a snoot at the powers that be. William Warburton almost gloated at its academic discomfiture, writing to a friend:

I am sorry to find what has lately passed in the two Universities. Makes Ld Halifax's saying of the Churchmen and Dissenters too applicable to them, That one spit in the King's face, & the other in his mouth. But there are some, who have redeemed the honour of yours [Cambridge], which is not so in the other place.[112]

---

[108] T. Leigh to Duchess of Chandos [12 Dec. 1748], Balliol Coll. Archives and Manuscripts, MS 403. The 3rd Duke of Marlborough gained brief popularity in Oxford for a false report that he was at pains to deny, 'viz. that I proposed to the Duke of Newcastle at Cambridge as toast, the University of Oxford; whereas I did not at that time wish very well to either University.' Marlborough to Henry Fox, Blenheim, 13 July 1749, Holland House papers, BL Add MS 51386 f. 48.

[109] See Chapter 8, pp. 29–32.

[110] John W. Draper, *William Mason. A Study in Eighteenth-Century Culture* (New York, 1924), 29, 169. It went into three editions. Mason had written in 1749 the *Ode for Music*, performed in the Senate House at the installation of Newcastle as chancellor.

[111] Pittock, *The Ascendancy of Taste*, 176. For Warton's evergreen readiness to spoof Cambridge see Lynch, *Loving Literature*, 66. 'A Gentleman of Cambridge' also produced *The Praises of Isis* (1755), an 'elegant' compliment to Oxford, as one periodical put it. *Monthly Review*, XII (1755), 107–9.

[112] To Thomas Balguy, 27 Nov. 1750, Uncatl. MS. Letters between the Revd. Mr Warburton and Dr Taylor from the Year MDCCXXVIII [Harry Ransom Center, University of Texas at Austin], Vol. 2, no. 1. Warburton was an Hon. Cambridge MA (1728) and had his own grudges against Oxford.

THE UNIVERSITY AS SEEN FROM OUTSIDE 509

For an Oxford man to masquerade as a Cambridge outsider in a literary publication potentially allowed for a sharper and more credible level of criticism of an Oxford institution or practices than might pertain if the writer was known to be an 'insider'. But it was not straightforward to keep one's identity concealed in this academic goldfish bowl. Thus when A 'Cambridge Soph' wrote a pamphlet on *The Conduct of—[Exeter] College* after the 1754 Oxfordshire election it was soon decided that the nom de plume had failed to hide a member of Oxford Convocation.[113] There were occasional, allegedly dispassionate efforts to weigh up the merits of the two English universities. Those so engaged included the Dean of Jesus College, Cambridge, Benjamin Newton (d. 1787), who, in 1754, offered advice in 1754 to a friend who asked him to express a preference. He found in favour of Cambridge and made several charges against Oxford for its examination practices.[114] Such an exercise had limited value. Given the enduring rivalry (as yet without an outlet in organised sporting contests), there were constantly shifting perceptions of academic prowess, with some Cambridge scholars considering that emergence of the Cambridge mathematics tripos in the course of the eighteenth century (a substitute for logic) gave their university a march over Oxford. Naturally, such a view was contested.[115] The Cambridge professor and reformer, Richard Watson, per contra, saw his university holding an advantage elsewhere. He claimed: 'If in anything we are superior to Oxford, it is in this, that our scholastic disputations in philosophy and theology are supported with seriousness and solemnity'.[116] Watson had several Cantabrigian supporters of subscriptional and curricular reform in the last quarter of the century, but the challenge to drive an agenda forward anything other than piecemeal was close to insurmountable, especially after the French Revolution.[117] At any rate, Cambridge graduates were more widely ready to admit the need to proceed in that direction than were their Oxford equivalents. And well-wishing Whig outsiders that included Bishop William Warburton assuredly did. As he told a physician friend and former neighbour, a product of St John's College, Cambridge, in 1756:[118]

---

[113] Stride, *Exeter College*, 123.

[114] [Benjamin Newton], *The Names in the Cambridge Triposes, from 1754 to 1807,... prefaced by a short letter, on the comparative merits of the two universities, Oxford and Cambridge*, Bath, 1808), cited in C. Stray, 'From oral to written examinations: Cambridge, Oxford and Dublin 1700–1914', *History of Universities*, 20/2 (2005) 76–130, at 90–1, 98; C. Fell-Smith, rev. Robert D. Cornwall, 'Newton, Benjamin (bap. 1722, d. 1787), Church of England clergyman', *ODNB*, online edn., 2004.

[115] See John Gascoigne, 'Mathematics and meritocracy: the emergence of the Cambridge Mathematical School', *Social Studies of Science*, 14 (1984), 547–84, at 571.

[116] ed. Watson, *Anecdotes of the life of Richard Watson*, I. 35. He saw it latterly threatened by late dining and an audience absence.

[117] Frida Knight, *University Rebel. The Life of William Frend* (London, 1971).

[118] Uncatl. MS. Letters between the Revd. Mr Warburton and Dr [Robert] Taylor from the Year MDCCXXVIII, no. 35, 25 May 1756, Harry Ransom Center, University of Texas at Austin.

'Do not pride yourself that you are in a better way than the Oxonians. They are in the right Road (Religion) tho' indolent of pursuing their journey, they stop to pick straws, you push your way with vigour, . . . You are of real weight & strength, if you would exert yourself, to reform what is so extremely amiss.—And it is time to begin—'.

But it would be erroneous to conceive those political differences and intellectual rivalries precluded cooperation—the customary mutuality of academic 'incorporation' of each other's graduates saw to that.[119] It went on in the normal course of things most years. It was thus not uncommon for young or intending clerics to take a BA at Cambridge and then their MA (or BCL) by incorporation at Oxford in order to obtain a College living (more plentiful than in Cambridge, with many conveniently situated in the Oxford diocese).[120] Degree-giving ceremonies in both Universities were habitually occasions when exceptional recognition could be given to those from the sister institution whose career or writings could be endorsed. Thus the doughty Cambridge champion of theological orthodoxy, Daniel Waterland, and his brother, Theodore, both became incorporated DDs at Oxford in 1724 when Delaune delivered a 'large encomium' in his honour.[121] Poetry collections were compiled and published displaying the work of talented versifiers from both universities, such as *Oxford and Cambridge Miscellany Poems* (1709) (which often appeared missing title pages and an indication of authorship). And with many families likely to have or have had sons at both Oxford and Cambridge, there was ample social association as a basis from which undergraduates from both might project themselves through literary offerings to the world outside. One resultant enterprise was *The Student, or the Oxford and Cambridge Monthly Miscellany*, publication of which began on 31 January 1750 and continued for twenty issues into 1751 before the writers moved on and the initiative wilted.[122]

---

[119] MS Rawl. J. 4°.25 Members of Cambridge University incorporated at Oxford 1690–1744 [also gives TCD incorporations]. Numbers varied anywhere from one in 1716 and 1742 to thirty-three in 1712 (when eight graduates of TCD also joined). There were none in 1702, 1734, 1741. See also MS Rawl. J. 4°.26, 'An Index of the names of members of the University of Cambridge afterwards incorporated into the University of Oxford since the Year MDCXCI', (another index of names gives Oxford enrolments at Cambridge). In 1738 the University Senate at Cambridge enacted a Grace with the power of Statute that gave notice no BA from any other University could proceed MA except those who had resided in Cambridge for the major part of six several terms after such determination. For Scottish and Irish incorporations at Oxford see Chapter 9, pp. 95, 102, 104.

[120] The process could also happen in reverse. Of the 500 clergy surveyed by Viviane Barrie-Currien, *Clergé et pastorale en Angleterre au XVIIIe siècle. Le diocèse de Londres* (Paris, 1992), in the London diocese she found forty-one, or 8.2%, had been at both Oxford and Cambridge. Ibid., 120–1.

[121] R. T. Holtby, *Daniel Waterland 1683–1740. A study in eighteenth century Orthodoxy* (Carlisle, 1966), 5. Jeremiah Seed, *The happiness of the good* (London, 1741) for Oxford's recognition of Waterland's standing as an apologist. Waterland is examined in Robert G. Ingram, *Reformation without end. Religion, politics and the past in post-Revolutionary England* (Manchester, 2018), 25–82.

[122] See letter from the Proprietors to Thomas Warton (?), 17 Jan. 1751, ed. Fairer, *Correspondence of Thomas Warton*, 19. The magazine included a series of letters from Cambridge purporting to be written by a female student. *The Oxford Magazine, or the Oxford Museum* was another instance of a periodical originating in Oxford intended for a wider public, published between 1768 and 1776.

THE UNIVERSITY AS SEEN FROM OUTSIDE   511

It was quite a serious production, intended to display the intellectual capacities of the student body to an educated readership at large. An exemplar of a scholar who looked easily beyond mere institutional loyalty was the Cambridge pedagogue and scholar, Samuel Parr, who had many Oxford friends and supporters. He thought its members 'very good people' in some ways, though generally 'too orthodox in religion, too rampant in loyalty, and too furious in politics'.[123] In return, Oxonians took care not to expose themselves by incautious comments or imputed impoliteness about his politics and his opinions. Parr's admiration for accurate scholarship and integrity of character always trumped party-political considerations. He and Martin Routh, President of Magdalen College after April 1791, were friends from some years earlier and remained so until Parr's death in 1825, despite all their differences. When Routh was elected, Parr wrote:

> Believe me, Mr President, there is not under the canopy of heaven one human being who rejoices more cordially than I do at your appointment...I long to make you a most profound bow, and to give your hand a most hearty shake in your palace;...[124]

Trinity College Dublin alumni were seldom courted by Oxford. There was an acceptance of dependency on both sides that made the English university too ready to presume an intellectual supremacy. It may have contributed to Edmund Burke's cautious attitude to Oxford and its to him in the early 1790s. Burke found himself in favour with Anglican divines in and beyond Oxford after his critique of the French Revolution in *Reflections* made some amends for his opposition to the American War and membership of the Fox-North Coalition in a career that had included public criticism of the University.[125] From Hertford College, Griffith Griffiths, Archbishop Moore's domestic chaplain, reported that there was 'one opinion' and 'one voice' in the college about Burke's book. 'All agree in saying that the brilliancy of the work is equalled only by the importance of its Tendency'.[126] In late 1790, just weeks after *Reflections* appeared in print,[127] an address from resident Masters of Arts to the Vice-Chancellor urged the award to Burke of a

---

[123] *New Monthly Magazine*, 16 (1826), 486, quoted in Warren Derry, *Dr Parr. A Portrait of the Whig Dr Johnson* (Oxford, 1966), 114.

[124] ed. John Johnstone, MD, *The Works of Samuel Parr, LL.D* (8 vols., London, 1828), vii, 645.

[125] See Chapter 7, p. 91.

[126] 12 Nov. 1790, Houghton Library, Harvard University, MS Eng 961(7), Edmund Burke papers. For Griffiths see *GM*, 80 (1796), 619. The new-found apparent warmth of the University towards one whom it had previously kept at arm's length was ruefully noted in Foxite quarters, how 'Oxford, which so long adored the meridian splendour of despotism', now hailed Burke as 'the champion of [the] remnants of Toryism'. Anonymous, *Parallel between the Conduct of Mr Burke and that of Mr Fox, in their late Parliamentary Contest, in a Letter to the Former* (London, 1791), 12.

[127] Burke took care to flatter the universities for their part in the civilising process whereby young clergy were attached to their noble and genteel coevals: 'By this connexion we conceive that we attach our gentlemen to the church; and we liberalize the church by an intercourse with the leading characters of the country'. Edmund Burke, *Reflections on the Revolution in France. A Critical Edition*, ed. J. C. D. Clark (Stanford, CA, 2001), 264.

DCL by diploma (the greatest mark of distinction available to the University). The recommendation was narrowly rejected by the hebdomadal board on 8 December and Burke received only 'the unauthorised compliments of a baffled minority'.[128] Burke's sponsors (with Thomas Burgess of Corpus Christi at their head) still had work to do if they wanted to persuade majority academic opinion that he had become a staunch ally of the Anglican establishment, and it did not help that, anti-Revolutionary though he may have been, he was also the perceived principal persecutor of Warren Hastings and an eloquent critic of the narrow basis of Anglican ascendancy in Ireland.[129] In late 1792, Edward Tatham of Lincoln (then senior proctor) tried again, but the Heads of Houses declined to reopen the issue by the wider margin of fourteen votes to three.[130] It helped Burke's cause that the Portland faction grew ever closer to the Pitt government in Parliament and, by extension, to Oxford University, and Burke attended in person when Portland was installed as Chancellor in July 1793.[131] The duke wanted Burke to accept an honorary doctorate on that occasion but, ever sensitive about perceived slights, the latter considered it a lesser degree than the one by diploma originally proposed, and it passed at his behest to his son Richard Burke.[132] It was only a temporary contretemps and Burke's influence in Portlandite Oxford was great for the last three years of his life, as when the Duke nominated French Laurence to the Regius Chair of Civil Law on Burke's recommendation in 1796.[133]

Graduates of Scottish universities tended largely to accept that Oxford's distinctiveness owed much to its historical origins and the contrasting pedagogic traditions of England and Scotland. Not so Adam Smith, Glasgow graduate and Snell Exhibitioner, who had experienced Oxford at first hand and had not been impressed.[134] He devoted part of the section 'Of the Expence of the Institutions for the Education of Youth' in the *Wealth of Nations* to comparing the alleged idleness of salaried college tutors whose students were tied to them with the vigour of Scottish professors whose voluntary students paid them fees. Oxford,

---

[128] ed. Countess of Minto, *Life and Letters of Sir Gilbert Elliot, First Earl of Minto from 1751 to 1806* (3 vols., London, 1874), II. 153. See also *GM*, 61 (1791), 99–100, 210. The award was recommended in *The Times*, 8 Dec. The voting of Heads of Houses on the suggestion was reportedly very close: 7 votes anti to 6 pro. The episode is illuminated in Ian Harris, 'The Authentication of Burke's Reflections: Church, Monarchy and Universities, 1790–91', *History of Political Thought* 43 (2022), 81–130. Harris emphasises the prominence of the Corpus connection in putting the case for Burke's degree. There was additional pressure on Oxford to be generous in the light of Trinity College Dublin's award *nem. con.* to Burke of an honorary LL.D earlier in 1790.

[129] Discussed in Nigel Aston, 'A "Lay Divine": Burke, Christianity, and the Preservation of the British State, 1790–1797', in ed. N. Aston, *Religious Change in Europe 1650-1914: Essays for John McManners* (Oxford, 1997), 185–212, at 197–200.

[130] OUA: Minutes, Dec. 1792, WP/y/24/2.

[131] eds. T. W. Copeland et al., *The Correspondence of Edmund Burke,* (10 vols., Cambridge, 1958–78), VII. 224, 227–8.

[132] Robert Bisset, *The Life of Edmund Burke...* (London, 1798), 547–8; Sir Gilbert to Ly Elliot, 9 July 1793, in ed. Minto, *Life and Letters*, II. 153–4; James Prior, *Memoirs of the life and character of the Right Hon. Edmund Burke* (London, 1824), 365; Green, *Lincoln College*, 364n.

[133] Burke, *Correspondence*, IX. 147.   [134] Chapter 9, pp. 98–100.

THE UNIVERSITY AS SEEN FROM OUTSIDE 513

by comparison with Glasgow, had been slow to bring in modern improvements in philosophy, but the constitution of the latter university facilitated such a change because 'the teachers, depending upon their reputation for the greater part of their subsistence, were obliged to pay more attention to the current opinions of the world'.[135] Similarly the classical scholar, Professor Andrew Dalzel, in train with his sixteen-year-old Edinburgh pupil, Lord Maitland (later 8th Earl of Lauderdale) in 1775 for the latter to be entered on the books at Trinity College. Dalzel may have enjoyed a convivial Oxford common room at Trinity but he claimed to be shocked at how 'very little study goes on at Oxford except among a few book-worms that shut themselves up, and do not associate with others'.[136]

One of those Scottish professors whom Smith acclaimed took an altogether more positive view of Oxford. This was the intensely Anglophile James Beattie, significantly an Aberdonian professor (King's College), with many Anglican friends in that one-time Scottish episcopalian heartland in the north-east.[137] His *An Essay on the Nature and Immutability of Truth in Opposition to Sophistry and Scepticism*, published in 1770 and directed principally at David Hume, won him admirers in Oxford and all across England.[138] Beattie crossed the border in 1773 in search of a pension (he was successful) and, by the end of his stay, thanks in large measure to Elizabeth Montagu, he had met most of the bishops and toyed seriously with taking holy orders in the Church of England. Though he eventually decided against such a course, it did not preclude a highly placed squadron of Oxford academics including Beattie on the personal list of honorands to be recognised by Lord North, the new Chancellor of the University, at his first degree ceremony that July. There were some last-minute alarms that a Doctor's degree would be opposed in Convocation (on the grounds that Beattie was a Presbyterian), and the plan was amended to bestow an honorary DCL instead. He duly received it in person along with Sir Joshua Reynolds and North's political henchman, Henry Thrale (d. 1781; matric. University College), the brewer, and reported that 'the applause of the Theatre was so loud and so long continued as plainly showed that the Spectators took a very particular concern in my

---

[135] Discussed in Rivers, *Reason, Grace, and Sentiment*, II. 258–9.

[136] Cited in Cosmo Innes, *Memoir of Andrew Dalzel, professor of Greek in the University of Edinburgh* (Edinburgh, 1861), 14. Maitland went on to Glasgow University from Trinity; Dalzel was Professor of Greek at Edinburgh University, 1779–1805. He kept up an amicable correspondence with some Trinity fellows shortly after his residency in college.

[137] Beattie complained that the Aberdeen professorial system failed to encourage the formation of sound morals or promote the interest of true learning. In his own teaching he adopted some of the pedagogical techniques he associated with Oxbridge colleges, including class discussions, in order to foster the moral and intellectual improvement of his students. Wood, *The Aberdeen Enlightenment*, 125.

[138] Bishop Warburton reported that Sir John Eardley-Wilmot (Lord Chief Justice of Common Pleas, 1766–71) '. . . had occasion to go to Oxford, advised the heads of Houses, to have it in their care, that all the youth committed to their trust, should be directed to study Mr Beattie's book'. Warburton to Lord Hailes, 21 Feb. 1772, NLS, Newhailes MS 25295, f.152.

514 ENLIGHTENED OXFORD

success'.[139] Beattie was, for one, in no doubt that an 'English university is the best place on earth for study', not least because at Oxford and Cambridge study of the classics was more intensive than at Scotland's equivalents, and 'the French philosophy... is seldom held in very high estimation', and 'a regard to religion is fashionable'.[140] Another famous Scot, though of a different philosophical disposition than Beattie, was the Scottish judge and scholar of linguistic evolution, James Burnett, Lord Monboddo (1714–99) (educated at Aberdeen, Edinburgh, and Groningen), who used to visit Oxford regularly, and there found a range of interest in his work. Monboddo had a healthy respect for Oxford, where his followers included Thomas Burgess of Corpus Christi and George Huntingford, fellow of New College and future Warden of Winchester College.

An Edinburgh graduate, James Boswell, was in Oxford more frequently than Beattie, and he came to relish his visits. His curiosity about the University was fuelled both by his awareness of Samuel Johnson's time at Pembroke and by the circle of Oxford friends Johnson had constructed since his youth. Boswell thus had a ready introduction into Oxford society via a different route from Beattie's, with a favourable pre-visit impression of Oxford in 1768 confirmed by the civility shown to him by Robert Chambers, Johnson's host.[141] It was just the start. When he returned in 1776 he benefitted from the friendship that Johnson had with Adams of Pembroke, Wetherell of University College, Horne of Magdalen, and Warton of Trinity. The celebrity duo were so fêted that they had to decline a dinner with Edward Bentham and the canons of Christ Church as they were already engaged at University College, '... it being St Cuthbert's day, which is kept by them as a festival, as he was a saint of Durham, with which this college is much connected'.[142] He returned with Johnson in 1784 for a final visit only months before the latter's death that December.

Boswell seems never to have appeared bitter about not having attended Oxford as a student. That was not so for Samuel Johnson's beloved London friend,

[139] Beattie to Elizabeth Montagu, 12 July 1773, in ed. R. J. Robinson, *The correspondence of James Beattie* (4 vols., Bristol, 2004), II. 222. See also same to Sir William Forbes, 17 July 1773, ibid., II. 224–5; N. Aston, 'James Beattie in London in 1773: Anglicization and Anglicanization', in ed. Stana Nenadic, *Scots in London in the Eighteenth Century* (Lewisburg, PA, 2010), 139–61, at 145. Beattie cultivated his Oxford friends after his degree award and when in England visited them when he could, usually lodging with his old friend James Williamson of Hertford. 'I have several agreeable acquaintances;' he told Forbes, 'and the place, you know, is wonderfully well contrived for literary amusement'. Beattie to Forbes, 7 July 1781, NLS Fettercairn ACC 4796 box 94.

[140] Beattie to Elizabeth Montagu and to the Duchess of Gordon, 15 Oct. 1773 and 8 Aug. 1788, in William Forbes, *An account of the life and writings of James Beattie* (2 vols., London, 1996, first pub. in 3 vols., Edinburgh, 1807), II. 170, 370; Wood, *The Aberdeen Enlightenment*, 129, 213. The Dublin and Edinburgh graduate, Oliver Goldsmith, also praised the English universities. In *An Enquiry into the Present State of Polite Learning in Europe* (1759), Goldsmith claimed that Oxford (and Cambridge), unlike Edinburgh, provide actual learning and inspire greatness. *Collected Works of Oliver Goldsmith*, ed. Arthur Friedman (5 vols., Oxford, 1966), I. 333–4.

[141] ed. Birkbeck Hill, rev. Powell, *Boswell's Life of Johnson*, II. 47.

[142] 20 Mar. 1776, ibid., II. 445.

THE UNIVERSITY AS SEEN FROM OUTSIDE   515

Richard Savage, earlier in the century. Savage was a mass of grudges and resentments, and the universities were not excluded from his animus. A non-graduate himself, as his scurrilous satire 'The Progress of a Divine' (1735) showed, he marked them down as nepotistic nurseries: 'Mark how a country Curate once could rise; /Tho' neither learn'd, nor witty, good, nor wise! /Of Innkeeper, or Butcher, if begot, /At Cam, or Isis bred, imports it not'.[143] Another non-Oxonian, Percival Stockdale (1736–1811), man of feeling, prolific minor author and cleric, was at any rate a graduate, even if he had Savage's delusions of grandeur. He was convinced that his output was being deliberately marginalised by the arbiters of the polite literary world, and he blamed his family's lack of money for his first significant failure: a university education at St Andrews rather than at Oxford, one that permanently denied him influence and status. In 1794, while recuperating from a post-chaise accident near Oxford, he wrote 'Verses Addressed to Oxford', a poetically imagined alternative life:

> Oh! had my ardent, and aspiring youth/Felt in thy hallowed groves, important truth;/Inhaled, in them, the God's inspiring ray;/Caught the strong thought, and waked the glowing lay;/Then, reason, fancy, happily combined,/And tuneful diction, had my verse refined:/Then would thy liberal sons have raised my fame;/And high above my merit, fixed my name.[144]

For all the criticism from outsiders that Oxford attracted on the grounds of its narrow curriculum and its inert fellows, Stockdale's plaintive sentiments of regret at never having been an Oxford graduate indicate a pang that (unusually for him) was not laced with bitterness. He recognised the difference Oxford might have conferred on him, the high personal price payable for remaining outside the gates.

iv) Insiders as outsiders

The obvious category of insiders who were outsiders (at least as far as not being technically members of the University) were the considerable numbers of servants—women as well as men—who worked as butlers, cooks, gardeners, porters, scouts, waiters in hall, and in many other roles.[145] And they worked

---

[143] ed. C. Tracy, *Poetical works of Richard Savage* (Cambridge, 1962), 191.

[144] *The poetical works of Percival Stockdale* (2 vols., London, 1810), II. 377–8, quoted in Adam Rounce, *Fame and failure 1720–1800. the unfulfilled literary life* (Cambridge, 2013), 157. See also H. Weinbrot, 'Samuel Johnson, Percival Stockdale, and brick-bats from Grubstreet', *HLQ*, 56 (1993), 105–34.

[145] Brockliss (2), 228–9, 287n. Some domestic staff were employed privately by fellows and gentle-men commoners. Not all Houses were wary of employing women. At Worcester, a woman—one Eleanor Cradock—was listed in accounts as working in the kitchen in 1717, only a few years after its foundation.

516   ENLIGHTENED OXFORD

hard. As George Colman the younger described the duties of a scout at Christ Church in 1780: 'He undergoes the double toil of Boots at a well-frequented Inn, and a Waiter at Vauxhall, in a successful season.'[146] Many of them were fiercely loyal to the establishment that employed them and worked there from generation to generation. It was also commonplace, as at Balliol, for several members of a family to be employed concurrently.[147] Colleges usually acted quickly against undergraduates who were abusive towards servants either verbally or physically: John Pelling, later rector of St Anne's, Westminster, and Tutor and Senior Censor at Christ Church, was in 1695 suspended for six months from his Studentship and confined to the library for beating a porter; later, Francis Delaval, hothead scion of the Northumberland landed family, was sent down outright from Oxford because of a fracas that had ended in the death of a college servant.[148] No college could afford that sort of adverse publicity. The social gradations among servants were as various as they were among the students and dons whom they attended, and the goodwill of upper servants in particular was not to be taken for granted. Some of them had the franchise and it was a recurrent Whig hope that colleges favourable to the 'New Interest' might influence such servants to vote for their candidates. Cooks and butlers, in particular, were prized assets, men of influence within a college community. Under the manciple and butler at Magdalen there were, by 1767, three cooks helped by a kitchen woman and a kitchen boy, all entitled to various perquisites beyond their stipends;[149] James Langford, cook at Jesus College for over fifty years, merited an obituary in the *Gentleman's Magazine* (1794).[150] A century earlier, the butler of University College, John Pricket, was, it has been argued, 'the first College servant to emerge as a character in his own right'. His influence with the Master, Arthur Charlett, was widely known and its extent and character debated. One unsuccessful candidate for a fellowship at the College blotted his copybook irrevocably when he allegedly called Pricket 'Pimp Master generall to the Lodgings'.[151] Apart from servants, at Christ Church there were also the twenty-four 'poor' male inhabitants of the Almshouses that the college maintained at its own expense; the bedesmen were familiar and respected figures within its precincts.[152]

In every generation there are Oxford graduates whose time at the University was less satisfying in some respects than those of most of their contemporaries. Joseph Butler (1692–1750), for instance, one of the greatest intellectual presences

---

[146] R. B. Peake, *Memoirs of the Colman family,...* (London, 1841), 35.

[147] Jones, *Balliol College*, 134ff.

[148] Ch. Ch. Archives, cited in Money, *The English Horace*, 202; Delaval, matric. Ch. Ch., 1747. Foster, III. 361.

[149] ed. Ursula Aylmer, *Oxford food. An anthology* (Oxford, 1995), 167–8.

[150] *GM*, 64, I (1794), 387. Thanks to Colin Haydon for this information.

[151] Darwall-Smith, *University College*, 229, 230. Ibid., 318–19 for more details of individual servants at the College.

[152] Curthoys (1), 57–67, 98; Curthoys (3), 111.

THE UNIVERSITY AS SEEN FROM OUTSIDE 517

in the mid-century Church, was an Oxford product yet found it 'deeply uncongenial' in a manner that his friend Secker (another former Dissenter) never did and, for all the contemporary acclamation given to his *Analogy* and his *Sermons preached at the Rolls Chapel*, eighteenth-century Oxford never took Butler to heart.[153] His known disdain for his education, his Presbyterian origins, his rational version of the faith (he was insistent that the case for revelation stood or fell according to its consonance with reason), his moderate Whiggism were all excuses enough.[154] Butler, no more than other lukewarm Oxford graduates, was never publicly critical of his alma mater, neither did he reposition himself as an insider turned outsider. Where there was overt disassociation, it was likely to be because of changed personal circumstances, often compounded by an enduring distaste, but its expression remained private. Thus, in 1691, Humphrey Prideaux, Archdeacon of Suffolk, prominent as a tutor in Oxford before the Revolution and currently in possession of the rectory of St Clement's in the city, would not contemplate the offer of the chair in Hebrew and the stall in Christ Church that went with it. As he explained to a friend:[155]

> As to Dr Pocock[e]s place, it was offered me and I refused it, and that for two reasons: the first is, I nauseate that learning, and am resolved to loose no more time upon it; and the 2nd is, I nauseate Christ Church; and, further, if I should goe to Oxford again I must quit whatever advantage I have here [the living of Saham Toney, Norfolk] , and ye advantage would scarce[ly] pay for ye remove,

But there were enough publicly dissonant voices in the course of the century to catch the notice of one commentator, who remarked 'many who have resided in them [the English universities], and have afterwards acquired celebrity, frequently join in the censure and the satire that is thrown out against these seats of learning'.[156] And when such people were as socially prominent as John Wesley, Vicesimus Knox, and Edward Gibbon, the damage they were capable of inflicting on the public standing of Oxford was considerable and long-lasting. Graduates with Whig sympathies in the earlier Hanoverian period were never short of well-

---

[153] He complained that he was obliged to 'mis-spend so much time here [in Oxford] attending frivolous lectures and unintelligible disputations, that I am quite tired out with such a disagreeable way of trifling;' Letter to Samuel Clarke, *c*. Sept. 1717, in ed. D. E. White, *The Works of Bishop Butler* (Rochester, NY, 2006), 27. Paul Seaward notes the importance for Butler of the patronage and friendship of Edward Talbot (fellow of Oriel, 1712–15), Seaward, 'A Society of Gentlemen', in ed. Catto, *Oriel*, 219–46, at 216–17, 245.

[154] Butler was 'recovered' by Oriel Oxonians towards the end of the century, led by John Eveleigh. Ernest Nicholson, 'Eveleigh and Copleston', in ed. Catto, *Oriel*, 256–60. For his influence on the Noetics see Nockles, 'Oriel and Religion', in ibid., 291–327. See generally E. C. Mossner, *Bishop Butler and the age of reason* (London, 1936, repr. Bristol, 1990).

[155] 12 Oct. 1691, ed. Thompson, *Letters of Humphrey Prideaux*, 150. He subsequently regretted his decision.

[156] Wendeborn, *A View of England*, II. 141.

518   ENLIGHTENED OXFORD

worn horror stories of the University's intolerant and disloyal Tory politics and its intellectual slackness. The most renowned was perhaps Pitt the Elder. His failure to derive signal benefit from his studies at Trinity College left him no friend to Oxford. As late as 1754, he was ready in the House of Commons to present Oxford as a sink of Toryism and Jacobite loyalties without adducing much evidence for his charge beyond the notorious *Redeat* speech of William King five years previously.[157] Such abuse was calculated to stick and stay in the public consciousness far longer than praise of the estimable qualities of the University and the variety of political sympathies to be found inside it. It also incidentally revealed much about the capacity of ex-insiders to present themselves as somehow 'victims' of an Oxford education, men with varying levels of vindictiveness looking for a degree of revenge and deploying the rhetorical capacities which their Oxford education had gifted them against it.[158]

There were plenty of disgruntled Whigs in Oxford in George I's reign doing their best to obtain ministerial recognition, and what more conspicuous sign of martyrdom could there be than expulsion from the University? Such was the fate of Nicholas Amhurst of St John's College (1697–1742), defender of Benjamin Hoadly, discloser and indicter of named academics' sexual antics in his anonymous *S's Revenge: a satire on the Oxford Toasts* (London, 1718), expelled on charges of libertinism and misconduct. He revenged himself on the authorities with élan by producing the most copious of all the press attacks on Oxford in his *Terrae-Filius* essays of 1721.[159] Amhurst may have had grounds for bitterness but he overcame them sufficiently to produce a brilliantly plausible insider's view for metropolitan consumption of this allegedly alienated, disloyal institution, chockfull of papists who wanted to live under a popish king, all delivered in what W. R. Ward justly deemed 'sparkling style'. His parting shot was more specifically targeted at the college heads in his *Oculus Britanniae; an Heroi-Panegyrical Poem on the University of Oxford* (London, 1724), though not without a trace of good humour.[160] His fate undoubtedly sharpened his sense of the academic ideals that he expected his former University to embody.[161]

Amhurst was six years older than John Wesley, whose politics and religion were more typical of 1720s Oxford than Amhurst's. Wesley's educational and (to a large extent) spiritual formation owed much to Christ Church and Lincoln College.[162]

---

[157] Jeremy Black, *Pitt the Elder* (Cambridge, 1992), 4–5, 104. See also Chapter 7, p. 5, n. 12.

[158] For Jeremy Bentham's loss of faith and criticism of Oxford, see Clark, *Our Shadowed Present*, 125–6.

[159] There were fifty-three essays in all. See [Amhurst] ed. William E. Rivers, *Terrae-Filius, or, The Secret History of the University of Oxford (1721; 1726)* (Newark, DE, 2004). It was banned by the University on its first appearance. Amhurst was later editor-in-chief for Bolingbroke's *The Craftsman*.

[160] Ward, *Georgian Oxford*, 79–80, 95.

[161] Cf. Rivers, in 'Introduction', to his edn. of the *Terrae-Filius*, 41–2.

[162] Rack, *Reasonable enthusiast*, 66, 68–9. For the origins of the Holy Club, ibid., 83–90. Also Richard P. Heitzenrater, *The elusive Mr Wesley* (Nashville, TN, 1984), and Green, *The young Mr Wesley, passim.*

THE UNIVERSITY AS SEEN FROM OUTSIDE 519

His experience of his own tutors at the former was satisfactory and, as a don himself, he proved diligent and painstaking. But, by the mid-1730s, approaching the era of the Aldersgate Street conversion experience, he was fast losing such sympathy for an Oxford that he had come to believe was an institution whose Christian values were overlaid by worldliness and sloth. He made ready to express his impatience in no uncertain terms. The university sermons on 'Salvation by Faith' (11 June 1738) and the 'Almost Christian' (25 July 1741) were largely unexceptionable, but the aspersions cast on the spiritual apathy of senior members of the University in 'Scriptural Christianity' (St Mary's Church, 24 August 1744) were so pronounced that news of his outburst spread quickly across Oxford and beyond.[163] As a former vice chancellor told his patron:[164]

> Same Wesley the Field Preacher was pleased to entertain us in an extraordinary manner at St Mary's on Ba[r]tholomew Day. He fell foul upon both City & University & found there was not one Xtian amongst us all. Heads of Colleges all bad. Fellows worse & young men worst of all being perjured every one of them. The Vice Chr had his Sermon...

For all that Wesley felt he had no choice but to speak thus, his homily was outrageously pointed with more than a hint of self-righteousness. The University authorities, understandably, never asked him to preach there again, but he professed unconcern. 'I preached, I suppose, the last time at St Mary's,' he wrote in his journal, 'Be it so; I have fully delivered my soul.'[165] Despite his detachment from the establishment thereafter, Wesley refrained from abusing Oxford University himself and would not sanction criticism of it among his followers.[166] He was perhaps conscious that he could never completely disassociate himself from his experiences there. For as Henry Rack has justly claimed, his emphasis as an evangelist on perfectionism originated in the University. Other signs and mannerisms were evident. Thus he habitually styled himself a fellow (or, later) 'late Fellow' of Lincoln College; used Oxford logic in his many controversies; habitually adopted a *de haut en bas* tutorial manner in relations with preachers and followers,[167] advising them in 1746 to think of themselves 'as young students at the university' and to read for many hours a day.[168] Wesley admitted to his

---

[163] There had been a foretaste that Wesley was aggravating opinion when, in 1742, he was 'in a manner hiss'd out of the Pulpit by the Lads' in St Mary's Church. Salmon, *The foreigner's companion*, 25.

[164] Shippen to Lord Noel Somerset, Oxon., 2 Sept. 1744, Badminton Muniments, FmJ 2/32/11 11.

[165] ed. Curnock, Wesley, *Journal*, III. 147.

[166] He tacitly acknowledged its primary importance as a bastion against Trinitarian revisionism of the kind commonly associated with Rational Dissent. G. M. Ditchfield, 'John Wesley, heterodoxy, and Dissent', in *Wesley and Methodist Studies*, 10 (2018), 109–31.

[167] Rack, *Reasonable enthusiast*, 104–5. See also Heitzenrater, *The elusive Mr Wesley*, 423, 426.

[168] 'The early conferences, 1746', in *The works of John Wesley: Vol. 10: The Methodist societies: the minutes of conference*, ed. Henry D. Rack (Nashville, TN, 2011), 179–80.

520   ENLIGHTENED OXFORD

brother in 1772 the appeal of being an Oxford Methodist again, saying of his past: 'I did then walk closely with God and redeem the time', but when he walked around Christ Church in 1778, Wesley still insisted to himself that its occupants lacked the key ingredient for happiness, 'the experimental knowledge of God'.[169] Brother Charles who, in his youth, was quick to take offence at the lack of righteousness in others, was generally somewhat less charitable towards Oxford and its disconnection in his eyes from heavenly values. Christ Church, he once wrote to John, 'is certainly the worst place in the world to begin a reformation in'.[170] His *Intercession for the University* begins thus:[171]

> Teacher divine, with melting eye
> Our ruined Seats of Learning see,
> Whose ruling scribes Thy truth deny,
> And persecute Thy saints and Thee,
> As hired by Satan to suppress
> And root up every seed of grace.

And continues in much the same vein for five verses in condescending dismissiveness of these 'sinks of desperate wickedness'.

Links between Methodism and the University may have ebbed to very little by the 1770s, yet John Wesley never rekindled the disdainful dismissal of Oxford and its values that had marked his final sermon in St Mary's three decades previously. Despite his many disparaging references to the nobility and gentry coupled with his appeal to the poor, Oxford was always for him an essential bastion of the constitution.[172] It was left to Edward Gibbon (1737–94), at the end of his life, to articulate insinuating criticism of the University and its teachers while he was an undergraduate at Magdalen in 1752–3 that slyly, inimitably damaged it. As David Womersley has convincingly argued, Gibbon was heavily influenced in what he had to say by other public critics of their old university, the don and subsequently headmaster, Vicesimus Knox (1752–1821) prominent among them. Knox, a

---

[169] ed. Curnock, Wesley, *Journal*, VI. 6, 213. Vivian Green considered that 'His love for Oxford remained undimmed', quoting inter alia from his *Plain Account of Kingswood School* (1781) in which he wrote, 'I love the very sight of Oxford; I love the manner of life; I love and esteem many of its institutions', *The Young Mr Wesley*, 289–90. Nevertheless, as Rack points out, the *Plain Account* was critical of the Oxford tutorial system, with Wesley much influenced by the teaching and curriculum practices of the Dissenting Academies and the Pietist establishment at Jena. *Reasonable Enthusiast*, 357–8.

[170] Sir Keith Feiling, *In Christ Church Hall* (London, 1960), 54–5.

[171] 'Hymns of Intercession' (1758), cited in Hulton, *The Clerk of Oxford*, 310–11.

[172] N. Aston, 'Wesley and the social elite of Georgian Britain', *BJRL*, 85 (2003), 123–36; M. Edwards, *John Wesley and the eighteenth century: a study of his social and political influence* (London, 1955), 47. Hugh Trevor-Roper disparagingly called him that 'great enemy of the Enlightenment.' *History and the Enlightenment* (New Haven, CT, 2010), 2–3.

THE UNIVERSITY AS SEEN FROM OUTSIDE 521

persistent and well-informed educational commentator, went much further in calling for change than Gibbon was ready to do.[173]

Knox's publications became progressively more critical of the state of academic pedagogy. In 1781, his *Liberal Education* praised the universities and only talked loosely of the desirability of 'a few public alterations'. In 1788, when the essays in *Winter Evenings, or Lucubrations on Life and Letters* appeared, the disposition was less amiable. The fictional protagonist of Essay fifty six, one Jack Hearty, was pictured as falling into bad company, running up debts, and getting minimal instruction. Oxford, it seemed, had a lot to answer for. In a second essay in the collection, the seventy second, 'On the Superiority of the English Universities, as places of Education, . . .' Knox showed himself prepared to be confrontationally critical. He asked whether 'any of the great literary works of this day, in any department, [are] produced by the university?'[174] Had he given offence to his old Oxford friends through such taunts? He professed indifference: 'I ask no favours of them, I want no indulgence'.[175] And he wanted thoroughgoing reformation of the institution, knowing the difficulty that upheavals would bring but concluding that that education had to be useful and that it was unpersuasive to dismiss action as politically dangerous when ' . . . the universities are so much degenerated by the lapse of ages, . . .'.[176] Knox's publications of the 1790s showed him trying desperately to advocate moderate reform (he steered clear of critiquing the curriculum) despite the long shadow cast by the French Revolution, but his underlying commitment to reformist Whiggism lay unconcealed in *The Spirit of Despotism* (1795). It may well be that the line-by-line rebuttal Knox had received back in 1790 in a tract written with the 'mild and amiable Earnestness of an Affectionate Son'[177] had deterred him from an unseasonable resumption of his one-man campaign against perceived academic anachronisms.

Gibbon, too, was ready to cast himself for posterity as firmly, aggressively, the outsider:

To the University of Oxford I acknowledge no obligation; and she will as cheerfully renounce me for a son, as I am willing to disclaim her for a mother.

---

[173] Womersley calls Knox ' . . . Gibbon's *doppelgänger* . . .', one who [in his *Winter Evenings: or lucubrations on life and letters,* published in 1788] took a path 'which Gibbon might have chosen, but which in fact he declined—a circumstance which might explain the claim such a book could have exerted upon Gibbon's attention' . . . *Gibbon and the "Watchmen of the Holy City"*, 321. For Knox see Michael J. Hofstetter, *The Romantic Idea of a University. England and Germany, 1770-1850* (Basingstoke, 2001), 16–20.

[174] Knox, *Winter evenings*, II. 574.   [175] Ibid., II. 578.

[176] Ibid., II. 352. He continued in the same vein in *A letter to the Right Hon. Lord North, Chancellor of the University of Oxford* (London, 1789). This was annexed to the 10th edn. of *Liberal education.*

[177] This was 'Philalethes', *A Letter to the Rev. Vicecimus [sic] Knox on the subject of his animadversions on the University of Oxford* (Oxford, 1790). He styled himself a 'resident member'.

522 ENLIGHTENED OXFORD

Such words in the *Memoirs* have a cultural potency that has proved impossible to dispel entirely. It is still impossible to write about eighteenth-century Oxford without a sense that however much Gibbon's words are contextualised and rationalised they will never cease to be alluringly persuasive or offered as a point of reference. Never mind that he was a precociously learned fourteen-year old when he came up and untypical of the student body as a whole, such considerations were not part of his mature acetic judgement.[178] Rather, he was retrospectively delighted that his youthful brief conversion to the Catholic faith had led to his removal from the University, and 'the gates of Magdalen College were for ever shut against my return'.[179] It may be that the largely aggrieved clerical response (still far from silent on the publication of the last volumes in 1788) to the *Decline and Fall* partly induced Gibbon's strictures,[180] but he was regularly revisiting and reworking his six draft unpublished manuscript versions of his *Memoirs,* and trying to see his fourteen months at Oxford within the sequence of his whole life. David Womersley has persuasively argued that Gibbon was drawing on an established idiom of writing about Oxford and deployed many of its tropes himself, less transcribing 'at a distance of some forty years, the emotions of the moment', more a case of 'concocting a career for himself from the available contextual materials, and then draping it around a spare (and therefore versatile) factual framework'.[181] Oxford, like the rest of Gibbon's life in what amounted to an unfinished autobiography, appears in highly polished cameo.

Gibbon was gracious enough to say nothing on the subject of his Oxford education in his lifetime, and that notorious section of his *Memoirs of my Life and Writings* did not appear until 1796, two years after his death, along with the rest of the volume constructed from the manuscript variants by his literary executor, Lord Sheffield.[182] The latter made some gestures to avoid both libel and insensitivity when the *Memoirs* was published, but only partly mitigated

---

[178] Pocock, *Barbarism and Religion,* I. 43–9, for Gibbon at Oxford. He wanted to learn Arabic and spent his first long vacation planning and writing a few pages of *The Age of Sesotris,* a chronological study intended to show that the Egyptian king was a contemporary of Solomon's. BL Add MS. 36248, f.9.

[179] *Memoirs,* 87.

[180] For 'An Oxford confederacy' of Henry Davis, James Chelsum, and Thomas Randolph see Pocock, *Barbarism and Religion,* I. 353, 356. And the more moderate appraisals of his history emanating from Cambridge are considered in J. A. W. Bennett, 'Gibbon and the Universities', *The Cambridge Review,* xcix (1976), 15–18.

[181] *Gibbon and the "Watchmen of the Holy City",* 284. Gibbon did concede in his *Memoirs* the likelihood from his own knowledge that the last forty years had brought academic improvements. Gibbon read extensively while at Magdalen.

[182] Authoritatively discussed in D. Womersley, 'Gibbon's *Memoirs*: autobiography in time of revolution', in eds. D. Womersley, J. Burrow, and J. Pocock, *Edward Gibbon* (Oxford, 1997), 347–404; Womersley, *Gibbon and the "Watchmen of the Holy City",* 257–332. Each version contained 'discrepant contents and divergent tendencies', ibid., 332. Sheffield's role in constructing the posthumous image of Gibbon cannot be exaggerated.

THE UNIVERSITY AS SEEN FROM OUTSIDE 523

Gibbon's arraignment of his Magdalen tutor, Thomas Winchester, of whom the author had originally written:

> Instead of guiding the studies, and watching over the behaviour of his disciple, I was never summoned to attend even the ceremony of a lecture; and, except one voluntary visit to his rooms, during the eight months of his titular office, the tutor and the pupil lived in the same college as strangers to each other.[183]

In Sheffield's edition, care was taken to limit the derogatory reference by asterisking Winchester's surname: 'Dr —— well remembered that he had a salary to receive, and only forgot that he had a duty to perform'.[184] Sheffield also defensively inserted this footnote:

> ' [I] have further to observe, that I have not met with any person who lived at the time to which Mr Gibbon alludes, who was not of opinion that his representation, at least of his own college, was just:...but every man, acquainted with the former and present state of the University, will acknowledge the vast improvements which have of late been introduced into the plan and conduct of education in the University.[185]

Sheffield's version of Gibbon, under the influence of the French Revolution, was still less strident than it might have been.[186]

It did not go unanswered. James Hurdis, Fellow of Magdalen and Professor of Poetry since 1793, offered *A word or two in vindication of the University of Oxford, and of Magdalen College in particular, from the posthumous aspersions of Mr Gibbon* (London, 1800), a low-key response that explained much of Gibbon's animus in terms of his coming to Oxford prematurely:

> It is wonderful that in penning his opinions of our English University the Historian should not have recollected that they were the opinions of a boy, who by his own confession was not sufficiently improved to be able to judge of matters so important.

---

[183] Gibbon, *Memoirs*, 83.

[184] Gibbon, ed. J. B. Bury, *Autobiography of Edward Gibbon [originally edited by Lord Sheffield]* (Oxford, 1907), 53. John Loveday, Winchester's contemporary, observed, in his defence: 'It is sad the feelings of a discontented child, swollen through thirty years to an outrageous animosity, should have prevailed rather than the solid, honest loyalty of Thomas Winchester'. Markham, *John Loveday*, 67–8. For an ingenious attempt to connect the intellectual values of Gibbon and Winchester see Doolittle, 'William Blackstone, Edward Gibbon and Thomas Winchester', 59–76.

[185] ed. Bury, *Autobiography of Edward Gibbon*, 54–5n.

[186] Womersley also argues that, in his various versions, Gibbon diluted the extent of his criticism of Oxford. *Gibbon and the "Watchmen of the Holy City"*, 303, 309. 'When he set about editing the Memoirs, Sheffield wanted to present Gibbon as what, in his experience, Gibbon had been: Namely, an opponent of democracy who yet had had little in common with Burke'. Ibid., 236.

524 ENLIGHTENED OXFORD

Hurdis also reminded his readers that it had become a perilously close step to pass from perceived social utility to revolutionary objectives: 'If the mere plea of inutility were admitted as sufficient cause of deprivation, estates and offices would soon be in a continual transfer at the will of the factious and dissatisfied, and society would be a mere whirlpool of revolution'.[187] These were sentiments from which Gibbon, had he lived, might have found it hard to dissent.[188] And his view of Oxford might also have been less qualified had he while in residence, like most of his slightly older contemporaries, been more susceptible to the considerable presence of women in and around the city.

v) The female presence in Oxford

Our Oxford ladies reign o'er youthful hearts;
In their own native, naked charms they shine,
Smug chamber-maids and semsptresses divine,
Smart laundresses on Saturdays so clean,
And bed-makers on every day between,...

>   Philo-Musus, Oculus Britanniae: An heroi-panegyrical
>   poem on the University of Oxford (London, 1724), 49.

...as for Women I have not seen one since I left London. There does not seem to be one under 50 in or bout this place—of old women there are abundance, at least 10 or 20 in every College—so judge what a kind of life one must lead—not so much as one even to talk to—.

>   Lord Fitzmaurice to Sir James Caldwell, 8 Apr. 1755,
>   JRUL, Bagshawe Muniments, B3/14/45.

Lord Fitzmaurice had not looked hard enough. Women were actually everywhere in Oxford, but it is primarily from the male perspective rather than from their own surviving testimonies that they have been viewed.[189] Where they do survive, primary sources written by women are therefore of exceptional value for the

---

[187] Hurdis, *Vindication*, 7, 40.

[188] That formidable Cambridge man, Samuel Parr, in 1800 preached his Spital Sermon replying to the censures of Thomas Gray on Cambridge and Gibbon on Oxford and produced long lists of their alumni conspicuous for their learning and ability. See Parr, *Works*, II. 541–6. As his biographer observed, Parr 'was aware there was a case to be made, and no advocate could have gone to greater trouble in calling up witnesses'. Derry, *Dr Parr*, 220.

[189] The subject has been broadly treated in Midgley, *University Life*, 'Women and Love', 75–90. At the end of the eighteenth century Oxford was the only major English town not to have a majority of women. Corfield, *The Impact of English Towns*, 99; Mary Prior, 'Women and the urban economy: Oxford 1500–1800', in ed. M. Prior, *Women in English society, 1500–1800* (London, 1985), 93–117.

THE UNIVERSITY AS SEEN FROM OUTSIDE   525

vantage point offered.[190] The extent to which, other than formally, they were 'outsiders', is far from being *une question mal posée*. Oxford as an urban centre had as significant a female presence as any other comparable English town and a high proportion of those who lived there interacted with the University, among them: Heads of Houses and canons of Christ Church had wives who lived in University accommodation and who could be seen on a regular basis in and around the colleges;[191] at a lower social level, most colleges employed a limited number of female servants as laundresses and bedmakers (at Christ Church, there was Mrs Showwell, employed by the college to show the Guise collection of Pictures to visitors).[192] But, as the epigraph to this section suggests, in a town full of young men, women in Oxford, especially young women, needed to be on their guard against the wiles of college students and extra careful of their behaviour in order to preserve their reputations.

Women were not, by definition, members of the University, and no one seriously contended that Oxford should follow the University of Bologna's example and appoint a woman to a Professorship.[193] Which is not to say that the University could not offer informal support for scholarship and creativity to female intellectual 'outsiders'.[194] Elizabeth Elstob (1683–1756) was one of the greatest of early eighteenth-century Saxon scholars, best known for her Anglo-Saxon dictionary, which came out in 1715. This landmark occasion was the

[190] One invaluable source is the recently edited *Memoirs of the City and University of Oxford in 1738...* [Oxford Historical Society, ns. 47] ed. G. Neate (Woodbridge, 2018), written by Elizabeth Sheppard, a young woman who called herself 'Shepilinda'. Her father, William Sheppard, was from a comfortably off Oxfordshire family at Great Rollright, and a Hart Hall alumnus. Her sparky personality and acute observation were supplemented by influence and money, and she had two cousins who were Gentleman Commoners at University College.

[191] Uniquely, the Wardens of Wadham could not marry until an Act of 1806 permitted the connubial state, and James Gerard had resigned as Warden in 1783 on the failure of his petition to Parliament for relief from the foundress's injunction. See Gerard to Lord North, 16 Nov. [1786?], North [Sheffield Park] Papers, BL Add. MS. 61869, f. 163.

[192] See the print of 1807 of her by Thomas Rowlandson after John Nixon. At Corpus Christi female bedmakers were barred under both Founder's statutes and the Visitor's statute, and laundresses could not come beyond the lodge. Fowler, *Corpus Christi*, 49. At Wadham in 1698 some of the fellows presented a comprehensive indictment to the Visitor, instancing the employment of female bedmakers, and easy access into the college for townsmen and women via the King's Arms. Davies, 'Decline and Revival', 38. At Magdalen, by the mid-century, 'bed-makers' were again almost exclusively male. Darwall-Smith, 'The Monks of Magdalen', 295. Brockliss attributes much of the decline in servitor numbers to the increase in female bedmakers. Brockliss (2), 228–9.

[193] There is just one female privileged person listed in *Alumni Oxonienses*: Catherine Slatford, a carrier, matriculated on 18 July 1723. It would appear to be, on the face of it, an anomalous entry. For Lady Mary Wortley Montagu's appreciation of Maria Gaetana Agnesi, nominated to a chair at Bologna on Pope Benedict XIV's nomination in 1750, see Margaret R. Hunt, *Women in Eighteenth-Century Europe* (Harlow, 2010), 298–9. Agnesi was reportedly too shy to offer lectures.

[194] What Katharine Glover has written of Scotland might equally be applied to Oxford: '...the prominent role of formal institutions like universities in the Scottish Enlightenment need not necessarily be viewed as entirely detrimental to women; rather, the central position of the universities in Scotland's principal burghs may have created social climates more amenable to women's acquisition of learning than existed elsewhere'. Glover, *Elite Women and Polite Society in Eighteenth-Century Scotland* (Woodbridge, 2011), 169–70.

Fig. 10.3 Mrs Showwell, the Woman who shows General Guise's Collection of Pictures at Oxford, Thomas Rowlandson, hand-coloured etching, 1807 (The Metropolitan Museum of Art, New York: The Elisha Whittelsey Collection, The Elisha Whittelsey Fund, 1959).

THE UNIVERSITY AS SEEN FROM OUTSIDE 527

culmination of her work on the English Saxon clergy and of all the editions that had been published earlier by the University Press. She owed something to her elder brother, William Elstob (1673–1715; Fellow of University College, 1696), another Saxonist,[195] but her superior talent (she was proficient in eight languages) stood out in its own right.[196] Elstob was as perhaps as close to being a de facto member of Oxford University as any woman became in this era and was actually described as such in at least one instance.[197] Her academic achievement owed much to an Oxford-based community of Old English scholars that trained and supported someone who was doing cutting-edge work, but she could have no formal institutional vantage point of her own.[198]

The *Westminster Magazine* in the 1770s argued that learned ladies should be eligible for honorary Oxford degrees, but there was no serious attempt to make this so.[199] Intelligent women dedicated to literary pursuits knew all too well that they were shut out of a formal higher education, so made the best of this frustration. They might, for instance, call without scandal on male supporters, especially when the latter were married. That indefatigable proponent of religious virtue and the constitutional status quo, Hannah More, a regular visitor to Oxford,[200] frequently took tea with George Horne and his family in the President's lodgings at Magdalen, and was well-known to William Adams and his daughter at Pembroke.[201] Where such women were members of clerical

---

[195] William Elstob was educated at Eton and St Catherine's Hall, Cambridge, but reputedly came to Oxford as a commoner (initially to Queen's) because the Cambridge air did not agree with his consumptive constitution. See George Hickes to Arthur Charlett, 23 Dec. 1712, *Letters written by eminent persons*, I. 243, where he recommends Elizabeth to the University for patronage, and to Charlett in particular. See also Darwall-Smith, *University College*, 223. In fact, Elstob's later life (she unsuccessfully opened a school in Evesham) was marked by financial hard times because of William's decease in 1715. She later relied on another scholar in the provinces, George Ballard (1705/6–1756) to gain access to books and texts. Leonie Hannan, *Women of letters. Gender, writing and the life of the mind in early modern England* (Manchester, 2016), 52–3, 74–80, 172–3; Douglas, *English scholars*, 75–6.

[196] Hannan, *Women of letters*, 70–4 Norma Clarke, 'Elizabeth Elstob (1674–1752): England's first professional woman historian", *Gender & History*, 17 (2005), 210–20; M. Gretsch, 'Elizabeth Elstob: a scholar's fight for Anglo-Saxon studies', *Anglia*, 117 (1999), 163–200, 481–524.

[197] Edward Rowe Mores, *A dissertation upon English typographical founders and founderies* (London, 1778), 28.

[198] It says much for her originality that when Swift's *Proposal for Correcting the English Tongue* came out in 1712, she appears to have been the only person who attacked it not on political grounds, but on the grounds of his ignorance about the English language.

[199] See J. Brewer, *The Pleasures of the imagination. English culture in the eighteenth century* (London, 1997), 78. A female student was imagined by undergraduate journalists in *The Student, or the Oxford Monthly Miscellany* 2 (1750), 49–52.

[200] On one such visit in 1782 she was delighted to have Samuel Johnson as her 'Cicerone' and to be having dinner with him and Thomas Warton as well as '...some other Savans as of much learning I suppose, but of less wit'. 18 June 1782, in eds. E. and F. Anson, *Mary Hamilton...From Letters and Diaries 1756 to 1816* (London, 1925), 116–18.

[201] Anne Stott, *Hannah More. The First Victorian* (Oxford, 2003), chap. 5 and 135–6. She wrote thus after a call: 'Mrs Garrick and I both thought he did us honour and pleasure by giving us as much of his time as he cou'd spare.' To Sarah Adams, 9 May 1785, Houghton Library, Harvard University, MS Hyde 8 (2).

528 ENLIGHTENED OXFORD

families they could take advantage of 'a range of social activities based in parishes and cathedral closes, not to mention access to libraries; [and] an emphasis on serious reading of theology, philosophy, and history, as well as belles lettres'[202] that made them able to socialise on a basis of intellectual equality with male graduates in their households.

One such was Mary Jones (1707–78), 'one of the most intelligent and amusing women writers of her period',[203] the daughter of a cooper, who was postmistress of Oxford at her death. She had lived in the city all her life with her brother Oliver (1705–75), the Precentor of Christ Church (1736), and subsequently Senior Chaplain.[204] Jones published her *Miscellanies in Prose and Verse* (Oxford, 1750) by subscription, and there were no fewer than two thousand names listed when it appeared.[205] These unpretentious poems were acclaimed for their verve, humour (engagingly found in 'Soliloquy on an Empty Purse' and 'Holt Waters'), and self-deprecation;[206] she was also capable of producing a stately elegy to Lord Aubrey Beauclerk, serving with Admiral Edward Vernon, and killed fighting the Spanish at Boca Chica in the defeat at Cartagena in 1741.[207] She was both respected and liked within (by Joseph Spence) and well beyond (Samuel Johnson, who called her the 'Chantress') her brother's coteries at the House. The gifted Catherine Talbot (1721–70) found Jones's work occasionally indelicate.[208] Talbot was the ward of archbishop Thomas Secker (who encouraged her early interest in the classics, English and French literature, and history), and was less proximate to the University than Jones. She fantasised about the pleasures of an academic life as contained in her unpublished 'The Borlaciad' (1743) in four cantos, an allegory of Oxford and Cambridge, casting herself as its heroine.[209] She looked on her learned friend, Elizabeth Carter (1717–1806), as a college don, one who would be eminently eligible to instruct

---

[202] Clarissa Campbell Orr, 'The Sappho of Gloucestershire: Sarah Chapone and Christian feminism', in ed. Deborah Heller, *Bluestockings now! the evolution of a social role* (London, 2016), 91–110, at 96.

[203] ed. Roger Lonsdale, *Eighteenth-century women poets* (Oxford, 1990), 155–6.

[204] Deborah Kennedy, *Poetic sisters. Early eighteenth-century women poets* (Lewisburg, PA, 2013), 163–203.

[205] '... in extent and weight Mary Jones's subscription list is unparalleled'. 'Books Published by Subscription', *Notes and Queries*, 6 Sept. 1879, 198, quoted in Kennedy, *Poetic Sisters*, 171.

[206] For instance, Mary Scott in 1774: 'To Oxford next the Muse transported turns,/Where Jones with all a poet's ardour burns;/Jones, in whose strains another Pope we view,/Her wit so keen, her sentiments so true.' *The Female Advocate* ..., int. G. Holladay (repr. Los Angeles, CA, 1984).

[207] See Paula R. Backscheider, *Eighteenth-century women poets and their poetry. Inventing agency, inventing genre* (Baltimore, MD, 2005), 273–4, for the Beauclerk elegy. The first prose essay in the *Miscellanies in Prose and Verse* is about a woman student in Oxford who receives an honorary degree and a key to the Bodleian Library, Kennedy, *Poetic Sisters*, 169.

[208] ed. M. Pennington, *A series of letters between Mrs. Elizabeth Carter and Miss Catherine Talbot, from the year 1741 to 1770* (2 vols., London, 1808), II. 86–7.

[209] Luton & Bedfordshire Archives, Lucas papers, L30/21/3/10 & 12. On the place of Latin and Greek in female education see M. Cohen, '"To think, to compare, to combine, to methodise": girls' education in Enlightenment Britain', in eds. S. Knott and B. Taylor, *Women, gender, and Enlightenment* (Basingstoke, 2005), 224–42.

THE UNIVERSITY AS SEEN FROM OUTSIDE   529

at a 'university of ladies'.[210] This imagined academy was a far cry from the real Oxford, but it is testimony to how much the University's cultural associations could inspire the female imagination.

Talbot was far from disconnected from that world: she was the friend of Lady Mary Gregory (c.1720–62, youngest daughter of Henry Grey, 1st and last Duke of Kent), who married David Gregory, future Dean of Christ Church, in 1743, and kept abreast of Oxford developments through him.[211] She was also a significant member of the Whiggish Yorke-Hardwicke circle, and a presence at Cuddesdon (and later, Lambeth) whenever Secker was in residence.[212] Talbot duly became the pupil and friend of many on the bishops' bench in the 1740s and 1750s.[213] There was a genuine respect in academic quarters for learned women—especially if they were drawn from the ranks of the peerage. A case in point was Margaret, 2nd Duchess of Portland (d. 1785), Robert Harley's granddaughter, resident at Bulstrode Park, thirty-five miles towards London out of Oxford. Her knowledge of shells was such that the University dedicated a comprehensive book on conchology to her.[214]

Catherine Talbot was almost unofficially attached to the University, but one could get even closer. All of Oxford's Chancellors in this period were married, if not always happily married. Conjugal disharmony explains the rare visits to Oxford of Mary, Duchess of Ormond, wife of the 2nd Duke (and aunt of the High Tory 2nd Duke of Beaufort), as well as her husband's premature loss of office consequent on his flight to France in 1715. Not that she was wanting for male admirers, as a laudatory notice of the duchess after her death intimated:[215]

[210] ed. Pennington, *A series of letters*, II. 186 (26 Nov. 1754); II: 351 (17 Sept. 1760); Beth Kowaleski-Wallace, 'Two Anomalous Women: Elizabeth Carter and Catherine Talbot', in eds. F. M. Keener and S. E. Lorsch, *Eighteenth-century women and the arts* (Westport, CT., 1988), 19–27, at 26. Carter tutored her nephew for Oxford entry. See M. Bignold, 'Letters and learning', in ed. R. Ballaster, *The history of British women's writings, 1690-1750*, vol. 4, *The history of British women's writing* [J. Batchelor and C. Kaplan, gen. eds.], (Basingstoke, 2010), 181.

[211] See her letters (1750–7) to her sister Jemima, Marchioness Grey, daughter-in-law of Lord Chancellor Hardwicke, Bedfordshire & Luton Archives, L30/9/50/1–43. Horace Walpole cattily described Lady Mary as 'nothing less than a monster' and Gregory as one 'whose talents would have been extremely thrown away in any priesthood, where celibacy was one of the injunctions'. Walpole, *Memoirs of the Reign of George II*, I. 46.

[212] In 1758 she declined George Berkeley the younger's offer of marriage but remained friends with him and his future wife for the rest of her life. Sylvia Harcstark Myers, *The Bluestocking Circle. Women, friendship, and the life of the mind in eighteenth-century England* (Oxford, 1990), 216–21. See also S. Staves, 'Church of England Clergy and Women Writers', in eds. N. Pohl and B. A. Schellenberg, *Reconsidering the Bluestockings* (San Marino, CA, 2002/3), 81–103, at 83–6, 93, 96; Myers, *The Bluestocking Circle*, 159–60.

[213] Staves, 'Church of England Clergy and Women Writers', 85.

[214] Beth Fowkes Tobin, *The Duchess's Shells: Natural History Collecting in the Age of Cook's Voyages* (New Haven, CT, 2014). It was familiarity with the Duchess that reassured Tories when it came to the selection of her son, the 3rd Duke, as Chancellor, in 1792. M. Pelling, 'Collecting the world: female friendship and domestic craft at Bulstrode Park', *JECS*, 41 (2018), 101–20; A. M. Baker, 'The Portland family and Bulstrode Park', *Records of Buckinghamshire*, 43 (2003), 159–78, at 169.

[215] *A short memorial...of Princess Mary, Duchess of Ormonde* (s.n., 1735), 9. The apostrophe tactfully said nothing about her penchant for the gaming table, which had played its part in the spectacular collapse of the Duke's fortune.

A virtuous young Lady of rank and Beauty is a publick Blessing, she civilizes the Souls of her Admirers more than all their Academical Institutions, and fires them to aim at a proper Similitude of Accomplishments. Innocence, Purity and Honour appear so persuasive in the Fair-One, that it is no Wonder if she daily increases the Number of their Votaries, and brings them fresh Accessions of Homage.

Subsequent Chancellors' wives—Elizabeth, Countess of Arran, Mary, Countess of Westmorland (d. 1778, a member of the 2nd Duchess of Portland's 'Bulstrode circle'), Diana, Countess of Lichfield (d. 1779), and Anne, Lady North (Countess of Guilford after 1790) (d. 1797)—also kept their distance, usually appearing on ceremonial occasions and entertaining, but not much more.[216] Their appearance would do nothing to lessen their husbands' popularity and their presence was sought. Thus Lord North deliberately deferred his visit as Chancellor to the Ashmolean museum until the summer of 1775 when the measles that had erupted in his household had gone and Lady North and one of his daughters could accompany him.[217] On a day-to-day basis the predominant role for women in eighteenth-century Oxford fell by default to the wives and female relations of the Heads of Houses and canons of Christ Church.

To them fell on regular occasion the crucial role of hostess when their husband's patron's friends were in Oxford and housekeeping and culinary skills could make all the difference. When the Hebrew Professor, Thomas Hunt, sent Gregory Sharp a present of Lowth's poetry Lectures he invited Sharp to visit at Christ Church and used his wife's custard-making skills as an additional incentive.[218] A racy choice made in the by definition limited academic marriage market could sustain Oxford-wide interest for months: Professor John Potter's 1709 marriage to Elizabeth Venner, the granddaughter of Thomas Venner, the Fifth Monarchist, executed as a traitor in 1661, aroused no end of scandalous comment well beyond Oxford.[219] To be the wife of a canon professor or a college Principal brought a woman into the corporate life of the University of which she could never be formally a member and, as a presiding female presence inside her spouse's lodgings, she had scope to become a force not just in her family but within a very male academic society.[220]

---

[216] The 3rd Duke of Portland became a widower a month prior to his installation as Chancellor.

[217] To Thomas Harris, 23 Apr. 1775, Hants RO, 9M73/G537/2.

[218] 24 Feb. 1753, Bodl. Ms Eng. lett. d. 146, f. 37. Mrs Hunt was an untypical canon's wife. She had fallen pregnant by Hunt when he was a tutor at Hart Hall and she was a laundress. He married her and enjoyed domesticity. Hearne, XI. 59, 16 May 1732.

[219] 'The Christ Church men, I apprehend, will make work with him upon this marriage', wrote Humphrey Prideaux. ed. Thompson, *Letters of Humphrey Prideaux*, 202–3. 11 July 1709.

[220] It was not always a wife who presided: Mary Waldo kept house for her uncle, Dr Theophilus Leigh, for nearly forty years at Balliol College. Markham, *John Loveday*, 359–60.

THE UNIVERSITY AS SEEN FROM OUTSIDE 531

And when the woman was relatively young and good-looking, undergraduate interest could be intense, as it was in the case of Dean Bagot's wife. One acclaimed her thus:[221]

> ...I was at the Deanery; Mrs Bagot very politely having invited me to an elegant concert and supper—Her style of singing is wonderful; she seems sensible; and her manner is captivating; but neither her singing, her conversation, nor her manner, pleased me half as much, as her attentions to the Dean;—...Did you ever see them together? did you ever hear her call him 'Lewis'? No one of her songs had half the melody in it of that little word 'Lewis'—the company of the Deanery was numerous, and well chosen.

In at least one instance, the Master's wife was reported to have an active tutorial role. It occurred at University College where Thomas Cockman's wife acted as 'Nurse & Tutoress' to Thomas, Lord Deerhurst (d. 1744) and his brother, the Hon. George Coventry (d. 1809, later 6th Earl of Coventry).[222]

Some of these women became well-known well beyond the college, especially if their husband became Vice Chancellor. At one extreme was the wife of Dr Michael Marlow, last Vice Chancellor of the eighteenth century (elected 1798), known for her kindness but more for a social stiffness that led to some styling her 'the Duchess of Freezeland'. At the other, Mrs Mary Fothergill, wife of the President of Queens' and niece of Lord Chancellor Hardwicke (Thomas died in 1796), who walked at a distance behind her spouse, the gap steadily increasing the further they travelled from the College, so that they were known as Orpheus and Eurydice. What contemporaries would have known as 'petticoat rule' could also be detected in some colleges. Queen's at one time was a case in point where, to quote one contemporary, 'the Grey Mare is the Better horse', testimony to the dominance of Mary Smith over her husband the Provost.[223] Other females could be decidedly cutting about the appeal of Heads of House's choice of wives. The witty 'Shepilinda', busy assessing the eligibility of any unmarried College Head in the late 1730s, agreed that Warden Niblett at All Souls was married to a 'fine Wife' but then added a deadly qualifier—'who was ever yet a moving Dumpling'.[224]

---

[221] Charles Thomas Barker to G. H. Glasse, 24 Feb. 1779, Houghton Library, Harvard University, MS Hyde 61 (8.11). She was Mary Hay, niece of the earl of Kinnoull, whom Bagot had married in 1771.

[222] 'Shepilinda' thought it extremely odd for these two 'to be bred up at the Apron Strings of an Old Woman whose greatest qualifications are being Mistress of Quadrille, a Curtsey & washing her hands in the Mid[d]le of Dinner.', *Memoirs*, 26.

[223] 'Mrs Smith Rules the College', ibid., 44, 45. Appearances may have been deceptive. Woodforde observed of Fothergill as V-C: 'He is an exceedingly good kind of a Man, and seems very fearful of doing anything that is disagreeable'. ed. Hargreaves-Mawdsley, *Woodforde at Oxford*, 215, (15 Apr. 1774).

[224] Ibid., xv, xix, 23. This was Elizabeth née Whitfield.

532   ENLIGHTENED OXFORD

Widows of college heads could not expect to remain in residence if their husbands predeceased them, and their fate could be harsh. The highly respectable widow of Samuel Dennis of St John's (he died in 1795) removed to Holywell Street but was eventually impoverished by her spendthrift clergyman son and had no choice except to leave for the Widows' College at Bromley, Kent. Others looked for supportive roles in gentry or clerical families, women such as the stiff-mannered Ann Cawley, the widow of Principal Ralph Cawley (d. 1777) of Brasenose, who acted as private tutor to Cassandra and Jane Austen in 1783–4 where, encouraged by their brother James, she took the two girls on sightseeing tours around '... many dismal chapels, dusty libraries, and greasy halls, ... '.[225] And, invariably, these ladies had families, who were also adjuncts of their father's collegiate life. Daughters seldom wanted for undergraduate admirers. The very pretty Grace Gardiner (1716–77), only surviving child of the Warden of All Souls and former vice chancellor, was a popular presence in the 1730s with many of the younger Fellows at St John's in particular. As her friend, Elizabeth Shepherd, wrote:

> 'But sure Miss Gard'ner gained the prize
> On her was fixt each gownsmans eyes.'[226]

At Magdalen, of George Horne's three daughters, Maria, Felicia, and Sarah, it was Maria who was known for her beauty and her beaux would hang around the College entrance on the off-chance of seeing her pass from the President's lodgings to the chapel.[227] On some evenings they thought themselves duty bound to visit the lodgings and Felicia Horne recalled: 'They were frightened & my father was worried & we girls tittered'.[228]

Students met females all over Oxford, but it tended to be in the taverns, coffee-houses, market, and shops of the city.[229] There was a degree of informal mixed-sex sociability inside academic precincts, but its operation remains to be systematically explored. Females of status and connection, probably with male relations in colleges, appear to have presented few problems gaining entrance. They might already be known to undergraduates through family networks and such visitors

---

[225] Irene Collins, *Jane Austen and the clergy* (London, 1993), 35.

[226] 'Upon our Rare Consort', in *Memoirs*, 71, 88.

[227] Cox, *Recollections*, 163, 164, 165, 199–200. Felicia later recalled these happy years in the lodgings with their father, one who united 'so much real religion with so much cheerfulness, humour—and I may add *fun*.' Magd. Coll. MS 1028, f. 5. For Dick the cat sharing the Hornes' family life see George to Sarah Horne, 16 Aug. 1786, CUL MS Add. 8134/K/3.

[228] Magd. Coll. MS 1028, f. 3.

[229] In their interaction with young women in the town, male students understandably tended to sound the note their parents might wish to hear. One promised not to have any acquaintance with 'the Oxford Ladies', writing, 'my mind is utterly alienated I assure you from the insipid Conversation of inn keeper's daughters and such ... which all here go under one common denomination of Ladies'. Feb. 9th [1744?] W. Lee to L. C. J. Lee, Beinecke Library, Yale University, Lee Box 3, Folder 2.

THE UNIVERSITY AS SEEN FROM OUTSIDE   533

afforded a welcome relief to the normal routines of student life.[230] Women like Elizabeth Sheppard could be found inside academic spaces including common rooms, indeed might be encouraged to visit by college members. At New College one day in the late 1730s she and her friend 'Scrip' went up the narrow stairs to the organ loft where the organist, Richard Church, considered that 'our Scrip sat down like a Fairy Queen in a Cowslip & she sang & play'd most harmoniously'.

But if flirtation with females of social standing was admissible, it was a short and easy step to the transgressive when less reputable women intruded themselves into academic spaces. Soon after the Sheldonian opened, Thomas Isham noted the old Oxford character known as 'Mother Louise' in the gallery, but 'as soon as she was observed she sent the whole theatre into a roar of laughter'.[231] Women of 'Mother Louise's age often functioned as brothel Madams, for prostitution in the town, the walks, and certainly on university premises was a problem throughout this era that the authorities never resolved.[232] Women strolling in the grounds of Merton College in 1718 could recognisably be described as 'vanity fair', thereby reducing Christian and Faithful's encounter with a Satanic town to the temptation of abandoning one's studies to take a prostitute out for a stroll.[233] The sight caused scandal in many quarters and one pamphlet of 1779 sent to the Vice Chancellor [Horne], the Proctors, and every common room daringly urged a radical solution: the recognition of permitted brothels.[234] It was not acted on.

An excess of caffeine or alcohol might occasionally lead to violence when sexual appetites were not satisfied. Mr Bugge's coffee shop in St Clement's was popular with students partly because the owner's wife and unmarried sister were supposed to be loose women. After drinking all day on New Year's Eve 1727 three gentlemen commoners of Queen's—Godfrey Copley, William Pennington, and Charles Bowles—went on to Bugge's coffee-house but left unsatisfied. They tried to grab a barber's maid in the street, beat up her master when he stepped in, and then attacked an apprentice.[235] Like female servants across the country, women working in colleges had to be on their guard against unwanted advances or suffer the

---

[230] This interconnection through kinship and marriage is treated in Chapter 12.

[231] ed. G. Isham, *The Diary of Thomas Isham of Lamport, 1671–73*, trans. N. Marlow (London, 1971), 220–2, July 1673.

[232] Fully discussed in Midgley, *University Life*, 78–83. The vice-chancellor as a magistrate had the power to commit prisoners to the city goal. These were mainly prostitutes committed (until a statutory change in 1824) on detection as 'rogues and vagabonds'.

[233] See K. Milne, *At Vanity Fair. From Bunyan to Thackeray* (Cambridge, 2015).

[234] 'The passions of young men in such a seminary *will* be gratified. It is to be Questioned whether connivance at the crime, under certain limitations and conditions were not preferable to compelling young men either to the ruinous expences of *London* and other expeditions, or to injure their constitutions by means of the Dregs of Prostitution that remain in the University'. *The Cruelty, Injustice, and Impolicy of the present mode of Information and Punishment relative to Prostitution Established in the University* (Oxford, 1779), iv.

[235] Hearne, 8 Jan. 1728, IX. 390. The matter was referred back to the University authorities by the town officers for action. OUA; Chancellor's court papers, CC Papers; Court Act Book Hyp/A/57.

Fig. 10.4 University, Thomas Rowlandson, after James Brydges Willyams, hand-coloured etching, 1802 (The Metropolitan Museum of Art, New York: The Elisha Whittelsey Collection, The Elisha Whittelsey Fund, 1959).

consequences. These might be beyond their control in a male-dominated environment. In October 1720, the sixteen-year-old Sarah Smith at Queen's was locked in the college kitchens until she owned up to the identity of her unborn child's father. It was a student, predictably, and Queen's, with some sensitivity, offered a douceur of twenty guineas to any local man who would take her as his bride. The bridegroom was the sixty-year-old landlord of the village inn at Stanton St John who died only three years later.[236] Students themselves were very conscious that sexual desperation was linked to the homosocial context in which they found themselves. As one told his better-off army friend in 1746: 'The worst of it is we have very little of the Ladies Company, except Sappho, Lydia, the Dryades & c. who tho' they may arise warm ideas, afford but cold embraces'.[237]

The pursuit of women was not limited to very young men. There were also informal liaisons between college fellows and women unconnected with the

---

[236] Hearne, 11 Oct. 1720, VII. 176. Predatory male conduct is a feature of John Cleland's fictitious *Memoirs of an Oxford Scholar. Containing, His Amour with the beautiful Miss L—, of Essex* (London, 1756), which includes the attempt (101) of 'Mr Busy' to rape a milkmaid.

[237] Richard Heber to Charles Hotham, Brasenose, 22 Oct. 1746, Hotham Papers, Hull History Centre, 4/1/46.

THE UNIVERSITY AS SEEN FROM OUTSIDE 535

University. For instance one fellow of Merton, described by one as 'a deformed rich gentleman', for years was 'familiar' with the beautiful Mrs Bradgate, landlady of the Three Tuns after her husband's death in 1729, 'a fine, stately, beautifull, large young Woman, but very proud and empty of sense, ... [and] a great Company Keeper, ...'.[238] More mature women about town might have an eye on the material advantages accruing from spending leisure hours with dons. As one fictional witness avowed: 'Believe me, Sir, we scorn to look or speak to an Under-graduate, when engag'd in a Pleasure-Boat with the Fellows of Baliol; there's glorious living, good Ham and Chickens, sparkling Wines, ravishing Musick, then we can sip and tip and smack our Lips all round with some Satisfaction.'[239] Female servants got closest of all to them and, sometimes, an affair could lead to a happy marriage, as was the case for Sarah Adkins, the 'large and comely laundress' (as Hearne described her), whom Thomas Hunt, the future professor, wed.[240]

Female pulchritude was a highly prized asset in any men-only corporate body and Oxford was no exception.[241] College authorities would usually step in to forestall junior members' making a clandestine wedding with a completely unsuitable bride and, while reputable girls from the town could be tempted to set their caps at the wealthy and titled, they rarely succeeded in their ambition. One unknown versifier of the 1720s instanced the case of 'Vanessa', one Miss Dolly Freeman:[242]

> 'Fond of Patrician Blood and proud of Place
> In vain she dy'd her Hair, she stain'd her face,
> And edg'd each Arrow at his Idol'd Grace.
> Her charms possess'd ye Wanderer fled away,
> And left ye rifled Fair to Grooms a Prey.
> Thus Abigails enjoy'd are left forsaken,
> The Chaplains Fee to save his Lordships Bacon.'

When a well-known 'beauty' was in town it incited no end of curiosity, someone like Mary Chetwynd, of whom it was said: 'This Lady *when* single putt both our Universitys into a general Combustion like a Comet.'[243] Or the playwright Samuel

---

[238] ed. Linnell, *The Diaries of Thomas Wilson DD*, 74; Hearne, X. 85, 9 Jan. 1729.

[239] *The Oxford Toast's Answer to the Terrae Filius's Speech, ...* (London, 1733), 20.

[240] See this Chapter, p. 93.

[241] For a mock-heroic appreciation of the attractive young women to be found in Oxford see [John Dry], *Merton walks, or the Oxford beauties, a poem* (Oxford, 1717).

[242] Durham University Library, Add MS 1543 Commonplace book, a poem in couplets c.1720 about the young ladies of Oxford and their affairs (with marginal identification of the main characters). 'His Idol'd Grace' is possibly the 3rd Duke of Beaufort.

[243] William Stukeley to Maurice Johnson, 29 Nov. 1719, eds. Honeybones, *Correspondence*, 37. She was later Lady Blundell [I].

Fig. 10.5 Love and Learning, or the Oxford Scholar, Benjamin Smith, after Thomas Rowlandson, hand-coloured etching, 1786 (The Metropolitan Museum of Art, New York: The Elisha Whittelsey Collection, The Elisha Whittelsey Fund, 1959).

Foote's estranged wife, Polly, a celebrity visitor of 1758, who featured in *The Oxford Sausage*:[244]

---

[244] 'On Miss Polly Foote's unexpected arrival at Oxford, and speedy flight from thence in 1758', [Warton], *The Oxford sausage*... (new edn., Oxford, 1772), 101–5, at 103; Green, *Oxford during the last century*, 60. This is a provisional identification. For Mary Foote, see Ian Kelly, *Mr Foote's Other Leg* (London, 2012), 24–5, 26, 38–9.

THE UNIVERSITY AS SEEN FROM OUTSIDE 537

See Churches are foresaken too,
If Polly does not grace a Pew,
  To keep grave Heads from sleeping:
Mad H—tch—ns—n—ns rave in vain,
The sad deserted Seats remain
  For 'Prentice Boys to weep in'.

Dons and undergraduates alike were always looking to add names to their long lists of 'toasts'. Those of the 1720s included Grace Gardiner and Cassandra Leigh, niece of Theophilus Leigh, Master of Balliol College, and later married to Sir Edward Turner, 2nd Bt., of Ambrosden.[245] Lady Catherine ('Kitty') Hyde (1701–77), the Whiggishly inclined 3rd Duchess of Queensberry, and sister of Lord Cornbury MP, the slightly eccentric beauty was another favourite of these years, especially at newly founded Worcester College with its first Principal, Richard Blechinden.[246]

At Trinity there were periodic poetic interludes when one of the Fellows was elected Poet Laureate for the year. His duty was 'to celebrate in a copy of English verses a Lady, likewise annually elected, and distinguished by the title of Lady Patroness'.[247] There was at least a literary sheen to this adoption, much less at one of the great social occasions of the Oxford year, the High Borlace meeting. Each year a (male) Comptroller was selected and a (female) patroness. In 1748, as a fascinated and well-informed Theophilus Leigh recounted, the latter was Miss Sukey Cope (the younger daughter of Sir Jonathan Cope, 1st Bt., once a leading Oxfordshire Jacobite), and it was her task to receive the homage of this well-lubricated society of peers, baronets, and gentlemen (plus academic hangers-on) gathered for the races in Port Meadow and the Assemblies, Balls, and Consorts of Musick that were also laid on for them.[248] The selection could be freighted with political significance. When the 'Old Interest' elected the sister of young Sir Thomas Stapleton to serve as the patroness for the High Borlace in 1753 (she was chaperoned by Lord Lichfield), her appointment was correctly sized up by the Whig Lady Susan Keck. She at once suspected that this 'social' appointment was intended as a statement of gentry support for her brother's political ambitions within the county.[249]

---

[245] Bodl. MS Ballard 29, f. 130; Hulton, *The Clerk of Oxford*, 263–4, 292 for female toasts. Toasting, it has been said, constituted 'declarations of remembrance, respect, status, and generosity'. Peter Clark, *British Clubs and Societies 1580–1800: the origins of an associational world* (Oxford, 2000), 163–4.

[246] A. H. Barrett, 'Richard Blechinden: the first Provost of Worcester College, Oxford', *Oxoniensia*, 51 (1986), 139–69, at 162. There is a spirited, imaginative presentation of the Duchess at the time of the '45 in John Buchan's 1923 novel *Midwinter*.

[247] Hearne, XI. 287n., 25 Dec. 1733.

[248] Theophilus Leigh to Lydia, Dcss of Chandos, 22 Aug. 1748. Balliol Coll. Archives and Manuscripts, MS 403, f. 68.

[249] Elaine Chalus, '"That epidemical madness": Women and electoral politics in the late eighteenth century', in eds. E. Chalus and H. Barker, *Gender in eighteenth-century England: roles, representations, and responsibilities* (London, 1997), 151–78, at 159.

538 ENLIGHTENED OXFORD

Beauty was all very well and had its own form of celebrity, but Oxonians looking for patronage could not afford to ignore well-placed ladies connected to the University whose good offices they sought. The number of women with lucrative livings in their gift was considerable and they could come to the rescue of Oxonians looking around for preferment in decades when it was otherwise scarce, such as the 1730s. The Oxford historian Walter Harte, the son of a Nonjuror and Vice-Principal of St Mary Hall,[250] received Gosfield, Essex, in 1734 through the beneficence of its patron, the widow of John Knight, later Lady Nugent.[251] Similarly, with politics, party devotees stood ready to welcome the involvement of elite women whose intervention might achieve results. The most renowned at mid-century was Lady Susan Keck (1706–55) of Great Tew, someone well-known in university Whig circles. Her connection with Thomas Bray at Exeter College was vitally important to the success of the 'New Interest' in the notorious election of 1754.[252] Oxford was always ready to receive female benefactions.

Thus when Sarah née England, the widow of former President and Vice Chancellor, William Holmes, died in 1750, two years after him, her personal wealth made all the difference to funding the Holmes Building at St John's.[253] If gifts of money or objects of *vertù* were exceptional or the woman was a peeress with political influence, the donor could be publicly acclaimed by a grateful academy, none more generously than Henrietta Louisa, (1st) Countess of Pomfret (1698–1761): three days of festivities were held to honour her in 1756

---

[250] Walter Harte was commended by Johnson for his *History of Gustavus Adolphus* (London, 1759), and described as 'a man of the most companionable talents he had ever known'. ed. Birkbeck Hill, rev. Powell, *Boswell's Life of Johnson*, II. 120. See also Black, *Charting the Past*, 150.

[251] *The London Magazine* 4 (1735), 91. It was celebrated in verse by Richard Savage, in ed. Tracy, *Poetical Works*, 187–8:

> While by mean arts, and meaner patrons rise
> Priest, whom the learned, and the good despise;
> This sees fair KNIGHT, in whose transcendent mind,
> Are wisdom, purity, and truth enshrin'd.
> As modest merit now she plans to lift,
> Thy living, *Gosfield*, falls her instant gift.
> 'Let me' (she said) 'reward alone the wise,
> And make the church revenue virtue's prize'.
> She sought the man of honest, candid breast,
> In faith, in works of goodness, full exprest;
> Though young, yet tut'ring academic youth
> To science, moral, and religious truth.
>   She sought where the disinterested friend,
> The scholar sage, and free companion blend;
> The pleasing poet, and the deep divine:
> She sought, she found, and HARTE, the prize was thine.

[252] E. Chalus, 'The rag plot: the politics of influence in Oxford, 1754', in eds. R. Sweet and P. Lane, *Women and urban life in eighteenth-century England* (London, 2017) 43–64, where Chalus also draws attention to the political activities in the town of non-elite women. See also Chap. 9, pp. 43–4.

[253] R. H. Adams, *Memorial inscriptions in St John's College, Oxford* (Oxford, 1996), 47ff.

THE UNIVERSITY AS SEEN FROM OUTSIDE   539

on the occasion of her award of highly prized statuary to the University.[254] Lady
Pomfret was herself an inspiration to Anglican bluestockings hovering on the
fringes of Oxford in her concern for female education. As Catherine Talbot put it:

> I believe Lady P. to be a very good woman, and have for many years respected
> her highly. I know no one who has educated so many daughters so excellently
> well, . . .[255]

Beyond the women who resided in the city were the female travellers drawn out of
curiosity to see its sights and form an impression of them. The intrepid Celia
Fiennes was well-pleased. She was entertained at supper in Corpus Christi College
in 1694 and ate 'their very good bread and beare . . . '.[256] They could often make the
most intelligent comparisons from the sheer breadth of their travels, for instance
Amelie Murray comparing the churches and colleges to the cityscape of
Cologne.[257] Or Dorothy Richardson, a regular traveller and tourist around the
country, fascinated by Oxford, its buildings and facilities, especially concerts at the
Holywell room.[258] Such leisured women might have no other connection with
Oxford, but perhaps the majority of females who visited did so because of and
through the males in their family who were or had been members of the
University, for instance, Gilbert White's female relations visiting Oxford in his
Proctorial year (1752–3).[259] At Magdalen, as President Horne put it, perhaps half
seriously, to one of the male Lovedays: 'I wish we had good fellowships for your
sisters, who are charming girls, and have enlivened us here for some days'.[260]

Gentry women understood the importance of university attendance and might
well be instrumental in placing their sons in a particular college with a particular
tutor.[261] They might well desire to make his acquaintance personally and he,
undoubtedly, would want to meet them, and could increasingly expect quizzing
about academic achievement, as parents construed success as a form of honour to
themselves and the family.[262] When mothers and fathers visited, it might be that

---

[254] ed. Harcourt, *The Harcourt Papers*, III. 87. For 'Gratitude', a poem addressed to her by William
Thompson, see Queen's College MS 476, f. 158. For one visitor's enjoyment of the occasion see ed.
Donald Gibson, *A Parson in the Vale of Whitehorse: George Woodward's Letters from East Hendred
1753-1761* (Gloucester, 1982), 84–6. See Chapter 12 for the background to the bequest.

[255] C. Talbot to Mrs Carter, 3 Dec. 1761, in ed. Pennington, *A series of letters*, I. 508.

[256] ed. Griffiths, *Diary of Celia Fiennes*, 26.

[257] To Ly George Murray, 20 Oct. 1764, NAS 234/Box 49/3/285.

[258] JRUL, Eng. MS. 1122, f. 94, Journals, 14 May 1772.

[259] Richard Mabey, *Gilbert White: A biography of the author of the Natural History of Selborne*
(London, 1986), 64, for details. His scientific life had begun at Oxford. See Robert Fox, 'Science at Oriel',
in ed. Catto, *Oriel College*, 645–77, at 653.

[260] Horne to Dr John Loveday (the younger), 3 Nov. 1779. Magd. Coll. MS. 1034/i/5.

[261] French and Rothery, *Man's Estate*, 95.

[262] Thus Henrietta Acland expressed to her son her 'satisfaction' at 'great credit' earned by his
coming second in an essay competition at Oxford. Devon RO, 1148M Add36/899, 1 Jan. 1806, quoted
in ibid., 96.

540   ENLIGHTENED OXFORD

they would be accompanied by young women who had Oxford beaux or were on the lookout for eligible husbands—or already had one and were going to flirt anyway, like Jane Austen's cousin, Eliza, Comtesse de Feuillide, who, in August 1788, visited Jane's brothers James and Henry, in residence at St John's. She reported that they

> ...were very elegantly entertained by our gallant relations at St John's, where I was mightily taken with the Garden & longed to be a *Fellow* that I might walk in it every Day, besides I was delighted with the Black Gown and thought the Square Cap mighty becoming.[263]

The personal constructions of 'Oxford' by these young women visitors could depend all too easily on whether they found a lover there, but there was a more serious motive, too. The University wanted to cater for women in new ways. In 1765 Thomas Hornsby delivered a course of lectures and electrical experiments 'for the Entertainment of ladies and others', apparently a continuation of those started by his predecessor, Nathaniel Bliss, and they were packed out despite the high admission price of half a crown per head.[264] A popular public lecturer would always attract a high percentage of females and that was the case, for instance, with Joseph White's Bampton Lectures of 1784, which, Samuel Parr reported: '...give equal satisfaction to the beaux, the belles and the doctors; the church is crowded in the most extraordinary manner'.[265]

There were always plenty of polite female visitors on festival days such as those celebrating the Pomfret benefaction, many brought there by curiosity aroused by their male relations, a possibility imaginatively reconstructed by the mid-century novelist, Eliza Heywood, in her *Betsy Thoughtless*:

> ...one evening, as the family were sitting together, some discourse concerning Oxford coming on the tapis, Mr Francis spoke so largely in the praise of the wholesomeness of the air, the many fine walks and gardens with which the place abounded, and the good company that were continually resorting to it, that Miss Betsy cried out, she longed to see it, - Miss Flora said the same.

In due course off they went, flattered but also slightly defensive about the attention they received from Oxford students, and looking to see how ladies more accustomed to living amongst a male majority managed. The lesson was apparent:

---

[263] Letter to Philadelphia Walter, Aug. 1788, in *Austen papers, 1704–1856*, ed. R. Austen-Leigh, (University Microfilms International, Ann Arbor, MI, 1980), 133.

[264] Ruth Wallis, 'Cross-Currents in Astronomy and navigation', 223. The Tower in the Old Schools quadrangle was used. The recently widowed Mrs Bliss joined Hornsby in organising the event. Gunther, *Early Oxford Science*, II. 277, n.13; Fauvel, Flood and Wilson, *Oxford Figures*, 147, 148.

[265] Parr, *Works*, I. 220.

THE UNIVERSITY AS SEEN FROM OUTSIDE 541

The ladies of Oxford are commonly more than ordinarily circumspect in their behaviour, as indeed it behoves them to be, in a place where there are such a number of young gentlemen, many of whom pursue pleasure more than study, and scruple nothing for the gratification of their desires.[266]

There were actually twin perils for these young ladies. On one side there were the student would-be Lotharios, on the other a boorish minority among younger male citizens, perhaps the worse for drink and probably at a remove from the Oxford service economy that benefited financially from the extra business that these seasonal visitors brought into the city. When Sir Francis Dashwood from nearby West Wycombe brought two ladies into Oxford in 1747 to be joined by the Master of Balliol, they, 'very particular (chiefly I think in dress) as they walk'd the streets [were] ... us'd uncivilly by some rude townsmen'.[267]

Such elite visitors found the allure impossible to resist, and they kept coming in ever-increasing numbers, usually returning home with favourable narratives of their time in Oxford. There were particular festival occasions when the female presence was especially strong: on the installation of a new Chancellor, and at the Act, or Encaenia.

vi) Installations, acts, and Encaenias

... the doors of the Sheldonian Theatre are thrown open for almost a whole week, it is no wonder that London once more empties itself into this magnificent reservoir, and that all ranks and degrees of people are assembled to see the doctors in scarlet, and to attend the Lectures of TERRAE-FILIUS.

Terrae-Filius, No. 2, July 6, 1763, in Colman,
Prose on Several Occasions, I. 243.

The state which Oxford especially displayed on solemn occasions rivalled that of sovereign princes.

Macaulay, *The History of England*, ed. Firth, II. 924.

Outsiders poured into Oxford on these great academic holidays when Convocation met at the Sheldonian Theatre to enjoy the festival atmosphere while members of the University, outwardly respecting the ostensibly dignified nature of the occasion, were no less bent on recreation and showing themselves at

---

[266] Eliza Haywood, *The History of Miss Betsy Thoughtless* (1751), ed. Beth Fowkes Tobin (Oxford, 1997), 46, 60.

[267] Theophilus Leigh to Lydia, Dcss of Chandos, 21 [Nov. 1747], Balliol Coll. Archives and Manuscripts, MS 403, f. 39.

542 ENLIGHTENED OXFORD

their best.[268] The end of the academic year ushered in what a young Oxonian in 1779 called 'gay week' in Oxford when, as he boasted to his friend, there were 'women in swarms'.[269] Oxford became a summer locus where the sexes mingled easily and women of wealth and rank brought their own female servants along and were tempted to use the services of itinerant couturiers, hairdressers, and other consumer providers who followed them temporarily into the city's precincts. These celebrations were excellent public-relations opportunities in which all parties could, in different ways, show themselves at their best, often their uninhibited best, in the feastings, festivities, and frolics that accompanied the formalities. And the inns, taverns, coffee-houses of the city, plus private individuals, indeed anyone who had a bed to let (at an inflated price), were well-placed to make a tidy profit.

The installations of new Chancellors were generally splendid affairs that could last up to a week, usually longer than royal visits, which could be either attenuated or less than full-hearted on either side (as with William III in 1695) or a private, last-minute visit (as with George III in 1785) that gave the academic authorities insufficient time to prepare an elaborate menu of events. If the installations of the two Butler brothers, the 2nd Duke of Ormond and the Earl of Arran, in 1688 and 1715 respectively, were hurried affairs because of national exigencies, the University made up for it later in the century: the festivities that accompanied the installations at Encaenia time (early July) of Westmorland (1759), Lichfield (1763), North (1773), and the Duke of Portland (1793) as Chancellor were on a lavish scale that brought in the crowds to enjoy the academic carnival.[270] Lichfield's (5 July 1763) coincided with the Peace of Paris, ending the Seven Years' War, and contained a musical Ode in his honour representative of the genre:[271]

RECITATIVE: Hark! Hark! From ev'ry Tongue loud Accents rise;/Applause on Wing now mounts the vaulted Skies./CHORUS: Isis, with all her Choir, this Hour/Her Guardian hails, reveres his power;/Ordain'd her Empire to sustain,/ And rule where Kings have learn'd to reign./AIR; The Muses in his Praise rejoice;/ They echo to the Publick Voice:/ Minerva's Sons glad Homage pay,/ And to be happy court his sway. CHORUS repeated.

---

[268] Recent scholarly interest in the performative nature of University ritual, ceremonial, and spectacle is reflected in the essays in ed. Richard Kirwan, *Scholarly self-fashioning in the Early Modern University* (Farnham, 2013).

[269] Charles Thomas Barker to G. H. Glasse, 4 July 1779, Houghton Library, Harvard University, MS Hyde 61 (8.18).

[270] For Westmorland's magnificent event see Chapter 6; for North's *GM* 43 (1773), 350–2; ed. Ralph S. Walker, *James Beattie's London Diary: 1773* (Aberdeen, 1946), 67–71.

[271] OUA: NW.1. 6 (1).

THE UNIVERSITY AS SEEN FROM OUTSIDE 543

Portland's was perhaps the grandest of all, as it was turned into a patriotic celebration of British martial values vis-à-vis Revolutionary France (the country had been just six months at war) that was reflected in many of the verse declamations that marked the event. One delivered by the twenty-three-year-old rising star (just elected as Pittite MP for Newtown), George Canning, captured the attention. Its exordium offers an accurate flavour of the occasion:[272]

> 'While Britain rous'd by Gallia's fanatick pride,
> Joins the fierce war, & turns the battle's tide:
> The cause of Europe strengthens with her arms,
> Guides with her counsel, with her spirit warms:
> Oxford meanwhile within these hallow'd walls,
> To peaceful pomp her letter'd offspring calls;
> Oxford, who late o'er North's lamented bier,
> In splendid sorrow pour'd the pious tears;
> Now to new themes awakes the willing Muse,
> Now with fresh zeal her solemn rites renews;
> & fondly proud to fill her vacant chair
> With kindred virtue—places Bentinck there'.

Convocation met over three days in very hot weather, so much so that with people fainting and crowds uncomfortable in stifling conditions, the Duke cut short the proceedings. The windows of the Sheldonian were deliberately nailed down by the Heather Professor of Music, Philip Hayes, so that his setting of a Robert Holmes's Ode might be heard to full effect, and it led to a fracas when students in the galleries began to smash the glass with their caps so they could let in air, despite the cries of the Professor not to do so. In 1793 as on earlier occasions, pickpockets abounded and mingled with the crowds during 'Installation-week'. They went artfully about their business and could look very plausible, with some well-practised London villains wearing MA gowns in the Theatre. When a suspicious proctor asked one of them for the name of his college he replied. 'Oh! I belongs to St Malens's.' The reply was judged satisfactory.[273]

The University authorities did their best to control and order the proceedings and were ready to take action to prevent them turning outright into a charivari. It was this concern that brought about the transmutation of the potentially riotous—and certainly subversive—'Act' into the politer Encaenia, that centred more exclusively on giving thanks for founders and benefactors and on degree giving. The summer Act was essentially a rite of passage for those leaving the university

---

[272] Lewis Way to a friend at Glasgow University, Sept. 1793, Hants RO, 75M91/B19/1. Canning's were reportedly the only verses interrupted during the recital by applause.
[273] Cox, *Recollections*, 14, 15.

544 ENLIGHTENED OXFORD

and those receiving higher degrees. It was the traditional Oxford mode of marking the end of the academic year with verse declamation ('the Exercise'),[274] the conferment of honorary degrees, concerts and parties, plus a sanctioned speech by the anonymous figure of the *Terrae Filius*, a kind of lord of misrule who was given a platform to make a long speech in English marked by mockery, scurrility, scandal, and wit, that was one of the highlights of the event. This irreverent ritual was a well-established part of the programme.[275] The problem was that the *Terrae Filius* all too often departed from the script that had been cleared in advance and delighted his auditors with slanderous comments at the expense of leading figures within the University. And, still worse, be politically inflammatory in sensitive times. It was this last concern that led Vice Chancellor Gardiner to ban the *Terrae Filius* outright from taking part in the 1713 Act from concern that he would offer a Jacobite version and vision of Oxford that the hebdomadal board was desperate to avoid.[276]

Concerns about the role of the *Terrae Filius* had been smouldering away since the late seventeenth century. Henry Aldrich kept a tight control on the Act of 1693 and the *Terrae Filius* was not summoned in 1700. But it was not seen as an irrevocable demise. He popped up again at the Act of 1703 performing in a macaronic mixture of Latin and English,[277] and there were widespread expectations that he would reappear at the great festival Act of 1713 (the first since 1703) that was Oxford's official celebration of the Peace of Utrecht and a conspicuously Tory (though not at all a Jacobite) occasion.[278] Gardiner had other plans: the *Terrae Filius* would take no part in the proceedings. For him the centrepiece consisted of the various academic addresses on this gala occasion and the

---

[274] It was humorously presented as 'the modern Athens' by Alicia D'Anvers in *The Oxford Act* (London, 1693):

> 'Now the full-buttoned Youth appear,
> And squeakings fill the Theatre:
> Their parts well-conned say over prettily,
> Nay, humour all things wondrous wittily:
> The prettiest littlest harmless Baubles.
> Young unfledged Lords and callow Nobles;
> ...One sings, though in Heroicks oddly,
> A Catalogue of the New Bodley;
> While from another you may hear
> Our swingeing the French Fleet last year'.

[275] Kristine Haugen, 'Imagined universities: public insult and the *Terrae Filius* in early modern Oxford', in eds. Anne Goldgar and Robert Frost, *Institutional culture in early modern Europe* (Leiden, 2004), 317–43. For the comically subversive within a court setting see B. K. Otto, *Fools are everywhere. The court jester around the world* (Chicago, IL, 2001).

[276] W. T. Gibson, 'The suppression of Terrae filius in 1713', *Oxoniensia*, 54 (1989), 410–13.

[277] Haugen, 'Imagined Universities', 339.

[278] There were official national celebrations with fireworks of the Utrecht Treaty and the end of the war on 7 July 1713. eds. Renger de Bruin & Maarten Brinkman, *Peace was Made here. The Treaties of Utrecht, Rastatt and Baden 1713-1714* (Utrecht, 2013), 66, 176.

THE UNIVERSITY AS SEEN FROM OUTSIDE 545

Fig. 10.6 Frontispiece to Nicholas Amhurst's 'Terrae-Filius', William Hogarth, print, 1726 (The Metropolitan Museum of Art, New York: Harris Brisbane Dick Fund, 1932).

546   ENLIGHTENED OXFORD

full-blooded Latin tributes paid to the Queen.[279] It was no doubt some compensation to lesser attendees that Colley Cibber and the Drury Lane theatre company were allowed back into residence (they had been banned in 1710), offering a daily performance in late June, ensuring that the city was crammed with visitors.[280] As Arthur Charlett reported:

> The Town has been so exceeding full this Act beyond what was ever known before, I think, that [t]here was too great a Hurry & Confusion for us to be able to doe as we ought, either for the Satisfaction of our friends or the Reputation of the University. Friday's performance was to the Satisfaction of Every One; but ye Great Crowd on Monday was a little too Mobbish—[281]

The 1713 Act turned out to be the last prior to that of 1733, a less fraught affair that celebrated the visit of the Prince of Orange and was a determined attempt by the University to mend political fences with the Hanoverian crown. After 1733 there were no more Acts at all. Instead, taking advantage of the generous bequest of Nathaniel, Lord Crew, most summers the University staged Encaenias that still offered an ambitious and entertaining festival culture but with a minimal reduced risk of any form of sanctioned academic subversion (unofficial efforts were another matter): the *Terrae Filius* was gone for good. But it was impossible to stop the exhibition of good humour and high spirits from the predominantly youthful presence in the galleries.[282] At the Encaenia of 1752 there were rounds of applause for William King and the University's new MP, Sir Roger Newdigate, but when the name of the Whig John Burton was mentioned there were catcalls and boos. And it was never possible to keep revellers from coming into the Sheldonian who might still be the worse for wear from wining and dining rather too well.[283] Thus during the Encaenia of 5 July 1774, James Woodforde saw how, during a performance of Handel's *Hercules*, 'Mr Woodhouse a Gent. Com: of University College was very drunk at the Theatre and cascaded in the middle of the Theatre'.[284] Other bathetic moments could occur in the procession on the way to the degree ceremony, when the weather could wreak havoc with the best-laid plans, as one undergraduate rather gleefully reported to his mother in the 1770s:[285]

---

[279] Details in *Academiæ Oxoniensis comitia philologica in Theatro Sheldoniano Decimo Die Julii A. D. 1713. celebrata: in honorem serenissimæ Reginæ Annæ pacific* (Oxford, 1713).

[280] In 1703 the Act had attracted the celebrated Thomas Betterton, the veteran actor and dramatist, where he had declaimed a verse 'Prologue to the University of Oxford'. *Oxford and Cambridge Miscellany Poems*, ed. E. Fenton, (London, 1709), 150–2. See also Nichols, *Lit. Anec.*, VIII. 164.

[281] Charlett to William Dobson, President of Trinity College, Bodl. MS Ballard 21, f. 192.

[282] For Durkheim's notion of 'collective effervescence', a ritually induced passion or ecstasy that cements social bonds and forms the ultimate basis of religion.

[283] R. G. Owen to his mother, NLW, Brogyntyn MS 1391.

[284] ed. Hargreaves-Mawdsley, *Woodforde at Oxford*, 235-6. Performances of works by Handel (often by London-based musicians) remained at the core of the Encaenia concert repertoire. Thus at the 1752 festivities just mentioned, *Messiah*, *Acis & Galatea*, and *Israel in Egypt* were all on the programme.

[285] Walter Stanhope to Mrs Ann Stanhope, WYAS (Bradford), Spencer-Stanhope MSS, Sp/St/6/1/77.

THE UNIVERSITY AS SEEN FROM OUTSIDE 547

We have had a Member of ye College here to take ye Degree of a Doctor in Physick, upon which ye whole Society, as is usual, attended him in their robes, when, (horrible to tell) when we were all trick'd out, some in new wigs, some in silken array, & others in humble crape, just at ye moment ye Bells announced ye Beginnings of ye Procession a windy shower, big with envy, & malice, attack'd our flank, & Overthrew all our splendour.

The formal rituals and proceedings of Convocation gathered at Encaenia remained centred on the Sheldonian Theatre with the Public Orator the master of ceremonies. He may aptly be viewed as a modern-day Director of Development for the University, using rhetoric, or in the service of the eighteenth-century equivalent of public relations. The Orator led participants and audience through the events in good order, presenting degree honorands and prizewinners in a Latin style that was seldom too florid and dressed with a salty wit that was seldom lost on attendees. It helped maximise impact if the Public Orator, apart from being an accomplished Latinist and a dramatic performer in his own right, was sufficiently idiosyncratic to make individuals want to attend Encaenia just to watch him at work year after year. It was also vital to strike the right political note and two names stand out in this regard: Digby Cotes, the Public Orator from 1712 (Principal, Magdalen Hall, 1716–45), was diplomatic enough to tailor his speeches so as not to annoy Whigs looking for excuses to be outraged without compromising his own principled Toryism; while, much later in the century, William Crowe (1745–1829), BCL, Public Orator for four and a half decades (1784–1829), whose fine voice and mellifluous Latinity commanded attention, played down his own moderate Whiggism so as not to discountenance the majority of University members.[286] His predecessor in the post, Dr King, had taken no such pains to conceal his Jacobite sympathies.

Visitors and University members alike were expected to watch and appreciate the public recital of mainly Latin prose and verse with eight to ten declamations by undergraduates and BAs given each day. It was, to quote Dame Lucy Sutherland, a 'marathon affair',[287] but it gave an opportunity for young men to make what was, in effect, their debut in public life, and the University was unabashed about pushing into prominence on the occasion youths of the highest rank irrespective of talent, such as the nineteen-year-old 5th Duke of Beaufort at the Encaenia of

---

[286] Cotes was rector of Coleshill, Warwickshire, in the gift of his kinsman, the High Tory moral exemplar William, 5th Lord Digby of Geashill. Hamilton, *Hertford College*, 123. For Crowe see Cox, *Recollections*, 229. He had written verses for the installation of Lord North as Chancellor in 1773 that included favourable reference to the Whig 'martyrs' of the 1680s, Algernon Sidney and William, Lord Russell, that were prudently omitted upon the rehearsal, 'lest his Lordship should have been too much puzzled, and have fancied himself in the Senate house at Cambridge instead of the Sheldon Theatre'. Charles Thomas Barker to G. H. Glasse, 30 Nov. 1779, Houghton Library, Harvard University, MS Hyde 61 (8.23). This faux pas did not prevent Crowe from later becoming Public Orator.

[287] Sutherland, *The University of Oxford in the Eighteenth Century*, 23. An increasing number were written and performed in English in the second half of the century.

548   ENLIGHTENED OXFORD

July 1763, the occasion for the University to signify lavishly its approval of government policy in closing the Seven Years' War with the controversial Peace of Paris.[288] The families gathered around would, of course, have happily heard all the other speakers go through their paces until the moment came when their own boy took to the stage. The quality varied appreciably, perhaps reflecting reluctance on the part of many participants.[289] How far they knew that many of those delivered by noblemen and gentlemen commoners were often written for them by tutors (or tutors were in some way involved in the progress of composition) cannot be known.[290] Many, but not all, for the ability to write Latin verse was a highly prized accomplishment and students from Westminster School excelled particularly at it.[291] Among them (though an Old Etonian) was Richard, Viscount Wellesley (later 2nd Earl of Mornington), who came to Oxford known at school for his flair in writing Horatian lyrics. He won the Chancellor's Prize for Latin verse in 1780 with an elegy on Captain James Cook that was recited in the Sheldonian that July.[292] As throughout the century, Oxford verse writers had an eye on contemporary events that would have a relevance and a resonance for a mixed assemblage.[293] Events like Encaenia were fundamental to preserving the vitality of the panegyric as a primary rhetorical genre. Likewise Pindar's Olympic Victory Odes acted as an inspiration in these declamations. The Christ Church alumnus, Gilbert West's, 1749 collection of the Greek poet's Odes remained in print throughout the century and suggested their thematic adaptability to modern times, as further betokened by the popularity of Thomas Gray's Pindaric Odes of the 1750s, which tried to attain a sublimity far removed from the quotidian.[294]

---

[288] *GM* 33 (1763), 348; Godley, *Oxford in the Eighteenth Century*, 192–3, 277.

[289] 'No verses can be so bad but they will deserve a place in Academic compositions, which the youth are forced to make as unwillingly as turn spit currs enter into the wheel.' Rev Edward Vernon, of Redmile, Leics., to his son, Rev Edward Vernon, Rector of St George's Bloomsbury, 23 Apr. 1736, BL Stowe MS 748, f. 147. Vernon was actually referring to verses offered at Cambridge to honour the marriage of the Prince of Wales with Princess Augusta of Saxe-Gotha but the sentiment would be just as applicable to Oxford.

[290] Bodl. MS. Don. e. 53 lists some reciters and authors from the 1733 Act.

[291] Bill, *Christ Church*, 247–8.

[292] The Prize was first offered in 1768 and the annual competition, on a different subject, aroused much interest. Wellesley was encouraged to enter by his tutor at Ch. Ch., William Jackson. Iris Butler, *The eldest brother. The Marquess Wellesley 1760–1842* (London, 1973), 35. Bradner, *Musae Anglicanae*, 302–4. He was still writing in Latin after his retirement from public life in the 1830s.

[293] This panegyrical opportunity occasionally allowed poets of promise first to show their mettle. For instance, the exceptional Anglo-Latin poet, Anthony Alsop, whose 1693 Act song, *Britannia*, celebrated recent British successes at Barfleur and La Hogue in the Nine Years' War against Louis XIV. Money, *The English Horace*, 61.

[294] Martin Price, 'Sacred to Secular: Thomas Gray and the cultivation of the Literary', in H.D. Weinbrot and M. Price, *Context, Influence, and Mid-Eighteenth-Century Poetry: Papers presented at a Clark Library seminar 21 March 1987* (Los Angeles, 1990), 41–78. West regretted how far short of the original the so-called Pindaric odes of his own day went, William Congreve excepted. P. Wilson, 'The Knowledge and Appreciation of Pindar in the Seventeenth and Eighteenth Centuries', Oxford D. Phil., 1974, esp. 240–54. David Fairer, '"Love was in the next Degree": lyric, satire, and inventive modulation', *JECS*, 34 (2011), 147–66, for the problems and scope of Pindaric verse in the eighteenth century.

THE UNIVERSITY AS SEEN FROM OUTSIDE 549

The granting of honorary degrees, usually in the form of a Doctorate of Civil Law (the DCL), was a common feature of Installations, Acts, and Encaenias alike.[295] These were used by Chancellors (in whose gift they primarily lay) and canvassed at the hebdomadal board less to reward academic and/or public distinction than to flatter potential benefactors, reward political loyalty, and honour friends and county magnates.[296] Thus Chancellor Ormond, the toast of most Oxonians, encountered no resistance when he requested that the University make his indispensable personal secretary, Benjamin Portlock, a DCL before he left England with the Duke on the Cadiz expedition of 1702.[297] Degree recipients often received lavish hospitality within Oxford and sometimes returned the favour, like Martin Warren in 1730, who 'made a great & most splendid supper upon acct of his proceeding Dr in Physick & had near 150 with him & all the 1st quality of the place, Duke of Bedford, marquis of Blandford 6 or 7 Barts & other Country Gentlemen without number'.[298] Until the reign of George III, government-supporting Whigs were unlikely to figure on the list of honorands. Thus, during Queen Anne's Bath progress of 1702 that brought her to Oxford, she agreed to the creation of eleven Tory DCLs as opposed to just one Whig (the 6th Duke of Somerset).[299] Similarly, in the 1740s, degrees were lavished on Opposition politicians.[300] It was only when the Duke of Portland was installed in July 1793 that Whigs were awarded Oxford doctorates in any number, no less than sixty-five honorary degrees at that protracted meeting of Convocation in broiling weather.[301] The 3rd Duke's father had himself been given one at a convocation especially convened in March 1755, when he was in Oxford to see his son and heir at Christ Church.[302] But then, the 2nd Duke was the grandson of Robert Harley.

With some honourable exceptions (such as Sir Joshua Reynolds and James Beattie, the Aberdonian philosopher and poet), Portland's predecessor as Chancellor, Lord North, filled his installation list in July 1773 with individuals who might be useful to him in Parliament via the conferment of an Oxford gown, men such as the brewer, MP for Southwark, and friend of Samuel Johnson, Henry Thrale.[303] Though he received one himself, Johnson was scathing in *A Journey to*

---

[295] For foreign recipients see Chapter 11.

[296] Bill, *Christ Church*, 178–81. For supposedly deserving clerics see OUA: NEP/subtus/30/Reg Bk, Register of Convocation 1776–93. See OUA: NW/1/5 *Formulae used at Presentations for DCL Honoris Causa* for the years 1761–97. There are pertinent comments on 'Honorary Degrees at Oxford, how generally bestowed', in *GM* 61, II (1791), 893–5.

[297] HMC, *Ormonde MSS*, VIII. xl.

[298] Euseby Isham to Sir Justinian Isham, 9 July 1730, NRO, Isham 2641.

[299] Bucholz, 'Queen Anne and the limitations of Royal Ritual', 310.

[300] Ward, *Georgian Oxford*, 164.   [301] Cox, *Recollections*, 14.

[302] Bodl. MS Top Oxon. d.174, f. 209. For Lord Titchfield's (the future 3rd Duke's courtesy title) purported reputation as the pride of the University, see Edward Young to the Duchess of Portland, 29 July 1756, HMC, *Bath MSS*, I. 323.

[303] Curley, *Sir Robert Chambers*, 149.

550   ENLIGHTENED OXFORD

The Western Islands about the way in which the honorary degree system operated.[304] He was not alone in being unimpressed: North had tried to incentivise the young Charles Fox by including him on his list, but Fox was not interested and saw it as not much better than bribery. It was reported that he 'said he was not worth a single guinea, and he fear'd the University would not Tick, so declined it.'[305] On the other hand, Edmond Halley was so immensely proud of the DCL he was awarded in 1710 that he finally adopted the prefix 'Professor' rather than the 'Captain' he had previously insisted on retaining. Refusal could function as a form of political thumb-giving.[306] It said much of Richard Willis, a typical Whig prelate and former chaplain of William III, promoted Bishop of Gloucester in 1714 and Lord Almoner in 1717, that he was content to be a mere Lambeth DD, and never donned the scarlet and black of its Oxford equivalent.[307]

Fox was unimpressed with this offer; Warburton and Burke were, as has been seen, decidedly stung by the refusal of one. Both were, in their different ways, defenders of the religious establishment and Christian orthodoxy and the University was, by and large, at pains to recognise the merits of such individuals. It was, perhaps, the most positive use of the honorary degree system. Beattie was a case in point. Another, earlier in the century, was John Walker. He was awarded the DD in 1714 on the grounds of both academic and confessional merits for his writings against the dissenting author Edmund Calamy, notably his *The Sufferings of the Clergy during the Late Rebellion*, drawing attention to those Anglicans who had been deprived during the Civil Wars and the English Republic of the 1650s. It was a riposte to Calamy's account of those ministers who had lost their posts in the Church in 1662 following the Restoration of Charles II.[308] Walker stood up to Dissent; two of those who took up the cudgels against arch-rationalisers of Christianity, disinclined to say anything about the divinity of Christ, one of them in this case being the Cambridge don, Conyers Middleton, were also recognised by the conferment of an honorary degree.[309] So was someone like Thomas Townson, who received a DD in 1779 for a clear restatement of Biblical orthodoxy in his *Discourses on the Four Gospels*. It was constructed around the central thesis that the Evangelists wrote their Gospels in the order contained in

---

[304] 'The indiscriminate collation of degrees has justly taken away that respect which originally claimed as stamps, by which the literary value of men so distinguished was authoritatively denoted. That academical honours, or any others should be conferred with exact proportion to merit, is more than human judgment or human integrity have given reason to expect.' *A Journey to The Western Islands*, ed. Peter Levi (Harmondsworth, 1984), 44.

[305] Mrs Harris to Thomas Harris, 14 July 1773, Hants RO, 9M73/G1260/22.

[306] Gribbin, *Out of the Shadow of a Giant*, 270–1.   [307] Wells, *Wadham College*, 116–17.

[308] John Seed, *Dissenting Histories. Religious Division and the Politics of Memory in Eighteenth-Century England* (Edinburgh, 2008), 26.

[309] These authors were William Dodwell (1709–85) and Thomas Church (1707–56). Pocock, *Barbarism and Religion*, I. 45; V. 229, 365. For the importance of Middleton as a rationalising polemicist see Ingram, *Reformation without end*, 161–80.

THE UNIVERSITY AS SEEN FROM OUTSIDE   551

the Bible, each written with a special purpose and a design as assigned to them by the early Fathers and the tradition of the Church.[310]

vii) Conclusion

Educated non-Oxonians of both sexes generally had some view of Britain's oldest university, whether favourable or critical. It impinged, it mattered, they were drawn to see it, and to look on as dons and graduates went about their work or their pleasures. The University had long accepted that it was on the tourist map and the businesses of the city reaped the benefits of this constant through traffic. Though restrictions on admission remained on academic grounds, women were a constant feature of the urban and academic scene, both residents and visitors, for Oxford participated in a general European trend whereby '...academic institutions in the eighteenth century gave the appearance of being less opposed than previously to the presence of women,...'[311] And those who had never been there in person could choose, if they liked, to read novels in which it featured and watch plays in which its inhabitants—and very often their politics—were sent up. Members of the University doubtless laughed as much as any at their dramatic depiction. After all, these were often written by Oxford graduates as a kind of payback for disappointment or disgruntlement and not to accept these offerings in good humour only invited more of the same. And those who had never been there could associate themselves at a distance with Oxford and its perceived values. For example, the Derby stocking-maker Benjamin Parker (c.1700–47?) felt able to write and have published works on physico-theology and natural philosophy for a local, aspirational audience. And he was orthodox in his theology and proud to link himself with Oxford. He dedicated the second volume of his *Philosophical Meditations* (Birmingham, 1738) to the 'reverend doctors and masters of colleges of the famous University of Oxford', while the third edition was 'revised and corrected by a gentleman of the university of Oxford'.[312]

Alumni disdain was another matter, capable of seriously compromising institutional prestige by dint of decrying practice and personnel deemed inimical to progress, Whiggishly defined. Did the strictures make any difference? A disappointed John Wesley drifted away from the University's orbit and, to his credit, showed no inclination to repeat his celebrated strictures of the 1740s. Edward Gibbon (who spent just over a year in the place) took care not to say anything about Oxford in his lifetime and, in the various parts of his

---

[310] Townson, 'Discourses on the Four Gospels', in *Works*, I. 27–8.

[311] Maria Rosa di Simone, 'Admission', 297.

[312] See P. A. Elliott, *The Derby philosophers. Science and culture in British urban society, 1700–1850* (Manchester, 2009), 24–7.

Autobiography, offered reflections that were actually *au courant* anyway and stung a lot less than they might have done. As Gibbon would have granted towards the end of his life, Oxford University was less complacent than its critics liked to imagine, and its uncompromising resistance to the values of the French Revolution both reflected and led national opinion. In its combination of opposition to root-and-branch institutional remodelling and willingness to implement significant curricular and pedagogical changes, Oxford exhibited in its own manner the resilient foundations of the Hanoverian order in England as it variously equipped the governing elite to defend British values in person, on paper, and from the pulpit. For this was, above all, a confident cultural institution capable of adaptation without sacrificing its historical inheritance and the need to honour its past. The critical outsiders could say their piece; its supporters far outnumbered them.

11

Oxford and the wider world

The European connections and imperial involvements of the University

Oxford's centuries-old reputation as a centre of learning and a University whose foundation was only preceded by Bologna's guaranteed it notice among the learned and the polite across Europe. Though its continuing attachment to a formal curriculum with scholastic roots was commonly noted, this regard for historical continuity was more often acknowledged than rudely derided. Oxford was hardly alone in eighteenth-century Europe in validating its present-day standing by reference to the time-honoured statutes, customs, and conventions; equally, Oxford, as a classic *ancien régime* institution, proved capable over time of adapting its inherited structures and practices without either fanfare or the casting aside of a culture rooted in the English past. Even if, arguably, it was less an embodiment of Enlightenment than most Scottish universities, it was far from being *unenlightened*. If Oxford was not primarily a centre for progressive ideas (unlike, for instance, Prussian universities such as Halle, that 'were the main conduits through which the Enlightenment found its way into public life'[1]), it was an indisputable centre for an admixture of ideas, both 'ancient' and 'modern'. The interaction of Oxford graduates with their counterparts in continental Europe, travelling, working, studying as it might be, overall gave a flattering impression of the University's part in their social fashioning, while Oxford dons were generally welcomed, irrespective of any religious differences, in libraries, academies, and even salons from Paris to St Petersburg, Stockholm to Naples. In the reverse direction, Europeans travelled to Oxford, a few matriculating as youthful members of the University, others joining in early or middle career, attracted by the collegiate life, academic initiatives, the Church of England, or a combination of all three. Guests and hosts alike shared in the common culture of eighteenth-century elites, rooted in antiquity and enriched in the Renaissance, one whose continuing importance can hardly be overstated. And the prestige that an honorary Oxford degree conferred was coveted by European princes throughout

---

[1] T. C. W. Blanning, *The Culture of Power and the Power of Culture. Old Regime Europe 1660–1789* (Oxford, 2002), 199.

Enlightened Oxford: The University and the Cultural and Political Life of Eighteenth-century Britain and Beyond.
Nigel Aston, Oxford University Press. © Nigel Aston 2023. DOI: 10.1093/oso/9780199246830.003.0012

554   ENLIGHTENED OXFORD

the century and Convocation was skilled in turning such occasions into festive publicity exercises.[2]

The attachment of foreign scholars and the mutual homage exchanged with princes were part of the complex processes of cultural transfer that were expressed not only through physical presence but in international epistolary networks;[3] these constituted varying testimonies to the University's claims to a place of honour in the Republic of Letters, a cultural construction whose existence some would argue either merged or collapsed into Enlightenment *tout court* in the course of the century. The extent to which that occurred is considered later in this chapter. The point made here is that Oxford preserved its mediatory status as an educational centre that was ready to embrace moderate intellectual change while, for the most part, disdaining novelty in the form of either irreligion or anti-monarchism. Its achievement in acting as an intellectual preservative drew upon it much disdain from *bien pensants* around the close of the century, but those in France and elsewhere who came to see what they had lost through political rupture were ready to admit Oxford's centrality to the intelligent defence of Church and state in England. This commitment had earlier, in the 1770s, put the University at odds with the rebellious American colonists and contributed to a decline in the number of 'Americans' completing their education as Oxford undergraduates. Nevertheless, even as the number of students from the colonies fell away, so the awareness of domestic students about opportunities in imperial administration surged. From at least the Seven Years' War, British governments needed talented graduates to both advise them on running the expanding empire and act at first hand in that capacity. Oxford's expanding imperial role thus came to be as much a dimension of its eighteenth-century character as the consolidation of its European connections.

i) Oxonians in Europe and beyond

I fancy our Governor [the Dean of Christ Church], nor any of the ministry,... could tell the names of the tenth part of the Protestant Universities, so little have we to do with them.

William Stratford to the 2nd Earl of Oxford, HMC, Portland MSS, VII. 389. 6 Nov. 1724.

---

[2] Discussed in Chapter 10, pp. 124–7.

[3] Complex both in terms of the role played by the receiving culture and of the extent to which transfer implies change. See the essays in eds. A. Thomson, S. Burrows, E. Dziembowski, and S. Audidière, *Cultural transfers: France and Britain in the long eighteenth century* (Oxford, 2010). There is much recent literature on the importance of international networks; see, for instance, P.-Y. Beaurepaire, *La plume et la toile. Pouvoirs et réseaux de correspondence dans l'Europe des lumières* (Arras, 2002). And 'Cultures of Knowledge: Networking the Republic of letters 1550–1750' [web].

OXFORD AND THE WIDER WORLD   555

Like other Britons from élite (and, increasingly, non-élite) backgrounds, Oxford students and graduates were regular travellers in Europe for recreational and educative purposes, usually a varying combination of purposes, but the sense in which élite young men travelled *because* they had attended university is uncertain—with one notable exception. In 1715 John Radcliffe had left substantial funds for the establishment of Travelling Fellowships in Medicine, two tenable for up to ten years, with the primary purpose of continental travel with a view to studying medicine, with a stipend of £300 annually.[4] These were often awarded to mature alumni and, though their pedagogical uses were not neglected, the Fellowship also offered many socialising opportunities. John Monro (1715–91), for instance, of St John's, was elected a Travelling Fellow by the University in 1741 and spent a decade on the continent studying medicine and exhibiting a taste for the fine arts and engravings, as well as Jacobite intrigue.[5] Otherwise, it appears that institutional attempts (as opposed to individual persuasion) to encourage Oxford students and graduates to travel or prepare them for their Grand Tour (beyond proximity to their like-minded peers) were insignificant.[6] Very occasionally, the particularly gifted with the right political connections would be encouraged to travel by servants of the Crown. The young Joseph Addison, Fellow of Magdalen, was regarded with such favour by the Whig 'Junto' ministers that he received a disbursement of funds from the Civil List to meet some of the costs of an extensive four-year Grand Tour to France, Italy, Switzerland and Holland that he commenced in August 1699. It was semi-official for he was 'sent from the University by King William, in order to travel and qualify himself to serve His Majesty'. He took with him copies of his new edition of the two Oxford volumes *Musarum Anglicanarum Analecta* (1692, 1699) that contained his own Latin verses and those of the young Christ Church and Magdalen poets, his contemporaries. Addison intended to distribute it as a

---

[4] The holders were 'to spend half their time' 'in parts beyond the sea, for their better improvement'. The text of the will is given in Guest, *Radcliffe*, app. See also B. J. B. Nias, *Dr John Radcliffe: A Sketch of his Life with an Account of his Fellows and Foundations* (Oxford, 1918), 45–6. Between 1714 and 1760 Corpus was awarded four out of a total of eleven Radcliffe Fellows elected. Charles-Edwards and Reed, *Corpus Christi College*, 239–40; Darwall-Smith, *University College*, 241. While on his last Oxford visit, Samuel Johnson said that there was little profit from Radcliffe Scholars looking for a career in medicine visiting European countries 'for all that is known there is known here', but that they should be sent out of Christendom to be resident in what he called 'barbarous nations'. Reported for 10 June 1784 in ed. Birkbeck Hill, rev. Powell, *Boswell's Life of* Johnson, IV. 293. He had in mind as barbarous' lands Peru (and adjacent provinces of the Spanish Empire in the Tropical Andes) for Peruvian Bark, and the Ottoman Empire for inoculation.

[5] He was appointed Physician to Bethlem Hospital 1751–91. ed. John Ingamells, *A Dictionary of British and Irish travellers in Italy 1701-1800* (compiled from the Brinsley Ford Archive) (New Haven, CT, 1997), 668; Costin, *St John's College*, 199.

[6] At the moment, there is very little attempt amongst scholars to link the different stages of élite education of boarding school/private tutor, Oxford/Cambridge, and then the Grand Tour. I am grateful to Sarah Goldsmith for articulating this insight. For a Travelling Fellowship awarded by Corpus Christi for a maximum of three years see Charles-Edwards and Reid, *Corpus Christi College*, 238n.

556 ENLIGHTENED OXFORD

badge of his scholarly accomplishment and personally capitalise on the interest it had already attracted.[7]

In a prize essay submission on its advantages and disadvantages, John Scott (the future Lord Chancellor Eldon) argued that while it was important for the aspiring politicians among them to acquire some knowledge of foreign constitutions, '... we need not be sent abroad to exercise a study wch has been long & successfully cultivated at home'.[8] Scott's relatively plebian background made his comment somewhat untypical and for most Oxonians who did travel abroad it functioned as a key tool within elite strategies of pan-European networking that could create lasting ties of friendship that transcended national tensions. Oxonian journeys might in fact be often no more than a short sight-seeing dash across the Channel undertaken during the long vacation. As one put it in 1773: 'Our College [Ch.Ch.] is quite frenchified, most of our members having been this summer'.[9] And there could be common points of convergence on arrival, such as Wilson's coffee-house in Paris (which served English drinks and food) where they could be assured of meeting fellow countrymen.[10] Other itineraries might be much longer and build on college friendships. Thus the 3rd Lord Holland (Charles James Fox's nephew) went with his contemporary Lord Granville Leveson-Gower to Naples in 1794 so that they could 'like true English men' lodge with Oxford friends. 'There is', he went on, 'absolutely a Christ Church colony here at present'.[11] The academic migration that was a common feature of medieval university life operated on a much smaller scale by the 'long' eighteenth century. Nevertheless, some graduate Grand Tourists continued their education by undertaking formal study at different continental universities (invariably Protestant), academies, or tutors.[12] Some joined the many Scots to be found in the United Provinces. Thus Joseph Atwell (elected Rector of Exeter College in 1733) studied at Leyden for a time, like other Devon men.[13]

While few would take a full degree abroad, joining for a semester or two was relatively common. Thus as part of a three-year sojourn in Europe in the early 1750s, the future Premier, Frederick, Lord North and his half-brother, the 2nd

---

[7] Smithers, *Joseph Addison*, 32, 42, 44–5. Addison had two meetings with Malebranche and another with Boileau in Paris. Ibid., 53.

[8] Beinecke Library, Yale University, Osborn Shelves c373, Common Place book, 23–34, at 37.

[9] Richard Perryn to James Bland Burges, Bodl., Bland Burges Papers: Dep. Bland Burges, 18/1.

[10] One earlier traveller, a medical student, became caught up in a discussion at Wilson's about the relative merits of Oxford and Cambridge. Edward Browne, *Journal of a Visit to Paris in the Year 1664*, ed. G. Keynes (London, 1923), 9–10, 14, 16, 22.

[11] BL Bowood Papers, Vol. 36, Lord Holland to Lord Lansdowne, 21 Jan. [1794?] f. 106 [fragment before start of letter proper]. He later reported to his uncle: 'I am sorry to say that our little Christchurch Colony [that included the Pittite, Lord Boringdon] here is not composed of people who agree much in the necessity of preserving what liberty we have, and of securing its continuance with interest to our posterity.' f. 108, Naples, 15 Mar. 1794.

[12] However, Perraton, *A History of foreign students in Britain*, 35, estimates that a mere 2% of Oxonians in this era travelled abroad in search of teaching.

[13] Stride, *Exeter College*, 106.

OXFORD AND THE WIDER WORLD   557

Earl of Dartmouth, were sent to the University of Leipzig, studying international law; there they joined a prestigious faculty whose members 'considered it their mission to prepare ... young men for high governmental office'.[14] Their tutor was Johann Jakob Mascov, whose *Principia Iuris Publici Imperii Romano-Germanici* was widely respected across Europe, and took part with other students in the discussions that followed his lectures. Elsewhere in Germany, Oxford students were prominent among young Englishmen in heading for the Georg-August-Universität in Göttingen, south of Hanover (founded as recently as 1737),[15] a new academic establishment that became a centre for the dissemination of English influences. During its heyday under George III—with his interest in scholarship and the preservation of religion—Göttingen became something of Britain's 'imperial university', with 228 British graduates attending between 1763 and 1800.[16] In the absence of a regular court in Hanover, the University acquired a surrogate courtly role, and functioned as a kind of noble finishing school for German, British, and Russian aristocratic students, as well as a centre for modern scholarship.[17]

Many dons throughout the century followed their pupils from Oxford to the continent as their Grand Tour 'bear-leaders', acting as tutors, chaperones, and guardians to their charges (though, seemingly, without any encouragement or facilitation on the part of the University), helping them (often vainly) to gain a gentlemanly polish of taste and virtù, reporting back to their parents with an understandable hope that a job well-done might lead to a lucrative benefice as the tutor-student relationship was over time transmuted into one of client-patron.[18] Thomas Townson (1715–92), Fellow of Magdalen, made Italian journeys in three decades: in 1743–5 with William Drake; in 1751–2 with William Bagot, and in 1768–9 with William Drake the Younger.[19] His Nonjuring friend, Edward Holdsworth, once of Magdalen himself, tried to compensate for the loss of his

---

[14] C. D. Smith, *The early career of Lord North*, 58. Both North's and Dartmouth's sons in their turn undertook the Grand Tour. Ingamells, 600, 712.

[15] At its opening the French instructor Antoine Rougemont, in an oration, grandiloquently compared the rule of George II to the *pax Romana* and promised that new Horaces and Virgils would arise in the fledgling academy. J. von Stackelberg, 'Klassizismus und Aufklärung—der Blick nach Frankreich', in *Zur geistigen Situation der Zeit der Göttinger Universitätsgründung 1737. Eine Vortragsreihe* (Göttingen, 1988), 167–86.

[16] Biskup, 'The university of Göttingen and the Personal Union', 138–9; G. M. Stewart, 'British students at the University of Göttingen in the eighteenth century', *German Life and Letters*, 33 (1979–80), 24–41, at 30. See also H. Wellenreuther,'Göttingen und England im 18. Jahrhundert', in Norbert Kamp, et al., eds., *250 Jahre Vorlesungen an der Georgia Augusta 1734–1984* (Göttingen, 1985), 30–63, and, for a more subdued view than Biskup's, D. Collet, 'Creative misunderstandings: circulating objects and the transfer of knowledge within the personal union of Hanover and Great Britain', in *German Historical Institute London Bulletin*, 36 (2014), 3–23.

[17] Charles E. McClelland, *State, Society, and University in Germany 1700–1914* (Cambridge, 1980).

[18] For a good example see N. Aston, 'Thomas Townson and High Church Continuities and Connections in Eighteenth-Century England', *BJRL*, 2021, 53–69.

[19] Ingamells, *Dictionary*, 949. It was Bagot's father, Sir Walter Bagot, who offered Townson the family living of Blithfield, Staffs., in 1749.

558   ENLIGHTENED OXFORD

fellowship income by making a business out of bear-leading. Townson was not alone in developing a taste for travel. Thus William Sherard, botanist and fellow of St John's, served as tutor to several noblemen heading for the continent in the 1690s, culminating in a grant of travel leave in 1695 when he departed for France and Italy with Wriothesley, Lord Tavistock (heir of William, Lord Russell, the Whig 'martyr' in the Rye House Plot), later 2nd Duke of Bedford.[20] The presence of educated young noblemen and gentlemen with their erudite tutors welcomed as equals in the palaces and *hôtels* of Italy, France, and Germany underlined the mobility of the European élites and constituted an enriching component of the Republic of Letters.[21] Travelling tutors might take some personal credit for giving their charges capacity to mix, on occasion, in those circles. It might do their chances of preferment from the parents further good to offset any lowering of their profile in college caused by two or three years' absence as a 'bear-leader'.

Protracted excursions with pupils might be the prelude for tutors to further continental journeying in the interests of amity and scholarship, extending contacts with the learned abroad. On his three Grand Tours into Italy during his years as Professor of Poetry, Joseph Spence was able to undertake research, set up various interviews in Turin, probably gain access to the royal archives of Savoy, and attend Herman Boerhaave's physiology lectures at Leiden;[22] having been awarded a DCL (1719) and ordained a deacon in the Nonjuring Church, Richard Rawlinson's travels (1720–6) saw him registered at three universities (Leiden, Utrecht, and Padua) and add appreciably to his trophies as a collector and ship home manuscripts, books, statuary, paintings, and coins.[23] Travellers seem generally ready to place Oxford—and Anglicanism—within Catholic contexts where appropriate.[24] Thus Secker's Lambeth Librarian, Andrew Coltée Ducarel (1713–85: Trinity and St John's, 1731), in his antiquarian tour of 1752 around northern France, experienced and appreciated at first hand the historical links between dioceses in Normandy (where he had been born) and the Church of England.[25]

---

[20] Costin, *St John's College Oxford*, 159. He also accompanied the future statesman, the 2nd Viscount Townshend, to the Low Countries. ed. Andrew W. Moore, *Norfolk and the Grand Tour* (Norwich, 1985), 85. The College gave him further 5 years travel leave in 1697.

[21] For an emphasis on these trans-national presences see Antoine Lilti, *The World of the Salons. Sociability and Worldliness in eighteenth-century Paris*, trans. Lydia G. Cochrane (Oxford, 2015); Pierre-Yves Beaurepaire, *Le mythe de l'Europe française au XVIII siècle. Diplomatie, culture et sociabilités au temps des Lumières* (Paris, 2007).

[22] Spence had only served two years as Professor of Poetry when he left on his first and longest continental tour with Lord Middlesex. Spence insisted to a friend that he went as a companion and not as tutor. Ingamells, 881; Chapter 6, p. 61, n. 138.

[23] He was also received by 'James III' and Clementina Sobieska and even paid a visit to the young Prince of Wales. An essential purpose of his Tour was to offer a Jacobite *hommage*. Tashjian, 'Richard Rawlinson', 1–2, 28, 31–4.

[24] For interest and involvement in Roman Catholic religious ceremonies on the continent see Brant, *Eighteenth-Century Letters and British Culture*, 240–1.

[25] See his 'anonymous' *A Tour through Normandy,...* (London, 1754); Rosemary Sweet, *Antiquaries. The Discovery of the Past in Eighteenth-Century Britain* (London, 2004), 252. Letters to

OXFORD AND THE WIDER WORLD 559

Earlier, in 1737, the highlight of William King's travels in France was a meeting with the Archbishop of Auch, Cardinal Melchior de Polignac (1661–1742), for two reasons: first, the Cardinal (French ambassador to the Stuart court in Rome 1724–32) was supportive of the Stuart dynasty and the personal friend of 'James III', whom he had once spoken of electing 'as king of Poland'; second, for his attempted refutation of Lucretius in Latin verse, the *Anti-Lucretius, sive de Deo et Natura*. King was immediately at his ease with this 'elegant and polite scholar', for he 'had a most engaging affability, and a peculiar art and manner of obliging every man, who was introduced to him, to lay aside all restraint. I had not been with him a quarter of an hour, when I found myself as easy as if I had been educated in his family'.[26]

Academic engagement on the continent was increasingly seen as a means of securing professorial preferment back in Oxford. John Sibthorp, having made many botanical discoveries in the south of France, read a memoir to the Royal Society of Montpellier on fifty species not mentioned in a local flora compendium and, having been made a member of the Montpellier Society (widely considered the sister academy of Paris) was hopeful that these external achievements would be enough to get him a chair.[27] Then there were the independently wealthy, whose scholarly interests were disconnected from academic ambition, such as the philanthropically minded Joseph Wilcocks (1724–91), son of the Dean of Westminster, learned in Roman history and archaeology, who undertook serious antiquarian work in Italy after graduating from Christ Church, and was allegedly known to Pope Clement XIII as 'the blessed heretick'.[28]

Some scholarly Oxonians travelled well beyond Italy. Richard Chandler (1738–1810), who became an important international figure, was the first Briton to journey extensively for the Dilettanti Society in Greece and Turkey (1766–8)

Loveday in Robin Myers, 'Dr Andrew Coltée Ducarel (1713–1785): a pioneer of Anglo-Norman studies', in eds. Robin Myers and M. Harris, *Antiquaries, Book Collectors and the Circles of Learning* (Winchester, 1996), 45–70.

[26] Greenwood, *King*, 76–7; King, *Political and Literary anecdotes*, 10–11. King wryly noted: 'The Cardinal observing that during dinner I drank only water, and being told I never drank any other liquor, said, turning to me, "Whilst I was ambassador at Rome, and since my return to France, I have entertained more than five hundred of your countrymen"'. For Cardinal Polignac in Rome, see Edward Corp, *The Stuarts in Italy 1719–1766. A Royal Court in Permanent Exile* (Cambridge, 2011), 70, 72–4, 246.

[27] Sibthorp to his father Humphrey Sibthorp, Montpel[l]ier, 23 Mar. 1783, Lincolnshire Archives, 3 Sibthorp 3. He succeeded his father as Sherardian Professor of Botany in 1784 and undertook further travels in Italy and Greece during the mid-1780s for plant specimens. He took with him the botanical artist Ferdinand Bauer (1760–1826), whom he had met in Vienna, to illustrate the flora that he hoped would make him famous. His early death at the end of his second expedition to Constantinople and Greece may have resulted from the effects of dysentery, compounded by tuberculosis. On his travels he collected 3000 botanical species. H. Tregaskis, *Beyond the Grand Tour. The Levant Lunatics* (London, 1979), 29–32; S. Harris, *The Magnificent Flora Graeca: How the Mediterranean came to the English Garden* (Oxford, 2007); J. Black, *A brief history of the Mediterranean* (London, 2020), 141.

[28] For 'some account of the Author' see W. Bickerstaffe, *Roman Conversations; or, A short description of the antiquities of Rome*, ed. Weeden Butler the Elder (2nd edn., London, 1797).

which resulted in a compelling travelogue (published 1775–6) and an edition of hitherto unknown inscriptions which he had collected (*Inscriptiones antiquae, pleraeque nondum editae, in Asia Minori et Graecia collectae*, 1774).[29] Chandler was following in some illustrious Oxonian footsteps, notably those of Thomas Shaw (1694–1751)—'a Great Virtuosa & has brought many Curiositys with him out of Egypt'.[30]

Starting his career as chaplain to the English factory at Algiers in 1720,[31] Shaw travelled widely in the Islamic Middle East down to 1732 and made archaeological discoveries and careful observations on all aspects of life, and survived robbery and kidnap. His *Travels, or, Observations Relating to Several Parts of Barbary and the Levant* (2 vols., Oxford, 1738) was initially well-received and became a standard work of reference for decades, despite Richard Pococke attacking it for inaccuracies in *Description of the East* (2 vols., London, 1743–5).[32] Shaw was important for his critique of classical and Arabic texts about North Africa and in the 1730s his company was particularly sought out by foreign *érudits* visiting Oxford.[33] And before Shaw, Edmund Chishull (1671–1733), a Whig Fellow of Corpus Christi, went from the college not to a rural living in England, but to the chaplaincy of the English Factory at Smyrna, which he held from 1698 to 1702. Chishull used his position to travel extensively in Turkey, publishing notes of his journeys, transcribing inscriptions, as well as *Antiquitates Asiaticae* (London, 1728), a major advance in the study of ancient epigraphy.[34]

For university dons there could be a fascination in encountering monastic communities (usually Benedictine) not too dissimilar in ethos and organisation from their own colleges, where celibacy and learning went hand in hand; many

---

[29] Fellow of Magdalen, 1770–80; senior Proctor, 1772; DD, 1773. Published *Marmora Oxoniensia* (1763), an illustrated record of the Arundel marbles commissioned by the University; *Ionian Antiquities*, 1769. Held livings in Hants. and Berks. after 1779. R. Churton, 'Account of the Author', in R. Chandler, *Travels in Asia Minor and Greece*, ed. R. Churton (2 vols., Oxford, 1825); Darwall-Smith, 'The Monks of Magdalen', 316–17.

[30] 'Shepilinda', *Memoirs*, 45.

[31] For the Chaplains of the Levant Company and their pronounced High Church tendencies see Zwierlein, *Imperial Unknowns*, 163–73; J. B. Pearson, *A biographical sketch of the chaplains to the Levant Company, maintained at Constantinople, Aleppo and Smyrna, 1611–1706* (Cambridge, 1883).

[32] His *Travels* listed 640 species of plants and won him fame as a naturalist. It was translated into French, German, and Dutch. Kelly, *St Edmund Hall*, 58–9.

[33] See especially Zwierlein, *Imperial Unknowns*, 188–9, 240–7, 288–90. Zwierlein judges Shaw to be 'one of the most learned geohistorical and natural historical observers of North Africa' of his age (240); Z. Zizi, 'Thomas Shaw (1692–1751) à Tunis et Alger missionnaire de la curiosité européenne', thèse de doctorat, Université de Caen 1995 (ANRT Lille). He was elected FRS in 1734.

[34] Chishull was in due course a candidate for the Presidency of the College on the death of Thomas Turner in 1714. Charles-Edwards and Reid, *Corpus Christi College*, 224–5, 238, 241. Before Chishull and Shaw, there was no Oxford figure who had the familiarity with the near East that could compare to that possessed by John Covel [Colvill] (1638–1722), Vice-Chancellor of Cambridge University twice (1688–9; 1708–9) and Master of Christ's College, 1688–1722. He served as chaplain at Constantinople between 1670 and 1676, travelled extensively in Asia Minor, and, at the very end of a long life, published an account of the Greek Church, based on decades of enquiries, information gathering, and his own notes. Zwierlein, *Imperial Unknowns*, 128–9.

Fig. 11.1 Rev. Thomas Shaw, unknown artist, oil on canvas (St Edmund Hall, Oxford).

eighteenth-century monasteries in Germany and France were at least as resourceful as Oxford in relating the enlightened ideas of the age to their distinctive intellectual inheritance, often embodied in their library holdings.[35] Access to such collections, wherever they were housed, was essential for the inspection and checking of manuscripts required for a reliable edition of a classical text, as Chandler sought in his travels in Switzerland and Italy (1785–7), collecting and collating materials for his new edition of Pindar.[36] He worked through Greek Testament manuscripts in the Vatican, but the papal authorities eventually curtailed his opportunities for completing his studies there.[37] Anglican scholars in successive generations also craved access to the major collections of manuscripts housed in the Sorbonne and the other libraries of greater Paris, and were seldom

---

[35] Ulrich L. Lehner, *Enlightened Monks. The German Benedictines 1740–1803* (Oxford, 2011); Derek Beales, *Prosperity and Plunder. European Catholic Monasteries in the Age of Revolution, 1650–1815* (Cambridge, 2003), 13–14; Beales, 'Edmund Burke and the Monasteries of France', *HJ*, 48 (2005), 415–36.

[36] Magdalen College, MC: F10, papers. The edition was never completed.

[37] W.W. Wroth, rev. R.D.E. Eagles, 'Chandler, Richard (bap. 1737–1810), classical scholar and traveller', *ODNB*, online edn., 2019.

562 ENLIGHTENED OXFORD

turned away.[38] Thomas Hunt, Professor of Hebrew, was in touch with Parisian *érudits* in the early 1750s (principally Dr Charles Gillot, physician of the faculty of the Sorbonne) over manuscripts and books to be found in the King of France's library for his own projected Egyptian History.[39] Benjamin Kennicott, the Hebraist, of Exeter College, benefitted from a prolonged stay in the capital in 1770–1, and extended conversations with the young Sorbonne biblical theologian Jean-René Asseline (later Bishop of Boulogne, 1789). These built on those of a decade earlier with the Abbé Jean-Baptiste Ladvocat (1709–65), Librarian and Hebraist at the Sorbonne, one of the most cultivated French clerics of his generation, and one equally intent on stabilising the Hebrew text of the Old Testament.[40]

Kennicott was not the last scholar to take advantage of the facilities put at the disposal of visiting Anglican clerics, generally acceptable to their Gallican counterparts in a manner that harder-line Protestants never could be. Thus in 1789—during the first months of the French Revolution—the former Bampton Lecturer, Robert Holmes, Fellow of New College and friend of James Woodforde, was hard at work in Paris—assisted by some recent Oxford graduates—as he continued his collation of the Septuagint (both the Rome and the Alexandrine copies).[41] Thanks largely to Viscount Stormont, the ally of Lord North and former envoy to France, Holmes gained friends at the highest level of French political society, including Suzanne Necker, the leading *salonnière* and wife of Jacques Necker, the first minister, whose name opened most doors. She put him in touch with the classical scholar J-.B.-G, d'Ansse de Villoison (then preparing his great work on Greece, ancient and modern, that would never be published),[42] who showed Holmes additional Greek manuscript sources and took him to meet other colleagues able to assist in his collation. Villoison was impressed: 'c'est un homme plein de connoissances, de critique d'ardent, de probité et de candeur. Je ne doute point que cette edition de septante ne soit un chef d'oeuvre... [et] seroit digne de

[38] For Samuel Johnson's visit to Saint-Cloud and other libraries in 1775 see eds. M. Tyson and H. Guppy, *The French journals of Mrs Thrale and Dr Johnson* (Manchester, 1932); R. Shackleton, 'Johnson and the Enlightenment', in *Johnson, Boswell, and their circle: essays presented to Lawrence Fitzroy Powell* (Oxford, 1965), 76–92, at 77–81; J. Clark, 'Samuel Johnson: The Last Choices, 1775-1784', in eds. J. Clark and H. Erskine-Hill, *The Politics of Samuel Johnson* (Basingstoke, 2012), 168–222, esp. 185–6.

[39] Bodl. Ms Eng. lett. d. 146, f. 9, Hunt to Gregory Sharp, 13 Apr. 1752. Hunt, revelling in this confessional openness, later asked Lord Baltimore (probably Frederick, the 6th Baron, 1731–71) if there were any Maronites in the city. (f. 20).

[40] For Ladvocat see L. Poinsinet de Sivry, *Le Nécrologe des hommes célèbres de France* (Paris, 1767). For Kennicott in Paris see William McKane, 'Benjamin Kennicott: an eighteenth-century researcher', *JTS*, 28 (1977), 445–64, at 447–8.

[41] Daniel Prince to Rev. Samuel Viner, 7 Aug. 1789, Gloucestershire Archives, Ellis & Viner Papers, D2227/6/3.

[42] In 1788 his *Venetus A* of Homer had appeared, based on his discovery a few years previously of a 10th-century manuscript of the *Iliad* in a Venetian library. Villoison's knowledge of manuscripts in Greece and other ex-Byzantine parts of the eastern Mediterranean was exceptional in the 1780s. Bon-Joseph Dacier, *Notice historique sur la vie et les ouvrages de Villoison* (Paris, 1806).

l'Angleterre et seroit fort utile à l'humanité et aux lettres'.[43] Such contacts testified to what William Jones of Nayland in 1777 called the 'more liberal communication between the learned of the English and Roman persuasions', one encouraged by a common threat from 'this atheistical opposition to all revelation'.[44] Jones's view that the learning of the *philosophes* was, on the whole, antipathetic to the interests of religion was widely shared in Oxford, fuelled by concerns about atheism resulting from the exposure to it of students and former students.[45] This deprecation ensured that contacts between dons and leading figures of the French Enlightenment were minimal.[46] Tellingly, the Abbé Raynal (1713–96), who apparently wished for an Oxford honorary degree, was refused one on the basis of his radical views, despite the fame of his bestselling but overtly anticlerical *Histoire des deux Indes* (1770) which, in later editions, contained enthusiastic support for the rebellious American colonists.[47] But such a putting of distance is far from decisive in considering Oxford in any sense unenlightened.

ii) Europeans in Oxford

> It is neither rich nor great, but it is all amiable, nay, and all magnificent; for its 25 Colleges may be call'd so many royal and stately Edifices.
>
> M. Misson, *Memoirs and Observations in his Travels over England*, trans. John Ozell (London, 1719), 202–3.

The disinclination of the *philosophes* to take particular account of Oxonians— John Locke apart—and Oxford itself was not widely shared among the great majority of learned, the curious, and the touristic in continental Europe. The

---

[43] d'Ansse de Villoison to Stormont, 1 Jan. 1789, Mansfield Papers, Scone Palace, Box 85, bundle 7. Villoison had been patronised by Stormont at least as early as 1780. Holmes looked to Henry Addington, the future Premier, as his principal patron. The latter would, in 1802, offer him the chair of Hebrew. Holmes to Addington, 9 July 1788, Devon RO, 152M/C1788/F28.

[44] [William Jones], *Observations in a Journey to Paris, by way of Flanders, in the Month of August 1776* (2 vols., London, 1777), I. 179. For Jones's francophilia see K. Turner, *British Travel Writers in Europe, 1750–1800. Authorship, gender and national identity* (Aldershot, 2001), 30.

[45] The anonymous author of the *World* no 205 (2 Dec. 1756) worried that 'the majority of our young travellers return home entirely divested of the religion of their country, without having acquired any new one in its stead'. Quoted in George C. Brauer, Jr., *The education of a Gentleman. Theories of Gentlemanly Education in England, 1660–1775* (New York, 1959), 180.

[46] For Horne's assault—as 'Nathaniel Freebody Esq' on Voltaire's religious views, see 'The Miscellany', *St James's Chronicle*, 3–5 Feb. 1767; N. Aston, 'The Dean of Canterbury and the Sage of Ferney: George Horne looks at Voltaire', in eds. W. M. Jacob and N. Yates, *Crown and Mitre. Religion and Society in Northern Europe since the Reformation* (Woodbridge, 1993), 139–61, esp. 154–5. In the 1770s Horne drew up the heads of a sermon, provisionally entitled 'We are not ignorant of his devices', that aimed to counter Voltaire's objections to Christianity decisively. CUL MS Add. 8134, B/1/313–19, undated.

[47] *GM* 61 (1791), II. 894.

564   ENLIGHTENED OXFORD

University's reputation for learning was a European commonplace and had been for centuries. Certainly, by Henry III's reign (1216–72) the presence of foreign scholars and students had been vital 'in cementing the notion of Oxford as a fully extended university as that was understood within the international academic community'.[48] Along with London, it was one of only two cities in the British Isles that rated a mention in the Abbé Bordelon's 1699 description of the Republic of Letters. Its prestige made it a magnet for non-domestic learned visitors, who might have encountered it first, imaginatively, via such marketing products as Anthony Wood's *Historia et antiquitates Oxoniensis* (1674);[49] by the mid-century, the market was explicitly catering for the less learned but still curious foreign visitor with a text such as *The Foreigner's Companion through the Universities of Cambridge and Oxford.*[50]

Throughout this time they came to Oxford to see the sites and gain an impression of the place that they could pass on to others.[51] Compliments could be flattering—to the point of hyperbole. One Cambridge don had heard a story that the French Huguenot, Admiral Du Quesne (1610–88), when he visited Oxford, declared that 'the Prospect from the Mount' in New College Gardens was 'so extremely magnificent,...[that] it was the equal to the principal view at Versailles'.[52] A century later, the young François, Duc de La Rochefoucauld d'Anville (1765–1848) was insistent: 'I don't believe that anywhere in the entire world you will find a university so magnificent as this and rarely will you come across a town so beautiful'.[53] His fellow countrywoman, the genteel, agreeable, educationalist and mistress of the Duc d'Orléans, Félicité de Genlis, making her first visit to England in 1785, was very keen to tour Oxford. Her *Adèle et Théodore* (1782)—a complete courtesy book in four volumes combining orthodox principles with Rousseau's new methods of education (while aspersing his doctrines)—had many admirers in the University, so much so that unfounded rumours circulated that a doctorate would be conferred on her.[54]

Other visitors were distinctly less impressed by different aspects of academic life. One French visitor of the early 1730s admitted that the physical setting of

---

[48] A. B. Cobban, *The medieval English universities to c.1500* (Aldershot, 1992), 44.

[49] Haugen, *Richard Bentley*, 54, 108.

[50] It made few concessions in terms of detail and historical background. See chap.10, p. 22.

[51] F.M. Wilson, *Strange Island. Britain through Foreign Eyes 1395–1940* (London, 1955), 60.

[52] Norfolk Archives, MC150/50 625 x 3, 'A Journal of my Expedition to Oxford in the Year 1759' [Rev Robert Le Grys a fellow of Caius College]. Du Quesne's grandson, Gabriel, became a naturalized British subject in 1711, and was Lt. Col. of the 1st Troop of the Grenadier Guards in 1717. W. K. Lowther Clarke, *Eighteenth Century Piety* (London, 1944), 54.

[53] N. Scarfe, *Innocent Espionage. The La Rochefoucauld Brothers' Tour of England in 1785* (Woodbridge, 1995), 136, dated 26 Mar. 1785. Having evidently read *The New Oxford Guide*, the Duc took in the false notion that the town was 'consecrated to the muses' by the Britons long before the Roman settlement of Bellositum [sic]. Ibid., 134.

[54] Magdi Wahba, 'Madame de Genlis in England', *Comparative Literature*, 13 (1961), 221–38. Genlis was so well-thought-of in England before the French Revolution that Queen Charlotte gave her permission to send her work to the Royal Library at Windsor. Ibid., 227.

OXFORD AND THE WIDER WORLD   565

Oxford 'far surpassed all that we had been led to expect in London...' but opined that if the Muses resided there 'secure from indigence', they also lived 'at ease'. And his verdict on the University's publication record was unflattering:

> The good books published in England rarely come from Oxford, but are wrote in London, and although the authors mostly have some degree in this University, they are not of the number of those who are paid generously to make it their residence.[55]

Another French lady, who complained that she had acquired a sore throat because of the inclement spring weather on her visit to the city, was horrified to find the Arundel marbles '...thrown carelessly to the bottom of a damp cellar' and wondered at this neglect. Was it possible, she speculated,

> ...that the English, in seeking for the precious remains of Greece and Rome, resemble conquerors or lovers, who are eager to acquire at a great expence the object of their wishes, and equally ready to neglect it when once it is in their possession?'[56]

Inspired by the example of the Anglophile king Stanislaw August Poniatowski (1764–95) (who, before his accession, had visited Professor Thomas Hunt in Oxford),[57] Oxford was very much on the aristocratic Polish tourist circuit.[58] Princess Izabela Czartoryski, visiting in 1790 with her son Jerzy Czartoryski, was shocked by the 'great liberty' granted to students: 'They are subject to no one, coming and going as they wish just by paying the porters [a] shilling an hour. Children of lords are singled out from the rest by their status and clothes. Truly, this is a great evil'.[59]

In many cases, foreign visitors sought to take away knowledge from Oxford's great manuscript libraries that could be of use in their own countries or make personal contact with its academics. It always helped if those in this category had a

---

[55] Abbé Prévost, *Adventures of a man of quality*, trans. Mysie E. I. Robertson (London, 1930), 170–1. The 'Man of Quality' was a technically fictional creation but his opinion on Oxford seems based on Prévost's own. In *Le pour et contre* (first published 1733, ed. Jean Sgard, Paris, 1969) there are details of his close association while in England between 1728 and 1734.with a Whig family and a pupil who was a Cambridge student with 'bonne opinion de tout ce qui vient de Cambridge'. Ibid., 54. For Prévost in England see Claire-Eliane Engel, *Figures et aventures du XVIIIe siècle: Voyages et découvertes de l'abbé Prévost* (Paris, 1939).

[56] Mme du Bocage, *Letters concerning England, Holland and Italy, translated from the French* (2 vols., London, 1770), I. 58. She visited in 1750 before the Pomfret bequest and better housing for the marbles. See Chapter 12.

[57] Markham, *John Loveday*, 438.

[58] His sister Ludwika visited Oxford in 1767 on her travels in England. R. Butterwick, *Poland's Last King and English Culture. Stanislaw August Poniatowski 1732–1798* (Oxford, 1998), 131.

[59] *Diary of Princess Izabela Czartoryski from Travels around England and Scotland in 1791*, ed. A. Whelan, trans. A. Whelan and Z. Zygulski, Jr. (Warsaw and Torun, 2015), 65.

letter of introduction like that Henry Newman (Secretary of the SPCK 1708–43) wrote to George Fothergill at Queen's on behalf of the Danish Bishop of Aarhus, Johannes Ocksen (b. 1667):[60]

> He has travelled through Germany and France, and takes England in his way home, with which he seems not a little pleas'd, so far as he has seen it. He is a Lover of Letters and Learned Men, and therefore you will excuse the liberty I take of recommending him to yr advice for passing a few days at Oxford, in the best manner to give him an idea of ye illustrious University.

And where they were not forthcoming, it could make all the difference in terms of what foreign visitors were able to see, even when they held ducal rank like the young La Rochefoucauld in 1785:

> We were expecting letters of recommendation for Oxford that [a] friend was due to send to us here . . . , but either they were lost in the post or our friend forgot about them . . . and so we had to leave without having come near to satisfying our curiosity as to the precise way young men study in the universities.[61]

In a Europe where university library facilities were inadequate (partly because of an absence of endowed funding) the Bodleian proved a considerable magnet.[62] A report of 1697 extolled it as the 'glory of our university and kingdom in its kind', an attraction that drew 'hither strangers even from countries beyond the seas to their benefit and to the honour and profit of the nation'.[63] Among several Lutherans who wanted to see Bodleian manuscripts was Erik Benzelius the younger, university librarian at Uppsala and married to the sister of the mystic Emanuel Swedenborg. These opportunities were also highly prized by savants from Roman Catholic polities who would be disqualified from matriculation, men such as Francesco Bianchini, prominent in the small scientific community of Rome in the early eighteenth century. Though a right-hand

---

[60] MS. 473 Queen's College, 26 Sept. 1733; L. W. Cowie, *Henry Newman: An American in London, 1708–1743* (London, 1956); Nicholas Hope, *German and Scandinavian Protestantism 1700-1918* (Oxford, 1995), 155–6.

[61] Quoted in Scarfe, *Innocent Espionage*, 137.

[62] Brockliss (2), 303, pointedly notes that 88% of volumes ordered up at the Bodleian in Dec. 1708 came from requests made by seven foreign scholars. As late as 1789 only four of twenty-two French universities had a central university library. For a survey of the European library situation, see Ridder-Symoens, 'Management and resources', in ed. de Ridder-Symoens, *Universities in early modern Europe*, 195–202.

[63] 'Some Thoughts concerning the Bodleian Library' (7 June 1697), BL MS Harl. 7055, ff. 42–3, quoted in Israel, *Radical Enlightenment*, 129. The report warned against failing to keep up purchasing momentum. In his well-known visit of the late summer of 1710, Zacharias von Uffenbach speculated that Wolfenbüttel had more books, though he felt the Bodleian had more manuscripts. eds. W. H. Quarrell and W. J. C. Quarrell, *Oxford in 1710, from the Travels of Zacarias Conrad Von Uffenbach* (Oxford, 1928), 4.

man of Pope Clement XI (1700–21), Bianchini had international contacts with Leibniz and the English astronomer John Flamsteed. He came to Oxford in 1713 from France at the end of a diplomatic mission, taking advantage of the Peace of Utrecht to visit the University after attending the Royal Society and meeting Newton three times.[64] Enquiries about specific documents or objects came into the University regularly from foreign savants. Thus the French astronomer Jean Sylvain Bailly (later Mayor of Paris during the French Revolution) wrote in 1777 requesting permission to view various astronomical manuscripts.[65]

Oxford was able to attract even crowned heads of state. The young Peter I of Russia much desired to visit the city and did so incognito (with a huge wig to conceal his face). In April 1698 he toured the Bodleian and the Sheldonian led by the landlord of Golden Cross Inn; when his identity was revealed at the Ashmolean Museum by the students and townsfolk who had hemmed him in, he rushed back to London with his visit cut short.[66] He had still managed to see the town hall, the Sheldonian, the new chapel of Trinity College (the only collegiate building that he visited), and the Ashmolean, where the attendant, William Williamson, reported he was 'a very uncouth fellow' with dirty scratched hands.[67] There was no time for Peter to receive a degree from Oxford. That was not the case with George III's brother-in-law, Christian VII of Denmark (1749–1808), who undertook a grand tour of Europe in 1768–9—also incognito. Oxford granted him an honorary doctorate in September 1768 (so did Cambridge) that in equal parts did honour to King George and reflected King Christian's popularity with the British public at that time. Various personages from his retinue were also comparably honoured out of respect to their sovereign.[68]

A foreign monarch's personal representative could also be eligible. Ezekiel, Freiherr von Spanheim, despatched by Frederick I, the newly minted King of Prussia, was one such. Spanheim (1629–1710), resident in London during most of

---

[64] Hans Gross, *Rome in the Age of Enlightenment. The post-Tridentine syndrome and the ancien regime* (Cambridge, 1990), 254.

[65] Magdalen College, MC: PR29/C1/1, 26 Aug. 1777 (there was a supportive letter from his Portuguese colleague, Jean Hyacinthe de Magellan, FRS). See also MS 534, MS 471.

[66] Luttrell, *Brief Historical Relation*, IV. 361, 8; Charlett to Charles Boyle, 12 Apr.1698, in ed. Emily Charlotte, countess of Cork & Orrery, *The Orrery papers* (2 vols., London, 1903), I. 20; A. G. Cross, *Peter the Great through British eyes: perceptions and representations of the Tsar since 1698* (Cambridge, 2000), esp. 28 n.53, 29 n. 55.

[67] Quoted by Leo Loewenson, 'Some details of Peter the Great's stay in England in 1698. Neglected English materials', *Slavonic and Eastern European Review*, 40 (1962), 431–43. It was reported that on the morning of his tour he was nursing a hangover from consuming two bottles of vodka the previous evening.

[68] Edward Hooper to James Harris, 20 Aug. 1768, Hants RO, MS 9M73/G329/12; Green and Roberson, *Studies in Oxford history*, 299; Ulrik Langen, 'The meaning of incognito', *The Court Historian*, 7 (2002), 145–55, at 146–7. Some of his Danish entourage were also honoured. The visit was before Christian became mad and Queen Caroline Mathilda was embroiled with her lover, the royal doctor, Johann Friedrich Struensee.

Fig. 11.2 Duc de Nivernais, Allan Ramsay, oil on canvas, c.1763 (© National Trust).

the War of the Spanish Succession was both a scholar (appointed FRS, 1679) and a diplomat, who had published the first volume of his numismatic treatise, *Dissertationes [Disputationes] de praestantia et usu numismatum antiquorum* in Rome as far back as 1664, a magisterial folio showing the uses of coins and medals for the study of all aspects of ancient history. A new edition came out in London in 1706 and Spanheim sent a copy of it to Oxford with a Latin inscription thanking the University for the conferment of his degree.[69] Another ambassador honoured by the University was that lettered Anglophile aristocrat, the Duc de Nivernais, who assisted in the negotiation of the Treaty of Paris, which controversially ended the Seven Years' War in 1763.

By offering the Duc a DCL, the authorities were signalling their endorsement of Lord Bute's peace policy, all part of the University's charm offensive towards the young George III.[70] More usually, it was simply a matter of the Vice-Chancellor

---

[69] Anthony Alsop wrote a Latin poem in honour of the occasion. David Money, *The English Horace*, 89. He was buried in Westminster Abbey.

[70] D. Roche, 'The English in Paris', in eds. C. Charle, J. Vincent, and J. Winter, *Anglo-French Attitudes. Comparisons and transfers between English and French intellectuals since the eighteenth century* (Manchester, 2007), 78–97, at 88.

OXFORD AND THE WIDER WORLD 569

and senior academics extending hospitality when foreign envoys and their distinguished guests came calling, as they regularly did, sometimes with a full party, like that of September 1786 when the Archduke [Ferdinand Karl] and Archduchess of Austria (Maria Beatrice, Princess of Modena and Reggio), along with the Imperial Ambassador, the Venetian resident, the Neapolitan ambassador, and other princely guests visited. They were conducted to several public buildings and colleges, before going on to Blenheim, Stowe, and Nuneham, coming back to the University for an inspection of the observatory.[71]

Oxford had earlier done its best with the physically unprepossessing William IV, Prince of Orange, George II's future son-in-law and (after 1747) Stadtholder of the United Provinces.[72] He was received on his visit to Oxford in late February and early March 1733 with a lavish hospitality that the King himself was never inclined to solicit or receive. Based with his household in the Christ Church Deanery, the Prince was determined to see as much as he could—and show himself affable and accessible to the city and the county as well as the University. He heard prayers in the cathedral, rushed over to Blenheim, on his return was received by the mayor, recorder, aldermen, and common council at the Council chamber, and dined in public at the Deanery, where the High Sheriff and grand jury were presented to him. There was much more to come: a procession to the Sheldonian from Peckwater quadrangle with degrees for himself and most of his party, a speech by the Public Orator, and an elegant reply back, with clapping from an estimated 4,000 people in the gallery. Then to the Bodleian, the Picture Gallery, the Divinity School, and the Ashmolean Museum, where he was conducted around by Professor James Bradley, who showed him 'several experiments in natural philosophy'. That night, while the Prince dined with William Holmes, then Vice-Chancellor, at St John's, the whole town was illuminated. The visit was a spectacular success on both sides and did Oxford's standing with the court no harm in furthering—perhaps unexpectedly—George II's desire to reattach the House of Orange to British strategic interests through a renewal of the dynastic tie.[73] Other princes related to the Hanoverian royal family wanted to see Oxford all down the century.

---

[71] Bodl. MS Top Oxon. d.174, f. 221, 16 Sept. 1786; *GM*, 56 (1786), II. 803; Green, Oxford during the last century, 123. The Archduke was the 4th son of the Empress Maria-Theresa. The couple were on a private visit to George III and his family. Diary of Thomas, 1st Earl of Ailesbury, in HMC, *Ailesbury MSS*, (London, 1898), 269–74.

[72] They were married exactly a year later. He shared with his strong-willed wife (and cousin), Anne, the Princess Royal, a wide range of intellectual and musical interests. Veronica P. M. Baker-Smith, *A Life of Anne of Hanover, Princess Royal* (Leiden, 1995).

[73] BL Add MS 33052, Newcastle Papers, ff. 140–2; Herbert Rowen, *The Princes of Orange. The Stadholders in the Dutch Republic* (Cambridge, 1988), 158–9. Holmes's career also benefitted. He was named a royal chaplain in 1734; appointed the second Regius Professor of Modern History, 1736; Dean of Exeter, 1742 onwards. Costin, *St John's College*, 184. There was a volume of commemorative poetry to mark the visit and the nuptials, *Epithalamia Oxoniensia* (Oxford, 1734).

George III's nephew, for instance, Frederick, the Crown Prince of Denmark (the future Frederick VI), passed through in 1793 and on his return expressed his appreciation with a gift to the University.[74]

It was the fame of its scholarship that attracted the learned in every generation to move from several parts of Europe to settle in Oxford and enrol at the university—so long as they technically subscribed to the Thirty-Nine Articles.[75] Peter Stahl, for instance, came from west Prussia to lecture on mining and metallurgy and to teach analytical chemistry;[76] the Parisian John Gagnier (1670?–1740) to lecture in Hebrew in succession to Rabbi Levi in 1710. Gagnier owed this preferment to the (Whig) Bishop of Worcester, William Lloyd, who surveyed the workings of the University from nearby Sunningwell Rectory (where his relations held the living). Lloyd had to battle hard with Vice-Chancellor Lancaster, who felt that enough foreigners had been appointed to academic posts. Lloyd put up forty shillings per quarter to pay Gagnier a living wage, while 'most of the colleges having subscribed forty shillings a year each, to have one of their Society alwaies learning of him, some have subscribed four pounds, and they send him two scholars'. The same source admitted that 'My Lord is ye greatest encourager of this good design of making ye Hebrew tongue become more universal, . . . '.[77]

In a related field, Bishop Lloyd patronised the former Lutheran John [Johannes] Ernest Grabe (b. 1666, attended Königsberg University) who fled Prussia to be welcomed in Oxford in 1697 (he had already been received into the Church of England at Hamburg). There he used his supportive university contacts in the academic and publishing worlds to pursue an ambitious programme of religious scholarship.[78] His first Oxford patron and mentor was John Mill, the Principal of St Edmund Hall, the accomplished New Testament scholar who had previously assisted the young Richard Bentley to show his academic paces. The holding of a chaplaincy at Christ Church between 1700 and 1703 (he had been ordained

---

[74] John Wills, Wadham College, to the Duke of Portland, 6 Mar. 1793, John Wills's Letter book, Balliol College Archives and Manuscripts, Jenkyns VI.A (2), f. 19.

[75] Learned non-Christians who could not matriculate also found Oxford a place of refuge and employment. For Ignatius Dumay, a French Jew in Oxford who assisted Kennicott, associated with the Hutchinsonians, and was valued as a writing master in Oxford, see Robert M. Andrews, *Lay Activism and the High Church Movement of the late Eighteenth Century. The Life and Thought of William Stevens, 1732–1807* (Leiden, 2015), 122–34.

[76] H. Kellenbenz, 'German Immigrants', in ed. C. Holmes, *Immigrants and Minorities in British Society* (London, 1978), 63–80, at 69. See also ed. P. Panayi, *Germans in Britain since 1500* (London, 1996).

[77] Benjamin Marshall, scholar in Arabic at Christ Church, nephew of Bishop Lloyd, in Hartshorne MSS, Corpus Christi College, Cambridge, f. 160, 16 Jan. 1710, quoted in A. Tindal Hart, *William Lloyd 1627–1717. Bishop, Politician, Author and Prophet* (London, 1952), 170.

[78] Nicholas Keene, 'John Ernest Grabe, Biblical learning and religious controversy in early eighteenth-century England', *JEH*, 58 (2007), 656–74; G. Thomann, 'John Ernest Grabe (1666–1711): Lutheran syncretist and Anglican patristic scholar', *Review of English Studies*, 43 (1992), 414–27.

Fig. 11.3 Johann Ernest Grabe, Francis Bird, marble monument, 1726, south transept, Westminster Abbey (Copyright: Dean and Chapter of Westminster).

deacon in 1700) and association with St Edmund Hall via Mill both cemented Grabe's connection with the University and brought him an additional income. It was only appropriate that his 1700 edition of Justin Martyr's *First apology* (a text explaining the faith to 2nd-century pagans) should be dedicated to his patron

572 ENLIGHTENED OXFORD

Henry Aldrich.[79] Grabe was involved as a liturgist and linguist in the publication of the German translation of the Book of Common Prayer at Frankfurt-an-der-Oder in 1704, but had no success in having Prussian bishops consecrated by their English counterparts, thereby securing the apostolic succession.[80] He had better luck in gathering subscriptions from across the continent for his edition of the Septuagint with scholars in France, Italy, Sweden, and Prussia sending him variant readings from manuscripts.[81]

Grabe's interest in fostering Anglican-Lutheran ecumenism was not new. In the early 1680s, Daniel Ernst Jablonski, that 'indefatigable apostle of union' within and beyond the dominions of the electorate of Brandenburg, was in Oxford, where, influenced by John Fell, William Sancroft, Henry Compton, and William Wake, he became impressed by the Cyprianic concept of the episcopate as the basis of unity in the Church, and kept up the pressure on Frederick I of Prussia to consider an Anglican-Prussian Church union as one strand in a project for a coming-together of all Evangelical Churches.[82] During the Harley ministry of 1710–14, the plan was taken up again by Oxford High Churchmen and Tories such as George Smalridge, but it fell victim to the latter's insistence that the Prussians receive episcopacy into their Church, the deaths of leading sponsors on both sides in 1712–14, and Prussian fury at British unilateral pursuit of peace with France in the Utrecht negotiations.[83]

After William Wake became archbishop in 1715, he tried to revive confessional interest in a pan-Protestant penumbra, looking first this time to Swiss religious leaders. Among them was the manuscript expert Pastor Ami Lullin (1695–1756), from a patrician Genevan family, who held membership of the SPG during his residency in England (1719–21), when he was a regular visitor to the Bodleian

---

[79] Keene, 'John Ernest Grabe', 660–1.

[80] G. Every, 'Dr Grabe and his manuscripts', *JTS*, 8 (1957), 280–92, at 281. Grabe was in touch with Anglicans inspired by the Greek Church and attended the oratory of Edward Stephens. As befitted a friend of the Nonjuror, George Hickes, he advocated an unambiguous emphasis on the sacrifice of bread and wine in the Holy Communion service. See ed. G. Thomann, *J. E. Grabe's liturgies: two unknown Anglican liturgies of the seventeenth century* (Nuremberg, 1989); Bryan D. Spinks, *Liturgy in the age of reason. worship and sacraments in England and Scotland 1662–c.1800* (Farnham, 2008), 113–16. For his syncretic High Church piety C. F. Secretan, *Memoirs of the life and times of the pious Robert Nelson* (London, 1860), 220–2.

[81] Keene, 'John Ernest Grabe', 664. He died before it appeared. A Christ Church colleague, William Stratford, thus lamented his passing to Edward, Lord Harley: 'No man in Europe can finish the Septuagint as he has begun it, ... His loss looks somewhat ominous as to the Arian heresy, which is openly revived. Had he lived he had effectually quashed it, by exposing the forgery of those constitutions on which it is chiefly grounded by Whiston'. Letter of 27 Oct. 1711, in HMC, *Portland MSS*, 64–5.

[82] N. Sykes, *Daniel Ernst Jablonski and the Church of England. A study of an essay towards Protestant union* (London, 1950), 5, 8, 13. Oxford gave an honorary degree to his teacher Dr Adam Samuel Hartmann in 1680. Ibid., 13. See also M. Schmidt, 'Ecumenical activity on the continent of Europe in the seventeenth and eighteenth centuries', in eds. R. Rouse and S. C. Neill, *A History of the Ecumenical Movement 1517–1948* (3rd edn., Geneva, 1986), 73–112, at 109–120.

[83] R. Barry Levis, 'The failure of the Anglican-Prussian ecumenical effort of 1710–1714', *Church History*, 47 (1978), 381–99. There were further attempts in 1716 and after prompted by Wake. Sykes, *Wake*, II. 60–80.

OXFORD AND THE WIDER WORLD   573

Library.[84] Wake knew of Lullin's presence and his endorsement of the project for a Union of Protestant Churches in the early 1720s. It was encouraged by George I, but aroused less enthusiasm in Oxford.[85] Individual Swiss intellectuals were never deterred from visiting Oxford and the University by its High Church character, and it no doubt helped pave the way for others that one of them, the mathematician Nicolas Fatio (1664–1753), a Fellow of the Royal Society at twenty-three, had been Lord Arran's tutor.[86] The University was just about comfortable with overlooking their Presbyterianism, increasingly accompanied as it was by a more generous form of Calvinism that often spilled over into non-Trinitarianism as the century wore on. Their scholarly needs were still respected.

Shortly after Lullin had gone back to Geneva, on 13 April 1725, John William Thomson, a Calvinist humanist, Court chaplain at the Reformed Burgkirche in Königsberg (part of the new kingdom of Prussia) from 1707, registered as a reader at the Bodleian and matriculated at St Edmund Hall three months later, drawn thither by the University's library facilities and its reputation for Platonic scholarship.[87] His edition of the *Parmenides* was published in Oxford in 1728, as well as his own *The First Principles of the Sciences or Natural Theology*, arguing for the compatibility of natural religion and revelation.[88] Another German, Johann David Michaelis (1717–91), part of an extended scholarly family, was attracted to the University during his eighteen months' tour of England in 1741–2 by the fame of the great Hebraist, Robert Lowth. He was so impressed by hearing Lowth's second series of lectures, *De Sacra poesi Hebraeorum*, that he produced an inexpensive, annotated edition of Lowth's *Praelectiones* in 1758–62 that introduced his hero to many new continental readers.[89] Thomson came to use Oxford's libraries,

---

[84] Béat de Fischer, 'Swiss in Great Britain in the eighteenth century', in eds. W. H. Barber, J. H. Brumfitt, R. A. Leigh, R. Shackleton, and S. S. B. Taylor, *The age of Enlightenment. Studies presented to Theodore Besterman* (Edinburgh/London, 1967), 350–74, at 359. He was Professor of Ecclesiastical History at the Academy of Geneva from 1737. See Victoria C. Miller, 'William Wake and the Reunion of Christians', *Anglican and Episcopal History* 62 (1993), 7–35.

[85] Bénédict Pictet, Professor of Theology at the Geneva Academy from 1687 to 1724, and father and son François Turretin (1623–87) and Jean-Alphonse Turretin (1671–1737), were key figures within Reformed Orthodoxy, promoting the scheme of Union over many years from Geneva. M. I. Klauber, 'Reformed Orthodoxy in Transition: Bénédict Pictet and Enlightened Orthodoxy in Post-Reformation Geneva', in ed. W. F. Graham, *Later Calvinism. International Perspectives* (Kirksville, MS, 1994), 93–113; M. C. Pitassi, 'L'Apologétique Raisonnable de Jean-Alphonse Turretini', in eds. O. Fatio and M. C. Pitassi, *Apologétique 1680–1740: Sauvetage ou naufrage de la théologie* (Geneva, 1990), 180–212.

[86] Scott Mandelbrote, 'Fatio, Nicolas, of Duillier (1664–1753), mathematician and natural philosopher', *ODNB*, online edn., 2016.

[87] The Hall unusually allowed its members unrestricted admission to its library. Paul Morgan, 'Oxford college libraries in the eighteenth century', *BLR*, 14 (1992), 228–36. For access to Oxford libraries see Ian Philip, *The Bodleian Library in the seventeenth and eighteenth centuries* (Oxford, 1983), 70; Philip, *Oxford libraries outside the Bodleian* (Oxford, 1973), 118–22.

[88] See Zebrowski, 'A Calvinist Humanist from Königsberg', 113, who argues that Thomson 'sought good theology through good philology, and offered Plato as witness to reason and natural religion'.

[89] Legaspi, *The death of scripture*, 107, 116; Deconinck-Brossard, 'England and France in the Eighteenth Century', 160. Michaelis declared that only a boor or ignoramus could fail to appreciate poetic translations of the Bible. Legaspi, *The Death of scripture*, 123.

574 ENLIGHTENED OXFORD

Michaelis to hear Lowth lecture;[90] the utterly distinctive George Psalmanazar came to teach. He was, by origins a Frenchman educated by Franciscan and Dominican monks, forged a certificate claiming Irish origins, then reinvented himself as a Japanese person to try and raise cash. Though he was ingenious enough to create an alphabet and bits of a language (he also claimed he was from Formosa, modern Taiwan), none of it was sufficient to rescue him from destitution. But he stayed with the persona, and was actually invited by Henry Compton, Bishop of London, to come to Oxford to teach Formosan to potential missionaries. This was at a time when books about the Formosans were in vogue, for all their fictitious claims, and his fabulous account of that island (*An Historical and Geographical Description of Formosa*, 1704) sold well. Psalmanazar kept up the hoax until his death and made money, though he was only resident at Christ Church for a few months before deciding it was expedient to refresh his novelty value elsewhere.[91]

Scholars and charlatans apart, students, too, enlisted at Oxford, from a desire to learn the English language, mix with a foreign—crucially Protestant—élite, and return culturally enriched and cosmopolitanly inclined.[92] Paths from eastern Europe to England were well trodden by the close of the seventeenth century with, interestingly, Calvinists rather than Lutherans more disposed to despatch their sons thither,[93] supplemented by a steady flow of Scandinavian students from around the same date.[94] There was also considerable interest in Oxford from students coming from an Orthodox religious background. With no universities named as such until the Empress Elizabeth founded Moscow University in 1755,[95] a state commission was set up in 1764 in Russia to select suitable students to be

[90] He later claimed he had been more impressed by the Lutheran court preacher in London, Friedrich Michael Ziegenhagen, than by the Oxford dons during his England trip. Biskup, 'The university of Göttingen', 153.

[91] Delbourgo, *Collecting the World*, 224–5, 398. Psalmanazar enjoyed Oxford. Writing from London to Rev Samuel Reynolds [Balliol College], 9 Nov. *c*.1706, he enclosed verses written in a coffee-house acclaiming Ormond for nominating Lancaster as V-C and aligning his ducal interests with Oxford's. Houghton Library, Harvard University, MS Eng 1473. See M. Keevak, *The Pretended Asian: George Psalmanazar's Eighteenth Century Formosan Hoax* (Detroit, MI, 2004); P. G. Adams, *Travelers and Travel liars 1660–1800* (New York, 1962, repr. 1980), 93–7.

[92] See generally Perraton, *A History of foreign students*, *passim*. The number of continental students at Oxford never rose above one per cent. H. de Ridder-Symoens, 'Mobility', in ed. Ridder-Symoens, *Universities in early modern Europe* 416–48, at 429.

[93] Nicholas Hans, 'Polish Protestants and their connections with England and Holland in the 17th and 18th centuries', *Slavonic and East European Review*, 37 (1958–9), 196–220. For Johannes Uri, a Hungarian scholar in Oxford in the late 1760s, see Ingram, *Secker*, 269.

[94] Perraton, *A History of foreign students*, 33.

[95] Moscow University was initially dominated by German professors, who outnumbered the students in early decades. See eds. V. V. Ponomareva and I. V. Khoroshilova, *Universitet dlia Rossii: Vzgliad na istoriiu kul'tury XVIII stoletiia* (Moscow, 1997) (I am grateful to Simon Dixon for this reference). The St Petersburg Academy of Science (1724) also functioned as a higher-educational institution, while theological education remained in the hands of the Orthodox Church. E. Donnert, *La Russie au siècle des Lumières* (Leipzig, 1986), 54–96; J. C. McClelland, *Autocrats and Academics. Education and Culture in Tsarist Russia* (Chicago, IL, 1979), 5–28; W. Frijhoff, 'Patterns', in ed. de Ridder-Symoens, *Universities in early modern Europe*, 43–110, at 48–9, 55–6, 59–60.

OXFORD AND THE WIDER WORLD   575

beneficiaries of the intellectual contacts with western academic institutions that Catherine II was bent on establishing (at least as much as she was courting favoured *philosophes*). She chose Oxford as well as Göttingen, Leiden, Paris, Strasbourg, and Jena, as a suitable destination for the dozen or so young Russians she planned to send abroad annually to gain a university education.[96] A number were registered in the colleges for the study of Greek, Hebrew, French, moral philosophy, and mathematics, the first four arriving in 1765–6. Several abandoned their studies because of debt or illness, but two Russian students were awarded MAs by diploma in 1775,[97] and there was a trickle of sons from the Russian aristocracy going to Oxford thereafter.[98]

Some of them conspicuously benefitted from their time at the University and gave much back, as Thomas Hornsby, Savilian Professor of Astronomy, acknowledged when he gave Vasily Nikitich Nikitin (1737–1809) of St Alban Hall a letter in Latin to take back to St Petersburg praising his contribution to the observation of the transit of Venus.[99] As this Russian presence indicated, the oaths which hindered non-Anglicans from either matriculating or taking degrees could, it appears, be circumvented when occasion demanded, though awards were not uncontested.[100] That Anglophile monarch, Stanislaw Poniatowski, king of Poland, Catherine's one-time lover, was happy to see a handful of Polish students study at either Oxford or Cambridge, and the fact that they were Roman Catholics proved an easy barrier to surmount. One Wasowicz returned home in 1768 with letters recommending him to his sovereign from the Vice-Chancellor of Oxford, David Durell, and Thomas Hornsby. Shortly afterwards, two other royal scholars, Zukowski and Glazer, were sent off to Oxford.[101] These contacts alerted leading Polish-Lithuanian academics to some of Oxford's modern facilities. The astronomers Fr Marcin Odlanicki Poczobutt (rector of Vilnius University 1780–99, a former Jesuit and an FRS from 1771) and the younger Jan Sniadecki (first a professor in Kraków, later himself rector of Vilnius University) expressed great

[96] Leipzig was soon added to this list: it was there that the future critic of social conditions in Russia, Alexander Radishchev, went in 1766. I owe this reference to Simon Dixon.

[97] These were Nikitin and Prokhor Ignat'evich Suvorov. ed. Goudie, *Hertford College*, 36.

[98] A. G. Cross, 'Russian students in eighteenth-century Oxford (1766–75)', *Journal of European Studies*, 5 (1975), 91–110; G. R. V. Barratt, 'Vasily Nikitin: a note on an eighteenth-century Oxonian', *Eighteenth-Century Studies*, 8 (1974–5), 75–99; Isabel de Madariaga, *Russia in the Age of Catherine the Great* (London, 1981), 502. A.G. Cross, *"By the Banks of the Thames": Russians in Eighteenth-century Britain* (Newtonville, MA, 1979), 319–35, gives a checklist of Russians in Britain, 1700–1800.

[99] Nikitin had the responsibility of supervising the other Russian students in Oxford. He was also a Freemason who attended the Alfred Lodge in the city. ed. Goudie, *Hertford College*, 35–6.

[100] James Woodforde noted the opposition to the bestowal of MAs by diploma on one occasion in Convocation: 'There were many *non Placets* from many Parts of the House, therefore the Proctors took each Members Voice by which the *Placets* had the Majority—I was a *Placet*. The Convocation House was very full on the Occasion'. ed. Hargeaves-Mawdley, *Woodforde at Oxford*, 286 (2 June 1775). Nikitin was one of two Russians receiving his degree.

[101] Butterwick, *Poland's Last King*, 234. By that date, Poland had for Oxonians outgrown its late seventeenth-century association with Whiggism suggested by its elected monarchy. See, for instance, the opening of Dryden's poem *The Medall, a satire against sedition* (1682).

576 ENLIGHTENED OXFORD

interest in the astronomical observatory as an extension of their fascination with William Herschel's discoveries at Slough.[102] Poczobutt was King Stanislaw's astronomer, director of the Vilnius Astronomical Observatory, and regularly in England for the purchase of astronomical equipment.

Students from Russia or the Orthodox East were seen by many High Churchmen as welcome in Oxford on three principal grounds: the suffering many had endured through living in the Ottoman Empire; their commitment to a patriarchal Catholic faith that rejected Roman primacy and had its own patristic tradition dear to many Anglicans; and the possibilities of ecumenical cooperation between Canterbury and Constantinople.[103] Though the Nonjuror schism weakened the number of established Anglicans who set store by contacts with Orthodoxy,[104] Benjamin Woodroffe (1638–1711), Canon of Christ Church since 1672, was prepared to take an initiative. It was one that had been originally suggested by Joseph Georgirenes, Metropolitan of Samos, to Archbishop Sancroft in 1682 on the basis of having twelve Greek students trained in the doctrines of the Church of England.[105]

A decade later, Woodroffe, appointed Principal of Gloucester Hall from 1692, revived the scheme and probably issued *A Model of a College to be settled in the University for the Education of some Youths of the Greek Church* around this time.[106] It proposed twenty youths from Greece aged fourteen to twenty, to be based at Gloucester Hall under Woodroffe as 'President and Head of the Greek College at Oxford'.[107] Neither Sancroft (before his deprivation) nor Compton, Bishop of London (subsequently) could accomplish anything quickly but then, in

---

[102] I am grateful to Richard Butterwick-Pawlikowski for this information.

[103] Diarmaid MacCulloch archly notes, 'After the Church of England had developed a High Church wing unique [to] Protestant Churches, those involved were interested in finding a respectably ancient alibi for their sacramentalist and sacerdotalist views which saved them from being accused of papist subversion, so Orthodoxy looked a promising milieu to explore'. *JEH*, 55 (2004), 410. For the relative ignorance in England of the theology of the Eastern Greek Church see Zwierlein, *Imperial Unknowns*, 118–42. Zwierlein points up the importance of Henry Dodwell's interest in the Greek Church while he was in post at Oxford before the Revolution of 1688. Ibid., 129–33, 137, 161.

[104] Eastern bishops were disconcerted to be told Nonjurors were outside the establishment; they also had problems with the Nonjuring bishops' insistence on ecclesiastical autonomy from the state. For their 1716 attempt at submission to the Patriarch of Jerusalem see ibid., 141, 171–2.

[105] There was at that date no express mention of Oxford. E. D. Tappe, 'The Greek College at Oxford, 1699–1705', in ed. P. Doll, *Anglicanism and Orthodoxy 300 years after the 'Greek College' in Oxford* (Oxford, 2006), 153–74, at 155. For the Greek perspective, V. N. Makrides, 'Greek Orthodox compensatory strategies towards Anglicans and the West at the beginning of the eighteenth century', in ibid., 249–88.

[106] Tappe, 'The Greek college', App. A, in ibid.

[107] He was thus described in a letter to Callinicus, Patriarch of Constantinople, dated 14 Mar. 1695. Lambeth MS. 951, f.1, quoted in E. Carpenter, *Protestant Bishop, Being the Life of Henry Compton, 1632–1713 Bishop of London* (London, 1956), 362. More details in Tappe, 'The Greek College', 159–60. Woodroffe encouraged foreigners to come to Gloucester Hall. His first student was a Frenchman. In 1703 the antiquary Edmund Chishull met a young Hungarian in Debrecen, Hungary, who had recently resided at Gloucester Hall. E. Chishull, *Travels in Turkey and back to England* (London, 1747), 106, quoted in ibid., 159.

OXFORD AND THE WIDER WORLD 577

early 1699, the Greek students came to Oxford—but not for long.[108] They were treated badly, and soon, tired of their poor accommodation, moved to Paris to enjoy Gallican hospitality instead, but not before Neophytus, Archbishop of Philippopolis, 'Exarch of all Thrace and Drovogia', received an honorary DD on 2 September 1701, with one speech of welcome delivered by Woodroffe and one in reply from the Archbishop 'all in plain proper hellenistick Greek'.[109] There was also the issue of the instruction the students had received. In 1706, Francis Prossalentis of Corfu—a former student—published a memoir of his time, in which he reportedly claimed the young Greeks were taught that the sign of the cross, the honouring of icons, keeping of fasts, and the Body and Blood of Christ in the Holy Liturgy were all 'Latin inventions'.

For whatever reason, the Oxford experience was so dispiriting that the Patriarch of Jerusalem, Gabriel III/Dositheus, in 1705 banned all further Greek students from going to there on pain of excommunication.[110] Even so, some of the Greeks retained in interest in the Church of England as they had experienced it in Oxford. For instance, Georgios Homeros, a schoolmaster at Smyrna, who had studied at the Greek College (he was in Oxford for a total of thirteen years), asked for books in Anglican theology to be sent out to him in 1713–14 so that he could introduce his own pupils to it.[111] And other prelates resident in Ottoman territories were undeterred from establishing contact with Oxford scholars. In July 1707 an Armenian was received in Oxford 'with a cargo of those books he has printed in his own language for the promoting of piety and learning'. With the help of Thomas Turner, President of Corpus Christi, he raised a subscription of £300 towards costs, an indicator of the extent of interest across the University in this exotic churchman.[112] Thereafter mutual fraternisation faded away until much

[108] 'The young Graecians are run away from Gloster Hall', William Adams to Thomas Tanner, quoted in J. A. W. Bennett, 'Oxford in 1699', *Oxoniensia*, 4 (1939), 147–52, at 149. In fact some remained for a few years longer. An ode in Greek hexameters was addressed to Queen Anne in Aug. 1702 by Simon Homerus, the senior Greek student. Tappe, 'The Greek college', 164.

[109] Ibid., App. B; E. Thwaites to Charlett, Bodl. MS Ballard 13, art. 22, quoted in ed. G. Williams, *The Orthodox Church of the East in the eighteenth century, being the correspondence between the Eastern Patriarchs and the Nonjuring Bishops* (London and Cambridge, 1868), xxii. Thwaites noted, 'He commended the English nation for hospitality; the Church of England, the University, the Chancellor's civility to him, the Vice-chancellor's kindness, & c., in very round periods'. Others in his entourage were honoured and they subsequently received comparable degrees from Cambridge.

[110] S. Runciman, *The great Church in captivity: a study of the patriarchate of Constantinople from the eve of the Turkish conquest to the Greek War of Independence* (Cambridge, 1968), 300–4, 310–18; J. Pinnington, *Anglicans and Orthodox. Unity and subversion 1559–1725* (Leominster, 2003), 100, 107; Tappe, 'The Greek college', 169. For Edward Stephens (*c*.1633–1706), latterly a Nonjuring lawyer and philo-Orthodox, and his schemes for a Greek College in Oxford that predated the Gloucester Hall project, and lodgings and accommodation for Greek students in London after the Woodroffe scheme flagged, see ibid., 163–4; H. A. N. Hallam, 'The anonymous pamphleteer: a checklist of the writings of Edward Stephens (1633–1706)', *BLR*, 18 (2005), 502–31; Carpenter, *Protestant bishop*, 363; Tappe, 'The Greek college', 164.

[111] Zwierlein, *Imperial Unknowns*, 170.

[112] Robert Nelson to Arthur Charlett, 22 May 1707, Ascension Day, in Walker, *Letters written by Eminent persons*, II. 167; Bishop Henry Compton to Charlett, n.d. [1707], Bodl. MS Ballard 9, f. 62.

578   ENLIGHTENED OXFORD

later in the century when Graeco/Ottoman ties resumed through the person of
Adamantios Korais (1748–1833), born at Smyrna, then resident in Amsterdam
before moving to Paris in 1789. In the west, this leading classicist was known as
Adamance Coray, and sought the resurgence of Greece as an independent nation.
He was for many years in correspondence with the Clarendon Press, received a
regular stipend from Oxford, and was even considered for a chair at the
University. All this despite Britain being at war with France.[113]

iii) Oxford and the Republic of Letters

The University took its place in the 'Republic' for granted. In its origins it was the
Respublica litterarum sacrarum, a self-conscious community of European scholars
exchanging ideas and developing strategies for mining the scriptures, patristic
texts, and Church history.[114] And though, at the turn of the eighteenth century,
'sacred letters' retained pride of place in any unofficial scholarly hierarchy, other
disciplinary endeavours that bound together the learned were recognised as
deserving of honour for they represented an effort to embrace a vernacular,
more public world.[115] The 'Republic' was by definition an entity whose citizens
were self-selected and subscribed to a set of humane values that transcended
confessional and dynastic allegiance, though it undoubtedly had its own hierarchies, prejudices, and enmities.[116] In certain circumstances, war for instance, allegiance would be subordinated to considerations of national loyalty but, on the
whole, so long as this polity was taken to subsist (as it did through to the 1740s at
least) Oxford men were proud to participate. Learned friendships at a distance
with their counterparts on the continent were the most obvious sign of individual
membership of this 'Republic', making up what one writer has recently called 'an
invaluable information highway for scholarly enterprise'.[117] And the continued

[113] See ed. Paschalis M. Kitromilides, *Adamantios Korais and the European Enlightenment* (Oxford,
2010).
[114] D. K. Shuger, *The Renaissance Bible: scholarship, sacrifice, and subjectivity* (Los Angeles, CA,
1994), 12–17. See also Anthony Grafton, 'A sketch map of a lost continent: the Republic of Letters', in
his *Worlds made by words: scholarship and community in the modern West* (Cambridge, MA, 2009),
9–34; Marc Fumaroli, *La République des Lettres* (Paris, 2015).
[115] M. Ultee, 'The Republic of Letters: learned correspondence 1680–1720', *Seventeenth Century*,
2 (1987), 95–112.
[116] Andrea Rusnock, 'Correspondence networks and the Royal Society, 1700–1750', *BJHS*, 32
(1999), 155–69, notes, aptly, that 'Hierarchy, centralization and social status shaped the form and
content of science by correspondence' (169).
[117] Keene, 'John Ernest Grabe', 664. See also K. L. Haugen, 'Academic charisma and the old regime',
History of Universities, 22/1 (2007) 76–130, at 219–23; eds. H. Bots and F. Waquet, *Commercium
litterarium: forms of communication in the Republic of Letters* (Amsterdam, 1994). Moyra Haslett has
perceptively noted the 'apparent paradox' whereby 'a virtual community becomes more significant than
a literal community'. Haslett, 'Swift and Conversational Culture', *Eighteenth-Century Ireland*, 29
(2014), 11–30, at 12.

OXFORD AND THE WIDER WORLD   579

use of Latin by the Chancellor's Secretary (for so long William King) in much of the University's official correspondence with continental institutions of higher education was another token of this learned fraternisation.[118] As was, at a less official level, the routine offering by John Hudson of Oxford of review copies of books published by the University Press to continental learned journals, early in the century.[119]

Individuals could, of course, be singled out for recognition of services rendered to the world of letters through an eminent publication, especially when the author's political stance aroused Oxonian sympathies. Thus Andrew Michael Ramsay's 1730 DCL *honoris causa* was quite an achievement for a Scottish Frenchman, a Catholic convert, and Freemason, someone courted by the Royal Society.[120] Onlookers could speculate whether it was more for his bestselling utopian *Voyages de Cyrus* (1727, 4th edn., 1730) that he received his degree—or for his Jacobite loyalism.[121]

In fact it was primarily his *Essay upon Civil Government* that was republished in 1732 so that it could be included in the University's polemical armoury, along with other works perceived to refute Locke's claims regarding civil society.[122] Collective academic amity could also be expressed through sign and ritual, like the Encaenia-style ceremony held in Oxford in commemoration of the King of Prussia's new University of Frankfurt-an-der-Oder in 1706. Degrees were awarded, and George Smalridge (deputy Professor of Divinity) gave an encomium on Grabe, made DD on the occasion. Grabe was given 'a Ring, signifying that the University of Oxford and Francfurt were now joyn'd together and become two Sisters, and that they might be more firmly united together as well in Learning as in Religion', whereupon Smalridge kissed Grabe.[123] This was a visible mapping-out exercise of the 'Republic' within England that could operate in the reverse

---

[118] Greenwood, *William King*, 13.

[119] Haugen, *Richard Bentley*, 130. Brockliss (2), 303, notes that Hudson was a regular correspondent of Lorenzo Alessandro Zacagni, the Vatican Librarian (1657–1712).

[120] He is reported to have said on the occasion that '... our buildings at Oxford [were] good, but too much crowded'. Spence, *Observations*, I. 454.

[121] Hearne, X. 264; G. Glickman, 'Andrew Michael Ramsay (1686–1743), the Jacobite court and the English Catholic Enlightenment', *Eighteenth-Century Thought*, 3 (2007), 293–329. Ramsay's syncretic religious world is treated in M. Baldi, *Philosophie et politique chez Andrew Michael Ramsay* (Paris, 2008), his Jacobitism in Andrew Mansfield, *Ideas of monarchical reform. Fénelon, Jacobitism and the political works of the Chevalier Ramsay* (Manchester, 2015), 172–3. Livesey, *Civil society and empire*, 119, considers links between Ramsay and the prominent Jacobites Lord Forbes of Pitsligo, and Nathaniel Hooke.

[122] Mansfield, *Ideas of monarchical reform*, 162; Clark, *English Society* (1985), 152–3. The degree award had led to regular correspondence between Ramsay with King and Carte. Ramsey to Carte, 22 Nov. 1736, Bodl Carte MSS. 226, f. 419.

[123] Hearne, I. 235 (26 Apr. 1706). For Grabe, see this chapter and A. Tindal Hart, *The Life and Times of John Sharp Archbishop of York* (London, 1949), 269. He was highly regarded by contemporaries. For instance, Hickes to Charlett, 10 Nov. 1711: 'He was certainly the greatest man in divine literature, as well as the greatest example of Christian piety, of this age, and as St Ignatius said of St Paul, I wish I may be worthy to sit under his feet in heaven'. Walker, *Letters written by Eminent persons*, II. 221.

Fig. 11.4 Frontispiece, *Voyage de Cyrus*, Chevalier Ramsay (Bodleian Libraries, University of Oxford).

direction. For instance, a delegation went from Cambridge University in 1706 to attend the inauguration of the new university at Frankfurt. With an eye on the future, only the Cambridge delegation called at the Hanoverian court en route.[124]

Oxford, with its hopes over-centred on Queen Anne and averse to looking too far ahead, sent no comparable party to either bid for dynastic favour or consolidate academic fraternity. Yet Oxford's external outreach is not to be underestimated, though it has been overlain through scholarly concentration on the growth of learned (particularly 'scientific') societies since the mid-seventeenth century, often enjoying royal patronage and based in capital cities. Certainly, societies made up of self-organising groups of scholars and scientists based in cities as diverse as London, Oxford, Dublin, and Boston were flourishing c.1700,[125] but a high proportion of their members consisted of men with university qualifications and positions. In extending and cherishing their contacts with foreign savants,

---

[124] See Andrew Hanham, 'Caroline of Brandenburg-Ansbach and the "anglicisation" of the House of Hanover', in ed. C. Campbell Orr, *Queenship in Europe, 1660–1815. The Role of the Consort* (Cambridge, 2004), 276–99, at 284; BL Add MS 7075, ff. 73–99.

[125] J. McCleelan, *Science reorganized: scientific societies in the eighteenth century* (New York, 1985), 57.

they were not necessarily subordinating their academic status to the societal one. The two went together in the processes of cultural transfer and the structuring of the Republic of Letters. With confessional loyalties (especially those between Anglicans and Catholics) seen as having marginal consequences by the mid-century, there was rarely any shortage of energy in trying to develop new sorts of academic and amicable contacts. Thomas Hunt, Professor of Hebrew, thus commended Gregory Sharp in 1753 (Master of the Temple, 1763–71, and a Cambridge graduate) for his efforts:

> The Correspondence you have establish'd with the Academies you mention will be very useful, as it will be a means of letting you know what is doing by learned Foreigners, which is a piece of literary knowledge, which I think we much want in this Island.[126]

If there was one exception to this breadth of outreach during the years between the Revolution and the accession of George I, it was contacts with Switzerland. Oxford for much of that era continued to entertain a hearty suspicion of Geneva as the original stronghold of Calvinism. Twice in the later years of Henry Compton's tenure of the see of London (1700 and 1705) did this Tory bishop receive complaints from several professors and then the pastors of the city about poetry produced in Oxford, the latter 'approved of the University and under its Name offered to the Queen by the Title of *Strena Oxononiensis*'. Bishop Compton, on the second occasion, pressured the University to be gracious, and the reply of 12 February 1706, signed by George Cooper, Notary Public, more or less emolliently talked of not condemning ' . . . the Reformed Churches, which by an irresistible Necessity, were forced to recede from the primitive form of Episcopal Government, . . .' Polite letters were exchanged between the University and the Pastors for a little longer but there was only a show of rapprochement.[127] It was not until the early Hanoverian era, encouraged by George I and facilitated by the decline of rigorous Calvinist attitudes within the Swiss Churches, that any qualms about dealing with Swiss scholars (often pastors) as fellow members of the Republic of Letters gradually dissipated.

That 'Republic' contained innumerable networks of scholarly communication, many of which flowed to and around Oxford. Sometimes the services of a British envoy or a member of his entourage would be sought to open up contacts. Thus Thomas Hunt required the good offices of the Rev Dr John Jeffreys, British embassy chaplain in Paris, to try and secure the cooperation of the Sorbonne

---

[126] Bodl. Ms Eng. lett. d. 146, f. 49, Aug 1753.

[127] Carpenter, *Protestant Bishop*, 346–9; Compagnie de Pasteurs et Professeurs de l'Eglise et de l'Académie de Genève, *Several Letters from the Pastors of the Church of Geneva, to the Archbishop of Canterbury, the Bishop of London, and the University of Oxford; with their answers . . . Translated from the Latin and the French* (London, 1707).

582 ENLIGHTENED OXFORD

savant, Charles Gillot (a considerable Latinist), in setting up a series of learned exchanges.[128] Not content with requesting the young James Harris (envoy-extraordinary to the British embassy in Berlin) to procure access for one of his assistants to all royal and other manuscripts in Berlin, Kennicott went on to have Harris add the name of Frederick the Great to the subscription list for his magnum opus on the basis that '...the Learned at Berlin [are]...strong in favour of my work;...'[129] Robert Holmes sought Henry Addington's aid as one of the 'friends of sacred Learning' to act as a go-between in Florence so that payment could be rendered to Angiolo Maria Bandini, Keeper of the Grand Duke's Library, who was collating for him all the Greek manuscripts of the Septuagint that the Library contained. He noted that 'Lord Hervey is Envoy at Florence: and if I know how to obtain his Lordship's consent to make payments, as they shall become due to Bandini, and to forward collations to me in any of the dispatches he may send to this country; my difficulty in this respect would be at an end'.[130]

It could be simply a matter of gift-giving, a goodwill gesture of largesse, whereby a presentation copy set up or reinforced friendly links that rested on mutual obligation and gratitude.[131] Thus when in 1787 Lord North, as Chancellor, learnt that the bibliophile Charles-François-Simeon de Vermandois de Rouvroy de Saint Simon Sandricourt, Bishop of Agde (1759–94) in south-west France, stood in need of editions of Euripides, Theocritus, and Cicero, he asked his friend Anthony Storer to use the good offices of William Eden (on ambassadorial duties at Versailles), to forward Oxford textual editions to the Bishop as a personal present.[132] A gift offered at the highest level by a foreign court to the University could potentially benefit Britain's international standing when graciously received. In 1775, at a tricky time in relations with the Bourbon powers as rebellion erupted in British North America, the chaplain at the British Embassy in Madrid, Robert Darley Waddilove, enquired of Vice-Chancellor

---

[128] Bodl. Ms Eng. lett. d. 146, 8 Aug 1753, ff. 51, 57–9. Hunt promised he would even talk to Lord Macclesfield, PRS, about making Gillot FRS next time he saw that peer. Hunt to Jeffreys, 19 Oct. 1753, f. 63.

[129] Kennicott to Harris, 23 Dec. 1772, Hants RO, 9M73/G142; same to same, 11 Mar. 1773, Hants RO, 9M73/G158/144. Kennicott planned, if Frederick II was willing, to lay his proposals before the German Electoral Princes, including the three ecclesiastical Electors.

[130] Holmes to Addington, St Giles', Oxford, 9 July 1788, Devon RO 152M/C1788/F28. Holmes was another scholar who intended to make use of Sir James Harris, his old Winchester College school contemporary, hoping that Harris (by this date envoy in St Petersburg) would facilitate access to the Septuagint MSS that Holmes knew to be in the city.

[131] For contextual background on gifts within the intricacies of diplomatic exchange see F. Heal, The Power of Gifts: Gift Exchange in Early Modern England (Oxford, 2014) and, classically, M. Mauss, The Gift: The Form and Reason for Exchange in Archaic Societies, trans. W. D. Halls (London, 1990). See Françoise Waquet, Respublica academica. Rituels universitaires et genres du savoie (xvii–xxi siècles) (Paris, 2010) for an essay on gifts in an academic context.

[132] Storer to Eden, 11 May 1787, in ed. Bishop of Bath & Wells, The Journal and Correspondence of William, Lord Auckland (4 vols., London, 1861), I. 420. North may have felt it appropriate not to contact Eden directly in the light of the latter's celebrated desertion of the Opposition in 1785.

OXFORD AND THE WIDER WORLD   583

Thomas Fothergill whether Oxford would graciously receive the gift of a volume of the works of Sallust translated into Spanish by Don Gabriel, 4th son of Carlos III, king of Spain. It was at once accepted, and the University returned a letter of thanks to the king for his gifts to the Bodleian and praising his son for his learning. Spain did not declare war against Britain for another four years.[133] Even when there was no pressing diplomatic onus, Convocation was ever ready to be steered towards offering thanks for a gift, such as the books relating to the discoveries at Herculaneum sent on by Carlos of Naples (Carlos VII) in 1755, aware of the excitement they had kindled at Oxford.[134] One Oxford appointment was due directly to the growth by the mid-century of international circles devoted to the cultivation of natural history. This was the placing of Johann Jakob Dillenius of Giessen in the new Sherardian chair of botany, a nomination made in 1728 on his death by William Sherard, (he had put aside funds to endow the professorship) who had seven years earlier attracted Dillenius from Germany, to become the first President of the London Botanical Society.[135]

At the heart of the 'Republic' was the passing on of information adjudged useful to learned colleagues. After the French philosopher and Newtonian scientist Pierre-Louis Moreau de Maupertuis had returned from his Lapland expedition of 1736 to measure the shape of the Earth, he contacted James Bradley in Oxford with a request that he communicate to the Royal Society information that, in the light of his visit, the flatness of Earth appeared more considerable than Newton deemed it and that gravity increased towards the Pole and diminished more towards the Equator.[136] Or it might be simply scholar nurturing and encouraging scholar. The career of Thomas Burgess, one of the University's brightest hopes in the 1780s, was thus nourished by his correspondence with Daniel Albert Wyttenbach (1746–1820), a German Swiss classical scholar, exponent of rigorous textual criticism in classical studies, whose own connections with Oxford were originally mediated by John Randolph.[137] Wyttenbach was Professor of Greek, History, and Philosophy at the University of Amsterdam for twenty years from 1779, and gained renown for his edition of Plutarch. The first (four) volumes were the *Moralia* (1795–6) and, thanks to the Burgess link, they were published by the Clarendon Press.[138]

---

[133] 9 July 1775, Bedfordshire & Luton Archives, Wrest Park (Lucas) MSS, L30/14/292/1–4.

[134] Bodl. MS Top Oxon. d.174, f. 209.

[135] R. Houlbrooke, *Britain and Europe 1500–1700* (London, 2011), 296.

[136] Letter of 27 Sept. 1737 enclosed in one from Colin MacLaurin to James Stirling.

[137] A. J. Brothers, 'Burgess and the Classics: A Letter of April 1792', 41–50; M. Smith, 'Thomas Burgess, Churchman and Reformer', 5–40, both in ed. N. Yates, *Bishop Burgess and his World. Culture, Religion and Society in Britain, Europe and North America in the Eighteenth and Nineteenth Centuries* (Cardiff, 2007). Burgess made research visits to Holland and Paris in 1784 and 1787.

[138] R. Darwall-Smith, 'Daniel Wyttenbach and the Clarendon Press', in ed. L. Van der Stockt, *Plutarchea Lovaniensia: a miscellany of essays on Plutarch* (Louvain, 1996), 53–77.

584 ENLIGHTENED OXFORD

Most virtual roads led not to Amsterdam but to Göttingen, for Thomas Biskup '...*the* university of the age of Enlightenment, ...'[139] a constant focus for creative cultural exchange with Britain (and Oxford in particular), staffed by a professoriat that saw their English partners as members of an international community of scholars. And some reformist observers came to view this new creation as producing students of a much higher calibre than its older English counterparts. As an anonymous newspaper writer put it in 1799:

> Oxford & Cambridge, sisters two/With prejudice begotten in,/Your tasselled Commoners should embue/Their minds with knowledge from the/University of Gottingen[140]

Nevertheless, Oxford academics were regularly honoured in Göttingen, certainly after the Anglo-Hanoverian union became comprehensively acceptable to Oxford opinion after *c*.1760. Thus, for example, both Lowth (a correspondent of the German dramatist and philosopher, Gotthold Ephraim Lessing) and Kennicott were elected into Göttingen Royal Society of Sciences in 1766; exactly two decades later, Thomas Hornsby, Professor of Astronomy, and Edward Waring, his Cambridge counterpart, received the same award.[141] A linchpin of the connection was the theologian Johann David Michaelis, 'the most accomplished Orientalist of the eighteenth century', crucial mediator of English scholarship to the German-speaking world, and one who found favour with George III and Queen Charlotte.[142] He corresponded with Kennicott on textual variations and with Lowth on Hebrew poetry, for both of them had a fund of information unobtainable elsewhere.[143] Mutual admiration did not preclude mutual sniping: Michaelis eventually fell out with Kennicott when he criticised the latter's Bible edition for being based on too narrow a source, while Kennicott, offering page-by-page

---

[139] Biskup, 'The university of Göttingen', 159. He argues that 'It was *British* scholarship which benefited most from the Gottingen connection, ...', ibid., 143. For the predominance of Britons among western Europeans going to Göttingen and Halle see N. Hammerstein, 'Die deutschen Universitäten im Zeitalter der Aufklärung', *Zeitschrift für historische Forschung*, 10 (1983), 73–89.

[140] 'Iterumque iterumque', from the *Morning Herald* 2 Apr., 1799, Lincs Archives, BNLW 4/8/1/130. It went on: 'Johnson and Milton ye can shew/or tell the graves they're rotting in,/But what are they to Kotzebue/Who studied morals at the/University of Gottingen'. For a favourable comparison of Oxford and its students with their German equivalents see *Letters of Baron Bielfeld, containing Original Anecdotes of the Prussian Court for the last Twenty Years, trans. from the original German by Mr Hooper* (4 vols., London, 1768–70), IV. 176–80.

[141] Hornsby's reputation in Germany was well-established. Georg Christoph Lichtenberg from Göttingen, after visiting Hornsby at the Observatory and marvelling at the capacities of his telescope, told his friend Johann Christian Schernhagen: 'Can you imagine ... a telescope through which stars of the fifth, and even of the sixth, magnitude can be seen, sometimes in broad daylight, at four o'clock on a summer afternoon. This can be done with Mr Hornsby's transit instrument.' Kew, 17 Oct. 1775, in *Lichtenberg's visits to England as described in his letters and diaries*, trans. Margaret L. Mare and W. H. Quarrell (Oxford, 1938), 99.

[142] Legaspi, *The death of scripture*, 5, 37–45, 81.

[143] For these comments see Biskup, 'The university of Göttingen', 140, 143, 146.

OXFORD AND THE WIDER WORLD   585

comments 'on this new [1778] edition of the Goettingen Professor', complained to Lowth that he had been 'shamefully' misrepresented on several pages.[144] The *Index nominum* to Kennicott's two folio volumes gives an idea of the extent of his interchange of ideas across national and denominational frontiers. Michaelis's name was there. As was the French Oratorian Fr Charles François Houbigant (*c*.1686/7–*c*.1783/4), perhaps the chief Biblical scholar of eighteenth-century France (he published a four-volume edition of the Pentateuch in 1753) and Kennicott's regular correspondent. He also wanted to emerge with the genuine Hebrew text of the Bible, though without collating as many original manuscripts as Kennicott. It was on the latter's brows that the learned world agreed to place the laurels.[145]

However strained they might be by individual rivalries and *odium theologicum*, such connections sharpened a sense of institutional mutuality that was as much for bad times as for good. Oxford and Oxonians showed a constant readiness to offer help to continental centres of learning fallen into difficulty. It was usually more a gesture than a full-scale rescue package, like the five guineas offered to the University of Debrecen in Hungary in 1756 by the common room of Corpus Christi.[146] Individuals within the University might take the initiative in making the case for particular charities. Few causes appeared worthier in the early 1730s than the persecuted Protestants of Salzburg, many of whom came to Britain as refugees. Prompted by the SPCK, which sent a copy of an appeal to every Oxford college, the Rev. Thomas Wilson of Christ Church (son of the Bishop of the Sodor & Man) and Joseph Smith, Provost of Queen's, brought their plight to the attention of the hebdomadal board with a view to encouraging generous giving.[147] This was a case of confessional solidarity with continental Protestantism that had many precedents, whereas the arrival of penurious scholar-clergy in Oxford sixty years later had none. They were Gallican Catholics driven out of their presbyteries by a principled refusal to swear an oath to the Civil Constitution of the Clergy (1790–1) as the French Revolutionaries demanded.[148] The Vice-Chancellor was a founder member of the Wilmot Relief Committee while colleges and individuals were quick to offer them some level of practical relief: £1,123 had been raised by

---

[144] This was Michaelis's German translation of the Bible with notes that appeared between 1773 and 1792. Ibid., 146n.; Beinecke Library, Yale University, Osborn Files 8319, Kennicott to Lowth, Windsor, 17 Aug 1778.

[145] Deconinck-Brossard, 'England and France in the Eighteenth Century', 155, 160.

[146] 22 June 1756, Fowler, *Corpus Christi College*, 288.

[147] Henry Newman to George Fothergill, 23 June 1733, Queen's College MS. 473; ed. Linnell, *Diaries of Thomas Wilson*, 63, 94, 85, 95, 107. For the background see M. Walker, *The Salzburg Transaction. Expulsion and Redemption in Eighteenth-Century Germany* (Ithaca, NY, 1992); W. R. Ward, *The Protestant Evangelical Awakening* (Cambridge, 1992), 308–9.

[148] Dominic Aidan Bellenger, '"Fearless resting place": the Exiled French Clergy in Great Britain', in eds. K. Carpenter and P. Manse l, *The French Emigrés in Europe and the struggle against Revolution, 1789-1814* (Basingstoke, 1999), 214–29.

586   ENLIGHTENED OXFORD

the end of 1792 within Oxford for the Gallican clergy in England.[149] Having mostly come to England without any books, the University also in time acted to satisfy some of their spiritual needs. Convocation in March 1796 thus voted that 2,000 copies of the New Testament in Latin should be produced by the University Press for their use.[150] Neither were they forgotten in death. The Warden of New College paid out of his own pocket for the burial at Dorchester abbey of the Abbé Thoumin des Valpons, formerly Archdeacon and Vicar General of the diocese of Dol.[151]

There is a strong case for seeing the hospitality offered in Oxford to learned refugees from the Revolution as following naturally from convergent paths trodden for upwards of a century in defence of the Christian faith as central to the health, security, and identity of the polity in France as in England.[152] Dale K. Van Kley, for instance, arguing that devout Catholicism (as he calls it) was 'a catalyst in the creation of a mode of political thought that, well before...the French Revolution, preached the need for a union between absolute thrones and a single papal altar' finds Anglo-Saxon counterparts among Anglican leaders he calls 'latter-day Laudians', such as Horne and Horsley, 'who came up with a comparable ideology uniting Hanoverian throne and Anglican miter against the twin menace of religious dissidence and political radicalism'.[153] The analogy is at best a rough fit but it is rightly suggestive of a sense of common problems facing orthodox churchmen and indicative of the defences they were busy constructing as antidotes to the cultural incertitude and anxiety of the 1770s and 1780s.[154] An attack on the established Church was deemed in these quarters inseparable from an attack on the Crown. That was the reading Horne and his allies attached to the campaign for repeal of the Test and Corporation Acts in the late 1780s and would see confirmed by the way events played out in France during the 1790s. It was

---

[149] See Dominic Aidan Bellenger, *The French Exiled Clergy in the British Isles after 1789* (Bath, 1986), 31. Funds continued to be raised thereafter, St John's College, for instance, collecting a further 30 guineas for their relief in 1796. Coll. Reg. viii. 31, cited in Costin, *St John's College*, 240.

[150] Vice-Chancellor to Bp de la Marche of St Pol de Léon (the leader of the exiled clergy in England), 1 May 1796, in which he stated his pleasure at cooperating 'in your pious Endeavours to cherish & promote the Studies & investigation of the Grounds of the Christian Faith'. John Wills's Letter book, Balliol College Archives and Manuscripts, Jenkyns VI.A (2), f. 146; Cox, *Recollections*, 11, 21.

[151] B. Stapleton, *Catholic Missions in Oxfordshire* (London, 1906), 247–8.

[152] cf. F. Deconinck-Brossard, 'A vast body of evidence may lead to the conclusion that devotional literature and religious books circulated widely in European ecclesiastical circles, across national borders and denominational frontiers'. 'The Art of Preaching' in ed. J. van Eijnatten, *Preaching, sermon and cultural change in the long eighteenth century* (Leiden, 2009), 95–130, at 107.

[153] Van Kley, 'Religion and the age of "Patriot Reform"', in *JMH*, 80 (2008), 252–95, at 287.

[154] Didier Masseau, 'Quelques réflexions sur la crise de l'apologétique à la fin de l'Ancien Régime', in ed. Nicolas Brucker, *Apologétique 1650–1802. La nature et la grâce* (Berne, 2010) [*Recherches en littérature et spiritualité*, vol. 18, ed. Gérard Nauroy]), 375–90. Cf. Justin Champion, who sets up a case for theological instability and some of the continuities between France and England in '"May the last king be strangled in the bowels of the last priest": Irreligion and the English Enlightenment, 1649-1789', in eds. T. Morton and N. Smith, *Radicalism in British literary culture, 1650–1830. From Revolution to Revolution* (Cambridge, 2002), 29–44.

OXFORD AND THE WIDER WORLD 587

comparable to arguments adopted in France by those defending the rights of the Gallican episcopacy against richériste lower clergy, aggressive in asserting their status, such as Le Corgne de Launay, anti-Jansenist professor at the Sorbonne, who deemed the Puritans' assault against Anglican episcopacy in 1640 the prelude to a drama that could only have ended with the trial and execution of Charles I.[155]

Central to the classic Anglican and Gallican self-definition in the long eighteenth century was affirming the pre-eminence of the episcopate and the sovereign's temporal power.[156] Oxonians were to the fore in the three decades after the Revolution of 1688 in establishing the resemblances to William Wake's research on medieval councils which had drawn on the Gallican historiographical tradition (Mabillon especially), and with Joseph Bingham looking at common ecclesiastical origins in the early Christian centuries. As Bruno Neveu put it, 'On both sides of the Channel, for half a century at least, a kind of brilliant era of ecclesiastical erudition opened up'.[157] Both Churches appealed to the Fathers as foundational, but Oxford scholars were at pains to articulate a rationale that was distinguishable from Roman Catholic doctrines of tradition. In this they followed the lead of Henry Dodwell, for all that he had resigned his posts and joined the Nonjurors in 1691. In the end, much depended on which of the Fathers one chose to follow, Gallicans preferring those of the fourth and fifth centuries, Dodwell and his followers the ante-Nicene ones.[158] One classic apology for the position of the Church of England on its patristic understanding can be found in the *Defensio ecclesiae Anglicanae* (1707, 1708), the work of the liturgist William Nicholls (1664–1712), a former Fellow of Merton, deliberately composed to inform continental scholars of formularies of the Church of England that attracted much attention in learned circles across the Channel.[159]

Theological developments at Oxford and the Sorbonne tended to take part in isolation and formal contacts between the two were necessarily limited because of confessional barriers. It might have been otherwise had Archbishop Wake's hopes for some kind of rapprochement between the Anglican and Gallican Churches come to fruition during the Regency of Philippe, Duc d'Orléans (1715–22), when the French Church rekindled the sense of its liberties that

---

[155] See his *Les droits de l'épiscopat sur le second ordre, pour toutes les fonctions du ministère ecclésiastique* (n.p., 1760), 3–5, quoted in Van Kley, 'Religion and the Age of "Patriot Reform"', 287.

[156] McManners, *Church and Society in Eighteenth-Century France*, I. 7–94; Georges Ascoli, *La Grande-Bretagne devant l'opinion française au xvii siècle* (2 vols., Paris, 1930), I. 408ff., II 314–17.

[157] Bruno Neveu, *Erudition et religion au xvii et xviii siècles* (Paris, 1994), 223 (my translation). Neveu instances the praise extended by Bishop Bossuet on behalf of the French clergy, communicated to George Bull (later Bishop of St David's) for his *Defensio fidei Nicaenae* of 1685.

[158] Jean-Louis Quantin, *The Church of England and Christian Antiquity. The Construction of a Confessional Identity in the 17th Century* (Oxford, 2009), 369, 382, 390, 398, 401–2.

[159] Wells, *Wadham College*, 121. Nicholls took his BA at Wadham in 1683, then moved to Merton. He became a Canon of Chichester in 1707. His later produced his *Comment on the Book of Common Prayer* (1710). Robert D. Cornwall, 'Nicholls, William (1664–1712), theologian', *ODNB*, online edn., 2006. Cf. Edmund Chishull, *The Orthodoxy of an English Clergy-Man, . . .* (London, 1711).

588 ENLIGHTENED OXFORD

had so lately, as it seemed to many, been encroached on by the papacy following the publication of the Bull *Unigenitus*. Correspondence with Gallican leaders was initiated in 1716 by Joseph Wilcocks (fellow of Magdalen College 1703–22) but, for a variety of reasons, not least political expediency, Wake did not much deploy High Church clergy in this exercise in outreach and the result was a marginalisation of Oxford luminaries in the exchanges that arguably hindered his diplomacy.[160]

Jansenism inevitably complicated the picture and Oxonian interests in the disputes that periodically rocked the Gallican Church in the first half of the century remain to be systematically mapped though appear to be thin.[161] Pascal was increasingly recognised as a keen psychologist and religious philosopher on account of his *Pensées*, translated by Basil Kennett, briefly President of Corpus Christi College.[162] Other founding Jansenists also attracted notice: Thomas Turner, Kennett's predecessor, possessed a copy of Antoine Arnauld's *De la fréquente communion*, while William Wake had a copy of the edition printed at Lyon in 1683.[163] There were occasional contacts in the present day, as in 1729 when the Jansenist Abbé Etemare visited England in 1729 and met several savants and examined their libraries.[164] The influence of Jansenism within Anglicanism was more for its mystical tendencies than for its Augustinian theological politics.[165] John Wesley translated about one third of Saint-Cyran's *Instructions chrétiennes* while George Horne was a constant reader of Pierre Quesnel, whose method of writing he adopted for his own *Commentary on the Book of Psalms*.[166] He thoroughly approved of the New Testament written with a plain commentary by one 'who had a great talent in speaking to the heart'.[167] Edward Gibbon also owed an immense debt to Jansenism in the shape of the great historian Le Nain de

---

[160] Jacques Gres-Gayer, *Paris-Cantorbéry 1717–1720: le dossier d'un premier oecuménisme* (Paris, 1989); Sykes, *Wake*, I. 257, 279, 299; Norman Sykes, 'Ecumenical Movements in Great Britain in the Seventeenth and Eighteenth Centuries', in eds. Ruth Rouse and Stephen C. Neill, *A History of the Ecumenical Movement 1517–1948* (3rd edn., Geneva, 1986), 123–67, at 154–8. Wilcocks, a Whig high churchman, became a king's chaplain and was made Bishop of Gloucester in 1721, both sure indicators of his court politics after 1714. E.I. Carlyle, rev. Richard Sharp, 'Wilcocks, Joseph (1673–1756)', *ODNB*, online edn., 2011.

[161] In 1725, there were Whig estimates that two-thirds of the French clergy were Jansenists. Gabriel Glickman, 'The church and the Catholic community', at 235. For the under-examined Whig press interest in Jansenism see Blanning, *The culture of power*, 15n.

[162] Palmer, *Jansenism and England*, 62.

[163] Palmer, *Jansenism and England*, 58. Even the Whig bishop Gilbert Burnet praised Jansen's industry as a translator of St Augustine. Ibid., 60n., 203, 210–11. For Jacobites and Jansenism see Glickman, *The English Catholic Community*, 186.

[164] Neveu, *Erudition et religion*, 288.

[165] See Palmer, *Jansenism and England*, 56. Ruth Clark, *Strangers and Sojourners at Port Royal* (Cambridge, 1932), 262, 264, notes that William Law the Nonjuror was a reader of Jansenist books. The influence of Jansenism on contemporary English Catholicism is considered in Glickman, *The English Catholic Community*, 15–16, 175–88, 224–9, 238–9, 249–51.

[166] See *A Commentary on the Book of Psalms* (2 vols., Oxford, 1790 edn.), Preface, ix, xi, xvi.

[167] Letter written to a lady in 1758. Horne, *Works*, I. 231.

OXFORD AND THE WIDER WORLD   589

Tillemont, whose influence in the construction of *The Decline and Fall* cannot be exaggerated.[168]

Inasmuch as it was considered at all, there was a recognition that mainstream Gallicanism manifested a religious spirit well-disposed to High Church *iure divino* clericalism divested of deference to the curia. A particular Gallican favourite was Pierre-François Le Courayer, late canon regular and Librarian of Ste. Geneviève in Paris, author of *Dissertation sur la validité des ordinations des Anglais* (1723), who received an Oxford DD by diploma in 1727 in absentia for writings on the apostolic legitimacy of the Anglican clergy and his translations of anti-papal writings.[169] He also translated the influential Fra Paolo Sarpi's *Istoria del Concilio Tridentino* into French, and published a memoir of Sarpi in 1736.[170] By that date Le Courayer had managed to capture the attention of Queen Caroline for his anti-ultramontane sympathies and that in itself did Oxford's standing no harm.[171] His writings played their part in ensuring that curiosity about things Gallican was thereafter periodically reignited.[172]

By the 1740s, academic patristic studies may have been in decline but the old Republic of Letters recognisably persisted for the remainder of the century, and from it had arisen into healthy, independent, and predominant existence what may for convenience be termed the European Enlightenment in all its variety.[173] Given the internationalist dimension to many of its networks of epistolary exchange, Oxford's intellectual life at mid-century unavoidably stood in relation to that movement and, to an underestimated extent, partook of its complex cosmopolitanism and sponsorship of innovation.[174] Oxford had a capacity for

---

[168] David Jordan, 'Le Nain de Tillemont: Gibbon's "sure-footed mule"', *Church History*, 39 (1970), 483–502; B. Young, 'Gibbon and Catholicism', in eds. K. O'Brien and B. Young, *The Cambridge companion to Edward Gibbon* (Cambridge, 2011), 147–66, at 154–9. See also J-L Quantain, 'The reception of Tillemont in England before Gibbon,' in eds. J.-L. Quantain and J.-C. Waquet, *Papes, princes, savants dans l'Europe Moderne. Mélanges a la Memoire de Bruno Neveu* (Geneva, 2007, 287–311. Edward Gibbon later recorded that he read Pascal's *Provincial Letters* 'almost every year' and modelled his satirical style upon them. *Memoirs*, 100.

[169] He attended the Act of 1733 and made a speech thanking the University for the degree received earlier. Godley, *Oxford in the eighteenth century*, 191.

[170] The memoir was translated into English by the young Samuel Johnson and published in the *Gentleman's Magazine*. Da Maria, *Johnson*, 44. See Colin Haydon, 'Le Courayer, Pierre-François (1681–1776), Roman Catholic priest and religious controversialist', *ODNB* online edn., 2006.

[171] Bishop John Potter gave Lincoln College library a copy of Le Courayer's later *Relation historique* in 1729. Green, *Lincoln College*, 293n. For Le Courayer's many High Anglican friends. Nichols, *Lit. anecdotes*, II. 39f.

[172] For Thomas Hunt's apparent interest in the condemnation of the doctoral thesis of the Abbé de Prades and the perspective it offered on the intellectual life of the Gallican Church in the early 1750s see letters from Arthur Ashley Sykes, esp. that dated 18 Feb. 1752 in Bodl. Ms Eng. lett. d. 146, f. 7. See generally J. D. Burson, *The rise and fall of theological Enlightenment. Jean-Martin de Prades and ideological polarization in eighteenth-century France* (Notre Dame, IN, 2010).

[173] Lorraine Daston, 'The ideal and reality of the Republic of Letters in the Enlightenment', *Science in Context*, 4 (1991), 367–86, considers the interplay between the ideal and the reality of the Republic of Letters. For discussion of whether the Enlightenment can be considered a new phase in the development of the Republic of Letters, see Robertson, *The case for the Enlightenment*, 38ff.

[174] Calhoun, 'Imagining solidarity', 172.

change and adaptation to be seen in most European universities, not least in its pioneering—though far from uncritical—adoption of Newtonian natural philosophy.[175] Yet, equally, many of the volumes produced by the University stood in creative tension towards the Enlightenment, as was bound to be the case in an institution that insisted on the creative and continuing power of tradition.

In that it was far from alone, as the Enlightenment held no monopoly on intellectual life anywhere in Europe and a high proportion of the intellectual elite were 'decidedly unenlightened in their mental outlook'.[176] And, as suggested above, many Oxford academics were alert to the threat to the established ecclesiastical—and therefore educational—order by the anticlerical preferences of most *philosophes* and their followers, those who had a facility for both engaging with national opinion and communicating their intellectual interests across frontiers and language barriers.[177] At least, by comparison with some of its southern European counterparts, the University could be confident that any externally proposed university reform scheme for structural or curricular changes based on renewal of the statutes, or one sponsored by government—(unlikely though that was)—would receive short shrift.[178] Oxonians had few incentives to embrace the institutional and societal retuning that advanced thinkers were prepared to recommend elsewhere in the later eighteenth century. That disclaimer did not in itself signify either intellectual retardation or a lack of interest in cultural outreach, as the willingness of the University's graduates to take up opportunities in Britain's growing empire betokened.

iv) Oxford and the British Atlantic: emerging imperial involvements

In the course of the eighteenth century, as the British government's involvement in administering the country's expanding empire increased, so graduates across the country had new opportunities to make a career and a fortune.[179] A military

---

[175] Gascoigne, 'The role of the universities in the Scientific Revolution', 246.

[176] Brown, 'Was there an Irish Enlightenment?', 63. Brown concludes: '...the Enlightenment itself was peripheral to the mainstream of intellectual life in eighteenth-century Europe', ibid., thus echoing Jonathan Clark's scepticism. See, for example, his 'The Enlightenment: catégories, traductions et objets sociaux', in eds. G. Laudin and D. Masseau, *Lumières*, special issue 17–18 (2011), 19–39, and the essays in his *Our shadowed present*.

[177] Robertson, *The case for the Enlightenment*, 38.

[178] For instance, at the University of Coimbra in Portugal, a royal statute of 1772 regulated university life in minute detail. Jurisprudence became more important than theology, ecclesiastical alignment was played down, and preferential treatment for Jansenist ideas was given. Notker Hammerstein, 'Relations with authority', in ed. de Ridder-Symoens, *Universities in Early Modern Europe*, 114–53, at 134. See also Frijhoff, 'Patterns', in ibid., 75–7. For a study of teaching in the Catholic universities of Piedmont, where civil rulers were anxious to control education without alienating the ecclesiastical hierarchy, Patrizia Delpiano, *Il trono e la cattedra. Instruzione e formazione dell'élite nel Piemonte del Settecento* (Turin, 1997).

[179] For legal opportunities in India see Chapter 4.

background was usually required for imperial governors, but the social and academic connections that an Oxford education offered were also important elements in the mix. The trend had been inaugurated well before the 1763 Peace of Paris. Some graduates had élite colonial origins, none more so than Christopher Codrington (1668–1710), from a Barbadian family of planters and a respected servant of the Revolution state. As a fellow of All Souls College, Codrington became the protégé of the long-serving Secretary-at-War, William Blathwayt, fought at the siege of Namur in 1695, and went out to be Governor of the Leeward Islands. In politics he was a moderate Whig who dutifully attended William III on his visit to Oxford in 1695 and, in learning, an acquaintance of Malebranche's and a friend of Locke's. Yet Codrington was also a Christ Church product, someone who had been taught by Smalridge and Atterbury, a man who read the Fathers, who admired St Basil and was compared to him in the address at his funeral. His friends on all sides lauded his laying aside for philanthropy so much of the personal wealth derived from his colonial holdings. All Souls was his enduring beneficiary: he gave £6,000 in his will to the building of a new library by Nicholas Hawksmoor with two-thirds of that sum earmarked for the purchase

Fig. 11.5 Christopher Codrington, Sir James Thornhill, oil on canvas (by permission of the Warden and Fellows of All Souls College, Oxford).

of books.[180] Codrington also bequeathed funds for the foundation of a missionary college on monastic lines in Barbados, further evidence of Oxford influence and High Church fascination with a revival of the religious life in the Church.[181] It was to be supported by two sugar plantations (based on slave labour) and run by the Society for the Propagation of the Gospel (SPG). As has been recently argued, the SPG's experience of managing the plantations safely while also encouraging slaves to be baptised pushed its members—many of whom were Oxford graduates—towards propounding a pro-slavery apologetic.[182] But, by the 1780s, an influential section of University opinion was moving in an abolitionist direction. Thomas Burgess of Corpus Christi College appealed directly to the public with his *Considerations on the Abolition of Slavery*, etc. (1789). Christian principle and rational argument, he insisted, imposed on the clergy the duty of inculcating in their people the necessity of its abolition.[183]

The first servants of empire the University provided tended to be clerics rather than civil servants, those who might look for preferment in the established Church overseas or even function as missionary pioneers. Such was the vision of Jesus College's alumnus, Sir Leoline Jenkins, Secretary of State to Charles II, 1680–4 (d. 1685). In his will he made provision for two [Leoline] missionary fellows, who would be obliged 'to go to sea in any of His Majesty's fleets when they or any of them are thereunto summoned by the Lord High Admiral of England'. Failing that call, they were to be ready to be nominated by the bishop of London '...to go out into any of His Majesty's plantations there to take upon them a cure of souls'.[184] The first two men were appointed in 1702. Already, by that date, Oxford-educated ordinands were responding to the challenge of ministering in British colonies where Anglican churches had none of the prior advantages of establishment and had to compete to make their voice heard in a confessional free market in which majority opinion remained suspicious of their presumed intolerant intentions.

That was particularly the case in British North America, where Henry Compton, Bishop of London, had begun to exercise his jurisdiction over the

---

[180] Mandelbrote, 'The Vision of Christopher Codrington'; V. T. Harlow, *Christopher Codrington 1668–1710* (Oxford, 1928).

[181] Peter F. Anson, *The Call of the Cloister: religious Communities and kindred bodies in the Anglican Communion* (London, 1955), 22. Thanks to Peter Doll for this reference. The educational plan developed only fitfully.

[182] Codrington was in that minority of West Indian masters who favoured the conversion of enslaved people. George Smalridge was Codrington's Oxford tutor and his brother, John Smalridge, was Codrington's plantation manager, supported by the SPG for twenty years. He had many Catholic connections across the Atlantic world. See Travis Glasson, *Mastering Christianity. Missionary Anglicanism and Slavery in the Atlantic World* (Oxford, 2012), 143–5. Thanks to Peter Walker for this reference.

[183] M. Smith, 'Thomas Burgess, Churchman and Reformer', in ed. N. Yates, *Bishop Burgess and his World. Culture, Religion and Society in Britain, Europe and North America in the Eighteenth and Nineteenth Centuries* (Cardiff, 2007), 5–40, at 30. For Sir William Dolben, see Chapter 8.

[184] Baker, *Jesus College*, 22.

OXFORD AND THE WIDER WORLD   593

communities in America from the 1670s,[185] and gave his support to the Oxford graduate Thomas Bray's Society for the Propagation of the Gospel, whose Charter was granted in 1701.[186] The SPG proved to be critical for Anglican life in a swathe of colonies, for it provided colonial churches with clergy (many of them Oxford graduates) and, additionally, a formidable number of colonial governors were SPG members.[187] And, as is well-known, the great Oxford-educated revivalists and rivals, John Wesley and George Whitefield, were quick to see the scope for evangelism in the thirteen Colonies. Whitefield particularly made frequent Atlantic crossings before his death in 1770 and used the long voyages to study with an intensity he had not given it since leaving Pembroke College.[188]

Some Oxford-educated men came from families already settled in the colonies and they frequently brought back to America the sentiments they had imbibed at the University, the High Church layman, John Checkley, a native of Boston and bookshop owner, for instance. An inveterate controversialist, he viewed himself as a Bostonian Sacheverell and, in 1719 (the same year in which he refused the oaths to George I and was fined), he underwrote the reprint and publication of Charles Leslie's *The religion of Jesus Christ the only true religion* (1697). It underlined the extent to which colonial factions had been absorbed into the British 'rage of party';[189] clergy and laity moving from England to take up residence in North America (Virginia was especially favoured as a place of settlement)[190] in the eighteenth century all too often reinforced the lines of fissure. Oxonians were relatively few compared to those proceeding from Scotland. Thus between 1680 and 1740 some 443 college- or university-educated men settled in the Chesapeake, with Oxford and Cambridge sending only 153 of them.[191] There were never

[185] Arthur Lyon Cross, *The Anglican Episcopate and the American colonies* (New York, 1902), 8–33; G. Yeo, 'A case without parallel: The Bishops of London and the Anglican Church overseas, 1660-1748', *JEH*, 44 (1993), 450–73; Carpenter, *Protestant bishop*, 250–98. For the background see J. Woolverton, *Colonial Anglicanism in North America* (Detroit, MI, 1976); James Bell, *The imperial origins of the king's Church in early America, 1607–1783* (Basingstoke, 2004).

[186] H. P. Thompson, *Thomas Bray* (London, 1954).

[187] Listed in an appendix in Bell, *Imperial origins.*

[188] 'Fancied myself all this Day in my little Cell at Oxford: for I have not spent so many Hours in sweet Retirement since I left the University. The Pleasure I felt was inexpressible'. Whitefield, *A Journal of a Voyage from London to Savannah in Georgia . . .* (London, 1738), 13.

[189] E. Slafter, *John Checkley; or, The evolution of religious tolerance in Massachusetts Bay* (Boston, MA, 1897); David Parrish, *Jacobitism and anti-Jacobitism in the British Atlantic World 1688-1727* (London, 2017), 99, 151–64. Parrish argues that there was nothing inherently Jacobite in what Checkley wrote but he that he was relentlessly provocative. He studied in Oxford but appears never to have matriculated.

[190] In 1661 an unsuccessful proposal was made to Gilbert Sheldon (bishop of London) to set up 'Virginia fellowships' in Oxford and Cambridge under which the fellows would move to Virginia for a minimum of seven years. P. S. Haffenden, 'The Anglican Church in Restoration colonial policy', in ed. J. M. Smith, *Seventeenth-Century America: essays in colonial history* (Chapel Hill, NC, 1959), 166–91, at 180.

[191] T. M. Devine, *Scotland's Empire 1600-1815* (London, 2003), 164–5. Between 1745 and 1775 eighteen clerics served in North America who had received their training in Britain and Ireland, among them six from Oxford, one more than from Cambridge. F. S. Mills, *Bishops by ballot. an*

594   ENLIGHTENED OXFORD

enough clergy to cater for the pastoral demands in British North America created by population growth, with Anglican congregations increasing at a staggering rate: from about fifty *c*.1700 to over 300 half a century later.[192] Not that this trend prevented dissenting colleges spreading their influence in the colonies, despite Secker in the 1760s working to tighten the reins of control.[193]

Several Oxonians sought out teaching positions in American institutions with strong connections to the established Church, such as the College of William & Mary in Williamsburg, whose first two Presidents, William Dawson (1743–52) and William Stith (1752–55), were both graduates of the Queen's College; of the Instructors in moral philosophy at William & Mary on the eve of the Revolution all but one were Oxford graduates (the content of their teaching is hard to ascertain).[194] Among them, support for a locally based episcopacy was strong but not invariable, and there was an underlying diversity characteristic of Virginian Anglicanism.[195] In 1771, Thomas Gwatkin, a Professor of the College in natural history and philosophy from 1769 and a Jesus College matriculand, was one of those dissenting from a College proposal for an American episcopate, on the grounds of the likelihood of civil violence in the tense times that had followed the passing of the Stamp Act.[196]

Further north, King's College, New York, as its name suggested, became the principal centre for royalist sentiments. The talented Oxonian High Churchman, Myles Cooper (Queen's College), was personally selected by Archbishop Secker to succeed Samuel Johnson as President of King's in 1763 and, after making his presence felt at the convention of episcopal clergymen for the Atlantic colonies (New York, New Jersey, Pennsylvania, Connecticut, Delaware) meeting in

---

eighteenth-century ecclesiastical revolution (New York, 1978), 8–9. For the shortage of clergy in Virginia see J. R. Gunderson, 'The search for good men: recruiting ministers in colonial Virginia', *Historical Magazine of the Protestant Episcopal Church*, 48 (1979), 465–72. Dell Upton, *Holy things and profane: Anglican parish Churches in colonial Virginia* (New Haven, CT, 1986), 171–3, notes the slightly subordinate social status of the clergyman as 'a gentleman's gentleman' in the colony, a likely disincentive for Oxford graduates to move there.

[192] P. J. Marshall, *The making and unmaking of empires. Britain, India, and America c.1750–1783* (Oxford, 2005), 40.

[193] Peter Choi, 'Whitefield, Georgia, and the Quest for Bethesda College', in eds. G. Hammond and Ceri Jones, *George Whitefield*, 224–40, at 233–4.

[194] C. Canby, 'A note on the influence of Oxford University upon William and Mary College in the eighteenth century', *W&MQ*, new series, 21 (1941), 243–7. The Bishop of London held the right of appointment to professorships. See generally David W. Robson, *Educating Republicans: The [William & Mary] College in the era of the American Revolution, 1750–1800* (London, 1985). For the argument that the College organisation owed as much to the Edinburgh example see J. Herbst, *From crisis to crisis. American college government 1636–1819* (Cambridge, MA, 1982), 33–4, 36, 260.

[195] See generally Ingram, *Religion, reform, and modernity*, 234–59; John K. Nelson, *A blessed company. parishes, parsons, and parishioners in Anglican Virginia 1690–1776*, (Chapel Hill, NC, 2001).

[196] Ibid., 257–8; Rhys Isaac, *The transformation of Virginia 1740–1790* (Chapel Hill, NC, 1982), 184–5, 185n. He was untypically anticlerical and, interestingly, does not appear to have taken his degree at Oxford. ibid., 198.

OXFORD AND THE WIDER WORLD 595

late 1766,[197] became the lead controversialist for the Anglican and Loyalist causes, organising the clergy of the middle colonies, and visiting those in the south three times to help rally support for a colonial episcopate.[198] Archbishop Secker recognised how much Oxford doctorates brought prestige to the colleges of the recipients and to the Church of England in America and the hebdomadal board of the University was quick to follow its metropolitan's promptings. Thus when William Samuel Johnson (Samuel Johnson's son) came to England in 1767 as Connecticut's colonial agent, Oxford gave him an honorary degree in recognition of his father's advocacy of an American episcopate.[199]

With the reliable Cooper at the helm, and King's College petitioning the Crown, the North government was enthusiastic about turning it into an American Oxford within a network of colleges that together would form a university for the province, partly as a means of cementing relations between Britain and the peripheries.[200] The time was not available to them. Across the thirteen Colonies, Oxford-educated clerics were to the fore in retaining and proclaiming their personal loyalty to the Crown after war erupted in 1775, despite the foreseeable risk of deprivation and loss of income.[201] Once momentum had passed to the insurgents, where the British army went, they followed. Thus after the retaking of Charleston in 1780, two Welshmen were—briefly—inserted into the rectories of the city's two main parishes, Edward Jenkins to St Michael's, and Robert Cooper (of Jesus College) to St Philip's.[202]

[197] Efforts to set up the convention (attended by about one-third of the region's clergy) were initiated by the New Jersey priest, Thomas B. Chandler (1726–90) in an effort to obtain an American episcopate. The convention remained in existence after the first meeting. Mills, *Bishops by ballot*, 42–4, 84.

[198] J. J. Ellis, *The New England mind in transition: Samuel Johnson of Connecticut, 1696–1772* (New Haven, CT, 1973); Peter Doll, *Revolution, religion, and national identity. Imperial Anglicanism in North America, 1745–1795* (Cranbury, NJ, 2000), 192; Robert M. Calhoon, *The loyalists in revolutionary America, 1760–1781* (New York, 1973), 259–60. For Cooper in Oxford after the War had started see Chapter 7.

[199] Ingram, *Religion, reform, and modernity*, 221. Other recipients included Henry Caner (1766) and William Smith for their defence of the Church, ibid., 217, 221; W. D. MacRay, 'Honorary Oxford degrees conferred on New England clergy in the eighteenth century', *Notes and Queries*, 7th Ser. VI (July 1888), 61–2. There was competition for doctoral degrees between the Anglican clergy in America, who received them from Oxford, and the Presbyterian and Congregationalist clergy who looked to the Scottish universities (e.g. Jonathan Mayhew, Charles Chauncy) (thanks to Peter Walker for this information).

[200] E. Countryman, *A people in revolution. The American Revolution and political society in New York, 1760–1790* (New York, 1989), 240–2; J. Herbst, 'The American Revolution and the American university', *Perspectives in American History*, 10 (1976), 279–355, esp. 301–9; David C. Humphrey, *From King's College to Columbia, 1746–1800* (New York, 1976), 126–39. It only became a university after the colonies had declared independence.

[201] University members were conscious of the need to succour materially distressed loyalist clergy. St John's College, for instance, donated £200 towards their relief in 1776. Costin, *St John's College*, 212.

[202] George Smith McCowen, Jr., *The British Occupation of Charleston, 1780–82* (Columbia, SC, 1972), 126–7. Robert Cooper returned to England in exile after the British evacuated Charleston. In the end, over half the colonial American Anglican clergy broke their oath to George III. N. L. Rhoden, *Revolutionary Anglicanism: The Colonial Church of England clergy during the American Revolution* (Basingstoke, 1999), 24, chaps. 4 and 5; Woolverton, *Colonial Anglicanism in North America*, 35.

596   ENLIGHTENED OXFORD

Until the Revolutionary Wars began, élite American families from Anglican backgrounds habitually sent their boys to the ancient English universities as part of the process of appropriate socialisation. Young Carolinians from Charleston tended, usually, to attend school locally. Such was not the case for the Pinckney brothers, from a family of large-scale planters: when their father moved to London in 1753 to serve as South Carolina's agent, both Charles Cotesworth Pinckney (1746–1825) and his younger brother, Thomas (1750–1828), came with him. They attended Westminster School before Christ Church, and the Inner Temple afterwards.[203] But American numbers at Oxford fell in the mid-century as colonial institutions expanded and gained prestige.[204] For instance, in George II's reign, South Carolina sent very few students to Oxford, with the last one from Charleston entering the University in 1772. And the final colonial American to be sent to England for education was Scrope Bernard (born in Pestel Amberg, New Jersey), who matriculated at Christ Church in April 1775.[205]

American-born Oxford graduates fought on both sides during the Revolutionary War, with a preponderance enlisting with the Loyalists, including William Wragg, of the South Carolina association; with the 'rebels' could be found William Henry Drayton, Chief Justice of South Carolina;[206] James Jones Wilmer, Swedenborgian, army chaplain and later chaplain to the United States Senate, and James Bowdoin, of Massachusetts, minister designate to Spain.[207] Charles Pinckney was colonel of the first South Carolina regiment and fought at Germantown and Brandywine as George Washington's aide-de-camp before suffering imprisonment when Charleston fell to the British besiegers in 1780; Thomas Pinckney was seriously wounded and captured during the battle of Camden and, during the British occupation of Charleston in 1780–2, suffered the sequestration of his estates.[208] Neither memories of his upbringing nor his friends on the loyalist side could persuade him to abandon the cause: 'my heart is

---

[203] M. R. Zahniser, *Charles Cotesworth Pinckney: Founding Father* (Chapel Hill, NC, 1967); Charles Cotesworth Pinckney, *Life of General Thomas Pinckney* (Boston, MA/New York, 1895), 22–4; Feiling, *In Christ Church Hall*, 88–96, for a summary of the Pinckney brothers' careers before and after the American Revolution.

[204] By mid-century there were more young men from West Indian plantation families (such as Banastre Tarleton, later Commander of the British Legion in the American War, who went to University College) than North Americans going to British universities. Andrew Jackson O'Shaughnessy, *An Empire Divided. The American Revolution and British Caribbean* (Philadelphia, PA, 2000), 19–27.

[205] To call him a 'a colonial American' is stretching the term. His father, Francis Bernard, was Governor of New Jersey, 1758–60, a Ch. Ch. graduate, and the recipient of an Hon. DCL in 1772.

[206] W. M. Dabney and M. Dargan, *William Henry Drayton and the American Revolution* (Albuquerque, 1962), 175.

[207] 'Colonial Americans in Oxford and Cambridge', repr. from W. Connely, *The American Oxonian*, Jan. 1942, 11, 13, 16.

[208] McCowen, G. S., Jr., *The British Occupation of Charleston*, 70–1. He was exchanged in 1781 and fought alongside Lafayette at Yorktown.

altogether American, and neither severity, nor favour, nor poverty, nor affluence can ever induce me to swerve from it'.[209]

After the Peace of Versailles was signed in 1783 and American Independence was recognised, a steady trickle of United States citizens continued to matriculate at Oxford, among them the young Daniel Horry, whose grandmother, Eliza Lucas Pinckney (herself the daughter of a British officer who became Lieutenant-Governor of Antigua before buying estates in Carolina), reminded him that as a 'Gentleman commoner at an English University' he could acquire 'one of the greatest advantages in life a Liberal Education'.[210] And, in the post-war consolidation of Empire, the encouragement of colonial attendance at English universities was not discarded. Thus in 1790, following the decision of the Nova Scotia legislature to establish King's College in Halifax the year before, Lord Grenville (Home Secretary) devised a detailed plan to provide British North American scholars with exhibitions to the English universities to train them for holy orders.[211] This new King's College was staunchly Anglican in its affiliations and its foundation owed much to the energy of Charles Inglis (first Bishop of the colony, 1787–1816, a loyalist awarded an Oxford DD in 1778), who was keen to model it on Oxford.[212] So, too, was Sir Thomas Strange (1756–1841) an old Christ Church alumnus and Chief Justice of Nova Scotia from 1789 to 1797, who even wanted to call it Christ Church and in 1790 consulted Dean Jackson on designs for the college buildings. On behalf of members of King's College, in 1793 Strange approached the Dean and Chapter of Christ Church with advice on stocking their public library. Jackson responded constructively with a list of 137 titles he thought would be useful, including classical texts, sermons, polyglot Bibles, and John Pearson's *Exposition of the Creed*. His recommendations for scientific volumes ranged from Hippocrates to Newton, and there were many suggestions for geography, law, and modern history.[213] These fostering connections between colonial higher educational establishments and the 'mother university' would become commonplace during the nineteenth century.

v) Conclusion

Despite its tight confessional standards of admission, Oxford was ready to welcome a wide range of Europeans into its precincts and expected its own graduates

---

[209] Letter of 30 June 1780 quoted in ibid., 71.

[210] Letter of 18 Feb. 1787, Pinckney Papers, quoted in ibid., 122.

[211] Doll, *Religion, revolution, and national identity*, 250–2. These never materialised as the funding was ploughed into encouraging attendance at the College itself.

[212] Brian Cuthbertson, *The First Bishop: a Biography of Charles Inglis* (Halifax, NS, 1987), chap. 9.

[213] Beryl L. Anderson, 'An Eighteenth Century List of Books for a Public Library in Halifax', unpublished typescript, Nova Scotia Archives, MG 100, vol. 86/53. I am grateful to Judith Curthoys for her extensive help in tracking down this paper.

in return to feel comfortable abroad, partly because their education (both official and unofficial) offered them access to a common European culture that united their equivalents across the continent. The University's academic life was not divorced from what was happening elsewhere in the world; its scholars formed part of entangled multiple, ocean-spanning networks and it was a commonplace that what was happening in other centres of learning influenced what was done in Oxford—and vice versa. Though Oxford, like all eighteenth-century universities, was challenged by the rise of new learned societies and novel forms of intellectual sociability, its values were never as distinct from those of the moderate Enlightenment as its opponents liked to suggest. If, as has been argued, 'curiosity' had generally been recognised as a virtue by the 1740s, it was reflected within this Anglican bastion and found outlet in a range of contacts and cooperation. Not the least of those—for all Oxford's 'Tory' loyalties—was taking advantage of the ways the Anglo-Hanoverian union provided a unique transnational framework for scholarly exchange.[214] Thus, using the model of a pluralised enlightenment, Oxford's place within a pan-European context is best seen as both embodying and mediating the various fault lines running through eighteenth-century thought. Those could equally be found in a British Atlantic context. Young men weaned on a classical curriculum were able to celebrate British military and naval achievements, the same curriculum which, arguably, helped determine the allegiance of the Pinckney brothers and others to George Washington in the 1770s. An increasing number of those who took holy orders looked to practise their ministry in the Empire,[215] while others were sufficiently inspired by the glories of ancient empires to undertake service in Britain's.[216] These were precisely the kind of outcomes one might have expected from Oxford's varied and multiform educative witness.

---

[214] Biskup, 'The university of Göttingen', 132–3.

[215] Opportunities for mission work in India were limited before the 1790s though Joseph White, in his 1784 Bamptons, 'Mahometism and Christianity', had urged the propagation of the faith in the subcontinent. P. Carson, *The East India Company and Religion, 1698–1858* (Woodbridge, 2012), 21.

[216] cf. Colley, *Britons*, 167–8.

12

Insider trading

Family, friendship, connection, and culture beyond the University

...could we but revive ancient discipline, and make young gentlemen carry away a little of what they are sent to us for, viz. good learning, good manners, a reasonable insight into the grounds of their religion, and a habit of obedience to their superiors, I am persuaded, that neither they, nor their parents, would think they had lost their time amongst us, or complain, or make them what the Town calls fine gentlemen.

> Bishop John Hough to Arthur Charlett, 27 Feb. 1699, quoted in John Wilmot, *The Life of the Rev. John Hough, DD* (London, 1812), 145.

Oxford University's impact on eighteenth-century England and Wales was primarily the product of informal association. The University's physical presence was generally admired, the well-being and direction of its intellectual culture less so, and its politics could be divisive, but it was the varied interaction of Oxford graduates with each other and with outsiders that explains the enduring centrality of this 'greatest of clerical seminaries' at the heart of national life.[1] At Oxford, the sons of the ruling elites had the opportunities generally begun at school 'to forge relationships between themselves that were one of the keys to the perpetuation of their rule'.[2] It amounted to a form of insider(s) trading but it was one that was largely taken for granted, fed off ties of kinship and friendship, and offered what could turn out to be lifelong support networks.[3] Of course, there were winners and

---

[1] The phrase is G.V. Bennett's. *Tory Crisis*, 144.

[2] Cannon, *Aristocratic Century*, 33–4. Oxford and Cambridge educated a greater proportion of the British elite than comparable higher-educational institutions in Germany and France. L. Brockliss, 'The European university in the age of revolution, 1789–1850', in HUO VI, 77–133, at 83, 119.

[3] C. Kadushin, *Understanding social networks: theories, concepts, and findings* (Oxford, 2012) is useful. Other title dealing generally with this subject in an eighteenth-century setting is Naomi Tadmoor, *Family and friends in eighteenth-century England: household, kinship, and patronage* (Cambridge, 2001). The latter offers (216–36) a Sussex case study in political 'friendship'. The importance of patronage in launching many a career began *inside* the University, as it did, for instance, with Samuel Parker, elected a Fellow of Merton College in August 1789. A relation noted: '..., he before had Lord Craven's Exhibition £25 per Ann. & the Duke of Beaufort's £25 per Ann. An Instance

---

Enlightened Oxford: The University and the Cultural and Political Life of Eighteenth-century Britain and Beyond.
Nigel Aston, Oxford University Press. © Nigel Aston 2023. DOI: 10.1093/oso/9780199246830.003.0013

losers in this important stratum of social activity with its inevitable transactional dimension, but in a society where government and professional life were inseparable from personal connection, the importance of association as the basis of its modus operandi went unchallenged until the 1790s at the earliest.

This chapter examines selected aspects of connection and culture beyond Oxford to explore and explain how insiders, through their own social interactions, gave the University exceptional leverage at most levels of eighteenth-century society. It brings unapologetically centre-stage the issue of patronage and power-brokerage with its multiple points of access and degrees of involvement whose foundation was the patron-client relationship and the nebulous concepts of influence and interest that informed it.[4] This relationship had a dynamic that could be complicated by neediness or ambition that could extend in both directions plus an essential *de haut en bas* aspect that friendship sometimes softened. As George Bubb Dodington, Prince Frederick's follower, put it at mid-century:

> Service is obligation, obligation implies return. Could any man of honour profess friendship, accept the offer of his friend's whole services, suffer those offers to be carried into execution, avail himself of their utility, and then tell him he could not or would not make him any return? Could there be such a character?[5]

Even when Tory Oxonians were frozen out from royal bounty for so much of the first half of the century, those among them at the highest levels of society with funds and favours to support the disinherited often stepped into the gap to offer support to their fellow collegians. Academic loyalties were never lightly discarded.[6] It was not just amity that encouraged varying bonds of commitment. They could be kept oiled by successive generational attendance at a particular college, while choice of spouse could be occasioned by a college friendship that

---

of the great things [that] can be done for a decent behav'd young man, with friends to speak a word for him. But where friends cannot speak, as little can be done as they deserve'. Daniel Prince to Rev. Samuel Viner,Oxford, 7 Aug. 1789. Glos Archives, Ellis & Viner Papers, D2227/6/3.

[4] Patronage, as Elaine Chalus has noted, 'pervaded the eighteenth-century domestic, cultural, social, and economic domains,' *Elite women in English political life*, 107. She tellingly observes that it has fallen out of historical fashion as a topic, ibid., 108. See also Glover, *Elite women and polite society in eighteenth-century Scotland*, 114n. For step models of patronage such as the 'ladder of patronage' and 'pagoda of patronage' see L. P. Curtis, *Anglican Moods of the Eighteenth Century* (np, 1966). S. N. Eisenstadt and L. Roniger, *Patrons, clients and friends. Interpersonal relations and the structure of trust in society* (Cambridge, 1984), sets out several sociologically informed comparative studies of interpersonal relationships and their connections to the institutional matrices within which they develop. See also ed. C. Clapham, *Private patronage and public power. Political clientelism in the modern state* (London, 1982).

[5] ed. Henry Penruddocke Wyndham, ed., *The Diary of the late George Bubb Dodington, Baron of Melcombe Regis...* (London, 1828), 162. For a contemporary warning against the scope for exploitation see Generosus, *The nature of patronage, and the duty of patrons, consider'd in three letters published in the Weekly Miscellany...* (London, 1735).

[6] For Tory families' 'cultural debt to Oxford', sustaining them during the reigns of the first two Georges, see Colley, *In Defiance of Oligarchy*, 290.

had brought access to a wider family network.[7] Where consanguinity was not an element, association was invariably fostered through the possession of a college living or simply the tenancy of a college estate. Whatever an individual's motivation in emphasising Oxonian loyalties, they were likely to be stimulated through social gatherings in London and the major provincial centres, events that tended to develop a more formal organisation as the century wore on. As Peter Clark has well observed: 'society members often provided the sinuous highway of communication, on to which, other looser or more informal branches were grafted'.[8] In these settings, allegiance was assumed, emphasised, confirmed, and strengthened. And, in the other direction, ambitious dons wanted to make polite, political, and public connections that might work to their advantage.

If there was one profession to which the University looked as foremost in its loyal following it was the clerical one. Some clergy used relative isolation as an opportunity for intellectual production that added lustre to Oxford's reputation and the extent of their achievement should not be underestimated. Often former college fellows as well as graduates, Oxford contacts in remote parishes could help keep alumni priests from sinking into rural stagnation and mental atrophy. They could gossip and grumble together and keep each other abreast of likely vacancies in the Church. In the first half of the century, they helped keep the Tory cause alive in the provinces at some cost to their career prospects; in the second half, when times were more propitious as the University's relations with the Crown stabilised, they were loyalist standard-bearers for 'Church and King' values out of conviction as much as for personal advantage. As individuals, clergy could function as one-man academic cells; in conjunction with each other, they commonly made up the core components of provincial associational culture with an Anglican intellectual edge, often but not always willing to include Dissenters in their midst (certainly from the second third of the century the trend was there), and making up a neglected foil to rival confessional cultural groupings intent on commending constitutional change.[9] For clergy with an Oxford degree, the ultimate sign of their institutional loyalty was to leave a bequest to their college or to the whole University, though, as the century wore on, Oxford had to compete for funds with an ever-increasing number of philanthropic societies.[10] What sums they could offer were often small. The biggest donors tended to come from the laity: the

---

[7] For the shift from consanguineal to conjugal bonds as the centre of family relations see R. Perry, *Novel Relations: The Transformation of Kinship in English Literature and Culture 1748–1818* (Cambridge, 2004). The operation of one such family network—the Hebers—can be followed in ed. R.H. Cholmondeley, *The Heber Letters* supplemented by J. McManners, *All Souls and the Shipley Case* (Oxford, 2001); idem., 'Bishop Heber and Early Nineteenth-Century Churchmanship', in eds. Green and Horden, *All Souls under the Ancien Régime*, 324–40.

[8] Clark, *British Clubs and Societies*, 453–4.

[9] And, as Rosemary Sweet has said, the parish priest acted as 'a mediating figure between centre and locality and [was] essential in the network of communication that supported the construction of the eighteenth-century state'. Sweet, *Antiquaries*, 51.

[10] Langford, *Public Life and the Propertied Englishman*, 490–5.

lawyers, the physicians, the gentry, and the nobility, those with cash or chattels to spare or no expectant heir apparent ready to contest any windfall outside the family. Generally, the colleges were becoming adept at fund-raising in the eighteenth century and the largest ones like Christ Church tended to be the most proficient at it and to net the largest gifts, not least because their alumni tended to be among the University's wealthiest. Requests for contributions towards the cost of new buildings could raise significant sums in well-directed appeals to the pockets and generous nature of graduates. But legacies were often unexpected or against the odds, a token of goodwill and an indicator of contented Oxford memories founded on friendships that had lasted a lifetime, a remittance intended to foster the same sentiments in succeeding generations.

i) Patronage and power brokerage

> The University borrows its complection from its patrons, and the moon her light from the sun, ...
>
> *Terrae-Filius*, no. 4, 257, July 8, 1763.

The reaction against an essentially Namierite understanding of eighteenth-century power politics as explicable primarily in terms of clientage and patronage networks has been long-lasting and difficult to displace, and does much to explain the movement of historians away from political history for the last generation.[11] It may be time to restate and reinstate the importance of these networks within the wider framework of Georgian socio-political connections, more inclusively defined, and, for our purposes, within Oxford contexts.[12] University and college patronage in relation to Church benefices, chaplaincies, and other offices and properties in their gift intersected with networks operated by other regional power brokers in Church and state.[13] These could be used (especially before 1760) to support a distinctive cultural nexus that might run counter to Whiggish values

[11] That said, the work of historians such as Chalus, Glover, Sweet, and Campbell Orr, indicating the opportunities open to elite women within the patronage system, have recently helped to refresh the study of high politics within widened contexts.

[12] Roger Emerson, in *Academic Patronage in the Scottish Enlightenment*, demonstrates the centrality of patronage for the flowering of thought in eighteenth-century Scotland under the successive political direction of the 11th Earl of Mar, the Squadrone, the 3rd Duke of Argyll, Lord Bute, and Henry Dundas. Emerson argues that what was happening in Scotland was also occurring in other parts of Europe where, in relatively autonomous localities, elite patrons also shaped things as they wished them to be.

[13] Hirschberg reckoned that 6.7% of all Church livings were in the patronage of educational bodies and that this figure grew in the century after 1660. D. R. Hirschberg, 'The government and Church patronage in England, 1660–1760', *JBS*, 20 (1980), 109–39, esp. 124–7. Christ Church was the largest single patron in the diocese of Oxford with 8.4% out of a total scholastic and collegiate patronage of 29.2% (including St John's College, Cambridge, and Eton College). Marshall, *Church Life in Hereford and Oxford*, 75–6. For chaplaincies, see Gibson, *A Social History of the Domestic Chaplain*.

INSIDER TRADING 603

and become predominant in any neighbourhood where the social reach of a magnate was marked. For such a patron to show his loyalties to the University and the Tory cause as a key incentive to inducing the same preferences in aspirational clients was a sign of elite defiance at a juncture when the Hanoverian state was deliberately exclusionist in its use of patronage. It also offered a lifeline to individuals who, on leaving Oxford, could only practicably hope to sustain their own disdain of the oligarchic Whig order through the income afforded by an office in the gift of a peer, country gentleman, or another corporate body sympathetic to Tory leanings.

It was not only Oxford Tories who benefitted from noble patronage.[14] Moderate Whigs had their champions and one need look no further than Blenheim for what was on offer there by mid-century to aspirational dons and clerics. Sarah, Duchess of Marlborough, was not the only duchess to become directly involved in the patronage stakes. Her granddaughter-in-law, Elizabeth, the wife of the 3rd Duke, followed in her footsteps, lobbying the Duchess of Newcastle for the appointment of Dr John Kelly as Professor of Physick (i.e. Medicine) at Oxford in 1758–9, while her husband did the same with the Duke. Newcastle promptly saw George II and granted the request.[15] The Marlboroughs had many chaplaincies in their gift. The cultural agency of chaplains had many aspects and was potentially highly interactive: to take up a chaplaincy to a private notable enhanced the status of both in mutual bonds of reciprocity and obligation.[16] A chaplaincy inside the Pembroke family gave an appointee potentially an exceptional springboard to preferment at the heart of the University. The earls as Visitors of Jesus College could become involved in appointments to the Principalship and it was the 8th Earl's familiarity with John Wynne as his chaplain that did much to ensure the latter became Head of House there in 1715, when Lord Pembroke was asked to adjudicate in a contested election.[17]

Another great family with Welsh origins (though without the Pembrokes' hereditary status) was consistently involved with Oxford. Throughout the decades covered by this book, successive Dukes of Beaufort and other members of the extended Somerset family poured money into Oxford, patronised some of its most

---

[14] Or who hoped to benefit. *The Loiterer. A Periodical Work in Two Volumes* (Oxford, 1790), issue 11, Apr. 1789, features the fictional Luke Lickspittle, who fails to gain a living from his 'tuft-hunter' noble friends.

[15] Marlborough to Newcastle, 14 Nov. 1758, BL Add MS 32885, f. 330; Newcastle to Marlborough, 15 Nov. 1758, ibid., ff. 344. See also http://www.oxfordhistory.org.uk/doctors/regius_professors/kelly_john.html

[16] eds. H. Adlington, Tom Lockwood, and Gillian Wright, *Chaplains in early modern England. Patronage, literature and religion* (Manchester, 2013). See also W. Gibson, 'Patterns of nepotism and kinship in the eighteenth-century Church', *Journal of Religious History*, 14 (1987), 382–9; Gibson, 'Nepotism, family, and merit: the Church of England in the eighteenth century', *Journal of Family History*, 18 (1993), 179–90; Gibson, '"Unreasonable and Unbecoming": Self-recommendation and place-seeking in the Church of England, 1700–1900', *Albion*, 27 (1995), 43–63.

[17] Gibson, 'A Whig Principal of Jesus'. See also Chapter 6.

talented graduates, and fostered Tory sociability. The road between Oxford and Badminton was always a well-travelled one. The Beauforts came back to court in the 1760s after several decades of distance with the good offices of the monarchy once again behind them. With extensive landholdings centred around their main English estate at Badminton in south Gloucestershire, others in Glamorgan, and along the England-Wales border adjoining their old seat at Raglan, the Beauforts had a princely powerbase as patrons and, coupled with their supreme rank in the peerage, could afford to operate at a remove from the post-1689 establishment as implacable opponents of Whiggism.[18] The 1st Duke (the dukedom dated from 1682) was not prepared to compromise his loyalty to James II, gave up all his offices, and passed the 1690s in retirement as a Nonjuror, an accurate indicator of the Somerset family's uncompromising High Churchmanship.[19] The title passed to his grandson in 1700. He was not actually educated at Oxford; the University came to him in the shape of William Sherard, the botanist and fellow of St John's College. Sherard spent much of 1700-2 at Badminton as tutor to the 2nd Duke combining pedagogic duties at the great house with service as college bursar,[20] preparing his charge for public life, and the leadership of one of the greatest High Tory connections in the country (a predominantly Oxford-educated one). By the time the Harley ministry was formed in 1710, Beaufort's forte for boozy male socialising was well-established, and his 'Board of Brothers' (founded in 1709)—like-minded good fellows of the 'honest' party—was a smaller, less long-lived version of the more celebrated Whig Kit-Kat Club. There was an attempt to observe some of the proprieties. Thus the Board ordered 'That all bumpers be excluded the board except one to Church & Queen to avoid excess & reproach'.[21]

Beaufort held court office under Harley from 1712 as Captain of the Band of Gentlemen Pensioners, but predeceased Queen Anne, dying aged only thirty in May 1714.[22] His ill-disguised Jacobite proclivities were accordingly never put to the test at her passing and in its aftermath. Thus on the eve of a Succession that would be disastrous for the party in obtaining Crown patronage, the Tories lost one of their greatest patrons and protectors, whose electoral influence, which extended to six counties and at least a dozen boroughs, exceeded that of any other

---

[18] Jenkins, 'Jacobites and Freemasons', 393.

[19] He was placed under house arrest on a charge of high treason during the Assassination Plot of 1696. E. Cruickshanks, 'Attempts to Restore the Stuarts, 1689–96', in eds. E. Cruickshanks and Edward Corp, *The Stuart Court in Exile and the Jacobites* (London, 1995), 1–13, at 11. See Molly McClain, *Beaufort: The Duke and his Duchess, 1657–1715* (New Haven, CT, 2001), 188–200.

[20] Costin, *St John's College*, 159–60. His fellowship was terminated in 1703.

[21] BL Add. MSS. 49360, minutes, 1 Dec. 1710. See generally Geoffrey Holmes, *British Politics in the Age of Anne* (London, 1967), 296–7. There were about thirty Tory MPs and peers as full brothers or 'adopted nephews'. The Board's secretary was the Duke's Oxford client, Thomas Yalden DD, fellow of Magdalen. Rules to be observed by the Brotherhood, and list of members Feb. 1709/10, Badminton muniments, FmH 4/5.

[22] By 1714 Beaufort's loyalty had been given without reserve to Bolingbroke. Holmes, *British Politics in the Age of Anne*, 270.

Tory magnate.[23] The ducal power of appointment to offices in the Church had been on the same scale: five prebendaries in the see of Exeter, plus twenty-seven and a half livings (sixteen of them in the dioceses of St David's or Llandaff), all largely filled by Oxford men.[24] The 2nd Duke's benign link to Oxford had meanwhile been personally confirmed by the University's grant of an honorary DCL upon him in 1706, bestowed by his uncle, the Duke of Ormond;[25] it was left to his other uncle—and the University's Chancellor after 1715—Lord Arran—to take personally under his wing his two surviving male heirs, the 3rd Duke of Beaufort (1707–45) and his younger brother, Lord Noel Somerset, later the 4th Duke. The former was entered on the books in 1720 at what was by then an exceptionally tender age—thirteen—for matriculation. William Denison, his tutor, brought him triumphantly to Oxford, and University College under that smooth operator, Arthur Charlett, cosseted him, even considering moving the dinner hour forward one hour to midday to suit the Duke's preference.[26] All was well at the College in Charlett's lifetime but, on his death in 1722, Beaufort family influence was shamelessly put at the disposal of Denison to have him elected to the vacant Mastership.[27] The contested result eventually obliged Denison to vacate the Master's lodgings, but only after interminable legal wrangling that damaged the University's reputation beyond Oxford,[28] weakened University College academically until the mid-century, and exhibited the extensive damage that patronal influence, when exercised uncompromisingly on behalf of one cherished client, could do.[29] Even so, in *not electing* Denison, the college was taking a huge gamble in risking ducal favour. It duly passed to Oriel College which, in the 3rd Duke's will, was endowed with several exhibitions that otherwise would have come to his old college.[30]

---

[23] It has been estimated that the Beauforts had electoral influence in at least ten western counties c.1710–60, but ducal minorities (1714–28; 1756–65) weakened Beaufort and Tory interests alike. Jenkins, *The making of a ruling class*, 160, 165, 172.

[24] John Cannon, *Aristocratic Century. The peerage of eighteenth-century England* (Cambridge, 1984), 63, 64, and n., using figures derived from Browne Willis's *A Survey of the cathedrals . . . with an account of all the churches and chapels in each diocese, etc.* (3 vols., London, 1742).

[25] The 2nd Duke of Ormond married in 1685, as his second wife, Lady Mary Somerset, Beaufort's aunt (d. 1733).

[26] Hearne, VII. 182; HMC, *Portland MSS*, VII. 280, cited in Darwall-Smith, *University College*, 244, 315. When Cambridge tried to poach him in 1721, the Vice Chancellor, Robert Shippen (a fellow Jacobite), turned out to greet the 3rd Duke on his return to Oxford, bells were rung, and a great dinner held in honour of the Somerset family. Hearne, VIII. 24.

[27] Darwall-Smith, *University College*, 250–1. Shippen was also pro-Denison, or 'chief stickler', in Ward's phrase. *Georgian Oxford*, 115.

[28] It also cost Denison substantial legal fees. He wrote from Oxford on 4 Nov. 1733 asking Lord Noel Somerset to smooth his way to draw some money from the 3rd Duke rather than personally troubling him with such a supplication. His solicitor had sent him his 'frightful bill' £503 15s 8d, of which he had paid about half and asked him for a credit till next Lady Day. Badminton Muniments, FmJ 2/11.

[29] As late as 1728, the Duke was urging the Heads of Houses to take the case of the University's visitatorial rights to the courts. Ward, *Georgian Oxford*, 115. See also Chapter 6.

[30] Seaward, 'Politics and Interest, 1660–1781', 188.

606   ENLIGHTENED OXFORD

Many dons courted the 3rd Duke's favour—and though he was created DCL in 1725 in recognition of his rank and good offices with regard to the University[31]— he turned out to be something of a disappointment in his lifetime to Tory supporters who looked to him for a lead. While there was no doubting his ardent Jacobitism (on display during his Grand Tour of 1726-7),[32] the Duke's taste ran more to the hunting field and connoisseurship than either politics or estate management, and he could be neglectful of well-intentioned clerical supplicants.[33] Above all (as was apparent during his student years), he had inherited his father's love of the bottle and his health suffered accordingly.[34] His last years were weighed down with an expensive divorce suit,[35] and he died prematurely, on the eve of the '45.[36] Even during his lifetime, the political drive in his family was exercised by his younger brother, Lord Noel Somerset (matric. Univ., 1725),[37] who duly succeeded as 4th Duke.

As befitted the changed times post-Culloden, the new master of Badminton was a more temperate Jacobite than his predecessor; by the mid-1750s he saw that the Tory future might well lie in developing ties with Pitt the Elder and invited him to

[31]   GEC, II. 54.

[32]   While resident in Rome during the summer of 1726 he held receptions for the Jacobite community and for Maria Clementina Sobieska's birthday ('James III's' wife) and put on a grand entertainment to mark the anniversary of the Stuart Restoration in 1660. J. Black, *Italy and the Grand Tour* (New Haven, CT, 2003), 144. He also met 'James III' at the Villa Borghese most days and had access to the private staircase at the Palazzo del Re to see the 'king' in his private apartment. Corp, *The Stuarts in Italy*, 168–72; L. Lewis, *Connoisseurs and Secret Agents in Eighteenth Century Rome* (London, 1961), 82. For suspicions of his Jacobite intrigues in Paris, 1727, see J. Black, *France and the Grand Tour* (Basingstoke, 2003), 109.

[33]   For example, the curate Thomas Payne, on the death of his father (who had received ducal favour), and recalling that the Duke's younger brother, Lord Noel, had given him repeated assurances of his good offices while he was at university, was obliged to write to the Duke to put himself under his protection, '& to my Ld Noel, to beg his Lordships assistance in bringing it about'. Chelsea, 25 June 1744, Badminton Muniments, FmJ 2/32 f. 16. It was not until 1752 that he received the living of Sopworth, Wilts.

[34]   '...young as he is, he will drink and swear with any cocker in England....', reported Dr Stratford to Lord Oxford, HMC, *Portland MSS*, VII 374, 23 Feb. 1724. Beaufort's health had never been good, even as an undergraduate. When he caught a cold in the summer of 1724 from dabbling in the water, George Clarke noted: 'Pain & illness will convince even Dukes that they are not exempt from the common accidents to mortal man'. Nicholas Papers, BL Egerton MS 2540, f. 289, to Edward ['Ned'] Nicholas, MP Surrey, 2 July 1724. He later suffered from gout and digestive problems. 3rd Duke to Lord Noel Somerset, 7 Jan. 1740, Badminton Muniments, FmJ 2/22/3, with its reference to 'us Bath people'.

[35]   There were accusations of impotence—and ducal demonstration to the contrary! L. Stone, *Broken Lives. Separation and Divorce in England 1660-1837* (Oxford, 1993), 117–38, esp. 133–5.

[36]   Mary Delany observed, 'he was unhappy in his constitution and unhappy in his circumstances, though possessed of great honours and riches; his brother is qualified to make a better figure,... *Autobiography and Correspondence*, II. 344. He was still thought of as a candidate for the Chancellorship in 1743, when a vacancy was expected. Ward, *Georgian Oxford*, 258.

[37]   He later left and entered himself on the books at Brasenose because of his unhappiness at the extrusion of Denison from the Mastership of University College. He kept in touch with developments at the latter through his friendship with George "Jolly" Ward (Fellow, 1708–33), 'the most outrageously Rabelaisian figure whom the College ever elected to a Fellowship', in Darwall-Smith's estimation. *University College*, 234.

dine at Badminton in October 1754 (while the latter was taking the waters at Bath).[38] It was said by one obituarist—with some justice—that:[39]

> His speeches were much approved of, and altho' ministerial influence was during the whole time he was in Parliament too strong to be checked by the arguments however weighty and forcible of a few men of honor, yet they did good, and shewed the Public that Corruption was not the universal bent of the English Nation.

He knew Oxford well, became a Radcliffe trustee, and found the affection was two-way.[40] Beaufort was no sluggard in doing what he could for his protégés, taking care in awarding the chaplaincies in his gift and recommending the many he could not satisfy to other patrons.[41] His influence was also exercised in the heart of the University, on behalf, for instance, of Robert Leybourne, DD, Principal of St Alban Hall and nephew of the Shippen brothers, for whom he lobbied Lord Arran in 1753 when there was expected to be a vacancy in the headship of Hertford College.[42] The 4th Duke was a figure of some national importance—'steady and upright in his public actions'[43]—whose death in 1756 shocked his political ally and the University's future High Steward, Lord Lichfield, and had party as well as patronage consequences. As the latter, mourning his friend and wondering at the formation of the Pitt/Devonshire ministry, told William Pulteney, Earl of Bath, he was going to Parliament 'to see what may happen from this Change of hands. What are they about?—are we likely to have any National Good? If not, adieu to old England'.[44]

Henry, the 5th Duke (1744–1803), carried on his family's patronal interaction with Oxford University and enhanced its worth through the recovery of a degree of power brokerage in public life on the basis of a Beaufort return to court duties for the first time since Queen Anne's death. The retreat into the interior for the Duke, as for so many Tory families, was finally over in the 1760s. George III and Queen Charlotte welcomed the family back with posts in the

---

[38] Clark, *The dynamics of change*, 122. Beaufort's politics are further discussed in Chapter 8.

[39] 'A true character of Charles Noel 4th Duke of Beaufort' [prob by the Duchess], Badminton Muniments, FmK 1/2/12.

[40] 'He was a zealous advocate of the University of Oxford & beloved and admired by all the principle Members of it'. Ibid.

[41] Badminton Muniments, FmJ 2/7, Memoranda book. He was also ready to listen to importunities from his family. For instance, the 5th Earl of Coventry asked the duke (when still Lord Noel) on behalf of his great aunt, Anne, Lady Coventry (died 1763), to 'use your interest' with Dr Shippen at Brasenose on behalf of a particular candidate for a college fellowship. He duly did so. Badminton Muniments, FmJ 2/22/18, 17 Jan. 1741.

[42] Beaufort to Leybourne, 1 May 1753, BL Egerton MS 2618, f. 231. The Duke warned that it was always possible the founder of Hertford had the power of naming his successor. The Principalship of Magdalen Hall was held by Beaufort's client, William Denison, 1745–56, after he had lost his battle at University College. OUA: CC Papers 1731/13:15. Leybourne became Arran's chaplain.

[43] Badminton Muniments, FmK, 1/2/12.

[44] Ditchley, 13 Nov. 1756, Glos. RO, D1833 F1, f. 24.

608 ENLIGHTENED OXFORD

royal household,[45] without the Duke being expected to dilute a devotion to the Crown that had for two previous generations manifested itself as Jacobitism. It says much that Thomas Nowell, the controversial Oxonian preacher and professor, was the 5th Duke's Glamorgan client.[46] Nowell came to public notice around the time that the twenty-eight-year-old Beaufort was mounting a challenge to Lord North for the Chancellorship, in 1772. The Duke's rehabilitation had actually made him too dependent on the Crown for some old-fashioned Oxford voters; others saw the expediency of preferring the premier to the peer.[47]

Oxonians still continued to be ready to head for Badminton at the slightest pretext. The Duchess's mother, the witty and engaging Fanny Boscawen (the Hon. Mrs. Edward Boscawen), visiting the family seat in the summer of 1779, found her pleasure in a quiet family reunion, enhanced when 'My favorite Mr [John] Price of the Bodleian Library [was] sent for to meet me'.[48] The Duke's sincere churchmanship (he rebuilt the parish church at Badminton in 1785 at his own expense)[49] and commitment to his family stood at a remove from raffish Whig society in that decade, and had won him enough University admirers and followers to make him adjudge standing a second time for the Chancellorship in 1792 was worthwhile. Fanny Boscawen canvassed numerous Oxford voters, calling in family favours in support of her son-in-law:

> I am going to write to Lord Onslow at Clandon to get a certain Dr Turner of Merton, a friend of his, and I am so zealous that I shall never lose an opportunity of trying, in which I find lights and lights that I should not have expected. One tells me of a Master of Arts, another suggests a Doctor of Laws, ... '[50]

The bid failed since the full weight of government—and Christ Church—influence was put behind the 3rd Duke of Portland. Beaufort saw the direction of the tide and withdrew with some grace in order to ensure the peace of the University.[51]

---

[45] He was Master of the Horse to Queen Charlotte, 1768–70, resigning when the Grafton ministry fell. The Duke refused the Lord Chamberlainship in 1783, as he believed George III had broken his promise to give him the Garter. Horace Walpole, Journals of George III [MS], p. 5, Lewis Walpole Library, Yale University. He was eventually awarded the Order in 1786.

[46] Jenkins, 'Jacobites and Freemasons', 403.

[47] Beaufort's weak candidature was withdrawn at the last moment. Ward, Georgian Oxford, 258–9.

[48] Mrs Boscawen to Fanny Sayer, 23 June 1779, quoted in C. Aspinall-Oglander, Admiral's Widow. Being the Life and Letters of the Hon. Mrs. Edward Boscawen From 1761 to 1805 (London, 1942), 96. Price (1735–1813, BA, Jesus College, 1757; Bodley's Librarian, 1768–1813), was'...always ready to communicate information to his friends and literary men and from the rich stores of which he had the care.' Bodl MS Top Oxon. d.174, f. 233. David Vaisey, 'Price, John (1735-1813), librarian', ODNB, online edn., 2004.

[49] B.F.L. Clarke, The building of the eighteenth-century church (London, 1963), 60.

[50] Letter, 12 Aug. 1792, quoted in Aspinall-Oglander, Admiral's Widow, 152. 'Dr Turner' is likely to be George Turner (d. 1797), matric. Merton College 1753, BA 1756, MA 1762, DD 1783, vicar of Culham, Oxon. He was appointed Archdeacon of Oxford in 1783 while Onslow's client, John Butler, was Bishop of Oxford. Foster, IV. 1449.

[51] Hants RO, Carnarvon Papers, 75M91/A17/6, Portland to Porchester, 21 Aug. 1792.

For all the Bentinck family's hereditary Whiggery, the Duke of Portland quickly consolidated and extended his reach as an Oxford patron during Pitt's wartime ministry. Much was due to the good offices of Dean Jackson, but it helped that his estate at Bulstrode Park was only just over the county boundary in Buckinghamshire. With Portland mostly away in London on demanding Home Office duties in wartime (he was Secretary of State from 1794 to 1801) and preferring to go further away to his main estate at Welbeck Abbey when he had opportunity for leisure, he allowed easy-to-reach Bulstrode to become both an academic and a ministerial retreat. In 1797, for instance, it was made available for the use of William Windham, Secretary-at-War, and Speaker Henry Addington, as well as for Oxford's Vice Chancellor.[52] Here networks intersected, connections were formed (or not), and promises of patronage made in a setting located with symbolic aptness halfway between Oxford and Westminster.[53] Because of the crisis generated domestically by the French Revolution, Portland had the opportunity to make himself an insider in 1792–4 on a scale none of the Beaufort dukes had managed. Apart from his own Bentinck family offerings, he was the point of access to Home Office and University patronage combined.[54] No Oxonian with half an ambition in the 1790s could afford to ignore him or fail to identify with the Duke's political pedigree and ancestral associations that, historically, could not be more different from the Beauforts'. In the last years of the century, however, there was nothing much to distinguish the loyalism of the Portland Whigs from the Oxford Tories.

The scale of ducal patronage was on a different level from that in the gift of most Oxford patrons, those who might look first, when a family living fell vacant, to offer it to a student contemporary or perhaps to a Fellow despairing of finding a college benefice. Such networks remain to be fully recovered, but an appropriate place to begin would be with the Midlands gentry, a rich source of patronage for Oxford graduates in good and bad times. Families like the Digbys, the Bagots, and the Dolbens were largely cold-shouldered by the Whig establishment before the 1760s, and they did what they could to help clergy clients find curacies or chaplaincies when Toryism, churchmanship, and intellectual preferences made getting a career under way problematic unless principle was compromised. At Coleshill in Warwickshire resided that archetype of Tory virtues, the 5th Lord Digby of Geasehill [I] (1661–1752), a Magdalen man (DCL, 1708), exemplary in his charity and support for Oxford High Churchmen including Nonjurors, among

---

[52] Nottm UL, Pw F 6255, Portland to Dr. French Laurence, 13 July 1797. Scrope Berdmore (Warden of Merton) and Edmund Isham (Warden of All Souls) both held the Vice-Chancellorship in 1797.

[53] This use of Bulstrode was foreshadowed when University leaders were splendidly entertained by the Duke there shortly prior to his installation, with Lord Stormont, Lord Malmesbury, Bishop Smallwell of Oxford, Sir William Scott, Burke, the wealthy young plantation owner Charles Rose Ellis (1771–1845), and William Windham among the other guests. Bodl. MS Top Oxon. d.174, f. 233.

[54] See Chapter 8, pp. 41, 81–2.

Fig. 12.1 5th Lord Digby of Geashill, Sir Godfrey Kneller, attrib., oil on canvas, 1715 (Reproduced by kind permission of the President and Fellows of Magdalen College).

them the pious John Kettlewell (1653-95) and later, the poet and educationalist, Edward Holdsworth.[55]

They held his livings, educated his sons (who all predeceased him), and were set an irreproachable example of integrity by their patron.[56] One practical way patrons like Digby could help was by funding increased endowments for livings in their gift. Digby did so for the rectory of Over Whiteacre, where his constant supporter in good works, Thomas Bray (later founder of the SPCK and SPG), had been installed in 1685.[57]

In a later generation, few did as much as Sir Roger Newdigate, MP, did for the University over three decades, he who, through his own rebuilding work at his

---

[55] William E. Burns, 'Kettlewell, John (1653-1695), nonjuring Church of England clergyman and theological writer', *ODNB*, online edn., 2016.

[56] L. Digby, *My Ancestors, Being the History of the Digby & Strutt Families* (London, 1928), 59, 61; Howard Erskine-Hill, The *Social Milieu of Alexander Pope: lives, example, and the poetic response* (New Haven, CT, 1975), 132-65; GEC, IV. 354-5. It was a loss to the Tory cause in Parliament that he could not be persuaded to stand for the University in the by-election of 1703. http://www.histparl.ac.uk/volume/1690-1715/member/digby-william-1661-1752

[57] He held the rectory of nearby Sheldon after the holder became a Nonjuror in 1690. Thompson, *Thomas Bray*, 3-4, 9.

Warwickshire seat, inspired 'the web of Gothic endeavour spreading from Arbury Hall',[58] and was indefatigable in attending to local matters in the north of the county, (which included placing men of capacity in parishes). Among them was his old friend and Gibbon's tutor at Magdalen, Dr Thomas Winchester, incumbent of Astley (whose stipend was made up by local contributions).[59] The patron-client relation could always sour. Thus Winchester's curate, one Walters, in 1767 circulated material in Oxford that started criticism of Newdigate's parliamentary conduct. Understandably piqued, Sir Roger, turned the tables on Walters by observing that he had breached the express condition of his appointment to say the offices in their liturgical sequence: 'on Saints days & Holy days, he suffer'd the Holy Week to pass without prayers, even on Good Friday.' Newdigate further told the Vice-Chancellor that when Walters was reminded of what was expected of him 'he flatly & rudely told me I might expect what I pleas'd [but] he would not do it.'[60]

It was not far from Arbury into Staffordshire and the Bagot family seat at Blithfield, held successively by Sir Walter Bagot, 5th Bt., High Tory with Jacobite leanings and his son, Sir William, a fervent churchman and defender who, with Newdigate, was vociferous in the Commons for maintaining the legal status quo of the Church of England when the pressure was on in 1772.[61] The family living at Blithfield was reserved as a place of refuge for Oxonians of the same kidney, though, like Newdigate, the Bagots expected their appointees to be dedicated pastors (or at least to appoint curates who would do so for them). The rectory was held between 1749 and 1758 by Thomas Townson, though he moved north across the county boundary to Malpas (Cheshire) in 1752 to take possession of the lower mediety benefice at the disposal of his former tutee, William Drake.[62]

---

[58] Oliver Cox, 'An Oxford college and the eighteenth-century Gothic Revival', *Oxoniensia*, 77 (2012), 117–35, at 135.

[59] Astley was a perpetual curacy. Newdigate hoped that Winchester would accept his offer of the parish in 1757 but said '...I wish [it] was better worthy of you'. 10 Mar. 1757, ed. White, *Newdigate correspondence*, 91. For legal squabbles in the late 1760s over the curate's income and legal charges allegedly owing to Newdigate see ibid., App. B.

[60] See Wetherell to Newdigate, 11 Dec. 1767, Warks. RO, Newdegate of Arbury, B2332. He went on, '...can my good constituents at Oxford think or expect...that I could sit quietly down with such a person as my table companion after this,...'. Newdigate was absolutely insistent that clergy in his living performed their duty and when they did not do so to his satisfaction he put his case before them and asked them to resign. See the instance of the Rev. John Rennie, a wartime refugee from Georgia and undertaking—or not doing—duty at Astley and Chilvers Coton. Newdigate to Rennie, 27 Apr. 1782, ed. White, *Newdigate correspondence*, 229–31; n.d., 253–4. When Rennie eventually did vacate the vicarage of Chilvers Coton, Newdigate appointed the Rev. G. Ebell Jr. simply on the basis of his Oxford education and Oxford endorsements. Ibid., [Mar. 1786], ibid., 238. I have been unable to discover the first name of the Rev. Mr Walters.

[61] In the new atmosphere of George III's reign, the bestowal of a barony on Sir William Bagot in 1780 on North's recommendation and the appointment to the Deanery of Christ Church of his brother Lewis in 1777 was not greatly out of the ordinary. GEC, I. 374; www.histparl.ac.uk/volume/1754–1790/member/bagot-william-1728–98

[62] See Chapter 11, p. 11.

Arbury–Blithfield–Malpas was one Midlands axis.[63] A more self-contained one had Finedon in central Northamptonshire as its nucleus. It was here that the High Church Dolben family resided. Oxford amply compensated the Rev. Sir John Dolben, the 2nd Baronet, for the absence of the Crown largesse he might have anticipated as the son of an archbishop of York - but for the Hanoverian succession in 1714. At that date, though still under thirty, Dolben was already Sub-Dean of the Chapels Royal, but found himself soon discarded as a suspect Tory placeman by Whig ministers with their own followers to feed. Balliol, his old college, chose him as its Visitor; Lord Crew, Bishop of Durham, secured him one of the best prebends in the cathedral, and made him one of his five executors.[64] When not in residence in the north, Dolben made Finedon a civilised centre of musical culture and High Church values, working to ensure that his parochial and diocesan influence was exercised on behalf of young Oxford Tories who shared his values. It was thus no surprise to find that, towards the close of Sir John's life (1750–5), William Jones (of Nayland) was curate at Finedon and his fellow Hutchinsonian, George Horne, delivered his first sermon from its pulpit.[65] Sir John Dolben's successor in the baronetcy was a layman, his eldest son, William, who, no less dedicated to the well-being of the University, represented it in the Commons for over two decades, and quietly preserved Finedon as a High Church bastion, indeed one with an Evangelical edge, reflected in his own commitment to the humanitarian regulation of the slave trade.[66]

The number of personal livings in the hands of the Bagots, the Dolbens, and the like was relatively small by comparison with what some diocesan bishops from an Oxford background might have on offer for old college connections, quite apart from the chaplaincies in their gift. This route provided another clientage corridor through which many graduates travelled in the course of the century, supplementing what colleges and private patrons had at their disposal.[67] And with Oxford men receiving more mitres in George III's reign, the opportunities for episcopal patronage rose to a level not seen since the later Stuarts. When

---

[63] The families socialised on a regular basis; see, for instance, Lady Bagot looking forward to a Saturday dinner at Arbury, 'if you will be troubled with such revellers as we...' To Sir R. Newdigate, 2 Nov. 1788, Warks. RO, Newdegate of Arbury, CR136/B/2650.

[64] Such was the general respect for Sir John Dolben that he ended his career at Durham as Vice-Dean. ed. Hughes, *Letters of Spencer Cowper*, 118, 150, 163.

[65] NRO, Finedon Parish Registers. He appears to have left on Dolben's decease in 1755.

[66] The Slave Trade Act 1788 28 Geo. III, c. 54 (known as Dolben's Act) was the first legislation to regulate the shipping of slaves. In his speech of 9 May 1788, *PH*, 27, col. 606, he noted 'that venerable body' [Oxford University] had proposed 'by the distribution of religious books, and other means' to take steps towards 'the improvement of the minds of the African slaves,...'

[67] The bishops of Exeter had the meagre total of seventeen in their diocese. The archbishops of Canterbury were exceptional in presenting to 105 benefices, well above the next highest of Bangor (61). Gregory, *Restoration, Reformation and Reform*, 37. In 1835 only 11.6% of advowsons across the country were in episcopal hands. G. F. A. Best, *Temporal Pillars. Queen Anne's Bounty and the Ecclesiastical Commissioners of the Church of England* (Cambridge, 1964), 345;Virgin, *The Church in an age of negligence*, 173–4, 179–80.

William Markham was translated from Chester to the metropolitan see of York in 1777 he gave up the Deanery of Christ Church but immediately began to use archiepiscopal patronage for the benefit of his former collegians, especially Chapter members.[68] They took their place in the queue next after his sons and other male relations, and did well over the twenty-nine years he held the see. Thus Cyril Jackson (his next but one successor as Dean of Christ Church) was awarded the well-endowed rectories of first Carlton-in-Lindrick (Notts.), then Kirkby-in-Cleveland (NR Yorks.).[69] Such a nomination of a former Common Room colleague was an accurate indication that patron-client relations often rested on previous amicable association rather than clinical calculation of mutual interest.

ii) Family, friendship, and academic loyalties

> ... those individual friendships, which are the most pleasing, the most permanent, and the most beneficial, that human nature and human life admit.
>
> William Barrow, *An Essay on Education; in which are particularly considered the merits and the defects of the discipline and instruction in our Academies* (2 vols., London, 1804), [Bampton Lecturer, 1799], II. 305.

> ... the only thing that ever made you like Oxford was the company of some friends that you was very fond of...
>
> Charles Arbuthnot, Vienna, to John Sneyd, 26 May [1788], Houghton Library, Harvard University, John Sneyd correspondence, MS Eng 742

Oxford loyalties were frequently the product of early upbringing, absorbed by a boy within a family setting well before he was of an age to attend a particular college. The strong continuity of masculine values was a given in this period in which familial traditions could be presumed to override other influences.[70] There would be a presumption of attending the University that would be present first in the home and then in his schooldays, and it would only falter as a consequence of personal incapacity or major changes in a family's personal or material

---

[68] The Abps of York had fifty-five advowsons to livings, just 6% of the diocesan total. Daniel Cummins, 'The clergy database as a tool for academic research: a study of the parochial patronage of the Archbishops of York c1730–1800', in eds. R. C. E. Hayes and W. J. Sheils, *Clergy church and society in England and Wales c.1200–1800. Borthwick texts and studies*, 41 (2013), 163–74, at 165.

[69] Ibid., 166–9.

[70] H. French and M. Rothery, '"Upon your entry to the world"; Masculine values and the threshold of adulthood among landed elites in England, 1680–1800', *Social History*, 33 (2008), 403–22.

614   ENLIGHTENED OXFORD

circumstances. Motives were undoubtedly varied. Fathers might be privately keen to relive their own collegiate experience vicariously through their sons;[71] this would afford an excuse to be in contact again with a former tutor; tutors in turn might use parental contact (especially with gentry families) to nurture personal or institutional benefits; a particular college might recommend itself because of its reputation on one head or another. In 1696 the London bookseller, Richard Lapthorne, was thus pleased that his son was going to Pembroke College because it was governed in person by the Bishop of Bristol [John Hall] and noted that Pembroke was 'one of the best for sobriety and order and I am very glad that it is my sons lot to bee there'.[72] Of course, the experience of Oxford life might have been so unfortunate or unhappy that an individual might want to forget it and not commend it to his own sons or nephews. Or, he could decide that, rather than reject attendance at Oxford altogether (or send the boy to Cambridge), advise enrolment at a different college or hall. Otherwise, generational associations with individual colleges on the basis of family attendance imparted a dynastic dimension to being an Oxonian, who would, after graduation, be expected to make the same endorsement to his own male descendants.[73]

Entry to a particular college could simply be on the basis of the linear descent from the founder and other dignitaries of the college. By the early nineteenth century, sixteen out of twenty-four Oxford colleges and halls had engrafted foundations with preference for founders' kin. All Souls was the most celebrated because of its vulnerability to the claims of descendants of its founder, Archbishop Walter Chichele.[74] On the intending student's side, proofs of academic genealogy had to be forthcoming or someone with a better claim might instead gain entry. As a place-seeker at Corpus Christi College was advised by Henry Sacheverell in 1704: 'to render your claim sufficient there must be a disproof of the pretensions of others'.[75] Short of comprehensively querying the applicant's natal bona fides and even taking him to court, colleges could struggle to do much about it. They certainly tried the various options as opinion against the privilege of founders' kin began to harden. Various attempts were made to impose restrictions to prevent

---

[71] New accommodation could be a lure, as at Christ Church, as Peckwater Quad was constructed. Canon Stratford reported to Lord Harley: 'My Lord Berkeley [4th Lord Berkeley of Stratton, Chancellor of the Duchy of Lancaster] brought his son [John, later 5th Baron] hither yesterday, and we have notice of so many noblemen and gentlemen that design to come to us shortly that we are under great difficulties how to provide rooms for them. We are going to finish as fast as we can the third side of Peckwater, though we do it upon credit'. 14 July 1713, HMC, *Portland MSS*, VII. 154.

[72] eds. R. J. Kerr and I. Coffin-Duncan, *The Portledge papers ... 1687–1697* (London, 1927), 220, quoted in French and Rothery, '"Upon Your entry onto the world"'.

[73] For families offering 'a sort of readymade network', see I. K. Ben-Amos, *The culture of giving: informal support and gift-exchange in early modern England* (Cambridge, 2008), 47.

[74] Squibb, *Founders' kin*, 15. Appendix one gives details of these privileges at Oxford Colleges and Halls, 134–44.

[75] To Edward Willson, 13 Sept. 1704, Staffs RO D1178/2, unfoliated papers, quoted in Woolf, *The social circulation of the past*, 79.

the academically undistinguished taking up places. but the case of Wood v. All Souls College (1723) established that the provisions of statutes relating to founders' kin must be literally obeyed.[76] Not that the ruling prevented Fellows—fortified by having Blackstone's *Collateral Consanguinity* (1750) to guide and justify them—from still rejecting candidates for alleged lack of learning. Many appeals to the not unsympathetic Visitor (the Archbishop of Canterbury) followed.[77] One way to squeeze out the unqualified and keep down the numbers of Chichele's kinsmen was to postulate the widest possible interpretation of kindred, and that was exactly what Benjamin Buckler's *Stemmata Chicheleana* (1765, supp. 1775) offered.[78] There was recognition that if founders' kin was educationally anomalous, outright abolition was out of the question in a society where the entitlements of birth were a social given.

Even where founders' kin was not technically applicable, familial associations with particular colleges were enduring. Examples abound. The Fothergills from Westmorland were perhaps the most prominent of families from the far north-west of England who nurtured connections with Queen's in every generation while remaining rooted in their own home parish of Ravenstonedale.[79] George Fothergill ('Old Snod') in the course of the 1720s progressed from being a Taberdar and Poor Child to a fellowship and kept a watchful eye on the progress of his younger brother, Thomas, and other relations, while personally building up what Thomas called a 'very fine stock of pupils'.[80] He made few trips back to the family residence at Lockholme, in what was a large parish, but gave generously to the rebuilding of Ravenstonedale church, and furnished it with a chalice and patten in 1743.[81] Thomas himself (1715–96, 'Old Customary'), who served as provost between 1767 and 1796, was admitted as tenant of Lockholme on his eldest brother's death in 1783, but it was Queen's that was his real home throughout his life.[82]

In Northamptonshire, the association of the Isham family (from a higher social bracket than the Fothergills, holding a Charles I baronetcy) with Lincoln College

---

[76] Burrows, *Worthies of All Souls*, 383–4.   [77] See Chapter 6.

[78] Burrows, *Worthies of All Souls*, 47.

[79] See Fothergill letters, MS 737/1–6, Queen's College, Oxford; Richard Fothergill, *The Fothergills. A First History* (Newcastle, 1998); Catherine Thornton and Frances Mclaughlin, *The Fothergills of Ravenstonedale. Their Lives and their Letters* (London, 1905).

[80] Thomas Fothergill was delighted to tell his parents that George was 'highly esteemed by the most distinguished men' in Oxford. Cumbria Record Office (Kendal), WDX 94/acc. 165 (n.d.). George was also esteemed by his eldest brother Richard, who called him '... strict, regular & exemplary in his piety. As well bred & accomplished as a courtier, as reverend & venerable as an apostle.' Richard to Thomas Fothergill, (n.d., c. 1760), Cumbria Record Office (Kendal), WDX 94/acc. 165.

[81] Fothergill, *The Fothergills*, 40. When meeting with friends with a Ravenstonedale background and talking about fundraising for the church, he noted ruefully that '... tho' everybody seemed to wish well to the design, I did not discover or observe in them any forwardness to contribute towards it, and so the talk of it passed off'. To his parents, 22 July 1751, Cumbria Record Office (Kendal), WDX 94/acc. 165.

[82] Fothergill, *The Fothergills*, 42. R. H. Hodgkin lays much of the blame for what he considered the decline of Queen's on its two Fothergill Provosts. *Six centuries of an Oxford College*, 153, 160.

Fig. 12.2 Rev. George Fothergill, Principal St Edmund Hall, 1751–60, unknown artist, oil on canvas (St Edmund Hall, Oxford).

was at least as emphatic. Usually the eldest son went into Parliament, one of the younger ones became a don, most of them attended Lincoln, and they married into neighbouring gentry families with comparable ties to the University.[83] With the ancestral seat only fifty miles north of Oxford, it was feasible for Euseby Isham (elected Rector of Lincoln in 1731) to be also incumbent of Lamport (from 1730), where he built the elegant rectory designed by Francis Smith of Warwick.[84] He had a deep affection for his home, and was never happier than when in residence on his living, where he saw restoration work on the church through to completion.[85] Euseby—or 'Eusy' as his relations familiarly referred to him—was a sociable man and liked to bring his family back to Oxford with him when opportunity offered. His sister Edmunda ['Munda'] Isham told her brother, Sir

---

[83] For Isham family pride in its heraldry and lineage see Matthew Craske, *The Silent Rhetoric of the Body. A History of Monumental Sculpture and Commemorative Art in England, 1720–1770* (New Haven, CT, 2007), 445.
[84] Colvin, *Dictionary of British Architects*, 889.
[85] Green, *Lincoln College*, 309. Movement of his books between the two sites became problematic. See his request for a wagon to convey his books to Lamport. E. Isham at Oxford to Sir J. Isham at Lamport, 30 Apr. 1730, NRO, Isham Papers, 2640.

Edmund, about a grand ball held locally, attended by Sir John Dolben [of Finedon], noting that 'Bro. Eusy was at lamport during the Bar^{nts} Stay, and has invited a Party of us to Oxford, ... '[86] Such social recreations offered opportunities for what might be deemed 'extended Oxford families' to socialize, and from them often resulted those ties of wedlock which reinforced connections with each other and, by extension, to particular colleges and the University as a whole, all part of the way in which was fostered 'a greater degree of cultural cohesions among elites' that 'crystallized their self-awareness as a ruling class'.[87] The local nexus was always prominent. Thus at Lincoln College, Isham's successor, Michael Robinson (author of *Short Treatise on the Globes*, 1752) had a sister, Mary, who married Sir John Danvers of Culworth, Northamptonshire, as his third wife and it was his nephew, Sir Michael Danvers, who awarded Robinson the valuable living of the same village in 1765.[88]

Friendship, too, could be a motivator in confirming academic loyalties, and might give rise to a recognition in later years of how much of an individual's progress through life had come about through sharing a common Oxford experience with congenial contemporaries. As Richard Polwhele, the Cornish antiquarian, observed with no small gratitude:[89]

At Christ Church I have succeeded in forming connexions the most valuable— connexions which probably through life will soothe my cares, and heighten my enjoyments.

Through those connections could arise passions that might last for life. Thus Coplestone Warre Bampfylde (1720–91), a fine amateur artist and gardener of Hestercombe House near Taunton, was friends at Oxford with the portraitist Richard Phelps of Porlock (1718–85), who had been, like Sir Joshua Reynolds, the apprentice of Thomas Hudson. Without that early contact with Phelps at St John's College, Bampfylde's artistic commitment would never have developed as it did.[90] Particular friendships forged while at the University could be the result of previous recommendation but, whatever their origin, they might well continue when Oxford was left behind. As one new graduate told a friend at Glasgow University in 1793:

---

[86] Brixworth, 29 Jan. n.d., NRO, Isham Papers, 2517.

[87] Nicholas Henshall, *The Zenith of European Monarchy and its Elites. The Politics of Culture, 1650–1750* (Basingstoke, 2010), 64; H. de Ridder-Symoens, 'Training and Professionalization', in W. Reinhard, *Power Elites and State Building* (Oxford, 1996), 149–72, at 159–60.

[88] Green, *Lincoln College*, 351. Robinson owed his fellowship (1720) to Lord Crew, his father having been Rector of Eydon close to Crew's seat at Steane; his sermons were printed after his death.

[89] Richard Polwhele, *Traditions and Recollections* (London, 1826), 88.

[90] P. White, *A Gentleman of Fine Taste. The Watercolours of Coplestone Warre Bampfylde* (Taunton, 1995).

Fig. 12.3 Richard Roundell and others on the banks of the Isis, a view of Oxford beyond, John Hamilton Mortimer, oil on canvas, c.1765 (Dorfold Hall Events Limited). Roundell (matric. Univ. Coll., 1760) is seated; the Hon. Thomas Noel (matric. BNC, 1763, later 2nd Viscount Wentworth) is to his right; Henry Dashwood (matric. BNC, 1763, later 3rd Bt., of Kirtlington Park, Oxon.) is in the centre; and Walter Ramsden Beaumont Hawksworth (later Fawkes) (matric. Univ. Coll., 1764), later Fawkes) to his left.

> 'Birch, as you probably know, is gone into a regiment of Dragoons:... He was only a short time at Oxford, but quite long enough to be esteemed by all who knew him. I cultivated his acquaintance as being a friend of yours, for (as in mathematics), those who are friends to the same person, ought to be friends to one another,...'[91]

Such recent graduates might holiday together discovering that amity trumped political differences. This was the case for two Christ Church men, the protégés of Cyril Jackson: Henry, 3rd Lord Holland (the nephew of Charles James Fox) and the 'extremely good natured' John, 2nd Lord Boringdon (1772–1840), also the friend of George Canning and an embryonic Pittite.[92] At the other end of their

---

[91] Lewis Way to anon., Sept. 1793, HRO, 75M91/B19/1.
[92] Lord Holland (in Alicante) to the Countess of Upper Ossory, 28 July 1793, NLI, Fitzpatrick MSS. 8012 (8).

lives, two eighteenth-century Oxonians, between them MP for the University for above half a century, were bound together by a rich tapestry of associations and, as widowers and still vigorous, continued to take pleasure in each other's company, their estates, and what these represented, as the county drifted back into war with Napoleonic France in 1803. What Dolben called, after another stay at Arbury, Newdigate's 'noble & hospitable roof, preeminent as it is in genuine Gothic Grandeur, primitive Regularity, & warm old English benevolence...', was both an expression of thanks and a recognition of values at risk in a renewed global contest.[93]

Just to mention time spent together could, by bringing those days back to memory, generate personal fulfilment in the present for the two individuals who had shared them. There could be a real nostalgic edge to Oxford recollected in tranquillity. One verse epistle from a former Christ Church student who recalled times when 'BAGOT smil'd Applause, nor JACKSON frown'd', in places almost anticipates Matthew Arnold in its evocation of Oxford and the surrounding countryside, as in the lines:[94]

> 'How oft, as less excursive Fancy mov'd,
> Not unimpeded by our Gowns we rov'd –
> (Our careless Gowns that vaunted no Degree)
> And climbed the Hill, and hail'd Joe Pullen's Tree;
> Or winded thro' our own contiguous Glade,
> Or Merton waving wild its bowering Shade.'

It might be enough to state, as one writer recalled in 1691, 'Thou and I were chums [i.e. chamber fellows] together at Brasenose College', and leave the rest to return to memory unbidden.[95] An unexpected letter from a college contemporary might both bring back memories of times in Oxford decades previously and provide an impetus to reconnect in turn with other matriculands of a given cohort, as much out of curiosity as from any search for present benefits. Bishop Lowth's son, the Rev. Robert Lowth, thus wrote affectionately in 1822 to the dramatist and wit, George Colman the Younger, reminding him of their days together at Christ Church back in 1781 when Bagot was Dean, a moment when the future Foreign Secretary William, Lord Grenville, future Governor-General of India, Marquess Wellesley, future Colonial Secretary, the 3rd Earl Bathurst, and future Speaker, Charles Abbot, Lord Colchester, were all in residence.[96] Colman was delighted:

---

[93] Dolben to Newdigate, 25 Apr. 1803, Warks. RO, B3728.

[94] *Epistle to a College Friend, written in the country some years after the author had left the university* (London?, 1785?).

[95] Quoted in Keith Thomas, *The Ends of life. Roads to fulfilment in early modern England* (Oxford, 2009), 199–200.

[96] Colman the Younger, *Random Records*, I. 277–81, 303–4.

620 ENLIGHTENED OXFORD

Had a man been "bearing fardels" for half a century, till his jaundiced mind could perceive nothing in this world but "envy, hatred, and all uncharitableness", such a kindly letter as the foregoing might present an antidote to his misanthropy, and bring back his affections to his fellows.[97]

Past Oxford ties could also be a useful lever to call in favours in the present day, as one obscure Irish baronet tried with the 1st Earl of Ilchester, brother of the powerful Henry Fox. After apologising for troubling the Earl after a thirty-year interval, he asked a favour for his third son, who was a cornet in General John Campbell's 14th regiment, sugaring the request with '... memories of the intimacy your Lordshp once permitted me to have wth you; and the many merry happy days and nights we spent together, at Christ Church and Balliol Colleges'.[98]

A sense of what one owed might have burnt with a steady flame with minimal stimulation from others, and from an early date. Witness the measured but heartfelt comments of a recent graduate, William Gilpin [son of the recorder of Carlisle], writing to Provost Smith in 1746:

> Whenever I think or speak of Queen's, my first thoughts are always sentiments of gratitude; and indeed I must have an uncommon share of a hateful vice were it otherwise. The absence in the country indulged me before my residence; my immediate selection after it; an exhibition, to which I had no manner of claim; a taberdarship, which the indulgence of the College alone gave me a title to, with a great many other favours, have already laid me under such obligations, as perhaps few have been bound by.[99]

Comparable instances can be multiplied, for many alumni both wanted to stay in touch with their alma mater and were conscious of a debt, in terms of social and patronal capital acquired, that could not be paid off but should simply be acknowledged with gratitude, as one ex-scholar of Worcester College turned Hertfordshire parson tried to do with his old Provost:

> I cannot forget the continued favours you shewed me when I lived at Worcester College, and others confer'd since; but to Remember you, as I do, in my Devotions is all the Gratitude I can boast of. The rest degenerates into mere Impertinence and makes me trouble you as I do now.[100]

---

[97] Ibid., I. 387.

[98] Sir Edward O'Brien to Ilchester, 25 Jan. 1761, BL Holland House Papers Add MS 51349, f. 113.

[99] 28 Nov. 1746, Queen's College, MS. 473.

[100] Rev Thomas Ringer, of Wymondley, Herts., to Warden Blechinden, 30 Sept. 1732, Worcester College Archives, B1/1/20. For gifts to Worcester College in the decades after its foundation see Richard Smethurst, 'Benefactors, Endowment and Finances', in eds. J. Bate and J. Goodman, *Worcester, portrait of an Oxford college* (London, 2014), 46–58.

The letter suggests a warm, filial-paternal affection between student and Head of House. Indeed, relations between the dons, 'noblemen', and gentlemen commoners were often close and not easily discarded. They would get to know each other quite well with an emerging sense of what each might do for the other, an exchange, as it were, of an education for patronage.[101] To act as 'bear-leader' on a continental Grand Tour offered such opportunities, and so did pre-graduation excursions around Britain in the long vacation, of the sort undertaken by Richard Newton, Principal of the brand-new Hertford College, in company with well-off undergraduates. Only too conscious of the need to boost income, Newton manoeuvred to keep gentleman commoners from taking the relatively easy road to a BCL degree, and required them to go through the same rigorous course of studies as the rest of the College, paying, as they thus did, double fees.[102] Cyril Jackson, Dean of Christ Church, was peerless in his cultivation of his pupils at every stage in their later life, and visited many of them in London or during the summer vacations on their estates.[103] So was his younger brother William, the future Bishop of Oxford. His familiarity with the Dartmouths and their family began in the early 1770s as a tutor at Christ Church.[104]

At an institution such as Christ Church, where the occupants of the cathedral canonries (appointed by the Crown) determined the flavour of the 'House', favours could be called in early. Thus a very recent graduate, Lord Finch (later 7th Earl of Winchilsea) was contacted by Bishop Smalridge late in 1715 to support Richard Newton's appointment to a canonry as '... one who have unasked been please'd to shew Ye self a Friend & patron to Christ Church, & one whom therefore I can safely depend that you will go on to be so, when we very much want Yr patronage'.[105] It mattered considerably that Finch was a newly promoted Lord of the Treasury and might help avert the appointment of a 'foreigner', i.e. a non-Christ Church appointee. Smalridge recognised that Christ Church, a Tory bastion in the new Whig dispensation, was all too aware the House needed all the friends it could get and saw the tactical uses of being quick off the mark in congratulating William Wake on his translation from Lincoln to Canterbury,

---

[101] For care taken in an earlier era among Cambridge tutors about organising work for gentry in a future rural setting see Victor Morgan, 'Cambridge University and "The Country" 1560–1600', in eds. Stone at al, *The University in Society*, I. 183–246, at 226–31.

[102] Hamilton, *Hertford College*, 76, 80.

[103] Jackson used his trips to London for the election of Westminster scholars to Christ Church to hobnob with the great and good in the capital. ed. Jupp, *The Letter-Journal of George*, 108. For his career advice to the young Canning, ibid., 43n. At Oxford Canning was awarded the Chancellor's medal and college prize for Latin verses. D. Marshall, *The rise of George Canning* (London, 1938), 22.

[104] He was writing regularly to Viscount Lewisham (Harrow and Christ Church, later the 4th Earl) while he was on his continental travels, e.g. 3 Nov. 1776, Staffs., RO, D(W) 1778/V/852. See also Ingamells, 600.

[105] Bp of Bristol to Lord Finch, Ch. Ch., 6 Nov. 1715, LLRO DG7/Bundle 24, Box 4950. Newton had to wait until 1752 for his canonry when it was recommended for him by Henry Pelham. Hamilton, *Hertford College*, 82–3.

622 ENLIGHTENED OXFORD

pointing out that he was the first Houseman to hold the primacy.[106] Wake replied in a vein that brilliantly illuminates collegiate expectations of prominent alumni:

> How far it may be in my power to be serviceable to Christ Church, the place of my education, I cannot foresee. This you may be assured; that as I always with pleasure remember my beloved college, and heartily bless God that I was bred in it, so I will never be wanting in my true endeavours for its service, as far as my other obligations of duty elsewhere will permit me to use them.[107]

There were several means of nurturing a warm regard for Oxford at a distance apart from kinship, friendship, and variations in academic paternalism. Individuals might be obligated in later life simply through the tenancy of a college estate or presentation to a college living.[108] Sometimes it was possible to combine a rural living and a college post. Thus Richard Radcliffe, vicar of Colsterworth, elected bursar of Queen's in 1776, divided his year between Oxford and his Lincolnshire parish, one hundred miles apart.[109] There would likely be regular trips to Oxford from all points of the compass, especially in activities directed towards securing a post or a property, or when legal disputes blew up and a college was unavoidably involved. Graduates would converge at election times, the perfect opportunity to gossip and catch up with each other's news and compare notes on the present state of the University by comparison with their time in residence. John Parfect, an Oriel graduate and former fellow in holy orders who had moved to the City of London,[110] proudly informed Sir Roger Newdigate, a decade after the latter's election success, of the basis of his dutiful outings back to Oxford:

> As to myself, I have been resident in this City above 12 years, visit College as often as the business of it, & the interest of our alma mater require; & never did i go with more readiness, or return with more spirit, than about ten years ago now. Your cause call'd me thither, & your triumph grac'd my Return back. My absence from college, & various Commissions have swell'd my correspondence to a considerable size, . . . [111]

The mechanics of travelling to Oxford could themselves open the way to clerkly socialising, as the Rev Robert Le Grys, a fellow of Caius College, Cambridge, recounted. En route, at Buckingham, he met a cleric [John Risley] 'who was going from Northampton to Oxford, on account of a Living belonging to

---

[106] Smalridge to Wake, 20 Dec. 1715, Ch. Ch., Wake MS, XV. ff. 38–40; same to same, 29 Dec. 171, Ch. Ch., Wake MS, XV. f. 41.

[107] 24 Dec. 1715, Ch. Ch., Wake MS, XV. f. 24.   [108] See the discussion in Chapter 9.

[109] ed. Evans, *Letters of Richard Radcliffe and John James*, 37.

[110] Foster, III. 1064: CCEd Person ID: 1645.

[111] Clement Lane, Lombard St., 15 Dec. 1761, Warks. RO, B2034.

New College, ... ' The two men got on so well that Risley introduced him to others in his circle.[112] Most colleges had a limited stock of livings and first preference tended to go to Fellows. It was thus always important for well-wishers to be alert for vacancies in their locality and report opportunities for additional patronage as they arose back to their friends in Oxford. As Henry Felton, the Principal of St Edmund Hall, did in 1738. He heard from the 3rd Duke of Rutland advising that the parish of Woolsthorpe with Stainworth, Lincolnshire (close to the family seat at Belvoir Castle) was vacant and that the living was at the disposal of Queen's College. Felton told Provost Smith to seize the moment, with the rather fussy caveat that 'All I am concerned for, is, that some Gentleman will take it, who will make himself acceptable to his Grace, ... '.[113]

Over the century, Oxford associational culture for alumni gradually added a more formalised dimension, but this owed less to the University or the colleges than to individual initiatives. Clubs and Societies were an established feature of eighteenth-century British culture, with instances in the metropolis for resident Welshmen or Yorkshiremen,[114] and these were something of a model for Oxonians who felt moved to meet recreationally and keep friendships warm and college loyalties well-defined, often building on convivial social and political connections first made in clubs and societies at the University.[115] Thus an annual anniversary meeting in London of men educated at either Winchester or New College began in 1758 and was held until 1800, first at the 'Crown and Anchor' in the Strand, then at Willis's Rooms and elsewhere. There was a good dinner, plenty to drink, and a chance to sing familiar associational songs such as 'Dulce Domum' and 'Omnibus Wykehamicis'.[116] From a more modest establishment, former pupils of Ealing school who had gone on to Oxford would meet regularly in the capital to renew the association of their undergraduate days, and men from other schools did similarly.[117] A prominent private individual could often take the lead

---

[112] 'A Journal of my Expedition to Oxford in the Year 1759', Norfolk Archives, MC150/50 625 x 3.

[113] MS. 473 Queen's College. Felton was chaplain to three successive dukes of Rutland. There is a sense in this letter of why Hearne deemed him 'a poor, vain, halfstrained, conceited man' (IX. 371). The Rev. William Atkinson was appointed to the rectory. CCEd Person ID: 5514.

[114] Newton E. Key, 'The political culture and political rhetoric of County Feasts and Feast Sermons, 1654-1714', *JBS*, 33 (1994), 223–56. Oxford city and county natives normally resident in the capital dined annually (at first separately, then together) in Oxford every year (226).

[115] Clark, *British Clubs and Societies*, 67–8. For instance, Whigs meeting in the Constitution Club, or the Tory wine club that met on 18 August annually to drink the Pretender's health and confusion to the Constitution Club's Whigs. Davis, *Balliol College*, 165–6. For the Red Herring Club, see Chapter 9. Thomas Warton the Elder and his son successively belonged to the Jelly Bag Society, a secret literary society that gathered at the Three Tuns tavern, Oxford, to compose epigrams and drink. Lynch, *Loving Literature*, 99–101. There were also the Nonsense Club, Free Cynics, and Arcadians in the early eighteenth century, but little is known in detail about their activities. In 1762 there were fourteen friendly societies, eight learned groups, seven drinking or dining clubs, and fourteen others, political, ethnic, or sporting. Hibbert and Hibbert, *Encyclopedia of Oxford*, 95–6.

[116] Hale, 'Music and Musicians', in eds. Buxton and Williams, *New College*, 276.

[117] Charles Knight, *Passages of a Working Life during half a Century; with a Prelude of Early Reminiscences* (3 vols., London, 1864), I. 55.

organisationally. Charles, 4th Earl of Orrery, the focus of the Phalaris controversy of the 1690s, maintained a lifelong association with his Christ Church contemporaries, sponsoring a lavish dinner 'every winter' for them in the 1710s and keeping up the connection into the next decade.[118] Such gatherings offered a less ritualised alternative to occasional College Feasts and commemorations held in Oxford and were managed by members rather than college officers.[119] Another influential model was the University College Club, founded by the Scott brothers, Robert Chambers, and Jacob, 2nd Earl of Radnor, in 1792. Primarily for lawyers, it was also enticing for College graduates who had enjoyed the academic and social *esprit de corps* fostered throughout Nathan Wetherell's long Mastership. It was intended to invoke the spirit of those early days and provide a both informal and private setting in which to discuss contemporary issues, principally the French Revolution, from a loyalist perspective. It was emblematic of their collective pride in their past that the bust of King Alfred was prominent at their gatherings.[120] And then there was the popularity of Freemasonry with Oxford graduates and the opportunities for beneficent sociability such gatherings offered, building on a culture of personal giving most colleges had been quick to nurture.[121]

iii) Clericalist culture beyond Oxford: individual endeavours

'I have a notion that at Oxford, if they are good Scholars, they contract High notions of themselves, which wear off when they come to live with the rest of the world'.

Lady Stafford to Lord Granville Leveson Gower, 14 May 1787.
Granville Leveson Gower, *Private Correspondence,* I. 8.

Members of the University College Club were primarily lawyers, littérateurs, and politicians, but it was, above all, the clergy whose individual and corporate ties to Oxford helped define them professionally, pastorally, and politically. Their presence in parishes across the country symbolised the reach not just of the Established Church but of the University of Oxford and confirmed the importance of the University in their formation. They were 'Oxford' in the localities and that character

---

[118] See Swift, *Journal to Stella,* ed. Williams, 408-9, 15 Mar. 1712; Smith, Jr., 'Charles Boyle, 4th Earl of Orrery', 488. For a fictional account of an annual London dinner held by Oxford graduates see Thomas Holcroft, *The Adventures of Hugh Trevor,* ed. Seamus Deane (first published 1797, Oxford, 1973), 396-402. For the Oxfordshire Club of 1753-5 and the sponsoring of dinners in the capital by both 'Old' and 'New' Interest see Robson, *Oxfordshire Election,* 58-9.

[119] For details of a gaudy at Brasenose held in the early 1770s see Crook, *Brasenose College,* 112.

[120] John Wilmot, *Memoirs of the life of the Right Honorable Sir John Eardley Wilmot, Knt.* (2nd ed., London, 1811), 123-4; Curley, *Sir Robert Chambers,* 65; Bourguignon, *Sir William Scott, Lord Stowell,* 38-9; Darwall-Smith, *University College,* 329. See also Chap. 8, pp. 99-100.

[121] The first Oxford Masonic lodge was set up in 1769 by the 5th Duke of Beaufort, and there were cultural connections with Jacobitism. Crook, *Brasenose College,* 150-3.

attracted loyalty and disdain in equal measure. Where they were resident in their parishes, their social status (especially as incomes rose over the century) was largely assured, pastoral duties could be undertaken personally or in whole or part delegated to a curate, but the opportunities for the intellectually inclined were limited. Many of them were ex-Fellows who had married, moved to the countryside, and encountered problems of either social or intellectual isolation or both.

One remedy was to hand, for many country parsonages operated as ad hoc research centres in eighteenth-century England.[122] Beneficed clergy usually had, should the inclination take them, sufficient leisure hours to commit themselves to one or more scholarly projects that both provided a relief from the demands of parish ministry and testified to the lasting imprint of their years at Oxford. At a time when there was no such thing as a research degree, an incumbency was often the closest Georgian England had to a funded opportunity for early career researchers. Publication was generally the objective, but many of these men left behind enough piles of accumulated notes and half-finished manuscripts to suggest that much of the gratification had come from the enterprise itself rather than a search for fame.[123] This persistence in learned pursuits could also lead to engagement in intellectual controversy by pamphlet or published sermon that might flare up into more vituperative exchanges along party lines. But that hazard was also a means of reconnecting them into networks they might have feared had been left permanently behind.

However remote from Oxford their physical distance, it was always open to graduates to return when they had opportunity, to work in the Bodleian or one of the college libraries, or bring their families with them to enjoy the sights and memories of old times.[124] It could bring forth almost rhapsodical emotions, as with the University College alumnus, Samuel Swire:[125]

---

[122] Cf. William McKelvey, noting ecclesiastical contexts for the 'invention' of English literature, observed that it was 'to a great extent shaped by parsons scribbling in their manses'. *The English Cult of Literature: Devoted Readers, 1774–1880* (Charlottesville, VA, 2006). Cf. Macaulay's reflection on the isolation of the parish clergy: 'Even a keen and strong intellect might be expected to rust in so unfavourable a situation'. *History of England*, ed. Firth, I. 318. Cf. Bishop Horsley's complaint to the clergy of the Rochester diocese about those who shut up their books after leaving University. *The Charge of Samuel... Bishop of Rochester to the Clergy of his diocese... at his primary visitation in... 1796, etc.* (London, 1796), 10. Moans about the intellectual sloth and lightweight reading tastes of many country clergy were nothing new. See, for instance, [Rev] John Clubbe, A *Letter of Free Advice to a Young Clergyman* (2nd edn., London, 1765); 31; Eusebius, Vicar of Lilliput [Joseph Robertson], *Observations on the late Act for augmenting the salaries of curates, in four letters to a friend* (London, 1797), 5.

[123] A case in point is Edward Williams (1762–1833), Pembroke, MA 1787; fellow of All Souls; perpetual curate of Battlefield and Uffington, Salop, 1786–1833, who left MSS on the history and antiquities of Shropshire. CCEd Person ID: 2567; G.C. Baugh, 'Shropshire', in eds. C.R.J. Currie and C.P. Lewis, *A Guide to English county histories. A tribute to C. R. Elrington* (Stroud, 1994), 336–47, at 343.

[124] John B. Radner, *Johnson and Boswell. A Biography of Friendship* (New Haven, CT, 2013), 178.

[125] Glos Archives, D2227/6/3, 16 Dec. 1805, Melsonby [N.R. Yorks.], 16 Dec. 1805. Dr Samuel Swire to Samuel Viner. Melsonby was a University College living that he held 1787–1816. Swire's parting

... reached old Alma Mater just as the lamps were beginning to be lighted up—In that sweet Place, which I saw with infinite pleasure, we staid one week—hearing sermons—attending Cathedral Prayers—seeing sights—eating & drinking incessantly—reading learned lectures—strutting about in a scarlet gown and swearing at no small rate—my happiness suffered some abatement when ever I came in sight of Merton or Corpus—...

Individual clergy were never at a remove from the University's cultural influence except by their own volition. Family reasons could also be decisive. After the incumbent of Castle Cary, father of the diarist James Woodforde, Fellow of New College, died in 1771, the latter soon relinquished his Somerset curacies on the appointment of his uncongenial cousin, Frank Woodforde, to the benefice. The latter had made it clear that he would serve the living of Ansford himself, 'which notice of my leaving the Curacy is I think not only unkind but very ungentlemanlike... Far be it from me to expect any favour at all from that house. All their actions towards me are bad...'.[126] And so James Woodforde came back to Oxford in December 1773, using New College as a base for his travels over the next few months, and his best and most likely source of patronage.[127] The strategy paid off. Within eighteen months (Dec. 1774), he had accepted the New College living of Weston Longville, Norfolk, where he remained until his death in 1803.

Those clergy who held benefices in Oxfordshire and adjacent counties might find their own parsonages more conducive to writing than remaining in college. Benjamin Holloway, the Hutchinsonian divine, did much of his best work while holding the rectories of Middleton Stoney (c.1730–59) and Bladon (1736–9), including *Originals physical and theological* (1751), *The Primaevity and Pre-eminence of the sacred Hebrew, above all other Languages, vindicated...* (1754), the latter directed against the Oxford Hebraist, Thomas Hunt.[128] Though originally a graduate of St John's College, Cambridge, Holloway was quickly assimilated into Oxford life, published with the University Press, and became a hero of the mid-century generation of Hutchinsonians, described by one enthusiastic undergraduate in 1749 as 'the greatest Scholar this Day in Europe'.[129] Holloway lost no opportunity of proclaiming the significance of what his master, John Hutchinson, had to say. In an advertisement to one of his own sermons originally preached in Woodstock, he affirmed this commitment with this admonition:

---

words are a reminder that Oxford could hold memories preferably not recalled. For Swire who was a Fellow of University College, 1766–88, see CCEd Person ID: 37781. For the living of Melsonby, Darwall-Smith, *University College*, 233, 326, 331.

[126] ed. Beresford, *The Diary of a Country Parson*, I. 118, 19 July 1773. He was also sub-Warden of New College and served as Pro-Proctor in 1774. He continued to reside at New College until Feb. 1776.

[127] See ed. Beresford, *The Diary of a Country Parson*, I. 119–42.

[128] See Chapter 8, p. 87 n. 226.

[129] 'Waggenseil' [G. Horne?] to Dr Fairfax, 17 Nov. 1749. Kent Archives, U23 C21/6.

were those writings so generally read as they deserve, and the original scriptures studied as they ought to be; by so many gentlemen as we have among us otherwise excellently learned, and orthodox; either, such strange books, as have, of late disturb'd the Church, would never be writ, or would be refuted with very little trouble.[130]

Interestingly, given his theological leanings and Tory inclinations, Holloway had been selected to deliver that sermon at an archidiaconal visitation in the Oxford diocese. The choice may have been motivated less by contentious divinity than his persona grata status at Blenheim with Sarah, Duchess of Marlborough (he acted as tutor to her favourite grandson, John, later 1st Earl, Spencer). During her twenty-two year widowhood, her importance as a patroness could not be overlooked, even by clergy with Holloway's views.[131] In search of models for the Duke's tomb at Blenheim, she had begun to visit Oxford regularly from the mid-1720s, behaved graciously, and patronised local tradesmen. A little coterie of university clergy attended wherever she went, cringing to her, it was said, as if they had been her footmen.[132] Holloway may well have been among them.

Holloway was a celebrity (though on a smaller scale than his supporters might have wished) and a presence in the University. Other clergy experienced acute pangs that, for all their achievements in their own eyes, for all that they had once been recognised in Oxford, in later life the alma mater had not done a stroke to lift them out of what one disgruntled priest called living 'in the midst of rustic HEATHENS'. The Whig, Dr John Free, complained that even during the national crisis of 1745-6, he (in his own words), 'a noted and approved Preacher in one of the Universities', had to make the melancholy reflection that even only for such a Term as this, all his Service, all his Piety, all his Innocence of Life, tho' in the Notice, and under the Eye, of his Superiors, pass quite unregarded'.[133] Certainly, in the first half of the century, the majority of Oxford educated parish clergy were Tories by persuasion and liable to do what they could to recommend the 'honest' cause to their parishioners (especially at election times). Where a parson of Whig persuasion,

---

[130] Benjamin Holloway, *The Commemorative Sacrifice. A Sermon preached at the Visitation* [George Rye, DD, Archdeacon of Oxford] *holden at Woodstock, Friday, October 8th, 1736* (Oxford, 1737).

[131] He dedicated several of his theological tracts to members of the Marlborough family. Sir Henry Ellis, *Original Letters of Eminent Literary Men of the Sixteenth, Seventeenth, and Eighteenth Centuries* (London, 1845), 320. Patronage in the Oxford diocese was concentrated in the hands of a few powerful magnates, headed by the dukes of Marlborough. McClatchey, *Oxfordshire Clergy*, 5.

[132] Harris, *A Passion for Government*, 269, 467. For the tetchy quarrel between the bps of Bristol (Bradshaw, Dean of Christ Church) and Oxford (John Potter) as to who should consecrate Blenheim chapel see Stratford to Oxford, 14 Oct. 1728, HMC, *Portland MSS*, VII. 467.

[133] *Sermons preached before the University of Oxford*, ix. Free worked hard to make his name during the Jacobite scare preaching loyalty and producing an *Imitation of Horace, Book IV. Ode 5* 'Humbly inscribed to his Royal Highness the Duke of Cumberland upon his defeat of the Rebel Army in Scotland'. *Poems, and Miscellaneous Pieces formerly written by John Free, DD* (London, 1751), 45–50. His courting of Cumberland was fruitless. Ward, *Georgian Oxford*, 167–8, 282.

628 ENLIGHTENED OXFORD

such as Walter Evans, the curate at Brailes, Warwickshire, a Welshman from Jesus College, attempted to indoctrinate his unsympathetic parishioners with his own trenchant anti-Catholicism bound up with his own Whiggishness, it merely triggered a counterproductive backlash in a village where, overall, both Catholics and Protestants wanted conciliation, not confrontation, in the later eighteenth century.

The more fortunate could be invited back to share again in academic life at first hand, and it was a great mark of collective esteem when an invitation to deliver the Bampton Lectures (after they began in the 1780s) was extended to one whose intellectual capacities had continued to mature at a distance. One striking instance was Richard Shepherd (1732?–1809) (MA, Corpus Christi, 1757), whose rise was assured after he had become chaplain to Bishop Thomas Thurlow (brother of Edward, Lord Thurlow, Lord Chancellor 1778–83; 1783–92). Though Archdeacon of Bedford from 1783, Shepherd's periodic production of theological and devotional works earned him appointment as Bampton Lecturer in 1788 on the subject of 'The Ground and Credibility of the Christian Religion'.[134] Intellectual capacities as demonstrated by having been a former University Prize winner raised a man's prospects of delivering the Bamptons, as with William Barrow (1799), who gained the Chancellor's English Essay prize in 1778, and Charles Hall (1798) (a pupil of Dean Cyril Jackson's), who achieved the same distinction in 1784 after having secured the Chancellor's Prize for Latin Verse in 1781. Barely less telling could be holding a living not very far from Oxford, as with Robert Gray (1796), vicar of Faringdon, Berkshire (and a protégé of Bishop Shute Barrington's), and William Finch (1797), who held the St John's College living of Tackley in north Oxfordshire.

Shepherd's steady publication record instances what could be done outside a University milieu (he moved to take up parishes in Suffolk in 1792). Most counties had at least one savant in every generation in a range of disciplines, for whom their Oxford academic affiliation was a constant source of reference and pride. In the natural sciences, Gilbert White (1720–93), Fellow of Oriel (1744),[135] author of the extraordinarily influential *The Natural History of Selborne* (1789), composed most of the letters that constitute its backbone at The Wakes, his family property in that Hampshire village. Early friendships complemented existing family connections with the University. Schooled by Thomas Warton the Elder (then vicar of Basingstoke), White knew his sons Joseph and Thomas from a tender age and, at Oriel, John Mulso, a bishop's son, became a close friend and correspondent.[136] White made annual trips to Oxford most Aprils during the 1740s and it was a

---

[134] These included *Reflections on the doctrine of materialism and the religious purposes to which modern philosophers have applied it* (2nd edn., London, 1779), and *Free examination of the Socinian exposition of the prefatory verses of St John's Gospel* (1781). He was a FRS and a regular correspondent of Sir Joseph Banks. W. P. Courtney, 'Shepherd, Richard (1731/2–1809), Church of England clergyman and theological writer', rev. Emma Major, *ODNB*, online edn., 2004.

[135] He was admitted as a commoner at Oriel in 1739. His grandfather had been a fellow of Magdalen, but his uncle Charles (Oriel 1710–14) may have swayed his choice. Mabey, *Gilbert White*, 34.

[136] Ibid., 34–9.

INSIDER TRADING 629

mark of his standing that, unusually for a non-resident, he was appointed as Junior Proctor in 1752. White was a candidate for the Oriel Provostship in 1757 and his disappointment at not being elected ended—acrimoniously—his prospects of permanent residence in the city, much to his disappointment.[137] Oxford friends were important visitors to him in Hampshire. In August 1769, Richard Skinner of Corpus Christi and William Sheffield of Worcester (Keeper of the Ashmolean Museum, 1772–95), stayed with him for a fortnight, and delighted him by appearing to know the identity of every living creature they encountered in their walks. Such involvements kept his spirits from faltering. Skinner's failure to visit the previous year had made him lament that '...I must plod on by myself, with few books and no soul to communicate my doubts or discoveries to'.[138]

White eventually subdued his career ambitions within Oxford, but Edward Lye (1694–1767), 'the most competent Saxonist' of his day,' had none.[139] His shyness as a scholar made him prefer to hole up in a Northamptonshire parsonage (vicar of Little Houghton, 1721–50) than remain in Oxford (BA, Hart Hall, 1716) and give from a distance a firmer sense of direction at mid-century to studies in his field.[140] In the late 1730s he commenced compilation of an Anglo-Saxon and Gothic dictionary which he despaired of publishing.[141] Archbishop Secker made a subscription to that end in 1765, others followed. Thirty sheets had been published at the time of his death, and the rest followed posthumously in 1772. From time to time his friends pleaded with him to come occasionally to Oxford and assist young researchers interested in the Scandinavian languages:[142]

[137] He was non-resident perpetual curate at Moreton Pinkney, Northants., and also held the curacy of Farringdon, Hants. He became curate-in-charge of Selborne from Oct. 1784. Ibid., 70–6, 196. For the Oriel tie, Seaward, 'An Anglican foundation', 203, 208–9, 232–7.

[138] To Joseph Banks, 21 Apr. 1768, *The natural history and antiquities of Selborne*, ed. T. Bell, (2 vols., London, 1877), II. 241. Learned, informed contacts were central to White's observational and reflective natural history. As the 'Advertisement' to his volume put it, the 'pleasing information' and 'intelligent communications' of 'a circle of gentlemen' had added much to his happiness.

[139] Sweet, *Antiquaries*, 203, 205.

[140] Margaret Clunies Ross, 'Re-evaluating the work of Edward Lye, an eighteenth-century septentrional scholar', *Studies in Medievalism*, 9 (1997), 66–79. Lye had an extensive correspondence with Swedish clergy and librarians, including Erik Benzelius (the younger), Abp of Uppsala (d. 1744), whose notes and version of the Gothic Gospels were published by Lye at Oxford.

[141] He edited and published the two vols. of the seventeenth-century Saxonist Franciscus Junius (the younger)'s *Etymologicon linguae Anglicanae* through Oxford University Press in 1743. It was used extensively by Samuel Johnson in compiling his own Dictionary. Philip, 'Oxford and scholarly publication', 132.

[142] Francis Wise to Lye, 10 Sept. 1754, BL Add MS 32325, f. 117. With what success the plea was received is unknown. Cf. Thomas Hunt writing a decade later:

'I hope you will be able to get a Curate soon, that you may be at liberty to make a visit to your friends at Oxford, who will all be very glad to see you, but none more so than those you have at Christ Church'. 12 Oct. 1763, ibid., f. 203.

630 ENLIGHTENED OXFORD

> As you are at the head of this sort of learning, it would be but kind in you to spend a few weeks among us now & then, and set us forward by your example. It is a duty you owe to the commonwealth of learning,...

Other parsons inclined to serious literary pursuits studied more recent vernacular literature. Thus John Upton (1707–60), fellow of Exeter, 1728–36, MA 1732, edited Spencer's *Faerie Queen* (1758) while holding benefices in the south-west of England.[143]

What Lye accomplished in Anglo-Saxon studies, so John Toup arguably surpassed in Classics, one whom, in Charles Burney's judgment, was one of the seven greatest classical scholars of the century. Toup, a parish priest in Cornwall, was deservedly popular with the Oxford University Press delegates. They published his edition of Longinus's *On the sublime* (1778) and paid for his memorial tablet in his parish church.[144] More accessible, perhaps with a wider readership, was Christopher Pitt (1699–1748), of New College, a Dorset rector, recognised as a poet and translator of Virgil's *Aeneid* (1740), the first to appear after the completion of Pope's *Iliad* (Pitt had Pope's blessing) and one that proved deservedly popular with compilers of anthologies.[145] An individual did not have to be ordained or even an Oxford graduate for his academic endeavours in the Classics to be honoured by the University and, as it were, incorporated within it. Benjamin Heath (1704–66), the book collector, was town clerk of Exeter between 1752 and 1766 and received an hon. DCL in 1762 for his published notes on Aeschylus, Sophocles, and Euripides (1762).[146]

Among antiquarians, few had a greater sense of what they owed to Oxford than Browne Willis (1682–1760), who, though a minor north Buckinghamshire landowner himself, was essentially a clerk, though not in holy orders,[147] and would not take the oath to the Hanoverian dynasty.[148] His departure from public life (he had served briefly as MP for Buckingham, 1705–8) was his making as a scholar, one all

---

[143] For John Upton, see E. C. Marchant, rev. S. J. Skedd, 'Upton, James (1671–1749), Church of England clergyman', *ODNB*, online edn., 2008.

[144] Nichols, *Lit. anecdotes*, II. 345–6. *The Critical Review*, 47 (1779), 403 called Toup a critic 'who is to Longinus, what Longinus was to Homer'. Bishop Warburton was one of many learned appreciators of Toup's *Emendationes in Suidam* (1760). He is alleged to have once asked Bishop Keppel of Exeter what he had done for Toup. 'Toup, who is Toup?', Keppel responded. 'A poor curate in your diocese', said Warburton, 'but the first Greek scholar in Europe'. Evans, *Warburton and the Warburtonians*, 195–6; Ogilvie, *Latin and Greek,* 72. See also Chapter 4, p. 32.

[145] Robin Sowerby, *The Augustan art of poetry: Augustan translation of the classics* (Oxford, 2006), chap. 1; M. Thackeray, 'Christopher Pitt, Joseph Warton, and Virgil', *Review of English Studies*, 43 (1996), 43 (1992), 329–46, at 334–6.

[146] W. P. Courtney, 'Heath, Benjamin (1704–1766), literary scholar and collector', rev. Ian Maxted, *ODNB*, online edn., 2004.

[147] He believed in clerical celibacy and would have banned married clergy. J. G. Jenkins, *The dragon of Whaddon, being an account of the life and work of Browne Willis (1682–1760). Antiquary and historian* (High Wycombe, 1953), 33. See also Sweet, *Antiquaries*, 243–6.

[148] Ibid., 81n.

too conscious of the devastation inflicted by the Reformation and Civil Wars on the built heritage of the English Church and anxious to stabilise the written record by recording, chronicling, and moralising crossly against those who had permitted ruination.[149] As Catherine Talbot archly recorded of this unapologetic High Churchman, he would undertake '... any journey properly undertaken that will bring him to some cathedral on the Saints day to which it is dedicated'.[150] His field work went directly into an extensive illustrated publication, *A Survey of the Cathedrals* (published in several volumes, 1716–27) and other comparable antiquarian works. He also poured money into building, repairing, and beautifying the churches in his gift, taking care to acknowledge the Oxford connection, as at Fenny Stratford, in suitably inserted armorial crests.[151] His efforts stretched his resources to the limit, and he came at intervals to Oxford to solicit donations for church conservation. His friend, Thomas Hearne, standing before the ruined church of Hogshaw, Buckinghamshire, knew what was owed to him: 'God send us more Willis's that may be of service to our poor, distracted, and afflicted church...' As a loyal Christ Church man, he was customarily present in Oxford every St Frideswide's Day; As he once told Arthur Charlett with reference to Wolsey, 'I should think myself exceeding fortunate could I make a real discovery of the Cardinal's ashes...'[152] Willis was generous to the University even in his lifetime with his regular his gifts of books, manuscripts, and coins, for which he was appropriately recognised with an honorary degree in 1749 (DCL).[153]

In its accuracy and perception, the vitality of antiquarian scholarship such as Willis's in his and other subject areas reflected its roots in the University and the formative academic influence of tutors, evidenced in such mid-century scholars as Francis Wise and the self-taught Saxonist, George Ballard (1706–55).[154] Those who stayed on to secure fellowships and, eventually, college livings, had, in the study of local history and antiquities, a means of keeping intellectual ossification at bay once in residence at their country parsonages. Others already had a passion for the study of their locality before they came up to Oxford. Notable among them was the Cornish antiquarian and expert in mineral specimens, William Borlase (1696–1772), unsurprisingly the product of Exeter College. Back in the far west, as vicar of Ludgvan from 1722, his career culminated in the Oxford publication of his

---

[149] See his letter dated 1713 complaining of spleen against the monks in Burnet's *History of the Reformation*. For High Church embarrassment over Henry VIII's destruction of abbeys and monasteries, Alexandra Walsham, *The reformation of the landscape. Religion, identity & memory in early modern Britain & Ireland* (Oxford, 2011), 272.

[150] Catherine Talbot, writing in 1739, quoted in ibid., 91.

[151] Jenkins, *Dragon of Whaddon*, 55–74 for details.

[152] Ibid., 191. Another Houseman, Bishop Trelawny of Winchester, commissioned the sculptor Grinling Gibbons to make a statue of Wolsey to be placed in a niche in the passage to the hall stairs only to find that, when executed, it looked the wrong way for the niche in which it was intended to stand. HMC, *Portland MSS*, VII. 38, 7 July 1711; VII. 249, 28 Feb. 1719.

[153] Jenkins, *Dragon of Whaddon*, 67, 79, 100, 138ff. For Willis's esteem for Oxford, ibid., 216.

[154] Sweet, *Antiquaries*, 204. For Wise see Chapter 9.

632 ENLIGHTENED OXFORD

impressive *Observations on the Antiquities, Historical and Monumental, of the County Cornwall* (1754), *Observations on the Ancient and Present State of the Islands of Scilly* (1756), election as an FRS in 1750, and an Oxford LL.D. in 1766.[155] He subsequently donated a generous collection of fossils, antiquities to the Ashmolean Museum.[156] Borlase was always ready to encourage younger scholars who ventured west to Cornwall one of whom, Thomas Pennant, recalled how, in the mid-1740s, Borlase, 'that able and worthy man' encouraged him in his passion for minerals and fossils, and communicated ' to me every thing worthy my notice on the subject'.[157]

Whatever the original inspiration, British antiquarianism fed (not least through the renaissance in local history writing) a wider public interest in the nation's cultural roots and identity. Though their organisation was idiosyncratic,[158] Robert Plot's natural histories of Oxfordshire (1677), and Staffordshire (1686) had set a benchmark for subsequent scholars attempting to emulate his example for their own towns and counties, not least because of the field work he had undertaken.[159] John Whitaker (1735–1808: fellow of Corpus Christi College, 1763), several decades later, worked on an urban history, though his *History of Manchester* (2 vols, 1771–5) was a much broader text containing the author's learned ruminations on British identity in the Roman period and its aftermath. He was so determined to rescue the reputation of the Ancient Britons that he insisted Manchester had been a town even before the Romans invaded. Whitaker was not a tractable man, and the strongly speculative side of his work, while not hurting his sales figures, bemused fellow antiquarians and attracted the notice of another Oxford author, Edward Gibbon.[160] By the late 1770s, he had moved to a remote coastal part of south-west Cornwall and turned his attention to the

---

[155] Borlase's interests developed from natural history to encompass archaeology and topography, John Walker, 'Cornwall', in eds. Currie and Lewis, *English county histories*, 85–90, at 87–8. The *Observations* also revealed a considerable and necessarily speculative interest in Druids. Richard Polwhele, another Oxonian, published a three-volume history of the county in 1803 after he moved from a Devon to a Cornish parish.

[156] Borlase's extensive correspondence is in the Morrab Library, Penzance.

[157] Pennant, *The Literary Life of the late Thomas Pennant, Esq., by Himself* (London, 1793), 1.

[158] Spence, *Observations*, II. 1032, quoted Henry Felton *c.*1730, who wrote that 'Plot was very credulous, and took up with any stories for his *History of Oxfordshire*: 'A gentleman of Worcestershire was like to be put into the margin, for [having] one leg rough, and the other smoothed (shaved), had not he discovered the cheat to him'. See also M. B. Campbell, *Wonder & Science. Imagining Worlds in Early Modern Europe* (Ithaca, NY, 1999), 101–9, who notes (103) that 'Despite Plot's Baconian loyalties, wonders seem to spring up at his every footfall'.

[159] The emphasis in the Oxfordshire volume was strongly on natural history; archaeology was the focus for Staffordshire. Michael Hunter, *John Aubrey and the world of learning* (London, 1975), 70, 100, 111. And, generally, Stan A. E. Mendyk, *'Speculum Britanniae'. Regional study, antiquarianism, and science in Britain to 1700* (Toronto, 1989), 192–205; Stan A. E. Mendyk, 'Robert Plot: Britain's "Genial Father of County Natural Histories"', *News and Records of the Royal Society of London*, 39 (1985), 159–77. E. W. Gilbert argued that, thanks to Plot, natural history became the dominant element in regional studies.

[160] Womersley, *Watchmen of the Holy City*, 337–8, for their acquaintance.

antiquities of that county[161]—with little appreciable difference in either technique or temerity. His character and temperament was well summed up by a neighbouring cleric:

> He is a man of a good deal of learning, but litigious & perpetually involved in Law-suits with his parishioners, particularly the Squire of his parish; they have even gone to logger heads & fisty cuffs.[162]

Resident at the rectory of Ruan Lanihorne for thirty-one years from 1777, Whitaker's career nicely illustrates the possibilities of scholarship at a distance from either the University or the metropolis, and the eccentric turn it could easily take.[163]

It also indicates the ready recourse to polemic that stranded Oxonian savants often favoured, as they tried to combine scholarship and High Churchmanship in philippics that often assumed the worst about the moral drift of contemporary society far away from their parishes.[164] But, through the press, their sermons and minor literary efforts in defence of the Church could often reach a wide public, as the High Anglican controversialist, schoolmaster and priest, John Hildrop (1682–1756: matric, St John's College, 1698), showed. A pupil and then headmaster of Sacheverell's old school, Marlborough Grammar School, Hildrop was eventually ordained and moved to livings in the gift of his patron Lord Bruce (later 2nd Earl of Ailesbury), finishing his career as parish priest of Wath in the North Riding. But he had an audience far beyond his Yorkshire parish via his occasional but lengthy submissions in the 1730s to the *Weekly Miscellany*, a periodical established to confront and rebut a variety of challenges to orthodoxy.[165] He supplemented them with witty longer pieces such as *An Essay for the better Regulation and Improvement of Free-Thinking. In a Letter to a Friend* (1739). Here Hildrop, following Swift, playfully adopted the persona of a contemporary *esprit libre*, and detailed the advantages to freethinkers if they organised themselves more effectively so as to qualify for legal indulgence by the state. It was

---

[161] He produced *The ancient cathedral of Cornwall historically surveyed* (2 vols., London,1804), which was an account of the church of St Germans. G. C. Boase, *Bibliotheca Cornubiensis* (3 vols., London, 1874–82), II. 867–70.

[162] W. J. Temple to James Boswell, 8 Aug. 1786, Beinecke Library, Yale University, MS. Yale (C 2842). Temple later told Boswell that Whitaker '...apes Johnsons manner very awkwardly'. To Boswell, 5 Nov. 1793, ibid., Yale (C 2944). See also R. Polwhele, *Biographical sketches in Cornwall* (3 vols., Truro, 1831), III. 167.

[163] Sweet contends that Whitaker was more a polemicist than an antiquarian. *Antiquaries*, 5, 6, 20, 177–8, 146–7, 186, 196, 358.

[164] eds. Walsh, Haydon, Taylor, *The Church of England: from Toleration to Tractarianism*, 20, for parish priests leading the fight against infidelity and immorality.

[165] For the increase in religious periodical publication as part of a press search for new markets see Black, *The English Press 1621–1861*, 87. Some of the leading papers sponsored by parties targeted clergy in the expectation they would relay news at local level. B. Harris, *Politics and the Rise of the Press: Britain and France, 1620–1800* (London, 1996), 31–4.

634 ENLIGHTENED OXFORD

typical of his style and caught public notice. His old University duly rewarded Hildrop for his efforts with a BD and a DD on 9 June 1743.

His contemporary, Arthur Collier (1680–1732: matric. Pembroke & Balliol, 1697), made occasional forays into controversial divinity from his Wiltshire rectory at Langford Magna (1704–32) but put his principal energies into philosophy. Collier was a long-time student of Descartes and Malebranche and, with the *Clavis Universalis, or a New Enquiry After Truth* (1713) produced a text that independently articulated the idealistic metaphysics of Bishop Berkeley, though with less originality and finesse in explanation and exposition. He much later produced *A Specimen of True Philosophy* (1730), a philosophical commentary on the opening chapter of Genesis, and planned a large work that would be a commentary on the most considerable passages in Scripture.[166] The Oxford clerical diaspora also used its learned leisure time to good effect in the applied sciences. A classic instance would be that of Edward Saul, former fellow of Magdalen, who was preferred to the rectory of Harlaxton, Lincolnshire, in 1706 and held it for a subsequent forty-eight years. Inspired by his attendance at Keill's lectures, he produced an important work on the barometer in 1730 encouraged by his patron, the 3rd Duke of Rutland, a latecomer to learning himself and a nobleman with many livings in his gift that he looked to offer from preference to the scholarly.[167]

iv) Clerical culture beyond Oxford: associational

> [The University is] 'a Nursery wherein ye Sprouts of the Royal Foundation are to be cherish'd a While, til they are fit to be transplanted (in greater maturity) to their Original Soil'.
>
> Bp William Nicolson to Bp William Wake, 17 Sept. 1711,
> BL Add. MS 6116, f. 30

Such individuals, in their distinctive ways, made an underestimated contribution to mainstream cultural life in eighteenth-century England and beyond, and demonstrated that the Oxonian academic imprint was enduring and capable of application in a range of genres. And, invariably, the sociable ones among them

---

[166] Charles J. McCracken, *Malebranche and British Philosophy* (Oxford, 1983), 191–204. See also S. Brown, 'The Critical Reception of Malebranche, from his own time to the end of the eighteenth century', in ed. S. Nadler, *The Cambridge Companion to Malebranche* (Cambridge, 2000), 262–87; R. Benson, *Memoirs of the Life and Writings of the Rev. Arthur Collier, MA* (London, 1837); Richard Glauser, 'Arthur Collier', in eds. Yolton et al., *Dictionary of eighteenth-century British philosophers*, I. 218–22.

[167] Saul, *An historical and philosophical account of the Barometer, or Weather Glass* (London, 1730). See also this Chapter, p. 45.

kept up their earlier contacts and, in person or by post,[168] extended them in ways which facilitated personal intellectual enterprise, fostered friendships, lessened their sense of solitude, and encouraged mutual creativity.[169] It served to foster a dynamic, distinctly Anglican provincial associational culture that could be open to outsiders, but has largely gone either unrecognised or underestimated by historians intent on looking for signs of intellectual vitality primarily in Dissenting communities.[170] These many enterprises helped to secure the Church's status as not dependent exclusively on legal protection of its rights and privileges but underpinned by highly educated clergy, capable of studies that reflected academic aptitude and that were also, in increasing numbers, accessible and relevant to the educated world at large. These could have a cumulative national impact across dispersed settings because of the easy dissemination of print culture and thus the fruits of what might be reimagined as an Oxford micro-enlightenment could be transmitted.

One area of formal association was through membership of a cathedral chapter. Their clergy were key personnel in the defence of the Church and, for every one drone, there were any number of prebends and canons active either locally or nationally, from the pulpit and in the press, as articulate representatives of the Establishment, who were far from unaffected by or hostile to the ideals and values of the moderate Enlightenment, and brought with them into these distinctive milieus the imprint of Oxford. By and large, they admitted the need to justify their privileged status through their works. Many prebendaries found holding a stall gave them an opportunity to continue their scholarly activities and publish undistracted by the small change of University life; their presence confirmed a growing recognition of the significance of cathedrals in the provision of education.[171] With some notable exceptions such as the Six-Preacherships at Canterbury, in the generality of sermons preached in a cathedral, minster, or major parish church, scholarly rigour was less requisite than congregational

---

[168] See Lindsay O'Neill, *The Opened Letter. Networking in the Early Modern British World* (Philadelphia, PA, 2015). In France, attention has shifted significantly to provincial correspondence networks. See L. W. B. Brockliss, *Enlightenment and the Republic of Letters in Eighteenth-Century France* (Oxford, 2002).

[169] Gary Bennett nicely described the clerical profession as 'in large measure an extension of the universities' function into innumerable parishes spread throughout the country', 'University, society and Church', 360–1.

[170] Seeing provincial science as largely a Dissenters' preserve is misleading. In places like Bath, Bristol, Derby, and Leeds it was as least as much in the hands of Anglicans.

[171] For the prebendaries of Canterbury and their contribution to learning see the assessment in Gregory, *Restoration, Reformation and Reform*, 55–60; Gregory, in eds. P. Collinson, N. Ramsay, and M. Sparks, 'Canterbury and the *Ancien Régime*: The Dean and Chapter, 1660–1828', in *A history of Canterbury Cathedral* (Oxford, 1995), 204–55, at 219–23, 252–3; S. and S. Lehmberg, 'Writings of Canterbury Cathedral clergy, 1700–1800', *Anglican and Episcopal History*, 73 (2004), 53–77. For the cathedrals and education see G. Horne's *The character of true wisdom, and the means of attaining it* (Oxford, 1784). The matter of cathedrals as centres of learning in the long eighteenth century is an understudied subject. eds. D. Marcombe and C. S. Knighton, *Close encounters: English cathedrals and society since 1540* (Nottingham, 1991) is a serviceable introduction to post-Reformation capitular history.

636   ENLIGHTENED OXFORD

accessibility. In those settings, the preacher could function as a vessel for the dissemination of political loyalty and theological orthodoxy in troubled times; if their more important or controversial offerings were published, Chapter members could expect to find their words (when printed) attracting attention well beyond the original auditors. Chapter appointments were accordingly critical. It was not uncommon for heads of colleges to combine their function with decanal office that made them concurrently heads of cathedral chapters. Thus two major luminaries of the University in George III's reign, George Horne and Nathaniel Wetherell, were awarded the Deaneries of Canterbury (1781) and Hereford, respectively, by Lord North as Premier, in part prompted by Charles Jenkinson, that useful half-minister, half-courtier, and key link between the royal closet and the cabinet.[172] At Gloucester, by royal letters patent confirmed by Act of Parliament in 1713, the next vacant prebend was annexed for ever to the Mastership of Pembroke College upon his election.[173]

The varieties of provincial intellectual culture in the eighteenth century were remarkable, often distinctively Anglican and Tory in flavour and linked with the University through patronage and college membership. These tended to revolve around urban centres of varying sizes and tradition: cathedral cities, county or market towns, places of resort, and centres of sociability for Oxford-educated clergy, loci beyond their rural parishes where they could gather and meet other professional men, perhaps college contemporaries, hear sermons, and dine together, perhaps at the expense of the diocesan bishop or archdeacon at a Visitation or a charity dinner.[174] How easily the social and the scholarly, the formal and the informal, intersected is well seen in the activity of someone such as the High Church John Lewis (matric. SEH, 1701, rector of Great Chalfield, Holt, and Atworth in Wiltshire from 1713), a keen scholar who kept up his reading, carefully prepared his sermons, and lectured once a month at Tetbury (Glos.). But Lewis did not hide himself with his books. He shot and went coursing, and it is estimated that between 1710 and 1724 he had over 170 social contacts, dining with and receiving visits from the gentry, tenant farmers, and the clergy (no less than fifty-seven of his colleagues in holy orders, the majority of them Oxford men).[175]

---

[172] Chapter 6, pp. 39, 55; Darwall-Smith, 'Monks of Magdalen', 266; Darwall-Smith, *University College*, 292, 295.

[173] *Fasti*, VIII, 36. Pembroke Masters might also hold other posts. For instance, William Adams (Master, 1775–89) was also Archdeacon of Llandaff from 1777, and the effective head of the cathedral (there was no dean until the mid-19th century). He was conscientious in the discharge of all his responsibilities. B. M. Lodwick, 'William Adams, a distinguished eighteenth-century archdeacon of Llandaff,' *Morgannwg*, 52 (2008), 30–50. Similarly, the holder of the Lady Margaret Professorship of Divinity received a canonry at Worcester.

[174] See, generally, ed. Peter Clark, *Country towns in pre-industrial England* (Leicester, 1981). For James Woodforde's enjoyment of the dinner provided by Bishop Lewis Bagot at Norwich on 7 Nov. 1783 see ed. Beresford, *Diary of a Country Parson*, II. 103–4.

[175] Donald A. Spaeth, *The Church in an age of danger. Parsons and parishioners, 1660–1740* (Cambridge, 2000), 50–1, 54, 55n.

At Melksham, also in Wiltshire, in the 1720s, a group of ten priests made up the so-called Clergy Club, assembling at least monthly between March and October for dinners, either at an inn such as the George at Melksham or in their parsonages. These were High Church Tories and their socialising did not exclude matters of common concern, such as offering each other mutual advice on tithes and devising electoral strategies, as on 2 May 1722, when they dined with John Ivory Talbot, MP, and helped prepare for the general election, the first since the Triennial Act reached the statute book.[176] More purely social than political, the widespread creation of lending libraries (sometimes specifically for clergy) was a bonus for country parsons feeling the deleterious effects of solitude. The initiative was pioneered by well-meaning, well-placed laymen like the 5th Lord Digby in north Warwickshire in the 1690s, who encouraged the clergy of his neighbourhood to meet for common counsel and encouragement, read and exchange books, and talk over the pastoral challenges facing them. Predictably, they also chewed over the news with each other and gossiped. Comparable was the Book Club at Beccles in Suffolk. It had forty members in the 1770s; they paid a subscription of one guinea per annum.[177]

Opportunities for socialisation could be occasioned by more formal duties that would bring county society together. The presence of Oxford graduates (both lay and clerical) among the Justices of the Peace assembled in Quarter or Petty Sessions could be assumed. In less populous counties, the Bench could be dominated by men from one college as, in Cumberland and Westmorland, those from Queen's College. In the 1690s these included John, 1st Viscount Lonsdale, Sir George Fletcher, Sir Christopher Musgrave, and Sir William Fleming, committed well-educated churchmen all of them, who kept up correspondence with old Oxford friends and Queen's fellows past and present.[178] The arrival of the King's judges on Assize was generally marked by a sermon in a cathedral or major parish church that offered scope for reflection on themes of justice, civil order, and obligation to the powers ordained of the Lord that underlined the status of the clergy as moral guides and was used by some as an opportunity to parade their learned credentials. In corporations (through which much government patronage tended to be channelled) the presence of a priest attending the Mayor in the performance of his office offered a further chance for prominence and, indeed, junketing. At Reading, as in other towns, the installation in office and due departure of the Mayor was marked by a feast attended by gentry,

---

[176] Their candidate for the county, Richard Goddard, was returned in a by-election in Nov. 1722. Ibid., 55; eds. R. B. Pugh and E. Crittall, *The Victoria history of Wiltshire*, vol. 5, (London, 1957), 200.

[177] Thompson, *Thomas Bray*, 23. For some clergy readers of fiction and book clubs in Northamptonshire see Jan Fergus, *Provincial readers in eighteenth-century England* (Oxford, 2007) 51, 56.

[178] Hodgkin, *Queen's College*, 126. In 1694 no less than four prebends of Carlisle Cathedral came from Queen's. Ibid., 126n. Musgrave represented Oxford University in Parliament, 1698–1700.

638   ENLIGHTENED OXFORD

clergy, and townsmen of any 'tolerable fashion', as mayor John Watts had observed in 1728.[179]

Meeting in person afforded scope for the exchange of ideas, the discussion of work in progress, and possible opportunities for the publication and circulation of their books and pamphlets. Implicit in these activities was, more often than not, the provincial defence of Anglicanism and the values associated with it against the challenges of Nonconformity, indifference, and outright hostility. Learned societies tended towards the High Church, flirted with a Nonjuring line as an opportunity to manifest disagreement with elements of natural philosophy or politics. They often exhibited an interest in mathematical puzzles, and were keen on music and poetry. Oxford-educated clergy and other graduates were also quick to position themselves in responsible positions on the hospital boards and trusts, encouraging that active benevolence the Established Church did much to inculcate. Subscriptions and legacies were encouraged; annual sermons and festivals raised additional funds; bishops were encouraged to be presidents and patrons of infirmaries.[180] Above all, patients could receive the ministrations of the Church via the hospital chaplaincies (chapels were usually provided in the new buildings). In many cities, such as Bristol, Norwich, Leicester, and Nottingham, where Protestant Dissenters were numerous, the strategy could be considered part of a competition for cultural power between the confessions—often with political consequences. But cooperation could be fostered where mutual regard existed. Thus the inaugural sermon for the Northampton Infirmary was preached in 1744 by Richard Grey, Rector of Hinton-in-the-Hedges, a friend of that eirenic Dissenter, Philip Doddridge.[181]

Of course, there were innumerable variations, dependent on time and place. The character of the locale and range of different urban milieus helped determine the ease with which Anglican notables could set the tone. Where Dissenters were strong and party politics divisive, as in Queen Anne's reign or during the American War of Independence, a restatement of Anglican values as part of a defence of the confessional status quo might be considered a counter-revolutionary initiative. Or it might be that the presence in the vicinity of a 'freethinker' could often incite the local clergy and others to issue a counterblast. In 1715 the Welshman Thomas Morgan (d. 1743) (appointed a Dissenting minister in 1716) took up residence in Marlborough and published sermons and pamphlets in 1719 and 1720 (particularly *The nature and consequences of*

---

[179] ed. K.G. Burton, *The Memorandums of John Watts Esq., Mayor of Reading 1722-23 and 1728-29*, (London, 1950).

[180] Langford, *Polite and commercial people*, 134–7; Roy Porter, 'The gift relation: philanthropy and provincial hospitals in eighteenth-century England', in eds. L. Granshaw and R. Porter, *The Hospital in History* (London, 1989), 149–78; C. Stevenson, *Medicine and magnificence: British hospital and asylum architecture, 1660-1815* (New Haven, CT, 2011); Adrian Wilson, 'Conflict, consensus and charity: politics and the provincial voluntary hospitals in the eighteenth century', *EHR*, 111 (1996), 599–619.

[181] M. Deacon, *Philip Doddridge* (Northampton, 1981), 123.

enthusiasm consider'd, in some short remarks on the doctrine of the Blessed Trinity, London, 1719) that were sufficiently anti-Trinitarian to resemble a form of freethinking that upset churchmen for he favoured what he called a 'Christian Deism'.[182] These writings elicited from John Hildrop his *Reflections upon reason* (London, 1722) under the pseudonym of 'Phileleutherus Britannicus'.[183] He took exception to Morgan's insistence that there was no aspect of Christianity that could not be known through human reason, thereby eliminating any dimension of mystery.

Hildrop's standing in Marlborough was confirmed by his place in an informal local Anglican network with friendship as well as clientage underpinning it. More formalised Church of England-based clerical and lay societies survived vigorously (or otherwise) in the provinces throughout George III's reign. Two national organisations that had local representatives were the SPCK and the SPG, primarily mission-centred, but marked by an indelible Anglicanism that Oxford-educated clergy had no wish to play down, especially in the case of the SPG. Masonic lodges in the provinces were also dominated by a clerico-lay elite whose charitable values, while loosely Whiggish and progressive, cannot be considered as any kind of threat to the status quo in Church and state.[184] Dissenters were not excluded, though their numbers tended to come from the upper echelons of urban society and the semblance of social equality in the lodges amid a numerically predomin-ant Anglican landed and professional elite neutralised any radicalising instincts.

On the one hand there were the intellectually ambitious, confessionally exclu-sive, socially conservative societies built around a hegemonic Anglicanism that represented a serious cultural alternative to the preferences of Dissent and Dissenters. These found classic provincial format in the Gentlemen's Societies founded in Spalding (1709) and Peterborough (1720).[185] On the other there were social units with a scholarly or didactic purpose, where religious allegiance was largely an irrelevance and which tended to be favoured by non-Anglicans, of which the Lunar Society within the 'Midlands Enlightenment' is the best-known example.[186] Anglicans, however, were not excluded, many participated actively in

---

[182] Peter Harrison, 'Morgan, Thomas (d. 1743)', *ODNB*, online edn., 2004.

[183] Hildrop being relatively unknown at this date, some critics and readers attributed the work to Francis Gastrell, the Tory Bishop of Chester.

[184] As Paul Monod has noted, 'It remains unclear,... whether the lodges simply attracted Whigs or helped to shape them.' 'A disunited brotherhood?: Secrecy, publicity, and controversy among British Freemasons of the eighteenth century', *ECS*, 50 (2017), 440–2, at 440.

[185] Michael Honeybone, 'The Spalding Gentlemen's Society: the communication of science in the East Midlands of England 1710–1760' (Ph.D. thesis, Open University, 2001), and the introduction to *The correspondence of the Spalding Gentlemen's Society 1710–1761*, eds. D. and M. Honeybone (Woodbridge, 2010).

[186] R. E. Schofield, *The Lunar Society of Birmingham, a Social History of Provincial Science and Industry in Eighteenth-Century England* (Oxford, 1963); R. Porter, 'Science, provincial culture and public opinion in Enlightenment England', *BJECS* 3 (1980), 20-46, at 28–39; Jenny Uglow, *The Lunar Men*; P. M. Jones, *Industrial Enlightenment: science, technology and culture in Birmingham and the*

640 ENLIGHTENED OXFORD

these several 'conversable worlds' and the many unlikely social intersections they contained. They thereby showed an enlightened commitment to the ideal of toleration and, by displaying a side of the Established Church waspish critics were uneasy about acknowledging, helped disarm their complaints and perpetuate its academic predominance nationally. Cyril Jackson of Christ Church was thus a friend of Matthew Boulton, the West Midlands industrialist and leading Lunar man, and often came down to Birmingham from Oxford to attend Society meetings. He was there, for instance, on 3 August 1789 in company with two unnamed guests, probably Oxford natural scientists, James Thomson and Thomas Beddoes.[187] Boulton and Jackson got on well, so did Jackson and James Watt. Jackson was clearly intrigued by industrial developments afoot in Birmingham and district and visited the Soho quarter at least twice (Sept. 1791, 6 July 1799).[188] The Lunar Men were aware of the influence the Dean wielded, and of his willingness to supply letters of recommendation to Matthew Boulton. When they needed more patents to implement the change from beam-acting engines into rotary motion, Jackson was the obvious man to lobby.[189] However, after the French Revolutionaries moved towards displacing the monarchy from 1791 onwards and many English rational Dissenters (usually with Unitarian sympathies) kept up their commitment to the reform cause and sponsored branches of the Society for Constitutional Information (with urban-based reformers elbowing aside the county gentry), confessional cooperation was compromised. When delegates from the Midlands and the north went to the French National Convention in 1792, loyalists were aghast. As the Rev. Robert Wilmot of Morley put it, from Derby they have 'actually sent two persons to the national convention of France to invite the French over to this country to create the same anarchy here which is there triumphant'.[190]

Until the caesura of the 1790s, there are clear limits to considering distinctively Anglican organisations in provincial England as a counterbalance to other societies locally organised, where sociability and religious orthodoxy were less strictly conjoined. As Roy Porter pointed out as long ago as 1980, presenting 'Anglicans and nonconformist culture as if they were utterly polarized is also a false

---

West Midlands 1760–1820 (Manchester, 2013). For philosophical groups in Derby and their social diversity see Elliott, *The Derby Philosophers*, 58–64; R. P. Sturges, 'The membership of the Derby Philosophical Society, 1783–1802', *Midland History*, 4 (1978), 212–29.

[187] The Library of Birmingham, Archives & Heritage, MBP 280. I am grateful to Peter Jones for this reference.

[188] Thanks to Peter Jones for this information.

[189] It may have been with Jackson's encouragement that Boulton insisted in 1791 his son should attend Hornsby's lectures in Oxford. A. E. Musson and E. Robinson, *Science and technology in the industrial revolution* (Manchester, 1969), 145–6, 176. There is no record of Boulton's son matriculating.

[190] Quoted in C. Kerry, *Smalley in the County of Derby: its history and legends* (London, 1905), 42–3. For the background E. Fearn, 'Derbyshire reform societies, 1791–93', *Derbyshire Archaeological Journal*, 88 (1968), 47–59 and, generally, A. Goodwin, *Friends of Liberty: the English Democratic Movement in the Age of the French Revolution* (London, 1979), 136–267.

hypostasis'.[191] Men and women could still be members of both, and it could make strategic sense when, post-1689, the Church of England was the Established Church, or rather strictly, the national one. Likewise in the metropolis, where the impact of Oxonians on learned institutions based there should not be underestimated. They played their part in the eighteenth century in reasserting their place in the deliberations of the Royal Society where, c.1790, no less than ten per cent of the membership was still in holy orders. And, where learned culture could not flourish by personal presence, contact at a distance was sustained by Oxford authors either seeking the active assistance of graduates in all parts of the kingdom or through subscription. Robert Plot was again a trendsetter. Having shown the possibilities in the 1670s of coordinating learned activity in the provinces by corresponding with local naturalists and sending out printed questionnaires, after the Revolution he hoped to use volunteers to collect a mass of data from which to write the natural history of all the counties in England through the good offices of Oxford graduates. He raised contributions, but nothing came of his efforts.[192] Similarly, when Edmund Gibson undertook to produce a vastly enlarged edition of Camden's *Britannia* in the 1690s he found a pool of contributors willing to revise each county, and a gratifyingly large readership.[193] Invitation to subscribe to a forthcoming publication was far from being a passive activity and suggested much about authorial enterprise; with Robert Dodsley's practical aid, Joseph Spence collected a subscription list of no fewer than 717 names for *Polymetis*, headed by the Prince of Wales, plus eighteen Dukes, Lord Chesterfield, Alexander Pope, Mark Akenside, and Edward Young.[194] A list of subscribers to any number of volumes published by Oxonians in the course of the century generally functioned as a reliable indicator of more than intellectual curiosity. It underlined loyalties, both personal and political, and much remains to be learnt from the relationship of the subscribers to each other and to the author.[195]

---

[191] 'Science, Provincial Culture and Public Opinion', 24.

[192] ed. R. T. Gunther, *Early science in Oxford*, XII: *Dr Plot and the correspondence of the Philosophical Society of Oxford* (Oxford, 1939); Michael Hunter, *Science and society in Restoration England* (Cambridge, 1981), 54, 79; Michael Pafford, 'Robert Plot', *History Today*, 20 (1970), 112–17.

[193] Mayhew, *Enlightenment geography*, 100–1. Sweet, *Antiquaries*, 12, for widespread use of lists of queries.

[194] Solomon, *The rise of Robert Dodsley*, 108. Twenty college libraries also subscribed, mainly Oxford ones.

[195] For one attempt at this see Richard Sharp, '"Our common mother, the Church of England"; Nonjurors, High Churchmen, and the evidence of subscription lists', in eds. Paul Monod, Murray Pittock, and Daniel Szechi, *Loyalty and Identity. Jacobites at Home and Abroad* (Basingstoke, 2010), 167–79. Sharp argues for the importance of subscription lists to show '... the continuing contribution made by well-informed orthodox religious conviction to the formation and definition of Tory political identity...' embracing both Nonjurors and High Churchmen. Ibid., 177, 179. For authors superintending their own subscriptions see Yale, *Sociable knowledge*, 168–204.

v) Lasting association: the culture of bequests and legacies

There could be no more tangible token of loyalty to Oxford from its alumni than the monies its constituent parts constantly received in the form of gifts, bequests, and legacies. It was nothing new in itself. The University corporately, and every college individually, honoured 'founders and benefactors'. Their names were familiar to most undergraduates from frequent recitation on official occasions and at commemorative services: benefactors were remembered in the Bidding Prayer at University sermons at St Mary's Church where, on the first day of full term and on the Sunday before Encaenia, a comprehensive list of founders was read out.[196] That some among those who listened to these recitations to wish to have their own names thus brought to posterity's notice would be unsurprising.

Fig. 12.4 Statue of John Radcliffe, 1747, Michael Rysbrack (Bodleian Libraries, University of Oxford).

---

[196] Buxton and Gibson, *Oxford University ceremonies*, 113, 115. Within colleges, a pious remembrance of founders went deep within some individuals. Thus Ralph Churton, Fellow of Brasenose and a future archdeacon and author, wanted to complete his life of the College's founders before 'I accept a living from their society'. Letter of 1 Apr. 1790, Houghton Library, Harvard University, MS Eng 731, 9/8.

They could see just how far the University would go in honouring its most bountiful sons in the lavish funeral rites granted to that extraordinary benefactor, Dr John Radcliffe, in 1714, in recognition of the immense funds he had left for buildings (including £40,000 to house his science library), his charities, and his trusts, gifts that kept his name in daily use among Oxford residents of every kind.[197]

As the University tended to arouse affection from its graduates, its officials and governors were correspondingly practised in the art of wheedling funds out of old members. Incentives for generosity varied, the terms and conditions of use similarly, and there could be much work for lawyers on both sides, but the regularity with which private funds poured in suggests both a public recognition of the University's worthiness as a recipient and an individual's personal recognition of what he owed in the course of his life to Oxford's formative influence and, quite possibly, the enduring connections that flowed from it. Fame might prompt, vanity certainly did, but this substantial gift culture is not reducible to egotistical satisfaction, a drawing attention to oneself as a conspicuous donor. Those who had benefitted from a scholarship themselves at matriculation might want to extend the benefits that they had enjoyed themselves. Such sentiments inspired the Rev James Phipps, Rector of Elvetham near Winchfield, Hants, a former Tesdale scholar at Pembroke College, to bequeath on his death in 1773 his entire fortune towards the purchase of four advowsons principally for the benefit of Tesdale scholars and the increase of their stipends.[198]

The basic motive of enhancing the intellectual life of the University was an obvious incentive for scholars who wanted to offer their collections of manuscripts and books for the use of future generations, none more generous than the great collector and Nonjuring bishop, Richard Rawlinson (d. 1755), with his gifts to the Bodleian and St John's College Library.[199] But legacies in intellectual property accrued to every college. To single one out: Richard Warner of Woodford, Essex (d. 1775) gave 4,000 books to Wadham, with an emphasis on the botanical plus a choice collection of English literature to be expected from a wealthy, would-be editor of Shakespeare.[200] The endowment of a scholarship, the bequest of land or a personal library, or simply a contribution towards fundraising for a new building (the Peckwater Quadrangle and library at Christ Church in the 1710s and the New Building at Magdalen two decades later are celebrated instances of old members digging deep into their pockets),[201] served practical ends, the enduring

---

[197] For the text of Radcliffe's will see Guest, *Dr. John Radcliffe*, app. B.

[198] Macleane, *Pembroke College*, 201.

[199] Costin, *St John's College*, 203. For the Rawlinson endowment for an appointment in Anglo-Saxon studies see Chapter 4.

[200] These include a sixteenth-century Venetian edition of Horace's works that has been lately identified as belonging to John Donne: Hugh Adlington, 'Close reader. John Donne's Horace', *TLS* Jan. 16 2015; Wells, *Wadham College*, 145.

[201] The Ch. Ch. library had a total cost of £15,517 of which £13,312 came from 306 members. The fundraising took until 1779, sixty-three years, to complete. Curthoys (2), 128–35.

Fig. 12.5 The library, Christ Church, Oxford (© Governing Body, Christ Church, Oxford).

fruits of an associational culture that was originally nurtured in a convivial academic society. One extraordinary gift offered in that spirit was the capacious punch bowl with a ten-gallon capacity given by the Jacobite Sir Watkin Williams Wynn to Jesus College. Distinguished visitors were generally offered a ladleful of its contents 'to Drink Sr Watkins health which by all honest Jovial Tory Topers, is reciev'd With great Glee,...'[202]

The willingness of alumni to stump up funds when cultivated and requested played a neglected part in preserving the University's cultural pre-eminence nationally and internationally, especially as funds from the Crown and its agencies were reluctantly given before 1760. The authorities were not beyond playing fast and loose with what came down to them. Thus the great-grandchildren of Edward Hyde, 1st Earl of Clarendon, left his papers to the University in 1751 so that the proceeds of publishing them could fund a riding academy, which their ancestor had reckoned as essential for a gentleman's education. The University opted to do nothing, accumulated the interest, and did not finally spend the money until the setting up of the Clarendon Laboratory in 1872.[203]

---

[202] Helen M. Clifford, *A Treasured Inheritance. 600 years of Oxford College Silver* (Oxford, 2004), 27ff; 'Shepilinda', *Memoirs*, 15.

[203] *The Miscellaneous Works of...Edward Earl of Clarendon* (2nd edn., London, 1751), 325–6; Carter, *History of O.U. Press*, I. 362; Thomas, *The Ends of life*, 50, considers this protraction to be to Oxford's 'eternal shame'. George Colman, masquerading as *Terrae-Filius*, reported that a 'facetious' Lincoln College cleric 'of uncommon parts,' hoping that the profits of the last collection of the

Some of the benefactions, notably the Radcliffe bequest, were spectacular. Many substantial gifts came from wealthy bachelor fellows, for instance, Ralph Bathurst (who had so tastefully rebuilt the College's chapel) spent more than £5,000 of his estate on Trinity College in and after his lifetime. Of course, the majority of gifts from Oxford graduates were relatively small-scale; but, cumulatively, they could make a considerable difference to a college's relative standing within the University. Or even create a new college. When Sir Thomas Cookes (died 1701), of Bentley Pauncefoot, Worcestershire, left a confused bequest of £10,000 for the foundation of a new establishment with strong ties to his home county, there was an understandable if unseemly rush to persuade his family of a suitable home for his largesse. Balliol wanted this benefaction; Gloucester Hall was also in contention. Eventually, after much acrimony and pamphleteering, and the blatant intervention of Lord Keeper Harcourt in 1712 (by a decree in Chancery, he set aside the University's preference for the money to go to Magdalen Hall), Gloucester Hall prevailed, and Worcester College was instituted in 1714.[204]

A new lectureship, the construction of a library, the commission of new silverware, all these enhanced collegiate prestige even if they only occasionally attracted notice outside Oxonian circles. Building on a grand scale, however, constantly brought the University attention, with the Radcliffe Camera opened in 1749, the fruit of its greatest benefactor, and Gibbs's architectural masterpiece, acclaimed by the cognoscenti from its opening.[205] Emulation could work wonders. The brilliant, unstable, Philip, 1st Duke of Wharton (1698–1731), had his ear burnt by his companion the poet, Edward Young, to complete the building work at All Souls College, and glimpsed a chance of going beyond Dr Radcliffe with a benefaction that would see Hawksmoor's designs brought to completion. Wharton and the All Souls dons got on well, £250 was immediately forthcoming, and the Duke was honoured by the fellowship with a laudatory Latin inscription placed on the north side of the quadrangle:

The Most Noble Prince Philip Duke of Wharton caused this building to be erected at his own expense, to adorn with his munificence the Muses he had cultivated with scholarship, in the year of our Salvation 1720.

Clarendon papers would be used for a riding school, foresaw 'great advantage to the church-militant, from our Doctors in Divinity being taught to ride the Great horse, . . .' *Terrae-Filius,* Number 4, July 8, 1763. *Prose on Several Occasions,* I. 262.

[204] L. S. Sutherland, 'The foundation of Worcester College', *Oxoniensia,* 44 (1979), 62–80, at 62; Emma Goodrum, 'The foundation of Worcester College', in eds. Bate and Goodman, *Worcester,* 32–7. Harcourt's chaplain (1710), Richard Blechinden, became the first Provost of Worcester. Barrett, 'Richard Blechinden', 142.

[205] Stephen Hebron, Dr *Radcliffe's library: the story of the Radcliffe Library in Oxford* (Oxford, 2014), 59; Tyack, *Oxford. An Architectural Guide,* 167–71.

Fig. 12.6 Sir Thomas Cookes Contemplating the Bust of King Alfred, Robert Edge Pine, oil on canvas (The Provost and Fellows of Worcester College, Oxford).

The £250 was, in fact, the first and last sum that the young Duke could afford to spend, and the college subsequently had to sue his executors to obtain the balance from his estate, which was finally awarded in 1751 through the efforts of Blackstone.[206]

Major building projects could stand or fall according to the generosity of benefactors, either individual or collective. The Christ Church alumnus and Archbishop of Armagh, Richard Robinson (1709–94), financed the construction of the small but fashionable Canterbury Quadrangle (1773–83), an early masterpiece of the up-and-coming architect, James Wyatt, that cost the prelate £6,000.[207]

Canterbury Quad was a compact design, whereas Magdalen in the 1730s planned a vast new addition to the College, a grand colonnaded quadrangle. The scheme was lavishly illustrated for fundraising purposes; and an appeal was circulated among the old members by Edward Butler (1686–1745), a fellow and

---

[206] Stratford to Lord Harley, 4 Aug. 1720, HMC, *Portland MSS*, VII. 279; Edward Harley, jnr., to Abigail Harley, 2 Aug. 1720, ibid. V. 601; Burrows, *Worthies of All Souls*, 397–8; Lewis Melville, *The life and writings of Philip Duke of Wharton* (London, 1913), 108–9.

[207] Curthoys (2), 147–51; Malcolmson, *Primate Robinson*, 2, 45; Chapter 9, pp. 114, 116.

Fig. 12.7 Canterbury Gate, Christ Church, Oxford before rebuilding, John Baptist Malchair, pencil and watercolour, 1775 (© Governing Body, Christ Church, Oxford).

future President who, in 1720, had given £100 to start a building fund; alumni were expected to bear the cost of what became just the one-sided range known as the New Building, with the Nonjuror and respected former fellow, Edward Holdsworth (1684–1746), the presiding architectural force.[208]

Alumni were solicited at the beginning of this era as much as they were a century on. At Trinity College President Ralph Bathurst was busy in the early 1690s fund raising for his great project of a new chapel (consecrated 1694). He sent out to alumni delineations of the whole design together with reminders of the decree *de gratiis collegio rependendis* (decree about repaying favours to the College). Trinity Colleges who had been made bishops were importuned, and replied with donations of varying generosity, while the fellows, including the

---

[208] Colvin, *Unbuilt Oxford*, 78–85; Darwall-Smith, 'The Monks of Magdalen', 350–2; Christine Ferdinand, *An Accidental masterpiece. Magdalen College's New Building and the people who built it* (Oxford, 2011). Early occupants of these spacious sets were expected to pay for the cost of furnishing the rooms, including cornices, plaster, paint, shelving, chimneypieces, locks, and shutters. Thus William Howe, gent. commoner (matric. 1742) had to reimburse the College £54 4s 6d for his wainscoting plus £7 for nails and hinges. For the various plans post-1791 to complete the Great Quadrangle, see Colvin, *Unbuilt Oxford*, 85–98.

Fig. 12.8 A Perspective View of the New [Canterbury] Gate at Christ Church (Oxford Almanack, 1781) (© Governing Body, Christ Church, Oxford).

bursar, travelled widely with letters urging old members to be generous. As they were.[209] At Oriel, old members paid for Wyatt's new library built quickly between 1787-86 to house the overflow of books previously collected by the college and to house the fine country house library with titles of 'unusual magnificence' gifted to it by Edward, 5th Lord Leigh (1742-86), lately High Steward of the University, who lapsed into lunacy and died prematurely with no male heir.[210] And the supervention of death upon an anticipated major benefactor could either halt or retard college expenditure, as with repairs to Christ Church Hall in 1714 for which it was hoped the 1st Viscount Weymouth (1640–1714, matric. 1657) would finance plans. As Canon Stratford reported the news: 'I am afraid Lord Weymouth has not made provision for our hall. The surveyor has been here and settled all and

[209] Hopkins, *Trinity*, 155.
[210] Mark Purcell, '"A Lunatick of Unsound Mind": Edward, Lord Leigh (1742–86), and the refounding of Oriel College Library', *BLR*, 17 (2001), 246–60; E. Nicholson, 'Eveleigh and Copleston: the pre-eminence of Oriel', in ed. Catto, *Oriel College* (Oxford, 2013), 247–90, at 250–4; M. Bool, 'The buildings of Oriel', in ibid., 549–96, at 560–6; Robinson, *Wyatt*, 206–8. For the Leigh family and its Oxford connections M. Rothery and J. Stobart, 'Inheritance events and spending in the English country house: the Leigh family of Stoneleigh Abbey, 1738–1806', *Continuity and Change*, 27 (2012), 379–407, at 387.

was to have made his report the day Lord Weymouth fell ill'.[211] For colleges with limited endowments like Hertford a slump in alumni legacies was no trivial matter. During Bernard Hodgson's long Principalship (1775–1805), when it had ceased to attract gentlemen commoners, the last substantial bequest came in 1777 when John Cale of Barming, Kent, left it his library, fortunately finding the funding for the librarian's £30 annual emolument.[212]

It was understandable that the University should be considered a primary repository for artistic bequests by those with no surviving immediate family, uninterested collateral descendants, or heirs they found downright uncongenial. Thus when the 4th Earl of Orrery fell out with his son John, Lord Boyle, he decided to make over his select and valuable library to his old college, Christ Church. Or the head of a family who took pride in an individual ancestor's eminence within the University might wish to make a gift.[213] Such was the motive of the 8th Earl of Pembroke when he donated a statue of William Herbert, the 3rd Earl (d. 1630) to the University in 1723.[214] Though the Pembrokes' ancestral seat at Wilton House might be an exception, public display in Oxford's spaces generally offered a more fitting site than a private mansion.

A family could always decide that an endowment should properly have remained in their custody and legally contest a bequest. Such was the case at Christ Church which, under a deed of 1760, was seven years later controversially awarded a major gift of 200 largely Italian Old Master paintings and 2,000 drawings by General John Guise (1683–1765), discerning connoisseur and adviser to Frederick, Prince of Wales. His heirs planned to hold back part of the collection, counsel for the executors arguing,

> . . . that that the pictures in dispute had been bought after the date of the Will; but besides it seemed evident from alteration in the General's style of Purchase, that they could not be design'd for the University. For since he had exchanged the Offering of the Wise Men for Jupiter and Leda such a Present was unsuitable to ye Youth of the Place, as well as the character of graver Divines.

Counsel for Christ Church argued, as plausibly as they could, turning that claim on its head against the executors:

> '. . . the General could never design the Contemplation of naked Limbs and losse attitudes for his Heir, or to debuch the morals of his family by lascivious Representations—. No, these were manifestly intended for the [. . .] of Christ

---

[211] Stratford to Lord Harley, HMC, *Portland MSS*, VII. 197, 29 July 1714.
[212] Hamilton, *Hertford College*, 92.
[213] ed. Countess of Cork & Orrery, *The Orrery Papers*, I. xxvi.
[214] BL Egerton MS 2618, 19 Apr. 1723, f. 223, Univ. of Oxford to Pembroke acknowledging the gift. The 3rd Earl founded the eponymous college and was Chancellor from 1616 to his death.

650 ENLIGHTENED OXFORD

Church; not wanton Gazers, but Connoisseurs, who [...] them with learned eyes; and, who had Prudence and Discernment sufficient to know, when to produce them, and when to lock them.[215]

In such an instance as the Guise Bequest, when a gift to a college was queried publicly and where the legacy was large-scale and culturally significant, its conferral aroused curiosity, excitement, and envy all over the country publicly, through press reports, and privately, via oral and personal contacts among former collegians, some of whom might (as colleges would hope) be encouraged to be likewise bountiful in their giving.

The paintings and drawing arrived in 1767 and were displayed in the lower library, with a catalogue of the collection published in 1776. They were unequalled in any contemporary Oxford collection, and enabled Christ Church to introduce art into Oxford education without any necessity of travelling on to Italy and, no less significantly, they constituted the first public art gallery in Britain.[216] More usually, colleges received individual art objects from its alumni, not an entire collection. Thus James Clutterbuck Smith, an Oriel graduate, bought a canvas called 'Portrait of six Tuscan poets' (c.1544) reputedly by Vasari, in London in 1790 and donated it to his college the same year.[217] And with all the new constructions going on in the centre of Oxford there were many wall spaces to be filled, including 'Golgotha' (the meeting place of the hebdomadal board in the Clarendon Building). What could be more suitable to their interior than the portraits of the Earls of Rochester and Clarendon bequeathed by George Clarke, MP? [218]

Those who gifted prestige items to the University during their lifetime expected, with some justification, to be noticed and that convention could be fully tested when the gift-giver was a woman. There was some concern that the University was slow to react in the 1750s to the offering made by Henrietta Louisa, the Dowager Countess of Pomfret, the wealthy widow of the 1st Earl (died 1753), a redoubtable lady endowed with a keen architectural interest and whimsical taste, whose connection with Oxford was of long standing, partly because her husband, her son, and her father the 2nd and last Lord Jeffreys of Wem (1673–1703, son of James II's notorious Lord Chief Justice), had all been educated there.[219] After the 1st Earl's death in 1753 she never returned to the family seat at Easton Neston, Northants. However, when her debt-encumbered son, the 2nd Earl, auctioned off 135 marble statues and fragments that had been part of the great seventeenth-

[215] Hants RO, Malmesbury MSS 9M73/165R, F[rancis] Rowden to James Harris, 20 Apr. 1767; N. Aston, *Art and Religion in Eighteenth-Century Europe* (London, 2009), 141–2; ed. Butler et al., *Christ Church, Oxford*, 69.

[216] Thanks to Jacqueline Thalmann, Curator, for confirmation.

[217] It was placed in the inner common room. *A New Pocket Companion for Oxford* (Oxford, 1810), 121.

[218] Bodl. MS Top Oxon. d. 174, f. 151.

[219] Her mother was a Catholic convert. For Lady Pomfret's qualities, see Queen's College MS 476, f. 157, Bernard Brougham to the Countess, 10 July 1746.

century Arundel Marbles collection,[220] encouraged by her friend Sir Roger Newdigate and his wife, she bought them at sale from her two youngest daughters and, after an interval, generously bestowed them on Oxford.[221] She was motivated in her bequest by a desire to reunite the collection (purchased by her father-in-law, William, Lord Leominster) with the bulk of the Arundel Marbles which had come to the University in 1667, and by a wish to honour her immediate ancestors.[222] Nothing, however, happened immediately afterwards, something of an embarrassment when Cambridge had intimated how acceptable the gift would have been to them.[223] William Blackstone of All Souls confided to Newdigate:

> To say ye Truth, entre nous, I think our great men here, from a coldness of constitution natural to those advanced in years, did not receive ye notice of this inestimable Donation with that Rapidity of Gratitude which it demanded, nor seem to have Virtu enough to set a proper value upon it; having heard it insinuated more than once from that Quarter, that several of ye statues were maimed. You will laugh at this, as I do; & not have upon this account a worse opinion of ye taste of your Constituents, when I assure you that the insensibility of our Chiefs is amply compensated by ye zeal, almost mounting to rapture, which is expressed by ye whole Body of ye University.[224]

Part of the problem lay in the University's inability to decide where to put the bequest;[225] it was not until the Encaenia of 1756 that Lady Pomfret was invited to the University and acclaimed, though, of course, she could not, as a woman, be awarded an honorary degree.[226]

Both the Guise and Pomfret bequests were always intended for pedagogic purposes. As the indenture of the Pomfret grant stated, the transfer would act

---

[220] Warks RO, Newdegate of Arbury Papers, CR 136/B2976, Catalogue of the Antique Marbles given by the Countess of Pomfret to the University of Oxford; M. Vickers, *The Arundel and Pomfret Marbles in Oxford* (Oxford, 2006); D. E. L. Haynes, *The Arundel Marbles* (Oxford, 1975).

[221] D. L. Dudley, 'Henrietta Louisa Jeffreys, Oxford and the Pomfret Benefaction of 1755: Vertu made Visible', (Ph.D., University of Victoria, 2004); Sarah Freeman, 'An Englishwoman's home is her castle: Lady Pomfret's house at 18 Arlington Street', *The Georgian Group Journal*, 20 (2012), 87–102, at 87–90. See also S. Houfe, 'Antiquarian inclinations: diaries of the Countess of Pomfret—II', *CL*, 31 Mar. 1977, 800–2.

[222] Sir Roger Newdigate, her kinsman, acted as intermediary in the negotiations and, in his letter of 13 Feb. 1755, nudged the Vice Chancellor into an appropriate response with the words, '... there could be no sort of Honour or Regard which the University would not readily shew towards those noble Persons and Herself for so great and generous a Benefactress'. Quoted in John Gutch, *The history & antiquities of the colleges and halls in the University of Oxford...* (2 vols., Oxford, 1786–90), I. 808.

[223] Sir Roger to Lady Newdigate, London, 15 Feb. 1755, Warks RO, Newdegate of Arbury Papers, CR136/B2980.

[224] Blackstone to Newdigate, All Souls College, 27 Feb. 1755, Warks RO, Newdegate of Arbury Papers, CR136/B2982.

[225] Westmorland as Chancellor offered £500 to cover the cost of installing the collection in and around the library at the Oxford Physic Garden. This effort proved unsuccessful, and the collection was initially housed in the old School of Logic. Berry, 'Collecting at Oxford', 80–1.

[226] Chapter 10, pp. 82–95.

652   ENLIGHTENED OXFORD

'for the further encouragement of the Study of Antiquity and the polite Arts in the same [University].'[227] That was all very well, but the practical problem of where precisely to house them proved never easy to resolve. Few were as solicitous for the well-being of the University during the century than its long-serving MP, Sir Roger Newdigate. Having no son of his own to inherit his estate may have intensified his wish to be generous to his alma mater and offer objets d'art as part of a plan to create a museum of ancient sculpture in the Radcliffe Library, newly opened but standing empty. He gave casts of the Belvedere Apollo and the Medici Venus to the Bodleian in the 1750s then, in 1777, two marble candelabra acquired on his second grand tour two years earlier (excavated by Gavin Hamilton in 1769 and restored by Piranesi) were installed in the Camera. But his hopes for a Radcliffe (or even a Newdigate) Museum were dashed because the University considered that what would have been the centrepiece of any such public space— the Arundel marbles—were, in many cases, in too much of a fragmentary state.[228] If both the Pomfret and the Guise bequests were intended in the first instance for the use of the refined and the classically educated, the gift of the young Joseph Banks tapped into public fascination for South Sea exploration and confirmed Oxford's importance as an obvious centre for displaying what had been collected. It was almost certainly to John Parsons, first Lee's Reader in anatomy (1742–85), that Banks sent hundreds of artificial curiosities he and Solander had collected on James Cook's ship *Endeavour*. These were housed first at the Anatomy School, whose completion Parsons had overseen, and they were accessible to a potentially wider public.[229]

The objects in the Pomfret Bequest pointed attention to the donor and under-lined the status of the museum and the college as a site of refined display as well as of learning but served no charitable purpose. Several Oxford bequests did so and drew attention to a neglected aspect of associational culture: improving the lot of those within a college's circle whose material needs were appreciable. The poorer clergy were an obvious object of support for well-disposed Oxonians who wanted to emulate—on a smaller scale—the example set by the generosity of Queen Anne in 1704 in setting up the eponymous 'Bounty', intended to supplement the revenues of priests in livings that generated scanty incomes (less than £80 per annum).[230] Robert South, canon of Christ Church, who died two years after the last Stuart monarch, had shown his concern for the material and educational well-being of his Islip parishioners for thirty-eight years, and in death identified other objects for his charity. He left his Kentish Town and Caversham estates to Christ Church, and a

---

[227] Gutch, *History and Antiquities*, I. 809.

[228] Cf. D. C. Kurtz, *The Reception of Classical Art in Britain: An Oxford Story of Plaster Casts from the Antique* (Oxford, 2000), 118.

[229] They included the thirty weapons, tools, and textiles from Tahiti and New Zealand rediscovered at the Pitt-Rivers Museum in 2002.

[230] W. R. Le Fanu, *Queen Anne's bounty, a short account of its history and works* (London, 1921).

fund was established thereby to support financially the incumbents of the college's livings in their daily ministry.[231]

The University's sense of its vulnerability in the new Whig world was one factor in explaining one of Oxford's greatest trophy bequests of the whole century, that willed to it as part of Nathaniel, Lord Crew's, complicated and comprehensive settlement.[232] There was another obvious motive at work here that was commonly replicated: Crew was the last of the direct male line. The most foolproof way by which he could perpetuate his name was through the endowments to which it would be attached. When his will was read in Convocation on 12 July 1722 (at the height of the Atterbury Plot crisis), it was learnt that the former bishop of Durham had left Oxford £200 per annum to be used as the Chancellor, masters and scholars should think fit. It was a gratifyingly substantial sum, though not so exceptional that it was likely to make the Bishop's name lasting currency. That was achieved through the award of much lesser sums: £10 for an annual entertainment for the heads of houses, doctors, professors, proctors, at Encaenia and, more particularly, £20 per annum for the Public Orator and Professor of Poetry to make speeches commemorating benefactors in the 'public theatre' on the same occasion. In helping to further marginalise the possibility of a return of the *Terrae Filius*, whom Vice Chancellor Gardiner had banned in 1713, Lord Crew proposed a polite alternative that would enshrine his active benevolence via an annual public mention.[233] At the same time, his 'entertainment' encouraged the very kind of associationalism that would generate solidarity, good-will, amity—and funds—for the whole University.[234]

Lord Crew's association with Oxford (with Lincoln College pre-eminently), went back to the Restoration, and he had held some of its some of its most senior offices. Those individuals elected to the University Chancellorship were expected to do what they could to follow up the impressive example set by some of their predecessors, such as William Laud, whose patronage and munificent donation of books and manuscripts had helped make Oxford the main seat of biblical learning in Britain. Though they knew the difference a major gift could make to academic life and Oxford's international reputation, the cancellarial eighteenth-century record is disappointing. The 2nd Duke of Ormond and Lord Arran between them held the Chancellorship for seventy consecutive years, but the Duke's debts and confiscated estates yielded nothing from him but the family papers

---

[231] Curthoys (4), 49, 95. There was also a clause in his will leaving £200 to be shared by twenty Nonjurors who had been ejected from their livings because of their principles. Reedy, *Robert South*, 10.

[232] C. J. Stranks, *The Charities of Nathaniel, Lord Crewe and Dr. John Sharp 1721-1976* (Durham, 1976), esp. 6–8.

[233] Whiting, *Nathaniel Lord Crewe*, 322, 326–7. The Will is printed in ibid., App. 1, 332–58.

[234] OUA: WPα/60/3, Statutes *c.*1725 [n.d.], for the Creweian benefaction. The administration of a bequest might, according to the terms of the will, initially be left to a trusted client. Thus Richard Grey (Crewe's former chaplain) in the 1730s maintained an interest in the proper administration of the Bishop's benefaction. Gibson, *Domestic chaplain*, 79.

for the Bodleian (used devotedly by the historian Thomas Carte), while Arran was relatively cash-strapped in his efforts to stabilise the Butler family fortune—inasmuch as that could be done—and left only a full-length portrait. Lord Arran's childless state (a not uncommon incentive to leave large bequests to the alma mater) was thus offset by impecuniosity. His successor, the 7th Earl of Westmorland, shared the first condition but not the second, and he was in office for too brief a time (three years) to give the University any hope of a lasting memorial that would take precedence over his various Fane family obligations. George Lee, 3rd Earl of Lichfield (d. 1772), knowing that his earldom would expire on his brother's death, did rather better by Oxford by establishing the Lichfield Clinical Professorship (to the Radcliffe Infirmary) to ensure his title a longer existence. He devised his house and furniture at in Berkeley Square on the death of his wife, with £4,256 produced clear at the sale after deductions.[235] Lichfield wanted to be associated with a medical initiative that underlined his personal regard for good and useful causes; with Lord North the customary pattern reasserted itself. Death overtook him in 1790 when he had barely succeeded as 2nd Earl of Guilford and enjoyed an income that his father's longevity had thitherto denied him. With many sons and daughters to provide for, there was no prospect of either the University (or Trinity College in particular) doing well out of his estate.

vi) Conclusion

An Oxford education offered its beneficiaries access to a world of connections both formal and informal that would likely be primary to their social and professional existence throughout their lives. Students were at Oxford, to quote Laurence Brockliss, 'to make contacts and acquire a cultural veneer of varying degrees of thickness',[236] but the process of building up this social capital obligated them, in the first instance to their college, and then to the University at large. There was an essential mutuality to membership of the University reflected, at one level, in the unavoidably transactional dimension of patronage in whichever dimensions these flowed, in another to the unseen bonds of affection that membership was intended to foster. That usually took the form of male friendships nurtured at Oxford (often originating at school) as a foundational aspect of that homosociability that characterised almost the entire institutional operation of Hanoverian Britain. But it also not infrequently led to the creation of new inter-family connections through marriage in a manner that could also strengthen

---

[235] Bodl MS Top Oxon. d.174, f. 214. John Parsons was elected to the Chair in Convocation on 19 June 1780. See Chapter 5, pp. 66–8.
[236] Brockliss (2), 161.

political affinities and affiliations.[237] It was a particularly important mechanism of securing kinship solidarity (and therefore political ties) for outcast Tories in the reigns of George the First and Second that built on shared *mentalités* and allegiances. As Linda Colley put it:[238]

> Traditional but still relevant political and religious attitudes sustained Tory politicians quite as much as did their cultural debt to Oxford, and their families' extensive inter-marriage.

The patronage networks in those decades, however, that produced the most material rewards were Whig in character, and they became increasingly dominant—and difficult to resist for careerists—in Oxford. They were entrenched in colleges such as Exeter, Wadham, and Merton, but also took powerful hold elsewhere, for instance in Christ Church, thanks to royal patronage of the Dean and Chapter. The former tutor of a Cabinet minister could reasonably anticipate patronal recognition at some point even if that took decades, as it did for Henry Pelham, when Premier, to get his former tutor, Richard Newton of Hart Hall, a canonry of Christ Church.[239] By no means all Whig nexuses were Pelhamite ones: John, 2nd Earl Granville (1690–1764), a Christ Church product, court Tory turned court Whig, was a nationally pre-eminent politician much admired by many Oxonians despite—or more likely because of—the Pelham brothers' antipathy towards him. The likelihood of Oxford dons benefitting from having former pupils governing the state (high during Anne's reign) increased incrementally with each passing decade thereafter until it became assured under George III. It was only personal disinclination that made Cyril Jackson, the great panjandrum of Oxford University in this era, refuse to accept any offers made to him. Jackson's exceptional talent for networking was far from being merely mercenary and that presumption should hold good for the majority of tutors embedded in the patronage state of which Oxford was but one (very significant) component. For these it flowed in many cases from a wider, pastoral sense, the generational concern of an older man for a younger one originally articulated in a college setting, or on the Grand Tour, and might be expressed in nothing more than occasional calls or just epistolary contact.

Associational ties between Oxford graduates could be found across the nation. College feasts, provincial gatherings in urban centres, estate visits by college stewards or heads of house were proven ways of maintaining contact with Oxford and with each other for lay and clergy alumni. These links were not

---

[237] The ties of kinship are stressed in J. S. Chamberlain, 'Portrait of a High Church clerical dynasty in Georgian England: the Frewens and their world', in eds. Walsh, Haydon, and Taylor, *From toleration to Tractarianism*, 299–316, esp. 308.

[238] Colley, *In defiance of oligarchy*, 323.   [239] See this chapter, p. 42, n. 105.

656 ENLIGHTENED OXFORD

necessarily sustained evenly and regularly throughout adulthood; college connections might be rediscovered later in life and ties with the college (or just with the University) confirmed and renewed by striking up a friendship with a fellow alumnus who was not necessarily one's own contemporary. Parish clergy, in particular, many of whom felt acutely a sense of intellectual isolation, seem to have found social links based on earlier academic associations helpful in promoting personal well-being. In any given region, clerics grouped together in the name of friendship and mutual support for meeting at large-scale social events, including races and dinners. Thus on the first Tuesday of each month at St Laurence's Church, Reading, clergy had a sermon known as 'The Lecture', after which a clerical dinner followed supported by a society of the clergy.[240] Contacts between them based on shared political loyalties intensified when an election to Westminster loomed, for the clergy in most localities made up an electoral force on which party campaigning strategies could be partly constructed. Most parish priests took a pronounced interest in national affairs and paid close attention to any legislation that affected them. Yet many of them preferred scholarship to politics and the extent to which a country parsonage could be no less conducive to study and publication than an Oxford college in the long eighteenth century is striking. One might plausibly argue that, in relative rural isolation, the pastoral demands on clergy were rather less than on active tutors inside Oxford and, the lack of ready access to libraries apart, enhanced the scope for literary productiveness. Nevertheless, the inspiration and interest in an area of study was commonly kindled in the University and return visits to Oxford by its graduates for whatever reason were willingly undertaken and invariably prompted an emotional recognition of an original academic debt.

It was a sentiment likely to inspire a willingness to offer supportive funds in one's lifetime or a legacy after one's death. Oxonian wealth, both University and collegiate, rested historically on what it had been freely given over the centuries by benefactors. The alma mater expected her sons to dig deep into their pockets in every generation and winning gifts and bequests remained a primary preoccupation of the whole foundation in the eighteenth century. The University generally excelled at stimulating the intent, though it could fumble the handling of proffered personal largesse. The most spectacular coup was the acquisition of the Pomfret marbles in 1755, though it only highlighted the problem of where to put them, a consideration that had almost deterred Lady Pomfret from bestowing them in her lifetime in the first place. And Oxford increasingly had to compete for funds as the number of charitable institutions supplicating for them increased. Individuals tended to apportion funds proportionately and Oxford benefactors from well-established landed backgrounds were generally generous to a range of good

---

[240] Charles Coates, *The History and Antiquities of Reading* (London, 1802).

causes. Thus that staunch Oxonian, Sir Edmund Isham, 6th Bart., Fellow of Magdalen (1720–36), a judge advocate of the Admiralty court (1731–41), Tory MP for Northamptonshire 1737–72, gave £1,000 towards the building of Magdalen College library, but was also, on his own patrimony, the founder of village schools for Lamport and Hanging Houghton on his own estate.[241] Don, lawyer, landowner, Member of Parliament, Isham symbolised in his own career those diffuse values of duty, obligation, and connection that were nurtured by the Isham family's generational connections with the University of Oxford. On him as on its other graduates, for better or for worse, Oxford left its imprint in a manner that makes unsupportable G. M. Trevelyan's contention that 'the country houses, the Dissenting Academies, and the Scottish Universities did more than Oxford and Cambridge to nourish the widely diffused English culture of that period...'.[242]

[241] ed. Sir G. Isham, *A Rugby Headmaster's Letters to a Parent in the Early eighteenth century* (Northampton, 1952), 3. None of his elections to Parliament were contested.

[242] Quoted in Felix Markham, *Oxford* (London, 1967), 129.

Conclusion

Oxford variations on an Enlightenment theme

> these noble Foundations and Monuments of the Vertue of our Ancestors, are in their very Nature directly opposed to Tyranny and unlimited Power, since as *Ignorance* is a natural Consequence of *Slavery, Arts and Sciences* may be properly called the Eldest Daughters of LIBERTY.
>
> *The Englishman*, 19–2 Dec. 1713.

> ...should those venerable monuments of the wisdom and piety of our ancestors ever fall into disrepute, I question not that the blow will be nationally felt, in the religion, the morals, and the literature of this country.
>
> George Gregory, *Essays Historical and Moral*, Essay XIV. Of Education (London, 1785), 280.

Whatever its claims to intellectual distinction during the long eighteenth century, the University of Oxford—at once a Church seminary, a finishing school for the lay elite, and a property-owning corporation—was at the heart of the established order irrespective of the latter's dynastic character. It was uneasily so until 1760, more comfortably thereafter, and even had a Jacobite dispensation replaced a Williamite or a Hanoverian one, such would have been no less the case. Loyalty was a central Oxford value and therefore discomfort with the Revolution settlement and all that flowed from it was necessarily going to inaugurate years of uncertainty, disengagement, and disenchantment with the revamped regime for a large proportion of the University's membership. Yet this was never at the cost of complete detachment from the rest of the polity where, in an era of personal and institutional mutability, what Oxford represented and demonstrated in terms of an intelligent respect for the past, both antiquity and more recent times, was as prized in some quarters as it was derided in others. Whig administrations were not comfortable dealing amicably with any other than their political friends and well-wishers inside the University and, in the end, inattention, rather than new regulations imposed from the centre, was their preferred approach towards Oxford on the *quieta non movere* principle. But it was that disconnection, that mutual wariness, that contributed to the internalisation of much of the

---

Enlightened Oxford: The University and the Cultural and Political Life of Eighteenth-century Britain and Beyond.
Nigel Aston, Oxford University Press. © Nigel Aston 2023. DOI: 10.1093/oso/9780199246830.003.0014

University's life at mid-century. Oxonians were quick to diagnose the malaise and to be alarmist about the symptoms but their capacity for compellingly countering them was never fully on show, the result of external political pressures, internal divisions, and plain wrongfootedness.

In retrospect, these years of stasis (as distinguished from atrophy), precipitated in large measure by an absence of government favour in the form of even-handed patronage, amounted to a relatively short hiatus between the greater dynamism of the first and last three decades of the eighteenth century. At no point, however, should Oxford be considered intellectually at a clear remove from what one might call the moderate Enlightenment, a description consonant with Niall O'Flaherty's excellent point that '... schematic definitions of enlightenment tend to scythe through the tangled web of alliances and affinities that comprised intellectual debate in eighteenth-century Britain'. This moderate trajectory was built and expressed incrementally on and in existing institutions, and was never confined to a set of influential ideas that encouraged improvements and progression: it also encompassed justifications for hesitating to displace existing dispensations. What in retrospect appears the plotting of a steady course balancing Enlightenment and Counter-Enlightenment discourses that preserved the cultural authority of churchmen may have been articulated within an Anglican framework, but it was never closed off from external influences, for, as Michael Brown has recently emphasised, modes of Enlightenment transcended particular confessions.[1] And any sense that the Christian religion was anything other than central to enlightened intellectual activity in this century has virtually disappeared from contemporary scholarship.[2] For if the underlying task of Oxford academic life, broadly defined, was to restate truths grounded in religion that had some sort of resonance in wider society, that did not preclude scholarly clerics from being any less concerned for human betterment than their sceptical counterparts. And that concern began with the Bible, stabilising and protecting the text but in the light of the latest scholarship, as Benjamin Blayney's *Authorized Version* (1769), prepared for the Clarendon Press, sought to do. Oxford divines were ready to build on the insights from their learned predecessors while putting their own distinctive gloss on them and adapting them to contemporary circumstances. Merely that they were operating within the apparent confines of the academy does not disqualify their work as somehow 'unenlightened'. The Church in England was, after all, at the centre of intellectual activity nationally.

[1] M. Brown, *The Irish Enlightenment, passim*. Cf. J. Champion, '"May the last king be strangled in the bowels of the last priest": Irreligion and the English Enlightenment, 1649–1789', in eds. T. Morton and N. Smith, *Radicalism in British literary culture, 1650–1830. From Revolution to Revolution* (Cambridge, 2002), 29–44, at 43.

[2] J. G. A. Pocock, 'The Re-Description of Enlightenment', *Proceedings of the British Academy*, 125 (2004), 101–17; Jonathan Sheehan and Dale K. Van Kley, 'Review Essay: God and the Enlightenment', *AHR*, 108 (2003), 1061–80; Sheridan Gilley, 'Christianity and Enlightenment: An Historical Survey', *History of European Ideas*, 1 (1981), 103–21.

660   ENLIGHTENED OXFORD

The majority of University men were not revivalists and were correspondingly sceptical about religious reform movements. Thus they shared the general distaste of the educated classes for Methodism as an enthusiastic, irrational movement damaging to good order in Church and state, and the mature John Wesley would find no ready welcome in Oxford for either himself or his followers. Not that this made them impervious to the impulse to call the nation to faith but to do it without 'enthusiasm' within the well-trodden boundaries of the liturgy and mature spiritualities of the Established Church. Yet Wesley's High Church family background made him a classic Oxford product of his time with concerns and anxieties that were not unique to him. Oxonians of that kidney were preoccupied in their defence of the Established Church after 1689—and again after 1714—with the question of where that Church, conceived as a divinely ordained and ordered spiritual creation, fitted into a revised national polity, and it was not easy to articulate a vision that accorded with Whig values. That mismatch arguably tempted pious Oxford churchmen to turn inwards and search, in Wesley's case, for personal purification through grace, while the majority gave outward vent to their frustrations, as with the insistence on the integrity of the sacraments that powered the campaign against Occasional Conformity in Anne's reign.

Despite party splits and internal divisions based on ideologies as much as personalities,[3] the bedrock of Oxford Anglicanism never ceased to be credal orthodoxy and the multiple challenges confronting it. Here was a cause which in time could unite moderate Whigs with their Tory counterparts. Take Thomas Secker, the long-serving, bishop of Oxford, of whom it has been well-said that he 'wanted orthodoxy promulgated in sermons, from the pulpits of the remotest parish churches to those of the greatest cathedrals'.[4] And he knew that it could not be done without well-educated, pastorally minded young clergy drawn from the cadres of those who each year took holy orders after graduating at Oxford. Despite an overriding belief that Christianity was a reasonable religion, even prominent Whigs in the University, such as John Conybeare, were counselling against excessive reliance on reason as early as the 1720s.[5] A sense of how much deism and natural philosophy were undermining the doctrine of the Trinity existed in every decade from the 1690s to the 1790s and the most talented could be tempted into heterodoxy: the career of Samuel Clarke was a clear warning of what could go amiss. In the second half of the century anti-Trinitarians were prominent among those criticising the existing English translations of the Bible and had some formidable protagonists in their ranks. Joseph Priestley, for one, seemed person-ally intent on demolishing the whole religious establishment in the 1780s, as

---

[3] Stephen Hampton has noted the elusive search for consensus at either end of the seventeenth century: 'Later Stuart Anglicanism was no more marked by theological consensus than early Stuart Anglicanism'. *Anti-Arminians*, 273.

[4] Ingram, *Religion, Reform and Modernity*, 85.

[5] See his sermon preached at Whitehall, 1726, Bodl. MS Eng. Th. e 49, ff. 61r, 64r.

CONCLUSION   661

though he were a Gunpowder plotter. As one former Oxford vice chancellor, George Horne, observed concerning Priestley's sermon on 'Free enquiry':[6]

> ...the author spoke of this Powder-plot against the Church of England with as much certainty, as if he had *held the lantern.*

Horne was to the fore in meeting this challenge; he and other clerical colleagues wrote and lobbied hard to hold the line on Anglican privileges that would have been compromised by any repeal of the Test and Corporation Acts, but a perception remained, on the eve of the French Revolution, that orthodox academics were underperforming in taking the fight to their critics. The bishop of Lichfield, Richard Hurd, sensed this in a letter to the Scottish jurist and Christian apologist, Lord Hailes:

> There are undoubtedly many of our clergy, equal to this task, but we want zeal & industry. At the same time the irreligious party, both abroad & at home, are unaccountably active.[7]

It may be that churchmen, Oxonians among them, were too expectant that governments would always act to protect the confessional status quo, whatever experience had taught them. The price to be paid across Europe was acceptance that the Church's institutional voice was to be restricted. In England, even after the accession of George III, it is significant that Oxford divines never considered the resuscitation of the Church's Convocation as a realistic objective and recognised that even having a Chancellor as Premier, in the person of Lord North, was no guarantee that the coterminous interests of the University and the Church would be his priority.

The loyalty of Oxonians to the University as much as to the monarchy and the Church played a neglected part in ensuring an underlying academic stability for the University that made possible creative intellectual opportunities for those in Oxford who wanted to take them. And many deliberately did, and make their reputation in the wider literary world, as the examples of Joseph Addison at the beginning of this era and Thomas Warton towards its close suggest. They courted a large readership and wrote in the vernacular, whereas a figure such as Robert Lowth found acclaim and attention as word got out about the insight and

---

[6] W. Jones, *Memoirs of the Life, Studies, and Writings of the Right Reverend George Horne, D.D., late Lord Bishop of Norwich* (London, 1795), 144.

[7] Hurd to Hailes, NLS, Newhailes MS25297, ff. 19–20, 2 Nov. 1776. The extent to which doctrinal orthodoxy had been vindicated in the later eighteenth century should not be underestimated. Even Richard Watson, the reformist Bishop of Llandaff and Professor of Chemistry at Cambridge, held fast to the miracles of the Virgin Birth and Resurrection of Christ. *Anecdotes of the Life of Richard Watson,* I. 24.

662 ENLIGHTENED OXFORD

originality of his lectures on Hebrew poetry in the 1740s.[8] Authors in the still vigorous (at least until the mid-century) Anglo-Latin literary tradition could expect less notice from the public outside. Which is not to say that there was none, especially if such verse disclosed witty academic and personal point-scoring. History writing at Oxford spilled over into contemporary controversies, arguably a sign of its vigour. To recover the Church of England's history had a missional dimension, one which justified its apostolic integrity against the claims of both Dissent and Roman Catholicism. Patristic knowledge and tradition in Oxford was well-established *c.*1700 as 'part of a broader reinvention of the Church of England by Anglican divines in the mid-seventeenth century, a process that wove episcopacy further into the Anglican understanding of the constitution of a national church'.[9] But it became less fashionable as party contestation within the Established Church receded after *c.*1725 and High Church Oxonians were sidelined by the hierarchy. Controversy, even party controversy, generated scholarship within the *érudit* tradition as the dispute over the rights of Convocation emphasised where Oxford men figured on both sides of the debate. But, after the Bangorian Controversy had precipitated the prorogation of Convocation, interest in the question faded away. Much the same may be said over more secular histories. Thus Rochester's Tory and royalist contextualisation of his father's *History of the Great Rebellion* generated much heat in Anne's reign, but ceased to do so after her death. Thomas Carte's later *History of England* was an attempt at offering an intelligent Tory narrative of the English past, but it suffered equally from incompletion and a conspicuous absence of ministerial approval.

The fostering of medieval scholarship by Nicolson, Gibson, and Kennett (all moderate Whigs, interestingly enough) in the period from the 1690s to the 1730s was insufficient to ensure its continuation. Editions of the Church Fathers and ancient English chroniclers (including the Oxford edition of George Hickes's acclaimed *Thesaurus*) suddenly became unfashionable, and the University was perhaps slow to adjust and adapt. The establishment of a Regius Professorship in Modern History in 1724 famously did not prompt the subject's flourishing. David Gregory, the first holder of the chair, complained:

the methods of education in our universities have been in some measure defective, since we are obliged to adhere so much to the rules laid down by our forefathers...the old scholastic learning has been for some time despised, but not altogether exploded, because nothing else has been substituted in its place.[10]

---

[8] Stephen Prickett does not minimise the scale of Lowth's achievement: 'To Lowth we owe the rediscovery of the Bible as a work of literature within the context of ancient Hebrew life', Prickett, *Words and the Word: Language, Poetics, and Biblical Interpretation* (Cambridge, 1986), 105.

[9] J. Spurr, '"A special kindness for dead bishops": The Church, History, and Testimony in Seventeenth-Century Protestantism', *HLQ*, 68 (2005), 313–34, at 317–18.

[10] 24 May 1728, TNA (PRO), SP 36/6, f. 227.

CONCLUSION 663

But, in articulating his difficulty (and not doing much to resolve it), Gregory overlooked the intellectual adaptability of colleagues in other nascent disciplines, such as Law, where there was much going on—despite the survival of scholasticism. William Blackstone was not the first in Augustan Oxford to interest himself in the contemporary common law and its origins. But his capacity for authoritatively articulating it (and that as a moderate Tory) in his lectures and in the *Commentaries* inspired any number of Oxford-educated lawyers and saw him recognised as Britain's foremost constitutional commentator in his own lifetime.[11] In the next generation, (Sir) William Jones, of University College, another brilliant jurist, 'a scholar, a lawyer, and a man of genius' as Edward Gibbon acclaimed him,[12] built on Oxford's existing tradition of scholarship in Oriental languages, to raise the status of Persian as a literary language, and master Sanskrit with publications that caught the attention of the learned across Europe. More locally, Oxford turned itself into a nationally recognised music centre with some of the best performers keen to play in the city, either in the Sheldonian or in the new Holywell Music Room and, in William Hayes, produced one of the most accomplished native composers of the century. The University's record in the humanities, while by no means outstanding in the 'long' eighteenth century, deserves respect for what was achieved in terms of individual scholarly accomplishments (and their wider impact), despite considerable official detachment and curricular constraints. It also confirmed that the foundation of new professorships, including the Chair of Comparative poetry set up in 1708 and endowed by Henry Birkhead (a former fellow of All Souls), was no guarantee in itself that their holders would perform diligently, let alone with distinction.

Much the same might be said of Oxford's record in the natural sciences, where its invariably unfavourable comparison to Cambridge requires revision. It may be the case until well into the eighteenth century that the Oxford intellectual environment was 'dominated by the task of defending the Established Church by recourse to the traditional weapons of Aristotelian logic and knowledge of the Church Fathers', but that commitment did not preclude Oxonians from pursuing interests in the 'new sciences', as their numbers in the Royal Society and figures such as Robert Boyle and Halley indicated.[13] They drew on sources of inspiration beyond Newton that both reflected the somewhat reduced place traditionally given to mathematics in the curriculum by comparison with Cambridge, and indicated a corporate independence of outlook that owed more to dispassion than

---

[11] Macaulay noted wryly that Blackstone's *Commentaries* were read with applause in a setting where books had been publicly burned eighty years earlier for 'the damnable doctrine that the English monarchy is limited and mixed' and applauded 'a salutary change' in what he called 'political science'. *History of England*, II. 556–7.

[12] *Decline and Fall*, III. 822n.

[13] Gascoigne, 'Ideas of Nature', 290. Gascoigne overlooks the underlying point that to defend the Church was not unenlightened if the Church was held to show the way to truth.

664 ENLIGHTENED OXFORD

to cussedness. And Oxford had its own Newtonian moment early in the century through the inspirational presence of Gregory and Keill, whose achievement has been nicely summed up thus: 'Gregory did for the heavens what Keill did for the terrestrial world: he rendered Newtonian celestial mechanics teachable'.[14] But that Newtonian moment had largely ended by the 1730s. And this faltering cannot be detached from unease among the orthodox that too many of its apologists (perhaps even Newton himself and, certainly, his minor followers outside the Universities) were compromised by heresy or outright unbelief. The perception was explicable given that, at this date, science itself was essentially a theological project, and its practice and its use in defence of the faith could not be casually hazarded. It also helps to explain the rise and appeal of Hutchinsonianism among academics for whom theology and physics should be mutual handmaidens rather than disciplinary rivals.

Their antagonism towards Newton personally was not the majority view within the University at mid-century as Newtonianism became more diverse and interests shifted towards astronomy, chemistry, and medicine and, gradually, some teaching spaces for them were made available. This new direction of travel was in part a belated response to and recognition of the public's fascination with these subjects, that sites of natural knowledge were many and various in a commercial society, and that science was 'a commodity consumed in a wide variety of public locations'.[15] In other words, the University would have to develop an adaptability to external market forces operative in the natural sciences if it did not wish to be marginalised by outsiders with suspect academic credentials but popular credibility and endorsement. Academic exclusivism was never going to achieve much and members of the University who were demonstrating the practical application of sciences tended to welcome the admittance of outsiders into their lectures and laboratories. This was, in part, a response to the reputation of some of its best-known practitioners. In astronomy, James Bradley's status as a teacher and practitioner built on Halley's earlier. Between them, from 1705 until 1760 they gave Oxford a lustre that bears comparison with that of the heyday of the 1650s on the eve of the formation of the Royal Society.[16]

The difficulty of achieving this kind of cultural turn should not be underestimated for, as Steven Shapin has noted, 'During the eighteenth century no version of the character of the man of science was immune to polite imputations of abstruseness, pedantry, and incivility'.[17] And Oxford was a gentlemanly society par excellence. Those tensions were always there, dramatically visible during the 1790s when the University in effect expelled the outstanding chemist, Thomas

---

[14] Feingold, *The Newtonian Moment*, 43.
[15] Fissell and Cooter, 'Exploring Natural Knowledge', 133.
[16] Chapman, 'Pure research and practical teaching', 210.
[17] 'The image of the man of science', in ed. Porter, *Eighteenth-century science*, 159–83, at 173.

CONCLUSION 665

Beddoes, because of his refusal to tone down his radical political sympathies or indicate that his fascination with gases was any less subversive than Joseph Priestley's.[18] Beddoes's behaviour was adjudged as more resembling that of a rational dissenter in an Academy rather than a loyal Anglican Oxonian. That there could be no place for a chemist of his capacities in the 1790s is a reminder that intellectual excellence inside the University was compromised when it was not associated with some show of religious and political conformity.

The removal of Beddoes was actioned by the University authorities at the highest level, for senior officer-holders knew that, whatever their personal misgivings, to be excessively confrontational with the government of the day was likely to incur ill will or outright retribution. Most placed the well-being of the University before their own political preferences and cultivated the influential and the powerful. It was that necessity that made the office of Chancellor so much more than a mere Oxford figurehead. Arran, after some initial fumbling, soon settled into a role as a seasoned *politique*; he may not have had the cavalier ebullience of his brother, Ormond, but, in straitened times for Tories after 1715, his longevity and his caution were more useful assets. Ironically, it was the tenure of Lord North, the Premier-Chancellor, that was the more unsettling. National policy formation was always going to take priority over academic group interest, as with the Toleration Act 1779; and then, as a result of his junction with Fox in 1783, North went into opposition, while the University quickly saw the sense of aligning itself with Pitt the Younger. It fell to Chancellors to nominate to the Vice-Chancellorship and, by and large, they chose well. Aldrich, Gardiner, Niblett, Randolph, Wetherell, and Horne bear favourable comparison with their counterparts in any century, for they discharged their internal duties resourcefully and proved more than capable of effective external lobbying when the interests of the University were judged to require it. All of them had decided political views, but they also had a capacity for pragmatism without appearing to be unsubtle time-servers.

Heads of Houses and senior tutors were more likely to wear the political colours of their foundation more flagrantly. That was particularly the case before the accession of George III, after which it was rare to find a Principal who was uncomfortable with the political status quo. For the most part, their impact beyond the University (and certainly outside Oxfordshire) was not pronounced, though there were exceptions: Nathan Wetherell, through his ties to Charles Jenkinson, was highly influential behind the scenes, but on nothing like the scale of Cyril Jackson, Dean of Christ Church for over a quarter of a century, whose influence on policy and appointments in the 1790s and 1800s (especially after the Portland Whigs joined Pitt's administration in 1794) was as immense as

---

[18] Ibid., 175–6.

666 ENLIGHTENED OXFORD

it was discreet. Christ Church was a royal foundation, where the sovereign was Visitor, and there was never any question in Jackson's time of embroiling the royal personage in any internal wrangling of the sort that had racked the House while Atterbury was Dean (1711–13). Most colleges were, at some point or other, caught up in unseemly, protracted contests that dragged in their Visitor, a figure of potentially decisive importance. The unfavourable publicity that the dispute over the Mastership of University College generated in the 1720s was publicly damaging but at least it underlined that the Visitatorial system, requiring the intervention of a figure half in and half out of the University, was in good working order. Bishops of Oxford had less scope for direct action. Nevertheless, the fact that they might hold chairs in the University, as with John Potter, or were well-in with ministers, as with Thomas Secker, gave them opportunities (not always taken) for what amounted to a constructive ministry of reconciliation within the University around which moderate opinion could rally.

Primary to the duty of successive diocesan bishops was to be persuasive within the University about the duty of loyalty to the Crown and the person of the monarch in possession. Given Oxford's record during the first Civil War (1642–6) the need should not have existed but the traumas, first, of the Catholic intrusions of James II, followed by the lesser one of the Williamite settlement, made Oxonian loyalty problematic: the break in the hereditary succession and the fraught issue of oath-taking that ensued saw to that. The exile of James II and the (possibly temporary) end of hereditary monarchy was the high price that Oxford, like the majority of the Church of England, was willing to pay for the perpetuation and (they trusted) protection of Anglican privileges. But these continued fragile and the Church was weakened by the loss of a sizable proportion of its present and future leadership cadre in the Nonjurors plus the concessions to Protestant Dissenters in the legislation of 1689. While Oxford was never anything other than an impeccably royalist institution in this era, its loyalism could not be taken for granted between 1689 and 1702 and 1714 and 1760. It did its best to be gracious to William III; it owed the King a debt of thanks as a deliverer, after all. But there was no love lost between the King and the University, as his rather abrupt visit of 1695 confirmed. Anne's accession ended this cautious distance and promised a return to royal beneficence last on offer during the Tory reaction of the early 1680s. That was not to be but, despite any disappointment, and although moderate Toryism had its defenders and exponents in the University, majority opinion was all too ready to look on the sovereign as entitled by birth no less than by statute to the throne. It preferred not to contemplate the Queen's death, with its associated questions of legitimacy and allegiance, and the necessary endorsement of one potential successor over the other that followed from them.

There was, in effect, not much Tory advance in developing monarchical ideology in these twelve years (1702–14) when the focus was more on the prevention of further concessions to Protestant Dissenters rather than reducing those that had been conceded. This defensively minded protection of the Church was prioritised after 1714, when it became patent that George I would not promote Tories in the new Anglo-Hanoverian state. For a brief interval, and born out of desperation, a sizable body of opinion inside Oxford took the Jacobite option very seriously. Measuring the extent of a movement that by definition was treasonable and operated covertly is impossible, one driven not so much by affection for 'James III' personally, more by a sense that a Catholic king was at least as likely to uphold the Church of England as a Lutheran one. For many inside Oxford, its loose profession was compatible in a Vicar of Brayish sense with loyalty to the regime in place, functioning less as a genuine commitment than as a rhetoric of disgruntled opposition for clergymen failing to get the prebends and deaneries that they considered they deserved and educated laity deprived of other places and preferment. Inasmuch as there was a 'Jacobite' interval, between the beginning of the '15 and the inglorious collapse of the Atterbury Plot, it was short, though Whig politicians had some success for years afterwards in presenting any (Tory) discourses about monarchy as ones about Jacobitism. Such 'spin' eventually became stale and unconvincing, and scarcely overlaid the point that neither George I nor George II was much interested in the well-being of the University of Oxford. University leaders were careful to give the appearance of unambiguous loyalty, with addresses and commemorative verses produced as royal occasion demanded, and such public events as the 1733 visit of the Prince of Orange sparked a show genuine affection for him and his royal bride, the Princess Royal. For an interval, academic hopes centred on a better future once Prince Frederick of Wales came into his inheritance, though they were only realised in the decades after 1760 when the University offered to George III an unconditional regard that was reciprocated.

Whig ministers between 1689 and 1760 may have encouraged their political allies to play the Jacobite card against Oxford but, on a day-to-day basis and, putting the rhetoric aside, a stable working relationship between a given administration and the University had much to commend it for both sides. The regime was precarious, there were genuine security issues, and the failure of the Atterbury Plot appeared to confirm the pointlessness of overt backing for the Stuart cause. For the Whigs, techniques of watchfulness and manipulation varied according to what seemed to them the wider requirements of the polity. How far should intervention go? How best was it to be done? Was it to be management or revenge? These were the questions facing ministers and the ones that the University authorities were required to negotiate.

Significantly, even after the Atterbury Plot had confirmed Oxford's links with Jacobite subversion, the ministry opted for conciliatory gestures such as the endowment of the Regius Professorship in Modern History, rather than reviving their predecessors' plans for a royal Visitation. Sensing a cowed readiness to toe the line, the Northern Secretary, Lord Townshend urged on the King a right use of

668 ENLIGHTENED OXFORD

the 'present Disposition' of the clergy and two universities; these would be 'Points of Consequence to ye Peace, Ease & Security of Your M[ajesty]s Government', but 'further Encouragements' were needed to make 'those Great bodies firm friends'.[19]

Townshend, like most ministers after 1714, was a Cambridge product, and tacitly recognised that Cambridge was not the problem, which was why government patronage and favours tended to be bestowed in that direction. Oxford, semi-officially out of favour as it was for decades, was less part of a state Church apparatus that, in its higher reaches, had become a branch of Walpole's political machine—and was so with the complicit acquiescence of Edmund Gibson, himself originally a distinguished Oxford scholar. Conciliation did not involve favouring moderate Oxford Tories, despite the overt or tacit acceptance of the Revolution settlement pretty much across the whole University. Arguments among Tories only gave the advantage to their opponents. Resourceful academic operators such as Dr William King caused ripples outside Oxford, but he could unsettle as much as he could inspire within it. It was precisely because Oxford tended to be kept at arm's length by ministers that the Whig Church interest in the University was built up to only a limited degree, a situation that reflected both the resilience and appeal of Toryism for private patrons and clients alike, as well as indicating that Whig patrons on the whole did not make this objective a priority. Of course, there were numerous loyal Whigs in Oxford during the early Hanoverian years, but it is striking how they failed to produce any new twists in Whig apologetics and preferred instead to be the often pettifogging creators of a victim culture quick to run to ministers. They did so conspicuously in the jumpy 1740s with the resurrection of the Jacobite challenge to the regime and its apparently continuing appeal to some within the University despite the decisive result at Culloden. Back came the old bogey of a Visitation scare and the ramping up of rhetoric on both sides that only calmed down after the divisive Oxfordshire election of 1754 was over and the formation of a Pitt–Newcastle government brought the nation together to fight the Seven Years' War.

Over time, unsettled relations with the government were bound to have an impact on the intellectual life of the University and create an impression of 'under-performance', as political intrigue and management engrossed the attention of academic leaders who might, in more propitious times, have given it to the arts and sciences. W. R. Ward wrote of 'the sacrifices made to politics in these years' and his judgement that the University had little choice in the matter remains persuasive, that these were 'sacrifices which the University, as a school of the Church in a time when political and ecclesiastical disputes were not readily distinguished, could hardly avoid making'.[20] After 1760 more of the king's ministers were likely to be Oxford graduates and relations between the University and

---

[19] Lord Townshend to George I [draft], c.1723, HMC, *Weston Underwood MSS*, 430.
[20] Ward, *Georgian Oxford*, 129.

CONCLUSION 669

the government were placed on a very even keel. Even Pitt the Younger, though MP for Cambridge University as well as Premier, took pains to ensure that the elder establishment received a proportionate share of Crown patronage, not least in appointments to bishoprics. This new stability did nothing to diminish Oxonian interest in national politics.

Oxford was in an important sense an agency of the state and crucial to the cultural formation of its elites, so no government could be disinterested in relation to it. The marginalisation of Oxford c.1714-60 was a backhanded token of how much disquiet the University caused in ministerial circles and the extent to which its internal instability had the potential to affect the country at large. It reminds us that core and peripheries are not merely spatial concepts; they are intricately linked to power relationships. Through a property portfolio that extended across England and Wales, the colleges were in touch with thousands of tenants maintaining an umbilical connection between the University and the rest of the country. Within the city of Oxford itself, the academic and municipal authorities largely cooperated, by comparison with previous centuries, and the sharing of space was seldom contentious. Both, for instance, sponsored the urban renewal schemes that changed the face of the city centre in the reign of George III. Oxford was also the capital and centre of gravity for the county and for the wider region; most Oxfordshire grandees were connected to the University by propinquity, kinship, and interest. Two of them, Lords Lichfield and North, were successively its Chancellor, while the arrival in the first decade of the century of the most illustrious family of them all—the Marlboroughs at Blenheim—tilted the balance of University as well as county politics and was played out in successive generations. Oxonian preferences and predilections flowed readily to and from the University to schools across England. The governing bodies of New College and Winchester College or Christ Church and Westminster School were porous and interchangeable, but it was the steady number of Oxford graduates who took up teaching in grammar and comparable private schools (most in holy orders) that were arguably the main agencies of transmission. These were likely to encourage the next wave of male adolescents to pursue an Oxford education (perhaps through scholarships linking a college to a particular school or geographical area) and, more generally, through their broadly defined Tory views, upheld an Oxonian ethos that their pupils were more than likely to register.

If Wales had no university of its own, the absence of any campaign to provide one may be taken as evidence that in Jesus College, Oxford offered sufficient opportunities for the sons of the Principality's gentry and middling sort to obtain a lettered education and appropriate acculturation. Significantly, when, in 1822, St David's College was founded in Lampeter for the training of ordinands who might lack the funds to come to Oxford, the initiative came from Thomas Burgess, Bishop of St Davids since 1803 but, as a younger man, one of the leading lights

670 ENLIGHTENED OXFORD

of Oxford.[21] Institutional connections between Oxford and Trinity College Dublin had been intimate since the latter's foundation in 1592 but they loosened somewhat in the eighteenth century after the two ceased to share the same Chancellor—the 2nd Duke of Ormond—following his flight in 1715, and Trinity embraced Establishment Whiggism. Nevertheless, many Irish families from preference sent their sons to Oxford rather than Trinity or, at least, despatched them there after an initial time at the one Irish university. They shared, of course, a common Anglicanism and this confessional attachment was a barrier, though not an insuperable one, to academic exchange and interplay between Oxford and the Scottish universities. Comparisons between them too readily assume an Oxford inferiority that takes inadequate account of contrasting national educational and social divergences. Scottish universities may have been 'Enlightened', but to discount Oxford as the opposite is to insist on a tight definition of 'Enlightenment' that goes against the drift and direction of contemporary scholarship. That said, the relationship between Oxford (and Cambridge) and their Scottish counterparts could be uneasy. It was soured at the end of this period by a series of vitriolic exchanges in the press and pamphlets in which each variously impugned the teaching methods and scholarship of the other.[22]

The varied image its products gave of Oxford created an impression of the University that helped outsiders formulate their own view of it as an institution, and these 'readings' are indispensable in creating a rounded picture in contemporary constructions of 'Oxford'. Most literary perspectives played along with the well-established stereotypes of worldly students looking to outwit cranky, hard-drinking tutors remote from their charges, but at least there was an underlying good humour to it: this was what the ancient universities were supposed to be like and audiences expected it. The subversion was gentle, arguably more so than that to which the University subjected itself through the coruscating and frequently vitriolic rigolade of the *Terrae Filius* at the 'Act'. Eighteenth-century literary productions might conflate English undergraduate identities into a common 'Oxbridge' brand but the cultural and political differences between the two universities were not lost on their respective graduates. The rivalry was sharpened by changing perceptions of how much (or how little) official favour the sister institutions enjoyed and opportunities for displays of *schadenfreude* individually and collectively were seldom ignored. And, of course, at this date there was no scope for organised sporting competition within which to exhibit expressions of one-upmanship. Yet each year Oxford graduates were incorporated as members of Cambridge and vice versa and it was customary for the right sort of Cantabrigian

---

[21] See the essays in ed. Nigel Yates, *Bishop Burgess and his world. Culture, religion and society in Britain, Europe and North America in the eighteenth and nineteenth centuries* (Cardiff, 2007)).

[22] Brockliss, 'The European university in the age of revolution, 1789–1850', HUO VI, 77–133, at 126–8; A. Briggs, 'Oxford and its critics, 1800–35', HOU VI, 134–45, at 134–5.

CONCLUSION 671

academic talent to receive appropriate recognition in Oxford, as when Daniel and Theodore Waterland both became DDs at Oxford.[23]

Oxford and Cambridge had this at least in common: they were legally Anglican institutions from which Protestant Dissenters were excluded. These were perhaps the most continuously vehement critics of the University, less because they wished for their congregations to be admitted as students than because Oxford was the spokesman, bulwark, and arch-representative of that exclusive Anglicanism they wished to dissipate. This antipathy appeared patent to High Church Oxonians. As William Jones (of Nayland) put it: 'In the eyes of all reasonable men, the Church of England could want but little defence, in a literary way, against an adversary so enflamed with political hatred against it,...'[24] Jones had in mind the efforts of Priestley in the 1780s to target Oxford as part of his wider, formidably organised agitation to secure the repeal of the Test and Corporation Acts, but the resentment at confessional and educational privilege was present in successive generations. Thus Robert Molesworth (a TCD graduate), a friend of Dissenters, one for whom education was the 'foundation of the publick liberty', worked hard for three decades after the Revolution of 1688 to persuade his fellow Whigs to introduce statutory changes to bring the English universities to heel, lambasting 'the narrow spiritedness, and not enduring of contradiction, which are generally contracted by a monastick life', and blaming Oxford for self-interest, the survival of scholasticism, and the entrenchment of Toryism. This recurrent type of critique was never enough to persuade ministers to act, despite Dissenters usually receiving support from an Anglican minority within Oxford, concurring that some legal concessions for fellow Protestants should be negotiated.

There was never any prospect of Oxford admitting women to any kind of academic status, and yet women were everywhere in the city: as wives and daughters of heads of Houses, college servants, working in taverns, coffee-houses, or as prostitutes, or just visiting as tourists or the friends and relations of males in residence. Amid the hierarchies of inclusion and exclusion their omnipresence was taken for granted and appreciated. Thus Charles Burney's remark to Hester Thrale of '...how Charming a place wd Oxford be, if they had but the sense & Politeness of Italy, & gave Degrees to learned Ladies!' had a serious edge to it.[25] There were ample opportunities for dons and students to engage with women at work and in social life, and the presence of females in large numbers could be a real incentive to attend an event in the first instance. Oxford races were an obvious magnet in this regard and members of the University were quick to regale friends with appreciative news of the women seen or encountered there.[26] But one should

---

[23] See Chap. 10, p. 54.   [24] Jones, *Memoirs of Horne*, 144.
[25] To Mrs Thrale, 6 Nov. 1778, in ed. Ribeiro, *The letters of Charles Burney*, I. 260.
[26] See, for instance, Thomas Townson to Rev Richard Congreve, Sept. 1738, Congreve Papers, Staffs. RO, D1057/M/I/14/1–37.

672 ENLIGHTENED OXFORD

not disregard the extent to which women were vulnerable to male aggression or detraction, often sexually motivated, as with these comments of Robert Shippen to his patron regarding the notorious 1744 sermon in which John Wesley had castigated the spiritual laxness of the whole University:[27]

> The Vice Chr had his Sermon. He came hither in his coach & four with three fair sisters in it & Near 100 of his followers at St Mary's...went away the next with his 3 godly whores & a great Retinue.

Shippen's acetic note reflected the perspective of an ageing Oxford insider whose Jacobite principles were barely concealed, one who had seen temporisers and the less scrupulous make the running. Other graduates, too, ended up—to lesser or greater degrees—adopting the voice and vision of outsiders, ready to disassociate themselves from their own University because of its perceived deficiencies. Celebrated examples abound. Thus Nicholas Amhurst, the author of the *Terrae-Filius*, the embittered humorist, revenged himself by some telling japes and jibes that his friends in the Whig press readily circulated. He was happy to compare Oxford heads of houses with the directors of the South Sea Company. John Wesley, the great Oxford revivalist of the 1730s, in the next decade had prematurely ruptured the connection between Methodism and its birthplace (Whitefield, it may be noted, was more charitable).[28] Nevertheless, Wesley was honest enough to admit that he had once been an insider with warm early Oxford associations that were too indelible to deny. Arguably, the same was the case with Edward Gibbon, who, in his *Memoirs*, spoke from beyond the grave to offer a damning picture of his college half a century previously, yet there are indicators that before his death in 1794 Gibbon wanted to temper his critique (along lines that were duly discharged by his friend and executor, John, Lord Sheffield). Another contemporary critic, Vicesimus Knox, also toned down his earlier fault-finding. Both men, in the light of the French Revolution, had come to share with the bulk of the population a sense of what the country stood to lose from any hasty, externally brokered remodelling of its premier educational institutions.

The survival of the British state during the French Revolutionary and Napoleonic Wars ensured that its universities also endured, but not unaltered, for the pressures generated by war and the concomitant need to ensure social stability led to examination and curricular changes within Oxford that, it has been

---

[27] Shippen to Lord Noel Somerset, Oxon., 2 Sept. 1744, Badminton Muniments, FmJ 2/32 f. 11.

[28] See the touching account of his college days by Whitefield in *A short account of God's dealings with the Reverend Mr George Whitefield, AB, late of Pembroke-College, Oxford. From his infancy, to the time of his entering holy orders* (London, 1740).

argued, were motivated by the need for closer monitoring of the student body.[29] And, increasingly, thoughtful dons were sketching out further substantive plans for change such as those contained in Henry Kett's *Elements of General Knowledge* (London, 1802) that envisaged the University moving towards a modernised, multi-disciplined education. Those wars also deprived Oxford in large measure from that fruitful scholarly interaction with continental academics and students that, it has been argued here, are an overlooked aspect of the eighteenth-century University's life. The cosmopolitan Scottish universities were plugged into western European networks and had been so since their foundation. No less so, and more variously (because it had less of a problem with non-Protestants) was Oxford a site of international encounter and exchange. For confessional reasons, foreign Protestants were unlikely to be qualified for formal admittance to membership of the University, but this does not appear to have precluded them from taking part at a distance in exchanges with Oxford scholars, or even sitting in on lectures. Most eighteenth-century German universities were state initiatives intended to operate on pragmatic and irenic lines, and it may be that scholars from those lands initially presumed Oxford operated comparably (which, up to a point, it did). Johann David Michaelis, that admirer of the English universities and their teachers (and Lowth in particular), regarded them as national institutions loosely resembling the latest educational powerhouse of the Anglo-Hanoverian polity— Göttingen. In a sense he was right, for just as the latter existed to benefit the state, so (despite appearances, at times) did Oxford, however much religion and scholarship were historically its raison d'être.

Roman Catholic and Orthodox scholars were in practice equally drawn to Oxford out of curiosity, for its library resources, or just because of that amity which was foundational to the Republic of Letters and made it more than a networking exercise. Oxonians, in turn, whatever their misgivings about 'Popery' in general, could see beyond the trappings of Catholicism and had no hesitation in taking advantage of the hospitality on offer by the learned in Catholic countries, including monastic communities. The resemblances between the colleges and halls of Oxford (and their celibate inhabitants) and the religious houses of mainland Europe were too pronounced not to be mutually explored when opportunity offered at first hand.

English clerics and laity could meet their continental counterparts confident that their mutually comparable social standing would minimise confessional discrepancy and discordance. And they could likewise—accurately—presume that letters of invitation presented to potential foreign hosts would open doors and operate in their favour. Such practices made up an aspect of that system of patronage and clientage that remained fundamental to the functioning of English

---

[29] Ellis, *Generational Conflict and University Reform*. She argues that these trends pre-dated the French Revolution.

society and which Oxford graduates would have taken for granted, not least because the University rested on it both in its internal operations and via its connections externally to Church and state. Oxford was far from anomalous in that regard: patronage was the rule across British higher education. The characteristic feature of the Scottish universities was the tendency of professors to hire their own sons and relatives, sometimes converting a chair into a heritable or vendable estate. Thus in 1714, ten out of seventeen of Glasgow University's staff were related to each other; by the 1790s the entire faculty of St Mary's College at St Andrews was composed of the related families of Hills and Cooks.[30]

Academic merit and achievement represented valuable cultural capital, but it could not displace the social capital that individuals either brought with them to Oxford as undergraduates or acquired while in residence as a result of associational involvements. Established social networks of family and friends were fundamental to the character of the University, representing a kind of generational link that recognised the value of attendance at Oxford as formative in nurturing peer connections that might be expected to last the best part of an individual's life. And, in their turn, undergraduates might be expected to develop an affection for their own college (if not for the University as a whole) that would work to its material advantage through benefactions and bequests. Without this kind of generosity from its old members, the eighteenth-century University would have been unable to function, and the fiscal deficit would certainly have prohibited the architectural renewal of its buildings that so distinguished it materially. These actions should be seen as part of a complex rhetoric inherent in gift culture in which a loin of venison, assistance with repairs, a letter in a friend's own hand, or even an embrace could be deemed performative gifts. Loyalty to one's college helped a young man acquire a sense of the wider uses of loyalty, as to the monarch and the Established Church, and the legal requirement to take oaths at matriculation and graduation only served to sharpen an awareness that one was obligated to respect the constitutional status quo even as duty prompted the mature adult to participate in its functioning. The University prepared its students to serve in the Church, increasingly so in the state, and for them to have turned against it would have been a form of matricide visited upon their alma mater. For the vast majority, there was never any chance of that happening, owing in large measure to old associations and early friendships formed.

An Oxford education fostered individuals who in later life could be relied on to compete hard for prominence not just in the schools, but in urban corporations, in charitable foundations, and on hospital boards. It bonded most of its beneficiaries and, while there would be a minority glad to put their student years behind them, the majority could in later life use common collegial membership as a means of

---

[30] See Emerson, *Academic Patronage in the Scottish Enlightenment*.

building up friendships (particularly where it could be presumed graduates of particular colleges had firm political views). That was certainly the case within the professions but, whereas lawyers on circuit were inherently clubbable as they moved around together, clergy could be isolated in remote parts of the countryside. In those circumstances, continuing or new connections to their Oxford contemporaries could stave off the loneliness that many of them seem to have experienced. Thomas Hearne's huge national correspondence network, for one, must therefore have kept up morale among Tory malcontents who could also feed on the gossip he transmitted to some of them. Yet solitude or domesticity offered scope for intellectual creativity of one sort or another and many Oxford graduates took advantage of it, despite the problems that the scarcity of well-stocked libraries in their vicinity could pose. They were part of a provincial intellectual culture in Georgian England that was, to an unrecognised degree, distinctively Anglican and Tory in flavour and connected directly with the University.

Those who stayed in Oxford as fellows and had livings within a comfortable distance of the University were not faced with that difficulty and also had an opportunity to register the opinions of ordinary parishioners that could feed to advantage into academic exchanges. Thus William Crowe, BCL, Public Orator 1784–1829, used to walk the sixty miles between Oxford and his [New College] living at Alton Barnes in Wiltshire (which he held continuously for forty-two years) and developed a familiarity with most of the farmers and many of the artisans en route.[31] It is a vivid instance of how open the associational culture of the University was to the world outside, and parishes presided over by former or current members of the University provided means of mutual inter-connection whose importance can easily be overlooked.

As Public Orator, Crowe was, in a sense, the voice of Oxford, but, as this book has sought to show, there was a rich diversity of voices in eighteenth-century Oxford (though there could be a dominant note and its enemies could readily project one for it). The University was historically supposed to function as one of the great pillars of the constitution, but the Revolutionary settlement unsettled that dynamic and, under the first two Georges particularly, what Oxford graduates said and what they symbolised could be vexatious in the extreme to Whig ministers and other power brokers in Church and state. Party warfare here, compared to the rest of England, went on longer and more intensively and it was exacerbated by academic envy of those who were enjoying favour and Oxford's propinquity to the capital. Yet, in educating its male elite for rule and forming future parish clergy, the University all the while fed the needs of the polity

---

[31] Cox, *Recollections*, 230. There were precedents. Edward Lhuyd used to say that he preferred talking with shepherds and colliers in Wales to academic debate in Oxford and London. Yale, *Sociable knowledge*, 96.

676 ENLIGHTENED OXFORD

and facilitated rather than hindered the growing professionalisation of the state.[32] And its graduates in state and Church defended that existing order (at no juncture, an unreformed one) capably, variously, and vocally at the close of the century in the protracted struggle for survival with France.

Oxford was a university rooted in the past, and yet, in many regards, it looked to the future, and showed itself careful of adaptation in incremental ways. It may never have had that charisma associated with celebrity professors, scholarly journals, and massive libraries that made Hanoverian Göttingen the epicentre of the academic German Enlightenment, yet Lowth and Thomas Warton, Keill and Hornsby, Kennicott and Blayney, Blackstone and Sir William Jones merited and secured international notice while the Bodleian attracted scholars from across Europe. Likewise, the print culture of Oxford, though offering a smaller stage for cultural engagement than London's, presents a vantage point on Enlightenment currents to be set alongside those of Edinburgh or Dublin. Eighteenth-century Oxford was never an archetypal Enlightenment centre. It was too clerical, too conservative, and too centrifugal for that, but its forgotten diversity was itself a token of Enlightenment, its contrapuntal, liminal contribution to that international phenomenon[33] The motives and intentions of its members, who participated locally, nationally, and internationally in a vast complex of debates, varied as much as the ideas they put forward so that the University of Oxford resists final intellectual classification in this era. But the institution itself possessed an authoritative status grounded in its history with a standing and influence in, across, and beyond the polity that, in the 'long' eighteenth century, commanded notice.

[32] In that sense, at least, Lucy Sutherland's claim that the 'cards were heavily stacked against the University as an institution in the eighteenth century' was an exaggeration. *The University of Oxford in the Eighteenth Century*, 13.

[33] Cf. R. Butterwick, 'Peripheries of the Enlightenment: an Introduction', in eds. Butterwick et al., *Peripheries*, 1–16.

Bibliography

Unpublished primary sources

Aberdeen University Library
MS 3320/6/97
MS 3320/6/111

Badminton Muniments
FmH 4/4; FmH 4/5
FmJ 2/7; 2/11; 2/32; 2/34
FmJ 2/22/3; 2/22/29; 2/22/59
FmJ 2/32/11
FmK 1/2/12; 1/3/36.
FmL 4/2/1

Balliol College Archives and Manuscripts
Theophilus Leigh Letters
Jeremiah Milles Diary
Jenkyns papers, VI.A (2)

Bedfordshire and Luton Records and Archives
Wrest Park (Lucas) Papers:
L30/9/50/1–43; L30/14/292/1–4; L30/21/3/10 and 12
L230/14/315/17

Beinecke Rare Book and Manuscript Library, Yale University
Balguy Correspondence, OSB MSS 127
Boswell Collection, C 2842, C 2944, L 154.
Lee Papers: Box 3, Folder 2

Beinecke Rare Book and Manuscript Library, The James Marshall
and Marie-Louise Osborn Collection
Osborn MS Fc 80, Diary of Edward Pigott, *c.*1764–1785 (2 vols.)
OSB file 7942
OSB file 8319
OSB file 16852
Osborn Shelves, c 373
Osborn Shelves, c 509
Osborne Shelves, fc 24
Osborn Shelves, fc 142

678 BIBLIOGRAPHY

Birmingham City Archives & Heritage Service, Birmingham
Matthew Boulton Papers: MBP 280

Bodleian Library, Oxford
Add. MS a.269
MS Ballard
Bland Burges Papers: Dep. Bland Burges
MS Bodley
MS Bradley
Carte MSS
MS Dep. C.577
MS Don. e. 53
MSS D.D. Dashwood (Bucks.) A.4/2
MS Eng. C.
MS Eng. lett.
MS Eng. Misc.
MS Eng. Th.
G.A. Oxon.
Gough Oxf.
MS North
MS Radcliffe Trust
MS Rawlinson
MS Sherard
MS Smith
MS Top

Borthwick Institute for Archives, University of York
Will and codicils of Lady Elizabeth Hastings: LEF/4
MS Bp C. & P. VII/175/2

Brasenose College Archives, Oxford
R. W. Jeffery, 'An Oxford Don Two Hundred Years Ago', unpub. MS, MPP 56F4/10

The British Library, London
Berkeley Papers
Blenheim papers
Bowood Papers
Carewe Papers
Chichester Papers
Colbatch Correspondence
Douglas Autobiography (Egerton MS)
Dropmore Papers
Egmont Papers
Ellis Papers
Fox Papers
Hardwicke Papers
Holland House Papers
Journals of an Irish cleric, 1761, 1772

Kennett's Collections (Lansdowne MS)
Liverpool Papers
Lye Papers
Newcastle Papers
Nicholas Papers (Egerton MS)
Nicolson Letters
North [Sheffield Park] Papers
O'Conor Letters
Stepney Papers
Warburton Papers (Egerton MS)
Thomas Warton the younger Letters
Wilkes Papers
William Cole's Collections
Windham Papers

Cambridge University Library
MS Add. 6301
MS Add. 8134
MS Add. 9317

Chatsworth House
MS FCH/6/22

Christ Church, Oxford
Dean and Chapter MSS (D&C)
Dean's Register
MS lii.b.i, 'Annual visitation of Dr. M. Lee's anatomical theatre, accounts etc. 1796–1860'
Wake MS

Cornwall Record Office, Truro
Scrapbook of Catharine Davies: DG 25.

Cumbria Record Office (Kendal)
Fothergill Papers: WDX 94/acc. 165

Devon Heritage Centre, Exeter
152M/C1788/F28
1148M Add36/899

Durham University Library
Add MS 419
Add MS 1543

East Suffolk Record Office, Ipswich
Pretyman Papers: HA 119

East Sussex Record Office, Lewes
SHR830A, Travel diary of Mary Shiffner

680   BIBLIOGRAPHY

Exeter College, Oxford
Bray MSS

Glamorgan Record Office, Cardiff
D/DKT/1/7

Gloucestershire Archives, Gloucester
Ellis & Viner Papers: D2227/6/3
D1833 F1

Hampshire Record Office, Winchester
Carnarvon of Highclere Papers
Malmesbury Papers
Normanton Papers

Harry Ransom Center, University of Texas at Austin
Uncatalogued MS. Letters between the Revd. Mr Warburton and Dr Taylor (later Sir Robert
    Taylor) from the Year MDCCXXVIII

Hertfordshire Archives and Local Studies, Hertford
Ashridge Papers: AH1934–1936
Panshanger Papers: D/EP F57, F62, F138

Houghton Library, Harvard University
Edmund Burke papers
John Sneyd correspondence
MS Eng 731.9/8
MS Eng 1473
MS Harvard Theatre Collection
MS Hyde 8 (2); 61.

Hull History Centre
Hotham Papers

Huntington Library and Archives, San Marino, California
Black family Papers
Jerningham Papers

Jesus College, Oxford
JCOA PR. PARDO/1

John Rylands Library, University of Manchester
Bagshawe Muniments
Eng. MS 1122

Kent History and Library Centre, Maidstone
U23 C21/6; U23 C21/8

BIBLIOGRAPHY 681

Leicestershire, Leicester, and Rutland Record Office
Finch Papers: D57, DG7

Lambeth Palace Library
Moore Papers Vol. 6
Secker Papers Vols. 2, 7
MS 941/42
MS 2186

Lewis Walpole Library, Farmington, Yale University
Horace Walpole, MS Journals of George III

Lincolnshire Archives Office, Lincoln
Berkeley Diaries
Sibthorp Papers
BNLW 4/8/1/130

Magdalen College, Oxford
Drake MSS
MC: F10
MC: PR29/C1
MS 534, 571, 1028, 1034, 4990

Museum of the History of Science, Oxford
MS Ashmole
MSS Museum
MSS Radcliffe

National Archives of Scotland, Edinburgh
Leven & Melville Muniments
Montrose Muniments
Robertson of Lude Muniments
GD18/5542
PA 10: Records of the Committee of Visitaion of Scottish Universities 1690

National Library of Ireland, Dublin
Fitzpatrick MSS
MS 2456

National Library of Scotland, Edinburgh
Delvine Papers [Earl of Southesk]
Fettercairn Papers
Gleig Papers
Newhailes MS
Saltoun Papers

National Library of Wales, Aberystwyth
Badminton MSS
Bettisfield MSS

Brogyntyn MS
Glynllifon Estate Papers
Ottley Correspondence (Pitchford Hall)
Penrice & Margam MSS

Norfolk Archives, Norwich
MC55/23
MC150/50

Northamptonshire Record Office, Northampton
Dolben (Finedon) collection
Finedon Parish Registers
Isham MSS

Northumberland Archives, Woodhorn
SANT/BEQ/4/16/084/B

Nottingham University Library
Portland Papers

Oxford University Archives
Beddoes Papers
CC Papers
MS Conv. Reg. Bd 3; MS Conv. Reg. Bd 31; MS Conv. Bg 34; MS Conv. Bh 35; MS Conv. Reg. Bi
NEP/*subtus*/30, Reg. Bk
NW/1/1; NW/1/5; NW.1.6(1); NW/1/29
SP/D/9
UD/23/1
WPa/22/1/30; WPa/60/3; WPb/2/2
WPy/22/1p; WP/y/24/2; WPy/28/8/37; Wpy/82/8/37

Oxfordshire Archives
DIL XXIII/a-j
MS Oxf. Dioc. e.6, e.7, e. 8

Public Record Office of Northern Ireland, Belfast [PRONI]
D623/A/37/21
D2092/1/9
T2905/22/102

The Queen's College, Oxford, Library and Archives
MS 473
MS 476
MS 737/1–6

Scone Palace, Perth
Mansfield Papers, Box 85, bundle 7.

BIBLIOGRAPHY 683

Staffordshire Record Office, Stafford
Bagot MSS
Congreve Papers
Dartmouth MSS

Surrey History Centre, Woking
Brodrick MSS
Onslow Papers

The National Archives, Kew, Surrey [TNA (PRO)]
Home Office Papers
Pitt Papers
State Papers
War Office Papers

Warwickshire Record Office, Warwick
Newdigate Diary
Newdegate family of Arbury Papers

Plymouth and West Devon Record Office
Saltram Papers

Westminster Abbey Muniments
64856A

West Sussex Record Office, Chichester
John Hawkins Papers
Petworth House Archives

West Yorkshire Archive Service [WYAS] (Bradford)
Spencer-Stanhope Collection

West Yorkshire Archive Service [WYAS] (Calderdale)
RP 2404; RP 2477

West Yorkshire Archives Service [WYAS] (Leeds)
Vyner MSS
Abstract of Lady Elizabeth Hasting's will: LD 235, 236, 239

Worcester College Archives, Oxford
B1/1/20

Published primary sources

1. Newspapers and Periodicals
Anti-Jacobin
British Weekly Mercury

684 BIBLIOGRAPHY

The Englishman
European Magazine
The Flying Post
General Evening Post
Gentleman's Magazine
Historical Register
Jackson's Oxford Journal
London Chronicle
London Evening Post
London Gazette
The London Magazine
Mists's Weekly Journal
Monthly Review
Morning Post
New Monthly Magazine
Oxford University Calendar
The Oxford Magazine, or the Oxford Museum
Public Advertiser
St James's Chronicle
St James's Evening Post
Town and Country Magazine or Universal Repository
The Student, or the Oxford and Cambridge (added from no. 6) Monthly Miscellany
Universal Chronicle or Weekly Gazette
Whitehall Evening Post

2. Diaries, Journals, Memoirs, Correspondence, and Contemporary Publications

Historical Manuscripts Commission
HMC, *Ailesbury MSS* (London, 1898).
HMC, *Ancaster MSS* (London, 1907).
HMC, *Bath MSS* (5 vols., London, 1904–80).
HMC, *Buccleuch and Queensberry (Montagu House) MSS* (2 vols., London, 1897–1903).
HMC, *Carlisle MSS* (London, 1897).
HMC, *Downshire MSS* (6 vols., London, 1924–95).
HMC, *Egmont diary* (3 vols., London, 1920–23).
HMC, *Fortescue MSS* (3 vols., London, 1892–99).
HMC, *House of Lords MSS, 1693-1695* (New Series), I (London, 1900).
HMC, *Kenyon MSS* (London, 1894).
HMC, *M. L. S. Clements MSS* (London, 1913).
HMC, *Onslow MSS* (London, 1895).
HMC, *Ormonde MSS* (New Series), VIII (London, 1920).
HMC, *Portland MSS* (10 vols., London, 1891–1913).
HMC, *Stopford-Sackville MSS* (2 vols., London, 1904–10).
HMC, *Stuart papers* (7 vols., London, 1902–23).
HMC, *Townshend MSS* (London, 1887).
HMC, *Weston Underwood MSS* (London, 1885).
Abbot, Charles, *The diary and correspondence of Charles Abbot, Lord Colchester, Speaker of the House of Commons 1802-1817*, ed. Lord Colchester (3 vols., London, 1861).
Abingdon, Earl of, *Thoughts on the letter of Edmund Burke, Esq.* (6th edn., Oxford, 1777).
A Citizen, *A candid remonstrance* (London, 1764).

BIBLIOGRAPHY 685

Adam, Thomas, *Private thoughts on religion, ... extracted from the diary of the Rev. Thomas Adam*, ed. James Stillingfleet (2nd edn., York, 1795).

Adams, William, *The nature and obligation of virtue. A sermon preached in the parish church of St Chad, Salop, ...* (London, 1754).

Adams, William, *An essay on Mr Hume's essay on miracles* (London, 1752).

A gentleman of Oxford, *The new Oxford guide: or, companion through the University* (Oxford, 1759).

Agutter, William, *The difference between the death of the righteous and the wicked, illustrated in the instance of Dr Samuel Johnson and David Hume, Esq. A sermon* (London, 1800).

[Aiken, John], *England delineated; or, a geographical description of every county in England and Wales: ... for the use of young persons* (2nd edn., London, 1788).

[Allan, G.], *A sketch of the life ... of Richard Trevor, Lord Bishop of Durham* (Darlington, 1776).

Almon, John, *The parliamentary register* (17 vols., London, 1775–80).

[A.M.], *A letter from a member of the University of Oxford, to a gentleman in the country; containing a particular account of a watch-plot* (London, 1754).

[Amhurst, N.] *A letter from a student in Grub-street, to a Reverend high-priest in Oxford. Containing an account of a malicious design to blacken him and several of his friends ...* (London [1720]).

[Amhurst, N.] *Oculus Britanniae; an heroi-panegyrical poem on the University of Oxford* (London, 1724).

[Amhurst, N.] *Terrae-Filius, or, the secret history of the University of Oxford (1721; 1726)*, ed. William E. Rivers (Newark, DE, 2003).

Anonymous, *An answer to the address of Oxford University* (London, 1710).

Anonymous, *A Collection of papers, designed to explain and vindicate the present mode of subscription required by the University of Oxford* (Oxford, 1772).

Anonymous, *College-wit sharpen'd: or, the head of a house, with, a sting in the tail ...* (London, 1739).

Anonymous, *The cruelty, injustice, and impolicy of the present mode of information and punishment relative to prostitution established in the University* (Oxford, 1779).

Anonymous, *The election magazine, or the Oxfordshire register ...* (Oxford, 1753).

Anonymous, *Epistle to a College Friend, written in the country some years after the author had left the University* (London?, 1785?).

Anonymous, The gentleman and lady's pocket companion for Oxford (London, 1747).

Anonymous, *The muses' fountain clear, or the dutiful Oxonian's defence of his mother's loyalty to His present Majesty King George* (London, 1717).

Anonymous, *Parallel between the conduct of Mr Burke and that of Mr Fox, in their late Parliamentary contest, in a letter to the former* (London, 1791).

Anonymous, *A new pocket companion for Oxford* (Oxford, 1810).

Anonymous, *Reasons for a royal Visitation. Occasion'd by the present great defection of the clergy from the Government* (London, 1717).

Anonymous, *Reasons humbly offered to the House of Commons against the bill now depending for restraining the disposition of lands ... as far as relates to the University of Oxford* [London] (1736?).

Anonymous, *Some plain reasons humbly offer'd against the bill now depending in Parliament & c.* (London, 1736).

Anonymous, *The Spiritual Intruder unmask'd: in a letter from the orthodox in White-Chappel to Dr Shippen* (London, 1716).

686 BIBLIOGRAPHY

Anonymous, *State-amusements, serious and hypocritical, fully exemplified in the abdication of King James the Second, to which is added a true list of the members of both universities that amused his Majesty... with some select copies of amusing verses, taken out of those two famous volumes, intitul'd, Strenae Natalitiae...* (London, 1711).

Anonymous, *The Oxford Toast's Answer to the Terrae Filius's Speech, ...* (London, 1733).

Anonymous, *A treatise concerning oaths and perjury* (London, 1750).

Anonymous, *The tryal of Dr Henry Sacheverell* (London, 1710).

Anonymous, *University loyalty: or, the genuine explanation of the principles and practices of the English clergy, as established and directed by the decree of the University of Oxford, past in their convocation 21 July 1683. and republish'd at the trying of Dr. H. Sacheverell* ...(London, 1710).

Anonymous, *The University Miscellany, or more burning work for the Oxford Convocation* (London, 1713).

Anonymous, *Verses on the coronation of their late Majesties King George II and Queen Caroline, October 11, MDCCXXVII* (London, 1761).

Anderson, R., *Memoirs of the life and writings of John Potter* (Edinburgh, 1824).

Angeloni, B. [John Shebbeare], *Letters on the English nation* (2 vols., London, 1755).

Anson, E. and F., eds., *Mary Hamilton...from letters and diaries 1756 to 1816* (London, 1925).

Arblay, Madame d', *Diaries and letters*, ed. Charlotte Barrett (7 vols., London, 1854).

Arbuthnot, John, *Correspondence of John Arbuthnot*, ed. Angus Ross (Munich, 2006).

Archer, Edmund, *A Sermon preach'd at the parish church of St Martin October the 21st 1712. At the anniversary meeting of the Mayor, aldermen, and other trustees, for the charity schools of the City of Oxford* (Oxford, 1713).

Arnold, Thomas, *Sketches from the Carte Papers* (Dublin, 1888).

Ashburner, Edward, *A sermon at the ordination of the Rev. Sir Harry Trelawny, Baronet, and A.B.(late of Christ Church, Oxford)...preached at Southampton, April 22, 1777... Together with an introductory discourse, and questions...Sir Harry Trelawny's answers, and confession of faith...* (Southampton, 1777?).

A short memorial...of Princess Mary, Dutchess of Ormonde (s.n., 1735).

A Society of Gentlemen, *The loyal mourner for the best of princes: being a collection of poems sacred to the immortal memory of her late Majesty Queen Anne* (London, 1716).

Aspinall-Oglander, C., *Admiral's widow. being the life and letters of the Hon. Mrs. Edward Boscawen from 1761 to 1805* (London, 1942).

[Atterbury, Francis], *A letter to a convocation-man* (London, 1697).

Atterbury, Francis, *Sermons on several occasions...published from the originals by Thomas Moore* (2 vols., London, 1723).

Atterbury, Francis, *The epistolary correspondence of the Right Reverend Francis Atterbury, DD.*, ed. J. Nichols (2nd edn., 4 vols., London, 1789–90).

Auckland, Lord, *Journal and correspondence*, ed. Bishop of Bath & Wells (4 vols., London, 1861).

[Austen, George, ed., at al.], *The loiterer. A periodical work in two volumes* (Oxford, 1790).

Ayliffe, John, *The ancient and present state of the University of Oxford* (2 vols., London, 1714).

Ayliffe, John, *The case of Dr Ayliffe* (London, 1716).

[Bagot, L.], *A defence of subscription to the 39 Articles, as it is required in the University of Oxford;...'* (Oxford, 1772).

[Thomas Baker], *An Act at Oxford* (London, 1704).

BIBLIOGRAPHY   687

Bandinel, James, *Eight lectures preached before the University of Oxford in the year 1780...* (Oxford, 1780).

Barker, Charles Thomas, *On the use of history* (Oxford, 1836).

Barker, G. Russell and Alan H. Stenning, *Record of old Westminsters* (2 vols., London, 1928).

Barrow, William, *An essay on education; in which are particularly considered the merits and the defects of the discipline and instruction in our academies* (2 vols., London, 1804).

Beattie, James, *The correspondence of James Beattie*, ed. R. J. Robinson (4 vols., Bristol, 2004).

Belsham, Thomas, ed., *Memoirs of the late Reverend Theophilus Lindsey, MA....* (London, 1812).

Belsham, W., *Memoirs of the reign of George III... to the commencement of the year 1799* (6 vols., London, 1801).

Benson, R., *Memoirs of the life and writings of the Rev. Arthur Collier, MA* (London, 1837).

Bentham, E., *Reflexions upon the nature and usefulness of logick as it has been commonly taught in the schools* (1740, Oxford, 2nd ed., 1755).

Bentham, E., *An Introduction to moral philosophy* (Oxford, 1745).

[Bentham, E.], *A letter to a Young Gentleman of Oxford* (London, 1749).

Bentham, E., *A letter to a Fellow of a College* (Oxford, 1749).

Bentham, E., *An introduction to logick (scholastick and rational)* (Oxford, 1773).

[Bentham, E.], *The honor of the University of Oxford defended against the illiberal aspersions of E[dmun]d B[urk]e Esq.* (London, n.d.) [1776].

[Bentham, E.], *De tumultibus Americanis...* (Oxford, 1776).

Bentham, Jeremy, *Works*, ed. John Bowring (11 vols., London, 1843).

Bentley, Richard [with Hody, Humphrey], *Epistola ad Joannem Millium* (London, 1691).

Bentley, Richard, *A dissertation upon the epistles of Phalaris with an answer to the objections of the honourable Charles Boyle, Esq.* (London, 1699).

ed. Beresford, J., *The Diary of a Country Parson: The Reverend James Woodforde. 1758-1781* (5 vols., London, 1924–31).

Bickerstaffe, W., *Roman conversations; or, a short description of the antiquities of Rome*, ed. Weeden Butler the Elder (2nd edn., London, 1797).

Bielfeld, Baron, *Letters... containing original anecdotes of the Prussian court for the last twenty years, trans. from the original German by Mr Hooper* (4 vols., London, 1768–70).

Bingham, George, *Dissertations, essays, and sermons, to which are prefixed memoirs of his life, & c. by his son Peregrine Bingham, LL.B* (2 vols., London, 1804).

Biographia Britannica, eds. W. Oldys and A. Kippis (6 vols., London, 1747–66).

Birch, Thomas, *The history of the Royal Society of London* (4 vols., London, 1756–7).

Bisset, Robert, *The life of Edmund Burke...* (London, 1798).

Blackstone, W., *Considerations on copyholders* (London, 1758).

Blackstone, W., *Commentaries on the laws of England* (originally published Oxford, 1765–9), gen. ed. W. Prest. Book 1: *Of the rights of persons*, ed. David Lemmings (Oxford, 2016).

Blacow, Richard, *A letter to William King, LL.D. Principal of St Mary Hall in Oxford. Containing a particular account of the treasonable riot in Oxford in Feb. 1747* (London, 1755).

Bloxam, J.R., *A register of the presidents, fellows... of St Mary Magdalen College* (7 vols., Oxford, 1853–85).

Boase, G. C., *Bibliotheca Cornubiensis* (3 vols., London, 1874–82).

688   BIBLIOGRAPHY

Bocage, Mme du, *Letters concerning England, Holland and Italy, translated from the French* (2 vols., London, 1770).

Bodleian Library, *A catalogue of the several pictures, statues, and busto's, in the picture gallery, adjoining to the Bodleian Library* (Oxford, 1759).

Bond, Donald F., ed., *The Spectator*, (5 vols., Oxford, 1965–87).

Boswell, James, *London journal 1762–1763*, ed. Gordon Turnbull (Harmondsworth, 2010).

Boswell, James, *The life of Samuel Johnson*, ed. George Birkbeck Hill, rev. L. F. Powell (6 vols., Oxford, 1934–50).

Boulter, Hugh, *Foundation of submission to our governors considered: a sermon preached at St Olave's, Southwark, 26 November, 1715* (London, 1715).

Boulter, Hugh, *Letters written by His Excellency Hugh Boulter, D.D., Lord Primate of all Ireland & c.* (2 vols., Oxford, 1769).

Bourne, Robert, *A syllabus of a course of chemical lectures, read at the Museum, Oxford, in seventeen hundred ninety four* [Oxford, 1794].

Boyer, Abel, *The history of the reign of Queen Anne* (London, 1733).

Boyer, Abel, ed., *The political state of Great Britain* (60 vols., London, 1711–40).

Boyle, Charles, *Dr. Bentley's dissertations on the Epistles of Phalaris...examin'd* [with the assistance of F. Atterbury, G. Smalridge, R. Freind, J. Freind, and A. Alsop] (London, 1698).

Boyle, John, Earl of Orrery, *Remarks on the life and writings of Dr. Jonathan Swift...in a series of letters from John Earl of Orrery to his son* (London, 1752).

Bradley, James, *Miscellaneous works and correspondence*, ed. S. P. Rigaud (Oxford, 1832).

Bray, Gerald, ed., *Records of Convocation*, (20 vols., Woodbridge, 2005–6).

[Bray, Thomas], *Mr Boot's apology for the conduct of the late H—gh S—f* (Oxford, 1754).

Brewster, John, A *Memoir of the late Reverend Hugh Moises* (Newcastle, 1823).

Browne, Edward, *Journal of a visit to Paris in the year 1664*, ed. Geoffrey Keynes (London, 1923).

Brydges, Sir Egerton, *The autobiography, times, opinions, and contemporaries of Sir Egerton Brydges* (2 vols., London, 1834).

[Buckler, Benjamin], *Reflections on the impropriety and inexpediency of lay-subscription to the XXXIX Articles in the University of Oxford* (Oxford, 1772).

[Buckler, Benjamin], *The alliance of religion and learning considered: a sermon preached before the Right Honourable John Earl of Westmorland, Chancellor, and the University of Oxford, at St Mary's, on Act Sunday, viii July 1759* [Eph. 2:21] (Oxford, 1759).

Bugge, Thomas, *An observer of observatories. The journal of Thomas Bugge's tour of Germany, Holland and England on 1777*, eds. K. M. Pedersen and P. de Clercq (Aarhus, 2010).

Burgess, Thomas, *The divinity of Christ proved from his own declarations attested and interpreted by his living witnesses, the Jews. A sermon preached before the University of Oxford at St Peter's, February 28th 1790* (Oxford, 1790).

Burke, Edmund, *Reflections on the revolution in France. A critical edition*, ed. J. C. D. Clark (Stanford, CA, 2001).

Burke, Edmund, *Correspondence*, eds. T. W. Copeland et al. (10 vols., Cambridge, 1958–78).

Burke, Edmund, *Thoughts on the cause of the Present Discontents*, ed. F.G. Selby (London, 1951, originally pub. 1902).

Burnet, Gilbert, *History of his own time*, ed. M. Routh (6 vols., Oxford, 1833).

Burney, Charles, *A general history of music* (4 vols., London, 1776–89).

BIBLIOGRAPHY 689

Burney, Charles, *Memoirs of Dr Charles Burney 1726-1769*, eds. S. Klima, G. Bowers, and K. S. Grant (Lincoln, NA, 1988).

Burney, Charles, *The letters of Charles Burney*, Vol. 1, *1751-1784*, ed. A. Ribeiro, SJ (Oxford, 1991).

Burrows, M., ed., 'Table-talk and papers of Bishop Hough, 1703-1743', in *Collectanea. Second Series* [OHS, 16] (Oxford, 1890), 380-416.

Burton, John, *The genuineness of Ld. Clarendon's history of the rebellion printed at Oxford vindicated. Mr Oldmixon's slander confuted* (Oxford, 1744).

Burton, K. G., ed., *The memorandums of John Watts Esq., Mayor of Reading 1722-23 and 1728-29* (London, 1950).

Bury, Arthur, *The danger of delaying repentance; set forth in a sermon preached to the University, at St Mary's Church on Oxford, on New Year's Day, 1691/2* (London, 1692).

[Butler, John], *An address to the cocoa-tree, from a Whig* (London, 1762).

Butler, John, *A sermon preached at the ordination held at Ch. Ch. Nov. 21. 1779. By John Lord Bishop of Oxford* (Oxford, 1779).

Butler, Joseph, *Works*, ed. D. E. White (Rochester, NY, 2006).

Butler, Weeden, *Some account of the life and writings of the Reverend Dr George Stanhope* (London, 1797).

Byng, John, 5th Viscount Torrington, *The Torrington diaries (1781-94)*, ed. C. Bruyn Andrews (4 vols., New York, 1935-8).

Byrom, John, *Miscellaneous poems* (2 vols., Manchester, 1773).

Calendar of state papers domestic: William and Mary, 1695 addenda 1689-1695, ed. W. J. Hardy (London, 1908).

[Campbell, John], *The case of the Opposition impartially stated* (London, 1742).

Canning, George, *The Letter-Journal of George Canning, 1793-1795*, ed. Peter Jupp [Camden, 4th series, 41] (London, 1991).

Cardwell, Edward, *Synodalia. A collection of articles of religion, canons, etc. for the year 1547 to the year 1717* (2 vols., Oxford, 1842).

Carroll, William, *Spinoza reviv'd...* (Oxford, 1709).

Carte, Thomas, *An history of the life of James, Duke of Ormond* (originally published 1736, 6 vols., Oxford, 1851).

Cary, John, *Cary's traveller's companion, or, a delineation of the turnpike roads of England and Wales* (London, 1791).

Chandler, Richard, ed., *The history and proceedings of the House of Commons from the Restoration to the present time* (14 vols., London, 1742-4).

Chandler, Richard, *Travels in Asia Minor and Greece*, ed. R. Churton (2 vols., Oxford, 1825).

Chesterfield, 4th Earl of, *Letters from Lord Chesterfield to Alderman George Faulkner, etc.* (London, 1777).

Dobrée, B., ed., *The letters of Philip Dormer Stanhope, 4th Earl of Chesterfield* (6 vols., London, 1932).

Chishull, Edmund, The Orthodoxy of an English Clergy-Man,... (London, 1711).

Chishull, Edmund, *Antiquitates Asiaticae* (London, 1728).

Chishull, Edmund, *Travels in Turkey and back to England* (London, 1747).

Cholmondeley, R. H., ed.,The *Heber letters: 1783-1832* (London, 1950).

Clarke, *The Georgian era: memoirs of the most eminent persons, who have flourished in Great Britain, from the accession of George the First to the demise of George the Fourth* (4 vols., London, 1832-4).

690 BIBLIOGRAPHY

Clavering, Robert, *A sermon preach'd before the Lords Spiritual and Temporal... on Saturday, January XXX. 1730* [*The great duty and happiness of living quiet and peaceable*] (London, 1731).

Clayton, Mary, ed., *A portrait of influence. Life and letters of Arthur Onslow, the great Speaker* [Parliamentary History: Texts & Studies 14] (London, 2017).

[Cleland, John], *Memoirs of an Oxford scholar. containing, his amour with the beautiful Miss L—-, of Essex* (London, 1756).

Clubbe, [Rev] John, *A letter of free advice to a young clergyman* (2nd edn., London, 1765).

Coates, Charles, *The history and antiquities of Reading* (London, 1802).

Cobb, John, DD [Fellow of St John's], *Eight sermons preached before the University of Oxford in the year 1783* (Oxford, 1783).

Cobbett, William, *The Parliamentary History of England, from the Earliest Period to the Year 1803* (36 vols., London, 1806–20).

Cocks, Sir Richard, *The Parliamentary diary of Sir Richard Cocks 1688–1715,* ed. D. W. Hayton (Oxford, 1996).

Cokayne, G.E., and Vicary Gibbs, *The complete peerage...* (13 vols., London, 1913–59).

Colman, George, the Elder, *The Oxonian in town. A comedy* (London, 1767).

Colman, George, the Elder, *Prose on several occasions; accompanied with some pieces in verse* (3 vols., London, 1787).

Colman, George, the Younger, *Random records* (2 vols., London, 1830).

Compagnie de Pasteurs et Professeurs de l'Eglise et de l'Académie de Genève, *Several letters from the pastors of the Church of Geneva, to the Archbishop of Canterbury, the Bishop of London, and the University of Oxford; with their answers... Translated from the Latin and the French* (London, 1707).

Conybeare, John, DD, *A defence of reveal'd religion against the exceptions of a late writer, in his book, intituled,* Christianity as old as the Creation (2nd edn., Oxford, 1732).

Conybeare, John, DD, *True patriotism. A sermon preach'd before the Honorable House of Commons...* (London, 1749).

Conybeare, John, DD, *Sermons* (2 vols., London, 1757).

Cooper, Myles, *National humiliation and repentance recommended and the causes of the present rebellion in America assigned* (Oxford, 1777).

Cork & Orrery, Emily Charlotte, Countess of, ed., *The Orrery papers* (2 vols., London, 1903).

Cotton, H., *Poetical remains of French Laurence, DCL, MP, and Richard Laurence, DCL, Archbishop of Cashel* (Dublin, 1872).

Cowper, Spencer, *Letters of Spencer Cowper Dean of Durham 1746–47,* ed. Edward Hughes, [Surtees Society, vol. clxv] (Durham/London, 1956).

Cox, G. V., *Recollections of Oxford* (London, 1870).

Coxe, William, *Memoirs of the life and administration of Sir Robert Walpole* (3 vols., London, 1798).

Coxe, William, *Memoirs of John, Duke of Marlborough* (3 vols., London, 1818–19).

Coxe, William, *Memoirs of the administration of the Right Honourable Henry Pelham...* (2 vols., London, 1829).

Croft, George, *A plan of education, delineated and vindicated... and a short dissertation upon the stated provision and reasonable expectation of public teachers* (Wolverhampton, 1784).

Croly, George, *The life and times of His late Majesty, George the Fourth* (London, 1830).

Cugoano, Ottobah, *Thoughts and sentiments on the evil and wicked traffic of the slavery* (London, 1787).

BIBLIOGRAPHY 691

Cumberland, Richard, *Memoirs* (2 vols., London, 1807).

Czartoryski, Izabela, *Diary of a princess from travels around England and Scotland in 1791*, ed. A. Whelan (trans. A. Whelan and Z. Zygulski, Jr. (Warsaw and Torun, 2015).

Dacier, Bon-Joseph, *Notice historique sur la vie et les ouvrages de Villoison* (Paris, 1806.

Dallaway, James, ed., *Letters of the late Thomas Rundle* (2 vols., Gloucester, 1789).

Dalton, John, *Two sermons preached before the University of Oxford at St Mary's, on Sept 15th, and Oct. 20th, 1745, and now publish'd for the use of the younger students in the two universities* (Oxford, 1745).

D'Anvers, Alicia, *The Oxford Act* (London, 1693).

Dawes, Richard, *Miscellanea critica* (Cambridge, 1745).

Defoe, Daniel, *A tour through the whole island of Great Britain*, ed. P. Rogers (Harmondsworth, 1971).

Delany, Mary, *The autobiography and correspondence of Mary Granville, Mrs Delany*, ed. Lady Llanover (3 vols., London, 1861).

Devonshire, (4th) Duke of, *The Devonshire diary. William Cavendish fourth Duke of Devonshire, memoranda on state affairs 1759-1762*, eds. Peter D. Brown and Karl W. Schweizer [Camden, 4th Ser., 27] (London, 1982).

Dibdin, Thomas Frognall, *Reminiscences of a literary life* (London, 2 vols., 1836).

Dickens, L. and M. Stanton, eds., *An eighteenth-century correspondence: being letters ... to Sanderson Miller, Esq of Radway* (London, 1910).

Disney, J., *Memoirs of the life and writings of Arthur Ashley Sykes* (London, 1785).

Doddridge, Philip, *Letters to and from the Rev. Philip Doddridge, DD*, ed. T. Stedman (Shrewsbury, 1790).

Dodsley, Robert, *The correspondence of Robert Dodsley 1733-1764*, ed. James E. Tierney (Cambridge, 1988).

Dodwell, Henry (the younger), *Christianity not founded on Argument ... In a Letter to a young Gentleman at Oxford* (London, 1742).

Dodwell, William, *Sermon on the practical influence of the doctrine of the Holy Trinity* (Oxford, 1745).

Dodwell, William, *Two sermons on 1 Pet, ii. 15 on the nature, procedure, value and effects of a rational faith considered; In two sermons preached before the University of Oxford, 11 March and 24 June 1744* (Oxford, 1745).

[Dry, John], *Merton walks, or the Oxford beauties, a poem* (Oxford, 1717).

[Ducarel, Andrew], *A tour through Normandy, ...* (London, 1754).

Durell, David, *Critical remarks on the books of Job, Proverbs, Psalms, Ecclesiastes, and Canticles* (Oxford, 1772).

Edgeworth, R. L., *Memoirs of Richard Lovell Edgeworth, Esq.*, ed. Maria Edgeworth (3rd edn., London, 1844).

Eland, G., ed., *Shardeloes papers of the seventeenth and eighteenth centuries* (Oxford, 1947).

Elliot, Gilbert, *Life and letters of Sir Gilbert Elliot, first Earl of Minto from 1751 to 1806*, ed. Countess of Minto (3 vols., London, 1874).

Elliot, N., *The atheist* (Oxford, 1770).

Ellis, Sir Henry, *Original letters of eminent literary men of the sixteenth, seventeenth, and eighteenth centuries* (London, 1845).

England, *An Attempt to state the accounts of receipts and expenses relative to the Oxford Paving Act: with remarks* (Oxford, 1774).

Eusebius, Vicar of Lilliput [Joseph Robertson], *Observations on the late Act for augmenting the salaries of curates, in four letters to a friend* (London, 1797).

692 BIBLIOGRAPHY

Evans, M., ed., *Letters of Richard Radcliffe and John James of Queen's College, Oxford 1753–1783* [Oxford Historical Society, 9] (Oxford, 1888).

Farington, Joseph, *The Farington diary, by Joseph Farington, RA*, Vol. 1, *1793 to 1801*, ed. J. Greig (London, *c.*1922).

Felton, Henry, *The Christian faith asserted against deists etc.* (London, 1732).

Fielding, Henry, *'Jacobite's journal' and related writings*, ed. W. B. Coley (Middletown, CT, 1975).

Finch, William, *The objections of infidel historians and other writers against Christianity, considered in eight sermons* (Oxford, 1797).

Forbes, Sir William, *An account of the life and writings of James Beattie* (2 vols., London, 1996, first pub. in 3 vols., Edinburgh, 1807).

Force, Peter, ed., *American Archives...*, (4th ser., 6 vols., Washington, 1837–46).

J. Foster, *Alumni Oxonienses, the members of the University of Oxford, 1715–1886...* (4 vols., Oxford and London, 1887–8).

Fox, Charles James, *The speeches of the Rt. Hon. C. J. Fox in the House of Commons*, ed. J. Wright (6 vols., London, 1815).

Francis, Philip, *The Francis letters...*, eds. B. Francis and E. Keary (2 vols., London, 1910).

Free, DD, John, *A volume of sermons preached before the University of Oxford* (London, 1750).

Free, DD, John, *Poems, and miscellaneous pieces formerly written by John Free, DD* (London, 1751).

Freinshemius, John, *Threnodia, or an elegy on the unexpected and unlamented death of the [Master] of B[alliol], faithfully done into modern English...* (Oxford, 1753).

[Froud, John], *Daphnis: Or, a Pastoral Elegy upon the unfortunate and much-lamented Death of Mr Thomas Creech* (London, 1700).

Gardiner, Bernard, *A plain relation of some late passages at Oxford* (Oxford, 1717).

Generosus, *The nature of patronage, and the duty of patrons, consider'd in three letters published in the Weekly Miscellany...* (London, 1735).

George III, *The correspondence of King George the Third*, ed. Sir John Fortescue (6 vols., London, 1927–8).

Gibbon, Edward, *Autobiography of Edward Gibbon [originally edited by Lord Sheffield]*, ed. J. B. Bury (Oxford, 1907, repr. 1978).

Gibbon, Edward, *Memoirs of my life*, ed. Betty Radice (Harmondsworth, 1984).

Gibbon, Edward, *The history of the decline and fall of the Roman Empire*, ed. David Womersley (3 vols., Harmondsworth, 1994).

Gibson, Donald, ed., *A parson in the Vale of Whitehorse: George Woodward's letters from East Hendred 1753–1761* (Gloucester, 1982).

Gibson, Edmund, *The charge of Edmund Lord Bishop of Lincoln, at his primary visitation, in the year 1717* (London, 1717).

Gilbert, R., *Liber scholasticus* (London, 1829).

Goldsmith, Oliver, *Collected works*, ed. Arthur Friedman (5 vols., Oxford, 1966).

Gregory, P.S., *Records of the Family of Gregory* (London, 1886),

Griffith, Thomas, *The evils arising from misapply'd curiosity. A sermon preached before the University of Oxford, 9 March 1760* (Oxford, 1760).

Griffiths, John, *The Statutes of the University of Oxford codified in the year 1636* (Oxford, 1888).

Gutch, J., *Collectanea curiosa; or miscellaneous tracts, relating to the history of England and Ireland,...* (2 vols., Oxford, 1781).

BIBLIOGRAPHY   693

Gutch, J., *The history & antiquities of the University of Oxford and of the colleges and halls* (2 vols., Oxford, 1786–90).

Halley, Edmond, *Correspondence and papers*, ed. E. F. MacPike (Oxford, 1932)

Hampton, James, *A parallel between the Roman and British constitution ...* (London, 1747).

Hansard, T.C., ed., *The Parliamentary Debates from the Year 1803 to the Present Time* (22 vols., London, 1812).

Harcourt, E. W., ed., *The Harcourt papers* (14 vols., Oxford, 1880–1905).

Hargreaves-Mawdsley, W. N., ed., *Woodforde at Oxford, 1759–1776* (Oxford, OHS., 21, 1969).

Harley, Edward, 3rd Earl of Oxford and William Hay, 'William Hay's Journal', in *Tory and Whig. The parliamentary papers of Edward Harley, 3rd Earl of Oxford, and William Hay, MP for Seaford 1716–1753*, eds. S. Taylor and C. Jones (Woodbridge, 1998).

Harris, James, First Earl of Malmesbury, *Diaries and correspondence*, ed. 3rd Earl of Malmesbury (4 vols., London, 1844).

Harris, Richard L., ed., *A chorus of grammars: the correspondence of George Hickes and his collaborators on the "thesaurus linguarum septentrionalium"* (Toronto, 1992).

Hartshorne, A., ed., *Memoirs of a royal chaplain, 1729–1763. The correspondence of Edmund Pyle, DD ...* (London, 1915).

Harwood, Edward, *A view of the various editions of the Greek and Roman Classics, with remarks* (2nd edn., London, 1778).

Hastings Wheler, George, *Hastings Wheler family letters 1693–1704. Lady Betty Hastings and her brother* (2 vols., London, 1929).

Hawkins, William, *Discourses on scripture mysteries, ...* (Oxford, 1787).

Hawkins, William, *Poems on various subjects* (Oxford, 1781).

Haywood, Eliza, *The history of Miss Betsy Thoughtless* (1751), ed. Beth Fowkes Tobin (Oxford, 1997).

Hearne, Thomas, *Ductor historicus; or, a short system of universal history, and an introduction to the study of it* (London, 1714).

Hearne, Thomas, *Reliquiae Hearnianae*, ed. J. Buchanan-Brown (London, 1857; rev. 1966).

Hearne, Thomas, with R. Rapin, *Instructions for History* (London, 1680).

Hearne, Thomas, *Ductor historicus; or, A short system of Universal History, and an Introduction to the study of it* (London, 1714).

Hearne, Thomas, *Remarks and collections of Thomas Hearne*, eds. C. E. Doble, D. W. Rannie, and H. E. Salter [Oxford Historical Society] (11 vols., Oxford, 1885–1921).

Heitzenrater, R., ed., *Diary of an Oxford Methodist: Benjamin Ingham 1733–1734* (Durham, NC, 1985).

Herbert, Lord, ed., *Pembroke papers (1780–1794), letters and diaries of Henry, tenth Earl of Pembroke and his circle* (London, 1950).

Hervey, John, Lord, *Some materials towards memoirs of the reign of King George II*, ed. R. Sedgwick (3 vols., London, 1931).

Hickes, William, *Oxford jests, refined and enlarged* (London, 1671).

Hiscock, W. G., ed., *David Gregory, Isaac Newton and their circle: extracts from David Gregory's memoranda 1677–1708* (Oxford, 1937).

Hoadly, Benjamin, *The <u>Oxford</u> decree: being an entire confutation of Mr Hoadly's book, of the <u>original of government</u>; taken from the <u>London Gazette</u>* (London, reprinted 1710).

Holcroft, Thomas, *The adventures of Hugh Trevor*, ed. Seamus Deane (first published 1797, Oxford, 1973).

Holdsworth, Winch, *A defence of the doctrine of the resurrection of the same body* (London, 1727).

694 BIBLIOGRAPHY

Holloway, Benjamin, *The commemorative sacrifice. A sermon preached at the Visitation* [George Rye, DD, Archdeacon of Oxford] *holden at Woodstock, Friday, October 8th, 1736* (Oxford, 1737).

[Holloway, Benjamin], *Experimental philosophy asserted and defended against some attempts to undermine it* (London, 1740).

Holloway, Benjamin, *Remarks on Dr Sharp's pieces on the words Elohim and Berith* (Oxford, 1751).

Holloway, Benjamin, *The Primaevity and Pre-eminence of the sacred Hebrew... vindicated from the repeated attempts of the Reverend Dr Hunt to level it with the Arabic, and other Oriental dialects* (Oxford, 1754).

Holt, Edward, *The public and domestic life of his late Gracious Majesty George the Third* (2 vols., London, 1820).

Honeybone, D. and M., eds., *The correspondence of William Stukeley and Maurice Johnson 1714-1754* [Lincoln Record Society, vol. 104] (Woodbridge, 2014).

Honeybone, D. and M., eds., *The correspondence of the Spalding Gentlemen's Society 1710-1761* (Woodbridge, 2010).

Horn, Joyce, M., *John Le Neve. Fasti ecclesiae Anglicanae 1541-1857, vo. 8. Bristol, Gloucester, Oxford and Peterborough dioceses* (London, 1996).

Horne, George, *A fair, candid and impartial state of the case between Sir Isaac Newton and Mr Hutchinson* (Oxford, 1753).

Horne, George, *An apology for certain gentlemen...* (Oxford, 1756).

Horne, George, *A view of Mr Kennicott's method* (London, 1760).

Horne, George, *The Christian king* (Oxford, 1761).

[Horne, George], *A letter to the Right Hon. The Lord North, Chancellor of the University of Oxford, concerning subscription to the XXXIX Articles* (Oxford, 1773).

Horne, George, *A letter to Adam Smith LL.D. on the life, death, and philosophy of his friend David Hume... By one of the people called Christians* (2nd edn., Oxford, 1777).

Horne, George, *The character of true wisdom, and the means of attaining it* (Oxford, 1784).

Horne, George, *The duty of contending for the faith. A sermon preached at the Primary Visitation of the Most Reverend John, Lord Archbishop of Canterbury, in the Cathedral and Metropolitical Church, on Saturday, July 1st, 1786* (Oxford, 1786).

Horne, George, *Letters on infidelity* (2nd edn., Oxford, 1786).

[Horne, George], *A letter to the Rev. Dr Priestley. By an undergraduate* (2nd edn., Oxford, 1787).

Horne, George, *A Commentary on the Book of Psalms* (2 vols., Oxford, 1790 edn.).

Horne, George, *Sermons on various subjects and occasions* (London, 1793).

Horne, George, *Memoirs of the life, studies and writings of the Right Reverend George Horne, D.D., late Lord Bishop of Norwich*, ed. W. Jones (2nd edn., 6 vols., London, 1799).

[Horne, George], *Works*, ed. W. Jones (6 vols., London, 1809).

Horsley, Samuel, *The charge of Samuel... Bishop of Rochester to the clergy of his diocese... at his Primary Visitation in... 1796, etc.* (London, 1796).

Hulton, Samuel F., *The clerk of Oxford in fiction* (London, 1909).

Hunt, Thomas, *Observations on several passages in the book of Proverbs*, ed. Benjamin Kennicott (Oxford, 1775).

Hunt, Thomas, *De antiquitate, elegantia, utilitate, linguae arabicae, oratio* (Oxford, 1739).

[Hurdis, James], *A word or two in vindication of the University of Oxford, and of Magdalen College in particular, from the posthumous aspersions of Mr Gibbon* (London, 1800).

Hyde, Edward, *The miscellaneous works of... Edward Earl of Clarendon* (2nd edn., London, 1751).

BIBLIOGRAPHY   695

Hyde, Henry, Earl of Clarendon, *The correspondence of Henry Hyde, Earl of Clarendon, and his brother Laurence Hyde, Earl of Rochester, with the diary of Lord Clarendon from 1687 to 1690*...ed. S. W. Singer (2 vols., London, 1828).

Ilchester, Earl of, ed., *Letters to Henry Fox Lord Holland*... (London, 1915).

Innes, Cosmo, *Memoir of Andrew Dalzel, professor of Greek in the University of Edinburgh* (Edinburgh, 1861).

Isham, G., ed., *A Rugby headmaster's letters to a parent in the early eighteenth century* (Northampton, 1952).

Isham, G., ed., *The diary of Thomas Isham of Lamport, 1671-73*, trans. N. Marlow (London, 1971).

J. K., *Dr Sacheverel's progress from London, to his Rectory of Salatin [Selattyn] in Shropshire* (London, 1710).

Jackson, C., ed., *The diary of Abraham de la Pryme, the Yorkshire antiquary* (Surtees Society, 54), (Durham, 1870).

Johnson, Samuel, *Letters*, ed. R. W. Chapman (3 vols., Oxford, 1952).

Johnson, Samuel, *Yale edition of the works*, gen. eds. A. T. Hazen and J. H. Middendorf (23 vols., New Haven, CT, 1958).

Johnson, Samuel, *The Latin & Greek poems. Text, translation & commentary*, ed. Barry Baldwin (London, 1995).

Johnson, Samuel, *A dictionary of the English language: an anthology*, ed. D. Crystal (Harmondsworth, 2005).

Jones, C. and G. Holmes, eds., *The London diaries of William Nicolson, Bishop of Carlisle 1702-1718* (Oxford, 1985).

[Jones, William [of Nayland]] *An essay on the first principles of natural philosophy* (Oxford, 1762).

Jones, William [of Nayland], *A discourse on the English constitution; extracted from a late eminent writer, and applicable to the present times* (London, 1776).

Jones, William [of Nayland], *Observations in a journey to Paris, by way of Flanders, in the month of August 1776* (2 vols., London, 1777).

Jones, Revd. William, *Diary, 1777-1821*, ed. O. F. Christie (London, 1929).

Jones, Sir William, *Letters*, ed. Garfield Cannon (2 vols., Oxford, 1970).

Jones, Sir William, *Selected poetical and prose works*, ed. Michael J. Franklin (Cardiff, 1995).

Jucker, N.S., ed., *The Jenkinson Papers: 1760-1766* (London, 1949).

Junius, *Letters of Junius*, ed. John Cannon (Oxford, 1978).

Keill, John, *An introduction to the true astronomy: or, astronomical lectures, read in the Astronomical School of the University of Oxford* (London, 2nd edn., London, 1721).

Keill, John, *Introductio ad veram physicam* (1701, Eng. trans. 1736).

Kennicott, Benjamin, *The state of the printed Hebrew text of the Old Testament considered* (2 vols., Oxford, 1753).

[Kennicott, Benjamin], A friend to Mr Kennicott, *A letter to Dr King occasion'd by his late apology,*... (London, 1755).

Kennicott, Benjamin, *Christian fortitude* (Oxford, 1757).

Kennicott, Benjamin, *Vetus Testamentum Hebraicum*, etc. (2 vols., Oxford, 1776–80).

Kenyon, J. P., ed., *The Stuart constitution, 1603-1688: documents and commentary* (1st edn., Cambridge, 1966).

Kett, Henry, *A representation of the conduct and opinions of the primitive Christians*... (Oxford, 1791).

Kielmansegge, Count Frederick, *Diary of a journey to England in the years 1761-1762* (London, 1902).

696 BIBLIOGRAPHY

King, Dr. William [of Christ Church], *The Transactioneer, with Some of His Philosophical Fancies: In two dialogues* (London, 1700).

King, Dr. William [of Christ Church], *The original works in verse and prose* (3 vols., London, 1776).

King, William [of St Mary Hall], *A poetical abridgement both in Latin and English of the Rev. Mr. Tutor Bentham's letter to a young gentleman of Oxford...* (London, 1749).

King, William [of St Mary Hall], *Political and literary anecdotes of his own times* (London, 1818).

Knight, Charles, *Passages of a working life during half a century; with a prelude of early reminiscences* (3 vols., London, 1864).

Knox, Vicesimus, *Liberal education, or a practical treatise on the methods of acquiring useful and polite learning* (London, 1781).

Knox, Vicesimus, *Essays moral and literary* (2 vols., 9th edn., London, 1787).

Knox, Vicesimus, *Winter evenings: or lucubrations on life and letters* (3 vols., London, 1788).

Knox, Vicesimus, *A letter to the Right Hon. Lord North, Chancellor of the University of Oxford* [annexed to the 10th edn. of *Liberal Education*] (London, 1789).

Landon, James, *A sermon [on 1 Pet. II. 17] preached before the University of Oxford, etc.* (Oxford, 1800).

Langhorne, John, *Letters on the eloquence of the pulpit* (London, 1765).

Launay, Le Corgne de, *Les droits de l'épiscopat sur le second ordre, pour toutes les fonctions du ministère ecclésiastique* (n.p., 1760).

Le Clerc, Jean, *An historical vindication of the naked gospel, recommended to the University of Oxford* (London, 1690).

Le Clerc, Jean, *The life of Dr Burnet, late Bishop of Sarum...* (London, 1715).

Le Neve, John, *Fasti ecclesiae Anglicanae 1541-1857*, vol. 8. *Bristol, Gloucester, Oxford and Peterborough dioceses,* ed. Joyce M. Horn (London, 1996).

Leveson Gower, Lord Granville, *Private correspondence 1781 to 1821*, ed. Castalia, Countess Granville (2 vols., London, 1916).

Lichtenberg, G. C., *Lichtenberg's visits to England as described in his letters and diaries,* trans. Margaret L. Mare and W. H. Quarrell (Oxford, 1938).

Lindsey, Theophilus, *Letters (1723-1808),* ed. G. M. Ditchfield (2 vols., Woodbridge, 2007, 2012).

Linnell, C. L. S., ed., *The diaries of Thomas Wilson, DD, 1731-37 and 1750: son of Bishop Wilson of Sodor & Man* (London, 1964).

Locke, John, *The correspondence of John Locke,* ed. E. S. de Beer, (8 vols., Oxford, 1976–89).

Lockhart, George, *The Lockhart Papers: containing memoirs and commentaries upon the affairs of Scotland from 1702 to 1715,* ed. Anthony Aufrere (2 vols., London, 1817).

Loveday, John, of Caversham, *Diary of a tour in 1732 through parts of England, Wales, Ireland and Scotland* (Edinburgh, 1890).

[Lowth, Robert], A late professor in the University of Oxford, *A letter to the Right Reverend author of the divine legation...* [William Warburton] (London, 1766).

Lowth, Robert, *Lectures on the Sacred Poetry of the Hebrews,* trans. G. Gregory, (2 vols., London, 1787).

Lowth, Robert, sometime Bishop of London, *Sermons and other remains of Bishop Robert Lowth,* ed. Peter Hall (London, 1834).

Luttrell, Narcissus, *A brief historical relation of state affairs from September 1678 to April 1714* (6 vols., Oxford, 1857).

Macaulay, T.B., *The History of England from the Accession of James the Second,* ed. C.H. Firth (6 vols., London, 1913–15).

Mackenzie, Eneas, *A descriptive and historical account of the town and county of Newcastle Upon Tyne* (Gateshead, 1827).

Maclaurin, Colin, *An account of Sir Isaac Newton's philosophical discoveries* (2nd ed., London, 1750).

Maclaurin, Colin, *The collected letters*, ed. S. Mills (Nantwich, 1982).

Mallet, D., ed., *The works of Henry St. John, Lord Viscount Bolingbroke* (5 vols., London, 1754).

Maurice, Peter, *The true causes of the contempt of Christian ministers* (London, 1719).

M. G., *Mercurius Oxoniensis, or the Oxford intelligencer, for the year of our lord 1707* (London, 1707).

Miege, G., *The present state of Great Britain and Ireland...* (London, 1719).

Miller, Edmond, *An account of the University of Cambridge, and the colleges there* (London, 1717).

[Miller, James], *The humours of Oxford* (Dublin, 1730).

Misson, M., *Memoirs and observations in his travels over England*, trans. John Ozell (London, 1719).

Monkhouse, Thomas, ed., *State papers collected by Edward, Earl of Clarendon...from which his History of the Great Rebellion was composed* (3 vols., Oxford, 1767–86).

More, Hannah, *Memoirs*, ed. W. Roberts (4 vols., London, 1834).

Moritz, Carl, *Journeys of a German in England in 1782*, trans. R. Nettel (London, 1965).

Mossner, E.C., and Ian Simpson Ross, eds., *The Glasgow Edition of the Works and Correspondence of Adam Smith, Vol. 6. Correspondence* (2nd edn., Oxford, 1987).

Napleton, John, *Considerations on the public exercises for the first and second degrees in the University of Oxford* (Oxford?, 1773).

Nares, Robert, *Principles of government deduced from reason, supported by English experience, and opposed to French errors* (London, 1792).

Neve, Timothy, *Eight sermons preached before the University of Oxford in the year 1781...* (Oxford, 1781).

Neville, Sylas, *Diary 1767-1787*, ed. B. Cozens-Hardy (London, 1950).

Newcome, William, *An attempt towards an improved version, a metrical arrangement, and an explanation of the twelve minor prophets* (Dublin, 1785).

Newte, Thomas, *Prospects and observations; on a tour in England and Scotland: natural, oeconomical, and literary* (London, 1791).

[Newton, Benjamin], *The Names in the Cambridge Triposes, from 1754 to 1807,... prefaced by a short letter, on the comparative merits of the two universities, Oxford and Cambridge* (Bath, 1808).

Newton, Isaac, *Correspondence*, eds. H. W. Turnbull et al. (7 vols., London, 1959–77).

Newton, Richard, *A series of papers on subjects the most interesting to the nation in general and Oxford in particular...* (London, 1750).

Nichols, John, *Illustrations of the literary history of the eighteenth century* (8 vols., London, 1817–58).

Nichols, John, *Literary anecdotes of the eighteenth century* (9 vols., London, 1812–15).

No academic, *An appeal to the members of the University of Oxford relating to the Rev. Dr White's Bampton Lectures* (London, 1789).

Oldfield, Thomas H.B., *An entire and complete history, political and personal of the boroughs of Great Britain History of Boroughs* (2 vols., London, 1792).

Oxford and Cambridge miscellany poems, ed. E. Fenton (London, 1709).

Oxford Council Acts 1752-1801, ed. M. G. Hobson (Oxford, 1962).

Parker, William, *The scripture doctrine of predestination stated and explained* (Oxford, 1759).

698 BIBLIOGRAPHY

Parr, LLD, Samuel, *Works*, ed. John Johnstone, MD (8 vols., London, 1828).

Peake, R. B., *Memoirs of the Colman family,...* (London, 1841).

Pellew, Hon. G., *The life and correspondence of Lord Sidmouth* (3 vols., London, 1847).

Pennant, Thomas, *The literary life of the late Thomas Pennant, Esq., by himself* (London, 1793).

Pennington, M. (ed.), *A series of letters between Mrs. Elizabeth Carter and Miss Catherine Talbot, from the year 1741 to 1770* (2 vols., London, 1808).

Peshall, Sir John, *The history of the University of Oxford, to the death of William the Conqueror* (Oxford, 1772).

Philalethes, *A letter to the Rev. Vicecimus [sic] Knox on the subject of his animadversions on the University of Oxford* (Oxford, 1790).

Philanthropos, *A second plain and humble address to the clergy of all orders in Great-Britain* (York, 1731).

Philips, John, *Poems*, ed. M. G. Lloyd Thomas (Oxford, 1927).

Phillips, Sir Richard, ed., *Addisoniana* (2 vols., London, 1803).

Philo-Musus, *Oculus Britanniae: an heroi-panegyrical poem on the University of Oxford* (London, 1724).

Piozzi, Hester Lynch, *Anecdotes of the late Samuel Johnson during the last twenty years of his life* (London, 1786).

Pitcairn(e), Archibald, *The phanaticks*, ed. John MacQueen (originally 1691, new edn., Woodbridge, 2012).

Polwhele, R., *The follies of Oxford: or, cursory sketches on a university education* (London, 1785).

Polwhele, R., *Traditions and Recollections* (London, 1826).

Polwhele, R., *Biographical sketches in Cornwall* (3 vols., Truro, 1831).

Pope, Alexander, *Works*, eds. W. Elwin and W. J. Courthorpe (10 vols., London, 1871–89).

Potter, Francis, *A sermon preached before the University of Oxford...on the present rebellion* (London, 1745).

Potter, John, *A sermon [on 2 Chron. ix. 8] preach'd at the coronation of King George II, and Queen Caroline,... Oct. 11, 1727* (London, 1727).

Powys, Mrs Philip Lybbe, *Passages from the diaries of Mrs Philip Lybbe Powys of Hardwick House, Oxon. AD 1756 to 1808*, ed. E. J. Climenson (London, 1899).

Prévost, Abbé, *Adventures of a man of quality*, trans. Mysie E. I. Robertson (London, 1930).

Price, Richard, *Evidence for a future period of improvement in the state of mankind...in a discourse delivered on Wednesday the 25th April 1787, at the meeting-house in the old Jewry London...* (London, 1787).

Prideaux, Humphrey, *The true nature of imposture fully display'd in the life of Mahomet... offered to the consideration of the deists of the present age* (Oxford, 1697).

Prideaux, Humphrey, *The life of the Reverend Humphrey Prideaux, D.D., Dean of Norwich, with several tracts and letters...* (London, 1748).

Priestley, Joseph, *Theological and miscellaneous works of Joseph Priestley, LLD FRS & c.*, ed. J. T. Rutt (25 vols., New York, 1817–31).

Priestley, Joseph, *Letters to Dr Horne...young men, who are in course of education for the Christian ministry, at the universities of Oxford and Cambridge* (Birmingham, 1787).

Pütter, Johann Stephan, *Versuch einer academischen gelehrten-geschichte von der Georg-August Universität zu Göttingen* (4 vols., Göttingen, 1765–1838).

Quarrell, W. H. and W. J. C. eds., *Oxford in 1710. From the travels of Zacharias Conrad von Uffenbach* (Oxford, 1928).

BIBLIOGRAPHY   699

Randolph, Thomas, *An enquiry into the sufficiency of reason in matters of religion...* (Oxford, 1738).

Randolph, Thomas, *The Christian's faith. A rational assent. In answer to a pamphlet, entitled, Christianity not founded on argument* (London, 1744).

Randolph, Thomas, *Party zeal censur'd. In a sermon preached before the University of Oxford, at St Mary's, on Sunday, January 19. 1752* (Oxford, 1752).

Randolph, Thomas, *A vindication of the doctrine of the Trinity from the exceptions of a late pamphlet entitled an essay on spirit &c.* (Oxford, 1753).

Randolph, Thomas, *The use of reasoning in matters stated and explain'd* (Oxford, 1762).

Randolph, Thomas, *The prophecies and other texts, cited in the New Testament, compared with the Hebrew original, and with the septuagint version* (Oxford, 1782).

Randolph, John, *Heads of a course of lectures* (Oxford, 1784).

[Rawlinson, Richard], Philoxon, *A full and impartial account of the Oxford riots* (London, 1715).

Reynolds, Frederick, *The life and times of Frederick Reynolds* (2 vols., London, 1826).

Richardson, J., *A Grammar of the Arabick Language* (London, 1776).

Ritson, Joseph, *Observations on the three first volumes of the History of English Poetry. In a familiar letter to the author* (London, 1782).

Rowe Mores, Edward, *A dissertation upon English typographical founders and founderies* (London, 1778).

[Salmon, Thomas], *The Life and reign of her late Excellent Majesty Queen Anne* (London, 1738).

Salmon, Thomas, *The present state of the universities and of the five adjacent counties* (London, 1744).

Salmon, Mr, *The Foreigner's companion through the universities of Cambridge and Oxford, and the adjacent counties* (London, 1748).

Saul, Edward, *An historical and philosophical account of the barometer, or weather glass* (London, 1730).

Savage, Richard, *Poetical works*, ed. C. Tracy (Cambridge, 1962).

Scott, Mary, *The female advocate...*, int. G. Holladay (London, 1774, repr. Los Angeles, CA, 1984).

Secker, Thomas, *Eight charges...a Latin speech intended to have been made at the opening of the Convocation in 1761* (London, 1769).

Secker, Thomas, *The autobiography of Thomas Secker, Archbishop of Canterbury*, eds. J. S. Macauley and R. W. Greaves (Lawrence, KA, 1988).

Secker, Thomas, *Oratio quam coram Synodo Provinciae Cantuariensis anno 1761...in the records of Convocation*, ed. G. Woodbridge (Woodbridge, 2006), xii. 315–25.

Secretan, C. F., *Memoirs of the life and times of the pious Robert Nelson* (London, 1860).

Seed, Jeremiah, *The happiness of the good* (London, 1741).

Sharpe, R., ed., *Roderick O'Flaherty's letters to William Molyneaux, Edward Lhwyd, and Samuel Molyneaux, 1696–1709* (Dublin, 2013).

Shepherd, Richard, *Reflections on on the doctrine of materialism and the religious purposes to which modern philosophers have applied it* (2nd edn. London, 1779).

Shepherd, Richard, *Free examination of the Socinian exposition of the prefatory verses of St John's Gospel* (London, 1781).

Shepherd, Richard, DD, Sermons on Several Occasions (London, 1803).

'Shepilinda' [Elizabeth Sheppard], *Memoirs of the City and University of Oxford in 1738...* [Oxford Historical Society, ns. 47], ed. G. Neate (Woodbridge, 2018).

700 BIBLIOGRAPHY

[Shore, A. M.], *A letter to the Rev. Dr. Cooper on the origin of civil government* (London, 1777).

A sincere wellwisher to our universities, *Free thoughts upon university education; occasioned by the present debates at Cambridge* (London, 1749).

Sivry, L. Poinsinet de, *Le nécrologe des hommes célèbres de France* (Paris, 1767).

Smalridge, George, *Miscellanies* (London, 1715).

Smith, Adam, *An Inquiry into the Nature and Causes of the Wealth of Nations*, ed. W.B. Todd (2 vols., Oxford, 1976).

Smith, W. J. ed., *The Grenville papers* (4 vols., London, 1852–3).

[Some Oxford Electors], *A letter to the right honourable Henry Lord Viscount Cornbury, occasioned by a letter from his Lordship to the Vice-Chancellor of Oxford in Convocation* (London, 1751).

Spence, Joseph, *Polymetis, or an enquiry concerning the agreement between the works of the Roman poets, and the remains of the ancient artists* (London, 1747).

Spence, Joseph, *Observations, anecdotes, and characters of books and men collected from conversation*, ed. James M. Osborn (2 vols., Oxford, 1966).

Spencer, N., *The complete English traveller, or a new survey and description of England and Wales* (London, 1771).

Squire, S., *Remarks upon Mr Carte's specimen of his general history of England:...*(London, 1748).

[Statutophilus] *An impartial bystander's review of the controversy concerning the wardenship of Winchester College* (London, 1759).

Steele, Richard, *Tracts and pamphlets*, ed. R. Blanchard (Baltimore, MD, 1944).

Stirling, A. M. W., *The annals of a Yorkshire house from the papers of a macaroni and his kindred* (2 vols., London, 1911).

Stockdale, J., *Debates and Proceedings... during the Sixteenth Parliament of Great Britain* (19 vols., London, 1785–90).

Stockdale, Percival, *Poetical works* (2 vols., London, 1810).

Stukeley, William, *Family memoirs*, ed. W. C. Lukis (3 vols., Durham, 1882–7) [Surtees Society, vols. 73, 76, 80].

Swift, Jonathan, *A vindication of His Ex[cellenc]y the Lord C[arteret]...*(Dublin, 1730).

Swift, Jonathan, *Journal to Stella. Letters to Esther Johnson and Rebecca Dingley, 1710-1713*, ed. Abigail Williams (Cambridge, 2013).

Talbot, William, *A sermon [on Ps. cxviii. 24, 25] preach'd at the coronation of King George, ...October the 20th, 1714* (London, 1714).

Tatham, Edward, *Oxonia explicata et ornata. Proposals for the disengaging and beautifying the University and City of Oxford* (Oxford, 1773).

Tatham, Edward, *A sermon suitable to the times* (London, 1792).

[Tatham, Edward], *Oxonia purgata, consisting of a series of addresses on the subject of the new discipline in the University of Oxford* (London, 1812).

[Tatham, Edward], *A new address to the free and independent members of Convocation* (Oxford, 1810).

Teignmouth, Lord, *Memoirs of the life, writings, and correspondence of Sir William Jones* (2 vols., London, 1804).

Temple, W. J., *Diaries of William Johnston Temple 1780–1796*, ed. Lewis Bettany (Oxford, 1929).

Thornton, Catherine, and Frances Mclaughlin, *The Fothergills of Ravenstonedale. Their Lives and their Letters* (London, 1905).

Thicknesse, Philip, *Memoirs and anecdotes* (3 vols., London, 1788–91).

Thompson, Edward Maunde, ed., *Letters of Humphrey Prideaux sometime Dean of Norwich to John Ellis sometime Under-Secretary of State 1674–1722* (Camden Society, London, 1875).

[Thomson, William], *A tour in England and Scotland, in 1785/By an English gentleman* (London, 1788).

Thoresby, Ralph, *The Diary of Ralph Thoresby*, ed. J. Hunter (2 vols., London, 1830).

Tickell, Thomas, *The poetical works*, ed. C. Cooke (London, 1796).

[Toland, John], *Reasons for enabling Protestant Dissenters to bear public office* (London, 1717).

[Toland, John], Patricola, *The state-anatomy of Great Britain. Containing a particular account of its several interests and parties*...(9th edn., London, 1717).

'Tom Pun-Sibi', *Ars punica, sive flos linguarum: the art of punning; or, the flower of languages; in seventy-nine rules: for the farther improvement of conversation and help of memory* (Dublin, 1719; repr. London, 1720?).

Towle, Matthew, *The young gentleman and lady's private tutor* (Oxford, 1771).

Townson, Thomas, *Works*, ed. R. Churton (2 vols., London, 1810).

[Trapp, Joseph?], *The character and principles of the present set of Whigs* (London, 1711).

Trapp, J., *The nature, folly, sin, and danger of being righteous over-much* (London, 1739).

Trapp, J., *The true spirit of the Methodists, and their allies...fully laid open* (London, 1740).

Trelawny, H., *A letter from the Rev. Sir Harry Trelawny, Bt., to the Rev. Thomas Alcock, vicar of Runcorn and of St Budeaux* (London, 1780).

Tyson, M., and H. Guppy, eds., *The French journals of Mrs Thrale and Dr Johnson* (Manchester, 1932).

University of Oxford, *Judicium et decretum Universitatis Oxoniensis latum in Convocation habita Jul. 21, an 1683, contra quosdam perniciosos libros & propositiones impias* (Oxford, 1683).

University of Oxford, *Academiæ Oxoniensis comitia philologica in Theatro Sheldoniano decimo die Julii A. D. 1713. celebrata: in honorem serenissimæ Reginæ Annæ pacific* (Oxford, 1713).

University of Oxford, *Epithalamia Oxoniensia* (Oxford, 1734).

University of Oxford, *Gratulatio academiae Oxoniensis*...(Oxford, 1736).

Verney, Margaret Maria, Lady, ed., *Verney letters of the eighteenth century from the MSS at Claydon House* (2 vols., London, 1930).

Vernon, James, *Letters illustrative of the reign of William III from 1696 to 1708, addressed to the Duke of Shrewsbury*, ed. G. P. R. James (3 vols., London, 1841).

Voltaire, *Letters concerning the English nation*, ed. Nicholas Cronk (Oxford, 1994).

Voltaire, *Philosophical letters or, letters regarding the English nation* [trans. Prudence L. Steiner], ed. John Leigh (Indianopolis, IN, 2007).

Wakefield, G., *Memoirs of the life of Gilbert Wakefield, BA, formerly fellow of Jesus College, Cambridge. Written by himself* (2nd edn., 2 vols., London, 1804).

Walker, J., ed., *Letters written by eminent persons in the seventeenth and eighteenth centuries* ...(2 vols., London, 1813).

Walker, Ralph S., ed., *James Beattie's London Diary: 1773* (Aberdeen, 1946).

Walpole, Horace, *Memoirs of King George II*, ed. John Brooke (3 vols., New Haven, CT, 1985).

[Warburton, William], *Letters from a late eminent prelate to one of his friends* (2nd edn., London, 1809).

Ward, Robert E., John F. Wrynn, SJ, and Catherine Coogan Ward (eds.), *Letters of Charles O'Conor of Belanagare. A Catholic voice in eighteenth-century Ireland* (Washington, DC, 1988).

Warton, Thomas, *The life of Ralph Bathurst* (Oxford, 1761).

702 BIBLIOGRAPHY

[Warton, Thomas], *A companion to the Guide, and a guide to the Companion: being a complete supplement to all the accounts of Oxford hitherto published* (3rd edn.., London, 1762?).

[Warton, Thomas], *The Oxford sausage...* (new edn., Oxford, 1772).

[Warton, Thomas], *Poetical works*, ed. Richard Mant (5th edn., Oxford, 1802).

[Warton, Thomas], *Correspondence of Thomas Warton*, ed. D. Fairer (Athens, GA, 1995).

Watson, Richard, ed., *Anecdotes of the life of Richard Watson, Bishop of Llandaff* (2 vols., London, 1817).

Watts, I., *Logick, or The Right Use of Reason...* (London, 1724, numerous later edns.).

Watts, I., *The improvement of the mind: or a supplement to the art of logick* (London, 1741).

Wendeborn, G. F. A., *A view of England towards the close of the eighteenth century* (2 vols., London, 1791).

Wesley, John, *Journal* (8 vols., London, 1916, repr. 1938).

Wesley, John, *Letters*, ed. J. Telford (8 vols., London, 1931).

Wesley, John, *The bicentennial edition of the works of John Wesley*: Vols 1-4: *Sermons*, ed. Albert C. Outler (1984-7) (Oxford, 1975-83; Nashville, TN, 1984).

Wesley, John, *The bicentennial edition of the works of John Wesley: Journal and Diaries*, vol. II (1738-1743), ed. W. R. Ward and R. P. Heitzenrater, (Nashville, TN, 1990).

Wesley, John, *The bicentennial edition of the works of John Wesley: Journal and Diaries*, vol. III (1743-1754), eds. W. R. Ward and R. P. Heitzenrater, (Nashville, TN, 1991).

Wesley, John, *The bicentennial edition of the works of John Wesley*: Vol. X: *The Methodist Societies: the minutes of Conference*, ed. Henry D. Rack (Nashville, TN, 2011).

Whitaker, Edward W, *Sermons on education* (London, 1788).

White, A. W. A., ed., *The correspondence of Sir Roger Newdigate of Arbury Warwickshire* [Dugdale Society Publication, xxxvii] (Hertford, 1995).

White, Gilbert, *The natural history and antiquities of Selborne*, ed. T. Bell (2 vols., London, 1877).

White, Joseph, *A revisal of the English translation of the Old Testament recommended* (Oxford, 1779).

Whitefield, George, *A journal of a voyage from London to Savannah in Georgia...* (London, 1738).

Whitefield, George, *A short account of God's dealings with the Reverend Mr George Whitefield, AB, late of Pembroke-College, Oxford. From his infancy, to the time of his entering holy orders* (London, 1740).

Whitefield, George, *Letter to the Reverend Dr Durell, Vice Chancellor of the University of Oxford* (London, 1768).

Williams, George, ed., *The Orthodox Church of the East in the eighteenth century, being the correspondence between the Eastern Patriarchs and the Nonjuring Bishops* (London and Cambridge, 1868).

Willes, John, *The speech that was intended to have been spoken by the Terrae-Filius* (London, 1713).

Willis, Browne, *A Survey of the cathedrals... with an account of all the churches and chapels in each diocese, etc.* (3 vols., London, 1742).

Wilmot, John, *Memoirs of the life of the Right Honourable Sir John Eardley Wilmot, Knt.* (2nd ed., London, 1811).

Wilmot, John, *The life of the Rev. John Hough, DD* (London, 1812).

Wingfield Griffiths, E., ed., *Through England on a side saddle in the time of William and Mary, being the diary of Celia Fiennes* (London, 1888).

Wood, Anthony à, *Wood's antient and present state of the City of Oxford*, ed. Sir John Peshall (London, 1773).

Wood, Anthony à, *History of the University of Oxford* (3 vols., Oxford, 1792–6).

Wood, Anthony à, *Athenae Oxoniensis*, ed. P. Bliss (4 vols., London, 1813–20)

Wood, Anthony, *Wood's history of the City of Oxford. Vol. 1: the City and suburbs,* Andrew Clark (ed.), (Oxford, 1889).

Wood, Anthony, *The life and times of Anthony Wood, antiquary, of Oxford, 1632–1695, described by Himself,* ed. Andrew Clark, (5 vols., Oxford, 1891–5).

Wood, T., *A vindication of the proceedings of the University of Oxford* (Oxford, 1703).

Wood, T., *New institute of the imperial or civil law* (London, 1704).

Wood, T., *Some thoughts concerning the study of the laws of England in the two universities* (London, 1708).

Wood, T., *An Institute of the Laws of England* (London, 1720).

Woolley, David., ed., *The Correspondence of Jonathan Swift, D.D.,* (5 vols., Frankfurt am Main, 1999–2007).

Wyndham, Henry Penruddocke, ed., *The Diary of the late George Bubb Dodington, Baron of Melcombe Regis...* (London, 1828).

Wynne, John, *An abridgement of Mr Locke's Essay concerning Human Understanding* (first published 1696, 3rd edn., London, 1731).

Wyttenbach, Daniel Albert, *Bibliotheca critica* (3 vols., Amsterdam, 1779–1808).

Young, Arthur, *An historical dissertation on idolatrous corruptions in religion* (2 vols., London, 1734).

Selected secondary sources

The following list aims to be a broadly comprehensive coverage of sources cited in the text.

1. Books

Adams, P. G., *Travelers and travel liars 1660–1800* (New York, 1962, repr. 1980).

Adams, R. H., *Memorial inscriptions in St John's College, Oxford* (Oxford, 1996).

Addison, William Innes, *The Snell exhibitions: from the University of Glasgow to Balliol College, Oxford* (Glasgow, 1901).

Adlington, H., Tom Lockwood, and Gillian Wright, eds., *Chaplains in early modern England. Patronage, literature and religion* (Manchester, 2013).

Albert, W., *The turnpike road system in England 1663–1840* (Cambridge, 1972).

Alderson, W. A. and A. C. Henderson, *Chaucer and Augustan scholarship* [University of California Publications in English 35] (Los Angeles, CA, 1970).

Allan, David, *Making British culture. English readers and the Scottish Enlightenment, 1740–1830* (New York/Abingdon, 2008).

Anderson, C. A. and M. Schnaper, *School and society in England: social backgrounds of Oxford and Cambridge students* (Washington, DC, 1952).

Anderson, Robert D., Michael Lynch, and Nicholas Phillipson, *The University of Edinburgh: an illustrated history* (Edinburgh, 2003).

Andrews, Robert M., *Lay activism and the High Church movement of the late eighteenth century. The life and thought of William Stevens, 1732–1807* (Leiden, 2015).

Andrews, S., *Unitarian radicalism. Political rhetoric, 1770–1814* (Basingstoke, 2003).

Anson, Peter F., *The call of the cloister: religious communities and kindred bodies in the Anglican Communion* (London, 1955).

Arberry, A. J., *Asiatic Jones: the life and influence of Sir William Jones* (London, 1946).

704 BIBLIOGRAPHY

Ascoli, Georges, *La Grande-Bretagne devant l'opinion française au xvii siècle* (2 vols., Paris, 1930).

Aston, Nigel, 'The Dean of Canterbury and the sage of Ferney: George Horne looks at Voltaire', in W.M. Jacob and N. Yates, eds., *Crown and mitre. Religion and society in Northern Europe since the Reformation* (Woodbridge, 1993), 139–61.

Aston, Nigel, 'A "lay divine": Burke, Christianity, and the preservation of the British state, 1790–1797', in N. Aston, ed., *Religious change in Europe 1650–1914: essays for John McManners* (Oxford, 1997), 185–212.

Aston, Nigel, 'Bidlake, John (1755–1814), schoolmaster and Church of England clergyman', *ODNB*, online version (2004). https://www.oxforddnb.com/view/10.1093/ref:odnb/9780198614128.001.0001/odnb-9780198614128-e-2366

Aston, Nigel, 'Dolben, Sir William, third baronet (1727–1814), politician and slavery abolitionist', *ODNB*, online version (2004). https://www.oxforddnb.com/view/10.1093/ref:odnb/9780198614128.001.0001/odnb-9780198614128-e-7780

Aston, Nigel, 'From personality to party: the creation and transmission of Hutchinsonianism, c.1725–1750', *Studies in the History and Philosophy of Science*, 35 (2004), 625–44.

Aston, Nigel, 'Moore, John (bap. 1730, d. 1805)', *ODNB*, online version (2008). https://www.oxforddnb.com/view/10.1093/ref:odnb/9780198614128.001.0001/odnb-9780198614128-e-19131

Aston, Nigel, *Art and religion in eighteenth-century Europe* (London, 2009).

Aston, Nigel, 'James Beattie in London in 1773: Anglicization and Anglicanization', in Stana Nenadic, ed., *Scots in London in the eighteenth century* (Lewisburg, PA, 2010), 139–61.

Aston, Nigel, 'Petty and Fitzmaurice: Lord Shelburne and his brother', in N. Aston and C. Campbell Orr, eds., *An Enlightenment statesman in Whig Britain: Lord Shelburne in context* (Woodbridge, 2011), 29–50.

Aston, Nigel, 'The Established Church', in William Doyle, ed., *The Oxford handbook of the Ancien Régime* (Oxford, 2011), 285–301.

Aston, Nigel, 'Whitaker, Edward William (bap. 1752, d. 1818)', *ODNB*, online version (2012). https://www.oxforddnb.com/view/10.1093/ref:odnb/9780198614128.001.0001/odnb-9780198614128-e-29219

Aston, Nigel, 'The Great survivor: Charles Butler, Earl of Arran and the Oxford Chancellorship, 1715–1758, in R. Darwall-Smith and P. Horden, eds., 'Oxford: the forgotten century', *History of Universities* XXXV, 1 (2022), 348–69.

Aston, Nigel and Benjamin Bankhurst, eds., *Negotiating toleration. Dissent and the Hanoverian succession, 1714–1760* (Oxford, 2019).

Aston, Nigel, 'Dual loyalties? John, 7th Earl of Westmorland, Jacobitism, and the Leicester House connection', unpublished paper.

Austen-Leigh, R. A., *The story of a printing house; being a short account of the Strahans and Spottiswoodes* (2nd edn., London, 1912).

Ayling, Stanley, *George III* (London, 1972).

Aylmer, Ursula, ed., *Oxford food. An anthology* (Oxford, 1995).

Backscheider, Paula R., *Eighteenth-century women poets and their poetry. Inventing agency, inventing genre* (Baltimore, MD, 2005).

Baer, Marc, 'Burdett, Sir Francis, fifth baronet (1770–1844), politician', *ODNB*, online version (2009). https://www.oxforddnb.com/view/10.1093/ref:odnb/9780198614128.001.0001/odnb-9780198614128-e-3962

Bagster-Collins, Jeremy F., *George Colman the Younger, 1762–1836* (New York, 1946).

Baker, C. H. Collins and Muriel I. Baker, *The life and circumstances of James Brydges, first Duke of Chandos* (Oxford, 1949).

Baker, Frank, *A charge to keep. An introduction to the people called Methodists* (London, 1947).

Baker, J. H., *Monuments of endlesse labours. English canonists and their work, 1300–1900* (London, 1998)

Baker, J. N. L., *Jesus College Oxford 1571–1971* (Oxford, 1971).

Baker-Smith, Veronica P. M., *A life of Anne of Hanover, Princess Royal* (Leiden, 1995).

Baldi, M., *Philosophie et politique chez Andrew Michael Ramsay* (Paris, 2008).

Bamborough, J. B., 'William Lisle Bowles and the riparian muse', in W.W. Robson, ed., *Essays and poems presented to Lord David Cecil* (London, 1970), 93–108.

Barker, G. F. Russell, *Richard Busby DD (1606–1695)* London (1895).

Barnard, L. W., 'The Use of the Patristic tradition in the late seventeenth and early eighteenth centuries', in R. Bauckham and B. Drewery, eds., *Scripture, tradition and reason. A study in the criteria of Christian doctrine. Essays in honour of Richard P. C. Hanson* (Edinburgh, 1988), 174–203.

Barnard, T., 'Improving clergymen, 1660–1760', in A. Ford, J. McGuire, and K. Milne, eds., *As by law established. The Church of Ireland since the Reformation* (Dublin, 1995), 136–51.

Barnard, T., *A new anatomy of Ireland. The Irish Protestants, 1649–1770* (New Haven, CT, 2003).

Barnard, T., *Making the grand figure. Lives and possessions in Ireland, 1641–1770* (New Haven, CT, 2004).

Barnard, T., 'Protestantism, ethnicity and Irish identities, 1660–1760', in T. Claydon and I. McBride, eds., *Protestantism and national identity: Britain and Ireland, c.1650–1850* (Cambridge, 2004), 206–35.

Barnard, T., '"Almoners of Providence", the clergy, 1647 to c.1780', in T.C. Barnard and W. G. Neely, eds., *The clergy of the Church of Ireland 1000–2000* (Dublin, 2006), 78–105.

Barnard, Toby and Jane Fenlon, eds., *The Dukes of Ormonde, 1610–1745* (Woodbridge, 1999).

Barratt, J., *Cavalier capital: Oxford in the English Civil Wars* (Solihull, 2016).

Barrie-Currien, Viviane, *Clergé et pastorale en Angleterre au XVIIIe siècle. Le diocèse de Londres* (Paris, 1992).

Barton, J.L., 'Legal Studies', in *HUO* V, 593–605.

Bate, J. and J. Goodman, eds., *Worcester, portrait of an Oxford college* (London, 2014).

Batey, Mavis, *Oxford gardens. The University's influence on garden history* (Amersham, 1982).

Beales, D., 'Religion and culture', in T.C.W. Blanning, ed., *The eighteenth century. Europe 1688–1815* [Short Oxford History of Europe] (Oxford, 2000), 131–77.

Beales, D., *Prosperity and plunder. European Catholic monasteries in the age of revolution, 1650–1815* (Cambridge, 2003).

Beattie, Lester M., *John Arbuthnot: mathematician and satirist* (Cambridge, MA, 1935).

Beaurepaire, Pierre-Yves, *La plume et la toile. Pouvoirs et réseaux de correspondence dans l'Europe des lumières* (Arras, 2002).

Beaurepaire, Pierre-Yves, *Le mythe de l'Europe française au XVIII siècle. Diplomatie, culture et sociabilités au temps des Lumières* (Paris, 2007).

Beddard, R. A. P. J., 'Jane, William (bap. 1645, d. 1707)', *ODNB*, online version (2009). https://www.oxforddnb.com/view/10.1093/ref:odnb/9780198614128.001.0001/odnb-9780198614128-e-14650

706   BIBLIOGRAPHY

Beddard, R.A., 'James II and the Catholic Challenge', in *HUO* IV, 907–54.

Bell, James, *The imperial origins of the King's Church in early America, 1607–1783* (Basingstoke, 2004).

Bellenger, Dominic Aidan, *The French exiled clergy in the British Isles after 1789* (Bath, 1986).

Bellenger, Dominic Aidan, '"Fearless resting place": the exiled French clergy in Great Britain', in K. Carpenter and P. Mansel, eds., *The French emigrés in Europe and the struggle against revolution, 1789–1814* (Basingstoke, 1999), 214–29.

Ben-Amos, I. K., *The culture of giving: informal support and gift-exchange in early modern England* (Cambridge, 2008).

Bending, Stephen, '"The true rust of the barons' wars": gardens, ruins and the national landscape', in M. Myrone and L. Peltz, eds., *Producing the past. Aspects of antiquarian culture and practice 1700–1850* (Aldershot, 2001), 83–94.

Bennett, G. V., *White Kennett, 1660–1728, Bishop of Peterborough. A study in the political and ecclesiastical history of the early eighteenth century* (London, 1957).

Bennett, G. V., 'King William III and the episcopate', in G.V. Bennett and J. D. Walsh, eds., *Essays in modern English Church history in memory of Norman Sykes* (London, 1966), 104–32.

Bennett, G. V., 'Conflict in the Church', in Geoffrey Holmes, ed., *Britain after the Glorious Revolution, 1689–1714* (London, 1969), 155–75.

Bennett, G. V., 'Patristic tradition in Anglican thought, 1660–1900', in Gassmann, Günther, and Vajta Vilmos, eds., *Tradition in Luthertum und Anglikanismus: Oecumenica 1971–2* (Gütersloh, 1972), 63–87.

Bennett, G. V., *The Tory Crisis in Church and state 1688–1730. The career of Francis Atterbury, Bishop of Rochester* (Oxford, 1975).

Bennett, G.V., 'Loyalist Oxford and the Revolution', in *HUO* V, 9–30.

Bennett, G.V., 'Against the tide: Oxford under William III', in *HUO* V, 31-60.

Bennett, G.V.,'The Era of Party Zeal 1702-1714', in *HUO* V, 61–98,

Bennett, G.V., 'University, society and Church 1688-1714', in *HUO* V, 359–400.

Bennett, J. A., 'Equipping the Radcliffe Observatory: Thomas Hornsby and his instrument makers', in R.G.W. Anderson, J. A. Bennett, and W. F. Ryan, eds., *Making instruments count* (Aldershot, 1993), 232–41.

Best, G. F. A., *Temporal pillars. Queen Anne's bounty and the ecclesiastical commissioners of the Church of England* (Cambridge, 1964).

Bevilacqua, Alexander, *The republic of Arabic letters. Islam and the European Enlightenment* (Cambridge, MA, 2018).

Bignold, M., 'Letters and learning', in R. Ballaster, ed., *The history of British women's writings, 1690–1750,* vol. 4, *The history of British women's writing* [J. Batchelor and C. Kaplan, gen. eds.], (Basingstoke, 2010).

Bill, E. G. W., *Education at Christ Church Oxford 1660–1800* (Oxford, 1988).

Bishop, M., 'Wesley and his Kingswood schools', in John Lenton, ed., *Vital piety and learning: Methodism and education—papers given at the 2002 Conference of the Wesley Historical Society* (Oxford, 2005), 16–24.

Biskup, Thomas, 'The University of Göttingen and the personal union, 1737–1837', in Brendan Simms and Torsten Riotte, eds., *The Hanoverian dimension in British history, 1714–1837* (Cambridge, 2007), 128–60.

Black, E. C., *The association. British extraparliamentary political organisation 1769–1793* (Cambridge, MA, 1963).

Black, Jeremy, *The English press in the eighteenth century* (London, 1987).

BIBLIOGRAPHY 707

Black, Jeremy, *Pitt the Elder* (Cambridge, 1992).

Black, Jeremy, *British diplomats and diplomacy 1688–1800* (Exeter, 2001).

Black, Jeremy, *The English press 1621–1861* (Stroud, 2001).

Black, Jeremy, *France and the grand tour* (Basingstoke, 2003).

Black, Jeremy, *George III. America's last king* (New Haven, CT, 2006).

Black, Jeremy, *Charting the past. The historical worlds of eighteenth-century England* (Bloomington, IN, 2019).

Black, Jeremy, *A brief history of the Mediterranean* (London, 2020).

Blanning, Tim, *The culture of power and the power of culture. Old regime Europe 1660–1789* (Oxford, 2002).

Blanning, Tim, *The romantic revolution* (London, 2010).

Bolton, F. R., *The Caroline tradition of the Church of Ireland* (London, 1958).

Bonwick, C., 'English Dissenters and the American Revolution', in H.C. Allen and R. Thompson, *Contrast and connection: bicentennial essays in Anglo-American history* (eds.) (Athens, OH, 1976), 88–112.

Bonwick, C., *English radicals and the American Revolution* (Chapel Hill, NC, 1977)

Bool, M., 'The buildings of Oriel', in Jeremy Catto, ed., *Oriel College* (Oxford, 2013), 549–96.

Bots, H. and F. Waquet, eds., *Commercium litterarium: Forms of communication in the Republic of Letters* (Amsterdam, 1994).

Bourguignon, Henry J., *Lord Stowell: judge of the High Court of Admiralty, 1798–1828* (Cambridge, 1997).

Boutin, P., *Jean-Théophile Desaguliers. Un Huguenot, philosophe et juriste, en politique* (Geneva, 1999).

Bradley, Henry, 'Blayney, Benjamin (1727/8–1801), Hebraist and Church of England clergyman', rev. P. Carter, *ODNB*, online version (2013). https://www.oxforddnb.com/view/10.1093/ref:odnb/9780198614128.001.0001/odnb-9780198614128-e-2628

Bradley, James E., *Religion, revolution, and English radicalism. Nonconformity in eighteenth-century politics and society* (Cambridge, 1990).

Bradner, Leicester, *Musae Anglicanae: A history of Anglo-Latin poetry, 1500–1925* (New York, 1940).

Braithwaite, H., *Romanticism, publishing and Dissent. Joseph Johnson and the cause of liberty* (Basingstoke, 2003).

Brant, Clare, *Eighteenth-century letters and British culture* (Basingstoke, 2006).

Brant, Clare, *Balloon madness. flights of imagination in Britain, 1783–1786* (Woodbridge, 2017).

Brauer, George C., Jr., *The education of a gentleman. Theories of gentlemanly education in England, 1660–1775* (New York, 1959).

Brewer, J., *The Pleasures of the imagination. English culture in the eighteenth century* (London, 1997).

Briggs, Asa, 'Oxford and its critics, 1800-1835', in *HUO* VI, 134–45.

Brink, C. O., *English Classical scholarship. Historical reflections on Bentley, Porson and Housman* (Cambridge, 1985).

Brockliss, L. W. B., 'The European University in the age of revolution, 1789-1850', in *HUO* VI, 77–133.

Brockliss, L. W. B., *Enlightenment and the Republic of Letters in eighteenth-century France* (Oxford, 2002).

Brockliss, L. W. B., 'Science, the universities, and other public spaces: teaching science in Europe and the Americas', in Roy Porter, ed., *Eighteenth-century science* (*Cambridge History of Science*, Vol. 4) (Cambridge, 2003), 44–86.

BIBLIOGRAPHY

Brockliss, L.W.B., ed., *Magdalen College, Oxford. A history* (Oxford, 2008).

Brockliss, Lawrence, *The University of Oxford. A History* (Oxford, 2016).

Brockliss, L. W. B., G. Harriss, and A. Macintyre, *Magdalen College and the Crown: Essays for the tercentenary of the restoration of the college 1688* (Oxford, 1988).

Brooke, John, *The House of Commons 1754–1790. Introductory survey* (Oxford, 1968).

Brooke, John Hedley, 'The God of Isaac Newton', in John Fauvel, Raymond Flood, Michael Shortland, and Robin Wilson, eds., *Let Newton be!* (Oxford, 1988), 169–83.

Brooke, John Hedley, *Science and religion. Some historical perspectives* (Cambridge, 1991).

Brothers, A. J., 'Burgess and the Classics: a letter of April 1792', in Nigel Yates, ed.,, *Bishop Burgess and his world*, 41–50.

Brown, Michael, 'Was there an Irish Enlightenment? The case of the Anglicans', in Richard Butterwick, Simon Davies, and Gabriel Sánchez Espinosa, eds., *Peripheries of the Enlightenment* [SVEC 2008: 01] (Oxford, 2008), 49–64.

Brown, Michael, *The Irish Enlightenment* (Cambridge, MA, 2016).

Brown, Peter, *The Chathamites. A study in the relationship between personalities and ideas in the second half of the eighteenth century* (London, 1967).

Brown, S., 'The critical reception of Malebranche, from his own time to the end of the eighteenth century', in S. Nadler, ed., *The Cambridge companion to Malebranche* (Cambridge, 2000), 262–87.

Browning, R., *Political and constitutional ideas of the Court Whigs* (Baton Rouge, LA, 1982).

Bullard, P. and A. Tadié, eds., *Ancients and moderns in Europe: comparative perspectives* [Oxford University studies in the Enlightenment] (Oxford, 2016).

Bullock, F. W., *A history of training for the ministry of the Church of England in England and Wales from 598 to 1799* (St Leonards-on-Sea, 1969).

Bulman, W. J., *Anglican Enlightenment. Orientalism, religion and politics in England and its empire, 1648–1715* (Cambridge, 2015).

Bulman, W. J., 'Introduction: Enlightenment for the culture wars', in W.J. Bulman and R. G. Ingram, eds., *God in the Enlightenment* (New York, 2016), 1–41.

Bumpus, J. S., *History of English cathedral music, 1548–1889* (London, 1908).

Burns, Arthur, 'English "church reform" revisited, 1780–1840', in A. Burns and J. Innes, eds., *Rethinking the age of reform: Britain 1780–1850* (Cambridge, 2007), 136–62.

Burns, Robert, 'William Adams', in J.W. Yolton, J.V. Price, and J. Stephens, eds., *Dictionary of eighteenth-century British Philosophers*, I. 4–6.

Burns, R.M., *The Great Debate on Miracles* (Lewisburg, PA, 1981).

Burns, William E., 'Kettlewell, John (1653–1695), Nonjuring Church of England clergyman and theological writer', *ODNB*, online version (2016). https://www.oxforddnb.com/view/10.1093/ref:odnb/9780198614128.001.0001/odnb-9780198614128-e-15491

Burrows, D. and R. Dunhill, *Music and theatre in Handel's world: the family papers of James Harris 1732–1780* (Oxford, 2002).

Burrows, Montagu, *Worthies of All Souls: four centuries of English history, illustrated from the College archives* (London, 1874).

Burson, J. D., *The rise and fall of theological Enlightenment. Jean-Martin de Prades and ideological polarization in eighteenth-century France* (Notre Dame, IN, 2010).

Butler, C., J. Curthoys, and B. Young, eds., *Christ Church, Oxford, a portrait of the house* (London, 2006).

Butterfield, Herbert, *George III, Lord North and the people 1779–1780* (London, 1949).

Butterwick, R., *Poland's last king and English culture. Stanislaw August Poniatowski 1732–1798* (Oxford, 1998).

Buxton, John, and Penry Williams, eds., *New College, Oxford 1379–1979* (Oxford 1979).

Buxton, L. H. Dudley and Strickland Gibson, *Oxford University Ceremonies* (Oxford, 1935).

Cadilhon, F., J. Mondot, and J. Verger, eds., *Universités et institutions universitaires européennes au XVIIIe siècle: Entre modernisation et tradition* (Talence, 1999).

Calhoon, Robert M., *The loyalists in Revolutionary America, 1760–1781* (New York, 1973).

Cameron, H. C., *Sir Joseph Banks. The autocrat of the philosophers* (London, 1952).

Campbell, G., *Bible. The story of the King James Version 1611–2011* (Oxford, 2010).

Campbell, J. L. and D. Thomson, eds., *Edward Lhuyd in the Scottish Highlands 1699–1700* (Oxford, 1963).

Campbell, M. B., *Wonder & science. Imagining worlds in early modern Europe* (Ithaca, NY, 1999).

Campbell Orr, Clarissa, 'The Sappho of Gloucestershire: Sarah Chapone and Christian Feminism', in Deborah Heller, ed., *Bluestockings now! The evolution of a social role* (London, 2016), 91–110.

Cannon, G., *The life and mind of Oriental Jones: Sir William Jones, the Father of Modern Linguistics* (Cambridge, 1990).

Cannon, John, *Lord North. The noble lord in the blue ribbon* (London, 1970).

Cannon, John, *Aristocratic century. The peerage of eighteenth-century England* (Cambridge, 1984).

Cannon, John, 'Jenkinson, Charles, first Earl of Liverpool (1729–1808), politician', *ODNB*, online version, (2013). https://www.oxforddnb.com/view/10.1093/ref:odnb/9780198614128.001.0001/odnb-9780198614128-e-14737

Carlyle, E.I., rev. Richard Sharp, 'Wilcocks, Joseph (1673-1756)', *ODNB*, online edn., 2011.

Carpenter, A. T., *John Theophilus Desaguliers. A natural philosopher, engineer and Freemason in Newtonian England* (London, 2011).

Carpenter, Edward, *Thomas Sherlock 1678–1761* (London, 1936).

Carpenter, Edward, *Thomas Tenison Archbishop of Canterbury. His life and times* (London, 1948).

Carpenter, Edward, *Protestant bishop, being the life of Henry Compton, 1632–1713 Bishop of London* (London, 1956).

Carson, P., *The East India Company and religion, 1698–1858* (Woodbridge, 2012).

Carswell, John, *The old cause. Three biographical studies in Whiggism* (London, 1954).

Carter, Harry, *A history of Oxford University Press, Vol. 1: To the year 1780* (Oxford, 1975).

Carter, Jennifer, 'British Universities and revolution, 1688–1718', in Paul Dukes and John Dunkley, eds., *Culture and Revolution* (London, 1990), 8–21.

Caudle, James Joseph, 'Preaching in Parliament: patronage, publicity and politics in Britain, 1701–60', in L.A. Ferrell and P. E. McCullough, eds., *The English sermon revised: Religion, literature and history, 1600–1750* (Manchester, 2000), 235–65.

Chalus, Elaine, '"That epidemical madness": Women and electoral politics in the late eighteenth century', in E. Chalus and H. Barker, eds., *Gender in eighteenth-century England: roles, representations, and responsibilities* (London, 1997), 151–78.

Chalus, Elaine, *Elite women in English political life, c.1754–1790* (Oxford, 2005).

Chalus, Elaine, 'The rag plot: the politics of influence in Oxford, 1754', in R. Sweet and P. Lane, eds., *Women and urban life in eighteenth-century England* (London, 2017) 43–64.

Chamberlain, J. S., 'Parish preaching in the long eighteenth century', in K.A. Francis and William Gibson, eds., *The Oxford handbook of the British sermon 1689–1901* (Oxford, 2012), 47–62.

Chamberlain, J. S., 'Portrait of a High Church clerical dynasty in Georgian England: the Frewens and their world', in John Walsh, Colin Haydon, and Stephen Taylor, eds.,

The Church of England c.1689–c.1833. From toleration to Tractarianism (Cambridge, 1993), 299–316.

Champion, Justin, *The pillars of priestcraft shaken. The Church of England and its enemies* (Cambridge, 1992).

Champion, Justin, 'Pere Richard Simon and English Biblical criticism, 1680–1700', in J. Force and D. S. Katz, eds., *Everything connects. In conference with Richard H. Popkin. Essays in his honor* (Leiden, 1999), 38–61.

Champion, Justin, '"May the last king be strangled in the bowels of the last priest": irreligion and the English Enlightenment, 1649–1789', in T. Morton and N. Smith, eds., *Radicalism in British literary culture, 1650–1830. From revolution to revolution* (Cambridge, 2002), 29–44.

Champion, Justin, *Republican learning: John Toland and the crisis of Christian culture* (Manchester, 2003).

Champion, Justin, '"My kingdom is not of this world": The politics of religion after the Restoration', in N. Tyacke, ed., *The English revolution c.1590–1720* (Manchester, 2007), 185–202.

Chaney, Edward, 'The Grand Tour and the evolution of the travel book', in Andrew Wilton and Ilaria Bignamini, eds., *Grand Tour. The lure of Italy in the eighteenth century* (London, 1996), 95–7.

Chapman, Allan, *Dividing the circle: the development of critical angular measurement in astronomy 1500–1800* (Chichester, 1995).

Chapman, Allan, 'The first professors', in John Fauvel, Raymond Flood, and Robin Wilson, eds., *Oxford figures: eight centuries of the mathematical sciences* (2nd edn., Oxford, 2013), 92–113.

Chapman, Allan, 'Edmond Halley', in John Fauvel, Raymond Flood, and Robin Wilson, eds., *Oxford figures: eight centuries of the mathematical sciences* (2nd edn., Oxford, 2013), 140–64.

Chapman, Allan, 'Oxford's Newtonian school', in John Fauvel, Raymond Flood, and Robin Wilson, eds., *Oxford figures: eight centuries of the mathematical sciences* (2nd edn., Oxford, 2013), 166–71.

Chapman, Allan, 'Thomas Hornsby and the Radcliffe Observatory', in John Fauvel, Raymond Flood, and Robin Wilson, eds., *Oxford figures: eight centuries of the mathematical sciences* (2nd edn., Oxford, 2013), 202–20.

Chapman, Hester W., *Queen Anne's son. A memoir of William Henry, Duke of Gloucester 1689–1700* (London, 1954).

Charles-Edwards, Thomas, and Julian Reid, *Corpus Christi College, Oxford. A history* (Oxford, 2017).

Chesser, R. and D. Wyn Jones, eds., *The land of opportunity: Joseph Haydn and the British* (London, 2013).

Chico, Tita, *The experimental imagination. Literary knowledge and science in the British Enlightenment* (Stanford, CA, 2018).

Choi, Peter, 'Whitefield, Georgia, and the quest for Bethesda College', in Geordan Hammond and David Ceri Jones, eds., *George Whitefield* (Oxford, 2016), 224–40.

Christie, C., *The British country house in the eighteenth century* (Manchester, 2000).

Christie, I. R., *Stress and stability in late eighteenth-century Britain. Reflections on the British avoidance of revolution.* [The Ford Lectures 1983–84] (Oxford, 1984).

Clapham, C., ed., *Private patronage and public power. Political clientelism in the modern state* (London, 1982).

BIBLIOGRAPHY 711

Clark, Elizabeth A., 'From Patristics to early Christian studies', in Susan Ashbrook Harvey and David G. Hunter, eds., *The Oxford handbook of early Christian studies* (Oxford, 2008), 7–41.

Clark, Sir George, *Elsfield church and village* (Oxford, 1975).

Clark, J. C. D., *The dynamics of change. The crisis of the 1750s and English party systems* (Cambridge, 1982).

Clark, J. C. D., *English society 1688–1832. Ideology, social structure and political practice during the ancien regime* (1st edn., Cambridge, 1985).

Clark, J. C. D., *Samuel Johnson, literature, religion and English cultural politics from the Restoration to Romanticism* (Cambridge, 1994).

Clark, J. C. D., *English society 1660–1832. Religion, ideology and politics during the ancien regime* (2nd edn., Cambridge, 2000).

Clark, J. C. D., 'Religion and political identity: Samuel Johnson as a Nonjuror', in J. Clark and H. Erskine-Hill, eds., *Samuel Johnson in historical context* (Basingstoke, 2002), 79–145.

Clark, J. C. D., *Our shadowed present. Modernism, postmodernism and history* (London, 2003)

Clark, J. C. D., The eighteenth-century context', in W.J. Abraham and J. E. Kirby, eds., *The Oxford handbook of Methodist studies* (Oxford, 2009), 3–29.

Clark, J. C. D., 'Samuel Johnson: the last choices, 1775–1784', in J. Clark and H. Erskine-Hill, eds., *The politics of Samuel Johnson* (Basingstoke, 2012), 168–222.

Clark, J. C. D., *From Restoration to reform. The British Isles 1660–1832* (London, 2014).

Clark, J. C. D., '"God" and "the Enlightenment"', in William Bulman and Robert Ingram, eds., *God in the Enlightenment* (Oxford, 2016), 215–35.

Clark, J. F. M., 'Kidd, John (1775–1851), physician', *ODNB* online version (2007). https://www.oxforddnb.com/view/10.1093/ref:odnb/9780198614128.001.0001/odnb-9780198614128-e-15511

Clark, Peter, ed., *Country towns in pre-industrial England* (Leicester, 1981).

Clark, Peter, *British clubs and societies 1580–1800: the origins of an associational world* (Oxford, 2000).

Clark, Ruth, *Strangers and sojourners at Port Royal* (Cambridge, 1932).

Clark, William, *Academic charisma and the origins of the research university* (Chicago, IL, 2006).

Clarke, B. F. L., *The building of the eighteenth-century church* (London, 1963).

Clarke, John, 'Warden Gardiner, All Souls, and the Church, c.1688–1760', in S. Green and P. Horden, eds., *All Souls under the Ancien Régime,* 197–213.

Clarke, John, 'Warden Niblett and the Mortmain Bill', in S. Green and P. Horden, eds., *All Souls under the Ancien Régime,* 217–32.

Clarke, M. L., *Greek studies in England* (Cambridge, 1945).

Clarke, M.L., 'Classical Studies', in *HUO* V, 513–34.

Clarke, T., 'Nurseries of sedition?: The Episcopal congregations after the revolution of 1689', in J. Potter, ed., *After Columba—after Calvin, community and identity in the religious traditions of North East Scotland* (Aberdeen, 1999), 61–9.

Claydon, T., *William III and the Godly Revolution* (Cambridge, 1996).

Claydon, T., 'The sermon, the "public sphere" and the political culture of late seventeenth-century England', in Lori Anne Ferrell and Peter McCullough, eds., *The English sermon revised* (Manchester, 2000), 208–34.

Claydon, T., *William III* (Harlow, 2002).

Claydon, T., *Europe and the making of England 1660–1760* (Cambridge, 2007).

712   BIBLIOGRAPHY

Clayton, Tim, 'Clarke: father and son', in S. Green and P. Horden, eds., *All Souls under the Ancien Régime*, 117–31.

Clifford, Helen M., *A treasured inheritance. 600 years of Oxford College silver* (Oxford, 2004).

Coffey, John, *Persecution and toleration in Protestant England, 1558–1689* (London, 2000).

Cohen, M., '"To think, to compare, to combine, to methodise": girls' education in Enlightenment Britain', in S. Knott and B. Taylor, eds., *Women, gender, and Enlightenment* (Basingstoke, 2005), 224–42.

Colley, Linda, *In defiance of oligarchy. The Tory Party 1714–1760* (Cambridge, 1982).

Colley, Linda, *Britons. Forging the nation 1707–1837* (New Haven, CT, 1992).

Collins, Irene, *Jane Austen and the clergy* (London, 1993).

Colvin, Howard, *Unbuilt Oxford* (New Haven, CT, 1983).

Colvin, Howard, *A Dictionary of British architects 1600–1840* (3rd edn., New Haven, CT, 1995).

Connell, Philip, *Secular chains. Poetry and the politics of religion from Milton to Pope* (Oxford, 2016).

Conner, Patrick, *Michael Angelo Rooker 1746–1801* (London, 1984).

Connolly, S. J., *Religion, law, and power. The making of Protestant Ireland 1660–1760* (Oxford, 1992).

Conway, S., *Britain, Ireland, & Continental Europe in the eighteenth century. Similarities, connections, identities* (Oxford, 2011).

Cook, Alan, *Edmond Halley. Charting the heavens and the seas* (Oxford, 1998)

Cookson, J. E., *The British armed nation 1793–1815* (Oxford, 1997).

Cooper, C. H. and J. W., *Annals of Cambridge* (5 vols., Cambridge, 1842–1908).

Cooper, Thompson, 'Schomberg, Alexander Crowcher (1756–92), poet and writer on jurisprudence', rev. Rebecca Mills, *ODNB*, online version (2004). https://www.oxforddnb.com/view/10.1093/ref:odnb/9780198614128.001.0001/odnb-9780198614128-e-24818

Coppola, Al, *The Theater of experiment. Staging natural philosophy in eighteenth-century Britain* (Oxford, 2016).

Corbett, E., *A history of Spelsbury* (Banbury, 1962).

Corfield, P. J., *The impact of English towns 1700–1800* (Oxford, 1982).

Corley, T. A. B.,'Valpy, Richard (1754–1836), schoolmaster', *ODNB*, online version (2006). https://www.oxforddnb.com/view/10.1093/ref:odnb/9780198614128.001.0001/odnb-9780198614128-e-28057

Cornwall, Robert D., *Visible and apostolic. Constitution of the Church of England in High Church Anglican and Non-Juror thought* (Newark, DE, 1993).

Cornwall, Robert D., 'Charles Leslie and the Political Implications of Theology', in W. Gibson and R. Ingram, eds., *Religious identities in Britain, 1660–1832* (Aldershot, 2005), 27–42.

Cornwall, Robert D., 'Nicholls, William (1664–1712), theologian', *ODNB*, online version (2006). https://www.oxforddnb.com/view/10.1093/ref:odnb/9780198614128.001.0001/odnb-9780198614128-e-20116.

Corp, Edward, *The Stuarts in Italy 1719–1766. A royal court in permanent exile* (Cambridge, 2011).

Costin, W. C., *The history of St John's College, Oxford, 1598–1860* (Oxford, 1958) [Oxford Historical Society, new series, 12].

Countryman, E., *A people in revolution. The American Revolution and political society in New York, 1760–1790* (New York, 1989).

Courtney, W. P., 'Heath, Benjamin (1704–1766), literary scholar and collector', rev. Ian Maxted, *ODNB*, online version (2004). https://www.oxforddnb.com/view/10.1093/ref: odnb/9780198614128.001.0001/odnb-9780198614128-e-12829

Courtney, W. P., 'Shepherd, Richard (1731/2–1809), Church of England clergyman and theological writer', rev. Emma Major, *ODNB*, online version (2004). https://www.oxforddnb.com/view/10.1093/ref:odnb/9780198614128.001.0001/odnb-9780198614128-e-25336

Courtney, W. P., 'Lombard, Daniel (1678–1746), Church of England clergyman and author', rev. Philip Carter *ODNB*, online version (2013). https://www.oxforddnb.com/view/10.1093/ref:odnb/9780198614128.001.0001/odnb-9780198614128-e-16952

Cowan, Brian, *The social life of coffee. The emergence of the British coffeehouse* (New Haven, CT: 2011).

Cowan, Brian, 'The spin doctor: Sacheverell's trial speech and political performance in the divided society', in Mark Knights, ed., *Faction displayed: reconsidering the impeachment of Dr Henry Sacheverell* (London, 2012), 28–46.

Cowie, L. W., *Henry Newman: an American in London, 1708–1743* (London, 1956).

Cragg, G. R., *Reason and authority in the eighteenth century* (Cambridge, 1964).

Craig, John, 'Sermon reception', in P. McCullough, H. Adlington, and E. Rhatigan, eds., *The Oxford handbook of the early modern sermon* (Oxford, 2011), 179–93.

Cranston, Maurice, *John Locke: a biography* (London, 1968).

Craske, Matthew, *The silent rhetoric of the body. A history of monumental sculpture and commemorative art in England, 1720–1770* (New Haven, CT, 2007).

Crook, J. Mordaunt, *Brasenose. The biography of an Oxford college* (Oxford, 2008).

Cross, A. G., *"By the banks of the Thames": Russians in eighteenth-century Britain* (Newtonville, MA, 1979).

Cross, A. G., *Peter the Great through British eyes: perceptions and representations of the Tsar since 1698* (Cambridge, 2000).

Cross, Arthur Lyon, *The Anglican episcopate and the American colonies* (New York, 1902).

Crossley, Alan, ed., *VCH Oxon.*, IV. *The City of Oxford* (London, 1979).

Crossley, Alan, 'City and University', in *HUO* IV, 105–35.

Cruickshanks, Eveline, *The Glorious Revolution* (Basingstoke, 2000).

Cruickshanks, Eveline, 'Attempts to restore the Stuarts, 1689–96', in E. Cruickshanks and Edward Corp, eds., *The Stuart court in exile and the Jacobites* (London, 1995), 1–13.

Cruickshanks, Eveline, *Political untouchables. The Tories and the '45* (London, 1979).

Cruickshanks, Eveline and Howard Erskine-Hill, *The Atterbury plot* (Basingstoke, 2004).

Curley, T. M., *Sir Robert Chambers: law, literature, and empire in the age of Johnson* (Madison, WI, 1998).

Curtis, L. P., *Anglican moods of the eighteenth century* (n.p. [Archon], 1966).

Curtis, Mark, *Oxford and Cambridge in transition, 1558–1642. An essay on changing relations between the English universities and English society* (Oxford, 1959).

Curthoys, Judith, *The Cardinal's college: Christ Church, chapter and verse* (London, 2012).

Curthoys, Judith, *The stones of Christ Church. The story of the buildings of Christ Church, Oxford* (London, 2017).

Curthoys, Jusith, *The King's cathedral. The ancient heart of Christ Church, Oxford* (London, 2019).

Curthoys, Judith, *Cows & curates. The story of the land and livings of Christ Church, Oxford* (London, 2020).

Cuthbertson, Brian, *The first bishop: a biography of Charles Inglis* (Halifax, NS, 1987).

714 BIBLIOGRAPHY

Dabney, W. M., and M. Dargan, *William Henry Drayton and the American Revolution* (Albuquerque, NM, 1962).

Danker, Ryan, *Wesley and the Anglicans: political division in early evangelicalism* (Downers Grove, IL, 2016).

Darwall-Smith, R. 'Daniel Wyttenbach and the Clarendon Press', in L. Van der Stockt, ed., *Plutarchea Lovaniensia: a miscellany of essays on Plutarch* (Louvain, 1996), 53–77.

Darwall-Smith, Robin, *Univ. A history of University College Oxford* (Oxford, 2008).

Darwall-Smith, R., The Monks of Magdalen, 1688–1854', in L. W.B. Brockliss, ed., *Magdalen College, Oxford*, 253–386.

Davidson, M., *Medicine in Oxford* (Oxford, 1953).

Davies, C. S. L., 'Decline and revival: 1660–1900', in C. Davies and J. Garnett, eds., *Wadham College* (London, 1994), 36–55.

Davies, C. S. L., 'Thistlethwayte, Robert (bap. 1690, d. 1744), college head and subject of sexual scandal', *ODNB*, online version (2008). https://www.oxforddnb.com/view/10.1093/ref:odnb/9780198614128.001.0001/odnb-9780198614128-e-74037

Davies, C., and J. Garnett, eds., *Wadham College 1610-2010* (London, 2009).

Davies, Sir L. T. and A. Edwards, *Welsh life in the eighteenth century* (London, 1939).

Davies, Mark J., *King of all balloons. The adventurous life of James Sadler the first English aeronaut* (Stroud, 2015).

Davis, H. W., *A history of Balliol College*, rev. R. H. C. Davis and Richard Hunt (Oxford, 1963).

Day, C.J., 'The University and the City', in *HUO* VI, 441–76.

Deacon, M., *Philip Doddridge* (Northampton, 1981).

Dean, W., *Handel's dramatic oratorios and masques* (2nd edn., Oxford, 1990).

Dearing, T., *Wesleyan and Tractarian worship. An ecumenical study* (London, 1966).

de Bruin, Renger and Maarten Brinkman, eds., *Peace was made here. The treaties of Utrecht, Rastatt and Baden 1713-1714* (Utrecht, 2013).

Deconinck-Brossard, F., 'The churches and the '45', in W.J. Sheils, ed., *The Church and war* [Studies in Church History, 20] (Oxford, 1983), 253–62.

Deconinck-Brossard, F., 'England and France in the Eighteenth Century', in S. Prickett, ed., *Reading the text. Biblical criticism and literary theory* (Oxford, 1991), 136–81.

Deconinck-Brossard, F., 'The art of preaching' in J. van Eijnatten, ed., *Preaching, sermon and cultural change in the long eighteenth century* (Leiden, 2009), 95–130.

Delbourgo, James, *Collecting the world. The life and curiosity of Hans Sloane* (Harmondsworth, 2017).

Delpiano, Patrizia, *Il trono e la cattedra. Instruzione e formazione dell'élite nel Piemonte del Settecento* (Turin, 1997).

DeMaria, Jr., Robert, *The life of Samuel Johnson. A critical biography* (Oxford, 1993).

Dennison, Matthew, *The first iron lady. A life of Caroline of Ansbach* (London, 2017).

Derry, Warren, *Dr Parr. A portrait of the Whig Dr Johnson* (Oxford, 1966).

Deutsch, O.E., *Handel: A Documentary Biography* (London, 1955).

Devine, T. M., *The Scottish nation 1700-2000* (Harmondsworth, 1999).

Devine, T. M., *Scotland's empire 1600-1815* (London, 2003).

Dewhurst, K., ed., *Oxford medicine. Essays on the evolution of the Oxford Clinical School to commemorate the bicentenary of the Radcliffe Infirmary 1770-1970* (Oxford, 1970).

Dickie, S., *Cruelty & laughter. Forgotten comic literature and the unsentimental eighteenth century* (Chicago, IL, 2011).

Dickinson, H.T., *The Politics of the People in Eighteenth-Century Britain* (Macmillan Press, Basingstoke, 1994).

Ditchfield, G. M., 'Ecclesiastical policy under Lord North', in J. Walsh, C. Haydon, and Stephen Taylor, eds., *The Church of England c.1689–c.1833. From toleration to Tractarianism* (Cambridge, 1993), 228–46.

Ditchfield, G. M., *George III. An essay in Monarchy* (Basingstoke, 2002).

Ditchfield, G. M., 'Feathers Tavern petitioners (act. 1771–1774)', *ODNB*, online version (2005). https://www.oxforddnb.com/view/10.1093/ref:odnb/9780198614128.001.0001/odnb-9780198614128-e-93823

Ditchfield, G. M., 'Joseph Priestley and the complexities of Latitudinarianism in the 1770s', in I. Rivers and D. L. Wykes, eds., *Joseph Priestley, scientist, philosopher, and theologian* (Oxford, 2008), 144–71.

Dobbs, Betty Jo Teeter and Margaret C. Jacob, *Newton and the culture of Newtonianism* (Atlantic Highlands, NJ, 1995).

Doll, Peter, *Revolution, religion, and national identity. Imperial Anglicanism in North America, 1745–1795* (Cranbury, NJ, 2000).

Doolittle, I.G., 'College Administration', *HUO* V, 227–68.

Doolittle, Ian, 'William Blackstone, Edward Gibbon and Thomas Winchester: the case for an Oxford Enlightenment', in W. Prest and A. Page, eds., *Blackstone and his critics* (London, 2018), 59–75.

Douglas, D., *English scholars 1660–1730* (London, 1939).

Downes, Kerry, *The architecture of Wren* (London, 1982).

Downey, James, *The eighteenth century pulpit: Butler, Berkeley, Secker, Sterne, Whitfield and Wesley* (Oxford, 1969).

Drage, Sally, 'A reappraisal of provincial church music', in D. Wyn Jones, ed., *Music in eighteenth-century Britain* (Aldershot, 2001), 172–90.

Draper, John W., *William Mason. A study in eighteenth-century culture* (New York, 1924).

Drury, John, ed., *Critics of the Bible 1724–1873* (Cambridge, 1989).

Duchesne-Guillemin, J., *The Western response to Zoroaster* (Oxford, 1958).

Duncan, Dennis, *Index, A History of the. A Bookish Adventure* (Harmondsworth, 2021).

Durey, Michael, *William Wickham, master spy* (London, 2009).

Edelstein, Dan, *The enlightenment. A genealogy* (Chicago, IL, 2010).

Edwards, Elizabeth, *English language poetry from Wales* (Cardiff, 2013).

Edwards, M., *John Wesley and the eighteenth century: a study of his social and political influence* (London, 1955).

Ehrman, John, *The Younger Pitt. Vol. 2. The reluctant transition* (London, 1983).

Ehrman, John, *The Younger Pitt. Vol. 3. The consuming struggle* (London, 1996).

Eisenstadt, S. N. and L. Roniger, *Patrons, clients and friends. Interpersonal relations and the structure of trust in society* (Cambridge, 1984).

Elliott, Paul A., *The Derby philosophers. Science and culture in British urban society, 1700–1850* (Manchester, 2009).

Elliott, Paul A., *Enlightenment, modernity and science. Geographies of scientific culture and improvement in Georgian England* (London, 2010).

Ellis, Aytoun, *The penny universities: a history of the coffee houses* (London, 1956).

Ellis, Heather, *Generational conflict and university reform. Oxford in the age of revolution* (Leiden, Boston, MA, 2012)

Ellis, J. J., *The New England mind in transition: Samuel Johnson of Connecticut, 1696–1772* (New Haven, CT, 1973).

Ellis, K., *The Post Office in the eighteenth century. a study in administrative history* (Oxford, 1958).

Elmarsafy, Ziad, *The Enlightenment Qur'an: the politics of translation and the construction of Islam* (Oxford, 2009).

716 BIBLIOGRAPHY

Emerson, Roger L., 'Lord Bute and the Scottish universities 1760–1792', in K. W. Schweizer, eds., *Lord Bute. Essays in re-interpretation* (Leicester, 1988), 147–79.

Emerson, Roger L., *Professors, patronage and politics. The Aberdeen universities in the eighteenth century* (Aberdeen, 1992).

Emerson, Roger L., 'Politics and the Glasgow professors, 1690–1800', in A. Hook and R. B. Sher, eds., *The Glasgow Enlightenment, 1690–1800* (East Linton, 1995), 21–39.

Emerson, Roger L., *Academic patronage in the Scottish Enlightenment: Glasgow, Edinburgh and St Andrews universities* (Edinburgh, 2008).

Emerson, Roger L., *An Enlightened duke. The life of Archibald Campbell (1682–1761), Earl of Ilay, 3rd Duke of Argyll* (Kilkerran, 2013).

Emery, F., *Edward Lhuyd, FRS, 1660–1709* (Cardiff, 1971).

Erskine-Hill, Howard, *The social milieu of Alexander Pope: lives, example and the poetic response* (New Haven, CT, 1975).

Evans, A. W., *Warburton and the Warburtonians. A study in some eighteenth-century controversies* (London, 1932).

Fairer, David, 'Oxford and the Literary World', in *HUO* V, 779–805.

Fara, P., 'Faces of genius: images of Isaac Newton in eighteenth-century England', in G. Cubitt and A. Warren, eds., *Heroic reputations and exemplary lives* (Manchester, 2000), 57–81.

Fara, P., *Newton. The making of genius* (London, 2002).

Farooq, Jennifer, *Preaching in eighteenth-century London* (Woodbridge, 2013).

Fasnacht, R., *A history of the city of Oxford* (Oxford, 1954).

John Fauvel, John, Raymond Flood, and Robin Wilson, eds., *Oxford figures: eight centuries of the mathematical sciences* (2nd edn., Oxford, 2013).

Fawcett, T. J., *The liturgy of comprehension, 1689: an abortive attempt to revise the Book of Common Prayer* (London, 1973).

Feather, John, 'A Learned Press in a Commericial World', in ed. Ian Gadd, *The History of Oxford University Press*. Vol. 1. *Beginnings to 1780,* (Oxford, 2013), 243–79.

Feiling, Sir Keith, *A history of the Tory party 1640–1714* (Oxford, 1924).

Feiling, Sir Keith, *The second Tory party 1714–1832* (London, 1938).

Feiling, Sir Keith, *In Christ Church hall* (London, 1960).

Feingold, M., 'Mathematical sciences and new philosophies', in HUO IV, 359–48.

Feingold, M., *The Newtonian moment. Isaac Newton and the making of modern culture* (New York, 2004).

Fell-Smith, C., 'Newton, Benjamin (bap. 1722, d. 1787), Church of England clergyman', rev. Robert D. Cornwall, *ODNB*, online version (2004). https://www.oxforddnb.com/view/10.1093/ref:odnb/9780198614128.001.0001/odnb-9780198614128-e-20049

Feola, Vittoria, 'The ancients "with" the moderns: Oxford's approaches to publishing ancient science', in P. Bullard and A. Tadié, eds., *Ancients and moderns in Europe,* 19–35.

Feola, V. and S. Mandelbrote, 'The learned press: geography, science and mathematics', in ed. Gadd, *The History of Oxford University Press,* 1. 317–57.

Ferdinand, Christine, *An accidental masterpiece. Magdalen College's New Building and the people who built it* (Oxford, 2011).

Fergus, Jan, *Provincial readers in eighteenth-century England* (Oxford, 2007).

Ferguson, J. P., *Dr. Samuel Clarke: an eighteenth century heretic* (Kineton, 1976).

Findlay, D. and A. Murdoch, 'Revolution to reform: eighteenth-century politics, c.1690–1800', in E.P. Dennison, D. Ditchburn, and M. Lynch, eds., *Aberdeen before 1800: a new history* (East Linton, 2002), 267–86.

Firby, Norah Kathleen, *European travellers and their perception of Zoroastrians in the 17th and 18th centuries* (Berlin, 1988).

Fischer, Béat de, 'Swiss in Great Britain in the eighteenth century', in W.H. Barber, J. H. Brumfitt, R. A. Leigh, R. Shackleton, and S. S. B. Taylor, eds., *The age of Enlightenment. Studies presented to Theodore Besterman* (Edinburgh/London, 1967), 350–74.

Fissell, Mary and Roger Cooter, 'Exploring natural knowledge. Science and the popular', in ed. R. Porter, *Eighteenth-century science*, (*Cambridge History of Science*, Vol. 4) (Cambridge, 2003), 129–58.

Fitzmaurice, Lord, *Life of William Earl of Shelburne* (2nd edn., 2 vols., London, 1912).

Fitzpatrick, M. H., 'Enlightenment', in I. McCalman, ed., *An Oxford companion to the Romantic age: British culture 1776–1832* (Oxford, 1999), 299–310.

Fitzpatrick, M. H., 'Heretical religion and radical political ideas in late eighteenth-century England', in E. Hellmuth, ed., *The transformation of political culture: England and Germany in the late eighteenth century* (Oxford, 1990), 339–72.

Fletcher, Anthony, *Gender, sex, and subordination in England 1500–1800* (New Haven, CT, 1995).

Fletcher, D. H., *The emergence of estate maps. Christ Church Oxford, 1600 to 1840* (Oxford, 1995).

Flood, R. and J. Fauvel, 'John Wallis', in John Fauvel, Raymond Flood, and Robin Wilson, eds., *Oxford figures: eight centuries of the mathematical sciences*, 114–39.

Flood, Warden, *Memoirs of the life and correspondence of Henry Flood* (Dublin, 1838).

Folkenflik, Robert, 'Johnson's politics', in Greg Clingham, ed., *The Cambridge companion to Samuel Johnson* (Cambridge, 1997), 102–13.

Foord, Archibald S., *His Majesty's Opposition 1714–1830* (Oxford, 1964).

Foote, Yolanda, 'Mendes da Costa, Emanuel (1717–1791), naturalist', *ODNB*, online version (2008). https://www.oxforddnb.com/view/10.1093/ref:odnb/9780198614128.001. 0001/odnb-9780198614128-e-58513

Force, James E., *William Whiston. Honest Newtonian* (Cambridge, 1985).

Force, James E., 'The breakdown of the Newtonian synthesis of science and religion: Hume, Newton, and the Royal Society', in J. Force and R.H. Popkin, eds., *Essays on the context, nature, and influence of Isaac Newton's theology* (Dordrecht, 1990), 143–64.

Forshall, F. H., *Westminster School. Past and present* (London, 1884).

Fothergill, Richard, *The Fothergills. A first history* (Newcastle, 1998).

Fowler, M., *Blenheim. Biography of a palace* (Harmondsworth, 1989).

Fowler, Thomas, *The history of Corpus Christi College* (Oxford, 1893).

Fox, Adam, *John Mill and Richard Bentley. A study of the textual criticism of the New Testament 1675–1729* (Oxford, 1954).

Fox, Robert, 'Science at Oriel', in ed. Catto, *Oriel College*, 645–77.

Frank, Bruce, '"The excellent rehearser": Charles Leslie and the Tory party, 1688–1714', in J.D. Browning, ed., *Biography in the 18th century* (London, 1980), 43–68.

Franklin, Michael J., *Sir William Jones* (Cardiff, 1995).

Franklin, Michael J., 'Gagnier, John (c.1670–1740)', *ODNB*, online version (2004). https://www.oxforddnb.com/view/10.1093/ref:odnb/9780198614128.001.0001/odnb-9780198614128-e-10278

Franklin, Michael J., *Orientalist Jones* (Oxford, 2011).

French, Henry and Mark Rothery, *Man's estate. Landed gentry masculinities c.1660–c.1900* (Oxford, 2012).

Friedman, Terry, *James Gibbs* (New Haven, CT, 1984).

Frijhoff, Willem, 'Patterns', in H. de Ridder-Symoens, ed., *Universities in early modern Europe*, 43–110.

718 BIBLIOGRAPHY

Frijhoff, Willem, 'Graduation and careers', in H. de Ridder-Symoens, ed., *Universities in early modern Europe*, 355–416.

Fumaroli, M., ed., *La querelle des anciens et des modernes, xviie–xviiie siecles* (Paris, 2001).

Fumaroli, M., *La République des Lettres* (Paris, 2015).

Gallagher, Noelle, *Historical literatures. Writing about the past in England, 1660–1740* (Manchester, 2012).

Gascoigne, John, *Cambridge in the age of the Enlightenment. From the Restoration to the French Revolution* (Cambridge, 1989).

Gascoigne, John, 'Church and state allied: the failure of parliamentary reform of the universities, 1688–1800', in A.L. Beier, D. Cannadine, and J. M. Rosenheim, eds., *The first modern society. Essays in English history in honour of Lawrence Stone* (Cambridge, 1989), 401–29.

Gascoigne, John, 'The role of the universities in the Scientific Revolution', in David C. Lindberg and Robert S. Westman, eds., *Reappraisals of the scientific revolution* (Cambridge, 1990), 207–60.

Gascoigne, John, 'Ideas of nature', in R. Porter, ed., *Eighteenth-century science, (Cambridge history of science*, Vol. 4) (Cambridge, 2003), 285–304.

Gaukroger, Stephen, *The collapse of mechanism and the rise of sensibility: science and the shaping of modernity, 1680–1760* (Oxford, 2011).

Gee, Austin, *The British volunteer movement, 1794–1814* (Oxford, 2003).

Geraghty, Anthony, *The Sheldonian Theatre: architecture and learning in seventeenth-century Oxford* (New Haven, CT, 2013).

German, K., 'Jacobite politics in Aberdeen and the '15', in P. Monod, M. Pittock, and D. Szechi, eds., *Loyalty and identity. Jacobites at home and abroad* (Basingstoke, 2010), 82–97.

Gibbon, A. M., *The ancient free grammar school of Skipton in Craven* (Liverpool, 1947).

Gibson, A. G., *The Radcliffe Infirmary* (London, 1926).

Gibson, W., *A social history of the domestic chaplain* (Leicester, 1997).

Gibson, W., *The Church of England 1688–1832. Unity and accord* (London, 2001).

Gibson, W., *Enlightenment prelate. Benjamin Hoadly, 1676–1761* (Cambridge, 2004).

Gibson, W., 'Altitudinarian equivocation: George Smalridge's churchmanship', in W. Gibson and R. Ingram, eds., *Religious identities in Britain, 1660–1832* (Aldershot, 2005), 43–60.

Gibson, W., 'The British sermon 1689–1901: quantities, performance, and culture', in K. Francis and W. Gibson, eds., *The Oxford handbook of the British sermon 1689–1901* (Oxford, 2012), 3–30.

Giles, Paul, 'Enlightenment historiography and cultural civil wars', in S. Manning and F. Cogliano, eds., *The Atlantic Enlightenment* (Aldershot, 2008), 19–35.

Gillam, S. G., ed., *The building accounts of the Radcliffe Camera* (Oxford, 1958).

Glasson, Travis, *Mastering Christianity. Missionary Anglicanism and slavery in the Atlantic world* (Oxford, 2012).

Glassey, Lionel K. J., *Politics and the appointment of Justices of the Peace, 1675–1720* (Oxford, 1979).

Glauser, Richard, 'Arthur Collier', in Yolton, Price, and Stephens (eds.), *Dictionary of eighteenth-century philosophers*, I. 218–22.

Glickman, Gabriel, 'The Church and the Catholic Community', in G. Tapsell, ed., *The later Stuart church, 1660–1714* (Manchester, 2012), 217–42.

Glickman, Gabriel, *The English Catholic community, 1688–1745* (Woodbridge, 2009).

Glover, Katharine, *Elite women and polite society in eighteenth-century Scotland* (Woodbridge, 2011).

BIBLIOGRAPHY   719

Glover, R., *Britain at Bay. Defence against Bonaparte, 1803–14* (London, 1973).

Godley, A.D., *Oxford in the eighteenth century* (London, 1908).

Goldgar, Anne, *Impolite learning: conduct and community in the Republic of Letters, 1680–1750* (New Haven, CT, 1995).

Goldie, Mark, 'The Non-Jurors, episcopacy, and the origins of the Convocation controversy', in E. Cruickshanks, ed., *Ideology and conspiracy: aspects of Jacobitism, 1689–1759* (Edinburgh, 1982), 15–35.

Goldie, Mark, 'Priestcraft and the birth of Whiggism', in Nicholas Phillipson and Quentin Skinner, eds., *Political discourse in early modern Britain* (Cambridge, 1993), 209–31.

Golinski, Jan, *Science as public culture. Chemistry and Enlightenment in Britain, 1760–1820* (Cambridge, 1992).

Goodrum, Emma, 'The foundation of Worcester College', in J. Bate and J. Goodman, eds., *Worcester, portrait of an Oxford college* (London, 2014), 32–7.

Goodwin, A., *Friends of liberty: the English democratic movement in the Age of the French Revolution* (London, 1979).

Gottlieb, E. and J. Shields, eds., *Representing place in British literature and culture, 1660–1830: From local to global* (Farnham, 2013).

Goudie, A., ed., *Seven hundred years of an Oxford college: Hertford College, 1284–1984* (Oxford, 1984).

Gourlay, A. B., *A history of Sherborne School* (Winchester, 1951).

Grafton, Anthony, *Worlds made by words: scholarship and community in the modern West* (Cambridge, MA, 2009).

Graham, J. A. and B. A. Phythian, *The Manchester Grammar School 1515–1965* (Manchester, 1965).

Greaves, R., 'Religion in the University 1715-1800', in *HUO* V, 401–24.

Green, David, *Sarah, Duchess of Marlborough* (London, 1967).

Green, J. B., *John Wesley and William Law* (London, 1945).

Green, John Richard, *Oxford during the last century* (Oxford, 1859).

Green, J. R. and G. Roberson, *Studies in Oxford history, chiefly in the eighteenth century*, ed. C. L. Stainer [OHS, 51] (Oxford, 1901).

Green, S.J.D., and Peregrine Horden, eds., *All Souls under the Ancien Régime. Politics, learning, & the Arts, c.1600-1850* (Oxford, 2007).

Green, V. H. H., *The young Mr Wesley. A study of John Wesley and Oxford* (London, 1961).

Green, V.H.H., *Religion at Oxford and Cambridge* (London, 1964).

Green, V.H.H., 'The University and Social Life', in *HUO* V, 309–58.

Greenwood, David, *William King. Tory & Jacobite* (Oxford, 1969).

Gregg, Edward, *Queen Anne* (London, 1980).

Gregory, J., 'Canterbury and the *Ancien Régime*: The Dean and Chapter, 1660–1828', in P. Collinson, N. Ramsay, and M. Sparks, eds., *A history of Canterbury Cathedral* (Oxford, 1995), 204–55.

Gregory, J., *Restoration, reformation and reform, 1660–1828. Archbishops of Canterbury and their diocese* (Oxford, 2000).

Gregory, J., 'Standards of admission to the ministry of the Church of England in the eighteenth century', in T. Clemens and Wim Janse, eds., *The pastor bonus. Papers read at the British-Dutch Colloquium at Utrecht, 18–21 September 2002* (Leiden, 2004), 283–95.

Gregory, J., 'In the Church I will live and die: John Wesley, the Church of England and Methodism', in W. Gibson and R. Ingram, eds., *Religious identities in Britain, 1660–1832*, 147–78.

720 BIBLIOGRAPHY

Gres-Gayer, Jacques, *Paris-Cantorbéry 1717–1720: le dossier d'un premier oecuménisme* (Paris, 1989).

Gribbin, J. and M., *Out of the shadow of a giant. Hooke, Halley and the birth of British science* (London, 2017).

Griffin, Dustin, *Patriotism and poetry in eighteenth-century Britain* (Cambridge, 2002).

Grist, E., 'Pierre Des Maizeaux and the Royal Society', in A. Thomson, S. Burrows, E. Dziembowski, and S. Audidière, eds., *Cultural transfers: France and Britain in the long eighteenth century*, 33–42.

Guerlac, H., 'Where the statue stood: divergent loyalties to Newton in the eighteenth century', in E.R. Wasserman, ed., *Aspects of the eighteenth century* (Baltimore, MD, 1965), 317–34.

Guerrini, Anita, 'Ether madness: Newtonianism, religion, and insanity in eighteenth-century England', in P. Theerman and A. Seeff, eds., *Action and reaction* (Newark, DE, 1993), 232–54.

Guerrini, Anita, Newtonianism, medicine and religion', in Ole Peter Grell and Andrew Cunningham, eds., *Religio Medici: religion and medicine in seventeenth-century England* (Aldershot, 1996), 293–313.

Guerrini, Anita, 'Nicholls, Francis [Frank] (bap. 1699–? 1778), anatomist and physician', *ODNB*, online version (2004). https://www.oxforddnb.com/view/10.1093/ref:odnb/9780198614128.001.0001/odnb-9780198614128-e-20109

Guest, I., *Dr John Radcliffe and his trust* (London, 1991).

Gunn, J. A. W., *Beyond liberty and property: the process of self-recognition in eighteenth-century political though*t (Kingston/Montreal, 1983).

Gunther, R. T., *Oxford gardens* (Oxford, 1912).

Gunther, R. T., *Early science in Oxford* (14 vols.) (Oxford, 1923–45)

Guthrie, Neil, *The material culture of the Jacobites* (Cambridge, 2013).

Haakonssen, K., ed., *Enlightenment and religion: rational Dissent in eighteenth-century Britain* (Cambridge, 1996).

Habermas, J., *Between naturalism and religion*, trans. C. Cronin (Cambridge, 2008).

Hackman, Willem, 'Mathematical instruments', in J. Fauvel, R. Flood, and Robin Wilson, eds., *Oxford figures: eight centuries of the mathematical sciences*, 74–90.

Hadfield, A., *Lying in early modern English culture. From the oath of supremacy to the oath of allegiance* (Oxford, 2018).

Haffenden, P. S., 'The Anglican Church in Restoration colonial policy', in J.M. Smith, ed., *Seventeenth-century America: essays in colonial history* (Chapel Hill, NC, 1959), 166–91.

Hale, Paul R., 'Music and musicians', in J. Buxton and P. Williams, eds., *New College, Oxford*, 267–93.

Halliday, Paul D., 'Finch, Heneage, first Earl of Aylesford (1648/9–1719, lawyer and politician', *ODNB*, online version (2008). https://www.oxforddnb.com/view/10.1093/ref:odnb/9780198614128.001.0001/odnb-9780198614128-e-9435

Hamer, John, Lord, *A memorial of the parish and family of Hanmer in Flintshire* (London, 1876).

Hamilton, James, *Turner's Britain* (London, 2003).

Hamilton, S. G., 'Dr Newton and Hertford College', in M. Burrows, ed., *Collectanea,* 3rd Ser. (Oxford, 1896).

Hamilton, S. G., *Hertford College* (London, 1903).

Hammerstein, Notker, 'Relations with authority', in H. de Ridder-Symoens, ed., *Universities in early modern Europe*, 114–53.

Hampton, S., *Anti-Arminians: the Anglican Reformed tradition from Charles II to George I* (Oxford, 2008).

BIBLIOGRAPHY 721

Hanbury, H. G., *The Vinerian Chair in English legal education* (Oxford, 1958).

Hankins, Thomas L., *Science and the Enlightenment* (Cambridge, 1985).

Handley, Thomas, 'Carte, Thomas (bap. 1686, d. 1754)', *ODNB*, online version (2015). https://www.oxforddnb.com/view/10.1093/ref:odnb/9780198614128.001.0001/odnb-9780198614128-e-4780

Handley, Stuart, 'Aldrich, Henry (1648–1710)', *ODNB*, online version (2004). https://www.oxforddnb.com/view/10.1093/ref:odnb/9780198614128.001.0001/odnb-9780198614128-e-314

Handley, Stuart, 'Harcourt, Simon, first Viscount Harcourt (1661?–1727), lawyer and politician', *ODNB*, online version (2004). https://www.oxforddnb.com/view/10.1093/ref:odnb/9780198614128.001.0001/odnb-9780198614128-e-12244

Handley, Stuart, 'Ellis, John (1646–1738), government official', *ODNB*, online version (2008). https://www.oxforddnb.com/view/10.1093/ref:odnb/9780198614128.001.0001/odnb-9780198614128-e-8702

Hanham, Andrew, 'Caroline of Brandenburg-Ansbach and the "Anglicisation" of the House of Hanover', in Clarissa Campbell Orr, ed., *Queenship in Europe, 1660–1815. The role of the consort* (Cambridge, 2004), 276–99.

Hanham, Andrew, 'Parker, Thomas, First Earl of Macclesfield (1667–1732), Lord Chancellor', *ODNB*, online version (2009). https://www.oxforddnb.com/view/10.1093/ref:odnb/9780198614128.001.0001/odnb-9780198614128-e-21341

Hanham, Andrew, 'Bromley, William (bap. 1663, d. 1732), Speaker of the House of Commons', *ODNB*, online version (2011). https://www.oxforddnb.com/view/10.1093/ref:odnb/9780198614128.001.0001/odnb-9780198614128-e-3515

Hannan, Leonie, *Women of letters. Gender, writing and the life of the mind in early modern England* (Manchester, 2016).

Hans, N., *New trends in education in the eighteenth century* (London, 1951).

Harding, Alan, *The Countess of Huntingdon's connexion. A sect in action in eighteenth-century England* (Oxford, 2003).

Harford, J. S., *The life of Thomas Burgess, DD, FRS, FAS, & c., late Lord Bishop of Salisbury* (2nd edn., London, 1841).

Harlow, V. T., *Christopher Codrington 1668–1710* (Oxford, 1928).

Harmsen, T., *Antiquarianism in the Augustan age: Thomas Hearne 1678–1735* (Oxford, 2001).

Harris, Bob, *Politics and the rise of the press: Britain and France, 1620–1800* (London, 1996).

Harris, Bob, *Politics and the nation. Britain in the mid-eighteenth century* (Oxford, 2002).

Harris, Frances, *A passion for government. The life of Sarah Duchess of Marlborough* (Oxford, 1991).

Harris, S., *The magnificent flora Graeca: how the Mediterranean came to the English garden* (Oxford, 2007).

Harris, Tim, *Politics under the later Stuarts. Party conflict in a divided society 1660–1715* (Harlow, 1993).

Harris, Tim, 'Incompatible revolutions?: the Established Church and the revolutions of 1688–9 in Ireland, England and Scotland', in Allan Macinnes and J. Ohlmeyer, eds., *The Stuart kingdoms in the seventeenth century: awkward neighbours* (Dublin, 2002), 204–25.

Harris, Tim, *Revolution. The great crisis of the British monarchy, 1685–1720* (Harmondsworth, 2006).

Harris, Tim, 'Scotland under Charles II and James VII: in search of the British causes of the Glorious Revolution', in T. Harris and S. Taylor, eds., *The Final crisis of the Stuart monarchy. The revolutions of 1688–91* (Woodbridge, 2013), 109–32.

722 BIBLIOGRAPHY

Harrison, Colin et al., *John Malchair of Oxford. Artist and musician* (Ashmolean Museum, Oxford, 1998).

Harrison, Peter, *The territories of religion and science* (Chicago, IL, 2015).

Hart, Vaughan, *Nicholas Hawksmoor. Rebuilding ancient wonders* (New Haven, CT, 2002).

Hatton, Ragnhild, *George I. Elector and King* (London, 1978).

Haugen, Kristine Louise, *Richard Bentley. Poetry and Enlightenment* (Cambridge, MA, 2011).

Haugen, Kristine Louise, 'Imagined universities: public insult and the Terrae Filius in early modern Oxford', in Anne Goldgar and Robert Frost, eds., *Institutional culture in early modern Europe* (Leiden, 2004), 317–43.

Haydon, Colin, *Anti-Catholicism in eighteenth-century England. A political and social study* (Manchester, 1993).

Haydon, Colin, 'Le Courayer, Pierre-François (1681–1776), Roman Catholic priest and religious controversialist', *ODNB*, online version (2006). https://www.oxforddnb.com/view/10.1093/ref:odnb/9780198614128.001.0001/odnb-9780198614128-e-6442

Haydon, Colin, 'Two Hundred Years: From "The Glorious Revolution" to the Tercentenary c.1688–c.1871', in eds. F. Heal, R. Darwall-Smith, R.J.B. Bosworth, and C. Haydon, *Jesus College Oxford of Queen Elizabethes Foundation. The first 450 Years* (London, 2021).

Hayes, John, *Rowlandson watercolours and drawings* (London, 1972).

Haynes, D. E. L., *The Arundel marbles* (Oxford, 1975).

Hayton, David, 'The "Country" interest and the party system, 1689–1720', in C. Jones, ed., *Party and management in Parliament 1660–1784* (Bath, 1984), 37–85.

Hayton, David, 'The High Church party in the Irish Convocation, 1703–1713', in H.J. Real and H. Stover-Leidig, eds., *Reading Swift: papers from the 3rd Münster symposium on Jonathan Swift* (Munich, 1998), 117–40.

Hayton, David, 'Dependence, clientage and affinity: the political following of the second Duke of Ormonde', in T. Barnard and J. Fenlon, eds., *The Dukes of Ormonde* (Woodbridge, 2000), 211–42.

Hayton, David, *Ruling Ireland, 1685–1742. Politics, politicians and parties* (Woodbridge, 2004).

Hayton, David, 'Irish Tories and victims of Whig persecution: Sacheverell fever by proxy', in M. Knights, ed., *Faction displayed,* 80–98.

Hayton, David, *The Anglo-Irish experience, 1680–1730. Religion, identity and patriotism* (Woodbridge, 2012).

Heal, F., *The power of gifts: gift exchange in early modern England* (Oxford, 2014).

Hebron, Stephen, *Dr Radcliffe's library: the story of the Radcliffe Library in Oxford* (Oxford, 2014).

Heighes, Simon, *The life and works of William and Philip Hayes* (New York, 1995).

Heitzenrater, Richard P., *The elusive Mr Wesley* (Nashville, TN, 1984).

Heitzenrater, Richard P., 'Wesley and education', in S.J. Hels, ed., *Methodism and education from roots to fulfilment* (Nashville, TN, 2000), 1–13.

Henderson, B. W., *Merton College* (London, 1899).

Henriques, U. R. Q., *Religious toleration in England, 1787–1833* (London, 1961).

Hepworth, Brian, *Robert Lowth* (Boston, MA, 1978).

Hibbert, C., with E. Hibbert, *The encyclopedia of Oxford* (London, 1988).

Hicks, Philip, *Neoclassical history and English culture. From Clarendon to Hume* (Basingstoke, 1996).

Highet, G., *The Classical tradition* (Oxford, 1949).

Hinchliffe, E., *Appleby Grammar School—from Chantry to comprehensive* (Appleby, 1974).

Hiscock, W. G., *A Christ Church miscellany: new chapters on the architects, craftsmen, statuary, plate, bells, furniture, clocks, plays, the library and other buildings* (Oxford, 1946).

Hiscock, W. G., *Henry Aldrich of Christ Church, 1648–1710* (Oxford, 1960).

Hodgkin, R.H., *Six centuries of an Oxford college. A history of the Queen's College 1340–1940* (Oxford, 1940).

Hofstetter, Michael J., *The Romantic Idea of a University. England and Germany, 1770–1850* (Basingstoke, 2001).

Hole, Robert, 'British counter-revolutionary popular propaganda in the 1790s', in Colin Jones, ed., *Britain and revolutionary France: conflict, subversion and propaganda* (Exeter, 1983), 59–83.

Hole, Robert, *Pulpits, politics and public order in England 1760–1832* (Cambridge, 1989).

Hole, Robert, 'English sermons and tracts as media of debate on the French Revolution 1789–99', in M. Philp, ed., *The French Revolution and British popular politics* (Cambridge, 1991), 18–37.

Hole, Robert, 'Randolph, John (1749–1813)', *ODNB*, online version (2004). https://www.oxforddnb.com/view/10.1093/ref:odnb/9780198614128.001.0001/odnb-9780198614128-e-23120

Holmes, Geoffrey, *British politics in the age of Anne* (London, 1967).

Holmes, Geoffrey, 'Harley, St John and the death of the Tory party', in G. Holmes, ed., *Britain after the Glorious Revolution 1689–1714* (London, 1969), 216–37.

Holmes, Geoffrey, *The trial of Doctor Sacheverell* (London, 1973)

Holt, P. M., 'The treatment of Arab history by Prideaux, Ockley, and Sale', in B. Lewis and P. M. Holt, eds., *Historians of the Middle East* (Oxford, 1962), 290–302.

Holtby, R. T., *Daniel Waterland 1683–1740. A study in eighteenth century Orthodoxy* (Carlisle, 1966).

Hone, Joseph, *Literature and party politics at the accession of Queen Anne* (Oxford, 2017).

Hopkins, Clare, *Trinity. 450 years of an Oxford college community* (Oxford, 2005).

Hopkins, D., *Conversing with antiquity. English poets and the Classics from Shakespeare to Pope* (Oxford, 2010).

Hoppit, Julian, *A land of liberty? England 1689–1727* (Oxford, 2002).

Horn, D. B., *The British diplomatic service 1689–1789* (Oxford, 1961).

Horwitz, H., *Revolution politicks: the career of Daniel Finch, second Earl of Nottingham, 1647–1730* (Cambridge, 1968).

Houlbrooke, R., *Britain and Europe 1500–1700* (London, 2011).

Hourani, A., *Islam in European thought* (Cambridge, 1991).

Hudson, Wayne, *The English deists: studies in early Enlightenment* (London, 2009).

Hughes, R., *Haydn* (rev. edn., London, 1974).

Hughes, W. J., *Wales and the Welsh in English literature* (London, 1924).

Hulton, Samuel F., *The clerk of Oxford in fiction* (London, 1909).

Humphrey, David C., *From King's College to Columbia, 1746–1800* (New York, 1976).

Hunt, Arnold, *The art of hearing: English preachers and their audiences, 1590–1640* (Cambridge, 2010).

Hunt, David, 'Cartwright, Edmund (1743–1823), Church of England clergyman and inventor of a power loom', *ODNB*, online version (2015). https://www.oxforddnb.com/view/10.1093/ref:odnb/9780198614128.001.0001/odnb-9780198614128-e-4813

Hunt, J., *Religious thought in England from the Reformation to the end of the last century* (3 vols., London, 1870–3).

Hunt, Lynn, Margaret C. Jacob, and Wijnand Mijnhardt, eds., *The book that changed Europe. Picart & Bernard's religious ceremonies of the world* (Cambridge, MA, 2010).

724 BIBLIOGRAPHY

Hunt, Margaret R., *Women in eighteenth-century Europe* (Harlow, 2010).
Hunt, William, 'Browne, Joseph (1700–1767), college head', rev. S. J. Skedd, *ODNB*, online version (2004). https://www.oxforddnb.com/view/10.1093/ref:odnb/9780198614128.001.0001/odnb-9780198614128-e-3685
Hunter, Ian, *Rival Enlightenments: civil and metaphysical philosophy in early modern Germany* (Cambridge, 2001).
Hunter, Michael, *John Aubrey and the world of learning* (London, 1975).
Hunter, Michael, *Science and society in Restoration England* (Cambridge, 1981).
Hunter, Michael, *Establishing the new science: the experience of the early Royal Society* (Woodbridge, 1989).
Hunter, Michael, *Science and the shape of Orthodoxy: intellectual change in late seventeenth-century Britain* (Woodbridge, 1995).
Hunter, Michael, *Boyle: between God and science* (New Haven, CT, 2009).
Hunter, Paul, *Before novels: the cultural contexts of eighteenth-century English fiction* (New York, 1992).
Hutton, R., *Charles II. King of England, Scotland, and Ireland* (Oxford, 1989).
Hylson-Smith, K., *Evangelicals in the Church of England, 1734–1984* (Edinburgh, 1988).
Ihalainen, Pasi, 'The Enlightenment sermon: towards practical religion and a sacred national community', in Joris Van Eijnatten, ed., *Preaching, sermon and cultural change in the long eighteenth century* (Leiden, 2009), 219–60.
Ihalainen, Pasi, 'The sermon, court, and Parliament, 1689–1789', in K. Francis and W. Gibson, eds., *Oxford handbook of the British sermon 1689–1901*, 229–44.
Ilchester, Earl of, *Lord Hervey and his friends* (London, 1950).
Iliffe, Rob, 'Philosophy of science', in R. Porter, ed., *Eighteenth-century science* (*Cambridge history of science*, Vol. 4) (Cambridge, 2003), 267–84.
Impey, O. and A. MacGregor, eds., *The origins of museums. The cabinet of curiosities in sixteenth- and seventeenth-century Europe* (Oxford, 1985).
Ingamells, John, ed., *A Dictionary of British and Irish travellers in Italy 1701–1800* (compiled from the Brinsley Ford Archive) (New Haven, CT, 1997).
Ingram, Robert G., 'William Warburton, divine action, and Enlightened Christianity', in W. Gibson and R. Ingram, eds., *Religious identities in Britain, 1660–1832*, 97–117.
Ingram, Robert G., *Religion, reform and modernity in the eighteenth century: Thomas Secker and the Church of England* (Woodbridge, 2007).
Ingram, Robert G., *Reformation without end. Religion, politics and the past in post-Revolutionary England* (Manchester, 2018).
Innes, J., 'Politics and morals: the reformation of manners movement in later eighteenth-century England', in E. Hellmuth, ed., *The transformation of political culture*, 57–118.
Isaac, Rhys, *The transformation of Virginia 1740–1790* (Chapel Hill, NC, 1982).
Israel, Jonathan, *Radical Enlightenment. Philosophy and the making of modernity 1650–1750* (Oxford, 2001).
Israel, Jonathan, *Democratic Enlightenment. philosophy, revolution, and human rights 1750–1790* (Oxford, 2012).
Jackson, Clare, 'The later Stuart church as "national church" in Scotland and Ireland', in G. Tapsell, ed., *The later Stuart Church*, 127–49.
Jacob, Margaret C., *The Secular Enlightenment* (Princeton, NJ, 2019).
Jacob, Margaret C., *The Newtonians and the English Revolution, 1689–1720* (London, 1976).
Jacob, W. M., *The clerical profession in the long eighteenth century, 1680–1840* (Oxford, 2007).
James, F. G., *Lords of the ascendancy. The Irish House of Lords and its members 1600–1800* (Dublin, 1995).

BIBLIOGRAPHY 725

Jarick, J., ed., *Sacred Conjectures: The Context and Legacy of Robert Lowth and Jean Astruc* (New York, 2007).

Jay, M., *The atmosphere of heaven: the unusual experiments of Dr Beddoes and his sons of genius* (New Haven, CT, 2009).

Jenkins, G. H., *The foundations of modern Wales 1642–1780* (Oxford, 1993).

Jenkins, J. G., *The dragon of Whaddon, being an account of the life and work of Browne Willis (1682–1760). Antiquary and historian* (High Wycombe, 1953).

Jenkins, Philip, *The making of a ruling class. The Glamorgan gentry 1640–1790* (Cambridge, 1983).

Jenkins, Philip, 'The Anglican Church and the unity of Britain: the Welsh experience, 1560–1714', in S. Ellis and S. Barber, eds., *Conquest & union. Fashioning a British state 1485–1725* (Harlow, 1995), 115–38.

Johnson, Joan, *Princely Chandos. James Brydges 1674–1744* (Stroud, 1984).

Johnson, J. W., *The formation of English Neo-Classical thought* (Princeton, NJ, 1967).

Johnson, Margot, 'Talbot, William (1659–1730), bishop of Durham', *ODNB*, online version (2004). https://www.oxforddnb.com/view/10.1093/ref:odnb/9780198614128.001.0001/odnb-9780198614128-e-26945

Johnston, Kenneth R., *Unusual suspects. Pitt's reign of alarm & the lost generation of the 1790s* (Oxford, 2013).

Johnstone, H. Diack, 'Music and drama at the Oxford Act of 1713', in S. Wollenberg and S. McVeigh, eds., *Concert life in eighteenth-century Britain* (Aldershot, 2004), 199–218.

Jones, C., '"Venice preserv'd; or a plot discovered": the political and social context of the peerage bill of 1719', in C. Jones, ed., *A pillar of the Constitution: the House of Lords in British politics, 1640–1784* (London, 1989), 79–112.

Jones, George Hilton, *The main stream of Jacobitism* (Cambridge, MA, 1954).

Jones, John, *Balliol College. A history, 1263–1939* (2nd edn., Oxford, 1988).

Jones, P. M., *Industrial Enlightenment: science, technology and culture in Birmingham and the West Midlands 1760–1820* (Manchester, 2013).

Jupp, Peter, *Lord Grenville 1759–1834* (Oxford, 1985).

Jüttner, Siegfried, and Jochen Schlobach, eds., *Europäische Aufklärung (en). Einheit und nationale Vielfalt* (Hamburg, 1992).

Kadushin, C., *Understanding social networks: theories, concepts, and findings* (Oxford, 2012).

Kahn, D., *The codebreakers: the comprehensive history of secret communication from ancient times to the Internet* (London, 1996).

Katz, D. S., 'Moses's *Principia*: Hutchinsonianism and Newton's Critics', in J.E. Force and R.H. Popkin, eds., *The books of nature and scripture: recent essays on natural philosophy, theology and Biblical criticism in the Netherlands of Spinoza's time and the British Isles of Newton's time* (Dordrecht, 1994), 201–11.

Kearney, H., *Scholars and gentlemen. Universities and societies in pre-industrial Britain 1500–1700* (London, 1970).

Keevak, M., *The pretended Asian: George Psalmanazar's eighteenth century Formosan hoax* (Detroit, MI, 2004).

Kellenbenz, H., 'German immigrants', in C. Holmes, ed., *Immigrants and minorities in British society* (London, 1978), 63–80.

Kelly, J.N.D., *St Edmund Hall. Almost seven hundred years* (Oxford, 1989).

Kelly, James, *Henry Flood. Patriots and politics in eighteenth-century Ireland* (Dublin, 1998).

Kemp, Betty, *Sir Francis Dashwood: an eighteenth-century independent* (London, 1957).

726   BIBLIOGRAPHY

Kennedy, Deborah, *Poetic sisters. Early eighteenth-century women poets* (Lewisburg, PA, 2013).

Kennedy, G., 'Adam Smith on religion', in C.J. Berry, M. P. Paganelli, and C. Smith, eds., *The Oxford handbook of Adam Smith* (Oxford, 2013), online version. https://academic.oup.com/edited-volume/38582

Kent, John, *Wesley and the Wesleyans: religion in eighteenth-century Britain* (Cambridge, 2002).

Kenyon, J. P., *Revolution principles. The politics of party 1689–1720* (Cambridge, 1977).

Kenyon, J. P., *The history men: the historical profession in England since the Renaissance* (2nd edn., London, 1983).

Ketton-Cremer, R. W., *Humphrey Prideaux* (Norwich, 1955).

Kidd, C., *Subverting Scotland's past. Scottish Whig historians and the creation of an Anglo-British identity, 1689–c.1830* (Cambridge, 1993).

Kilburn, Matthew, 'The Fell Legacy 1686–1755', in ed. Gadd, *The History of Oxford University Press,* 1. 107–38.

Kilburn, Matthew, 'The Blackstone Reforms 1755–1780', in ed. Gadd, *The History of Oxford University Press,* 1. 139–58.

Kirwan, Richard, ed., *Scholarly self-fashioning in the early modern university* (Farnham, 2013).

Kitromilides, Paschalis M., ed., *Adamantios Korais and the European Enlightenment* (Oxford, 2010).

Knight, Frida, *University rebel. The life of William Frend* (London, 1971).

Knight, Roger, *Britain against Napoleon. The organization of victory 1793–1815* (Harmondsworth, 2013).

Knights, Mark, ed., *Representation and misrepresentation in later Stuart Britain. Partisanship and political culture* (Oxford, 2005).

Knights, Mark, ed., *Faction displayed: reconsidering the impeachment of Dr Henry Sacheverell* (London, 2012).

Knox-Shaw, H., J. Jackson, and W. H. Robinson, *The observations of the Reverend Thomas Hornsby, DD* (Oxford, 1932).

Kowaleski-Wallace, Beth, 'Two anomalous women: Elizabeth Carter and Catherine Talbot', in F.M. Keener and S. E. Lorsch, eds., *Eighteenth-century women and the arts* (Westport, CT, 1988), 19–27.

Kramnick, Jonathan Brod, *Making the English canon: print-capitalism and the cultural past, 1700–1770* (Cambridge, 1999).

Kroll, R., *The material world: literate culture in the Restoration and early eighteenth century* (Baltimore, MD, 1991).

Kubrin, D., 'John Keill', in Charles C. Gillespie, ed.-in-chief, *Dictionary of scientific biography* (16 vols., New York, 1970–80), VII, 275–7.

Kurtz, D. C., *The reception of classical art in Britain: An Oxford story of plaster casts from the antique* (Oxford, 2000).

Lacey, Andrew, *The cult of King Charles the Martyr* (Woodbridge, 2003).

Lalor, Stephen, *Matthew Tindal, freethinker. An eighteenth-century assault on religion* (London, 2006).

Landau, Norma, *The Justices of the Peace 1679–1769* (Berkeley, CA, and London, 1984).

Landon, H. C. Robbins, *Haydn: chronicle and works* (5 vols., London, 1976–80), III. *Haydn in England 1791–1795.*

Langford, Paul, 'Tories and Jacobites 1714–1751', in *HUO* V, 107–22.

Langford, Paul, *A polite and commercial people. England 1727–1783* (Oxford, 1989).

Langford, Paul, 'The English clergy and the American Revolution', in E. Hellmuth, ed., *The transformation of political culture: England and Germany in the late eighteenth century* (Oxford, 1990), 275–308.

Langford, Paul, *Public life and the propertied Englishman 1689–1798* (Oxford, 1991).

Langford, Paul, *Englishness identified. Manners and characters 1650–1850* (Oxford, 2000).

Lathbury, Thomas, *A History of the Convocation of the Church of England* (2nd edn., London, 1853).

Leask, Ian, 'The undivulged event in Toland's Christianity Not Mysterious', in Hudson, W., D. Lucci, and J. R. Wigelsworth, eds., *Atheism and deism revalued. Heterodox religious identities in Britain, 1650–1850* (Farnham, 2014), 63–80.

Ledger, A. P., *A Spencer love affair. eighteenth-century theatricals at Blenheim Palace and beyond* (Fonthill, 2014).

Le Fanu, W. R., *Queen Anne's bounty, a short account of its history and works* (London, 1921).

Legaspi, Michael C., *The death of scripture and the rise of Biblical studies* (New York, 2010).

Lenman, B., *The Jacobite Risings in Britain 1689–1746* (London, 1980).

Lepper, Charles, *The Crypt School Gloucester 1539–1989* (Gloucester, 1989).

Leppert, R., *Music and image. Domesticity, ideology and socio-cultural formation in eighteenth-century England* (Cambridge, 1988).

Lessenich, Rolf P., *Elements of pulpit oratory in eighteenth-century England* (Cologne, 1972).

Levine, A., ed., *Early modern skepticism and the origins of toleration* (Lanham, MD, 1999).

Levine, Joseph M., *Dr Woodward's shield. History, science, and satire in Augustan England* (Berkeley, CA, 1977).

Levine, Joseph M., *The battle of the books: history and literature in the Augustan age* (Ithaca, NY, 1991).

Levitin, D., *Ancient wisdom in the age of the new science: histories of philosophy in England, c.1640–1700* (Cambridge, 2016).

Lewis, B., 'Gibbon on Muhammad', in G.W. Bowerstock, J. Clive, and S. R. Graubaud, eds., *Edward Gibbon and the decline and fall of the Roman Empire* (Cambridge, MA., 1977), 61–73.

Lewis, J. Saunders, *A school of Welsh Augustans, Being a study in English influences on Welsh literature during part of the 18th century* (Wrexham/London, 1924).

Lewis, L., *Connoisseurs and secret agents in eighteenth century Rome* (London, 1961).

Lilti, Antoine, *The world of the salons. Sociability and worldliness in eighteenth-century Paris,* trans. Lydia G. Cochrane (Oxford, 2015).

Lim, Paul C. H., *The crisis of the Trinity in early modern England* (Oxford, 2012).

Lincoln, A., *Some political and social ideas of English Dissent, 1763–1800* (Cambridge, 1938).

Little, Bryan, *James Gibbs 1682–1754* (London, 1955).

Littleton, C. G. D., 'Ancient languages and new science: the Levant in the intellectual life of Robert Boyle', in A. Hamilton, M. H. van den Boogert, and B. Westerweel, eds., *The republic of letters and the Levant* (Leiden, 2005), 151–71.

Livesey, James, *Civil society and empire. Ireland and Scotland in the eighteenth-century Atlantic world* (Yale, CT, 2009).

Lloyd, D. J., *Country grammar school: history of Ludlow Grammar School* (Ludlow, 1977).

Lockmiller, D. A., *Sir William Blackstone* (Chapel Hill, NC, 1938).

Lonsdale, Roger, ed., *Dr Charles Burney. A literary biography* (Oxford, 1965).

Lonsdale, Roger, ed., *Eighteenth-century women poets* (Oxford, 1990).

728 BIBLIOGRAPHY

Loudon, Jean, 'Frewin, Richard (1680/1–1761)', *ODNB*, online version (2008). https://www.oxforddnb.com/view/10.1093/ref:odnb/9780198614128.001.0001/odnb-9780198614128-e-10182

Lowther Clarke, W.K., *Eighteenth Century Piety* (London, 1944).

Luce, J. V., *Trinity College, Dublin. The first 400 years* (Dublin, 1992).

Lyles, Albert M., *Methodism mocked: the satiric reaction to Methodism in the eighteenth century* (London, 1960).

Lynall, Gregory, *Swift and science. The satire, politics, and theology of natural knowledge, 1690–1730* (Basingstoke, 2012).

Lynch, Deidre Shauna, *Loving literature. A cultural history* (Chicago, IL, 2015).

Lyons, Sir Henry, *The Royal Society, 1660–1940: a history of its administrations under its charters* (Cambridge, 1944).

Mabey, Richard, *Gilbert White: a biography of the author of the Natural History of Selborne* (London, 1986).

McAdoo, H.R., *The spirit of Anglicanism: a survey of Anglican theological method in the seventeenth century* (London, 1965).

MacGregor, A., *Tradescant's Rarities: essays on the foundation of the Ashmolean Museum 1683, with a catalogue of the surviving early collections* (Oxford, 1983).

MacGregor, A., and A. J. Turner, 'The Ashmolean Museum', in *HUO* V, 639–58.

Mack, E. C., *Public schools and British opinion 1780 to 1880* (London, 1938).

Mack, Maynard, *Alexander Pope. A life* (New Haven, CT, 1985).

Mackail, J. W., *Henry Birkhead and the foundation of the Oxford Chair of Poetry* (Oxford, 1908).

Macleane, Douglas, *Pembroke College* (London, 1900).

McClain, Molly, *Beaufort: the Duke and his Duchess, 1657–1715* (New Haven, CT, 2001).

McClatchey, Diana, *Oxfordshire clergy 1777–1869* (Oxford, 1960).

McCleelan, J., *Science reorganized: scientific societies in the eighteenth century* (New York, 1985).

McClelland, Charles E., *State, society, and university in Germany 1700–1914* (Cambridge, 1980).

McClelland, J. C., *Autocrats and academics. Education and culture in Tsarist Russia* (Chicago, IL, 1979).

Macleod, Emma Vincent, *A war of ideas. British attitudes to the wars against revolutionary France, 1792–1802* (Aldershot, 1998).

McCracken, Charles J., *Malebranche and British philosophy* (Oxford, 1983).

McDowell, R. B., and D. A. Webb, *Trinity College Dublin 1592–1952. An academic history* (Cambridge, 1982).

McGrath, Alistair, *In the beginning. The story of the King James Bible and how it changed a nation, a language and a culture* (London, 2001).

McInelly, Brett C., 'Whitefield and his critics', in G. Hammond and D. Ceri Jones, eds., *George Whitefield*, 150–66.

McKelvey, J. L., *George III and Lord Bute: the Leicester House years* (Durham, NC, 1973).

McKitterick, David, 'Wantonness and use. Ambitions for research libraries in early eighteenth-century England', in R. G. W. Anderson, M. L. Caygill, A. G. MacGregor, and L. Syson, eds., *Enlightening the British: knowledge, discovery and the museum in the eighteenth century* (London, 2003), 37–48.

McLynn, F., *Charles Edward Stuart. A tragedy in many acts* (London, 1988).

McMahon, D., *Enemies of the Enlightenment: the French Counter-Enlightenment and the making of modernity* (New York, 2001).

McManners, John, *Church and society in eighteenth-century France* (2 vols., Oxford, 1998).

McManners, John, *All Souls and the Shipley case* (Oxford, 2001).

McManners, John, 'Bishop Heber and early nineteenth-century churchmanship', in S. Green and P. Horden, eds., *All Souls under the Ancien Régime*, 324–40.

Makrides, V.N., 'Greek Orthodox compensatory strategies towards Anglicans and the West at the beginning of the eighteenth century', in ed. P. Doll, *Anglicanism and Orthodoxy 300 years after the 'Greek College' in Oxford* (Oxford, 2006), 249–88.

Malcolm, Noel, 'The study of Islam in early modern Europe: obstacles and missed opportunities', in P. Miller and F. Louis, eds., *Antiquarianism and intellectual life in Europe and China, 1500-1800* (Ann Arbor, MI, 2012), 265–88.

Malcolmson, A. P. W., *Archbishop Charles Agar: churchmanship and politics in Ireland, 1760-1810* (Dublin, 2002).

Malcolmson, A. P. W., *Primate Robinson 1709-94: 'a very tough incumbent in fine preservation'* (Belfast, 2003).

Mandelbrote, Scott, 'The Bible and national identity in the British Isles, c.1650–c.1750', in T. Claydon and I. McBride, eds., *Protestantism and national identity. Britain and Ireland, c.1650–c.1850* (Cambridge, 1998), 157–81.

Mandelbrote, Scott, 'The Bible and its readers in the eighteenth century', in Isabel Rivers, ed., *Books and their readers in eighteenth-century England: new essays* (London, 2001), 35–78.

Mandelbrote, Scott, *Footprints of the lion. Isaac Newton at work* (Cambridge, 2001).

Mandelbrote, Scott, 'Eighteenth-century reactions to Newton's anti-Trinitarianism', in J.E. Force and S. Hutton, eds., *Newton and Newtonianism. New studies* (Dordrecht, 2004), 93–111.

Mandelbrote, Scott, 'Robert Clavering (1675/6-1747), orientalist and Bishop of Peterborough', *ODNB*, online version (2004). https://www.oxforddnb.com/view/10.1093/ref:odnb/9780198614128.001.0001/odnb-9780198614128-e-5554

Mandelbrote, Scott, 'Pierre Des Mizeaux: history, toleration, and scholarship', in C. Ligota and J.-L. Quantin, eds., *History of scholarship: a selection of papers from the seminar on the history of scholarship held annually at the Warburg Institute* (Oxford, 2006), 385–98.

Mandelbrote, Scott, 'The Vision of Christopher Codrington', in S. Green and P. Hordern, eds., *All Souls under the ancien régime* (Oxford, 2007), 132–74.

Mandelbrote, Scott, 'Biblical scholarship at Oxford in the mid-eighteenth century: Local contexts for Robert Lowth's *De sacra poesi hebraeorum* (1753)', in John Jarrick, ed., *Sacred conjectures: the context and legacy of Robert Lowth and Jean Atruc* (New York/London, 2007), 3–24.

Mandelbrote, Scott, 'Early Modern Natural Theologies', in Russell Manning with J.H. Brooke and Fraser Watts, eds., *Oxford Handbook of Natural Theology* (Oxford, 2013), 75–99.

Mandelbrote, Scott, 'Fatio, Nicolas, of Duillier (1664-1753), mathematician and natural philosopher', *ODNB*, online version (2016). https://www.oxforddnb.com/view/10.1093/ref:odnb/9780198614128.001.0001/odnb-9780198614128-e-9056

Manning, Bernard Lord, *The Protestant Dissenting deputies*, O. Greenwood, ed., (Cambridge, 1952).

Manning, J. A., *The lives of the Speakers of the House of Commons...* (London, 1851).

Mansbridge, Albert, *The Older Universities of England. Oxford & Cambridge* (London, 1923).

Mansfield, Andrew, *Ideas of monarchical reform. Fénelon, Jacobitism and the political works of the Chevalier Ramsay* (Manchester, 2015).

730 BIBLIOGRAPHY

Mant, R., *History of the Church of Ireland from the Reformation to the revolution . . .* (2 vols., London, 1840).

Manuel, Frank E., *The religion of Isaac Newton* [The Fremantle Lectures 1973] (Oxford, 1974).

Marchant, E. C., 'Upton, James (1671–1749), Church of England clergyman', rev. S. J. Skedd, *ODNB*, online version (2008). https://www.oxforddnb.com/view/10.1093/ref:odnb/9780198614128.001.0001/odnb-9780198614128-e-28009

Marcombe, D. and C. S. Knighton, eds., *Close encounters: English cathedrals and society since 1540* (Nottingham, 1991).

Markham, Felix, *Oxford* (London, 1967).

Markham, Sarah, *John Loveday of Caversham 1711–1789. The life and tours of an eighteenth-century onlooker* (Salisbury, 1984)

Marshall, Ashley, *The Practice of satire in England 1658–1770* (Baltimore, MD, 2013).

Marshall, D., *The rise of George Canning* (London, 1938).

Marshall, E., *The early history of Woodstock Manor and its environs* (Oxford, 1873).

Marshall, John, *John Locke, resistance, religion and responsibility* (Cambridge, 1994).

Marshall, John, 'Locke, Socinianism, "Socinianism" and Unitarianism', in M. A. Stewart, ed., *English Philosophy in the Age of Locke* (Oxford, 2000), 111–82.

Marshall, John, *John Locke, toleration and early Enlightenment culture* (Cambridge, 2006).

Marshall, P. J., 'Warren Hastings as scholar and patron', in A. Whiteman, J. S. Bromley, and P. G. M. Dickson, eds., *Statesmen, scholars, and merchants: essays in eighteenth-century history presented to Dame Lucy Sutherland* (Oxford, 1973), 242–62.

Marshall, P.J., 'Oriental studies', *HUO* V, 551–64.

Marshall, P. J., *The making and unmaking of empires. Britain, India, and America c.1750–1783* (Oxford, 2005).

Marshall, P. J. and G. Williams, *The great map of mankind. British perceptions of the world in the age of Enlightenment* (London, 1982).

Marshall, W. M., *George Hooper 1640–1727 Bishop of Bath and Wells* (Milborne Port, 1976).

Marshall, W. M., 'The Dioceses of Hereford and Oxford, 1660–1760', in J. Gregory and J. S. Chamberlain, eds., *The national Church in local perspective. The Church of England and the regions, 1660–1800* (Woodbridge, 2003), 197–221.

Marshall, W. M., *Church life in Hereford and Oxford 1660–1760. A study of two sees* (Lancaster, 2009).

Martin, G.H., and J.R.L. Highfield, *A history of Merton College, Oxford* (Oxford, 1997).

Martin-Jones, David, *Conscience and allegiance in seventeenth-century England,: the political significance of oaths and engagements* (Rochester, NY, 1999).

Mather, F. C., *High Church prophet. Bishop Samuel Horsley (1733–1806) and the Caroline tradition in the later Georgian Church* (Oxford, 1992).

Matytsin, Anton M., 'Whose light is it anyway? The struggle for light in the French Enlightenment', in Anton M. Matytsin and Dan Edelstein, eds., *Let there be Enlightenment. The religious and mystical sources of rationality* (Baltimore, MD, 2018), 62–85.

Mauss, M., *The gift: the form and reason for exchange in archaic societies*, trans. W. D. Halls (London, 1990).

May, James E., 'Young, Edward (bap. 1683, d. 1765)', *ODNB*, online version (2015). https://www.oxforddnb.com/view/10.1093/ref:odnb/9780198614128.001.0001/odnb-9780198614128-e-30260

Mayhew, R., 'Gibbon's geographies', in Karen O'Brien and Brian Young, eds., *The Cambridge companion to Edward Gibbon* (Cambridge, 2018), 41–61.

Mayhew, R., *Enlightenment geography: the political languages of British geography, 1650–1850* (London, 2000).

BIBLIOGRAPHY 731

Mayo, T.F., *Epicurus in England (1650–1725)* (Dallas, TX, 1934).

Mee, J. H., *The oldest music room in Europe: a record of eighteenth-century enterprise at Oxford* (London, 1911).

Melville, Lewis, *The life and writings of Philip Duke of Wharton* (London, 1913).

Mendyk, Stan A. E., *'Speculum Britanniae'. Regional study, Antiquarianism, and science in Britain to 1700* (Toronto, 1989).

Mercer, C., 'The vitality and importance of early modern Aristotelianism', in T. Sorell, ed., *The rise of modern philosophy. The tension between the new and traditional philosophies from Machiavelli to Leibniz* (Oxford, 1993), 33–67.

Middleton, R.D., *Dr Routh* (Oxford, 1938).

Midgley, Graham, *University life in eighteenth-century Oxford* (New Haven and London, 1996).

Miller, John, *Cities divided: politics and religion in English provincial towns, 1660–1722* (Oxford, 2007).

Mills, F. S., *Bishops by ballot. An eighteenth-century ecclesiastical revolution* (New York, 1978).

Minowitz, P., *Profits, priests and princes. Adam Smith's emancipation of economics from politics and religion* (Stanford, CA, 1993).

Mitchell, L.G., 'Politics and Revolution 1772-1800', in *HUO* V, 163–90.

Mitchell, L.G., *Charles James Fox* (Oxford, 1992).

Mitchison, R., *Agricultural Sir John. The life of Sir John Sinclair of Ulbster 1754–1835* (London, 1962).

Money, D. K, *The English Horace: Anthony Alsop and the tradition of British Latin Verse* (London, 1998).

Money, D. K, 'Free flattery or servile tribute? Oxford and Cambridge commemorative poetry in the seventeenth and eighteenth centuries', in J. Raven, ed., *Free print and non-commercial publishing since 1700* (Aldershot, 2000), 48–66.

Money, D. K, 'The Latin Poetry of English gentlemen', in L. B. T. Houghton and G. Manuwald, eds., *Neo-Latin poetry in the British Isles* (London, 2012), 125–41.

Monod, P., *Jacobitism and the English people 1688–1788* (Cambridge, 1989).

Monod, P., 'A voyage out of Staffordshire', in J.C.D. Clarke and H. Erskine-Hill, eds., *Samuel Johnson in historical context*, 11–43.

Montluzin, Emily Lorraine de, *The Anti-Jacobins, 1798–1800: the early contributors to the Anti-Jacobin review* (Basingstoke, 1987).

Moore, James, Ian Macgregor Morris, and Andrew Bayliss, eds., *Reinventing history. The Enlightenment origins of ancient history* (London, 2008).

Moore, Norman, 'Austin, William (1754–1793), physician', rev. Claire L. Nutt, *ODNB*, online version (2004). https://www.oxforddnb.com/view/10.1093/ref:odnb/9780198614128.001. 0001/odnb-9780198614128-e-919

Morgan, Victor, 'Cambridge University and "The Country" 1560–1600', in Stone et al., eds., *The University in Society*, Vol. 1, 183–246.

Morgan, Victor, [with a contribution by C. Brooke], *A history of the University of Cambridge*, Vol. 2, *1546–1750* (Cambridge, 2004).

Mori, J., *William Pitt and the French Revolution 1785–1795* (Edinburgh, 1997).

Morris, Marilyn, *The British monarchy and the French Revolution* (New Haven, CT, and London, 1998).

Morris, Peter J. T., 'The eighteenth century: chemistry allied to anatomy', in R. J. P. Williams, A. Chapman, and J. S. Rowlinson, eds., *Chemistry at Oxford. A history from 1600 to 2005* (London, 2009), 52–78.

Morris, Peter J. T., *The matter factory. A history of the chemical laboratory* (London, 2015).

732 BIBLIOGRAPHY

Mortier, Roland, *Clartés et ombres du siècle des Lumières: études sur le XVIIIe siècle littéraire* (Geneva, 1969).

Mortimer, S., 'Great Tew circle (*act.* 1633–1639)', *ODNB*, online edn., 2007.

Mortimer, S., *Reason and religion in the English Revolution* (Cambridge, 2010).

Mossner, E. C., *Bishop Butler and the Age of Reason* (London, 1936, repr. Bristol, 1990).

Murray, A., ed., *Sir William Jones 1746–1794: A commemoration* (Oxford, 1998).

Myers, Robin, 'Dr Andrew Coltée Ducarel (1713–1785): a pioneer of Anglo-Norman studies', in Robin Myers and M. Harris, eds., *Antiquaries, book collectors and the circles of learning* (Winchester, 1996), 45–70.

Myers, Sylvia Harcstark, *The bluestocking circle. Women, friendship, and the life of the mind in eighteenth-century England* (Oxford, 1990).

Nenadic, Stana, *Lairds and luxury. The Highland gentry in eighteenth-century Scotland* (Edinburgh, 2007).

Neufeld, M., *The Civil Wars after 1660: public remembering in late Stuart England* (Woodbridge, 2013).

Neveu, Bruno, *Erudition et religion au xvii et xviii siècles* (Paris, 1994).

Newman, Aubrey, *The Stanhopes of Chevening. A family biography* (London, 1969).

Newman, Steve, '"The maiden's bloody garland": Thomas Warton and the elite appropriation of popular song', in P. Fumerton, A. Guerrini, and K. McAbee, eds., *Ballads and broadsides in Britain, 1500–1800* (Farnham, 2010), 189–205.

Nias, J. B., *Dr John Radcliffe: a sketch of his life with an account of his fellows and foundations* (Oxford, 1918).

Nicholson, Eirwen E. C., 'Sacheverell's harlots: non-resistance on paper and in practice', in M. Knights, ed., *Faction displayed*, 69–79.

Nicholson, E., 'Eveleigh and Copleston: the pre-eminence of Oriel', in J. Catto, ed., *Oriel College*, 247–90.

Nicolson, Marjorie, and Nora M. Mohler, 'The scientific background of Swift's "Voyage to Laputa"', in A. Norman Jeffares, ed., *Fair Liberty was all his cry. A tercentenary tribute to Jonathan Swift 1667–1745* (London, 1967), 226–70.

Nockles, P. B., *The Oxford Movement in context: Anglican High Churchmanship 1760–1857* (Cambridge, 1996).

Nockles, P.B., '"Lost causes and ... impossible loyalties": the Oxford Movement and the University', in HUO VI, 195–268.

Nockles, P.B., 'Oriel and Religion', in ed., Catto, ed., *Oriel College*, 291–327.

Norgate, G. Le G., 'Milles, Thomas (1671–1740), Church of Ireland Bishop of Waterford and Lismore', rev. Julian C. Walton, *ODNB*, online version (2004). https://www.oxforddnb.com/view/10.1093/ref:odnb/9780198614128.001.0001/odnb-9780198614128-e-18754

Norton, David, *A history of the Bible as literature* (2 vols., Cambridge, 1993).

Norton, David, *The King James Bible. A short history from Tyndale to today* (Cambridge, 2010).

Nouvo, Victor, 'Locke's theology', in M.A. Stewart, ed., *English philosophy in the age of Locke* (Oxford, 2000), 183–215.

Nuttall, G. F., *Philip Doddridge, 1702–51: his contribution to English religion* (London, 1951).

Oates, J., *Jacobitism in eighteenth century English schools and colleges* [The Royal Stuart Society, Paper LXXII] (London, 2007).

O'Brien, Karen, 'The history market in eighteenth-century England', in Isabel Rivers, ed., *Books and their readers in eighteenth-century England: new essays* (London, 2001), 105–34.

O Ciardha, Eamon, *Ireland and the Jacobite Cause, 1685–1766. A fatal attachment* (Dublin, 2004).

Ogilvie, R. M., *Latin and Greek: a history of the influence of the classics on English life from 1600 to 1918* (London, 1964).

O'Gorman, Frank, *The Whig Party and the French Revolution* (London, 1974).

O'Gorman, Frank, *Voters, patrons and parties. The unreformed electorate of Hanoverian England, 1734–1832* (Oxford, 1989).

O'Gorman, Frank, 'Pitt and the Tory reaction to the French Revolution, 1789–1815', in H. T. Dickinson, ed., *Britain and the French Revolution, 1789–1815* (Basingstoke, 1989), 21–37.

Okie, L., *Augustan historical writing: histories of England in the English Enlightenment* (Lanham, NY, and London, 1991).

Ollard, R., *Clarendon and his friends* (Oxford, 1988).

Ollard, S. L., *The six students of St Edmund Hall* (Oxford, 1911).

Olson, Mark K., 'Whitefield's Early Theological Formation', in G. Hammond and D. Ceri Jones, eds., *George Whitefield*, 29–45.

Olson, Richard, 'Tory-High Church opposition to science and scientism in the eighteenth century: the works of John Arbuthnott, Jonathan Swift, and Samuel Johnson', in John G. Burke, ed.,, *The uses of science in the age of Newton* (Berkeley, CA, 1983), 171–204.

O'Neill, Lindsay, *The opened letter. Networking in the early modern British world* (Philadelphia, PA, 2015).

Oslington, P., ed., *Adam Smith as theologian* (London & New York, 2011).

Ousby, Ian, *The Englishman's England. Taste, travel and the rise of tourism* (London, 2000).

Ovenell, R. F., *The Ashmolean Museum, 1683–1894* (Oxford, 1986).

Overton, J. H., *History of the Nonjurors* (London, 1902).

Owen, J. B., *The rise of the Pelhams* (London, 1957).

Oxfordshire County Council, *The Oxfordshire Election of 1754*, Record Publication No. 6 (Oxford, 1970).

Palmer, Bernard, *Serving two masters. Parish patronage in the Church of England since 1714* (Lewes, 2003).

Palmer, Thomas, *Jansenism and England. Moral Rigorism across the Confessions* (Oxford, 2018).

Panayi, P., ed., *Germans in Britain since 1500* (London, 1996).

Pantin, W. A., *Oxford life in Oxford archives* (Oxford, 1972).

Pares, Richard, *King George III and the politicians* (Oxford, 1953).

Parker, M. F., *Scattered notices of Shirburn Castle, Oxfordshire* (London, 1887).

Parrish, David, *Jacobitism and anti-Jacobitism in the British Atlantic world 1688–1727* (London, 2017).

Partington, G. and Adam Smyth, eds., *Book destruction from the medieval to the contemporary* (Basingstoke, 2014).

Patterson, D., 'Hebrew Studies', in *HUO* V, 535–50.

Patterson, M. W., *Sir Francis Burdett and his times* (2 vols., London, 1931).

Paulson, R., *Rowlandson. A new interpretation* (London, 1972).

Pearson, J. B., *A biographical sketch of the chaplains to the Levant Company, maintained at Constantinople, Aleppo and Smyrna, 1611–1706* (Cambridge, 1883).

Pécharman, Martine, 'From Lockean logic to Cartesian(ised) logic: the case of Locke's <u>Essay</u> and its contemporary controversial reception', in P. Bullard and A. Tadié, eds., *Ancients and moderns in Europe*, 73–95.

Perraton, H., *A history of foreign students in Britain* (Basingstoke, 2014).

734   BIBLIOGRAPHY

Perry, R., *Novel relations: the transformation of kinship in English literature and culture 1748-1818* (Cambridge, 2004).

Perry, T. W., *Public opinion, propaganda, and politics in eighteenth-century England. A study of the Jewish Naturalization Act of 1753* (Cambridge, MA, 1962).

Petrie, Sir Charles, *George Canning* (London, 1946).

Petter, H. M., *The Oxford almanacks* (Oxford, 1974).

Philip, Ian, *Oxford libraries outside the Bodleian* (Oxford, 1973).

Philip, Ian, *The Bodleian library in the seventeenth and eighteenth centuries* (Oxford, 1983).

Phillips, Mark Salber, *Society and sentiment. Genres of historical writing in Britain, 1740-1820* (Princeton, NJ, 2000).

Phillipson, Nicholas, *Adam Smith. An enlightened life* (Harmondsworth, 2010).

Phillipson, N., 'The Making of an Enlightened University', in Robert D. Anderson, Michael Lynch, and Nicholas Phillipson, *The University of Edinburgh: an illustrated history* (Edinburgh, 2003), 51-102.

Philp, M., ed., *The French Revolution and British popular politics* (Cambridge, 1991).

Piggott, S., *William Stukeley* (Oxford, 1950).

Piggott, S., 'Antiquarian studies', in *HUO* V, 757-78.

Pinckney, Charles Cotesworth, *Life of General Thomas Pinckney* (Boston, MA,/New York, 1895).

Pincus, S., *1688. The first modern revolution* (New Haven, CT, 2009).

Pinnington, J., *Anglicans and Orthodox. Unity and subversion 1559-1725* (Leominster, 2003).

Pittock, Joan, *The ascendancy of taste. The achievement of Joseph and Thomas Warton* (London, 1973).

Pittock, Murray, *Poetry and Jacobite politics in eighteenth-century Britain and Ireland* (Cambridge, 1994).

Pittock, Murray, *Inventing and resisting Britain. Cultural identities in Britain and Ireland 1685-1789* (Basingstoke, 1997).

Pittock, Murray, 'The culture of Jacobitism', in J. Black, ed., *Culture and society in Britain, 1660-1800* (Manchester, 1997), 124-45.

Pittock, Murray, *Jacobitism* (Basingstoke, 1998).

Pocock, J. G. A., 'Clergy and commerce: the conservative Enlightenment in England', in R.J. Ajello et al., eds., *L'Età dei lumi: studi storici sul settecento europeo in onore di Franco Venturi* (2 vols., Naples, 1985), I, 523-65.

Pocock, J. G. A., *Barbarism and religion* (6 vols., Cambridge, 1999-2015).

Popkin, Richard H., 'Polytheism, deism, and Newton', in James E. Force and R. H. Popkin, eds., *Essays on the context, nature and influence of Isaac Newton's theology* (Dordrecht, 1990), 27-42.

Porter, R. and M. Teich, eds., *The Enlightenment in national context* (Cambridge, 1981).

Porter, R., 'The Enlightenment in England', in R. Porter and M. Teich, eds., *The Enlightenment in national context*, 1-48.

Porter, R., 'The gift relation: philanthropy and provincial hospitals in eighteenth-century England', in L. Granshaw and R. Porter, eds., *The hospital in history* (London, 1989), 149-78.

Porter, R., *Enlightenment. Britain and the creation of the modern world* (Harmondsworth, 2000).

Porter, R., ed., *The Cambridge history of science. Eighteenth-century science* (Cambridge, 2003).

Poser, Norman S., *Lord Mansfield. Justice in the age of reason* (Montrea and Kingston, 2013).

BIBLIOGRAPHY 735

Powell, Martyn J., 'Simon, first Earl Harcourt (1717–1777), politician and administrator in Ireland', *ODNB* online version, 2006. https://www.oxforddnb.com/view/10.1093/ref: odnb/9780198614128.001.0001/odnb-9780198614128-e-12245

Prest, Wilfrid, 'Law, lawyers and rational Dissent', in K. Haakonssen, ed., *Enlightenment and religion*, 173–82.

Prest, Wilfrid, *William Blackstone. Law and letters in the eighteenth century* (Oxford, 2008).

Preus, J. Samuel, *Spinoza and the irrelevance of Biblical authority* (Cambridge, 2001).

Prickett, Stephen, 'Poetry and prophecy: Bishop Lowth and the Hebrew scriptures in eighteenth-century England', in David Jasper, ed., *Images of belief in literature* (New York, 1984), 81–103.

Prickett, Stephen, *Words and the Word: language, poetics, and Biblical interpretation* (Cambridge, 1986).

Prior, James, *Memoirs of the life and character of the Right Hon. Edmund Burke* (London, 1824).

Prior, Mary, 'Women and the urban economy: Oxford 1500–1800', in M. Prior, ed., *Women in English society, 1500–1800* (London, 1985), 93–117.

Proctor, Mortimer Robinson, *The English university novel* (Berkeley, CA, 1957).

Quantain, J.-L., 'The Fathers in seventeenth-century Anglican theology', in J. Backus, ed.,, *The reception of the Church Fathers in the west: from the Carolingians to the Maurists* (Leiden, 1996), 987–1008.

Quantain, J.-L., 'Anglican scholarship gone mad? Henry Dodwell (1641–1711) and Christian antiquity', in J.-L. Quantin and C. R. Ligota, eds., *History of scholarship. A selection of papers from the seminar on the history of scholarship held annually at the Warburg Institute* (Oxford, 2006), 305–56.

Quantain, J.-L., 'The reception of Tillemont in England before Gibbon,' in J.-L. Quantain and J.-C. Waquet, eds., *Papes, princes, savants dans l'Europe moderne. Mélanges à la mémoire de Bruno Neveu* (Geneva, 2007), 287–311.

Quarrie, P.R., 'The Learned Press: Classics and Related Works', in ed. Gadd, *The History of Oxford University Press*, 1. 371–84.

Quehen, Hugh de, 'King, William (1663–1712)', *ODNB*, online version (2008). https://www.oxforddnb.com/view/10.1093/ref:odnb/9780198614128.001.0001/odnb-9780198614128-e-15604

Rack, Henry D., *Reasonable enthusiast. John Wesley and the rise of Methodism* (London, 1992).

Radner, John B., *Johnson and Boswell. A biography of friendship* (New Haven, CT, 2013).

Raffe, A., *The culture of controversy: religious arguments in Scotland, 1660–1714* (Woodbridge, 2012).

Raffe, A., *Scotland in revolution, 1685–1690* (Edinburgh, 2018).

Rasmussen, D. C., *The infidel and the professor. David Hume, Adam Smith and the friendship that shaped modern thought* (Princeton, NJ, 2017).

Raven, James, 'Publishing and bookselling, 1660–1780', in John Richetti, ed., *The Cambridge history of English literature, 1660–1780* (Cambridge, 2005), 11–36.

Reade, A. L., *Johnsonian gleanings* (11 vols., London, 1909–52).

Realey, Charles B., *The early opposition to Sir Robert Walpole, 1720–1727* (Philadelphia, PA, 1931).

Redwood, John, *Reason, ridicule, and religion: the Age of Enlightenment in England, 1660–1750* (London, 1976).

Reedy, G., *Robert South (1634–1716). An introduction to his life and sermons* (Cambridge, 1992).

736 BIBLIOGRAPHY

Reid, C., *Imprison'd wranglers. The rhetorical culture of the House of Commons 1760–1800* (Oxford, 2012).

Rex, M. B., *University representation in England 1604–1690* (London, 1954).

Reynolds, J. S., *The evangelicals at Oxford 1735–1871* (Abingdon, 1975).

Rhoden, Nancy L., *Revolutionary Anglicanism. The colonial Church of England clergy during the American Revolution* (Basingstoke, 1999).

Ridder-Symoens, H. de, 'Training and professionalization', in W. Reinhard, ed., *Power elites and state building* (Oxford, 1996).

Ridder-Symoens, Hilde de, ed., *A history of the university in Europe. Vol. 2. Universities in early modern Europe (1500–1800)* (Cambridge, 1996).

Ridder-Symoens, H. de, 'Mobility', in H. de Ridder-Symoens, ed., *Universities in early modern Europe*, 416–48.

Rivers, I., *Reason, grace and sentiment. A study of the language of religion and ethics in England, 1660–1780* (2 vols., Cambridge, 1991–2005).

Rivers, I. and D. L. Wykes, eds., *Joseph Priestley, scientist, philosopher, and theologian* (Oxford, 2008).

Rivington, Septimus, *The publishing family of Rivington* (3rd ed., London, 1919).

Robb-Smith, A. H. T., *A short history of the Radcliffe Infirmary* (Oxford, 1970).

Robb-Smith, A. H. T., 'The life and times of Dr Richard Frewin (1681–1761): medicine in Oxford in the eighteenth century', [15th Gideon de Laune lecture, Worshipful Society of Apothecaries of London, 19 Apr. 1972]. Available at http://practitioners.exeter.ac.uk/wp-content/uploads/2014/11/Frewin.pdf. Accessed 08/08/2022.

Robbins, Christopher, *The Earl of Wharton and Whig party politics 1679–1715* (Lewiston, NY, 1991).

Roberts, B. F., *Edward Lhuyd: the making of a scientist* (Cardiff, 1980).

Roberts, Charlotte, *Gibbon and the shape of history* (Oxford, 2014).

Robertson, Charles Grant, *All Souls college* (London, 1899).

Robertson, John, *The case for the Enlightenment. Scotland and Naples 1680–1760* (Cambridge, 2005).

Robertson, John, *The Enlightenment. A very short introduction* (Oxford, 2015).

Robins, Brian, 'The catch and glee in eighteenth-century provincial England', in S. Wollenberg and S. McVeigh, eds., *Concert life in eighteenth-century Britain*, 141–60.

Robson, David W., *Educating Republicans: The [William & Mary] College in the era of the American Revolution, 1750–1800* (London, 1985).

Robson, R. J., *The Oxfordshire election of 1754: a study in the interplay of city, county and university politics* (London, 1949).

Rocher, R., *Orientalism, poetry, and the millennium: the checkered life of Nathaniel Brassey Halhed* (Delhi, 1983).

Rogers, Ben, 'The House of Lords and religious toleration in Scotland: James Greenshield's appeal, 1709–11', in *Studies in Church history, 56: the Church and the law*, R. McKitterick, C. Methuen, and A. Spicer, eds., (Cambridge, 2020), 320–37.

Rogers, Pat, *Pope and the destiny of the Stuarts. History, politics, and mythology in the age of Queen Anne* (Oxford, 2005).

Rohr, Deborah, *The careers of British musicians, 1750–1850* (Cambridge, 2001).

Ronan, C. A., *Edmond Halley: genius in eclipse* (London, 1970).

Roos, Anna Marie, 'Fossilized Remains: The Martin Lister and Edward Lhuyd Ephemera', in V. Keller, Anna Maria Roos, and Elizabeth Yale, eds., *Life, death, and knowledge-making in early modern British scientific and medical archives* (Leiden and Boston, 2018), 150–72.

Rose, Craig, *England in the 1690s. Revolution, religion and war* (London, 1999).

Rose, Jacqueline, *Godly kingship in Restoration England: the politics of the royal supremacy, 1660–1688* (Cambridge, 2011).

Rose, Jacqueline, 'By law established: the Church of England and the royal supremacy', in G. Tapsell, ed., *The later Stuart Church*, 21–45.

Ross, Ian Simpson, *The life of Adam Smith* (Oxford, 1995).

Rothblatt, Sheldon, *The modern university and its discontents. The fate of Newman's legacies in Britain and America* (Cambridge, 1997).

Rounce, Adam, *Fame and failure 1720–1800. The unfulfilled literary life* (Cambridge, 2013).

Rousseau, G. S., *Enlightenment borders: pre- and post-modern discourses: medical, scientific* (Manchester, 1991).

Rousseau, G. S., 'Privilege, power and sexual abuse in Georgian Oxford', in George Rousseau, ed., *Children and sexuality: From the Greeks to the Great War* (Basingstoke, 2007), 142–69.

Rowlinson, John S., 'Chemistry comes of Age: the 19th century', in R. J. P. Williams, A. Chapman, and J. S. Rowlinson, eds., *Chemistry at Oxford. A history from 1600 to 2005* (London, 2009), 79–130.

Rowse, A. L. *The later Churchills* (London, 1958).

Roy, I., 'The city of Oxford, 1640–1660', in R.C. Richardson, ed., *Town and countryside in the English Revolution* (Manchester, 1992).

Roy, I. and D. Reinhart, 'Oxford and the Civil Wars', in HUO IV, 687–732.

Rudd, Niall, 'Samuel Johnson's Latin poetry', in L. B. T. Houghton and G. Manuwald, eds., *Neo-Latin poetry*, 105–24.

Rudolph, *Common law and Enlightenment in England, 1689–1750* (Woodbridge, 2013).

Rupp, Gordon, *Religion in England, 1688–1791* (Oxford, 1986).

Russell, C. F., *A history of King Edward VI School Southampton* (Cambridge, 1940).

Sack, James J., *The Grenvillites, 1801–29. Party politics and factionalism in the age of Pitt and Liverpool* (Urbana, IL, 1979).

Sack, James J., *From Jacobite to Conservative: reaction and Orthodoxy in Britain c.1760–1832* (Cambridge, 1993).

Salter, H. E., *Oxford City properties* (Oxford, 1926).

Salter, H.E., and M.D. Lobel, eds., *VCH Oxon.*, III., *The University of Oxford* (London, 1954).

Sargeaunt, John, *Annals of Westminster School* (London, 1898).

Scarfe, N., *Innocent espionage. The La Rochefoucauld brothers' tour of England in 1785* (Woodbridge, 1995).

Schaffer, S., 'Comets & idols: Newton's cosmology and political theology', in Paul Theerman an Adele F. Seeff, eds., *Action and reaction: proceedings of a symposium to commemorate the tercentenary of Newton's Principia* (Newark, DE, 1993), 206–31.

Schmidt, M., 'Ecumenical activity on the continent of Europe in the seventeenth and eighteenth centuries', in R. Rouse and S. C. Neill, eds., *A history of the ecumenical movement 1517–1948* (3rd edn., Geneva, 1986), 73–112.

Schofield, R. E., *The Lunar Society of Birmingham, a social history of provincial science and industry in eighteenth-century England* (Oxford, 1963).

Schofield, R. E., *The enlightened Joseph Priestley. A study of his life and work from 1773 to 1804* (Philadelphia, PA, 2004).

Searby, Peter, *A history of the University of Cambridge,* Vol. 3: *1750–1870* (Cambridge, 1997)

Seaward, P., 'Politics and interest, 1660–1781', in J. Catto, ed., *Oriel College*, 160–92.

738   BIBLIOGRAPHY

Seaward, Paul, 'A society of gentlemen', in J. Catto, ed., *Oriel College*, 219–46.

Seed, John, *Dissenting histories. religious division and the politics of memory in eighteenth-century England* (Edinburgh, 2008).

Sell, Alan P., *John Locke and the eighteenth-century divines* (Cardiff, 1997).

Shackleton, R., 'Johnson and the Enlightenment', in Lawrence Fitzroy Powell, *Johnson, Boswell, and their circle: essays presented to Lawrence Fitzroy Powell in honour of his eighty-fourth birthday* (Oxford, 1965), 76–92.

Shackleton, R., *British scholarship and French literature: an inaugural lecture* (Oxford, 1981).

Shapin, S., *The scientific revolution* (Chicago, IL, 1997).

Shapin, S., 'The image of the man of science', in R. Porter, ed., *Eighteenth-century science (Cambridge history of science*, vol. 4) (Cambridge, 2003), 159–183.

Sharp, Richard, '"Our common mother, the Church of England"; Nonjurors, High Churchmen, and the evidence of subscription lists', in eds. Paul Monod, Murray Pittock, and Daniel Szechi, *Loyalty and Identity. Jacobites at Home and Abroad* (Basingstoke, 2010), 167–79.

Sharp, Richard, 'Trapp, Joseph (1679–1747), Church of England clergyman and writer', *ODNB*, online version (2004). https://www.oxforddnb.com/view/10.1093/ref:odnb/9780198614128.001.0001/odnb-9780198614128-e-27666

Sharp, Richard, 'Tanner, Thomas (1674–1735)', *ODNB*, online version (2006). https://www.oxforddnb.com/view/10.1093/ref:odnb/9780198614128.001.0001/odnb-9780198614128-e-26963

Sharpe, K., *Rebranding rule. The Restoration and revolution monarchy 1660–1714* (New Haven, CT, 2013).

Sheldon, R. D., 'Beeke, Henry (1751–1837), writer on taxation and finance', *ODNB*, online version (2004). https://www.oxforddnb.com/view/10.1093/ref:odnb/9780198614128.001.0001/odnb-9780198614128-e-1952

Shepherd, C. M., 'Newtonianism in the Scottish universities in the eighteenth century', in R. H. Campbell and Andrew S. Skinner, eds., *The origins and nature of the Scottish Enlightenment* (Edinburgh, 1982), 62–85.

Sheps, Arthur, 'Sedition, vice, and atheism: the limits of toleration and the Orthodox attack on rational religion in late eighteenth-century England', in R. Hewitt and P. Rogers, eds., *Orthodoxy and heresy. Essays from the DeBartolo conference* (Lewisburg, PA, 2002), 51–68.

Sher, R. B., *Church and university in the Scottish Enlightenment. The moderate literati of Edinburgh* (Princeton, NJ, 1985).

Sher, R. B., 'Science and medicine in the Scottish Enlightenment', in P. Wood, ed., *The Scottish Enlightenment. Essays in reinterpretation* (Woodbridge, 2002).

Shurlock, Barry, *The Speaker's chaplain and the master's daughter. A Georgian family & friends* (Winchester, 2015).

Simcock, A. V., *The Ashmolean Museum and Oxford science, 1683–1983* (Oxford, 1984).

Simmons, J. S. G., *French publications acquired by the Codrington Library, 1762–1800* (Oxford, 1978).

Simmons, Jack, *Parish and empire: studies and sketches* (London, 1952).

Simone, Maria Rosa di, 'Admission', in H. de Ridder-Symoens, ed., *Universities in early modern Europe*, 285–325.

Sinclair, H. M. and A. H. T. Robb-Smith, *A short history of anatomical teaching in Oxford* (Oxford, 1950).

Sirota, Brent S., '"The leviathan is not safely to be angered": The Convocation controversy, country ideology and Anglican High Churchmanship', in J.B. Stein and S. G. Donabed, eds., *Religion and the state: Europe and North America in the seventeenth and eighteenth centuries*, (Lanham, MD, 2012), 41–61.

Sirota, Brent S., *The Christian monitors. The Church of England and the age of benevolence, 1680–1730* (New Haven, CT, 2014).

Siskin, Clifford, *The work of writing: literature and social change in Britain, 1700–1830* (Baltimore, MD, 1998).

Slafter, E., *John Checkley; or, the evolution of religious tolerance in Massachusetts Bay* (Boston, MA, 1897).

Slinn, Sara, *The education of the Anglican clergy 1780–1839* (Woodbridge, 2017).

Smethurst, Richard, 'Benefactors, endowment and finances', in J. Bate and J. Goodman, eds., *Worcester, portrait of an Oxford college*, 46–58.

Smiles, Sam, *The image of antiquity: ancient Britain and the Romantic imagination* (New Haven, CT, 1994).

Smith, C. D., *The early career of Lord North the Prime Minister* (London, 1979).

Smith, D.N., *Warton's History of English Poetry* (London, 1929).

Smith, Lawrence B., 'Boyle, Charles, fourth earl of Orrery (1674–1731)', *ODNB*, online version (2008). https://www.oxforddnb.com/view/10.1093/ref:odnb/9780198614128.001.0001/odnb-9780198614128-e-3124

Smith, M. G., *Fighting Joshua. A study of the career of Sir Jonathan Trelawny, Bart., 1650–1721, Bishop of Bristol, Exeter and Winchester* (Redruth, 1985).

Smith, M., 'Thomas Burgess, churchman and reformer', in N. Yates, ed., *Bishop Burgess and his world*, 5–40.

Smith, R. J., *The Gothic bequest: medieval institutions in British thought, 1688–1863* (Cambridge, 1987).

Smithers, P., *The life of Joseph Addison* (Oxford, 1968).

Snyder, J. R., *Dissimulation and the culture of secrecy in early modern Europe* (Berkeley, CA, 2009).

Solomon, Harry M., *The rise of Robert Dodsley, creating the new age of print* (Carbondale, IL, 1996).

Somerset, Anne, *Queen Anne. The politics of passion. A biography* (London, 2012).

Sorkin, David, *The religious Enlightenment. Protestants, Jews, and Catholics from London to Vienna* (Princeton, NJ, 2008).

Southern, R.W., 'From Schools to University', in *HUO* I, 1–36.

Sowerby, Robin, *The Augustan art of poetry: Augustan translation of the Classics* (Oxford, 2006).

Spadafora, David, *The idea of progress in eighteenth-century Britain* (New Haven, CT, 1990).

Spaeth, Donald A., *The Church in an age of danger. Parsons and parishioners, 1660–1740* (Cambridge, 2000).

Spain, Jonathan, 'Fane, John, seventh earl of Westmorland (bap. 1686 – d. 1762), army officer and politician', ODNB, online version (2009). https://www.oxforddnb.com/view/10.1093/ref:odnb/9780198614128.001.0001/odnb-9780198614128-e-9134

Sparrow, E., *Secret Service. British agents in France 1792–1815* (Woodbridge, 1999).

Speck, W. A., *Tory & Whig. The struggle in the constituencies, 1701–1715* (London, 1970).

Speck, W. A., 'Politicians, peers, and publication by subscription, 1700–1750', in Isabel Rivers, ed., *Books and their readers in eighteenth-century England* (Leicester, 1982), 47–68.

Speck, W. A., *Robert Southey. Entire man of letters* (New Haven, CT, 2006).

Speck, W. A., 'The current state of Sacheverell scholarship,', in Knights, M., ed., *Faction displayed*, 16–27.

740 BIBLIOGRAPHY

Spinks, Bryan D., *Liturgy in the age of reason. Worship and sacraments in England and Scotland 1662–c.1800* (Farnham, 2008).

Spurr, John, *The Restoration Church of England, 1646–1689* (New Haven, CT, 1991).

Spurr, John, *The laity and preaching in post-Reformation England* [Friends of Dr Williams's Library sixty-sixth Lecture] (London, 2013).

Squibb, G. D., *Founders' kin. Privilege and pedigree* (Oxford, 1972).

Stackelberg, J. von, 'Klassizismus und Aufklärung—der Blick nach Frankreich', in *Zur geistigen Situation der Zeit der Göttinger Universitätsgründung 1737. Eine Vortragsreihe* (Göttingen, 1988), 167–86.

Stansfield, D., *Thomas Beddoes MD. 1760–1808: chemist, physician, democrat* (Dordrecht, 1984).

Starkie, Andrew, *The Church of England and the Bangorian controversy, 1716–1721* (Woodbridge, 2007).

Starkie, Andrew, 'Contested histories of the English Church: Gilbert Burnet and Jeremy Collier', in P. Kewes, ed., *The uses of history in early modern England* (San Marino, CA, 2006), 329–47.

Staves, S., 'Church of England clergy and women writers', in N. Pohl and B. A. Schellenberg, eds., *Reconsidering the bluestockings* (San Marino, CA, 2002/3), 81–103.

Stephen, Jeffrey, 'English liturgy and Scottish identity: the case of James Greenshields', in Allan I. Macinnes and D. J. Hamilton, eds., *Jacobitism, Enlightenment and empire* (London, 2014), 59–74.

Stevenson, C., *Medicine and magnificence: British hospital and asylum architecture, 1660–1815* (New Haven, CT, 2000).

Stewart, A. G., *The academic Gregories* (Edinburgh, 1901).

Stewart, Larry, *The rise of public science: rhetoric, technology, and natural philosophy in Newtonian Britain, 1660–1750* (Cambridge, 1992).

Stewart, Larry, 'The Trouble with Newton in the eighteenth century', in J.E. Force and S. Hutton, eds., *Newton and Newtonianism*, 221–37.

Stone, L. et al., eds., *The university in society*. Vol. 1: *Oxford and Cambridge from the 14th to the early 19th century* (Princeton, NJ, 1974).

Stone, L., 'The Size and Composition of the Oxford Student Body 1580-1909', in Stone et al., eds., *The University in Society*, Vol. 1, 3–110.

Stott, Anne, *Hannah More. The first Victorian* (Oxford, 2003).

Stranks, C. J., *The charities of Nathaniel, Lord Crewe and Dr. John Sharp 1721–1976* (Durham, 1976).

Stray, C., ed., *Oxford Classics: teaching and learning, 1800–2000* (Oxford, 2007).

Stride, W. K., *Exeter College* (London, 1900).

Stroumsa, Guy G., *A new science. The discovery of religion in the age of reason* (Cambridge, MA, 2010).

Stuart-Buttle, Tim, 'Gibbon and Enlightenment history in Britain', in Karen O'Brien and Brian Young, eds., *The Cambridge companion to Edward Gibbon*, 110–27.

Stubbs, J. W., *The history of the University of Dublin* (Dublin, 1889).

Surtees, W. E., *A sketch of the lives of Lords Stowell and Eldon* (London, 1846).

Sutherland, L. S., *The University of Oxford in the eighteenth century: a reconsideration* (Oxford, 1973).

Sutherland, L.S., 'The origin and early history of the lord almoner's professorship in Arabic at Oxford', *BLR*, 10 (1978–82), 166–77.

Sutherland, L. S., 'William Blackstone and the legal chairs at Oxford', in R. Wellek and A. Ribeiro, eds., *Evidence in literary scholarship: essays in memory of James Marshall Osborn* (Oxford, 1979), 230–5.

BIBLIOGRAPHY 741

Sutherland, L.S., 'Political Respectability 1751–1771', in *HUO* V, 129–62.

Sutherland, L.S., 'The administration of the University', in *HUO* V, 205–26.

Sutherland, L.S., 'The curriculum', in *HUO* V, 469–92.

Sutton, Geoffrey V., *Science for a polite society. Gender, culture, & the demonstration of Enlightenment* (Boulder, CO, 1995).

Sweet, Rosemary, *The writing of urban histories in eighteenth-century England* (Oxford, 1997).

Sweet, Rosemary, *The English Town 1680–1840. Government, Society and Culture* (Harlow, 1999).

Sweet, Rosemary, *Antiquaries. The discovery of the past in eighteenth-century Britain* (London, 2004).

Sykes, Norman, *Edmund Gibson, Bishop of London, 1669–1748: a study in politics and religion in the eighteenth century* (Oxford, 1926).

Sykes, Norman, *Church and state in England in the eighteenth century* (Cambridge, 1934).

Sykes, Norman, *Daniel Ernst Jablonski and the Church of England. A study of an essay towards Protestant union* (London, 1950).

Sykes, Norman, *William Wake. Archbishop of Canterbury* (2 vols., Cambridge, 1957).

Sykes, Norman, 'Ecumenical Movements in Great Britain in the Seventeenth and Eighteenth Centuries', eds. R. Rouse and Stephen C. Neill, *A History of the Ecumenical Movement*, 123–67

Szechi, Daniel, *The Jacobites, Britain and Europe 1688–1788* (Manchester, 1994).

Szechi, Daniel, 'Jacobite politics in the age of Anne', in C. Jones, ed., *British politics in the age of Holmes. Geoffrey Holmes's British politics in the age of Anne 40 years on* (London, 2009), 41–58.

Tadmoor, Naomi, *Family and friends in eighteenth-century England: household, kinship, and patronage* (Cambridge, 2001).

Tappe, E. D.,'The Greek College at Oxford, 1699–1705', in P. Doll, ed., *Anglicanism and Orthodoxy 300 years after the 'Greek College' in Oxford* (Oxford, 2006), 153–74.

Tarbuck, Derya Gurses, *Enlightenment Reformation. Hutchinsonianism and religion in eighteenth-century Britain* (London, 2017).

Tashjian, G. R., 'Richard Rawlinson: a biographical study', in G.R. Tashjian, D. R. Tashjian, and B. J. Enright, eds., *Richard Rawlinson: a tercentenary memorial* (Kalamazoo, 1990), 83–5.

Taylor, Stephen J., '"Dr. Codex" and the Whig "Pope": Edmund Gibson, Bishop of Lincoln and London, 1716–1748', in R.W. Davis, ed., *Lords of Parliament. Studies, 1714–1914* (Stanford, CA, 1995), 9–28.

Taylor, Stephen J., 'The Government and the Episcopate in the mid-eighteenth century: the uses of patronage', in Charles Giry-Deloison and Roger Mettam, eds., *Patronages et clientélismes 1550–1750 (France, Angleterre, Espagne, Italie)* (Lille/London, 1995), 191–207.

Taylor, Stephen J., 'Bishop Edmund Gibson's proposals for church reform', in S. Taylor, ed.., *From Cranmer to Davidson. A Church of England miscellany* (Woodbridge, 1999), 169–202.

Taylor, Stephen J., 'Un état confessionel? L'Eglise d'Angleterre, la constitution et la vie politique au XVIIIe siècle', in Alain Joblin et Jacques Sys, eds., *L'identité Anglicane* (Arras, 2004), 141–154.

Thackeray, A. D., *The Radcliffe Observatory, 1772–1972* (Oxford, 1972).

Thomann, G., ed., *J. E. Grabe's liturgies: two unknown Anglican liturgies of the seventeenth century* (Nuremberg, 1989).

742   BIBLIOGRAPHY

Thomas, D. O., *The honest mind: the thought and work of Richard Price* (Oxford, 1977).

Thomas, Keith, *The Ends of life. Roads to fulfilment in early modern England* (Oxford, 2009).

Thomas, Peter D. G., *Lord North* (London, 1976).

Thomas, Peter D. G., *George III. King and politicians 1760–1770* (Manchester, 2002).

Thompson, Andrew C., *George II. King and Elector* (New Haven, CT, 2011).

Thompson, H. L., *Christ Church* (Oxford, 1900).

Thompson, H. P., *Thomas Bray* (London, 1954).

Thompson, Robert, 'Goodson, Richard (c.1655–1718)', *ODNB*, online version (2008). https://www.oxforddnb.com/view/10.1093/ref:odnb/9780198614128.001.0001/odnb-9780198614128-e-10984

Thompson, R. S.,'English and English education in the eighteenth century', in J.A. Leith, ed., *Facets of education in the eighteenth century*, [SVEC 167] (Oxford, 1977), 66–85.

A.S. Thomson, A., S. Burrows, E. Dziembowski, and S. Audidière, eds., *Cultural transfers: France and Britain in the long eighteenth century* (Oxford, 2010).

Thorne, Roland, 'Lee, George Henry, third earl of Lichfield (1718–1772), ODNB, *ODNB*, online version (2006). https://www.oxforddnb.com/view/10.1093/ref:odnb/9780198614128.001.0001/odnb-9780198614128-e-16286

Thwaites, W., 'Oxford's food riots', in A. Randall and A. Charlesworth, eds., *Markets, market culture and popular protest in eighteenth-century Britain and Ireland* (Liverpool, 1996), 137–62.

Tickell, R. E., *Thomas Tickell and the Eighteenth Century Poets (1685-1740)* (London, 1931).

Tilmouth, M., 'The beginnings of provincial concert life in England', in C. Hogwood and R. Luckett, eds., *Music in Eighteenth-Century England. Essays in Memory of Charles Cudworth* (Cambridge, 1985), 1–19.

Tindal Hart, A., *The life and times of John Sharp Archbishop of York* (London, 1949).

Tindal Hart, A., *William Lloyd 1627–1717. Bishop, politician, author and prophet* (London, 1952).

Tompson, R. S., *Classics or charity? The dilemma of the 18th century grammar school* (Manchester, 1971).

Toomer, G. J., *Eastern wisedome and learning. The study of Arabic in seventeenth-century England* (Oxford, 1996).

Townsend, J., *The Oxfordshire Dashwoods* (Oxford, 1922).

Townsend, W. C., 'Life of Lord Stowell', in *The lives of twelve eminent judges of the last and of the present century* (2 vols., London, 1846), II. 279–365.

Tracy, Clarence, *A portrait of Richard Graves* (Toronto, 1987).

Treadwell, Michael, 'The stationers and the printing acts at the end of the seventeenth century', in John Barnard and D. F. McKenzie, eds., *The Cambridge history of the book in Britain. Vol. IV: 1557–1695* (Cambridge, 2002), 755–76.

Trevor-Roper, H., 'The religious origins of the Enlightenment', in H. Trevor-Roper, *Religion, the Reformation and social change: the crisis of the seventeenth century* (London, 1967).

Trevor-Roper, H., *Catholics, Anglicans and Puritans* (London, 1987).

Trevor-Roper, H., *History and the Enlightenment* (New Haven, CT, 2010).

Tuckwell, W., *Reminiscences of Oxford* (London, 1900).

Turner, G.L.'E., 'The physical sciences', in HUO V, 659–81.

Turner, K., *British Travel Writers in Europe, 1750–1800. Authorship, gender and national identity* (Aldershot, 2001).

Tweddle, Ian, 'Stirling, James (1692–1770), mathematician and mine manager', *ODNB*, online version (2004). https://www.oxforddnb.com/view/10.1093/ref:odnb/9780198614128.001.0001/odnb-9780198614128-e-26530

Tweedie, C., *James Stirling. A sketch of his life and works along with his scientific correspondence* (Oxford, 1922).

Tyack, G., *Oxford. An architectural guide* (Oxford, 1998).

Tyacke, N., *Aspects of English Protestantism, c.1530–1700: Politics, culture, and society in early modern Britain* (Manchester, 2001).

Tyacke, N., 'From Laudians to Latitudinarians: a shifting balance of theological forces', in G. Tapsell, ed., *The Later Stuart Church*, 46–70.

Uglow, Jenny, *The lunar men: the friends who made the future 1730–1810* (London, 2002).

Upton, Dell, *Holy things and profane: Anglican parish churches in colonial Virginia* (New Haven, CT, 1986).

Vaisey, David, 'Price, John (1735–1813), librarian', *ODNB*, online version (2004). https://www.oxforddnb.com/view/10.1093/ref:odnb/9780198614128.001.0001/odnb-9780198614128-e-22757

Vandermeersch, Peter A., 'Teachers', in H. de Ridder-Symoens, ed., *Universities in early modern Europe*, 210–55.

van Ostade, Ingrid Tieken-Boon, *The bishop's grammar. Robert Lowth and the rise of prescriptivism* (Oxford, 2011).

Varley, E. A., *The last of the Prince Bishops: William Van Mildert and the High Church movement of the early nineteenth century* (Cambridge, rev. edn., 2002).

Vaughan, J., *The English guide book c.1780–1870: an illustrated history* (Newton Abbot, 1974).

Vickers, M., *The Arundel and Pomfret Marbles in Oxford* (Oxford, 2006).

Virgin, Peter, *The Church in an age of negligence. Ecclesiastical structure and problems of Church reform 1700–1840* (Cambridge, 1989).

Vulliamy, C. E., *The Onslow family 1528–1874 with some account of their times* (London, 1953).

Walker, Christopher J., *Reason and religion in late seventeenth-century England. The politics and theology of radical Dissent* (London, 2013).

Walker, John, 'Cornwall', in C. J. R. Currie and C.P. Lewis, eds., *A Guide to English county histories. A tribute to C. R. Elrington* (Stroud, 1994), 85–90.

Walker, M., *The Salzburg transaction. Expulsion and redemption in eighteenth-century Germany* (Ithaca, NY, 1992).

Walsh, J. D., 'The Origins of the evangelical revival', in G.V. Bennett and J. D. Walsh, eds., *Essays in modern English Church history in memory of Norman Sykes* (London, 1966), 132–62.

Walsh, M., 'Literary scholarship and the life of editing', in I. Rivers, ed., *Books and their readers in eighteenth-century England*, 191–216.

Walsham, Alexandra, *Charitable hatred. Tolerance and intolerance 1500–1700 in England* (Manchester, 2006).

Walsham, Alexandra, *The reformation of the landscape. Religion, identity & memory in early modern Britain & Ireland* (Oxford, 2011).

Waquet, Françoise, *Latin or the empire of a sign: from the sixteenth to the twentieth centuries*, trans. J. Howe (London, 2001).

Waquet, Françoise, *Respublica academica. Rituels universitaires et genres du savoir (xvii–xxi siècles)* (Paris, 2010).

Ward, W. R., *Georgian Oxford. University politics in the eighteenth century* (Oxford, 1958).

744 BIBLIOGRAPHY

Ward, W. R., *Victorian Oxford* (London, 1965).

Ward, W. R., *The Protestant evangelical awakening* (Cambridge, 1992).

Waterman, A. M. C., *Political economy and Christian theology since the Enlightenment: essays in intellectual history* (Basingstoke, 2004).

Watney, V. J., *Cornbury and the forest of Wychwood* (London, 1910).

Watts, Michael R., *The Dissenters* (3 vols. Oxford, 1978–2015).

Weber, William, *The rise of musical classics in eighteenth-century England. A study in canon, ritual, and ideology* (Oxford, 1992).

Webster, C., *The great Instauration: science, medicine and reform 1626–1660* (London, 1975).

Webster, C., 'The medical faculty and the physic garden', in *HUO* V, 683–723.

Weinbrot, H., *Britannia's issue. The rise of British literature from Dryden to Ossian* (Cambridge, 1993).

Weinbrot, H., *Literature, religion, and the evolution of culture 1660–1780* (Baltimore, MD, 2013).

Weld, C. R., *History of the Royal Society* (2 vols., London, 1848).

Wellek, R., *The rise of English literary history* (Chapel Hill, NC, 1941).

Wellenreuther, H., 'Göttingen und England im 18. Jahrhundert', in Norbert Kamp, et al., eds., *250 Jahre Vorlesungen an der Georgia Augusta 1734–1984* (Göttingen, 1985), 30–63.

Wells, Joseph, *Wadham College* (Oxford, 1898).

Whatton, W. R., *The history of Manchester School . . .* (2 pts., Manchester, 1825).

Whitaker, A. P., *James Hurdis. His life and writings* (Chichester, 1960).

White, G. Cecil, *A versatile professor. Reminiscences of the Rev. Edward Nares, DD* (London, 1903).

White, P., *A gentleman of fine taste. The watercolours of Coplestone Warre Bampfylde* (Taunton, 1995).

White, R., ed., *Nicholas Hawksmoor and the replanning of Oxford* (Oxford and London, 1997).

White, R. J., *Dr. Bentley. A study in academic scarlet* (London, 1965).

Whiteley, Peter, *Lord North. The Prime Minister who lost America* (London, 1996).

Whiting, C. E., *Nathaniel Lord Crewe Bishop of Durham (1674–1721)* (London, 1940).

Wigelsworth, Jeffrey R., 'Fashioning identity in eighteenth-century politics: the case of John Toland', in David A. Valone and Jill Marie Bradbury, eds., *Anglo-Irish identities, 1571–1845* (Lewisburg, PA, 2008), 59–83.

Wigelsworth, Jeffrey R., *Deism in Enlightenment England. Theology, politics, and Newtonian public science* (Manchester, 2009).

Wigelsworth, Jeffrey R., *Selling science in the age of Newton. Advertising and the commoditization of knowledge* (Aldershot, 2010).

Wigelsworth, Jeffrey R., '"God can require nothing of us, but what makes for our happiness:" Matthew Tindal on toleration', in W. Hudson et al., eds., *Atheism and deism revalued: heterodox religious identities in Britain, 1650–1850* (Farnham, 2014), 139–55.

Wigelsworth, Jeffrey R., *All Souls College, Oxford in the early eighteenth century: piety, political imposition, and legacy of the Glorious Revolution* (Leiden, 2018).

Wilbur, E. M., *A history of Unitarianism in Transylvania, England and America* (Cambridge, MA, 1952).

Wilkinson, David, *The Duke of Portland. Politics and party in the age of George III* (Basingstoke, 2003).

Williams, A., *Poetry and the creation of a a Whig literary culture 1681–1714* (Oxford, 2005).

Williams, B., *Stanhope: a study in 18th-century war and diplomacy* (Oxford, 1932).

Williams, C. F. A., *Degrees in music* (London, 1893).

Williams, Penry, 'From the Reformation to the era of Reform, 1530–1850', in J. Buxton and P. Williams, eds., *New College*, 44–72.

Wilson, C., *Epicureanism at the origins of modernity* (Oxford, 2008).

Wilson, F. M., *Strange island. Britain through foreign eyes 1395–1940* (London, 1955).

Winch, Donald, *Adam Smith's politics: an essay in historiographic revision* (Cambridge, 1978).

Wing, William, *Oxfordshire in the eighteenth century, and the county election of 1754* (Bicester, 1881).

Winn, James Anderson, *Queen Anne. Patroness of arts* (Oxford, 2014).

Withers, Charles J., *Placing the Enlightenment. Thinking geographically about the age of reason* (Chicago, IL, 2007).

Wojcik, Jan W., 'The theological context of Boyle's things above reason', in M. Hunter, ed., *Robert Boyle reconsidered* (Cambridge, 1994), 139–55.

Wollenberg, S.L.F., 'Music and musicians', in *HUO* V, 865–88.

Wollenberg, S., *Music at Oxford in the eighteenth and nineteenth centuries* (Oxford, 2001).

Wollenberg, S., '"So much rational and elegant amusement, at an expence comparatively inconsiderable": The Holywell concerts in the eighteenth century', in S. Wollenberg and S. McVeigh, eds., *Concert life in eighteenth-century Britain*, 243–59.

Wollenberg, S., '"Thus we Kept Away Bonaparte:" music in Oxford at the time of the Napoleonic Wars', in M. Philp, ed., *Resisting Napoleon: The British response to the threat of invasion 1797 to 1815* (Aldershot, 2006), 173–204.

Womersley, David, 'Gibbon's *Memoirs*: autobiography in time of revolution', in D. Womersley, D., J. Burrow, and J. Pocock, eds., *Edward Gibbon* (Oxford, 1997), 347–404.

Womersley, David, *Gibbon and the 'watchmen of the Holy City'. The historian and his reputation 1776–1815* (Oxford, 2002).

Wood, A. S., *Thomas Haweis 1734–1820* (London, 1957).

Wood, Paul, ed., *The Aberdeen Enlightenment. The arts curriculum in the eighteenth century* [Quincentennial Studies in the history of the University of Aberdeen] (Aberdeen, 1993).

Woodland, Patrick, 'Meredith, Sir William, third baronet, (bap. 1724, d. 1790), politician' *ODNB*, online version (2004). https://www.oxforddnb.com/view/10.1093/ref:odnb/9780198614128.001.0001/odnb-9780198614128-e-18580

Woolf, Daniel, *The Social Circulation of the Past. English Historical Culture 1500–1730* (Oxford, 2003).

Woolf, Daniel, 'Historical writing in Britain from the late middle ages to the eve of Enlightenment,' in J.Rabasa, M. Sato, E. Tortarolo, and D. Woolf, eds., *The Oxford history of historical writing. Vol. 3: 1400–1800* (Oxford, 2012), 473–96.

Woolverton, J., *Colonial Anglicanism in North America* (Detroit, MI, 1976).

Worden, Blair, 'Cromwellian Oxford', in *HUO* IV, 733–72.

Wordsworth, C., *Social life at the English universities in the eighteenth century* (London, 1874).

Worsley, G., *Classical architecture in Britain: the heroic age* (New Haven, CT, 1995).

[Wrangham, F.], *A brief history of the Free Grammar School at Leeds* (Leeds, 1822).

Wright, Austin, *Joseph Spence. A critical biography* (Chicago, IL, 1950).

Wroth, W.W., rev. R.D.E. Eagles, 'Chandler, Richard (bap. 1737–1810), classical scholar and traveller', *ODNB*, online version (2019). https://www.oxforddnb.com/view/10.1093/ref:odnb/9780198614128.001.0001/odnb-9780198614128-e-5108.

Wykes, D. L., 'The contribution of the Dissenting academy to the emergence of rational Dissent', in Haakonssen, K. (ed.), *Enlightenment and religion* (Cambridge, 1996).

746 BIBLIOGRAPHY

Yale, Elizabeth, *Sociable knowledge. Natural history and the nation in early modern Britain* (Philadelphia, PA, 2016).

Yates, Nigel, *Buildings, faith and worship: the liturgical arrangement of Anglican Churches 1600–1900* (Oxford, 1991).

Yates, N., ed. *Bishop Burgess and his world. Culture, religion and society in Britain, Europe and North America in the eighteenth and nineteenth centuries* (Cardiff, 2007).

Yates, Nigel, *Eighteenth-century Britain. Religion and politics, 1714–1815* (Harlow, 2008).

Yates, Nigel, *Liturgical space: Christian worship and church buildings in Western Europe 1500–2000* (Aldershot, 2008).

Yilmaz, Levent, *Le temps moderne: variations sur les anciens et les contemporains* (Paris, 2004).

Yolton, John W., John Valdimir Price, and John Stephens, eds., *The Dictionary of eighteenth-century British philosophers* (2 vols., Bristol, 1999).

Yolton, J., 'Edward Bentham', in J. W. Yolton, J.V. Price, and J. Stephens, eds., *Dictionary of eighteenth-century British philosophers*, I. 76–7.

Yolton, J., *John Locke and the way of ideas* (Oxford, 1956).

Yolton, J., 'Schoolmen, Logic and Philosophy', in *HUO V*, 565–92.

Yorke, P. C., The *life and correspondence of Philip Yorke, Earl of Hardwicke, Lord High Chancellor of Great Britain* (3 vols., Cambridge, 1913).

Young, B. W., *Religion and Enlightenment in eighteenth-century England: theological debate from Locke to Burke* (Oxford, 1998).

Young, B. W., *The Victorian eighteenth century: an intellectual history* (Oxford, 2007).

Young, B. W., 'Gibbon and Catholicism', in K. O'Brien and B. Young, eds., *Cambridge companion to Edward Gibbon*, 147–66.

Zagorin, P., *Ways of lying: dissimulation, persecution and conformity in early modern Europe* (Cambridge, MA, 1990).

Zagorin, P., *How the idea of religious toleration came to the West* (Princeton, NJ, 2003)

Ziegler, Philip, *Addington. A life of Henry Addington First Viscount Sidmouth* (London, 1965).

Zimmermann, D., *The Jacobite movement in Scotland and in exile, 1746–1759* (Basingstoke, 2003).

Zwierlein, Cornel, *Imperial unknowns. The French and British in the Mediterranean, 1650–1750* (Oxford, 2016).

2) Articles

Aslet, William, 'James Gibb's autobiography revisited', *The Georgian Group Journal*, 25 (2017), 113–130.

Aston, Nigel, 'Horne and heterodoxy: the defence of Anglican beliefs in the late Enlightenment', *EHR*, 108 (1993), 895–919.

Aston, Nigel, 'Wesley and the social elite of Georgian Britain', *BJRL*, 85 (2003), 123–36.

Aston, Nigel, 'From personality to party: the creations and transmission of Hutchinsonianism, c.1725–1750', *Studies in the History and Philosophy of Science*, 35 (2004), 625–44.

Aston, Nigel, 'Queen Anne and Oxford: the royal visit of 1702 and its aftermath', *JECS*, 37 (2014), 171–84.

Aston, Nigel, 'Thomas Townson and High Church continuities and connections in eighteenth-century England', *BJRL*, 97 (2021), 53–69.

Baird, John D., 'Whig and Tory panegyrics: Addison's The Campaign and Philips's Blenheim reconsidered', *Lumen*, 26 (1997), 163–77.

BIBLIOGRAPHY 747

Baker, A. M., 'The Portland Family and Bulstrode Park', *Records of Buckinghamshire*, 43 (2003), 159–78.

Barber, Alex, '"Why don't those lazy priests answer the book?" Matthew Tindal, censorship, freedom of the press and religious debate in early eighteenth-century England', *History*, 98 (2013), 680–707.

Barber, Alex, 'Censorship, salvation and the preaching of Francis Higgins: A reconsideration of High Church politics and theology in the early eighteenth century', *PH*, 33 (2014), 114–39.

Barnard, L. W., 'Joseph Bingham and the early church', *Church Quarterly Review*, 169 (1968), 192–205.

Barratt, G. R. V., 'Vasily Nikitin: a note on an eighteenth-century Oxonian', *Eighteenth-Century Studies*, 8 (1974–5), 75–99.

Barrett, A. H., 'Richard Blechinden: the first provost of Worcester College, Oxford', *Oxoniensia*, 51 (1986), 139–69.

Beales, D., 'Edmund Burke and the monasteries of France', *HJ*, 48 (2005), 415–36.

Bell, H. E., 'The Savilian professors' houses and Halley's observatory at Oxford', *Notes and Records of the Royal Society*, 16 (1961), 179–86.

Bennett, G. V., 'Patristic authority in the age of reason', *Oecumenica: Jahrbuch für ökumenische Forschung* (1971/2), 72–87.

Bennett, J. A. W., 'Oxford in 1699', *Oxoniensia*, 4 (1939), 147–52.

Bennett, J. A.W., 'Gibbon and the universities', *The Cambridge Review*, xcix (1976), 15–18.

Black, J., 'Parliament and the political and diplomatic crisis of 1717–18', *PH*, 3 (1984), 77–102.

Black, J., 'Regulating Oxford: ministerial intentions in 1719', *Oxoniensia*, 50 (1985), 283–5.

Bromley, J. S., 'Britain and Europe in the eighteenth century', *History*, 66 (1981), 394–412.

Bucholz, R. O., 'Queen Anne and the limitations of royal ritual', *JBS*, 30 (1991), 288–323.

Burrows, D., 'Sources for Oxford Handel performances in the first half of the eighteenth century', *Music & Letters*, 61 (1980), 177–85.

Cairns, J. W., 'Blackstone, an English institutist: legal literature and the rise of the nation state', *Oxford Journal of Legal Studies*, 4 (1984), 318–60.

Canby, C., 'A note on the influence of Oxford University upon William and Mary College in the eighteenth century', *W&MQ*, n.s., 21 (1941), 243–7.

Cannon, John, 'The Parliamentary representation of the City of Oxford 1754–90', *Oxoniensia*, 10 (1960), 102–8.

Carter, Philip, 'Polite "persons": character, biography and the gentleman', *TRHS*, 6th ser., 12 (2002), 333–54.

Chalus, Elaine, '"My Lord Sue": Lady Susan Keck and the great Oxfordshire election of 1754', *PH*, 37 (2013), 443–59.

Chapman, A., 'Pure research and practical teaching: the astronomical career of James Bradley, 1693–1762', *Notes and Records of the Royal Society of London*, 47 (1993), 205–12.

Chartier, R., 'Student populations in the eighteenth century', *BJECS* 2 (1979), 150–62.

Chartier, R. and J. Revel, 'Université et société dans l'Europe modern: position des problèmes', *Revue d'histoire moderne et contemporaine*, 25 (1978), 353–74.

Christie, I. R., 'The Tory Party, Jacobitism and the '45: a note', *HJ*, 30 (1987), 921–31.

Clark, J. C. D., 'Providence, predestination and progress: or, did the Enlightenment fail'?, *Albion*, 35 (2003), 559–89.

Clark, J. C. D., 'The Enlightenment: catégories, traductions et objets sociau', in G. Laudin and D. Masseau, eds., *Lumières*, special issue 17–18 (2011), 19–39.

748 BIBLIOGRAPHY

Clark, J. C. D., 'Secularization and modernization: the failure of a "grand narrative"', *HJ*, 55 (2012), 161–94.

Clarke, Norma, 'Elizabeth Elstob (1674–1752): England's first professional woman historian', *Gender & History*, 17 (2005), 210–20.

Clarke, T., 'The Williamite episcopalians and the Glorious Revolution in Scotland', *Records of the Scottish Church Historical Society*, 24 (1990), 35–51.

Coffey, John, 'Milton, Locke and the new history of toleration', *Modern Intellectual History*, 5 (2008), 619–32.

Cole, C., 'Carfax conduit', *Oxoniensia*, 29–30 (1964–5), 142–66.

Coleman, C., 'Resacralizing the world: the fate of secularization in . . . historiography', *JMH*, 82 (2010), 368–96.

Colie, R., 'Spinoza in England 1665–1730', *Proceedings of the American Philosophical Society*, 107 (1963), 183–219.

Collet, D., 'Creative misunderstandings: circulating objects and the transfer of knowledge within the personal union of Hanover and Great Britain', in *German Historical Institute London Bulletin*, 36 (2014), 3–23.

Colley, Linda, 'The apotheosis of George III: loyalty, royalty and the British nation 1760–1820', *P&P*, 102 (1984), 94–129.

Colvin, H. M., 'The architects of All Saints Church, Oxford', *Oxoniensia*, 19 (1954), 112–16.

Connely, W., 'Colonial Americans in Oxford and Cambridge', repr. from *The American Oxonian*, Jan. 1942.

Cornwall, Robert, 'The search for the primitive Church: The use of Early Church Fathers in the High Church Anglican tradition, 1680–1745', *AEH*, 59 (1990), 303–29.

Cox, Oliver, 'An Oxford college and the eighteenth-century Gothic revival', *Oxoniensia*, 77 (2012), 117–35.

Cranfield, G. A., 'The London Evening Post and the Jew Bill of 1753', *HJ*, 8 (1966), 16–30.

Creasy, J., 'Some Dissenting attutudes towards the French Revolution', *Transactions of the Unitarian Historical Society*, 13 (1966), 155–67.

Crosland, M., 'The image of science as a threat: Burke versus Priestley and the "Philosophic Revolution"', *BJHS*, 20 (1987), 277–307.

Cross, A. G., 'Russian students in eighteenth-century Oxford (1766–75)', *Journal of European Studies*, 5 (1975), 91–110.

Crum, M., 'An Oxford music club, 1690–1719', *BLR*, 9 (1974), 83–99.

Cunningham, A., 'Gettting the game right: some plain words on the identity and invention of science', *Studies in History and Philosophy of Science*, 19 (1988), 365–89.

Daniel, G., 'Edward Lhuyd: antiquary and archaeologist', *WHR*, 3 (1966), 345–59.

Daston, Lorraine, 'The ideal and reality of the Republic of Letters in the Enlightenment', *Science in Context*, 4 (1991), 367–86.

Davies, C. S. L., 'Problems of reform in eighteenth-century Oxford: the case of George Wyndham, Warden of Wadham, 1744–77, *Oxoniensia*, 79 (2014), 61–75.

Ditchfield, G. M., 'The Parliamentary struggle over the Test and Corporation Acts, 1787–1790', *EHR*, 89 (1974), 551–77.

Ditchfield, G. M., 'Parliament, the Quakers and the tithe question 1750–1835', *PH*, 4 (1985), 87–114.

Ditchfield, G. M., 'The subscription issue in British parliamentary politics, 1772–9', *PH*, 7 (1988), 53–64.

Ditchfield, G. M., 'Ecclesiastical legislation during the ministry of the Younger Pitt, 1783–1801', *PH*, 19 (2000), 64–80.

Ditchfield, G. M., 'William Tayleur of Shrewsbury (1712–96): A case study in eighteenth-century lay religious leadership,' *Enlightenment and Dissent*, 26 (2015), 3–23.

Ditchfield, G. M., 'John Wesley, heterodoxy, and dissent', *Wesley and Methodist Studies*, 10 (2018), 109–31.

Doll, Peter, 'The idea of the primitive church in High Church ecclesiology from Samuel Johnson to J. H. Hobart', *AEH*, 65 (1996), 6–43.

Doyle, T., 'Jacobitism, Catholicism, and the Irish Protestant Elite, 1700–1710', *Eighteenth-Century Ireland*, 12 (1997), 28–59.

Durey, Michael, 'William Wickham, the Christ Church connection and the rise and fall of the security service in Britain, 1793–1801', *EHR*, 121 (2006), 714–45.

Eagles, C. M., 'David Gregory and Newtonian science', *BJHS*, 10 (1977), 216–25.

Eagles, Robin, 'Frederick, Prince of Wales, the "court" of Leicester House and the "patriot" opposition to Walpole, c.1733–1742', *The Court Historian*, 21 (2016), 140–55.

Eastwood, D., 'John Reeves and the contested idea of the Constitution', *JECS*, 16 (1993), 197–212.

Edwards, N., 'Edward Lhuyd and the origins of early medieval Celtic archaeology', *Antiquaries Journal*, 87 (2007), 165–96.

Elliot, P. and S. Daniels, 'The "school of true, useful and universal science"? Freemasonry, natural philosophy and scientific culture in eighteenth-century England', *BJHS*, 39 (2006), 207–29.

Emerson, R. L., 'Scottish universities in the eighteenth century, 1690–1800', *SVEC*, 167 (1977), 453–74.

English, J. C., 'John Hutchinson's critique of Newtonian heterodoxy', *Church History*, 68 (1999), 581–97.

English, J. C., 'John Wesley and Isaac Newton's "system of the world"', *Proceedings of the Wesley Historical Society*, 48 (1991), 69–86.

Evans, F. B., 'Platonic scholarship in eighteenth-century England', *Modern Philology*, 41 (1943), 103–10.

Every, G., 'Dr Grabe and his manuscripts', *JTS*, 8 (1957), 280–92.

Falvey, J., 'The Church of Ireland episcopate in the eighteenth century', *Eighteenth-Century Ireland*, 8 (1993), 103–14.

Feather, John, 'British publishing in the eighteenth century: a preliminary subject analysis', *Library*, 6th ser., 8 (1986), 32–46.

Firth, Sir C., 'Modern history in Oxford, 1724–1841', *EHR*, 32 (1917), 3–12.

Fitzpatrick, Martin, 'Toleration and truth', *Enlightenment & Dissent*, 1 (1982), 3–31.

Force, J., 'Hume and the relation of science to religion among certain members of the Royal Society', *JHI*, 45 (1984), 517–36.

Fox, Adam, 'Printed questionnaires, research networks and the discovery of the British Isles, 1650–1800', *HJ*, 53 (2010), 593–621.

Frace, Ryan K., 'Religious toleration in the wake of revolution: Scotland on the eve of Enlightenment (1688–1710s)', *History*, 93 (2008), 354–75.

Frank, R. G., 'Science, medicine and the universities of early modern England: background and sources. Part 1', *History of Science*, 11 (1973), 194–216.

Freeman, Sarah, 'An Englishwoman's home is her castle: Lady Pomfret's house at 18 Arlington Street', *The Georgian Group Journal*, 20 (2012), 87–102.

French, H. and M. Rothery, '"Upon your entry to the world:" masculine values and the threshold of adulthood among landed elites in England, 1680–1800', *Social History*, 33 (2008), 403–22.

750 BIBLIOGRAPHY

Friesen, John, 'Archibald Pitcairne, David Gregory and the Scottish origins of English Tory Newtonianism, 1688–1715', *History of Science*, 41 (2003), 163–91.

Friesen, John, 'Christ Church Oxford, the ancients-moderns controversy, and the promotion of Newton in post-revolutionary England', *History of Universities*, XXIII/I (2008), 33–66.

Gascoigne, John, 'Politics, patronage and Newtonianism: the Cambridge example', *HJ*, 27 (1984), 1–24.

Gascoigne, J., 'Mathematics and meritocracy: the emergence of the Cambridge mathematical school', *Social Studies of Science*, 14 (1984), 547–84.

Gascoigne, J., 'Anglican latitudinarianism and political radicalism in the late eighteenth century', *History*, 71 (1986), 22–38.

Gascoigne, J., 'From Bentley to the Victorians: the rise and fall of British Newtonian natural theology', *Science in Context*, 2 (1988), 219–56.

Gascoigne, J., The eighteenth-century scientific community: a prosopographical study', in *Social Studies of Science*, 25 (1995), 575–81.

Gascoigne, J., 'Science, religion and the foundations of morality in Enlightenment Britain', *Enlightenment and Dissent*, 17 (1998), 83–103.

Gascoigne, J., 'The Royal Society and the emergence of science as an instrument of state policy', *BJHS*, 32 (1999), 171–84.

Gibbs, F.W. and W. A. Smeaton, 'Thomas Beddoes at Oxford', *Ambix*, 9 (1961), 47–9.

Gibson, S., 'Francis Wise, BD, Oxford antiquary, librarian and archivist', *Oxoniensia*, 1 (1936), 173–95.

Gibson, W., A Welsh bishop for a Welsh see: John Wynne of St Asaph', *The Journal of Welsh Ecclesiastical History*, 1 (1984), 28–43.

Gibson, W., 'Patterns of nepotism and kinship in the eighteenth-century Church', *Journal of Religious History*, 14 (1987), 382–9.

Gibson, W., 'A Whig principal of Jesus', *Oxoniensia*, 52 (1987), 204–8.

Gibson, W., An eighteenth-century paradox: the career of the decipherer-bishop Edward Willes', *JECS*, 12 (1989), 69–76.

Gibson, W., 'The suppression of Terrae Filius in 1713', *Oxoniensia*, 54 (1989), 410–13.

Gibson, W., 'Nepotism, family, and merit: the Church of England in the eighteenth century', *Journal of family history*, 18 (1993), 179–90.

Gibson, W., '"Unreasonable and Unbecoming": self-recommendation and place-seeking in the Church of England, 1700–1900', *Albion*, 27 (1995), 43–63.

Gibson, W., 'The election of Lord Grenville as Chancellor of Oxford University in 1809', *Oxoniensia*, 61 (1996), 355–68.

Gibson, W., 'William Talbot and Church parties, 1688–1730', *JEH*, 58 (2007), 26–48.

Gibson, W., 'Muscipula and Hoglandia, Sacheverell's literary battle, 1709–1711', *Welsh Journal of Religious History*, 7 & 8 (2012–13), 39–50.

Gibson, W., '*Strenae Natalitiae*: ambivalence and equivocation in Oxford in 1688', *History of Universities*, XXXI/1 (2018), 121–40.

Gillam, Stanley, 'Humfrey Wanley and Arthur Charlett', *BLR*, 16 (1999), 411–29.

Gilley, Sheridan, 'Christianity and Enlightenment: an historical survey', *History of European Ideas*, 1 (1981), 103–21.

Glickman, G., 'Andrew Michael Ramsay (1686–1743), the Jacobite court and the English Catholic Enlightenment', *Eighteenth-Century Thought*, 3 (2007), 293–329.

Glickman, G., 'Parliament, the Tories and Frederick, Prince of Wales', *PH*, 30 (2011), 120–41.

Glyn, Lynn B., 'Israel Lyons: a short but starry career. The life of an eighteenth-century Jewish botanist astronomer', *Notes and Records of the Royal Society of London*, 56 (2002), 275–305.

Goldie, M., 'The roots of true Whiggism 1688–94', *History of Political Thought*, 1 (1980), 195–236.

Goldie, M., 'The revolution of 1689 and the structure of political argument', *BIHR*, 83 (1980), 473–521.

Goldie, M., 'John Locke and Anglican royalism', *Political Studies*, 31 (1983), 61–85.

Greig, M., 'Burnet and the Trinitarian controversies of the 1690s', *JEH*, 44 (1993), 631–51.

Greig, M., 'Heresy Hunt: Gilbert Burnet and the Convocation controversy of 1701', *HJ*, 37 (1994), 569–9.

Gretsch, M., 'Elizabeth Elstob: a scholar's fight for Anglo-Saxon studies', *Anglia*, 117 (1999), 163–200, 481–524.

Groot, Jerome de, 'Space, Patronage, procedure: the court at Oxford, 1642–46', *EHR*, 117 (2002), 1204–27.

Grote, S., 'Review essay: religion and Enlightenment', *JHI*, 75 (2014), 137–60.

Guerrini, Anita, 'John Keill, George Cheyne, and Newtonian physiology, 1690–1740', *Journal of the History of Biology*, 18 (1985), 247–66.

Guerrini, Anita, 'The Tory Newtonians: Gregory, Pitcairne, and their circle', *JBS*, 25 (1986), 288–311.

Gunderson, J. R., 'The search for good men: recruiting ministers in colonial Virginia', *Historical Magazine of the Protestant Episcopal Church*, 48 (1979), 465–72.

Gurses, Derya, 'Academic Hutchinsonians and their quest for relevance, 1734–1790', *History of European Ideas*, 31 (2005), 408–27.

Haig, Robert L., 'New light on the King's printing office 1680–1730', *Studies in Bibliography*, 8 (1956), 157–67.

Hallam, H. A. N., 'The anonymous pamphleteer: a checklist of the writings of Edward Stephens (1633–1706)', *BLR*, 18 (2005), 502–31.

Hammerstein, N., 'Die deutschen Universitäten im Zeitalter der Aufklärung', *Zeitschrift für historische Forschung*, 10 (1983), 73–89.

Hancock, David Boyd, '"The cabal of a few designing members": the presidency of Martin Folkes, PRS, and the Society's first charter', *Antiquaries Journal*, 80 (2000), 273–84.

Hans, Nicholas, 'Polish Protestants and their connections with England and Holland in the 17th and 18th centuries', *Slavonic and East European Review*, 37 (1958–9), 196–220.

Harmsen, T., 'Bodleian imbroglios, politics and personalities, 1701–1716: Thomas Hearne, Arthur Charlett, and John Hudson', *Neophilologus*, 82 (1998), 149–68.

Harris, B., 'The London Evening Post and mid-eighteenth-century British Politics', *EHR*, 110 (1995), 1132–56.

Harris, Ian, 'The Authentication of Burke's <u>Reflections</u>: Church, Monarchy and Universities, 1790–91', *History of Political Thought* 43 (2022), 81–130.

Harrison, Peter, 'Newtonian science, miracles, and the laws of nature', *JHI*, 56 (1994), 531–53.

Haslett, Moyra, 'Swift and conversational culture', *Eighteenth-Century Ireland*, 29 (2014), 11–30.

Haugen, K. L., 'Academic charisma and the old regime', *History of Universities*, 22/1 (2007) 76–130.

Hayes, R., 'A forgotten Irish antiquary: Chevalier Thomas O'Gorman 1732–1809', *Studies: An Irish Quarterly Review*, 30 (1941), 587–96.

752 BIBLIOGRAPHY

Herbst, J., 'The American Revolution and the American university', *Perspectives in American History*, 10 (1976), 279–355.

Hesse, C., 'Towards a new topography of enlightenment', *European Review of History*, 13 (2006), 499–508.

Hicks, P., 'Bolingbroke, Clarendon, and the role of Classical historian', *ECS*, 20 (1987), 445–71.

Hirschberg, D. R., 'The government and Church patronage in England, 1660–1760', *JBS*, 20 (1980), 109–39.

Hitchin, Neil W., 'The politics of English Bible translation in Georgian Britain', *TRHS*, 6th ser., 9 (1999), 67–92.

Holmes, G., 'Science, reason, and religion in the age of Newton', *BJHS*, 11 (1978), 164–71.

Holt, P. M., 'Edward Pococke (1604–91), the first Laudian Professor of Arabic at Oxford', *Oxoniensia*, 56 (1991), 119–30.

Hone, Joseph, 'Politicising praise: panegyric and the accession of Queen Anne', *JECS*, 37 (2014), 147–58.

Horne, C. J., 'The Phalaris controversy: King versus Bentley', *Review of English Studies*, 22 (1946), 289–303.

Houfe, S., 'Antiquarian inclinations: diaries of the Countess of Pomfret—II', *CL*, 31 Mar 1977, 800–2.

Hudson, N., 'What is the Enlightenment? Investigating the origins and ideological uses of an historical category', *Lumen*, 25 (2006), 163–74.

Hunter, Ian, 'Secularization: the birth of a modern combat concept', *JMIH*, 12 (2015), 1–32.

Innes, J., 'Jonathan Clark, social history and England's "Ancien Regime"', *Past and Present*, 115 (1987), 165–201.

Jenkins, J. P., 'Jacobites and Freemasons in eighteenth-century Wales', *Welsh History Review*, 9 (1978), 391–406.

Johnstone, H. Diack, 'Handel at Oxford in 1733', *Early Music*, 31 (2003), 248–60.

Jones, H. S., 'The foundation and history of the Camden chair', *Oxoniensia*, 8–9 (1943–4), 170–92.

Jordan, David, 'Le Nain de Tillemont: Gibbon's "sure-footed mule"', *Church History*, 39 (1970), 483–502.

Keene, Nicholas, 'John Fell: education, erudition and the English Church in late seventeenth-century Oxford', *History of Universities*, 18 (2003), 62–101.

Keene, Nicholas, 'John Ernest Grabe, Biblical learning and religious controversy in early eighteenth-century England', *JEH*, 58 (2007), 656–74.

Kelen, Sarah A., 'Cultural capital: selling Chaucer's "Works", building Christ Church, Oxford', *The Chaucer Review* 36 (2001), 149–57.

Key, Newton E., 'The political culture and political rhetoric of county feasts and feast sermons, 1654–1714', *JBS*, 33 (1994), 223–56.

Klein, Lawrence E., 'Addisonian afterlives: Joseph Addison in eighteenth-century culture', *JECS*, 35 (2012), 101–18.

Knights, M., 'The Tory interpretation of history in the rage of parties', *HLQ*, 68 (2005), 353–73.

Kuhn, A. J., 'Nature spiritualised, aspects of anti-Newtonianism', *Journal of English Literary History*, 41 (1974), 400–12.

Langen, Ulrik, 'The meaning of incognito', *The Court Historian*, 7 (2002), 145–55.

Langford, Paul, 'Old Whigs, old Tories and the American Revolution', *Journal of Imperial and Commonwealth History*, 8 (1980), 123–7.

Lawrence, P. D. and A. G. Molland, 'David Gregory's inaugural lecture at Oxford', *Notes and Records of the Royal Society*, 55 (2001), 185–90.

Lehmberg, S. and S., 'Writings of Canterbury Cathedral clergy, 1700–1800', *AEH*, 73 (2004), 53–77.

Leighton, C. D. A., 'Hutchinsonianism: a counter-Enlightenment reform movement', *Journal of Religious Studies*, 23 (1999), 168–84.

Leighton, C. D. A., '"Knowledge of divine things": a study of Hutchinsonianism', *History of European Ideas*, 26 (2000), 159–75.

Leighton, C. D. A., 'AntiChrist's revolution: some Anglican apologists in the age of the French wars', *Journal of Religious History*, 24 (2000), 125–42.

Leighton, C. D. A., 'Ancienneté among the Non-jurors: a study of Henry Dodwell', *History of European Ideas*, 31 (2005), 1–16.

Leighton, C. D. A., 'The Non-jurors and their History', *Journal of Religious History*, 29 (2005), 241–57.

Levere, T. H., 'Dr Thomas Beddoes at Oxford: radical politics in 1788–1793 and the fate of the Regius Chair in Chemistry', *Ambix* 28 (1981), 61–9.

Levere, T. H., 'Dr Thomas Beddoes: science and medicine in politics and society', *BJHS*, 17 (1984), 187–204.

Levere, T.H., 'Dr Thomas Beddoes: chemistry, medicine and the perils of democracy', *Notes & Records of the Royal Society*, 63 (2009), 61–9.

Levis, R. Barry, 'The failure of the Anglican-Prussian ecumenical effort of 1710–1714', *Church History*, 47 (1978), 381–99.

Levitin, Dmitri, 'Matthew Tindal's *Rights of the Christian Church* (1706) and the church-state relationship', *HJ*, 54 (2011), 717–40.

Lodwick, B. M., 'William Adams, a distinguished eighteenth-century archdeacon of Llandaff', *Morgannwg*, 52 (2008), 30–50.

LoGerfo, J. W., 'Sir William Dolben and "the cause of humanity": the passage of the slave trade regulation act of 1788', *ECS*, 6 (1973), 431–51.

Loewenson, Leo, 'Some details of Peter the Great's stay in England in 1698. Neglected English materials', *Slavonic and Eastern European Review*, 40 (1962), 431–43.

Lucas, Paul, 'Blackstone and the reform of the legal profession', *EHR*, 77 (1962), 456–89.

Lucas, Paul, 'A collective biography of the students and barristers of Lincoln's Inn, 1680–1804: A study in the "aristocratic resurgence" of the eighteenth century', *JMH*, 46 (1974), 227–61.

Lupton, Christina, 'Creating the writer of the cleric's words', *JECS*, 34 (2011), 167–83.

Lux, David S. and Harold J. Cook, 'Closed circles or open networks? Communicating at a distance during the scientific revolution', *History of Science*, 36 (1998), 179–211.

MacGregor, Arthur, 'William Huddesford, (1732–1772): his role in reanimating the Ashmolean Museum, his collections, researches and support network', *Archives of Natural History*, 34 (2007), 47–68.

MacGregor, Arthur, 'Edward Lhuyd, museum keeper', *WHR*, 25 (2010), 51–74.

McKane, William, 'Benjamin Kennicott: an eighteenth-century researcher', *JTS*, 28 (1977), 445–64.

McMullin, B. J., 'The "vinegar Bible"', *The Book Collector*, 33 (1984), 53–65.

McNally, P., '"Irish and English interests": national conflict within the Church of Ireland episcopate in the reign of George I', *Irish Historical Studies*, 29 (1995), 295–314.

MacRay, W. D., 'Honorary Oxford degrees conferred on New England clergy in the eighteenth century', *Notes and Queries*, 7th Ser. VI (July 1888), 61–2.

754 BIBLIOGRAPHY

McCormack, Matthew, 'Rethinking "loyalty" in eighteenth-century Britain', *JECS*, 35 (2012), 407–21.

Mahoney, J., 'The Classical tradition in eighteenth-century English rhetorical education', *History of Education Journal*, 9 (1985), 93–7.

Manning, D., 'Theological enlightenments and ridiculous theologies: contradistinction in English polemical theology', in *Religion in the Age of Enlightenment*, 2 (2010), 209–41.

Mather, F. C., 'Church, parliament and penal laws: some Anglo-Scottish interactions in the eighteenth century', *EHR*, 92 (1977), 540–72.

Mayhew, Robert, 'Edmund Gibson's editions of Britannia: dynastic chorography and the politics of precedent, 1695–1722', *Historical Research*, 73 (2000), 239–61.

Mendyk, Stan A. E., 'Robert Plot: Britain's "genial father of county natural histories"', *News and Records of the Royal Society of London*, 39 (1985), 159–77.

Mijers, Esther, 'The Netherlands, William Carstares, and the reform of Edinburgh University, 1690–1715', *History of Universities*, 25 (2011), 111–42.

Miller, Victoria C., 'William Wake and the Reunion of Christians', *Anglican and Episcopal History* 62 (1993), 7–35.

Mischler, Gerd, 'English political sermons 1714–1742: a case study in the theory of the "Divine Right of governors" and the ideology of order', *JECS*, 24 (2001), 33–61.

Mitchell, A., 'Character of an independent Whig—"Cato" and Bernard Mandeville', *History of European Ideas*, 29 (2003), 291–301.

Money, D. K., '"A diff'rent-sounding lyre: Oxford commemorative verse in English, 1613–1834', *BLR*, 16 (1997) 42–92.

Money, John, 'Joseph Priestley in cultural context: philosophic spectacle, popular belief and popular politics in eighteenth-century Birmingham', *Enlightenment and Dissent*, 8 (1989), 69–89.

Monod, Paul, 'A disunited brotherhood?: secrecy, publicity, and controversy among British Freemasons of the eighteenth century', *ECS*, 50 (2017), 440–2.

Monod, Paul, 'Jacobitism and country principles in the reign of William III', *HJ*, 30 (1987), 289–310.

Morgan, Paul, 'Oxford College libraries in the eighteenth century', *BLR*, 14 (1992), 228–36.

Morton, Alan Q., 'Science lecturing in the eighteenth century', special issue of the *BJHS*, 28 (1995).

Munby, Julian, 'James (not John) Green (1729–1759), engraver to the University', *Oxoniensia*, 62 (1977), 319–21.

Musgrave, C., 'Arbury Hall, Warwickshire', *CL*, 8, 15 and 29 Oct. 1953.

Namier, Lewis, 'Country gentlemen in parliament 1750–1783', *History Today*, Oct. 1954, 676–88.

Neve, M. and Porter, R., 'Alexander Catcott: glory and geology', *The British Journal for the History of Science*, ix (1977), 37–60.

Newman, Aubrey, 'Leicester House politics, 1748–51', *EHR*, 76 (1961), 577–89.

Newman, Aubrey, 'Leicester House politics, 1750–60, from the papers of John, second earl of Egmont', *Camden Miscellany, XXIII*, 4th ser., 7 (1969), 85–228.

Nockles, P. B., 'A disputed legacy: Anglican historiographies of the Reformation from the era of the Caroline divines to that of the Oxford Movement', *BJRL*, 83 (2001), 121–167.

Pafford, Michael, 'Robert Plot', *History Today*, 20 (1970), 112–17.

Pailin, David, 'The confused and confusing story of natural religion', *Religion*, 24 (1994), 199–212.

Pelling, M., 'Collecting the world: female friendship and domestic craft at Bulstrode Park', *JECS*, 41 (2018), 101–20.

Petrie, Sir Charles, 'The Elibank plot, 1752–3', *TRHS*, 14 (1931), 175–96.

Philip, I. G., 'The court leet of the University of Oxford', *Oxoniensia*, 15 (1950), 81–91.

Philip, I. G., 'Oxford and scholarly publication in the eighteenth century', *BJECS*, 2 (1979), 123–37.

Pittock, Joan, 'Thomas Warton and the Oxford chair of poetry', *Eng. Studies*, 62 (1981), 14–33.

Pocock, J. G. A., 'Conservative Enlightenment and democratic revolutions: the American and French cases in British perspective', *Government & Opposition*, 24 (1989), 80–105.

Pocock, J. G. A., 'Enthusiasm: the anti-self of Enlightenment', *HLQ*, 60 (1998), 7–28.

Pocock, J. G. A., 'The re-description of Enlightenment', *Proceedings of the British Academy*, 125 (2004), 101–17.

Porter, Roy, 'Science, provincial culture and public opinion in Enlightenment England', *BJECS*, 3 (1980), 20–46.

Prys-Jones, A. G., 'Carmarthenshire and Jesus College, Oxford', *The Carmarthenshire Antiquary*, 4 (1962), 16–25.

Pugh, R. K., 'Post-Restoration Bishops of Winchester as Visitors of Oxford colleges', *Oxoniensia*, 43 (1978), 170–87.

Pumfrey, S., 'Who did the work? Experimental philosophers and public demonstrators in Augustan England', *BJHS*, 28 (1995), 131–56.

Purcell, Mark, '"A lunatick of unsound mind": Edward, Lord Leigh (1742–86), and the refounding of Oriel College Library', *BLR*, 17 (2001), 246–60.

Quarrie, Paul, 'The scientific library of the Earls of Macclesfield', *Notes and Records of the Royal Society*, 60 (2006), 5–24.

Raffe, Alasdair, 'Presbyterians and Episcopalians: the formation of Confessional cultures in Scotland, 1660–1715', *EHR*, 125 (2010), 570–98.

Rees, E. and G. Walters, 'The dispersion of the manuscripts of Edward Lhuyd', *WHR*, 7 (1974), 148–78.

Robinson, E., 'Thomas Beddoes, M.D., and the reform of science teaching at Oxford', *Annals of Science*, 9 (1955), 137–41.

Rogal, S. J., 'Thomas Tickell's *Prospect of Peace*', *Illinois Quarterly*, 35 (1973), 31–40.

Rogers, Pat, 'Book subscriptions among the Augustans', *TLS*, 15 Dec. 1972, 1539–40.

Roos, Anna Marie, 'Taking Newton on tour: the scientific travels of Martin Folkes, 1733–1735', *BJHS*, 50 (2017), 569–601.

Rose, Craig, '"Seminarys of faction and rebellion": Jacobites, Whigs and the London charity schools, 1716–1724', *HJ*, 34 (1991), 831–56.

Rosenfeld, S., 'Some notes on the players in Oxford 1661–1713', *Review of English Studies*, 19 (1943), 366–75.

Ross, Margaret Clunies, 'Re-evaluating the work of Edward Lye, an eighteenth-century septentrional scholar', *Studies in Medievalism*, 9 (1997), 66–79.

Rothery, M. and J. Stobart, 'Inheritance events and spending in the English country house: the Leigh family of Stoneleigh Abbey, 1738–1806', *Continuity and Change*, 27 (2012), 379–407.

Rousseau, G. S. and D. A. B. Haycock, 'Voices calling for reform: the Royal Society in the mid-eighteenth century, Martin Folkes, John Hill, and William Stukeley', *History of Science*, 37 (1999), 377–406.

Rowlinson, J. S., 'John Freind: physician, chemist, Jacobite and friend of Voltaire's', *Notes & Records of the Royal Society*, 61 (2001), 109–27.

Rusnock, Andrea, 'Correspondence networks and the Royal Society, 1700–1750', *BJHS*, 32 (1999), 155–69.

756 BIBLIOGRAPHY

Schaffer, Simon, 'Natural philosophy and public spectacle in the eighteenth century', *History of Science*, 21 (1983), 1–43.

Schofield, R. E.,'An evolutionary taxonomy of eighteenth century Newtonianisms', *Studies in Eighteenth-Century Culture*, 7 (1978), 175–92.

Sharp, Richard, 'The Oxford installation of 1759', *Oxoniensia*, 56 (1991), 145–53.

Shaw, H. Watkins, 'The Oxford University Chair of Music, 1627–1947, with some account of Oxford degrees in music from 1856', *BLR*, 16 (1998), 233–70.

Sheehan, Jonathan, and Dale K. Van Kley, 'Review Essay: God and the Enlightenment', *AHR*, 108 (2003), 1061–80.

Sherburn, G., 'The fortunes and misfortunes of *Three Hours after Marriage*', *Modern Philology*, 24 (1926–7), 91–109.

Shuttleton, D., '"A modest examination": John Arbuthnot and the Scottish Newtonians', *JECS*, 18 (1995), 47–62.

Sirota, Brent S., 'The Trinitarian crisis in Church and state: religious controversy and the making of the postrevolutionary Church of England, 1687–1702', *JBS*, 52 (2013), 26–54.

Smith, D. E., 'John Wallis as a cryptographer', *Bulletin of the American Mathematical Society*, 24 (1917), 82–96.

Snobelen, S. D., 'Caution and, conscience, and the Newtonian reformation: the public and private heresies of Newton, Clarke, and Whiston', *Enlightenment and Dissent*, 16 (1997), 151–84.

Snobelen, S. D., 'Isaac Newton, heretic: the strategies of a Nicodemite', *BJHS*, 32 (1999), 381–419.

Sorrenson, Richard, 'Towards a history of the Royal Society in the eighteenth century', *Notes and records of the Royal Society of London*, 50 (1996), 29–46.

Sorrenson, Richard, 'Did the Royal Society matter in the eighteenth century?', *BJHS*, 32 (1999), 130–2.

Sola Pinta, V. de, 'Sir William Jones and english literature', *Journal of the London School of Oriental Studies*, 11 (1946), 686–94.

Sparrow, E., 'The alien office', *HJ*, 33 (1990), 361–84.

Spurr, John, 'The Church of England, comprehension and the Toleration Act of 1689', *EHR*, 104 (1989), 927–46.

Spurr, John, '"A special kindness for dead bishops": the church, history, and testimony in seventeenth-century Protestantism', *HLQ*, 68 (2005), 313–34.

Stewart, G. M., 'British students at the University of Göttingen in the eighteenth century', *German life and letters*, 33 (1979–80), 24–41.

Stewart, Larry, 'Samuel Clarke, Newtonianism, and the factions of post-Revolutionary England', *JHI*, 42 (1981), 53–72.

Stewart, Larry, 'Public lecture and private patronage in Newtonian England', *Isis*, 77 (1986), 47–58.

Stewart, Larry, 'Seeing through the Scolium: religion and reading Newton in the eighteenth century', *History of Science*, 34 (1996), 123–64.

Stones, L., 'The life and career of John Snell (c.1629–1679)', *Stair Society Miscellany*, 2 (1984), 148–85.

Stray, C., 'From oral to written examinations: Cambridge, Oxford and Dublin 1700–1914', *History of Universities*, 20/2 (2005) 76–130.

Strong, E. W., 'Newtonian explications of natural philosophy', *JHI*, 17 (1957), 49–83.

Sturges, R. P. 'The membership of the Derby Philosophical Society, 1783–1802', *Midland History*, 4 (1978), 212–29.

Susato, R., 'Taming the "tyranny of priests": Hume's advocacy of religious establishments', *JHI*, 73 (2012), 273–93.

Sutherland, L. S., 'The origin and early history of the lord almoner's professorship in Arabic at Oxford, *BLR*, 10 (1978–82), xx.

Sutherland, L. S., 'The Foundation of Worcester College', *Oxoniensia*, 44 (1979), 62–80.

Sweet, R., 'Freemen and independence in English borough politics c.1770–1830', *P&P*, 161 (1998), 84–115.

Tapsell, Grant, 'Laurence Hyde and the politics of religion in later Stuart England', *EHR*, 125 (2010), 1415–48.

Taylor, Stephen J., 'Sir Robert Walpole, the Church of England and the Quakers Tithe Bill of 1736, *HJ*, 28 (1985), 51–77.

Taylor, Stephen J., 'The factotum in ecclesiastical affairs? The Duke of Newcastle and the Crown's ecclesiastical patronage', *Albion*, 14 (1992), 409–33.

Thackeray, M., 'Christopher Pitt, Joseph Warton, and Virgil', *Review of English Studies*, 43 (1992), 329–46.

Thomann, G.,'John Ernest Grabe (1666–1711): Lutheran syncretist and Anglican patristic scholar', *Review of English Studies*, 43 (1992), 414–27.

Thomas, P. D. G., 'Jacobitism in Wales', *WHR*, 1 (1962), 279–300.

Thomas, P. D. G., Sir Roger Newdigate's essays on party, c.1760', *EHR*, 102 (1987), 394–400.

Thomas, P. D. G., 'Politics in the age of Lord North', *PH*, 6 (1987), 47–68.

Thwaites, W., 'The assize of bread in eighteenth-century Oxford', *Oxoniensia*, 51 (1986), 171–81.

Tompson, R. S., 'The English grammar school curriculum in the 18th century: a reappraisal', *British Journal of Educational Studies*, 19 (1971), 32–9.

Townend, G. M., 'Repeal of the occasional conformity and schism acts', *PH*, 7 (1988), 22–44.

Toynbee, Paget, 'Horace Walpole's Delenda est Oxonia', *EHR*, 42 (1927), 95–108.

Trowell, S., 'Unitarian and/or Anglican: the relationship of Unitarianism to the Church from 1687–98', *BJRL*, 78 (1996), 77–101.

Turner, A. J., 'Mathematical instruments and the education of gentlemen', *Annals of Science*, 30 (1973), 51–88.

Tyack, G., 'The making of the Radcliffe Observatory', *The Georgian Group Journal*, 10 (2000), 122–40.

Tyack, G., 'Gibbs and the Universities', *The Georgian Group Journal* 27 (2019), 57–78.

Tyacke, N., 'From *Studium Generale* to modern research university: eight hundred years of Oxford history', *History of Universities*, XXX/1–2 (2017), 205–25.

Ultee, M., 'The Republic of Letters: learned correspondence 1680–1720', *Seventeenth Century*, 2 (1987), 95–112.

Vallance, Edward, 'Women, politics, and the 1723 oaths of allegiance to George I, 1723', *HJ*, 59 (2016), 975–99.

van den Berg, J., 'The Leiden professors of the Schultens family and their contacts with British scholars', *Durham University Journal*, 75 (1982–3), 1–14.

Van Kley, Dale K., 'Religion and the age of "patriot reform"', *JMH*, 80 (2008), 252–95.

Varley, F. J., 'The Oriel College lawsuit, 1724–6', *Oxoniensia*, 6 (1941), 56–69.

Wahba, Magdi, 'Madame de Genlis in England', *Comparative literature*, 13 (1961), 221–38.

Wallis, Ruth, 'Cross-currents in astronomy and navigation: Thomas Hornsby FRS (1733–1810)', *Annals of Science*, 57 (2000), 219–40.

758   BIBLIOGRAPHY

Walsh, M., 'Profession and authority; the interpretation of the Bible in the seventeenth and eighteenth centuries', *Literature and Theology*, 9 (1995), 383–98.

Walters, G. and F. Emery, 'Edward Lhuyd, Edmund Gibson, and the printing of Camden's *Britannia*, 1695', *Library*, 5th series, 32 (1977), 109–37.

Ward, A., 'The Tory view of Roman history', *Studies in English Literature 1500–1900*, 4 (1964), 413–56.

Ward Jones, P. and D. Burrows, 'An inventory of mid-eighteenth-century Oxford musical hands', *Royal Musical Association Research Chronicle*, 35 (2002), 61–139.

Weinbrot, Howard, 'Samuel Johnson, Percival Stockdale, and brick-bats from grubstreet', *HLQ*, 56 (1993), 105–34.

Werrett, Simon, 'Introduction: rethinking Joseph Banks', *Notes and Records of the Royal Society*, 73 (2019), 425–9.

White, G., 'Humphrey Humphreys, Bishop of Bangor and Hereford 1648–1712', *Anglesey Antiquarian Society and Field Club* (1949), 61–76.

Wigelsworth, J. R., 'A sheep in the midst of wolves: reassessing Newton and English deists', *Enlightenment and Dissent*, 25 (2009), 260–86.

Wilson, A., 'Conflict, consensus and charity: politics and the provincial voluntary hospitals in the eighteenth century', *EHR*, 111 (1996), 599–616.

Wintle, M., 'Islam as Europe's "other" in the long term: some discontinuities', *History*, 101 (2016), 42–61.

Wollenberg, Susan, 'Music in eighteenth-century Oxford', *Proceedings of the Royal Musical Association*, 108 (1981–2), 69–99.

Wollenberg, Susan, 'Handel in Oxford: The tradition c.1750–1850', *Göttinger Händel-Beiträge*, 9 (2002), 161–76.

Woolley, R., 'James Bradley, third astronomer royal', *Quarterly Journal of the Royal Astronomical Society*, 4 (1963), 47–52.

Wyland, R. M., 'An Archival study of rhetoric texts and teaching at the University of Oxford', *Rhetorica*, 21 (2003), 175–95.

Yeo, G., 'A case without parallel: the bishops of London and the Anglican Church overseas, 1660–1748', *JEH*, 44 (1993), 450–73.

Yohannan, J., 'The Persian poetry fad in England, 1770–1825', *Comparative Literature*, 4 (1952), 137–60.

Zebrowski, Martha K., 'John William Thomson's 1728 edition of Plato's "Parmenides": a Calvinist humanist from Königsberg reads Platonic theology in Oxford', *JECS*, 30 (2007), 113–31.

3) Unpublished Theses

Albers, Jan Maria, 'Seeds of contention: society, politics, and the Church of England in Lancashire, 1689–1780', Ph.D. thesis (Yale University, 1988).

Ansell, Richard, 'Irish Protestant travel to Europe, 1660–1727', D.Phil. thesis (Oxford University, 2014).

Berry, David A., 'Collecting at Oxford: a history of the University's museums, gardens, and libraries', D.Phil. thesis (Oxford University, 2 vols., 2004).

Bowles, G., 'The place of Newtonian explanation in english popular thought, 1687–1727', D.Phil. thesis (Oxford University, 1977).

Byrne, Michael, 'Alternative cosmologies in early eighteenth-century England', Ph.D. thesis (University of London, 1998).

Caudle, James Joseph, 'Measures of allegiance: sermon culture and the creation of a public discourse of obedience and resistance in Georgian Britain, 1714–1760', Ph.D. thesis (Yale University, 1996).

Clarke, T. M., 'The Scottish Episcopalians 1688–1720', Ph.D. thesis (Edinburgh University, 1987).

Dudley, D. L., 'Henrietta Louisa Jeffreys, Oxford and the Pomfret Benefaction of 1755: vertu made visible', Ph.D. thesis (University of Victoria, 2004).

Engel, D., 'The ingenious Dr King', Ph.D. thesis (University of Edinburgh, 1989).

Findon, J. C., 'The Nonjurors and the Church of England, 1689–1716', D.Phil. thesis (Oxford University, 1979).

Fisher, John, 'Astronomy and patronage in Hanoverian England: the work of James Bradley, third Astronomer Royal of England', Ph.D. thesis (University of London, 2004).

Honeybone, Michael, 'The Spalding Gentlemen's Society: the communication of science in the East Midlands of England 1710–1760', Ph.D. thesis (Open University, 2001).

Murray, Nancy U., 'The influence of the French Revolution on the Church of England and its rivals, 1789–1802', D.Phil. thesis (Oxford University, 1975).

O'Brien, Paula J., 'The life and works of James Miller, 1704–1744, with specific reference to the satiric content of his poetry and plays', Ph.D. thesis (University of London, 1979).

Smith, Lawrence Berkley, Jr., 'Charles Boyle, 4th Earl of Orrery, 1674–1731', Ph.D. thesis (Edinburgh University, 1994).

Smith, Valerie, 'Rational Dissent in England c.1770–c.1800: definitions, identity and legacy', Ph.D. thesis (University of Kent, 2017).

Stevens, Ralph, 'Anglican responses to the Toleration Act, 1689–1714', Ph.D. thesis (Cambridge University, 2014).

Swift, A. K., 'The formation of the library of Charles Spencer, 3rd Earl of Sunderland (1674–1722): a study in the antiquarian book trade', D.Phil. thesis (2 vols., Oxford University, 1986).

Taylor, S., 'Church and state in England in the mid-eighteenth century: The Newcastle years 1742–62', Ph D. thesis (University of Cambridge, 1987).

Townend, Graham M., 'The political career of the 3rd Earl of Sunderland', Ph.D. thesis (Edinburgh University, 1985).

Trowles, T. A., 'The musical ode in Britain, c.1670–1800', D.Phil. thesis (Oxford University, 1992).

Wilson, P., 'The knowledge and appreciation of Pindar in the seventeenth and eighteenth centuries', D. Phil. thesis (Oxford University, 1974).

Zizi, Z., 'Thomas Shaw (1692–1751) à Tunis et Alger missionnaire de la curiosité européenne', thèse de doctorat (Université de Caen, 1995) (ANRT Lille).

4) Other materials

The Heather Professor of Music, 1626–1976: exhibition in the divinity school October 1976 (Bodleian Library, Oxford, 1976).

CD notes by Anthony Rooley and Simon Heighes to Hayes, *The Passions*, Schola Cantorum Basiliensis (2010)

A. M. Roos: 'The Oxford Philosophical Society and the Royal Society: a meeting of minds?', podcast 23 July 2013 http://podcasts.ox.ac.uk/oxford-philosophical-society-and-royal-society-meeting-minds Accessed 26/08/2022.

5) Selected online links

The Taylor Institution Library

http://blogs.bodleian.ox.ac.uk/taylorian/2014/11/13/history-of-the-taylor-institution-library-and-its-collections/ Accessed 26/08/2022

BHO: Alumni Oxoniensis 1500–1714

https://www.british-history.ac.uk/alumni-oxon/1500–1714/ Accessed 26/08/2022

760 BIBLIOGRAPHY

Physicans, surgeons, apothecaries, dentists, 1621–1860
www.oxfordhistory.org.uk/doctors/index.html Accessed 26/08/2022
Lord Lieutenants of Oxfordshire
www.oxfordhistory.org.uk/people_lists/oxon_lord_lieutenants/index.html Accessed 26/08/2022
Church of England database: CCEd Person ID
Payne, Reider, 'George Pretyman, bishop of Lincoln, and the University of Cambridge 1787–1801', http://theclergydatabase.org.uk/cce_a3-html/ Accessed 26/08/2022
Sterk, Anna, https://history.lincoln.ac.uk/2018/12/11/cultural-assimilation-of-portuguese-jews-in-18th-century-london-and-portugal/.
Dissenting Academies online
www.qmul.ac.uk/sed/religionandliterature/dissenting-academies/dissenting-academies-online/
'Cultures of Knowledge: Networking the Republic of letters 1550–1750' [web].
http://emlo-portal.bodleian.ox.ac.uk/collections/?catalogue=edward-lhwyd Accessed 26/08/2022
https://artsandculture.google.com/story/emanuel-mendes-da-costa-1717-1791-the-royal-society/mAWBb0daZKtiIA?hl=en
https://history.lincoln.ac.uk/2018/12/11/cultural-assimilation-of-portuguese-jews-in-18th-century-london-and-portugal/.

Index

For the benefit of digital users, indexed terms that span two pages (e.g., 52–53) may, on occasion, appear on only one of those pages.

Abbey Leix, Co. Laois 474–5
Abbot, Charles, 1st Lord Colchester 394n.164, 619
 MP for the University 394–5
Abd al-Latif of Baghdad 174–5
Abel, Karl Friedrich 191–2, 432
Aberdeen 461–2
 University of (King's College and Marischal
  Colleges) 44n.120, 171–2
 curriculum 72
 Oxford connections 462–3, 465, 467–8
 purges after '15 Rebellion 69–70, 364–7,
  462–3
 Visitation after 1688 Revolution 69–70
Aberford, Yorks. 448–9
Abergavenny School 455–6
Abingdon, Earls of, see Bertie, and Venables-Bertie
Abjuration, Act of 303, 315–16; see also oaths
abolitionism 590–2
'Abulcasis' (al-Zahrawi) 174–5
Académie Politique 369–70
Académie Royale des Inscriptions et Belles-
  Lettres 182
Academies, Dissenting, see Dissenters, Protestant
Acland, Henrietta 540n.265
Acland, John 261n.65
actors 25; see also strolling players
Acts, see Oxford, University of
Adair, James 394–5
Adam, Robert 32
Adams, Fitzherbert 62
Adams, George (the elder) 227–8
Adams, George (the younger) 227–8
Adams, William (of Pembroke College) 527–8
 Archdeacon of Llandaff 636n.174
 admirer of Locke 194–5
 friend of Richard Price 497n.56
 friend of Samuel Johnson 514
 on moral law 172–3
 orthodoxy questioned 172n.209
 writes against Hume 171–2, 194–5, 210n.67
Adams, William (of Northants.) 424n.32
Addington, Henry 242n.199, 380–1,
  408–9, 608

administration (1801–4) 259–60
 reduces secret service funding 402–3
Addison, Joseph 136
 journalist and dramatist 135–6
 Latinist 135–6
 national influence of 135–6, 135n.19,
  661–2
 Oxford, and 135–6, 135n.19, 197n.322
 Pleasures of the Imagination 424–5
 Secretary of State 136
 travels in Europe 555–6
Admiralty, the 241–2
Adolphus, Prince 341–2
Adventures of Oxymel Classic, Esq: Once an
  Oxford Scholar, The 490–1
Aelfric, Abbot of Eynsham 153–4
Aeschylus 162–3, 630
Agar, Charles, Archbishop of Cashel, 1st Earl of
  Normanton 471, 475n.305
Agnesi, Maria Gaetana 527n.196
Agutter, William 171–2
Aiken, John 494
Ailesbury, Earl of, see Bruce
Aix-la-Chapelle, Treaty of (1748) 291–2,
  334, 508
Akenside, Mark 640–1
Alday, Paul 192
Alcock, Nathan[iel]
 career 224n.131
 declines Regius Professorship of
  Medicine 223–4
 lectures in anatomy and chemistry 223–4
Aldrich, George Oakley 242–3, 243n.202
Aldrich, Henry 27–8, 27n.48, 35–6, 66–8,
  71n.89, 136, 137n.28, 223, 269–70,
  282–3, 315–16, 404–5, 405n.209
 architecture, and 28–31, 29nn.52,53,
  474–5
 clerical politician 404–5
 Artis logicae compendium (1691) 167–8,
  194–5
 composer 186–7
 history writing, and 145–6

762   INDEX

Aldrich, Henry (*cont.*)
  mathematics tutor 219
  moderate Toryism 317–18, 404–5
  nurtures future Tory leaders 404–5
  Oxford University Press, and 54–5
  patron 570–2
  Phalaris controversy, and 160, 195–6
  Wesminster connections 66–8, 404–5
Algiers 162
Alfred, King 153–4
  and foundational myth 247; *see also*
    University College
Alien Office 402
Allgemeine Bibliothek der biblischen
    Litteratur 127–9
All Souls College
  Wardens, *see* Finch, Leopold; Gardiner
  benefactions 590–2, 645
  brought into disrepute by Tindal 62–3, 63n.53
  buildings 31, 645
  Codrington Library 32
  civil law taught at 410–11
  fellowship holding rules 64n.54
  Founders' Kin 286, 614–15
  Visitor, involvement in College affairs
    285–6
Alsop, Anthony 71n.89, 132–3, 160–1, 191,
    458n.208, 507, 549n.296, 569n.72
Altham, Roger 361–2
Alton Barnes, Wilts. 675
Ambrosden, Oxon. 426–7, 438
America, British North 10
  American students at Oxford 554, 596–7
  Anglican presence in 592–5
  Convocation endorses coercion of
    (1775) 346–7
  Declaration of Independence 345–6
  growing opposition to the war among
    University members 347
  loyalists in 39, 594–7
  Oxford and 39, 41–2, 180–1, 345–7, 357, 554,
    592–7, 594n.196
  refugee clergy welcomed in Oxford 346–7,
    347n.204
  relief fund for refugee clergy 376–7, 595
  Revolution 19–20, 76–7, 266–7, 596–7
Amhurst, Nicholas 42–3, 152–3, 167n.178,
    331–2
  disgruntled Whig 518
  edits *The Craftsman* 518n.162
  expelled from the University 518
  Oculus Britanniae 518
  Terrae-Filius essays 331–2, 518, 672
Amiens, Peace of (1802–3) 354, 402–3

Anacreon 165n.175
anatomy school, Old Schools quadrangle
    223–4; *see also* Bodleian Library,
    Christ Church
Ancient Britons, Society of 460–1
Ancients and Moderns 5–6, 161n.146; *see also*
    Cambridge, University of, 'Republic of
    Letters'
  fusion of two concepts 72–3, 215–16
  in France 55n.13
  Oxford defence of the 'Ancients' 55–6,
    159–62, 195–6, 507
Anglesey, Earl of, *see* Annesley
Anglicanism, *see* Church of England
Anglo-Latin verse 5–6, 132–3, 141, 661–2
Anglo-Saxon studies, *see* Oxford, University of
Anne, Princess Royal, later Princess of
    Orange 294–5, 570n.75, 666–7
Anne, Queen 7–8, 18–19, 21, 33–5, 39–40,
    65–6, 124–5, 136, 146n.72, 193–4,
    276–7, 299–300, 315–16, 357,
    580–1, 666; *see also* Tories
  accession 316–17, 361–2
  before her accession 306–7
  commitment to the Established Church
    307–8, 355
  death lamented 308, 313n.57, 320
  discussion as to her title 318
  political significance of her death 318, 362–3
  statues of in Oxford 318n.79
  visits Cambridge University 307n.30
  visits Oxford 1702 307–8, 420–1, 549
  wary of high Tories 155–6, 307–8,
    316–17, 361–2
Annesley, Arthur, 5th Earl of Anglesey 430–1,
    431n.67
Ansford, Somerset 626
anticlericalism 46–7, 74–5, 203–5, 213–14;
    see also Enlightenment
Antigua 597
anti-Catholicism, *see* Roman Catholics
Anti-Jacobin 140–1
antiquarians and antiquarianism; see also *érudits*,
    history
  popular with Oxford graduates in the
    provinces 158–9, 193–4, 630–3
  popular with Tories and Nonjurors 160n.142
  unfashionable 157–8
Apethorpe, Northants. 253
Apollonius Rhodius 163
Appleby Grammar School 454–5
Arabic, 175n.226; *see also* Oxford, University of,
    Laudian Chair of Arabic
  chairs in elsewhere 174n.222

Arbury Hall, Warwickshire 33n.72, 278–9, 389–90, 610–11, 618–19
Arbuthnot, Charles 60n.39, 461
Arbuthnot, John 60–1, 60n.39, 461
Arches, Dean of 285–6
Archives, University 176n.233
    Keepers of, *see* Swinton, Wise
Aretaeus 222–3
Argyll, dukes of, *see* Campbell
Arianism 116–18, 123–4, 239
Arius 84–6
Aristotelianism 72–3, 199
    at Oxford 165n.176, 167–8, 167n.178, 194–5, 200, 201n.21, 217–19, 238–9, 379
Armagh, Archbishops of, *see* Boulter, Stone, Robinson, Newcome
Arnauld, Antoine 588–9
Arne, Thomas 187–8, 192
Arnold, Samuel 187–8
Articles, Thirty-Nine 19–20, 83–4, 203, 256–7, 376–7, 465–6, 570; *see also* Church of England
Arundel marbles 341–2, 565, 650–1
Ashe, St George 468–9
Ashmolean Museum 6–7, 157–8, 216–17, 530
    Keepers 226n.139, *see* Plot, Lhuyd, Parry, Whiteside, Huddesford (William), Sheffield
    Under-Keeper, *see* Massey
    collections updated 225–6
    contents 216–17
    donations to 225–6
    foundation 216–17
    laboratory at 217–19
    lectures at 217–19, 227–8, 233
    public admission numbers 226n.140
Asseline, Jean-René 560–2
Assize sermons 361–2, 637–8
Association, Articles of (1696) 64–5, 384–5, 413n.255, 431–2
Association to preserve the constitution in Church and State (1745) 262–3, 291–2, 305, 325, 334, 371–2
Association movement (early 1780s) 348
Association for the Preservation of Liberty and Property against Republicans and Levellers 351n.226
Association, City (of Oxford) and University (1798) 353; *see also* Oxford Loyal Volunteers and City Volunteers
Astley, Warks. 610–11, 611n.59
Astorga, Emanuele d' 188n.284
Astronomers Royal, *see* Flamsteed, Halley, Bradley

Athalia, see Handel
Athanasian Creed 115–16
Athanasius, St 84–6, 203
Athens 32, 180
Atholl, duke of, *see* Murray
Atterbury, Bishop Francis 27–8, 64–5, 134, 201n.17, 282–3, 289, 355, 415–16, 472–3, 590–2
    Dean of Carlisle 269–70
    Dean of Christ Church 92–4, 94n.70, 223, 259–60, 269–70, 270n.94, 272–4, 405, 665–6
    Bishop of Rochester and Dean of Westminster 269–70, 405
    alliance with Harley 405
    alliance with Bolingbroke 405
    and Convocation dispute and revival 63–4, 156–7, 405, 406n.214
    and Phalaris controversy 160–2
    as preacher 92–4
    exiled 146–7
    fails to write a History 146–7
    in the House of Lords 396–7
    sermons published 98–9, 99n.96
    support for in Oxford 97
    trial 401–2
Atterbury Plot 248–50, 308–10, 320, 322–3, 368–9, 401–2, 435, 653, 666–8; *see also* Arran
Atwell, Joseph 332–3, 556
Atworth, Wilts. 636–7
Aubrey, John 63n.48
Augsburg League, War of (1689–97) 58–60, 65–6, 360–1, 412, 549n.296
Augusta of Saxe-Gotha, Princess of Wales 325, 413, 548n.292
Augusta, Princess, daughter of George III 341–2
Augustus, Prince 341–2
Austen, Cassandra 531
Austen, Jane 531, 539–40
Austin, William 184n.267, 229, 229n.159
Austria, Ferdiand Karl, Archduke of 567–8
Austrian Succession, War of the (1740–8) 324
Avignon 248n.3
Avison, Charles 192
Aylesford, Earl of, *see* Finch, Heneage
Ayliffe, John 331–2, 331n.138

Bach, C.P.E. 187–8
Bach, J.C. 192, 432
Bacon, Francis, 1st Viscount St Albans 166–7, 239–41
Bacon, John 32

764   INDEX

Badcock, Samuel 502–3
Badminton, Glos. 603–4, 607–8
Bagot family 10–11
Bagot, Bishop Lewis
 Dean of Christ Church 256–7, 271–2, 295–6,
  379, 611n.61, 619
 Bishop of Bristol, later Norwich 271–2,
  636n.175
 defends the Established Church 117–18,
  256–7, 257n.44
 Tory politics 271–2
Bagot, Sir Walter, 5th Bt. 611
Bagot, Sir William, 6th Bt., 1st Lord Bagot
  557–8, 611
Bagot, née Hay, Mary 485
Bagshot Park, Surrey 250–1, 271n.100
Baker, Thomas
 An Act at Oxford 486–8
Baker, William
 Warden of Wadham College 275–6
 client of 1st Duke of Marlborough 275–6,
  330n.133
 receives bishopric 275–6, 333
Ballard, George 25–6
Baillardeau, Louis 142
Bailly, Jean Sylvain 566–7
Bainbridge, Richard 452
Baldwin, Richard 468–9
Ballard, George 527n.198, 631–2
Balliol College 8–9; see also Snell exhibition
 Masters, see Hunt, Joseph; Leigh; Parsons
 building work at 31–2
 Greaves Exhibition 447–8
 lectureship endowed by Richard Busby
  283–4
 school connections 450–1
 Scots at 465–7
 Tory character of 467–8
 Visitorship 283–4, 287
balloon flights, see Sadler
Bampton Lectures 78–9, 105–6, 115,
  118–20, 122, 127–9, 454–5, 628
Bampfylde, Coplestone Warre 617
Banbury 257n.48
Bandinel, James 119–21, 120n.192, 121n.195
Bandini, Angiolo Maria 581–2
Bangor, Bishops of, see Humphreys, Hoadly,
  Baker, Ewer, Moore
Bangorian Controversy 80–1, 94–5, 276n.123,
  328, 661–2
Banks, Sir Joseph, 1st Bt. 233–4, 242n.197,
  651–2
Banner, Richard 371n.62
Barbados 590–2

Barker, Charles Thomas 43n.116
Barming, Kent 647–9
Barnard, Toby 474–5
Barnes, Rev. Frederick 352
Baron, John 363n.17
 and reform of the universities 367n.39
Barrington, John, 1st Viscount
  Barrington [I] 478
Barrington, Bishop the Hon. Shute 127n.217,
  343n.187, 628
 Canon of Christ Church 348
 Visitor of Balliol College 287
 supporter of Biblical scholarship 87–8
Barrow, William 338, 628
Baskett, John 81–2
Bastard, John Pollexfen 391–3
Bate, Julius 210n.66
Bath, Earl of, see Pulteney
Bathurst, Henry, 3rd Earl Bathurst 619
Bathurst, Ralph 91, 645, 647–9
'Battle of the Books', see Ancients and Moderns
Bauer, Ferdinand 560n.29
Bayle, Pierre 177n.237
Beales, Derek 47n.140, 76n.109
Beattie, James 467–8
 Aberdeen professor 513–14, 514n.139
 An Essay on the Nature and Immutability of
  Truth in Opposition to Sophistry and
  Scepticism 513–14, 514n.140
 Anglophile 513–14
 arch critic of Hume 171–2, 513–14
 awarded Oxford DCL 513–14, 549–50
 enjoyment of Oxford visits 514n.141
 The Minstrel 179
Beauclerk, Lord Aubrey 527–8
Beaufort, Dukes of 1; see also Somerset
 connections to Oxford 603–4
 ecclesiastical patronage 604–5
 electoral influence 605n.23
 estates 603–4
Beaufoy, Henry 257, 500–1
Beccles, Suffolk
 Book Club at 636–7
Beddoes, Thomas 6–7, 225
 Cyril Jackson an early patron 231–2
 denied a professorship on political
  grounds 232–3, 238–9, 664–5
 foreign languages familiarity, and 143, 231–2
 leaves Oxford 232
 links with dissenters 231–2
 popularity of his lectures 231–2
 reader in chemistry 231–2, 231n.169
 sympathies for the French Revolution 232,
  233n.176

INDEX   765

Bedford, Duke of, *see* Russell
Bedford
  Archdeacon of, *see* Shepherd
  School 446–7, 452
Bedouins 180–1
Beeke, Henry 151n.101
Behn, Aphra 165n.172
Bellarmine, Cardinal Robert 41n.103
Bellini, Lorenzo 216–17
Benedictines 16–17, 17n.16
Bennett, G.V. (Gary) 405, 635n.170
Bentham, Edward 514
  sub-dean of Christ Church 102
  and Durham canonry 334n.153
  assessment of 171n.205, 194–5
  critical of disputations 167–8
  endorses Locke 170
  moderate Whig credentials 102, 301–2, 334
  offers lectures 102–3, 129
  published writings 102, 168–70, 298
  Regius Professor of Divinity 102,
    102n.109, 348
  supports repression of the American
    colonies 346–7, 374
  Whitehall preacher 334
Bentham, Jeremy 132n.6, 304n.19, 518n.161
Bentinck, Lord Edward 27n.46
Bentinck, née Harley, Margaret, 2nd Duchess of
  Portland 371n.64, 527–8, 530
Bentick, William, 2nd Duke of Portland 549
Bentinck, William Cavendish-, 3rd duke of
  Portand 230n.161, 353–4
  alliance with Cyril Jackson 407–8
  Chancellor of the University 26–7, 141n.53,
    258–9, 272–4, 351–2, 359–60,
    377–9, 511–12, 608
    installation 1793 189–91, 258n.53, 259,
      542–3, 549
  Christ Church graduate 26–7, 402, 550n.305
  Home Secretary 259–60, 354, 378–9,
    395–6, 472
  intelligence services, and the 402
  Nottinghamshire magnate 243n.202
  patron of Oxford Whigs 267, 348–9,
    378–9, 549
  political career 258–60, 259n.55, 378–9
  proposes Burke for honorary degree 511–12
  presents Volunteer colours 1798 353
Bentinck, William Henry Cavendish-Scott-, 4th
  duke of Portand 403n.196
Bentley, Richard 55–6, 164, 570–2
  Boyle lecturer 241
  Oxford critics of 160–2, 195–6, 207, 207n.48
  Phalaris controversy, and 160, 162n.153

plans for new edition of Greek New
  Testament 84–6
time in Oxford 163n.157
Whig politics 161–2
Benucci, Francesco 189–91
Benzelius the younger, Erik, Archbishop of
  Uppsala 566–7, 629n.141
Berdmore, Scrope 609n.52
Berkeley, Bishop George 98n.89, 633
Berkeley, George, the younger 113, 462–3,
  529n.215
Berkeley, George Monk 424–5
Berkeley, John, 5th Lord Berkeley of
  Stratton 251n.17, 614n.71
Berks., Archdeacon of, *see* Dodwell, William
Berlin 581–2
Bernard, Francis 597n.210
Bernard, Scrope 596
Bertie, Hon. Albemarle 132–3
Bertie, Hon. Charles 391n.153, 432n.70
Bertie, James, 1st Earl of Abingdon 418–19
  Lord-Lieutenant of Oxfordshire 431–2
  dismissed as 431–2, 436
Bertie, Hon. Peregrine 418–19
Bertie, Willoughby, 3rd Earl of Abindon 429,
  431–2, 432n.71
Bertie, Willoughby, 4th Earl of Abingdon
  debts 432
  minor patron of Kennicott 348
  musical composer and patron 432
  Pittite 440–1
  Whig politics 348, 418–19, 432, 440–1
Bessarion 162
Betterton, Thomas 138n.40, 546n.283
Betty, Joseph 94–5
Beverley Grammar School 443–4
Bianchini, Francesco 566–7
Bible; *see also* Oxford, University Press
  Authorized Version 1611 81–2, 660–1
  British identity, and 83n.18
  distribution 90
  marketing and profits from 81–2
  monarchy and 89, 89n.54
  New Testament in Latin 585–6
  Oxford biblical scholarship 82–90, 89n.54,
    127–9, 659
  Quarto Bible 1798 81–2
  revision of AV attempted 82–9, 83n.16
  Vinegar Bible 81–2
Bicester 352
Biddlecombe, William 192
Bidlake, Dr John 454–5
Billington, Elizabeth 189–91
Bilson-Legge, Henry 139n.42

766   INDEX

Bingham, Joseph
  adjudged guily of anti-Trinitarianism 62,
    123–4
  patristic scholarship 123–4, 123n.202, 587
Bird, John 227–8
Birkhead, Henry 138n.39, 663
Birmingham 182–4, 639–40
  1791 riots 502
Biskup, Thomas 583
Bisse, Thomas
  Chancellor of Hereford cathedral 454–5
Black, Jeremy 108n.136, 145n.67
Black, Joseph 225, 231–2, 502
Blackall, Offspring 202–3
Blackburne, Francis 117–18, 496–7
  The Confessional 496
Blackstone, James 352
Blackstone, Sir William 94, 102–3, 180–1, 347,
    373, 410, 646, 676
  Collateral Consanguinity 614–15
  Commentaries 326–8, 327n.121, 345–6, 663
  consulted by ministers 398–9
  court politics in 1760s 413–14, 413n.258
  first Vinerian Professor of English Law
    410–11, 413–14
  influences future George III's
    education 346n.199
  Laudian statutes, and the 16–17
  lauds George III's constitutional grasp 346
  national standing 413–14, 663
  Pomfret marbles, and 651
  proposed edition of Cicero's works 146n.73
  reform of Oxford University Press 54–5, 89,
    89n.55
  Solicitor General to Queen Charlotte 413–14
  Tory politics of 413–14, 439n.109
Blacow, Richard 311–12, 325, 336, 371–3,
    414n.261, 429
  Canon of Windsor 336n.158
Bladon, Oxon. 626
Blandford, Marquess of, *see* Marlborough,
    5ᵗʰ Duke of
Blanning, Tim 45n.126
blasphemy, bill against 1721 117
Blathwayt, William 590–2
Blayney, Benjamin 676
  Vice-Principal Hertford College 84n.22
  Oxford Bible 1769 83–4, 84nn.21,22,24,
    87–8, 659
  Professor of Hebrew 84n.22
  translates Jeremiah and Lamentations 88–9
Blechinden, Richard 270n.94, 537, 646n.206
Blencowe, William
  All Souls College, and 400, 400n.186

  commits suicide 400
  official Decypherer 400
  Whig politics 400
Blenheim, battle of 329
Blenheim Palace (Blenheim 'House') 418, 669;
    see also Dukes of Marlborough
  1ˢᵗ duke and duchess take up
    residence 330n.131
  amateur theatricals at 429
  chapel consecration 627n.132
  cost 428n.48
  visitors to 493, 493n.41, 567–8
  George III visits 342
Bletchingdon, Oxon. 425–6, 430–1
Bliss, Nathaniel 221n.113, 224, 540
Blithfield, Staffs. 279, 611
Blundell's School, Tiverton 450–1
'Board of Brothers' 603–4, 604n.21
Bodleian Library 4–5; *see also* anatomy school
  Librarians of, *see* Hudson, Hyde (Thomas),
    Price (John)
  sub-librarian, *see* Hearne
  admissions 54n.7, 574n.90
  books burnt outside 40–1, 318
  foreign visitors to 53–4, 472, 566–7, 567n.64,
    572–4, 676; *see also* Oxford, University of
  Old Schools Quadrangle 40–1, 227–8
  Oriental manuscripts in 182
  purchase of 'Enlightenment' and scientific
    texts 54–5
  research library 53–5
Boerhaave, Herman 223–4, 558–9
Bolingbroke, Viscount, *see* St John
Bologna, University 525–7, 553–4
Bonaparte, Napoleon
  First Consul 402–3
Bordelon, Abbé 563–4
Boringdon, Lord, *see* Parker, John
Borlase, William
  antiquarian publications 631–2
  donations to the Ashmolean Museum
    225–6, 631–2
  minerologist 631–2
Boscawen, Frances ('Fanny'), the Hon.
    Mrs. Edward Boscawen 607–8
Bossuet, Bishop 588n.161
Boston, MA 580–1, 593–4
Boswell, James 344n.196, 464, 495–6
  enjoyment of Oxford visits 514
Botanical Society of London 582–3
Boulter, Hugh
  Dean of Christ Church 270–1
  Bishop of Bristol 270
  Archbishop of Armagh 271, 474

anti-Jacobite 270n.98, 474
  Whig politics 270–1, 474
Boulton, Matthew 225n.137, 502, 639–40
Bounty, Queen Anne's 652–3
Bourne, Robert
  'chemical reader' 233
  lectures 233
Bouverie, Pleydell-, Jacob, 2ⁿᵈ Earl of
  Radnor 623–4
Bowdoin, James 596–7
Bowles, William Lisle 140–1
Boyce, William 192
Boyle Lectures 70–1, 71n.87, 106–7, 160, 202–3,
  202nn.26,27, 241
Boyle, Charles, 4ᵗʰ Earl of Orrery
  bequest of scientific instruments and library to
    Christ Church 224, 649
  hosts dinners for alumni 623–4
  Phalaris controversy, and 160, 397, 470
  Tory leader in House of Lords 397
Boyle, John, 5ᵗʰ Earl of Orrery 147–8,
  206n.41, 649
Boyle, Hon. Robert 70–1, 160, 215–16,
  663–4
Boyne, battle of the (1690) 60–1, 65–8
Bracegirdle, Anne 138n.40, 162
Brackley, Northants. 413
Bradley, James
  Savilian Professor of Astronomy 221–2,
    221n.116
  Astronomer Royal 221–2, 241–2
  client of Earls of Macclesfield 212–13,
    221nn.114,116
  importance of his work 221n.120, 664
  meets the Prince of Orange 569–70
  Newtonianism, and 221–2, 583
  popular Oxford lecturer 221–2
Bradshaw, William
  Bishop of Bristol 333
  Dean of Christ Church 271n.101, 332,
    332n.142, 369–70
Brailes, Warks. 627–8
Braisbridge, Rev. William 465
Braithwaite, Thomas 282–3, 446–7
Brand, Rev. John 449–50
Brandenburg, electorate of 572; see also Prussia
Brandywine, battle of (1777) 596–7
Brasenose College
  Principals of, see Shippen; Cawley; Cleaver,
    William
  benefactions to 448–9
  connections to schools on north-west
    England 447–8, 448n.156
  gaudy at 624n.119

Jacobite culture at 447–8
  panegyric on James II at 58n.24
Braunston, Northants. 442
Bray, Thomas (SPG founder) 592–3, 609–10
Bray, Thomas (academic) 306, 336
  client of 1ˢᵗ Earl Harcourt 431n.65
  ecclesiastical preferments 430n.59
  1754 Oxfordshire election 438–9,
    439n.107, 508
Brewood School, Staffs. 443–4
Bridgeman, Sir Francis 58n.24
Brighton 341n.173
Bristol, Bishops of 270, see Ironside, Hall,
    Robinson, Smalridge, Boulter, Bradshaw,
    Butler, Conybeare
  Corporation 452
  Deans of, see Royse
  Grammar School 452
British Museum 53–4
'Broad Bottom' ministry 1744–6 324
Brockliss, Laurence 1–2, 6–7, 654–5
Bromley, William 320–1, 355, 404n.206,
  415–16
  Address to George I 320–1
  Atterbury, and 406n.214
  career 316n.67, 382–5, 395, 405n.210
  Country party politics 1690s 315–16
  Harleyite and Tory leader in
    Commons 300n.34, 302–4
  on Lord Arran 250–1
  refuses office after 1714 386
  supporter of James Greenshields 461–2
Bromley (the younger), William 381–2
Bromley, Kent 531
Brooke, Henry 96–7
Brookes, Thomas 312n.52
Brothers Club 218n.102
Brown, Michael 659
Browne, Isaac Hawkins 259n.56
Browne, Joseph
  Provost of Queen's College and Vice-
    Chancellor 391n.153
  and accession of George III 339
Bruce, Thomas, Lord, 2ⁿᵈ Earl of Ailesbury 633
Brudenell-Bruce, Thomas, 2ⁿᵈ Lord Bruce of
    Tottenham 253
Brussels 332–3
Brydges, Henry, Earl of Carnarvon, later 2ⁿᵈ
    Duke of Chandos 278, 278n.136
Brydges, Hon. Henry, Archdeacon of
    Rochester 283–4
Brydges, James, 1ˢᵗ Duke of Chandos
    201n.17, 278
  influence at Balliol College 283–4

768 INDEX

Brydges, James, 1st Duke of Chandos (*cont.*)
  musical interests 191
  patron of Desaguliers 208–9, 209n.56
Buckingham, Duke of, *see* Sheffield
Buckingham, Marquess of, *see* Grenville
Buckler, Bejamin 105n.123, 439–40
  Stemmata Chicheleana 614–15
Budgell, Eustace 64n.54
Bugge, Thomas 227–8, 228n.149
Bull, Bishop George 587
Bulman, William J. 46n.135
Bulstrode Park, Bucks. 258n.53, 527–8, 608,
  609n.53
Burdett, Sir Francis, 5th Bt. 380n.102
Burford, Oxon. 95–6, 476–7
Burgess, Thomas 78
  Bishop of St Davids 669–70
  admires writings of Lord Monboddo 513–14
  foreign research visits 584n.141
  intellectual eminence 583
  keen on Burke receiving honorary
    degree 511–12
  revival of Greek studies, and 165–6
  writes against slavery 590–2
Burke, Edmund 37, 232, 339n.164
  leading Rockingham Whig 347
  on Oxford University's importance 39–40,
    512n.129
  critic of its support for the American
    War 346–7, 511–12
  Reflections on the Revolution in France
    408–9, 511–12
  University opinion of 511–12
  refused DCL by diploma 511–12, 512n.130
  declines degree 1793 511–12
Burke, Richard 511–12
Burleigh Hall, Leics. 262
Burlington House, *see* London
Burnet, Gilbert 103n.111, 106–7, 158n.136, 318,
  329n.128
  in favour with William III 58–60
  disliked by Tories 68
  tutor to William, Duke of Gloucester 306n.26
  Jansenism, and 588n.167
Burnett, James, styled Lord Monboddo 513–14
Burney, Charles
  as composer 187–8
  William Crotch, and 186
  Haydn, and 189
  on women at Oxford 671–2
Burney, Charles (the younger) 165–6
Burney, Fanny 342, 342n.183
Burrows, Donald 188
Burton, Daniel 289n.173

Burton, John
  classicist 164–6
  publicly hissed 546
  sympathetic to Locke 170
  Whig politics 301–2
Bury, Arthur 61–2, 117, 282, 282n.150; see also
  The Naked Gospel
Busby, Dr Richard 283–4
Bute, Earl of, *see* Stuart
Butler, Charles, 1st Earl of Arran 280, 604–5
  public career 248–52, 395–6
  Chancellor of Oxford 146–7, 248–52,
    260–1, 269–70, 294–5, 308,
    397–8, 468–9, 542, 607, 665
  Jacobite inclinations and awards 248–50,
    250n.8
  later tempered 250–1, 261–2
  Atterbury Plot, and the 248–50, 250n.8,
    309–10, 368–9
  High Steward of Westminster 250–1
  Ranger and Keeper of Bagshot Park 250–1
  patron of Thomas Carte 146–7
  sense of family obligation 250
  Ormond Irish family estates restored 251n.14,
    309–10, 653–4
  does not use the Ormond ducal title 251n.14
  reputation for charity 250–1
  longevity 250–1
  verdicts on 251n.17
Butler, Edward
  Vice-Chancellor 262
  family and politics 262
  Magdalen College benefactor 646
  MP Oxford University 381–2
Butler, Elizabeth (née Crew), Countess of
  Arran 250–1, 530
Butler, James, 1st Duke of Ormond
  Chancellor of Trinity College, Dublin 468–9
  Chancellor of Oxford 468–9, 470n.277,
    479–80
Butler, James, 2nd duke of Ormond 384–5, 404–5
  Captain-General of the Army 65–6,
    188n.286
  Chancellor of Trinity College, Dublin 65n.62,
    669–70
  Chancellor of Oxford 39, 248, 294–5,
    306–7, 395–6, 468–9, 479–80, 542, 665
  loyal to his cousin William III 65–8,
    306–7, 360–1
  Lord-Lieutenant of Ireland 472–4
  popularity among University members 248,
    248n.3, 427, 549
  presents loyal address to George I 1714
    320–1

flight 1715 65–6, 248–50, 308, 321–2, 362–3, 472–3, 529
  in exile 248n.4, 250
  as patron 65n.62, 549
  debts 248n.3, 653–4
Butler, James 250n.11
Butler, John, Bishop of Oxford 297
  Archdeacon of Surrey 292–3
  becomes Bishop of Oxford 292–3
  on his powers within the University 288n.171
  relations with Christ Church chapter 289, 293–4
  cultivates University opinion 293–4
  scholarly patronage 293–4
  on Edward Gibbon 293–4
  translated to Hereford 293–4
  politics 293–4
Butler, Bishop Joseph 122, 122n.198, 170
  Analogy of Religion 170–3
  distant relationship to Oxford 194–5, 516–17, 517n.156, 518n.157
Butler, Mary (née), Duchess of Ormond (wife of 2nd Duke) 250, 250n.9, 529–30
Butler, Richard 250n.11
Butler, Somerset Hamilton, 8th Viscount Ikerrin, 1st Earl of Carrick [I] 250n.11
Butler, Col. Thomas 250n.10
Butterwick, Richard 56n.14
Byng, Hon. John 186n.271
  on Oxford 494n.44
Byrom, John 298

Cadiz expedition (1702) 549
Cahir, Barons [I] 250n.11
Calamy, Edmund 367, 550–1
Calder & Hebble Navigation 443
Cale, John 647–9
Cambridge, University of 3–4, 10, 13–15, 39–40, 461, 579; *see also* Revolution 1688
  colleges and halls, *see* Clare, Trinity
  Botanic Garden 233n.181
  Chancellors, *see* Newcastle, Grafton
  Lucasian Professorship, *see* Whiston
  Regius professorships created 1724 322–3, 370n.56
  adaptability 43–4
  Arabic studies in 174–5, 174n.222, 176n.232
  cultural spaces in 45–6
  curriculum reform 509
  defence of the 'Moderns' 55–6, 159–61
  dissenters, and 56n.17, 500–1
  importance of 53
  Irish students at 21n.25
  latitudinarian theology popular in 110, 509
  mathematics centre 222, 509
  Nonjurors at, *see* Nonjurors
  relations with and views of Oxford 9, 507–11, 670–1
  tutor-student relations 621n.101
  Whigs in 83–4, 348–9
  early Hanoverian loyalism and Crown favour 2, 18–19, 42–3, 65–6, 204–5, 328, 337, 356–7, 365n.25, 507
  possible visitation of 368, 415–16
  address on Peace of Aix-la-Chapelle 507–8
  address on accession of George III 339
  favoured by Pitt the Younger 377
  Volunteers in French Revolutionary Wars 353n.235
Cambridge, University Press 81 2
Camden, William 152n.107, 153, 494
Campbell, Colen 251
Campbell, George 465
Campbell, John, 2nd duke of Argyll 70
Campbell, Archibald, 1st Earl of Islay, later 3rd Duke of Argyll 70, 367, 375, 466–7
  critic of Oxford University 467n.266
Camperdown, Battle of 353–4
Caner, Henry 596n.204
Canning, George 272–4, 402, 618–19
  academically distinguished 621n.103
  influence of Cyril Jackson on 403n.195, 410n.240
  Portland installation, at 543
Canterbury, Archbishops of, *see* Chichele, Laud, Sancroft, Tillotson, Tenison, Wake, Potter, Herring, Secker, Cornwallis, Moore
  as Oxford College Visitor, *see* All Souls, Merton
  cathedral prebendaries 635–6, 636n.172
  deans of, *see* Stanhope, Horne
  prebendaries of, *see* Marlow
  diocesan clergy 339n.165
Careswell, Edward 441–2
Carey, Henry 136n.23
Cardigan, Archdeacon of, *see* Williams (John)
Carlisle
  Archdeacons of, *see* Law (John)
  Bishops of, *see* Law (Edmund), Douglas (John)
  Deans of, *see* Atterbury
  prebends of 638n.179
Carlos III, King of Spain 582–3
  as King of Naples 582–3
Carlos of Naples, *see* Carlos III of Spain
Carlton-in-Lindrick, Notts. 612–13
Carnegie, Sir David., 4th Bt. 24
Carnarvon, Earl of, *see* Brydges
Caroline divines 123–5

770 INDEX

Caroline of Ansbach, Queen (previously Princess of Wales) 31n.58, 136, 248–50, 270n.97, 322–4, 330–1, 333, 589
Carrick, Earl of, *see* Butler (Somerset Hamilton)
Carroll, William 63n.51
Carstares, William 70
Cartagena 423–4, 527–8
Carte, Thomas 308n.35
  history writings 147–9, 193–4, 661–2
  reception 148–9, 149nn.90,91
  patronage 147–8, 653–4
  Jacobitism 148–9
Carter, Elizabeth 527–8
Carter, George 284–5, 333, 333n.146
Carter, Ian 54–5
Carter, Thomas 402
Carteret, John, 2nd Lord Carteret of Hawnes, later Earl Granville 372–3, 413
  Lord-Lieutenant of Ireland 474–5
  opponent of Walpole and the Pelhams 370–1, 655
  patron of Christ Church 474–5
  his learning 35–6
Cartesianism 72, 200, 211n.68
Cartwright, Edmund 242–3, 243n.202
Cary, Lucius, 2nd Viscount Falkland 299
Cashel
  Archbishop of, *see* Agar
  Archdeacon of, *see* Perceval
Castle Cary, Somerset 626
Castle Durrow, Co. Laois 475–6
Castle Durrow, Lord, *see* Flower
Cato, see Addison
Catcott, Alexander Stopford 452
  Hutchinsonian 452
cathedrals
  scholarship and preaching in 635–6, 636n.172
  Oxonian Deans 635–6
Catherine II, Empress of Russia
  sends Russian students to Oxford 574–6
Cavendish, Lord Henry 251
Cavendish, William, 1st Duke of Devonshire 330–1
Cavendish, William, 2nd Duke of Devonshire 251, 330–1, 367
Cavendish, William, styled Marquess of Hartington, later 3rd Duke of Devonshire 330–1, 363
Cawley, Anne 531
Cawley, Ralph 531
Celsus 222–3
Chalgrove, battle of (1643) 299n.2

Chambers, Robert 180, 410–11, 412nn.250,251, 514, 623–4
Chambers, Sir William 32
Champion, Justin 63n.48, 587n.158
Chandler, Richard 559–62, 560n.31
Chandler, Thomas B. 595n.202
Chapel Royal 187–8
chaplaincies 279–80, 603; *see also* clergy
  royal chaplaincies and Oxford appointees 404n.206
Chapman, Joseph 341–2, 342n.185
Charlbury, Oxon. 253
Charles I 17–18, 298–9, 304–5, 339n.165, 355, 400, 586–7
  commemoration as 'martyr' 125–7, 127n.218, 146–7, 261–2, 262n.67, 299, 310–11, 344–5, 389–90, 390n.151, 426–7
Charles II 36, 146–7, 253, 299, 360–1, 434–5
Charleston, SC 595–7
Charlett, Arthur 544–6
  Oxford University Press, and 54–5
  Pro-Vice-Chancellor 363, 403–4
  relationship with University College butler 515–16
  university reform, and 368
  Westminster connections 66–8, 398–9, 403–4, 404n.205
  Church preferment 404n.206
  loses office as a King's chaplain 321–2
  loses office as a Justice of the Peace 321–2, 364n.20
  as a correspondent 54–5, 403–4
  satirised 132–3, 404n.203
  moderate Toryism 315–18, 355
  vague Jacobite tendencies 312n.53, 403–4
  and 3rd Duke of Beaufort 604–5
  death 279–80
Charlotte of Mecklenburg-Strelitz, Queen 254, 340n.169, 345–6, 430–1, 435
  visits Oxford 341–2, 349
Charlotte, Princess Royal, daughter of George III 341–2
Charterhouse 407n.220
Chatham, Earl of, *see* Pitt the Elder
Chatterton, Thomas 167n.180, 179
Chaucer, Geoffrey 134, 134n.15
Charnock, Robert 67n.69
Charles, Charles 596n.204
Checkley, John 593–4, 594n.193
Cheere, Henry 31n.58
Chelmsford 339n.165
Chelsum, James 522
Cherwell, River 424–5

Chester
Bishops of, *see* Dawes; Gastrell; Markham; Porteus; Cleaver, William
Chesterfield, Earl of, *see* Stanhope
Chetwynd, Mary 535–6
Chichele, Archbishop Henry 286, 614–15
Childs, Sir Josiah 27n.49
China 177n.239
Chishull, Edmund 132–3, 559–60, 561n.36
Chislehampton, Oxon. 425–6
Christ Church cathedral, Dublin 473–4
Christ Church (Oxford) 35–6, 137n.28, 201n.17, 207, 342, 455–6
    Deans of, *see* Fell, Aldrich, Atterbury, Smalridge, Boulter, Bradshaw, Conybeare, Gregory, Markham, Bagot, Lewis, Jackson (Cyril)
    sub-Deans, *see* Bentham
    Chaplains of, *see* Grabe; Free;
    Stewards, *see* Massey
    Studentships, types of available at 445–6, 446n.144
    Dr Lee's Readership in Anatomy 226n.138, 242–3
    alleged excessive influence within the University 394–5
    appointment to Deanery and Canonries 269–70, 273n.113, 292, 655
    relation to the *see* of Bristol
    Visitor of 283–4, 665–6
    Westminster School connections 445–6, 446n.145
    curriculum reform, and 39–40
    graduates in government employment 259–60, 402–3
    graduates in House of Commons 379
    Newtonianism at 205n.37
    noblemen at 404n.208
    rhetorical education of students 379
    accommodation at 26–8
    almshouses 476–7, 515–16
    Canterbury Building 33–5
    Canterbury Quadrangle and Gate 32, 475–6, 646
    cathedral 91–2, 287–9, 297, 341–2, 395–6
    fire in Hall 1720 322–3
    Lee Building (Anatomy School) 229–31, 230n.162
    library 31, 31n.60, 227–8, 643
    Peckwater Quadrangle 27–8, 27n.48, 31, 319n.86, 474–5, 614n.71, 643
    picture gallery 524–5, 650
    choral foundation 79n.2, 182–4, 186
    ecclesiastical patronage 602n.13

perpetual curacies in gift of 425–6
land ownership and benefactions 441–3
patronal and policy connections with government 259–60, 295n.209, 402–5, 407–8
Tories at 136, 270–2, 332
Jacobite presence 309n.40
Whigs at 271–2, 332, 337
court allegiance in George III's reign 348
Earls of Abingdon, and 432n.68, 446n.144
Irish students at 470n.282, 472n.289, 473n.290, 475–6
Christie, Ian R. 389–90
Christian belief
    in civil society 79–80, 129–30
    reasonable 121–2
    limits of reason 122
Christian VII, King of Denmark 567
Christianity not Mysterious 62–5; *see also* Toland
Christology controversy 1690s 61–2
Church, Richard 532–3
'Church in Danger' 108–9, 498–9; *see also* Sacheverell
Church of England 4–5, 62, Chapter 3 passim;
    see also Convocation, Erastianism, Evangelicals, High Church, Low Church, 'Oxford Movement', Protestant Succession 1714, Revolution of 1688
    alliance with the state 43, 124–7, 661
    clergy, cultural isolation of 10, 601–2
    Comprehension 58–60, 68, 404–5
    Justification by faith, doctrine of in 81n.9
    ministry in the Empire 592–4
    privileges and legal monopolies 19–20, 36
    Welsh clergy in 460–1
    Whig character and sympathies of the hierarchy after 1689 68, 148–9, 155–6, 299–300, 306–7, 360–1, 370–1, 668
    loyalist preaching 1790s 350–1, 352n.228, 601–2
Churchill, John, 1ˢᵗ duke of Marlborough
    John 136, 308, 361–2
    Commander-in-Chief of allied forces 1702–12 427
    royal grant of Woodstock manor 427
    major patronal influence 84n.26, 275–6, 329
    limited popularity and influence in the University 248, 316–17, 330n.132, 427
    and county politics 427, 437
    few benefices in his gift 330n.133
    and chaplaincies 603
    in exile 188n.286, 431–2
    tomb at Blenheim 627

772   INDEX

Churchill, Sarah, (1st) Duchess of
    Marlborough 289n.177, 437–8
  Groom of the Stole and Mistress of the
    Robes 427
  dominance at Queen Anne's court 316–17
  as patron 603
  preference for Whigs at Oxford
    University 330n.131
  clerical following 627
  attitude to Blenheim Palace 427
  death 429, 477–8
Church, Thomas 551n.312
Churton, Ralph 643n.198
Cibber, Colley 25, 544–6
Cicero 144–5, 146n.73, 379, 582–3
Cimarosa 192
Civil Constitution of the Clergy 118–19; see also
    French Revolution
Civil War, English 5–8, 17–18, 73–4, 146–7,
    193–4, 233–4, 304–5, 550–1, 630–1
  and Oxford 298–9, 666
Clare, Earl of, see Fitzgibbon
Clare Hall, Cambridge 199, 274n.118
Clarence, William, Duke of 454–5
Clarendon, Earls of, see Hyde
Clarendon Building 32, 81–2, 82n.11, 650
Clarendon Laboratory 644
Clarendon Press, see Oxford University Press
Clark, Jonathan 304n.22, 313, 340n.168,
    413–14
Clark, Peter 600–1
Clarke, George 386–8, 650
  Fellow of All Souls College 31
  MP for the University 31, 309–10, 381–2,
    384–6, 386n.124, 387n.129, 395
  career in government 384–5
  moderate Tory 355, 383–4
  architect 28–32, 31n.59, 333
  bequest to Worcester College 281–2,
    387–8
Clarke, Samuel 98–9, 107–8, 116, 129–30,
    130n.227, 170
  friend of Newton 202–3
  Boyle lecturer 202n.26
  heterodoxy 202–3, 203n.29, 660–1
  censured in Convocation 203n.29
  not preferred in the Church 202–3
Clarke, Samuel [Esquire Bedel] 490
Clavering, Robert
  career 318n.80
  praises George II and Queen Caroline 333
Claverton 141
Claydon, Tony 91n.60
Clayton, Bishop Robert 103–4

Cleaver, Euseby
  Bishop of Ferns, later Archbishop of
    Dublin 272n.110, 409n.237
Cleaver, William
  Principal of Brasenose College 272–4,
    272n.111, 295–6
  appointed Bishop of Chester 267n.85
  possible translation to Oxford 409n.237
  close to the Grenvilles 272–4, 378n.95
  later Toryism 274
Clement XI, Pope 566–7
Clement XIII, Pope 558–9
clergy, Anglican
  antiquarianism, and 631–2
  associational culture in localities 634–41,
    655–6, 675
  chaplaincies 279–80
  dissenting challenges locally 638–9
  election times, at 655–6
  Justices of the Peace 637–8
  parochial presence 396n.168, 624–5
  pastoral efficiency 394–5
  polemic, engagement in 633, 638–9
  rural isolation 107–8, 127–9, 624–5, 625n.122,
    674–5
  scholarship and publications 107–8, 195–6,
    625, 628–9, 655–6, 658
  scientific popularisation, and 206–8, 633
  support for repression of rebellious American
    colonists 345n.198
  ties to Oxford 239–41, 627–8, 674–5
  use of lending libraries 636–7, 674–5
clergy, French émigré 232
Clerical Residency Act 1803 394–5, 396n.168
Cleveland, Archdeacons of, see Blackburne
Cleveland, Duchess of, see Palmer
Clogher, Bishop of, see Clayton
Clubs 600–1, 623–4, 636–7; see also
    Cycle of the White Rose, Red
    Herring Club
Cobb, John 79, 122
Coalition 1783, see Fox, North
  University attitudes towards 348–9
Cobham, Viscount, see Temple
Cockman, Thomas 322–3, 531
Codrington, Christopher 132–3, 164, 361n.7
  career 590–2
  benefactions 590–2
  and slavery 590–2, 593n.186
Coffey, John 74–5
Coimbra, University of 592n.182
Coke, Col. John 352
Colchester, Lord, see Abbot
Coleridge, Samuel Taylor 140–1

Coleshill, Warks. 609–10
Colley, Linda 655
Collier, Arthur
  philosophical works 633
Collier, Jeremy 155–6
Collins, Anthony 172
Collins, William 136–7, 140, 184–5, 446–7
Colman, George (the elder) 338, 645n.205
  journalism 193, 344n.193
  The Oxonian in Town 489–90
Colman, George (the younger) 379, 465, 515–16,
  619–20
Cologne 33–5, 539
Colsterworth, Lincs. 622
Combe, Oxon. 426–7
Common Prayer, Book of (1662) 83–4, 91–2,
  496–7
  state services in 91–2, 125–6
  1552 edition 572n.83
  attempted revision 1689 58–60
  use in Scotland 461–2
  German translation of 570–2
'Common Sense' philosophy 168–72
Commonwealth, *see* Interregnum
Comprehension, *see* Church of England
Compton, Bishop Henry 28–31, 58–60, 59n.33,
  572–4, 576, 580–1, 592–3
Conduitt, John 199n.6
  Tory politics 315n.65
  botanical bequest to Oxford 234n.182
Confucius 172
Congreve, William 549n.297
Coningsby, Dr George 261–2, 262n.67
Connecticut 594–5
Connoisseur, The 193
Constantinople 124–5
Convention Parliament (1689) 57–8, 318
Convocation (of the Church of England) 5,
  58–60, 404–5; *see also* Aldrich,
  Atterbury
  campaign for revival of (1690s, 1700s) 63–4,
  315, 329, 360–1
  of 1701 64–5
  powers contested 155–7, 405, 661–2
  disputatious sittings 155–6
  suppressed 1717 79–80, 157–8, 364
  later notions of revival 89, 370, 661
  in Ireland 472–3, 474n.298
Convocation (University of Oxford) of 19n.20,
  420–1
  decrees of 1683 and 1685 on non-
    resistance 40–1, 318
  reaffirms subscription on matriculation
    1772 256n.42

address of 1710 condemned in
  Parliament 317n.75, 318
address on establishment of Regius
  Professorship of Modern History
  369–70
on status of sons of Scottish and Irish
  peers 475–6
on response to accession of George III 339
and the American War 346–7
award of honorary degrees to foreigners
  553–4
Conybeare, Jemima 336n.156
Conybeare, John
  Principal of Exeter College 276
  Dean of Christ Church 128n.221, 271
  Bishop of Bristol 271, 271n.104
  client of Edmund Gibson 271
  patronised by 1st Earl of Macclesfield 433n.76
  Whig in politics 271–2, 276, 301–2, 333–4,
    356–7
  praise of George II 336nn.155,156
  writings 110, 127, 128n.221, 271
  as a theologian 110n.144, 660–1
  opposed to heterodoxy 116, 276n.125
  esteems Locke 170–1
  friend of Alexander Pope 483–4
  sermons published posthumously 336n.156
  reputation 127
Cook, Captain James 547–8, 651–2
Cooke, John 341–2, 349–50, 427n.47
  Justice of the Peace 427
  his charitable giving 476–7
Cooke, Rev. Theophilus Leigh 352
Cookes, Sir Thomas, 2nd Bt. 645
Cooper, Anthony Ashley, 1st Earl of
  Shaftesbury 40–1
Cooper, Anthony Ashley, 3rd Earl of
  Shaftesbury 166–7
Cooper, George 581
Cooper, Myles 346–7, 594–5
Cooper, Robert 595, 596n.207
Cope, Sukey 537
Cope, Sir Jonathan, 1st Bt. 537
Copenhagen, University of 227–8
Coppola, Al 486
Copyright Act (1710) 136
Coray, Adamance, *see* Korais
Corbiere, Anthony 401–2
Corelli, Arcangelo 192
Corfu 576
Cornbury Park, Oxon. 434n.81
  bought by 1st Earl of Clarendon 433–4
  dons entertained at 433–4
  sold by Hyde family 433–4

774 INDEX

Cornbury, Viscount, *see* Hyde
Cornbury Plot 386–7
Corneille 143–4
Cornelius Nepos 165n.175
Cornwallis, Archbishop the Hon. Frederick
  rules on Founders' Kin at All Souls 286
  uninterested in new Biblical translations 88,
    89n.52
Corpus Christi College
  Presidents of, *see* Turner, Mather, Randolph
    (Thomas), Cooke (John)
  building work at 31–2
  chapel 91
  college estates 442
  George III visits 341–2
  support for Burke 512n.130
  women servants at 527n.195
Cosi fan tutte 189–91
Costard, George 498–9
Cotes, Digby 547, 548n.289
Cotesbach, Leics. 107–8
Cotton, Sir John Hynde, 3rd Bt. 324
Counter-Enlightenment, *see* Enlightenment
Counter-Revolution, *see* French Revolution
Country party politics 315–16, 324, 347, 389–90;
    see also Tories
Covell [Colvill], John 561n.36
Coventry 264–5
Coventry, Anne, (2nd) Countess of
    Coventry 607n.42
Coventry, George, 6th Earl of Coventry 531
Coventry, Thomas, styled Lord Deerhurst 531
Coventry, William, 5th Earl of 607n.42
Cowley, Hannah 488n.19
Cowper, Hon. Spencer 280
Cowper, William, 1st Earl Cowper 332, 366n.32
Cowper, William 140
Cradock, Eleanor 516n.148
Cramer, Wilhelm 191–2
Craven, William, 6th Lord Craven 348, 436,
    437n.96
Crawford, Earl of, *see* Lindsay
Creech, Thomas
  edition of Lucretius 164, 165n.172, 165n.174
  suicide 164
Crew, Nathaniel, Bishop, 3rd Lord Crew of
    Steane 109n.141, 248–50, 310–11, 391–3,
    611, 617n.88
  Rector of Lincoln College 436
  entertains University members at Steane
    Park 436
  benefactor to the University 436n.90,
    546, 653
Critical Review 127–9

Croft, George 120
  career as a teacher 443–4
  educational author 443–4
Croft, William 186n.272, 187–8
Crotch, William 186, 186n.272, 187n.279,
    354n.237
Crouch, Isaac 113, 425–6, 675
Crowe, William 547, 548n.289
Cruickshanks, Eveline 398n.179
cryptography 400
Cuddesdon, Oxon. 287–8, 291–2, 292n.189,
    527–8
Cugoano Ottobah 394n.161
Cullen, William 231–2
Culloden, battle of 251, 311–13, 325, 668; *see also*
    '45 Rebellion
Culworth, Northants. 615–17
Cumberland, William, Duke of 313n.56, 325,
    627n.133
Curll, Edmund 64n.54
Cycle of the White Rose 458
Czartoryski, Princess Izabela 565

da Costa, Emanuel Mendes 236–8, 237n.188,
    238n.189
Dalrymple, Sir David, 3rd Bt., styled Lord
    Hailes 661
Dalton, John 44, 78
Dalzel, Andrew 512–13
Danvers, Henry, 1st Earl of Danby 233–4
Danby, Earl of, *see* Danvers
D'Anvers, Alicia 544n.277
  Academia, or the Humours of Oxford 490
Danvers, Sir John, 3rd Bt. 615–17
D'Anvers, Knightley 490
Danvers, née Robinson, Mary, Lady 615–17
Danvers, Sir Michael, 5th Bt. 615–17
Dartmouth, Earls of, *see* Legge
Darwall-Smith, Robin 264n.76
Darwin, Charles 465
Darwin, Erasmus 465
Dashwood, Sir Francis, 2nd Bt. 251, 541
Dashwood, Sir James, 2nd Bt. 419n.3, 437–8,
    438n.98, 440–1, 478
Daventry academy 497–8, 498n.61
Davis, Henry Edward 293–4, 523n.183
Davy, Major William 182
Dawes, James 371–2
Dawes, Richard 165–6
Dawes, Archbishop Sir William, 3rd Bt. 31n.58,
    108n.136, 395–6
Dawson, William 594
Debrecen, University of 585–6
Defoe, Daniel 494

Delaune, William 510–11, 670–1
Lady Margaret Professor of Divinity 94–5, 103–4
President of St John's College 286n.163
Vice-Chancellor 316–17
ally of Lord Harcourt 260–1
debt problems 103–4, 286n.163
publications 103–4
Delaval, Francis 515–16
Delegates, *see* Oxford University Press
Demosthenes 379
demy, *see* Magdalen College
Denbighshire 455–6
Denison, William
career 280n.143
client of Beaufort family 279–80, 604–5
attempts to become Master of University College 279–80, 280n.144, 604–5
Principal of Magdalen Hall 279–80
Dennis, Samuel 341–2
Vice-Chancellor 343, 440–1
widow of 531
Derby 311–12, 311n.51, 312n.52, 639–40
Derry, Bishop of, *see* Hickman
Desaguliers, John Theophilus
lectures in Oxford and London 200, 208–9
popularises Newtonianism 208–9
neglectful parish priest 208–9
significance 209n.56
Descartes 166–7, 207n.49, 216–17, 633
Des Maizeaux, Pierre 432–3, 433n.75
Devonshire, Dukes of, *see* Cavendish
Dibdin, Thomas Frognall 16
Digby of Geashill [I], William, 5th Lord 548n.289, 609–10, 610n.56, 636–7
Dilettanti Society 559–60
Dillenius, Johann Jakob
Sherardian Professor of Botany 233–4, 582–3
Dinwiddy, John 19n.21
Discourse on Church Government, see Potter
Dissenters, Protestant; *see also* Socinians, subscription controversy
prominence after Revolution of 1688 315–17, 360–1, 368–9, 498–9, 666
attitudes towards in Oxford 115–18, 266–7, 483, 496–502
perceived danger to the Established Church 146n.72, 398, 496–551
critics of Oxford University 496–8, 501, 503, 671
amity towards the University 1727–60 498–9
civil rights of 19–20, 73–4, 105n.123
campaign to extend 115–18, 398

cultural association with Anglican clergy 601–2, 639–41
divisions among 9, 118
non-Trinitarians 73–4, 116
Relief Act 1779 19–20, 256–7, 266–7, 376–7, 389–90
schools and academies 64–5, 143–4, 461, 497–8
science, and 233, 635n.171, *see also* Priestley
Whig loyalties 56, 73–4
sympathetic to French Revolution 639–40
in North America 593–4, 596n.204
Ditchley Park, Oxon. 253, 267n.84, 434–5, 493
Dittersdorf, Carl Ditters von 192
Dixon, George 505
Doctors' Commons 410–11
Doddridge, Philip 498–9, 638
Dodington, George Bubb 624
Dodsley, Robert
and Oxford authors 131, 640–1
Dodwell, Henry
Camden Professor 151–2
Nonjuror 67n.65, 406n.213
Orthodox Church 576n.106
patristics, and 587
Dodwell, Henry, the younger 122
Dodwell, Archdeacon William 110, 123n.200, 551n.312
Dol, diocese of 585–6
Dolben, Rev. Sir John, 2nd Bt. 109n.141, 615–17
Visitor of Balliol College 292–3, 391–3, 450–1, 612
Canon of Durham 310–11, 612, 612n.64
financial support for Bishop Atterbury in exile 310–11
musical tastes 611
Dolben, Sir William, 3rd Bt. 8, 395, 618–19
MP for the University, 1768, 1780–1806 292–3, 391–5
defender of the Church Establishment 391–3
opposes relaxation of subscription 376, 500–1
pro-slave trade regulation and abolition 391–3, 394n.161, 612, 612n.66
1780 General Election, and 182n.259
votes for Fox's East India Company bill 257n.46
Don Gabriel of Spain 582–3
Donowell, John 33–5
Doomsday Book 343
Dorchester abbey, Oxon. 585–6
Dorset, Dukes of, *see* Sackville
Douglas, Catherine, née Hyde, 3rd Duchess of Queensberry 434n.81, 537

776 INDEX

Douglas, Bishop John 277–8
  Snell exhibitioner 467–8
  ecclesiastical career 467–8
Dr Lee's Readership in Anatomy, *see* Christ Church
Drake, Sir Francis 248n.3
Drake, George 277–8, 467–8
Drake, William (the elder) 278–9, 557–8, 611
Drake, William (the younger) 557–8
Drayton St. Leonard, Oxon. 425–6
Drayton, William Henry 596–7
Drelincourt, Anne, Viscountess [of]
    Primrose 314n.61
Dromore, Bishops of, *see* Newcome
Drury Lane theatre and company 25, 486–8,
    544–6
Dryden, John 165n.172
Dublin
  Archbishops of, *see* Cleaver
  Philosophical Society 215–16, 474–5, 580–1
Ducarel, Andrew Coltée 558–9
Dumay, Ignatius 570n.78
Duncan, Adam, 1st Viscount Duncan 353–4
Duncan, William 167
Dundas, Henry 232
Dunning, John 347
Duns, Berwickshire 467–8
Dunster, Thomas
  Whig politics as Warden of Wadham
      College 329n.127
  sympathetic to Locke 170n.199
  visits Blenheim palace 330n.131
Durell, David
  Morley Scholar at Pembroke
      College 448n.159
  Principal of Hertford College 87–8
  Vice-Chancellor 83–4, 505, 575–6
  client of Archbishop Secker 87–8
  Biblical scholar 87–8, 113
Durey, Michael 402–3
Durham
  Bishops of, *see* Crew, Butler, Trevor, Thurlow
      (Thomas), Barrington, Van Mildert,
  Deans of, *see* Cowper (Spencer)
  cathedral chapter 147–8, 292
  University of 16–17
  'duumvirs', *see* Godolhin; Marlborough,
      1st Duke of
Du Quesne, Admiral 563–4, 564n.54

Ealing school 623–4
Eardley-Wilmot, Sir John 514n.140
East India Company 438
  and Oxford 181–2
  and Persian language 173–4, 181

Eastlake, Charles Locke 454–5
Easton Neston, Northants. 650–1
Echard, Laurence 149n.91
Eden, Robert 410–11
Eden, William 582–3
Edgcumbe, James
  Principal of Exeter College 276n.125
Edgeworth, Richard Lovell 233n.176, 470–1
Edgeworthstown, co. Longford 470–1
Edinburgh 479–80
  Town Council 70
  University of 44–5, 199, 225, 231–2
    Visitation after 1688 Revolution 70
    medical teaching at 222, 229
Edward II 442
Edwards, Jonathan
  University posts 106–7
  reluctance to eject Nonjurors 67n.65
  Locke, and 168–70
  writings 106–7
Edwards, John 199n.6
Egmont, Earls of, *see* Perceval
Egerton, Henry 168–70
Egremont, Earl of, *see* Wyndham
Egypt 174–5
Eldon, Earl of, *see* Scott, John
Elizabeth I 136–7, 325–6, 434–5
Elizabeth, Princess 341–2
Elizabeth, Empress of Russia 574–5
Elliot, Sir Gilbert, 1st Lord Minto 152n.111
Elliot, N., shoemaker 424–5
Ellis, Heather 45–6
Ellis, John 384–5, 385n.123
Ellis, Bishop Welbore, Dean of Christ Church,
      Dublin 473–4
Ellis, Welbore, 1st Lord Mendip 471
Elsfield, Oxon. 426–7
Elstob, Elizabeth 134n.13, 154–5, 508n.108
  Anglo-Saxon scholar 525–7
  critiques Swift's scholarship 527n.201
Elstob, William 525–7, 527n.198
Ely, Bishops of, *see* Turner (Francis)
Emerson, Roger 69n.80, 602n.12
émigrés 142–3; *see also* French Revolution
Enlightenment: *see also* Oxford, University of,
      Pocock, J.G.A.
  variously characterised and defined 44–5,
      45n.122, 46–7, 74–6, 589–90, 659
  relationship to the Republic of Letters 589–90,
      590n.177
  its place in intellectaul life assessed 592n.180
  light metaphor 74–5, 75nn.104,105
  anticlericalism, and 204
  heresy, as 47n.140

radical texts 41–2, 176–7, 266–7
utility, and 211–12
sub-categories 45–6
  'Anglican Enlightenment' 11–12, 55–6, 76
  Arminian Enlightenment 62
  'civil enlightenment' 56n.15
  Counter-Enlightenment 45–6, 76, 77n.113,
    113, 241–2
  'English Enlightenment' 14–15, 53, 57n.20,
    60–1, 74–5, 129–30
  French Enlightenment 562–3
  Irish contexts 45n.124
  'Medical Enlightenment' 6–7
  'Midlands Enlightenment' 639–40
  'moderate Enlightenment' 74–6, 110, 659
  'religious Enlightenment' 45–6
  Russian contexts 45n.124
  Scottish Enlightenment 69–70, 76n.111,
    468n.271, 553–4, 669–70
  'theological Enlightenment' 45–6
Epicureanism 165n.172
epistolary networks 554
Ernest, Prince 341–2
Erasmus 165n.175
Erastianism 155
érudit scholarship 157–8, 661–2; *see also* history
Etemare, Abbé 588–9
Eton College 446, 446n.149, 479
  Montem ceremony at 479
Euclid 201n.17
Europe
  Oxford scholarly contacts with 46, 553–4
  Oxford graduates and scholars in 10, 553–63,
    557n.14
Euripides 162, 164n.163, 582–3, 630
Evangelicals 19n.21, 183n.262
  in Oxford 113, 504–5; *see also* St Edmund Hall
Evans, Caleb 500n.72
Evans, Walter 627–8
Eveleigh, John
  career 455n.194
  curriculum reformer 454–5
Evelyn, John 165n.172
Evenlode valley 426–7
Ewer, Bishop John 98
Excise Bill (1733) 310–11, 370–1
Exclusion Crisis (1678–81) 40–1, 299
Exeter 40–1
  Bishop of, *see* Lavington
Exeter College
  Rectors of, *see* Bury, Conybeare, Atwell,
    Edgcumbe, Webber
  building work at 31–2
  Whig character 111, 276, 332–3, 337

and Oxfordshire election (1754) 263–4, 336,
  438–40, 440n.114
Eyre, Chief Justice in 436
Eyre, John 506n.101
Eyston, Charles 114n.163

Faber, G.S. 113n.156
Fairer, David 131, 194
Fane, John, 7th Earl of Westmorland
  army officer 251
  opposed to Walpole and the Pelhams 251,
    340n.169
  antipathy towards George II 339
  links to Leicester House and Prince
    Frederick 313
  turns Jacobite 251, 253
  High Steward of the University 251, 313n.57
  Chancellor 251, 337, 395–8, 653–4
  installation 189n.292, 251, 313, 326–8, 542
  and accession of George III 339
  muddles address to 1761 180, 340
  tries to kiss Lady Sarah Lennox 340n.169
  architectural patron 251, 252n.20
Fane, Mary (née Cavendish), Countess of
  Westmorland 251, 530
Fanshawe, John 102
Farington, Joseph 34n.74
Farquhar, George
  Sir Harry Wildair 489
Fatio, Nicolas 572–3
Fazakerley, Nicholas 387–8
Feathers Tavern petition, *see* subscription
  controversy
Feiling, Sir Keith 170n.197
Fell, Bishop John 27n.48, 59n.30, 572
  and Oxford University Press 53–5
  and Arabic teaching 175n.226
Felton, Henry
  client of Manners family 622–3, 623n.113
  defends Clarendon's *History* 147n.79
  critic of Newton 204
Fenny Stratford, Bucks. 630–1
Fenton, Thomas 163
Feola, Vittoria 215–16, 238–9
Fermor, Henrietta Louisa, née Jeffreys, Countess
  of Pomfret 538–9, 650, 656–7
Fermor, William, 1st Lord Leominster 650–1
Ferns, Bishop of, *see* Cleaver
Feuillide, Eliza, Comtesse de 539–40
Fiddes, Richard 107–8, 108n.135
fideism 122
Fielding, Henry 325
Fiennes, Celia 494, 539
Fifteen ('15) Rebellion 270, 308, 321–2, 363–4

778 INDEX

Fifth Monarchists 375
Filmer, Sir Robert 13–14, 148–9, 318
Finch, Lady Charlotte 277–8, 340–1
Finch, Daniel, 2nd earl of Nottingham 58–60,
66–8, 67n.66, 270n.96, 276, 382–3, 411–12
Finch, Daniel, 8th earl of Winchlisea & 3rd Earl of
Nottingham 621–2
Finch, George, 9th Earl of Winchilsea & 4th Earl of
Nottingham 277–8, 340–1
Finch, Hon. Heneage, 1st Lord Guernsey, later 1st
Earl of Aylesford
career 382–3
MP Oxford University 382–3, 403–4, 411–12
as parliamentarian 412
cooperates with Williamite regime 411–12
barony awarded 403–4
Finch, Hon. Leopold 300n.10, 383n.116
Finch, William 115, 115n.170, 628
Findlater, Earl of, see Ogilvy
Findlay, Robert 463n.246
Finedon, Northamptonshire 109n.141, 391–3, 611
Fingal 179
Fisher, Blencombe 64n.54
Fisher, Henry 457
Fitzgibbon, John, 1st Earl of Clare 471–2
Fitzmaurice, Lord, see Shelburne
Fitzmaurice, Hon. Thomas 465
Fitzroy, Augustus Henry, 3rd Duke of
Grafton 180–1, 255n.37, 348, 375
Flamsteed, John 219, 566–7
Fleming, Sir William, 1st Bt. 637–8
Fletcher, Andrew, styled Lord Milton 466–7
Fletcher, Sir George, 2nd Bt. 637–8
Flood, Henry 470–1
Florence 581–2
Flower, Col. William, 1st Lord Castle Durrow
[I] 475–6
Foley, Paul 315–16
Foley, Thomas, 2nd Lord Foley 253, 325–6
Folkenflik, Robert 304n.22
Folkes, Martin 221n.114
President of the Royal Society 212–14
awarded Oxford doctorate 213–14, 238
Masonic commitment 213n.77
reputation for irreligion 212–13, 212n.76
Fontenoy, battle of 467–8
Foote, Polly 535–7
Formosa 573–4
Forty-Five ('45) Rebellion 21, 301–3, 416
attitudes towards in Oxford 95–6, 262–3,
294–5, 311–12, 324
Addresses to George II during 262–3, 324–5;
see also Association to preserve the
constitution in Church and State

Fothergill, George 21–4, 97–8, 615
Fothergill, Mary, née Billingsley, wife of
Thomas 531
Fothergill, Richard 449–50
Fothergill, Thomas
Provost of Queen's College 449–50, 615
Vice-Chancellor 265–6, 389–90, 582–3
Foucault, Michael 46–7
Founders' Kin 614–15; see also All Souls College
Fox, Charles James 257, 418–19
disdain for Oxford University 379n.98
refuses honorary degree 549–50
Coalition with Lord North 1783 257–8,
259n.55, 348–9, 511–12
Foxite followers during the French
Revolution 301–2, 351–2, 377–8
Fox, Henry 413–14
Fox-Strangways, Stephen, 1st Earl of
Ilchester 620
Foxe, Bishop Richard 442
Frampton, Matthew 78
France; see also French Revolution, Gallicanism
universities in 15
anti-Gallican feeling towards 95–6
Frankfurt-an-der-Oder
University of and Oxford 570–2
Franklin, Benjamin 347n.208
Fraser, James 185n.268
Frederick, Prince of Wales 251, 311–12, 435,
640–1, 649, 666–7
his monarchical outlook 314–15
cultivates Tories 301–2, 311–12, 325–6, 336
following in Oxford 325–6, 356–7, 371–2, 508
predeceases George II 301–2, 313, 325–6,
326n.116, 336, 373–4; see also Augusta of
Saxe-Gothe; Leicester House Circle
Frederick, Crown Prince of Denmark 569–70
Frederick I, King of Prussia 567–8, 572
Frederick II (the Great) of Prussia 581–2
Free, John 95–6, 311n.51, 439n.106, 451–2,
627–8, 627n.133
Freemasons, see Masons
Freiberg 189–91
Freind brothers 223
and Phalaris controversy 160–1
Freind, John
career summarised 218n.102
classicist 218n.102
chemical lectures 217–19
learned in medicine 219n.103
Newtonian and High Churchman 209,
217–19
implicated in Atterbury Plot 218n.102
donation to Christ Church 229–31

Freind, Robert 404–5
  scholastic career 446, 446n.147
Freke, William 61n.42
French Revolution 19–20, 36–8, 258, 623–4,
    639–40, 672; *see also* Civil Constitution of
    the Clergy, clergy, French *émigré*;
    September Massacres
  Oxford and 19–21, 36–7, 41–2, 76–7, 115,
    140–1, 225, 232–3, 267–9, 268nn.88,89,
    301–2, 350–2, 357–9, 585–7, 672–3, 675–6
  Counter-Revolution 140–1
  Revolutionary War 259–60, 271–2, 352–4,
    377–8, 402, 409, 543
Frewin, Richard 223
Friesen, John 203n.28, 205n.37
Fry, Thomas 113n.156

Gabriel III/Dositheus, Patriarch of
    Jerusalem 577–8
Gagnier, Jean
  Arabic teaching 173–4, 175n.226
  writings on the Prophet Muhammad 176–7,
    178n.242
  patrons 570
  reputation 178n.242
Galen 222–3, 223n.126
Galland, Antoine 177
Gallicanism 76, 100–2, 114–15, 156–7, 589;
    see also Jansenism, Oxford, University of
  patristic studies, and 587
  conversations regarding union with
    Anglicans 587–8
  similar opponents to the Church of
    England 586–7
Garden, James 69–70, 70n.82
Gardiner, Bernard 355, 382–3
  controversial Warden of All Souls
    College 285–6, 383–4, 400
  Founder's Kin at All Souls 286
  Tindal, and 62–3
  stifles Jacobitism as Vice-Chancellor 307–8,
    361–3, 543–6
  Harleyite 308n.34, 317–18, 412–13
  loses office as a Justice of the Peace 321–2,
    364n.20
  George I, and 308, 320–1, 369–70
Gardiner, Grace 479, 531–2, 537
Garrick, David 485–6
Garsington, Oxon. 426n.38
Gascoinge, John 14–15, 48–9, 664n.14
Gassendi 207n.49
Gastrell, Francis 202–3, 202n.27, 276–7,
    639n.184
  Bishop of Chester 395–6

Gay, John 386–7
Gaza, Theodorus 162
Gazzaniga, Giuseppe 192
Geddington 105–6
General Turnpike Act 1773 493
Geneva
  pastors of 581
Genlis, Félicité de 563–4
Gentleman's Magazine 127–9, 193, 195n.315
Gentlemen's Societies 639–40
George I 7–8, 65–6, 155n.124, 270n.97, 307–8,
    330–1, 362–3, 462–3
  attitudes in the University towards the king
    and his governments 261–2, 304–5,
    308–10, 320–2, 356–7, 415–16
  University Addresses to 320–3, 355–6,
    369–70, 666–7
  'treasonable' suspicions of Oxford
    University 260–1, 308, 666–7
  benefactions to 322–3
  will not employ Tories 666–7
  visits Cambridge University 320n.87
  rumours of visit to Oxford 320n.87
  reform of the universities, and 366n.32
  visits to Hanover 276, 308, 321n.91
  confessional reunion, and 572–3
  Swiss Protestants, and 581
George II 7–8, 17–18, 136, 262n.67, 569–70
  as Prince of Wales 308, 396–7
  brief welcome for Tories on his
    accession 310–11, 323–4, 323n.103
  ignores them thereafter 323–4
  visits Cambridge University 320n.87, 323–4
  and Oxford University 291–2, 309n.39,
    311–12, 320, 324–6, 338n.161, 356–7,
    666–7
  University Addresses to 323–4, 334, 338–9,
    338n.161, 355–6, 508, 666–7
  qualified distaste for the king and his
    governments in Oxford 251, 323–4,
    371–2
  Chancellor of Trinity College, Dublin 468–9
  longevity 313, 325–6
George III 8, 227–8, 354, 395, 655; *see also* Tories
  as Prince of Wales 274–5, 301–2, 313
  accession 17–18, 39, 125–6, 326–8, 338–9,
    340n.168, 416
  Oxford delegations on his accession, marriage,
    and coronation 251, 339
  University Addresses to 339, 342, 342n.181,
    348–50
  Tories welcomed to court 339, 375
  unconcerned about Jacobitism 314n.62
  'a Patriot King' 343–4

780 INDEX

George III (cont.)
model of a Christian king 344–5, 357
enemy of 'party' 339n.163
as book collector 343n.186
loyalty felt towards 36–7, 253, 298–9, 313, 338–41, 343–4, 348–51, 358–9
Oxford in favour with 80–1, 264–5, 292–3, 301–2, 357, 375
prefers to Cambridge 341n.176
visits to Oxford 341–2, 349, 502
encouragement of learning 343, 343n.187
Latin verses offered to 344n.192
involvement in appointment to Oxford Regius chairs 343
Regency Crisis 1788–9 349, 357
Oxford loyalty to during 349–50
popularity during the French Revolution 301–2, 349, 357
an 'old Whig' 379n.101
George IV 258–9, 271–2
birth 340–1
education 340–1
George of Denmark, Prince 384–5
Georgirenes, Joseph, Metropolitan of Samos 576
Gerard, James 525n.194
Germantown, battle of (1777) 596–7
Germany
universities in 16–17
Biblical scholarship in 140
Gibbon, Edward 41–2, 120, 632–3
on the dons of Magdalen College 314n.59, 520–1
as Oxford outsider and critic 9, 196n.318, 517–18, 520–1, 551–2
lasting impression of his aspersions 522
Decline and Fall and Oxford history writing 193–4
debt to Jansenist authors 588–9, 589n.172
erudition, and 158–9
Christianity, and 144–5
his Vindication 293–4
briefly a Catholic 522
plans to study Arabic 174n.218, 522n.181
Arabic literature, on 196
endorsement of [Sir] William Jones 182n.261
his Memoirs 522–3, 672
critics of 144–5, 193–4
attitudes towards in Cambridge 523n.183
on accession of George III 339n.164
Gibbons, Grinling 631n.153
Gibbs, James 32, 114–15, 115n.167
rebuilding of Ditchley Park 434–5
Radcliffe Camera/Library 645

Gibson, Bishop Edmund 105–6, 128n.221, 270–1, 486–8
at Oxford 153
Anglo-Saxon scholarship 153–4, 155n.124, 662
writings and editions 153, 156–7
editor of Camden's Britannia 458–9, 640–1
Bible, and the 83–4
chaplain to Archbishop Tenison 153
Convocation dispute 156–7
moderate Whig 329
Walpole's principal ecclesiastical adviser 328, 368–71, 668
university policies 369–70
end of alliance with Walpole 271, 370–1
Giddy, Edward 191, 485–6
Giessen 582–3
gift giving, culture of 582–3, 642–57, 674; see also Oxford, University of
Gillot, Charles 581–2
Gilpin, William 620
Glamorgan
gentry in 455–6
Beaufort estates in 603–4
Glasgow, University of 44–5, 225, 512–13
Calvinist tradition at 467
pro-Williamite 70
Visitations 70, 70n.84, 366–7
its graduates at Oxford 465–7
patronage at 673–4
Glorious Revolution, see Revolution of 1688
Gloucester 184–5
Bishops of, see Warburton; Deans of, see Jane; Duke of, see William
cathedral 442
Crypt School 445
Gloucester Hall
and foundation of Worcester College 645
Principal of, see Woodroffe, Benjamin
Glyndwr, Owain 455–6
Glynne, Sir William, 2nd Bt. 426–7
Goady Marwood, Leics. 242–3
Godolphin, Francis, 2nd Earl of Godolphin, previously Viscount Rialton
MP for Oxfordshire 437
Lord-Lieutenant of Oxfordshire 437
Godolphin, Sidney, 1st Earl of Godolphin 361–2
Goldgar, Anne 194
Goldie, Mark 300n.9, 406n.213
Goldsmith, Oliver 514n.142
Golding, Dr Christopher 446–7
Goodson, Richard (senior) 182–4, 186–7, 186n.272
Goodson, Richard (junior) 182–4, 186

INDEX 781

Gordon, Thomas 368
Görtz-Gyllenborg correspondence 401–2
Gosfield, Essex 538
Göttingen, Georg-August-University of 574–5, 672–3, 676
British links 46, 556–7, 584
Oxford students attend 556–7
George II visits 320n.87
Enlightenment 584, and the
Royal Society of Sciences at 584–5
Gouge Trust 460–1
Gower, Lord, *see* Leveson-Gower
Grabe, John [Johannes] Ernest
career 570–2
ecumenist 572
churchmanship 572n.83
awarded DD 579
patrons in Oxford 570–2
publications 570–2
edits Septuagint 570–2
death lamented 573n.84, 583n.136
Graf, Friedrich Hartmann 187–8
Grafton, Duke of, *see* Fitzroy
Graham, James, 1st Duke of Montrose 198–9
grammar schools, *see* schools
Grand Tour
Oxford tutors and students on 278–9, 557–9, 621
Grantham, Earl and Countess of, *see* Nassau
Granville, Earl, *see* Carteret
Granville, John 316n.68
Graves, Richard 141
Gray, Robert 628
Gray, Thomas 547–8
Great Chalfield, Wilts. 636–7
'Great Rebellion', *see* Civil War
Great Tew, Oxon. 438–9
Great Tew circle 299
Greaves, Richard L. 102–3
Greek College at Oxford 124–5, 576; *see also*
Orthodox Church
Green, James, 34n.76
Green, Vivian 520n.172
Greene, Robert 199
Greenshields, James 461–2, 462n.240
Greenwich 221–2
Observatory 241–2
Gregory, Professor David 60n.39, 200, 217–19, 485–6, 663–4
Professor of Mathematics at Edinburgh
University 70–1, 202n.22
Episcopalian, an 70–1
Savilian Professor of Astronomy 70–1
curriculum reform, and 16–17

Fellow of the Royal Society 70–1
Newtonian 70–1, 71n.89, 209, 213–14, 241–2
publications 71n.90, 201n.18
reputed atheist 70–1
reputed Jacobite 71n.90
Gregory, Dean David 31n.60, 252n.22
Professor of Modern History 149–51, 662
Dean of Christ Church 150n.95, 292, 527–8
modern language teaching 142
Oxford curriculum and its reform
149–50, 446
Whig politics 149–51
Gregory, née Grey, Lady Mary 527–8, 529n.211
Grenville, George 313, 348, 375, 406–7
Grenville, George Nugent-Temple-, 1st Marquess
of Buckingham, 2nd Earl Temple
143n.59, 267n.85, 272–4, 398–9
Grenville, William Wyndham, 1st Lord
Grenville 258–9, 259n.56, 273n.112
as Oxford student 272–4, 619
Chancellor of Oxford 115, 248, 259–60,
261n.59, 272n.109
Church reform, and 272–4
Nova Scotia higher education, and 597
Grey, Charles, 2nd Earl 17–18, 391–3
Grey, Richard 638, 654n.236
Griffith, Thomas 79n.5, 80
Griffiths, Griffith 511–12
Guernsey, Lord, *see* Finch, Heneage
Guilford, Earls of and Barons, *see* North
Guise, General John
artistic bequest to Christ Church 649–50
Gwatkin, Thomas 594, 595n.201

Habermas, Jürgen 48n.143
Hackney academy 497–8
Hafez 177, 179, 179n.246, 180n.250
Hailes, *see* Dalrymple
Hale, Sir Matthew
History of the Common Laws of England 410
Halifax, Yorks. 443
Halifax, Nova Scotia
King's College 597
Halhed, Nathaniel 181
Hall, Charles 628
Hall, John
Master of Pembroke College 329, 613–14
Lady Margaret Professor 329n.128
doubts about his episcopal
ordination 329n.128
made Bishop of Bristol 329
Halle, University of 553–4
Halley, Edmond 199n.6, 217–19, 663–4
work in mathematics and astronomy 219

782 INDEX

Halley, Edmond (*cont.*)
  solar eclipse 1715 239
  observatory 219, 220n.111
  patron 433n.76
  fails to secure Savilian chair of Astronomy
    1692 70–1
  appointed Savilian Professor of Geometry 219
  DCL 549–50
  Astronomer Royal 433n.76
  alleged unbelief 215–16, 239
Halley's Comet 210
Halton, Timothy 28–31
Hambleden, Buckinghamshire 403–4
Hamburg 187–8, 570–2
Hamilton, Gavin 651–2
Hamilton, James, 6th Duke of Hamilton 438–9
Hammerstein, Notker 14–15
Hampden, John 299n.2
Hampton, James 325n.113
Hampton, Stephen 81n.9, 130n.227, 660n.3
Hampton Lucy Grammar school,
  Warwickshire 447–8
Handel, George Frederick (Georg
  Friedrich) 138n.40, 546
  in Oxford 1733 188–9
  enduring influence at 188–9, 192
Hanging Houghton, Northants. 656–7
Hanmer, Sir Thomas, 4th Bt. 404–5,
  405nn.209,210
Hannes, Sir Edward 27–8
  career 216n.96
Hanover, Electors of, *see* George I, George II
Hanoverian Succession, *see* Protestant
  Succession
Harcourt, Elizabeth, (2nd) Countess
  Harcourt 341–2
Harcourt, George, 2nd Earl Harcourt 341–2,
  430–1
  and the University 431n.66
Harcourt, Simon, 1st Viscount
  Harcourt 361n.11, 645
  legal career 412–13
  Country party politics 1690s 315–16
  cultivates High Church clergy 405
  chief defence counsel for Sacheverell at his
    trial 318, 412–13
  arguments deployed there 318, 319n.81
  Oxford University politics, and 269–70,
    361–2, 477–8
  Atterbury, and 406n.215, 412–13
  Bolingbroke, ally of 412–13
  joins the Whigs 322–3, 368, 386, 430–1,
    430n.62
  University benefactor 430n.62

Harcourt, Simon (son) 358–9, 412–13
Harcourt, Simon, 1st Earl, 2nd Viscount
  Harcourt 431n.65
  royal household appointments 430–1, 435
  firm Whig 430–1, 431n.63
  'New Interest' 438
  Oxford University, wary of 430–1
Harcourt interest 260–1
Hardwicke, Earl of, *see* Yorke
Hare, Francis, Bishop of St Asaph 451
Harefield, Middlesex 390n.148
Harlaxton, Lincs. 633
Harley, Edward, 2nd Earl of Oxford &
  Mortimer 154–5, 270n.94, 276–8
Harley, Edward, 3rd Earl of Oxford &
  Mortimer 397–8, 397n.176, 398n.177,
  399n.181
Harley, Robert, 1st Earl of Oxford &
  Mortimer 107–8, 154–5, 174–5, 271, 549
  Country party politics 1690s 315–16
  Tory leadership 1700s 403–5
  ministry 1710–14 187–8, 259–60, 269–70,
    307–8, 318, 358–9, 383–4, 400
  choice of title 361–2
  Oxford University, and 361–2, 361nn.10,11
  impeachment 276–7, 321–2, 396–7
Harley, Hon. Robert 390n.148
Harley, Roger 4th Earl of Oxford &
  Mortimer 397
Harris, James, the elder 79n.3
Harris, (Sir) James, 1st Earl of Malmesbury
  581–2, 583n.134
Harris, Tim 299n.7
Harrison, Peter 6–7
Harrison, Sedgwick 64n.54
Harrow School 177
Hart Hall 200, 208–9, 274
  Principals, *see* Newton, Richard; *see also*
    Hertford College
  Vice-Principals, *see* Marten
Harte, Walter 538, 538n.253
Hartington, Marquess of, *see* 3rd Duke of
  Devonshire
Hartmann, Dr Adam Samuel 573n.85
Harwood, Edward 498–9
Hastings, Lady Elizabeth ('Betty')
  benefactions to Queen's College 448–9
  her will 449nn.165,166
Hastings, Selina, Countess of Huntingdon 505,
  505n.99
Hastings, Warren 174n.219, 181–2, 410–11,
  511–12
Haugen, Kristine Louis Haugen 160–2
Havant 123–4

Haweis, Thomas 112–13, 504–5
Hawes, Matthew 96n.82
Hawkesbury, Lord, *see* Jenkinson
Hawkins, Thomas 25n.36
Hawkins, William 115–16, 120, 140n.48
 Professor of Poetry 140
 playwright 140n.49
 authority on classical Greek drama 162–3
Hawksmoor, Nicholas 28–32, 333, 590–2
Haydn, Joseph 187–8, 191n.301
 awarded Oxford degree 187–9, 192, 432
 concerts in Oxford 189
 his music performed there 192
Haydon, Benjamin 454–5
Hayes, Philip 184–5, 189n.292, 192, 543
Hayes, William 184–6, 188–9, 341–2, 663
 career 184–5
 compositions 184–5, 189n.292
Hayton, David 321n.91
Hayward, Thomas 442–3
Headbourne Worthy 123–4
Headley, Henry 140–1
Hearne, Thomas 55n.13, 152–3, 400, 674–5
 Jacobitism 144–5, 304–5
 Nonjuror 355–6
 attitudes to Roman Catholics 114n.163,
  157n.133
 publications 144–5, 157–8, 159n.141, 164
 critic of John Potter 101n.103
 critic of Handel 188
 on William Bromley 386
 friend of Browne Willis 630–1
Heath, Benjamin 630
Heber family 601n.7
Hely-Hutchinson, John 470
Henley, Robert, 1st Earl of Northington 372n.69
Henley-on-Thames 381–2
Henry I 325–6
Henry III 563–4
Henry V 135–6
Henry VIII 156–7, 269–70, 287–8
Herbert, Hon. Henry 465
Herbert, Thomas, 8th Earl of Pembroke &
  Montgomery 162, 198–9, 199n.3, 249n.5
 as (hereditary) Visitor of Jesus College 283–4,
  284n.158, 603
 donates statue to the University 649
Herbert, William, 3rd Earl of Pembroke 649
Herculaneum 582–3
Hereford
 Bishops of, *see* Ironside, Egerton (Henry),
  Butler, John
 Deans of, *see* Webber, Wetherell
Herring, Archbishop Thomas 358, 372–3

Herschel, William 575–6
Hertford College; *see also* Hart Hall Principals,
 see Newton, Richard; Durell; Hodgson
 Vice-Principals, *see* Blayney, Newcome
 foundation 274
 centre of Biblical scholarship 87–8, 87n.41
 Whig leanings 337
 bequests to 647–9
 Edmund Burke, and 511–12
Hervey, John, styled Lord Hervey 581–2
Hesiod 163
Hestercombe House, Somerset 617
Hey, John 117–18
Heywood, Eliza 540
Hickes, Bishop George
 Nonjuror 54–5, 153–4
 concerns about Newtonianism 202n.22
 publications 54–5, 153–4, 662
 friend of Grabe 572n.83
Hickes, William
 Oxford Jests, Refined and Enlarged 490
Hickman, Bishop Charles 473–4
Higgins, Francis 472–3
Higgins, Ian 109n.137
'high and dry', *see* High Churchmen
High Borlace 477–8, 537
'high flyers', *see* High Churchmen
History of the Great Rebellion, see Hyde
High Churchmen 68, 73–4, 111, 114–15, 155–6,
  258n.51; *see also* Oxford, University of
 in ascendancy 1710–14 99–100, 125
 excluded after 1714 362–3
 Hutchinsonianism, and 113
 Jesus College, at 458
 Ireland, in 472–5
 Orthodox Church, and 576n.106
 religious orders, and 590–2
 aghast at Henrician dissolution of the
  monasteries 631n.150
Higson, John 505
Hildrop, John 452
 publications 633, 638–9
 schoolmaster 633
 academic honours 633
Hinton-in-the-Hedges, Northants. 638
Hinton St. George, Somerset 300n.10
Hippocrates 222–3, 223n.126, 597
history, ancient; *see also* Oxford, University of
 intellectual standing of 151–2
history, medieval; *see also* Oxford, University of
 reduced interest in 157–9
history, modern; *see also* Oxford, University of
 character of 144–51
 elite formation, and 144–7

784 INDEX

history, modern (*cont.*)
  'philosophical history' 146n.70, 148–9
Hitchin, Neil 83n.16, 88nn.45,46
Hoadly, Bishop Benjamin 116, 318, 446–7,
    458, 518
  Whig polemicist 40–1
  censure of 41n.106
  *The Original and Institution of Civil
    Government* 40–1
  'My Kingdom is not of this World'
    sermon 364
Hoadlyite/ism 330–1, 368–9
Hoare, Joseph 430–1, 431n.65
Hobbes, Thomas 41n.103, 207n.49
Hodges, Walter 209–10
Hodgson, Bernard 647–9
Hody, Humphrey
  Professor of Greek 157n.133, 162
  Archdeacon of Oxford 158n.136
  Biblical scholar 84–6
  Whig sympathies and supporters 157n.133,
    158n.136
  works with Richard Bentley 163n.157
Hogarth, William 486–8
Hogton, Sir Henry, 6th Bt. 376–7
Holdsworth, Edward 31, 262n.69, 304–5, 557–8,
    609–10
  Magdalen College building schemes, and 646
  Muscipula Sive Cambro Muo Machia 457
Holdsworth, Winch 168–70
Holland, Lord, *see* Vassall Fox
Holland, John
  Whig politics 275–6
Holland, *see* United Provinces
Holloway, Benjamin
  Hutchinsonian author and apologist 209–10,
    210nn.63,65, 626–7
  critical of other Hebraists 175n.226, 626
  Oxfordshire livings held 626
  close to Sarah, Duchess of Marlborough 626,
    627n.131
Holmes, Geoffrey 71n.87, 382–3, 386
Holmes, Robert 87–8, 543
  funding of his Biblical manuscripts
    research 343n.187
  visits Paris 562–3
  manuscripts in Florence 581–2
  Addington his patron 563n.45, 581–2
Holmes, Sarah, née England 538–9
Holmes, William
  Vice-Chancellor 262, 294–5
  Regius Professor of Modern History 149–51,
    151n.103, 262
  royal chaplain 262

Dean of Exeter 570n.76
enetrtains the Prince of Orange 569–70
Holt, Wilts. 636–7
Holt, LCJ, Sir John 360–1
Holwell, William 164–5
'holy alliance', *see* Newtonianism
Holy Club, *see* Methodists
holy orders, bill to end college fellows taking
    1709 383–4, 396–7
Holyoake, Henry 479n.321
Holroyd, John Baker, 1st Lord Sheffield
    522–3, 672
Home Office 259–60
Homer 140, 163
Homeros, Georgios 577–8
Hooke, John 452n.183
Hooke, Robert 215–16
Hooper, Bishop George 306n.26, 369n.54
Horne, Bishop George 43–4, 120, 295–6,
    527–8, 539
  family 532, 533n.230
  vice-chancellor 106–7, 265–7
  concerns for students 172
  Dean of Canterbury 106–7, 266–7, 635–6
  High Churchman 106–7
  admiration for Scottish Nonjurors 462–3
  defence of throne and altar alliance 586–7
  acclaims George III 344–5
  Hutchinsonian, as 110, 113, 210, 265–6
  writings 106–7, 266–7
  journalism 109, 109n.140
  sermons 118–19, 612
  condemns 'free enquiry' 42n.107, 266–7
  anti-Priestley 118–19, 500–1, 660–1
  attacks Voltaire's religious views 564n.48
  critical of Locke 171n.202
  critical of Newton 209n.59, 210–11, 211n.71
  interest in Jansenism 588–9
  writes against Hume 171–2, 173nn.211,213,
    266–7
  Samuel Johnson, and 514
Hornsby, Thomas 34n.76, 236–8, 429, 676
  Savilian Professor of Astronomy 226–7
  Radcliffe Observer 226–7
  career summarised 227n.143
  client of 2nd Earl of Macclesfield 227n.142,
    432–3
  celebrity 226–8, 585n.145
  observations, *see* Venus, transit of
  lectures 227–8, 231n.166, 645
  Göttingen, connection to 584–5
  Russian students, and 575–6
Horry, Daniel 597
Horse Guards 251

INDEX 785

Horsley, Samuel
  writes against Priestley 118–19
  becomes Bishop of St Davids 294n.207
  defence of throne and altar alliance 586–7
  admiration for Scottish Nonjurors 462–3
  on Volunteers 353n.235
hospitals
  clergy involvement in preaching and fund
    raising for 638
Houbigant, Fr Charles François 584–5
Hough, John
  President of Magdalen College, Bishop of
    Oxford 287–9, 289nn.173,175, 295–6
Howe, William 648n.210
Huddesford, George
  Vice-Chancellor 225–6, 263–4, 264n.75
  and Oxfordshire election 1754 263–4
Huddesford, William
  Keeper of the Asmolean Museum 225–6
  updates collections 225–6
  sponsors publications 226
Hudson, John
  Bodleian Librarian 454–5
  classicist 164, 499
  continental connections 578–9
  friend of John Woodward 486n.11
Hudson, Thomas 617
Hughes, David 354
Hume, David 44–5, 465
  history writing, and 144–5
  Oxford's responses to his philosophical
    writings 171–2
  upholds religious establishment in
    England 79n.4
Hume, Bishop John 112–13, 292, 292n.193
Humphreys, Bishop Humphrey 458–9
Hunt, Arnold 96–7, 96n.81, 98n.92
Hunt, Joseph 278n.136, 283–4
Hunt, née Adkins, Sarah 534–5
Hunt, Thomas 177
  chaplain to 1st earl of Macclesfield 176n.229
  relations with 2nd and 3rd Earls 213n.81
  Professor of Arabic 173–5
  Regius Professor of Hebrew 175nn.224,228,
    176n.234
  criticised by Hutchinsonians 173–4, 210,
    210n.66
  contacts with foreign scholars 560–2, 562n.41,
    581–2, 590n.176
  endorsement of [Sir] William Jones 182n.261
  Polish sovereign visits 565
  admirer of Philip Doddridge 498–9
  preacher, as a 96–7
  supports 'New Interest' 439n.104

domestic life 530, 531n.221
Hunter, Ian 56n.15
Hunter, John 451
Hunter, Michael 53–4, 54n.3
Hunter, William 224n.130
Huntingdon, Selina, Countess of, see Hastings
Huntingford, George 513–14
Hurd, Richard 661
Hurdis, James
  Professor of Poetry 140, 141n.51
  censures Gibbon 140, 523
Hurley, Oxon. 57
Husbands, John 134–5
Hutcheson, Francis 168n.186, 170
Hutchinson, John 13–14, 113, 210
  writings published 209–10
Hutchinsonianism 454–5
  contents 76, 113
  supreme regard for Hebrew 173–4
  anti-Newton 113, 210
  critical of Kennicott 87n.39, 113
  popularity in Oxford 76, 110, 113, 209–12,
    452, 663–4
  manifestation of counter-Enlightenment,
    as a 241–2
Hutton, James 226n.138
Hyde, Edward, 1st Earl of Clarendon 74n.100
  and Great Tew circle 299
  minister of Charles II 299
  History of the Great Rebellion 32n.66, 73–4,
    145–7, 146nn.71,74, 147n.78, 150–2,
    193–4, 661–2
  bequest to the University 644
Hyde, Henry, 2nd Earl of Clarendon 58–60,
    59n.29, 382–3, 411–12, 433–4
Hyde, Henry, 2nd Earl of Rochester & 4th Earl of
    Clarendon
  High Steward of the University 320–1, 433–4
Hyde, Henry, Viscount Cornbury and Baron
    Hyde of Hindon 325–6; see also
    Cornbury Plot
  MP for the University 386–90, 395
  and 'James III' 386–7, 387n.132
  abandons Jacobitism 386–7
  political career 386–7
  peerage in acceleration 386–7, 387n.136
  defence of Clarendon's History 146–7
  fails to write his own History 146–7
Hyde, Laurence, 1st earl of Rochester 59n.29,
    384–5
  Cornbury Park transferred to 433–4
  opposed to Comprehension (1689) 58–60
  takes oaths to William and Mary 58–60
  Tory politics of 315n.65, 404–5, 411–12

786   INDEX

Hyde, Laurence, 1st earl of Rochester (*cont.*)
  summoning of Convocation, and (1701) 315
  edits his father's *History* 73–4, 145–6, 146n.72
  in office during Anne's reign 361–2, 404–5, 473–4
Hyde, Thomas 156n.127, 177
  Professor of Arabic 173–4
  Regius Professor of Hebrew 175n.224
  Bodley's Librarian 175n.224
  publications 174–5
  linguisitic talents 174–5
  recognition of the importance of Chinese culture 177n.239
  Zoroastrianism, and 174–5
  influence and reputation 177nn.237,238

Ihalainen, Pasi 128n.224
Ilchester, Earl of, *see* Fox
Ikerrin, Viscount, *see* Butler, Somerset Hamilton
India 590n.179
Indulgence, Declaration of 1688 496–7
Inglis, Bishop Charles 597
Ingram, Robert G. 57n.20, 86n.33
Inns of Court 461
  graduate numbers at 410, 410n.243
Interregnum (1650s) 37–8, 65–6, 73–4, 215–16, 358
invasion attempt (1759) 338–9
Ireland 8–9
  Irish students in Oxford 21, 21n.25, 469–72, 475–6
  possible links with United Irishmen 472
  Oxford clergy in the Church of Ireland 472–5
  Anglo-Irish cultural interaction at Oxford 475–6, 479–80
Irish Brigade 472
Ironside, Bishop Gilbert 57, 57n.22
Isham, Sir Edmund, 6th Bt. 262–3, 615–17, 656–7
Isham, Edmund (Warden of All Souls College) 609n.52
Isham, Edmunda 615–17
Isham, Euseby 95–6
  Vice-Chancellor 262–3
  Rector of Lincoln College 615–17
  Northamptonshire family 262–3, 615–17
  advises Arran 263n.72
  diplomatic conduct during the '45 Rebellion 262–3, 292n.191, 294–5, 311n.51
  appearance 263n.72
Isham, Sir Justinian, 4th Bt. 452
Isham, Thomas 533
Islam, *see* Qu'ran, Oxford, University of
Islay, earl of, *see* Campbell

Islip, Oxon. 92–4, 425–6, 652–3
Israel, Jonathan 14–15, 16n.9, 74–5
Italy
  universities in 15

Jablonski, Daniel Ernst 572
Jackson, Cyril 7, 273n.113, 353–4, 435–6, 475–6
  sub-preceptor to George, Prince of Wales 340–1
  remains in contact with the Prince thereafter 341n.173
  appointed Dean of Christ Church 259n.55
  tutor, as 277–8, 278n.134
  livings held 612–13
  connections with Westminster School 621n.103
  college land management 443
  declines major preferment 271–2, 293n.197, 409, 410n.238
  politics 407–9
  influence in government circles 272–4, 295–6, 398–9, 407–9, 416
  amity with Portland 407–9, 608
  sponsors election of Portland as Chancellor 1792 258–9, 259nn.55,56, 294–5
  ditto Lord Grenville 1809 272n.109
  powerful academic politician 258–9, 271–2, 359–60, 407–9, 655
  critics of his influence 297n.212
  curriculum reformer 454–5
  educates students with a view to state service 271–4, 379, 402
  revival of Greek studies, and 165–6
  mathematician and botanist 225, 233n.177
  character 407–8, 410n.239
  life style 226n.138
  travels 409, 621
  cordial relations with Dissenters 409, 502
  friends in the Lunar Society 639–40
  King's College, Halifax, NS, and 597
Jackson, William 549n.295
  Regius Professor of Greek 162
  Bishop of Oxford 409n.237
  Cyril Jackson's view of 409n.237
  close to the Dartmouth family 621, 621n.104
Jackson, William (University printer) 98, 417
Jackson's Oxford Journal 98, 417
  founded 264n.74
  advertisements in 452
  concerts advertised in 191–2
  Pittite in 1750s 326–8
Jacob, Margaret, C. 53n.1

Jacobinism 6–7
  Jacobitism 3–4; *see also* Fifteen ('15)
    Rebellion, Forty-Five ('45) Rebellion,
    'Old Interest'
  Oxford, in 7–8, 17–19, 39, 42–3, 48–9, 95–6,
    114–15, 262–3, 304–13, 338–9, 355–6,
    400, 483–4, 666–7
  after the '45 Rebellion 263–4, 311–13, 325–8,
    338–9, 371–4, 668
  moribund after 1760 264–5, 375
  presence in Oxford scholarship 131–3
  school masters, and 451
  liquor, and 312n.53
  in Oxfordshire 96n.80
  in Scotland 69n.80, 462–3
  in Wales 455–6
  in Ireland 472–3
James I 125
James II and VII 7–8, 58–60, 125, 146–7,
    299–300, 365n.25, 496–7
  'abdication' 17–18, 36–7, 57–8, 306–7
  exile in France 306–7
  in Ireland 60–1
  death 315–16
  Oxford, and 36, 38, 53, 57–8, 66–8, 114–15,
    260–1, 306–15, 358, 373n.76, 666; *see also*
    Magdalen College
James Edward Stuart, 'James III' 57–8, 65–6, 125,
    248–50, 250n.8, 266, 270n.98, 300–1, 303,
    305–8, 462–3, 666–7; *see also* Abjuration,
    Act of
  'accession' 1701 315–16
  invasion hopes in Anne's reign 400
  communicates with the English universities
    (1715) 309n.42
  residence in Italy 309–10
  possible King of Poland 558–9
  death 375
James, John 143
James, Robert 142n.56
James, Thomas 445n.137
Jane, William 58–60, 59n.30, 100–2, 404–5
  Dean of Gloucester 64n.58
  neglectful professor 64–5, 64n.58
  politically ambitious 64–5
Jansen, Cornelius 588n.167
Jansenism 588–9, 588n.165, 589n.169
Japan 573–4
Jebb, John 496n.55
Jebb, Samuel 499
Jeffreys of Wem, John, 2nd Lord 650–1
Jeffreys, Edward 60–1
Jeffreys, Dr John 581–2
Jena, University of 574–5

Jenkins, Edward 595
Jenkins, Sir Leoline 592
Jenkinson, Charles, 1st Lord Hawkesbury, later
    1st Earl of Liverpool 312n.52, 635–6
  background 406n.217
  career as a minister 406–7
  candidate for a University seat 1768 390–1
  character 406n.217
  confidante of George III 265–6, 406–7,
    407n.223
  Oxford University politics, and 264–5, 406–7
  patron and friend of Nathan Wetherell 295–6,
    406–7, 406n.218
  other University connections 348
  association with Jones of Nayland 407n.220
  peerage 406–7
Jenkinson, Sir Robert, 5th Bt. 312n.52
Jenkinson, Robert Banks, 2nd Earl of
    Liverpool 274
Jenner, Thomas
  President of Magdalen College 103–4
  Lady Margaret Professor 103–4
Jesus College 8–9, 417–18, 455–6
  Principals 106–7, *see* Wynne, Thelwall, Pardo,
    Owen, Hughes, Hoare
  election of 1712 283–4
  hereditary lay Visitor, *see* Pembroke, Earl of
  Leoline fellows at 592
  plebian students at 455–6
  cook at 515–16
  political character of 458
  intellectual life after Lhuyd 460–1
  Welsh connection 455–6, 456n.201, 458,
    669–70
  Whig character 332–3
  land ownership 442
  livings in gift of 457
  student enlistment in Oxford University
    Volunteers 352n.230
Jewish Naturalisation Act 1753 373–4, 438–9
John III, King of Poland 217n.99
Johnson, Samuel 46–7, 99n.95, 194–5
  school 451
  Pembroke College, and 134–5, 142n.56,
    304n.22
  later visits to Oxford 514
  banter about Cambridge 507, 508n.108
  on honorary degree awards 549–50
  possible Jacobite 304n.22, 451
  Literary Club 180
  his poetry 135n.17
  Lives of the Poets 136–7
  modern languages familiarity 142n.56
  on Methodism 505

788 INDEX

Johnson, Samuel (*cont.*)
  on quacks 208
  on Archbishop Secker 291n.187
  deathbed compared to Hume's 171–2
Johnson, Samuel (Principal of King's College,
    New York) 594–5
Johnson, William Samuel 594–5
Jones, Charles 361–2
Jones, Inigo 28–31
John, Jones (Balliol College historian) 297
Jones, John (of Oundle school) 452
Jones, Mary
  poetry 527–8
  popularity and esteem 527–8, 528nn.208,209
Jones, Oliver 527–8
Jones, Richard, 1st Earl of Ranelagh [I] 251n.14
Jones, William (of Nayland) 562–3
  High Churchman and Hutchinsonian 209,
    344–5
  curate at Finedon 612
  critic of experimentalism and Newton 209–10
  on Dissenters, on 671
  endorses non-resiatnce 345
  regard for the Nonjurors 344–5
Jones, William (of Abergavenny) 455–6
Jones, [Sir] William 5–6, 676
  publications and translations in Oriental
    languages 177–80, 180nn.251,253, 663
  studies in Sanskrit 180–1, 663
  on cultural transmission, on 180
  lack of interest in Christian apologetics 180–1,
    183n.262
  international standing 177, 180–2, 193,
    196, 663
  poetic influence 179
  academic endorsement 180n.252
  defence of Oxford scholarship 185n.269
  republican Whig sympathies 180–1,
    182n.259, 183n.263, 347n.209, 355
  parliamentary candidature 1780 182n.259,
    347, 390–1
  lawyer 180–1, 196, 410–11
  government employment, and 181, 410–11
journalism
  academic involvement in 274–5
  clerical involvement in 108–9, 276n.123
  student involvement in 193, 510–11
  patriotic, of the 1790s 351–2
Journal littéraire de La Haye 200
Junius (the younger), Franciscus 629n.142
Junto Whigs 156–7, 315, 329, 360–2, 382–4, 400;
    see also Whigs
Jurieu, Pierre 282
Jurin, James 213–14

Justinian's *Digest* 60–1
  Institutes 410–11
Justin Martyr 570–2

Keble, John 18n.18
Keck, Anthony 438–9
Keck, Lady Susan 438–9, 537
Keene, Henry 32, 226–7, 228n.148, 229–31
Keighley 443
Keill, James 461
Keill, John 208–9, 633, 676
  comes to Oxford 461
  pupil of David Gregory 70–1
  Savilian Professor of Astronomy 70–1
  official Decypherer 400
  Newtonian 200, 200n.11, 209, 213–14, 241–2,
    663–4
  academic eclecticism 200
  personal life 201n.16
  publications 200n.13, 201n.17, 201–2, 217–19
Kelly, John 603
Kendal 450
Kendal, Duchess of, *see* Schulenburg
Kennet & Avon Canal 443
Kennett, Basil 588–9
Kennett, White 63n.48, 318
  Oxfordshire parish priest 426–7
  Bishop of Peterborough 1718 332
  Bible, and the 83–4
  Convocation dispute, and 156–7
  historian and antiquarian 146–7, 426–7,
    426n.43, 662
  Whig in politics 329, 426–7
  receives doctorates 330n.130
Kennicott, Benjamin 676
  Radcliffe Librarian 348
  Hebraist and Old Testament scholar 86–7
  Biblical revision, and 86–9
  secures access to manuscripts abroad 581–2,
    583n.134, 584–5
  stay in Paris 560–2
  connection to Göttingen 584–5
  supported by Archbishop Secker 86–7
  funding of his research 343
  classical editions 165n.175
  critics of 87n.39, 210
  Whig in politics 336–7, 438–9
  Whitehall preacher 336n.158
Kent
  Lord-Lieutenant of 300n.10
Keppel, Bishop the Hon. Frederick 630n.145
Ker, John, 1st Duke of Roxburgh 198–9
Kett, Henry
  Bampton Lecturer 120

critic of Locke 168–70
curriculum modernisation 672–3
historian 41–2
Kettlewell, John 609–10
Kew 313
Kidd, John 242–3, 243n.202
Kilcash, co.Tipperary 250n.10
Kilkenny 471
Killaloe, Bishop of, *see* Lindsay
Kilton, Somerset 447–8
King, John 402
King, Peter, 1st Lord King 198–9
King, William
  lawyer and satirist 207, 207nn.46,48
King, Dr William 264n 75, 306, 546, 668
  Principal St Mary Hall 96–7, 261n.62, 274–5
  secretary of Lord Arran 260–2, 274–5
  Public Orator 324, 547
  controversial figure 96–7
  candidate for the University seat, 1722 General
    Election 274–5, 309–10, 385
  Redeat speech on opening of Radcliffe
    Library 114–15, 188–9, 311–13,
    312–13nn.54–56, 336n.154, 373, 429,
    517–18
  Commemoration address 1754 313n.57
  last Oration (1763) 341, 343–4
  Oxfordshire election (1754) 439–40
  Jacobitism 274, 309–10, 324, 558–9
  travels abroad 558–9
  meets Prince Charles Edward Stuart 313,
    373–4
  loyal to George III 274–5, 313
  disillusioned with Tory leadership
    cadre 327n.122
  literary productions 274–5, 334n.153
King's College, Aberdeen, *see* Aberdeen,
    University of
King's College, Cambridge 496
King's College, New York 346–7
'King's Friends' 348, 406–7
Kingswood 505
Kippis, Andrew 118
Kirkby-in-Cleveland, NR Yorks. 612–13
Kirtlington, Oxon. 437–8
Kit-Kat Club 603–4
Knights, Mark 327n.119
Knox, Vicesimus 40n.99
  critic of Oxford University 39–40,
    143–4, 167, 443–4, 517–18, 521, 672
  Gibbon's *doppelgänger* 521n.176
  headmaster 444n.134
  applauds George III 349
  publications 521

Königsberg
  University 570–2
  Burgkirche 573–4
Korais, Adamantios (Adamance Coray) 577–8

Ladvocat, Abbé Jean-Baptiste 560–2
Lamb, Matthew
  Principal of Magdalen Hall 257n.48
Lamb, William, 2nd Viscount Melbourne 17–18
Lambeth Palace 152–4
Lampeter, St David's College 669–70
Lamport, Northants. 615–17, 656–7
Lancaster, William
  Vice-Chancellor 317–18, 382–3, 570
  Marlboroughs, client of the 427, 429n.51
  Sacheverell, and 317–18, 317n.77
  Whig interest, and the 429n.51
  architect, as 28–31
Langford, James 515–16
Langford Magna, Wilts. 633
Langford, Paul 206–7, 308, 339n.163, 349n.215
Langhorne, John 90
Lapland 583
Lapthorne, Richard 613–14
Lardner, Nathaniel 423–4
La Rochefoucauld d'Anville, Duc de 563–4
latitudinarianism 68; *see also* Low Church
Laud, Archbishop William 79–80, 339n.165,
    653–4
Lauderdale, Earl of, *see* Maitland
Launay, Le Corgne de 586–7
Laurence, French 410–11, 511–12
Laurence, Richard 483
Lavington, Bishop George 330–1
Lavoisier, Antoine Laurent 229–31, 231n.170
Law, Bishop Edmund
  Arian tendencies 116–18
Law, Archdeacon John 454–5
Law, William 589n.169
Lawson, Charles 452
learned societies
  in relationship to the universities 54n.3, 64–5,
    580–1; *see also* Royal Society
Lechmere, Sir Nicholas 367, 368n.45
Le Clerc, Jean 62n.46, 168–70
Le Courayer, Père Pierre-François
  anti-papal and other writings 589
  High Church favourite 589
  receives Oxford honorary degree 589, 589n.173
Lee, Diana, née Frankland, (3rd) Countess of
    Lichfield 267n.84, 530
Lee, Edward, 1st Earl of Lichfield
  marriage 434–5
  Nonjuror 434–5

790 INDEX

Lee, Frances, née Hales, (2nd) Countess of Lichfield 434–5
Lee, George, 3rd Earl of Lichfield, previously Viscount Quarendon 325–6
  family background 253
  awarded DCL 434–5
  MP for Oxfordshire 253
  High Steward of the University 1760–62 253, 607
  Chancellor of Oxford University 1762–72 253, 254n.31, 395–6, 669
  installation as 542
  accession of George III, and 339
  positions held at court 253
  presents portrait of George III to the University 343–4
  Radcliffe trustee 229–31, 260–1
  bequest to the University 229–31, 653–4
  High Borlace, at the 537
  reputation as a toper 253–4
Lee, Dr George
  legal career 413
  Leicester House loyalties 413, 413–14nn.257–259
Lee, George Henry, 2nd Earl of Lichfield 434–5
Lee, Sir Henry 434–5
Lee, Matthew
  Readership in anatomy 229–31, 231n.164
  benefactions to Christ Church 229–31, 445–6
Lee, (Hon.) Robert, 4th Earl of Lichfield 267n.84
Lee, William 143
Leeward Islands 590–2
Legge, William, 1st Earl of Dartmouth 383–4
Legge, William, 2nd Earl of Dartmouth 435–6
  High Steward of Oxford University 349–50, 398
  student in Germany 556–7
Legge, George, 3rd Earl of Dartmouth 254–5
Legge, Hon. William 435–6
Legh, Peter 260–1
Le Grys, Robert 622–3
Leibniz, Gottfried Wilhelm 72n.92, 200, 203n.28, 217–19, 566–7
Leicester House Circle 251, 313, 325–6, 336; see also Fredrick, Prince of Wales
Leiden, University of 72n.94, 223–4, 235n.183, 558–9, 574–5
  Professorship in Arabic 174n.222
  Oxford graduates in 248n.3, 556
Leigh, Cassandra 537
Leigh, Edward, 5th Lord Leigh
  High Steward of Oxford University 398
  bequest to Oriel College 224, 225n.135, 647–9

Leigh, Theophilus 31–2, 508, 537
  Master of Balliol College 283–4
  rebuilding at 31–2
  life of the College, and 284n.160
  Scottish students at, and 467
  follower of Prince Frederick 325–6
  and 1754 Oxfordshire election 438–9, 440n.111
  Justice of the Peace 427, 439n.110
Leipzig, University of 556–7, 575n.99
Lenman, Bruce 69–70
Lennox, Lady Sarah 340n.169
Leominster, Lord, see Fermor
Leslie, Charles 40–1, 59n.29, 105–6, 109n.137, 344–5
  as a journalist 108–9
  The religion of Jesus Christ the only true religion 593–4
Lessing, Gotthold Ephraim 584–5
Leveson-Gower, Lord Granville 556
Leveson-Gower, John, 2nd Lord and 1st Earl Gower 324, 397–8
Levi, Rabbi 570
Lewis, John 636–7
Lewis, Matthew 407–8
Leybourne, Robert 607, 607n.42
Lhuyd, Edward 458n.208, 674n.30; see also Jesus College
  Keeper of the Ashmolean Museum 458
  publications 226, 458–9
  Archaeologia Britannica 459–61
  'Parochial Queries' 458–9
  Red Herring Club founder 457
  travels 459–60, 460n.224
  achievment 459–60
Licensing Act, lapsing of the 1695 40–1, 57n.20, 108–9, 315
  impact on Oxford University 57
Licensing Act (1737) 485–6
Lichfield 182–4
  Grammar School 451
Lichtenberg, Georg Christoph 585n.145
Ligonier's Horse 325
Lincoln, Bishops of, see Wake, Gibson, Reynolds, Pretyman
Lincoln College
  Rectors of, see Crew, Adams, Fitzherbert, Isham (Euseby), Robinson (Michael), Tatham
  benefactions from Bishop Crew 436, 449–50
  connections to east Midlands and Northumbria 449–50
  dispute with the Bishop of Oxford 291–2
  evangelical fellows at 113n.156

Lindsay, Thomas, Bishop of Killaloe 472–3
Linday, William, 18th earl of Crawford 69–70
Lindsey, Theophilus 117–18, 120, 496–7
  critic of Horne 501n.80
  Essex Street chapel 496–7
  view of the Anglican clergy 502
  Vindiciae Priestleianae 501
Linley, Elizabeth 189–91
Linnaeus, Carl 233–4
Linnean Society 233–4, 235n.184
Lister, Martin 226
Little Houghton, Northants. 629
Liverpool, Earls of, *see* Jenkinson
Livy 164
Llandaff, bishops of, *see* Barrington, Watson
  archdeacon of, *see* Adams
Lloyd, Bishop William 570–2
Locke, John 166–7, 198–9, 579, 590–2
  Student of Christ Church 40–1, 41n.103
  flight abroad 40–1
  connection with Newtonian science 72
  limited endorsement in Oxford 72–3, 168–70,
    172–3, 194–5
  reputed irreligion and heterodoxy 63n.51,
    168–70, 170n.198
  reputation 72n.96, 135–6
  respect for in Europe 563–4
  rehabilitation 160–71, 239–41
  Scottish students, respect for in Europe 466–7,
    563–4
  statue of 172n.207
  Essay on Human Understanding 72, 168–71
  Two Treatises of Government 40–1
Loggan, David 33–5, 34n.79
Lombard, Daniel 330–1
London; *see also* Westminster
  Bishops of, *see* Compton, Robinson, Sherlock,
    Lowth, Randolph (John)
  Berkeley Square 653–4
  book trade in 5–6, 131, 134–5
  Burlington House 267–9
  City connections with the University of
    Oxford 275
  'Crown and Anchor' 623–4
  Downing Street, 10 255
  Grosvenor Street 250
  Lincoln's Inn 408–9
  Pall Mall 251
  Pantheon 32
  Pleasure Gardens, *see* Ranelagh, Vauxhall
  St Albans Tavern 397–8
  St Bartholomew's Hospital 229n.159
  St George's church, Hanover Square 91
  St James's Palace 339, 355–6

St Paul's Cathedral 98n.91, 204, 289
  Deans, of, Sherlock, William; Butler;
    Secker 62, 117
  University of 16–17
  Vauxhall Gardens 191–2
  Whitechapel 261n.64
  Willis's Rooms 623–4
London Evening Post 109, 110n.142
Longditude, Board of 241–2
Longinus 630
Longleat, Wiltshire 403–4
Lonsdale, Earls and Viscounts, *see* Lowther
Lord's Day Observance Act 396n.169
Loughborough, Leics. 262
Louis XIV 153–4
Louis XV 463–4
Loveday, John 142, 524n.187
Lovelace, John, 3rd Baron Lovelace 57
Low Church 68
Lowth, Robert 83–4, 106, 140n.45, 180, 267n.85,
    424–5, 676
  Professor of Poetry 84–6, 138
  Hebrew scholar 86–7, 113, 138–40, 177
  lectures 138–9, 139nn.42,43
  supporter of Biblical revision 86–9
  Bishop of Oxford, later London
    292–3, 297
  freedom of enquiry, on 80
  moderate Whig 118, 292–3
  Short Introduction to English Grammar 134,
    134n.13, 194
  international impact and reputation 138, 140,
    141n.50, 193, 573–4, 661–2
  connection to Göttingen 584–5
Lowth, Rev Robert (son of the Bishop) 619
Lowther, Sir James, 1st Earl of Lonsdale
    409n.236
Lowther, John, 1st Viscount Lonsdale 637–8
Loyal Brotherhood, Honourable Board
    of 397–8
Lucretius 164, 558–9
Lucy, Dr William 447–8
Ludgvan, Cornwall 631–2
Ludlow Grammar School 447–8
Lullin, Pastor Ami 572–3
Lunar Society 225n.137, 443, 502, 639–40
Lutheranism 572
Luxmore, Charles 371–2
Lye, Edward 156n.130
  Anglo-Saxon scholarship 629, 629n.142
  international contacts 629n.141
  reluctant Oxford returnee 629–30
Lyme Park, Cheshire 260–1
Lyons, Israel 233–4, 236n.185, 391n.153

792 INDEX

MacCulloch, Diarmaid 576n.106
Macdonald of Sleat, Sir James, 8th Bt. 463–4, 464nn.251,252
McGann, Jerome J. 180n.253
Mackenzie, Sir George 60–1
Maclaurin, Colin
    Newtonian mathematician 199, 199n.6
McLynn, Frank 312n.53
Macpherson, James 179
Mabillon, Jean 587
Macclesfield, Earls of, see Parker
Mackworth, Sir Digby, 3rd Bt. 353n.231
Magdalen College
    Presidents of, see Hough, Butler, Jenner, Horne, Routh
    'New Building' 31, 643, 646, 648n.210
    choral foundation 79n.2, 182–4, 186
    chapel used for ordinations 290n.181
    college servants 515–16
    women servants 527n.195
    water meadows 424–5
    James II, and 57n.21, 289
    pro-Stuart sentiments at 314n.59
    relationship of Sacheverell to 317n.76
Magdalen Hall
    Principals of, see Cotes, Denison, Lamb
    benefaction to 447–8
Maine, Jonathan 91
Maitland, James, Lord Maitland, later 8th Earl of Lauderdale 512–13
Malchair, John 33–5, 34nn.76,78
Malebranche 590–2, 633
Malmesbury, Earl of, see Harris
Malcolm, Sir Noel 176n.230
Mallet, David 278
Malpas, Cheshire 106, 611
Malpighi, Marcello 216–17
Manchester 262–3
    Grammar School 447–8, 452
    History of Manchester 632–3
Mandelbrote, Scott 202n.26
Manilius 165n.172
Manners, John, 3rd Duke of Rutland 147–8, 622–3, 633
Manners, Lord William 442
Manning, David 48n.144, 75n.105
Mansell, Thomas, 1st Lord Mansell of Margam 458–9
Mansfield, LCJ, 1st Earl of, see Murray
Mara, Gertrude Elizabeth 189–91
Marengo, Battle of 402–3
Maria Beatrice, Archduchess of Austria, Princess of Modena and Reggio 567–8
Maria-Theresa, Empress of Austria 463–4

Marischal College, see Aberdeen, University of
Markham, Archbishop William 104n.116, 259n.56
    Bishop of Chester, later Archbishop of York 271–2, 612–13
    earlier career and Westminster School 271–2, 446, 452, 470–1
    Dean of Christ Church 151–2, 271–2, 272n.106, 295–6, 446
    revival of Greek studies at 165–6
    Irish connections 470–1
    rift with Edmund Burke 346–7
    patron, as 612–13
Marlborough, Dukes of, see Churchill, Spencer
Marlborough 638–9
    Grammar School 448–9, 452, 633
Marlow, Michael
    Vice-Chancellor and client of Duke of Portland 267–9, 269n.91
    and riots winter 1799–1800 354
    his wife 531
Marmion, Shackerley 486
Maronites 560–2
Marriage of Figaro 189–91
Marsh, Richard 199n.6
Marshall, Benjamin 572n.80
Marten, William 304–5
Mary II, Queen 36, 59n.29, 66–8, 315n.66;
    see also William III
    statue of at University College 321n.92
Maryland 347n.204
Mascov, Johann Jakob 556–7
Mason, William 507–8, 508n.111
Masons 223–4, 623–4
    Oxford, in 631n.151
    Oxfordshire, in 478
    provincial Lodges 639
    Royal Society, at the 212–13, 213n.80
    Whiggish tone 639n.185
Massey, Richard Middleton 304–5
Matching, Essex 460–1
Mather, John
    President of Corpus Christi College 442
    Vice-Chancellor 261–2, 369–70
    Tory politics 361–2
Maupertuis, Pierre-Louis Moreau de 583
Maurice, Henry 66–8
Maurice, Peter 94–5, 95n.73, 458
Mayhew, Jonathan 596n.204
Mead, Richard 223–4
Meadowcourt, Richard
    tutor, as a 280–1
    Whig loyalties 280, 310–11
    steward of the Constitution Club 330–1
    canon of Worcester 281

INDEX   793

Melbourne, *see* Lamb
Melksham, Wilts.
  Clergy Club at 636–7
Mells, Somerset 452
Members of Parliament (MPs), *see* Parliament
Mendip Hills 443
Mendip, Lord, *see* Ellis
Merchant Taylors School 450–2
Meredith, Sir William, 3rd Bt. 376, 377n.88,
    390n.150
Mereworth Castle, Kent 251, 253
Merionethshire 460–1
Merrick, James 498–9
Merton College
  Wardens, *see* Holland
  Visitor 275–6, 285–6, 329, *see* Archbishop of
    Canterbury
  visitatorial commission 1737 285–6
  Whig character 111, 275–6, 275n.122,
    276n.123, 329, 332, 337
  prostitutes in grounds 533
Methodists; *see also* Wesley, John
  Oxford origins 112–13, 503–4
  Holy Club 112n.149, 423–4, 519n.165
  within the University 112–13, 484–5,
    503–6, 660
  in the city of Oxford 504, 504n.93
  divisions among 9, 504–5
  ridicule of 141, 503–4
  growth of nationally 503–4
Mews, Bishop Peter 282–3
Michaelis, Johann David 573–4
  Oxford, in 573–4, 574n.93
  admiration for Lowth 573–4, 672–3
  relations with Kennicott 584–5
  scholarship 573–4
Middlesex, Earl of, *see* Sackville
Middleton, Conyers 550–1
Middleton Stoney, Oxon. 209–10, 626
Middleton Winterslow, Wilts. 441–2
Mill, John
  Principal St Edmund Hall 84–6
  Biblical scholar 84–6, 84n.26, 499
  parson at Bletchingdon 425–6
  patron of younger scholars 570–2
  politics 84n.26
Millar, John 149
Miller. Rev. James
  The Humours of Oxford 486–8
  criticised 486–8
Milles, Jeremiah 278n.133
Milles, Bishop Thomas 162
  Regius Professor of Greek 162, 163n.160
  career summarised 163n.160

Milton, Lord, *see* Fletcher
Milton, John 136–7
Minto, Lord, *see* Elliot
ministers and Oxford 9, 13–14, 46–7, 290–2, 294–5
Mirza 177
Mitchell, Leslie 293–4
Moises, Rev. Hugh 449–50
Molesworth, Sir John, 5th Bt. 390n.150
Molesworth, Robert, 1st Viscount Molesworth [I]
    364–5, 671
Molesworth, Walter 136n.22
Molyneaux, Dr Samuel 470n.278
monasteries 560–2
Monboddo, Lord, *see* Burnett
Money, David 58n.23
Monkhouse, Thomas 147n.78
Monmouth, Duke of, *see* Scott
Monmouthshire 455–6
Monod, Paul Kléber 310n.43
Monro, John 555–6
Montagu, Elizabeth 179, 513–14
Montagu, Lafy Mary Wortley 490–1
Montesquieu 174–5
  Lettres Persanes 177
Montgolfier brothers 232n.172
Montpellier Society 558–9
Montrose, Duke of, *see* Graham
Moore, John, Archbishop of Canterbury,
    previously Bishop of Bangor
  patronised by 4th Duke of Marlborough
    348, 429
  stall at Christ Church 429
  Founders' Kin at All Souls 287n.168
  and slave trade 394n.159
Mordaunt, Sir Charles, 6th Bt. 390n.150
More, Hannah 106–7
  regular visitor to Oxford 527–8,
    528nn.203,204
Morgan, David 398n.179
Morgan, Rev. John 460–1, 461n.230
Morgan, Thomas 638–9
Moritz, Pastor Carl 34n.74
Morley, Derbys. 639–40
Mornington, Earl of, *see* Wellesley
Mortmain Act 1736 292–5, 370–1
  university opposition to 387–8, 389n.146,
    397–8, 413
Moscow University 574–5, 575n.98
Moses 210, 212–13
Moss, Charles
  Bishop of Oxford 289
Mostyn, Sir Roger, 3rd Bt. 276
Moyer [Lady] lectures 204
Mozart, Wolfgang Amadeus 186

794 INDEX

Mulso, John 628–9
Murray, Amelie 539
Murray, David, Viscount [of] Stormont, later 2nd
    Earl of Mansfield 463–4, 562–3
Murray, James 500n.72
Murray, John, 1st duke of Atholl 70n.81
Murray, William, 1st Earl of Mansfield, LCJ
    413–14, 463–4, 465n.253
Museum oxoniense literarium 165–6
Musgrave, Sir Christopher, 4th Bt. 637–8
Musgrave, Samuel 164n.163
mysticism 122

Naked Gospel, The 61–2, 117
Namur, Siege of 361n.7, 590–2
Naples 10, 556
Napleton, John 39–40
    examination reforms, and 167–8
    Locke, critical of 171n.202
Nares, Lady [Georgina] Charlotte, née
    Spencer 429
Nares, Edward 429, 430nn.59,60
Nares, Robert 350–1
    loyalist 1790s 351n.226
    British Critic 350–1
natural religion 239–41, 241n.194
Nassau, Henrietta de, née Butler, Countess of
    Grantham 250
Nassau, Henry de, 1st Earl of Grantham 250
Necker, Jacques 562–3
Necker, Suzanne 562–3
Nelson, Horatio, 1st Viscount Nelson 353–4
Nelson, Robert 101n.103, 476–7
Neophytus, Archbishop of Philippopolis 576,
    577n.112
Nether Winchendon 436, 437n.95
Neve, Timothy
    Lady Margaret Professor 105–6
    Bampton Lecturer 105–6, 120, 120n.192
Neveu, Bruno 587
Neville, Sylas 490n.26, 495n.50
Newcastle, Duke of, *see* Pelham-Holles
Newcastle-on-Tyne
    Royal Grammar School 449–50
Newchurch, Isle of Wight 465
New College
    Wardens, *see* Braithwaite, Purnell, Hayward
    contest for Wardenship (1703) 282–3
    building work at 31–2
    choral foundation 79n.2, 182–4, 186,
        186n.271
    declamations at 379
    fellowships at 446–7
    Founders' Kin at 446–7

gardens 563–4
land management 442–3
New College School 447n.150
links to Bedford School 446–7
links to Winchester College 446–7, 623–4
Whigs in 330–1
alumni gatherings 623–4
livings 626
Newcome, Archbishop William
    Vice-Principal Hertford College 87–8, 379
    Biblical scholar 87–8
    death 409
Newdigate, Sir Roger, 5th Bt. 8, 126–7, 278–9,
    437–8, 546, 618–19, 622
    disdain for party labels 389–90
    MP for the University 389–91, 391n.153, 395,
        406–7, 413–14
    opposes relief for Dissenters 257n.44, 264–5,
        376, 389–90
    proud of his University College
        connection 390n.152
    friend of Nathan Wetherell 264–5, 390n.152
    relations with Lord North 391n.153
    thanked by the University for his
        parliamentary services 389–90
    influential in Warwickshire 610–11
    criticised 610–11
    insists on discharge of clerical duties 611n.59
    architectural and aesthetic interests 32,
        33n.72, 389–90
    Pomfret marbles, and 650–1, 651n.225
    sculptural bequest to the University 651–2
Newdigate Prize 390n.148
New Inn Hall 410–11, 412n.250
    Principals of, *see* Blackstone, Sir William
Newman, Aubrey 326n.114
Newman, Henry 565–6
Newman, John Henry 16–17, 17n.16, 18n.18,
    92–4
Newmarket 470–1
Newsham, James 278
newspapers, *see* journalism
Newte, Thomas 38
Newton, Benjamin 509
Newton, Sir Isaac 597
    personal authority 217–19, 239–41
    public offices held 198–9
    President of the Royal Society 212–13
    standing in Cambridge University 70–1,
        71n.86, 194–5, 199
    Anglicanism, and 14–15, 204n.31
    latitudinarianism, and 205n.39
    religious heterodoxy 199, 203–5, 203n.30
    physics 204–5

Principia 70–1, 203n.30
'ancient wisdom', and 204–5
interest in prophecy 204
Observations on the Prophecies of Daniel, and the Apocalypse of St John 204
death and burial 198–9, 199n.5
critiques of 204
cultural icon 199
European fame 198–9
Whig appropriation 213–14
Newtonianism 1, 4–5, 204n.32
Cambridge University, in 14–15, 70–1, 204–6
Oxford University, in 6n.10, 72, 200–6, 209–10, 213–14, 217, 239–42, 589–90, 663–4
cultural hegemony 241–2
'holy alliance' of physics and religion 204–5
Newton, Richard
University reformer 274, 274n.117, 373n.77
collegiate ambitions for Hart Hall 274
relations with undergraduates 621
political affilations 274
Henry Pelham his pupil 274, 274n.118
Philip Doddridge, admirer of 498–9
Christ Church canonry 621n.105, 655
'Newtonian Revolution' 53, 214n.83; see also *science*
its physics and their uses 76, 203n.28, 206–7
popularised 206–7, 209
fashionable 202–3
anxieties generated by 201–2, 203n.28, 204–5, 209, 210n.65, 213–14, 239; see also Hutchinsonians
Royal Society, and the 205–6
Scotland, in 72
Newtown (Isle of Wight) 543
New York
King's College 594–5, 596n.205
Niblett, née Whitfield, Elizabeth 531
Niblett, Stephen
and the Mortmain Act 1736 387–8
cultivates Frederick, Prince of Wales 325
Nicephorus 158n.136
Nicholl, John 446
Nicholls, Frank 223–4, 224n.130
Nicholls, William 587, 588n.163
Defensio ecclesiae Anglicanae 587
Nicholson, Margaret 341–2
Nicolini 138n.40
Nicolson, William
Anglo-Saxon scholarship 153–4, 662
Nile, Battle of the 353
Nine Years' War, see Augsburg League, War of
Nikitin, Vasily Nikitich 575–6, 576n.102

Nivernais, Duc de 567–8
Nonjurors 17–18, 58–60, 59n.29, 80–1, 124–5, 158n.136, 299–300, 315, 344–5, 434–5, 461–2, 666
Cambridge, at 66–8, 67n.65
Oxford, at 67n.65, 70–1, 75–6, 152–3, 304–5, 361–2
Scotland, in 68–9, 461–3
attitudes towards Roman Catholics 155–6, 157n.133
non-resistance and passive obedience 7–8, 36, 57–8, 59n.30, 125, 126n. 215, 299–300, 305, 344–5
relations with Orthoxdox Church 576
Normandy 558–9
Normanton, Earl of, see Agar
Norris, Thomas 189–91
North, née Speke, Anne, Lady North, later 2nd Countess of Guilford 530
North, Francis, 1st Baron Guilford 435
Francis, 2nd Lord Guilford 435
North, Francis, 3rd Lord and 1st Earl of Guilford 254, 375, 435–6, 436n.89, 438
North, Frederick, Lord North (2nd earl of Guilford after 1790) 98, 389–90; see also Trinity College
student in Germany 556–7
Chancellor of Oxford University 1772–90 254–5, 264–5, 406–7, 530, 582–3, 653 4, 665, 669
installation 255, 513–14, 542, 548n.289, 549–50
First Minister 1770–82 254, 267, 348–9, 375–7, 407n.223
Coalition 1783 and after 257, 348–50, 376–7, 665
character 254–5
Anglicanism, his 255, 257n.44
defence of the Church and the University assessed 256–7, 256n.42, 257, 257n.43, 264–5, 294–5, 358–9, 375–7, 661
North, William, 6th Lord North & Grey 435
Northampton Infirmary 638
Northington, Earl of, see Henley
North Somerset Canal 443
Norton, Sir Fletcher 126–7
Norwich, bishops of, see Bagot, Horne; dean of, see Prideaux
Nottingham, earl of, see Finch
Nova Scotia 597
bishop of, see Inglis
Nowell, Thomas
Professor of Moder History 150
Principal of St Mary Hall 348–9

796 INDEX

Nowell, Thomas (*cont.*)
  Public Orator 126–7
  sermon on Charles I censured 126–7,
    127n.217, 127n.219, 344–5
  Welsh connections 126n.216
  client of 5th Duke of Beaufort 607–8
  receives no royal patronage 344n.196
  supports 1783 Coalition 348–9, 441n.117
Nugent, Lady 538
Nuneham Courtenay 341–2, 430–1, 567–8
  estate purchased by Harcourt family 430–1
  Carfax Conduit moved to 430–1
Nutt, Richard 109

oaths and oath taking 302–4, 302n.15, 305,
  315; *see also* Oxford, University of;
  Abjuration, Act of
  Oath of Allegiance 303
  Oath of Suremacy 303
Observatory, *see* Radcliffe Observatory
Occasional Conformity 109, 305, 307–8, 358–9,
  364, 382–3, 396–7, 660
Ockley, Simon 174–5, 176n.232
Ocksen, Johannes 565–6
[O']Connor, Bernard 216–17, 217n.99
O'Flaherty, Niall 659
O'Flaherty, Roderick 460n.222
O'Gorman, Chevalier Tómas 472
Ogilvy, James, 7th Earl of Findlater, styled Lord
  Deskford 424–5
Old Corps Whigs, *see* Pelhamites
Oldfield, Anne 486–8
'Old Interest', *see* Oxfordshire
Oldmixon, John 146–7, 147n.79
Old Norse, *see* Oxford, University of,
  Anglo-Saxon studies at
Old Schools quadrangle, *see* Bodleian Library
Onslow, Arthur 277n.131, 357n.244,
  370, 414
Onslow, George, 4th Lord Onslow 293–4
Orange, House of 53, 53n.1, 248–50; *see also*
  William III, William IV
Oriel College
  Provosts of, *see* Royse, Carter, Hodges,
    Eveleigh
  establishing identity of Visitor 284–5
  library and fundraising for 647–9
  Whig influences evident in 329, 333
  Beaufort endowment 455–6, 604–5
  Glamorgan matriculands at 457n.203
  Gloucester cathedral, and 442
Orléans, Philippe, Duc'd (the Regent) 587–8
Ormond, Duke of, *see* Butler
Orrery, Earls of, *see* Boyle

Orthodox Church 124–5; *see also* Greek College
  students at Oxford 576–8, 673
  valued by high churchmen 576
  Nonjuring bishops, and 576n.107
orthodoxy
  legally vindicated in Bury affair 282
  appeal of 129
  predominant ideal of 110
  case made for 115–16, 127–9
  threat to in 1770s and 1780s 586–7
Ossian 179
Ossory, Bishop of, *see* Vesey
Otmoor, Oxon. 426–7
Ottoman Empire 173–4, 576
Otway, Thomas 165n.172
Oundle School 452
Over Whiteacre, Warks. 609–10
Ovid 164
Owen, Humphrey 457
Oxford, Archdeacons of, *see* Hody, Baker,
  Randolph (Thomas), Turner (George)
Oxford, Bishops of 7, 287–94, 395–6, 665–6
  see Fell, Parker, Hough, Secker, Hume (John),
    Lowth, Butler (John), Smallwell,
    Randolph (John), Jackson (William),
    Moss; *see also* Oxford, diocese of
  value of the see 287–8
  relations with the University 287–94, 297
Oxford, city of 8–9
  Alfred Masonic Lodge 576n.102
  Assize of Bread 419–20, 476–7
  Barbers, Company of 420n.12
  built environment improvements 33–5
  catch clubs 187n.277
  cathedral, *see* Christ Church
  charity schools 476–7
  Christ Church meadows 232n.172
  churches of
    All Saints 28–31, 291–2
    St Clements 110n.143, 433n.76, 516–17
    St Martin's, Carfax 127–9
    St Mary's 62, 91–4, 419–20, 423
    St Mary Magdalen 112–13, 504–5
    St Michael's 291–2
    St Peter's-in-the-East 92n.65, 430n.59
  citizens 25–6, 127–9
  city council 33–5, 127–9, 354; *see also*
    Corporation
  City Lecturers 127–9
  City Loyal Volunteer Corps 353n.231, 354
  coffee houses 25–7, 26n.40, 61, 97, 98n.89, 533–4
  Corporation
    constitution 418n.2
    councillors 423–4

council chamber 341–2, 569–70
financial problems 418–19, 423n.22
relations with the University 418–25, 669
court leet 420n.11
guides to 493–6
   *A companion to the Guide, and A guide to
      the Companion* 494–5
   The New Oxford Guide 494
   A Pocket Companion for Oxford 493–4
high stewards of, *see* Dashwood, Sir James,
   Earls of Abingdon, Rowney
locations/streets within
   Bocardo 423–4
   Broad Street 435–6
   canal 8–9
   Carfax 32n.65, 354, 421
   Castle, *see* Prison
   debtors' prison, *see* Bocardo
   East Gate 421
   Folly Bridge 33–5
   Friar Bacon's Study 33–5
   Golden Cross Inn 567
   Hall's tavern 191
   Headington (Quarry) 233–4, 236–8
   High Street 28–31, 235n.183, 421, 494
   Holywell cockpit 478
   Holywell Music Room 13, 25–6, 182–5,
      191–2, 353n.233, 539
   Hythe Bridge 266n.80
   King's Head tavern 191, 423n.26
   market 264n.76, 421
   Magdalen Bridge 421
   Martyrs' memorial 18n.18
   New College Lane 224n.133
   North Gate 421
   Port Meadow 353–4, 478
   Prison 229–31, 423–4, 476–7
   Radcliffe Square 32
   St Clement's 533–4
   St Ebbe's Lane 424–5
   St Giles 229, 423
   Shotover Hill 233–4, 354
   Three Tuns 534–5, 623n.115
   town hall 25
   Woodstock Road 226–7
Market Committee 421
Members of Parliament, *see* Rowney; Lee, Hon.
   Robert; Stapleton; Wenman, Viscount;
   Bertie, Peregrine; Spencer, Lord Robert
Mileways Act 1771 33–5
military occupation 308, 325, 363–4,
   364nn.18,19
musical centre 182–92
Paving Commission 421

physicians in 222–3
population numbers 27–8, 28n.50
race meetings 478–9, 537, 671–2
rebuilding 32, 421
riots (1702, 1799–1800) 354, 420–1
sexual violence in 533–4
taverns 25–6, 25n.33
theatre, absence of 25
visual depiction of 33–5
women residents 524–5, 525n.192
Oxford, University of; *for specific bodies, buildings
   and institutions existing within the
   University, see independent listings* (eg
   Bodleian Library)
academic dress 423–4
Act Sunday 91–2
Acts 57–8, 134–5, 182–4, 186n.272, 379, 483;
   see also *Terrae Filius*
   1688 57–8
   1703 186–7, 544–6
   1713 187–8, 307–8, 308n.35, 543–6
   1733 188, 294–5, 370, 546, 548n.293
   music at 186–8, 543–4
   Cambridge presence at 507
adapatbility 11–12, 38, 43–4, 72–7, 553–4, 676
anatomical studies at 223–4, 224n.132,
   229–31; *see also* Christ Church
ancient history at 151–2, 193–4; *see also*
   Camden Professor
Anglo-Saxon studies at 153–5, 193–4, 525–7
apologetics, published 100, 119–20
Arabic studies, *see* Oriental studies
architectural rebuilding 27–35, 34n.74, 48–9
artists and Oxford settings 491–2
astronomy at 200, 221–2, 226–31
attitudes towards graduates from other
   universities 506–15
benefices in gift of 425n.36
bequests and benefactions to 10–11, 601–2,
   642–54, 656–7, 674
Biblical scholarship at, *see* Bible
book burning in 40–1, 61n.42, 318
botany at 217, 233–4
Britishness, nurturing of 463–4, 479–80
Chancellors 7, 37–8,
   installation 542
   powers and influence 248, 258, 260, 294–5,
      395–6, 665
   wives of 529–30
   as benefactors 653–4
   see Ormond, Duke of, Arran, Earl of,
      Westmorland, Earl of, Lichfield, Earl of,
      North, Lord, Portland, Duke of, North,
      Grenville, Lord

798 INDEX

Oxford, University of (*cont.*)
Chancellor's Court 261n.65, 331–2, 420–1
Chancellor's Prize for Latin verse 132n.5,
547–8
Chancellor's Secretary, *see* King, Dr William
charitable giving 476–7
chemistry at 217–19, 229–33, 229n.157,
231n.168, 242–3
choral tradition maintained 186; *see also*
Christ Church. Magdalen College, New
College
civil law at 410–11, 411n.246
civil society, and 38, 247, 398–9
classical literature and controversies at
159–66, 195–6
clerical character of 358, 362–5
clubs in 623n.115
Constitution Club 330–1, 363, 623n.115
Jelly-Bag Society 136–7, 623n.115; *see also*
Clubs
colleges and halls, *see* colleges (of Oxford
University)
college bursars 442–3
college chapels 91–2, 91n.61
college Visitors 7, 281–7, 296–7, 658
common law at 410–11
compared with Cambridge 494, 496, 506
concerts 186–91
constitution, place in the British 36–42, 76–7,
79–80, 377–8, 416, 675–6
corporate inertia 11–12
cosmopolitanism 21, 45–6, 589–90
court leet 419–20
critics of 1n.1, 42, 514–24, 554, 670–1; *see also*
Gibbon, Knox, Smith (Adam)
cultural and social spaces in 45–6, 48–9,
61, 97
curriculum 11–12, 16–17, 19–20, 39–40, 131,
149, 672–3
decentralised 20
depicted in literature and the fine arts 9,
485–92
disloyalty, alleged 65–6, 308, 328, 483–4;
see also rioting
dissenters, attitudes towards, *see* Dissenters,
Protestants
diversity within membership 76–7, 676
divine right, notions of at 125
doctoral degrees for colonial clergy 594–5,
596n.204
elite formation and cohesion, and 43, 53,
151–2, 152n.111, 195–6, 247, 351–2,
615–17, 669, 675–6
empire and 5–6, 10, 181–2, 196, 554, 590–8

Encaenias 9, 134–5, 483, 543, 546
1756 651
1763 341, 547–8
1773 183n.263, 343–4, 344n.193
1789 189–91
rhetorical performance at 379, 546–8,
548n.292
music at 186–91, 524n.187, 546
English literary and language studies 5–6,
131–41, 194
and the Enlightenment 2–4, 11–12, 38, 44–9,
55–6, 72–7, 131, 239–41, 461–2, 553–4,
562–3, 589–90, 597–8, 634–5, 676
Esquire Bedel, *see* Clarke
European scholars and universities,
relationship to and interaction with 10,
46, 48–9, 114–15, 553–63, 585n.144, 597–8
European visitors to 16, 563–4, 673
examinations 39–40, 167–8
foreign languages teaching 369–70
foreign matriculands 570, 574–5
foreign visitors to 33–5, 34n.74, 53, 189–92
fund raising in war and peace 352, 352n.228,
353–4, 601–2
Gallican clergy welcomed 115, 585–6
geology at 236–8
general elections and 358–9, 390–1
government and 8, 13–14, 18–19, 42–3, 48–9,
142, 241–2, 259–60, 358–9, 398–409, 665,
668–9
graduate connections and careers 10–11, 21,
43, 193, 259–60, 359–60, 590–2, 609–10,
613–14, 654–6, 674
graduates, conjugal bonds between 539–40,
600–1, 615–17, 654–5
graduate friendships 617–19, 655–6
graduate identity 127–9
graduate interactions in Continental
Europe 553–4, 597–8
graduate returnees to Oxford 622–3, 625, 655–6
graduates with legal careers 410–14
Greek studies 162–6
Hebrew studies 173–4
hebdomadal board 258–9, 261n.65, 650
heterodoxy, attacks on 116–18; *see also*
Dissenters; Socinians
High Churchmen in 68, 80–1, 110, 121,
124–5, 201–2, 316–17, 462–3, 660–2;
see also orthodoxy
High Steward 7, 58–60, 253n.28, 398, *see also*
Hyde, Henry, Clarendon, 2nd Earl of,
Hyde, Henry, Rochester, 2nd Earl of,
Westmorland, Earl of, Lichfield, Earl of,
Dartmouth, Earl of

history of 16
historians associated with, *see* history
History of the University 1–2
homosexuality at 26n.45, 332–3
honorary degrees 549, 549n.299, 630
incorporation at 465, 468–9, 510–11, 670–1
independent political tradition valued 339
industrialisation, and 225, 242–3
instruments, scientific, in 224–32
intellectual challenges 64–5, 73–4
intellectual importance 48–9, 53, 127–9
intellectual life 53–6, 79–80, 129–30, 196–7, 205–6, 483–4, 668–9
intelligence gathering and national security, involvement in 398–9, 402–3, 407–8; *see also* cryptography
international prominence and reputation 16, 39–40, 53, 196–7, 672–3
Islam, studies in at 176–7, 196; *see also* Qu'ran
land ownership 8–9, 441–3
Latin, instruction in 131, 138
lectures 119–20, 238–9; *see also* Bampton Lectures
female attendance at 613–14
legacies to, *see* bequests
legal culture at 410–11
litigious character 281–2
livings in gift of colleges 622–3
logic, teaching of 167–8
mathematics at 219–22
matriculation
foreigners doing so 570
subscription on 256, 256n.42
parliamentary motion to amend 376, 390n.150
medicine at 222
medieval studies at 152–9, 193–4, 662; *see also* Anglo-Saxon studies
Members of Parliament (MPs) for the University 359–60, 380–1, 394n.164, 415–16, *see* Finch (Heneage), Trumbull, Glynne, Whitelocke, Bromley, Clarke (George), Hyde, Henry, Lord Cornbury, Bromley (the younger), Butler (Edward), Palmer, Newdigate, Dolben (Sir William), Page, Scott (Sir) William, Abbot
Methodism in, *see* Methodists
ministers and 8, 13–14, 19–20, 42–3, Chapter 8 *passim*, 658–9
modern history writing and 144–51, 193–4; *see also* Professors of Modern History
modern languages teaching 142–4, 144n.62, 194

monarchy and 17–20, 37–8, 43–4, Chapter 7 *passim*, 658–9, 666–7
motto 74–5
music studies and scene 5–6, 182–92, 196–7, 663
degrees in 182–4, 186n.272, 187–8
national connections, outreach, and impact 48–9, 127–31, 138, 141, 161–2, 193–4, 196–7, 241–2, 300–2, 455–76, 479–80, 661–2, 669
natural history at 217; *see also* botany
Nonjurors at, *see* Nonjurors
nostalgia for 619
numbers at 450–1, 483–4
oath-taking in 7–8, 18–19, 58n.28, 66–8, 105n.123, 302–5, 674; *see also* matriculation
Old English studies, *see* Anglo-Saxon studies at
ordinands 96–7, 127–9, 173–4, 660–1; *see also* clergy, parish
arts of preaching, and 96–7, 96n.82
lectures offered to 102–3, 105–6, 129
Oriental studies at 131, 173–82, 196
origins 37–8
outsiders 9, 193, 241–2; Chapter 10 *passim*, 670–2
Oxford University Volunteers 352
Parliamentary Elections at 381–2, 390n.148; *see also* Members of Parliament
1751 397, 413–14
1780 182n.259
patriotism 39
patronage and clientage 10–11, 48–9, 247, 276–81, 295–6, 359–60, 600, 602–3, 609–10, 612–13, 621–2, 673–4
periodical literature, depiction in 490–1
Persian, studies in at 174n.219, 177–80, 182
philosophy and metaphysics at 166–73, 195–6; *see also* Aristotelianism
plebians at, *see* servitors, numbers
poetic performances at 134–5, 134n.16
poetic representations of 490
poetry collections published 510–11
political economy at 151n.101
preaching at, *see* sermons
prestige 53, 75–6
'privileged persons' [tradesmen] 420–1
privileges 58n.28
Proctors 267–9, 341–2, 369–70, 389–90, 419–20
Professors, *see* Professorial chairs
prostitution problem 533
Public Orator 92–4, 119–20, 126–7, 324, 547, 569–70, *see* Cotes, King (Dr William), Nowell, Crowe (William)

800 INDEX

Oxford, University of (*cont.*)
  Radcliffe Travelling Fellows 164n.163,
    436n.89, 555–6, 555n.5
  Radcliffe Trustees 226–7, 229–31
  readership, Tomlins 223–4
  reforms, post-1800 19–20, 20n.22, 76–7, 672–3
  regions, and the 8–9, 417, 669
  Registrar 419–20, *see* Fisher
  religion and the constitution, relationship to
    and defence of 12, 15–16, 19–20, 39–44,
    46–9, 55–6, 68, 72–4, 76–7, 77n.114,
    Chapter 3 passim, 350–2, 355, 357,
    375–7, 496–7, 508, 554, 660–1, 666,
    672–3; *see also* apologetics, sermons
  religious observance and worship 4–5, 79n.2
  remodelling of proposed 38, 364–7; *see also*
    Royal Visitations
  Republic of Letters and 61, 554, 557–8,
    578–85, 673
  reputation of 1–2, 10, 14–15, 14n.2, 42
  research at 39–40, 54–5
  Revolution, and, *see* French Revolution
  rhetorical training of students 379
  rioting in George I's reign 308, 362–4
  rioting in George II's reign 371–2
  Roman Catholics in 17–18, 36, 250, 673
  Royal Visitations of 8, 18–19, 358–9, 370n.58,
    372–3, 397–8, 508, 667–8; *see also*
    Universities Bill(s) 1717, 1719
  royal visits to, *see* Anne, Queen; George III
  scholastic thought, and 55–6, 72–3
  schools, reations with 417–18, 443–51, 669;
    see also school masters
  science in 6–7, 16–17, 46, Chapter 5 *passim*,
    663–5
    chemistry 6–7
    and the state 12
  Scots in 60–1, 461–8, 669–70, *see also*
    Scotland
  scouts, *see* servants, college
  Select Preacher(s) 92n.65
  Sheldonian Theatre 57–8, 66–8, 135–6, 184–5,
    186n.273, 188–9, 192, 306–7, 316–17,
    341–2, 494, 533, 546
  sermons, University
    arrangements for 91–4, 642–3; *see also*
      Oxford, St Mary's church
    quality and style of 92–4, 96–7
    controversial content 94–6, 496
    charity 98
    publication 98–100
    publicity for 98
    reception 96–7
    disseminated 97

servants, college 423–4, 483–4, 484n.1,
  515–16, 524–5, 533–5
servitors 484, 484n.1
social stability, and 131
statutes, Laudian (1636) 3–4, 53–4, 92–4,
  172–3, 196–7, 222–3
student numbers 14–16
student societies 267–9, 268n.89
students and Crown service 35–6, 272–4;
  see also government
students' educational formation 35–6
students' love lives 532–4
students' national origins 21
students' social life 21–5
Terrae Filius 188–9, 307–8, 308n.35,
  344n.193, 507, 543–6, 670–1
theatrical performances 25, 544–6
  depictions of the University on stage 485–90
theologians
  leading figures among 106–8, 110
  neglected by historians 100
  qualities of 100
torpor, alleged 14–16, 15n.8, 16–17, 45–6
tourists and visitors to 493–6
town-gown relations 423–5, 476–7
tradition, and 38, 46–7, 72–3, 127, 196–7, 247
'treasonable' politics 260–1; *see also* George I
Toryism in 4–5, 7–8, 12, 39–41, 48–9, 73–4,
  124–5, 155–6, 248, 256n.40, 274, 291–2,
  300–2, 306–28, 355, 378–9, 379n.100,
  413–14, 416, 602–3, 609–10, 654–5, 666–8
tradesmen, matriculated 420–1
Turkish, teaching of, *see* Oriental studies
tutors and tutorials 21–4, 46–7, 53–4,
  128n.223, 159, 170–1, 276–81, 296,
  449–50, 547–8, 621, 630–2, 655, 670–1;
  see also Grand Tour
Vice-Chancellor, office, duties, and powers 7,
  91–4, 260, 264–5, 269–70, 665, *see*
  Edwards, Aldrich, Adams, Fitzherbert,
  Lancaster, Delaune, Braithwaite, Gardiner,
  Baron, Shippen, Mather, Butler (Edward),
  Holmes (William), Niblett, Isham (Euseby,
  Purnell, Huddesford (George), Randolph
  (Thomas), Browne (Joseph), Durell,
  Wetherell, Fothergill (Thomas), Horne,
  Dennis, Chapman, Cooke, Wills
war and 39, 39n.96
Whigs in and attitudes towards the
  University 4–5, 7–8, 18–19, 36, 40–2,
  57–8, 65–6, 73–4, 125, 155, 253, 258–60,
  269–70, 275–6, 300–3, 310–11, 326–37,
  339, 348, 356–7, 362–3, 380–1, 390–1,
  416, 498–9, 655, 667–8

wit and waggery in 136–7, 140–1, 161–2, 490–1
wives of vice-chancellors and heads of
	Houses 531
women and 9, 25–6, 483, 524–42, 551, 671–2
Oxford University Press; *see also* Bible
	Delegates 33–5, 34n.78, 53–4; *see also* Aldrich,
		Charlett
	Clarendon Press 331n.138
	reform of 54–5, 90; *see also* Blackstone
	Authorized Version of the Bible, copyright
		in 81–2, 89
	leased 81–2
	publications, range of 53–4, 90, 90n.56, 194
	Anglo-Saxon publications 154–5
	Arabic editions 174–5
	editions of classical texts 163
	foreign languages, and 143–4
	sermons published 98–100
Oxford Act, The 544n.277
Oxford Almanack 491–2
Oxford canal 264–5, 264n.75, 266n.80
Oxford, diocese of
	livings in with academic patrons 602n.13
	magnate dominance of patronage 627n.131
Oxford, Earls of, *see* Harley
Oxford Loyal Volunteers 353–4
Oxford Magazine, or the Oxford Museum,
	The 511n.123
Oxford Mileways Acts (1771, 1781) 421
'Oxford Movement' 17–18, 100, 503–4
Oxford Parliament (1681) 299
Oxford Philosophical Society 215–17, 216n.94
'Oxford' Symphony no. 92, *see* Haydn
Oxfordshire 8–9, 425–41
	Lord-Lieutenants of, *see* Marlborough, 4th
		Duke of; 1st and 2nd Earls of Abingdon;
		Wharton, Marquess and Earl of; 2nd Earl
		of Godolphin
	Members of Parliament for, *see* Rialton,
		Viscount; Lee, George, Viscount
		Quarendon; Dashwood, Sir James; Turner,
		Sir Edward; Parker, Viscount; Wenman,
		4th Viscount; Spencer, Lord Charles
	nobility and gentry resident in 427–41, 477–8,
		see also High Borlace
	degrees awarded to 477–8
	clergy in 291–2, 425–6, 478, 626, 675
	Jacobitism in 310n.47, 312n.52, 477–8
	turnpike roads in 493n.38
	dinners for those living in London 623n.114
	Oxfordshire Club 624n.118
	political divisions in 427–41
	'New Interest' 263–5, 276, 336, 406–7, 430–1,
		437–41, 515–16, 538

'Old Interest' 253, 263–4, 301–2, 313, 355–6,
	375, 389–90, 437–41, 537; *see also*
	Jacobitism
1754 Election 263–4, 291–2, 373–4, 406–7,
	413–14, 437–40, 509, 668
Elections after 1754 440–1
University of Oxford involvement in
	above 263–4, 336, 437–41, 669;
	see also Exeter College; Huddesford,
	George

Padua 223–4
	University of 558–9
Page, Francis 257, 264–5, 380–1, 390–1,
	391n.153, 392n.156, 394–5
Paget, Thomas 452
Paine, Thomas
	The Rights of Man 232
Paley, William 172–3, 194–5
Palmer, Barbara, Duchess of Cleveland 434–5
Palmer, Peregrine 380–1
panegyric, survival of the 547–8
Papacy 115
Pardo, Thomas 451, 458n.214
Pares, Richard 406–7
Parfect, John 622
Paris, Treaty of (1763) 547–8, 567–8, 590–2
Parker, Benjamin 551
Parker, George, 2nd Earl of Macclesfield
	astronomical interests 212–13, 432–3
	President of the Royal Society 213, 432–3
	and Oxford University, and 212–13, 432–3
	proponent of 'New Style' calendar 214n.82
	1754 Oxfordshire election, and 438
Parker, John, 2nd Lord Boringdon 618–19
Parker, Samuel
	Bishop of Oxford 289
Parker, Samuel (Fellow of Merton
	College) 599n.3
Parker, Thomas, 1st Earl of Macclesfield
	176n.229, 221n.114, 291–2, 477–8
	prosecution of Sacheverell 366–7, 432–3
	and reform of the universities 366–7, 366n.32,
		367n.40, 432
	Cambridge connections 366n.31
	questionable religious orthodoxy 432–3
	radical intellectual associations 432–3
	astronomical interests 433n.76
	disgraced 432–4
Parker, Thomas, 3rd Earl of Macclesfield (styled
	Viscount Parker before succession to the
	earldom) 213n.81
	candidate in Oxfordshire Election 1754
		291–2, 438

802 INDEX

Parliament; *see also* Oxford, University of, Members of Parliament
  MPs educated at Oxford and Cambridge 43, 379, 463–4
  and Oxford University 8, 19–20, 58n.28, 415–16
  peers and the defence of University interests 395–8
Paris 10, 235n.183
  Luxembourg Palace 28–31
  Ste-Geneviève, church of 589
  Sorbonne 560–2, 574–5, 581–2, 586–7
  libraries in 164n.163, 560–2
Paris, Peace of (1763) 313, 542, 547–8
  Oxford address on 340–1
Parr, Samuel
  friends at Oxford 510–11
  impressed by Cyril Jackson 272
  impressed by William Scott 151–2
  publicly defends the English universities 525n.191
Parris, F.S. 84n.21
Parry, David 457
Parsis 174–5
Parsons, Isaac 287
Parsons, James 88n.43
Parsons, John
  first Lichfield Clinical Professor 229–31, 655n.237
  Lee Reader in anatomy 651–2
  anatomical lectures 229–31
  assists Joseoh White with Bampton Lectures 502
Pascal, Blaise 588–9
patristics 123–4, 452, 661–2
  decline of studies 123–4, 124n.206
  revived interest in 120, 123–4
  shared passion with Gallican scholars 587
Payne, Thomas 606n.33
Payne, William 59n.33
Pearce, Zachary 433n.77
Pearson, John 597
Peckard, Peter 117–18
Peerage Bill (1719) 364
Pegge, Sir Christopher 242–3, 242n.199
Peisley, Benjamin 254n.33
Pelham, Henry
  Oxford connections 274, 274n.118, 655
  attitude towards Oxford University 294–5, 371–2
  contemplates legal action against Oxford University 263–4
Pelham-Holles, Harriet, née Godolphin, (1st) Duchess of Newcastle 603

Pelham-Holles, Thomas, 1st Duke of Newcastle 101n.101, 150–1, 250–1, 313n.56, 328, 339, 367, 378–9, 398–9
  Chancellor of Cambridge University 274n.118, 294–5, 334, 371, 508
  attitude towards Oxford University 371–4
  as Church 'manager' 371
  loses office 1762 340–1
Pelhamites 324–6, 334, 371–2, 415
  followers in Oxford 336
Pelling, John 515–16
Pembroke College
  Masters of, *see* Hall (John), Adams (William)
  Channel Islands connections 447–8
  Gloucester connections 445, 635–6
  Welsh connection 455–6
  Bishop Morley scholarships 447–8
  Tesdale scholarships 643
Pembroke, Earl of, *see* Herbert
Pembrokeshire 455–6
penance, sacrament of 129–30
Pennant, Thomas 631–2
Pepper, General John 363–4
Perceval, John, 1st Earl of Egmont 312n.52
Perceval, John, 2nd Earl of Egmont 380–1, 413n.257
Perceval, Archdeacon William 472–5
Percy, Thomas 179
Perronet, Vincent 504
Pestel Amberg, NJ 596
Peter the Great, Tsar 567, 568n.70
Peterborough 639–40
  Bishops of, *see* Kennett, Clavering, Terrick
Phalaris Controversy 5–6, 131, 161–96, 162n.154, 195–6; *see also* Ancients and Moderns
Petty-Fitzmaurice, William, 2nd Earl of Shelburne, previously styled Viscount Fitzmaurice 411–14, 445–6, 465, 524
Petworth, Sussex 272n.110
Phelps, Richard 617
Philips, John 136
Phillipa of Hainault 135–6
Phillips, Sir John, 6th Bt. 455–6
philosophes 562–4; *see also* Enlightenment
Phipps, Sir Constantine
  receives honorary degree 1714 321–2, 321n.91
Phipps, James 643
Physic (later Botanic) Garden 233–4, 233n.181, 234n.182, 424–5
Pictet, Bénédict 573n.88
Piedmont 592n.182
Piers, Henry 504
Pigott, Edward 227

INDEX 803

Pinckney, Charles Cotesworth 596–8
Pinckney, Eliza Lucas 597
Pinckney, Thomas 596–8
Pincus, Steve 53n.1, 68
Pindar 163, 547–8, 549n.297, 560–2
Piranesi 651–2
Pitcairne, Archibald 72, 72n.94
  The Phanaticks 485–6
Pitt, Christopher
  cleric and classicist 630
Pitt the Elder, William, 1st Earl of Chatham
    389–90, 606
  alleges disaffection in Oxford 301n.12, 517–18
  disconnected from the University 375
  in government 607
  political dominance during the Seven Years'
    War 326–8, 338–9
  Oxford allegiance to his wartime
    'Patriotism' 340–1, 374
Pitt the Younger, William 7, 125–6, 232, 257–8,
    395, 406–9
  MP for Cambridge University 377
  and Oxford University 294–5, 376–7, 668–9
  defence of the Anglican establishment 377
  patronage disposal 267, 267n.85, 377
  resignation 1801 259–60, 402–3
Pius VI 115
Plato 164–5
  at Oxford 165n.175, 573–4
Plautus 454–5
players, strolling, 25–6, 25n.38; *see also* actors
Plomer, John 479n.321
Plot, Robert 216n.94, 458–9
  Professor of Chemistry 216–17
  Keeper of the Ashmolean Museum 216–17
  career summarised 216n.96
  edits *Philosophical Transactions of the Royal
    Society* 216–17
  his county histories 632–3, 632n.160
  as information gatherer 640–1
  alleged credulity 632–3
  Lhuyd critical of 459n.219
Plutarch 583
Plymouth Grammar School 454–5
Pocock, J.G.A. 11–12, 57n.19, 61n.42, 162n.151,
    193–4
  and the Enlightenment(s) 44n.119, 48–9,
    48n.143, 61–2, 124n.206
  on Gibbon 159
Pococke, Edward 173–5, 182, 517
Pococke, Richard 454–5, 559–60
Poczobutt, Fr Marcin Odlanicki 575–6
Polignac, Cardinal Melchior de, Archbishop of
    Auch 558–9, 559n.28

Poland
  students in Oxford 575–6
  republican past 576n.104
politeness 424–5
Polwhele, Richard 617, 632n.156
Polybius 165n.170, 325n.113
Pomeroy, Arthur 470–1
Pomfret, Countess of, *see* Fermor
Pomfret marbles 341–2, 550–1, 650–1, 652n.227,
    656–7
Pope, Alexander 135–6, 135n.21, 136, 140, 149,
    386–7, 486, 630, 640–1
  view of Oxford 197n.322
  declines honorary degree 483–4
  Lady Arran, and 251n.15
'Popery', *see* Roman Catholics
Porson, Richard 162
Porter, Roy 53n.2, 76n.112
Porteus, Beilby
  Bishop of Chester 639n.183
Portland, 3rd duke of, *see* Bentinck
Portland Whigs 258–60, 407; *see also* Bentinck,
    Fox, Windham
Portlock, Benjamin 549
Porto Bello 423n.26
Post Boy 207n.45
Potter, née Venner, Elizabeth 530
Potter, Francis 95–6, 334
Potter, Thomas, Bishop later Archbishop 62–3,
    104–6, 332, 590n.175
  background 100–2, 289n.174
  marriage 530
  chaplain to Archbishop Tenison 100–2
  client of William Wake 289n.174
  scholarly interests 102, 162–3
  Regius Professor of Divinity 94–5, 100–2,
    101n.102, 102n.105, 289, 289n.177, 329
  Discourse on Church Government 100–2,
    101n.103
  Bishop of Oxford 100–2, 289–91, 297, 395–6,
    665–6
  declines candidature for Christ Church
    Deanship 292
  amity with the royal family 289n.174
  preaches at George II's coronation 102n.104,
    125, 333, 333n.147
  translated to Canterbury 100–2
  as Visitor 285–6
Powys, Mrs Philip Lybbe 425
Prades, Abbé des 590n.176
preaching, *see* sermons
predestination, debate on 113n.153
Presbyterianism
  in Scotland 68–70, 69nn.78,79, 461–3

804   INDEX

Preston, battle of (1715) 309n.41
'Pretender, the Old', *see* James Edward Stuart,
   'James III'
Pretyman, Bishop George 125–6, 267, 267n.85,
   273n.113, 377, 408–9
Prévost, Abbé 564–5, 565n.57
Priaulx, Matthew 446–7
Price, John 607–8, 608n.48
Price, Richard 118
   'Rational Dissenting' leadership 500–1
   objectives 500n.75
Pricket, John 515–16
Prickett, Stephen 662n.9
Prideaux, Humphrey 41n.103, 365n.28
   dislike of Christ Church 517
   declines chair of Hebrew 516–17
   university reform proposals 365–6
   on the Toleration Act 57
   biography of the Prophet Muhammad 176,
      178n.241
'priestcraft' 79–80, 118–19
Priestley, Joseph 118, 120, 257n.48, 496–7
   writings and polemics 118–19, 500–2, 501n.79
   his theology 498n.62
   anti-Trinitarian 118–19
   'Rational Dissenting' leadership 500–1
   opposition to in Established Church 118–19
   'gunpowder' image 500–1, 660–1
   critic of Oxford University 497–8, 500–2, 671
   views of in Cambridge 501n.81
   as a chemist 229–31, 231n.166, 232, 664–5
Primrose, Viscountess, *see* Drelincourt
Principia, see Newton
Prior, Matthew 218n.102
prisca philosophia 200
Professorial chairs
   Birkhead Professor of Comparative Poetry,
      138, 141, 663, *see* Trapp, Warton,
      Thomas (the elder), Spence, Lowth,
      Hawkins (William), Warton, Thomas
      (the younger), Randolph, (John), Hurdis
   Camden Professor of History 193–4, *see*
      Dodwell, Frewin, Warneford, Scott
      (William), Warton, Thomas (the younger)
   Professor of Chemistry 233n.177, *see* Plot,
      Hannes, Austin
   Professor of Experimental philosophy, *see*
      Hornsby
   Heather Professor of Music 182–7, *see*
      Goodson, Richard (senior), Goodson,
      Richard (junior)
   Lady Margaret Professor of Divinity 104n.119,
      see Hall, Delaune, Jenner, Randolph
      (Thomas)

Laudian Professor of Arabic 5–6, *see* Pococke,
      Hyde, Wallis, Hunt (Thomas), White
   Lichfield Professor of Clinical Medicine
      653–4, *see* Parsons, Wall
   Lord Almoner's Professor of Arabic 173–4;
      see also Gagnier
   [Rawlinson] Professor of Anglo-Saxon 155
   Regius Professor of Civil Law 410–11, 411n.246,
      see Brooke, Wenman, Laurence
   Regius Professor of Divinity 100–2, *see* Jane,
      Potter, Fanshawe, Bentham, Wheeler,
      Randolph (John), Van Mildert
   Regius Professor of Greek 162, *see* Hody,
      Milles, Thwaites, Shaw, Fanshawe,
      Jackson (William)
   Regius Professor of Hebrew 91–2, *see* Pococke
      (Edward), Hyde, Clavering, Hunt,
      Blayney, White
   Regius Professor of Medicine 222–3, 223n.126,
      see Woodforde, Kelly, Pegge, Kidd
   Regius Professor of Modern History 142,
      149–50, 322–3, 369–70, 662, 667–8, *see*
      Gregory (Dean David), Holmes (William),
      Spence, Nowell, Beeke, Nares (Edward)
   Savilian Professor of Astronomy 215–16,
      221n.114, *see* Gregory, Keill, Bradley,
      Hornsby
   Savilian Professor of Geometry 215–16, *see*
      Wallis, Halley, Bliss, Smith (John),
      Robertson (Abraham)
   Sedleian Professor of Natural Philosophy,
      see Bertie (Charles), Browne, Wheeler,
      Hornsby
   Sherardian Professor of Botany 233n.177,
      see Dillenius, Sibthorp (John)
   Sibthorpian Professor of Rural Economy 233–4
   Vinerian Professor of English Law 410–11,
      411n.249, *see* Blackstone (Sir William),
      Chambers (Robert), Wooddeson,
      Blackstone (James)
   Whyte's Professor of Moral Philosophy
      166–7, 194–5, *see* Thwaites
Prossalentis, Francis 576
Protestant Interest, Act to Strengthn 1718 364
Protestant Succession 1714
   character of the Established Church, and 36
   Oxford, and 36, 41–2, 48–9, 75–6, 125, 132–3,
      299–300, 304, 330–1, 358, 362–3
   Tories and 361–2
Prujean, John 224n.133
Prussia 567–8, 570
   bishops in 570–2
   Anglo-Prussian Church union planned 572,
      573n.86

Pryse, Walter 477–8
Psalmanazar, George 573–4, 574n.94
public schools, *see* schools
Pulteney, William, 1st Earl of Bath 363–4, 370–1,
    467–8, 607
pulpits 91, 91nn.60,61; *see also* sermons
Purcell, Daniel 191
Purnell, John
    client of the Beaufort family 447n.154
    and 1748 riots 263–4, 371–2, 446–7
    Winchester College Wardenship, and 446–7

Quadring, Gabriel 507
Quakers bill 1722 395–6, 397n.171
Quakers' Relief Act 387–8
Quaker Relief bill (1797) 394–5
Quarendon, Viscount, *see* Lee
Queen Anne's Bounty 370–1
Queensberry, Duchess of, *see* Douglas
Queen's College 21–4
    Provosts, *see* Halton, Lancaster, Smith
        (Joseph), Browne
    rebuilding work 333
    chapel 31n.58, 91
    cupola at entrance 31n.58
    statue of Queen Caroline 333
    donation received from Queen Caroline 333
    Library 28–31
    battelers at 449–50
    'Poor Boys' at 449–51
    Bridgeman exhibitions 447–8
    Hastings exhibitions, terms of 448–9
    connections to the north of England 448–51
    headmasters from 454–5
    panegyric on James II at 447–8
    centre of Anglo-Saxon studies 153–4
    alumni affection for 620
Quesnel, Pierre 588–9
Qur'an 176–7

Rack, Henry 504, 519–20
Radcliffe, Dr Anthony 27n.49
Radcliffe, Dr John 32, 226–7, 387–8, 642–3, 645
Radcliffe, Richard 622
Radcliffe Infirmary 6–7, 98, 223, 229–31, 238–9,
    241–2, 478
    annual meeting for 188–9
Radcliffe Library (later Radcliffe Camera) 3–4,
    148–9
    design 32, 114–15, 645
    financed 32n.66
    opening 1749 188–9, 302–3, 311–12, 336,
        507–8: *see also* King (Dr William)
    contents 651–2

manuscripts given to 185n.268
Librarians, *see* Wise, Kennicott, Hornsby
Radcliffe Observatory
    design 32, 226–7
    sculptural details 227n.146
    construction and opening 226–7, 264n.76
    cost 228n.148
    equipment 226–7, sculptural details 227n.147
    visitors to 227–8, 341–2
Radishchev, Alexander 575n.99
Radnor, Earl of, *see* Bouverie
Raftor, Catherine, aka 'Kitty' Clive 486–8
Raglan 603–4
Ramsay, Andrew Michael 579
Randolph, Bishop John 292–3, 353
    Professor of Poetry 105–6, 140
    Regius Professor of Divinity 105–6, 106n.126,
        292–3
    lectures 105–6, 129
    publications 105–6, 110
    outreach 105–6
    client of Lord Grenville 274n.114
    Bishop of Oxford 409n.237
    declines Irish primacy 1800 293n.197
    active in the House of Lords on behalf of the
        University 292–3
    at Blenheim 429
Randolph, Thomas
    Lady Margaret Professor 103–5
    President of Corpus Christi College
        104–5, 442
    Archdeacon of Oxford 104–5
    client of Thomas Potter 289n.177
    character 103–4
    view of scripture 83–4
    publishes regularly 103–4, 110
    reason, and 122n.199
    critic of *Decline and Fall* 523n.183
    tepid Whig 103–4, 111, 326–8
    1754 Oxfordshire election, and 438–9
Ranelagh, Earl of, *see* Jones
Ranelagh Gardens 191–2
Rational Dissenters, *see* Dissenters,
    Protestant
Ravenstonedale, Westmorland 615
Rawlinson, Christopher 153–4
Rawlinson, Richard 148–9, 155, 157n.133,
    210n.66, 403–4
    Jacobite and Nonjuror 558–9
    traveller and collector 558–9
    Oxford bequests 643
Raynal, Abbé 562–3
Reading
    Grammar School 454–5

806 INDEX

Reading (*cont.*)
  mayor and corporation 637–8
  clergy at St Laurence's church 655–6
Red Herring Club 423n.26, 457, 458n.211
Redi, Francesco 216–17
Redwood, Sir John 42–3
Reeves, John 394n.160
Reformation 17–18, 37–8, 155–6, 186
Regency Crisis 1788–9, *see* George III
Rehearsal 108–9; *see also* Leslie
Reid, Christopher 380n.102
Reid, Thomas 465
Reims 216–17
Relief Act [Scotland] (1792) 462–3
'Remitters' 398n.179
Rennell, Thomas 201–2, 202n.24
Republic of Letters 61, 133, 165–6, 193, 589–90;
  see also Oxford, University of
Revolution of 1688 3–5, 7–8, 40–1, Chapter 2
    passim, 146–7, 152–3, 161–2, 201–2,
    213–14, 337, 377–8, *see also* Convention
    Parliament
    Oxford and 12, 17–18, 36–7, 41–2, 48–9,
      Chapter 2 *passim*, 147–8, 299–300, 315,
      351–2, 355, 361–2, 378–9, 666, 675–6
    Cambridge and 68–9, 299–300
    in Ireland 472–3
Reynolds, Sir Joshua 513–14, 549–50, 617
Reynolds, Bishop Richard 333
Richards, George 460–1
Richards, Thomas, of Llanfyllin 457
Richardson, Dorothy 539
Richardson, John 182
Richmond Lodge, Surrey 250n.12
Richter, Franz Xaver 192
Ridley, Sir Matthew White, 2nd Bt. 26–7
Rights of the Christian Church Asserted, The
    62–3, 63n.50; *see also* Tindal
  condemnation and burning of 62–3, 317n.75
  impact of 62–3
  replies to 62–3
Riot Act 354, 363
Risley, John 622–3
Ritson, Joseph 136–7
Rivington, Charles 98–9
Rivington, John 98–9
Roberts, Thomas 31n.60
Robertson, Abraham 467–8
Robertson, Charles 465–6
Robertson, John 3–4, 44–5, 45n.123, 46n.134
Robertson, William 145–6, 146n.74, 149
Robinocracy, *see* Walpole, Sir Robert
Robinson, Michael 615–17, 617n.88
Robinson, Archbishop Richard

architectural patron and benefactor 474–6,
    477n.311, 646
Robinson, Bishop John 66n.63, 234n.182, 436n.90
Robinson, Thomas 163
Rochester
  Archdeacon of, *see* Brydges
  Bishops of, *see* Sprat, Atterbury
Rochester, earl of, *see* Hyde, Laurence
Rockingham, Marquess of, *see* Watson-
    Wentworth
Roman Catholics; *see also* Gallicanism; Oxford,
    University of
  attitudes towards in Oxford 114–15,
    114n.163, 259–60, 378–9, 394–5, 407,
    472, 673
  Emancipation of 19–20, 259–60, 272–4,
    378–9, 402–3, 407, 471
  English 14n.2, 18–19, 95–6
  on the continent 558–9
  anti-Catholicism 95–6, 95n.78
Rooke, Admiral Sir George 248n.3, 316–17, 427
Rooke, Giles 411n.249
Rooker, Edward 491–2
Rooker, Michael Angelo 491–2
Ropsley, Lincs. 442
Rotherfield Greys, Oxon. 427n.45, 478
Rougemont, Antoine 557n.17
Roussea, Jean-Jacques
  educational ideas 563–4
Routh, Martin 36–7
  and patristic revival 123–4
  admired by Samuel Parr 510–11
Rowlandson, Thomas 491–2
Rowney, Thomas 229, 312n.52, 419n.3
Roxburgh, Duke of, *see* Ker
Royal College of Physicians 222–3, 235n.183
Royal Proclamation against Seditious Writings
  and Publications (1792) 232, 258
Royal Proclamation against Vice and Immorality
  1787 396n.169
Royal Society 53–4, 180, 198–200, 238, 579
  Presidents of, *see* Newton, Sloane, Folkes,
    Macclesfield (2nd Earl)
  foundation 215–16
  founding members 212n.73
  Philosophical Transactions 211–12
  Copley Medal 211–12
  turn towards applied science at 211–12
  shifts away from Christian orthodoxy 212–13
  clergy membership 640–1
  Oxford concerns regarding and relations
    with 207, 211–14, 239, 663–4
Royse, George 329
Ruan Lanihorne, Cornwall 632–3

INDEX 807

Rule, Gilbert 69n.79
Rugby School 445n.137, 452, 479n.321
Runcorn, Cheshire 95–6
Rundle, Thomas 201–2, 202n.24
Russell, John, 4th Duke of Bedford 326n.116
Russell, William, styled Lord Russell 548n.289,
  557–8
Russell, Wriothesley, 2nd Duke of Bedford, styled
  Marquess of Tavistock 557–8
Russia
  students from at Oxford University 574–6,
    576n.103
Rutherforth, Thomas 170
Rutland, Duke of, see Manners
Rycote Park, Oxon 418–19, 431–2
Ryder, Sir Dudley 371–2
Rye House Plot 40–1, 557–8
Ryswick, Treaty of 68n.71

St Alban Hall
  Principal, see Leybourne
  Vice-Principal of, see Free
  St Albans, Archdeacon of, see Horsley
St Albans
  Viscount, see Bacon
St Andrews
  Archbishop of 69–70
  University of 462–3
    Chancellor 70n.81
    purged of Episcopalians after 1688
      Revolution 69–70, 69n.80
    Visitation after Hanoverian
      succession 366–7
    patronage at 673–4
St Asaph, Bishops of, see Wynne, Hare, Tanner,
  Shipley
St Basil 590–2
St Bees School 449n.164
St Cecilia's Day 189n.293
St Cuthbert 514
Saint-Cyran, Abbé de 588–9
St Cyril of Alexandria 162
St Davids, Bishop of, see Bull, Squire, Willes
  (Edward), Smallwell, Horsley, Burgess
St Edmund Hall
  Principals of, 248, see Mill, Felton, Shaw, Dixon
  Vice-Principals, see Crouch, Higson
  numbers at 505
  Methodists expelled from 112–13, 505
St Frideswide 630–1
St Germain-en-Laye 306–7
St James's Chronicle 109
St John, Henry, 1st Viscount Bolingbroke
  259–60, 269–70, 318, 361–2

in office 1710–14 361–2, 383–4
  flight 1715 321–2
  and history writing 145n.68, 146–7, 149n.92
St John Chrysostom 123–4
St John's College, Oxford 229
  Presidents, see Delaune, Holmes, Dennis, Marlow
  restricted Fellowships at 450–1
  land ownership and benefactions 441–2
  Holmes Building 538–9
  headmasters from 452
  George III visits 341–2
  royal portraits given to 342n.178
  charity to American loyalist clergy 596n.206
  fund raising for émigré clergy 586n.153
  fund raising in French Revolutionary
    war 352–3
  benevolence gifts to the urban poor 476–7
  links to Lee family of Ditchley 434–5
St John's College, Cambridge 449n.164, 626
St Mary Hall
  Principals of, see King, Nowell,
  Vice-Principals of, see Coningsby, Harte
Saint-Maur, Congregation of, see Benedictines
St Paul's cathedral, see London
St Petersburg 10
  Academy of Science 575n.98
St Pol de Léon 586n.154
St Scholastica's Day Riot and annual
    commemoration 419–20, 420n.9
Sa'di 179n.246, 180
Sacheverell, Henry 36, 40–1, 109, 125, 262, 318,
    355, 362–3, 382–3, 614–15
  career pre-1709 317n.74, 452
  'False Brethren' sermon 1709 99–100, 361–2,
    498–9
  his trial 317–18
  gift for publicity 317–18
  exceptional sermon sales 99–100
  sermons ordered to be burnt 40–1, 62–3
  in Oxford after the trial 317–18
  kept at a distance by senior University
    figures 317–18, 355
Sack, James J. 313n.58
Sackville, Charles, Earl of Middlesex, later 2nd
    Duke of Dorset 279n.138, 558n.24
Sackville, Lionel, 1st Duke of Dorset 279n.138
Sacy, Silvestre de 182
Sadler, James
  laboratory technician 231–2
  balloonist 231–2, 232n.172
Sale, George 176–7
Salisbury 182–4, 192
  Bishops of, see Burnet, Talbot, Douglas
  seminary at 103n.111

808 INDEX

Sallust 582–3
Salmon, Thomas 494n.49
   The Foreigner's Companion Through the
     Universities of Cambridge and
     Oxford 494, 563–4
Salomon, Johann Peter 189
Salzburg 585–6
Sancroft, Archbishop William 152–3, 572, 576
Sandby, Paul 491–2
Sandricourt, Charles-François-Simeon de
     Vermandois de Rouvroy de Saint Simon,
     Bishop of Agde 582–3
Sanskrit 181, 185n.268, *see also* Jones, [Sir]
     William
Sarpi, Fra Paolo 589
Sarti, Giuseppe 192
Saul, Edward 633
Savage, Richard 514–15
Schism Act 1714 364, 396–7, 405
Schomberg, Alexander Crowcher 411n.247
schools 8–9, 443–51
   donations to 454–5
   masters and teachers in 8–9, 417–18,
     451–5, 479
     Oxford connections 451, 454–5, 479, 669
     prestige, growing 452
   grammar schools
     curriculum in 443–4, 445n.139, 479
     numbers of 444n.134, 450–1
     poorer boys at 449–50, 449n.167
   private schools 450–1
   public schools 443–4, 450–1
     curriculum in 443
Schulenburg, Melusine von der, Duchess of
     Kendal 366n.32
science, dissemination of; *see also* Newton,
     Newtonianism
   popularised 206–9
   advertised 207n.45
   dubious character of popularisers 207–8,
     242–3
Scotland 5; *see also* Enlightenment,
     Presbyterians
   Episcopalians in 8–9, 60–1, 60n.38, 68–9,
     461–3, 462n.236
   Parliament 69–70
   Revolution 1688 68–9
   universities 8–9, 15–16, 45–6, 149, 512–15,
     673; *see also* Aberdeen, Edinburgh,
     Glasgow, St. Andrews
   Investigative commissions into 60–1, 68–9,
     462–3
   Scots in Oxford 461–8, 479–80, 669–70
   social elite and English education 463–4

'Scotophobia' 463–4, 475–6
Scott, James, Duke of Monmouth 300n.10
Scott, John, 1st Earl of Eldon 272n.109, 394–5,
     413–14, 556, 623–4
Scott, Sir William, 1st Lord Stowell 8, 180,
     413–14, 623–4
   tutor at University College 278
   Edward Gibbon endorses 394–5
   as Camden Professor 151–2
   lectures in vernacular 151–2
   MP for the University 380–1, 394–5
   defender of the Established Church 394–5
   judicial career 394–5, 396n.167, 410–11
Scripture Doctrine of the Trinity 129–30; *see also*
     Clarke, Samuel
Secker, Bishop later Archbishop Thomas 102,
     334, 504–5, 629
   as Bishop of Oxford 289, 289n.174, 297,
     395–6
   Dean of St Paul's 289
   relationship with Oxford University 86,
     290–1, 292n.195, 373–4, 483, 500–1,
     516–17, 665–6
   Whig politics of 86, 291–2, 438
   in opposition to Walpole 395–6
   client of Lord Hardwicke 291–2
   Biblical revision, and 86, 88
   education of ordinands, and 102–3, 103n.112,
     660–1
   Enlightenment, and the 86n.33
   America, and 593–5
   bluestockings, and 527–8
secularism 46–7, 47n.139
Selborne, Hants. 628–9
Selwyn, George 340n.169
September Massacres 232
Septennial Act 1716 364
'Septentrionalists' 153–4
sermons; *see also* Oxford, University of, Assizes
   characeristics of 96n.83
   composition 100n.100
   politics of 361–2
   reception of by the laity 96n.81
   popularity as publications 98–100, 100n.99,
     127–9
   preached during the French Revolution
     350–1
servants, in Oxford colleges and halls
   enlist as Volunteers 1790s 352
Settlement, Act of 1701 80–1, 299–300, 307–8,
     315–16, 355
Seven Years' War 5–6, 39, 181, 326–8, 340–1,
     374, 389–90, 547–8, 567–8, 668
Seward, Anna 192

Seymour, Charles, 6th Duke of Somerset 371, 508, 549
Seymour, Sir Edward, 4th Bt. 58n.26, 412
Seymour, Sarah, (4th) Duchess of Somerset 448–9
Shackleton, Robert 143–4
Shaftesbury, Earls of, see Cooper
Shakespeare, William 140n.49
Shapin, Stephen 233
Shardloes, Bucks. 278–9
Sharp, Granville 463n.246
Sharp. Gregory 530, 580–1
Sharp, John, Archbishop of York 452
Sharp, Richard 314nn.59,61
Shaw, John 163
Shaw, Richard
  Regius Professor of Greek 162
  travels in North Africa and the Middle East 162, 559–60
  writings 559–60, 560n.34
Sheffield, John, 1st Duke of Buckingham 319n.86
Sheffield, William 628–9
Sheffield, Lord, see Holroyd
Shelburne, Earl of, see Petty-Fitzmaurice
Sheldon, Archbishop Gilbert 306n.26, 594n.194
Sheldon, Ralph 304–5
Shepherd, Richard
  Archdeacon of Bedford 628
  Bampton Lecturer 120
  publications 628n.135
Sheppard, Elizabeth 525n.193, 531–3
Sher, Richard B. 45–6
Sherard, William 233–4, 233n.181, 582–3
  widely travelled 235n.183, 557–8, 558n.22
  tutor of 2nd Duke of Beaufort 603–4
Sherborne School 445, 452
Sheridan, Richard Brinsley 189–91, 394n.160
Sheridan, Thomas 490
Sherlock, Bishop Thomas 372–3
  Vindication of the Corporation and Test Acts 377
Sherlock, William 62, 62n.47, 92–4, 117
Shipley, Bishop Jonathan 347n.208
Shipley Moor, Yorks. 443
Shippen, Robert 369–70, 605n.26
  Vice-Chancellor 260–2, 436n.90
  rector of Whitechapel 261n.64
  later influence 262n.67
  character 261nn.60,65
  Jacobite politics 260–1, 261n.63
  on John Wesley, on 672
Shippen, William 260–1, 387–8
Shipton-under-Wychwood 312n.52

Shirburn Castle, Oxon. 212–13, 213n.81, 221n.116, 226–7, 432–3
Shore, John, 1st Lord Teignmouth 183n.262
Showwell, Mrs 524–5
Shrewsbury, Duke of, see Talbot
Shrivenham, Berks. 478
Shropshire 259n.56
Sibthorp, Humphrey 233–4
  Sherardian Professor of Botany 233–4
Sibthorp, John
  Sherardian Professor of Botany 233n.177, 560n.29
  lectures 233–4
  publications 233–4, 237n.187
  establishes Sibthorpian Professorship or Rural Economy 233–4
  international significance 233–4, 558–9, 560n.29
Sicily 161n.147
Sidney, Algernon 548n.289
Sidney, Sir Philip 463–4
Simeon, Charles 113n.157
Simon, Père Richard 84–6
  reception of his writings in England 85n.28
Simone, Maria Rosa di 15–16
Sinclair of Ulbster, Sir John, 1st Bt. 464
Skinner (the younger), Bishop John 462–3
Skinner, Richard 628–9
Skipton [Ermysted's] Grammar School 452
Slatford, Catherine 527n.196
slave trade 391–3, 395, 590–2
  Oxford University, and 612n.66; see also abolitionism
Slave Trade Regulation Act (1788) 391–3
Sloane, Sir Hans 458
  President of the Royal Society 212–13, 217
  importance 217
  critique of 207
Slough 575–6
Smallwell, Bishop Edward 26–7, 289
  Christ Church connections 293–4
  as Bishop of Oxford 293–4, 409
  previously Bishop of St Davids 293–4
  client of the 3rd Duke of Portland 293–4, 294n.206
Smalridge, George 27–8, 71n.89, 107–8, 579, 590–2
  and the Phalaris controversy 160–1
  Dean of Christ Church 269–70, 405, 621–2
  Bishop of Bristol 270
  Lord High Almoner 270, 321–2
  deputy Regius Professof Divinity 64n.58, 100–2
  moderate Tory 100–2, 270, 321n.90, 322, 355, 385

810   INDEX

Smalridge, George (*cont.*)
  laments Queen Anne's death 320
  in the House of Lords 396–7
  invites George I to Christ Church 321–2
  cultivates Archbishop Wake 621–2
  reform of the universities, and 367n.39
  Whig pleasure at his loss of favour 321n.92
  possible heterodoxy 322n.95
  ecumenist 572
  death 322
Smalridge, John 593n.186
Smart, Christopher 140
Smellie, William 224n.130
Smith, Adam
  Snell exhibitioner 467
  Oxford critic 42–3, 42n.110, 467–8, 468n.270,
    512–13
  compares unfavourably to Scottish
    universitities 512–13
  his intellectual formation and the
    University 468n.269
  pupils of 465
  attacked for amity with Hume 171–2
  Wealth of Nations 512–13
  suspected Christian indifference 42n.110,
    468n.270
Smith of Warwick, Francis 615–17
Smith, James Clutterbuck 650
Smith, John 6n.12, 467–8 [Savilian Professor]
Smith, John [Tomlins reader] 223–4
Smith, Joseph 91, 333, 449n.166, 450–1, 585–6
Smith, Mary 531
Smith, Matthew 452
Smith, Robert 206n.40
Smith, William 596n.204
Smollett, Tobias
  Peregrine Pickle 490–1
  The expedition of Humphrey Clinker 458
Smyrna 235n.183, 559–60, 577–8
Snell exhibition 8–9, 417–18, 462–3, 465–6,
    466n.262, 467n.263, 467–8
  see also Balliol College
Sniadecki, Jan 575–6
Sobieska, Maria Clementina 606n.32
societies, provincial musical 186, 188n.282
Society for Constitutional Information
    639–40
'Society for Promoting Primitive
    Christianity' 201–2
Society for the Promotion of Christian
    Knowledge [SPCK] 81–2, 90, 99n.95,
    176–7, 424n.29, 585–6, 639
Society for the Propagation of the Gospel
    [SPG] 590–3, 638–9

Socinianism 61–2, 116–18, 129–30, 376–7;
  see also Unitarianism
Solander, Daniel Charles 651–2
Somers, John, 1st Lord Somers 155n.124, 315,
    360–1, 368
Somerset
  Christ Church collieries in 443
Somerset, Duke of, *see* Seymour
Somerset, Charles, Marquess of
    Worcester 27n.49
Somerset, Henry, 1st Duke of Beaufort 250,
    603–4, 604n.19
Somerset, Henry, 2nd Duke of Beaufort
  nephew by marriage of 2nd Duke of
    Ormond 308n.33
  High Tory 603–4
  Jacobite sympathies 604–5
  as patron 604–5
  honorary Oxford degree 604–5
Somerset, Henry, 3rd Duke of Beaufort
  at University College 279–80, 604–5
  his Jacobitism 398n.179, 606
  Grand Tour 606n.32
  endows scholarship at Oriel College 455–6
  possible Chancellorship candidate 606n.36
Somerset, Henry, 5th Duke of Beaufort 457n.203
  character 607–8
  at the 1763 Encaenia 547–8
  as courtier 607–8, 608n.45
  candidature as Chancellor 1772, 1792 258,
    607–8
  masonry 631n.151
Somerset, Henry, 6th Duke of Beaufort,
    previously Marquess of Worcester 380–1
  candidature as Chancellor 1809 272n.109
Somerset, Noel, 4th Duke of Beaufort 280,
    313n.56, 325–6
  at University College 279–80, 604–5, 606n.37
  moves to Brasenose 606n.37
  defender of the University's interests 397–8, 607
  Radcliffe trustee 607
  awarded DCL 397–8
  patron of Thomas Carte 147–8
  his Jacobitism 397–8, 398n.179, 606, 606n.32
  meets Prince Charles Edward Stuart 373–4
  service in Lords as Tory leader 397–8, 607
  death 607
Somner, William 153–4
Sophia of Hanover, Princess 330–1
Sophocles 162–3, 454–5, 630
Sorbonne, *see* Paris
South Carolina 596–7
South, Robert 92–4, 425–6, 445–6
  charitable bequest 652–3, 653n.233

INDEX   811

Southampton
    Grammar School (King Edward VI) 454–5
Southern, Sir Richard 37–8
Southey, Robert
    sympathies for French Revolution 140–1,
        233n.179
    not admitted to Christ Church 233n.179
    facetious verses 141n.53
South Molton, Devon 502
South Sea Bubble 368
Spadafora, David 199
Spalding, Lincs. 639–40
Spanheim, Ezekiel, Freiherr von 567–8
    Prussian diplomat 567–8
    Dissertationes [Disputationes] de praestantia et
        usu numismatum antiquorum 567–8
    receives Oxford DCL 567–8
Spanish Succession, War of the 426–7
Spence, Joseph
    Professor of Poetry 131, 150n.99
    Professor of Modern History 150
    prebend of Durham 278–9
    on vernacular literature 134
    on the Grand Tour 278–9, 558–9
    London connections 131
    publishes *Polymetis* 640–1
    admires Mary Jones's poetry 527–8
Spencer, Charles, 3ʳᵈ Earl of Sunderland 270,
    281, 308, 362–3, 415
    education in Holland 367
    son-in-law of 1ˢᵗ Duke of Marlborough 282–3
    anticlericalism 384n.119
    Sunderland-Stanhope ministry 331–2,
        364, 368
    death 368–9
Spencer, Charles, 3ʳᵈ Duke of Marlborough 429,
    429n.54, 437–8, 508n.109
Spencer, Lord Charles 440–1, 478
Spencer, Elizabth, née Trevor, (3ʳᵈ) Duchess of
    Marlborough 603
Spencer, George, 4ᵗʰ Duke of Marlborough
    Lord Chamberlain 429
    Lord-Lieutenant of Oxfordshire 429
    Oxford city politics, and 418–19
    at Oxford races 478
    Oxfordshire politics 440–1
    possible candidature for Oxford
        Chancellorship 258–9
    cordial relationship with Oxford
        University 342, 430n.57
    friend of George III 348, 418–19, 429
    royal family visits 342
    taste for a quiet life 429, 429n.56
    amateur astronomer 429

Spencer, George, 5ᵗʰ Duke of
    Marlborough 342n.184
Spencer, George, 2ⁿᵈ Earl Spencer 378–9
Spencer, John, 1ˢᵗ Earl Spencer 627
Spencer, Lord Robert 418–19
Spenser, Edmund 136–7
Spinoza 62–3, 63n.51, 176–7
Sprat, Thomas
    Bishop of Rochester and Dean of
        Westmisnter 93n.66
Squire, Bishop Samuel 149n.90
Stackhouse, John 235n.184
Stadhampton, Oxon. 425–6
Stahl, Peter 570
Stamitz, Johann 192
Stamp Act (1765) 373, 394
Stanhope, George
    Dean of Canterbury 106–7
    incorporated at Oxford 107n.131
    Boyle lecturer 201–2
    writings 106–7
Stanhope, James, 1ˢᵗ Earl Stanhope 281, 362–3
    briefly at Oxford 367
    soldiering 361n.7
    in office 1714 415
    for Sunderland-Stanhope ministry, *see*
        Sunderland
    death 368–9
Stanislaw August Poniatowski, king of
    Poland 565, 575–6
Stanhope, Philip Dormer, 4ᵗʰ Earl of
    Chesterfield 163n.158, 328,
        372–3, 640–1
Stanhope, Walter 24
Stanton Harcourt, Oxon. 430–1
Stanton St John, Oxon. 533–4
Stapleton, Sir Thomas, 5ᵗʰ Bt. 478, 537
Steane Park, Northants. 436
Steele, (Sir) Richard 197n.322, 361n.7, 362–3,
    404n.203, 474n.301
    The Lying Lover 489
Stephens, Edward
    his oratory 572n.83
    and Orthodox Church 578n.113
Stephens, Lewis 164n.168
Sterne, Laurence 44
Stillingfleet, Bishop Edward 161–2, 163n.157,
    283n.154
Stirling, James 72n.92, 462–3
Stith, William 594
Stockdale, Percival 514–15
Stone, Archbishop George 474
Storace, Nancy 189–91, 192n.302
Storer, Anthony 582–3

812 INDEX

Stosch, Baron Philip von 387n.132
Stowe, Buckinghamshire 493, 567–8
Stowell, Lord, *see* Scott, Sir William
Strafford, Earl of, *see* Wentworth
Stratford, William 195n.316, 270n.94, 271, 276–8, 369–70, 647–9
  loses office as a King's chaplain 321–2
Stratford-on-Avon 493
Strange, Sir Thomas 597
Strasbourg, University of 574–5
Stormont, Lord, *see* Murray
Stroumsa, Guy G. 174–5
Stuart, Prince Charles Edward 251, 262–3, 310–13, 324, 338–9, 360, 373–4
  unsuitable kingly qualities 313
  uninterested in Oxford University 313n.57
  converts to Anglicanism 326–8
  death 462–3
  see also Forty-Five Rebellion
Stuart, John, 3rd Earl of Bute 251, 253, 301–2, 340–1, 375, 406–7, 567–8
Student, or the Oxford and Cambridge Monthly Miscellany, The 510–11
Stukeley, William 212–13, 212n.76
subscription controversy 1770s 104–5, 105n.123, 117–18, 118n.186, 126–7, 256, 264–5, 305, 375–7, 496–7, 500–1; *see also* Dissenters, Protestant
subscription to publications 640–1
Succession, Act of (1701) 18–19
Suffolk, Archdeacon of, *see* Prideaux
Sunderland, Earl of, *see* Spencer
Sunningwell, Berks. 570
Surat 174–5, 185n.268
Surrey, Archdeacons of, *see* Butler, John
Sussex, Earl of, *see* Yelverton
Sutherland, Dame Lucy 125n.209, 547–8
Swansea 455–6
Swedenborg, Emanuel 566–7
Sweet, Rosemary 601n.9
Swift, Jonathan 35–6, 218n.102, 386–7, 490
  matriculates at Hart Hall 207n.49
  pride on his Oxford incorporation 470n.281
  satires on science 207, 207n.49
  on Oxford in the 1730s 323–4
Swinton, John 176n.233
Swire, Samuel 625–6
Switzerland
  Church reunion, and 572–3, 573n.88
  Oxford dislike of Calvinism in 581
  Swiss visitors to Oxford 572–3
Sykes, Norman 500n.69
Szechi, Daniel 307n.32

Tacitus 145–6
'Tackers', *see* Occasional Conformity
Talbot, Catherine 539, 630–1
  ward of Archbishop Secker 527–8
  familiarity with the bishops 527–8
  'The Borlaciad' 527–8
Talbot, Charles, 1st Duke of Shrewsbury 360–1
Talbot, Charles, 1st Lord Talbot of Hensol 370
Talbot, Edward 517n.156
Talbot, John Ivory 636–7
Talbot, William
  Bishop of Oxford (later Salisbury) 289–91, 289n.178, 297
  Dean of Worcester 289
  Whig politics 291n.184
  preaches at the coronation of George I 333n.147
Taman, William 420n.13
Tanner, Bishop Thomas
  All Souls, and 63n.53, 154n.116
  Anglo-Saxon scholarship 153
  writings 153, 154nn.117,118
  Whig politics 153
Tarleton, Banastre 597n.209
Tate, Mary 262
Tatham, Edward 226–7
  critic of the curriculum 167–8
  critical of Cyril Jackson 297n.212
  keen on Oxford urban improvement 423
  on Catholics 116n.172
  Oxfordshire parish priest 426–7
  Oxonia Explicata et Ornata 423
  proposes Edmund Burke for honorary degree 511–12
  unpopular 167–8
Tatler, see Addison
Tayleur, William 496–7
Taylor, Michael Angelo 143–4
Taylor, Sir Robert
  endowment for modern languages teaching 143–4
Teignmouth, Lord, *see* Shore
Temple, Richard, 1st Viscount Temple 251
Temple, Sir William, 1st Bt. 160
Temple, Rev. William Johnston 495–6
Tenducci, Giusto Ferdinando 189–91
Tenison, Archbishop Thomas 62–3, 62n.47, 84–6, 153, 270, 329, 400
  Visitation of All Souls College (1710) 285–6
Terrae Filius, see Oxford, University of
Terrick, Bishop Richard 125–6
Test Act 1673 and Corporation Act 1661 19–20, 36, 118–19, 126–7, 305, 364
  attempts at repeal 1730s 478

INDEX 813

attempts at repeal 1787, 1790 257, 377, 398, 500–1, 586–7, 661
repeal 1828 496–7
Tetbury, Glos. 636–7
Thame, Oxon. 431–2, 438, 478
Thelwall, Eubule 457
Thetford, Bishop of, *see* Hickes
Theocritus 162–3, 164n.164, 165n.172, 499, 582–3
Thistlethwayte, Robert 332–3
Thomas, Henry 330–1
Thomson, James 202n.24, 639–40
Thomson, John (geologist) 226n.138
Thomson, John William 164–5
matriculates 573–4
Platonic scholarship 573–4
Thoresby, Ralph 154–5, 156n.129
Thornhill, Wilts. 448–9
Thornowitz, Henry 261n.65
Thornton, Bonnell 193
Thousand and One Arabian Nights 177, 179n.247
Thrale, Henry 513–14, 549–50
Thrale, Hester 507
Three Choirs Festival 182–5
Three Hours after Marriage 486
Thucydides 145–6, 164
Thurlow, Edward, 1st Lord Thurlow 294n.207, 628
Thurlow, Thomas, Bishop of Durham 628
Thwaites, Edward 54–5, 153–4, 155n.122, 454–5
Thynne, Thomas, 1st Viscount Weymouth 403–4, 404n.205, 647–9
Tickell, Thomas 135–6, 135n.21, 136nn.22,24
Tillemont, Le Nain de 588–9
Tillotson, Archbishop John 58–60, 84–6, 98–9, 329
Tilly, William 361–2
Tindal, Matthew 62–3, 115–16, 127
Christianity as Old as the Creation 172, 173n.216, 271
followers in Oxford 64n.54
opponents 100–2, 127
influence 172–3
Titchfield, Marquess of, *see* Bentinck
Toland, John 115–16, 172, 360
Irish background 472
Oxford, in 62–3, 63n.48, 472
reform of the English universities, and 364–7
connection with Locke 72n.96
Newtonianism, and 202n.22
client of 1st Earl of Macclesfield 432–3
toleration, religious 53, 56, 75–6
Toleration Act (1689) 56–7, 56n.16, 57n.20, 497–8

Toleration Act (1712, Scotland) 461–2
Tonbridge School, Kent 444n.134
Toomer, G.J. 176
Tories, *see also* Jacobitism; Oxford, University of
Revolution of 1688, and the 299–300, 300n.9, 315
divided over Comprehension 1689 58–60
in government 68–9
William III, and 315–16
in Anne's reign 316–20
Hanoverian Toryism 318, 327n.123, 362–3
divisions in 1714 318
out of favour with the early Hanoverians 276–7, 308, 321–8, 355–6, 362–3, 666–7
after fall of Walpole 324, 324n.107
political withering 1750s 326–8, 327n.124, 338–9
favour towards and with George III 111, 339n.164, 349n.215; *see also* George III
Toulmin, Joshua 500n.72
Toup, Jonathan 164n.164
scholarship and publications 630
Towle, Matthew 424–5
Townesend, William 28–31, 31n.58
Townshend, Charles, 2nd Viscount Townshend 262, 270, 362–4, 368–9, 373–4, 415, 668
university reform, and 365–6, 370n.58, 667–8
Townshend, Charles (died 1767) 389–90
Townson, Thomas
Grand Tour 'bear leader' 278–9, 557–8
declines Regius Professorship of Divinity 106
patronal connections 278–9
publications 106
awarded doctorate 550–1
Tractarianism, *see* 'Oxford Movement'
Tradescant, John 216–17
Trafalgar, Battle of 354
Transactioneer, The 207, 207n.48
Trapp, Joseph
Professor of Poetry 138, 162–3, 187–8
Tory apologist in Anne's reign 318
chaplain to Bolingbroke 318
oration 1714 on Phipps's honorary degree 321n.91
lectures 138n.40
playwright 138n.40
pamphleteer 138
gives Lady Moyer lecture 204
critic of Newton 204n.33
attacks Methodists 503–4, 504n.91
Trelawny, Sir Harry, 7th Bt. 496–7, 497n.59

814 INDEX

Trelawny, Bishop Sir Jonathan, 3rd Bt. 123–4, 315n.65
  on powers of a college Visitor 281
  powers legally vindicated in Bury affair 282
  as Visitor of Trinity College 286–7
  commissions statue of Cardinal Wolsey 631n.153
Trenchard, John 368
Trevecca 505
Trevelyan, G.M. 656–7
Trevor, John Morley 278–9
Trevor, Hon. Richard 278–9
  Bishop of Durham 251
  candidate for the Chancellorship 1759 251, 337
Trevor, Hon. Robert 381n.110
Trimnell, Charles 282–3
Trinitarianism 116–17, 375, 462–3, 496–7;
    see also orthodoxy
  Oxford University a bulwark of 110, 117, 129–30, 520n.169, 572–3, 660–1
Trinity College, Cambridge 17–18, 159, 206n.40, 507
  graduates in House of Commons 379
  Westminster School, and 445–6, 446n.145
  comparisons to Oxford 494, 496
Trinity College, Dublin 8–9, 21n.25, 60–1, 417–18, 479–80
  Chancellor of, *see* Ormond
  Provosts of, *see* Ashe; Baldwin, Hely-Hutchinson
  Oxford connections 468–73, 511–12, 669–70
  Whig character 468–9, 472–3, 669–70
  instellectual stagnation 470
  United Irishmen at 473n.292
  awards Burke honorary degree 512n.130
Trinity College, Oxford 136–7
  Presidents, *see* Bathurst, Chapman
  Visitor 286–7
  chapel and its financing 91, 567, 645, 647–9
  common room life at 512–13
  Poet Laureate at 537
  land ownership 442
  links to the North family 254, 417–36; *see also* Wroxton Abbey
Trumbull, Sir William, Kt. 66–8, 384–5, 395
  elected MP for the University 306–7, 382–3
  Secretary of State for the Nothern Department (1695–7) 66–8, 382–3
Tuam, Archbishop of, *see* Vesey
Turin 558–9
Turner, Sir Edward, 2nd Bt. 32, 291–2, 438, 438n.101, 537
Turner, Bishop Francis 275n.121

Turner, George 608, 608n.50
Turner, J.M.W. 491–2
Turner, Thomas
  President of Corpus Christi College 275
  connections to the City of London 275
  Nonjuring sympathies 275, 275n.121
  helps an Armenian student 577–8
  interest in Jansenism 588–9
Turretin, François 573n.88
Turretin, Jean-Alphonse 573n.88
Twells, Leonard 276n.125
Tyack, Geoffrey 32
Tyacke, Nicholas 239n.191
Tynte, Sir Charles Kemys, 5th Bt. 456n.199
Tyrrell, James 149n.91, 170n.199
Tyrwhitt, Thomas 134n.15, 164–5, 167n.180, 398–9

Uffenbach, Zacharias Conrad von 567n.65
Unigenitus, Bull 587–8
Union, Act of, with Ireland (1800) 19–20, 378–9, 407, 409, 471
universities
  in eighteenth-century Europe 15–16, 15n.6, 27n.49, 56, 672–3
  in Ireland and Scotland, *see* Trinity College, Dublin; Scotland
Unitarians 496–8, 502
United Irishmen 472
United Provinces 222, 227–8
United States, *see* America, British North
University Advowsons Act (1805) 292–3, 390n.147
University Almanack 98
Universities Act (1737) 25
Universities Act (1788) 25
Universities bill(s) (1717, 1719) 367–8
University College
  Masters of, *see* Charlett, Walker, Wetherell
  Visitor of 262n.67
  butler at 515–16
  civil law teaching at 410–11
  architecture 32
  Radcliffe Quadrangle 321n.92
  James II visits 57n.21
  tepid early Hanoverian allegiance 403–4
  internal disputes of 1720s 279–80, 280n.144, 284–5, 322–3, 604–5, 665–6
  [Sir] William Jones and 180–1
  graduates in House of Commons 379
  University College Club 410–11, 623–4
  King Alfred its alleged founder 16, 37–8, 623–4
  Durham connection 514
Upssala, Archbishop of, *see* Benzelius

Upton, John 630
Urry, John 134, 134nn.14,15
Usher, Dr Henry 472
Utrecht
    University 367, 558–9
    Treaty of (1713) 39n.96, 136n.22, 546n.281, 566–7, 572
    Act for the Peace (1713) 39n.96, 134–5, 362–3, 544–6

Vallance, Edward 310n.46
Valpons, Abbé Thoumin des 585–6
Valpy, Richard 454–5
Vanbrugh, Sir John 138n.40
Vanhal, Johanm Baptist 192
Van Mildert, Bishop William
    interest in geology at Oxford 236–8
    career summarised 239n.190
Vasari 650
Vassall Fox, Henry, 3rd Lord Holland 380n.105, 408–9, 556, 618–19
Vatican library 560–2
Vauxhall Gardens, see London
Venables-Bertie, Montagu, 2nd Earl of Abingdon 418–19
    Lord-Lieutenant of Oxfordshire 431–2
    loss of county influence 431–2
    loss of urban influence 432n.70
Venables-Vernon, George, 2nd Lord Vernon 457n.203
Venice 33n.73
Venner, Thomas 530
Venus, transit of 227–8, 433n.78
Verney, George, Dean of Windsor, and 12th Lord Willoughby de Broke 117
Vernon, Lord, see Venables-Vernon
Vernon, Admiral Edward 423–4, 423n.26, 527–8
Versailles, Peace of (1763) 597
Vesey, John, Archbishop of Tuam 471n.283
Vesey, Sir Thomas, 1st Bt., Bishop of Ossory 474–5
Vigo, battle of (1702) 248n.3
Villoison, J-.B.-G. d'Ansse de 165–6, 562–3, 563n.44
Vilnius University 575–6
Vincent, William 165–6, 233n.179, 446n.149
Viner, Charles 410–11
Virginia 593–4, 594n.196
    'Virginia fellowships' 594n.194
Vivian, John 150
Virgil 162–4, 195n.316, 630
Visitors, college, see Oxford, University of
Voltaire 176–7, 199
    and Newton 204n.35
Voss, Isaac 84–6

Waddilove, Robert Darley 582–3
Wadham College 25–6
    Wardens, see Dunster, Ironside, Baker, Thistlethwayte, Gerard, Wills
    celibacy imposed on 525n.194
    Whig character 111, 329, 329n.127, 337
    links to south-west England 445
    seventeenth-century science, and 215–16
    lecturer in Arabic at 184n.267
    sodomy at 26n.45
    women servants at 527n.195
    Warner bequest 643
Wake, Etheldreda 286
Wake, William, Bishop later Archbishop 62–3, 148–9, 212–13, 282n.149, 395–6, 572
    education at Christ Church 622
    as a historian 587
    uninterested in becoming Bishop of Oxford 287–8, 289n.173
    Convocation dispute, and 155–7
    Visitor of All Souls College 285–6
    reform of the universities, and 365–7, 367n.39
    conversations with Gallican leadership 587–8
    interest in Jansenism 588–9
    Protestant reunion, and 572–3
    averse to blasphemy 117
Wakefield, Gilbert 497–8
Waldo, Mary 531n.223
Wales 8–9
    Princes of, see Frederick, George III, George IV
    Princess of, see Caroline of Ansbach, Augusta of Saxe-Gothe
Wales, principality 455–61, 669–70
    cultural renaissance 460–1
    Grammar Schools in 479
    literary skills of students at Oxford 457
    their career paths 457
    students stereotyped 457
Walker, George 500n.72
Walker, John 304–5, 550–1
Walker, Obadiah 57n.21
Walker, Rev. Samuel 504–5
Wallis, John 62, 167–8
    work in mathematics and astronomy 219
    Savilian Professor of Geometry 215–16
    official cryptographer 219, 400
    Whig in politics 219
Wallis, John (Laudian Professor of Arabic) 174n.221, 176n.229
Wall, Martin
    Lichfield Professor of Clinical Medicine 231n.170
    lectures in chemistry 231–2, 232n.171

816 INDEX

Walpole, Horace 251n.17, 340n.169
Delenda est Oxonia 373n.76
Walpole, Sir Robert 310–11, 362–3
  relations with Oxford University, and 250,
    322–3, 368–71, 415
  ecclesiastical politics and appointments 271,
    368–9, 415
  in opposition (1717–20) 364
  Robinocracy, the 323–4, 415
  opposition to 395–6
  Scottish allies 70
  fall 1742 324, 334
Walton, John, *see* Stosch
Walwyn, Francis 410–11
Wanley, Humphrey 154–5, 156n.127
Wanstead, Essex 221–2
Wappenham, Northants. 426n.38
Warburton, Bishop William 13–14, 146n.74,
  630n.145
  attitude to Oxford University 483–4, 508, 510
  critic of Hume 171–2
  critic of Kennicott 87n.39
  critic of Wake and Kennett 158–9
Ward, George 606n.37
Ward, W.R. 102n.105, 264–5, 320n.88, 362–3,
  518, 668–9
Waring, Edward 584–5
Warneford, John 426n.38
Warner, Marina 179n.247
Warner, Richard 643
Warner exhibitions 58n.25
Warren, Martin 549
Warrington academy 497–8
Warton, Joseph 134, 136–7, 140, 446–7, 628–9
Warton, Thomas, the elder 138, 260–1, 323–4,
  323n.102, 623n.115, 628–9
Warton, Thomas, the younger 13, 131, 134, 140,
  157–8, 184–5, 264n.75, 344n.192,
  623n.115, 628–9, 676
  Professor of Poetry 136–8
  Camden Professor 151–2
  Trinity College bursar 442–3
  Poet Laureate 136–7, 349
  poetry 136–7, 137n.31
  lectures on Greek poetry 136–7, 138n.37,
    151–2, 162
  on Arabic literature 196
  humorous productions 136–7, 141, 494–5
  literary scholarship 136–7
  rivalry with William Mason 508
  Samuel Johnson, and 514
  William King's 'Redeat' speech, and
    (1749) 313
  influences 140–1, 661–2

penchant for public executions 423–4
prominence 194
Washington, George 596–8
Waterford, Bishop of, *see* Milles
Waterland, Daniel 170–1
  critic of Newton 204
  incorporation at Oxford 510–11, 670–1
Waterland, Theodore 510–11, 670–1
Wath, NR Yorks. 633
Watlington, Oxon. 432
Watson, George 209–10
Watson, Richard, bishop of Llandaff 10, 509,
  662n.8
Watson-Wentworth, Charles, 2nd Marquess of
  Rockingham 375, 408–9
  administration (1765–6) 378–9
Watt, James 225, 502, 639–40
Watts, Isaac 167–8, 498–9
  Logic, or The Right Use of Reason 498–9
Webber, Francis
  Principal of Exeter College 276
  Dean of Hereford 276, 440n.114
  Whig politics 276, 440n.114
Weedon, Northants. 354
Weekly Miscellany 633
Weil, Gustav 176–7
Welback Abbey 608
Wellesley, Richard, Viscount Wellesley, later 2nd
  Earl of Mornington 379, 547–8,
  549n.295, 619
Wells, Edward 107–8, 108n.134, 164, 165n.171
Welsted, Richard 163
Welton, Northants. 479n.321
Welwyn, Herts. 164
Wem, Shropshire 405n.209
Wenman, Philip, 3rd Viscount Wenman [I] 438
Wenman, Philip, 4th Viscount Wenman [I]
  440–1, 478
Wenman, Thomas 380–1
Wentworth, Thomas, 1st Earl of Strafford 321–2
Wesley, Charles 519–20
Wesley, John 106–7; *see also* Methodists
  Lincoln College tutor 112n.150, 504n.93,
    518–19
  High Church background 112–13, 660
  autocratic character 503–4
  beliefs 112–13
  conversion 518–19
  prison visiting 423–4
  preaching in Oxford 94, 94n.72, 112n.152,
    504, 518–19, 672
  critical of the University 517–19, 551–2, 672
  enduring imprint of Oxford on 519–20,
    520n.172, 672

later life visits to 519–20
seeks educated adherents 505–6, 519–20
Methodists expelled from St Edmund
    Hall 505
potential school master 452
admirer of Isaac Watts 498–9
American colonies, and the 592–3
Enlightenment, and the 521n.175
Hutchinsonianism, and 210, 211n.68
Jansenism, and 588–9
critics of 112–13, 503–4
celebrity status 505
Wesley, Samuel 132–3, 424n.29
West, Gilbert 499, 547–8
West Indies
    students from at Oxford 597n.209
West, Richard 163, 196n.318
Westminster Abbey 187–8
    Dean and Chapter 250–1
    Deans of, see Sprat, Atterbury
    Handel commemorations at 189–91
    Newton's funeral and burial 198–9
Westminster Confession of Faith 461
Westminster Hall 396–7
Westminster Infirmary 250–1
Westminster School 160, 251n.15, 271–2, 455–6,
    547–8
    reputation 445–6
    Christ Church connection 445–6, 669
Westmorland, Earl of, see Fane
Weston-on-the-Green, Oxon. 418–19
West Wycombe, Bucks. 541
Wetherell, Nathan 8, 379, 623–4
    Vice-Chancellor 264–5, 264n.76, 295–6, 406–7
    Dean of Hereford 264–5, 635–6
    Hutchinsonian 113, 264–5, 406–7
    encourages city of Oxford built
        improvements 421
    political networker 264–5, 295–6, 359–60,
        406–7, 416, 665–6
    supports [Sir] William Jones 180
    Samuel Johnson, and 514
    death 407
Weymouth, Viscount, see Thynne
Wharton, Philip, 1st Duke and 2nd Marquess of
    Wharton
    turns Jacobite 436
    benefactor of All Souls College 281–2, 645
    exile, bankruptcy, and death 436, 437n.97, 646
Wharton, Thomas, 1st Marquess and 1st Earl of
    Wharton
    Lord-Lieutenant of Oxfordshire 436
    Oxford city and county politics, and 418–19,
        436–7

Wheeler, Benjamin
    Regius Professor of Divinity 105–6, 129
    Sedleian Professor of Natural
        Philosophy 227–8
Whigs; see also Junto; Pelhamites; Walpole, Sir
    Robert
    Commonwealth Whigs 63–4, 64n.55, 73–4,
        347, 364
    Court Whiggery 328
    principles 63–4
    religious attachments 73–4, 114–15
    sympathetic to Dissenters 117, 364
    in Anne's reign 329
    political dominance after 1714 300–1, 308,
        320, 330–7, 355–6, 358, 362–3, 415
    split 1717–20 364, 368
    'Patriot' Whigs 146–7
    after Walpole's resignation (1742) 334, 336
    fading of party distinctions, and 1750s 326–8,
        338–9
    Old Whigs 389–90
    Rockingham Whigs 346–7
    ministry of 1830–41 17–18
    Tory attitudes towards Whigs 63–4
Whiston, William 70–1, 202n.23, 573n.84
    Newtonian follower 201–2
    visits Oxford 201–2
Whitaker, Edward W. 96n.84
Whitaker, John
    publications 632–3, 633n.162
    Cornish parson 633
    truculent 633
Whitby, Daniel 106–7
Whitchurch, Middx. 208–9
White, Gilbert 539
    Oxford career and connections 628–9
White, Joseph 88n.49
    Professor in Arabic 173–4
    Regius Professor of Hebrew 175n.224
    studies in Persian 182
    controversial Bampton Lecturer (1784) 120,
        120n.193, 176–7, 182, 502, 598n.215
    publications 174–5, 182
    reputation sullied 182, 502–3
Whitefield, George 112–13, 141, 456n.198,
    503–5, 503n.89, 592–3, 672
Whitehall Preachers 369–70, 369n.51
Whitelocke, Sir William 381–5, 403–4,
    412–13
Whiteside, John 217–19
Whitmore, John 371–2
Whole Duty of Man, The 423–4
Wickham, William 272–4
    Christ Church connection, and the 402

818 INDEX

Wickham, William (cont.)
  superintendent of aliens 402–3, 403n.199;
    see also Oxford, University of,
    intelligence gathering and national
    security
Wilberforce, William 391–3, 395
Wilcocks, Bishop Joseph 587–8, 588n.164
Wilcocks, Joseph (the younger) 558–9
Wilkes, John 347, 357, 375
Wilkins, David 153–4
Wilkins, John 215–16
Willes, Edward
  official Decypherer 401–2
  ecclesiastical rewards 401–2
  grandsons 401–2
Willett, John 361–2
William III 7–8, 250, 306–7, 337, 389–90
  journey to London 1688 300n.10
  accepts throne 57–8
  oaths taken to 302–3
  another Oliver Cromwell 58n.25
  Calvinist 68n.72
  coronation 57–8
  death of Queen Mary 67n.67
  in Ireland 60–1
  religious views 68n.72, 69n.79, 300n.11
  Whig supporters in the University
    156n.130, 329
  rebukes the University 62, 62n.47
  addresses from Oxford University 66–8,
    67n.69
  reception within Oxford University 57–8,
    58n.26, 68–9, 315–16, 666
  visits Oxford University 66–8, 67n.68, 182–4,
    306–7, 355, 542, 590–2, 666
  legacy 149n.90
William IV 16–17
William IV, Prince of Orange 262, 294–5;
    see also Anne, Princess Royal, Princess of
    Orange
  visits Oxford 569–70, 570n.76, 666–7
William, Prince, Duke of Gloucester (son of
    Queen Anne) 70–1, 219n.103, 306–8,
    306n.26, 315–16
William, Prince, Duke of Gloucester (brother of
    George III)
  visits Oxford University 350n.221
Williams, Edward 625n.123
Williams, John, Archdeacon of Cardigan 458–9
Williams, Moses 460–1
  Repertorium Poeticum 460–1
Williams, William 33–5
Williamsburg, VA 594
  William & Mary College 594, 595n.199

Williamson, James 467–8, 514n.141
Williamson, William 567
Williams-Wynn, Sir Watkin 3rd Bt. 387–8,
    458, 643
Willis, Browne
  antiquarian scholarship 630–1
  belief in clerical celibacy 630n.148
  church restoration 630–1
  Oxford loyalties 630–1
  charitable 630–1
Willis, Bishop Richard 132–3, 549–50
Willoughby de Broke, Lord, see Verney
Wills, John 25–6
  Vice-Chancellor 267–9
  client of the Duke of Portland 267–9
Wilmer, James Jones 596–7
Wilmot Relief Committee 585–6
Wilmot, Robert 639–40
Wilson, David B. 200
Wilson, Rachel 469
Wilson, Thomas 585–6
Wilson's coffee house, Paris 556
Wilton House, Wilts. 649
Winchester
  Archdeacons of, see Eden, Robert
  Bishops of, see Mews, Trelawny, Hoadly
  College 623–4
    Jacobitism at 451n.178
    links to New College 446–7, 669
    Wardens of 446–7
Winchester, Thomas 278–9, 279n.140, 522–3,
    610–11
Winchilsea, Earls of, see Finch
Windham, William 377–9, 394n.160, 608
  Secretary-at-War 407
  pro-Catholic Emancipation 407
Windsor, Deans of, see Verney, Douglas
Winstanley, Thomas 164–5
Wise, Francis 155, 426–7, 631–2
Withers, Charles J. 46
Wodehouse 1n.1
Wodrow, Robert 462n.236
Woide, Carl Gottfried 293–4
Wolsey, Cardinal Thomas 476–7, 630–1
Womersley, David 520–2
Wood, Anthony (à) Wood 33–5
  Historia et antiquitates Oxoniensis 563–4
Wood Eaton, Oxon. 232n.172
Wood, Thomas 410–11, 411n.248
Wooddeson, Richard 411n.249
Woodford, Essex 643
Woodforde, Frank 626
Woodforde, James 546, 562–3
  ministers to prisoners 423–4

musical interests of 193n.306
possible school master 452
Somerset curacies 626
at New College 626n.126
moves to Weston Longville 626
Woodforde, William 224n.130
Woodroffe, Benjamin 576
Woodroffe, Dr Charles 441–2
Woodstock, Oxon. 329, 477–8, 626
Woodward, John 486
Woolsthorpe with Stainworth, Lincs. 622–3
Wootton Bassett, Wiltshire 433–4
Worcester
  Bishops of, see Stillingfleet, Lloyd, Hurd
  cathedral 104n.119, 201, 104n.206
  Lady Margaret Professorship of Divinity,
    and 636n.174
Worcester College
  Provosts, see Blechinden
  foundation 20, 645
  architecture 31–2
  female servants at 516n.148
  affection for 620
  gifts to 621n.101
Worcester, Marquess of, see Somerset
Wordsworth, William 140–1
Worrall, David 24n.30
Worsley, Giles 29n.52
Wren, Sir Christopher 91, 91n.62, 215–16
Wrexham School 451
Wroxton Abbey 254
  North family seat 426–7, 435
Wyatt, James 32, 226–7, 475–6, 646–9
Wychwood Forest 312n.52, 433–4
Wykeham, Bishop William of 446–7
Wyndham, Charles, 3rd Earl of Egremont 272n.110

Wyndham, Sir William, 3rd Bt. 387–8
Wynne, Rev. Ellis 457
Wynne, John
  Principal of Jesus College 276, 283–4, 603
  named Bishop of St Asaph 276
  patrons 276; see also Finch, Mostyn,
    Pembroke
  Tory turned Whig 276
  diffuses knowledge of Locke 72
Wynne, John
  Fellow of Jesus College 298
Wytham, Berkshire; see also Abingdon,
    Earls of
Wyttenbach, Daniel Albert 164n.167, 165–6
  Oxford connections 583

Xenophon 164

Yalden, Thomas 604n.21
Yates, Richard 452
Yelverton, Talbot 1st Earl of Sussex 198–9,
    199n.3
Yolton, John 170
York, archbishops of
  see Sharp (John), Dawes, Markham
York, Frederick, Duke of 408–9
  visits Oxford 1799 353–4
  chaplain, see Nares, Robert
Yorke, Philip, 1st Earl of Hardwicke 290–2, 334,
    339, 360, 373–4, 397, 527–8
Young, Arthur 204
Young, Edward 136, 371n.64, 640–1, 645

Zacagni, Lorenzo Alessandro 579n.122
Ziegenhagen, Friedrich Michael 574n.93
Zoroastrianism 174–5, 177n.236